Introduction to Forensic Psychology

Court, Law Enforcement, and Correctional Practices

Third Edition

ELSEVIER *science & technology books*

Introduction to Forensic Psychology

Court, Law Enforcement, and Correctional Practices

Third edition

Stacey L. Shipley

North Texas State Hospital, Wichita Falls, TX, USA

Bruce A. Arrigo

University of North Carolina, Charlotte, NC, USA

AMSTERDAM • BOSTON • HEIDELBERG • LONDON • NEW YORK • OXFORD
PARIS • SAN DIEGO • SAN FRANCISCO • SINGAPORE • SYDNEY • TOKYO

Academic Press is an imprint of Elsevier

BP45

Academic Press is an imprint of Elsevier
32 Jamestown Road, London NW1 7BY, UK
225 Wyman Street, Waltham, MA 02451, USA
525 B Street, Suite 1800, San Diego, CA 92101-4495, USA

First edition 1999
Second edition 2005
Third edition 2012

British Library Cataloguing-in-Publication Data
A catalogue record for this book is available from the British Library

Library of Congress Cataloging-in-Publication Data
A catalog record for this book is available from the Library of Congress

ISBN : 978-0-12-382169-0

For information on all Academic Press publications
visit our website at elsevierdirect.com

Typeset by TNQ Books and Journals Pvt Ltd.
www.tnq.co.in

Printed and bound in United States of America

12 13 14 15 16   10 9 8 7 6 5 4 3 2 1

Working together to grow
libraries in developing countries

www.elsevier.com | www.bookaid.org | www.sabre.org

ELSEVIER   BOOK AID International   Sabre Foundation

12/31/13

Dedication

The book is dedicated to John St.Clair for his patience and support throughout this process. Thanks to him for this and many, many other things. I would also like to express my heartfelt thanks to my parents, Bob and Carol Shipley for their love, understanding, and encouragement when it was most required.

Finally, we are forever indebted to our colleagues, students and interns, both past and present, who have always challenged us to be better teachers, researchers, mentors, and practitioners.

Contents

PART I. Adult Forensics

Court and the Legal System: Criminal Forensic Evaluation

Court and the Legal System: Criminal Forensic Consultation

Court and the Legal System: Civil Forensics

Police and Law Enforcement

Corrections and Prison Practices

PART II. Juvenile Forensics

Court and the Legal System: Delinquent Conduct

About the Authors

STACEY L. SHIPLEY, Psy.D., obtained her doctorate in clinical/forensic psychology from California School of Professional Psychology in Fresno, California and obtained her Bachelor's Degree from St. Edward's University in Austin, Texas, with a Major in Psychology and a Minor in Criminal Justice. She completed her predoctoral internship at Milwaukee County Mental Health Complex in Milwaukee, Wisconsin, where she worked with the County Forensic Unit, conducting competency to stand trial evaluations. Additionally, she provided clinical services for child, adolescent, and adult inpatient programs. Her clinical and forensic training has focused on both adults and adolescents in inpatient, outpatient, and forensic settings.

Dr. Shipley is licensed by the Texas, North Carolina, and Iowa Boards of Psychology Examiners. She is the Director of Psychology at North Texas State Hospital, which includes both the Wichita Falls and Vernon Campuses. The Vernon Campus of North Texas State Hospital is the only maximum-security forensic hospital in the state. She specializes in the areas of forensic and clinical assessment, violence risk assessment, evaluating and treating maternal filicide offenders, and treatment for individuals who have been adjudicated by the courts as Not Guilty by Reason of Insanity. She also serves as a consulting expert witness, conducts assessments of competency to stand trial and sanity, as well as general psychological assessments of individuals in the criminal justice system. Dr. Shipley conducts police officer screenings in her community.

Dr. Shipley has presented professionally on competency to stand trial, maternal filicide, psychopathy, and the relationship between mental health and murder. She has published two articles in the *International Journal of Offender Therapy and Comparative Criminology*, exploring the construct of psychopathy and its clinical implications. She was first author of *The Female Homicide Offender: Serial Murder and the Case of Aileen Wuornos* (2004) published in Prentice Hall's Women in Criminal Justice Series. She has published the chapter "Serial killers and serial rapists: dichotomy or continuum — an examination of commonalities and comparison of typologies" in the 2008 edited book by R. Kocsis entitled: *Serial Murder and the Psychology of Violence* and published the chapter, "Perpetrators and victims: Maternal filicide and mental illness" in the 2007 and 2011 edited books by R. Muraskin entitled: *It's a Crime: Women and Justice*, 4th & 5th Editions. She coauthored "Sexual offenses against adults" in the 2011 edited book by M. McMurran and P. Sturmey entitled: *Forensic Case Formulation*. Dr. Shipley has most recently contributed three chapters to *Criminal Psychology — Three Volume Set* edited by J.B. Helfgott with an expected 2013 publication date. These chapters include: "Competency to stand trial: Legal foundations and practical applications," "Predatory and affective aggression: Calculated and explosive pathways to violence," and "Mental illness and violence: A misunderstood relationship."

Dr. Shipley has completed both the Violent Crime Behavior I and II trainings offered by the Academy Group, comprised of retired Supervisory Special Agents from the Behavioral Science Unit (BSU) or Behavioral Analysis Unit of the Federal Bureau of Investigation (FBI). Dr. Shipley was one of 12 that attended Violent Crime Behavior I in 2010, a two-week course offered by invitation only to professionals who are experienced in the investigation and evaluation of violent crimes, crime scenes, and offenders and addressed the motives, behavior, and crime scene characteristics of the violent criminal. She was one of five who attended Violent Crime Behavior II training in 2011, a one-week interactive program that combined major case presentations followed by small group workshops covering linkage analysis, crime scene reconstruction, statement analysis, crime scene analysis, and threat communications.

Photo courtesy of UNC Charlotte.

BRUCE A. ARRIGO, Ph.D., is Professor of Criminology, Law, and Society within the Department of Criminal Justice and Criminology at the University of North Carolina — Charlotte. In the College of Liberal Arts and Sciences, he holds additional faculty appointments in the Psychology Department and the Public Policy Program. In the College of Health and Human Services, he holds an appointment in the Department of Public Health Sciences. Professor Arrigo is also a Faculty Associate in the Center for Professional and Applied Ethics — a teaching, research, and service unit of the Philosophy Department, a senior member of the University Honors College, and a Faculty Affiliate of Wake Forest University's Bioethics, Health, and Society Program.

Dr. Arrigo began his professional career as a community organizer for and social activist on behalf of the homeless and marginally housed, users of (mental) health services, adult and juvenile ex-offenders, survivors of sexual assault, and abusers of licit/illicit drugs. Professor Arrigo's work with these constituencies culminated in his overseeing the novel social designing and implementation of affordable, single room occupancy (SRO) housing for a number of poor, low-income, and other disenfranchised citizens residing in Pittsburgh, PA. His civic engagement in this area also included developing and managing the facility's human welfare and social policy agenda. During his Directorship, this agenda addressed the unmet needs of thousands of under-served and non-served children, adults, and families living in the city of Pittsburgh.

Professor Arrigo was awarded the Ph.D. from the Pennsylvania State University in the Administration of Justice (specializing in law, mental health, and justice policy). He has additional graduate training in law, as well as advanced degrees in psychology and in sociology. He served as founding Director of the Institute of Psychology, Law, and Public Policy at the California School of Professional Psychology — Fresno (1996—2001), and as Chair of the Department of Criminal Justice at UNC — Charlotte (2001—2004).

Dr. Arrigo is a highly prolific, internationally acclaimed, and award winning researcher and scholar. He has authored more than 150 peer-reviewed journal articles, law reviews, chapters in books, and academic essays. He is also the (co)author or (co)editor of 29 volumes, published or in press. Selected recent books include *Psychological jurisprudence* (SUNY Press, 2004), *Theory, justice, and social change* (Springer, 2005), *Philosophy, crime, and criminology* (University of Illinois Press, 2006), *The terrorist identity* (NYU Press, 2007), *Revolution in penology: Rethinking the society of captives* (Rowman & Littlefield, 2009), and *The ethics of total confinement: A critique of madness, citizenship, and social justice* (Oxford University Press, 2011). Recent textbooks include *Ethics, crime and criminal justice*, 2nd edn. (Prentice Hall, 2012) and *Introduction to forensic psychology* (Elsevier, 2012).

Professor Arrigo's scholarship explores the normative, philosophical, empirical, clinical, and policy dimensions of various human justice and social welfare issues relevant to an understanding of: (1) law, mental health, and society; (2) theory, culture, and society; and (3) deviance, violence, and society. Dr. Arrigo was the Editor-in-Chief of the peer-reviewed quarterly, *Humanity & Society* (1996—2000); is founding and current Editor-in-Chief of the peer-reviewed publication, *Journal of Forensic Psychology Practice* (2000—Present); and serves on the Editorial or Advisory Boards of several (inter)national periodicals relevant to the disciplines of sociology/criminology, psychiatry/psychology, law/legal studies, and social/public policy. He also served as the founding Book Series Editor for *Criminal Justice and Psychology* (Carolina Academic Press) and *Critical Perspectives in Criminology* (University of Illinois Press).

Among his numerous honors and recognitions, Professor Arrigo is a past recipient of the Criminologist of the Year Award (2000), sponsored by the Division on Critical Criminology of the American Society of Criminology; an elected Fellow of the American Psychological Association (2002, Psychology — Law Division); and an elected Fellow of the Academy of Criminal Justice Sciences (2005). In 2005, his book, *The French connection in criminology: Rediscovering crime, law, and social change*, received the Book-of-the-Year Award from the Crime and Juvenile Delinquency Division of the Society for the Study of Social Problems. In 2007, he received the Bruce Smith Sr. Award (for distinguished scholarship), sponsored by the Academy of Criminal Justice Sciences. In 2008, he was the recipient of the First Citizens Bank Scholars Medal, the most prestigious research honor bestowed upon a single UNC — Charlotte faculty member annually. In 2012, he was the recipient of the Lifetime Achievement Award, from the Division on Crime and Juvenile Delinquency of the Society for the Study of Social Problems.

Dr. Arrigo has been a (co)principal investigator for a number of public, private, and corporate grants and contracts totaling approximately $3,000,000. Sources of funding support have included the Departments of HUD and FEMA, the Office of Criminal Justice Planning (CA), and the William Penn Foundation (PA). He has served as a consultant to various organizations and institutions including the Correctional Service of Canada, the National Institute of Justice, the Florida Psychological Association, and Savant Learning Systems. These consultancies have emphasized progressive social policy and practice, evidenced-based research and programming, and citizenship-oriented education and training.

Preface

Defining Forensic Psychology — What it is and is not

DeMatteo, Marczyk, Krauss, and Burl (2009) note that the practice of forensic psychology dates back to the early 1900s; however, it is only within the last 50 years that the field has significantly expanded. In 1969 the American Psychology-Law Society (AP-LS) was formed and played a role in the creation of Division 41 (Psychology and Law) of the American Psychological Association (APA) in 1981 (Grisso, 1991). In 1984, Division 41 was renamed the American Psychology-Law Society after the merger of Division 41 and the AP-LS (Grisso). Nevertheless, it was not until 2001 that the APA recognized forensic psychology as a specialty (APA, 2011).

According to the *Specialty Guidelines for Forensic Psychology* (APA, 2011; p. 1), forensic psychology is the "professional practice by any psychologist working within any sub-discipline of psychology (e.g., clinical, developmental, social, cognitive) when applying the scientific, technical, or specialized knowledge of psychology to the law to assist in addressing legal, contractual, and administrative matters." It is further noted that this includes (p. 1):

> *...all matters in which psychologists provide expertise to judicial, administrative, and educational systems including, but not limited to, examining or treating persons in antici-pation of or subsequent to legal, contractual, administrative, proceedings; offering expert opinion about psychological issues in the form of amicus briefs or testimony to judicial, legislative or administrative bodies; acting in an adjudicative capacity; serving as a trial consultant or otherwise offering expertise to attorneys, the courts, or others; conducting research in connection with, or in the anticipation of, litigation; or involvement in educa-tional activities of a forensic nature.*

While necessarily broad in definition in an effort to be inclusive rather than exclusive of non-clinical work, the practice of psychology is not considered forensic in nature "solely because the conduct takes place in, or the product is presented in, a tribunal or other judicial, legislative, or administrative forum" (APA; p. 1). For example, providing treatment to an individual who has been court ordered to attend treatment is not necessarily considered the practice of forensic psychology.

Forensic Psychology and the Justice System: An Overview

As described by Hall, Cook, and Berman (2010), there were two court cases which helped to propel the role of psychologists into the legal system. First, in *Brown v. Board of Education* (1954), the Supreme Court "relied on psychological research concerning the effects of segregation on school children" (p. 71). Subsequent to that, "in *Jenkins v. United States* (1962), the Court of Appeals for the District of Columbia determined that a psychologist could serve as an expert witness in diagnosing mental disorders, a role previously limited to physicians" (p. 71). As will be discussed in Chapter 1, there are also a number of other court cases which solidified the role of psychologists serving as an expert witness.

In working as a forensic psychologist, you may be called on to perform a variety of services. As noted by Frost, de Camara, and Earl (2006; p. 78):

> *Courts rely on mental health professionals to help decipher complex cases at the intersection of psychology and criminal law. When a defendant appears to have a mental disability, numerous legal questions come into play. If the defendant was impaired at the time of the alleged offense, the disability may support an insanity defense or mitigation in the sentencing phase of the trial. If the defendant is impaired at the time of the proceeding, competence concerns may delay a trial or an execution. Attorneys generally rely on mental health testimony to establish the nature and impact of a defendant's mental impairment.*

Ballard and Nyman (2009; p. 491) note that "the continued hybridization of law and psychology will ideally lead to empirically supported legal interventions. The goal is to turn interdisciplinary work into a practice that invigorates and informs both disciplines while making the lives of our clients measurably better."

Programs, Training, and Careers in Forensic Psychology

There are a variety of paths that an individual might take, all of which could conceivably lead to a career in forensic psychology. In order to be a knowledgeable and competent forensic psychologist one must master a number of skills, all of which require "considerable in-depth study, advanced and knowledgeable supervision, and experience in various forensic settings" (Clements & Wakeman, 2007; p. 54). The *Specialty Guidelines for Forensic Psychology* (APA, 2011; p. 4) note that the competence required to work as a forensic psychologist "can be acquired through various combinations of education, training, supervised experience, consultation, study, and professional experiences."

The most obvious way to obtain the necessary education and training to practice as a forensic psychologist is to attend a program which offers a specialization or emphasis in this area. Opportunities to obtain an education in forensic psychology exist at the Bachelor's, Master's, and doctoral (i.e., Ph.D. and Psy.D.) level. However, DeMatteo *et al.* (2009) note that despite the increase in the number of training programs in forensic psychology that are available, there is currently no consensus regarding core educational components. Many psychology departments now offer at least one course in law and/or forensic psychology, and at least one college, John Jay College of Criminal Justice, now offers a Bachelor of Arts in Forensic Psychology (DeMatteo *et al.*, 2009). It should be noted that as with any undergraduate degree in psychology, employment opportunities at the bachelor level are limited. At the graduate level, the *Guide to Programs in Forensic and Legal Psychology 2010–2011* (2nd edition; Adherhold, Boulas, & Huss, 2011) provides an overview of the graduate programs available in forensic and legal psychology. This includes master's, Psy.D., clinical Ph.D., non-clinical (i.e., research-based) Ph.D., and joint degree programs. The first joint degree program in law and psychology was developed in 1973 at the University of Nebraska (Bersoff, 1999; cited in DeMatteo *et al.*, 2009). Currently, there are over 50 graduate programs offering a specialization in forensic psychology and/or joint degree programs (i.e., a degree in psychology and a degree in law) in law and psychology (Adherhold, Boulas, & Huss). You might also be able to obtain training and educational experiences as an adjunct to a more general program. It should be noted that while there are graduate degrees available at the Master's level, it has been argued that the most efficient way to acquire the necessary skills is through the extensive study and collaboration that is required in a doctoral level psychology program (Clements & Wakeman, 2007). The reader is encouraged to review the Clements and Wakeman article for a more thorough discussion regarding the benefits of a doctoral education as a basis for the practice of forensic psychology.

In order to engage in the independent practice of psychology, an individual must be licensed by the state in which they intend to practice. In all 50 states, part of the requirements for obtaining a license is a one-year, predoctoral internship. According to the Association of Psychology Postdoctoral and Internship Centers (APPIC, 2011) website, in the United States there are 283 full-time internships in forensics/corrections as a major specialty area, 191 of which are APA accredited. Additionally, there are 117 full-time internships which offer forensics/corrections as a minor specialty area, 69 of which are APA accredited.

Opportunities to obtain training as a forensic psychologist have also become more widely available in the form of continuing education and postdoctoral specialization, and it has been noted that the specialization in a particular area of forensic psychology might be best accomplished at the postdoctoral level, after a core set of competencies has been obtained (DeMatteo *et al.*, 2009). Currently, there are 27 full-time forensics/corrections postdoctoral positions available in the United States, eight of those are accredited by the APA (APPIC, 2011). With regards to credentialing, some states require that individuals obtain training and obtain credentialing as a "forensic examiner" in order to ensure a minimum level of competence (Clements & Wakeman, 2007; DeMatteo *et al.* 2009; Frost *et al.*, 2007). On a national level, there is an opportunity to obtain board certification through the American Board of Professional Psychology (ABPP) in order to distinguish oneself as having expertise in forensic psychology (Clements & Wakeman, 2007; Cox, 2009; DeMatteo *et al.*, 2009). Board certification is available to doctoral level psychologists who are licensed to practice independently and have the appropriate education, training, and experience in the specialty area for which they are seeking certification (Cox, 2009). Interested individuals should visit the ABPP website (www.abpp.org) for more information.

As a forensic psychologist, there are a wide variety of career opportunities available. At the doctoral level, opportunities to work in academia, in a teaching and/or research capacity, are available. Clinically, there are opportunities for "private clinical and consultation practice, clinical practice within a forensic or correctional facility, or other clinical or consultation practice within the psychologist's domain of competence" (Clements & Wakeman, 2007; p. 61). This clinical work may be conducted within the confines of a private practice, jail, prison, or state hospital. It is important to note while some states allow psychologists to be licensed at the master's level, individuals licensed at this level are typically not allowed to practice independently and require supervision throughout their career and are typically unable to hold leadership or supervisory positions (Clements & Wakeman, 2007). Furthermore, many settings in which forensic psychology is practiced, such as prisons, exclusively employ doctoral level psychologists.

What's New in This Edition?

The purpose of *Introduction to forensic psychology* has always been to educate practitioners and academics about the complexities of police, court, and correctional work. These complexities have been clarified by noting where and how the insights and values of psychology can (and do) foster human justice and pro-social change for various stakeholders subjected to institutional and community-based decision-making by way of the criminal and civil justice systems. In this edition, this purpose is retained but made much more accessible to students. All controversies reviewed in this volume have been thoroughly updated, mindful of important clinical, legal, and social science developments. But, more importantly, each chapter is designed to connect with the next generation of forensic psychologists, non-clinical mental health specialists, legal experts, academic researchers, community advocates, and policy analysts. To accomplish this, the 3rd edition now consists of extensive (and new) pedagogy within each chapter. Examples include:

1. "Key Issues" that succinctly frame out and summarize the controversies examined in the chapter.
2. " International Issues" that clearly demonstrate the global reach of specific forensic psychological topics.
3. "Practice Updates" that cogently describe the routine problems of everyday clinical evaluation, diagnosis, treatment, and consulting.

4. "Ethical Issues" that systematically recount the everyday dilemmas practitioners confront when working with criminal justice agencies.
5. "Case Illustrations" that dramatically highlight how the lives of individuals have been (or could be) impacted by developments in psychology and law.
6. "Websites" that usefully assist readers in their efforts to learn more about forensic psychological themes and issues.
7. "Chapter Reviews" that intentionally draw attention to some of the more interesting and challenging aspects of the chapter's subject matter for the purpose of classroom discussion and review.

Acknowledgements

I am forever grateful to my coauthor Bruce Arrigo for bringing me along on this journey of writing and professional collaboration. He has inspired me to contribute to the field of forensic psychology by way of the written word, as well as my direct practice.

We would like to express gratitude to friends, family, and colleagues, who assisted in bringing this edition to completion. We appreciate the care with which Carolyn Holleyman, Copyeditor, reviewed the text and thanks to both Nikki Levi and Barb Makinster at Elsevier for their guidance, flexibility, and support throughout this project.

I'm particularly indebted to Kelly Warner, Jennifer Russell, Kyle Gullette, Ashley Holland, and Angela Hatcher for contributing as both writers and researchers to this edition. They were instrumental in the successful completion of this book. I also appreciate the contributions of Marcia Williams, Michelle Gorrell, James Peck, and Diana Bailey for their assistance with research and/or editing of text and images.

Many thanks to Jim Smith, Superintendent of North Texas State Hospital, for his commitment to high standards of practice and support of my publication efforts. I am grateful for the ongoing support of Lauren Parsons, my supervisor and an excellent model for what a strong, professional woman should be. I would also like to acknowledge Pat Wilson for her able guidance and useful suggestions throughout this process. Finally, but importantly, I would like to extend my sincere thanks to Deputy John Warner, Sheriff David Duke, Deputy Melvin Joyner, and the men and women of the Wichita County Sheriff's Department for their consultation and service to our community.

PART I

Adult Forensics

Court and the Legal System: Criminal Forensic Evaluation

Key Issues

Competency to Stand Trial
- The rationale behind competence to stand trial
- Competency standards
- Differentiating between competency and other dispositions

Psychological Tests and Forensic Assessment Instruments in the Courtroom
- The nature of psychological evidence in court
- The standards for evidence in court
- Trends of use and support for psychological tests

Mental State at the Time of the Offense: Not Guilty by Reason of Insanity (NGRI) and Guilty But Mentally Ill (GBMI) Verdicts
- Exploration of the "legal insanity" definition
- Analysis of landmark cases such as John Hinckley and Andrea Yates
- A brief discussion of the Guilty But Mentally Ill verdict and how it is applied in the courts

Violence Risk Assessment
- The evaluation of risk assessments
- The information gathered by the evaluator, what that information tells the evaluator, and how that information is used in the criminal justice system

Competency Restoration and Insanity Acquittees: The Maximum-Security Forensic Hospital
- Examine the dichotomous function of the Maximum-Security Forensic Hospital in providing treatment and a secure environment for criminal defendants adjudicated Incompetent to Stand Trial or NGRI for a felony offense
- Analysis of Internal Review Boards in a Maximum-Security Forensic Hospital
- Examination of the role of a forensic psychologist in a Maximum-Security Hospital

Adult Forensic Evaluation

Chapter Outline

Introduction to Forensic Psychology. DOI: 10.1016/B978-0-12-382169-0.00001-3

Overview

The role of psychology in the legal system is both diverse and expansive. In addition, new and/or emerging application areas are being discovered all the time. The adult forensic field is one domain where this particular focus is appreciable, particularly in the realm of forensic evaluation. The adult forensic arena encompasses all facets of criminal adjudication, from the pretrial stage to the post-conviction phase, where psychology's role in the court process is evident, necessary, and, ultimately, impactful. Psychologists are frequently called upon to answer difficult questions at the intersection of law and psychology. Answering psycholegal questions requires specialized training encompassing both psychological and legal principles.

In this chapter, five areas of forensic evaluation or practice are explored. These topics include (1) competency to stand trial; (2) psychological tests and forensic evaluation instruments; (3) mental state at the time of the offense (NGRI & GBMI); (4) violence risk assessment; and (5) competency restoration and insanity acquittees in maximum security forensic hospitals. These areas of practice demonstrate some of the most common and challenging specialized roles that exist for forensic psychologists in the court system.

In order for a person to be prosecuted, the individual must be competent to stand trial. What is the legal standard for competency to stand trial? What role does psychology play in furthering our understanding of competency? How does the "psycholegal" standard relate to one's capacity to stand trial? How do symptoms of mental illness or other impairments impact relevant legal functional capacities? What role does psychiatric diagnosis play in a determination of competency to stand trial? Do forensic tests provide accurate information about the personality, intelligence, ability, and psychopathology of an offender? Are such instruments and their findings legally admissible? What is the reliability and validity of testimony based on forensic assessments in the courtroom? Mentally ill defendants can be found guilty or not guilty. In addition, however, they can be found Not Guilty by Reason of Insanity (NGRI) or Guilty But Mentally Ill (GBMI). How does the legal system understand insanity and mental illness? What are the various tests or standards the court uses for insanity? How do NGRI and GBMI verdicts differ?

One type of forensic evaluation is violence risk assessment. In short, the question posed is whether the defendant presents a risk for future violent behavior. How accurately do risk-assessment instruments predict future dangerousness? Do evaluations tend to be over- or underinclusive and what are the implications for defendants? What is the constitutionality of using risk evaluations in a criminal case? What happens to a mentally ill defendant who has been adjudicated incompetent to stand trial or one who has been found NGRI? What type of setting accommodates their unique treatment needs? How does a maximum-security forensic hospital differ from a general clinical facility? What is the role of the forensic psychologist working in this setting? What ethical dilemmas arise with the provision of psychological services and forensic evaluation services in a secure hospital setting?

The five topics examined in this chapter, though limited in scope, nonetheless explore several critical areas of forensic psychology practice that dramatically reveal the interplay of law and psychology in the adult forensic arena. As the individual sections of this chapter explain, the policy implications for this continued trend necessitate that carefully trained specialists who understand the mechanics of law, the science of psychology, and the complexities of human behavior be called upon to assist the legal system. In part, as is suggested in the pages that follow, more and better research is therefore essential to accomplishing this end. Indeed, this level of training will ready the way for future generations of forensic specialists so that they can confront the challenges that await them in the adult forensic field.

Competency to Stand Trial

Introduction

Questions of competency in the legal system can be raised at any point throughout the proceedings of the criminal process. Such questions may be raised by the prosecution, the defense, or the judge. The most frequent application of the competency rule involves adjudicative competency. In addition, a number of other competency issues may be raised including competency to plead guilty, competency to confess, competency to waive the right to an attorney, competency to testify, and competency to be sentenced and executed. Psychologists answering psycholegal questions for the courts or those concerning psychology and the legal system have an obligation to be well versed in mental health law and the relevant literature.

The idea of competency to stand trial (CST) or competency to proceed has a long history, beginning in English common law. This allowed for an arraignment, trial, judgment, or execution of an alleged capital offender to be stayed if he or she "be(came) absolutely mad" (Hale, 1736, cited in Silten & Tullis, 1977, p. 1053). Mossman, Noffsinger, Ash, Frierson, Gerbasi, *et al.* (2007, p. S4), define competency to stand trial as "the legally determined capacity of a criminal defendant to proceed with criminal adjudication. Jurisdictional statutes and case law set out the criteria for competence to stand trial." It should also be noted that the terms "**adjudicative competency**" can be used interchangeably with CST. The precise meaning of competency assumes different forms, however, depending on the context for which it is addressed. In general, there is longstanding agreement that an individual should not be subjected to the processes of the legal system if he or she is unable to understand the nature and purpose of those proceedings and be able to participate meaningfully in their defense (Shipley, 2013). Further, it is important for defendants to be competent in order to ensure accurate results, maintain the dignity of the legal system, and justify the imposition of punishment (Weiss, 1997; Shipley, in press).

The laws addressing a defendant's competency to proceed to trial are to protect the **due process rights** of that individual (e.g., right to a fair and speedy trial; right to confront one's accusers). Our criminal justice system affords us the opportunity to be physically and mentally present to face our charges and accusers in a court of law. The adversarial nature of this system makes putting an incompetent defendant on trial comparable to a fight "in which the defendant, like a small boy being beaten by a bully, is unable to dodge or return the blows" (*Frith's Case*, 1790, as cited in Golding, 2008, p. 76).

This section is intended to be an introduction to CST and will provide a brief overview of the historical context, relevant case law, key elements of the CST interview, sources of evidence, opinion formulation, and written report. There are many unique and important areas related to CST that are either described briefly or that will be beyond the scope of this chapter (e.g., juvenile fitness to proceed, intellectually disabled defendants). For further analysis of competency to be sentenced and executed, refer to the section entitled "Incarcerating and Executing the Mentally Ill". The implications for forensic psychology, policy analysis and practice are also briefly discussed. High profile cases such as Ted Kaczynski (the Unabomber), Colin Ferguson (Long Island Railroad Massacre), and most recently Brian David Mitchell have created significant debate regarding issues related to CST.

Brian David Mitchell was alleged to have kidnapped Elizabeth Smart from her bed in 2002 and his case was in legal limbo for a number of years due to the conflicting expert opinions about his CST. This case will be used to demonstrate many of the core issues of adjudicative competency. The information in the case vignette is summarized from a number of public records sources, particularly Judge Atherton and Judge Kimball's decisions regarding CST in district and federal court respectively, which included aspects of the competency evaluations completed by the various experts (Shipley, 2013).

Brian David Mitchell

In 2002, Brian David Mitchell (now 56) kidnapped Elizabeth Smart at age 14 by knifepoint from her Salt Lake City home. Mitchell, a drifter and self-described prophet, who called himself Emmanuel, had done some handyman work at the Smarts' home. In March of 2003, nine months later, Brian David Mitchell and his now-estranged wife Wanda Barzee were arrested after they were spotted walking on a suburban street with Elizabeth Smart. At the age of 21, Elizabeth Smart testified in Mitchell's competency hearing in October of 2010, and indicated that she had been held captive in Utah and California after her abduction. Shortly after being kidnapped, Mitchell took her to a wooded area behind her home and performed a mock marriage ceremony with her, then raped her. She said that during the nine months of her captivity, no 24-hour period passed without her being raped by Mitchell. After his arrest, he was referred for a CST evaluation for bizarre beliefs and his unwillingness to discuss issues with his defense counsel.

Mitchell claimed to receive revelations from God that he felt compelled to act upon. However, at his later competency hearings and trial, witnesses, particularly Elizabeth Smart and Wanda Barzee, as well as other lay witnesses, testified that Mitchell's actions were manipulative and his alleged revelations occurred when he needed them to justify his actions for self-gratification. There was significant debate regarding the presence and extent of delusions potentially affecting his CST.

Mitchell was found incompetent to stand trial by Salt Lake City District Judge Judy Atherton on 26 July 2005. Mitchell was committed to a forensic hospital in Salt Lake City. Later, Judge Atherton denied a request to involuntarily medicate Mitchell. On 18 December 2006, he was again found incompetent to stand trial. Mitchell was indicted in federal court in 2008 on charges of kidnapping and unlawful transportation of a minor across state lines. New testimony was included in the federal competency hearing to include expert witness testimony, primarily Dr. Michael Welner, a forensic psychiatrist, as well as numerous lay witnesses, including Elizabeth Smart and individuals who cared for Mitchell in the Utah state hospital. The issue of having lay persons, including the alleged victim, testify at a competency hearing was hotly contested. The federal competency hearing began on October 2009, with Elizabeth Smart giving early testimony, and continued throughout November and December 2009.

In 2008, Dr. Richart DeMier, a court-appointed forensic psychologist from the U.S. Medical Center for Federal Prisoners in Springfield, Missouri, diagnosed Mitchell with schizophrenia, paranoid type. He said he believed Mitchell had a factual understanding of the legal proceedings but did not have a rational understanding and opined that he was incompetent to stand trial. Dr. DeMier indicated that Mitchell was not capable of making rational decisions about his criminal defense due to religious delusions such as the belief that he is going to be miraculously delivered from prison by God in two years' time.

Dr. Michael Welner, a forensic psychiatrist, indicated that Mitchell was not psychotic or delusional. He reported that beliefs that were being interpreted as delusional were not bizarre within the subculture of the Latter Day Saints' movements or Mormonism. His conclusions focused on Mitchell's twisting of religious beliefs to manipulate others. A criticism of Dr. Welner's findings include interpreting all of Mitchell's thoughts and behaviors as a result of an extremely malignant and often prejudicial combination of personality characteristics (i.e., antisocial, narcissistic, psychopathic, and sadistic).

On 1 March 2010, a federal judge ruled that Brian David Mitchell was competent to stand trial, making it possible for him to move forward with facing charges almost eight years after kidnapping Elizabeth Smart. U.S. District Judge Dale Kimball wrote in a 149-page ruling that Brian David Mitchell "does not presently suffer from a mental disease or defect that impedes his rational and factual understanding" of the proceedings against him. The ruling came after a 10-day competency hearing held for Mitchell in 2009, where experts who testified split in their opinions about Mitchell's competency.

In November 2010, Wanda Barzee pleaded guilty in federal court to kidnapping and unlawful transportation of a minor for her part of Elizabeth Smart's abduction. Brian David Mitchell's criminal trial on federal kidnapping charges began on 8 November, 2010, and after only a five-hour deliberation, the jury rejected the insanity plea and returned guilty verdicts on both counts on 10 December 2010.

Literature Review

To allow criminal court hearings or a trial to proceed while the defendant is psychologically incapacitated would prevent that individual from making decisions affecting their liberty. Melton, Petrila, Poythress, and Slobogin (2007) estimated that there are around 60,000 competency cases annually with 20% to 30% of those cases resulting in the defendant being found incompetent to stand trial. Grisso (2003) reports that attorneys have doubts about their clients' competence in approximately 10% to 15% of their criminal cases but raise the issue in only half of those cases. The increasing number of felony arrests results in rising numbers of competency referrals. Thus, the sheer number of individuals facing competency evaluations leaves CST as one of the most significant issues confronted in the fields of law and criminal or forensic psychology. Rogers and Johanson-Love (2009) describe the assessment of CST as "the most common pretrial focal point" in forensic psychology or psychiatry (p. 452).

The legal definition of CST was put forth by the Supreme Court in *Dusky v. United States* (1960). The *Dusky* standard requires the individual to have (1) "sufficient present ability to consult with a lawyer with a reasonable degree of rational understanding" and (2) "rational as well as factual understanding" of the general proceedings (*Dusky v. United States*, 1960, p. 402). However, the *Dusky* court was silent about what conditions may make a person incompetent to stand trial (*Dusky*, 1960). The *Dusky* court's attention was on defendant's "ability," not "willingness." The ambiguity of *Dusky* leaves the very definition and evaluation of CST in many jurisdictions vague and open to interpretation. Some legislatures and courts have attempted to develop guidelines for evaluators, but ample opportunities for variance remain.

Though competency standards vary somewhat from state to state, nearly every state has adopted some variation of *Dusky* (Grisso, 2003). Some courts and legislatures (e.g., Texas) have provided direction to evaluators but there is no uniform way to interpret *Dusky* (Roesch, Zapf, & Golding, 1999). In Texas, defendants are presumed competent and are found competent unless proved incompetent by a preponderance of the evidence. The purpose of raising the issue is to protect the due process rights of the defendant in question. He or she should be capable of being a rational, independent, decision maker and participant in the preparation and execution of their defense.

Clinicians who undertake forensic evaluations without the appropriate training for the specific psycholegal questions they are tasked to answer are working beyond the scope of their competence and could be misleading the **trier of fact**. The evaluation of adjudicative competency involves examining both mental status and psycholegal abilities. In the past 20 years, advances in the understanding of competency and the training of evaluators have been made, but not every state requires specialized forensic training for evaluators (Roesch, Zapf, & Golding, 1999; Mossman *et al.*, 2007).

Forensic experts are frequently called upon to assess for CST and to address the standards set forth in *Dusky v. United States* (Rogers, Grandjean, Tillbrook, Vitacco, & Sewell, 2001). In *U.S. v. Timmins* (9th Circuit, 2002), the court ruled that when offering an opinion about a defendant's competence to stand trial, evaluators must be careful to closely scrutinize the independent decision-making abilities of the defendant. The case demonstrated the necessity of utilizing a mental health expert to assist in a competency determination in part because "a lawyer is not a trained mental health professional capable of accurately assessing the effects of paranoid delusions on the client's mental process" (Osinowo & Pinals, 2003, p. 261). On the other hand, Melton *et al.* (2007) discuss the perils of courts relinquishing their role in making the ultimate decision on competency issues to experts. Specifically, they state, "Presumably, conclusory reliance on diagnosis or unsubstantiated opinion will exacerbate the tendency on the part of the courts and lawyers to avoid investigating the competency issue; this abdication in turn will ill serve defendants, who deserve a legal, not a clinical determination of competency (p. 136)."

Competency versus sanity

Competency to stand trial must be differentiated from the standard of insanity. Competency refers only to a defendant's *present* ability to function. For example, an individual may have been legally insane at the time he or she committed a crime, but perfectly competent to stand trial and be sentenced. Likewise, an individual who was legally sane during the commission of a crime may not be competent several months later when he or she faces criminal trial. Thus, insanity and adjudicative competence are entirely different legal constructs and, though often confused, must be considered as such. A competency evaluation centers on a patient's current mental state and abilities and, as a result, typically does not require as much collateral information as a sanity evaluation, which is retrospective (Mossman *et al.*, 2007). A sanity evaluation requires the evaluator to do their best to recreate or determine from a variety of sources the defendant's state of mind at the time of the crime.

Someone who is found incompetent to stand trial has not been tried, convicted, or sentenced for any wrongdoing, and the court must determine the defendant's competence before proceeding with any elements of this process. He or she is simply treated in an effort to restore his or her ability (if possible) to understand the charges, proceedings, and ability to assist his or her counsel in the trial. Grisso (2003, pp. 74–75) identifies five main stages for determining and disposing of adjudicative competence cases to include: (1) Requesting a competence determination (often called "raising the question"); (2) The competence evaluation stage; (3) The judicial determination of competence or incompetence; and in some cases (4) Disposition and provision of treatment, and (5) Rehearings on competence. If it appears that the defendant's incompetence is amenable to treatment, admission to a forensic treatment facility for restoration of trial competency is the most common disposition (Grisso, 2003). Follow-up competency evaluations by appropriately trained mental health professionals at the admitting facility will be required periodically to ascertain whether or not the defendant has improved amply to merit a return to court for another competency hearing.

Authors recommend that sanity and competency be conducted separately and that sanity evaluations are not conducted on incompetent defendants (Roesch, Zapf, & Golding, 1999; Melton *et al.*, 2007; Mossman *et al.*, 2007). Some state laws prohibit performing a sanity evaluation on a defendant who has been evaluated and recommended to be incompetent to stand trial; for example, the Texas Code of Criminal Procedure Article 46B.025 addressing competency evaluations states: "(c) An expert's report may not state the expert's opinion on the defendant's sanity at the time of the alleged offense, if in the opinion of the expert the defendant is incompetent to proceed." If a defendant is thought to be incompetent or incapable of rationally participating in their defense or legal proceedings, moving forward with an evaluation that could likely impact the ultimate disposition of their case is at the least ill advised.

Raising the question

Raising the issue of competency to proceed to trial creates an opportunity for a delay in the process (Roesch, Zapf, & Golding, 1999). In *Pate v. Robinson* (1966, p. 385), the United States Supreme Court ruled that a suitable hearing on CST must be held whenever there is a "bona fide doubt" about a defendant's competency. This is a low threshold and suggests that in order to protect all defendants' rights to a fair trial, many competent defendants may have to go through an evaluation to prevent the prosecution of a defendant who is incompetent to stand trial (Mossman *et al.*, 2007). When issues are raised by any party regarding CST, almost invariably the motions are granted by the courts, primarily to avoid a due process violation.

The role of mental illness

The concept of CST concerns not only the presence of mental illness, but also centrally the individual's ability to function as a defendant in light of the effects of his or her mental illness. A psychiatric diagnosis does not equal incompetence, which is a legal construct. Slovenko (2002, p. 421) cautions that psychiatric diagnosis may "play a role in the legal process but it is not always a *sine qua non* in the resolution of a legal matter." The primary concern, then, is whether the mentally ill defendant is capable of fulfilling his or her role as a defendant and to what extent their legal functional capacities are impaired. The knowledge and ability to do those things required by the court before and during the trial process are of primary importance (Grisso 2003; Melton *et al.*, 2007; Wolber, 2008).

For example, a diagnosis or symptoms of psychosis do not necessarily mean that a defendant is incompetent. It would be critical to ascertain the nature of the symptoms and if they would impact the individual's capacities such as being able to rationally understand their charges, work with their attorney, or prepare a defense. Do symptoms of psychosis (e.g., auditory hallucinations, delusions) intermingle with issues related to their case and the court system? For example, if a defendant experiences delusions that include the belief that his attorney is part of a government conspiracy to incarcerate him in order to steal all of his inventions, property, and money, he is unlikely to be able to rationally work with that attorney in preparing a defense (Shipley, 2013). The evaluator must consider if inappropriate behavior is volitional or driven by mental illness. The specific demands and circumstances of each individual case must be considered by the evaluator when formulating their opinion on CST.

Similarly intellectual and developmental disabilities do not necessarily mean that person is incompetent to stand trial. *Dusky* does not require that a mental disorder be present in order to find a defendant incompetent, but some state legislatures have done so. Texas statute indicates the evaluator must consider "whether the defendant has a diagnosable mental illness or is a person with mental retardation" and "the impact of the mental illness or mental retardation, if existent, on the defendant's capacity to engage with counsel in a reasonable and rational manner (Art. 46B.024)." *Godinez v. Moran* (1993) established that the States may adopt criteria for competence that are more structured than *Dusky*. It also interpreted *Dusky* as requiring a defendant to have decision-making capacities related to CST (e.g., whether or not to testify, what type of defense to put forward, etc.). This certainly impacts the types of questions forensic evaluators need to ask to form an opinion regarding CST.

Examples of how the three prongs of *Dusky* are examined include: (1) **Factual Understanding** – Conditions such as brain damage, dementia, intellectual disabilities, severe depression, and thought disorders are the most likely to potentially impact this area (Mossman *et al.*, 2007).

Asking follow up questions is important to ensure that a defendant is not just parroting answers without a conceptual understanding. (2) **Rational Understanding** — The evaluator has to determine whether symptoms impact the reality-based understanding of their legal situation, perceptions and decisions regarding it, as well as their logical participation in that process (e.g., a delusion that one is married to someone famous may not impact their rational competence; whereas, a delusion that one is the President of the United States and believes he can issue his own pardon and not face trial would). (3) **Ability to Assist Counsel** — Addresses the defendant's ability versus willingness to assist their counsel or the average attorney. A choice to not participate does not render one incompetent. The defendant needs to be capable of providing rational information to the attorney regarding defense strategy, cross-examining witnesses, considering the attorney's advice, considering plea options in consultation with their attorney, and the like. Rogers and Shuman (2005, p. 154) note that a number of defendants "make poor, emotionally based decisions that do not accurately capture the potential risks and benefits," but their faculties are not compromised by mental disorders.

In *Drope v. Missouri* (1975, p. 171), the Supreme Court enhanced the capacity to consult with one's attorney requirement in *Dusky*, stating that a defendant must be able to "assist in preparing his defense." Moreover, this case indicated that "a trial must always be alert to circumstances suggesting a change that would render the accused unable to meet the standards of competency to stand trial." In the U.S., the Sixth Amendment established a defendant's right to be represented by attorneys. However, U.S. law does not require criminal defendants to use lawyers in criminal proceedings (Mossman *et al.*, 2007). In *Faretta v. California* (1975), the Supreme Court held that the right to self-representation is implicit in the structure of the Sixth Amendment. A knowing and intelligent decision to represent oneself is required and the defendant must be competent to waive the right to counsel. However, legal knowledge is not essential and those proceeding pro se are commonly referred to as having "a fool for a client." A number of courts have held that active mental illness should not, alone, prevent someone from proceeding pro se. Nonetheless, courts have a responsibility to preserve the integrity of judicial process. In *Indiana v. Edwards*, 554 U.S. 164 (2008), the Supreme Court of the United States ruled that the standard for competency to stand trial was not connected to the standard for competency to represent oneself. The Court held that a criminal defendant who is competent to stand trial may also be found incompetent to represent himself during the same trial.

Conducting the CST evaluation

Statutes or case law provide that information gleaned during a competency evaluation cannot be used in the guilt/innocence phase of a criminal trial unless a defendant places their mental state into evidence either at trial (e.g., sanity defense) or sentencing (*Estelle v. Smith*, 1981; Golding & Roesch, 1988; Mossman *et al.*, 2007). Whether a court can convict a defendant based on information obtained in a competency evaluation became the subject of *Estelle v. Smith* (1981) and *Buchanan v. Kentucky* (1987). In *Estelle v. Smith*, the defendant had been convicted of murder and then faced sentencing before the jury that found him guilty. Based on a pretrial competency evaluation, the competency evaluator testified that Smith lacked remorse, was untreatable, and was at very high risk of committing future acts of violence, and the jury subsequently imposed the death penalty. Ultimately, a federal district court vacated the death sentence, after determining that the trial court made a constitutional error in allowing the psychiatrist's testimony based on the pretrial competency evaluation at the penalty phase. The Supreme Court upheld the finding. In *Buchanan v. Kentucky*, the Supreme Court expressly limited the protections described above to situations in which the defendant did not initiate the mental health evaluation or attempt to introduce psychological evidence at trial. When the defense raises the issue, the prosecution can use this psychological evidence in rebuttal.

The forensic evaluator will need to review relevant history, conduct a mental status examination, and most importantly evaluate competence-related capacities. The relevant police reports should be thoroughly reviewed prior to beginning the interview, and prior competency evaluations (if applicable) to determine what led to the initial finding of incompetency. At the start of a CST interview, the evaluator should provide a **forensic warning** or inform the defendant of the purpose and potential consequences of evaluation, who will get a copy of the report, and the overall **limits to confidentiality** (e.g., no doctor-patient confidentiality; may have to testify; information cannot be used in guilt/innocence phase except under conditions described above) (Shipley, 2013). The defendant's understanding of the nature and consequences of the evaluation should be assessed; for example, having him or her paraphrase the information provided to them. The evaluator should be familiar with the legal literature related to CST to ensure that the competency evaluation and the reports prepared for court be in accord with both the spirit and the letter of the law (Shipley, 2013; Melton *et al.*, 2007; Mossman *et al.*, 2007; Grisso, 2003).

When evaluating someone's CST, you are assessing their abilities related to their specific charge or each of their multiple charges. A criminal defendant with conspiracy to commit capital murder charges will have to function within a far more complex legal arena than the defendant with a misdemeanor trespassing charge. A lack of information about the charges does not equal incompetence. When a defendant claims no knowledge of the charges or other elements of court facts or procedures, providing brief tutorials about these concepts is not only allowed, but expected to determine if the defendant can benefit from instruction and demonstrate their ability to work appropriately with that information. Moreover, a number of legal findings have held that amnesia does not equal incompetence (e.g., *Ritchie v. Indiana*, 1984; *Wilson v. United States*, 1968; *Missouri v. Davis*, 1983; *Montana v. Austed*, 1982; *Morrow v. Maryland*, 1982). These decisions support the view that evaluators cannot reach a finding of incompetency based upon mental state alone, independent of the facts of the legal case (Mossman *et al.*, 2007).

The ultimate decision on CST belongs to the court, either a judge or jury depending upon the jurisdiction. Evaluators inform the court by offering for **adjudication** an opinion about whether or not the defendant is CST. More often than not, the court concurs with the evaluator. Once found incompetent, the trial is postponed or the charges are dismissed, usually without prejudice and a defendant's right to refuse treatment is more restricted (Roesch, Zapf, & Golding, 1999; Mossman *et al.*, 2007).

Psychological tests and competency evaluations

In a competency evaluation, the evaluator must consider if formal psychological testing is needed. A limited number of forensic assessment tools have been developed specifically for CST evaluations. However, there are criticisms that the reliability and validity of instruments have not been sufficiently tested and can't be used with confidence in the courtroom (Weiner, 2003). See the subsection on "Psychological Tests and Forensic Assessment Instruments in the Courtroom" for specific information on this issue, particularly regarding instruments designed for competency evaluations. **Malingering** will be discussed in the "Practice Update" section at the end of this chapter.

The written report

Because competency evaluations typically do not result in courtroom testimony, a written report usually is the evaluator's primary work product (Mossman *et al.*, 2007). The report's primary audience is made up of attorneys and judges rather than mental health professionals so it is important to use jargon-free language. Offer your opinion and carefully explain the reasoning process behind the opinion. Reports should be free of gratuitous comments about defendants' behavior, need for incarceration, violence risk, or lack of remorse (Mossman *et al.*, 2007).

CST evaluations become court documents and unnecessary information should be excluded from the report. According to Rogers and Shuman (2005, p. 168):

> *Psychosocial history is, at best, only peripheral to the current...assessment of competency to stand trial... Past information may be irrelevant to the referral issue and represent an ethical violation in its unnecessary violation of privacy.*

If there is medical or other personal information that is not directly relevant to adjudicative competency, do not include it (e.g., HIV status). The report should be a stand-alone document, which provides or reproduces the data needed to support the opinions that the evaluator expresses. In a quality report, the psychological data should be linked to the legal issue with a clearly articulated chain of reasoning.

Restoration of trial competency

How long can an incompetent individual be held in a psychiatric facility? Prior to *Jackson v. Indiana* (1972), it was not uncommon for incompetent defendants to be confined to psychiatric facilities for unlimited periods of time. At times, this period exceeded the sentence the individual would have faced if tried and convicted. Thus, it was not uncommon for the prosecution to raise questions concerning competency to essentially sentence an individual without the time and effort of a trial (Wrightsman, Nietzel, & Fortune, 1994). In *Jackson v. Indiana* (1972), the Supreme Court held that confinement indefinitely based upon one's incompetency to stand trial created a more stringent standard for release than those committed under civil statutes, constituting a violation of the Fourteenth Amendment's Equal Protection Clause and the right to due process. The *Jackson* decision indicated that if treatment could not restore a defendant to competence, the state must either initiate civil commitment proceedings or release the defendant. The proposed limits were defined as "…a reasonable period of time necessary to determine whether there is a substantial probability that [the defendant] will attain the capacity [competence] in the foreseeable future" (*Jackson v. Indiana*, 1972, pp. 737–738). The *Jackson* decision, however, was the first Supreme Court case to place legal limits, though imprecise and not well defined, on the commitment of such individuals. According to the *Jackson* decision, forensic evaluators must address in their reports whether or not those individuals determined to be IST have a substantial probability of regaining competency through treatment in the foreseeable future (Hubbard, Zapf, & Ronan, 2003). Except for an irreversible condition (e.g., a severe head injury) or a mental disorder that has proven treatment resistant, most defendants are restorable (Melton *et al.*, 2007). More recently, the *Indiana v. Davis* State Supreme Court decision has given some precedence for the dismissal of charges pending against those who have been found unrestorable and who have spent more time committed in a mental health facility than they would have been confined had they been found guilty (*Indiana v.* Davis, 2008*)*.

Since psychosis is the very frequent cause of impairments resulting in adjudicative incompetency, the need for psychotropic medications in their treatment for restoration is common. In *Sell v. US* (2003) the Supreme Court limited the right of a lower court to order involuntary psychiatric medication with the singular purpose of restoring a criminal defendant who is incompetent to trial competency. Specifically, the court held that medication is medically appropriate only when it is necessary and likely to restore the defendant to competency, unlikely to have side-effects that interfere with the defendant's ability to assist counsel in conducting a defense, and less intrusive treatments are unlikely to achieve substantially the same results. In 2005, after being found incompetent to stand trial in Utah District Court and committed to a forensic hospital, Judge Atherton denied a request to involuntarily medicate Brian David Mitchell.

Forensic Psychology and Policy Implications

The implications of adjudicative competency and developments for forensic clinicians are profound. Research in the area has shown that the expert opinions of psychologists or psychiatrists on the issue of competency are highly valued. It is uncommon for a judge to disagree with a mental health professional's recommendation (Nicholson & Kugler, 1991). Often a full competency hearing is not necessary if all parties involved including the defense attorney, prosecuting attorney, and the judge stipulate that they are in agreement regarding the determination of the defendant's competence or incompetence, and if they agree after taking into consideration the forensic evaluation results (Grisso, 2003). Thus, the mental health expert has the potential to significantly influence the future of the defendant being examined for CST. Involuntary medication to restore competency has significant policy implications. Often, an individual's competency may be restored following the administration of psychotropic medications. Questions then arise as to whether there is a justified basis for forcing medications on defendants in an effort to restore competency. Bullock (2002) explains that the defendant's interest in wanting to refuse medication is in conflict with the government's interest in obtaining an adjudication of the defendant's culpability in a criminal matter.

Regarding restoration to trial competency, evaluators should exercise caution in providing feedback to courts concerning the likely success of competency restoration. Evaluators must consider restoration issues: requirements for inpatient versus outpatient, the role of medications in competency restoration, and the likelihood to restore in the foreseeable future. Mossman *et al.* (2007) suggests the evaluator consider the following factors when speaking to restorability: (1) Whether the ICST results from a treatable disorder or deficit as opposed to a static and relatively irreversible (or even degenerative) condition such as dementia; (2) a defendant's previous psychiatric treatment and responses to treatment; and (3) a defendant's particular symptoms and current scientific knowledge about how well those symptoms respond to treatment. The two most common causes of incompetency to stand trial are psychosis and intellectual or developmental disabilities (Grisso, 2003; Mossman *et al.*, 2007).

Suggestions for Future Research

Perhaps the most controversial issue with regard to competency issues is exactly what constitutes a competent individual. Though cases such as *Dusky v. United States* (1960) shed light on the question, no distinct and specific conclusion has been reached by any court of law. This topic continues to receive substantial attention in both legal and social science literature. Given the inherent difference between individuals and the unique requirements of each legal situation, evaluators must consider these nuances alongside a somewhat ambiguous legal standard. Hubbard *et al.* (2003) express the need for continued research on characteristics of defendants not restorable to competency and those who are in order to improve our ability to accurately predict and classify them.

Another area in need of future consideration concerns involuntary confinement of incompetent individuals. Several proposals have been made to place limitations on the conditions under which this commitment should occur. Further, though the Court's decision in *Jackson v. Indiana* (1972) forbade unlimited confinement, it failed to define "reasonable period of time" and "substantial probability" (pp. 737–738). Thus, the Court has assumed some responsibility for the treatment of incompetent defendants. It has not, however, adequately resolved the issues with consideration of the best interest of the individual and the State (Bardwell & Arrigo, 2002). According to Pinals (2005, p.104), "Overall, competency restoration literature supports that between 80–90% of all defendants with mental illness will be able to be restored to competence, and generally this restoration has been achieved in a period of less than six months." Continued research is needed on the issue of effectiveness of restoration interventions or the ability of examiners to predict accurately restorability with different types of defendants.

Psychological Tests and Forensic Assessment Instruments in the Courtroom

Introduction

Psychological assessment is the use of standardized measures to evaluate the abilities, behaviors, and personal qualities of people (Gerrig & Zimbardo, 2002). Typically, psychological tests attempt to shed light on an individual's intelligence, personality, psychopathology, or ability. Traditionally, these tests were formed on clinical or psychiatric populations and were used primarily for diagnosis and treatment. However, with the increasing presence of forensic psychologists in the courtroom, these tests are being used to help determine legal questions or legal constructs. As a result, there is a growing debate over the utility of these tests in the courtroom. Currently, a limited number of **forensic assessment tools** have been developed specifically for forensic evaluations such as competency to stand trial or criminal responsibility (insanity). Critics argue that the reliability and validity of these instruments have not been sufficiently tested, indicating that future research is needed before these instruments can be used with confidence (Nussbaum, Hancock, Turner, Arrowood, & Melodick, 2008; Weiner, 2003; Borum & Grisso, 1995; Zapf, Green, & Rosenfeld, 2011).

According to Wakefield and Underwager (1993), the consequences of a forensic evaluation regarding criminal issues, such as competency to execute, or civil issues, such as child custody, are potentially immediate and severe. Additionally, Weiner (2003) warns that psychological assessment data are much more dependable for describing an individual's current characteristics or functioning, rather than predicting how they might behave, or speculating on what they have done, or been like, in the past. These researchers argue that in a clinical setting if a test is misused or if an inaccurate interpretation of a test is made, the most likely result is a correctable misdiagnosis or an ineffective treatment plan. The controversy over the careful selection and interpretation of assessment tools, as well as their legal limits, is at the forefront of the debate over the role of forensic psychologists in the courtroom. The following case illustration demonstrates the impact of psychological tests and the responsibility held by forensic psychologists in their administration and interpretation.

A father in a divorce and custody dispute was accused of tying up his 3-year-old son with a bicycle chain and then sexually abusing him. Both parents were evaluated by a psychologist. The father was tested and interviewed by the psychologist, who left the office, leaving him to finish his drawings. He took them home, finished them with the use of drafting instruments, and brought them to her office the next day.

The psychologist stated that the response style to the projective drawings suggested "obsessive—compulsive tendencies, high defensiveness and an intense need to control... [and] his rigidly defensive posture does not adequately bind the underlying anxiety and trepidation of doing poorly" (Wakefield & Underwager, 1993, p. 59). However, his Bender Visual Motor Gestalt Test results were completely normal. His House-Tree-Person (HTP) drawings were careful and detailed. He clearly attempted to do as good a job as possible. Given that his understanding was that these drawings would be interpreted to indicate whether he was an abuser, his choice to carefully complete them at home demonstrates an understandable effort to comply with the instructions and do the best job he could. None of this was noted in the report. There are no scientific data to support the interpretive comment quoted above. It is meaningless jargon with no connection to an empirical base.

Literature Review

Cases like the one presented by Wakefield and Underwager (1993) illustrate the potential for misuse or misinterpretation of psychological tests or other forensic assessment tools. This case illustration demonstrates the great care forensic psychologists must take in choosing, interpreting, and corroborating psychological tests with other relevant archival or **third-party information** (information gained from a party other than the original source). Forensic psychologists must address the issue of which assessment tools are appropriate in forensic settings. Conclusions reached by forensic psychologists can be challenged during cross-examination and are subject to close scrutiny in the legal arena (Hilsenroth & Stricker, 2004; Knapp & VandeCreek, 2001; Wakefield & Underwager, 1993). Hilsenroth and Stricker (2004) caution that for any instrument used in a forensic evaluation, examiners should be prepared to provide information on not only **reliability** (the stability or consistency of scores) and **validity** (the degree to which a test measures what it is intended to), but also **incremental validity** (the degree to which a measure explains or predicts a phenomenon of interest), **normative data** (the normal or average score for any given survey question across various levels of performance), ethnic diversity issues, specific applications, patterns of use, and clinical as well as forensic utility. They go on to explain that the quality of forensic evaluations, which include psychological tests, must meet the highest standard of practice and be able to withstand careful scrutiny in the adversarial system, particularly in the criminal courtroom. Therefore the primary focus of forensic assessment is on accuracy as opposed to a "therapeutic" focus in clinical settings (Hilsenroth & Stricker, 2004; Heilbrun, 1992; Acklin, 2002; Gacono, 2002). Forensic assessments are significantly different from traditional clinical assessments in terms of the psycholegal question, the goals, scope, limits of confidentiality, the role of the examiner, and the nature of the relationship with the examinee (Nies, 2005; Nicholson & Norwood, 2000; Melton Petrila, Poythress, & Slobogin, 2007).

Forensic assessments must also adhere to legal and ethical parameters of the referral question, and results and determinations must be communicated in a manner that is understandable to nonmental health professionals. Traditional psychological tests have seen widespread use in forensic contexts. However, their utility is being challenged. Currently, specialized forensic assessment instruments (FAIs) are being developed to address specific legal questions. The rigor by which these instruments have been validated has also come under fire. Forensic psychologists are questioning how to more effectively answer legal referral questions with the available assessment tools.

According to Heilbrun (1992), "the primary legal criterion for the admissibility of psychological testing is relevance to the immediate legal issue or to some underlying psychological construct" (p. 257; see also Faigman & Monahan, 2009). He states that the courts typically will not limit the use of psychological tests or forensic instruments if their relevance to the legal standard is shown. Heilbrun explains that relevancy can be demonstrated either by directly measuring a legal construct included in the forensic referral question or by measuring a psychological construct that is considered to make up part of a legal standard. For example, intelligence testing could be used to measure an individual's ability to understand the charges against him or her. He concludes that this relationship could be demonstrated through a written report or testimony (Heilbrun, 1992).

The broad range of legal issues requiring the assessment of a forensic psychologist is subject to a standard that is determined from either statutes or case law. Federal Rules of Evidence,

Rule 702 (Melton *et al.*, 2007) considers the admissibility of expert opinions, stating that the primary criterion is whether the opinion will assist the **factfinder** (judge or jury). Rule 703 indicates that evidence presented by mental health professionals in the legal setting must be reasonably relied upon by professionals in the field (Melton *et al.*, 2007; Faigman & Monahan, 2009).

In the past, the majority of courts required that evidence follow the Frye test or that the evidence be based on procedures that have achieved "general acceptance" within that particular profession (*Frye v. United States*, 1923, p. 1013). Critics charge that under the Frye test evidence that is novel yet reliable is excluded while unreliable evidence that has gained general acceptance is allowed (Faigman & Monahan, 2009; Melton *et al.*, 2007; Martin, Allan, & Allan, 2001). In 1993, the Supreme Court's decision in *Daubert v. Merrell* shifted the standard for the admissibility of evidence to focus on scientific validity, methodology, and the application of the expert opinion to the facts at issue.

Rogers and Johansson-Love (2009, p. 451) provide four guidelines under the *Daubert* test for evidence admissibility that can be summarized as follows: (1) Whether a theory or technique is scientific knowledge that will assist the **trier of fact** (a person, or group of persons who determines facts in a legal proceeding) will be whether it can be (and has been) tested; (2) whether the theory or technique has been subjected to peer review and publication; (3) in the case of a particular scientific technique, the court ordinarily should consider the known or potential rate of error; and (4) finally, "general acceptance" can have a bearing on the inquiry. Melton and his colleagues (2007) warn that if *Daubert v. Merrell* (1993) were strictly followed, a considerable amount of clinical testimony would not meet this threshold. They maintain that it would prevent the use of novel ways of thinking about human behavior that have relevance to the legal proceeding.

The Supreme Court has upheld rulings that a defendant can present "less reliable" evidence banned by a state statute (*Chambers v. Mississippi*, 1973; *Rock v. Arkansas*, 1987). The Court explained that a defendant's Fourteenth Amendment right to present evidence is paramount to the state's ability to ban such evidence. Heilbrun (1992) recognizes the potential for "…a similar approach to the admissibility of expert mental health testimony based on psychological testing, even if they were inclined to exclude some tests on the grounds of limited psychometric rigor" (p. 261).

Psychological tests and competency evaluations

An evaluator must consider if there is a need for formal psychological testing. What question needs to be answered? Can the capacities be directly observed? More information is not always better if the information is not valid for the issue at hand. The forensic evaluator has to consider whether or not the norms and psychometric properties are a good fit. A wrongly used psychological test or forensic assessment tool can lead to incorrect conclusions (Shipley, 2013).

A limited number of forensic assessment tools have been developed specifically for CST evaluations. However, there are criticisms that the reliability and validity of instruments have not been sufficiently tested and can't be used with confidence in the courtroom (Weiner, 2003). These instruments typically do not delve into the case specific issues that are often at the core of a defendant's lack of rational competency. When considering psychological testing in general, Skeem, Golding, Cohn, and Berge (1998) found that 70% of the relevant CST evaluations in their study did not articulate any relationship between assessment data and CST. The remaining 30% only provided ambiguous claims related to symptoms identified by testing and broad impairment in CST. Results of intelligence tests were only sometimes correlated to functional capacities related to competency. Projective, objective, and neuro-psychological test data were almost rarely or never associated with CST (Skeem *et al.*, 1998).

Administration of conventional psychological tests (e.g., MMPI-2) is unlikely to be a relevant or cost-efficient means of gathering information in most competency cases (Melton *et al.*, 2007); however, in a limited range of cases, when specific issues need explored such as malingering, testing may be useful (e.g., TOMM, SIRS, VIP, etc.). Additionally, if incompetency is suspected based on interview data related to potential cognitive/intellectual deficits, cognitive testing may be useful to corroborate the degree of intellectual disabilities or to assess the ability to consider alternatives and process information in a structured situation (Melton *et al.*, 2007).

Many forensic evaluators find that a thorough competency interview carefully structured around the psycholegal question, the defendant's relevant factual and rational understanding, as well as the necessary functional capacities, most closely approximates the attorney–client interaction. This well-structured, case specific competency interview can provide invaluable information about ability to participate in a meaningful interchange with their attorney. The evaluator must provide the linkage between the information or evidence described and the opinion on adjudicative competence, and, if relevant, describing any steps to be taken to compensate for difficulties a defendant may have.

Overall, research indicates use of standard forensic assessment instruments are, at best, screening instruments. The studies endorsing the use of these tools caution evaluators to understand the instrument's limitations. The assessment of CST should go beyond the data that can be gathered by these tools. The following provides a brief overview of two of the second-generation measures that use relatively standardized interview formats to examine *Dusky* related abilities (Melton *et al.*, 2007).

The *MacArthur Competence Assessment Tool – Criminal Adjudication* (Mac-CAT-CA) was a product of the MacArthur Adjudicative Competence Project (Poythress, Nicholson, Otto *et al.*, 1999). It is a 22-item test that takes 30 to 45 minutes to administer and it includes a hypothetical case and questions surrounding it. Moreover, it addresses a defendant's beliefs about his or her own case in one section of the test. Its validity, reliability, and ease of administration are good compared to other measures of adjudicative competence (Otto, Poythress, Nicholson *et al.*, 1998). Strengths include derivation from psycholegal theory of competence, assessment of multiple psycholegal abilities, assessment of the capacity to assimilate new information, standardized administration, objective criterion-referenced scoring, and availability of normed data for the purpose of comparison (Mossman *et al.*, 2007). Weaknesses include its focus on understanding factual rather than rational aspects; limited focus on the complexity of the defendant's case; a lack of formally addressing potential malingering and claims of amnesia, and those with severe thought disorders, major concentration problems, or serious memory impairment likely will be unable to complete an assessment with the instrument (Mossman *et al.*, 2007).

The *Evaluation of Competency to Stand Trial-Revised* (ECST-R) is a more recently developed tool by Rogers, Tillbrook, and Sewell (2004). It is a semi-structured interview with 46 items total. There are 18 items and three scales that speak to factual and rational understanding of criminal proceedings and consulting with counsel. There are also five scales for consideration of atypical presentation or feigning, considering rare symptoms and symptom severity (Rogers & Johansson-Love, 2009). Rogers and Johansson-Love (2009) describe the ECST-R's strong psychometric properties as compared to the Mac-CAT-CA. It should be noted that likely due to the relative newness of this instrument, most of the peer-reviewed articles available that examine the ECST-R are authored by one or more of its designers. Mossman *et al.* (2007, p. S43) note that evaluators "…should not overvalue the information that they provide…should interpret results of testing in light of all other data obtained from clinical interviews and collateral sources." Regarding forensic assessment tools, Golding (2008, p. 76) indicates "competency cannot be reduced to a precise set of operational definitions (like a score of such-and-such on a test, or the presence of a given symptom or diagnosis), but is by its nature open-textured…this is one of the main reasons why various proposals to operationalize competency, by means of nomothetic tests, often produce unsatisfactory or incomplete results."

According to Zapf, Green, and Rosenfeld (2011) three FAIs have been found to be acceptably reliable in evaluating competency to stand trial; the MacArthur Competency Assessment Test-Criminal Adjudication (MacCat-CA), the Evaluation of Competency to Stand Trial-Revised (ECST-R), and the Fitness Interview Test-Revised (FIT-R). The FIT-R is a semistructured interview intended screen for competency-related difficulties within the Canadian judicial context and does so using three sections; factual knowledge of criminal proceedings, appreciation of personal involvement and importance of consequences, and capacity to communicate with counsel and participate in defense (Nussbaum, Hancock, Turner, Arrowood, & Melodick, 2008).

Sanity evaluations

Researchers note that in many cases mental health professionals have the awkward task of trying to assess mental state at the time of the alleged offense (i.e., legal sanity) with instruments that assess current mental functioning (Weiner, 2003; Lanyon, 1986). These types of evaluations are done retrospectively and require other sources of data including police reports, medical or mental health records, psychosocial history from friends and family, and the like (Reid, 2006; Melton *et al.*, 2007; Weiner, 2003; Nicholson & Norwood, 2001; Heilbrun, 1992). Zapf, Green, and Rosenfeld (2011) point out criminal responsibility evaluations remain largely unstructured. They point out that the Rogers Criminal Responsibility Assessment Scales (R-CRAS) remains the only published measure intended to aid in these evaluations despite a lack of sufficient research support. Criminal responsibility evaluations are examining a defendant's mental state at the time of the offense. Standard psychological tests (e.g., MMPI-2, PAI, or MCMI-III) are examining some aspect of the individual's current functioning; therefore, these instruments would only be peripherally related to the psychological question of "sanity" at best.

According to Bartram and Coyne (1998), frequent misuse of standard psychological tests include deficits in psychometric knowledge, inappropriate use of norms, not maintaining the integrity of test results, not providing a comprehensive assessment, improper test use, and accuracy of scoring. In a survey of 152 doctoral level members of the American Psychology-Law Society (AP-LS) and the American Academy of Forensic Psychology (AAFP) Archer, Buffington-Vollum, Stredny, and Handel (2006) found that multiscale inventories such as the MMPI-2, PAI, or MCMI were the most commonly used (86% of sample participants) instruments in the forensic evaluation of adults. The Minnesota Multiphasic Personality Inventory-Second Edition (MMPI-2), Personality Assessment Inventory (PAI), and Millon

Clinical Multiaxial Inventory (MCMI) are instruments intended to measure psychopathology and personality characteristics. Intellectual or achievement tests such as the Wechlser Intelligence scales followed with 82.2% of participants indicating that they had used them. In assessing for the presence of malingering, 72% of participants reported using specialized tests, most commonly the Structured Interview of Reported Symptoms (SIRS) and the Test of Memory Malingering (TOMM); both of these tests are intended to detect feigned pathology in patients. In violence risk assessment evaluations, 64% of participants reported using instruments such as the Psychopathy Checklist-Revised (i.e., PCL, PCL-R); a measure of psychopathy (characterized by inability to form normal relationships, a lack of empathy, deception, and antisocial behavior). In the study sample, 57% of participants reported using specific instruments in the evaluation of competency or sanity with the MacArthur Competence Assessment Tool (MacCAT) being the most commonly used.

Melton *et al.* (2007) suggest there are limitations regarding traditional clinical methods in gaining accurate information from forensic populations. These researchers note the potential for malingering, defensiveness, and even normal forgetfulness. According to Melton *et al.* (2007), these instruments are more focused to specific legal criteria and have been tested on relevant legal populations. However, these researchers acknowledge that many of these instruments are conceptually flawed and lack empirical research. Forensic psychologists are left to determine the methodology of the various psychological tests and forensic assessment instruments available to them as well as their relevance to the legal question.

Forensic Psychology and Policy Implications

Research indicates that traditional psychological tests will continue to be used in forensic assessments. However, as more instruments are developed to address specific legal questions, their role will diminish. Lanyon (1986) points out that years ago traditional psychological instruments were considered adequate to answer all questions in the realm of neuropsychology, specifically, the presence or absence of organicity. He suggested that the area of forensic psychology would also develop its own psychometric instruments specific to the psycholegal question at hand. While such instruments have been developed during the past 25 to 30 years, advancement of forensic assessment instruments is needed to increase their utility. Future research is needed to further support the validity and reliability of these instruments.

Some researchers are calling for "…the development of an independent set of standards for the selection, administration, and interpretation of psychological testing in forensic contexts" (Heilbrun, 1992, p. 269). Given the frequency and nature of test misuse by evaluators, this is a justifiable proposition. In addition to adopting a set of standards regarding testing, increased or improved training in test usage is recommended. The case illustration of the father who is assumed to have sexually abused his child due to his "response style to the projective drawings" demonstrates the need for more accuracy in test administration and interpretation as well as corroborating data if possible in forensic contexts (Wakefield & Underwager, 1993, p. 57). The consequences of a custody dispute as well as accusations of sexual abuse could result in this father's loss of his child and possible incarceration. Contemporary instruments designed specifically for use in custody determinations also require much more research, particularly on their validity (Emery, Otto, & O'Donohue, 2005; Otto, Edens, & Barcus, 2000).

Forensic psychologists are continually trying to improve their effectiveness in the legal arena. Unfortunately, many criticisms have been leveled regarding the role of psychologists in the courtroom by legal professionals. The subjective and unreliable nature of the instruments used for assessment is a primary criticism. Techniques by which forensic psychologists can be more effective, persuasive, and credible in legal proceedings are being developed and put into practice.

Suggestions for Future Research

Clearly, the further development of methodologically sound forensic assessment instruments is needed. Those FAIs in current use are in need of additional research to determine their validity and reliability, especially when used with offenders of different cultural backgrounds. Research is also necessary to determine if these instruments produce any positive trends when used in forensic evaluations. In general, more empirical data are called for on the uses of psychological tests in forensic evaluations; which are more effective and with which type of evaluation? Additional research is needed to demonstrate if there is any substantial utility in using a measure of current functioning to speak to a mental state or behavior in the past or to predict characteristics or behavior in the future. The many differences between the fields of psychology and law, as well as expanded training opportunities, should be continually explored to better prepare forensic psychologists for entry into legal settings.

Mental State at the Time of the Offense: Not Guilty by Reason of Insanity and Guilty But Mentally Ill Verdicts

Introduction

The insanity defense has long been a debated issue within psychology, the legal system, and society in general. Melton, Petrila, Poythress, and Slobogin, (2007) have indicated the **Not Guilty by Reason of Insanity (NGRI)** or insanity defense is "a controversial and difficult issue in criminal law" (p. 4). While society and the law have historically been inclined to treat rather than punish mentally ill offenders, there are nevertheless a plethora of arguments that encourage an alteration in the legal system's present philosophy toward insanity and crime.

Such strong opposition to the defense of insanity is founded upon several notable cases in which societal perception was that justice was not done. The current more stringent standard of legal insanity has recently left many mental health professionals feeling that justice was also not done when Andrea Yates was found guilty and sentenced to prison after her first trial, rather than being found NGRI and placed in a maximum-security forensic hospital. Consider the following (Shipley, 2012, p. 81):

In January of 2005, after Andrea had already been incarcerated for four years with deteriorating mental health, a Texas appeals court overturned her conviction based on the misleading and prejudicial information provided by an expert witness for the prosecution, Dr. Park Dietz. She was granted a new trial with a much different outcome. The second trial resulted in a Texas jury finding her Not Guilty by Reason of Insanity. As much new information has come to light regarding Ms. Yates's mental illness and its impact on her ability to appreciate the wrongfulness of her actions, there seems to have been an appreciable shift in public opinion that the justice rendered for someone like Susan Smith is not justice for Andrea Yates. She was a woman in deep torment due to her illness and the loss of her children, who was in need of intensive psychiatric treatment and therapy, not the harshest of punishments handed down to the most violent of offenders.

There are several problems with the insanity defense as it stands. These problems encourage the perspective that such defenses should be at the very least modified, while other alternatives should be implemented.

One such alternative was established in the 1970s and is referred to as the **Guilty But Mentally Ill (GBMI)** verdict. Thus, GBMI is not a defense per se, but a verdict that is reached wherein the defendant is found guilty, but his or her need for treatment is acknowledged. Melville and Naimark (2002) indicated that 14 states to date have attempted to reduce NGRI verdicts by presenting the alternative verdict of GBMI. A review of the state statutes revealed that the 14 states that permitted the GBMI verdict did not require mitigation of sentence and that the verdict did not preclude the death penalty. Furthermore, the GBMI verdict resulted in more conditions, typically mandating treatment as a condition of parole based on the need to protect the public, "despite the well-established fact that mentally ill offenders have less recidivism than mentally normal criminals" (Melville & Naimark, 2002, p. 554). Moreover, this verdict does not ensure more comprehensive psychiatric treatment than what is afforded to all inmates.

The GBMI verdict, however, has also had its critics. Many are concerned that GBMI only serves to confuse jurors by appearing to offer an intermediate verdict that may result in more severe punishment than what would have resulted from a guilty verdict (Melton *et al.*, 2007). In addition to the proposal of a GBMI verdict and in response to the perceived inadequacy of the NGRI defense, several states have adopted other alternatives. Montana, for example, has completely eliminated the insanity defense. In this section, we explore the purpose of the insanity defense and the different variations of "insanity," tests for insanity, as well as several of the proposed alternatives.

On 30 March, 1981, John Hinckley, Jr. attempted to assassinate the then-President of the United States, Ronald Reagan. Hinckley was apprehended and, a little over a year later, went to trial for his actions. One of the psychiatrists in the case offered the opinion that Hinckley was unable to control himself (i.e., that he did not know what he was doing). Hinckley's attorneys invoked the defense of insanity. It was argued that Hinckley was driven to action by the movie "Taxi Driver" in which the lead character stalks and attempts to assassinate the President in an effort to "win over" the 12-year-old prostitute played by Jodie Foster. Hinckley is said to have seen the movie numerous times and become infatuated with the "hero" of the movie to the degree that he was driven to reenact the events of the movie in real life.

The expert witnesses (mental health professionals) in the case were in general agreement that Hinckley suffered from schizophrenia. Hinckley's defense argued that if someone can be so influenced by a movie as to reenact those events in his real life, he must not be in a rational frame of mind and therefore should not be held responsible for his actions. His attorneys agreed with the prosecution in conceding that Hinckley had planned the attack (therefore establishing premeditation and a presumably "sound" mind), yet they claimed his entire "plan" was based on the movie and that he was acting upon forces that resulted from a diseased mind. Several months later, the jury returned the verdict of NGRI.

Literature Review

The purpose of the insanity defense

It must first be noted that "insanity" does not refer to mental illness alone. It is a common misconception that "insane" equates "mentally ill" or "**psychotic**" (i.e., characterized by mood labiality, delusions, hallucinations, and violence) or "crazy." It is often thought that "the insane" are those seeking (or not seeking) help from the mental health profession. In fact, "**insanity**" is specifically a legal term that is not used in the psychological literature; yet, its precise definition has serious implications for the determination of an individual's status in the legal system (Finkel, 2006). *Black's Law Dictionary* (Garner, 2009) defines "**insanity**" as "any mental disorder severe enough that it prevents one from having legal capacity and excuses one from criminal or civil responsibility" (p. 319). Thus, insanity is a legal standard that must be differentiated from the medical and psychological conceptions of mental illness, psychosis, and the like. While the presence of a severe mental illness (e.g., psychosis) is often required for a finding of legal insanity, it alone is not sufficient. We explore this distinction later in this section.

The insanity defense is generally invoked by those considered to be of unsound mind at the time they committed their offense. Historically, society tends to hold criminals responsible for their actions. That is, we regard their crimes as having been committed by rational persons who have made a free choice concerning their actions. Naturally, society finds justice in punishing such offenders. In other cases, however, persons committing crimes are thought to be too irrational to have made a sound decision regarding criminal actions. In such cases, we have been reluctant to impose punishment on these individuals. In instances where persons have committed crimes without being aware of what they were doing; why they were doing it, or who may have been unable to control themselves; society often feels that these persons need not be held liable for their actions and, in some cases, are in need of compassion. Thus, the prevailing attitude has been that these individuals are in need of treatment rather than punishment. If not for a severe mental illness or misperception of reality, these individuals would not have committed the crime.

The American legal system is based upon the notions of morality and blameworthiness (Finkel, 2006; Winick, 2009). To be criminally responsible and therefore subjected to punishment for one's actions, one must be capable of making a moral decision regarding one's actions to be blameworthy. Theories of punishment are founded upon the idea that human beings are free to make rational decisions concerning their actions; therefore, they are to be held accountable for their actions. Insanity (i.e., mental disease or defect) is thought to interfere with free and rational decision making; subsequently, the presence of insanity does not allow for an individual to form "**criminal intent**." Such intent (i.e., *mens rea*) is necessary for a finding of blameworthiness under the American legal system. Howell (2004) notes that there is a three-step process that must take place prior to an accurate conclusion of NGRI. These three steps are: "(1) The examiner must be satisfied that at the time of the commission of the proscribed act the defendant had either a mental disease or defect (mental retardation) which was of substantial proportions; (2) Assuming the existence of a mental disease or defect, then the examiner must be satisfied that the crime was related to (or the product of) the mental disease or defect; and (3) Assuming the existence of both conditions listed in 1 and 2 above, then the examiner must be satisfied (as in the majority of the states now) that the mental disease or defect resulted in either a substantial lack of capacity to either appreciate the wrongfulness (sometimes criminality) of the conduct or to conform his or her behavior to the requirements of the law" (p. 222). It is generally held, then, that the insane offender is better served by rehabilitation versus punishment. If one is unable to make a rational decision about one's actions, punishment is unlikely to persuade one (or others) not to engage in similar behavior. In light of the questionable value of punishing the mentally ill, rehabilitation through hospitalization and psycho-medical treatment is generally considered to be in the better interest of the individual and society.

The historical basis of the insanity defense

The case of Daniel McNaughton is generally regarded as the historical origin of the insanity defense. McNaughton shot and killed the British Prime Minister's secretary in 1843. The jury found McNaughton to be insane at the time he committed the offense and acquitted him of the charges. The verdict in the McNaughton case was somewhat controversial at the time and consequently resulted in an official process of inquiry wherein English common law judges were given the task to determine the precise standards for competency. The first official test to determine a defendant's sanity developed out of these proceedings (Manchester, 2003; Melton *et al.*, 2007).

The test that came to be known as the McNaughton Test required clear proof that the individual was, at the time he or she committed the offense, under defect of reason resulting from a disease of the mind and that such a defect resulted in the individual not being able to recognize the nature and quality of his or her actions (or not knowing that such actions were wrong). The idea behind such a rule concerns the presence of *mens rea*. It is often thought that insane persons do not possess sufficient **mens rea** (criminal intent) to be found guilty for the crimes they commit. *Mens rea* along with **actus reus** (wrongful act) are the necessary components for criminal liability; therefore, the absence of necessary intention on the part of the actor justifies not punishing the individual. The McNaughton Test for insanity became the official determinant of sanity in Great Britain and its standard was adopted by the United States.

The McNaughton Test eventually expanded to include an "**irresistible impulse**" component. In such cases, an insanity defense was raised on the grounds that the person knew the nature and quality of their actions, knew that it was wrong, but whose mental disability resulted in an "overpowering compulsion," which did not enable the individual to resist the actions he or she undertook. The rationale for the "irresistible impulse" provision was that such a powerful compulsion was sufficiently strong enough so that the prospect of criminal punishment would not act as a deterrent and, thus, persons should not be held accountable for their actions. In 1954, Judge David Bazelon proposed an even broader test for insanity (*Durham v. United States*, 1954). Judge Bazelon opined that "an accused is not criminally responsible if his unlawful act was the product of mental disease or mental defect" (pp. 874–875). In reacting against the cognitive test of McNaughton and in consideration of the available psychological literature at the time, the **Durham Test** held that "[o]ur collective conscience does not allow punishment where it cannot impose blame" (pp. 666–667). In other words, we punish those committing criminal acts of their own free will and criminal intent (i.e., *mens rea*). Those persons whose actions are the result of a mental disease are not to be held morally responsible for their actions and, consequently, should not be punished as others.

Like the McNaughton Test, the Durham Test also sustained its share of criticism. As a result, the American Law Institute (ALI) proposed its own test for insanity. This test would be known as the **ALI Test**. The ALI Test holds that "a person is not responsible for criminal conduct if at the time of such conduct as a result of mental disease or defect he lacks substantial capacity either to appreciate the [wrongfulness] of his conduct or to conform his conduct to the requirements of the law" (Model Penal Code, Section 4.01, as cited in Melton *et al.* 2007 (p. 207), The ALI Test includes both a **cognitive component** (lack of appreciation for wrongfulness) and a **volitional component** (unable to control behavior) (Finkel, 2006). Thus, it is widely recognized as being advantageous over either the McNaughton or the Durham Tests. Further, the ALI Test's focus on "substantial incapacity" is thought more realistic than a necessary showing of total incapacity as is necessary with McNaughton.

Forensic Psychology and Policy Implications

After the verdict was reached in the Hinckley case, the issue of insanity assumed one of the more controversial roles in American legal history. The American public generally felt that justice had not been served in what they perceived as letting the man who attempted to assassinate the President "go free" (Manchester, 2003; H. Steadman *et al.*, 1993). In fact, Hinckley's acquittal, as with any successful insanity defense, is not grounds for immediate release back into society. Rather, the offender found not guilty by reason of insanity for murder is confined to a mental hospital for an indeterminate length of time. It is rare that such offenders are released from the hospital short of several years, and many remain there for most (if not all) of their lives if their mental illness is resistant to treatment. The criteria for release in these cases are far more restrictive than other cases of commitment (L. Wrightsman *et al.*, 1994; Mire *et al.*, 2007). In fact, it is not uncommon for an insanity acquittee to serve more time in a psychiatric hospital than he or she would have served in prison had the jury returned a guilty verdict. It was found that release criteria for individuals who have been found NGRI is far more stringent and extensive than those being released from a prison or jail setting. Mire *et al.* (2007) indicate that a patient's clinical and legal history play a large part in the release decision, as well as evaluation and treatment information. Release recommendations are strongly influenced by a patient's Psychopathy Checklist-Revised (PCL-R) scores and age of first crime, particularly given that psychopathy is a robust predictor of violence and recidivism.

Despite extensive criticisms of the narrowly defined McNaughton Test and previous attempts at reform, most states returned to this standard for the insanity defense in the wake of Hinkley's NGRI verdict (Manchester, 2003). This standard focuses on whether or not the defendant knew the difference between right or wrong but not other relevant issues of mental illness that are equally pertinent. Manchester (2003, p. 739) states: "The McNaughton test considers whether the individual was able to know that her actions were legally wrong and thus fails to account for irrational impulses and delusions that are common characteristics of many mental illnesses."

The primary beliefs of the public concerning the insanity defense are that criminals often employ the defense; many of these criminals are "set free" by naïve juries; those found NGRI are released back into society after the trial; and such persons present a threat to society, as they are dangerous and once again "on the streets" (Melton *et al.*, 2007). Public outcry, however misinformed it may be, places a tremendous amount of pressure on the justice system to revise its handling of these cases. In fact, the reality of the insanity defense is much different than the public generally believes. Speculation occurs around factors that may cloud the public and the jury's understanding and implementation of a NGRI plea (Finkel, 2006). Finkel (2006, p. 178) examines the influence of expert testimony in NGRI cases and found that the prosecutorial trend of converting an insanity case to a capital case "colors expert testimony," and examines whether this conversion "muddles culpability". An example would be the prosecution expert's testimony that was given in the 2002 case of Andrea Yates. Researchers on trial consultation (Colb, 2003; Denno, 2003; O'Malley, 2004) contend that the prosecution's psychiatric expert witness' testimony in this case made "inferences and conclusions [that] tipped the balance in favor of the guilty verdict, despite the fact that only he testified that Yates knew right from wrong, whereas five other experts testified that Yates 'did not know right from wrong…'" (Finkel, 2006, p. 179). The insanity defense is employed in only about nine out of every 1000 criminal cases, and, of these, it is successful in about 25% of these cases (Yates & Denney, 2008). The basis of the misconception that such acquittees "go free" is, perhaps, the use of the phrase "not guilty" with regard to the insanity defense. In response to such public outcry, some states have implemented the GBMI verdict. The primary difference with regard to the GBMI verdict concerns the finding of "guilty" rather than "not guilty" and the defendant is still considered fully culpable for the crime and is sentenced to a correctional institution. In states allowing for a finding of GBMI, the defendant generally pleads insanity, but the jury has the option of finding him or her GBMI rather than NGRI. In such cases, the defendant is sentenced for the crime committed, but spends the sentence in a hospital until sanity is restored. If and when such a time arrives that the defendant is perceived to have regained her or his sanity, the person is transported to prison to serve the remainder of the sentence. Time in the hospital is not credited as good time spent toward earlier parole. Generally speaking, the public is often less likely to oppose a finding of GBMI. Presumably, this perception of justice being served has, to some extent, a relationship to the fact that the offender has been found guilty of his or her crime in one way or another. Thus, had John Hinckley, Jr. been found GBMI rather than NGRI perhaps the public would have rested more contently. Yet, Manchester (2003) warns that this verdict reflects our ambivalence toward the mentally ill and numerous professional organizations such as the American Psychiatric Association and the American Bar Association have opposed the GBMI verdict.

There is sharp criticism of GBMI. Melville and Naimark (2002) contend that GBMI should be abolished on the grounds that it confuses and deceives jurors. They indicate that this verdict offers jurors a shortcut verdict, enabling them to avoid the difficult issues surrounding the insanity defense. It could be argued that the GBMI verdict is often used as a catch all, a sort of "yes—no decision" (Finkel, 2006. p. 194). Moreover, the majority of jurors do not adequately understand that the mental illness and treatment needs of a person found GBMI in no way guarantees that he or she will receive additional treatment in prison. These researchers point out that a GBMI verdict does not require mitigation of sentencing in any state, and this verdict does not prevent the death penalty (Melville & Naimark, 2002). In addition, each state imposes extra requirements on those convicted GBMI, most typically mandated treatment as a condition of their parole. Finally, Melville and Naimark (2002) report that the GBMI defendant is sentenced as fully responsible, sent to prison with the stigma of being mentally ill, and are often civilly committed at the end of their sentences. GBMI appears to represent the worst of both worlds and requires careful scrutiny by legislatures and policy makers in order to prevent a "double injustice" (Melville & Naimark, 2002, p. 554).

One of the more common criticisms of the insanity defense concerns its reliance on expert testimony. That is, the disposition of cases in which insanity is an issue is placed in the hands of psychologists and psychiatrists who ultimately may influence the jurors' opinions as to the defendant's mental state at the time of the offense. This controversy raises important issues regarding the extent to which psychology is and should be involved in the legal process. Critics argue that psychologists are often unsuccessful in evaluations of insanity. This criticism often stems from the fact that psychologists are asked to provide opinions, which are potentially extremely influential in court, on matters in which they hold little understanding. In other words, generalist or clinical psychologists are often untrained or undertrained in legal matters. This very point, perhaps, marks an intersection for the field of forensic psychology. Justice, it would appear, necessitates an understanding of both the legal and psychological disciplines when treating cases such as those employing the insanity defense. Until relatively recently, this cross-disciplinary training had been essentially nonexistent. With the advent of programs stressing both psychology and law (i.e., forensic psychology), the expertise to appropriately address these types of psycholegal questions in our criminal courts are being more effectively addressed.

Suggestions for Future Research

Given that criticism concerning the insanity defense often targets the role of psychology in the legal process, it seems necessary to ascertain the effectiveness of such involvement. In other words, are psychologists helping to inform justice? This raises important issues for future research in the field. In particular, it may be helpful to understand to what extent forensic psychologists can improve upon the merging of psychology practice and principles of the legal system. Does forensic psychology have something to offer that traditional psychology does not and what are the implications for education and training?

Additionally, the efficacy of insanity defense reform and proposals for reform must be examined in more depth. Does the current narrow standard for insanity address the complicated mental health related issues associated with women who experience postpartum psychosis and murder their children? More research and exploration into the nuances between legal and moral wrongfulness is needed, particularly regarding delusions or hallucinations that clearly impact a person's perception of moral wrongfulness.

As mentioned, several states have adopted alternative policies including the GBMI verdict. Future research into the average length of incarceration and hospitalization for those found GBMI would prove informative. Are individuals who are found GBMI spending more time institutionalized than if they were found Guilty or NGRI? Some states have taken it upon themselves to create their own standards for determining sanity. Are such alternatives more successful in the eyes of the law? The public? Justice? These questions are not nearing resolution and must be further examined in light of continuing developments. Longitudinal studies regarding the disposition of individuals found GBMI could help highlight the need for reform or the abolishment of this verdict.

Violence Risk Assessment

Introduction

Mental health professionals who work in the arena of forensic psychology are often asked to conduct **violence risk-assessment evaluations**. This type of assessment involves making predictions about an individual's likelihood of engaging in future violence. Empirical data are gathered from sources such as **demographic characteristics** (i.e., age, gender, socioeconomic status, ethnicity), level and history of past violence (i.e., criminal histories, sexual versus nonsexual offenders), psychiatric diagnosis (i.e. presence of personality disorder, or symptoms or presence of psychosis), any treatment received, the specific criterion being predicted (i.e., violent v. nonviolent behavior or different types of violent behavior), and environmental setting (i.e., if individual is in an institution versus being in the community) in order to complete a risk assessment (Yang, Wong, & Coid, 2010). In the criminal justice system, the sentencing hearing is a particularly common time for the court to ask a psychologist to generate an opinion about an individual's risk for reoffending. In this regard, a psychologist serving as an expert for the court can have a significant influence on the sentence imposed. With a consistent movement toward a more retribution-focused criminal justice system, risk assessments have been utilized more and more frequently in United States court systems.

Psychologists working in both correctional institutions and maximum-security hospitals are also conducting violence risk assessments to assist parole boards and **dangerousness review boards**, who consider insanity acquittees for release to less committing future violence is no better than chance. Past restrictive hospitals make more informed decisions relating to risk for future violence. However, there are a number of very serious issues involved in risk assessment that need to be addressed. One critical issue is the difficulty psychologists have with accurate prediction of future violent behavior. There are many legal and ethical issues that can arise from inaccurate predictions. In some instances, a clinician's opinion regarding an individual's likelihood of research indicated that prediction by mental health professionals from clinical judgment only accurately predicted future violence one third of the time (Monahan, 1981). Based on such knowledge, for the last three decades research in the area of risk assessment has emphasized improving the predictive models of violence utilized by clinicians who make such calculations. More recent research has demonstrated that with the continued development and use of **actuarial instruments** (i.e., instruments which have been statistically normed on a given population and allow a user to score an individual with regard to the presence/absence/degree of a certain trait or historical variable and then provide a quantitative measure of risk, such as "42% of individuals with a similar score reoffended violently within a ten year time period"), our ability to assess violence risk is improving (Moran, Sweda, Fragala, & Sasscer-Burgos, 2001; Skeem & Monahan, 2011).

Risk assessment techniques exist on a continuum, and may range from very structured, evidence-based approaches (e.g., actuarial measures such as the Historical-Clinical-Risk Management-20 [HCR-20], the Violence Risk Appraisal Guide [VRAG], Sex Offender Risk Appraisal Guide [SORAG]) to techniques that are completely unstructured (clinical interviews based primarily on the clinician's knowledge of the individual being evaluated and relevant risk factors) (Skeem & Monahan, 2011). Unstructured approaches are less effective than structured approaches (Skeem & Monahan, 2011). Currently, a few states have statutes that require specific instruments are administered in the risk assessment process; for example, Virginia's Sexually Violent Predator statute requires a specific instrument with a specific cutoff score on that instrument in order to continue the commitment process (Skeem & Monahan, 2011). Although the accuracy of predicting future violence has improved with the development of such instruments, the results of a recent **meta-analysis** (i.e., a research methodology in which the results of several studies examining similar hypotheses are statistically combined to determine the average effect of one variable on another, or effect size) indicate that these assessments are only moderately effective in terms of predicting future violence (Yang *et al.*, 2010). Specifically, these authors reviewed studies examining the accuracy of eight commonly-used actuarial risk measures, plus the Psychopathy Checklist – Revised (PCL-R – discussed in greater detail in the following sections), scores on which have been correlated with risk of future violence. The authors found that all of the instruments demonstrated moderate (i.e., above chance) levels of predictive accuracy with regard to risk of future violence, with the exception of one of the factors comprising the PCL-R (i.e., Factor 1, which captures personality-based aspects of psychopathy, such as superficial charm, grandiose sense of self-worth, lack of remorse, and emotional callousness). Factor 1 was the only aspect of any of the instruments that was below chance in terms of accuracy of prediction of future violence. Thus, despite the high stakes often involved in decisions related to violence risk (e.g., capital sentencing, whether to release patient or inmate, continued deprivation of civil liberties), our field's ability to accurately predict who will engage in future violence is still limited. The constitutionality of risk assessment, as well as the crucial role that psychologists play in making such predictions, has been examined in such landmark cases as *Barefoot v. Estelle* (1983). The following case illustration summarizes this case as well as the findings by the court.

Thomas Barefoot was convicted of first-degree murder and sentenced to death by a jury who based their opinion largely on the expert testimony of two psychiatrists. During Mr. Barefoot's sentencing hearing, the jury was instructed to consider whether "there is a probability that the defendant would commit criminal acts of violence that would constitute a continuing threat to society." If the jury found that such a probability existed, they were required to impose the death penalty on Mr. Barefoot. The jury listened to testimony by two psychiatrists, each of whom offered predictions as to Barefoot's likelihood for engaging in future violence. The conclusions by the two psychiatrists that Mr. Barefoot would continue to commit violent acts if he was not executed assisted the jury in delivering their decision that Mr. Barefoot did indeed deserve the death penalty. Mr. Barefoot challenged the constitutionality of risk assessment in an appeal to the United States Supreme Court. He argued that the expert testimonies of the psychiatrists were based on unreliable predictions. However, one of the psychiatrists who provided a risk assessment claimed that the accuracy of his prediction was "100% and absolute." Mr. Barefoot lost his appeal and the presiding Justice White stated that "the likelihood of a defendant committing further crimes is a constitutionally acceptable criterion for imposing the death penalty" (*Barefoot v. Estelle*, 1983, p. 880).

Literature Review

The case of *Barefoot v. Estelle* (1983) has repeatedly been used to illustrate the strength of the influence that psychological testimony has on jurors regarding an individual's perceived risk. While some debate surrounding the accuracy of risk assessment remains among psychologists and criminologists, certain issues are agreed upon by the vast majority of experts who research and conduct risk assessments. One such issue is that predictions of violence risk are never 100% accurate. Thus, the psychiatrist who offered an expert opinion in *Barefoot v. Estelle* was misleading jurors at best and perhaps not only made an inaccurate statement, but also an unethical one. This has serious implications given that mental health professionals who provide expert testimony in court regarding a risk assessment carry a great deal of weight in terms of the eventual sentence delivered (Melton *et al.*, 2007).

The research for violence risk assessments over more than the past three decades has increased the accuracy of predictions; however, years ago, the controversy was centered around the constitutionality of risk assessment (Skeem & Monahan, 2011). As illustrated by several cases, however, the courts have determined that risk assessments will continue to be allowed in court despite the debate regarding accuracy of predictions (*Barefoot v. Estelle*, 1983; *Schall v. Martin*, 1984; *United States v. Salerno*, 1987). Over time, the focus has shifted from whether clinicians can make accurate predictions about violence to researching ways in which the clinical models of prediction can be improved (Skeem & Monahan, 2011; Yang *et al.*, 2010).

Research has suggested that one way in which the predictive models of future violence can be improved is to use actuarial data as the premise for the prediction as opposed to clinical opinion. Miller and Morris (1988) state that **clinical prediction** is based on professional training and experience, whereas **actuarial prediction** is based on statistical models used to determine the commonalities between a particular individual and others with similar characteristics who have engaged in violent behavior. Research has consistently shown that actuarial methods are far more sophisticated in terms of predicting risk than clinical methods (Melton *et al.*, 2007; Quinsey *et al.*, 2006; Monahan, 2002; Harris, Rice, & Cormier, 2002; Moran *et al.*, 2001; Dernevik, Grann, & Johansson, 2002;). As noted by McGrath (1991), "it is imperative that decisions that can affect the liberty of offenders and the safety of the community are based not only on clinical experience but on empirical findings as well" (p. 331). However, limitations have also been noted with the use of actuarial data. For instance, the court system often has difficulty understanding information that utilizes statistical predictors (Melton *et al.*, 2007). Milner and Campbell (1995) suggested that a combination of actuarial and clinical methods will provide the most accurate risk assessment, and later researchers, including Monahan, Steadman, Silver, Appelbaum, Robbins *et al.* (2001), Quinsey, Harris, Rice, and Cormier (2006), and Monahan (2003), have conducted subsequent studies which continue to support the practice of combining these two methodologies to increase accuracy of prediction. While the literature remains controversial, there are certain factors that have consistently been shown to be significantly related to future violent behavior. Among such factors are the individual's score on the Hare Psychopathy Checklist, a history of criminal behavior, a history of substance abuse, and the age of the offender (Monahan *et al.*, 2005).

In the **MacArthur Risk Assessment Study**, Monahan, Steadman, Silver, Appelbaum, Robbins *et al.* (2001) evaluated over 1000 acute civilly committed patients at three mental health facilities in a variety of North American states and examined a wide variety of variables thought to be related to violent behavior. These researchers measured community violence by interviews with the patients, as well as by using collateral sources after their discharge in the community to include reviewing official records for the first 20 weeks after discharge and records after the first full year after discharge. Monahan (2002) described a number of specific risk factors that had a predictive relationship with violence. Despite much prior research that has found that men typically are more likely to be violent than women, results of this study suggested that the prevalence rates after one year were similar, but men were more likely to have been abusing substances and were less likely to have been adhering to prescribed psychotropic medications. The women who engaged in violent behaviors one year post discharge were more likely to have targeted family members and to have been violent in the home (Monahan, 2002). Prior violence and criminality was a strong predictive factor, as well as prior physical abuse as a child. High crime neighborhoods or the neighborhood context a patient was released into also had an effect. Diagnosis was also a significant factor; specifically, a co-occurring diagnosis of substance abuse or dependence was a key factor. A major mental disorder such as schizophrenia was less associated with violence than **Axis II personality disorders** (i.e., a class of mental disorders characterized by long-standing patterns of maladaptive behavior, emotion, and interpersonal functioning) or adjustment disorders.

The MacArthur Study revealed that within the major mental disorders, a diagnosis of schizophrenia was associated with lower rates of violence than a diagnosis of depression or bipolar disorder, but higher rates than a nondisordered comparison group from the community (Monahan, 2002). Psychopathy as determined by the **Hare PCL:SV** (screening version) added validity to a variety of other factors in predicting violence, including history of recent violence, substance abuse, and the like. Most of its predictive power appeared to be a result of the behavioral factor (Factor II) versus the more narcissistic and detached personality structure measured in Factor I. **Command** hallucinations (i.e., voices in one's head which instruct a person to engage in certain behaviors, e.g., performing violent acts) with violent content, violent thoughts, and anger were significant factors in increasing violence risk (Monahan, 2002). Other significant factors include individuals that exhibited poor impulse control, poor insight, noncompliance with treatment, and a low IQ score were also found to be at higher risk for future violence (Rocca, Villari, & Bogetto, 2006). The PCL:SV is a derivative of the **Hare Psychopathy Checklist-Revised (PCL-R)**, and scores on this measure have been associated with risk of future violence (Hare & Neumann, 2008). The PCL-R uses a semistructured interview, case history information, and specific scoring criteria to rate 20 items on a 3-point (0, 1, 2) scale based on the degree to which an individual displays personality or behavioral traits comprising **psychopathy** (i.e., a personality pattern marked by traits such as: emotional callousness, impulsivity, irresponsibility, criminal versatility, early criminal and antisocial behavior, lack of remorse, superficial charm, and a grandiose sense of self-worth) (Hare & Neumann, 2008).

Other studies have attempted to develop predictive models for specific types of offenders. Prentky, Janus, Barabee, Schwartz, and Kafka (2006) state that there are special considerations in conducting risk assessments for sexual offenders, such as assessing the individual's cognitive processes, their general lifestyle, their history of sexual deviance, as well as the unique presentation of mental illness among sex offenders, which may differ from the presentation of these symptoms in violent offenders. Moreover, as noted by Spehr, Hill, Habermann, Briken, and Berner (2010), risk assessments vary considerably depending on the specific type of sexual offender. Harris, Rice, Quinsey, Lalumiere, Boer, and Lang (2003) compared actuarial risk instruments for sex offenders for the prediction of violent and sexual reoffending using the **Violence Risk Appraisal Guide (VRAG)**, **Sex Offender Risk Appraisal Guide (SORAG)**, **Rapid Risk Assessment for Sex Offender Recidivism (RRASOR)**, and **Static-99**. All four instruments were found to predict violence, including sexual recidivism, with the VRAG and SORAG having some benefits. Overall, the predictive validity was higher for child molesters than for rapists, particularly for the Static-99 and the RRASOR. These researchers found that consistent with past research, those offenders with elevated scores in both psychopathy and sexual deviance were an exceptionally high risk group (Harris *et al.*, 2003). The **Static-2002**, a revision of the Static-99, has been found to be slightly more accurate than its predecessor in terms of risk prediction, though it has been criticized because of the cumbersome scoring system (Harris & Hanson, 2010).

As a result of greater risks associated with subtypes of offenders, mental health professionals who are not trained specifically in the assessment of sexual offenders are likely to draw erroneous conclusions regarding their risk. Yang *et al.* (2010) conducted a study and found that the risk assessments for sexual offenders were developed with males in mind. For example, the offense history, which is a good risk predictor for men in the United Kingdom, did not show the same reliability for a risk predictor for females in the United Kingdom (Yang *et al.*, 2010). Another common population for whom mental health professionals tend to conduct inaccurate risk assessments is the mentally ill. It has been suggested that this may be due to the illusory correlation between mental illness and violence or the belief that an individual is more dangerous simply because he or she is mentally ill (Monahan, 2002; Melton *et al.*, 2007; Friedman, 2006; Scott & Resnick, 2006; Elbogen & Johnson, 2009). Therefore, it is crucial for mental health professionals to truly have expertise with the specific population on whom they purport the ability to conduct risk assessments.

Risk assessments for specific populations, and in various settings, are becoming increasingly more common, such as assessments for workplace violence and violent terrorism (Skeem & Monahan, 2011). The **Fixated Threat Assessment Centre (FTAC)** was established in

October of 2006 to assess the individuals that have "intense, pathological fixations" on public figures (James, Kerrigan, Forfar, Farnham, & Preston, 2010). Within the first three years of operation, the Centre evaluated approximately 100 cases identified as moderate to high risk, 86% of which involved an individual suffering from a psychotic illness (James *et al.*, 2010). Through the triaging of cases and appropriate referrals for mental health treatment, hospitalization, and stabilization, 80% of the cases were successfully reduced to a "low" risk of future harm (James *et al.*, 2010). Another specific population that tends to be forgotten in predicting violence is individuals with intellectual disabilities. These individuals are four to five times more likely to commit a violent act, but it has been noted that their violence is predicted as well as, if not better, by the VRAG, HCR-20, or presence of psychopathy as classified by the PCL (Gray, Fitzgerald, MacCulloch, & Snowden, 2007). Indeed, in many cases in the seminal study on this issue, scores on these instruments were more predictive of violent and general reconvictions in an intellectually disabled population than in a population of mentally disordered offenders who were not intellectually disabled (Gray *et al.*, 2007). As they represent one of the fast growing populations in the United States prison system, and because traditional risk assessment measures have typically been normed using male populations, risk assessment literature is beginning to focus more on women, and more specifically, on women with severe mental illness (Abram, Teplin, & McClelland, 2003; Blum, 2007; Gondles, 2000; Greene, Pranis, & Frost, 2006; Lord, 2008; Parsons, Walker, & Grubin, 2001; Sacks, 2004; Teplin, Abram, & McClelland, 1996; Telpin, Abram, & McClelland, 1997). Results from this research indicate that, although women typically have lower recidivism rates than their male counterparts, factors associated with severe mental illness have a more detrimental impact on women than men (Cloyes, Wong, Latimer, & Abarca, 2010). This suggests that additional resources may need to be devoted to treating severe mental illness in female inmates in order to reduce violence risk.

Melton *et al.* (2007) provides guidelines for the most appropriate ways for mental health professionals to communicate the results of their risk assessments to the courts. The importance of refraining from using language which suggests that one's opinion is absolute is essential. They also suggest that experts present information to the court regarding the factors which have been empirically shown to enhance an individual's risk for violent behavior. Finally, mental health professionals are encouraged to provide the court with a statement as to the limitations of violence risk prediction (Melton *et al.*, 2007). These suggestions are in stark contrast to the method employed by the psychiatrist who testified in the *Barefoot v. Estelle* (1983) case.

In California, even those mental health professionals who are not accustomed to their work entering the legal system, have been faced with the issue of conducting risk assessments. In 1976, the landmark case of *Tarasoff v. Regents of the University of California* delivered a decision that requires therapists to take preventive measures if any reasonable therapist would believe that their client is likely to harm an identifiable victim in the near future.

Currently, most jurisdictions have a statute similar to that of Tarasoff in California (Melton *et al.*, 2007). Thus, this statute brought the issue of risk assessment into the lives of all therapists. In so doing, controversy exists among mental health professionals concerning the damage that this form of risk assessment has on the therapeutic process and the ethical principle of confidentiality between a therapist and his or her client. This controversy is further examined in the section entitled "Duty to Inform versus Client Confidentiality."

Forensic Psychology and Policy Implications

Experts have consistently agreed that predicting risk for future violent behavior is an extremely difficult task (Monahan, 2003; Elbogen & Johnson, 2009; Quinsey *et al.*, 2006). However, it is likely that the courts will continue to turn to psychologists to provide risk assessments, despite the difficulties noted in providing accurate predictions. The courts have repeatedly ruled that expert testimony is permissible regarding the predictions of violent behavior (*Barefoot v. Estelle*, 1983; *Schall v. Martin*, 1984; *United States v. Salerno*, 1987). With this in mind, it is crucial for the mental health professionals who provide risk assessments to the courts to uphold their ethical duty and acknowledge the limitations of their expertise in making such predictions.

Tolman and Mullendore (2003) compared the practice patterns of generally licensed psychologists with those of **specialist forensic diplomates** (i.e., psychologists who, in addition to being licensed, have undergone a rigorous certification process by specialty boards in which they must submit and defend work samples, as well as pass oral and written examinations in the area of forensic psychology) in providing risk assessments for the courts. Their results suggested that risk evaluations are frequently conducted by general clinicians, but forensic diplomates are more likely to use more modern actuarial risk instruments, are more aware of the scientific literature, and provide the court with more information about the scientific basis of their testimony (Tolman & Mullendore, 2003). Forensic psychologists, in general, who are specifically trained on these types of issues are much more likely to be aware of the relevant laws, the most recent relevant literature, and to have experience and training with specialized assessments with forensic populations (e.g., violence risk assessment, competency to stand trial evaluations, and mental state at the time of the offense evaluations rendering opinions on legal sanity). Considering the potential implications of probability statements about risk in the criminal courtroom, it appears that those who are forensically trained are better suited to conduct these evaluations. General clinicians who take on this type of work have an obligation to be familiar with relevant research and base their conclusions on solid empirical data relating to violence risk assessment.

Despite recent evidence that nine actuarial risk assessment tools are only moderately effective in predicting future violence (Yang *et al.*, 2010), many jurisdictions are drafting and implementing statutes which primarily rely on certain scores on these instruments in making decisions regarding **preventive detention** (i.e., the deprivation of an individual's freedom not as punishment for a crime, but in order to prevent the individual from committing future crimes, such as civil commitment of sex offenders who have been deemed at high risk for future acts of sexual violence or predation), though this is contrary to the intended use and application of these instruments, and such decisions, like risk assessment in general, should be based on all available data, rather than one particular score on a measure of risk.

In 2008, Governor David A. Paterson and New York City Mayor Michael Bloomberg announced new legislation that gave the Commissioner of the Office of Mental Health the authority to convene multi-agency, mental health incident review panels to investigate critical incidents that involve individuals with a mental illness (New York Office of the Governor, 2008). These incidents will include those where the individual with mental illness is harmed, causes harm to another individual, or becomes involved in violent incidents. The goal of this legislation was to ensure the improvement of the quality and consistency of care for individuals suffering from serious mental illness (New York Office of the Governor, 2008). The multi-agency review panel includes state and local officials, the appropriate community-based mental heath organization, social services, emergency, and law enforcement agencies. These agencies determine opportunities to prevent a similar incident from reoccurring by identifying factors that contributed to the incident. Then, the panel recommends administrative and legislative actions or changes to prevent future incidents and enhance public safety (2008).

As illustrated in the case of *Barefoot v. Estelle* (1983), there are decisions that juries make that require the risk assessment to be a primary consideration. Suppose for a moment that the jury's decision to sentence Mr. Barefoot to death was primarily the result of the testimony by a psychiatrist who claimed to be able to predict with 100% accuracy that imposing the death penalty was the only way to keep Mr. Barefoot from committing another violent crime. There are currently no clear provisions against an expert witness providing such testimony in court. Given the weight that the judge and jurors give to expert testimony regarding violence risk assessments, the criminal justice and the mental health systems would do well to place parameters around the predictions that can be offered in court.

A recent debate in the literature concerns whether risk assessment and risk reduction should be maintained as separate procedures and efforts, or whether these could be effectively integrated (Skeem & Monahan, 2011; Andrews, 2009; Baird, 2009). Proponents of separation (Baird, 2009) argue that the addition of treatment variables to risk assessment equations, which are currently useful, would dilute the predictive power of historical variables (e.g., history of past violence), while proponents of integration (e.g., Andrews, 2009), suggest that treatment-related variables also provide valuable information related to an individual's ongoing risk, and should be included in thorough assessment of violence risk. As this debate continues, information from the debate could have implications for public policy where violence risk prediction and prevention are tantamount (e.g., capital cases, sexually violent predator commitments, discharge procedures from state hospitals, etc.).

Findings from international efforts, such as the FTAC in the UK, suggest that society can best be protected, and offenders most effectively managed and their risk of violence reduced via the implementation of programs which combine law enforcement efforts and techniques with integrated mental health services (James *et al.*, 2010). Thus, future policies regarding the handling of individuals identified as high risk, particularly those with mental illness, should integrate the goals of these systems to every extent possible.

Suggestions for Future Research

To date, no predictive models exist which can predict future risk of violence with a high degree of certainty. Given that risk assessments continue to be commonly requested of forensic psychologists, it is imperative that research continues to explore factors which are associated with future violent behavior. The research has grown tremendously in the past 30 years on violence prediction and the accuracy of such predictions has improved. However, the predictive models that have been established thus far need to be tested in longitudinal studies across diverse populations of offenders. With the advancement of technology and the ability to look at the influence of genetics on violent behavior, research into treatment options aimed at reducing recidivism would be beneficial. Further research should also focus on developing tools for assessing subtypes of offenders (e.g., homicide offenders, individuals whose violence was prompted by symptoms of mental illness, individuals who commit violent acts while under the influence of substances, etc.), as well as developing norms for both males and females, in order to increase the accuracy with which predictions of violence in specific subgroups can be made. Additionally, the research addressing violence risk reduction is not as developed as violence risk prediction research. Therefore, it is recommended that future research efforts explore the causes of violence, which might uncover ways violence could be prevented (Skeem & Monahan, 2011). Moreover, research will need to address whether risk assessment and risk reduction techniques may overlap, and whether they can be addressed concurrently (Skeem & Monahan, 2011).

An additional area of research that has not received as much attention concerns the jurors' decision-making process regarding expert testimony of risk assessments. This would shed light on the impact that mental health professionals have when providing risk assessments to the court. The decisions of jurors could then be compared to the decisions of judges in this regard in order to establish whether the judge is better able to consider the limitations of risk assessments when rendering his or her final decision.

Competency Restoration and Sanity Acquittees: The Maximum-Security Forensic Hospital

Introduction

This section will address the dichotomous function of the maximum-security forensic hospital in providing both treatment and a secure environment for criminal defendants adjudicated incompetent to stand trial or NGRI for a felony offense. Psychologists who work in this setting have the delicate position of balancing their professional ethical obligations with the legal/forensic system. Individuals committed to this environment likely have a major mental illness requiring treatment, and have typically been committed by a criminal court or have been determined by a Facility Review Board (FRB) or an Internal Review Board (IRB) at a less restrictive hospital to be manifestly dangerous and in need of a more secure environment. This finding is usually due to a patient seriously assaulting other patients or staff. Psychologists working in this environment are charged with balancing the role of treatment provider for an offender population for part of their caseload with that of a forensic evaluator for others. If acting as a treatment provider, the forensic psychologist would not be able to provide the follow-up forensic evaluations for court (e.g., competency to stand trial evaluation).

Certainly, individuals who are court committed with violent felony charges, including anything from rape, child molestation, to multiple murder, have unique security and management issues beyond those typically found with general psychiatric patients. The goal of this setting is to make available ethical mental health treatment, while also creating a secure environment for all patients. Maintaining a secure environment also serves to protect the community. The potential for ethical abuses is high and the clientele are often at high risk for future and institutional violence.

The psychologist working at a maximum-security forensic hospital specializes in the provision of treatment and general diagnostic assessments for a high-risk and seriously mentally ill offender population, leads multidisciplinary treatment teams, and conducts forensic evaluations such as competency to stand trial and violence risk assessments. Koetting, Grabarek, Van Hasselt, and Hazelwood (2003, pp. 114–116) provide the following case examples to depict the types of psychopathology and offenses that illustrate insanity acquittees and incompetent offenders who are committed to forensic inpatient hospitals. Consider the following case illustrations:

Case One

J.T. was a 30-year-old Hispanic male diagnosed with chronic undifferentiated schizophrenia and polysubstance dependence, who had ridden his bike over to a security guard at a local school and asked for directions. He was then asked by the security guard to leave because he appeared disheveled and suspicious. After returning to the school later, he dismounted his bike, unzipped his pants, and began masturbating. Several students and school personnel witnessed the incident before he fled on his bike. After the crime, he denied exposing himself to those present. J.T. never completed high school, although prior psychological testing revealed average intelligence. He was born the third of six children and had been married and divorced at least once. His psychiatric and criminal histories included one suicide attempt, five psychiatric hospitalizations, treatment for crack cocaine and/or marijuana abuse, and three prior arrests on felony charges. There is evidence that he was intoxicated on marijuana at the time of the aforementioned offense. J.T. received Social Security Disability Income and lived with his mother at that time as well.

Case Two

L.M. was a white male in his mid-30s, diagnosed with paranoid schizophrenia, when he shot and killed his brother, sister, and sister-in-law on one occasion in 1966. He believed that they were poisoning him and stealing his money. He reported later that he was the former heavyweight champion of the world. Having served in the Air Force for less than five years, he also identified himself as Catholic with no children. A history of medication noncompliance, in addition to at least six prior psychiatric hospitalizations and prior treatment for substance abuse, were recorded. While on conditional release in the 1990s, he committed battery on a law enforcement officer, but was found not guilty by reason of insanity.

Literature Review

A maximum-security inpatient forensic hospital is typically a licensed state hospital with special security measures (Weinstein, 2002). The security measures are often substantial as most of the individuals committed to the institution have violent felony offenses such as arson, assault, rape, child molestation, and murder. Although a mental illness significantly influenced the thinking of L.M. at the time of the offense, he still posed a significant risk to society and required maximum-security management in order to protect society. Security measures may include: tall, razor wire fences, electronic perimeter controls, a large security staff, metal detectors and personal searches, strictly limited access to nonemployees, and no access to minors. Weinstein (2002) discusses the dual mission of the forensic hospital to include both caring versus management and treatment versus evaluation. To further complicate matters, the majority of individuals being involuntarily hospitalized in forensic hospitals are those found incompetent to stand trial and have not yet been tried and convicted. In 1969, after the passage of the Lanterman-Petris-Short Act in California, "the first restrictive civil commitment law"(Miller, 2005, p. 370), judges found it easier to commit an individual as incompetent to stand trial rather than pursuing a more difficult civil commitment procedure. Miller (2005) presented records from Metropolitan State Hospital in California, indicating that patients' commitments to the hospital as incompetent to stand trial grew from 20 in 1969 to 600 in 1970 with the trend of increasing numbers continuing to present. Melton, Petrila, Poythress, and Slobogin (2007) estimated that there are around 60,000 competency cases annually with 20% to 30% of those cases resulting in the defendant being found incompetent to stand trial. Studies indicate that defendants admitted to hospitals as incompetent to stand trial have increased over the years (Mossman *et al.*, 2007; Papapietro, 2008). Maximum-security forensic hospitals maintain a special relationship with the courts and legal system, as most persons admitted are committed through the criminal courts by a finding of NGRI or incompetency to stand trial.

Psychologists working in this setting also have a dual role that requires them in some instances to be a treatment provider, while in others to be a forensic evaluator. In order to comply with both ethical obligations as well as statutory requirements in some jurisdictions, psychologists must take care to only evaluate for competency those individuals that are not on their **treatment team** (i.e., a group of professional staff who take part in the care and treatment of the patients) or for whom they do not provide other treatment services such as individual or group therapy. The spirit of this separation of duties is to preserve the objectivity that is required for the forensic evaluator, particularly in light of the potential for court testimony and the scrutiny of cross-examination. This can sometimes be a difficult task depending on the psychologist-to-patient ratio on a particular unit and it may in some instances result in a referral to another unit psychologist or outside consultation.

Line staff or "treatment assistants" as defined by the state of New York, also have complicated multiple roles that involve both treatment and management. Weinstein (2002) indicates that despite the title, these individuals' duties include security responsibilities that appear to outnumber the treatment-related interactions. He cited the security responsibilities listed in a position description for a Security Hospital Treatment Assistant as to provide one to one patient supervision, chart patient behavior, and to "constantly monitor patients and provide safety through verbal and physical intervention, and, as a last resort, assist in the application of restraint" (Weinstein, 2002, p. 447). Employees of forensic psychiatric units are more likely to witness or experience threats or acts of serious physical violence by the patients with whom they work (Exworthy, Mohan, Hindley, & Basson, 2001; Haimowitz, Urff, & Huckshorn, 2006; Morrison, Morman, Bonner, Taylor, Abraham, & Lathan, 2002). Owens, Tarantello, Jones *et al.* (1998) noted that an investigation into the frequency and types of aggression and violent behavior encountered in a psychiatric acute care setting found that out of 174 patients, 1289 violent incidents were perpetrated. They noted that 78% of these incidents were committed against members of nursing staff, 4% against physicians, and 2% were against psychologists.

Overall, the use of seclusion and restraint is viewed as a necessary option for a severely psychotic patient, who, for example, is experiencing **psychotic agitation** (i.e., a period of agitation where hallucinations, delusions, and impaired insight are present), won't respond to verbal or less restrictive interventions, and is either harming or attempting to seriously harm staff, another patient, or themselves (Haimowitz, Urff, & Huckshorn, 2006). However, ethical dilemmas are inherent and the potential for misuse is present. Psychiatric hospitals across the country and internationally have embraced minimizing or eliminating the use of physical restraint altogether whenever possible.

Forensic psychologists working in this setting also engage in interactions that take place for the benefit of the patient's treatment and those that occur to meet the needs of the criminal justice system, particularly evaluations such as competency to stand trial, insanity defense assessments, and risk assessments for the purpose of evaluation for transfer to a **less restrictive hospital** (i.e., a non-maximum-security hospital that may allow increased privileges such as: weekend furloughs, contact visits, and off-campus food items) by a FRB, IRB, or Dangerousness Review Board (DRB). Pritchard (2011) indicates that while all patients admitted to hospitals as NGRI or incompetent to stand trial, have the potential for violence due to the nature of their crimes and their history of mental illness, IRB's may become complacent with their assessments if they are not careful to avoid personal biases. Research indicates that IRB evaluators must narrow their findings based on " (a) risk perception and acceptance; (b) the standards people use to make decisions; and c) some nonrational influences on group decision-making..." (Pritchard, 2011, p. 31).

The reader must be mindful that while most mentally ill individuals are not violent, those represented in a maximum-security forensic hospital are the minority and most have a history of violence. While in the hospital, the risk assessment and subsequent **risk management plan** (i.e., a plan that individually defines a patient's predisposition to violence and the steps to take to ensure safety) will help to facilitate safety and inform treatment. "Because the clinical and forensic review board includes members from all disciplines, the risk assessment also provides a vehicle for vertical integration of services as the patient moves toward less restrictive environments" (Moran *et al.*, 2001, p. 425).

In order to be discharged from an inpatient facility, the NGRI acquittee usually has the burden of proving in a court of law that he or she no longer requires hospitalization for their mental illness for public safety, and that he or she may be released into the community under a set of conditions (i.e., **conditional release**) (Manguno-Mire, Thompson, Bertman-Pate, Burnett, & Thompson, 2007). Mental health professionals are asked to provide expert opinions to the court about the probability of a patient's safe and successful reintegration into the community. This typically happens when a patient is going to potentially discharge from a less restrictive inpatient hospital. The IRB or DRB at a maximum-security forensic hospital, which is not affiliated with the court system, focuses on "**manifest dangerousness**" (i.e., is a risk for imminent harm to self or others in an institutional setting) and determines whether or not the patient can be transferred to a less-restrictive inpatient hospital. Once at a less restrictive inpatient hospital, the referring court must make the final decision about a patient's transition from a less restrictive hospital to the community.

Monson *et al.* (2001) examined the factors associated with NGRI acquittees maintenance of conditional release after discharge from the hospital. The medical and forensic records of 125

NGRI acquittees were reviewed. The results indicated that NGRI acquittees who were successfully released into the community tended to be White, with no previous criminal history, and were discharged to live alone or with their families. A statistical analysis indicated that minority status, substance abuse diagnosis, and a prior criminal history were the variables that significantly predicted conditional release revocation (Monson *et al.*, 2001).

More recently, Manguno-Mire, Thompson, Bertman-Pate, Burnett, and Thompson (2007) examined 91 patients from a maximum-security hospital who were deemed suitable for conditional release. Of the 91 patients, only 33% were recommended for conditional release under the current standards. This study indicated that 64% of those recommended were African-American, and 64% also had a diagnosis of schizophrenia and the prior commission of a violent crime. Of the 33% recommended for release, 39% also had a substance abuse disorder. Substance use disorders are commonly diagnosed along with other major mental illnesses in the NGRI patient. According to Manguno-Mire *et al.* (2007), in order for a patient to be deemed suitable for conditional release, the current standards indicate that the patient must demonstrate good insight and judgment, be amendable to treatment, and successfully complete the treatment process.

Criminal defendants are much more commonly committed to psychiatric hospitals after being adjudicated incompetent to stand trial for the purpose of restoration of trial competency (Mossman, 2007; Mueller & Wylie, 2007). The majority of these individuals are incompetent due to psychotic disorders and/or intellectual disabilities and less frequently due to mood disorders. Mueller and Wylie (2007) describe the process of inpatient competency restoration to include treatment for the underlying mental illness under the terms of *Jackson v. Indiana* (1972); specifically, the length of the commitment as it pertains to the progress towards restoration of competency. These individuals are simultaneously receiving didactic instruction to teach the incompetent defendant legal concepts and court procedures. Clearly the barriers to learning suffered by those with intellectual disabilities and the cognitive impairments experienced by those with schizophrenia can make this an arduous process. Competency to stand trial entails both factual and rational understanding. Therefore, a firm grasp of factual issues alone is insufficient if the defendant has paranoid delusions that directly impact his rational understanding of his charges or renders him unable to meaningfully participate in his defense. Considering that most jurisdictions in the U.S. require that the forensic examiner provide an opinion as to restorability, specific clinical data should be helpful in rendering this decision. The potential for malingering incompetency is also quite common and will be discussed in more detail in the "Practice Update" section of this chapter. Mossman (2007) estimates that each year between 50,000 to 60,000 defendants undergo evaluations for competency.

Mossman *et al.* (2007) suggest the evaluator consider the following factors when considering the issue of restorability: (1) Whether the ICST results from a treatable disorder or deficit as opposed to a static and relatively irreversible (or even degenerative) condition such as dementia; (2) a defendant's previous psychiatric treatment and responses to treatment; and (3) a defendant's particular symptoms and current scientific knowledge about how well those symptoms respond to treatment. The two most common causes of incompetency to stand trial are psychosis and intellectual disability (Nicholas & Kugler, 1991; Grisso, 2003; Mossman *et al.*, 2007). Except for an irreversible condition (e.g., a severe head injury) or a mental disorder that has proven treatment resistant, most defendants are restorable (Melton *et al.*, 2007).

Although the majority of individuals in secure forensic hospitals have a diagnosis in the **schizophrenic spectrum** (i.e., schizophrenia, schizoaffective, and schizophreniform disorders, or disorders characterized by the individual being out of touch with reality; for example experiencing delusions and/or hallucinations) (Koetting *et al.*, 2003), a substance abuse or dependence dual diagnosis is very common. J.T. in the case illustration exemplifies the **comorbidity** (i.e., the presence of two or more disorders at the same time) of substance abuse and other symptoms of mental illness. Personality disorders are also frequently diagnosed. D'Silva and Ferriter (2003) examined the frequency and pattern of substance use by mentally disordered offenders committing serious offenses, who were being housed in three high-security hospitals at any point between 1972 and 1998. Their results indicated that, overall, 18.6% of patients had used substances at the time of the offense and 38.3% reported regular substance use in the 12 months preceding detention. However, when comparing the trends from the early 1970s until the late 1990s the use of substances increased approximately threefold. The increasingly high prevalence of substance abuse in this population has important implications for the necessity of substance abuse (alcohol and drug) treatment programs in maximum-security forensic hospitals (D'Silva & Ferriter, 2003). This proves challenging because mentally ill offenders who are also addicted to substances are often resistant to treatment (Brown, Bennett, Li, & Bellack, 2011; Lurigio, Rollins, & Fallon, 2004).

Forensic Psychology and Policy Implications

Ethical issues such as confidentiality and informed consent are different in a forensic setting than in community treatment. Upon admission, the limits of confidentiality are typically explained to patients, and this should occur again at the commencement of any type of forensic evaluation, informing the patient of the nature and purpose of the evaluation and who will have access to the information gathered. When evaluations are court ordered, the same degree of patient consent is not required; however, the clinician should take steps to obtain it nonetheless.

In 1999, a civil rights class action suit was filed by Sidney Hirschfeld, Director of the Mental Hygiene Legal Service of the Second Judicial Department of New York against the Commissioner of the New York State Office of Mental Health and several administrators and clinical staff of Mid-Hudson Forensic Psychiatric Center (Poythress & Feld, 2002). In summary, the complaint alleged that in notifying the court that the defendant had been restored to competency, the report style used by New York's largest forensic psychiatric hospital stated confidential medical and psychiatric information in violation of the patient's privacy and confidentiality rights established by the 14th Amendment of the U.S. Constitution and state law. The defendants unsuccessfully argued that this release of information was in part justified based on the exception that "the interests of justice significantly outweigh the need for confidentiality" (as cited in Poythress & Feld, 2002, p. 53). The court's review of the Fitness Reports revealed that:

All of [the] treating doctors issued Fitness Reports which revealed extensive confidential information related to patients' psychiatric and medical treatment, including medical information about HIV, tuberculosis or hepatitis; sexual orientation and preference; and information regarding family histories of violence, mental illness, or substance abuse (p.5)" (as cited in Poythress & Feld, 2002, p. 53).

The New York case of *Hirschfeld v. Stone* (2000) highlights the difficulties encountered by the dual role inherent in the functioning of a forensic psychiatric hospital. Competency restoration, which is a legal mandate, had to be undertaken in a hospital that was also bound by laws that regulate medical and mental health records and was ultimately held liable for releasing too much information in their Fitness Reports to the referring courts (Poythress & Feld, 2002). Although the gathering of this information was necessary to provide adequate treatment, an individualized treatment plan and risk assessment, it was not relevant to address competency restoration in a report to be seen by the court designed to inform on a narrow legal issue. Although, currently, the ruling of *Hirschfeld v. Stone* only applies to the forensic hospital named in the suit, therefore mental health professionals working in these types of settings must be very aware of the fine lines that exist at the crossroads of psychology and law. While the community evaluator might have a lesser chance of having a treatment role inferred by the patient's hospital status, competency evaluators in the community or within an inpatient setting should target their assessment to the psycholegal question at hand.

The administrators of forensic hospitals must create their policies and procedure with both the ethics and laws related to mental health treatment and those specific to the criminal justice system. Generally, maximum-security forensic hospitals will have a legal advisor on retainer to consult regarding any ambiguous legal situations that may arise. Furthermore, the hospital usually has an ethics committee that is made up of a variety of professionals, both from within the organization and from the community, who can be consulted about a particular case or patient with regard to ethical dilemmas. The conclusions of the ethics committee are typically advisory only.

Haimowitz, Urff, and Huckshorn (2007) urge that all forensic hospitals maintain rigorous monitoring of the use of seclusion and restraint by both internal and external bodies in order to ensure protection and reduce and ideally extinguish the punitive element of the seclusion process. Another important ethical requirement should be staff training on multicultural issues, particularly due to the overrepresentation of minority groups in forensic psychiatric hospitals. This increased awareness could encourage a better understanding of how cultural diversity can impact the presentation of symptomatology and the delivery of mental health services. Staff should also be trained in **trauma informed care** (i.e., trauma-specific interventions designed specifically to address the consequences of trauma in individuals who have histories of physical and sexual abuse and other types of trauma-inducing experiences to facilitate healing). This is particularly relevant due to the large proportion of maximum-security patients who have been exposed to some sort of trauma in their lifetime (e.g., rape, sexual abuse, or family violence.

Training regarding maintaining appropriate professional boundaries with forensic patients is also strongly recommended. This is important for the treatment of the patient as well as the safety of the professionals and the staff caring for the patients. In the course of a patient's treatment, they are learning appropriate social skills to become productive in society. If the appropriate professional boundaries are not maintained, the treatment could be compromised. If professional boundaries are violated in a maximum-security hospital the safety of the treating staff is also at risk because of the criminalistic thinking patterns often associated with these types of patients.

Substance abuse is a very salient risk factor for future violence. The steady increase in the use of illicit substances both before and during the commission of violent crimes by mentally disordered offenders over the last 25 years highlights the absolute necessity of substance abuse treatment programs in maximum-security forensic hospitals. Additionally, defendants who are found NGRI for child molestation or rape are often sent to forensic hospitals that primarily treat their psychotic or mood disorders through prescribed psychotropic medications and **psychosocial rehabilitation groups** (i.e., goal-oriented treatment focused on guiding patients in functioning at the highest level possible independently). The danger here is if the **pedophilia** (i.e., the deviant sexual preference for young children), **criminal thinking errors** (i.e., thinking that leads to and/or justifies self-destructive and criminal behaviors), deviant arousal, deviant fantasies, and the like that lead to molestation or rape are not addressed, the individual will remain a significant threat to the community and will, perhaps, be a more organized sex offender upon release if their thought disorganization has improved. More forensic hospitals should implement sex offender treatment programs for those individuals with sexual offenses, who do not have legal charges pending or have been found NGRI and have stabilized enough to benefit from cognitive behavioral treatments. Additionally, forensic hospitals should have systems in place to provide a continuity of care with less restrictive hospitals and community providers for this issue.

Suggestions for Future Research

Future research is needed to examine the adjustment of insanity acquittees who are conditionally released from forensic hospitals into the community and the utility of diagnostic (e.g. PCL-R) and actual risk assessment tools (e.g. HCR-20; VRAG) in predicting success upon release or recidivism (Mueller & Wylie, 2007). Monson *et al.* (2001) encourage additional exploration into the issue of whether or not it is constitutional to remove an insanity acquittee from the community and rehospitalize them for behavior that is not the result of Axis I psychopathology. Further research into the factors examiners use to predict restorability will benefit both forensic evaluators as well as those who conduct competency restoration treatment. Manguno-Mire *et al.* (2007) also suggests that research into offender characteristics such as antipsychotic drug responses, duration of illness, and history of hospitalizations would provide valuable data into the improvements gained from treatment. This type of information will prove beneficial because presence of psychotic features and aggression often extend a patient's commitment due to the risk for future violence. Finally, Manguno-Mire *et al.* (2007) suggest further research into the effectiveness of treatment programs that utilize long-term, cognitive-behavioral treatment using techniques to address criminal thinking errors, along with substance abuse treatment, and psychiatric treatment with the goal of reducing recidivism for insanity acquittees on conditional release.

Regarding dually diagnosed individuals, additional research needs to be conducted regarding treatment strategies for the psychotic sexual offender. Researching the approaches that are utilized in a prison setting as compared to those of maximum-security hospitals would provide mental health professionals with data that will help to determine the most effective and safe methods of managing and treating this special population of offenders. Research on treatment programs that use cognitive-behavioral strategies but also incorporate a symptom management component would be beneficial. This is a seriously neglected portion of the sex offender population that is being cycled through the forensic hospital system. Koetting *et al.* (2003, p. 119) encourage more "in-depth, descriptive analyses of small groups of individuals who have committed **low base-rate, high magnitude offenses**" (i.e., Murder − a lethal but infrequent crime) to give more insight into the motivations and behaviors of these individuals. Continued research is needed on the impact of major mental illness and personality disorders, those impacted by anger and paranoia in particular, on violence perpetrated by mentally disordered offenders to further clarify the relationship and inform violence risk prediction (Bo, Abu-Akel, Kongerslev, Haahr, & Simonsen, 2011; Gilbert & Daffern, 2011).

Practice Update Section: Malingering and the Criminal Courts

The forensic psychologists working with the criminal court system face many challenges in educating the courts about the many psycholegal questions referred to them. Unlike their counterparts working in general clinical practice, forensic psychologists must be proficient in the assessment of malingering and be mindful for the potential of its occurrence. A diagnosis of malingering can have long-standing, negative connotations, and an opinion that a defendant is feigning or exaggerating can adversely affect his or her treatment in ensuing criminal proceedings (Mossman *et al.*, 2007). The DSM-IV-TR (APA, 2000) defines malingering as the "intentional production of false or grossly exaggerated physical or psychological symptoms, motivated by external incentives such as avoiding military duty, avoiding work, obtaining financial compensation, evading criminal prosecution or obtaining drugs" (p. 739). Criminal defendants may attempt to malinger mental illness in order to be found incompetent to stand trial and evade prosecution. Others will hope to give an exaggerated or falsified retrospective account of their mental illness at the time of the offense to support their insanity defense and some individuals will malinger mental illness to receive psychotropic medications or to avoid work or other responsibilities. A common misperception is that someone who is malingering mental illness is not, in fact, mentally ill. The symptoms of a mental illness can be exaggerated in a person whose disorder is in remission, while some individuals claim to have deficits or symptoms beyond their actual degree of impairment.

The true extent of feigning or exaggerating symptoms in order to be found incompetent is unknown (Hall & Poirier, 2001). Cornell and Hawk (1989) reported that out of 314 consecutive admissions to the Michigan Center for Forensic Psychiatry for pretrial evaluations, 8% were diagnosed by staff as malingering. Individuals motivated to fake incompetency are typically faking or exaggerating symptoms directed towards a mental disorder or cognitive impairments and those aimed at specific competency abilities. These specific competency abilities can include things such as: knowing the nature and process of the court proceedings; appreciating the possible consequences of the various legal options, and the ability to cooperate with one's attorney. Malingering can result in a finding of incompetence with recommendation for continued observation and treatment (Vitacco & Rogers, 2005; Mossman *et al.*, 2007; Hall & Poirier, 2001). The DSM-IV-TR (APA, 2000) recommends that malingering should be strongly suspected when an individual is: involved in a forensic evaluation, has an antisocial personality disorder, is being uncooperative with assessment or treatment, or there is a significant discrepancy between a person's reported distress and objective findings.

Understanding the relevant literature on the topic is important, as well as a good understanding of what are the typical presentations of symptoms such as auditory hallucinations or memory deficits associated with specific types of disorders. In addition, observing the defendant outside of the clinician's office in a forensic hospital setting will provide invaluable information. Far too often, the mentally disordered offender's presentation is markedly different in front of mental health professionals than during their other day to day activities. A psychologist who will be conducting a competency to stand trial evaluation has the ethical responsibility to inform the criminal defendant up front about the nature and purpose of the evaluation. The potential for secondary gain by presenting oneself in a less favorable light is immediately apparent for those motivated to malinger. If the defendant is being evaluated in a jail setting, interviewing security staff about the defendant's presentation is also very informative.

In conjunction with an interview, direct observation, and collateral sources, psychological testing can often provide important evidence to help support or reject a hypothesis of malingering. Diagnostic interviews alone are insufficient to reliably differentiate actual from malingered mental deficits, psychosis, or neurological impairment, particularly in a forensic criminal court context as compared to a medical one. The validity scales of objective instruments such as the Minnesota Multiphasic Personality Inventory-2 (MMPI-2) have long been used to serve as a red flag for possible malingering with dissimulation or invalidity being determined by exaggerated profiles and symptomatology (Kucharski & Duncan, 2007; Blau, 1998). According to Pope, Butcher, and Seelen (2006), the "test's wide use, extensive research base, and different ways of correctly identifying attempts to fake or cheat help account for courts usually finding MMPI-2-based testimony to be admissible (p. 129)." Other instruments have been developed to specifically address malingering; for example, the Structured Interview of Reported Symptoms (SIRS) was developed by Rogers, Bagby, and Dickens (1992) to differentiate honest response styles, irrelevant and inconsistent styles, defensiveness, and malingering. The SIRS reliably demonstrates hit rates for Honest Responders and Probable Feigners in both civil and criminal litigation circumstances (Kucharski & Duncan, 2007; Blau, 1998; Gothard, Viglone, Meloy, & Sherman, 1995). Green and Rosenfeld (2011) indicate that the SIRS is the most commonly used measure of feigning in forensic evaluations, and the results of the SIRS are frequently used in research settings to classify individuals as suspected malingerers or nonmalingerers. These authors examined 26 studies using the SIRS to identify feigning, and evaluated its effectiveness at differentiating malingerers from honest responders and the potential impact of moderating variables. They report that after nearly two decades of research, the published and unpublished literature regarding the validity of the SIRS continues to provide strong support for its utility in malingering assessments. They do caution that results of studies conducted since the initial validation studies indicate a substantial reduction in effect sizes and significant changes in observed specificity and sensitivity rates.

Lewis, Simcox, and Berry (2002) administered the SIRS and MMPI-2 to 55 men undergoing pretrial psychological evaluations for competency to stand trial or criminal responsibility in the federal system. Their findings indicated that both tests have potential utility as screens for malingering (Lewis *et al.*, 2002). The Test of Memory Malingering (TOMM) was designed to specifically assess for malingered memory deficits and has also received good empirical support (Iverson, Le Page, Koehler, Shojania, & Badii, 2007; Bauer, O'Bryant, Lynch, McCaffrey, & Fisher, 2007; Heinze & Purisch, 2001). Pivovarova, Rosenfeld, Dole, Green, and Zapf (2009) examined the accuracy of two measures of cognitive effort and motivation, the TOMM and the Validity Indicator Profile Verbal subtest (VIP-V; Frederick, 2003) using a simulation study design with psychiatric patients (n = 88) and community participants instructed to feign mental illness (n = 29). Both instruments were found to be useful in differentiating feigned from genuine psychiatric symptoms.

According to Hall and Poirier (2001), the majority of criminal defendants, including those with extensive criminal backgrounds, are cooperative with evaluations and do not try to exaggerate or minimize psychopathology. There are also occasions when the accused attempts to not cooperate (i.e., refusing to be interviewed or tested) in order to disrupt part or all of the evaluation. In these instances, the evaluator must determine if a lack of cooperativeness is volitional and for secondary gain or if it is stemming from a genuine symptom such as paranoia and delusional thinking. If a defendant is cooperative in the interview initially and then stops cooperating mid-evaluation, capacity v. willingness is again the issue. When a defendant will not cooperate with the evaluation, the evaluator must rely heavily on collateral sources (e.g., records, observations, collateral interviews). If methods are unavailable or are inconclusive, the defendant should be presumed competent to stand trial and returned to court as uncooperative (Shipley, 2013; Mossman *et al.*, 2007; Hall & Poirier, 2001).

Potential sources of evidence to support a diagnosis of malingering include: direct observation; psychological testing and/or specialized instruments for detecting malingering; medical, psychological, jail, and hospital records; interviews with family, friends, police, jail staff, hospital staff, and others who have had contact with the defendant (Mossman *et al.*, 2007). If a defendant is facing serious legal charges or is facing mandatory sentencing for multiple offenses, his or her motivation to malinger and avoid or delay prosecution would be much greater.

In at least two federal cases, a precedent has been set for malingering to be viewed as obstruction of justice, resulting in longer sentences. In these cases, the appellate courts have held that deliberate efforts to feign mental problems can be grounds for imposing a longer prison term under federal sentencing guidelines (Mossman *et al.*, 2007). In *U.S. v. Greer* (1998), a defendant's sentence was enhanced by 25 months as a result of his malingering, which was determined to be a willful attempt to obstruct justice. In *U.S. v. Binion* (2005) a sentencing enhancement was added based on the finding that the defendant was malingering and this was upheld in federal appeals court. This poses ethical questions for evaluators regarding what issues must be covered in the informed consent process (e.g., that a finding of feigning by the court may be considered obstruction of justice and lead to a harsher sentence).

Many of the symptoms reported to clinicians are subjective experiences and, as a result, there are no absolutes in assessing malingering. However, mental health professionals should use multiple sources of data collection if possible and base their findings on research regarding the form and content of psychiatric symptoms in genuine patients. The consequences for a finding of malingering can be substantial for the criminal defendant or forensic psychiatric patient so the evaluating clinician should take care in building his or her case before making this determination.

■ International Issues

The People's Republic of China (PRC) is seeing growth in forensic psychology (Hu, Yang, Huang, Liu, & Coid. 2010). These authors report that in the last 10 years, there has been an influx of admissions for the treatment of patients whose cases are forensic in nature or involve prisoners judged to be mentally ill. Hospitals known as **ankang hospitals** are similar to maximum-security hospitals in North America. These hospitals are under the supervision of the Public Security Bureau in China and there are approximately 25 of these institutions across China. These hospitals offer conventional psychiatric services as well as medical treatment services. Ankang Hospitals service civil commitments as well as criminal commitments and consist of a number of professional staff members (Hu, Yang, Huang, Liu, & Coid. 2010).

Forensic assessments in ankang hospitals are becoming commonplace and are similar to those of Western countries. Hu *et al.* (2010) conducted a national survey based on forensic assessment organizations (104 out of 143 facilities) and found a total of 16,980 cases were seen were forensic assessment in 2006. In this 10-year study, it was significant that like the United States, the number of forensic cases in the PRC has grown, and continues to grow. This study examined the differences in forensic practice in the PRC as compared to Western countries (Hu *et al.*, 2010).

The PRC has noticeable differences in forensic practice and assessment in content as well as practice. In China, the majority of hospital commitments or admissions are civil in nature compared to Western countries where the majority of involuntary commitments are criminal **forensic commitments** (i.e., a commitment to a mental health facility with criminal charges pending). In the U.S., the assessment of competency to stand trial is the most common pretrial question asked of forensic psychologists (Shipley, 2013; Rogers & Johanson-Love, 2009).

In China, the majority of assessments provided were civil and ranged from competency to make a will to assessing for the presence of a mental disorder. In contrast to the U.S., in China, it is commonplace for victims of sexual misconduct to be subjected to an evaluation to determine competency to consent to sexual intercourse (Hu *et al.*, 2010). Although this is not a new practice, it is becoming more frequent and is intended to determine if the woman has been a victim of a sexual offense. During the course of this evaluation, if the victim is found to be incompetent to consent to sexual intercourse, it could lead to criminal prosecution for the offender. The process only shifts from a civil matter to a criminal one, if the woman evaluated is found incompetent to consent to sexual intercourse. In the U.S., the victim is not subjected to this type of evaluation as the prosecution of the offender is based on the behavior of the offender and the criminal charges at hand. In the PRC, this type of assessment is aimed to replace the stigma associated with abused women in a family and to make this type of tragedy more sociably acceptable and less "shameful" (Hu *et al.*, 2010, p. 615). This type of evaluation increases the need for experts in forensic psychology in China.

Determining who is admitted to an ankang hospital is often the responsibility of law enforcement officers in the PRC. It is considered part of their duty to make decisions in the field based on their opinion of the mental status of the offender. They are expected to refer an individual for treatment at an ankang hospital if the officer believes that the offender displays behaviors that indicate mental illness may be present (Hu *et al.*, 2010). This type of system presents a noticeable strain to police officers in China, as it is the officer's duty to provide an accurate screening for mental illness prior to commitment.

Offenders in the PRC often face similar consequences to those of Western countries, as well as possessing similar characteristics. In their study, Hu *et al.* (2010, p. 610) identify the following typical offender characteristics: (1) older in age; (2) peasant farmers; (3) single or divorced persons; (4) low educational level; and (5) diagnosed with schizophrenia. Offenders who have committed a criminal act can face the death penalty if their charges are related to violence (homicide) or arson.

The ankang hospitals in China have a similar treatment design as the maximum-security hospitals in the U.S. In the United States, the patient receives care from various disciplines such as psychiatry, psychology, social work, and rehabilitation staff. In China, the treatment team consists of three professionals who all work in the same facility administering assessments (Hu *et al.*, 2010). In the U.S., an individual forensic psychologist or psychiatrist generates the forensic report. Like the U.S., forensic psychologists *do not* make recommendations to the court regarding sentencing, as that decision is left up to the court alone.

■

Related Websites

www.cbsnews.com/8301-504083_162-20074642-504083.html
CBS News article announcing Casey Anthony to be competent to stand trial.
www.reidpsychiatry.com/columns/Reid11-98.pdf
Article highlighting the importance of competency and evaluation procedures.
www.assessmentpsychology.com/testlist.htm
Website listing a number of common psychological tests and information on each.
http://faculty.ncwc.edu/mstevens/425/lecture02.htm
Website listing which states follow which standard for evidence, interpretations of Frye and Daubert, and the reliability factors of Daubert.
http://articles.cnn.com/2006-07-26/justice/yates.verdict
This website reviews the events surrounding the retrial of Andrea Yates.
www.law.cornell.edu/background/insane/insanity.html
This website defines and outlines standards for insanity and diminished capacity.
http://forensicpsychiatry.ca/risk/assessment.htm
This website gives a look at the psychiatric aspects of risk assessments by what factors influence determine risk factors.
www.psychology.heacademy.ac.uk/miniprojects/riskassessment/Violence%20RA/index.html
This site is a tool to teach individuals on how to conduct a risk assessment. From this site you will learn to determine when a risk assessment should be used, evaluate methods used to identify risk factors, and define key terms in the field of risk assessment and management.

Court and the Legal System: Criminal Forensic Consultation

Key Issues

Jury Selection
- The process of jury selection
- The voire dire process
- Juror biases and the CSI effect
- Psychological consultants in trial matters

The Forensic Psychologist as Expert Witness
- Discussion about qualifying as an expert witness
- Ultimate issue testimony
- Relevant case law
- Ethical considerations
- A discussion about the preferences of judges and attorneys for expert witnesses and their testimony

Intellectual Disability and Criminal Defendants: Implications for Capital Offenses and the Death Penalty
- The history and rationale of the death penalty as it pertains to mental retardation
- The clinical and state definitions of mental retardation
- State statutes regarding mental retardation evaluations
- Assessment considerations
- Implications and ethical considerations

Forensic Consultants in Criminal Mitigation
- Review of relevant legal standards regarding the role of mental health professionals in criminal mitigation
- Detailed discussion of the procedures involved in a mitigation evaluation
- Current controversies surrounding the role of mental health professionals in criminal mitigation

Adult Forensic Consultation

Chapter Outline

Introduction to Forensic Psychology. DOI: 10.1016/B978-0-12-382169-0.00002-5

Overview

Psychologists are frequently called upon for consultation in adult criminal court matters. The role of psychology in the legal system, and within the courtroom in particular, must withstand careful scrutiny due to the adversarial nature of this setting. The adult forensic arena can have life and death consequences, and having the essential training and experience to provide forensic consultation to the courts is critical.

In this chapter, four controversial areas of consultation for forensic psychologists are explored. These topics include (1) jury selection; (2) expert testimony; (3) intellectual disability and the death penalty; and (4) forensic consultants in criminal mitigation. The issues explored in this chapter explain where and how the adult forensic field routinely relies upon the psychological sciences to inform effective legal practice and sound judicial decision-making.

Jurors are an indispensable component of most criminal (and civil) cases. The selection process can significantly affect the desired outcome of a case. How do the psychological sciences contribute to the scientific selection of a jury? Is it possible to assemble, through the selection process, an impartial jury panel? How does the pretrial publicity of a high-profile case impact the jury pool? Both prosecuting and defense attorneys increasingly rely upon forensic experts with psychological assessment skills who can testify in court. Psycholegal questions in the criminal justice system necessitate that forensically trained mental health professionals educate or inform the court about relevant issues. It is critical for the forensic expert witness to understand both the underpinnings of human behavior and mental illness, but also the law applicable to the psycholegal question. Who is qualified to provide expert testimony? What types of issues warrant the evaluation and testimony of a forensic psychologist? What makes expert testimony more credible to jurors? Finally, what should the forensic mental health expert witness expect in the courtroom and what impact could her testimony have?

Psychologists are increasingly involved in educating juries about risk and mitigating factors that can impact sentences. What happens when a forensic consultant in a capital case finds information that does not support a lesser sentence or reduced culpability? What are relevant mitigating factors in criminal cases? The Supreme Court in *Atkins v. Virginia* (2003) held that executing the mentally retarded was unconstitutional. What impact has this ruling had for forensic evaluation and in the courtroom? How is intellectual disability measured and how is mental retardation defined in this context?

The four topics examined in this chapter are representative of the nuanced work that forensic psychologists can be called upon to perform in the adult criminal court arena. Responses to the problem of crime entail sophisticated, scientific solutions. Whether the questions asked involve mentally disordered defendants at different stages of the adjudication process, the vagaries of selecting jurors, or the potential impact of expert testimony, one thing is clear: psychology can and does impact what happens in the criminal courtroom and beyond.

Jury Selection

Introduction

The selection of jury members is one of the most important aspects of any given trial. The Sixth Amendment guarantees that "in all criminal prosecutions, the accused shall enjoy the right to a speedy and public trial, by an impartial jury." How then is an impartial jury selected? The last several decades have generated a substantial amount of criticism as to whether a jury can in fact be impartial, particularly with the rise in use of trial or jury consultants. After five decades of scientific research on juries and juror decision-making, there is much yet to learn on how factors such as pretrial publicity, inadmissible evidence, scientific evidence, and jury instructions influence juries (Daftary-Kapur, Dumas, & Penrod, 2010). Many factors, both sociological and psychological, can influence the means by which a juror reaches a decision about a defendant's guilt. The presumed impartiality of each juror is questionable, and several methods for assuring impartiality have been implemented. Each of these factors and methods must be considered by both the defense and the prosecution in selecting a final jury. This section examines these as well as other important questions concerning jury selection. Consider the hypothetical case of Jen:

Jen has been arrested and charged with felonious assault after police were called to a domestic dispute. Let us suppose that Jen has considered her plea bargaining options and decided against them, preferring instead to risk the trial process. She believes that she is completely innocent and that a jury of her peers will also see it that way. Thus, Jen has made the decision to place her future in the hands of the 12 jurors to be selected. Given this, it makes sense that Jen will want the jury to be composed of people most likely to find her innocent. The prosecution, on the other hand, will desire a jury composition that will be more likely to find her guilty. Jen and her defense counsel must now be concerned with how the members of the jury are selected and what, if anything, they can do to impact Jen's chance of acquittal. To further complicate matters, Jen happens to be a well-known public figure, and anyone who watches television has heard about her case. What are the defense's chances of finding a jury who has not already developed an opinion about the case? The media has been quick to suggest Jen's guilt, and polls have shown that the majority of the public believes her to be guilty even before the trial has begun. These are important considerations for the defendant in this case which will undoubtedly affect the outcome of the trial.

Some legal experts suggest that cases are won or lost during jury selection. High profile criminal cases such as that of O.J. Simpson, and most recently, the Casey Anthony case bring this debate to the forefront.

Casey Marie Anthony, mother of Caylee Anthony, was arrested on 16 July 2008, and was indicted on charges of first degree murder on 14 October 2008. According to Casey Anthony's father, George Anthony, Casey left the family's home on 16 June 2008, taking Caylee (who was almost 3 years old) with her. Casey did not have contact again with her parents for over a month and admitted that Caylee had been missing for 31 days. During the time, she did not report her child missing and was photographed drinking and participating in a hot body contest. On 11 December 2008, human remains were found in a plastic bag in a forested area near the Anthony home. Duct tape was found wrapped around the face of the toddler's skull with a heart shaped outline over the top of the tape approximately where the mouth would have been. Investigators later recovered heart shaped stickers in the Anthony home. On 19 December, the remains were confirmed to be those of Caylee Anthony. The death was ruled a homicide and the cause of death listed as undetermined. During the search for Caylee, Casey lied repeatedly to law enforcement personnel and claimed that Caylee had been kidnapped by her nanny, which police later confirmed never existed. The prosecution's case in Casey's trial relied heavily on circumstantial evidence (e.g., her behavior during the 31 days, a list of internet search terms on Casey's home computer including "chloroform," "neck-breaking," and "death"). The prosecution also relied upon relatively new techniques in forensic science to include "hair banding" from hair evidence from Casey's car trunk and opining that the hair was from Caylee after death. Another technique used in the Casey Anthony case is laser-induced breakdown spectroscopy which identified chemical compounds in the car trunk consistent with decomposition as well as chloroform. The defense argued that extracted DNA evidence from the hair recovered from the trunk could not definitively indicate whether the source was alive or dead. On 5 July 2011, Casey Anthony was found Not Guilty of first degree murder, aggravated manslaughter of a child, and aggravated child abuse. In the wake of the verdict, several jurors were interviewed by news agencies and reported that they could not return a guilty verdict because there was not enough evidence to support the prosecution's case. Many legal experts and lay persons believed that the circumstantial evidence was overwhelming and a conviction, at least on a lesser included charge, could and should have been reached. In the wake of this tragic case and surprising verdict, juror characteristics and decision-making are under a national spotlight.

Literature Review

The process of jury selection spans several stages, involving both the prosecution and the defense. In many high profile or high stakes cases, this process begins with attorneys utilizing the services of trial consultants (Fischoff, 2003; Lord, 2001; Moran, 2001; Strier, 2001). After an initial jury pool is chosen, a panel is selected for a voir dire hearing. At this hearing, each prospective juror is questioned by the judge and often the defense and prosecution. The voir dire is intended to identify and dismiss those who would be unable to render an impartial verdict. An individual may be dismissed by the judge alone or challenged for cause by the prosecution or defense. Challenges for cause address specific issues, such as the prospective jurors' relation to the defendant, exposure to media coverage of the case, or expressed personal biases about the defendant or case material. A potential juror can be challenged for cause on the basis of any of the following five criteria:

- They do not meet minimal juror requirements.
- They are incapable of being impartial.
- They have a mental or physical disability that leaves them incapable of serving.
- They adhere to beliefs that prevent them from finding the defendant guilty.
- They have had previous interaction with the defendant or are related to either attorney or the defendant (Petrila & Otto, 2003).

In addition, most jurisdictions allow the defense and prosecution of a certain number of peremptory challenges. These challenges may be used to dismiss a juror without having to provide a specific reason (*Swain v. Alabama*, 1965). Although peremptory challenges may not be used to dismiss a prospective juror solely because of his or her race (*Baston v. Kentucky*, 1986), the practice continues to be problematic as claims of systematic discrimination in jury selection are still forthcoming in appellate and supreme court cases (*Miller-El v. Dretke*, 2005; *Snyder v. Louisiana*, 2008). In 1994 the case of *JEB v. Alabama ex rel. TB* the U.S. Supreme Court ruled that peremptory challenges cannot be used to exclude jurors on the basis of their gender. This exception does not, as yet, extend to religion or national origin (L. Wrightsman *et al.*, 1994).

The voir dire process has been the focus of much interest in the field of forensic psychology. Consider the issue of pretrial publicity. "The threats posed by pretrial publicity to the defendant's right to a fair trial are clear (Daftary-Kapur, Dumas, & Penrod, 2010, p. 133). While many questions remain unanswered with regard to pretrial publicity, there is ample evidence that it can affect the jurors' ability to be impartial (Ruva, McEvoy, & Becker-Bryant, 2006; Hope, Memon, & McGeorge, 2004). Pretrial publicity can result in a change of venue. The location of a jury trial is changed if the defense or the state can prove that a fair trial is not possible in the county where the case is pending as a result of widespread publicity about the crime and/or defendant(s) (Petrila & Otto, 2003). The change of venue and much discussion about the Scott Peterson murder trial illustrates this complicated issue, particularly in light of the growing media saturation of high profile cases. Several remedies for such effects have been investigated, yet their effectiveness has not been well established. One of these remedies is the voir dire, or jury examination, process. The use of the voir dire process as a remedy for pretrial publicity assumes that upon extensive questioning by the prosecution, defense, and/or judge, the impact of pretrial publicity on that juror can be assessed. Thus, each juror could be examined for potential biases resulting from media exposure to the case and discarded from the pool if it is suspected that they will be unable to remain impartial in rendering a verdict. In theory, using extended voir dire to assess for biases should work. However, research in this area has failed to reach a conclusive status. Dexter *et al.* (1992) found that subjects who were exposed to pretrial publicity perceived the defendant as more culpable (guilty) and that subjects who were exposed to extensive voir dire (as opposed to minimal voir dire) perceived the defendant as less culpable (see also Hope, Memon, & McGeorge, 2004). It is safe to assume, then, that pretrial publicity has an impact on juror perceptions of culpability, and extended voir dire may be beneficial in these types of cases.

Pretrial juror bias, either pro-defense or pro-prosecution, has been shown to have a significant impact, particularly when more ambiguous evidence is presented (De La Fuente, De La Fuente, & Garcia, 2003). Research has also examined venirepersons' (those being considered in jury selection) evaluations of aggravating and mitigating circumstances (special circumstances that increase or decrease the severity of a crime) in capital trials by surveying 450 venirepersons from the 11th Judicial Circuit Court in Miami, Florida. The results revealed that death-qualified venirepersons (venirepersons who are not categorically opposed to the death penalty and do not believe it must be imposed in all capital cases), when compared to excluded persons, were more likely to endorse aggravating circumstances (Butler & Moran, 2007a; Butler & Moran, 2002). Additionally, death-qualified venirepersons are more likely to base their decisions on flawed science (Butler & Moran, 2007b) and are more easily swayed by victim impact statements (statements made by victims during sentencing phases of a trial or during parole hearings) than excluded persons (Butler, 2008).

A relatively new phenomenon that has gained attention in the field of forensic psychology is known as the "**CSI-Effect**," named after the popular television show and its multiple spin-offs about crime scene investigations and forensic science. Among other things, the best known hypothesis of the CSI effect is that it burdens the prosecution by creating unreasonable expectations on the part of jurors (Podlas, 2006; Schweitzer & Saks, 2007). The logic behind this hypothesis is that on television forensic evidence is presented in such a way that makes the jury's verdict clear and unmistakable. The problem with this expectation is that such a situation rarely, if ever, occurs. The end result is that the burden of proof changes from "beyond a reasonable doubt" to "beyond any and all doubt" (Podlas, 2006). In the case of Casey Anthony, a great deal of circumstantial evidence was presented by the prosecution and, yet, the jury returned a verdict of Not Guilty. It is possible that the circumstantial evidence and new forensic procedures were not sufficiently clear or scientifically accepted and understood well enough for a jury to agree upon a guilty verdict. Jurors who are affected by the phenomenon typically have inflated expectations of what type of evidence (e.g., DNA, fingerprints) must be present to return a verdict of guilty. Some research has supported the presence of this type of influence (Schweitzer & Saks, 2007), but other studies have failed to demonstrate the effect (Podlas, 2006; Tyler, 2006).

While some consultants rely solely on their instincts, others utilize sophisticated scientific research in jury selection consultation (Finkelman, 2010). In the 1970s, the concept of scientific jury selection was introduced. This notion examined whether social scientists could be employed by the defense to select the most favorable jurors in an effort to increase chances of acquittal. Generally, a telephone survey was used to interview people who met the same eligibility standards of prospective jurors. Questions concerning biographical information and general beliefs and attitudes about the defendant, which may influence their verdict, were posed. The interviewees were also presented a brief description of the case and questioned as to how they would vote if they were part of the jury (Abadinsky & Winfree, 1992). Scientific jury selection generally relies on community surveys to "identify demographic, personality, or attitudinal correlates of potential jurors' inclinations to vote guilty or not guilty in a particular case" (Kovera, Dickinson, & Cutler, 2003, p. 161).

By measuring sociological variables, general beliefs, and attitudes of those who could potentially be jurors, it could be determined how certain types of jurors would vote before the jury selection process began. Thus, the defense would be able to predict how members of the jury pool might vote based on personal characteristics in an effort to increase the probability of acquittal. Lawyer-conducted voir dire could be used to determine whether the potential jurors "fit" their desired profile. Moran (2001) indicates that the two leading professions taking part in trial consultation are psychology and communications; however, he warns that many consultants have limited or no pertinent professional training, specifically in jury selection or simulation. Furthermore, Strier (2001) cautions that the practice of trial consulting is virtually unregulated with no license required. There are no explicit standards of education, training, or ethics. Other research had noted that jury selection experts are not utilizing solid psychological principles and therefore are not being as effective as possible (Lord, 2001). The results of scientific jury selection have been noted to be modest at best, and it is generally believed that the success of such a process will continue to decrease in the future if better regulation of training and licensure are not created (Finkelman, 2010; Moran, 2001; Lord, 2001).

Forensic Psychology and Policy Implications

When considering jury selection, a number of controversial issues arise. One of the most pervasive concerns in the modern system of justice is whether a truly representative jury is possible. The effects of pretrial publicity, particularly in highly publicized cases (e.g., Scott Peterson, Michael Jackson, O.J. Simpson, Timothy McVeigh, Casey Anthony), create a situation where trying to find jurors who are impartial about the case is extremely unlikely and perhaps even futile. Thus, in many cases, defendants (and their legal representatives) leave their freedom in the hands of jurors who most likely have preconceived ideas or opinions about the case. The legal system permits some exposure to cases through the media, yet attempts to find those jurors who may be less biased than others in the pool. Consequently, the question of whether anyone can receive a truly *fair* trial by an *impartial* jury remains unanswered.

Steps to reduce jury bias, such as voir dire, may have some benefit. They allow for the exemption of jurors who are obviously biased or may show signs of being biased. One of the problems with the voir dire process is that both the defense and the prosecution are entitled to a certain number of dismissals. Consequently, any juror who is presumed to be a detriment to one side's case will be dismissed by the opposing counsel. A policy question arises when we address the voir dire process and the role of the defense and prosecution in that process. If each is concerned with finding jurors who favor, or who they presume will favor, their view, then the final product (selection of jurors) is not truly representative. All individuals will have some biases but the nature, extent, and their willingness to keep an open mind to the presentation of evidence is particularly important. Changing the venue of a jury trial is another way that jury impartiality is sought. However, there is a need to develop other cost-effective solutions to help overcome media-created biases (Daftary-Kapur, Dumas, & Penrod, 2010).

Research has shown that jurors have difficulties understanding the basic set of instructions provided by most courts, which provide the guidelines for their duties. Daftary-Kapur, Dumas, and Penrod (2010) discuss the importance of rewriting these instructions in ways to increase comprehensibility. Understanding scientific evidence presented in court can be even more challenging. Policies to better educate jurors and judges on issues relating to scientific evidence are needed (2010). Finally, clarifying the vague legal concept of "reasonable doubt" for juries to more easily interpret and apply in criminal cases could have far-reaching implications. Further clarifying the legal standard to jurors could help prevent its slippage into a concept perceived as beyond *any* doubt — a nearly impossible standard to attain. Jury consultants are in a position to try to predict which jurors are likely to interpret these concepts in a way that is favorable to their client(s).

Suggestions for Future Research

Given the varying results in peer-reviewed research studying the CSI effect, additional research should be undertaken to substantiate or refute the hypotheses presented or to determine under which set of circumstances are these effects more likely to be present. The results of such studies might help to determine what influence, if any, exists and the resultant implications for the jury selection process. Additional research on the effects of pretrial publicity in influencing jury bias is needed. The available research has shown some influence, yet the extent of that influence remains somewhat speculative. If researchers in fields such as forensic psychology are able to determine the type and extent of bias from pretrial publicity, greater steps can be taken to ensure juror impartiality. Further, the voir dire process leaves many questions unanswered. Its effectiveness is problematic, particularly when addressing extended voir dire. Research in the psychology of thought may provide some direction regarding this issue. Specifically, psychology has addressed how biases introduce themselves, why they exist, and why some individuals are able to look past bias-inducing experiences/thoughts, while others are not. This information, applied specifically to the legal system, could provide direction for research and possibly a remedy for the issue at hand. Along the same lines, future research should explore why some jurors are more successful in disregarding inadmissible evidence heard in court (Daftary-Kapur, Dumas, & Penrod, 2010). What cognitive processes are involved? How can problems or barriers with this be minimized? Continued research on the jury trial process will further our understanding about the factors that influence jury decision-making and drive jury selection consultation.

The Forensic Psychologist as Expert Witness

Introduction

The use of psychological and psychiatric expert witnesses flourished in the courtroom during the 1990s and shows no signs of diminishing (Coles & Veiel, 2001). Psychologists are called upon to provide expert testimony on specific psycholegal questions that have been put forth by the courts. This section will focus on the psychologist as an expert witness in the criminal court system, although, the guidelines apply generally to civil contexts as well. Please refer to Chapter 6, specifically, to the "Child Custody Evaluations" section for issues specific to that context. As described by Martone, Nemoianu, Shuarman, Singh, and Dolan Strano (2008, p. 858), an expert witness is an individual who, as a product of their "education, profession, publication, or experience" is considered to have specialized knowledge of a subject beyond that of the average person; thus, others may rely on the expert witness' opinion. Major areas that frequently require expert testimony are competency to stand trial, mental state at the time of the offense (**legal sanity**), assessment of violence risk, diagnosis and syndromes, sentencing at capital and non-capital cases, and relevant psychometric testing, as these are considered areas that require special knowledge and experience that is outside the purview of the jury. A psychologist may become involved in a forensic evaluation as a result of court appointment or as an employee of an attorney (Knapp & VandeCreek, 2001; Morgan, 2009). If a psychologist is hired by an attorney, his or her work may be considered under attorney client privilege, and some courts have ruled that the hiring attorney, after reviewing the report or findings of the clinician, may choose not to reveal that information in court (Knapp & VandeCreek, 2001). When the psychologist does appear in court no matter how they were initially retained, they then assume the role of expert witness.

A psychologist who is accustomed to the general clinical role as therapist would be in for a rude awakening with regard to the adversarial process involved with providing expert testimony in the criminal court system. Every opinion must be carefully formulated, supported by reasonable decision-making and accurate data, and will be subject to close scrutiny by opposing counsel.

The qualifications of an expert witness are also frequently questioned (Martone *et al.*, 2008). In a forensic setting, the expertise possessed by a doctoral level psychologist is not automatically treated with respect and the expert has to be prepared for challenges aimed at his or her training, knowledge, methodology, results, and opinions (Cramer, Brodsky, & DeCoster, 2009; Brodsky, 2004; Brodsky, Caputo, & Domino, 2002). Although confidence is important with regard to expert credibility, Cramer, Brodsky, and DeCoster's (2009) study suggests that if an expert appears to have manipulated confidence, they tend to lose credibility with jurors; for example, mock jurors possibly interpret "rapid rates of speech as being overly intense, unwillingness to admit uncertainty in conclusions as cocky, and forward-leaning posture as an excessive attempt to be persuasive" (p. 71). Qualification as an expert is up to the discretion of the presiding judge, based on the expert's education, training, and experience as well as its relevancy to the question before the court (Martone *et al.*, 2008; Knapp & VandeCreek, 2001). In some instances, both attorneys will stipulate to an expert's qualifications, particularly to one who has testified on a particular issue many times before.

Much debate has occurred within the professional community about whether or not psychologists should or should not testify on the **ultimate issue**. The ultimate issue is related to the legal question at hand, for example, whether or not a defendant's mental state at the time of the offense would reach the level of impairment necessary to qualify for a successful Not Guilty by Reason of Insanity (NGRI) verdict or if a defendant should be adjudicated as Incompetent to Stand Trial (IST). This issue depends on the presiding judge and the laws of the jurisdiction. Further complicating the matter is that concepts such as NGRI or IST are legal not mental health in nature and, as a result, defining these concepts is done by lawmakers, mental health and law scholars, and decisions by the courts (Yates & Denney, 2008). While the Supreme Court has established a definition for competency (i.e., *Dusky v. United States*, 1960) it has never established a particular standard for insanity or recognized this defense as a constitutional right (Yates & Denney, 2008). Many critics emphasize that testifying to this matter assumes the position of jury and puts the mental health expert in the role of single-handedly determining what is in the interest of justice (Martone *et al.*, 2008; Morgan, 2009; Tillbrook, Mumsley, & Grisso, 2003; Coles &Veiel, 2001). Consider the following case illustration (McSherry, 2001, pp. 13−14):

On 12 November 1990 in the Australian state of New South Wales, Andre Chayna, then aged 31, invited her sister-in-law, Cheryl Najim, to her house. While Najim was sitting at the kitchen table, reading a letter, Chayna made a frenzied attack upon her, first attempting to strangle Najim before cutting her throat and stabbing her until she was dead. Later that same day, Chayna went to the bedroom of her daughter, Sandy, and asked her to close her eyes while she read her a story. Chayna then stabbed her daughter in the throat, killing her. The bodies remained undiscovered until 3 days later when Chayna stabbed to death her second daughter, Suzanne, who had been away at camp when the first two killings occurred.

At her trial for murder, the prosecution argued that Chayna was motivated by jealousy and hostility to kill her sister-in-law and that she then killed her daughters to prevent her husband, with who she had a problematic relationship, from having custody of them when she was in jail.

Seven psychiatrists were called to give evidence at the trial. All had examined Chayna and all agreed that she was in a floridly psychotic state when she arrived at the jail. She was given medication and responded to treatment. However, the psychiatric evidence as to her state of mind at the time of the killings differed markedly. Each witness was invited, without objection, to state an opinion not only as to Chayna's condition at the time of the killings but also as to the applicability of the defenses of insanity (New South Wales follows the *McNaughton Rules*) and diminished responsibility (section 23A of the *Crimes Act* 1900 (NSW)).

Literature Review

Chayna was convicted of murder but her verdict was appealed and the Appellate Court substituted a verdict of manslaughter. Chief Justice Gleeson delivered the judgment of the Court of Criminal Appeal of New South Wales and criticized the practice of trial judges allowing expert testimony regarding the ultimate issue. He stated (cited in McSherry, 2001, p. 14), "Psychiatrists not only express expert opinions, but go on to give their conclusions on the ultimate issues in the case, and those conclusions come to be regarded as the most important, and perhaps the only important, features of their evidence. This can be a misleading impression." Similarly, in the United States, as described in Yates and Denney (2008, pp. 211−212):

> [The IDRA (Insanity Defense Reform Act of 1984)] restricted mental health professionals from providing an opinion in front of a jury on the ultimate issue of sanity and also, specifically, on the defendant's ability to appreciate the nature, quality, or wrongfulness of his or her behavior. This added limitation was based on the argument that mental health experts might have too much influence on the jury, because it was the jury's role to determine the ultimate issue. Experts are still allowed to testify to the mental status of the defendant at the time of the alleged offense, however (*United States v. Dubray*, 1988). Although experts are not allowed to testify directly to the ultimate issue, they are directed to provide the ultimate issue opinion in their written reports [Title 18, U.S.C. § 4247(c)(4)(B)].

Likewise, Yates and Denney note that one of the most controversial questions a forensic examiner is asked to address is criminal responsibility. Testifying on the ultimate issues and other pitfalls associated with providing expert testimony are equally relevant for psychologists. It is critical that psychologists who take on forensic evaluations are appropriately trained, qualify their opinions, and base their conclusions on accurate information.

Whether or not psychological expert testimony is admissible is subject to evidentiary rules and relevant case law. The Supreme Court Case *Daubert v. Merrell Dow Pharmaceuticals* (1993) set forth that expert testimony has demonstrable validity (Martone *et al.*, 2008; Slobogin, 2003; Shuman & Sales, 2001). This ruling held that trial judges should only allow expert scientific testimony when four requirements have been met: "(1) that the theory has or can be tested; (2) that the theory has been peer-reviewed; (3) that the potential rate of error is known; and (4) that the theory is generally accepted" (Martone *et al.*, 2008, pp. 858−859).

Judge Alex Kozinski, in writing for the Court, stated that the role of Court was "to analyze not what the experts say, but what basis they have for saying it" (*Daubert v. Merrell Dow Pharmaceuticals, Inc.*, 1993). The 1997 decision in *General Electric Co. v. Joiner* resulted in providing wider discretion to the trial judge in the application of the Daubert standard (Reed, 1999). Presently all federal courts and the majority of states have enacted some form of the Daubert standard. There was a split in the Circuit Courts of Appeals interpretation on whether the Daubert standard should apply only to hard scientific expert testimony or should include all expert witness testimony to include psychological expert testimony (Reed, 1999). However, the United States Supreme Court in *Kumho Tire Co., Ltd., et al. v. Carmichael et al.* (1999) concluded that the Daubert standard applies to all experts, even those who are not scientists, and that the trial judge's gate-keeping obligation applies to scientific, technical, or other specialized knowledge. The Court further clarified that a trial court may consider one or more of the specific factors mentioned in Daubert, but that this list "neither necessarily nor exclusively applies to all experts or in every case (pp. 1–2)" and that the test of reliability of testimony is flexible. Psychologists preparing to provide expert testimony can review common factors compromising this standard.

Groscup, Penrod, Studebaker, Huss, and O'Neil (2002) indicate that although there is a greater reliance on Daubert criteria in the years since the decision, only criteria related to the **Federal Rules of Evidence** (rules which govern court proceedings in the United States) are consistently related to the admissibility of expert testimony. "Rule 702 of the Federal Rules of Evidence states that 'if scientific, technical or other specialized knowledge will assist the trier of fact to understand the evidence or to determine a fact in issue, a witness qualified as an expert by knowledge, skill, experience, training or education may testify thereto in the form of an opinion or otherwise'" (as cited in Binder, 2002, p. 1819).

According to Snow and Weed (1998), general guidelines for expert witnesses include: (1) The expert testimony must provide information beyond the knowledge of the typical juror but in such a way that it is not beyond the juror's comprehension; (2) the testimony should be relevant and subject to the rules of evidence; (3) the testimony should be based on principles, methods, and techniques that have been proven to be reliable and valid; (4) the expert must be competent to do the evaluation and present relevant data; and finally (5) the factual presentation to the jury must be clear, concise, and understandable.

There are many ethical considerations for psychologists undertaking forensic evaluations likely to result in expert testimony. Knapp and VandeCreek (2001) suggest that the evaluating psychologist familiarize herself with courtroom procedures and the role of expert witness. Additionally, in order to comply with the *Specialty Guidelines for Forensic Psychologists* (2011) and APA's *Ethical Principles of Psychologists and Code of Conduct* (2010), the forensic psychologist should be mindful of competence or proficiency in the area of referral; **informed consent** (i.e., providing information to the individual being assessed prior to an evaluation) as to the nature and purpose of the evaluation and limits of confidentiality; documentation for the basis of conclusions; qualification of the limits of testimony provided; exclusion of statements by the defendant that could be self-incriminating in reports and/or testimony; and avoiding multiple relationships, such as conducting a forensic evaluation on someone for whom you also provide a treatment role (Knapp & VandeCreek, 2001). Individuals serving as an expert witness have an ethical obligation to perform their own examination and provide their own interpretation of all information available rather than accept the conclusions of other professionals regarding the mental status of a defendant (Morgan, 2009). Finally, an expert witness should be objective, as there will be many external pressures to overlook evidence that is contrary to his or her opinion, or to manipulate the available evidence to fit a particular position (Chappelle & Rosengren, 2001; Dvoskin & Guy, 2008; Goldstein, 1999). Being perceived as a "hired gun" will only hurt an expert's credibility (Chappelle & Rosengren; Dvoskin & Guy, 2008).

Perhaps the most feared or anxiety-provoking aspect of providing psychological expert testimony is the **cross-examination** (i.e., being questioned by the opposing attorney). Researchers offer guidelines for the expert witness to maintain composure and credibility during cross-examination and these will be briefly summarized (Dvoskin & Guy, 2008; Chappelle & Rosengren, 2001). The areas addressed included pretrial preparations, verbal behavior (e.g., speech, word choice), nonverbal (e.g., demeanor, eye contact, dress/attire), as well as the content and style of the actual testimony. The expert must be viewed as knowledgeable and credible by the jury, but not condescending or difficult to follow and understand. Pretrial preparation should include being familiar with all updated, relevant research on the pertinent issue, having your records in order, understanding court procedures, and meeting with the attorney who is going to call you on direct examination to be better prepared as to the nature of the questions to be asked. During the actual testimony, direct or cross, the expert should be concise and organized, and only answer the question that is asked. During the cross-examination, no matter how sarcastic or disrespectful counsel might become, it is critical that the expert witness does not argue and remain unrattled. The expert should listen carefully to questions asked, pause, breathe, and not be afraid to say, "I don't know." The expert witness will likely lose more credibility by attempting to snowball the jury than by admitting to the limitations of their expertise. An expert witness should present themselves as confident, poised, honest, and well-mannered. Dressing in professional attire, making eye contact with the jury, and consistency in one's testimony are all frequently cited elements of a more effective expert witness. Please refer to Chappelle and Rosengren's (2001) article titled *Maintaining Composure and Credibility as an Expert Witness During Cross-Examination* and Dvoskin and Guy's (2008) article titled *On Being an Expert Witness: It's not about you* for a much more in-depth analysis of the nuts and bolts of providing expert testimony.

Redding, Floyd, and Hawk (2001) presented a hypothetical insanity defense case to 59 trial court judges, 46 prosecuting attorneys, and 26 defense attorneys throughout Virginia in order to assess their preferences for types of forensic mental health testimony and for types of mental health experts. There is considerable scholarly evidence to support the utility of actuarial instruments or empirical data in educating the courts about a psycholegal question and much criticism about clinically focused testimony (e.g., diagnosis, interview findings, and psychological testing). However, in the present study, the judges and attorneys found the latter more useful. In a national survey of trial judges, Redding and Reppucci (1999, p. 50) found that judges and attorneys often did not appreciate the value of research evidence, believing instead that "**nomothetic research** (i.e., statistically based data) had no bearing upon individual cases." In fact, in Redding *et al.*'s (2001) study, they favored ultimate issue testimony and viewed research data, or statistically based data, as less helpful. This preference for ultimate issue testimony by mental health professionals occurred despite Virginia law and Federal Rule of Evidence 704, specifically prohibiting it. The study revealed, however, that more experienced attorneys gave much less credence to this type of expert testimony.

Redding *et al.* (2001) also found that judges, defense attorneys, and prosecuting attorneys had some differences in their preferences for types of expert testimony. Judges and prosecuting attorneys had the most similar preferences in types of testimony. Prosecutors were the least likely to favor theoretical or speculative information or testimony, most likely due to the potential mitigating effects. Defense attorneys were found to value clinical diagnostic testimony, as well as theoretical explanations for a defendant's behavior, and other speculative testimony related to exculpatory or mitigating circumstances (Redding *et al.*, 2001). Defense attorneys were the least likely to favor ultimate expert testimony. Participants in this study preferred the psychiatrist as expert witness, but this was followed closely by doctoral level psychologists, with other mental health professionals being far behind. Redding *et al.*'s (2001) study highlights the importance of the legal community better understanding the utility of social sciences and their place in the courtroom.

Forensic Psychology and Policy Implications

Redding *et al.* (2001) urge mental health professionals and social scientists to educate the courts and the bar about the dangers of ultimate issue testimony by mental health experts in criminal cases and the utility of actuarial and other research-based data in the courtroom. Additionally, psychological experts providing this type of testimony should take great care to explain its relevancy to the court in terms that are meaningful and understandable for individuals who are not trained in scientific methodology. The best expert witnesses are those who are excellent teachers and have prepared their information or message and present it in a way that has taken into consideration their audience.

Buchanan (2006) notes that despite the Federal Rules of Evidence, there is some inconsistency in whether or not experts are allowed to testify on the ultimate issue. Coles and Veiel (2001) warn that when expert testimony specifically addresses the ultimate issue, it has the potential to corrupt the whole trial process. Tillbrook *et al.* (2003) argue against testifying to the ultimate issue as there is "no basis in science or clinical knowledge for determining the degree of capacity that is required in order to reach the threshold of capacity associated with legal questions such as competency and criminal responsibility" (p. 77). These researchers fear to do so threatens the integrity of both the mental health professional and the adversarial system in the courtroom. Nevertheless, as Buchanan points out, there have been attempts to circumvent the prohibition of ultimate issue testimony by using such techniques as presenting hypothetical cases which mirror the case at hand. Yet some researchers (Rogers & Ewing, 2003) contend that uncategorically prohibiting ultimate issue testimony may have some untoward effect, and the courts have held that transparency in the rationale behind an expert's conclusion can minimize potential damage (Buchanan, 2006). Clearly, testifying about the ultimate issue is a topic that necessitates continued evaluation by both the mental health and legal communities.

Just as forensic psychology programs incorporate aspects of the legal system at the intersection of psychology and law, more law school curriculums should include training on social science evidence. Coles and Veiel (2001) also encourage attorneys to be more familiar with these issues in order to identify when an expert witness is overstating their position. These authors state, "There should be no poetic license in writing a professional report" (p. 623). The courts must be mindful of the potential for a criminal case to become a battle of the experts, particularly when the stakes are high. Martindale (2002) maintains that experts can frequently offer personal opinions, instead of expert opinions, while on the witness stand.

According to Olley (2009, p.139) expert testimony has become highly scrutinized in Atkins proceedings, making experience with "individuals with mild mental retardation, knowledge of the research on this population, and knowledge of the applicable laws and court procedures" absolutely critical. It is essential experts in this realm have a combination of knowledge and experience to provide the most valid and objective information to the court.

Suggestions for Future Research

A great deal of scholarly literature that focuses on the hired gun phenomenon has been written. However, Miller (2003) indicates that little has been written about attorneys who use expert witnesses to present the testimony of their clients without ever having to undergo cross-examination. He maintains that even though this is much less common, when it is determined to be admissible, it can be very problematic. The courts that have not allowed this type of testimony have typically ruled that the intent of the testimony was not to clarify diagnosis or elucidate psycholegal questions, but rather to avoid cross-examination. Furthermore, Miller (2003) encourages that this issue should be more closely examined in order to determine whether or not this type of testimony is allowed based on the medical records exception to the hearsay rules in the federal and state rules of evidence.

In an Australian study examining the level of agreement between expert opinions on competency and insanity in the New South Wales Office of the Director of Public Prosecutions, Large, Nielssen, and Elliott (2009) found little evidence of bias in expert opinions. Their study revealed a high level of agreement between experts regarding insanity, but only a modest level of agreement regarding competency. The authors suggest these results are indicative of the need for reform in both the way the criteria are applied and in the way in which the assessments are performed. Future research identifying issues which lead to these differing conclusions would be beneficial in establishing more standardized guidelines. Additionally, replication of this study in the United States would be beneficial in making the results even more relevant to these issues in U.S. courts.

Future research needs to take a closer look at the impact of ultimate issue testimony by mental health expert witnesses on juror decision-making. As more empirical and qualitative research explores the effect this type of testimony has on the judicial system, perhaps a more uniform approach could be agreed upon by both the mental health and legal systems. Additional research should also be conducted to further examine the effect of psychological expert testimony that does not directly speak to the ultimate issue. Also, this type of research, as well as the aforementioned research, should be compared to further illustrate the potential implications.

Intellectual Disability and Criminal Defendants: Implications for Capital Offenses and the Death Penalty

Introduction

Capital punishment has been one of the most hotly debated practices in the judicial system since the founding of this country. A recent Google search for the phrase "death penalty debate" resulted in over 4.6 million results; in comparison, a search for the phrase "gun control debate" returned about 2.8 million results. In 2009, 52 inmates (24 in Texas; six in Alabama; five in Ohio; three each in Georgia, Oklahoma, and Virginia; two each in Florida, South Carolina, and Tennessee; and one each in Indiana and Missouri) were executed nationwide (Snell, 2010).

At the intersection of psychology and the law, a multitude of controversial issues exists. Forensic psychology practice often requires the application of clinical knowledge within the context of a legal proceeding. One such instance is in the assessment of offenders for the presence of intellectual disability or mental retardation. This is an important issue that must be addressed in the legal system as the execution of the mentally retarded has been prohibited by a U.S. Supreme Court ruling (*Atkins v. Virginia*, 2002). In 2010, the American Association on Mental Retardation (AAMR; now the American Association on Intellectual and Developmental Disabilities, AAIDD) altered, not the definition, but the term favoring "Intellectual Disability" in place of "Mental Retardation" (AAIDD, 2010). This section presents the historical legal context of the intellectually disabled and the death penalty and the term "mental retardation" will primarily be used for the reasons to follow. Mental retardation remains a diagnostic category in the DSM-IV-TR and this construct is also referred to in many statutes and case law that will be referenced throughout this discussion. Varying definitions of mental retardation in the judicial system, court procedures involved, and a plethora of assessment-related issues can present a number of challenges for the forensic examiner. This section will provide the reader with a brief overview of five major areas: (1) the historical relationship between the death penalty and those with mental retardation; (2) the clinical and state definitions of mental retardation; (3) state statutes regarding evaluating for intellectual disabilities; (4) assessment considerations; and (5) implications and ethical considerations.

At approximately midnight on 16 August 1996, Daryl Renard Atkins and William Jones, armed with a semiautomatic handgun, abducted Eric Nesbitt, robbed him of the money on his person, and drove him to an automated teller machine in his pickup truck where cameras recorded their withdrawal of additional cash. They then took him to an isolated location where he was shot eight times and killed. Jones and Atkins both testified in the guilt phase of Atkins' trial. Each confirmed most of the details in the other's account of the incident with the important exception that each stated that the other had actually shot and killed Nesbitt. Jones' testimony, which was both more coherent and credible than Atkins', was obviously credited by the jury and was sufficient to establish Atkins' guilt. The prosecution ultimately permitted Jones to plead guilty to first degree murder in exchange for his testimony against Atkins. As a result of the plea, Jones became ineligible to receive the death penalty. Highly damaging to the credibility of Atkins' testimony was its substantial inconsistency with the statement he gave to the police upon his arrest. Jones, in contrast, had declined to make an initial statement to the authorities. In the penalty phase, the defense relied on one witness, Dr. Evan Nelson, a forensic psychologist who had evaluated Atkins before trial and concluded that he was "mildly mentally retarded." His conclusion was based on interviews with people who knew Atkins, a review of school and court records, and the administration of a standard intelligence test, which indicated that Atkins had a full scale IQ of 59. The jury sentenced Atkins to death (*Atkins v. Virginia*, 2002).

Literature Review

The death penalty has changed many times over the years by way of a number of Supreme Court appeals that predominately focused on the constitutionality of executing inmates. A complete review of all the Supreme Court cases relating to capital punishment is beyond the scope of this section; instead, it will focus on the cases most relevant to the execution of mentally retarded offenders. At one extreme, the systematic sterilization of mentally retarded individuals was implemented by law in 23 U.S. states, the first being Michigan in 1897 (French, 2005; Kevles, 1985). This practice, horrific by most modern standards, was upheld by the U.S. Supreme Court in the case of *Buck v. Bell* (1927) and continued until the civil rights movement of the 1960s. In the end, an estimated 65,000 people had been sterilized under these laws. Most often, the sterilization procedures were performed in homes for the mentally retarded or mentally ill, in prisons, and in hospitals (Kevles, 1985).

In *Penry v. Lynaugh* (1979), the first Supreme Court case dealing directly with the execution of a mentally retarded offender, the Court ultimately decided that the Eighth Amendment's prohibition of cruel and unusual punishment did not categorically exclude the mentally retarded from capital punishment. The Supreme Court's decision acknowledged that the Eighth Amendment's ban on cruel and unusual punishment defined "cruel and unusual" using standards common at the time of the writing of the Bill of Rights. However, the Court did recognize that societal standards and moral judgments concerning punishment do evolve over time and should be reflected by the country's legislature. The Supreme Court Ruling stated there was "insufficient evidence of national consensus against executing mentally retarded people" as only two states had passed legislation protecting this population from capital punishment (*Penry v. Lynaugh*, 1979, p. 8).

The most recent landmark case in the execution of the intellectually disabled was *Atkins v. Virginia* (2002). In *Atkins v. Virginia* (2002), the Supreme Court held that imposing capital punishment on offenders with mental retardation constituted a violation of the Eighth Amendment on the grounds that such executions are "cruel and unusual punishment." The Court's rationale for their decision was in part due to several states joining the ranks of those identifying capital punishment as inappropriate for offenders diagnosed with mental retardation. Additionally, the Supreme Court also cited the consistency of the trend; specifically, more states were passing legislation that prohibited the execution of mentally retarded offenders and none were reinstating this practice. The Supreme Court also questioned whether the imposition of the death penalty on the mentally retarded offender would satisfy the two main purposes of capital punishment: retribution and deterrence. For a summary of the *Penry* and *Atkins* cases, see Table 2.1.

As a result of the "victim's rights" movement and disillusionment with the concept of rehabilitation for offenders, retribution gained significant legitimacy as a goal of capital punishment. This was largely due to the belief that retribution promotes society's trust in the legal system and satisfies their need for retribution (Miller, 1990). However, the imposition of the death penalty can arguably only serve this purpose in cases where the offender's culpability justifies its application. Miller (1990) argues that the intellectual and behavioral difficulties characteristic of mental retardation precludes this level of culpability.

The deterrence rationale functions in two ways: (1) to prevent the offender from committing other crimes (**specific deterrence**); and (2) to discourage others from committing crimes

Table 2.1: Summary of Supreme Court cases relevant to the execution of mentally retarded offenders

Case	Decision	Rationale
Penry v. Lynaugh (1979)	The Supreme Court found that executing a mentally retarded offender did not constitute cruel and unusual punishment	Executing the mentally retarded would not be considered cruel and unusual punishment according to standards at the time of the writing of the Bill of Rights. There was not sufficient evidence that societal standards in the matter had changed
Atkins v. Virginia (2002)	The Supreme Court found that executing the mentally retarded would constitute cruel and unusual punishment	Sufficient evidence existed indicating that society viewed the execution of the mentally retarded as cruel and unusual. Executing the mentally retarded would not satisfy either of the two purposes of the death penalty: retribution and deterrence

(**general deterrence**). The general deterrence implies that an offender weighs his options and considers the possibility of receiving a death sentence. Miller (1990) suggests that this is highly unlikely in the case of the intellectually disabled offender as he or she may lack the capacity to engage in this process due to the limitations in foresight, logical reasoning, and strategic thinking among other deficits. Miller (1990) also points out that since some of these individuals have difficulty understanding their mortality, the death penalty cannot truly serve its deterrent purpose. For example, in the case of Morris Mason, a rapist and murderer with an intelligence quotient (IQ) between 62 and 69, Mr. Mason asked advice on what he should wear to his funeral while awaiting his execution.

In *Atkins*, the Supreme Court cited the mentally retarded offender's "diminished capacities to understand and process information, to communicate, to abstract from mistakes and learn from experience, to engage in logical reasoning, to control impulses, and to understand others' reactions" as sufficient to diminish the mentally retarded offender's culpability to a level at which neither the death penalty's retribution or deterrence rationales can be appropriately or morally applied (*Atkins v. Virginia*, 2002, p. 3).

Definitions of mental retardation, like many other diagnoses, differ depending on the source providing the definition. Nuances in meaning may seem like a matter of semantics, but the implications can be devastating. The varying clinical definitions of mental retardation and the statutory definitions imposed by the states are outlined below. For a comparison of the three major definitions of mental retardation, see Table 2.2.

Although in *Atkins* the Supreme Court found that those with mental retardation could no longer be subjected to the death penalty, they failed to provide the states with a definition of

Table 2.2: Comparison of the three current major definitions of mental retardation

	American Psychiatric Association	American Association on Intellectual and Developmental Disabilities*	American Psychological Association (DeMatteo, Marczyk, & Pich, 2007)
Intellectual functioning	Significantly subaverage intellectual functioning: an IQ of approximately 70 or below on an individually administered IQ test	Significant limitations in intellectual functioning	Significant limitations in general intellectual functioning (defined as two or more standard deviations below the mean)
Adaptive functioning	Concurrent deficits or impairments in present adaptive functioning in at least two of the following areas; communication, self-care, home living, social/interpersonal skills, use of community resources, self direction, functional academic skills, work, leisure, health and safety	Significant limitations in adaptive behavior as expressed in conceptual, social, and practical skills	Concurrent deficits in adaptive functioning
Age of onset	Prior to 18 years of age	Prior to 18 years of age	Prior to 22 years of age

*Note: The AAIDD definition uses the term intellectual disability in place of mental retardation.

mental retardation. Instead, the Court cited definitions provided by both the American Psychiatric Association (APA) and the AAMR (now the AAIDD) and tasked them with instating standards consistent with these definitions. The American Psychiatric Association's *Diagnostic and Statistical Manual of Mental Disorders-Fourth Edition-Text Revision* (DSM-IV-TR; 2000) defines Mental Retardation with the following three inclusion criteria:

A. Significantly subaverage intellectual functioning: an IQ of approximately 70 or below on an individually administered IQ test.
B. Concurrent deficits or impairments in present adaptive functioning (i.e. the person's effectiveness in meeting the standards expected for his or her age by his or her cultural group) in at least two of the following areas; communication, self-care, home living, social/interpersonal skills, use of community resources, self direction, functional academic skills, work, leisure, health and safety.
C. The onset is before age 18 years (DSM-IV-TR, 2000, p. 49).

This definition has remained unchanged since the publication of the DSM-IV-TR; however, the American Psychiatric Association definition may see some alteration with the publication of the DSM-V. The AAIDD's definition of mental retardation has developed in the years since

Atkins, which used the AAMR's 1992 definition (Schalock, Luckasson, & Shogren, 2007). This definition includes: subaverage intellectual functioning with concurrent limitations in two of 10 **adaptive skill areas** (communication, self-care, home living, social skills, community use, self direction, health and safety, functional academics, leisure, and work), and the manifestation of these before 18 years of age. In 2002, the AAMR definition was altered to read "Mental Retardation is a disability characterized by significant limitations both in intellectual functioning and in adaptive behavior as expressed in conceptual, social, and practical skills. This disability originates before age 18" (Schalock, Luckasson, & Shogren, 2007). As previously mentioned, in 2010, the AAIDD replaced "mental retardation" with the term "intellectual disability" (AAIDD, 2010). Although not cited by the Supreme Court in *Atkins* but still consistent with the national consensus, the American Psychological Association has also presented a definition of mental retardation, which differs slightly from the DSM-IV-TR and AAIDD definitions. This definition includes significant limitations in general intellectual functioning (defined as two or more **standard deviations** below the mean), concurrent adaptive functioning deficits, and an age of onset younger than 22 years of age (DeMatteo, Marczyk, & Pich, 2007). A standard deviation (SD) is a measure of the variability of a group of scores around a mean; since 95% of all results in a normal population fall within two SDs of the mean, two SD is considered an acceptable laboratory standard.

In a 2007 study, DeMatteo, Marczyk, and Pich found that the majority of states, specifically those that allow the death penalty, do not use criteria in their definitions of mental retardation that are entirely consistent with the preceding clinical standards (for a listing of state statutes, see Table 2.3). Specifically, of the 38 states permitting the death penalty, only four followed the DSM-IV-TR definition, six followed the AAMR definition, and one used the American Psychological Association's definition. The remaining 26 states used definitions that differ in either specificity or definitional elements. Of these states, 11 used all three elements (i.e., intellectual functioning, adaptive functioning, and age of onset) but did not operationally define any of them; and 16 states used all three elements but only defined one or two of them. Four of the states considered an IQ score below a specific cutoff score to be presumptive evidence of mental retardation regardless of age of onset or deficits in adaptive functioning. The remaining state, Kansas, used the AAMR definition, but added that "the sub-average intellectual functioning must substantially impair one's capacity to appreciate the criminality of one's conduct or conform one's conduct to the requirements of the law" (DeMatteo, Marczyk, & Pich, 2007, p. 787).

In addition to leaving the legal definition of mental retardation for the states to determine, the Supreme Court also tasked the states with setting the procedures to be followed in the determination of this diagnosis. According to Duvall and Morris (2006), only four states (i.e., AZ, CA, NV, and VA) have set procedures for conducting a psychological assessment in these cases. In the remaining states, the procedure is determined by the presiding judge on a case by case basis. As a result, some jurisdictions may only require a single assessment performed by

Table 2.3: Summary of statutory definitions of mental retardation for death penalty cases, related strict cutoff scores, and mandated assessments

State	Statutory definition; Cutoff scores; Number of mandated assessments
Arizona	Definition: "significantly subaverage general intellectual functioning, existing concurrently with significant impairment in adaptive behavior, where the onset of the foregoing conditions occurred before the defendant reached the age of 18" Strict cutoff score used: any score over 70 on a new assessment disqualifies as mental retardation Number of new assessments required: up to four within 68–90 days
Arkansas	Definition: "[s]ignificantly subaverage general intellectual functioning, accompanied by significant deficits or impairments in adaptive functioning manifest in the developmental period, but no later than age 18"
California	Definition: "significantly subaverage general intellectual functioning existing concurrently with deficits in adaptive behavior and manifested before the age of 18"
Colorado	Definition: "significantly subaverage general intellectual functioning existing concurrently with substantial deficits in adaptive behavior and manifested and documented during the developmental period. The requirement for documentation may be excused by the court upon a finding that extraordinary circumstances exist" Number of new assessments required: one or more
Connecticut	Definition: "significantly subaverage general intellectual functioning existing concurrently with deficits in adaptive behavior and manifested during the . . . period of time between birth and the 18th birthday" Strict cutoff score used: "significantly subaverage" defined as IQ "more than two standard deviations below the mean" (i.e., score of 69 or lower)
Delaware	Definition: "significantly subaverage general intellectual functioning ; . . . adaptive behavior is substantially impaired; [both] conditions . . . existed before . . . 18 years of age" Strict cutoff score used: "significantly subaverage" defined as IQ of 70 or below Number of new assessments required: one
Florida	Definition: "significantly subaverage general intellectual functioning existing concurrently with deficits in adaptive behavior and manifested during the period from conception to age 18" Strict cutoff score used: "significantly subaverage" defined as "performance that is two or more standard deviations from the mean" (i.e., score of 70 or lower) Number of new assessments required: two
Georgia	Definition: "significantly subaverage general intellectual functioning resulting in or associated with impairments in adaptive behavior which manifested during the developmental period"
Idaho	Definition: "significantly subaverage general intellectual functioning that is accompanied by significant limitations in adaptive functioning in at least two (2) of the following skill areas: [10 areas specified]. The onset of significant subaverage general intelligence functioning and significant limitations in adaptive functioning must occur before age eighteen (18) years" Strict cutoff score used: "significantly subaverage" defined as IQ of 70 or below

Continued

Table 2.3: Summary of statutory definitions of mental retardation for death penalty cases, related strict cutoff scores, and mandated assessments—cont'd

State	Statutory definition; Cutoff scores; Number of mandated assessments
Idaho (cont.)	Number of new assessments required: at least one ("upon request, the court shall order that the state's experts shall have access to the defendant [to] conduct an examination")
Illinois	Definition: "the mental retardation must have manifested itself by the age of 18. [A] low IQ must be accompanied by significant deficits in adaptive behavior in at least 2 of the following skill areas: [nine areas specified]"
Indiana	Definition: "before becoming twenty-two (22) years of age, [defendant] manifests: (1) significantly sub-average intellectual functioning; and (2) substantial impairment in adaptive behavior; that is documented in a court ordered evaluative report" Number of new assessments required: one
Kansas	Definition: "significantly subaverage general intellectual functioning . . . to an extent which substantially impairs one's capacity to appreciate the criminality of one's conduct or to conform one's conduct to the requirements of law Strict cutoff score used: "significantly subaverage" defined as "performance that is two or more standard deviations from the mean" (i.e., score of 70 or lower) Number of new assessments required: two
Kentucky	Definition: "significant subaverage intellectual functioning existing concurrently with substantial deficits in adaptive behavior and manifested during the developmental period" Strict cutoff score used: "significantly subaverage" defined as IQ of 70 or below
Louisiana	Definition: "significant limitations in both intellectual functioning and adaptive behavior as expressed in conceptual, social, and practical adaptive skills. The onset must be before the age of 18 years" Number of new assessments required: one ("state shall have a right to an independent psychological and psychiatric exam of the defendant")
Maryland	Definition: "significantly below average intellectual functioning, as shown by an intelligence quotient of 70 or below on an individually administered intelligence quotient test and an impairment in adaptive behavior; and . . . the mental retardation was manifested before the age of 22 years" Strict cutoff score used: "significantly below average" must be shown by IQ of 70 or below
Missouri	Definition: "significantly subaverage intellectual functioning with continual extensive related deficits and limitations in two or more adaptive behaviors [10 example behaviors cited], which conditions are manifested and documented before 18 years of age"
Nebraska	Definition: "significantly subaverage general intellectual functioning existing concurrently with deficits in adaptive behavior"
Nevada	Definition: "significant subaverage general intellectual functioning which exists concurrently with deficits in adaptive behavior and manifested during the developmental period" Number of new assessments required: one "by an expert selected by the prosecution"
New Mexico	Definition: "significantly subaverage general intellectual functioning existing concurrently with deficits in adaptive behavior"

Table 2.3: Summary of statutory definitions of mental retardation for death penalty cases, related strict cutoff scores, and mandated assessments—cont'd

State	Statutory definition; Cutoff scores; Number of mandated assessments
New York	Definition: "significantly subaverage general intellectual functioning existing concurrently with deficits in adaptive behavior which were manifested before the age of 18"
North Carolina	Definition: "significantly subaverage general intellectual functioning, existing concurrently with significant limitations in adaptive functioning, both of which were manifested before the age of 18"
South Dakota	Definition: "significant subaverage general intellectual functioning existing concurrently with substantial related deficits in applicable adaptive skill areas" with mental retardation "manifested and documented before the age of 18 years"
Tennessee	Definition: "significantly subaverage general intellectual functioning as evidenced by a functional intelligence quotient (I.Q.) of seventy (70) or below; [d]eficits in adaptive behavior; and [t]he mental retardation must have been manifested during the developmental period, or by eighteen (18) years of age" Strict cutoff score used: "significantly subaverage" must be evidenced by IQ of 70 or below
Utah	Definition: "significantly subaverage general intellectual functioning that results in and exists concurrently with significant deficiencies in adaptive functioning that exist primarily in the areas of reasoning or impulse control, or in both of these areas; and . . . the subaverage general intellectual functioning and the significant deficiencies in adaptive functioning . . . are both manifested prior to age 22" Number of new assessments required: at least two
Virginia	Definition: "significantly subaverage general intellectual functioning as demonstrated by performance on a standardized measure of intellectual functioning administered in conformity with accepted professional practice, that is at least two standard deviations below the mean, and . . . significant limitations in adaptive behavior as expressed in conceptual, social and practical adaptive skills" Strict cutoff score used: "significantly subaverage" defined as IQ "that is at least two standard deviations below the mean" (i.e., score of 70 or lower)
Washington	Definition: "significantly subaverage general intellectual functioning; . . . existing concurrently with deficits in adaptive behavior; and . . . both were manifested during the developmental period" Strict cutoff score used: "significantly subaverage" defined as IQ of 70 or below Number of new assessments required: one

Duvall & Morris, 2006, pp. 660–661.

one evaluator, while other jurisdictions may require multiple assessments within a set time period. For example, Arizona's procedures allow for up to four separate assessments by four different examiners within 68–90 days (Duvall & Morris, 2006). To further complicate matters, there is no requirement placed on the examiners to communicate with one another regarding what assessment instruments they used in their evaluation of the defendant. In these cases, it would be difficult to take into consideration the influence of such psychometric concerns as **test—retest reliability** (the degree to which a measure produces consistent results over several administrations) or **practice effects** (changes due to taking similar tests) (these subjects will be discussed in more detail later). Only seven states provide any guidance for the selection of assessment instruments for the evaluation of mental retardation (Duvall & Morris, 2006). Such guidance varies in specificity with Florida and Virginia requiring that the instrument be taken from a list of approved instruments (Fla. Stat § 921.137 [1]; Va. Code Ann. § 19.2-264.3:1.1[B, 1]). Duvall and Morris (2006) indicate that Virginia has the most specific guidelines for selecting an intelligence assessment instrument. For example, the Virginia Code states the following:

> *Assessment of intellectual functioning shall include administration of at least one standardized measure generally accepted by the field of psychological testing and appropriate for administration to the particular defendant being assessed, taking into account cultural, linguistic, sensory, motor, behavioral, and other individual factors (Va. Code Ann. § 19.2-264.3:1.1[B, 1]).*

The qualifications necessary to conduct a determination of mental retardation in the context of a capital case, as set forth by statutes, vary between states. Sixteen states are silent on the issue of who is qualified to provide an assessment of mental retardation in capital cases. Of the states with specified qualifications, the most basic requirements call for licensure, while others require experts in the field; though they fail to define what qualifies a practitioner as an "expert." It is necessary for mental health professionals to be aware of the relevant laws in their jurisdiction in order to be aware of the restrictions placed on their assessment, as well as how their assessment may be influenced by the court's procedures; for example, evaluating an offender who has already been tested by another practitioner.

Clinicians who have evaluated a defendant to determine the presence or absence of mental retardation can face significant challenges in court regarding their assessment of adaptive functioning and in the scoring and interpretation of test scores. The adaptive functioning prong of a mental retardation definition can be inappropriately assessed and misinterpreted in the courtroom. The AAMR (2002) explains that limitations in adaptive functioning should not be measured in a segregated environment such as a prison, but rather in their typical community environment, since some may function better in such a controlled environment. A frequently occurring debate in the assessment of adaptive functioning is the appropriateness of including the offender's behavior in prison, which is often assessed by interviewing correctional officers, as evidence of the degree of adaptive behavior present. In their 2007 study, Young, Boccaccini, Conroy, and Lawson reported that nearly all (90%) of the evaluators they interviewed believed that using correctional officers in the assessment process was appropriate, but few believed it was necessary. Several of the evaluators in the study explained that they treated correctional officers' reports with a great deal of caution, citing officers' tendencies to be biased and uninformed regarding mental retardation. Blume, Johnson, and Seeds (2009) argue that prison behavior is not a reliable measure of adaptive functioning. These behaviors may only appear to be adaptive strengths; for example, correctional officers may report that the offender in question regularly checks out multiple books, yet, the offender may be checking the books out for other inmates since he cannot read.

The question has also been raised as to whether an offender's behavior at the time of, and following, the crime should be considered in adaptive behavior evaluations. Though the Supreme Court ruled in *Tennard v. Dretke* (2004) that a defendant's criminal behavior did not need to be influenced by an intellectual disability, two state courts have argued that such behavior should be included in the assessment process. In Alabama, it is considered appropriate for fact finders to consider "post-crime craftiness" in their determination regarding mental retardation (*Clemons v. Alabama*, 2005). In *Ex parte Briseno* (2004), a Texas court found that determination of mental retardation evaluations should also consider the offender's behavior both at the time of the crime and after the crime. Proponents of using offense behavior indicate that criminal behavior, like any other behavior, can reveal useful information about one's ability to function effectively, and this behavior is likely to be well documented by police reports and witness statements. Those against this caution that mentally retarded individuals are easily persuaded, likely to acquiesce to authority figures, and lack the communication skills to correct others' misperceptions (Young, Boccaccini, Conroy, & Lawson, 2007). Furthermore, standardized and validated measures intended to measure adaptive functioning are not intended for use with criminal behavior.

Another issue in the assessment of adaptive functioning is the weight given to adaptive strengths. The AAIDD (2010) recognizes in their definition of mental retardation that individuals with mental retardation are unique, each having areas of adaptive limitations and often areas of strength as well. The assessment of adaptive functioning requires that the examiner weigh an individual's strengths and weaknesses within skill areas before determining whether an adaptive limitation exists in that area. When courts fail to engage in this careful process of consideration, they often resort to stereotypes (e.g., "intellectually disabled people don't..." statements) (Blume, Johnson, & Seeds, 2009). When courts rely upon stereotypes such as "Intellectually disabled people don't drive cars," there is ample opportunity to misclassify defendants based upon what they do or do not do. This type of reasoning is at odds with any of the definitions of mental retardation previously presented in that it represents an exclusionary criterion whereas the American Psychiatric Association, American Psychological Association, and AAIDD definitions use only inclusionary criteria (i.e., has an IQ of 70 or lower). These types of judgments may also reflect the operation of some biased or stereotyped beliefs. Blume, Johnson, and Seeds (2009) maintain that using criminal behavior in the evaluation of adaptive behavior can have a harmful influence by interjecting biases and stereotypes. Specifically, they cited a Tennessee case in which the court rejected the results of the Vineland and Independent Living Scale (a measure of adaptive functioning) as well as expert testimony, all of which supported a diagnosis of mental retardation. The court's ruling read, in part, as follows:

> In the legal setting, the court must not become so entangled with the opinions of psychiatric experts that we lose sight of the nature of the criminal offense itself. We must not turn a blind eye to the defendant's ability to use society to better his needs. There are mentally retarded persons who are criminals, but they tend to commit fairly primitive crimes, impulsive crimes, and sudden acts of violence. The more complex the crime, however, the less likely that the person is mentally retarded (*Van Tran v. Tennessee*, 2006).

Standardized measures of adaptive functioning would seem to be useful in evaluating offenders in capital cases; however, this may not be appropriate for incarcerated offenders. Offenders often do not have the opportunity to perform the behaviors that are included in the measures while incarcerated. Moreover, some pro-social behaviors in the community setting (where most adaptive functioning measures are meant to be used) may not be adaptive in the prison setting (Young, Boccaccini, Conroy, & Lawson, 2007).

The assessment of intellectual functioning is another area where clinical practice and the judicial system come into conflict. The use of the word "approximately" in definitions of mental retardation when referring to an IQ score of 70 is not inadvertent nor is it irrelevant. Its purpose is to allow for interpretation of the score while taking into account certain influential phenomena; most notably the **standard error of measurement**, the **Flynn effect**, and **practice effects**. Any measure of intelligence is subject to error whether due to the examiner's behavior, the examiner's presentation of the test, the environmental effects on the examinee, or a number of other factors. The **standard error of measurement** accounts for these influences by identifying a range of scores within which the examinee's true score is likely to be found. In the case of the Wechsler Adult Intelligence Scale (WAIS), the standard error of measurement is approximately five points. This means that if an examinee obtains a Full Scale IQ of 70, his true score likely lies between 65 and 75. The standard error of measurement takes on added significance in legal determinations as it can have life and death implications, especially in jurisdictions that treat IQ scores inappropriately. Some jurisdictions dismiss the standard error of measurement altogether by imposing set cutoff scores for intelligence. Other states do recognize that the standard error of measurement produces a range of IQ scores but do not allow for downward adjustment since, in their view, to do so is speculative as true score may be higher than the obtained one (Duvall & Morris, 2006). These practices are inconsistent with the definitions of mental retardation cited in *Atkins* which permit IQ scores from 70 to 75 to indicate subaverage intellectual functioning (Duvall & Morris, 2006).

Another factor further complicating intelligence assessment in mental retardation cases is a phenomenon known as the Flynn effect. The **Flynn effect** describes the tendency of intelligence measure scores to increase gradually over time following the norming process, which has been verified in multiple countries (Flynn, 1984, 1987). According to the Flynn effect, as soon as a test of intelligence has been normed on a population, the scores of individuals in that population will begin to rise over time. In the United States, this effect is of a magnitude of about 0.3 points per year, or three points every ten years, since the norming of the WAIS (Flynn, 1984, 1987). This may not seem like a significant increase; however, the cumulative effects can be alarming. When taken into consideration in a mental retardation assessment within the context of a capital case, the artificially elevated score obtained at the end of a norming period can make the difference between life and death when a specific cutoff score is imposed. The issue of the Flynn effect in capital cases came to light in the *Walker v. True* (2005) Federal Court of Appeals case. In this case, the court of appeals found that the trial court erred in not considering the Flynn effect in the defendant's claim of mental retardation. In their 2007 survey, Young, Boccaccini, Conroy, and Lawson described the familiarity of evaluators in their study with the Flynn effect. They reported that of the psychologists interviewed, about 62% were aware of the effect by name, 7.7% knew the effect but not its name, and about 23% were unaware of the effect or its name. Of the psychiatrists in the survey, none were aware of the effect by name and only about 29% were aware of the trend described by the Flynn effect. In the same study, seven evaluators reported that the Flynn effect had been brought up in at least one of the capital case evaluations they had participated in, typically in explaining varying scores obtained by defendants.

Practice effects can also exert a significant influence on mental retardation determinations. In the case of the WAIS-III, practice effects can contribute to a five point increase in a defendant's IQ when the same test is administered a second time within two to twelve weeks (The Psychological Corporation, 1997). These effects are necessary to consider in interpreting a defendant's obtained score when the same test has been used recently as the inflation in the score can mean the difference in a diagnosis that carries life or death consequences in a capital case.

Forensic Psychology and Practice Implications

The importance of a mental retardation determination in capital cases cannot be overstated. It can literally be the difference between life and death for a criminal defendant. Because a diagnosis of mental retardation has the power to protect an offender from the death penalty, there is a powerful incentive for them to feign or exaggerate intellectual disabilities (also known as malingering). Whenever there is significant secondary gain for an offender to malinger (e.g., facing the death penalty), the forensic evaluator must be aware of the potential for malingering and carefully examine the evidence presented regarding intellectual disabilities. The forensic psychologist must understand well the components of a mental retardation diagnosis, as well as the associated research regarding prevalence, presentation, and the like. Additionally, where appropriate, follow-up psychological testing, including tests specifically designed to help detect malingering, should be employed. As discussed further in other sections of this book, including the Practice Update Section of Chapter 1, if malingering is suspected, collateral data to include records and third party observations are critical in ruling it in or out; for example, school records and correctional officer observations can and should be utilized in the evaluation. The intent of the *Atkins* decision was to protect the rights of the intellectually disabled not to provide a defense strategy for a manipulative offender feigning symptoms or disabilities to avoid the ultimate punishment.

The widely varying definitions of mental retardation from state to state have been frequently pointed out as a problem, requiring evaluators to become very familiar not only with the statutory definition of mental retardation in their jurisdiction, but also with any relevant case law in that jurisdiction that may alter that definition (Duvall & Morris, 2006; DeMatteo, Marczyk, & Pich, 2007; Appelbaum, 2009). These varying definitions should also drive home the point to all mental health professionals that participate in these evaluations that their assessments are crucial to the fact finder's determination of whether a specific offender should be spared the death penalty under *Atkins*, which, in effect, places the practitioner in a pivotal role in the life or death decision.

Given the difficulty of assessing an offender's adaptive functioning in the prison setting and the lack of appropriately normed measures, Brodsky and Galloway (2003) propose that the best professional choice seems to be creating a "clinical synthesis of both preincarceration functioning and current functioning." Blume, Johnson, and Seeds (2009) conclude that in the evaluation of adaptive functioning, the facts of the crime should only be considered relevant when they are directly related to, and offset, the adaptive limitations claimed by the defendant. The most common practices in evaluating adaptive functioning among the evaluators in Young, Boccaccini, Conroy, and Lawson's (2007) study included reviewing records (educational and mental health), interviewing the defendant, and interviewing others that may provide descriptions of the defendant's behavior.

Young, Boccaccinni, Conroy, and Lawson (2007) emphasize that evaluators should be aware that there is no agreement among professionals concerning how the Flynn effect should alter any diagnostic conclusions. Flynn (2000) argued at one time against making any adjustments to individuals' obtained scores based on the Flynn effect since the trend it describes is subject to variability. However, in 2006, Flynn proposed a formula for converting IQ scores to compensate for the Flynn effect; a practice that has been supported by another expert in intelligence testing (Greenspan, 2006). Young, Boccaccini, Conroy, and Lawson (2007) still caution that the Flynn effect should serve as a method of explaining variations in test scores over time on different versions of the same test and that evaluators who consider the Flynn effect in their evaluations should be familiar with current Flynn effect research. It is recommended that examiners refrain from administering the same intelligence tests to the same person within a year in order to avoid the influence of practice effects.

The American Psychological Association's ethics code states that "Psychologists administer, adapt, score, interpret, or use assessment techniques, interviews, tests, or instruments in a manner and for purposes that are appropriate in light of the research on or evidence of the usefulness and proper application of techniques" (Standard 9.02(a); APA, 2002). Given the problems previously described that face evaluators in capital case mental retardation assessments, how can one serve their function ethically given the constraints placed on them? While evaluators could certainly refuse to produce assessments in states whose statutes conflict with psychological assessment practices, some authors provide explanations of how evaluators may perform their function ethically. For example, Duvall and Morris (2006) have pointed out that the American Psychological Association's ethics code itself provides some guidance to evaluators in Standard 1.02 which reads as follows:

If psychologists' ethical responsibilities conflict with law, regulations, or other governing legal authority, psychologists make known their commitment to the Ethics Code and take steps to resolve the conflict. If the conflict is unresolvable via such means, psychologists may adhere to the requirements of the law, regulations, or other governing legal authority (APA, 2002).

As they recommend, evaluators can satisfy their ethical responsibilities by adhering to the statutes in their jurisdiction while including in their reports and court testimonies what limitations exist in their findings based on recommended assessment practices.

Suggestions for Future Research

Due to the overwhelming secondary gain for a defendant facing capital charges in a death penalty state, continued research into malingering intellectual and developmental disabilities is recommended. Psychological tests specifically designed to detect the malingering of memory or other cognitive abilities or symptoms of psychosis could benefit from also being normed on a genuinely intellectually disabled population. Having more instruments normed in this manner increases their utility in evaluating both genuine and malingered deficits or psychiatric symptoms in a potentially intellectually disabled individual.

Given the frequency with which court decisions can alter how practitioners perform evaluations, it would be beneficial to continue studying court decisions that involve the evaluation of intellectual disability; especially those regarding the extent to which evaluators can include psychometric factors in their interpretations. Further research into the assessment of adaptive functioning in correctional institutions is needed. The focus of this research could be on establishing best practice guidelines for assessing adaptive functioning as well as developing and validating measures of adaptive functioning that can be reliably utilized within a correctional setting.

Examining the nature of stereotypes and biases of those within the legal system could also prove beneficial in educating judges, juries, and attorneys regarding the realities of intellectual disability. By doing so, it may be possible to minimize their tendency to draw inaccurate conclusions regarding intellectually disabled offenders. By studying the frequency with which psychometric issues play a pivotal role in intellectual disability determinations, it may be possible to build a case for altering statutes in jurisdictions that do not currently allow them to be considered in determinations.

Forensic Consultants in Criminal Mitigation

Introduction

Psychologists' involvement in the justice system has increased dramatically since the 1962 *Jenkins v. United States* decision that accepted psychologists as expert witnesses. In the wake of this decision, psychologists have been involved in every phase of the trial process, including pretrial, trial, sentencing, and appeals. Since the reinstatement of capital punishment in the United States in 1972 and the increased discretion afforded to judges and/or jurors in sentencing convicted criminals, **mitigating factors** (i.e., any evidence or information presented regarding a defendant or circumstances of a crime that may result in a reduced charge or a lesser sentence) have played an increasingly important role in the criminal justice system. Many mitigating factors may be psychological in nature or related to a defendant's mental state during the time leading up to an offense. As a result, judges, jurors, and attorneys often rely upon forensic mental health professionals to describe factors that may decrease a defendant's **culpability** (i.e., the degree to which a person may be held legally responsible for their actions). When mitigating the sentence is the goal, attorneys attempt to "humanize the client to the jury," and in capital cases, the goal is to "save the client's life" (Atkins, Podboy, Larson, & Schenker, 2007, p. 9). The scope of the roles of mental health experts may vary widely, depending on factors unique to the case, defendant, type of crime, and jurisdiction.

However, a review of criminal mitigation evaluations indicates that experts involved in mitigation work are most frequently asked the following questions: (1) Does the person have a mental disorder? (2) Is the person's legally relevant behavior caused by or the product of mental disorder rather than the product of the person's free choice? and (3) How will the person behave in the future? (Morse, 1978). The variety of mitigating factors is as diverse as criminal defendants and their crimes. It has been suggested that these factors typically fall into three broad categories (Connell, 2003): (1) cognitive functioning; (2) history of victimization or other evidence of emotional fragility which may increase an individual's risk of future violence; and (3) "catchall" categories that may be defined by a particular jurisdiction such as "other factors in the defendant's background, record, or character or any other circumstance of the offense that mitigate against the imposition of the death sentence" (18 U.S.C. 3592 § (a)(8)). Although the presence of mental illness may be evident even to the layperson, the testimony and findings of a mental health expert can assist the trier of fact in determining, as is required in many jurisdictions, the degree to which the actor's actions were the product of their illness (Barnard, 1997). It has been noted that statutorily-defined mitigators are "phrased in terms that invite clinical participation" (Melton, Petrila, Poythress, & Slobogin, 2007, p. 288). Twenty-two states have statutes guiding capital mitigation, which specifically identify future danger to others (a factor which mental health professionals are often called upon to assess) as a statutory aggravator, and two states (Oregon and Texas) actually require every capital jury to make a determination regarding a defendant's risk for future violence (Connell, 2003). As mitigation and/or sentencing evaluations have become more common, the literature regarding these evaluations has also expanded. The example below is followed by a discussion of the critical components of mitigation evaluations.

A Sample Mitigation Evaluation

What follows are excerpts from a deidentified sample evaluation of mitigating factors conducted by a psychologist. The report provides examples of topic areas covered in the evaluation, as well as the way in which information may be presented to the fact finder. These excerpts are taken from a sample report in an article by Marczyk, Heilbrun, DeMatteo, and Bell (2003, pp. 91–100).

Referral

John Doe is a 20-year-old African American male who is currently charged with murder and related charges. A request for a mental health evaluation to provide the defense with information relevant to sentencing, pursuant to 42 Ps. C.S.A. § 9711(e), was made by Mr. Doe's attorney.

Procedures

Mr. Doe was evaluated on two separate occasions for a total of approximately ten hours at the Correctional Facility, where he is currently incarcerated. In addition to a clinical interview, Mr. Doe was administered a structured screening instrument for symptoms of mental and emotional disorder (the Brief Symptom Inventory, or BSI), a standard test of current functioning in relevant academic areas (the Wide Range Achievement Test, 3rd edition, or WRAT-3), a test of current cognitive and intellectual functioning (the Wechsler Adult Intelligence Scale — revised edition, or WAIS-R), and a standard objective test of mental and emotional functioning (the Minnesota Multiphasic Personality Inventory, 2nd edition, or MMPI-2). Collateral phone interviews were conducted with Sally Smith, Mr. Doe's girlfriend of four years, and Jane Doe, Mr. Doe's mother. We also reviewed the arrest report and arrest history for Mr. Doe.

Prior to the evaluation, Mr. Doe was notified about the purpose of the evaluation and the associated limits of confidentiality. He appeared to understand the basic purpose of the evaluation, reporting back his understanding that he would be evaluated and that a written report would be submitted to his attorney. He further understood that the report could be used in a sentencing hearing, and if it were, copies would be provided to the prosecution and the court.

Relevant history

Historical information was obtained from collateral sources and from Mr. Doe (detailed history followed).

Current clinical condition

(This section detailed current mental status and psychological testing results.)

A Sample Mitigation Evaluation—cont'd

...Mr. Doe's mood throughout the evaluation was largely subdued and neutral, and his showed little emotional variability... Mr. Doe did not report experiencing any perceptual disturbances (auditory or visual hallucinations) or delusions (bizarre ideas with possible basis in reality), and his train of thought was clear and logical... As his cooperation with testing is questionable, Mr. Doe's MMPI-2 profile should be interpreted with caution... Acutely disturbed behavior tends to characterize inmates with this profile... Diagnostically, many individuals with his profile are considered to have severe Personality Disorders, and his response content is consistent with the antisocial features in his history...

Sentencing considerations

According to 42 Pa. C.S.A. § 9177(a)(2), any evidence relating to mitigating circumstances can be presented at the sentencing hearing. The following factors, as enumerated in 42 Pa. C.S.A. § 9177(e), can be considered as mitigating factors:

1. The defendant has no significant history or prior criminal convictions.
2. The defendant was under the influence of extreme mental or emotional disturbance.
3. The capacity of the defendant to appreciate the criminality of his conduct or to conform his conduct to the requirements of law was substantially impaired.
4. The age of the defendant at the time of the [offense].
5. The defendant acted under extreme duress, although not such duress as to constitute a defense to prosecution...or acted under the substantial domination of another person.
6. The victim was a participant in the defendant's homicidal conduct or consented to the homicidal acts.
7. The defendant's participation in the homicidal act was relatively minor.
8. Any other evidence of mitigation concerning the character and record of the defendant and the circumstances of the offense.

The mitigating factors that can be addressed through forensic mental health Assessment (factors 2, 3, 5, and 8) will be further discussed as they relate to Mr. Doe and the circumstances surrounding the alleged offense.

Influence of extreme mental or emotional disturbance

Although Mr. Doe's MMPI-2 profile suggests that he may be experiencing severe problems with his mental and emotional functioning, it may be that such problems are situationally triggered (that is, exacerbated by the conditions of prison incarceration). Nonetheless, his MMPI-2 profile, BSI responses, collateral interviews, and self-report suggest that Mr. Doe suffers from a long-standing adjustment problem in his relationships with other people and his home environment. Individuals with such profiles are often described as experiencing a number of psychological difficulties, and are frequently diagnosed with severe personality disorders. Mr. Doe denied all substance use on the day of the alleged offense.

Capacity to appreciate the criminality of conduct or to conform conduct to the requirements of the law

There is little about Mr. Doe to suggest that he would be unable to appreciate the wrongfulness of criminal acts such as homicide. He did not appear to be delusional (experiencing beliefs with little or no possible basis in fact), experiencing perceptual disturbances (typically seeing or

Continued

A Sample Mitigation Evaluation—cont'd

hearing phenomena not actually present), or grossly disturbed around the time of the offense, according to his own account. According to Mr. Doe's version of events, he was in the passenger seat of the car, and things "happened so fast" that there was little he could do about it. Mr. Doe also stated that he had no idea that his co-defendant was going to shoot the decedent.

Action under extreme duress or under substantial domination of another person

It is difficult to describe Mr. Doe's alleged actions in terms of possible domination by co-defendant, because (as just noted) he maintained that he was not aware that a shooting might have been contemplated and was not involved in any planning or execution of these acts. In other words, according to Mr. Doe, he was a passive bystander who happened to be in the passenger seat of the car when his co-defendant shot the decedent.

Other mitigating circumstances: character, record, and/or offense circumstances

There may also be other mitigating factors concerning Mr. Doe's character, his criminal record, and the circumstances surrounding the alleged offense. First, Mr. Doe apparently does not have a significant history of prior convictions, especially for violent offenses... Of particular importance is the nature of the prior offenses. Mr. Doe has never been charged with any violent offenses, or offenses involving weapons... Based on all sources considered for this evaluation, it appears that Mr. Doe's mother has not been actively involved in his life since an early age. He also reported that he fell under the influence of a gang at the age of ten because he "had to [in order to] survive." In addition, Mr. Doe reported that his mother began abusing cocaine when he was very young... Mr. Doe indicated that he had to provide for his family by selling drugs.

Conclusions

In the opinion of the undersigned, based on all of the above, Mr. Doe:

1. is apparently suffering from a personality disorder;
2. may have been suffering from some of the problems he currently reports around the time of the alleged offense;
3. has other mitigating factors concerning his character, criminal record, and the circumstances surrounding the offense;
4. has treatment/rehabilitation needs in the areas of substance abuse, training in the areas of anger control and interpersonal problem solving, academic achievement and vocational training, and psychological intervention for various maladaptive personality traits;
5. his amenability to interventions would appear somewhat mixed but generally limited, but if these interventions can be made successfully, his risk for future antisocial behavior may be decreased (Marczyk, Heilbrun, DeMatteo, & Bell, 2003, pp. 91–100).

Literature Review

Legal decisions regarding mitigation

Courts have long recognized the importance of considering individual circumstances when making sentencing determinations. In the landmark case of *Gregg v. Georgia* (1976), the Court made efforts to change the approach to mitigation in capital cases. The goal was to make the process less arbitrary by allowing jurors to consider the characteristics of a specific offender and their specific crime when determining an appropriate sentence. Following this decision, several additional cases further clarified the role of mitigating factors, including what may be considered a mitigating factor and even the particular roles psychiatrists and other mental health professionals may play in these types of cases. For example, in *State v. Michael* (1987), the defendant's death sentence was overturned on grounds the defense attorney erred by failing to investigate and discover substantial mitigating evidence regarding the defendant's mental condition. In *Eddings v. Oklahoma* (1982), the United States Supreme Court ruled that the sentencing court erred by not allowing consideration of the defendant's troubled family history as a mitigating factor. In a similar ruling, *People v. Morgan* (1999), the Court overturned a death sentence after finding that the defense attorney failed to investigate documentation of the defendant's organic brain damage, history of childhood abuse, and other mitigating evidence. In (*Wright v. Walls*, 2002), the Supreme Court held that the lower court erred by indicating that the introduction of mitigating evidence was simply a ploy to play on the sympathies of jurors. The ruling in *Hitchcock v. Dugger* (1987) provided for a defendant's right to introduce lack of criminal history as mitigating evidence; though a subsequent decision (*Delo v. Lashley*, 1993) held that defendants are not entitled to a presumption of no criminal history, but the burden of proof lies with the defense if lack of criminal history is to be considered as a mitigating factor, and their counsel must produce evidence indicating their lack of previous criminal behavior in such instances.

Information about a defendant's successful adjustment to incarceration without behavioral difficulties may also be presented as mitigating (*Skipper v. South Carolina*, 1986). The *Barefoot v. Estelle* (1983) decision held that psychiatrists may testify about a defendant's risk of future violence. Most recently, courts have required that when mitigation is pursued, efforts to discover "all reasonably available" mitigating evidence be made by defense counsel; likewise, the defense is required to make similar efforts to discover any evidence which may be used to rebut aggravating evidence (*Wiggins v. Smith*, 2003). Such rulings clearly establish the right of defendants to present mitigating evidence that could support a lighter sentence; thus, resulting in an increased demand for forensic consultants regarding these issues. Consequently, there has been an expansion of professional standards and research to guide practitioners who provide these services.

Uniqueness of mitigation evaluations

Mitigation evaluations differ from traditional psychological evaluations in many ways, and those conducting these evaluations should be familiar with these differences. For example, the referral questions often involve legal concepts and the subsequent results and possible testimony may be interpreted by a jury of laypeople. Traditional psychological assessment techniques may not be appropriate for use in mitigation or other evaluations for the court (Bursten, 1981; Connell, 2003; Melton *et al.*, 2007). Additionally, expert witnesses may experience subtle or blatant pressure to reach conclusions that support a particular outcome, particularly by the party that retained the expert (Connell, 2003). Experts, particularly in capital cases, must refrain from providing written materials or verbal testimony that directly indicate whether or not aggravating factors are outnumbered or justified by mitigating factors. Their role is to simply evaluate and address the presence or absence of such issues and then allow the fact finder to make a determination regarding the relative weight of these variables (Connell, 2003).

The mitigation evaluation differs from other forms of forensic assessment in its scope. These evaluations are typically more broad than other forensic evaluations (e.g., insanity, competency to stand trial), as the evaluator is asked to find "each and every" mitigating factor, which will require thorough investigation of the offender and their life circumstances from birth to the offense, and even their adjustment to incarceration beyond the offense (Connell, 2003, p. 327). Connell (2003, p. 327) notes that, in contrast to other forensic evaluations, such exploration "does not represent an absence of neutrality or objectivity on the part of the evaluator; in fact, it is essential to approach each potential mitigating factor with a posture of receptivity to evidence of its existence or its absence." Finally, in contrast to traditional diagnostic evaluations, a diagnosis alone may provide little helpful information to the court. Instead, the detailed **"psychobiography"** (i.e., a biographical account of an individual's life which analyzes the psychological makeup, motivations, or character of the subject) of the defendant may be the most important and relevant finding resulting from the evaluation; and diagnosis may even be contraindicated, as it may obscure more important and pertinent information (Connell, 2003).

Procedures in mitigation evaluations

When hired to be a mitigation expert, the goal of the evaluator is to help the jury "learn of the nexus between the troubled history and criminal behavior, or more particularly, the degree of autonomy in the defendant's life choices" (Connell, 2003, p. 322). Because traditional psychological tests will do little to assist the expert in making this connection, exemplary interviewing and information gathering techniques will be required of these experts (Connel, 2003). The array of factors which may lessen a defendant's responsibility is vast, and may include history of abuse, poverty, substance abuse, family **psychopathology** (i.e., the manifestation of mental illness, such as specific symptoms, including disturbances of mood, thought, or feeling), loss, unemployment, learning problems, and virtually any other psychological, social, or economic factor that may have contributed to the development of criminal behavior or the offense in question (Connell, 2003).

Informed consent

The first step in any psychological evaluation, including mitigation evaluations, is **informed consent** (i.e., the process of informing the individual of the process involved in the evaluation, as well as the possible uses of the information and any limits of confidentiality, and allowing the individual to ask questions as well as consult with legal counsel regarding whether and how to participate), and there are special issues which must be considered and addressed in these evaluations. As in every psychological evaluation, the expert must address the nature and purpose of the assessment, make arrangements regarding fees and who will pay them, and the reasons for the involvement of third parties (e.g., family members, attorneys, acquaintances, eyewitnesses). However, the mitigation evaluator must provide this information and obtain consent while maintaining awareness of the increased vulnerability of the defendant, particularly if the case is a capital offense (Connell, 2003). Extra time must be designated for the asking of questions, both by the defendant and legal counsel, and the expert must always consider the defendant's preferences and best interests, though actual consent will be obtained from the legal counsel (Connell, 2003). It should be explained to the defendant that the report (if one is produced) will be provided to his/her attorney, and the attorney will make decisions regarding whether and how it is introduced. Because mitigation includes a presumption of guilt, it is important that the examiner explain that their contact falls under the umbrella of his or her attorney client privilege since the expert has been retained by the defense; otherwise, the defendant, particularly if charged with homicide, may continue to maintain his/her innocence, limiting the evaluator's ability to obtain vital information.

Review of records in preparation for evaluation

Prior to meeting with the defendant for the formal assessment, the evaluator should obtain all relevant records from the retaining attorney (Atkins *et al.*, 2007). The minimally-required information should include: (1) a complete set of the crime reports concerning all offenses currently charged; (2) state and federal criminal records; (3) juvenile criminal history; (4) complete set of the offense reports for each and every arrest entry in the defendant's criminal history records; (5) court records of conviction for every adjudication, including psychological evaluations where they exist and are available; (6) District Attorney documents on previously filed cases against the defendant; (7) school records, including psychological testing results; (8) military records; (9) all psychological records, including court-appointed examination records; (10) jail medical and psychiatric treatment records; and (11) jail custody logs and prison records (Atkins *et al.*, 2007).

History interview

After consent has been obtained, the evaluation usually continues with a thorough review of the defendant's personal history from birth to the offense and to the time period of incarceration following the offense. The interviewer should inquire about "all of the history predating the present set of events" (Connell, 2003, p. 328), including prior convictions/ arrests, interactions with law enforcement, relationship difficulties, and any other idiosyncratic areas that might provide information regarding the defendant's development or character. If aggravating factors are uncovered during this investigation, such information will "help to round out one's appreciation for data that will be offered by the prosecution," and questions may be asked to "develop an understanding of how the defendant experienced or processed these events, how thinking and feeling were consequently altered, and how the bad acts or experiences shaped the eventual outcome" (Connell, 2003, p. 329). In other words, the mitigation investigation itself may uncover clues regarding aggravating evidence which may be utilized by the prosecution and information regarding a defendant's response to or experience of aggravating circumstances may be utilized to counter the presentation of such evidence.

It is generally recommended that the history interview proceed chronologically, beginning with the defendant's in-utero history and birth experience, including any complications or abnormalities. The interview should then cover the defendant's early childhood, family composition, early schooling, family socioeconomic status, and family relationships. At minimum, the interview should address common factors which contribute to violence, including: low IQ/learning disabilities, attention deficit hyperactivity disorder (ADHD), criminal modeling by a parent, peer rejection, childhood aggression, marital separation and conflict, child abuse, history of mental illness in the family, and parental absence and neglect (Atkins *et al.*, 2007). Information gleaned during this process will direct the examiner toward pertinent records, such as school, medical, and family mental health records in addition to providing the names of individuals who may be able to corroborate or elaborate on information provided by the defendant regarding his/her early years. This information will also assist the investigator in determining the nature of the defendant's emotional, intellectual, and psychological development, as well as provide the first clues to the defendant's level of emotional maturity at the time of the offense (Connell, 2003).

Inquiring about substance use

Depending on the circumstances and relevant statutes, substance use at the time of the offense or in the defendant's history may be considered either aggravating or mitigating. In order to do this, the evaluator must assess via direct interview and record review any familial history of substance use, types of substances used and periods of abstinence, previous treatment, typical amounts used, signs of dependence, and patterns of use in the time period preceding and during the offense.

The defendant's childhood

An expert's goal during this portion of the evaluation, as well as when providing written or verbal testimony, should be to "bring to life" (Connell, 2003, p. 331) the defendant's childhood for the jury. Information should be gathered regarding poverty, discrimination experienced by the defendant and/or members of his/her family, familial views regarding education, parental disciplinary techniques and parenting styles, familial views about the world as either a supportive or hostile environment, and detailed descriptions of the physical environments in which the defendant was reared. It is even recommended that evaluators visit the defendant's childhood home when possible, and photographs may be provided to bolster hypotheses regarding the defendant's upbringing and early life. A visit to the defendant's childhood neighborhood also affords the expert an opportunity to speak with teachers, coaches, or neighbors who can provide collateral information (Connell, 2003).

Character development

Haney (1995, p. 561) made the following statement about capital offenders:

> *There is increased recognition that the roots of violent behavior extend beyond the person-ality or character structure of those people who perform it, and connect historically to the brutalizing experiences they have commonly shared as well as the immediately precipitating situations in which violence transpires.*

In light of this information, it is important that examiners probing for the presence of mitigating factors explore the pathways that led a particular defendant to violence (Connell, 2003). While identifying aspects of the defendant's life relevant to the development of criminal or violent behavior, it is also important for the criminal mitigation specialist to search for information suggesting the defendant's capacity for goodness (e.g., acts of heroism, generosity, or other meritorious behavior), and accomplishments, including photographs of special events. The defendant's family and loved ones may also provide insight into how the defendant is perceived by those closest to him/her. These individuals can share memories describing their interactions with the defendant that can humanize him/her to the jury (Connell, 2003).

Psychological testing

Although historically viewed as not directly pertinent to specific mitigating factors (Heilbrun, 1992), psychological testing may offer data pertinent to the defendant's diagnostic history or diagnostic hypotheses generated by the examiner (Connell, 2003). Psychological tests should only be utilized if they are likely to be helpful in determining mitigating factors. Testing may be contraindicated for use with defendants where there is no indication of cognitive or emotional impairment. The pros and cons of using psychological testing in mitigation evaluations will be discussed in further detail in the implications section; however, it is generally recommended if formal testing is undertaken, it be comprised of objectively scored cognitive and personality measures (e.g., the Minnesota Multiphasic Personality Inventory-2 [MMPI-2], the Personality Assessment Inventory [PAI], the Wechsler Adult Intelligence Scale − IV [WAIS-IV], the Wechsler Memory Scale − IV [WMS-IV]) that bear directly on the **psycholegal question** (i.e., the reason for the solicitation of the evaluator's services, in this case, an evaluation for the presence of mitigating factors which may be present in the defendant's history or current presentation) at hand. Testing instruments selected should contain some **measure of impression management** (i.e., scales or items which have been normed on individuals instructed to display one or more problematic response styles, such as over- or under-reporting of symptoms, and allow the evaluator to determine if the respondent may be engaging in such distortion) or response style. As with any evaluation, the limitations of these instruments, as well as their applicability to the population being examined, must be stated (Connell, 2003).

Convergence of data

The importance of third party information cannot be understated, as defendants may be "invested in a portrayal that is not altogether accurate" (Connell, 2003, p. 337). Facts given by the defendant and others who may have motivation to portray circumstances in a particular way should be verified and checked against a review of records, prosecution files, medical and mental health records, academic records, prison records, and the defendant's criminal history (Reid, 2003; Heilbrun, Rosenfeld, Warren, & Collins, 1994). Collateral interviews should also be conducted when possible, and should include: arresting officers, crime scene investigators, corrections staff, eyewitnesses, family members, friends, teachers, clergy, employers, and coworkers (Connell, 2003). This standard of practice acknowledges and guards against the consciously or unconsciously introduced bias by those involved in a mitigation investigation (Atkins *et al.*, 2007).

Post-offense adjustment

Information regarding the defendant's ability to adjust to a structured environment that limits his/her access to drugs, weapons, or alcohol may provide data regarding potentially mitigating factors (Connell, 2003). For example, the quality of the defendant's interactions with peers and correctional staff may be assessed and compared to that of other individuals charged with or convicted of similar charges. Additionally, the prison or jail environment may provide opportunities for the defendant to engage in substance abuse or mental health treatment or academic/vocational training programs, which may not have previously been available. The defendant's responses to these programs provide the evaluator with information relevant to mitigation, including the defendant's motivation to engage in treatment, as well as indicators of the likely future effectiveness of such programs with that particular individual (Connell, 2003).

Presentation of findings

Once extensive data have been compiled, and opinions formed regarding the presence and impact of mitigating factors, the data must be presented in various forms. Typically, the first presentation of data occurs when the retained expert consults with the defense team informally, outside of open court (Connell, 2003). Although formal consultation with the defense team occurs at the conclusion of the evaluation, it is an ongoing process throughout the evaluation. Mitigation specialists are cautioned to not cross the line between keeping defense counsel informed and becoming too much of a member of the defense team, rather than an objective provider of information, as this could compromise an evaluator's objectivity or could give the appearance of advocacy on the part of a person who should be neutral and objective to the jury (Goldstein, 2001). As a result of this ongoing consultation, the defense team will determine whether or not they wish for the expert to provide a written report summarizing his/her findings. The expert should discuss their duty to present all data, regardless of whether it is supportive of a particular legal strategy, with the defense team, when discussing accepting the referral (Connell, 2003; American Psychological Association, 2002; Goldstein, 2001). If the defense team decides against the preparation of a written report, the expert may still be asked to produce an outline of probable testimony, including any visual aids (e.g., charts, graphs, photographs, awards, certificates, diplomas), which may be used to bolster testimony (Connell, 2003). Many courtrooms are now equipped with audio/visual equipment, and experts often use PowerPoint or similar software to clearly and concisely convey their findings.

General recommendations regarding mitigation evaluations

Connell (2003) has provided general recommendations for experts involved in mitigation consultation. She first recommends that evaluations be thorough and include exploration of all angles of a defendant's history, offense and criminal behavior, and current functioning in order to ensure that the expert develops a "comprehensive appreciation for all the facts of the case, both aggravating and mitigating" (p. 344). She then recommends that evaluators be objective and to provide adequate verification/corroboration of any opinions formed or testimony offered. Thirdly, evaluators should present their results in a "dispassionate, objective, and professional manner" (p. 345), and should present an "overall demeanor…of a resource to the court, not an advocate of a particular outcome" (p. 346). Limitations of any data must be clearly and directly stated, and evaluators should decline to answer questions for which there are not answers that are supported by theory and data. Finally, it is generally not acceptable for the evaluator to offer an opinion or recommendation about a particular sentence since this is typically left "strictly to the trier of fact" (p. 346), and runs counter to the role of the evaluator as a disinterested and objective third party.

Current controversies regarding mitigation consultation

Whether psychiatrists, psychologists, and other mental health professionals should be involved in capital cases on any level, including in mitigation evaluations, has historically been a controversial issue (Leong, Weinstock, Silva, & Eth, 1993). Some argue that any role in a capital case may be viewed by some as participation in an execution, and, therefore, counter to the ethical principles of these professions. In addition to this controversy, the "door opening" effect of such evaluations has come under criticism (Connell, 2003). Depending on jurisdictional regulations, discussing a defendant's actions during an alleged offense may open the door for prosecutors to discuss the alleged offense with the defendant as well, as in most jurisdictions, once the defense team broaches the topic of the alleged offense via an expert, the prosecution also will be provided an opportunity to discuss such information, including cross-examination of the expert and rebuttal testimony (Connell, 2003). Therefore, it is recommended that the expert discuss this matter in detail with defense counsel prior to asking a defendant any questions regarding the alleged offense. Mitigating evidence may be collected without discussing the defendant's actions during the alleged offense, allowing this potential conflict to be avoided altogether (Connell, 2003).

If a decision is made to discuss the alleged offense in detail, the following pros and cons must be weighed carefully by the evaluator and defense counsel. Pros of discussing the alleged offense in detail include: (1) supporting the evaluator's need to have a full, balanced, and comprehensive dataset from which to form opinions; (2) may be necessary to determine the level of the defendant's involvement in a crime; or (3) to ascertain the level of maturity displayed by a defendant (Goldstein, 2002; Connell, 2003). Regarding cons, failure to discuss the offense with the defendant leaves one vulnerable to attack by the prosecutor (Eisenberg, 2001). For example, during cross-examination, the prosecutor may well ask if an evaluator discussed the offense with the defendant, and could therefore pursue a line of questioning calling into the question the thoroughness of the evaluation, as well as the evaluator's ability to be objective without discussing all important aspects of the defendant's history, particularly an aspect so important to the current legal proceedings. On the contrary, Cunningham and Reidy (2001) have suggested that any information necessary to form such opinions may be obtained from investigative materials (e.g., police reports, witness statements). Finally, some researchers contend that the defendant may give a version of events that is not supported by available evidence, and such information may be unduly damaging when presented to a jury (Cunningham & Reidy, 2001).

Another controversy regarding sentencing evaluations concerns the role of formal psychological testing. Although these instruments may supply objective indicators of current pathology, response style, and the like (Connell, 2003), there are several considerations in test selection or if testing should be used at all (Cunningham & Reidy, 2001). For example, most instruments are not normed for criminal defendants, particularly those charged with capital murder. Other concerns include the following: (1) an individual's profile pattern may change over time; (2) personality assessment does not typically offer data concerning a defendant's past, which is often most relevant for mitigation; (3) personality assessment is typically of little use in predicting future violence within prison settings; and (4) personality assessment is likely to uncover evidence of personality disorders and descriptions of maladaptive traits that are rarely mitigating (Cunningham & Reidy, 2001).

Another issue causing debate involves how to handle criminal defendants, particularly homicide defendants, claiming amnesia for their alleged criminal offenses (Evans, 2006; Pyszaora, Barker, & Kopelman, 2003; vanOoursouw, Merckelbach, Ravelli, Nijman, & Mekking-Pompen, 2004). Claims of this nature have traditionally been viewed as possible **malingering** (i.e., exaggerating or fabricating symptoms of mental illness for the purpose of some secondary gain, in criminal cases, to avoid prosecution or lengthy sentences), yet, more recent evidence suggests that they are not predictive of malingering, but rather may be associated with substance use at the time of the offense (Stout & Farooque, 2008). Substance use can be viewed as either mitigating or aggravating depending upon the totality of the circumstances. Similarly, reports of dissociation by a defendant are often viewed as evidence of feigning or failure to take responsibility. The statutes of many jurisdictions fail to adequately address whether those with altered states of consciousness, such as those in a **dissociative state** (i.e., a state of consciousness in which there is a sudden, temporary alteration in the normally integrated functions of thought, feeling, and consciousness), are able to form criminal intent (Schiele, 2003). Thus, the interpretation of claims of amnesia and dissociation, as well as how this information should be presented to jurors, should be carefully considered.

Another controversy centers around the handling of high profile cases. Because mitigation evaluations frequently happen in the context of capital or other serious felony cases, examiners may face unique challenges. Although Reid (2003) recommends handling these cases the way one would handle any case by conducting a professional, comprehensive, objective evaluation that is sensitive to the referral question and the needs of the referral source, he also recognizes that "in prominent or controversial cases, it may be more difficult to adhere to the priorities and quality that one should come to expect in every case" (p. 390). More experienced and invested attorneys and the involvement of the media make these cases particularly challenging (Reid, 2003). Regarding the media, it is recommended that evaluators exercise caution when deciding whether to make statements or comments, and it is generally not recommended that the case be discussed at all while it is still ongoing (Reid, 2003). If a statement is given after the resolution of a case, the statement, like the expert, should be "objective and clear," and the expert should "understand that even your most reasonable statements are likely to be misconstrued" (Reid, 2003, p. 390). Mitigation evaluations, like all forensic evaluations, carry their own ethical, moral, and legal challenges. In their 1993 survey of forensic witnesses and consultants, Pfeifer and Brigham noted that the most troubling issues faced by these consultants involved the following: (1) accepting a case when they felt certain the defendant was guilty, and the evaluation was likely to help in their defense, possibly even assisting in the procurement of an acquittal; (2) determining if and how to handle media interviews; and (3) dealing with pressure from attorneys and others to provide testimony that supports only one opinion or only a limited portion of the available data.

Forensic Psychology and Policy Implications

As described above, forensic consultants involved in criminal mitigation face unique challenges. Although the Specialty Guidelines for Forensic Psychologists provide some guidance, there has historically been criticism of these guidelines with regard to their relative dearth, as authors have historically held that these guidelines are so aspirational in nature that they provide no "real-world" applicable recommendations for the detailed and thorough work often undertaken by forensic psychologists (Pfeifer & Briham, 1993). Additionally, these authors have suggested that case examples be provided as part of these guidelines, which could illustrate common ethical dilemmas and provide guidance to practitioners facing such issues (Pfeifer & Brigham, 1993). Although these criticisms have been repeatedly levied regarding these guidelines, the guidelines have not been updated to reflect the changes recommended in the literature. It has also been noted that mitigation evaluations often occur in cases that are resolved by a sentencing phase only, following a Guilty plea. Schiele (2003) has recommended against this practice, and has advocated for a complete guilt/innocence phase, followed by a sentencing phase where mitigating evidence may be introduced, if a verdict of guilt is obtained. This, the author argues, could protect the due process rights of defendants in these cases, as often a guilt/innocence phase allows the trier(s) of fact lengthier and more in-depth exposure to pertinent information regarding the defendant and his/her past. Additionally, the provision of a guilt/innocence phase prior to sentencing also upholds the defendant's right to challenge any and all evidence, including incriminating and mitigating evidence.

It has also been opined that mitigating evidence, particularly that of a psychological nature, has little practical meaning to most jurors, and it is recommended that care be taken by experts to present this information "with an eye toward the system in which it will be presented;" in other words, mental health experts should make efforts to explain jargon, as well as the relationship between relevant psychological variables and behavior, and to convey such information in concise ways which are easily understood by the layperson (Atkins *et al.*, 2007, p. 10). It has been noted that jury selection procedures in capital cases do not adequately allow consideration of a potential juror's ability and willingness to consider and weigh mitigating evidence. However, if defense counsel is aware of the specific mitigating factors that may be emphasized during proceedings, the defense attorney can attempt to screen out jurors who may be particularly reluctant to consider or accept this evidence. This, of course, would require the expert's involvement to begin much earlier in the process, and will also require the development of a good working relationship with retaining counsel (Atkins *et al.*, 2007). Also, because jurors are often skeptical of expert witnesses, where possible, data should be confirmed by third party sources, and this verification process should be conveyed to jurors to maximize the credibility of the witness (Atkins *et al.*, 2007). It has also been helpful for attorneys representing capital defendants to begin the introduction of mitigating evidence during the guilt/innocence phase, frequently by utilizing a defense strategy, such as diminished capacity, which may not result in successful acquittal, but nevertheless allows the jurors to receive the earliest and most in-depth exposure to mitigating factors related to the defendant's mental state, psychological functioning, or personal history (Atkins *et al.*, 2007). Finally, in light of historical evidence to suggest that specialized forensic training improves the quality of evaluations produced by experts (Melton *et al.*, 2007; Shipley, 2013), it is recommended that lawmakers include information regarding minimal qualifications of forensic mental health experts, to ensure that credible and relevant evidence is presented to the triers of fact. This is particularly important in cases that involve serious felonies or capital crimes.

Suggestions for Future Research

Research efforts in the area of criminal mitigation evaluations should continue to expound upon the literature covered in this section. Specifically, it has been recommended that future research should attempt to address what has been called a "lack of direction" for psychologists involved in this area of practice (Pfeifer & Brigham, 1993, p. 342). Additionally, although there has been much discussion of opposing viewpoints regarding current controversies in forensic work in general and mitigation work in particular, there is currently a dearth of empirical support for these viewpoints, and this should be a focus of future investigations. For example, future researchers would do well to elucidate the most effective ways in which information regarding mitigating factors may be communicated to attorneys, the courts, and the trier(s) of fact via experimental research, as well as surveys of the opinions of judges, jurors, and mental health experts regarding the utility and relevance of mitigation evaluations. Additionally, the criticisms which have been raised regarding the Specialty Guidelines for Forensic Psychologists should be incorporated into new, revised guidelines, which are more detailed, and could possibly include case examples and written samples for various types of evaluations, including mitigation evaluations.

Related Websites

www.aaidd.org/
Website for the American Association on Intellectual and Developmental Disabilities.
www.deathpenaltyinfo.org/intellectual-disability-and-death-penalty
Provides information about the death penalty and intellectual disability.
www.ap-ls.org/aboutpsychlaw/InfoPractitioners.php
Website of the American Psychology-Law Society, a division of the American Psychological Association, provides information on resources, training programs, etc. for practitioners and students.
www.megalaw.com/top/mentalhealth.php
Provides links to information regarding recent decisions from state and federal courts regarding the interpretation of mental health law.

Continued

Related Websites—cont'd

www.cayleedaily.com/
A website posting information from news sources covering numerous high-profile cases including Casey Anthony.
http://crime.about.com/od/current/a/scott.htm
A website providing information on the Scott Peterson case from multiple sources.
http://federalevidence.com/rules-of-evidence
Review the Federal Rules of Evidence as well recent cases and developments.
www.lawmall.com/jfk.mm/mm_daube.html
The Daubert Decision.

Court and the Legal System: Civil Forensics

Key Issues

Defining Mental Illness
- To analyze and understand key issues in law and psychology as they pertain to civil commitment
- Explore the legal concepts of mental illness and insanity
- To critically analyze the role of psychiatric diagnosis in the legal process and how it affects civil commitments.

Right to Refuse Treatment
- Civil rights issues of an individual's right to refuse treatment
- The Least Restrictive Doctrine, the Doctrine of Informed Consent, and competency of deciding treatment

Evaluating Psychiatric Work-Related Disability
- Social Security programs for mentally ill individuals who are unable to work due to mental illness
- Programs in place that help mentally ill individuals gain and maintain their employment

Duty to Inform v. Client Confidentiality
- Client confidentiality
- *Tarasoff* and "duty to warn"
- "Duty to warn" and HIV/AIDS

Victim—Offender Mediation
- Restorative justice and victim—offender mediation programs
- Effectiveness of mediation programs
- Arguments against victim—offender mediation

Civil Forensics

Chapter Outline

Introduction to Forensic Psychology. DOI: 10.1016/B978-0-12-382169-0.00003-7

Overview

The legal system assumes an important role in the adjudication of noncriminal matters impacting the lives of persons with mental illness. In addition, nonadjudicatory remedies affecting parties injured by offenders, or those emotionally suffering because of the pain they may have caused the public, represent alternative societal responses to the problem of crime and violence. Broadly defined, these are efforts designed to produce civil justice. Psychologists assist the court system or other administrative boards in determining how best to realize specific outcomes in this forensic area.

There are four civil justice issues examined in this chapter. These particular topics demonstrate the variety of avenues wherein forensic psychologists, invested in the effective operation of the formal civil and informal civil court system, influence overall decision-making. Subjects investigated include (1) defining mental illness; (2) the right to refuse (medical) treatment; (3) evaluating psychiatric work-related disability; (4) duty to inform versus client confidentiality; and (5) victim–offender mediation. Similar to other chapters in this textbook, emphasis is placed on presenting a breadth of topics to canvass. This allows one to consider the broader justice implications for the field (i.e., civil forensics) in relationship to the various roles of the psychologist or expert practitioner.

Persons with mental illness can be, under specified conditions, hospitalized against their will. What is the meaning of mental illness for lawyers and psychologists? How is the mental illness construct employed for purposes of involuntary commitment? Persons identified as psychiatrically disordered can, under the law, exercise their right to refuse (medical) treatment. To what extent can the mentally ill invoke this right in the context of antipsychotic medication? What role does one's informed consent play in the decision to refuse treatment? How do the legal and psychological communities endorse the individual autonomy of a mentally disordered citizen in the wake of one invoking a treatment refusal right? The law requires that the psychiatric care persons receive must occur in the most nonrestrictive environment possible so that the individual's liberty (e.g., freedom of movement) is protected. How does the "psycholegal" establishment operationalize this standard? Mentally ill individuals may be eligible for social security benefits. What is the difference between the clinical and legal definition of disability? Who is eligible for benefits and what role do psychologists play in this process?

In addition to formal courtroom outlets and legal mechanisms for advancing the aims of civil forensics, psychologists are called upon to promote the interests of justice in the informal legal system as well. Mental health clinicians are, on occasion, presented with clients who may act violently toward others. Psychologists are also entrusted with safeguarding the confidentiality of what their clients describe to them. What are the legal and ethical obligations and limits of mental health professionals when a client poses a threat to a third party? Are there circumstances in which client confidentiality can (and must) be breached? Increasingly, jurisdictions around the country are adopting the philosophy of restorative justice at the postconviction phase of a case. A key dimension to restorative justice is reconciliation through victim—offender mediation (VOM). How does VOM work? How can forensic psychologists assist in the restorative justice process? How does VOM promote the interests of reconciliation for offenders, victims, and the community of which both are a part?

The legal system has a vested interest in the resolution of noncriminal disputes that affect citizens who are users of mental health services or are victims of crime. When the tools of the psychological sciences are relied upon to address these matters, forensic experts are responding to issues of civil justice. The five controversies presented in this chapter reveal the degree to which psychologists influence outcomes in both the formal and informal court system. Clearly, this chapter demonstrates that citizens are impacted by the legal system in a number of noncriminal contexts and that trained forensic specialists assume vital roles in the process of determining how best to address these concerns. As a matter of policy, then, the civil forensic field, in relation to the legal system, presents the skilled practitioner with a different set of issues to understand and/or interpret versus its adult and juvenile counterparts.

Defining Mental Illness

Introduction

What exactly *is* **mental illness** and what is the significance of the concept for issues in law and psychology? While the mental health community has generally used the term "mental illness" somewhat haphazardly for purposes of diagnosis and treatment (International Association for Forensic and Correctional Psychology, 2010), it assumes greater significance when its legal relevance appears in a wide variety of contexts. Perhaps, most importantly, it is a prerequisite for **civil commitment** (i.e., a legal process to court-order an individual with symptoms of severe mental illness into treatment in a hospital) (as in the case of Gina below), and if mental illness impacts critical functional capacities designated in the law, it has implications for the insanity defense and trial competency as well. Mental illness can also have a dramatic impact on determining competencies, such as competency to stand trial, to execute a will, child custody, or to manage property (Shipley, 2013; Jones, Sheitman, Edwards, Carbone, Hazelrigg, & Barrick, 2011; Mossman, 2007; Johnstone, Schopp, & Shigaki, 2000). However, a diagnosis of a mental illness alone is insufficient to determine if someone is incompetent to perform a function as described in the law (e.g., competence to stand trial). The forensic evaluator must explain the functional deficits present for the specific competency in question, as a result of mental illness or some other condition (e.g., intellectual disability or a medical condition). For example, the plea of insanity was rejected by a jury in the case of Andrew Goldstein, a man with a history of schizophrenia, who pushed a woman to her death in front of a subway train in New York City (Barnes, 2000).

Further, the definition of mental illness becomes an issue *after* an individual is found incompetent or legally insane. The continued confinement of those found Not Guilty by Reason of Insanity (NGRI) is only permissible by law if a continued manifestation of mental illness exists. Individuals who are committed to a psychiatric hospital as incompetent to stand trial must still be demonstrating substantial functional deficits relating to their factual and/or rational understanding of court-related issues or in their ability to participate in their defense, as a result of mental illness.

Given the importance of the concept of mental illness in issues such as those described above, its legal definition and operationalization have significant consequences for psychology and the criminal justice system. The concern, however, is that the very definition of mental illness is rarely (or perhaps never) made precise by legislators, often resulting in broad, general descriptions. Despite the continuing controversy over the meaning of mental illness as a legal concern, legislators and courts have done very little to clarify the issue. The legal definition of "**insanity**" is different than the definitions of mental disorders/diagnoses commonly understood in the mental health arena. Slovenko (2002, p. 421) examines the question of whether or not psychiatric diagnosis should play a role in the legal process and concludes that it should, but it is "not always a *sine qua non*" or the essential condition in the disposition of a legal issue. We now turn to the concept of "mental illness" in more detail; specifically within the context of civil commitment and insanity defenses.

Gina Hampton is a 27-year-old musician in a large metropolitan area. Gina has a history of mental instability, with diagnoses of narcissistic and antisocial personality disorders as well as severe depression and occasional suicidal ideation. Recently, she was exposed to several stressful events, including the death of a close friend and the break-up of a 5-year relationship. Her friends and family have noticed her mental state worsening over the past few weeks and fear that she may present a danger to herself or those around her. Some suggest that she be placed in a psychiatric hospital for further observation. Gina, however, insists that she is "fine" and resists any attempt at psychological intervention. Unconvinced, her friends and family wonder under which conditions Gina may be hospitalized against her will, as they feel it would be in her best interest at this time. The involuntary hospitalization of Gina, however, requires a finding that she is "mentally ill" and presents an imminent danger to self or others. Given that she has recently engaged in several dangerous behaviors, jeopardizing her own safety as well as that of others, the primary question is whether she is "mentally ill" in the eyes of the law.

Literature Review

Civil commitment

The first substantive criterion for civil commitment or involuntary hospitalization is the presence of a mental impairment. Most jurisdictions define this as the existence of a "mental illness" or a demonstration that the individual is suffering from a "mental disorder". Recent research indicates that although the existence of mental illness is substantive criterion for civil commitment, it is not enough to force treatment (Testa & West, 2010). Legislation is being discussed that will decide if a "capacity test" will be needed when considerations are being made in regards to civil commitment, as well as involuntary medications (Buchanan, 2007; O'Brien, 2010). Consistent with basic due process, the Court has held that an individual who is not mentally ill cannot be involuntarily committed for civil purposes (see *Foucha v. Louisiana*, 1992). Since the existence of mental illness is a necessary prerequisite for civil commitment, the primary interest is then in the constitution of mental illness. What exactly must be found if an individual is to be hospitalized against his or her will?

Poletiek (2002) explored how psychiatrists and judges assess the dangerousness of mentally ill individuals being evaluated for civil commitment. Results indicated that judges more often define "**dangerousness**" as harming others, as compared to psychiatrists who more often include harm to self in the definition. Strachan (2008) explored the role of the government in civil commitments and the determination of dangerousness. What was found was that generally people are considered dangerous if they have a mental disorder. The role of *parens patriae* justifies providing care to an individual (in an incapacitated state) who is unable to seek out care independently. Werth (2001, p. 348) examined the civil commitment statutes of all 50 states and the District of Columbia to determine "(1) What is required for a person who is believed to be at serious and imminent risk of self-harm to be eligible for involuntary hospitalization; and (2) Whether an attempt to involuntarily hospitalize was required or was merely an option when the requirements in number (1) were met." The results indicated that 85% of the jurisdictions mandate that dangerousness to self be the result of a mental illness, and just two jurisdictions require attempts at involuntary hospitalization if a person is found to be an imminent risk of harm to self. A Canadian study found that individuals detained under civil commitment statutes were more likely to be male, diagnosed with schizophrenia, and already known to the criminal justice system, whereas those voluntarily committed were not (Crisanti & Love, 2001). Additionally, these researchers found that once hospitalized, involuntary patients stayed considerably longer than voluntarily admitted patients. In a study that examined the relationship between involuntary commitment and arrest (n = 1064 involuntary subjects; n = 1078 voluntary subjects), results indicated that subsequent criminal behavior was higher amongst those admitted under civil commitment legislation (Crisanti & Love, 2002).

States have had to face constitutional challenges to laws involving involuntary commitment, which have forced a significant change to commitment laws (Melton *et al.*, 2007). All state

laws require the presence of a mental disorder and the finding that the person is dangerous to self or others due to the mental disorder. Melton *et al.* (2007) cite one of the most specific of legislative attempts in Vermont to define mental illness as:

> *…a substantial disorder of thought, mood, perception, orientation or memory, any of which grossly impairs judgment, behavior, capacity to recognize reality, or ability to meet the ordinary demands of life, but shall not include mental retardation (p. 335).*

Such a proposal is far more precise than another statute, which reads, "a mentally ill person means a person whose mental health is substantially impaired" (Melton *et al.*, 2007, p.335). It is, however, still controversial as it relies on equally vague terms such as "substantial," "grossly impaired," and "ordinary demands of life." Many statutes have, however, attained some degree of success by excluding conditions such as mental retardation, substance abuse, and epilepsy (Melton *et al.*, 2007). Additionally, alcohol and substance abuse problems are generally not considered a mental illness for legal purposes. Thus, by excluding some mental impairment, the law has limited the scope of mental illness to some degree. The meaning of mental illness nonetheless remains open to individual interpretation. Who, then, interprets?

The consistent imprecision with and neglect for clearly defining the construct by the legislature has left the courts to "fashion a definition for the words 'mentally ill' …thereby fill [ing] the void in the statutory hospital law" (*Dodd v. Hughes*, 1965, p. 542). Several decades later and this statement remains true. With the responsibility of defining and assessing potential mental illness as it stands before them, the courts have further deferred to the profession of mental health (i.e., expert testimony by psychiatrists and psychologists) (Slovenko, 2002; Arrigo, 1993; Melton *et al.*, 2007; Strachan, 2008). This power given to, or, more appropriately, *dependent on*, the medical and mental health communities in the decision-making process persists, even though substantial research has documented a lack of consensus among professionals in matters of diagnosis (Perlin, 2005; Arrigo, 1993). Research has shown that psychologists and psychiatrists are not necessarily any more in agreement about what mental illness is than anyone else. There is a general consensus regarding criteria for a diagnosis in the mental health community, but there is often debate regarding whether or not a particular individual meets the criteria for a disorder. Thus, the failure to legally define mental illness may be, in part, a function of psychology and medicine's lack of precision in defining and describing it, particularly in the concrete fashion often necessitated in the law. For example, the **McNaughton standard** for the insanity defense used by many jurisdictions often doesn't clarify if the reference to the defendant's understanding or appreciation of the wrongfulness of his or her actions is referring to legal or moral wrongfulness. The case of Andrea Yates highlights this issue. She may have understood the legal wrongfulness of her actions, but her delusions rendered her unable to appreciate the moral wrongfulness of her actions. The severity of her post partum depression coupled with psychosis led to delusions that she was saving her children from eternal damnation.

Insanity defense

The various insanity defenses (tests) can only be used by individuals suffering from a mental disease or defect. In order to be "excused" from criminal behavior, the individual must not only be mentally ill, but the mental illness must directly cause a dysfunction which is relevant when the offense was committed (Melton *et al.*, 2007). When it is a psycholegal question, a specific diagnosis is not the central issue but the impact on functional capacities or ability to know the difference between right and wrong, and to conform one's behavior to the law. The functional impact of mental illness becomes the key issue. Melton *et al.* (2007) note that with mental illness being imprecisely defined, it would seem that "any mental disability that causes significant cognitive or volitional impairment will meet the threshold [of mental illness needed for insanity defenses]" (p. 335). The emphasis of "insanity," legally, is on the cognitive and/or volitional impact of the disorder on the defendant's thinking, feeling, and behavior at the time of the alleged offense. Historically, however, the successful insanity defenses have generally arisen from individuals who were suffering from a psychosis or intellectual disability. Studies suggest that 60–90% of defendants acquitted for reasons of insanity have been psychotic (Melton *et al.*, 2007).

Very few case opinions attempt to define mental disease or defect. The few cases that have, however, define the concept narrowly. In other words, the courts have shown a general disapproval of many conceptions of insanity including mildly psychotic individuals, dissociative disorders, and drug- and alcohol-induced insanity (Melton *et al.*, 2007). Further, the American Psychiatric Association (APA) has defined "mental disease or defect" in a narrow sense, suggesting it should only include "severely abnormal mental conditions that grossly…impair a person's perception or understanding of reality" (APA, 2010). Thus, the definition of mental disease or defect for purposes of insanity defenses varies from state to state and is probably more broadly defined than some have suggested.

Foucha v. Louisiana

The Supreme Court shed some light on the meaning of mental illness in the case
Foucha v. Louisiana (1992). While the case considered the extent to which an individual could
be confined *after* being found NGRI, it has some important implications for the meaning of
mental illness in civil commitment and insanity defense matters. The Court held that it would
be unconstitutional to detain an individual who was diagnosed only with antisocial personality
disorder. The primary issue was whether it was constitutional to continue to detain an
individual who had been acquitted but had recovered from his or her illness. The short answer
from the Court was "no." The more relevant issue, however, is the meaning of "mental illness."
While for purposes of involuntary commitment an individual must be shown to be mentally ill
and dangerous, the *Foucha v. Louisiana* case found that dangerousness and antisocial
personality disorder were not sufficient. Thus, the implication is that personality disorders, at
least antisocial personality disorder, do not constitute mental illness for purposes of
involuntary confinement. The Court did not justify this finding, leaving the issue unresolved.
Thus, the impact of the Court's decision in *Foucha* may be more apparent in future decisions.

Forensic Psychology and Policy Implications

The longstanding failure of the legislature and the courts to adequately define "mental illness"
leaves a number of issues for forensic psychological analysts and practitioners. Most
importantly, it leaves the decisions as to what constitutes mental illness and who is mentally
ill to the attending forensic examiner. Regardless of the specific (or general) reasons arguing
for or against psychology's involvement in the courtroom, its "expertise" is judged central to
civil commitment and mental illness affairs. Thus, the *legal* meaning of mental illness has
been "passed on" by the courts, only to be adopted by the "expert(s)" attending to the
particular circumstances of individual cases (i.e., the treatment team) (Arrigo, 1993). In all
likelihood this will continue. Thus, the meaning of mental illness becomes a significant issue
for forensic psychologists above all else.

Despite the disagreement among mental health professionals defining what mental illness is,
the legal system finds it appropriate to leave the decision in the hands of a select few individuals
in the mental health and/or medical field. The individuals, who are part of this defining, then,
would differ depending on the case in question. Thus, two individuals with identical mental
conditions may be found "mentally ill" and "not mentally ill" depending on the definer.
Unfortunately, since the courts rely almost entirely on disagreeing professionals to define
mental illness, someone like Gina may be involuntarily hospitalized in one city (or by one
treatment team) and not in another city (or by another team). In general, however, the medical
community has shown a preference for presuming mental illness. Given the medical
community's favor for *presumption* of illness when confronting uncertainty (Arrigo, 2002), it
is not unreasonable to assume that borderline cases are frequently labeled "mentally ill" for
legal (i.e., involuntary commitment) purposes. Thus, it would seem that forensic psychological

practitioners are over-inclusive in these matters. In other words, more nonmentally ill individuals are being involuntarily hospitalized than the truly mentally ill who are not.

The forensic psychology implications, then, are profound for individuals like Gina who are facing (potentially) legal intervention. While we must recognize individual freedom, liberty, and self-determination, we must also be concerned with more general matters of public safety and health. The line between the two is not clear, as evidenced in the law's failure to define mental illness. Thus, it is left to forensic psychology practitioners and policy analysts to determine where this line should be drawn. At this point, there is no correct answer.

Furthermore, cases such as Virginia Tech, Columbine, and the Unabomber remind us that the treatment of people who commit violent crimes is often difficult due to the prevalence of mental disorders and substance abuse, but the rarity with which it is associated with psychopathy and violence (Lurigio, 2007; Stout & Farooque, 2008). Often times those who suffer from mental illness turn to substance abuse as a sort of "self-medicating." The symptoms of the mental disorder are enhanced by the use of these drugs; often times this leads to violent or homicidal behavior. Stout & Farooque (2008) indicate that there is a distinct relationship between substance abuse and crime, and that people with "serious mental disorders" are at an elevated risk for violent behavior (p. 1218).

There is no determined future for Gina or others like her. If we know, however, that the legislature and the courts cannot define mental illness, psychology should at the very least assume the task of creating a *consistent* definition, one in which we could know what mental illness stands for in the legal context.

Suggestions for Future Research

As the future of mental illness in the legal system depends to a large degree on establishing an adequate psycholegal definition of mental illness, it is necessary that research be directed in such a way. While legislatures, courts, and even the American Psychological Association find it difficult to define mental illness, they have made many attempts; none seem to have proposed any conclusive interpretations. Thus, the varying definitions of mental illness across psychologists, psychiatrists, statutes, courts, and the like necessitate comparative analyses. Research may be directed at establishing commonalities between proposed definitions in an attempt to establish a single, definitive concept of mental illness. More importantly, perhaps, the effects of cases such as *Foucha* need to be analyzed to assess their future impact on other court and legislative decisions regarding mental illness and the law. Defining mental illness, however, is one problematic area of research. It is an area where a significant amount of inquiry has already been conducted; however, these studies have failed to solve the controversy. Thus, future case decisions and their implications in this area must be evaluated.

Research is also lacking in the area of analyzing current trends and the co-existence between violence prone mental illness, substance abuse, and psychopathic personalities. There is a rising trend in the assessment of risk for future violence. Many of these assessments address one or two of these prevailing disorders, but research into the prevalence of the three is lacking. Determining theoretical models to support the findings must also be researched and applied. The Developmental Theory of Delinquency (Bartol & Bartol, 2008) provides a foundation for a criminalistic lifestyle, but the presence of supporting theories on mental disorders that are prone to violent behaviors is lacking. Breaking down each factor contributing to violence and applying research in each specific area is absent in the literature and should be further examined. The very definition of mental illness has important implications for violence risk, civil commitment, and a number of other important areas where psychology intersects with the criminal justice system.

Right to Refuse Treatment

Introduction

The concept of personal liberty is, perhaps, the most treasured of all human rights in contemporary American society. The longstanding contention that lies at the historical core of American legal and social thought holds that the individual should have the right to decide what does or does not happen to his or her body and mind. During the time of the Civil Rights Movement, legislation for mental health was brought about that protected the civil liberties and increased patient rights, especially that of the right to refuse treatment (Hannon-Engel, 2011). If one becomes physically ill, for example, one can often choose not to receive medical treatment. The same should arguably apply to mental illness. The legal reality is, however, that this freedom from unwanted intrusion is not always enjoyed by the mentally disordered citizen. In fact, in some situations, individuals are subjected to psychological treatment against their will. Yet, the individuals most likely to refuse treatment are the ones who need treatment the most (Craigie, 2011; Wortzel, 2006). This is the controversy surrounding the "right to refuse treatment."

In the case of '*In Re Commitment of Dennis H.*' (Wis., 2002) (cited in Vitacco, 2003), the Wisconsin Supreme Court upheld Wisconsin's Fifth standard for civil commitment, based on the inability to make informed choices regarding medication or treatment. The Wisconsin Supreme Court contended that they were balancing the state's interest in protecting citizens unable to make informed decisions based on mental illness and their civil liberties. In this case, the constitutionality was upheld and the laws allowing for commitment of persons with mental illness who are incompetent to make treatment decisions were expanded (Vitacco, 2003).

While in Maryland, in the case of *Department of Health & Mental Hygiene v. Kelly*, 918 A.2d 470 (Md. 2007), the Court of Appeals of Maryland unanimously upheld the Circuit Court for Baltimore City's ruling that the state is required to prove that an involuntarily committed individual is a danger to themselves or to others before they are allowed to forcibly administer any medications. The courts in Maryland ruled that an individual is a danger to themselves and society because of their mental illness before that individual is forced to be medicated. In the ruling in *Morgan v. Rabun,* 128 F.3d 694 (8th Cir. 1997), the Eighth Circuit Court found that giving **psychotropic medications** (i.e., drugs which alter perceptions, emotions, or behavior; examples include antidepressants, antipsychotics, and antianxiety medications) did not violate individuals' **substantive** (i.e., basic fundamental constitutional rights and liberties; examples are the right to a speedy trial, right to challenge witnesses, and right to a lawyer present during questioning) or **procedural due process rights** (the process that protects substantive rights; for example, defense attorney following up with competency evaluation if competency is suspected to be an issue in current legal matters), because the hospital that admitted Mr. Morgan demonstrated he was showing imminently dangerous behavior.

Although questions of treatment refusal are relevant when considering the legal ramifications of *any* form of treatment, such questions are generally raised regarding psychotropic medications. The question of right to refuse antipsychotic medication has been called "the most important and volatile aspect of the legal regulation of mental health practice" (Perlin, Gould, & Dorfman, 1995, p. 111). Issues including personal autonomy of the individuals with mental illness to refuse medication, subjection to drugs which occasionally cause irreversible neurological side-effects, and questions of "informed consent" and "competency," as well as the "least restrictive alternative," all potentially become significant when confronting the right to refuse treatment. This section explores these concerns in the context of the right to refuse treatment.

Alyssa is a 34-year-old woman who has been diagnosed by her psychiatrist as suffering from a thought disorder. Her symptoms, including delusions and occasional auditory hallucinations, have become progressively worse over the past year-and-a-half. While there is no dispute as to whether Alyssa has a mental illness, she shows no signs of dangerousness to herself or others. Alyssa has been able to maintain a reasonably "safe" lifestyle and, although she is in a state of obvious mental discomfort, she is not a candidate for involuntary commitment at this time.

Following her diagnosis, her attending psychiatrist recommends that she be placed on Thorazine, an antipsychotic drug that may help to alleviate her symptoms. Following extensive consideration by Alyssa, she asks that the recommended treatment *not* be implemented. In other words, she asks not to be placed on Thorazine. Alyssa reached her decision after learning about the drug, finding that it often causes severe side-effects, which may be permanent. Alyssa decides that the risk is too high and she wishes to seek alternative treatment(s).

Upon learning of Alyssa's request, however, her psychiatrist questions her competence to make such a decision. He questions whether a reasonable person in need of psychiatric treatment could reach such a decision, as it would clearly not be in her best interest at this time. In light of her wishes and his concern, does Alyssa have a right to refuse medication? Does her psychiatrist have a right to involuntarily treat her as he sees fit? And, how exactly does the issue of competence come into play?

Literature Review

"The right to refuse treatment has been a controversial debate for the last 30 years, and is viewed as a battle between psychiatry and the legal system" (Perlin, 2005, p. 2). To fully understand its impact, one must consider the issue in light of a number of other important legal concerns; namely, the **Least Restrictive Alternative** (LRA) doctrine, competency issues, and the doctrine of **informed consent**. We briefly discuss each of these matters as they relate to the right to refuse treatment.

Least restrictive alternative doctrine and right to refuse treatment

For individuals in need of psychiatric attention, the right to refuse treatment becomes relevant within the context of the LRA doctrine. The LRA doctrine holds that individuals be placed in the least restrictive setting, when their condition necessitates state intervention. This doctrine also implies that the least restrictive *method* of treatment be employed. Thus, the goal is to treat the individual in a manner that is least intrusive upon his or her personal liberty (Sheehan & Burns, 2011; Lin, 2003; Atkinson, 2002). Some researchers are suggesting that the least restrictive alternative should also be interpreted to take into consideration the patient's views as well as clinicians and legislatures (Sheehan & Burns, 2011; Atkinson, 2002; Say & Thomson, 2003). Say and Thomson (2003, p. 542) state, "Health professionals are increasingly encouraged to involve patients in treatment decisions, recognizing patients as experts with a unique knowledge of their own health and their preferences for treatments, health states, and outcomes." However, these researchers point out that some doctors may wish to maintain the imbalance of power between themselves and their patients, and patients may be hesitant to share their preferences. Sheehan and Burns (2011) used data from structured interviews with 164 patients consecutively admitted to two psychiatric hospitals in Oxford, England. They found that the therapeutic relationship as well as the legal status (i.e., voluntary versus involuntary commitment) affected a patient's perception of coercion. A poor relationship with their treating clinician and involuntary commitment status resulted in the highest perception of coercion by patients. High levels of coercion were experienced by 48% of voluntarily and 89% of involuntarily admitted patients. Even voluntary hospitalization was viewed as more coercive when patients rated their relationship with the admitting clinician negatively (Sheehan & Burns, 2011).

Without question, the administration of any treatment could be regarded as an intrusion on personal liberty if the citizen did not wish to receive the treatment. For example, the administration of psychotropic medication(s) to alleviate symptoms may be regarded as necessary, but may also significantly affect the individual's mental functioning. In this instance, one may not wish to be subjected to certain primary effects and side-effects of medication. Thus, if a less restrictive alternative is available, it must be considered.

However, involuntary medication treatment is based on the assumptions that the medication will be effective in addressing the identified problem (i.e., impaired judgment, incapacity to make important decisions, and for the safety of the patient and community); the medications will help the individual control behaviors that may harm the individual themselves or others; the benefits outweigh the risks (i.e., side-effects, damage done by long-term use of the medication); options other than medication have been explored and found to be unsuccessful; the individual is noncompliant with treatment because they do not believe that they have a mental illness, and the medications will help the individual become stable and better assist them with living outside of an institution (Bassman, 2005).

Doctrine of informed consent

The doctrine of **informed consent** requires that persons be supplied adequate information concerning treatment prior to consenting. Thus, the individual is able to make a well-informed decision regarding the suggested treatment they may be receiving. Generally, adequate information consists of the risks and benefits of treatment, the potential side-effects, the chance of improvement both with and without the treatment, and any other treatments that may be available. The doctrine applies in a number of situations, including administration of medication, tests, and surgical procedures (Barnett, Wise, Johnson-Greene, & Bucky, 2007; Levy & Rubenstein, 1996). It is also important to view informed consent as a continuous necessity and to update the informed-consent agreement throughout treatment when significant changes to the treatment are offered (Barnett *et al.*, 2007).

While the doctrine of informed consent applies to the general adult public, it also applies to individuals with mental illness to the extent that they are competent to make such decisions. Thus, the existence of a mental disability alone does not take the right to make treatment decisions away from an individual. In order for such a right to be lost, the individual must be found incompetent by a court of law. While this seems simple enough, some controversial issues arise concerning the incompetent or civilly committed individuals with mental illness and their right to refuse treatment.

Competency

A **competent consent to treatment** requires that the individual make a reasoned decision to accept or refuse a proposed procedure. As noted, this generally means that the individual understands the treatment, its risks and benefits, and the potential alternatives. Thus, weight is not placed on the final decision itself, but rather on the manner in which the person came to such a conclusion.

An individual is not regarded as incompetent simply because his or her decision is not consistent with the majority of patients, is irrational, is not in the person's best medical interest, or is not consistent with the psychiatrist's recommendation. In the case of Alyssa, her refusal of antipsychotic medication, given the potential side-effects, is not an incompetent decision for the reasons mentioned above. Her choice must be assessed in light of what she considers a better quality of life (Levy & Rubenstein, 1996; Say & Thomson, 2003).

Thus, the standards for competency concerning the right to refuse treatment are similar to other competencies. While there is currently no standard test to determine competency, it generally follows that the individual must understand the implications of the treatment and be able to make a rational choice based on this understanding. If the individual is not competent to make such a decision, another important controversy arises. That is, who makes the decision in his or her place? Generally, this decision is made by a panel of psychiatrists who must decide if, in fact, the individual is not capable of making such a decision and whether the proposed treatment is in the individual's best interest. Treatment-related decisional capacity is a frequently debated issue that invokes the question of guardianship (Chopra, Weiss, Stinnett, & Oslin, 2003; Palmer, Nayak, Dunn, *et. al.*, 2002; Teaster & Roberto, 2002). An individual may be found to be incompetent to make his or her own treatment decisions by the judge, and a guardian may be appointed. The psychologist would then inform the patient about treatment in terms and language they are able to understand (Pinals, 2009). Teaster and Roberto (2002, p. 176), identified "third-party behavior, mental illness or personal behavior, and cognitive impairments or limitations" as the events most likely to precipitate guardianship.

Following the Court's decision in *Washington v. Harper* (1990), however, no finding of incompetency is necessary if the individual is judged to be "mentally ill" and either "gravely disabled" or poses a "likelihood of serious harm" to self or others (Slobogin, 1994, p. 687). Thus, similar to civil commitment law, individuals may not have a right to refuse treatment if it is in the state's best interest to protect the community. Mental health, law enforcement, and legal professionals are concerned that the criminal justice system is largely comprised of individuals with severe mental illness in need of treatment (Lamb, Weinberger, Marsh, & Gross, 2007). For further information, see the section "An Offender's Right to Refuse Treatment."

Forensic Psychology and Policy Implications

One of the prevailing controversies regarding the right to refuse treatment concerns its theoretical application versus its actual or practical application. In theory, the right was intended to place final decisions regarding the type and extent of treatment in the hands of the citizen rather than the medical or mental health professional (Craigie, 2011; Arrigo, 1996). In practice, however, the patient merely has the right to object to treatment decisions made by the attending clinician. In such cases, the decision may be reviewed by a team of clinicians to determine the appropriateness of the chosen treatment. Thus, in practice, the final decision concerning treatment of a person's mental illness and its consequent effect on the individual's personal liberty ultimately remain in the hands of the clinician or forensic expert. While the intention of the doctrine was to consider individual interests in the name of unwanted intrusions on personal liberty, some argue that the practice of mental health treatment essentially disregards this perspective and reinforces the power that the medical community holds over those judged to be mentally ill. Those providing mental health treatment must also consider protecting an individual whose judgment is so affected by the symptoms of their mental illness that they pose a risk to themselves or others.

Yet, in many cases, the mental health professional is concerned about the best interest of the patient, who if **decompensated** (i.e., decline in functioning or change in mental state; examples include psychotic thought processes, erratic behavior, or mood disturbance) may be incapable of rational decision-making for their own welfare. For example, a patient who was released from an inpatient psychiatric hospital into the community during the Texas summer heat died shortly thereafter from heat stroke on the streets. His inability to make rational decisions regarding his own personal welfare and lack of resources contributed to his death. It is very common to observe patients with **schizophrenia** (i.e., a psychotic disorder characterized by delusions, hallucinations, odd behaviors, and impaired thought process) in inappropriate dress, sometimes wearing several layers of clothing, when it is hot outside. Ideally, our communities would abound with resources for those diagnosed with mental illness. However, in reality, community resources are woefully inadequate and we must consider the welfare of those who are unable to adequately care for themselves. In many cases, mental health professionals are not the oppressors, but rather attempting to improve the quality of life, and in some instances sustain the physical life, of the mentally ill patient. Clinicians have the precarious position of balancing patient care with civil liberties.

Similarly, questions of competency are often raised only when acceptance or refusal of treatment differs from the opinion of the medical community. Decisions that are consistent with the psychiatrist, for example, are rarely questioned. In the case of Alyssa, the psychiatrist recommended Thorazine to treat her thought disorder. Had Alyssa concurred with the psychiatrist's recommendation, there would have been no issue regarding competency. Psychiatrists often accept a patient's consent without further considering if it is consistent with the physician's opinion. When a patient challenges the treatment recommendation, however, questions of competency are likely to be raised, particularly if they could compromise the health and safety of the patient and others. Often, it is thought that the individual lacks insight into his or her own condition and, thus, is not capable of making rational treatment decisions. In this instance, the individual may be subjected to a competency hearing to determine his or her capacity to make such a decision. Thus, the right to refuse treatment is often not a right at all, but rather a right to object and be subjected to a hearing. More recently, it has been proposed that in assessments of competence, the focus should be on the patient's capacity for the evaluative judgments that guide treatment decisions (Craigie, 2011).

Further, while considerable literature and public attention surround the "antitherapeutic" aspect of the right to refuse treatment, the "therapeutic" aspect must also be considered. Examples of the beneficial nature of the right to refuse treatment include judicial or administrative hearings (following the citizen's refusal of recommended treatment) to ensure that the mentally ill individual has the opportunity to fully present his or her case in a formal legal setting; the consequent procedures that help to prevent the inappropriate use of medications (e.g., for punishment or convenience); and the hearings that ensure that psychiatrists are not prescribing the wrong medication, wrong dosages, or ignoring concerns of the patient regarding side-effects (Perlin *et al.*, 1995). Thus, in addition to the negative or "antitherapeutic" aspects of the right to refuse treatment, forensic psychology must also consider the beneficial or therapeutic aspects of such a right.

Based on the need for standardizing the involuntary hospital admission, the European Commission funded a study in 12 European countries in order to develop European recommendations for good clinical practice in involuntary hospital admissions (Fiorillo, De Rosa, Del Vecchio, Jurjanz, Schnall, Onchev, Alexiev, *et al.*, 2011). These recommendations were developed through the collaboration of national leaders and key professionals. The final recommendations stressed the following needs: (1) to provide information to patients about the reasons for hospitalization and likely duration; (2) protecting patients' rights during hospitalization; (3) encouraging the involvement of family members; (4) improving the communication between community and hospital teams; (5) organizing meetings, seminars and focus-groups with users; (6) developing training courses for professionals on the management of aggressive behaviors, clinical issues regarding major mental disorders, the legal and administrative aspects of involuntary hospital admissions, and on communication skills.

Suggestions for Future Research

Some research has been conducted exploring treatment outcomes of refusers and differences between clinical and judicial reviews of petitions for involuntary medication (Perlin *et al.*, 1995). Overall, however, there is a lack of quality research concerning the various "therapeutic" and "antitherapeutic" effects of the right to refuse treatment (Craigie, 2011; Arrigo & Tasca, 1999). Thus, research on quality of life impacted after a decision to accept or refuse treatment, may be beneficial. As noted above, there is no standard test for competency. While competency to accept or refuse treatment stands as a major legal issue, it seems that a more direct confrontation of this issue is necessary. A standard that will allow treatment providers to respect a patient's right to refuse treatment as long as the individual is not incompetent to make treatment decisions and to realize when they are a danger to others and themselves seems reasonable on its face. However, determining what is actually protecting the rights and dignity of the patient, perhaps, when they are psychiatrically so unstable they are unable to make reality-based choices is a complex issue. In some cases, court-ordered medications or other forms of compelled treatment can help stabilize a patient who has a history of harming others, when symptoms of their mental illness go untreated. Craigie (2011) also recommends that the issue of involuntary treatment continues to be researched in cases of severe anorexia, where the patient's life hangs in the balance.

Further research into an antipsychotic treatment that will enhance medication compliance by having a combination of adherence-focused psychotherapy and mental illness education is needed (Schennach-Wolff, Jäger, Seemüller, Obermeier, Messer, *et al.*, 2009). This approach focuses on educating and supporting the patient in understanding the importance of continuing the appropriate treatment to maintain wellness and recovery. Further research into whether more medication education (i.e., what the medication name is, what the medication is to treat, and possible side-effects) would increase the likelihood of medication compliance would be beneficial to consumers and caregivers (Mills, Lathlean, Bressington, Forrester, Veenhuyzen, & Gray, 2011). Increased education on treatment goals and methods would allow the individual to be an active and central part of their recovery instead of just being the "treated." The dangerousness criterion for the right to refuse treatment is a controversial issue that needs continued exploration in order to better define the standard required by the courts.

Evaluating Psychiatric Work-Related Disability

Introduction

Many seriously mentally ill individuals are unable to maintain gainful employment due to the debilitating effects of their psychiatric symptoms (e.g., paranoia, severe depression, and panic attacks). The onset of mental illness prevents some individuals from learning vocational skills and chronic symptoms negatively impact their social and cognitive skills, emotions, and behavior in such a way that they are unable to support themselves through employment. Forensic psychologists working in the civil forensics arena are increasingly being asked to conduct **disability evaluations** (e.g., Social Security Disability Insurance evaluations) based on mental illness. Persistent, severe mental illness is one of the most common reasons for disability claims. Psychologists and psychiatrists are often asked to evaluate whether or not psychiatric symptoms are preventing an individual from functioning in a work setting (Enelow & Leo, 2002). Title I of the **Americans with Disabilities Act** (ADA) attempts to prevent through regulation employment discrimination against "qualified individuals with a physical or mental disability that substantially limits a major life activity" (cited in Gioia & Brekke, 2003, p. 302). According to Christopher, Boland, Recupero, Phillips (2010, p. 211), "The increasing frequency and societal cost of psychiatric disability underscore the need for accuracy in evaluating patients who seek disability benefits." Weber (2008) found that there are risks inherent in the examination for ADA claims. He indicated that evaluators may overstress the limitations of the individual, and this overstressing may actually make it more difficult for the individual to prove that he or she can actually perform essential job functions when reasonable accommodations are provided to maintain a steady income. Consider the following case illustration (Gioia & Brekke, 2003, p. 303):

Mr. E, a 24-year-old white man, was the only one of the four participants in group 3 to resume his job bagging groceries after his diagnosis of schizophrenia. He was also the only one to earn more than the minimum wage. His symptoms were initially job related. He believed he was receiving messages from the products he was bagging and that he had to perform actions by rhyming key words from the message. He stated that things got worse, "every decision was based on a sign."

> When these incidents began, Mr. E did not know what was happening to him. However, after his hospitalization he became aware of how severe his problems had become and how difficult it might be for him to return to work. He took a break from work and school to recuperate. However, his paranoid thoughts continued to be a daily presence. After two months Mr. E received a call from the store manager asking him to come back to work because the store was short staffed. ...Mr. E did return to work with a reduced hourly schedule, and along with his father he worked out an accommodation plan with the store manager.

Vocational rehabilitation programs (programs designed to help individuals with disabilities prepare, gain, and maintain employment) and employers who are willing to accommodate the mentally ill are far too rare. A study by Liu, Hollis, Warren, and Williamson (2007, p. 547) found that if illness-related barriers to gaining employment were removed in ways such as: "supporting effective job seeking, improving work-related skills and knowledge, and encouraging a partnership between case managers and participants," employment became an attainable option for the mentally ill individual. Furthermore, the **refractory symptoms** (fixed symptoms that do not respond to treatment, e.g., delusional systems) of some mentally ill people prevent them from working altogether. The stigma of mental illness and the fears and misconceptions regarding mental illness often preclude many employers from accommodating the mentally ill as they would the physically handicapped. The following section explores the role of mental health professionals in evaluating for disability based on mental illness and the issues and potential pitfalls of disability benefits.

Literature Review

Gold, Anfang, Drukteinis, Metzner, Price, Wall, Wylonis, and Zonana (2008), found that 48 to 66% of individuals with any disability were employed, and 32 to 61% of people with a severe mental illness were employed. Several empirically supported reasons for high unemployment rates for the group of severely mentally ill individuals include stigma and the belief that they are always violent, unreliable, unpredictable, and irrational (Marini, 2003; Hong, 2002). Employers are more skeptical about hiring those with mental illness than other disability groups (Marini, 2003; Corrigan & Kleinlein, 2005). Since 1935, the Social Security Administration (SSA) by way of the **Social Security Act** provides income to retired workers, disabled individuals, and families of deceased workers (Leo, 2002). The SSA defines "disability" as:

> *...the inability to engage in any substantial gainful activity by reason of any medically determinable physical or mental impairment which can be expected to result in death or which has lasted or can be expected to last for a continuous period of no less than 12 months. (Social Security Act, Section 223 (d), cited in MacDonald-Wilson, Rogers, & Anthony, 2001, p. 218).*

The SSA disability programs are made up of the **Social Security Disability Insurance (SSDI)** and **Supplemental Security Income (SSI)** programs (Leo, 2002). SSDI benefits are derived from a person's prior work (FICA payments), as compared to SSI benefits paid out from revenue funds of the U.S. Treasury. Individuals who receive SSI typically have very little or no previous work history. SSI provides a form of financial support for the marginalized and often indigent mentally ill. Individuals with psychiatric disabilities comprise the largest and most rapidly growing subgroup of beneficiaries of the SSA program (Drake, Skinner, Bond, & Goldman, 2009). Leo (2002) reported that over half of disability claimants have a mental disorder, with many being diagnosed with mental retardation. Out of the remaining mental impairments, schizophrenia accounts for one-third.

According to the SSA, disability prevents an individual from engaging in simple, repetitive work (Williams, 2010; Enelow & Leo, 2002). Characteristics essential to work such as attention and concentration, ability to relate to others, ability to adapt to change, and to effectively maintain **activities of daily living** (i.e., personal grooming and hygiene, maintaining personal area, and self-sufficiency) are seriously impaired. Factors affecting work performance such as attention and concentration can be assessed by observing the patient's ability to attend appropriately to their interview and their surroundings, and more formally, through psychological testing. Data sources involve interviewing the **claimant** (the individual applying for disability) as to their typical daily activities to ascertain their skill level, as well as any available third party or corroborating records or sources. The SSA may require formal psychological testing, for example, the Wechsler Adult Intelligence Test, Fourth Edition (WAIS-IV), to evaluate intellectual functioning or the degree of cognitive impairment, related to intellectual disability, dementia, or head injury (Enelow & Leo, 2002; Gold *et al.*, 2008). Other psychological tests that are useful for comprehensive neurological tests include the Halstead—Reitan Battery and the Luria—Nebraska Battery; these tests are useful for assessing cognitive functioning in disability cases involving dementia, stroke, head injuries, and neurological disorders with additional psychiatric symptoms (Melton *et al.*, 2007). These researchers state, if required for the disability claim, the SSA will often request and pay for the formal psychological testing.

In March 2008, the final draft of the Practice Guideline was approved by the Council of the American Academy of Psychiatry and The Law, which is a reflection of the "consensus of opinion among members and experts about the principles and practice applicable to the conduct of psychiatric disability evaluations" (Gold *et al.*, 2008, p. S3). Disability evaluations are the most common, nontherapeutic evaluation requested, but they are necessary in planning accommodations for ADA or in order to complete a Family and Medical Leave Act (FMLA) certification form (Gold *et al.*, 2008). Though there are no uniform standards of ethics that apply to the various disability evaluations, the American Academy of Psychiatry and the Law (AAPL) has published an ethics guideline that can apply to all types of forensic evaluations (American Academy of Psychiatry and the Law, 2005). This guide was developed by forensic psychiatrists who have experience conducting disability evaluations on a regular basis, and contain the following: (1) general aspects of a disability evaluation such as practical and ethics related topics and definitions of terms; (2) general guidelines for a disability evaluation; and (3) the common sources for disability evaluation referrals. Such referrals often are for SSDI, workers' or personal injury compensation, private disability insurance, and other specialized compensation and pension programs (Gold *et al.*, 2008).

The evaluator must consider whether or not this individual has the capacity to participate in simple, repetitive tasks or adapt to concrete routines. Enelow and Leo (2002, p. 294) identify several essential work functions for individuals to function in the competitive work force that are organized as either cognitive/intellectual functions or social functions. The six cognitive/intellectual functions include: (1) Ability to comprehend and follow instructions; (2) Ability to perform simple, repetitive tasks; (3) Ability to maintain a work pace appropriate to a given work load; (4) Ability to perform complex or varied tasks; (5) Ability to make generalizations, evaluations, and decisions without immediate supervision; and (6) Ability to accept and execute responsibility for direction, control, and planning. The two main social functions include: (1) Ability to relate to other people beyond giving and receiving instructions; and (2) Ability to influence others.

For example, **psychomotor retardation** (e.g., cognitive or processing speed slowing) due to depression could interfere with an individual's ability to keep up with the required pace at work (Enelow & Leo, 2002). These authors also contend that it is important to assess whether or not a patient can follow through with tasks in a timely fashion, maintain attendance, and be punctual. Certainly, if Mr. E in the case illustration had been observed **responding to internal stimuli** (i.e., talking to unseen others, losing concentration, appearing to see things that are not there) or talking to the groceries he was bagging, customers may have been frightened. Regarding social factors, the capacity to interact with others appropriately is critical. Communicating appropriately with coworkers, supervisors, consumers, and not exhibiting behavioral extremes would be an important component of maintaining gainful employment. Enelow and Leo (2002) further describe the necessity of social skills such as maintaining appropriate interpersonal space, using clear, goal-directed speech with rational and organized thoughts, dressing appropriately, maintaining personal hygiene, and above all else, not engaging in hostile or aggressive behaviors.

The evaluator or treating sources must be able to provide clinical information to the SSA in such a way that it can be applied meaningfully to essential work-related abilities (Williams, 2010; Enelow & Leo, 2002). They point out that the evaluator must consider that even if the individual is unable to perform prior work (e.g., accounting), that it does not necessarily preclude their ability to perform in other areas. If they can still work in some lesser skilled or different area, despite their mental illness, their claim will be rejected. SSI or SSDI does not indicate that you must be able to work at your prior level unless you are over the age of 55, which is considered of "advanced age." In that instance, the SSA presumes that you would be less adaptable to new job-related skills and you are not expected to take on a new line of work.

Criterion to be applied to the review of case material includes a determination of whether or not the claimant's earnings are substantial. If so, the disability claim is rejected. Beginning on 1 January 2001, wages are considered substantial if one's monthly earnings exceed $740 (Leo, 2002). Severity of psychiatric impairment is another criterion that is based on the chronicity or expected course and the effect on four areas of functioning to include: "activities of daily living, social functioning, concentration and adaptation, and frequency and duration of episodes or symptom exacerbation" (Leo, 2002, p. 286). Serious impairment of any two of these areas, or severe impairment in any one, will also qualify for substantial psychiatric impairment. The SSA provides listings of psychiatric impairments in terms of symptoms and behaviors based on DSM-IV criteria that presume disability. If the history, course, symptoms, and severity of the mental disorder, described by the treating clinician, are compatible with those provided in the listings, the claimant is awarded disability benefits. If the symptom or disorder is not one found in the listings, they are then evaluated to determine whether or not the impairments would prevent the claimant from returning to prior work, or if under the age of 55, performing any other work available (Enelow & Leo, 2002; Leo, 2002). The chronicity or continuation of residual symptoms of some mental disorders such as schizophrenia and affective and anxiety disorders for a minimum of two years, despite treatment, may still support the finding of a disability claim. A claim being rewarded is contingent upon compliance with treatment (e.g., attending psychotherapy and medication compliance) and little evidence for continued improvement (Leo, 2002). If awarded, disability benefits eligibility is typically reevaluated every three years.

A treating clinician may be asked to provide relevant clinical data on psychological impairments that affect vocational abilities, when a patient has filed a disability claim (Williams, 2010; Leo, 2002). According to the Social Security Administration (2001, p. 64-039), the treating mental health professional is "neither asked nor expected to make a decision as to whether the patient is disabled." After all, this is the ultimate issue to be decided by the SSA. Instead evaluators are asked to complete a disability-related evaluation by reviewing records and evaluating the claimant in order to form an opinion that helps make the decision of workplace accommodations, making changes in employment status, or authorizing health care benefits (Gold *et al.*, 2008). Just as a diagnosis of schizophrenia doesn't necessarily result in a finding of incompetency to stand trial, a clinically disabling condition does not necessarily result in the legal definition of disability (Leo, 2002; Druss, Marcus, Rosenheck, Olfson, Tanielian, *et al.*, 2001). After a disability claim has been filed with the SSA, the file is evaluated by a psychologist or psychiatrist hired by the SSA who acts as a disability reviewer (Leo, 2002). These evaluators will apply the legal standard to their paper review to determine eligibility. They will not reevaluate the patient. The ability to adjudicate the case is contingent upon the usefulness of the clinical information provided by mental health professionals and information provided by the claimant, particularly the report of the treating clinician (Leo, 2002).

Forensic Psychology and Policy Implications

There are many inconsistencies from region to region and state to state in awarding benefits. There is typically a 5 to 12 month waiting period for those applying for SSI/SSDI (Williams, 2010; Marini, 2003). Thirty-three percent of applicants are successful on their first attempt. Approximately 50% of those denied will appeal this decision, and after more records are collected, the SSA will conduct a second review with 15% on average being approved. Out of the 85% denied a second time, approximately 68% will appeal for a third time. At this point, an administrative law judge reviews the case and often a vocational expert is retained to assist the court in the evaluation. At this point, approximately 58% are successful (Marini, 2003). During the 2000 fiscal year, out of the 584,540 claims appealed, 16% were reconsidered by the SSA and 59% of those were awarded benefits after being heard by the administrative law judge (Leo, 2002). Five appeals are allowed with the final appeal being heard by the U.S. District Court. However, success rates drop off dramatically for the fourth appeal to approximately 4% (Marini, 2003). There are no firm guidelines on determining the degree to which mental impairments will affect vocational impairments and most decisions are very subjective.

Additionally, some of the guidelines for benefits to be awarded may penalize those mentally ill individuals who are managing to avoid hospitalization by adhering to their treatment. However, they may require a level of structure or supervision in a work environment that is not readily available, yet, still fail to clearly meet the severity and/or chronicity with marginal treatment outcomes criteria needed for initial eligibility or renewal. Furthermore, those individuals with improved functioning could be denied, yet the stress of a work environment could likely lead to decompensation, increased impairment, or the inability to maintain employment. It would be important for treating or evaluating clinicians to clearly document such limitations or necessary accommodations that would be necessary. When these risk factors could preclude successful employment, the treating clinician should carefully document the implications for vocational impairment.

More programs and policies focusing on the provision of job coaches, community case managers, and more intensive supervision in the work environment could keep many mentally ill individuals from falling through the cracks (Williams, 2010; Leo, 2002). The structure of this type of employment could help a mentally ill individual maintain their autonomy and dignity. Marini (2003, p. 39) reports that much research indicates the following strategies for placing and maintaining mentally ill individuals successfully in work environments as follows: "training available support systems to be aware of signs where medication noncompliance is occurring and to catch it early on; supported employment where follow-along contact is ongoing and natural coworker support at the work-site is strong; negotiating strong supervisor and coworker support as well as educating them about the disability; appropriate job matching; flex time work schedules where feasible; and positive feedback in addition to constructive feedback regarding work performance." An individual can have a disability evaluation to document the "lack of impairment or the ability to work despite symptoms" (Gold *et al.*, 2008, p. 85). Dewa and Lin (2000) also suggest early treatment through Employee Assistance Programs if available, to provide confidential on- and off-site mental health counseling, when the more subtle signs of mental illness begin.

Additionally, individuals lose their disability benefits when they are incarcerated or placed in a forensic hospital as incompetent to stand trial or not guilty by reason of insanity for committing a felony offense. Often, when the individual is released it takes some time and follow-up for their benefits to be reinstated. This period before reinstatement could increase the likelihood that they do not follow up with treatment, require emergency services, or reoffend and have new charges (Williams, 2010; Leo, 2002).

Suggestions for Future Research

MacDonald-Wilson *et al.* (2001) discuss the need for mental health professionals to have reliable and valid measures for work functioning. These researchers express the need for future research to evaluate old and new instruments to assess work capacity. This could enable a more standardized approach to a very imperfect and subjective system. Additionally, they also suggest longitudinal studies of current disability claimants who are both awarded and denied benefits. Continued research could help to alleviate the tremendous disagreement between evaluators about the essential domains of functioning, particularly with regard to clinical impairments (e.g., symptoms, diagnosis) versus functional impairments (e.g., social functioning, cognitive functioning) (MacDonald-Wilson *et al.*, 2001). Research should also explore the need for further training for forensic psychologists on evaluating for disability purposes. Future research should continue to explore the efficacy of varied strategies to successfully employ the mentally ill and to keep them engaged in their communities. Research should also look at the positive effects that employment has on the treatment of an individual with mental illness.

Duty to Inform v. Client Confidentiality

Introduction

Duty to inform, versus client confidentiality, stands as one of the more nebulous areas of forensic psychology today. The controversy generally involves a mental health professional's ethical and legal obligation to protect client confidentiality and his or her **duty to warn** or the responsibility of a professional to inform third parties or authorities if clients pose a threat to themselves or another identifiable individual. While the concept of confidentiality stands historically as one of the primary underpinnings of psychology, the legal ramifications of the duty to warn have caused substantial debate as to the limits of confidentiality. In short, the question is "when must and when should confidentiality be breached?"

The legal limits imposed on confidentiality are the result of the California Supreme Court's 1976 decision in *Tarasoff v. Regents of the University of California*. Generally, *Tarasoff* imposed an additional obligation on mental health professionals to consider the potential consequences of *not* releasing confidential information under certain circumstances. Thus, the ethically bound psychologist not only has the responsibility to uphold the value of confidentiality in his or her client relationships, but also must consider the interests of *other* individuals, organizations, and society in general in the process. Lee and Gillam (2000, p. 123) indicate that when considering the Tarasoff decision, psychologists must take into consideration the following relevant issues: "confidentiality, informed consent, ethical codes, identifiability of victims, level of dangerousness, and communicated threat."

In this section we explore more fully the concepts of confidentiality, the duty to warn or protect, and other relevant issues. We consider, in detail, the decision rendered in *Tarasoff* and its implications for psychological and forensic psychological practice. Further, we address a more recent controversy with regard to duty to warn: the implications of duty to warn for psychologists treating clients infected by the HIV virus or diagnosed with AIDS.

Peter is a 32-year-old man who recently began a therapeutic relationship with Dr. John to address issues of reported depression. Peter's depression appeared to Dr. John to revolve around several interpersonal issues that seemed to be common to all of Peter's relationships. After approximately 2 months of therapy, Peter told Dr. John that he was beginning to feel very secure in their therapeutic relationship and that there was something he needed to address. Peter then confessed that he was bisexual which, because he had not told anyone, caused him a great deal of stress. Peter further reported that his first homosexual encounter was about a year ago and he had since engaged in several short-term relationships with other men. While Peter enjoyed the company of men, he stated that he had every intention of continuing to date women. In particular, Peter noted an 8-month relationship with a woman named Michelle.

Dr. John and Peter continued to address this issue over the course of the next several months. One day, seeming particularly tense, Peter confessed to Dr. John that he had been diagnosed as HIV positive. He maintained that he had been tested "just to be safe" about a month ago and had been informed of the results about 2 weeks ago. Peter told Dr. John that he was concerned, but "it hadn't quite sunk in yet." Further, Peter stated that he was continuing to have unprotected sex with several of his companions because it was unlikely that he could infect others in such a short time. In particular, Peter said he did not want to inform Michelle. He had come to the conclusion that Michelle would end the relationship upon hearing the news, and Peter did not want this to happen.

Literature Review

The ethical principles of the American Psychological Association (2002) emphasize the psychologist's obligation to respect the privacy interests of the client. Maintaining confidentiality (assuring that a client's privacy will be protected) over the course of a relationship ensures that clients will feel free to engage more fully (i.e., fully disclose) with the psychologist (Kagle & Kopels, 1994; Young, 2009). Further, the establishment of confidentiality standards serves to protect the client from the negative effects of stigmatization (Stanard & Hazler, 1995). Thus, confidentiality, from its original intent to foster therapeutic relationships to its expanded consideration as an ethical responsibility, assumes a significant and necessary role in the effective psychologist—client relationship.

Confidentiality includes most information obtained over the course of a psychologist's contact with a client. Revealing confidential information is ethically acceptable only upon consent of the client or upon consent from the client's legal representative. Undermining the trust that is often difficult to build in the first place, violating standards of confidentiality may result in termination of the relationship, poor outcome, and/or malpractice suits against the psychologist (Kagle & Kopels, 1994; Koocher & Keith-Spiegel, 2008).

Over the years, confidentiality has become more difficult to maintain. The ability of the psychologist to protect privacy through confidentiality has been curtailed by a number of issues. Namely, these issues revolve around the court's expanding interest and involvement in professional decisions (Koocher & Keith-Spiegel, 2008). Clients must be made aware of the limits of confidentiality at the outset of the relationship and, additionally, must be made aware of the process of breaching confidentiality (APA, 2002). Thus, psychologists are often forced into onerous decisions, which necessitate the weighing of confidentiality against third-party interests in obtaining that information. This issue is, perhaps, most profound when violent or potentially violent clients are involved.

The "duty to warn," which has more recently invoked limits on client privacy and confidentiality rights, stems from the 1976 California Supreme Court case *Tarasoff v. Regents of the University of California*. In *Tarasoff*, client Poddar informed psychologist Dr. Moore over the course of their therapy that he intended to kill a woman when she returned from vacation. Taking the threats seriously, Dr. Moore consulted with his supervisors and campus police. Poddar did not meet the California standards for **involuntary civil commitment** (a legal process through which an individual with severe mental illness is provided treatment in a hospital (inpatient) or in the community (outpatient) against his or her will) and, thus, was not hospitalized. Further, the campus police detained Poddar briefly, yet released him after deciding that he presented no imminent and immediate harm. Two months later, after Tatiana Tarasoff returned from vacation, Poddar stabbed and killed her. Tarasoff's parents initiated lawsuits for wrongful death against Dr. Moore, his supervisors, campus police, and the Board of Regents, claiming that their daughter should have been made aware of the danger that Poddar posed. The defendants claimed that Tarasoff was not their patient and that warning her would have breached confidentiality. The California Supreme Court, in response to their defense, would forever change the way psychology and related fields view confidentiality. The Court held that:

> …*when a therapist determines, or pursuant to the standards of his profession should determine, that his patient presents a serious danger of violence to another, he incurs an obligation to use reasonable care to protect the intended victim against such danger* (Tarasoff v. Regents of the University of California, *1976, p. 34).*

The Court added that this duty would entail warning the intended victim or others who may alert the victim to the potential danger, notifying the police, and/or taking any other steps that may be necessary under the circumstances to protect the victim.

Following *Tarasoff*, a number of similar cases began to emerge in other parts of the country. In general, *Tarasoff* was used as the precedent case in the courts' rulings that therapists had a duty to warn third parties under certain circumstances (Felthous & Kachigian, 2001; Walcott, Cerundolo, & Beck, 2001; Kagle & Kopels, 1994; Quattrocchi & Schopp, 2005; Weisner, 2006; Yufik, 2005). Thus, the dilemma posed by confidentiality versus duty to warn has profound nationwide implications at this time. While some states had statutes that provided for the protection of confidentiality, *Tarasoff* caused many of these statutes to be amended, allowing for exceptions in cases where a danger to a third party was a factor. Thus, it generally stands that confidentiality should, or must be, breached when a therapist believes that disclosing information is necessary to protect others from a "clear, imminent risk of serious physical or mental injury, disease, or death" (Kagle & Kopels, 1994, p. 219). Since the Tarasoff decision, the courts have expanded the scope and role of a clinician's duty to protect with warnings only as one option for fulfilling this obligation (*Ewing v. Goldstein*, 2004; Koocher & Keith-Spiegel, 2008; Felthous & Kachigian, 2001; Walcott *et al.*, 2001). The precise implications of the duty to warn or protect, as presented in the following section, remain somewhat vague.

What if a therapist is warned by a client's family member? Does the therapist still have a duty to warn the intended victim? These were the questions posed in the case of *Ewing v. Goldstein* (2004).

Dr. David Goldstein had treated Geno Colello, a former Los Angeles police officer, for work-related injuries and the breakup of his 17-year relationship with a woman named Diana Williams. Dr. Goldstein received permission from Mr. Colello to speak with his father, Victor Colello. During their conversation, Victor told Dr. Goldstein that Geno was very depressed and seemed to have lost his will to live. He also went on to say that Geno was having a problem seeing Diana dating another man, and he was worried Geno might harm the other man. After being released from a hospital, Geno ceased communication with Dr. Goldstein and on 23 June 2001, shot and killed Keith Ewing, the man Diana had begun dating, before shooting himself (Koocher & Keith-Spiegel, 2008).

Keith Ewing's parents filed wrongful death suit against several defendants, including Dr. Goldstein. Initially, the case against Dr. Goldstein was dismissed on the grounds that his client had not disclosed anything directly to him. The California Court of Appeals, however, reinstated the case and opined that information communicated to a therapist by a client's family constitutes a client communication. What this means for therapists is that any information disclosed by a client's family that might indicate imminent risk for future violence must be treated as if the client had disclosed it themselves.

Forensic Psychology and Policy Implications

Before discussing the implications of Peter's case, let us examine several of the issues more broadly related to the "duty to warn." First, while courts have generally ruled that therapists have a duty to warn, the specifics of this duty have not been clearly elaborated. Court rulings have been inconsistent as to whether the duty is limited to specific victims or more generally to all third parties. In other words, exactly which third parties the therapist is responsible for protecting varies widely among jurisdictions (Kagle & Kopels, 1994; Mason, Worsley, & Coyle, 2010). Herbert (2002, p. 417) reported that 27 states mandate an actual duty to warn, but there is great disparity in the approaches leaving a "substantial burden of guesswork on clinicians." Several states and federal jurisdictions have even extended *Tarasoff* to include violence against property. As Koocher and Keith-Spiegel (2008) propose, whether the therapist knew or should have known that a client posed some danger is a key test of responsibility from both a legal and ethical perspective. Further, courts have generally not specified what this protection entails. What exactly a therapist must do to protect third parties remains extremely vague (Oppenheimer & Swanson, 1990). What has been suggested however, is that therapists would be wise to consult an attorney when they are unclear as to what standards apply in their jurisdiction (Koocher and Keith-Spiegel, 2008).

Moreover, questions remain about dangerousness and its prediction. One of the greatest difficulties pertaining to this is determining when a client is truly dangerous to a third party and when he or she is merely fantasizing (Oppenheimer & Swanson, 1990; Koocher and Keith-Spiegel, 2008). Is it asking too much of psychologists to be able to identify when a client may "really do" what he or she has brought to therapists' attention? If the therapist remains "on the safe side," he or she may be unnecessarily violating another's confidentiality rights. If that person does the opposite, he or she risks being held legally responsible for harm that may be inflicted upon another individual.

Additionally, how can we hold therapists responsible for the violent behavior of their clients, when predicting with a high degree of certainty whether a client will engage in a violent act is beyond the current ability of psychology (*Barefoot v. Estelle*, 1983; Levin, 2008; Monahan, 1981; Skeem & Monahan, 2011)? We must ask ourselves if holding the therapist legally responsible is justifiable when predicting future violent acts is so uncertain. Borum and Reddy (2001) suggest that evaluation of risk in these cases should be primarily fact-based and deductive, as compared to the more inductive risk assessment approach used for general violence recidivism. Tolman (2001, p. 387) argues that improving the training of professional psychology students to include more risk assessment education, relevant legal information, and conceptual models of potential patient violence will "improve clinical practice, reduce legal liability, and improve public safety."

Let us now return to the case of Peter. One of the most controversial aspects of the duty to warn involves the potentially violent sexual behavior of those infected with HIV. There are varying professional opinions as to the implications for psychologists of duty to warn with regard to client HIV infection. Some authors have pointed out that the sexual activity, not the person, is responsible for the risk; specifically the client's resistance to informing partners or using safe sexual practices (Kain, 1988; Koocher and Keith-Spiegel, 2008; D. Martin, 1989). Thus, because different types of sexual activity create different risks, the level of danger must be addressed with specific regard to the activity. For example, the therapist must consider whether the activity involves the exchange of bodily fluids and whether preventive measures (e.g., protected sex) are being taken (Koocher and Keith-Spiegel, 2008; Stanard & Hazler, 1995).

Others have suggested that the fatal nature of the disease creates a duty to warn, which surmounts any ethical obligations to confidentiality. These commentators recommend directly informing the client's sexual partners if the client refuses to do so, and, where unidentified partners are at risk, informing the appropriate authorities (Gray & Harding, 1988; Koocher and Keith-Spiegel, 2008). Regardless of the varying opinions, the majority of professionals seem to agree that HIV-positive clients engaging in high-risk behavior with uninformed partners are subject to *Tarasoff* (Stanard & Hazler, 1995). In other words, they are dangerous and steps must be taken to assure that, if a substantial threat exists, third parties are warned. Kain (1988) however, states that with regard to unidentified third parties, the "identifiable victim" criterion of *Tarasoff* is absent. Given this, he believes that breaching confidentiality in such situations is "highly questionable" (p. 224). In a more recent study, Huprich, Fuller, and Schneider (2003) conclude that there is still no clear professional standard for whether or not a clinician has a duty to warn the unknowing partner of an HIV-positive client.

Thus, with regard to HIV and duty to warn for psychologists, several important issues must be addressed. First, the nature of the threat — whether specific, identifiable third parties are present; the exact nature of the sexual behavior; whether there is an imminent danger to others; and which third parties or authorities to notify. Next, defining which behaviors put an individual at risk is difficult. Further, identifiable victims are often difficult to identify because the virus can lay dormant for many years (Stanard & Hazler, 1995). As Lamb, Clark, Drumheller, Frizzell, and Surrey (1989) note:

> Given the incomplete knowledge about the diagnosis and transmission of AIDS, there is little agreement as to who is likely to contract the disease from infected persons. Such a lack of certainty about the conditions under which the disease can be contracted make it even more difficult to identify a potential victim (p. 40).

Thus, while cases such as Peter's may seem reasonably clear, others are far more controversial. As with the transmission of most illnesses, it is nearly impossible to identify potential victims and make a risk assessment. Thus, HIV poses yet another difficult ethical and legal concern for psychologists to confront. To help therapists in this situation, Koocher and Keith-Spiegel (2008) suggest that therapists maintain a working knowledge of the medical research on HIV, including transmission risks, treatments, interventions, and laws governing professional interactions with HIV-positive patients. They also suggest that in situations in which an HIV-positive client presents a danger to others, they break confidentiality only as a last resort and only after notifying the client, explaining the decision, and asking for their permission.

Suggestions for Future Research

Many areas for future research have been addressed in this section. Generally, psychology is not efficient in assessing risk of future violence or determining under which conditions violent behavior is likely to occur. Like other areas of civil forensics, methods for more accurately predicting violence are necessary if psychology is going to remain in the position of interfering with individual civil rights. Further, we must better understand which third parties are best to contact if such a decision is reached or if information is disclosed by individuals other than the identified client. Clearly, as in the *Tarasoff* case, contacting certain third parties is often not enough, or possible, to ensure that an individual will be protected from potentially violent acts. For example, with a sexually promiscuous client who may be HIV positive, practitioners may not know the identity of individuals who may be at risk of contracting the virus from the client. With regard to HIV, as our knowledge of the illness continues to grow, we must continue to adapt our strategies for dealing with this condition in clinical and/or forensic situations. As previously noted, to identify potential victims and potentially violent behavior, we must know which individuals are at risk and under what conditions.

Victim—Offender Mediation

Introduction

Since 1990, the number of victim—offender mediation programs around the world has increased eightfold (VOMA, 2006). Growing for more than three decades, victim—offender mediation programs have spread throughout the United States and Europe, with programs in more than 1,200 communities (Umbreit & Armour, 2010; Uotila & Sambou, 2010; VOMA, 2006; Umbreit, Coates, & Roberts, 2000). According to Gerkin (2009), victim—offender mediation has continued to grow and develop into an alternative to a traditionally **retributive theory of justice** (e.g., considers that punishment is a morally acceptable response to crime). **Victim—offender mediation programs** (defined below) are emerging as one of the state's preferred **restorative justice** (e.g., focuses on repairing the harm caused by crime) approaches. Mediation programs for victims and offenders offer the victim an opportunity to play a role in determining the offender's punishment, explain to the offender the impact the crime had upon them, and give the victim closure after being violated. The program gives offenders an opportunity to voice their personal problems and explain their crime, avoid a possible harsher punishment such as imprisonment, and allows them to personalize their crime; that is, see first-hand the impact it had upon another human being. This personalization could ultimately reduce recidivism (Umbreit & Armour, 2010; Nugent, Umbreit, Wiinamaki, & Paddock, 2001). The goal of mediation programs is to provide a conflict resolution that is fair for both parties involved and to develop an acceptable reparation and/or restitution plan (Umbreit & Armour, 2010; Umbreit *et al.*, 2000).

Despite a variety in victim—offender mediation programs, most programs aim to achieve the same goals and have principles based on the concept of restorative justice (Shipley & Arrigo, 2004; Umbreit Coates, & Vos, 2001; Umbreit *et al.*, 2000; Severson & Bankston, 1995). Restorative justice is an age-old concept emphasizing that crime should be perceived as an act against individuals within the community, not only as an act against the state (Roach, 2000; Umbreit & Bradshaw, 1997). Most mediation programs are based on the same principles and follow the same process for mediation. First, either a victim or offender is referred to a mediation program. Second, each party is seen individually by an unbiased mediator who informs them about the process and the possible benefits of participating in such a program. Third, after each party agrees, the mediator schedules a joint meeting between the two parties. During this phase, both the victim and the offender are given the opportunity to talk to each other without interruption. Finally, some programs may have a follow-up phase in which the referral agency approves the restitution agreement and closes the case; approving the agreement may include making sure payments or services that were agreed upon are fulfilled (Joseph, 1996; Umbreit, 1993). The types of offender mediation programs and how they differ are discussed later in this section.

The following case illustration is a real situation in which victim—offender mediation was successfully utilized. This section uses this case to describe the types of victim—offender mediation programs and how they differ; to discuss the effectiveness of victim—offender mediation programs; and to address arguments against the appropriateness of such programs, including examples of how the following case could have been unsuccessful had circumstances been different.

Geiger was working as an auditor on the 11 a.m. to 7 p.m. shift that summer night when five men ages 18 to 21 entered the motel and demanded money. Geiger was punched and kicked, followed quickly by a pistol-whipping that knocked him to the ground. He jumped to his feet when he thought the crooks had left. Then he heard an explosion. The bullet tore into his chest, penetrating his right lung, breaking two ribs, and lodging in his stomach muscles. At the time of the robbery Geiger was a nationally ranked sprinter. Before the shooting he could do 100 meters in under 11 seconds; afterward, he could barely walk the distance. Facing unwanted publicity, motel management fired him.

At the trials of the black defendants, Geiger, who is white, was accused of racism and drinking and made to feel guilty. He felt left out and angry at a system that had victimized him a second time. He was depressed and he needed answers. He wanted to confront his shooter and tell him about the damage he had done, and he wanted an apology.

Geiger found answers to many of his questions in mediation. He found that the offender was a substance abuser, out of work, and on parole. He had planned a simple robbery. He hadn't intended to shoot Geiger but instead wanted to fire a warning shot. At the end of his session, Geiger shook hands with the man who shot him. "I saw the burden of guilt lifted from him and the anguish from me." Geiger testified on behalf of the man last February at his parole hearing. He was granted parole after serving 12 years of a 12- to 25-year term for first-degree robbery (Reske, 1995, pp. 1—3).

Literature Review

Types of victim—offender mediation programs

In the Middle Ages, a criminal act was punished by the criminal making reparations directly to the victim; this is the basis upon which victim—offender mediation programs are utilized today (Severson & Bankston, 1995). Currently, there are various types of mediation programs, which can differ in several ways. Some programs offer mediation after conviction of a crime but prior to sentencing, while others offer mediation upon parole and make restitution a condition of parole. In some programs the victim and offender meet face-to-face while in other programs they do not (Umbreit & Armour, 2010). In addition, programs may differ on the cases they accept; some programs may only accept juvenile cases while others accept adults (Kilchling & Loeschnig-Gspandl, 2000). Some programs only accept cases of violent crimes, while others accept nonviolent criminal cases (Umbreit & Armour, 2010; Uotila & Sambou, 2010). Finally, programs differ in who they use to mediate the cases, the model they utilize to run the program, and in their administration. Most programs use trained volunteers as mediators; however, other programs may use social workers or psychologists. Although some mediation programs are supported by religious agencies, others are run and financed by probation departments, private foundations, or in some other countries they are run by other governmental agencies (Uotila & Sambou, 2010; Joseph, 1996; Severson & Bankston, 1995).

The most commonly used model used to run victim—offender mediation programs is the Victim/Offender Reconciliation Program (VORP) model. The VORP model was developed in 1974 by the Mennonite Central Committee in Kitchener, Ontario, Canada (Umbreit & Armour, 2010; Umbreit & Bradshaw, 1997). In 1978, the United States' first victim—offender program was put together in Elkhart, Indiana (Reske, 1995). The Elkhart program, like most victim reconciliation programs nationwide, is based on the VORP model. Programs based on the VORP model provide face-to-face meetings between the victim and offender (Umbreit & Armour, 2010). Also, the VORP is usually a postadjudication program in which the offenders and their victims explore reconciliation and build a plan together for reparation (Roy, 1993; Severson & Blackston, 1995). Most likely, the program Geiger went through utilized the VORP model because he had a face-to-face meeting with his offender and because the mediation took place after the offender had served time in prison (postadjudication).

Despite the majority of reconciliation programs that utilize the VORP model, there are successful programs that do not. There are other successful programs that follow a different model. A restitution program in Kalamazoo County, Michigan, is operated by the Juvenile Probate Court, is a preadjudication program, and does not provide face-to-face meetings between the victim and offender; however, it does offer restitution to the victim similar to the VORP model. As of 03-31-10, the Ingham County/Lansing Restorative Justice Intervention Program was still active and intended to continue to use the principles of Balanced and Restorative Justice (BARJ) to provide a pre-adjudication solution to adolescent offenders (ages 10 through 17) for juvenile offenses such as truancy, curfew violations, failure to obey the lawful order of police/fire officer, furnishing false information to a police officer, fighting in public, loitering and disturbing the peace by loud noise, and disorderly conduct (Coalition of Juvenile Justice, 2009). It serves as a diversion program for juveniles who have been ticketed by the Lansing Police Department or the Lansing School Public Safety Officers or diverted from the prosecutor's office. Despite differences in this program and the VORP model, the Kalamazoo program has historically been found to be just as effective as the Elkhart, Missouri VORP model program (Roy, 1993). The longevity of the Ingham County/ Lansing Restorative Justice Intervention Program also speaks to its usefulness to the community.

Umbreit and Vos (2000, p. 265) presented two case studies that examined capital murder cases involving victim—offender mediation/dialogue sessions between surviving family members and two offenders about to be executed. These researchers concluded that this intervention brought some measure of relief and healing to those involved. Additionally, they suggested that more opportunities for these types of encounters be made available if "initiated and requested by victims and surviving family members of severely violent crime." However, opponents argue that this type of mediation does not fit the model of restorative justice in at least three critical ways (Radelet & Borg, 2000, p. 88): (1) There should be a "willingness and ability to change attitudes and understandings as a result of their communication." (2) "Restorative justice emphasizes recompense by the offender, actively taking steps to atone for the harm and injury he or she has caused." (3) "Restorative justice seeks to reduce the state's role in the justice process and to revitalize the ancient model in which victims, offenders, and communities all were actively involved in responding to crime and restoring peaceful relationships."

There are clearly many different types of victim reconciliation programs. A discussion of every type of program is beyond the scope of this section. However, it is important to be aware of how such programs differ, and how these differences can have an impact on the effectiveness of the program. Because there are so many victim reconciliation programs and because many of these programs differ, it is difficult to assess the effectiveness of these programs as a whole. However, research on the effectiveness of individual programs, as well as on the effectiveness of programs utilizing the VORP model, have been conducted.

Effectiveness of programs

Effectiveness of restitution programs is generally measured by program completion rates, the impact of restitution on lowering recidivism rates, and by victim satisfaction with the program (Umbreit & Armour, 2010; Nugent *et al.*, 2001; Roy, 1993; Umbreit & Bradshaw, 1997). For example, in the Geiger case, the mediation was considered successful because the offender and Geiger came to an agreement, the offender showed compassion, and Geiger felt satisfied by the meeting. However, program completion percentages vary from program to program. In an evaluation of a restorative justice program implemented by the Vermont Department of Corrections for nonviolent offenders, data suggest that the program is working. According to one researcher, the program is no less effective than the traditional retribution model of corrections and is freeing up space and resources to deal with more violent criminals (Hansen, 1997). Nugent *et al.* (2001) combined the data from four studies and ran a statistical analysis of the combination samples of 1298 juveniles, which indicated that victim—offender mediation participants' recidivism rate was 32% lower than nonparticipants. These researchers concluded that victim—offender mediation participation was related to significant decreases in delinquent behavior.

Research that has focused on victim satisfaction with the process has found high rates of victim satisfaction with reconciliation programs (Umbreit & Armour, 2010; Umbreit *et al.*, 2000; Umbreit & Bradshaw, 1997). When Geiger met his offender, it provided him closure to an occurrence which had a negative impact on his life. When an offender shows compassion, as in Geiger's case, many victims are satisfied with the program. According to Umbreit and Armour (2010), it is the victims who frequently benefit the most by the use of restorative justice practices. These authors also caution that there is not one model of restorative justice that fits all. To be effective, the model must be created in context, considering the type of offender and crime, as well as cultural and community norms and values (Umbreit & Armour, 2010).

Borton (2009) conducted a study examining victim—offender dialogue files archived by Ohio's Office of Victim Services (OVS). He found that victim—offender dialogue programs based on restorative justice theory have been shown to increase victim and offender satisfaction, decrease offender recidivism, and increase the rate of restitution. Data analysis on a sample (n = 212) of OVS completed and will-not-proceed files found offender race did not have a significant effect on dialogue completion rate (Borton, 2009). However, victim sex was found to have a significant effect on dialogue completion. Included are descriptive analyses of victims' stated motivations for seeking dialogue. This study found that victims who state specific motivations for participation in victim—offender dialogue were no more likely to follow through with the dialogue than those who did not.

Advocates for restorative justice believe that there is a reason why people commit crime again and again. One of these reasons is a lack of empathy for victims. With restorative justice, offenders are held accountable for their crimes, while the needs of some victims are met. Geiger needed an apology, and he received that and much more (Reske, 1995). In addition, his offender showed empathy and regret for what he did, which could have ultimately reduced the likelihood he would commit another crime of this nature. According to advocates for mediation programs, one of the benefits of mediation is that it allows offenders to become aware of the impact of their crimes and to see their victims as people rather than as objects (Umbreit & Armour, 2010; Reske, 1995). When offenders are able to see their victims as people and possibly have empathy for them, the likelihood of recidivism is reduced (Umbreit & Armour, 2010; Umbreit & Bradshaw, 1997). As a result, fewer offenders circulate through the prison system, helping to alleviate overcrowding. Also, mediation programs such as the one implemented in Vermont may aid in overcrowding issues simply by providing an alternative response to jail or prison.

Proponents for mediation programs suggest that prisons have become nothing more than "colleges for crime," which return to the public "meaner" and "craftier" criminals (Snyder, 2001; Evers, 1998; Severson & Bankston, 1995). These advocates suggest that the United States spends more on punishment and less on programs to prevent crime, and indicate that restorative justice is a program designed for prevention (Snyder, 2001; Evers, 1998). Restorative justice programs not only benefit victims, they benefit offenders as well (Borton, 2009). Proponents note that offenders need to be punished, but also need help; restorative justice can do both for some offenders (Borton, 2009; Shipley & Arrigo, 2004; Evers, 1998). However, other researchers are not so optimistic about restorative justice programs. They suggest that offenders often feel pressured into coming to an agreement during mediation and indicate such programs often do not benefit the offender (Brown, 1994; Joseph, 1996). Additionally, some offenders have little capacity for victim empathy and would only utilize such an opportunity to further victimize a surviving victim or family members.

Arguments against victim—offender mediation

Although most research is supportive of victim—offender mediation programs, some researchers note problems with the programs, resulting in debate about whether such programs should be utilized at all. The primary argument against mediation programs is whether true voluntariness exists for the offenders involved in the program (Brown, 1994; Joseph, 1996). Because many offenders are referred to mediation programs from the court, they participate because they feel it is required (Joseph, 1996). In addition, offenders may come to an agreement that they cannot afford or cannot complete because they fear if they do not come to an agreement in mediation they will be punished for noncompliance (Brown, 1994). In response, researchers who support victim—offender mediation programs suggest that giving the offender the opportunity to have a say in his or her punishment will more likely result in a punishment with which he or she can comply (Umbreit & Armour, 2010; Reske, 1995).

There are also arguments against restitution programs. Brown (1994) argues that such programs are a disservice to both victims and offenders. Victims may experience an injustice because reconciliation programs stress reconciliation before the victims "have the vindication of a public finding that the offender is guilty" (Brown, 1994, p. 3). However, this is not true for all programs; in Geiger's case, the offender was not only found guilty, he served 12 years in prison. Victim—offender mediation programs may pressure the victim into suppressing his or her anger and sense of loss through the assumption that his or her feelings can be expressed to the offender in merely a period of hours. These programs underserve the offender in several ways as well. First, the selection criteria are not related to the goals of the program. Second, such programs eliminate procedural protections, including the right to counsel. Third, programs attempt to gain advantages for the victims by using the threat of a pending criminal trial.

Some researchers argue against the use of victim–offender mediation programs for certain offenders such as sex offenders and domestic violence offenders. Women's rights advocates believe restorative justice may reduce progress battered women have made. However, the appropriateness of victim–offender mediation programs for certain populations does not appear to be as common. Mark Umbreit, the director of the Center of Restorative Justice and Mediation, does not recommend mediation for some sexual assault cases and domestic violence cases (Umbreit & Armour, 2010). Uotila and Sambou (2010) discuss the extra training required for those providing victim mediation services for intimate partner violence in Finland (see the Practice Update Section for more information). Proponents argue that in some cases, mediation can be beneficial for sexual assault incidents, and many programs require that sexual assault cases be victim initiated. Certainly, victim–offender mediation programs for primary psychopaths would be inappropriate due to the high risk of manipulation and further victimization of survivors and family members (Shipley & Arrigo, 2008; Shipley & Arrigo, 2004; Shipley & Arrigo, 2001).

Despite evidence which supports victim–offender mediation programs, these programs have not gone without dispute. There are few examples of cases which went wrong; however, they are sure to exist. For example, imagine if Geiger met the man who shot him and the man showed no remorse, guilt, refused to apologize, and did nothing but make excuses for his behavior. It is questionable whether Geiger would have experienced the closure he desired. In fact, such a meeting could have forced Geiger to relive some of the pain he had dealt with over the past 11 years. Clearly, there will always be problems with mediation programs, and there will always be instances where the program is unsuccessful. The question is whether the problems warrant giving up completely on such initiatives or warrant changing programs to be more effective. Because restitution programs threaten to alter the way in which some criminals are punished, there are clearly some policy implications for the existence of such programs.

Forensic Psychology and Policy Implications

A problem with victim–offender mediation programs is that they are run by many agencies. As a result, there are no set criteria about who can mediate, how offenders will be selected, and how the process of mediation should take place (Severson & Bankston, 1995). Umbreit and Armour (2010) caution that restorative justice models and victim mediation programs are very complex, and any persons or agencies wanting to create a program needs accurate information and appropriate training. In order for a program to both be effective and avoid causing greater harm, programs must be created and implemented with the needed data, training, and relevant education and experience of those involved.

According to Sherman and Strang (2007, p. 33), there are numerous variations of restorative justice to include: (1) "face-to-face conferences of victims, offenders and stakeholders; (2) face-to-face mediation (without supporters present); (3) indirect, 'shuttle diplomacy' mediation; (4) victim-absent discussions with offender and supporters about crime; (5) offender-absent discussions with victim and supporters about crime; (6) sentencing circles led by a judge (First Nations people in Canada)." Understanding the variations of the possible programs and which program is the best fit for the circumstances, victim, and offender is important for program success.

Many mediation programs rely on trained volunteers who know little or nothing about psychology or sociology. Several researchers suggest using trained professionals as mediators for these programs and that mediators should be required to have advanced training (Sherman & Strang, 2007; Umbreit & Armour, 2010). In addition, there is a need for policies based on research to be adopted for victim—offender mediation programs. Although some researchers have suggested policies that should be adopted, there is a need for research to be conducted in order to determine what guidelines create the most effective programs. One policy that most researchers do agree upon is a provision against mediation for certain domestic violence cases (Evers, 1998). It is essential that research on mediation programs and procedural guidelines be adopted immediately; the concept is becoming more popular and lawmakers are passing legislation to create restorative justice programs in states such as Vermont and Maine. The programs, however, are diverse and there are few guidelines that indicate how the programs could be successfully run. As demonstrated by the opponents of restorative justice programs, the negative effects of unsuccessful programs can be huge. Without guidelines based on research, it will be difficult to minimize the negative effects. A 2007 meta-analysis of all research projects concerning restorative justice conferencing or victim—offender mediation published in English between 1986 and 2005 found encouraging results, particularly for victims (Sherman & Strang, 2007). These results include the following:

- Greater ability to return to work, to resume normal daily activities, and to sleep.
- No cases of offenders verbally or violently abusing victims.
- Reduced fear of the offender (especially for violence victims).
- Lower perceived likelihood of another offense.
- Increased sense of security.
- Reduced anger towards the offender.
- Greater sympathy for the offender and the offender's supporters.
- Greater feelings of trust in others.
- Increased feelings of self-confidence.
- Reduced anxiety.

Sherman and Strang's (2007) study found that the only ethical basis for selectively allowing, or banning, restorative justice approaches is harm reduction. Additionally, they found that there is limited public familiarity with restorative justice approaches, and misconceptions about victim—offender mediation.

With prison overcrowding, it is more likely that many states will look for alternatives to traditional sentencing. States may begin to implement legislation for the development of restitution programs; they may be met, however, with opposition from the general public, whose attitudes have continued to trend toward the belief that punishment equals imprisonment. The public must be educated about the deficiencies of prisons and how these institutions financially impact them. Before legislation can be changed, society must become informed about alternatives to incarceration. As long as society equates imprisonment with punishment, politicians will continue to build prisons instead of invest in prevention programs. Perhaps the beginning of public education could occur through research results on the effectiveness of restorative justice programs. Because of the diversity of such programs, it is difficult to determine which aspects of various programs do or do not work. The growth of this approach and its influence on criminal justice systems has created a pressing need for professional support and continuing education for those who put restorative justice into action (VOMA, 2006).

Suggestions for Future Research

Further research on the effectiveness of victim—offender mediation programs is needed (Umbreit & Armour, 2010; Umbreit *et al.*, 2001). Although some studies have reported recidivism rates and program completion rates on individual programs, there is a need for more research that examines the benefits and consequences of all restorative justice programs in order for recommendations to be made for program guidelines (Sherman & Strang, 2007). Greater availability, along with information about victims' positive views about victim mediation programs, are likely to increase the number of victims willing to participate (Sherman & Strang, 2007). Also, additional research on long-term recidivism rates for those who participated in a mediation program is needed. These data are essential when states are enacting legislation to develop initiatives. If program developers do not have findings indicating which programs have successful long-term effects and therefore would serve as models to develop, then the development of these mediation programs will be no more successful than our overcrowded prisons at reducing recidivism. Both national and international program evaluations should continue in order to determine the effectiveness of these programs on dimensions such as victim satisfaction, community satisfaction, costs, and recidivism rates. Research should be clear on providing information on both programmatic successes associated with restorative justice, as well as the failures.

The case of Geiger is a clear illustration of how victim—offender mediation programs can benefit the victim and offender. However, the outcome of this case is not known. Quite possibly, the offender recidivated after his parole, perhaps this time shooting and killing an individual. There is no way to know this information for the majority of cases that have completed mediation programs, simply because long-term research on effectiveness is limited. Various studies indicate that victim—offender mediation programs do work. Studies demonstrate a high victim satisfaction rate and a recidivism rate no worse than those criminals who went through the traditional sentencing model. With prison overcrowding and the United States spending less on prevention and more on imprisonment, mediation programs appear to be promising.

Practice Update Section: Duty to Warn

The Tarasoff duty to warn or protect has been at the center of many debates and requires very well informed decision making. In many cases, the Tarasoff warnings exemplify the gray area that lurks between the concrete black and white world of perfect answers and textbook solutions. Ethics courses around the nation attempt to broach the conflict between legal and ethical duties and balancing the best interests of your client (e.g., confidentiality, etc.) as well as the safety of a foreseeable victim. In some states, for example Texas, there is no legal duty to warn. However, a clinician must take into consideration their more stringent ethical guidelines and do their best to adhere to them within the boundaries of the law. If a forensic psychologist finds him- or herself in a situation where, based on a careful risk assessment, clear and imminent danger exists to an identifiable victim, taking reasonable steps to protect the welfare of a potential victim appears justified, even when not mandated by law.

The Tarasoff case created a new legal duty to protect third parties from a mentally ill patient's "foreseeable violence" (Walcott, Cerundolo, & Beck, 2001, p. 325). The courts have initially expanded the scope of a clinician's duty to protect. However, subsequent cases began to substantially limit cases where Tarasoff warnings would apply. Some more recent cases have rejected a clinician's duty to warn. Furthermore, the creation of state statutes that codify the applicability and discharge of a Tarasoff duty to warn have also added to a limitation of the duty to protect. Finally, Walcott *et al.* (2001) have advocated for a "thorough, well documented assessment of risk of violence as the best means for addressing concern about potential legal liability." Individualized responses will be needed for the risk posed by individual patients.

What happens after a clinician contacts the police as a means of fulfilling their Tarasoff duty? Are law enforcement officers aware of a mental health professional's duty to warn or protect potential victims of a psychiatric patient or client? A survey of police officers' experience with Tarasoff warnings in two states revealed that many police officers have very limited experience with Tarasoff warnings (Huber, Balon, Labbate, Brandt-Youtz, Hammer, *et al.*, 2000). Out of 48 Michigan police stations and 52 South Carolina police stations surveyed, respondents at 45 stations reported receiving warnings from mental health professionals, with an average of 3.7 warnings a year. Only three respondents were familiar with the Tarasoff rulings. Out of the stations surveyed, only 24 had a specific policy on Tarasoff warnings and 27 stations responded that they would not warn a potential victim (Huber *et al.*, 2000). The duty to warn or protect has many potential moral, ethical, and legal implications for forensic psychologists. The preceding research highlights the boundaries of a mental health professional's ability to prevent potential violence. Psychologists are not law enforcement and cannot act in that capacity. If they have assessed clear and imminent danger and contacted law enforcement, as well as appropriately documented their actions, they may still be unsuccessful in preventing harm to the intended victim. However, if the responsible authorities fail to respond, then the moral and legal liability will likely shift to law enforcement. Psychologists are experts in risk assessment, not at enforcing laws and foiling crimes.

Weiner (2003) discusses two cases where the patients were criminally prosecuted as a result of Tarasoff warnings. In both cases, each individual was arrested while being evaluated as a patient in a locked psychiatric emergency service in a California hospital. Each individual was charged with "criminal threats," as defined by 422 of the California Penal Code. In both cases, the charge was a result of the Tarasoff warnings made by mental health professionals and the Tarasoff warning itself was the means by which the threat was carried to the intended victim (Weiner, 2003). While this is undoubtedly a more stringent application of law enforcement's response to Tarasoff warnings, the consequences in these instances weigh heavily with the patient. The failure to warn may have serious or even fatal consequences for a potential victim and legal ramifications for the clinician, whereas Tarasoff warnings may have serious legal implications for the patient, with a minimum of a loss of the therapeutic alliance. Expertise in violence risk assessment, the ethics code, and laws in one's state of practice, as well as good judgment should guide a psychologist's course of action.

■ International Issues: Restorative Justice

In Finland, the first mediation projects founded on the principles and ideals of restorative justice were started in the early 1980s (Uotila & Sambou, 2010). Prior to the time when the Act on Mediation in Criminal and Certain Civil Cases (10/15/2005) was enforced in 2006, mediation programs were provided by cities, municipalities, and non-governmental organizations. Victim—offender mediation practices varied, and there was limited guidance, training, and supervision by state authorities. The goal of this Act (10/15/2005) was to standardize the practice of mediation and enable evaluation of victim—offender mediation programs. Uotila and Sambou (2010) indicated that the evaluation of these programs is specifically important in order to create solutions to some of the issues raised regarding mediation in intimate relationship violence. The Act states that only police or prosecutors may initiate the process to refer a case that involves intimate relationship violence. Moreover, mediators/facilitators who specialize in intimate relationship violence cases are required to obtain further training in this area. The unique interpersonal dynamics involved in intimate relationship violence, and subsequent practice implications for victim—offender mediation, has been the subject of recent legislative action and standard of practice recommendations in Finland (Uotila & Sambou, 2010).

■

Related Websites

www.unccmh.org/clients-and-families/learn-about-mental-illness/a-family-guide/viii-legal-issues/right-to-refuse-treatment
This is a website for families of mental illness so the family can educate themselves on mental illness, and the individual's rights in treatment options.
www.antipsychiatry.org/wellstone.htm
This website gives both sides to the issue of forcing treatment for mentally ill individuals.
www.bu.edu/cpr/jobschool
This website is for psychiatric rehabilitation, with information for individuals with a mental illness who are in the work field as well as information for students.
www.reintegration.com/reint/employment/workplace.asp
This website is about the reintegration of individuals with mental illness, and getting the mentally ill into the workforce.
www.apa.org/ethics/code/index.aspx
The ethics code of the American Psychological Association.
www.aidshealth.org/about-hiv-aids/hiv-aids
Website with information on HIV/AIDS; symptoms, treatments, transmission, myths, etc.
www.voma.org
Website for the Victim—Offender Mediation Association (VOMA).
htpp://ssw.che.umn.edu/rjp/
Website for the Center for Restorative Justice and Mediation.
www.mvfr.org/
Website for Murder Victims' Families for Reconciliation

Police and Law Enforcement

Key Issues

Adult Criminal Profiling
- The criminal profiler
- The inductive and deductive approaches
- Characteristics and typologies of offenders

Use of Force
- "Fleeing Felon" law
- Factors of psychological and physical control
- Use of Force Continuum Scale
- Causes of excessive use of force

Suicide by Cop
- Motivations for suicide by cop
- Indicators of risk for suicide by cop
- Profile of perpetrator of suicide by cop

Coerced Confessions
- Due Process requirements
- The Threshold of Clarity Rule
- The Per Se Rule
- The Clarification Rule
- Tactics used by police
- The Reid Technique

The Police Personality and Pre-Employment Screenings
- Overview of the MMPI-2
- Traits portraying strengths and weaknesses of police

Critical Incidents Debriefing
- Debriefing methods
- The debriefing process
- Effectiveness of debriefing
- Barriers to successful implementation of debriefing programs

Adult Issues in Policing

Chapter Outline

Introduction to Forensic Psychology. DOI: 10.1016/B978-0-12-382169-0.00004-9

Overview

Traditionally, the fields of law enforcement and psychology have made for strained, if not strange, bedfellows. Policing by its very nature requires that officers responsibly exercise restraint and caution, be alert and suspicious, and exert power and force where appropriate. Psychology, by contrast, encourages considerable openness, reflection, and introspection. In short, the "protect and serve" function of policing does not seem easily incorporated with the "touchy-feely" sentiment of psychology. This notwithstanding, there are certainly a number of instances where the tools of psychology help officers interface with the public (for example, see the sections on police and the mentally ill, and police as mediators in domestic disputes).

In this chapter, five issues and/or controversies are examined, which explore different facets of this relationship. These issues/controversies include: (1) adult criminal profiling; (2) the use of force; (3) suicide by cop; (4) coerced confessions; (5) the police personality and pre-employment screenings; and (6) critical incidents debriefing. Clearly, there are a number of other domains where the psychological sciences impact the practice of policing; however, the selected topics were carefully chosen because they collectively suggest considerable breadth in forensic application. In other words, the adult issues in this section canvas a wide array of law enforcement psychology topics, which reflect the expanse of the field.

State and federal law enforcement personnel investigate crimes that are committed by very troubled individuals. This has led to the criminal profiling of offenders. What are the personality and behavioral characteristics that officers consider when evaluating the profile for a serial homicide killer, a mass murderer, a sex offender, or other seriously disturbed persons? How do these processes contribute to the apprehension of offenders?

Police officers, on occasion, use force. What are the psychological variables that impact the use of it, and what "dangerous" circumstances inform an officer's decision to use excessive and even deadly force? Police officers are responsible for eliciting information from suspects that may result in a confession. What psychological and sociological techniques, manipulative or otherwise, do law enforcement personnel employ to arrive at (in)voluntary confessions? How, if at all, do officers balance the suspect's right against self-incrimination with the precinct's, and/or the public's demand for apprehension of (factually) guilty criminals during the interviewing phase?

Police officers can, on occasion, confront dangerous citizens, aggressive suspects, and agitated groups. How, if at all, do exchanges such as these relate to the development of a police personality? Are officers susceptible to psychopathology? Can pre-employment (mental health) screening of officers assess for such characterological traits? Does cynicism and violence, as dimensions of law enforcement, draw certain individuals to this line of work?

Officers make decisions that can have lethal consequences. Suicide by cop is one example. How does it occur and how do officer cope with a victim-precipitated shooting? Additionally, when critical incidents materialize, psychologists employ debriefing strategies. How do they work and what challenges does the policing subculture present for such programs?

This chapter, therefore, demonstrates that psychology is very much a part of what happens in ongoing police practices. Interestingly, however, we know very little about the extent of its role in routine law enforcement. What we do know suggests that the implications for officers, for police departments, for suspects/offenders, for the public at large, and for communities in general need to be considered. More research on the identified controversies is needed, and better evaluations of how the adult issues in policing and psychology interface are essential. These conditions are necessary if we are to address the problem of crime and the search for justice at the crossroads of psychology and law enforcement.

Adult Criminal Profiling

Introduction

The area of forensic psychology dealing with **criminal profiling** is an increasingly popular one. A greater number of movies and prime-time television shows attempt to portray the glamorous and interesting process of profiling criminals (most often serial murderers). Torres, Boccaccini, and Miller (2006, p. 51) define criminal profiling as, "the process of using crime scene evidence to make inferences about potential suspects, including personality characteristics and psychopathology." Although much profiling is accomplished through intuitive processes possessed by law enforcement agents or their consultants, a scientific grounding does exist for profiling and is discussed in this chapter. The following vignette provides an example of a rape scenario presented by Hazelwood and Warren (2000, pp. 273–274) that provides several indicators that guide the investigator in creating a profile of the offender used to apprehend him.

The rape took place in the apartment of a young woman who was asleep when the rapist entered her home. He concealed his identity and held a knife to her throat as he assured her that he did not want to hurt her, and that if she was cooperative with him she may enjoy their evening together. After spending time undressing her and admiring her figure, the rapist noticed the tension of his victim and encouraged her to relax and he removed a bottle of lotion and some other provisions that he had brought along in his bag. After performing intimate sexual acts on his victim, she kicked him in his testicles. This angered the assailant and he questioned her reasons for kicking him as he felt he had not hurt her and could not understand why she would hurt him. The assailant, now enraged, proceeded to vaginally rape his victim and steal her identification. In examining the evidence, investigators were able to conclude that this offender's crimes were ritualistic in nature, linking him to six other attacks. On this crime scene, investigators located a video camera containing photos of the victim that he obtained while he was peeping on her. They obtained his "rape kit" which contained items that could be used to set the offender's mood and the mood that he perceived his victim should have. Intimate items such as lotion, condoms, and pornographic materials were all intended tools for his attack. They determined this offender was "Ritualistic" due to the fantasy that the assailant appeared to be fulfilling based on the evidence.

The following vignette provides an example of a "typical" serial murder scenario and gives a hypothesis or "profile" used to apprehend the murderer (Turco, 1990).

The homicide scene revealed a 21-year-old woman shot on each side of the head with a small-caliber weapon. She was found nude, lying face up on the stairway of her home and had been found sexually molested. Crime scene evidence led this author to the belief that she had been murdered while walking down the stairs. The investigation led to the comparisons of similar homicides in the area and "a profile" of the perpetrator was developed. We believed he was a young, athletic male with a casual acquaintance with his victims. We believed he was nonpsychotic and "organized" in his behavior. The detective team hypothesized that he was a "smooth-talker" and capable of easily winning a woman's confidence. This led to the "hunch" that he likely had good relationships with women, at least on a superficial basis. The possibility of "splitting" was entertained as a hypothesis in which we believed the perpetrator "divided" women into good (his friends) and bad (his victims). Investigators looked for physical patterns consistent with this hypothesis. This led to an examination of telephone records of public and private phones in the geographic vicinity of sequential homicides. This revealed a pattern of telephone calls to the same phone in another city. Interviews with the suspect and his girlfriend were arranged at the time of his arrest. Police learned that following each murder he telephoned his live-in girlfriend "just to talk." Examination of his telephone bills revealed collect calls made from the vicinity of previous homicides. He was an intelligent, good-looking psychopath who was later convicted of murder (p. 152).

Literature Review

The case illustrations given above demonstrate how a series of facts regarding a particular case can be used to develop a profile of a criminal based on their behaviors. According to Hazelwood, Ressler, Depue, and Douglas (2008), an "investigative profile" is provided upon request from an agency and it provides details to an investigation intending to "differentiate [the offender] from the general population" (p. 1). It's through the careful analysis of crime scene evidence, and witness testimony, that the profiler can provide useful information about "characteristics and traits" of the offender (p. 1). According to Woodworth and Porter (2000, p. 241), "A **criminal profiler** is a psychological consultant or investigator who examines evidence from the crime scene, victims, and witnesses in an attempt to construct an accurate psychological (usually concerning psychopathology, personality, and behavior) and demographic description of the individual who committed the crime." Despite the scientific grounding of criminal profiling and its increasing use in criminal investigations, many researchers contend that there is a paucity of empirical research to support its validity, and a lack of well-defined profiling framework that is empirically supported (Kocsis & Palermo, 2007; Snook, Eastwood, Gendreau, Goggin, & Cullen, 2007; Kocsis, 2003a; Kocsis, 2003b; Kocsis, Cooksey, & Irwin, 2002; Alison, Bennell, Mokros, & Ormerod, 2002; Davis & Follette, 2002).

According to the Federal Bureau of Investigation (FBI), profiling is defined as a technique which serves to identify the major personality and behavioral characteristics of an offender based on an analysis of the crime the offender committed. This process generally involves seven steps: (1) evaluation of the criminal act itself; (2) comprehensive evaluation of the specifics of the crime scene(s); (3) comprehensive analysis of the victim; (4) evaluation of preliminary reports; (5) evaluation of the medical examiner's autopsy protocol; (6) development of a profile with critical offender characteristics; and (7) investigative suggestions predicated upon construction of the profile (Kocsis, 2009; Douglas & Burgess, 1986). Cothran and Jacquin (2011) identify two approaches to criminal profiling that have proven to be helpful methods in this area. The **inductive approach** is based on a type of reasoning that would begin with the profiler observing a previous crime or taking information gathered from the crime scene and applying the appropriate theory, based on this information. The **deductive approach** avoids using "generalizations." This approach is based on information such as elements from a case that are considered key. This would include "weapons of choice, location, and placement of the body" (Cothran & Jacquin, 2011, p. 42). These authors also outline what makes one approach more desirable than the other. The deductive approach provides information that is not "over generalized, or "narrow," which has been sighted as a problem with the inductive approach, but provides a profile based on the offender's "thoughts, motivation, and behaviors before, after, and during the crime (p. 41)." This results in a more specific and original or distinct profile.

Douglas & Burgess (1986) equate the profiling process with that of making a psychiatric diagnosis. In this respect, data are obtained through assessment; situations are reconstructed; hypotheses are developed, formulated, and tested; and these results are reported back to the interested party. Researchers warn that although profiling can be a helpful tool in apprehending offenders, it should only be considered a working hypothesis due to the unique personality and behavioral characteristics of each offender (Hazelwood, 2009; Kocsis, 2009; Palermo, 2002). Palermo (2002) indicates that a profiler should have sound psychological and psychiatric knowledge, as well as investigative expertise.

The goal of any law enforcement agency is not only to enforce laws, but also to apprehend those who have broken the law. However, the latter part of this process is often difficult. Investigators must struggle with a multitude of evidence, reports, and inferences regarding each particular crime. Criminals are not often immediately apprehended, leaving the law enforcement agency to deal with a criminal at large. When the crime is serious enough, as in arson, rape, or murder, a psychological or criminological profile of the subject is obtained in order to facilitate apprehension.

Criminal profiling has conceivably existed since the inception of crime itself. Documented attempts of profiling such heinous killers as Jack the Ripper date back to the 1800s. The majority of modern literature focusing on profiling examines crimes such as murder, sexual offenses, and rape. These typologies are further broken down into subcategories. For example, murder is often subdivided into categories such as serial murder, sexual murder, and mass murder. Rape is often subdivided into Ritualistic and Impulsive (Hazelwood & Warren, 2009). Both professionals and nonprofessionals have made attempts at establishing profiles of those who have broken the law — each utilizing their own preferred school of thought. The FBI has done a great deal of research in the area of criminal profiling. Special agents in the FBI have developed, through archival and current case information, typical characteristics likely to be found in particular types of offenders. Woodworth and Porter (2000) found that the two approaches to crime scene and offender profiling which are the most promising include the holistic approach developed by the FBI that integrates aspects of the rational/deductive method and the empirical/inductive method, developed mostly by investigative psychologists.

In a study examining expertise in psychological profiling, Kocsis, Irwin, Hayes, and Nunn (2000) compared the accuracy of psychological profiles for a closed murder case created by individuals with varying degrees and types of expertise. The study compared the profiles generated by 5 professional profilers, 35 police officers, 30 psychologists, 31 university students, and 20 self-declared psychics. The results indicated that the professional profilers had a superior set of profiling skills as compared to all other groups. This is further substantiated by research completed by McGrath and Torres (2008) and defined this practice as an art, which is based on the application of experience, education, training, and skill by a professional. Furthermore, the psychologists performed better in some areas than the police officers and the psychics, which suggested that knowledge and insight into human behavior is possibly relevant to psychological profiling. Finally, the authors suggested that the psychic group did little more than rely on the social stereotype of a murderer in their profiles (Kocsis *et al.*, 2009). In an article that examined the conclusions of empirically derived studies on profiling expertise, Kocsis (2009; 2003b) found that professional profilers create a more accurate prediction of an unknown offender than other groups. More specifically, Kocsis (2009; 2003a) found that professional profilers tended to write more detailed profiles, which had more information about nonphysical attributes of the offender, and more information about the crime scene or the offender's behavior, at every stage of the crime. Hazelwood (2009) describes how a profile of a rapist can be obtained primarily through competent and informed interviewing of rape victims. He states that in profiling the rapist, three basic steps are critical: (1) careful interview of the victim regarding the rapist's behavior; (2) analysis of that behavior in an attempt to ascertain the motivation underlying the assault; and (3) a profile compilation of the individual likely to have committed the crime in the manner reported with the assumed motivation. A more recent study examining the homology of offender characteristics in rapists and their crime scene behavior found that rapists who offend in a similar way are not more similar with regard to age, socio-demographic features, or their criminal records (Beauregard, Lussier, & Proulx, 2007).

In establishing a profile of a rapist, Hazelwood describes how the rapist behaves within his environment relative to his personality structure. Behaviors are broken down into a number of categories and the victim is asked detailed information regarding the behavior in an attempt to classify the rapist. Three basic forms of behavior are exhibited by the rapist: physical (force), verbal, and sexual. For example, the rapist who dominates his victim primarily through the use of verbal degradation and threats may be portraying a personality characteristic consistent with an intense desire to emotionally harm his victim. This may be indicative of a recent break-up between the rapist and his girlfriend. The rape therefore serves as revenge on the girlfriend through the victim in order to satisfy a psychological need. Based on this information, profilers can then begin to formulate the type of personality profile which may use rape as a means of rectification and revenge.

Profiling victims can also give increased insight into a particular type of offender. Graney and Arrigo (2002) consolidate the criminological research on rape and the victimological research on victims to develop an increased understanding about the offender, his or her victims, and sexual crimes in general. Understanding a sexual offender's victim selection process could not only help prevent future victims, it could provide a better understanding of the offender, and potentially aid in his or her apprehension.

Other, more common techniques of profiling offenders come from gaining detailed information from a criminal population convicted of committing the same or similar crimes. These data are used to establish patterns or norms based on that particular type of offender. According to the FBI (1985b), individual development of offenders is based on two primary factors: the dominance of a fantasy life and a history of personal abuse. These factors are used to develop a working profile of a murderer. In-depth interviews of 36 sexual murderers revealed a number of characteristics typical of this type of offender. For example, the sexual murderer tends to be intelligent, good-looking, of average socioeconomic status, and an oldest son or first/second born. However, they also tend to have an attitude of devaluation toward people (having failed to form significant attachments), view the world as unjust, have an unstable or inconsistent view of authority and justice, and tend to have an obsession with dominance through aggression. These sexual murderers also tend to have few attachments outside their immediate families, tend to live in a created fantasy world in which they feel comfortable, and have a history of deviant behaviors. Based on these sets of characteristics, a profile can be developed (see Table 4.1).

As previously stated, certain criminals tend to receive the spotlight in regard to psychological/criminological profiling. Not surprisingly, these crimes are often the most serious, such as

Table 4.1: General characteristics, resultant attitudes and beliefs, and deviant behaviors of 36 sexual murderers

Background characteristics		
Family background	*Individual development*	*Performance*
Detachment	Dominance of fantasy	School failure
Criminality	History of personal abuse	Sporadic work record
Substance abuse		Unskilled
Psychiatric problems		Poor military records
Sexual problems		Solo sex
Resultant attitudes and beliefs		Deviant behaviors
Devaluation of victim society		Rape
World viewed as unjust		Mutilation
Authority/life viewed as inconsistent		Torture
Autoerotic preference		
Obsession with dominance through aggression		

Fantasy as reality.
FBI (1985a, p. 6).

homicide. It is therefore not surprising that the majority of research focuses on these criminals, since conceivably they are the most dangerous. Profiling sexual murderers seems to dominate the literature due to the nature of the crime itself. The sexual murderer often appears to be unmotivated and engages in a series of bizarre behaviors inconsistent with any other type of criminal typology.

Sexual murderers often have patterns to their crimes. It is because of these patterns that a system devised by the FBI allows characteristics of the offender to be indentified based on demographic and crime scene traits. These traits have broken down homicide into an organized and disorganized type (Minzi & Shields, 2007; FBI, 1985b). Each typology allows the law enforcement agent to create a profile of the murderer, thus expediting the arrest of the suspect (Tables 4.2 and 4.3).

Dividing sexual murderers into organized and disorganized types allows for more accurate profiling based on information obtained through arrests. The crime scene characteristics described in Table 4.3 enable the investigator to develop a profile based solely on behaviors exhibited at the scene of the homicide, thus allowing for a psychological profile and description based on these data.

Forensic Psychology and Policy Implications

A number of U.S. Supreme Court cases have dealt with the use of psychologists' and other mental health professionals' opinions regarding the "goodness-of-fit" of a criminal into

Table 4.2: Profile characteristics of organized and disorganized murderers

Organized	Disorganized
Average to above-average intelligence	Below-average intelligence
Socially competent	Socially inadequate
Skilled work preferred	Unskilled work
Sexually competent	Sexually incompetent
High birth order status	Low birth order status
Father's work stable	Father's work unstable
Inconsistent childhood discipline	Harsh discipline as child
Controlled mood during crime	Anxious mood during crime
Use of alcohol with crime	Minimal use of alcohol
Precipitating situational stress	Minimal situational stress
Living with partner	Living alone
Mobility with car in good condition	Lives/works near crime scene
Follows crime in news media	Minimal interest in news media
May change job or leave town	Significant behavioral change (drug/alcohol abuse, religiosity, etc.)

FBI (1985b, p. 19).

Table 4.3: Crime scene differences between organized and disorganized murderers

Organized	Disorganized
Planned offense	Spontaneous offense
Victim a targeted stranger	Victim/location unknown
Personalized victim	Depersonalized victim
Controlled conversation	Minimal conversation
Crime scene reflects overall control	Crime scene random and sloppy
Demands submissive victim	Sudden violence to victim
Restraints used	Minimal use of restraints
Aggressive acts prior to death	Sexual acts after death
Body hidden	Body left in view
Weapon/evidence absent	Evidence/weapon often present
Transports victim or body	Body left at death scene

FBI (1985b, p. 19).

a particular profile based on their assessment of the criminal. Much of this research stems from results obtained from the MMPI and mental status exams.

There have been numerous studies which describe a variety of issues related to the admissibility and inadmissibility of mental health professionals' expert opinions of profile fitting (Kocsis, 2009; Peters & Murphy, 1992). As of 1992, according to research by Peters and Murphy, every appellate court in the United States, with the exception of California, has ruled on the admissibility of expert testimony regarding the psychological profiles of child molesters. Research by Kocsis (2009) indicates that testimony of an expert witness as it pertains to profiling is approached with "trepidation" (p. 227). These appellate courts have consistently rejected the psychological profile concept as evidence either defending or attempting to help convict the child molester.

The psychological profile as court testimony has been used in child sexual abuse cases for three primary reasons: (1) to prove the defendant committed the crime; (2) to prove the defendant did not commit the crime; and (3) to solidify the credibility of the defendant. However, the primary reason the courts refuse to allow such evidence is because no matter how well a suspect may fit into the child molester profile, it can never prove whether the actual event took place (Peters & Murphy, 1992).

Future considerations involving the use of psychological/psychiatric testimony in relation to criminal profiles must involve continued research examining its efficacy in the court system. Policy implications will therefore depend on results obtained from developing future research in this field.

Suggestions for Future Research

More empirical research is needed to support the validity of crime scene and offender profiling. Research which assesses "fundamental merits" in regards to the validity and reliability of a profile is a constant need as it relates to profiling as a science (Kocsis, 2009, p. 227). The D.C. sniper case highlighted the weaknesses of offender profiles and the importance of remaining mindful of its limitations. Profiling is typically used in cold cases or investigations where the physical evidence (or leads) is limited. Research could help to refine the effectiveness of this investigative tool. There is clearly a need for careful, systematic evaluation of criminal profiles. More victimological research could also further inform accurate offender profiles (Graney & Arrigo, 2002). Continuing research in the capabilities of profilers as professionals in the art of behavioral analysis will also continue to contribute to this growing scientific area of crime. More research should be pursued with regard to analyzing what characteristics are shared by the most effective profilers. Additionally, clear guidelines as to what training is required to become proficient in investigative profiling is needed.

One could say that the future of criminological profiling has already arrived. In years past, investigators relied only on personal knowledge bases involving experience and wisdom. Inferences were drawn based on corroboration with peers and personal hunches. In the modern computer era, comprehensive and extensive computerized databases exist which allow thousands of variables to be cross-examined between criminals, crime scenes, and case details. Computerized searches look for specific patterns, consistencies, and inconsistencies, in order to determine the most likely course of action for law enforcement agents to act upon.

At the FBI's National Center for the Analysis of Violent Crime (NCAVC), experts in criminal personality profiling developed a computerized system of crime pattern analysis. This computerized system, termed VICAP (Violent Criminal Apprehension Program) uses a collection of crime pattern recognition programs to detect and predict the behavior of violent criminals. Future research is needed to examine the accuracy and reliability of such computer programs and to develop a method in which all law enforcement agencies could utilize a system on a cost efficient and practical level. Further, the development of a national database may bring large statistical power to such evaluations. Research examining these possibilities is certainly required.

Cothran and Jacquin (2011) identified differences in gender as it pertains to profilers. It is detailed in the work that female college students provide more accurate information in profiles than male students. With this in mind, future research should be done to determine if this holds true in the professional realm as well.

Research is also needed in order to determine the possible detrimental effects of criminal profiling. As mentioned, many courts do not allow for the inclusion of psychological profiles as evidence in courts. Will profiling a subject negatively persuade a jury to convict a potential felon if the profile is too broad or encompasses too many personality characteristics?

Use of Force

Introduction

The question of force used by police first came to attention in 1974, in Memphis, Tennessee, when a 15-year-old boy named Edward Garner broke into a home and stole 10 dollars and a purse. At the arrival of the police, Garner, who was unarmed, fled from the home and ran across the backyard. As the police began pursuit of the suspect, Garner reached a six-foot fence surrounding the yard. In an attempt to avoid police custody, he continued to flee and began to climb over the fence. The police officer, fearing that the suspect would get away if he made it over the fence, fired at the back of Garner's head and killed him.

The decision to use force in the apprehension of a citizen, whether it be excessive or deadly, ultimately rests in the hands of the police officer at the moment of conflict. Although the goal of the officer is always to resolve a conflict in the most peaceful manner, it is understood that there are situations in which a peaceful resolution is not possible. Guidelines are established to assist the officer, who at times must make a "split-second" decision as to the type of force necessary. In order to set these guidelines behind the use of force, it is first necessary to understand how dangerous situations in need of force unfold as well as the decisions that follow.

Literature Review

The history behind the police officer's right to use force dates back to common law under English rule. Known as the "fleeing felon" law, common law states that a police officer could use deadly force in situations that would protect the life of the officer or an innocent third party, to overcome resistance to arrest, or to prevent the escape of any felony suspect (Inciardi, 1993; Pursley, 1994). The loose generalization of the "fleeing felon" law leaves a series of questionable circumstances and issues that remain unaddressed due to the changing criminal activities of our present day. Our current legal system now classifies more crimes as felonies, which in turn allows for more felony-related crimes that are neither necessarily dangerous nor life-threatening. Furthermore, technology provides more effective means of communication and organization within police forces that can aid in the apprehension of criminals (Pursley, 1994).

Such unspecified circumstances established by the "fleeing felon" law were left to the discretion of the police jurisdiction. Many jurisdictions continued to use the common law guidelines until the landmark decision in *Tennessee v. Garner* (1985) that sought to outline the qualifications of the use of force in a constitutional frame. It was argued that the level of force the officer used against Edward Garner was extreme and unnecessary given the circumstances of the crime. Following *Tennessee v. Garner*, the use of force was restricted to circumstances where it is necessary to prevent the escape of a suspect who is believed to be a significant threat to the officer or others (Inciardi, 1993). "Objective reasonableness" is a standard created through the cases of *Tennessee v Garner* (1985) and *Graham v. Conner* (1989) that sets boundaries on the excessive use of force. However, there is no practical standard for excessive force, and it is usually determined on a case by case basis (Lee & Vaughn, 2010. p.194).

Within the creation of more defined standards of the use of force lies the exploration of the motives, behavior, and decision-making process that underlie such an action The Texas Commission on Law Enforcement Officer Standards and Education (2005, p. 7) has devised a list of factors that will allow the officer to maintain psychological and physical control. These factors are:

A. Demonstrated alertness.
B. Be emotionally in control.
C. Personal appearance and bearing.
D. If possible, maintain height advantage.
E. Triangle view (2 officers, 1 suspect).
F. Be over an arm's length from suspect.
G. Be prepared to step back.
H. Talking versus fighting.

Many social scientists have researched these aspects and have offered some insights that can serve as an aid in organizing such standards of force. In the past, the problems associated with the use of force were seen as the result of "a few bad apples" within the police community. Such an explanation is weighted in the view that many police officers possess a stereotypical aggressive and authoritative nature. This concept has received a great deal of attention due to the highly controversial Rodney King incident (see the following case illustration). Although the officers involved maintained that they acted according to police standards and that such force was necessary in the apprehension of King, the beating of Rodney King has been cited as a clear representation of the use of excessive force and stands to support the idea of the authoritative and aggressive police officer.

In the early morning hours of 3 March 1991, in a suburb of Los Angeles, police began a high-speed chase in pursuit of a suspect who was driving recklessly and believed to be dangerously intoxicated. The driver, Rodney King, led police on a chase that reached approximately 100 m.p.h. and ended when he reached an entrance to a park which had been closed off with a cable. After King, who was unarmed, stepped out of his car, police attempted to restrain him by striking him with a TASER gun and then followed by beating him repeatedly with their batons. King suffered multiple fractures, broken bones, and internal injuries. As this was occurring, a citizen who lived across from the park grabbed his video camera and proceeded to record the event. The tape was then sold to television stations, which broadcasted the tape nationwide. Initially the officers were acquitted in court, although upon appeal two of the four officers were convicted of excessive use of force. The King incident produced widespread public outrage that spawned numerous questions and concerns about police power and brutality.

Following the Rodney King incident, many police departments looked to establish a clearly defined set of guidelines for the use of excessive and deadly force. However, more recent explanations of force suggest it is impossible for such specified standards to be established and maintained because the act of force is based on a "split-second" decision that involves an immediate analysis of the situation by the police officer (Harris, 2009). Intense stress and the possibility of a life-threatening situation accompany such an analysis. Some experts believe that to expect an officer to make an appropriate decision under these circumstances is unrealistic. Consider the life and death situation that confronts a Texas police officer below and the immediate decisions made that could mean life or death for the officer and the offender.

On 2 April 2011, a veteran sergeant with the Conroe, Texas Police Department is shot and wounded when he responds to a domestic dispute involving an armed man. It appeared that the suspect in the altercation was emotionally involved with one of the witnesses on the scene. This witness was at work at the time of the incident. The police had been called as the suspect slashed the tires of all the other cars in the parking lot. When the sergeant arrived on the scene, the suspect was armed with a 410, double-barreled shotgun, and began closing distance between himself and the officer. He approached with his weapon leveled at the officer and appeared ready to fire. The officer prompted the suspect to drop his weapon over 16 times. The officer clearly stated several times that the situation could be resolved by other means. The suspect verbalized his intentions by stating "No!" to the officer numerous times. The officer radioed back to his dispatch office, telling them to have the witnesses move away from the window. The suspect did not comply and proceeded to fire on the officer, leaving him wounded with a gunshot to his eye. The other officers on the scene shot and killed the suspect. After being wounded, the officer makes reference to "all that tactical training." The officer was obviously confronted with a life-threatening situation and, in addition to his own safety, was concerned about the safety of innocent bystanders that influenced the resolution of this situation.

In contrast, there have been several studies that attempt to understand the process by which an officer makes his or her decision and the circumstances behind these decisions. Binder and Scharf (1980) researched the circumstances that evolved during a conflict and developed a four-phase model that describes the steps involved at the final decision to use deadly force. This model submits that "the violent police–citizen encounter is considered a developmental process in which successive decisions and behaviors by either police officer or citizen, or both, make the violent outcome more or less likely" (Binder & Scharf, 1980, p. 111). The model consists of the Anticipation Phase, Entry and Initial Contact Phase, Information Exchange, and Final Phase. Each phase describes the emotional as well as the environmental details as they unravel in a potentially violent situation. The Anticipation Phase is composed of the immediate involvement of the officer when he or she is first called to intervene and the information that is relayed as a result. Entry and Initial Contact includes what the officer is confronted with when arriving at the scene and the development of the crisis. The Information Exchange Phase consists of any verbal or nonverbal exchange of information between the suspect and the officer, which also contributes to the officer's assessment of the dangerousness of the situation. In the Final Phase, the officer makes the decision of whether to use force by incorporating the information received in the previous phases as well as any final action by the suspect or immediate threat.

As described, this model reflects the application of a series of decisions actively made by the police officer. The Texas Commission on Law Enforcement (2005) follows the "**Use of Force Continuum Scale**" as a tool to teach the officer when it is appropriate to elevate to the next level of force. It is devised in such a way that allows the officer to remain at one level of force above that of the suspect's resistance. It is noted that "excessive force results when the level of force is greater than the subject's level of resistance" (p. 18). Appropriate decisions are made when the police officer consciously evaluates the situation based on the development of the event. Many police departments have used a similar philosophy in developing a series of guidelines that establish a more definitive circumstance for the use of force. Such policies can aid the officer in making a rational decision in a time of great pressure.

Research examining the role of neighborhood context on police use of force has revealed that police officers are significantly more likely to use higher levels of force when they confront suspects in disadvantaged neighborhoods and in those areas with higher homicide rates (Harris, 2009; Terrill & Reisig, 2003). Lee and Vaughn (2010) contend that violent crime is more likely in cities with the largest discrepancies in employment status. This would weigh heavily on an officer's mind when they are performing their duties in these areas. Using the 1994 General Social Survey to examine effects of race, gender, and geographical region on support of various criminal justice policies, Halim and Stiles (2001) found that African Americans were less likely to support police use of force than their racial counterparts. This phenomenon is most certainly a major factor in strained relations between police officers and their minority constituents in disadvantaged communities. In a recent study, Theobald and Haider-Markel (2009) found that black suspects were less likely to perceive racism as a factor in use of force if a black officer is present. It was found that the same held true for white suspects and white officers.

Forensic Psychology and Policy Implications

One way to combat the chances of using force unnecessarily is by incorporating effective training programs that will prepare an officer in the event that such a quick decision must be made (Bohrer & Chaney, 2010). Developing extensive policies that outline the criteria that may necessitate the use of force can act as means of training police officers to recognize the key elements involved. These key elements include specific response levels on the part of the officer that must be evaluated during the course of the confrontation.

Bohrer and Chaney (2010) indicate that the use of force and the police investigation of the use of force have the potential to have significant and far reaching consequences for the public, the department, and the officers involved. Public perception of the use of deadly force by officers is shaped by *who* officers shot, media coverage, and can be influenced by "long-standing bias and mistrust of government. Documented cases of riots, property damage, and loss of life have occurred in communities where residents have perceived a police shooting as unjustified" (p. 3).

Providing officers with applicable response levels, such as appropriate dialogue and verbal direction with the citizen, appropriate means of restraint, and the use of weapons and incapacitation, can alleviate some of the intense pressure in that "split-second" decision. Harris (2009) argues that this "split-second decision" is based on an officer's "intuitive grasp" on the totality of the circumstances involved (p. 25). In his study, Harris (2009) identified circumstances that elevate the risk of an officer's use of improper force. In 39% of his population, there were indications of the suspect's blatant defiance of the officer's authority so demeanor plays a role in cases where improper force has been applied. The study also revealed that 27% of the cases with improper use of force involved an intoxicated suspect. Finally, it was found that class and gender played a larger role than race in this study with every victim of the improper use of force being a lower class male. Harris' study emphasizes the importance of examining suspect characteristics mentioned above, as well as various subject factors such as age, size, seriousness of crime, and weapon usage as compared to the officer's factors of size, number of officers present, an officer's defensive tactics, and legal requirements in developing departmental policies. Harris (2009) found that officers who are relatively young, inexperienced, and are male are more likely to engage in the improper use of force. As explored in the Edward Garner case, his youth, the fact that he was unarmed, and had not committed a dangerous crime would indicate under such a policy that deadly force was not appropriate within the context of the situation. Similarly, in the Rodney King case, an implication of policy could prevent questions as to the amount of force that is necessary to subdue a suspect. Such guidelines have been proven to be highly effective in the fast-paced discretionary decision making that is necessary in such an event.

Another effective means of preventing unnecessary use of force would be in the screening and counseling of those officers who reveal a greater propensity toward violence (Page & Jacobs, 2011; Miller & Barrett, 2008; Scrivner, 1994). Sugimoto and Oltjenbruns (2001) contend that law enforcement personnel who continue to work despite experiencing symptoms of Post-Traumatic Stress Disorder (PTSD) resulting from a critical incident may incur risks of reduced self-control, escalated use of force, and inappropriate behavior. This inappropriate behavior may manifest due to anger outbursts or irritability associated with their PTSD. Screening and counseling provisions would allow the police departments to gain more responsibility over the likelihood of an incident to occur, rather than to rely solely on the circumstances of the crime or on the suspect.

In addition, monitoring officers' behavior can also serve as a defense against the unnecessary use of force (Scrivner, 1994). By alerting supervisors to those officers who demonstrate behavior that suggests a risk for violence, intervention techniques can be performed early. In addition, monitoring officers in the field can provide a role model to other officers as well as aid in the enforcement of the policies established within the department. Lee and Vaughn (2010) devised a table (Table 4.4), that indicates cases in which the officers were held liable for damages. This table demonstrates what caused the officer to use excessive force and the result of the officer's actions.

Suggestions for Future Research

There is a great need for further research in the evaluation of the environmental aspects that lead to the need for force. As discussed, the environment in which the situation arises can determine the need for force and the potential outcome of such force. With a more complete understanding of how the environment develops, what role the environment plays, and how the environment can be manipulated for safety, we can hope to use force as a means to uphold justice with minimal conflict. Furthermore, there is a need to understand the psychological as well as the sociological aspects of the use of force. It is necessary to understand the emotional and cognitive functions of both the suspect and the police officer involved in such a crisis. It is essential to continue researching areas such as how gender and ethnicity relate to the use of force by officers. Harris (2009) expresses concern that research findings still indicate that the improper use of force is more often directed at certain kinds of people (e.g., antagonistic suspects, lower class, intoxicated, black, etc.). More research is recommended examining the interactions between the police and suspects, particularly with regard to suspect's resistance. Does the race of the officer engaging in use of force play a significant role? Future research should explore the relationship between the suspect characteristics and behavior (e.g., race, degree of compliance), as well as those of the responding officer. These environmental, sociological, and psychological applications can be beneficial in training police officers to recognize the scenarios that develop and can facilitate that final decision of whether or not to use force.

Finally, recent studies exploring the impact of the use of TASERS on police officers' use of force decisions indicate that officers armed with TASERS were significantly less likely to use pepper spray or a police baton, and most importantly, were less likely to discharge their firearm to respond to aggressive physical resistance (Sousa, Ready, & Ault, 2010). These authors recommend that the field would further benefit from studies examining why this is the case, providing more information about an officer's decision making. Additionally, as role playing scenarios have become more prominent in police training in recent years (Van Hasselt, Romano, & Vecchi, 2008), future research to help determine how well these role playing scenarios translate to real life situations is recommended (Sousa, Ready, & Ault, 2010).

Table 4.4: Types of excessive force and examples

Categories	Cases
Cases where the individual officer was to blame	
Use of deadly force against suspects who were surrendering to police authority	
Failure to control adrenaline overload resulting from hot pursuit	Killing a suspect lying on the ground (*Carr v. Castle*, 2003) Injuring a suspect with his hands up in the air (*Carter v. Chicago*, 2004; *Cooper v. Merrill*, 1990) Killing a suspect who stopped his vehicle (*Clark v. Nassau County, Florida*, 1991) Killing or injuring unarmed fleeing suspects (*Ayuso v. Amerosa*, 2008; *Davis v. City of Detroit*, 2006; *Fletcher v. District of Columbia*, 2005; *Jones v. Town of East Haven*, 2007; *Rudolph v. Jones*, 2002; *Whitfield v. Melendez-Rivera*, 2005)
Street justice	Killing a suspect after he was handcuffed by an officer who had chronic paranoid schizophrenia (*Graham v. Sauk Prairie Police Commission*, 1990) Killing a suspect who failed to follow police orders (*Moore v. Yost*, 1993)
Deadly use of force against uncooperative suspects	
Failure to handle suicide by cop situations	Use of force against citizens attempting to commit suicide (*Connors v. Town of Brunswick*, 2000; *Murphy v. Bitsolh*, 2004; *Sova v. City of Mt. Pleasant*, 1996)
Failure to consider suspect's intoxication	Killing a suspect with .24 percent blood alcohol level (*Bing v. City of Whitehall*, 2005)
Abuse of authority	Killing a citizen after a private altercation (*Ott v. City of Mobile*, 2001) Killing a suspect who refused to open the door (*Palva v. City of Reno*, 1996)
Failure to update legal developments	Injuring a citizen as a result of failure to apply the knock and announce rule (*Sledd v. Lindsay*, 1996) Killing a suspect while chasing fleeing suspect on foot with handgun drawn (*Collins v. Metcalfe*, 1997)
Split-second syndrome	Killing or injuring unarmed suspects by believing they were armed (*Brown v. Township of Clinton*, 2006; *Gilmere v. City of Atlanta, Georgia*, 1985; *Holland v. City of Houston*, 1999; *Johnson v. City of Richmond*, 2005; *McKnight v. District of Columbia*, 2006) Killing a suspect holding a pipe (*Brown v. Doe*, 1999) Killing non-dangerous drivers passing by officers (*Fields v. Nawotka*, 2008; *Luke v. Brown*, 2007; *Quade v. Kaplan*, 2008; *Scott v. Vasquez*, 2004; *Smartt v. Grundy County, Tennessee*, 2002; *Smith v. City of Wilmington*, 2007; *Willis v. Oakes*, 2006) Contagious shooting (*Parker v. Town of Swansea*, 2003)

Table 4.4: Types of excessive force and examples—cont'd

Categories	Cases
Cases where the individual officer was to blame	
	Killing a suspect 90 seconds after contact (*Allen v. Muskogee, Oklahoma*, 1997)
Reckless use of deadly force	
Misidentification of suspects	Friendly fire (*Small v. City of Philadelphia*, 2007; *Vaughn v. City of Orlando*, 2008; *Young v. City of Providence*, 2005)
Cases where the individual police officer was not liable	
Careless handcuffing	Injuring suspect while handcuffing with a gun drawn (*Dodd v. City of Norwich*, 1987; *Troublefield v. City of Harrisburg*, 1992)
Split-second decisions	When officers were threatened by a knife (*Bullard v. City of Mobile*, 2000; *Morais v. City of Philadelphia*, 2007; *Roy v. City of Lewiston*, 1994)
	When officers were threatened by a gun or vehicle (*Ali v. City of Louisville*, 2005; *Brown v. Forler*, 2007; *DeMerrell v. City of Cheboygan*, 2005; *Ellison v. City of Montgomery*, 1999; *Puston-Lounds v. Torres*, 2005; *Hassan v. City of Minneapolis, Minnesota*, 2007; *Hudspeth v. City of Shreveport*, 2006; *Jenkins v. Bartlett*, 2007; *Keller v. City of Portland*, 1998; *Long v. City and County of Honolulu*, 2007; *Myers v. Oklahoma County Board of County Commissioners*, 1998; *Snyder v. Trepagnier*, 1998; *Stackhouse v. Twp. Of Irvington*, 2007; *Venuti v. City of Elizabeth*, 2006; *Watson v. City of Long Beach*, 1996; *Watts v. City of Hartford*, 2004)
	When officers were experiencing physical threat to life (*Hickey v. City of New York*, 2006; *Merzon v. County of Suffolk*, 1991; *O'Toole v. Village of Downers Grove Police Department*, 1986; *Palmquist v. Selvik*, 1997; *Pena v. Leombruni*, 1999)
Not acting under color of law	An officer who was on medical roll as mentally unfit for duty shot and killed his neighbor (*Gibson v. City of Chicago*, 1990)
	An off-duty officer involved in a love triangle shot and killed his girlfriend's former boyfriend (*Hudson v. Maxey*, 1994)
	An off-duty officer shot and killed a security guard at an amusement park who asked him to leave because he was drinking beer in violation of the park's rules (*Turk v. McCarthy*, 1987)
Others	Voluntarily dismissed by plaintiffs who ultimately sued sheriff in her official capacity (*Whitewater v. Goss*, 2006)
	Chiefs in their individual capacity did not participate in the shooting (*Randle v. Panici*, 1991)

Suicide by Cop

Introduction

In the line of duty, police officers may face situations that require them to take lethal action. The most tragic of these instances can involve a person who is using law enforcement as the means to take their own life. Drylie and Violanti (2008) define **suicide by cop** as "an incident involving the use of deadly force by a law enforcement agent(s) in response to the provocation of a threat/use of deadly force against the agent(s) or others by an actor who has voluntarily entered the suicidal drama and has communicated verbally or nonverbally the desire to commit suicide" (p. 95). Other common terms that are used are victim-provoked shooting and victim-precipitated shooting (McKenzie, 2006). The officer is unknowingly being used as a tool in a suicide plan. Clearly, the effects of this scenario are potentially devastating to both the suicide by cop perpetrator and the responding police officer(s). Research has demonstrated that there are indicators that officers can use to help determine which scenes have the capacity to become a suicide by cop situation (Kingshott, 2009). According to Violanti and Drylie (2008), the phenomenon of suicide by cop has become a focus of research since the mid 1980s, but there are still many areas that require further study. How do officers identify persons and situations that are at greater risk of resulting in a suicide by cop? Are there approaches or trainings that contribute to better outcomes? What role do forensic/police psychologists play in educating and better preparing law enforcement for this possible life and death faceoff? How can psychologists debrief or counsel officers who have been involved in a suicide by cop? This section will define and examine the issue of suicide by cop, as well as address areas for future research. Consider the case of NY below:

NY was a 44-year-old, Hispanic male with an extensive history of problems. He had a background plagued with unstable relationships, violent behavior, anger issues, alcoholism, and a suicide attempt. On this mid-summer night, NY added another problem to his list. He allegedly shot a female and left her for dead in a multistory housing complex. Police arrived on the scene responding to a "shots fired" call. Upon arrival, they do a sweep of the area and find the female victim's lifeless body on the third floor. She was fully clothed, and her purse was still looped over her arm with shell casings surrounding her. Outside the building, officers encounter NY. NY was holding two firearms, one a pistol and the other a shotgun. Upon encountering NY, police began shouting a series of verbal commands to "drop the weapons," and NY responded verbally, "No!" while also shaking his head side to side indicating a negative response. At this point, NY is holding the shotgun barrel in his mouth and then suddenly says, "I can't do this." It is at this point he lowers the shotgun from his mouth and levels it at the responding officers. These officers respond with deadly force, killing NY. Upon examination, it is noted that NY had trace amounts of cocaine in his system and a blood alcohol level at 0.17% (Drylie, 2008, pp. 43–44).

Literature Review

Wolfgang (1959) pioneered the concept of suicide by cop, theorizing that individuals who engaged in "suicide by means of victim-precipitated homicide" reflected two death wishes: (1) the desire to kill the person who is frustrating him; and (2) the desire to kill himself. It is important to note that suicide is often a result of untreated or ongoing depression (p. 23). **Depression** is an abnormal feeling state that is marked by exaggerated feelings of loneliness and hopelessness. This despair can become so out of control that the perpetrator sees no other alternative (Kingshott, 2009). Kingshott (2009) also notes that there are clusters of depressive symptoms that are often present. These symptoms are emotional, cognitive, motivational, and somatic, and they "impact both dependently and independently on the individual" (p. 115).

In examining the prevalence of suicide by cop, Hutson, Anglin, Hardaway, Russell, Strote, Canter, and Blum (1998) analyzed 437 officer-involved shootings in the Los Angeles County Sheriff's Department. These shootings occurred between 1987 and 1997. It was determined by Hutson *et al.* (1998) that of these 437 shootings, 11% were suicide by cop cases. Drylie and Violanti (2008) noted that three elements must be present in order to consider a lethal use of force as a suicide by cop incident. These elements are: (1) the act is voluntary; (2) there is a threat; and (3) communication of suicidal intentions. In the vignette presented above, NY's situation contained all three of these crucial elements. First, the act was voluntary; he forced the officers into making a split-second decision based on his actions. Second, the officers were presented with a perceived threat; the victim leveled the gun at officers. Third, the communication of suicidal intentions was demonstrated to the officer, when the victim was holding the shotgun in his mouth. Without the presence of these elements, it would be hard to determine if the incident was truly a suicide by cop (Drylie & Violanti, 2008).

Individuals who initiate suicide by cop often display symptoms of a depressive disorder and the enlistment of the officer as an unwilling participant is a means to an end. Mohandie and Meloy's (2000) study explored the motivations for high risk behavior such as suicide and violence and identified two categories of motivations for suicide by cop incidents. The two categories were instrumental and expressive. The **instrumental category** includes purposeful and planned violent behavior as compared to the **expressive category** that characterizes suicidal behaviors as being caused by hostile impulsivity because an individual feels overwhelmed, frustrated, or threatened in some way (Mohandie & Meloy, 2000; Bresler, Scalora, Elbogen, & Moore, 2003). Instrumental motivations for suicide by cop incidents would be exemplified by statements such as, "I can't do it myself," or "Make sure my kids get the insurance money;" whereas expressive motivations would be demonstrated by statements such as, "My life is hopeless," or "Soldiers never surrender" (Bresler *et al.*, 2003, p. 1).

Drylie and Violanti (2008) further examined the reasons a person utilizes suicide by cop as the chosen mode of suicide in terms of instrumental or expressive categories. Examples of motives in the instrumental category include the individual seeking an escape from legal issues, the result of a failed relationship, or to remove the religious stigma that is attached to suicide. In the case of NY, it appears that his actions fit best in the instrumental category. He was facing imminent arrest for murder and did not want to be taken alive, but he was unable to take his own life. The expressive category is more a form of communication. This may be the subject's way of communicating the desperation, hopelessness, and sadness they are feeling as a result of the depression they are experiencing or situations they are facing. The subject may be fulfilling the "victim role," a need for power, or an expression of "rage or revenge" (2008; p. 29). Finally, the act of suicide by cop could be the person's way of bringing a personal problem to the foreground. The attention that the perpetrator creates acts as a platform for him or her to voice concerns, problems, and issues that have been building for a period of time. There may be a sense that creating this situation allows the perpetrator to be heard. Lord (2004) states that persons who prompt a suicide by cop often express a desire to die by the hands of an officer. In the case of NY, when he stated, "I can't do this," it appears to be the critical moment in which he decided that he wanted to die at the hand of an officer rather than his own. However, it still appears that his primary motive was instrumental — to avoid incarceration and punishment for the crime he had committed. Table 4.5 provides examples of common phrases or statements that perpetrators of suicide by cop use that suggest either instrumental or expressive motivations.

Table 4.5: Common statements of perpetrators of suicide by cop

Instrumental	Expressive
"I'm not going back to jail."	"My life is hopeless."
"I wanted her to come back to me."	"I am the ultimate victim."
"God won't forgive me if I do it, but He will if you do."	"Soldiers never surrender."
"Make sure my kids get the insurance money."	"I am important enough to be killed by the cops."
"I can't do it myself."	"This is worth dying for."

Adapted from Mohandie & Meloy, 2000, p. 384.

There are various behaviors that the suicide by cop victim will display when the decision has been made to engage officers in a victim-precipitated shooting. The categories listed above will also coincide with various behaviors that may indicate to the officer that the individual is at risk of suicide by cop. These behaviors include (Kingshott, 2009):

- **Hypervigilance (scanning):** a visual scanning of surroundings. The presence of police and negotiators is of little comfort to the subject.
- **Breathing pattern:** this change may be determined visually or audibly and act as a precursor to death. The research indicates that once the perpetrator has decided that suicide by cop is the answer, there is a notable change in the perpetrator's breathing pattern, which may be caused by the finality of the decision and the anticipation of death. This can be an important cue to the responding officers when taken in combination with other relevant risk factors that the situation could become a suicide by cop. It is one more factor for the officer to consider when assessing the situation and whether or not the person in question could be escalating to an act of violence.
- **Counting down or up:** this is when the subject begins to countdown. The counting may be accompanied by a rocking motion, which indicates a readiness to proceed with the suicidal action (Kingshott, 2009).

It is important for officers to receive the training necessary to help them recognize the observable signs that a suspect may be considering suicide by cop. The more familiar an officer is with the warning signs and behaviors, the more prepared he or she will be when they are in the field and are faced with this scenario. This knowledge and training will guide the officer when confronted with making the life or death split-second decisions that will change their life forever.

The research indicates a common variable in suicide by cop cases; specifically the verbalization of the desire to commit suicide (McKenzie, 2006; Lindsay & Dickson, 2000; Lord, 2004). This verbalization can be as clear cut as "I want to die tonight," or as vague as "I'm not going back to jail." The vagueness of the latter expression does not necessarily indicate that the perpetrator has intentions of suicide, but if the officer hears this phrase, it should raise the level of attentiveness to other behaviors that may indicate suicide is the goal.

This alone is not sufficient to label an incident as a suicide by cop, but it does help to differentiate it from other types of officer-involved shootings. As indicated in the vignette, NY did not verbalize intent to commit suicide; rather he showed this intent by placing the shotgun in his mouth.

Another event that has been identified as a common occurrence in suicide by cop is scripted behavior. Drylie (2008) points out that "the ability to measure whether or not the actions of the suicidal actor in the suicide by cop drama were voluntary rests in the principles of *script theory*" (p. 99). Script theory, as it pertains to suicide by cop, is a combination of circumstances and behaviors that communicate the intention of the perpetrator to carry out a suicide. For example, an individual is standing at his door with a shotgun in his hand and is verbalizing that he wishes to die. This would be considered a critical indicator of the situation's potential to go badly. The concept of script theory says that each scene will have a sort of script it follows. Drylie (2008) defines **script theory** as those cognitive thought processes which are rehearsed and provide a "mental representation" of those actions that are to be carried out (p. 100). Much of the research indicates that this sort of scripted or rehearsed behavior is a strong indicator that a perpetrator is considering suicide by means of cop. Although Drylie is the only one to give this phenomenon a name, many other researchers identify this type of behavior with similar descriptions (Mohandie & Meloy, 2010; Lindsay & Lester, 2008; Mohandie, Meloy, & Collins, 2009).

Further research by Kingshott (2009) provides a profile of what a suicide by cop perpetrator looks like. This profile includes:

- 96–98% of suicide by cop perpetrators are male.
- This perpetrator will experience difficulty doing anything that would make him responsible for his own death.
- He may have thought about suicide several times in the past.
- He may have attempted suicide in the past, the failure only adds to his feelings of inadequacy and worthlessness.
- Loss of hope.
- He believes that no one cares.

Because of the importance of police training on the topic of suicide by cop, there are several aspects for the officer to consider when approaching a scene. First, determine and interpret the person's actions and behaviors. In order to determine if the individual is exhibiting actions that could be deemed suicidal, the officer can look to the idea of script theory, and identify the presence or absence of characteristics described above. Perrou (2004) notes the importance of tactical training by law enforcement when handling these situations. As first responders, these individuals may "pose greater danger to the overall operation;" meaning without proper tactical training, the officer could somehow aggravate the circumstances, or cause the perpetrator to increase the level of imminent danger, or pose risk to innocent bystanders

(p. 231). Perrou (2004) also notes that these first responders often feel that it is necessary to engage the subject in conversation, which is considered a "rescue dynamic" (p. 231). This rescue mentality may be precisely what compels the subject to force the officer into shooting. This happens because the suicidal subject has become engaged with the officer, develops an "inverse relationship," which allows the suicidal subject to feel safe in having the officer carry out the suicidal plan (p. 231). Perrou (2004) also acknowledges that when a suicide by cop is unsuccessful, and the perpetrator actually fails at committing suicide, the officer tends to become gracious, secretly thanking the perpetrator for not harming himself, or the officer. Perrou (2004) suggests that this is a form of **Stockholm's Syndrome,** and it develops from engaging so closely and interacting on a personal level with the perpetrator. The officer will begin to identify with the perpetrator and his situation, and when the suicide attempt fails, the officer will feel a sense of relief for not having to take a life and for not sustaining any injuries.

Forensic Psychology and Policy Implications

Suicide is much more common than suicide by cop. Research indicates that many of the perpetrators of suicide by cop have an extensive documented history of mental illness (22%), suicide attempts (24%) and/or suicidal ideation (58%), and suicidal ideation with a plan (50%) (Arias, Schlesinger, Pinizzotto, Davis, Fava, & Dewey, 2008). Therefore, it would be important for officers to obtain mental health training in order to be better equipped to identify and interact with those individuals experiencing symptoms of mental illness, particularly those who are possible suicide by cop perpetrators. Although agencies provide mental health training to their officers, forensic psychologists are often called upon to assist in this training. The psychologist can provide more detailed and distinctive information to be used by the officers to identify mental illness and behavioral nuances that are precursors to a possible suicide situation. The benefits of mental health training for officers include increasing skills to deescalate crisis situations and giving the officers tools to help prevent them from having to take lethal action when responding to a scene. If the officer confronts a potential suicide by cop situation, knowing what to look for in the behavior of the perpetrator could make the difference between life and death.

Mental health training for officers will also provide insight to the officers in how they should deal with mentally ill offenders in any given situation, not only suicide by cop. Because of the impact such a scene could have on an officer, it is important that officers understand the implications of suicide by cop, not only legally, but emotionally. The officer who is provoked into killing a subject will have to face scrutiny from the legal system, the department from which they are employed, coworkers, and possibly the victim's family or remaining loved ones. The officer is forced to cope with taking another person's life — likely a person who was mentally ill. These can lead to post-traumatic stress disorder (PTSD) and depression. Because of the trauma associated with this type of incident, agencies may enlist the help of a forensic psychologist to provide its officers with mental health screenings. These assessments could take the form of personality testing or mental status testing. This would allow the agency to ensure that the officer's mental health is stable and he or she is fit for duty. Agencies may also enlist the help of a forensic psychologist to provide therapy to an officer that has been involved in a suicide by cop incident. Appropriate training on the aforementioned risk factors for a suicide by cop situation could better prepare police officers to react effectively in the moment. An understanding of warning signs and typical behaviors of perpetrators of suicide by cop gives officers more tools to deal with very difficult situations.

Some suicide by cop incidents will be unavoidable despite the best efforts of well trained officers. When this occurs, forensic psychologists working in law enforcement settings should be utilized in debriefing the involved officer, as well as providing counseling to address what has happened. These strategies contribute to the best emotional and legal outcome for the involved officers. The forensic psychologist will not only act as a buffer between the agency and the affected officer, but the psychologist will also provide support and validation to the officer who has been a part of a suicide by cop situation.

Suggestions for Future Research

Future research could provide more current information regarding the prevalence of suicide by cop incidents, although it is hard for agencies to accurately report suicide by cop incidents because there are no specific standards or reporting mechanisms that are recognized. It is suggested that research identifying specific factors needs to be created, and there is a need for a uniform definition of suicide by cop and a reporting mechanism that aligns with the Uniform Crime Report to accurately report these types of incidents (Drylie & Violanti, 2008, p. 96). It is also suggested by Drylie and Violanti (2008) that further research to explore and define the theoretical concepts, such as script theory, be completed in order to provide a uniform, general understanding of this phenomenon. Future research could examine the issue of suicide by cop internationally. Do international police agencies have similar prevalence rates for suicide by cop as the United States? Are the underlying issues of the perpetrator similar to those of the perpetrators in the United States? Forensic psychologists play a key role in cases of suicide by cop, not only in interpreting behavioral aspects of the crime scene, but in the aftercare of the officer involved. Research explaining the effect a suicide by cop scenario has on officers would provide a foundation that agencies could build upon to provide quality care for the officer to minimize the adverse consequences after these events. Assessing the officer's recovery and readiness to return to work would also provide information as to the length of time it takes after a suicide by cop situation for the officer to recover and be mentally fit to return to duty. The impact of a suicide by cop situation on an officer is great and this does not occur in a vacuum. Future research should also examine the effects on officers' family members who are in the position of witnessing their loved ones trying to understand and cope with the traumatic event. Rates of divorce and separation for the officers are another area to be explored. Are officers who have been involved in suicide by cop situations more likely to have marital problems resulting in divorce or separation? How are these officers coping with the trauma experienced?

Coerced Confessions

Introduction

No other piece of evidence is more damaging to a criminal defendant than a stated confession. Throughout history, confessions have been obtained in a variety of ways. Due process specifically states that interrogators may use certain tactics to obtain confessions, provided that the confession is voluntary and a product of an essentially free and unhindered person. However, many tactics employed by an interrogator do not fall within these guidelines and are therefore considered "coerced." This section outlines and discusses the legal definition of a **coerced confession**, its psychological and sociological bases and implications, and discusses some of the specific tactics used by investigators and interrogators in obtaining confessions. The following fictional vignette demonstrates a variety of interrogation issues, legal or otherwise.

Ned and Jake, desperate for cash and needing to obtain drugs to support their addictions, decide that robbing a downtown convenience store would be a quick and convenient way to obtain money. The two arrive in Ned's car, and it is decided that Jake will run into the store, hold up the convenience clerk, and make a quick escape. Upon entering the store, Jake becomes worried and apprehensive when he realizes that the store has approximately five other people inside. Nervously, Jake approaches the clerk, pulls a gun, and demands all the money in the cash register. The clerk, unwilling to be a victim of this type of crime any longer, pulls his own firearm out from under the counter and points it at Jake. In a panic, Jake fires, killing the store clerk. Hearing a shot fired, Ned also panics and quickly drives away, leaving Jake behind. Jake, seen by numerous eyewitnesses, flees into the night on foot, only to be apprehended later by the police who take him in to be questioned.

In the interrogation room, two officers enter and introduce themselves to Jake, who has been waiting for the officers for approximately 45 minutes in the isolated room. The officers, after offering Jake some water and/or use of the bathroom, quickly review Jake's Miranda rights. Jake listens and does not respond in any notable fashion. The officers then begin questioning Jake about the attempted robbery that took place earlier that evening. Jake, unwilling to give any information, states that he is innocent and wishes to speak with a lawyer. The officers tell Jake that the process can take place in one of two ways: cooperate and answer all questions immediately or cease questioning now and wait for legal counsel, thereby not cooperating with investigative procedures. Feeling somewhat intimidated, Jake concedes to answering more questions. Later, the officers come to another roadblock in Jake's testimony. He refuses to answer a question dealing with his accomplice. The officers state that if he implicates his friend in the murder of the clerk, the courts may reward his cooperation with leniency. Afraid and hopeful of a more lenient sentence, Jake admits full guilt and gives the name and description of his accomplice.

Would you consider the above confession to be coerced? If so, what specific techniques did you feel were inappropriate? If not, why not? The discussion to follow examines specific issues related to appropriate and inappropriate interrogation techniques. It also addresses the reason for these techniques' psychological power over many arrested subjects, as well as other topics related to coerced confessions.

Literature Review

According to police procedure and the Fifth Amendment, prosecutors cannot use statements obtained by a subject as evidence in court unless the arresting party has ensured that the subject's Miranda rights have been offered and explained. The courts believe that subjects pulled from their familiar environment and surrounded by potentially intimidating authority figures may reveal information that they otherwise would not give without the right to remain silent until counsel were available to them (*Davis v. United States*, 1994). Authority figures and unfamiliar environments could cause the subject to feel pressured making them more susceptible to revealing information. If the Miranda warning has been issued, and the interrogation follows proper standards and ethical guidelines, the resulting admission will have validity as it was not obtained through deception or pressure; therefore, making it a voluntary statement (Frumkin, 2010). When a suspect has been read his or her Miranda warnings, it is sometimes questionable whether or not he or she understood them and are able to make rational, independent decisions based on that information. The more vulnerable members of our society — the mentally ill, intellectually/developmentally disabled (IDD), and the young — are particularly at risk for manipulation and exploitation. In a study examining pre-adjudicative and adjudicative competency in juveniles and young adults, results indicated that Miranda competence and adjudicative competence were strongly related (Redlich & Drizin, 2007). Age and suggestibility were also related to Miranda competence. DeClue (2005) found that defendants with primary psychotic disorders had more impairment than defendants with affective disorders, substance abuse disorders, and no diagnosed major mental illness, in their understanding of interrogation rights, the nature of criminal proceedings, the possible consequences of those proceedings, and their ability to have a meaningful interchange with their attorneys.

As with many laws, ambiguity exists as to exactly when a subject requests counsel. For example, during an interrogation the subject states, "Maybe I should talk to a lawyer." Does the officer interpret this as a clear request to receive counsel? If so, the interrogator must immediately stop questioning and hold the subject until a lawyer is available. If not, has the officer breached the subject's Miranda rights, creating the possibility of coercing a confession?

Three basic rules exist to aid law enforcement agents in understanding whether a subject is requesting counsel. The first is termed **The Threshold of Clarity Rule** and states that the subject's request for counsel meets a "threshold of clarity." Under this rule, a subject must clearly demonstrate a request for counsel. As one may guess, this rule is itself somewhat vague and offers no specific guidelines stating what is "clear."

The second rule related to the right not to self-incriminate is termed the **Per Se Rule**. According to this rule, any reference to counsel during an interrogation session must result in the immediate cessation of questioning and the appointment of counsel to the subject. This rule has more clarity and leaves little question as to whether the subject is indeed requesting counsel.

Last, **The Clarification Rule** states that if a subject makes an ambiguous request for counsel, the officers may ask for further clarification. However, if the officers, in their request for clarification, continue to discuss the arrest, the law may be breached (*Davis v. United States*, 1994).

Once a subject's Miranda rights are read and the subject waives those rights or agrees to continue questioning until counsel arrives, the interrogator may then begin questioning the subject on matters related to the crime. Officers utilize a variety of techniques in interrogation to provide them with the most important, relevant information related to the crime. The majority of these techniques are psychological in nature. This differs from past interrogation techniques in that they are no longer deemed as violent or cruel (e.g., extinguishing a cigarette on a suspect's hand) (DeClue, 2005). As discussed in other portions of this book, the significant amount of stress felt by police often leads to an attitude of indifference or frustration. This results in tactics that ensure quick, albeit often inappropriate, justice. Given the variety of stressors and their severity, it is understandable why an officer may use underhanded tactics to obtain a confession, particularly from a suspect he or she believes is guilty.

For example, in the case study provided earlier, the suspect was clearly guilty of homicide and was identified by a variety of witnesses. The arresting officer, convinced that the subject is guilty, tries to expedite justice by bringing this criminal the punishment he deserves. Other cases may be encumbered with confusion and inconsistencies, and officers may then feel the need to use tactics to coerce a confession.

According to DeClue (2005), psychological science increases our understanding of why some people who initially claim innocence respond to interrogation procedures by confessing — sometimes to crimes they did not commit. Kassin (2008) described the three legal procedures that provide opportunities for a defendant to challenge confession evidence: "whether there was a knowing, intelligent, and voluntary Miranda waiver; whether the confession was coerced (involuntary); and whether the confession is unreliable" (p. 249). Kassin (2008) notes that police sometimes target innocent people for interrogation because of mistaken conclusions about truth and deception. Moreover, innocent people sometimes confess based on certain interrogation tactics and the dispositional (e.g., mood, personality traits, intelligence, etc.) suspect vulnerabilities. Dripps (1988) contends that many confessions are procured through manipulation, irrationality of the subject, and mistakes made by the subject during interrogation. Obviously, the courts need clear evidence of guilt if a subject is to be convicted of a crime. As stated previously, the most impressive and conclusive evidence one can obtain is a confession by the accused. This evidence must not come at the expense of the subject's personal autonomy; if personal autonomy were to be sacrificed, then unlawful tactics may as well be utilized to obtain the same end.

While one may be tempted to believe that police interrogations take place in prime-time television fashion, complete with 200-watt light bulbs, 8-hour grueling question-and-answer sessions, yelling in the face of the accused, and fist pounding, the reality is that the majority of interrogations normally do not take place in such a style. Leo (1996) describes, using observations from 122 interrogations involving 45 different detectives, the processes and tactics utilized during a variety of interrogation sessions incorporating everything from homicide to property crimes. His results indicate that, overall, coerced confessions occur less often than one may believe. However, he did state that he "…occasionally observed behavior inside the interrogation room − such as yelling, table pounding, or highly aggressive questioning − that straddled the margins of legality" (p. 270).

When Leo's results are broken down, we find that about 78% of the interrogated subjects ultimately waived their Miranda rights. In seven (4%) of the cases observed, the detective continued questioning the subject even after invoking their Miranda rights. The types of tactics used were: appealing to the suspect's self-interest (88%), confronting suspect with existing evidence of guilt (85%), undermining suspect's confidence in denial of guilt (43%), identifying contradictions in suspect's story (42%), behavioral analysis interview questions (40%), appealing to the importance of cooperation (37%), moral justifications/psychological excuses (34%), confronting suspect with false evidence of guilt (30%), using praise or flattery (30%), appealing to detective's expertise/authority (29%), appealing to the suspect's conscience (23%), and minimizing the moral seriousness of the offense (22%).

Less frequently used tactics were also implemented, possibly suggesting coercion: invoking metaphors of guilt (10%), exaggerating the facts/nature of the offense (4%), yelling at suspect (3%), accusing suspect of other crimes (1%), and attempting to confuse the subject (1%). In all, detectives used an average of 5.62 interrogation tactics.

Leo (1996), analyzing these data, states that according to his necessary conditions for coercion, police questioning involving coercive methods took place in only four (2%) of the cases. Further analysis of these four cases reveals that only psychologically coercive methods were used as opposed to physically coercive methods. In one case, detectives intentionally questioned a heroin addict suffering from acute withdrawal symptoms during the second day of his incarceration, knowing his symptoms were at their worst. In another case, the "good cop/bad cop" routine was utilized on a young gang member. One detective promised the youth's release if he cooperated, while the other stated that he would provide the prosecutor with incriminating information. The suspect provided the desired information and was subsequently released. All officers using coercive methods stated that they felt nothing could be lost by using coercive methods with these subjects, since they were treated essentially as informants or witnesses.

In a later study by Costanzo and Leo (2007), four types of false confessions were identified, two of which fall in the coerced category. These types include: (1) "*Instrumental-Coerced* false confessions occur, when as a result of a long or intense interrogation, suspects confess to crimes they know they did not commit" (p. 75); and (2) "An *Authentic-Coerced* false confession occurs when, as a product of a long or intense interrogation, suspects become convinced — at least temporarily — that they may have actually committed the crime" (p. 75). Costanzo and Leo (2007) caution that when considering person-situation risk factors that can lead to false confessions, the highest risk occurs when a psychologically vulnerable suspect is faced with a highly coercive interrogation.

Costanzo and Leo (2007, pp. 78–79) identify the **Reid Technique** as the most influential modern interrogation method that has been commonly used by numerous agencies. This technique is divided into nine steps that begins with direct confrontation and ends with a written confession and its foundation is five situational elements. If applied appropriately, this technique is considered to be effective in securing a confession. The five primary elements involved in the Reid Technique are:

1. **Control:** This involves removing familiar and comfortable stimuli. The key goal of this element is to "remove the psychological comfort of familiar surroundings."
2. **Social Isolation:** This element combined with the controlled environment will have a "psychological effect of disorienting and creating anxiety in the suspect."
3. **Certainty of Guilt:** Starting with a direct confrontation of guilt, it is the hope of the interrogator that the innocent suspect will respond with denial, and the guilty will perceive futility in the situation and admit to guilt.
4. **Minimization or Elimination of Culpability:** This element works to provide justifications for the alleged crime, and allow the suspect an out and an opportunity to "save face."
5. **Interpretation of Suspect Behavior:** The effectiveness of this element will depend on the reliability of the interrogator's training because it is based on the individual analysis of the suspect's behavior.

DiPietro (1993) describes a number of factors related to interrogation of subjects. He states that officers should assess the suspect's background and personal characteristics such as age, race, intelligence, and educational level before beginning interrogation. Certain subjects may be more conducive to coercive techniques, thus rendering a subsequent confession inadmissible if such techniques are used. Further, DiPietro states that some types of deceptive techniques are appropriate, given that they are not openly coercive, but that officers must not trick a subject into waiving his or her Miranda rights. He then gives a two-part definition of deception: (1) lies that relate to a suspect's connection to the crime; and (2) trickery that introduces extrinsic considerations. Perske (2000) explains that individuals with intellectual or other development disabilities are very susceptible to coerced or false confessions. He strongly recommends that mental health professionals or other types of human service workers are present, as soon as possible, during the interview process.

DiPietro (1993) also describes a number of interrogation techniques, which may, by some definitions, be considered coercive. The first of these are lies that connect the suspect to the crime. These include telling the subject that fingerprints were found at the crime scene when in fact they were not. Also, trickery that falsely introduces extrinsic evidence may also be considered coercive. This may include telling a subject that they will lose their welfare benefits if they are found guilty, but that leniency will be granted in exchange of cooperation. Another potentially coercive method is the effect of promises on voluntariness. This is a technique used in which an officer promises some sort of benefit to the subject in return for cooperation. Promises of leniency are also used in the facilitation of confessions, as are promises to tell higher authorities (such as the courts), that cooperation was given. Conceivably, a cooperative subject may be told that he or she will be treated less harshly if cooperation is given.

Promises of collateral benefits, such as the release of a family member or treatment for the subject's substance abuse problem, are also given. More specifically, the courts have found that promises to protect the accused, promises to protect the accused's family, and promises not to arrest the defendant are considered to be coercive. Finally, threats may be viewed as inherently coercive and are, therefore, not allowed in the interrogation process.

While the discussion thus far has focused mainly on coercive interviewing techniques, good interviewing techniques do exist and are encouraged in virtually all interrogation situations. The Reid Technique is the most commonly used interrogation model used in agencies today with approximately 300,000 interrogators trained to use this technique since 1974 (Costanzo & Leo, 2007).

Forensic Psychology and Policy Implications

A variety of policy implications exist for ensuring that confessions are not obtained through primarily coercive methods. Johnson and Hunt (2000, p. 17) recommend that entire police interrogations be electronically recorded, not only the resulting confession in order "to facilitate the court's task of determining the suspect's competence to waive constitutional rights and questions regarding the reliability of incriminating statements." Recently, more and more police departments have utilized video recorders in the interrogation room to provide the courts with real evidence of the interrogation process, should it be sought. Recent research shows the increase in departmental spending in regards to the installation of recording equipment. With questions of coercion, excessive force, and constitutional violations being called into question more frequently, agencies are finding it more costly to function without this type of equipment (Sullivan, 2010). This same author notes that laws and Supreme Court rulings are starting to implore all agencies to have access to recording technology. Other explorable policies may include a restructuring of the Fifth Amendment, making the currently ambiguous wording clearer. Clarification of this amendment would conceivably make coercion illegal and reduce appeals dealing with the interpretation of a detective's interrogation techniques.

DeClue (2005) notes that expert psychological or psychiatric testimony can assist courts in determining if confessions are voluntary and on the nature of interrogations. Thus, it is important for forensic psychologists working in this field to be very familiar with the aforementioned literature, particularly understanding the interplay between suspect, situation, and interrogator factors. Similar to other forms of expert testimony, the admissibility of expert testimony on false or coerced confessions is determined by the *Frye* standard, the *Daubert* standard, and Rule 702 of the Federal Rules of Evidence (Costanzo & Leo, 2007). The content of testimony involves educating the jury or judge about interrogation tactics and suspect factors that make them vulnerable to false confessions. Costanzo and Leo (2007) indicate that many false confessions elicited from coercion tend to follow a pattern of the suspect repeatedly denying involvement in the crime, yet, after a long, coercive interrogation, reluctantly offering a tentative admission of guilt, which is sometimes followed by the suspect recanting not long after leaving the interrogation room. These researchers recommend the following to help prevent coerced confessions: reform interrogation training, impose time limits on interrogations, videotape the entire interrogation process, place limits on deception and trickery used, require an appropriate adult when interviewing a vulnerable suspect, and seek expert testimony on interrogations and confessions (Costanzo & Leo, 2007). Implementing strategies to reduce coerced confessions is important as jurors can fail to discount even those confessions they see as coerced (Kassin, 2008).

Suggestions for Future Research

In more recent years, there has been an increase in the literature available regarding coerced confessions. Studies examining video-taped confessions and the psychological effects on the subject as well as on detectives' possible inhibition about being recorded are indicated. According to Kassin (2008), 20 to 25% of all DNA exonerations involve innocent prisoners who confessed. How many of those confessions were a result of coercive methods used by law enforcement? Future research should continue to focus on finding ways to improve the accuracy of confession evidence and its evaluation in the courtroom.

Personality characteristics associated with interrogators who routinely use coercive methods require further exploration. What types of personality traits make up a detective who uses coercive methods? Is it one who is "burned out" or grown overly cynical of the criminal justice system? Perhaps research investigating the level of experience required to become a routine interrogator should be examined.

What makes a particularly good interrogator? While the techniques used by certain detectives have been explored and examined, the actual characteristics associated with personality types have not. It may be that certain personality types will never, under normal conditions, develop good, efficient interviewing techniques.

What are the psychological after effects of the subject who has been coerced into giving a confession? Are there long-lasting psychological consequences of being deceived or tricked? What is the public's perception of coerced confessions? The public may feel that any means necessary to obtain justice are within reasonable limits. Others may feel that only the strictest of procedures should be followed, leaving little room for deviation. More research needs to be conducted to address what are acceptable methods by which to interrogate individuals with intellectual or developmental disabilities, particularly relating to high degrees of suggestibility coupled with subaverage intelligence. These topics and many more are available avenues for the continued study of coerced confessions. Interrogation must always take place; therefore the problem of coerced confession will continue.

The Police Personality and Pre-Employment Screenings

Introduction

Police officers hold a position that is replete with stress and responsibility. These officers face dangerous situations, aggressive suspects, and agitated citizens. Line officers must comply with their supervisors and uphold the law. These individuals are entrusted with a tremendous amount of power and with a great deal of discretion in how they use that power. As a result, various methods have been employed to assess the personality and any psychopathology exhibited by the officer candidates. Most frequently, psychological tests and civil service interviews are used to ascertain this information. Some researchers argue that this information is only detected through on-the-spot observation of on-the-street interactions (Harris, 2010; Toch, 1992). With the increasing media attention to cases of police brutality, there is a growing concern about the mental health screening of police officers. Are these cases examples of a few violence-prone men or are they more indicative of a "police personality" that pervades law enforcement? There exists a concern that the screening of officer candidates is insufficient at recognizing those officers who will be unable to cope with the responsibilities of the job. Consider the following case illustration.

Cameron's father had been a police officer and Cameron admired the "tough-guy" image and excitement that he perceived to be embodied in police work. He had always been outgoing and seemingly fearless. All of his friends and family knew that he would be an excellent candidate for law enforcement. Cameron applied for a job with the local police department. After what seemed like hours of psychological tests and panel interviews, Cameron was relieved to hear that he qualified to be on the police force. Being a new officer on his probationary period, he was eager to belong and to perform his duties to the utmost of his abilities. He had heard countless stories by the "veterans" about the difficulty of gaining compliance from a particular category of civilians. In addition, Cameron was warned that it was best to take a firm, consistent approach in dealing with this group as suspects. In his second month of duty, Cameron tried to obtain identification from a suspect who fit this description of "difficult" civilian. The suspect met his expectations by being belligerent and threatening. Cameron responded by being increasingly commanding and forceful. The conflict escalated into an altercation between the suspect and Cameron.

Literature Review

Conflicting conceptualizations of "police personality" are found in the literature. Some researchers contend that individuals with certain personality traits are drawn to police work (Cortina, Doherty, Schmitt, Kaufman, & Smith, 1992). Cameron's fearless attitude would seem to have led him to police work. These researchers hold that personality traits or any psychopathology present are detected during their initial screenings for the police academy. Harris (2010) explores the relationship between police officer experience and problem behaviors using internally generated complaints rather than citizen complaints and longitudinal data gathered from a large number of officers. Results suggest that combined patterns over time parallel those of citizen complaints from this same group of officers.

Other researchers maintain that although these individuals have similar occupational interests, it is really the police subculture of violence and cynicism that leads to particular actions such as excessive force or police brutality (Harris, 2010; Graves, 1996). In Cameron's case, it is difficult to determine if it was his personality characteristics alone or the influence of other officers that led to the violent interaction with a civilian. Yet others maintain that years of working with hostile civilians, occupational stagnation, and the loss of faith in our criminal justice system lead to personality and attitude changes in police officers. While some believe that one of these scenarios is dominant, other researchers contend that these influences can be interdependent. There is a growing controversy surrounding how to establish whether an individual is suitable for police work.

As many researchers have suggested, police officers are likely to share certain personality characteristics that may be assumed to help them in their work (Salters-Pedneault, Ruef, & Orr, 2010; Sellbom, Fischler, & Ben-Porath, 2007). Police officers encounter life-threatening situations, aggressive offenders, and have to answer to the community as well as to their supervisors (Kääriäienen, Lintonin, Laitinen, & Pollock, 2008). It is suggested that officers face the worst of society and then have to handle the most delicate of human crises with sensitivity. The unique stressors that officers face make emotional strengths and weaknesses the focus of screening procedures for officer candidates.

The research indicates that psychological assessment tools have been increasingly utilized in the past three decades as a means to screen and select police officer candidates (Sellbom, Fischler, & Ben-Porath, 2007; Beutler *et al.*, 1988). Historically, the Minnesota Multiphasic Personality Inventory (MMPI and MMPI-2) has been the psychological test that is most commonly used as a screening device in police officer selection (Beutler *et al.*, 1988; Cortina *et al.*, 1992; Kornfeld, 1995; Murphy, 1972). The MMPI is primarily a test of **psychopathology** or describing the development and symptoms/manifestations of mental or behavioral disorders and it is used most successfully when testing for this purpose (Graham, 2005). However, the literature suggests that these instruments are employed to determine which candidates are the most likely to fail during training or probationary periods (Sellbom, Fischler, & Ben-Porath, 2007; Detrick, Chibnall, & Rosso, 2001; Cortina *et al.*, 1992; Inwald, 2008; Murphy, 1972). In addition, they are used to suggest which candidates are most likely to use excessive force or misuse weapons while on duty. A 2007 study by Sellbom, Fischler, and Ben-Porath also found that several MMPI-2 scales (i.e., RC3, RC4, RC6, RC8, & Substance Abuse) showed promise in predicting police officer misconduct. Additionally, Detrick and Chibnall (2008) found significant relationships between moralistic and egoistic biases and the MMPI and the Inwald Personality Inventory (IPI) validity scales. In other words, recruits may be likely to present themselves as agreeable, sociable, and skilled in interpersonal interactions (moralistic) and as self-confident, competent, and action oriented (egoistic). Although historically researchers have maintained that efforts to correlate MMPI scores to job performance have not been effective (Cortina *et al.*, 1992), the MMPI-2 Revised Personnel System, 3rd Edition (2001), includes some specific items intended to predict work dysfunction. By identifying personality styles and any psychopathology, police departments hope to save time and money, as well as avoid any negative publicity or litigation that would ensue following an excessive force claim.

Cortina *et al.* (1992) noted that police officer candidates exhibit a distinguishable pattern on the MMPI. For example, these candidates' validity scales, which measure the accuracy of the test, usually show defensiveness or an unwillingness to acknowledge distress. The Psychopathic Deviate (Pd) scale is frequently elevated. Interestingly, the elevation of the Pd scale is typically seen in individuals who engage in criminal behavior. Interpretive possibilities for an elevated Pd score include: aggressive or assaultive behavior, substance abuse, or poor tolerance of boredom. A study by Kornfeld (1995), in which the MMPI-2 was administered to 84 police officer candidates, indicated low scores on scales 0 and 2. Male candidates had a low scale 5, while female candidates had an elevated scale 5. For a nonclinical sample, low scale 2 scores suggest that these individuals are less likely to worry, to have problems reaching decisions, and to worry about being rejected (Graham, 2005; Kornfeld, 1995). They are also more likely to be self-confident. A low scale 0 on the MMPI denotes an individual who is sociable, extroverted, and friendly (Graham, 2005; Kornfeld, 1995). A low scale 5 for a male indicates an extremely masculine presentation, with stereotypical masculine interests, and someone who is action oriented (Butcher, 2011; Graham, 2005; Kornfeld, 1995). A female with an elevated scale 5 could be a woman who has rejected the traditional feminine role, embracing more commonly masculine interests. Overall, Kornfeld (1995) found that these police officer candidates were psychologically well adjusted, comfortable with people, free of worry, and self-confident.

The MMPI-2 Revised Personnel System, 3rd Edition was revised in 2001 and is intended to aid psychologists evaluating candidates to fill high-risk, high-stress positions in order to potentially identify individuals who may be emotionally inappropriate for challenging public safety roles. The MMPI-2 Revised Personnel System, 3rd Edition presents more in-depth, occupation-specific information for six public safety fields. Using data from over 18,000 personnel cases, mean profiles were developed for a number of occupations including law enforcement. Five other important work-related dimensions can be assessed; Openness to Evaluation, Social Facility, Addiction Potential, Stress Tolerance, and Overall Adjustment.

The MMPI was not designed particularly for the selection of police officers, and some researchers have expressed concern over its use in this context (Cortina *et al.*, 1992).

In response to this concern, the Inwald Personality Inventory (IPI) was developed (Inwald, 2008; Detrick & Chibnall, 2002; Cortina *et al.*, 1992) and the MMPI-2 Revised Personnel System, 3rd Edition (2001) as described above was revised to also address these concerns. The IPI is a 310-item questionnaire that "…attempts to assess the psychological and emotional fitness of recruits as well as some of their job-relevant behavioral characteristics" (p. 20). In a validity study conducted by Inwald, Knatz, and Shusman (1983), the IPI was found to be superior to the MMPI in predicting job-relevant criteria such as absences, lateness, and derelictions (disciplinary interviews). However, according to Cortina *et al.* (1992), neither the MMPI nor the IPI could add much more than the Civil Service Exam, a multiple-choice exam testing cognitive ability, in predicting performance ratings and officer turnover rates. According to Inwald (2008), over time, studies have demonstrated that the IPI was a better predictor of poor job performance than were traditional tests of psychopathology like the MMPI-2. Inwald reports that antisocial behavior patterns and characteristics measured by the IPI have consistently predicted poor job performance for law enforcement officers (2008).

In a 2002 study, the IPI was administered to police officer candidates during a pre-employment screening and these scores were utilized in predicting applicant performance, as rated by supervisors after one year of active duty (Detrick & Chibnall, 2002). The results of the study indicated that IPI scales, including Family Conflicts, Guardedness, and Driving Violations, significantly predicted performance. Another study by Detrick, Chibnall, and Rosso (2001) examined the relationship between the IPI and the MMPI-2 as police officer screening tools. The MMPI-2 and the IPI were administered to 467 police officer candidates and moderate correlations were found with the clinical scales. However, substantial correlations were found with two validity scales. A defensive profile was noted on the MMPI-2 with elevations on the validity scales L and K. Additionally, Scales 2 (Depression) and 0 (Introversion) were low, while Scale 5 (Masculine/Feminine) were extreme (Detrick *et al.*, 2001; Weiss *et al.*, 2009).

Some researchers have called into question the possibility that police applicants could be coached to achieve more favorable scores on psychological tests and selection interviews. A study by Miller and Barrett (2008) sought to answer two questions: (1) could coached applicants achieve more favorable scores in psychological tests? and (2) if they would be more likely to be hired due to those scores? Their results indicated that the answer to the first question is in the affirmative as participants who received personality measure training scored significantly higher on measures of conscientiousness. Furthermore, their results also indicated that trained applicants, and even applicants that simply fake their responses, may increase their chances of being hired. Miller and Barrett also propose that in order to provide sufficient training to applicants one may only need as little as a few undergraduate psychology courses.

Eber (as cited in Lorr & Strack, 1994) obtained objective psychometric data on 15,000 candidates for positions in law enforcement agencies around the country. Using the Clinical Analysis Questionnaire, one of Eber's objectives was to determine a distinct police personality style that might explain the sporadic occurrence of excessive force or assaultive behavior in typically rational, stable, and professional officers. The Clinical Analysis Questionnaire consists of personality measure scales and 12 measures of psychopathology. Overall, the candidates were found to have very little psychopathology. They were less depressed, less confused, and less likely to engage in self-harm than the general population. However, they were more thrill seeking and had a disregard for social conventions based on these measures. Regarding their personality styles, Eber found that these candidates were self-disciplined, very tough-minded, and slightly independent.

Expanding on Eber's work, Lorr and Strack (1994) divided the police personality profile into three robust profile groups. The largest cluster was reflected as the typical "good" cop or those who are self-disciplined, are low in anxiety, extroverted, and emotionally tough. One in four candidates fell into a cluster that had relatively high levels of paranoia, schizophrenia, and psychasthenia (characterized by compulsions, obsessions, unreasonable fears, and excessive doubts), as well as high anxiety and lower self-control. Despite their relatively high occurrence compared to "good" cops, these occurrences of psychopathology were relatively low compared with the general population.

Arrigo and Claussen (2003) suggest that pre-employment screening should be utilized in the prediction, control, and prevention of police officer corruption. These authors examined the effectiveness of the IPI and the Revised-NEO Personality Inventory in evaluating antisocial behavioral proclivities and conscientious personality traits. They conclude that their use, in combination with appropriate administration, offers a reliable and valid predictor of good job performance (Arrigo & Claussen, 2003). Vasilopoulos, Cucina, and Hunter (2007) found that linear effects for specific personality scales, namely conscientiousness and emotional stability, served as better indicators of training performance than composite scores. In other words, high scores on these specific scales were more likely to predict better performance than a combined score. Their study also suggested a relationship between conscientiousness and training performance; specifically, those scoring high and low on the conscientiousness scale would perform more poorly than those with midrange conscientiousness scores. More recently, however, other researchers have found that police recruits often engage in **positive response distortion** or answering the questions in a certain way in order to present themselves in a more favorable light (Detrick, Chibnall, & Call, 2010). With respect to the NEO PI-R, Detrick, Chibnall, and Call (2010) found that positive response bias often results in a minimization of neuroticism scores (i.e., Anxiety, Hostility, Depression, Self-Consciousness, Impulsiveness, and Vulnerability to Stress subscales) and an inflation of agreeableness and conscientiousness (social desirability) scores. This type of response pattern poses a significant threat to the **validity or accuracy** of personality inventories in police selection.

Other researchers maintain that adverse psychological changes occur in officers after being on the job. A study conducted by Beutler *et al.* (1988) using the MMPI looked at 25 officers directly after recruitment, 2 years later, and, finally, 4 years later. These researchers found that the officers presented personality styles suggestive of substance abuse risk and stress-related physical complaints. In addition, they concluded that this risk increases with officers' time in service. In a recent study of the Personality Assessment Inventory (PAI), Weiss *et al.* (2008) found that while the instrument did not function overall as a predictor of performance, the Borderline Negative Relations subscale and Drug scale showed some promise in predicting the poorest functioning officers in their sample. Researchers maintain that, overall, this group is guarded and will be hesitant to seek mental health treatment (Page & Jacobs, 2011; Beutler *et al.*, 1998; Beutler, Storm, Kirkish, Scogan, & Gaines, 1985). Researchers also report that the alcoholism and suicide rates among police officers, by far, surpass those of the general population (Ballenger *et al.*, 2011; Russell & Beigel, 1982; Violanti *et al.*, 2009).

In a study undertaken by Saathoff and Buckman (1990), the most common primary diagnosis among 26 state police officers who requested, or were referred to, psychiatric services by their department was adjustment disorder, followed by substance abuse and then personality disorders. The majority of officers believed that there was a stigma attached to receiving mental health services. Despite infrequent occurrences, Saathoff and Buckman stress that the extremes of violence, homicide, and suicide must be taken into consideration with police officers, as they carry guns in the course of their duties.

Some researchers believe that the negative behavior displayed by some officers is related to a personality style that officers have when they join the force. However, other researchers maintain that incidents like police brutality stem from a belief system that forms as they begin to feel betrayed by the system and lose respect for the law (Harris, 2010; Sobol, 2010; Graves, 1996). These researchers explain that officers see the worst of society on a daily basis and begin to lose faith in others, trust only other officers, and suffer "social estrangement." Others have posited that it may be officers' loss of confidence in the average citizen and with supervisors that may cause them to become isolated from the community, loyalty to each other, and more likely to utilize independent measures in their work; thereby creating the code of silence (Terrill *et al.*, 2003; Kääriäienen, Lintonin, Laitinen, & Pollock, 2008). Some researchers contend that policepersons develop a survival personality defined by rigidity, increased personal restriction, and cynicism (Kroes, 1976; Saathoff & Buckman, 1990). Most of the research on police cynicism occurred in the late 1960s and mid-1970s (Graves, 1996). Cynicism is defined as a distrust in human beings and their intentions. According to Graves, "…cynicism is the antithesis of idealism, truth, and justice — the very virtues that law enforcement officers swear to uphold" (p. 16). He contends that cynicism is the precursor to emotional problems that lead to misconduct, brutality, and possibly corruption. In addition, he stresses the negative impact on officer productivity, morale, community relations, and even the relationship that the officer has with his own family.

Researchers have found that cynicism is more prevalent in large urban police departments, particularly with college-educated, lower ranking officers, during their first 10 years of service (Graves, 1996; Sobol, 2010). Graves suggests that the heavy demands of law enforcement lead to these incidents of burnout, stress, and cynicism. He contends that these factors also lead to unhealthy emotional responses such as a withdrawal from society and an antipathy to idealism, or a loss of respect for law and society.

Toch (1992) explains that there are "violent men" among the ranks of police officers. He further adds that while these men have certain fears, insecurities, and self-centered perspectives with which they enter the force, their brutality is often protected by a code of mutual support among officers. According to Toch:

> *In theory, aggressive police officers could be dealt with as dangerous deviants by their peers and by the administrator of their departments. Instead, they are seen as overly-forceful prac-titioners of a philosophy that comprises themes such as "lots of suspects are scumbags," "one cannot tolerate disrespect," "situations must be (physically) controlled," and "the real measure of police productivity is number of arrests" (pp. 242–243).*

Toch suggests that it is a fallacy to believe that the "police problem" is a function of personality disturbances among a small group of officers that can be detected during initial psychological screenings or a function of racial beliefs that can be eradicated by cultural sensitivity lectures. He contends that some officers have a proclivity to escalate interpersonal interactions into explosive situations. In addition, he maintains that this propensity for violence can only be identified through on-the-spot observations of their interactions on the street. Clearly, in Cameron's case, early detection of this type of behavior could prevent future abuses of citizens. In addition, his department could recognize the need for additional training in handling hostile situations without resorting to violence.

While the aforementioned studies center on personality profiles and psychopathology of police officers, a study by Kleider and Parrott (2009) has shed light on the possible role of working memory in an officer's decision to fire his weapon or aggressive shooting behavior. According to these authors, those with lower **working memory** capacities are more prone to making hasty shooting decisions. Due to these individuals' limited capacities, they are more likely to be overwhelmed by the multiple stimuli present, especially in threatening situations. By contrast, those with greater working memory capacities appear better able to attend to these multiple stimuli without becoming overwhelmed, and, subsequently, are better able to make judicious decisions regarding the discharge of their weapons.

Forensic Psychology and Policy Implications

Overall, it is clear that mental health professionals need to have a role in police training as well as to provide psychological services and evaluations after the occurrence of a critical incident or trauma. Many forensic psychologists specialize in the unique psychological dynamics of police work, the emotional needs of police officers, and the complexities of law enforcement organizations. In order for a mental health professional to be effective within an organization, they must understand the special needs or issues of their constituency, which in this case are police officers.

Page and Jacobs (2011) recommend that many police departments are in need of more mental health care providers. They propose that one possible option could be to establish some form of peer-support counseling in police departments. Peer-support counseling could be used in conjunction with intradepartmental programs for stress management, psychological interventions, and educational programs on the abuses of alcohol, and domestic violence prevention. Saathoff and Buckman (1990) recommend that when psychiatrists or psychologists conduct a psychological evaluation of officers, they should not be cajoled by the officer or the department into limiting the scope of their evaluation. Officers' continuing mental health counseling/education has endless implications for their own safety and the safety of the community. These researchers also suggest including officers' families in the mental health process in order to elicit critical information and to increase the level of support for that officer.

It is imperative for police departments to take all possible steps to reduce the stigma attached to psychological services for officers. Police supervisors should receive training to help them identify those officers in need of psychological referrals. These interventions should be encouraged and rewarded by supervisors and even made mandatory after critical events.

Regarding cynicism, Graves (1996) suggests that competent, principle-centered, people-oriented leadership can help to inspire and motivate employees and prevent negativity. In addition, these police leaders need to actively recognize the positive actions by police officers within the department as well as within the community. He also maintains that by having continuous training about the intent of rules of evidence, officers can be empowered within the criminal justice system rather than manipulated by it. Graves contends that a participatory management style that allows officers to have a voice increases their satisfaction with their jobs and reduces cynicism that flows out toward the community. Finally, he suggests that a realistic job preview should be offered to police officer candidates during recruitment. Kääriäinen, Lintonin, Laitinen, and Pollock (2008) suggest that providing police officers with clear and strict rules of conduct may help to increase their adherence to those rules.

With respect to pre-employment screening, Miller and Barrett (2008) caution that psychological testing in police selection may be influenced by training and preparation on how to improve their test scores. Where personality screening is utilized, Vasilopoulos, Cucina, and Hunter (2007) suggest using selection procedure that does not entail the selection of officers with the highest scores on certain personality factors to the exclusion of those with lower scores. Furthermore, Detrick, Chibnall, and Call (2010) caution that evaluators should also be aware of the impact of positive response distortions (e.g., faking good) in interpreting personality inventories as part of the police selection process. Given that recruits' scores on personality measures may be influenced by preparation or biased responding, it would also be prudent for evaluators to treat scores on personality measures with caution and consider them a part of the overall process and not the sole criterion for selection.

Toch (1992) suggests that rather than focus only on the individual recruit's personality style, their pattern of social interaction should be examined in order to assess the violence potential. He points out that it should be impressed upon young officers that they need to communicate to civilians the reasons for their actions. For example, Toch cites multiple incidents where police officers demand a certain response from a suspicious civilian, and that their increasingly authoritative and demanding demeanor contributes to the escalation of violence. Toch recognizes that the ambiguity in the power delegated to police officers frequently results in the abuse of those powers. He suggests that more guidance should be offered in handling discretion. Officers are bombarded with phrases like "reasonable force" without a clear understanding of their meanings or applicability in street situations. In the case illustration, Cameron was faced with a noncompliant suspect and no plan to counter the situation.

In order to confront these situations, researchers (Kääriäienen, Lintonin, Laitinen, & Pollock, 2008; Toch, 1992) suggest that officers should be provided with criteria of conduct with a realistic preparation for its use on the street. Specifically, directive, in-service training experiences rather than passive learning experiences are recommended. In addition, researchers suggest that while on their probationary periods, officers should be shadowed. During this shadowing procedure, when violence-producing situations are confronted, a resolution *should be* worked out and errors *should be* open to analysis and correction.

Suggestions for Future Research

The literature called for more objective or qualitative data on the mental disorders experienced by police officers. The categorization of the personality traits identified in the current research does little to elucidate the experience of police officers. Traditionally a guarded group, it is difficult to obtain an accurate indication of psychological functioning. Longitudinal studies of personality and mood changes could help to identify the effect of continued police service on the mental health of officers. Research into the effectiveness of peer-support services for police officers may provide a viable alternative to traditional counseling in departments without such resources. It would also be useful for future research to examine how frequently a police psychologist is utilized to provide counseling to on-duty officers and any trends in the purpose of the mental health contacts. Surveys of officers regarding the usefulness of these contacts could also further elucidate both the officers' perspectives on the effectiveness of the mental health contact(s), as well as officers' attitudes toward mental health professionals in their workplace.

Regarding the psychological assessment instruments used to screen officer candidates, Kornfeld (1995) reports the need for new normative data on the MMPI-2, especially for female and minority police officer candidates, to help promote fairness in the selection process. More research validating the use of interpretive systems such as the MMPI-2 Revised Personnel System is recommended. Additional research is needed to better understand the relevance of personality constructs for specific jobs and the impact of changing federal guidelines on employment testing (Camara & Merenda, 2000). Overall, more validation research needs to be done on the effectiveness of these various instruments or personality clusters in the prediction of job suitability. It would also be beneficial to increase the sensitivity to detecting faking good on personality-based selection instruments.

More research needs to be conducted on the notion that principle-centered, person-oriented leadership reduces cynicism among police officers. Program evaluations can be carried out in departments that implement these types of leadership styles and policies reflecting participatory management. Kääriäienen, Lintonin, Laitinen, and Pollock's (2008) study conducted in Finland, which examined the etiology or origin and development of the code of silence and police adherence to their code of conduct, should be replicated with a sample of police officers in the United States. Finally, departments that would implement the "shadowing" concept provided by Toch (1992) should be evaluated. This assessment would explore if incidents of excessive force or police brutality would be reduced by more directive evaluations of, and preparations for, violence-producing situations and training for violence-prone individuals. Evaluating the effectiveness of these various instruments or personality clusters in the prediction of job suitability is also necessary.

Critical Incidents Debriefing

Introduction

Law enforcement officers and other first responders work in stressful environments, and are repeatedly exposed to traumatic and dangerous situations, increasing their risk of both acute and chronic anxiety reactions. Such situations have been described as **critical incidents**, and reactions to these events can result in enormous cost to law enforcement agencies, in the form of increased absenteeism, turnover, and use of departmental resources, and decreased effectiveness. The critical incidents to which law enforcement officers may be exposed are as diverse as the officers themselves and the citizens whom they encounter; however, these incidents share common characteristics. Critical incidents are typically sudden and unexpected, have the potential to disrupt an officer's sense of control, disrupt beliefs, values, and basic assumptions about the ways in which the world, and the people within it, work, involve the perception of a life-damaging threat, and contain an element of physical and/or emotional loss (Maggio & Terenzi, 1993). Critical incidents to which law enforcement officers are frequently exposed include: line of duty death, multiple casualty situations, a child fatality, unusual situations involving death or serious injury of other officers or citizens, suicide of a colleague, death of a colleague, mutilated bodies, incidents involving public disorder, acts of terrorism, natural disasters, rape, assault, abuse, shootings, hostage situations, or the death of a partner while in the line of duty (Robinson & Mitchell, 1993; Brown & Campbell, 1994; Kirschman, 1997; Fay, 2000; Miller, 2008; LaFauci Schutt & Marotta, 2011).

As psychologists and other mental health professionals began to understand the potentially detrimental effects associated with repeated exposure to trauma, methods were developed in order to prevent such negative consequences, particularly in law enforcement and other first responders. As a result of these efforts, psychological debriefing was developed. First responders are often fatigued and ready to return to other tasks after a critical incident, and will often neglect the debriefing process if such efforts are not outlined as part of standard operating procedure (Thompson, 2004). However, such a process is critically important, as officers may be negatively impacted due to prolonged exposure to human suffering and/or life-threatening events. In order to address such concerns, the critical incident stress debriefing process was developed by Mitchell (1983) for use with firefighters involved in disaster work. This debriefing process, as outlined by Mitchell, involved witnesses of a disaster or incident (in this case, firefighters) meeting together to discuss their impressions and understanding of the event. The approach represents a systematic and structured forum in which those affected by critical incidents may process such events with a trained mental health professional.

This section will also focus on existing research regarding various methods of debriefing, including a brief history of the development of critical incident debriefing, descriptions of typical reactions by law enforcement officers exposed to critical incidents, characteristics of mental health professionals who are typically successful in working as debriefers, distinctions between traditional counseling and critical incident debriefing, barriers to the implementation of debriefing models, and research regarding the effectiveness of various debriefing strategies. The section will conclude with implications for agency policies, as well as directions for future research. Consider the vignette below involving an agent's experience in the FBI's Peer Support Program/Post Critical Incident Seminar (PCIS):

One agent who attended a PCIS was experiencing distress from a seemingly minor incident. During a surveillance, the suspect realized he was being followed and proceeded to drive at speeds in excess of 100 miles-per-hour. The suspect eventually pulled over on the highway, got out of his vehicle, and approached the agent. The agent identified himself and the suspect surrendered upon command. Despite the positive outcome, the incident still bothered the agent. At the PCIS the agent spoke about this incident and realized that the fear he had experienced stemmed from the accumulation of several past traumatic experiences. These included Vietnam experiences, being on-scene at two air disasters and engaging in several hostage negotiations. The agent recognized the connection between the successful pursuit/ arrest and these other situations where he faced his own mortality. With further discussion and peer support, the cumulative stress was resolved. Follow-up has shown the gains to be stable over the past two years (McNally, 1999, p. 113).

Literature Review

All debriefing methods have in common the goals of preventing negative reactions to trauma, teaching and reinforcing skills for team members, modeling what is taught to help first responders, helping individuals manage their own emotional responses and come to terms with the event, and returning first responders to a normal level of functioning (Thompson, 2004). As debriefing methods have been refined and specialized, groups other than law enforcement who may benefit from debriefing have been identified, and may include: bystanders and others exposed to the critical incident, family and friends of affected officers, and even those indirectly involved as members of a community surrounding an area where a critical incident has occurred (Thompson, 2004).

Much of the study of exposure to traumatic events has been focused on traumatic exposure in military personnel. Not surprisingly, critical incident debriefing also had its formal beginnings in the military. General Marshall, the chief historian of the U.S. Army during the Second World War, used and wrote about debriefing with his troops (Bisson, McFarlane, Rose, Ruzek, & Watson, 2000). In 1944, he published information regarding his debriefing process in his book, *Island Victory.* General Marshall recommended holding debriefings on the battlefield, in close temporal proximity to the traumatic event. He emphasized the time commitment required to effectively debrief soldiers, as he estimated that seven hours were needed to debrief one day of fighting (Marshall, 1944). Marshall's debriefing method was the first documented structured intervention focusing on individuals' grief, experiences, and expression of emotional responses (Bisson *et al.*, 2000). In the tradition of General Marshall's debriefing, in 1983, the FBI initiated its Peer Support Program/Post Critical Incident Seminars (PCIS), which was formed to explore post-shooting trauma and to neutralize the effects of the agents' reactions in a shooting incident (McNally, 1999). The protocol for the program consisted of a questionnaire, interview, group discussion, and follow-up interviews. Since its inception, there have been 37 PCISs with approximately 1000 total attendees. The PCIS is staffed by two Certified Employee Assistance Professionals, two mental health professionals, and an FBI chaplain (McNally, 1999). The program allows 25 attendees, who may include agents and their family members, and lasts four days (McNally, 1999). Since their inception, PCIS sessions have expanded to focus on events including death of a loved one, accidental shooting or death, depression, suicide or attempted suicide, homicide of a family member, severe car accidents, life-threatening diseases, hostage situations, sexual abuse, or major investigations involving multiple fatalities. The impact of the seminars is illustrated in the vignette above.

In June of 1995, the FBI implemented four regional critical incident stress debriefing (CISD) teams, in order to provide immediate response to the following types of critical incidents: death of an employee, spouse, or other family members, natural and man-made disasters and catastrophes, taking a life in the line-of-duty, suicide of an employee, spouse, or other family member, violent traumatic injury to an employee, death of a crime victim, witness and handling multiple fatalities, SWAT operations where dangers are present, hostage taking, barricaded suspect and negotiation, observing an act of corruption, bribery, or other illegal activity, and suspensions and/or threats of dismissal (McNally, 1999). The CISD teams consist of approximately 100 team members, the professional backgrounds of whom include mental health, chaplaincy, experience in police psychology and trauma, and service as bureau field staff (McNally, 1999). Over time, the bureau has witnessed a steady increase in the use of debriefings. During 1995, the first year the program was implemented, the agency conducted only a single debriefing (McNally, 1999). However, in the years following, debriefings increased to 18 in 1996, 29 in 1997, and 45 in 1998 (McNally, 1999). No current statistics were available to indicate the FBI's current usage of debriefings. However, such increases have also been observed more recently in the state of California, which observed an increase from only 14 requests for critical incident stress debriefings in 2008 to a record number of 33 such requests in 2009 (Ortiz, 2010). Several factors were theorized as contributing to this increase, including the failing economy and an increase in suicides among state employees, but nevertheless, critical incident debriefing appears to be an increasingly utilized method of addressing the traumatic stress to which law enforcement officials are exposed in carrying out their job duties.

Critical incident debriefing methods were developed with a common goal of preventing and/or decreasing problematic traumatic reactions, as well as providing an opportunity for mental health professionals to screen first responders who are experiencing or may be at increased risk for such reactions. Law enforcement officers may display a range of symptoms following exposure to a critical incident, from those displayed by members of the general population following a traumatic event to symptoms which are relatively unique to the police culture. In general, reactions to traumatic events, which may be displayed by law enforcement officers or members of the general population, include the following: psychic "numbing" (i.e., a feeling of being stunned, dazed, confused, apathetic), heightened physiological and emotional arousal, intense feelings of fear, anxiety, inability to relax, **survivor guilt** (i.e., a mental condition that occurs when a person perceives himself to have done wrong by surviving a traumatic event when others did not), emotional instability, irritability, sudden anger or aggression, or feelings of shock, resentment, helplessness, or hopelessness. Witnesses and survivors of trauma may also experience preoccupation with thoughts of the event, feel suspicious of others, exhibit an inability to make decisions and a shortened attention span, make efforts to isolate themselves, experience memory loss, engage in self-blame, or display overcontrolling behavior or impulsivity. Additional symptoms may include: feelings of tension, fatigue, sleep disturbance, nausea headache, impaired relationship, and feelings of denial, shame, regret, or guilt. In extreme cases, psychotic symptoms (e.g., delusions, hallucinations, disorganized speech or behavior) may result following exposure to a traumatic event (Dudley, Siitarinen, James, & Dodgson, 2009; Mueser, Lu, Rosenberg, & Wolfe 2010; Arseneault, Cannon, Fisher, Polanczyk, Moffitt, & Caspi, 2011; Thompson, 2004; Enhrenreich, 2002). In addition to these symptoms, law enforcement officers may be particularly prone to divorce, alcoholism, and suicide, following a critical incident (Patterson, 2001). In addition, police officers, mental health professionals, and first responders providing care to victims of trauma may experience **compassion fatigue** (i.e., a condition characterized by a gradual lessening of compassion over time in those who work directly with trauma victims), which may be marked by the following symptoms: feelings of powerlessness, impatience, decreased interest in activities or relationships, mistrust, survivor guilt, low self-esteem, physical pain, apathy, feelings of loneliness, or feelings of a loss of purpose (LaFauci Schutt & Marotta, 2011; Fay, 2000).

Recent research has examined the prevalence of various reactions following exposure to specific types of critical incidents (LaFauci Schutt & Marotta, 2011). In an early study, 8% of officers reported no symptoms following involvement in a shooting incident, while 46% self-reported symptoms of **post-traumatic stress disorder (PTSD)** (i.e., an anxiety disorder that can develop after exposure to a potentially life-threatening event, which may include symptoms of re-experiencing the trauma, avoidance of stimuli associated with the trauma, and increased arousal), and another 46% met diagnostic criteria for the disorder, as determined by a mental health professional (Ryan & Brewster, 1994). The importance of these findings has been emphasized, but more recent studies link the development of PTSD to negative outcomes, including depression, use of sick leave, decreased hardiness, and increased pathology following the incident (Matrin, Marchand, & Boyer, 2009). In addition, it has been noted that Caucasian race, less previous traumatic exposure prior to service in law enforcement, less traumatic exposure during law enforcement service, greater sense of self-worth, greater beliefs in the benevolence of the world, and greater social support are associated with a decreased risk for the development of PTSD (Yuan, Wang, Inslicht, McCaslin, Metzler, Henn-Haase, *et al.*, 2010). Although PTSD and related reactions have received much attention by researchers, officers' reactions to critical incidents have been proposed to fall broadly into two categories: operational and organizational responses (McCreary & Thompson, 2006), which were defined by Symonds (1970) as stressors associated with doing the job and stressors associated with the organization and culture within which they are performing their job, respectively. Interestingly, officers rated organizational stressors as significantly more challenging than operational stress (McCreary & Thompson, 2006).

Additionally, officers who are exposed to a death by suicide may experience denial, make efforts to search for meaning in the event, experience typical symptoms of grief, exhibit symptoms of depression, have increased anger, have intrusive memories of the event, withdraw from social life, experience guilt, and may identify with the person who committed suicide (Thompson, 2004; Kingshott, 2009; Drylie & Violanti, 2008). In contrast, officers who witnessed a shooting often reported that, despite their training, they had difficulty believing that the event was actually occurring; that they responded automatically based upon their training; that they felt a rush of adrenaline, fear, or both; that they questioned whether their actions were legally, procedurally, and morally correct; that they experienced the event in slow motion or through tunnel vision; experienced feelings that they were the "bad guy" and isolation from colleagues during subsequent investigations, and feelings of disconcertment regarding their own stress reactions (McNally, 1999; Kingshott, 2009; Drylie & Violanti, 2008). Given these responses, as well as the potential consequences and impact of the symptoms described above, debriefing methods ensure optimal functioning and psychological health of law enforcement officers. Other purposes of these methods, in addition to the mechanisms by which such methods are thought to accomplish these goals, are discussed below.

Brown and Campbell (1994) propose that, regardless of the specific model or techniques used, debriefing methods share common goals of establishing mutual support among those affected by critical incidents, providing education to those affected, allowing those affected to express emotional reactions to the traumatic incident, and establishing organizational support for those reactions. Miller (2008) recommends the proactive fostering of mental toughness and resilience as important protective factors in one's response to and recovery from traumatic events. Psychological debriefing, mental health counseling, and psychotherapeutic strategies are used to facilitate resilient recovery from critical incidents and traumatic events.

As research on debriefing has continued, the specific mechanisms by which it accomplishes its goals and purposes have been identified. Researchers have proposed that the opportunity for the victim to gain mastery of the disaster by actively redefining the experience and its consequences (Miller, 2008), and allowing integration of professional personal experiences brought on by the trauma, at both cognitive and emotional levels (Miller, 2008; Pannebaker & Susman, 1988) as possible mechanisms by which debriefing is effective. Debriefing also is effective inasmuch as it allows a formal method by which individuals can process a devastating event and reflect on the impact of the event (Thompson, 2004).

In addition to efforts by experts in the field of critical incident debriefing to identify mechanisms of its effectiveness, some studies have allowed the recipients of debriefings themselves to identify aspects of the intervention which they found most effective and helpful. A 2009 study by Halpern, Gurevich, Schwartz, and Brazeau determined that debriefing represents both an explicit and implicit acknowledgement of traumatic events by supervisors and law enforcement agencies, and those affected feel this is an important component of debriefing. Additionally, such efforts represent an acknowledgement of concern about the well-being of first responders, as well as a willingness to listen to their reactions and concerns, which can be helpful to those involved, as it emphasizes the value placed on the difficult work carried out by these individuals (Halpern *et al.*, 2009). Although experts seem to focus on the more formal and intentional aspects of debriefing, it appears that, in the eyes of the recipients of the intervention, the benefits are much more practical, and may include increased cooperation between agencies, or even the simple acknowledgement by supervisors and agencies of the difficulty of the work that law enforcement officials perform every day.

Although critical incident debriefing resembles traditional counseling, and utilizes techniques developed for use in long-term therapy with trauma survivors, debriefing methods differ from traditional counseling in many important ways. Perhaps the most important distinction is that debriefing is a single psychological crisis intervention, compared to therapy or counseling, which is typically ongoing and consists of multiple sessions (Tehrani & Westlake, 1994). As a crisis intervention, debriefing fosters a temporary dependency on the debriefer in order to foster a return to pre-incident functioning; traditional counseling methods typically discourage such dependency (Thompson, 2004). Further, in contrast to some forms of traditional counseling, debriefing is highly structured, and the debriefer maintains control of the process (Tehrani & Westlake, 1994). Finally, debriefing focuses on providing factual information in detail without allowing participants to be overwhelmed by emotion; in contrast to counselors or therapists, debriefers do not interpret or challenge the meaning of thoughts, feelings, or behavior (Tehrani & Westlake, 1994). In fact, more recent evidence suggests that emotional processing is not an essential component of effective debriefing (Watson, 2004).

The debriefing process

Several models of critical incident debriefing have been developed in the last 30 years and a small sample of these will be described below. These models are derived from the basic premises of crisis intervention in general, which include: *protecting* the safety, privacy, health, self-esteem, and emotional well-being of survivors, as well as those of helping professionals, *directing* individuals by helping them organize, prioritize, and plan, *connecting* individuals with helping professionals as well as with others who have endured the incident, *identifying* those who are at risk for severe problems as a result of the event, *referring* those affected to medical and mental health services, and *assessing* each person's emotional reactions, personal concerns, coping skills, and outlook for the future (Thompson, 2004).

Jeffrey Mitchell, of the Department of Emergency Health Services, University of Maryland, developed one of the most widely-used models of debriefing, the Critical Incident Stress Debriefing model, which is specifically designed for use with emergency response workers (Mitchell, 1988a, Mitchell, 1988b). Mitchell views debriefings as structured group discussions which allow individuals to express reactions to the incident and develop understanding of the event as well as of their own emotions. Mitchell's model begins with an introductory phase, which is designed to increase motivation of participants to involve themselves in the debriefing, and includes a rule setting component (Mitchell, 1988a). The second phase is the *fact* phase, the purpose is to develop a factual description of what actually occurred (Mitchell, 1983). Although emotions are acknowledged if they are spontaneously discussed during this phase, emotional processing is not the focus of this stage (Mitchell, 1983). The *thought* phase requires participants to discuss their thinking patterns during the incident, while the *reaction* phase focuses on participants' emotions (Mitchell, 1983). The *symptoms* phase provides a transition from a focus on participants' emotional reactions to a more cognitively oriented stage in which various trauma-related symptoms are discussed (Mitchell, 1983). In the *teaching* phase, facilitators provide information regarding typical symptoms and coping strategies for stress. This is followed by the *reentry* phase, in which participants are provided an opportunity to ask questions, a summary of the debriefing is provided, and the debriefing is closed (Mitchell, 1983).

The multiple stressor debriefing model was designed by Armstrong, O'Callahan, and Marmar (1991) for use with American Red Cross personnel and is the first model to focus on pretrauma strategies adopted by individuals to deal with stressful situations. The method entails four stages. The first stage focuses on disclosure of the events comprising the incident, while the second stage allows participants to consider feelings and reactions to the incident. In the third stage, coping strategies are discussed, with an emphasis on previous coping skills the individual has used in dealing with stressful events. Finally, in the termination stage, participants discuss what it will be like to leave the disaster, the positive work they have done, and the need to talk to significant others about feelings and experiences (Armstrong *et al.*, 1991).

The Critical Incident Stress Management (CISM) program, developed in 1997 by Everly and Mitchell, is one of the more versatile models, as it may be applied in either an individual or group format, and such groups may be larger than those used in other models, and may even include all members of an impacted community. The seven core components of CISM are described below. Precrisis preparation focuses on stress management education, stress resistance, and crisis mitigation training. Town meetings, community support programs, and informational briefings may be used to disseminate information regarding the incident. Defusing, which is a three-phase, structured small-group discussion, is provided within hours of the crisis, for the purpose of assessment, triage, and acute symptom management. The Mitchell model of critical incident stress debriefing is used beginning one to ten days after the incident to assess need for ongoing intervention, provide support, and mitigate acute symptoms. An individual component of treatment, and/or family crisis intervention or organizational consultation are provided to those assessed as being in need of these services. Finally, the model includes mechanisms to ensure referrals for follow-up care if participants deem it necessary (Everly & Mitchell, 1997).

Does debriefing work?

Recent research has focused on determining the effectiveness of debriefing in general, as well as comparing the effectiveness of various methods of debriefing. Although the results of such studies are mixed, overall, research suggests that debriefing is likely to have either a positive effect or no effect at all, though some studies suggest that debriefing may result in negative outcomes (Bisson *et al.*, 1997; Campfiled & Hills, 2001; Conlon *et al.*, 1999; Dolan *et al.*, 1999; Hobbs *et al.*, 1996; Mayou *et al.*, 2000; Lee *et al.*, 1996; Litz & Adler, 2005; Rose *et al.*, 1999; Sijbrandij *et al.*, 2006; Benner, 1994). To reduce the risk of negative impact caused by debriefing, Watson (2004) recommends that debriefing efforts not focus on emotional processing, and noted that debriefing may be particularly contraindicated in postdisaster settings involving mass trauma due to the chaotic nature of the postincident environment, the need for attention to pragmatic physical or material needs, possible cultural and bereavement issues, and multiple recovery trajectories based on complex variables (Watson, Friedman, Ruzek, & Norris, 2002). Additionally, it has been recommended that debriefing take place between 24 and 72 hours after the incident ends (Mitchell & Everly, 1993; Hodgkinson & Stewart, 1991; Pulley, 2000; Mayou *et al.*, 2000), as debriefings which occur within 24 hours of an incident are often not successful or helpful (Gist & Devilly, 2010), as victims may be too cognitively defended or shocked to discuss their feelings (Mitchell & Everly, 1993). Overall, research suggests debriefings that are the most likely to have positive effects on participants do the following: allow participants to process the factual aspects of the incident, normalize reactions to trauma, provide education regarding additional resources that may be utilized in the future, and occurs after the initial period of shock has dissipated.

The police subculture: barriers to successful implementation of debriefing programs

The culture of law enforcement agencies is often incompatible with mental health care in general and critical incident debriefing in particular. Research has noted that officers face social problems including hostile citizens, poverty, child abuse, violent crime, drug abuse, and gang activity, which may create dilemmas or conflicts among an officer's responsibilities as a public servant, demands of the organization for which the officer works, and their own personal beliefs and values (Kingshott, 2009; Drylie & Violanti, 2008; Goldstein, 1990). As a result of this unique perspective and set of responsibilities, a culture is often created in which officers believe that only other officers, and not mental health professional or other "outsiders," can understand their experiences. Such beliefs are thought to be exacerbated in the time period immediately following a critical incident. Such beliefs, according to Goldstein (1990), are one source of resistance to critical incident debriefing. Additionally, officers often engage in informal debriefing efforts with each other. Following an incident, it is not uncommon for responders to leave duty for anywhere from 30 minutes to an hour. During this time period, responders are often eating a meal or engaging in other activities with colleagues and provide a debriefing of sorts to one another (Halpern *et al.*, 2009). Such practices, particularly in light of the beliefs discussed by Goldstein, produce an environment that is not always receptive to formal debriefing processes led by mental health professionals.

Forensic Psychology and Policy Implications

Critical incident debriefers conduct their work in the aftermath of violent and traumatic incidents, and often are faced with strong emotions, less-than-ideal working conditions, and situations that may continue to threaten the safety and well-being of themselves and those who are being debriefed. As a result of these factors, individuals selected to conduct debriefings should be selected carefully, on the basis of the presence of many factors. Debriefers must be comfortable dealing with intense and raw emotions, should be mentally healthy themselves, should maintain positive and professional interactions with colleagues who also conduct crisis work, must be knowledgeable about community resources for the purpose of making referrals, and must be comfortable engaging in nonverbal actions that lend support to those being debriefed, such as providing tissues or offering hugs (Thompson, 2004). It is also recommended that debriefers possess awareness of their own "triggers" and vulnerable areas, monitor their own reactions, allow themselves to grieve in response to tragedy as well, develop realistic expectations of the rewards and limitations of being a helper, and balance crisis intervention with other professional activities (Thompson, 2004). With regard to training and education, Mitchell (1991) recommends that debriefers possess at least a master's degree in psychology or related field and should receive special training in crisis intervention, stress, post-traumatic stress disorder, and the debriefing process.

Because debriefers may themselves be exposed to aspects of critical incidents and their aftermath which may be traumatic, it is recommended that caregivers be debriefed at the end of their service. Such debriefings should occur shortly after the debriefing team's work is done and before its members disburse. They may be led by the team's leader, though an outside professional may be necessary in situations where exposure lasted a long time or was particularly difficult so that all team members may benefit from the debriefing process (Thompson, 2004).

Critical incident debriefing, when implemented skillfully and in ways which are informed by recent research findings, has been shown to be a powerful and cost-effective means through which agencies can address and prevent negative reactions to critical incidents by law enforcement personnel. Although implementation of such programs often requires additional initial investments of funds and time on the part of agencies that are often already strained with regard to these resources, the cost of implementation may be offset by reductions in absenteeism, turnover, and other negative consequences which may be related to chronic exposure to high stress incidents. Specific recommendations for agencies considering the implementation of a debriefing program are discussed below.

Administrators of law enforcement agencies should recognize that, despite interventions, not all officers will cope positively with a critical incident and that leadership during a crisis may come from "unexpected and nontraditional sources" (Maggio & Terenzi, 1993, p. 15), and should be open to this natural process in the aftermath of a critical incident. To facilitate organizational and individual recovery, agencies should make efforts to ensure that accurate information is disseminated, and that efforts are made to listen to those affected by the incident. Additionally, employees should be provided time alone in order to process the incident, if needed. This should include time away from work duties (Halpern *et al.*, 2009). Agencies should provide education about stigma with regard to mental health treatment and reactions to trauma in order to minimize resistance to crucial debriefings (Halpern *et al.*, 2009). Finally, a process for debriefing the debriefers should be standard operating procedure for any organization implementing a debriefing program (Thompson, 2004).

Suggestions for Future Research

Future research regarding critical incident debriefing should focus on further individualizing the procedures to increase effectiveness while limiting the negative impact on the consumers and providers. Additionally, the impact of the traits of the debriefer on therapeutic outcomes of debriefing should be examined, in addition to the impact of organizational leadership on the successful and effective implementation of debriefing. Further, research efforts should seek to determine the ways in which debriefing may be effectively applied to other professions and populations. Finally, as the number of women in law enforcement increases, future research should seek to identify how women's needs may differ from those of men in the aftermath of a critical incident (Fay, 2000).

Practice Update Section: Adult Issues in Policing

Psychology is inextricably intertwined in the interrogation process. For instance, interrogation strategies for a psychopathic murderer regarding the whereabouts of a victim's body would need to be designed to take into account their narcissism, callousness, and lack of empathy and remorse. Attempting to appeal to their sense of sympathy for the family, or the right of the victim to a decent burial, would be a futile effort. Appealing to their narcissism or implying that their crimes were unimpressive might yield better results in encouraging the accused to divulge details of the crime. A forensic or police psychologist could provide training or serve as a consultant to law enforcement, regarding the most effective strategies for interrogating different personality types or types of psychopathology. While in this type of case, the interrogation process could help lead to justice or closure for a family; however, improper interrogation strategies with the intellectually/developmentally disabled (IDD) can result in injustice for all parties.

Individuals with intellectual/developmental disabilities are, perhaps, the most grossly under-researched group with regard to their interaction with the police and legal system. The potential for rights infringement has been realized over and over again. The recent Supreme Court ruling that prohibits the execution of the IDD (*Atkins v. Virginia*, 2002) can be closely connected to the many injustices these individuals typically confront throughout the criminal justice system. The

American Association of Mental Retardation (2002, p. 13) provides a new definition describing this condition: "Mental retardation is a disability characterized by significant limitations both in intellectual functioning and in adaptive behavior as expressed in conceptual, social, and practical adaptive skills. This disability originates before age 18."

Although everyone is an individual and ability levels differ, research demonstrates that there are certain characteristics and cognitive limitations that are very common among the IDD. For example, these individuals are very susceptible to coerced confessions and are at a higher risk of being incompetent to understand their Miranda warnings. Moreover, IDD citizens are plagued by impulsive behaviors, poor planning and coping skills, and have a tendency to acquiesce in order to please those seen as authority figures (Everington & Keyes, 1999). Leading questions by law enforcement can result in exploitation. Those evaluating or interrogating individuals with intellectual/developmental disabilities should avoid leading questions and "yes or no" queries. Questioning that is sensitive to yes or no responses should be avoided. For example, the same question could be asked in two different ways, requiring a "no" answer in one instance but a "yes" response in another. This line of questioning could then be used to detect a pattern of acquiescence (Appelbaum, 1994). The IDD are particularly motivated to seek approval, especially from those in authority, even if it means giving incorrect or untruthful answers. They are very responsive to disapproval and will feel disempowered or unable to refuse the persistent demands of the officer pressing for a confession. Unable to truly conceptualize the long-term consequences of a confession, true or false, the IDD individual might accept blame from an accuser for their immediate approval, or for their removal from uncomfortable surroundings.

Further complicating the issue is the tendency for persons with intellectual/developmental disability to minimize or deny the severity of their deficits in an attempt to appear normal. An officer who has little knowledge of these issues might dramatically overestimate the intellectual capacities of a suspect. Compared to individuals with average IQs, the IDD have a limited capacity to reason, to consider consequences, and to make effective choices (Baroff, 1996). They have many expressive and receptive language deficits and have difficulty understanding directions or procedures (certainly complex legal rights), rapid speech, complex sentences, and more abstract concepts. The interrogation or interview should be conducted at a level commensurate to the suspect's cognitive level, with simple and concrete vocabulary. Information should be presented slowly, and repetition will likely be necessary. Rather than simply asking an IDD suspect if they understand what you have just read or told them, they should be asked to explain it back in their own words. Hypothetical situations are likely to be too abstract for them to effectively process. In order to facilitate the constitutional protections of the IDD, and to not encourage false/coerced confessions, law enforcement should use mental health consultants who are trained in working with this population. Police departments should expose their officers to the dangers and pitfalls of using standard interrogation techniques with the intellectually/developmentally disabled.

International Issues: Criminal Profiling

In North America, Canada, Australia, the United Kingdom, and Germany prosecutors are introducing profilers and profiles into court as evidence. Many European countries have developed their own approaches to criminal profiling and have established specialized academic research institutions and trained police units, such as the German Bundeskriminalamt, which implemented the first quality standards in 2003 (Meyer, 2002; Daéid, 1997). Austria, Scandinavia, and the United Kingdom also have specialized institutions and trained police units, and Switzerland recently adopted the computerized Violent Crime Linkage Analysis System (ViCLAS), and is now training its own case analysis specialists (Meyer, 2002; Winzenried, 1989; Winzenried, 1992). In Canada, attempts to introduce criminal profiling evidence, in terms of motivation and guilt or identity of the perpetrator, have not been successful (Meyer, 2007). In *R. v. Mohan*, the defense attorney wanted to introduce a psychiatrist's testimony that the profile of a typical offender in cases such as this would exhibit certain abnormal, pedophiliac characteristics, and the accused in the case did not possess these characteristics. The Supreme Court of Canada ruled that "there was no material in the record to support a finding that the profile of a pedophile or psychopath has been standardized to the extent that it could be said that it matched the suggested profile of the offender depicted in the charges" (Mohan, 1994, p. 4). In *R. v. Clark*, the Ontario Court of Appeal ruled that an expert in crime scene analysis could offer opinion evidence about what had occurred at the crime scene and how the crime was committed, but criminal profiling aspects to explain why the crime was committed or who committed the crime was generally inadmissible (Clark, 2004).

In Britain, criminal profilers are typically psychiatrists or psychologists, and they are involved in criminal investigations before trial, but are not usually involved in the pretrial, trial, or the sentencing phases (Gudjonsson & Copson, 1999). The Court of Appeals ruled in *R. v. Guilfoyle* that there was no identifiable way to test the reliability of the expert testimony of Professor David Canter, a psychologist, who had conducted a "psychological autopsy" on the deceased; the autopsy included Professor Canter examining the deceased's diary and post-mortem reports, in which he formed the opinion that the deceased had taken her own life (Guilfoyle, 2001). The Court of Appeals felt that there was no scientific tool to test the reliability and validity of this type of testimony.

In Australia, criminal profiling has had little success in being admissible in court as expert testimony. The Supreme Court of the Australian Capital Territory ruled that criminal profiling may aid the police in narrowing likely suspects but does not "justify a conclusion that its exponents may leap majestically over the limitations of modern psychology and psychiatry and give expert evidence as to the personality and conduct of a particular person," and the ruling continues on to state that a professional opinion is not likely to be formed on a person in which a psychologist or psychiatrist has never met nor seen interviewed (Hillier, 2003).

Dr. Thomas Mueller, a prominent FBI-trained Austrian policeman, who became a psychologist, has made progress in having a criminal profiler be used as an expert witness in a German courtroom. In the case of Roland K., Landgericht Nuernberg-Fuerth (1997), the criminal court, Landgericht, felt that Dr. Mueller's testimony about the offender being a retaliatory rapist and the crime being a sexual homicide was correct, and the court did not examine whether the testimony was scientifically sound or otherwise reliable because the court felt Dr. Mueller's credentials lent enough credibility to his testimony. Due to Dr. Mueller's testimony and the court having just enough circumstantial evidence, the offender was sentenced to 10 years in prison, which was the highest sentence under juvenile criminal law in Germany (Meyer, 2007). Though in another case in which Dr. Mueller testified that the murder of a 9-year-old girl was a mixed sexual homicide in accordance with the Crime Classification Manual from the FBI. Dr. Mueller went on to testify that the murderer had to know the apartment complex where the crime occurred, and that the offender had to have lived in the complex at some point before or during the crime. The Ladgericht was not convinced that these characteristics could not fit another individual, and the testimony did not convince the court whether the defendant had been correctly accused, therefore, the judge stated that he would be less likely to allow such testimony to be admitted in the future (Rueckert, 2004). Switzerland also struggles with the argument of profiling being scientifically supported.

In the Swiss courtrooms, no cases have yet been published in which criminal profiling has been introduced in a court of law (Meyer, 2007). Either the prosecution or the defense is able to bring up the possibility of using profile evidence to the judge, but it is the judge's discretion to evaluate and determine if the evidence will be admissible in court (Hauser, Schweri, & Hartmann, 2005; Webber, 2005). It is unlikely that a Swiss judge would allow the introduction of criminal profilers as expert witnesses because of the lack of success profiling has had in foreign countries' decisions (Hauser, Schweri, & Hartmann, 2005). Profiling is a tool law enforcement uses in order to narrow suspects and to find necessary and acceptable evidence to build a case (Meyer, 2007).

Italy has also recently begun debating the admissibility and utility of criminal profiling as expert testimony. Italy has problems with the perception and the practice of criminal profiling, and Italian law enforcement agencies are skeptical about criminal profiling's use due to perceptions that profiling is often inaccurate (Zappalá & Bosco, 2007). Italy does use criminal profiling in assisting with finding and using evidence to narrow possible offenders in a crime (Kocsis, 2003; Kocsis, 2006). Crime analysts in Italy do have a recognized role, yet these individuals are not necessarily psychologists or psychiatrists, but are often individuals that have a multidisciplinary background with knowledge in criminology and forensic sciences (Zappalá & Bosco, 2007). The United Sections of the Italian Supreme Court ruled in *Franzese* (2002) for the first time that profiling could be held as scientifically reliable and be admissible in court as evidence. The second case in which the United Sections of the Italian Supreme Court ruled in the case of Raso (2005) that "personality disorders that traditionally could not be regarded as the basis for a declaration of partial or total mental illness." Both of these cases deal with the concept of scientific evidence and point to the fact that the Italian judiciary is looking at the standards in which they hold that evidence (Zappalá & Bosco, 2007).

■

Related Websites

www.findlaw.com
Website will guide the reader to important case laws.
http://montgomerycountypolicereporter.com/?p=24706
Website shows video of the shooting in Conroe, Texas.
www.tcleose.tx.org
Training and standards website for police officers.
www.tcleose.tx.org http://www.badgeoflife.com
Police suicide prevention website.
www.passthepolicetest.com
Website offering tips on passing selection process.
www.policechiefmagazine.org
A website addressing issues for police officers.
http://icisf.org
Website of the International Critical Incident Stress Foundation, provides resources and information on recent debriefing efforts for natural and manmade disasters.
www.istss.org/Home.htm
Website of the International Society for Traumatic Stress Studies.

Corrections and Prison Practices

Key Issues

Offender's Right to Refuse Treatment
- Discuss and examine landmark cases that pertain to an offender's right to refuse treatment
- Examine informed consent and how it pertains to an offender's right to refuse treatment
- Explore treatment methods that may or may not be harmful, and how it affects those that are receiving involuntary treatment

Incarcerating and Executing the Mentally Ill
- Review of recent statistics regarding the rates and types of mental illness among incarcerated populations
- The development of specialty courts and other diversion programs to address this issue
- Practical, ethical, and moral issues pertaining to the execution of the mentally ill

Suicide Risk, Screening, and Crisis Intervention for Inmates
- Review of the literature on suicide of individuals who are incarcerated
- The need for correctional institutions to provide adequate mental health screenings, crisis intervention, and treatment in order to prevent suicide

Sex Offender Treatment
- Identify and discuss different treatment modalities for sex offenders
- Analyze the controversy surrounding sex offenses
- In-depth discussion as to the efficacy of sex offender treatment programs

Maintaining Boundaries with an Inmate Population
- Characteristics unique to the correctional/forensic environment which make staff in such settings particularly vulnerable to inmate attempts to violate personal and professional boundaries
- Types of boundary violations which may occur in these settings
- Recent statistics regarding the rates of sexual relationships between staff and inmates
- Methods inmates may use to violate the boundaries of staff
- Consequences of boundary violations
- Characteristics of both staff and inmates who are more likely to engage in boundary violations
- Strategies staff may use in avoiding boundary violations

Prison Violence

- Individual and situational factors contributing to prison violence
- Types of violence in correctional settings and characteristics of perpetrators and victims
- Programs intended to decrease prison violence

CHAPTER 5

Adult Issues in Corrections/ Correctional Psychology

Chapter Outline

Introduction to Forensic Psychology. DOI: 10.1016/B978-0-12-382169-0.00005-0

Overview

The adult prison population presents society with a complex set of issues and controversies requiring thoughtful, manageable, and effective responses. The assorted tools of the psychological sciences and the law are increasingly called upon to make sense out of difficult correctional questions affecting the lives of prisoners and the community of which they are a part. Thus, not only are the skills of the forensic/correctional professional utilized for purposes of evaluating, diagnosing, and treating inmates, they are also employed for purposes of understanding the correctional milieu itself.

This chapter describes a limited number of topics that are of considerable concern for psychologists working in prison settings or responding to matters of confinement for offenders. While certainly other subjects could have been investigated in this chapter, the issues explored represent some of the more controversial matters affecting correctional psychology today. These topics include (1) an offender's right to refuse treatment; (2) incarcerating and executing the mentally ill; (3) suicide, inmate screening, and crisis intervention; (4) sex offender treatment; (5) maintaining boundaries with an inmate population; and (6) prison violence.

The legal system has acknowledged that persons civilly committed for psychiatric treatment have, under specified conditions, the right to refuse medical intervention (see Chapter 3). Is the right to refuse treatment for persons criminally confined any different? What types of involuntary treatments do inmates typically refuse? What constitutional protections exist for offenders exercising their right to refuse treatment? Persons experiencing mental illness can be incarcerated and sentenced to death. What are the constitutional limits to executing the mentally ill? What role does a psychological competency evaluation play in a decision to carry out an execution? What moral and ethical dilemmas do psychologists confront when finding that a person is competent to be put to death? Suicides in jails and prisons occur at a higher rate than in the general population. Are correctional institutions doing enough to prevent potential suicides? Are the lack of institutional policies addressing comprehensive suicide prevention contributing to the suicide attempts and completions of detainees? Could inmate mental health screenings upon admission, treatment, and crisis intervention programs assist the mentally ill inmate and prevent suicides? Some incarcerated individuals are convicted of various sex crimes, including molesting or otherwise violating children. Psychologists with specialized training are relied upon to treat sex offenders. Do sex offender interventions work? Is the treatment beneficial? What impact, if any, does sex offender treatment have on recidivism (i.e., the prisoner's potential for future victimization).

In addition to the important role forensic psychologists assume regarding mentally ill prisoners, they also help determine how best to address related correctional dilemmas. Correctional officers and psychologists must be careful to maintain professional boundaries with inmates, many of whom are very street wise and have nothing but time to exploit their environments for their best interest. How do boundary violations or inappropriate relationships between staff and inmates occur? What professional, ethical, legal, and interpersonal effects can occur from violating rules and boundaries? Violence is a part of prison life. How do substandard correctional conditions impact prison violence? How is institutional life psychologically stressful for inmates? What is the relationship between prison violence and overcrowding?

The domain of adult forensics and corrections moves the psychologist into a more social arena in which to investigate noncriminal behavior, attitudes, beliefs, and so on pertaining to prisoners, correctional personnel, institutional practices, and the public's responses to them. Future investigators would do well to engage in research along these and similar lines of inquiry as it would substantially advance our knowledge of prisoners, correctional workers, and society's understanding of offender behavior. The adult correctional/forensic field is replete with an assortment of controversial issues or topical themes affecting prisoners and the institutions that house them. Psychologists help provide solutions to a number of these more vexing matters. Not only are forensic experts called upon to assess how best to deal with offenders who are mentally ill and in need of some form of therapeutic intervention, they help correctional facilities interpret the overall climate in which institutional problems surface, are resolved, and can be altogether avoided. As the individual sections of this chapter demonstrate, by its very nature there is a profound psychological dimension to any criminal confinement. Thus, well-trained correctional psychologists are sorely needed if the challenges that confront the adult prison population are to be thoughtfully, effectively, and efficiently addressed.

Offender's Right to Refuse Treatment

Introduction

The basic rights provided to citizens under most of the constitutional amendments have been extended to the inmates in our prisons. The source of the right to refuse treatment can be traced to case law beginning in the mid-1970s. During this time period, U.S. civil rights advocates, after successfully arguing for the rights of minorities, turned their attention to psychiatric patients. They argued for a greater recognition of the general rights of involuntary patients and for the specific right of these patients to refuse treatment. Since a voluntary patient cannot be treated against his or her will unless found incompetent to make treatment decisions, they reasoned that an involuntary patient should have a similar right. Since the late 1970s, an increasing number of state courts have recognized this common law principle as the doctrine of "informed consent." The state courts have not been receptive to countering arguments, namely, economic considerations about lowering treatment costs and the need of mentally ill patients to be treated. Involuntary competent patients are allowed the right to refuse treatment because state courts are creating laws that provide them with a review board or court to make treatment decisions in their best interest. In the case of *Sell v. United States* (2003) the Supreme Court addressed the issue of the constitutionality of forcing a "mentally ill criminal defendant" to take psychoactive medications in order to regain competency to stand trial (Bassman, 2005, p. 488). This decision held that the constitution does allow the government to force the administration of psychoactive medications under certain circumstances (i.e., dangerousness, risk of harm to self or others) against the will of the defendant. In the case of Charles Sell, it was found that these circumstances were not met, and Mr. Sell won his right to refuse treatment (Bassman, 2005).

An offender's right to refuse treatment raises significant questions in terms of constitutional law, and ethics (Freedman & Radden, 2006; Jarrett, Bowers, & Simpson, 2008; Arrigo & Tasca, 1999). When treatment is focused on changing the mind of the offender, the right to refuse treatment is based on the First Amendment right to free speech. The cruel and unusual punishment associated with experimental drugs and unstable treatment programs used with inmates has generated the controversial issue of the Right to Refuse Treatment doctrine. Bassman (2005) states, "the freedom to make poor choices is a privilege that is denied to the person who is labeled mentally ill" (p. 491). However, mandating experimental drugs for medical treatment addresses some different issues than court ordered antipsychotic medications. The *Washington v. Harper* (1990) case exemplifies the controversy of mandating antipsychotic medication.

In the case *Washington v. Harper* (1990), a prisoner's right to refuse treatment was in question. The Supreme Court decision considered the right of inmate Harper to refuse antipsychotic medication. The Department of Corrections for the state of Washington maintained a Special Offender Center to diagnose and treat convicted felons who were state prisoners and had serious mental disorders. Under the Washington Special Offender Center's policy, if a prisoner does not agree to treatment with antipsychotic drugs ordered by a psychiatrist, the prisoner is entitled to a hearing before a committee consisting of a psychiatrist, a psychologist, and another prison official, none of whom can be, at the time of the hearing, involved in the prisoner's treatment. Also, the prisoner can be subjected to involuntary treatment with the drugs only if the committee determines that the prisoner suffers from a mental disorder and is gravely disabled or poses serious harm to him- or herself, others, or their property.

Walter Harper had consistently taken antipsychotic medication for 6 years to curb his aggression and to silence voices he was hearing. In 1982, he refused his medication because of its side-effects. In 1988, the Washington Supreme Court agreed with inmate Harper, ruling that antipsychotic drugs could only be given to an involuntary inmate following a court hearing at which time the state was required to show that the medication was both necessary and effective. The Washington Supreme Court held that under the Fourteenth Amendment a state prisoner's interest in avoiding the groundless administration of antipsychotic drugs is not insignificant, since the forcible injection of medication into an unwilling person's body represents an indisputable interference with that person's freedom. Antipsychotic drugs can have serious, even fatal, side-effects, such as a severe involuntary spasm of the upper body, tongue, throat, or eyes; motor restlessness, a condition which can lead to death from cardiac dysfunction; and a neurological disorder characterized by involuntary, uncontrollable movements of various muscles.

The Washington Supreme Court's ruling was reversed and remanded in 1990 when the U.S. Supreme Court decided that the Constitution does not require a court hearing prior to a prisoner being involuntarily medicated. The Court held that the Fourteenth Amendment Due Process Clause permits the state to treat a prison inmate who has a serious mental illness with antipsychotic drugs against his will, if he is dangerous to him- or herself or others, and the treatment is in his medical interest. The Center's policy agreed with due process requirements because it protected others from potentially dangerous mentally ill inmates. The U.S. Supreme Court held that the Center's policy was acceptable because it applied exclusively to potentially dangerous mentally ill inmates who were gravely disabled or posed a threat to others. The Court held that the drugs could be given only for treatment and under the direction of a licensed psychiatrist. Therefore, the Due Process Clause did not require a judicial hearing before the state could treat a mentally ill prisoner with antipsychotic drugs against his or her will.

In the case of *Knecht v. Gillman* (1973), the court questioned the extent to which injections of the drug apormorphine could be used as an unwilling stimulus. The injections were oftentimes administered by a nurse without the presence of a doctor or specific authorization from a doctor. The United States District Court for the Southern District of Iowa, Central Division, dismissed the complaint and Knecht appealed. The Court of Appeals held that administering a drug which induces vomiting to nonconsenting mental institution inmates on the basis of alleged violations of behavioral rules constituted cruel and unusual punishment.

Written consent from the inmate, however, may obviate this situation's unconstitutionality. This applies if the written consent specifies the nature of treatment, purpose, risk, and effects as well as advises the inmate of his or her right to terminate consent at any time. The inmate must also be given the opportunity to cancel consent at any time, and the injection must be authorized by a physician and administered by a physician or nurse. Also, the fact that civil rights statutes do not specify the scope of judicial relief available in actions successfully sustained under them does not preclude federal courts from fashioning an effective equitable remedy.

Literature Review

One way to consider the issue of the right to refuse treatment is to examine the problems occurring with involuntary treatment on inmates. Perlin (2004) recognizes that the right to refuse treatment, and the debates that surround this topic make it one of the most controversial and highly debated issues in forensic psychiatry to date. For example, **behavior modification** centers on changing an offender's actions (Allen & Simonsen, 1989). One type of behavior modification is aversive conditioning for deviant sexual behavior. Territo (1989) indicates that **aversive conditioning** is the reduction or elimination of behavior patterns by associating them with unpleasant stimuli. Although these types of practices are not currently allowed in these settings, historically, nausea-inducing drugs were used extensively in early experiments in aversive conditioning. The drugs were primarily given by injection to induce vomiting during an undesirable behavior. This procedure is very unpleasant and traumatic to the offender. Historically, Territo (1989) also explained that in later experiments electric shock replaced drugs as an aversive stimulus. Some have argued that certain types of behavior modification programs are actually thinly disguised initiatives for furthering institutional objectives at the expense of prisoners.

With this in mind, a patient's right to informed consent is an important focus in the discussion about offender treatment. The doctrine of **informed consent** requires that persons be supplied adequate information concerning treatment prior to consenting. Thus, the individual is able to make a well-informed decision regarding the suggested treatment they may be receiving. Generally, adequate information consists of the risks and benefits of treatment, the potential side-effects, the chance of improvement both with and without the treatment, and any other treatments that may be available. The doctrine applies in a number of situations, including administration of medication, tests, and surgical procedures (Melton *et al.*, 2007). As a result, proponents of behavior modification are now using more sophisticated and humane treatment techniques with inmates. Nevertheless, as a protection, numerous institutional authorities have dropped the term "behavior modification" from the names of their treatment programs, knowing that the term carries negative connotations. A program that applies learning theory with the aim of altering criminal behavior is the **contingency management program**. A contingency is something that may or may not happen and management involves increasing the chances that it will happen. Agnetti (2009) indicates the aim of contingency management in a maximum-security setting is to increase the likelihood of occurrence of certain kinds of desired behaviors by reinforcing the behaviors when they occur. For example, participation in educational or vocational training programs, appropriate pro-social behavior, and prosperous interviewing for jobs are some of the behaviors that have been encouraged and rewarded in contingency management programs. Goodness and Renfro (2002) suggest that significant improvements are visible after **social learning principles** are part of the treatment milieu. In these types of programs, **tangible reinforcers** such as tokens, candy, soft drinks, and snacks can be increased, as well as privileges or access to desired activities such as watching television, making phone calls, exercising, and receiving extra visits from family members.

Another area of great contention is the state's right to involuntarily medicate a criminal defendant for the purpose of restoration of trial competency or to plead guilty (Bassman, 2005; Blackwood & Guyer, 2009; Morse, 2003).

> *When a defendant who has been adjudicated incompetent to stand trial invokes the right to refuse psychiatric treatment, the defendant's interest in being free from unwanted bodily intrusions is in conflict with the government's interest in obtaining an adjudication of the defendant's guilt or innocence in a criminal matter (Bullock, 2002, p. 1).*

While the individual's rights are compelling, researchers maintain that the state does have a right to restore trial competence through medicating the defendant charged with most crimes and that this and other remedies are available to ensure a fair trial (Bassman, 2005; Morse, 2003).

Forensic Psychology and Policy Implications

When an inmate's right to refuse treatment is legally quashed to the point that the prisoner becomes involuntarily medicated, as in the *Washington v. Harper* (1990) case, cruel and unusual punishment may occur. If an inmate is involuntarily medicated and a problem occurs with the medication, then the prisoner would have favorable grounds to initiate a lawsuit against the correctional facility. In other cases, class action litigation has been initiated for inadequate psychiatric or mental health treatment in correctional institutions (Freedman & Radden, 2006). In some cases, careful medication management and monitoring of the severely psychotic inmate can help prevent harm to the inmate or his or her peers, as well as dramatically improve the quality of life for the individual (e.g., reduction of auditory hallucinations, confusion, disorganized speech and thought process). According to Blackwood and Guyer (2009), some jurisdictions prefer the *Harper* decision to that of *Sell* when considering the dangerousness of an offender as a legal basis for forced medications likely due to apprehensiveness about forcing medications for the sole purpose of obtaining competency to stand trial. At the other end of the continuum from the involuntarily medicated inmate are the numerous inmates in correctional settings who are quite creative in their requests for medication or will feign symptoms of mental illness in an effort to obtain psychiatric medications for the mood-altering characteristics. Inmates with a history of substance abuse who are experiencing detoxification are particularly demanding in their pursuit of medication (Carr, Hinkle, & Ingram, 1991). Other inmates will feign symptoms of mental illness to avoid placement in the general population (Freeman & Alaimo, 2001). If an inmate's symptoms, diagnosis, or course of treatment is in question, correctional psychiatrists will frequently refer these inmates for an evaluation by correctional psychologists (e.g., assess for malingering, differential diagnosis).

Public policy makers must create stringent requirements and assurances that it is in the inmate's medical best interest before an inmate is medicated. As mentioned earlier, the *Knecht v. Gillman* (1973) case is one example of involuntary treatment leading to cruel and unusual punishment. Legal standards involving mental health care provisions are among the most composite regulations affecting jails, jail policy, and public policy today. Court decisions regarding the provision of medical care to jail detainees, criminal responsibility for an illegal act, and treatment of the mentally ill in jail play a vital role in legal standards related to the administration of mental health treatment and medication of prisoners. These matters also need to be considered.

Suggestions for Future Research

More research needs to be directed toward implementing safe regulations and procedures regarding inmate treatment administration. For example, a therapist has the ability to exert a high level of control over a prisoner. Experimental methods such as drug therapy and electric shock can change the behavior of an inmate in dramatic and often harmful ways. Unnecessary adverse side-effects may occur when these procedures are administered. The discomfort an offender experiences as a result of being forced to take medications can have an "antitherapeutic" effect that deserves further exploration. The offender may experience a complete loss of autonomy when forced treatment, and if trauma occurs as a result, the negative impact is even more significant (Bernstien, 2008). The potential outcomes of these circumstances warrant further attention in the literature. One example of an unstable and unpredictable treatment procedure is when the prison's needs are placed in priority over the needs of the inmate, and treatment programs are temporarily withheld because of prison activity or disciplinary behaviors. For instance, offenders who violate institutional rules may be placed in solitary confinement for a period of time without intervention. Treatment can be terminated when the needs of the institution are more important, causing the treatment to lose its effect and assist the offender. As a result, inmates lose confidence in the prison's therapeutic programming. In these instances, prisoners do not have faith in the correctional facility's promise to provide effective treatment because it can be discontinued based on the needs and financial status of the institution. The lack of prison industry and the presence of enforced inactivity have led to the development of treatment programs that fill time. The long-term value of such programs is questionable at best, and they are a topic of heated discussion, requiring further research. Unless some highly effective treatment programs are installed and supported by solid evaluation, intervention initiatives will be seriously jeopardized. As a result of failing to improve intervention programs for offenders, future appeals by the offender will not be aimed at the specific actions that brought the person to prison but, rather, will be targeted at the treatment programs themselves. Clearly, more research and testing need to be conducted in order to ensure that prisoners receive safe and effective treatment programs today, and in the future.

Incarcerating and Executing the Mentally Ill

Introduction

On any given day, approximately 1,255,700 mentally ill inmates are incarcerated throughout the United States in: state prisons (705,600 mentally ill inmates), federal prisons (70,200 mentally ill inmates), and local jail (479,900 mentally ill inmates) (James & Glaze, 2006). This number has increased dramatically since the mid-1990s, when approximately 100,000 mentally ill persons were incarcerated in prisons and jails throughout the United States (Penner & Oss, 1996). Strikingly, these data indicate that approximately 56% of state prisoners, 45% of federal prisoners, and 64% of jail inmates have experienced mental health symptoms within the last year (James & Glaze, 2006). The continued deinstitutionalization of state hospitals has led to an influx of mentally ill persons in the jail and prison systems, meaning that as many individuals who were once hospitalized are now incarcerated for their behavior (Raphael & Stoll, 2010; Torrey, Kennard, Eslinger, Lamb, & Pavle, 2010; Baillargeon, Binswanger, Penn, Williams, & Murray, 2009; Stefan & Winick, 2005). Contrary to public opinion, the mentally ill are typically arrested for non-violent offenses, which are directly connected to their not receiving adequate, comprehensive, and preventive mental health care and treatment (Stefan & Winick, 2005). Recent data indicate that the number of mentally ill individuals in prison or jails has exceeded the number of mentally ill individuals found in state and county inpatient psychiatric hospitals (Torrey *et al.*, 2010; Raphael & Stoll, 2010). It is estimated that 4 to 7% of the growth in incarceration rates in this country may be contributed to the effects of deinstitutionalization (Raphael & Stoll, 2010).

Despite the prevalence of mental illness in the criminal justice system, it is not uncommon for the mentally ill to receive little or no treatment during their incarceration. Only 34% of mentally ill state prisoners, 24% of mentally ill federal prisoners, and 17% of mentally ill local jail inmates had received treatment since their incarceration (James & Glaze, 2006). Perhaps even more disturbing is the staggering number of mentally ill individuals on death row. Although it is unconstitutional in the United States to execute a mentally ill person who is unaware of the nature or reason for his or her punishment, such individuals continue to be executed in the United States (Arrigo & Tasca, 1999; Perlin, 2008; Bordenave & Kelly, 2010) and other countries (i.e., Japan) (Kimietowicz, 2009). In addition to the legal issues that are raised by the unconstitutionality of such a practice, a number of psychological issues are raised as well. In order for the court to determine whether a particular mentally ill inmate is fit for execution, a mental health professional must conduct a competency for execution evaluation and provide an expert opinion as to the inmate's understanding of the nature and reason for his or her punishment (Zapf, 2007). Psychologists who conduct such evaluations are often faced with numerous ethical and moral dilemmas due to the literal life-and-death nature of their decision (Zapf, 2007). The following illustration of Monty Delk depicts a recent case involving the execution of a mentally ill person.

In November of 1986, Monty Delk, then 19, answered a newspaper advertisement for a sports car for sale. He phoned the owners and arranged for a meeting to see the car the next morning. While taking the car for a test drive, Delk shot the owner in the head with a sawed-off shotgun and then dumped the body in a ditch, stealing the car and the victim's wallet. The victim's body was discovered later that day. Meanwhile, Delk met a friend and asked the friend to accompany him to New Orleans. Delk and his friend were arrested three days later in Louisiana.

At his trial, Delk's estranged wife testified that Delk often contemplated robbery — murders like the one for which he stood accused, and that he routinely beat her. There is also information suggesting that Delk had confessed to others that he killed a man who disappeared in Florida in March of 1985, and he was considered the prime suspect in that murder until the time of his death. In May of 1988, Delk was convicted of capital murder and sentenced to death. The conviction and sentence were upheld by the Texas Court of Criminal Appeals in April of 1993.

During his incarceration on Texas' death row, Delk exhibited signs of mental illness, including showering without first removing his coveralls or using soap, and smeared himself with his own feces, exhibiting a personal odor so offensive that he had to be segregated from the other inmates so as to avoid making them ill, as well as claiming to be over 129 years old. Additionally, Delk reported having previously been a district judge and a submarine commander, as well as the president of Kenya and a physician who treated other inmates on his unit. He claimed to have been killed 150 times while in prison.

Delk's attorney indicated that he had difficulty communicating with Delk, and that Delk would babble incoherently. The attorney, John Wright, filed a motion claiming that Delk was Incompetent to be Executed. Prosecutors, on the other hand, claimed that Delk was coherent at his trial, and that he showed signs of being clever and manipulative. They cited evidence that Delk was able to remember personal information about correctional staff in order to threaten them, and that he chipped away at the blocks comprising his cell. In 1994, prison psychiatrists diagnosed Delk with malingering, and in 1997 a judge ruled that Delk was volitionally choosing not to communicate with counsel. His remaining appeals were denied, until Wednesday, 27 February 2002, the day before he was scheduled to be executed, when a U.S. District Judge ruled that Delk's mental condition needed to be examined. Texas Attorney General John Cornyn immediately announced that the ruling would be appealed to the 5th U.S. Circuit Court of Appeals the following day.

At approximately 2:00 on 28 February 2002, the Court ruled in favor of the State, and Delk was immediately transported to the Unit housing Texas' execution chamber. Delk's attorney appealed to the U.S. Supreme Court, a request which was denied. One half hour after this decision, Delk was strapped to the gurney and wheeled into the execution chamber. He yelled, "I've got one thing to say, get your Warden off this gurney and shut up! I am from the island of Barbados. I am the Warden of this unit. People are seeing you do this." At 7:47 pm, the warden signaled for the lethal injection to begin. After shouting more profanity, Delk blurted out, "You are not in America. This is the Island of Barbados. People will see you doing this." Delk then abruptly stopped speaking, and his mouth and eyes froze wide open. He was pronounced dead at 7:53 pm.

Literature Review

The case of Monty Delk is not an anomaly. It has been estimated that between 45 and 64% of the incarcerated population are mentally ill (James & Glaze, 2006). Moreover, according to the Bureau of Justice, an estimated 11.8% of state prison inmates, 7.8% of federal prison inmates, and 17.5% of local jail inmates suffer from a psychotic disorder (James & Glaze, 2006). International studies have estimated that between 2 and 40% of the incarcerated population has an **intellectual disability** (i.e., disorders involving limitations in mental functioning and in skills such as communicating, taking care of oneself, and social skills; this category includes diagnoses such as mental retardation) (Jones, 2007). In a study that examined the self-reported histories of psychiatric hospitalizations, 5.4% of state prison inmates, 2.1% of federal prison inmates, and 4.9% of local jail inmates reported being psychiatrically hospitalized in the year preceding their arrest (James & Glaze, 2006).

Butler, Andrews, Allnutt, Sakashita, Smith, and Basson (2006) found that there were markedly elevated prevalence rates for major mental disorders in Australian prisons with a very high comorbidity with substance use disorders, particularly when compared with the rates of these disorders in a community sample. These researchers concluded that the higher rates of mental illness and **comorbidity** (i.e., the simultaneous presence of two or more mental disorders) with substance abuse in the inmate sample demonstrates the need for specialized and more intensive services for these individuals. As depicted in the case illustration, **schizophrenia** is a psychotic disorder which is characterized by a detachment from reality, perceptual distortions, disorganized thoughts, odd or eccentric behavior, and delusional thinking that is often accompanied by paranoia (American Psychiatric Association, 2000). While schizophrenia is a chronic mental illness, it can often be less debilitating and kept somewhat under control when properly treated. However, an early investigation in Los Angeles County jails by the Department of Justice revealed that inmates who suffered from mental disorders such as schizophrenia oftentimes have to wait dangerously long periods of time before medication will be prescribed and frequently the medication will be improperly administered (Sherer, 1998).

With regard to other specific symptoms of mental illness, the high rates of **suicidal ideation** (i.e., thoughts of killing oneself) and **suicidal attempts** (i.e., behaviors which constitute an attempt to end one's life, such as overdosing on medications or other drugs, attempted hangings, etc.) among the incarcerated are of particular concern. Meltzer (2010) noted that 15% of male jail inmates and 25% of female jail inmates had attempted suicide in the 12 months preceding their incarceration, and many of these offenders make suicidal attempts or threats during their incarceration. It is common for inmates with mental illness not to receive proper treatment in jail or prison (Raphael & Stoll, 2010), and for mental illness to remain undetected in this population. Recent evidence from the Los Angeles County jails indicates that these problems have yet to be adequately remedied and may be continuing to worsen (Tiedeman & Ballon, 2009). Indeed, the stressful and inadequate conditions of jails and prisons may exacerbate the deterioration of inmates' mental conditions (Tiedeman & Ballon, 2009). Researchers recommend that the provision of mental health services in prisons should include adequate screening and triage, follow-up evaluations by mental health professionals, crisis intervention services, crisis beds, longer term residential treatment units, outpatient clinic services, inpatient services, and consultation services (Scott, 2010; Cohen & Dvoskin, 1992).

Some authors suggest that society's increasing incarceration of the mentally ill is related to the interactions of mental illness, substance abuse, poverty, unemployment, domestic violence, and contact with the criminal justice system (Henderson, 2007). Acknowledging the relationship between these factors is the recent development of **specialty courts** (i.e., courts designed to address the needs and unique issues pertaining to various classes of offenders, such as veterans, mentally ill offenders, nonviolent drug and alcohol offenders, juvenile courts, family courts, which are presided over by judges with special training and/or interest in a particular area, who develop and tailor specialized dispositions) (Grudzinskas, Clayfield, Roy-Bujnowski, Fisher, & Richardson, 2005). **Mental health courts** are one type of specialty court, in which offenders may be given the option of compliance with community based treatment programs as an alternative to incarceration (Grudzinskas *et al.*, 2005). There is some evidence that these courts can lessen the rates of incarceration of the mentally ill. However, they have been criticized by some who suggest that sentences and treatment mandates do not address the societal issues affecting these problems, but simply postpone the incarceration of the mentally ill until they either fail to comply or until the end of the judicially-mandated treatment period (Litschge & Vaughn, 2009; Grudzinskas *et al.*, 2005). At the end of the mandated treatment period, many will no longer have access to appropriate treatment. Additionally, these courts have been criticized for the often-lacking adversarial component, as this may constitute a violation of the due process rights of defendants in such courts (Grudzinskas *et al.*, 2005). To address these criticisms, Grudzinskas and colleagues (2005) recommend that mental health professionals, as well as attorneys trained in relevant mental health issues, participate in these courts in order to provide informed legal representation and individualized treatment plans, which minimize the likelihood of early treatment termination or non-compliance. According to Litschge and Vaughn (2009), unless the implementation and development of these courts occur in tandem with reform of the public mental health system, the courts will not be successful.

While incarceration of the mentally ill is controversial in and of itself, the issue is further complicated when mentally ill individuals commit capital offenses and face the death penalty. Every state that has a death penalty acknowledges that it is inhumane to execute an individual who is mentally incompetent and has adopted a law prohibiting such executions from occurring (Zapf, 2007; Melton, Petrila, Poythress, Slobogin, 2007). In the landmark case of *Ford v. Wainwright* (1986), the United States Supreme Court ruled that it was unconstitutional to execute a mentally ill death row inmate who did not understand the nature and reason for his execution. Despite such prohibitions, executions of the mentally ill continue to occur (see, e.g., Perlin, 2008; Bordenave & Kelly, 2010; Kmietowicz, 2009). In addition to the unconstitutionality of executing mentally ill inmates, there are a number of psychological issues that are raised as well. If a death row prisoner's mental stability is questioned prior to his or her execution, a psychologist or other mental health professional (e.g., psychiatrist) is called upon to conduct a competency-for-execution evaluation. Such an evaluation is requested in order to assist the court in determining whether the inmate has a mental illness that prevents him or her from understanding that he or she is going to be executed and the reason why (Melton *et al.*, 2007).

Research on the effects of long-term incarceration in supermax or solitary confinement environments (e.g., death rows) has demonstrated that deterioration of psychological functioning often occurs (Grassian & Friedman, 1986; Haney, 2003, 2006; Jackson, 2001; Arrigo & Bullock, 2008), and previously healthy individuals are not immune from such effects (Arrigo & Bullock, 2008). Such findings explain in part how an inmate who has endured a capital trial and sentencing phase, while maintaining competency, can become incompetent prior to the carrying out of their death sentence. Symptoms of long-term confinement in extremely restrictive conditions may include depression, difficulty in controlling impulses, psychosis, suicidal behavior, and self-mutilation (Haney, 2006). Although there is some research suggesting that long-term solitary confinement does not have the detrimental psychological effects described above, Arrigo and Bullock (2008) have noted that such studies were not adequately reflective of the conditions of secure isolation in this country.

There is oftentimes a great deal of skepticism associated with the reliability of psychologists' clinical diagnoses of mental illness. This skepticism has particular implications for the issue of competency for execution, which is already steeped in controversy. For example, in *Ford v. Wainwright* (1986), although three separate evaluators found Ford to be competent for execution, they all found him to be suffering from some sort of mental illness; yet, they could not agree on his diagnosis (Winick, 1992). This illustrates the fact that it is necessary but not sufficient for a death-row inmate to have a mental disorder to be found incompetent for execution. Examination of case law shows that neither mental illness (*Ford v. Wainwright*, 1986; *Garrett v. Collins*, 1992) nor mental retardation (*Penry v. Lynaugh*, 1989) in and of itself renders a person incompetent for execution. In a 2007 decision (*Panetti v. Quarterman*), the United States Supreme Court ruled that criminal defendants sentenced to death may not be executed if they do not understand the reason for their imminent execution, and that once an execution date has been set, the issue of competency to be executed may be raised, reaffirming the previous ruling in *Ford v. Wainwright*. Conducting competency-for-execution evaluations frequently poses a number of moral and ethical issues for psychologists. Melton *et al.* (2007) and others (see, e.g., Zapf, 2007) caution psychologists to examine whether their own belief systems would interfere with their objective assessment of an individual's competency for execution. Often, psychologists conducting such evaluations find themselves in a difficult position, given that their expert opinion can lead directly to an individual's execution. Moreover, if a psychologist finds a death-row inmate incompetent for execution, the individual's life is not automatically spared. In fact, in the years following the *Ford* decision, available literature suggests there have been only four cases in this country where a death-row inmate was found incompetent for execution (Radelet & Miller, 1992; Sisak, 2011; Levin, 2006). While it is possible there have been more, the numbers are clearly very small (Levin, 2006). In one such case, *Singleton v. State* (1991), the Court ruled of Singleton's incompetence.

On 10 February 2003, with a majority of six to four and one abstention, the federal appeals court in Saint Louis, Missouri, ruled that Charles Laverner Singleton, on death row since 1979 for the murder of a grocery store clerk, could be involuntarily administered antipsychotic medication to restore his competence for execution (Lancet, 2003). Mr. Singleton's mental health deteriorated in 1987, when he began manifesting delusions that his cell was inhabited by demons. He was diagnosed with schizophrenia and initially took medications voluntarily but was later compelled to take them based on the notion that he posed a danger to self and/or others. A habeas corpus petition was filed in 1999/2000, after his execution date had been set, challenging the constitutionality of competency restoration through involuntary medication for the purpose of execution (Lancet, 2003). His petition was denied but he was granted a stay of execution on appeal. During this decision, the court found that the antipsychotic medication was administered for the protection of the inmate and other inmates, rather than for restoration of competency (Heath, 2000). Lancet (2003, p. 621) identifies the *Singleton* case decision in 2003 as the first at the federal level to examine the question of treatment for the goal to make competent for execution and notes that in a dissenting opinion a Justice commented that "the medical community was being forced to practice in a manner contrary to its ethical standards."

In the second case of its kind, Gary Alvord was found incompetent for execution and, as of September, 2011, remains on death row. This case illustrates a second issue that is difficult for many psychologists who encounter death-row prisoners while working in the forensic arena. As in the case of Gary Alvord, if an inmate is found incompetent, he or she is sent to a state mental hospital to be restored to competency. Thus, the primary responsibility of a psychologist rendering treatment to a death-row inmate is to restore the inmate to competency so that the state can execute him or her. As might be expected, the psychologist often has ambiguous feelings about providing treatment under such circumstances. Similarly, individuals within the field of psychology have mixed feelings about the appropriateness of psychologists' involvement in capital cases. Brodsky, Zapf, and Boccaccini (2005) state that the decision to participate in a capital case at any stage of the process is a complex one and should be made with multiple factors in mind, on a case-by-case basis. These authors provide a decision tree to assist clinicians in this complicated and ethically tenuous process.

One such argument among those who believe that psychologists and psychiatrists should not treat those found incompetent to be executed pertains to weighing the costs and benefits of treatment. Opponents of such intervention believe that it is more detrimental to restore a death-row inmate to competency, since the result will be execution, than it is to withhold treatment from that individual (Heilbrun, Radelet, & Dvoskin, 1992). Second, those opposed to treating individuals found incompetent for execution acknowledge the potential adverse effects that such treatment could have on the clinician when he or she knows that rendering their services may result in the death of another human being (Heilbrun *et al.*, 1992). Ultimately, psychologists who choose to work in forensic and/or correctional settings must be mindful of the laws that pertain to the provision of psychological services in those contexts. If he or she feels either unwilling due to ethical concerns or unable due to lacking appropriate training to work in those settings, accepting a position at a correctional institution that houses death-row inmates would be ill advised.

Kimber (2005) recommends that states institute a "wait and see" approach, whereby the inmate's execution is stayed upon a finding of incompetence, and until the inmate no longer requires medication or treatment to maintain his or her competency to be executed, thereby eliminating or reducing the ethical dilemmas inherent in the involvement of mental health professionals in an execution or any related process. However, this isn't likely to be practical when many such instances are likely to necessitate medication or treatment to improve, particularly since the environmental conditions would go unchanged. Heilbrun (2005) offered an even more conservative recommendation, suggesting that death sentences should be automatically commuted upon a finding of incompetence.

Slobogin (2000, p. 667) identified three reasons why death sentences should never or rarely be imposed on individuals with mental illness: (1) execution of the mentally ill "violates equal protection of the law in those states that prohibit the execution of children (all states), or people with mental retardation" (now all states); (2) the majority of death sentences forced on the mentally ill are deprivations of life without due process of law, as a result of capital sentencing juries typically treating mental illness as an aggravating rather than a mitigating factor; and finally (3) even if the death sentence is valid, the Eighth Amendment will usually prevent the sentence being carried out because the sentenced mentally ill are incompetent under the *Ford* standard, or are made competent solely because of the unconstitutional administration of forced medication. The official text (passed 23—24 October 2000) of the American Psychiatric Association Board of Trustees (cited in Fava, 2001, p. 168) states:

> *The American Psychiatric Association endorsed the moratorium on capital punishment in the United States until jurisdiction seeking to reform the death penalty implement policies and procedures to assure that capital punishment, if used at all is administered fairly and impartially in accord with the basic requirements of due process.*

On the other hand, those who support treating incompetent death-row inmates believe that everyone has the right to receive psychiatric and psychological treatment if they so desire. However, this begs the question: Are incompetent individuals capable of providing informed consent (Kimber, 2005; McDonnell & Phillips, 2010)? For example, suspected or documented mental retardation is commonly used as a reason for examining a death-row inmate's competency for execution. In this country prior to 1998, 33 individuals with mental retardation have been executed, including those with the cognitive functioning of a 7-year-old child (Keyes, Edwards, & Perske, 1998). However, the 2002 *Atkins v. Virginia* decision has now rendered executing the mentally retarded unconstitutional. Lancet (2003) maintains that if cases such as *Singleton*'s proceed to the Supreme Court, the Court has an opportunity to build on the *Atkins* decision in protection of the mentally ill. Those in support of treating the incompetent argue that refusing to provide such treatment is nothing more than a protest against the death penalty, and although the principle of doing no harm applies in nonforensic settings, it is not as applicable to forensic treatment settings (Heilbrun *et al.*, 1992; McDonnell & Phillips, 2010).

One final issue that is raised in the controversy over treating mentally incompetent death-row inmates pertains to medication. As in the case of Monty Delk, a psychotic disorder such as schizophrenia is a common mental illness for which a competency-for-execution evaluation may be requested. Psychotic disorders are most commonly treated by some form of psychotropic medication. Therefore, death-row inmates who have been found incompetent for execution may be sent to a state mental hospital to be restored to competency through the administration of antipsychotic medication or be treated by correctional/forensic psychiatrist at the correctional institution. A problem that arises in cases such as these is the fact that individuals have the right to refuse treatment, including medication (*Washington v. Harper*, 1990). However, the United States Supreme Court in *Perry v. Louisiana* (1990) failed to resolve whether a death-row inmate possesses the right to refuse treatment (Winick, 1992), and the controversies regarding whether death-row inmates can refuse treatment continue to this day (see, e.g., Michelson, 2006; Cantor, 2005; Lerman, 2006; Entzeroth, 2008; Williams, 2006; Rolon & Jones, 2008).

Forensic Psychology and Policy Implications

There are a number of policy implications for the fields of criminal justice and mental health pertaining to the incarceration and execution of the mentally ill. There was a time in this country when mentally ill individuals were primarily housed in state mental hospitals (Raphael & Stoll, 2010). However, the deinstitutionalization of the mentally ill has in reality reinstitutionalized such individuals in the local jails and state prisons. Mentally ill persons who are homeless or who have been previously hospitalized are particularly vulnerable to subsequent incarceration (Henderson, 2007; Raphael & Stoll, 2010). Perhaps it is society's lack of appropriate means for caring for the mentally ill that leads to the incarceration of such individuals. Policy reform would do well to introduce alternative services to the mentally ill that would ensure that they received the proper treatment needed in order for them to function appropriately in society.

However, recent research has indicated that, although deinstitutionalization accounts for some of the increase in the incarceration of the mentally ill, it is not "the smoking gun behind the tremendous growth in incarceration rates" (Raphael & Stoll, 2010, p. 38). Rather, it has been noted that "shifts in sentencing policy occurring within most states" are also to blame for the increase in incarceration rates in general, as well as specifically with regard to the mentally ill (Raphael & Stoll, 2010, p. 38). In order to curb these disturbing trends, prevention efforts and reform in the treatment and placement of the incarcerated mentally ill is recommended. According to Raphael and Stoll (2010, p. 39), "the regimented, often predatory, environment common in U.S. prisons are not ideal setting[s] for treating mental illness. It is likely the case that the mentally ill are at elevated risk for assault and victimization while incarcerated, and likely receive insufficient mental health services." Such discrepancies and policies should be addressed by lawmakers.

According to Canton (2008), the once widely-held and simplistic view that **diversion techniques** (i.e., programs that attempt to intervene with the mentally ill early, prior to their becoming involved in the justice system via treatment and other efforts) alone will curtail this increasing problem is now considered outdated. Rather, Canton (2008) believes that these programs will be most effective when questions are asked and reassessed throughout the referral and diversion process to include the following: (1) What is it about this individual that seems to warrant referral to a diversion program based in mental health treatment? (2) Who is the best person to refer to? (3) Is the need for referral imminent, or can it wait until, for example, the prisoner is released? (4) Where could the assessment take place (e.g., outpatient, inpatient, correctional facility); and (5) what is the purpose or the desired outcome of making the referral (Canton, 2008)? Diversion and other prevention efforts might also do well to implement components specifically addressing issues compounded by poverty that may lead to criminal behavior. These factors may be particularly relevant for work with minorities, who are over-represented among the mentally ill and incarcerated populations (Hatcher, 2010; Henderson, 2007).

There is recent evidence that mentally ill offenders are quite able and willing to identify markers by which they will judge their own success post-release (Hatcher, 2010). This information should be incorporated on both the individual and societal level in order to ensure that society's needs are met and the public protected. In addition, this will ensure that issues important to offenders are addressed via diversion and other intervention programs, and ultimately increase the chances of successful integration into the community (Hatcher, 2010). Non-governmental agencies may be particularly adept at providing these services, as they are "often less constrained by institutional and political influences, are more flexible and able to react swiftly to changing social conditions" (Henderson, 2007, p. 77). Finally, programming should be developed to assist intellectually disabled offenders, as these offenders may typically be rejected by programs aimed at other types of mental illness (Jones, 2007). Historically, even programs designed for the intellectually disabled would exclude those with criminal histories.

Execution of the mentally ill holds significant implications for both the criminal justice and mental health systems. From a legal standpoint, the ruling of *Ford v. Wainwright* (1986) perhaps raised more questions than it answered. There is a lack of specificity in defining several issues which cross the divide between psychology and the law. For example, although an individual must have a mental illness in order to be rendered incompetent, the Court has yet to specify which mental illnesses or conditions (with the exception of mental retardation) can be used to exempt an individual from execution. As illustrated by several cases, this results in psychologists diagnosing death-row inmates as mentally ill, while still rendering them competent for execution.

Given the deleterious effects that long-term placement in solitary confinement may have on an offender's mental health, the following recommendations are offered regarding the secure housing of inmates (e.g., condemned inmates): (1) staff abuses of inmates in these units should be strictly prohibited and deterrent efforts, such as training and punitive measures for staff who violate these procedures, should be implemented; (2) the physical environment should be humane (e.g., clean, well-ventilated, exposed to natural light), and offenders should have control of the artificial lighting in their cells and access to personal belongings (e.g., reading material and space for exercise); (3) offenders should be afforded opportunities for normal and ongoing social interaction (e.g., when dining, exercising, participating in educational programming or religious services, as well as appropriately secure visits with family members); and (4) the duration of such conferment should be limited, and should never be indefinite (Arrigo & Bullock, 2008).

Finally, the Court has not yet ruled on the appropriate protocol to follow when psychologists disagree in their expert opinions regarding an inmate's competency for execution, presenting unique challenges to the judiciary. This area of practice is already wrought with ethical and moral dilemmas for psychologists and mental health professionals. Although professional agencies typically prohibit involvement in an execution, the behaviors which constitute such involvement are not readily agreed upon by experts. Guidance from lawmakers, licensing boards, and professional agencies could assist in clarifying these issues for practitioners. Finally, with so few cases in which death-row prisoners were found incompetent for execution, clear guidelines have not yet been established in terms of what to do with those deemed incompetent.

Suggestions for Future Research

There are a number of areas which need further exploration regarding the incarceration and execution of the mentally ill. Research is needed that compares mentally ill offenders who have been hospitalized with those who have been incarcerated in terms of their psychological symptomatology, as well as their risk to the community upon release. Such research would assist in understanding which environment provides the most benefit to the individual as well as to society. Additionally, research to determine the cost-effectiveness of preventive outpatient or residential mental health treatment as compared to the costs incurred following the incarceration of a mentally ill individual should be conducted. Such information could assist the development of laws and policies that will both provide proper care and treatment for those with mental illness and subsequently divert some of those at risk from a costly life of crime and incarceration. Such efforts should also continue to examine the effectiveness of mental health courts (Litschge & Vaughn, 2009).

Future research should also examine "feasible and humane alternatives to the use of segregated housing as a prison management tool," as well as developing and investigating the effectiveness of treatment programs for high-risk or difficult offenders who also have psychiatric illnesses (Arrigo & Bullock, 2008, p. 637). The effectiveness and impact of the policies and procedures of correctional institutions pertaining to the handling and management of mentally ill inmates should also be the subject of future empirical scrutiny (Clements, Althouse, Ax, Magaletta, Fagan, & Wormith, 2007).

Research that assesses the reliability of psychologists' expert opinions on death penalty cases would provide valuable information to the courts in determining the weight that should be given to such testimony. Moreover, it would be helpful to both the criminal justice and the mental health fields to have research available that identifies those factors, which account for the discrepancies among psychologists' opinions in capital cases. Finally, research could contribute significantly to operationalizing some of the legal terminology so that the legal standards could be appropriately applied to the practice of conducting competency-for-execution evaluations.

Suicide Risk, Screening, and Crisis Intervention for Inmates

Introduction

Jail and prison suicides continue despite the fact that many are both foreseeable and preventable (Knoll, 2010; Welch & Gunther, 1997). As prisons and jails keep filling up with the mentally ill, many correctional institutions still fail to implement proactive policies or programs for suicide prevention (Ax, Fagan, Magaletta, Morgan, Nussbaum, & White, 2007; Knoll, 2010; Vaughan & Stevenson, 2002). Growing litigation is compelling correctional institutions to provide adequate mental health screenings, **crisis intervention** (e.g., methods used to offer immediate, short-term help to individuals experiencing acute critical situations), and treatment for the prevention of suicide. Mental health care staff should be well trained because suicide risk assessments are a continuous and dynamic process (Daniel, 2006). Knoll (2010, p.1) states that "failing to adequately assess a patient's suicide risk deprives the clinician of the ability to identify, treat, and manage suicide risk." Welch and Gunther (1997, p. 229) maintain that "insufficient staff, maintaining inadequate training and supervision, deficient jail conditions, lack of written rules and procedures to screen and monitor potentially suicidal detainees, and overcrowding" are all factors involved in many jail suicides and subsequent litigation. Jails and prisons are filled with high-risk individuals to include those who abuse substances, the mentally ill, the indigent, young adults, and those facing a major life stressor.

In order to prevent suicide in our correctional systems, prevention and intervention programs are necessary. Once identified, special housing needs, mental health treatment, and increased supervision can be implemented for those inmates at risk of harming themselves. However, without proper identification, no preventive measures can be put into practice. Sometimes, even if properly screened, an inmate will deny a history of mental illness or current symptoms, or perhaps symptoms of mental illness were not manifesting at that time. The need for crisis intervention services in corrections is undeniable and is a major job duty for forensic/correctional psychologists. The case of Mr. M illustrates the importance of screening incoming inmates for mental health services and potential for suicide (Freeman & Alaimo, 2001, pp. 449–450).

Mr. M, a 26-year-old African American man charged with first-degree murder, had been jailed three times previously on drug charges. During intake, he was interviewed by a mental health specialist with a bachelor's degree who administered a primary mental health screening instrument. This questionnaire addresses various aspects of psychiatric history, drug and alcohol use, suicide history, and current risk of suicidal behavior, homicidal behavior, or both.

Mr. M reported no history of psychiatric treatment, but admitted to smoking upward of $150 of crack cocaine per day for the past 2 years. He also denied any history of suicide attempts and suicidal or homicidal ideation at intake. On closer questioning, the mental health specialist elicited that Mr. M was charged with murdering his mother. He spoke softly, appeared disheveled, and tears welled up in his eyes several times during the brief interview. Later he became mute and refused to answer further questions.

The mental health specialist conducted a secondary interview immediately. The secondary interview determined whether Mr. M should be referred for admission to the acute care psychiatric unit. A more in-depth assessment, the secondary interview includes questions about mental status and background information designed to both elicit risk factors for suicide and detect mental instability. Although Mr. M was unresponsive to secondary interview he was referred for admission to the acute care psychiatric unit based on his despondent behavior and the fact he was charged with murdering his mother. He also was considered high risk because of possible depression related to cocaine withdrawal. His disheveled appearance suggested possible underlying mental illness, an unstable living situation, and possible cognitive impairments related to substance withdrawal. These factors increase concerns about suicidal behavior.

Literature Review

The rate of suicides of incarcerated individuals is 47 deaths per 100,000 suicide attempts (Mumola, 2005), while in the general public the suicide rate is 11 deaths per 100,000 suicide attempts (American Association of Suicidology [AAS], 2006). According to Daniel (2006), the actual suicide rate of incarcerated individuals is unclear due to the under-reporting of suicides in correctional settings. This national study of jail suicides also found that most jails did not screen for suicide risk or mental illness and many individuals who completed suicide had been placed in isolation and killed themselves within 24 hours of their incarceration. The most common method of suicide was hanging (Hayes, 1989; Wortzel, Binswanger, Anderson, & Adler, 2009). While death by suicide is approximately the tenth leading cause of death in the overall population, it is a leading cause of death in correctional institutions (Baillargeon, Penn, Thomas, Temple, Baillargeon, & Murray, 2009; Cox & Morschauser, 1997). The suicide rates in Texas county jails from 2006 through 2007 averaged 18 suicides per 100,000 inmates (Baillargeon *et al.*, 2009). The highest rates were found in 1984 with 151 suicides per 100,000 inmates (Texas Commission on Jail Standards, 1996).

Most correctional institutions are ill equipped to identify and treat the numerous mentally ill offenders that are admitted daily. Some individuals with no prior history of mental illness also commit suicide soon after incarceration. Though an inmate may not have a history of suicidal ideation or thoughts, risk is still present because suicide is an impulsive behavior (Knoll, 2010). Often the suicide attempt or completion was precipitated by other factors such as intoxication and the shame or humiliation of being arrested for a crime. Durand, Curtiss, Burtka *et al.* (1995) indicate that factors such as intoxication, a history of depression or suicide attempts, and having been charged with murder or manslaughter are associated with high risk of suicide. As previously mentioned, the first 24 hours are the most related to the commission of suicide in a jail but suicide can be related to a variety of other factors. Freeman and Alaimo (2001) contend that the literature on jail suicides suggests that a number of combinations of situational factors, inmate adjustment and coping factors, and environmental or conditions of confinement are responsible for suicidal behavior. While there are often a number of precipitating factors, many researchers agree that incarceration itself is often traumatic and related to suicide (Knoll, 2010; Freeman & Alaimo, 2001; Hayes, 1998).

Two of the most salient factors for inmate suicide are the jail conditions and a personal crisis situation the detainee is facing (Knoll, 2010; Hayes, 1989). The factors related to conditions inherent in the jail include shame of incarceration, separation or isolation from family and friends, fear and distrust of their surroundings, a lack of control of the future, and the degrading features of the confinement. Other factors include inmate-to-inmate conflict and recent disciplinary action (Way, Miraglia, Sawyer, Beer, & Eddy, 2005). Researchers identify crisis situation factors that predispose inmates to suicide to include: excessive drinking and/or using drugs, severe shame over the conduct resulting in arrest, a recent loss, active mental illness, a history of past suicidal ideation or attempts, and an upcoming court date (Knoll, 2010; Hayes, 1989; Way *et al.*, 2005). Also, the stress (i.e., being separated from or finalizing a divorce) on relationships with significant others on the outside is also a contributing factor, enough so that the inmate has suicidal thoughts or attempts suicide (Way *et al.*, 2005). The individuals may have already been facing a crisis or may be experiencing a mental illness that contributed to the commission of the crime prior to being incarcerated.

Inmate suicide can also be explored by examining a detainee's vulnerability to stress (Bonner, 1992). A detainee may have lacked the capacity to cope with the stresses of incarceration or may have lost their capacity once confined. Once they have encountered more than they can bear, the result might be suicidal ideation, behavior, or completion. In addition to having difficulty coping with the immediate shock of incarceration, over time the stress may be exacerbated by victimization or conflicts within the institution, loss of relationships, continuing legal difficulties, and increasingly unstable emotions.

The Federal Bureau of Prisons (FBOP) has developed a standard protocol for suicide prevention that incorporates standards set by the American Correctional Association (Federal Bureau of Prisons, 2007). This program focuses on training staff, identification of inmates that are suicidal, as well as the referral, assessment, and intervention in the prevention of suicide. The FBOP has also utilized the Inmate Observer Program that trains inmates to provide constant observation for other inmates that are placed on suicide watch (Junker, Beeler, & Bates, 2005). This program is intended to provide peer support, provide a safe place where the inmate with suicidal ideation is able to talk to someone that is not in a position of authority, to reduce the opportunity for staff manipulation in some cases, and to give opportunities for the inmate observer to model healthy coping skills for an inmate on suicide watch (Junker *et al.*, 2005). This program has shown to reduce the number of hours that an inmate is placed on suicide watch compared to the number of hours when an inmate is being observed by staff (Junker *et al.*, 2005).

Welch and Gunther (1997) conducted a study to determine the areas of institutional policy and customs that were the most problematic with relation to jail suicide. Out of 77 cases examined, 52% cited inadequate training and supervision as the institutional problem most significantly related to suicide; 22% cited lack of policies and procedures for screening and monitoring potentially suicidal inmates; 21% specifically cited deficient jail conditions; 5% cited insufficient staff; and none of the cases cited overcrowding. Deficient jail conditions not only refers to placing suicidal inmates in isolation cells but also refers to physical characteristics of the institutions' architecture and design, particularly in the cells, that facilitate suicide, for example "an exposed light fixture (*Silva v. State; Thomas v. Benton County, Ark.*), a ceiling grate (*Natriello v. Flynn*), and a shower curtain rod (*Vega v. Parsley*)" (Welch & Gunther, 1997, p. 235). *Cabrales v. County of Los Angeles* specifically cited insufficient staff in the suit, whereas *Buffington v. Baltimore County* highlights the importance of not ignoring behavioral and psychological indicators (e.g., substance intoxication, severe depression, self-destructive behavior, delusional ideation) of suicide risk. Consider the following (p. 236):

In *Cabrales v. County of Los Angeles* (1989), for example, the decedent was examined by the institution's psychiatrists following a suicide attempt. The psychiatrist, however, concluded that the suicide attempt was merely a "gesture" to manipulate the staff. The decedent was no longer ruled a suicide risk and returned to the general population, where he committed suicide several days later. The plaintiff alleged that the institution deprived that decedent of adequate mental health services and supervision.

The jury found the jail commander and county liable because medical understaffing prevented psychiatrists from providing adequate assessments.

...As mentioned in *Buffington v. Baltimore County* (1990), the decedent, with a long history of depression and substance abuse, was arrested and placed in protective custody after leaving a suicide note and departing his home with several rifles and handguns. During the booking, the decedent admitted to the officer that he was planning to commit suicide. The decedent was placed in an isolation cell where he hanged himself by his trousers. Two officers were found liable for suicide.

Although suicides while in confinement should never happen, in reality they are a fairly rare event. Staff inaction to prevent suicide could result from a lack of training or in other cases the perception that some inmates are manipulative and are only "**gesturing**" without real intent to harm themselves (Welch & Gunther, 1997, p. 240). They may view **parasuicidal behaviors** or suicidal gestures/self-harming such as cutting and head banging without intent to kill themselves as attempts to get sympathy or attention. However, researchers stress the importance that these incidents should also be taken seriously because these actions can also lead to death. "Current research on suicidal gestures and attempts within the correctional setting is replete with evidence to view *all* threats of self-injury as potentially suicidal behavior" (NCIA, 1992, cited in Welch & Gunther, 1997, p. 240). Dear, Thomson, and Hills (2000, p. 160) found that "Prison staff cannot assume that prisoners who appear manipulative or report manipulative motives were not suicidal at the time of self-harming." Between 1999 and 2004 in the California Department of Corrections and Rehabilitation, 38% of 154 completed suicides had been determined to not be in need of mental health treatment by staff (Patterson & Hughes, 2008).

Having a central intake and screening program can help correctional staff classify detainees for housing and appropriate mental health services (Knoll, 2010; Way *et al.*, 2005; Snow & Briar, 1990). These researchers indicated that despite considerable research on risk factors associated with suicide, particularly for detainees, many jails do not have detoxification and mental health units. This can only serve to increase the risk for substance abusers suffering through withdrawal and suicidal ideation. Those with mental illness are misunderstood and their treatment needs often go unmet.

> *Environmental and service deficits accelerate the disorientation and decompensation of such inmates and result in unmeasurable human costs for the victim and severe management problems for the jail… In short, the mentally ill are not prepared to cope with jail life and jails are not prepared to cope with the mentally ill. Punishing their bizarre behavior with segregation or suspended privileges only increases their fear and suspicion. Suicide is one result (Snow & Blair, 1990, p. 154).*

Cohen and Dvoskin (1992) recommend that the delivery of mental health services in prisons should include screening and triage, follow-up evaluations, crisis intervention services, crisis beds, longer term residential treatment units, and outpatient clinic services (general population but with psychotropic medications, individuals and group therapy, and case management). Prisons must be able to screen incoming inmates to identify those who might need mental health treatment, suicide precautions, and/or special housing. Nonmental health staff to include nurses and correctional officers often conduct first level screenings. However, there should be a very low threshold for referral to a trained mental health professional (Masters or Doctoral level) for a follow-up evaluation. Additionally, crisis intervention services should be available for all inmates, not only those classified as mentally ill. Crisis intervention should be timely and adequate to prevent escalation of violence to self or others, as well to prevent further decompensation into more serious mental illness (Knoll, 2010; Way *et al.*, 2005; Cohen & Dvoskin, 1992).

There is a new approach in assessing suicidal ideation, planning, behaviors, desire, and intent in the Chronological Assessment of Suicide Events (CASE) (Knoll, 2010). Information gathered from this assessment is then used to evaluate risk and protective factors to determine the probability of suicide risk. This approach uses "**interviewing validity techniques**" that can increase the chance of obtaining accurate and reliable information (Knoll, 2010, p. 5). Supplemental tools such as the Beck Depression Inventory, the Beck Hopelessness Scale, or the Scale for Suicidal Ideations can be used as well (Knoll, 2010). Training for this method would be through macrotraining, or serial role playing (Shea & Barney, 2007). More information can be found in J. Knolls' (2010) article *Suicide in Correctional Settings: Assessment, Prevention, and Professional Liability* in the Journal of Correctional Health Care.

Forensic Psychology and Policy Implications

The lack of appropriate community mental health or other social service programs for persons with disabilities often contributes to the criminalization of the mentally ill, leaving jails and prisons to fill the gap in custodial care and services (Daniel, 2006; Vaughan & Stevenson, 2002; Snow & Briar, 1990). Class action litigation have obvious implications for correctional institution reform and proactive measures to prevent and reduce the risk of jail suicide. Researchers contend that important changes must be made in institutional policies affecting inadequate training and supervision, deficient jail conditions, the lack of adequate mental health screenings, treatment, and crisis intervention, as well as insufficient staff, particularly mental health professionals (Welch & Gunther, 1997; Knoll, 2010).

Consent decrees are another form of litigation where the court can order correctional institutions to be reformed in a particular area, for example, by implementing a comprehensive suicide prevention program. These changes can be very detailed and are judicially enforced and penalties are compulsory for noncompliance. Due to budgetary concerns and ideological differences, this path of institutional reform for the treatment of the mentally ill and/or suicide prevention is necessary in many instances. A consent decree in *Garcia v. Board of County Commissioners of the County of El Paso* (1985) resulted in the jail being compelled to create a comprehensive suicide prevention program to include intensive supervision to all admitted inmates during the first 24 hours of confinement. All inmates were required to undergo screening, including the completion of an in-depth questionnaire. Those inmates identified as "at-risk" were required to remain under active visual observation on either irregular intervals (no more than 15 minute checks) or constant supervision without interruption (Welch & Gunther, 1997). Mental health/medical staff will typically recommend this level of supervision for a high-risk inmate to help prevent suicide.

There is also empirical literature on suicide prevention in corrections that have taken a **psychological autopsy approach**, whereby characteristics of completed suicides by incarcerated individuals are examined (Leese, Thomas, & Snow, 2006; Mumola, 2005). Increasingly, the relevant literature is being reviewed in order to bring resources and support in suicide prevention and intervention efforts in correctional settings (Magaletta, Patry, Wheat, & Bates, 2008). Studies have shown that high-security offenders serving long sentences and offenders in segregated housing are a high-risk group in correctional settings for completed suicides (Magaletta *et al.*, 2008). However, data from the psychological autopsy approach may be limited because sample sizes are restrictive and create selection bias that can not be controlled statistically (Magaletta *et al.*, 2008).

Other consent decrees have resulted in written policies and procedures for institutions to provide "special needs" cells with a clear, unobstructed view of the inmate, which pass inspection by a suicide prevention expert. In addition, inmate screening, specialized training of correctional and mental health staff in suicide prevention have been mandated. The training of staff and having staff available is essential. Correctional psychologists should play a central role in training staff in the identification of high-risk individuals and situations, as well as suicide intervention techniques. Training correctional officers in identifying risk factors, as well as increasing the working relationship and communication between mental health staff and correctional officers, is one way to bolster suicide prevention (Cummings & Thompson, 2009; Daniel, 2006). The reality of the inmate to mental health professional ratios and their very limited contact requires that line staff, particularly correctional officers, are adequately trained in identifying those in need for a more in-depth screening or crisis intervention by mental health professionals. Many inmates are either missed during the initial mental health screening or their mental state deteriorates over the course of confinement. It will be essential that correctional staff be able to refer those individuals needing more evaluation or immediate crisis intervention to the appropriate medical and psychology staff. Correctional psychologists often are on-call for **crisis intervention** to further evaluate a detainee who is threatening suicide or who is exhibiting or experiencing bizarre or agitated behavior. Correctional/forensic psychologists must take a leadership role in implementing and monitoring the screening/ intake procedures for the correctional institution, as well as mental health treatment and crisis intervention.

Most likely due to their inability or reluctance to seek out mental health treatment during the early stages of their illness, many mentally disordered offenders' contact with mental health professionals in the community and criminal justice system is compelled by crisis (Vaughan & Stevenson, 2002). In both settings, a failure to provide continuity of care after the crisis is common. Mental health follow-up during their confinement is essential. Furthermore, after a period of incarceration and having had time to think about their situation and potentially emerge from the effects of drugs and alcohol, some individuals are more able to realize their need for mental health treatment and social support. Prison- or jail-based mental health treatment teams need to link the detainee to appropriate community resources before their release (Peters & Beckman; Tong & Farrington, 2006; Vaughan & Stevenson, 2002). Including a system of aftercare in the community to avoid a break in mental health care should be another piece in the chain of mental health services for detainees. "Finally, when all else fails, it is the police who are left to pick up the pieces, particularly in a crisis" (Vaughan & Stevenson, 2002, p. 19). In this instance, the cycle begins all over again.

Suggestions for Future Research

Additional research is needed to further identify risk factors specifically related to detainees. Data collection regarding the effectiveness of suicide prevention programs in correctional settings is also needed. Continued research on the provision of mental health services in jails and prisons and the preferred treatment modalities, based on effectiveness, could be very beneficial in improving the quality of treatment and the reduction of detainee suicides. Studies examining the impact of class action litigation and consent decrees on jail and prison administrators' attitudes toward mental health services are needed. Additionally, studies exploring the number and type of mental health policies and procedures that have been implemented in jails and prisons as a result of litigation could be very enlightening. A forensic/correctional psychologist, particularly one serving as a psychology director or having an administrative or consulting role, could use these data to educate wardens and other correctional administrators about the costs/benefits analysis to both the inmate and the institution of providing inadequate mental health services.

With the development of the CASE approach, further research is needed into its effectiveness in suicide prevention. Further research into the cost and accessibility of the training for mental health professionals in a correctional setting is also needed. Future studies should also focus on the benefits of providing mental health training to correctional officers that are in daily contact with inmates and are likely to have the first and most frequent opportunities to identifying early warning signs of suicide risk in order to help prevent suicides in a vulnerable population.

Sex Offender Treatment

Introduction

The most appropriate way of addressing sex offenders continues to be an issue debated among psychologists, criminologists, private citizens, and the legislature. The disposition options for convicted sex offenders are wide-ranging and include life imprisonment, civil commitment, chemical castration, and psychological treatment. Perhaps the area which has received the most attention from the fields of psychology and criminology is whether it is beneficial to provide treatment to sex offenders. Over the last 15–20 years, programs such as community notification, sex offender registration and specialized treatment programs within correctional and mental health settings have flourished, but programs aimed at successful intervention and reduction of recidivism have proven less successful (Harris & Hanson, 2010; Seto & Lalumière, 2010). This matter continues to be controversial even among the foremost experts in the field of sex offender research. On the one hand, some believe that sex offender treatment is beneficial (Thankker, Collie, Gannon, & Ward, 2008; Wheeler, George, & Stephens, 2005; Lee, 2003; Marques, 1999; Marshall, 2001), while there are some who do not (Beck, 2008; Binger, Bergman-Levy, & Asman, 2011; Quinsey, 1998). The method most often used in determining whether a particular treatment modality has been successful is the measure of recidivism. **Recidivism** (i.e., the act of repeating an undesirable behavior when negative consequences have already been experienced) is considered the best measure of treatment efficacy, since the primary goal of sex offender treatment is the reduction of future victimization (Beggs & Grace, 2011; R. Prentky & Burgess, 1990). Therefore, in exploring whether treatment of sex offenders is beneficial, it is essential to examine recidivism rates between those offenders who receive treatment and those who do not. The case of Jesse depicts a convicted sex offender incarcerated without treatment for a number of years for child molestation. Jesse knows that he will reoffend if released from prison because he is no better equipped to deal with his deviant behavior now than he was able to 10 years ago.

Jesse is a 36-year-old child molester who has been incarcerated for the past 10 years for molesting a 9-year-old boy. As his parole date approached, Jesse acknowledged that he did not know why he committed his offense in the first place and he was afraid that he would commit another offense if he was released. Jesse pleaded with the parole board not to release him.

The parole board recognized Jesse's plea as a sign of remorse and released him into the community. For 1 year, Jesse remained offense-free. Then one day a neighborhood boy visited Jesse for a piano lesson and Jesse reoffended.

When Jesse returned to prison, he learned about sex offender treatment. He wrote letters and spoke with prison officials requesting that he receive this treatment. The only response to Jesse's efforts was a prison chaplain who visited him weekly.

Literature Review

Jesse is perhaps a rare case in that he outwardly acknowledged that he would reoffend if he was released, and he believed that the only way to prevent reoffense was to remain incarcerated. Some experts would disagree with Jesse's position that remaining incarcerated was the only way in which to prevent a reoffense. This remains a controversial issue. In the 10 years that he was in prison, Jesse did not receive any treatment. It is possible that Jesse would not have reoffended if he had received the proper treatment to address his inappropriate sexual fantasies and behaviors.

Although numerous experts have shown that treatment does indeed reduce recidivism among sex offenders (McGrath, Cumming, Livingston, & Hoke, 2003; Beck, 2008; Birger, Bergman-Levy, & Asman, 2011), there has been a decrease in funding for sex offender treatment programs since the late 1980s (Leon, 2011). McGrath *et al.* (2003) examined the recidivism rates of 195 adult male sex offenders who were referred to a prison-based, cognitive-behavioral treatment program. Out of this sample, 56 of the offenders completed treatment, 49 entered treatment but did not complete, and 90 refused treatment services. After approximately six years, the sexual reoffense rate for the completed treatment sample was 5.4% as compared to 30.6% for the partial treatment, and 30% for the no-treatment groups. Those participants who had aftercare treatment and correctional supervision services in the community had even lower recidivism rates (McGrath *et al.*, 2003). The lack of funding and available treatment for sex offenders is, in part, due to public opinion that sex offenders cannot be successfully treated. The accuracy of such an opinion needs to be explored and is best accomplished through an examination of recidivism rates among sex offenders.

In a comprehensive study on the effectiveness of sex offender treatment, Alexander (1997) conducted a meta-analysis of 81 sex offender treatment studies involving 11,350 subjects. The results overwhelmingly show that sex offenders who received treatment while in prison have a lower rate of recidivism than do those offenders who did not receive treatment. Among the sex offenders who received treatment in prison, 9.4% reoffended, whereas those offenders who did not receive treatment had a reoffense rate of 17.6%.

A retrospective study that examined recidivism rates with sex offenders treated at a secure facility with a cognitive-behavioral program, as compared to an untreated correctional sample, found that successfully treated offenders were significantly less likely to reoffend (Scalora & Garbin, 2003). These researchers found that those who recidivated were significantly younger, single, had engaged in more victim grooming or less violent offending behavior, and had significantly more property crimes. Currently, more laws, programs and assessments that address **cognitive distortions** (i.e., exaggerated or irrational beliefs, such as the victim wanted to be sexually violated) through cognitive-behavioral therapy are gaining popularity due to the severity and brutality that often accompany these types of violent sexual crimes.

Differentiating between types of offenders has an impact on the effectiveness of treatment. Recidivism rates and response to treatment vary between types of offenders (e.g., rapists, child molesters, sexual sadists, etc.). Treatment programs for men who sexually offend against children are based on cognitive-behavioral principles and involve relapse prevention components (Shipley & Arrigo, 2011; Laws & O'Donohue, 2008). Beggs and Grace (2011) examined the effectiveness of sex offender treatment for men who sexually offend against children and found the following:

> *Measures of treatment change based on offender self-reports and structured clinical rating systems show convergent and predictive validity, which suggests that effective treatment that targets dynamic risk factors leads to a reduction in sexual recidivism (p. 182).*

Static risk factors for sexual reoffense are not typically subject to change (e.g., offense history, number of prior convictions for sexual offenses, preference for male or female victims, gender of offender). According to Beggs and Grace (2011, pp. 182–183), "**Dynamic risk factors** are variables that are related to recidivism and are amenable to change, at least in principle, for example, intimacy deficits, cognitive distortions, and impaired self-regulation."

In order to accurately examine the issue of treatment efficacy among sex offenders, it is imperative to differentiate the offenders and not address the entire sex offender population as a homogenous group. In this regard, numerous studies show that incest offenders have a very low rate of recidivism (Alexander, 1997; Hanson & Bussiere, 1996; Hanson, Steffy, & Gauthier, 1993). Referring again to Alexander's (1997) meta-analysis, the recidivism rate of treated incest offenders was 4.0%, whereas untreated incest perpetrators had a recidivism rate of 12.5%. For the incest-perpetrator population, it is apparent that treatment is quite effective in reducing future victimization. The comparison between treated and untreated rapists, however, does not provide encouraging results. Rapists who received treatment had a recidivism rate of 20.1% while untreated rapists had a reoffense rate of 23.7%. These findings clearly illustrate the point that treating sex offenders as a homogenous group will lead to erroneous conclusions regarding the effectiveness of treatment. Although representing a much less common type of sexual offender, the **sexual sadist** (e.g., individual who is sexually aroused and gratified through the emotional and/or physical suffering or torture of others) is the most likely to be lethal and least likely to respond to sex offender treatment (Shipley & Arrigo, 2008).

Wheeler, George, and Stephens (2005) found that relapse prevention applied to sexual offending is controversial. These researchers have identified a "**relapse cycle**" identified as a "progression of thoughts, feelings, and behaviors that precede the act of sexual offending" (p. 394). They have identified five observable factors that indicate a relapse to include: "chronic lifestyle imbalances and/or acute triggering events, seemingly unimportant decision (i.e., putting himself in a place where he has access to a potential victim), lapse (i.e., precursor activities), high-risk situations, and relapse (i.e., the occurrence of a new sexual offense)" (Wheeler, George, & Stephens, 2005, p. 395). McGuire (2000) found that sex offenders with adult victims show more impulsive-criminal trends in lapse behavior when compared to those with child victims. He found that the different categories of sex offenders relapse in different rates and manners. The empirical research shows that treatment is quite successful for incest perpetrators; however, it is less effective for rapists. Therefore, perhaps the question that needs to be addressed is not whether to treat sex offenders, but rather, what model of sex offender treatment is most effective for which type of sex offender?

Another area that has received a considerable amount of research attention pertains to the type of treatment that is most beneficial for sex offenders. Until very recently, the consensus among those who treat this population is that a cognitive-behavioral program which focuses on relapse prevention is the most effective (Beck, 2008; Thakker, Collie, Gannon, & Ward, 2008; Wheeler, George, & Stephens, 2005). Cognitive-behavioral therapy that focuses primarily on the offender's cognitive distortions is gaining popularity (Feelgood, Cortoni, & Thompson, 2005; Marcus & Buffington-Vollum, 2008). As mentioned previously, rapists tend to have a lower success rate in terms of reducing recidivism after treatment. Thus, instead of asking whether to treat sex offenders, perhaps the focus needs to be placed on which type of treatment program is most effective for this population. There is a considerable amount of current research, which lends support to the idea that cognitive-behavioral treatment, particularly when coupled with a relapse prevention component, can reduce recidivism in certain types of sex offenders.

Female sex offenders present with unique characteristics. A recent trend in the literature indicates that the rate of female sex offending is on the rise. Sandler and Freeman (2009) conducted a study using a sample of 1466 females convicted of a sexual offense in New York State and examined the following: (1) offending prior to the commission of the first sexual offense; (2) rates of recidivism following their first sexual offense conviction; and (3) factors associated with the probability of sexual recidivism. The study found that the recidivism rates of female sex offenders were lower than those of male sex offenders for all types of recidivism studied (i.e., any rearrest, felony rearrest, violent [including violent sexual] felony rearrest, and sexual rearrest). From their sample, Sandler and Freeman (2009) found that 29.5% were rearrested for any crime, 13.9% were rearrested for a felony, 6.3% were rearrested for a violent (including violent sexual) felony, and 2.2% were rearrested for a sexual offense. Results further indicated that many significant differences existed between the group of female sex offenders who sexually reoffended and the group who did not, including crime of first sexual conviction and measures of prior offending.

Wheeler, George, and Stephens (2005) point out that relapse prevention as a treatment strategy was not initially developed as a stand-alone treatment, but rather as one component combined with other interventions. Research (Laws, 2003; Polaschek, 2003) has discovered that the relapse prevention model incorporated in cognitive-behavioral sex offender treatment is not well suited to some types of sex offenders. This mode of sex offender treatment operated under the assumption that there was only a single model of relapse; a relapse was always triggered by negative emotions or events, all offenders were attempting to avoid offending, and that offending was the result of skills deficits (Ward & Hudson, 1998; Ward & Hudson, 2000). While the relapse prevention offense process model was once thought to be a one size fits all model, an alternative model focusing on the individual characteristics of the offender and offense patterns is gaining wider acceptance. Ward and Hudson (1998, p. 701) concluded that research has "provided evidence for the existence of diverse offense pathways containing a number of distinct phases and suggest that offenders vary in their goals, their capacity to plan offenses, and in the kinds of emotions they experience throughout the offense process."

Researchers (Wheeler, George, & Stephens, 2005; Ward & Hudson, 1998, 2000) present a self-regulation model for relapse prevention in sex offenders that take into account the individual differences in offenders; for example, some offenders are not triggered by a negative event, but rather are very planful and seek out offensive sex. Some offenders are not affected or influenced by social skills deficits and this would not be an appropriate focus of their sex offender treatment program. A cognitive-behavioral approach to address cognitive distortions, victim empathy, and addressing deviant sexual arousal are still critical components of sex offender treatment. However, researchers and practitioners recognize that certain components of treatment will be different for an offender who is under-regulated and is lacking cognitive planning and social skills, in addition to having deviant arousal patterns, problems with intimacy, and cognitive distortions, as compared to an offender who has cognitive distortions, dysfunctional schemas, deviant arousal, psychopathy, and loneliness (Shipley & Arrigo, 2011; Shipley & Arrigo, 2008; Feelgood, Cortoni, & Thompson, 2005; Marcus & Buffington-Vollum, 2008; Wheeler, George, & Stephens, 2008).

Despite the amount of psychological literature that illustrates the effectiveness of certain treatment modalities for particular types of sex offenders, the legislature continues to decrease funding for these treatment programs and exerts a great deal of energy supporting the **chemical castration** (i.e., the administration of drugs that are designed to reduce sex drive and sexual activity) of child molesters (Binger, Bergman-Levy, & Asman, 2011). There are a number of reasons why law enforcement, the legislature, and the public disregard the scientific research, demonstrating that rehabilitation of sex offenders is indeed possible. One criticism identified by individuals who believe that "nothing works" is the notion that a large number of sex offenses go undetected and therefore skew recidivism results. However, when addressing the issue of sexual offending, it unfortunately goes without saying that many sex offenders are not brought to the attention of the authorities. This is a commonly held assumption, even among those who believe in the efficacy of sex offender treatment (Masho, Odor, & Adera, 2005). Thus, the reported recidivism rates, reflecting an under-reporting of sex offenses, remain a valid consideration. It is important to keep in mind, however, that while the statistics underestimate actual victimization rates, this does not discount the vast discrepancy in the recidivism rates between those offenders who receive treatment and those who do not.

Forensic Psychology and Policy Implications

The issue of whether to treat sex offenders remains controversial. Perhaps one reason why this topic continues to be debated is that there are few subjects that raise as much emotion as the issue of child sexual abuse. It is understandable that many of the foremost leaders in the struggle to obtain stricter punishments for sex offenders are the parents of victims of child molestation. However, from a policy standpoint, it is important to bear in mind that even with the emotional disgust and rage exercised against sex offenders, they too are eventually released from prison. Given the research that supports the effectiveness of treatment for this population, consideration needs to be given to increasing rather than decreasing the funding for sex offender treatment programs. Withholding treatment from such individuals does not address the issue that is at the core of this controversy. Both those who treat sex offenders and those who seek to punish them have the common goal of reducing future victimization. Treatment programs that utilize cognitive-behavioral therapy and principles of relapse prevention models, focusing on cognitive distortions and deviant behaviors typical of sexual offenders continue to gain recognition (Donaldson & Abbott, 2011; First & Halon, 2008; Jackson & Richards, 2008; Palermo, 2007). It should be noted that certain types of sexual offenders, specifically **sexual sadists**, are consistently viewed as not responsive to or appropriate for sex offender treatment (Shipley & Arrigo, 2008).

Within the current criminal justice system, the vast majority of sex offenders are released from prison and returned to communities where potential victims reside. Recognizing this fact, it is important to question whether the public prefers to have sex offenders in their neighborhood who have received treatment or those who have not received any treatment whatsoever and, therefore, have not learned how to control their deviant sexual behavior. Another issue to consider regarding policy reform is the cost of incarceration versus the cost of treatment for sex offenders. Historically, Blanchette (1996) presented data illustrating that treating the average sex offender on an outpatient basis costs approximately $7000 per year less than incarceration. Subsequently, if treatment were successful for only for a small number of individuals, the cost-effectiveness of this approach is clear. Further, it cannot be overlooked that reducing recidivism by even a small amount spares numerous potential victims from suffering the devastating effects of sexual violence.

Another means by which legislators have attempted to prevent reoffense includes civil confinement for those who have served a prison sentence for a sexual offense, but who are evaluated to meet certain criteria such as being at a very high risk of violent sexual reoffense with questionable amenability to treatment. Approximately 20 states have developed **Sexually Violent Predator** civil confinement laws in the United States (Donaldson & Abbott, 2011; First & Halon, 2008). These laws state that a sex offender who has had multiple incarcerations for sexual offenses poses a risk for future violence, and has a mental disorder or personality disorder that makes them more likely to commit future acts of sexual violence, are subject to involuntary confinement in a state mental facility after they have served out their sentence for a sexual offense (Donaldson & Abbott, 2011; First & Halon, 2008; Jackson & Richards, 2008). These commitments are usually indefinite and require minimal review of the offender's progress in treatment (Donaldson & Abbott, 2011; First & Halon, 2008; Jackson & Richards, 2008). Offenses committed by those determined to be Sexually Violent Predators are often classified as **paraphilias**, which (Palermo, 2007, p. 497) defined as "deviant sexuality, such as pedophilia, exhibitionism, voyeurism, frotteurism, sexual masochism, sexual sadism, fetishism, transvestic fetishism, and zoophilia." Although these types of crimes do not occur frequently, when they do, several victims are left in the wake.

Suggestions for Future Research

In recent years, an abundance of psychological literature has addressed the issue of treatment efficacy for sex offenders. However, the fields of law and criminology have scarcely produced any research on this topic. Perhaps this is because professionals in the mental health arena are those who most often provide the treatment. However, it is essential for individuals working within the mental health and the criminal justice systems to find common ground on the issue if the goal of reducing victimization is to be actively pursued. As noted by Alexander (1997), when agencies become convinced that a cause is worthwhile and urgent, the money will be appropriately allotted. Therefore, it is necessary that research be conducted addressing the reluctance by legislatures to implement treatment programs for sex offenders. Perhaps there is a lack of communication between the respective disciplines, and, thus, research would do well to target educating the public, the legislature, and the prison system on the efficacy of sex offender treatment.

As assessment and treatment methods for sex offenders evolve, so must the research on the base rates of reoffending by released sex offenders, factors associated with different levels of risk, and impact of treatment on recidivism. The current literature on the topic of sex offender treatment is lacking in certain areas as well. The ineffectiveness of treatment with particular groups of sex offenders clouds public perception on the overall effectiveness of treatment. For this reason, research is sorely needed that addresses those sex offenders who do not respond well to existing treatment modalities. Specifically, limited studies assess how best to treat rapists, pedophiles, and exhibitionists.

Thakker, Collie, Gannon, and Ward (2008) suggest one way to assist law makers and improve the quality of sex offender evaluations is to provide information about the best standard of practice and finding some similarity and agreement in the application of assessing sex offenders. By doing so would provide important information and clarity to the many facets of sex offenses (i.e., child sexual offending, rape, etc.). The assessment of sex offenders, particularly those on probation or parole, often involves the use of **phallometric testing** using the **penile plethysmography** (i.e., measurement of changes in penile circumference in response to sexual and nonsexual stimuli, provides objective information about male sexual interests, including identifying deviant sexual interests) and **polygraph testing** (i.e., commonly known as a "lie detector test;" measure of physiological indices such as blood pressure, respiration, and skin conductivity as a person answers a series of questions to test for deception). Research into the efficacy of these measures of evaluation is lacking. Due to the intrusiveness of these measures, psychologists are encouraged to "provide clear rationales and evidence for their continued use" (Thakker, Collie, Gannon, & Ward, 2008, p. 376).

Future research needs to continue to focus on the heterogeneity of sex offenders in order to present a more accurate picture of what type of treatment works best for whom. Laws (2003) encourages more research into the self-regulation model and encourages researchers to not over-accept this model but to continue to explore and broaden the overall treatment approach to increase the efficacy for all types of sex offenders. Over the years, there has been an upward trend in females who sexually offend. There is a paucity of research regarding risk factors for these women. Research indicates the following factors may motivate women to commit sex offenses: a reenactment of sexual abuse, emotions, narcissism, extension of battered woman's syndrome, or as an accomplice to a male counterpart (Vandiver & Kercher, 2004). Future research is needed to explore the unique factors that contribute to sexual offending in women.

Maintaining Boundaries with an Inmate Population

Introduction

Professional boundaries have been defined as "the edge of appropriate, professional conduct" (Guthiel, 2005, p. 422), and this author also noted that what constitutes professional or appropriate conduct is highly dependent on the context in which a professional relationship is forged. Although maintaining professional boundaries is important in any setting, in correctional or forensic settings, the consequences of not doing so can be significant. It has been noted by some authors that unique characteristics of the correctional or forensic environment itself can elicit or even subtly encourage inappropriate behavior and relationships among inmates and staff. For example, correctional officers often rely heavily on inmates to perform or assist with institutional functions (e.g., housekeeping, custodial or maintenance tasks), tasks which will impact the officers' performance evaluations, thus creating an environment in which inmates are working closely with officers and reducing the power differential (Dial & Worley, 2008). Additionally, officers are often prohibited or discouraged from using physical means to coerce inmate obedience to requests or orders, creating situations where they use other forms of bargaining to persuade compliance (Dial & Worley, 2008).

Staff often work in close proximity to inmates, and prefer to get along with inmates in order to ease their workload and increase institutional safety (Dial & Worley, 2008; Blackburn, Fowler, Mullings, & Marquart, 2011). Additionally, inmates often lack access to things that they are highly motivated to obtain (e.g., sexual relationships, substances, preferred food or hygiene items), and many inmates have personality styles that make them more prone to violating boundaries with staff (Elliot & Verdeyen, 2003). It has been noted the adversarial environment of a prison where staff must interact daily with inmates who "will do almost anything to make their time more comfortable and convenient" (Elliot & Verdeyen, 2003, p. 14), contributes to staff manipulation. Factors including power struggles make correctional institutions a breeding ground for boundary violations. Although inmates may play a significant role in initiating or maintaining inappropriate relationships with staff, correctional staff, particularly mental health professionals, must take the ultimate responsibility for keeping boundaries clear and appropriate (Gutheil, 2005).

Troublesome or **inappropriate relationships between inmates and staff** have been broadly defined by Worley, Marquart, and Mullings (2003, p. 179) as:

> *personal relationships between employees and inmates/clients or with family members of inmates/clients. This behavior is usually sexual or economic in nature and has the potential to jeopardize the security of a prison or compromise the integrity of a correctional employee.*

As this definition implies, behaviors constituting boundary violations are diverse, and can result in effects ranging from slight to severe. Many authors distinguish between boundary crossings and boundary violations (Gutheil & Gabbard, 1993; Gerson & Fox, 1999; Atkins & Stein, 1993; Gutheil, 2005; Gabbard & Crisp-Ham, 2011; Seeman & Seeman, 2011). **Boundary crossings** are "transient, nonexploitative deviations from classical therapeutic or general clinical practice in which the treater steps out to a minor degree from a strict verbal psychotherapy" (Gutheil, 2005, p. 422). For example, offering a patient a tissue, visiting a patient at home due to their medical needs, or answering selected personal questions all represent boundary crossings, which do not usually constitute unethical or harmful behavior (Gutheil, 2005). **Boundary violations**, on the other hand, "constitute essentially harmful deviations from the normal parameters of treatment – deviations that do harm, usually through some sort of exploitation" (Gutheil, 2005, p. 422).

Although boundary crossings can certainly occur without leading to a boundary violation, boundary crossings can lead a professional down a slippery slope and result in eventual boundary violations. One of the most serious violations is the establishment of a sexual relationship with an inmate. According to recent statistics, approximately 2.8% of prison inmates and 2% of jail inmates report having a sexual relationship with a staff member while incarcerated (Beck, Harrison, Berzofsky, Caspar, & Krebs, 2010). Of these incidents, 47% involved female staff and male inmates; 43% involved male staff and female inmates; 8% involved male staff and male inmates, and 2% involved female staff and female inmates (Beck *et al.*, 2010). Even though this phenomenon may affect a minority of inmates, as detailed below, the consequences of such relationships can be deleterious to staff, inmates, and institutions. The following vignette illustrates the importance of maintaining boundaries with inmates, who are often potentially dangerous.

In 2009, a recently-released inmate was shot once in the chest in front of his grandparents' home. The inmate survived, though the bullet barely missed his heart. The shooter was later identified as his girlfriend. The couple met while the inmate was incarcerated at a local correctional institution for charges related to assaulting a female and carrying a concealed weapon. The shooter and girlfriend was a staff psychologist at the time of his incarceration, and had worked for the institution for approximately five years before she resigned after being confronted about suspicions regarding her relationship with the inmate.

As details of the story unfolded, it was revealed that the couple met while the inmate was incarcerated, and that when the inmate was released, he discharged to live in the psychologist's home. Although an investigation by the institution suggested that the two did not have sex at the facility while he was incarcerated, it was confirmed that the psychologist was directly involved in the treatment of the inmate, including individual therapy sessions. In subsequent interviews with prison officials and during an investigation by the state licensing board, the woman indicated that they first had intercourse the day of his release. Less than three weeks after the inmate's release, during an argument in which the psychologist claimed to have been assaulted by her partner and former patient, she produced a gun and shot him. The psychologist initially filed charges against the former inmate, but the District Attorney dropped these charges after discovering that the woman had continued her romantic relationship with the man, including allowing him to live with her. Following an investigation by her state's licensing board, the psychologist's license was revoked.

An expanding body of literature is developing, detailing methods used by inmates to manipulate staff, characteristics of inmates and staff who engage in inappropriate relationships, perceptions of boundary violations and violators, and strategies for those who work with individuals prone to con or manipulate others as a means to an end. These aspects of the literature, as well as implications for policy and directions for future research, are discussed in this section.

Literature Review

The types of behaviors constituting boundary violations are diverse. The literature identifies many such staff behaviors to include the following: (1) physical contact, which may include nonsexual touching such as pats or hugs, as well as sexual intimacy between staff and inmates; (2) discussing one's personal life with inmates; (3) breaches of confidentiality by mental health professionals regarding an inmate's treatment or assessment; and (4) initiating or permitting a financial relationship with an inmate (e.g., selling them contraband, giving or accepting gifts to or from an inmate) (Radden, 2001). This list, however, is not exhaustive, and boundary violations may "encompass almost any form of exploitation and/or any behavior likely to diminish the therapeutic effectiveness of the engagement" (Radden, 2001, p. 320).

There are also numerous behaviors by inmates that encourage or solicit boundary violations from staff. Cornelius (2009) describes how inmates often utilize various approaches, or masks, when attempting to manipulate staff. An inmate may attempt to portray themselves as a "good guy," who will exhibit confidence, tell those in authority what they want to hear, but will use the relationship or information for their own personal gain without concern for the consequences to the staff member (Cornelius, 2009, p. 58). Similar to the "good guy" is the "nice guy" who "will try to please everyone, and will cling to staff and volunteers. They will not tell the truth, but [will also be] 'back stabbers'" (p. 58). Cornelius also describes the inmate who presents themselves as naïve and uses "these traits to get their way," while, in reality, they are "cunning manipulators" (p. 58). According to Cornelius (2009, p. 58), inmates who wear the "illiterate dummy" mask appear low-functioning, hoping that people will excuse their behavior, but this act belies their true abilities and intent to deceive for secondary gain. He indicates that con men or women "are usually older and are very institutionalized and streetwise. They can wear any mask…and can manipulate" (p. 58). Another type described as preachers "use religion as a front and to justify behavior," and "are concrete thinkers" (Cornelius, 2009, p. 58). Finally, "Sam or Samantha Sentimental" will "appear to care for puppies, kittens, the elderly, family, and others," with the goal of "lower [ing] the staff's guard" (Cornelius, 2009, p. 58) and hopefully resulting in boundary violations that will benefit the inmate.

Manipulative behavior on the part of inmates may also serve the purpose of helping them get what they want when staff are initially not willing to give it, using dishonesty in order to get people to act in a way that they might not have if they had known the truth, maintain power and control over staff and others, avoiding their obligations and responsibilities, and attempting to make others feel guilty for the inmate's criminal actions and thoughts (Barnhart, 2007).

According to Dial and Worley (2008), inmates may work together to manipulate staff, and each inmate in a scheme may take on a unique role in its execution. For example, groups of inmates will often have an inmate or groups of inmates identified as an **observer**, who will watch and listen to the potential target of manipulation. They will pay especially close attention to body language and mannerisms. This person or persons will then provide information to other inmates, who will determine how vulnerable to manipulation a particular staff member may be. A second role inmates may play in a manipulation scheme is that of the **contact**. The contact attempts to obtain personal information regarding a staff member's life by paying close attention to conversations between employees and engaging the employee in seemingly meaningless discussions, which progress to soliciting more and more detail. The information is then conveyed to other inmates to assist in setting up the staff member for manipulation. **Runners** run the highest risk of being caught in the manipulation process, as they offer subtle suggestions to the staff regarding rule or boundary violations. Often, this takes the form of a request for seemingly harmless or insignificant contraband (e.g., hygiene items), and this inmate is often paid by other inmates for his or her services. The fourth role is that of the **turner**. The turner befriends an employee and ultimately uses that friendship in order to coerce the staff member to violate rules. First, the turner will get the staff member to break minor rules or engage in minor indiscretions. These indiscretions are later used as a **lever** to maintain control and power over the staff member and get them involved in more serious infractions. **Pointmen** stand guard while turners are receiving illegal favors. These individuals may distract other officers and staff members by acting aggressively or inappropriately (Dial & Worley, 2008).

Inmates may be very obvious in their attempts at deception, or they may be highly sophisticated. Inmates may lie by omission or voice an untruth with the specific intent to deceive. For example, an inmate may tell a chaplain that he needs time off from his job because of a death in his family, when no such death has occurred (Elliott & Verdeyen, 2003). An inmate lies by omission when he or she makes "a conscious attempt to leave out certain information that would be important for an audience to know" (Elliott & Verdeyen, 2003, p. 12). These types of lies are much more common. An example of such behavior is an inmate who returns from his job 30 minutes late, and tells an officer that he ran into his counselor and stopped to discuss his visiting list with her on his way back to the housing unit. The inmate did, in fact, talk to his counselor about a visiting list, but for less than a minute. The remaining thirty minutes was spent visiting friends at the prison's factory, signing up for a drug education program in the psychology department, and smoking cigarettes outside of his housing unit (Elliott &Verdeyen, 2003). **Dissimulation** is another form of deception in which an inmate deliberately distorts or misrepresents a psychological or physical symptom. For example, an inmate who requests a lower bunk because of a reported leg injury which prevents him from being able to climb into a higher bunk, when there is no such injury and the inmate is actually motivated by comfort and convenience, is engaging in dissimulation (Elliott & Verydeyen, 2003).

Inmates often spend a great deal of time and effort in the process of selecting a victim for manipulation. For example, they may target staff who appear weak, lenient, unconfident, or who are isolated from other staff members or sources of support (Cornelius, 2009). A staff member who is selected as a target may then be tested, a process through which inmates determine how far the employee will bend rules and policies, or how the employee will respond to covertly sexual statements, or "accidental" and nonsexual forms of touching. If the staff member allows minor rule violations, the manipulation efforts will then continue and increase in intensity. Such efforts are mixed with building up the ego of the staff by making statements such as, "you are the only therapist I've ever had who truly understands me" (Cornelius, 2009, p. 51). These statements may be accompanied by efforts by the inmate to perform odd jobs for the staff member, or perform simple ingratiating tasks, such as getting a cup of coffee for the staff member (Cornelius, 2009). The inmate may also attempt to garner sympathy and/or empathy from the staff member, by sharing stories from their past (whether true or not) in which the offender is a victim, or by crying in front of the employee. The offender may attempt to foster a "we versus them" mentality with the staff member, by telling the employee that supervisors or other employees were overheard criticizing the employee, and then telling the employee that, "we know you, they don't," or "How can [they] think that about you?" (Cornelius, 2009, p. 52). Inmates who are well-connected inside or outside of the prison may offer to protect the staff member from consequences of the boundary violations, or from attacks or threats by other inmates. A less direct technique used by inmates is that of starting a rumor about an employee. Although it may not be true, inmates do this in hopes that others will believe it, and the employee will become more isolated and more vulnerable to manipulation (Cornelius, 2009; Elliott, 2006). In a similar technique, an inmate may exploit existing tension between officers by playing on real situations in order to isolate and divide staff (Cornelius, 2009).

Other specific techniques utilized by inmates may include **extortion**, which includes using direct threats or intimidation to coerce an employee into violations of boundaries or rules (Elliott, 2006). An inmate using **disreputation** may criticize a staff member's authority and/or competence in hopes that the target will lose status in the eyes of peers and supervisors (Elliott, 2006). In implementing the technique of **negotiation,** an inmate may offer an employee valuable information (e.g., information about which inmates were involved in setting up a recent riot or staff assault) in exchange for additional privileges or accommodations (Elliott, 2006). **Splitting** occurs when inmates pit one staff against another, or groups of staff (e.g., disciplines, shifts, supervisors and subordinates) against each other (Elliott, 2006). An inmate may also attempt to utilize his or her **sphere of influence** by exploiting their own political, financial, or other personal resources to undermine staff authority and circumvent policies and procedures (Elliott, 2006). **Solidarity** is utilized when inmates make an organized attempt as a group to compel staff to undertake a course of action, or to abandon a course of action viewed as unfavorable by the inmates. Such efforts may be based on the inmates' geographic origin, ethnicity, religious affiliation, or gang membership (Elliott, 2006).

Researchers have also made recent efforts to identify characteristics of staff who are more vulnerable to manipulation and characteristics of inmates who are more likely to employ such techniques. For example, it has long been noted that new or inexperienced employees are most vulnerable (Elliott & Verdeyen, 2003). According to Barnhart (2007), this vulnerability can be attributed to the following factors: (1) New staff tend to be less hardened or familiar with rules, policies, and procedures than more experienced staff; (2) they may be quiet, timid, and seek to avoid conflict with inmates; (3) they may be very trusting of inmates and lack professionalism; (4) they may have not yet created meaningful relationships with their coworkers, making them isolated and vulnerable to manipulation; and (5) they may find it difficult to say no or take control during stressful situations. Other researchers have noted that correctional officers with boundary problems are more likely to have experienced problems in their personal and professional relationships in the time leading up to the violations (Worley & Cheeseman, 2006; Worley, Tewksbury, & Frantzen, 2010), or to have experienced feelings of social isolation, financial difficulties, and job-related problems (Worley & Cheeseman, 2006). Female staff in particular may be vulnerable to manipulation if they perceive themselves as being physically unattractive or exhibit low self-esteem (Worley &

Cheeseman, 2006). Finally, employees who use inmate slang or jargon, play favorites, ignore minor rule violations, have sloppy work habits, are easily distracted, display fear, nervousness, or indecisiveness, or provide inmates with personal information about themselves may be perceived by inmates as good targets for manipulation (Cornelius, 2009).

Research regarding characteristics of inmates who violate boundaries is more limited. However, a recent study by Dial and Worley (2008) indicates that offenders who violate boundaries are more likely to exhibit disparaging views of females within correctional settings (i.e., to believe that females are afraid of inmates, increase sexual tension in correctional settings, flirt and seek attention from inmates, use charm to control inmates, and are less able to control inmates than their male counterparts). This study also found that inmates who violated boundaries with staff were more likely to make efforts to get female staff to discuss their relationship problems with them, to masturbate in the view of female officers and staff, to manipulate females by using verbal flattery, to intimidate females with threats of harm, and to manipulate female staff by threatening to write a grievance about them (Dial & Worley, 2008).

In addition to these characteristics, inmates with traits of psychopathy are much more likely to violate boundaries with staff (Cornelius, 2009; Barnhart, 2007; Worley *et al.*, 2003; Worley *et al.*, 2010). This is particularly problematic for correctional systems, because these inmates, who often display high intelligence, superficial charm, and "likeable" personalities, may be more successful and make more sophisticated and subtle attempts to manipulate staff. Psychopathic and predatory inmates are also more likely to convince other inmates to manipulate staff, leaving the psychopathic inmate on the "fringe" of the manipulation effort, allowing him or her to often go undetected and avoid negative consequences associated with discovery while still benefitting from the "spoils" of the relationship (e.g., receiving contraband, information about staff to utilize in future manipulation efforts, etc.) (Cornelius, 2009).

The importance placed on maintaining boundaries with inmates is motivated by the serious consequences. Worley and colleagues (2010) found that boundary violations result in (1) negative staff-on-staff relationships; (2) negative staff-on-inmate relationships; (3) negative consequences for the inmate and/or inmate population; and (4) negative consequences for the staff member. Among the inmate population, boundary violators may be punished or stigmatized, or boundary violators who have protection from staff may victimize other inmates, and may have been provided with dangerous contraband by officers with which to carry out such victimization (Worley *et al.*, 2010; Cornelius, 2009). The staff member(s) engaging in boundary violations may lose their job, jeopardize their family relationships or the safety of their family members, and may even garner criminal charges against them. Serious boundary violations often receive media attention, and this may be a source of embarrassment for other employees and the institution as a whole (Worley *et al.*, 2010;

Cornelius, 2009). Mental health professionals working in correctional institutions who violate boundaries with inmates may experience other consequences, including damage to the therapeutic relationship with that inmate and other offenders who find out about the violation, suicide attempts by the therapist when the violation is discovered, civil lawsuits, loss or suspension of licensure, and complaints to professional societies such as the American Psychological Association against the practitioner (Guthiel, 2005).

The consequences of sexual misconduct with inmates are potentially the most serious. For example, mental health practitioners or other licensed individuals may be subject to civil suits for malpractice or harm to the offender/client (Simon & Shuman, 2011). Moreover, because offenders are legally unable to provide consent to sexual relationships, criminal sanctions may also be rendered against correctional employees who engage in sexual relationships with inmates, even if the offender willingly engages in the act(s) (Simon & Shuman, 2011). Federal law makes it a misdemeanor to engage in sexual activities with a federal prisoner; however, the federal law is significantly less stringent and "out of step" with state laws, as such behavior constitutes a felony in 43 of 50 states (Beck *et al.*, 2010, p. 1).

Recent research has also examined inmates' perceptions about staff rule violations. In a 2011 study, Blackburn and colleagues found that female inmates were particularly likely to view boundary violations by staff as problematic, and hypothesized that this may be due to the significant trauma histories typical of female inmates. They suggested that these female inmates may fear that staff, particularly male staff, may further victimize them. In a similar study by Worley *et al.* (2010), inmates provided statements regarding their perceptions of inappropriate relationships among staff and inmates, particularly female staff. One inmate stated, "It's unprofessional because these relationships make officers fight with each other over who's dirty and who's not… Also, because dirty officers act unprofessionally and break the law every time they bring in contraband or have sex with an inmate, this sets a bad example for all of the other offenders" (p. 351). Another female inmate from their sample reported, "These relationships between staff and inmates cause some officers to avoid any interaction with inmates, even if it's on a professional level. There are some officers that look at you strange, even if you're just asking for something legit like an I-60 [request to an official] or a Tylenol" (Worley *et al.*, 2010, p. 351).

Forensic Psychology and Policy Implications

Several strategies have been recommended to those working in correctional settings. Researchers suggest that the first line of defense against inmate manipulation strategies is for staff to recognize signs of manipulative behavior early on before they have become involved in the "con game" (Elliott & Verdeyen, 2003; Barnhart, 2007). One way of doing so is by developing a "red flag warning response," when the staff member feels compelled to do something they would not normally do and seeking consultation and supervision when these moments occur (Guthiel, 2005; Barnhart, 2007). If a mental health professional feels that a *boundary crossing* not violation is warranted, this should be preceded by three important steps: (1) the behavior should be examined to ensure that it still constitutes professional behavior; boundary crossings should never be unprofessional; (2) the behavior should be discussed with the inmate or patient; and (3) appropriate documentation, including documentation of any consultation or supervision, should be completed (Guthiel, 2005; Barnhart, 2007).

Additionally, the following strategies are recommended in order to identify manipulation attempts at the earliest possible point: (1) trust your intuition, or your "gut" when it tells you that something about an interaction with an inmate is just "not right"; (2) pay close attention to an inmate's normal behavior, so you will be aware of subtle changes to alert you that you may be being set up; (3) be aware of your own nonverbal behavior, particularly nonverbal behavior that may indicate that you are uncomfortable or unsure about a situation (Barnhart, 2007); (4) be honest and direct when talking with inmates (Barnhart, 2007); and (5) seek collateral information to confirm or disconfirm an inmate's story (Elliott & Verdeyen, 2003; Barnhart, 2007). Further, staff should never relay personal information to inmates, as this conveys a broken boundary and may allow the staff to be further set up for manipulation (Barnhart, 2007). For similar reasons, staff should never give anything to or accept anything from an inmate, no matter how seemingly trivial (Barnhart, 2007). Correctional psychologists can play a vital role in providing training to correctional officers about how psychopathic traits are particularly dangerous in inmates with regard to institutional violence, inappropriate staff relationships, and conning and manipulating other inmates, as well as staff. Supervising psychologists also a bear a large responsibility to ensure that staff psychologists are well-trained and supported in providing services to a challenging correctional/forensic population.

The previous strategies may assist employees in avoiding being manipulated; however, there are also times when an employee will realize that they have been manipulated. The following strategies may be helpful in doing "damage control" in such instances. According to Elliott and Verdeyen (2006), when staff realize that they are being deceived, it is recommended that they initially stall for time before providing a response. This allows them the opportunity to verify the inmate's story, reflect on the situation, and decide how best to handle it (Elliott & Verdeyen, 2006). It is also recommended that staff who have been manipulated or deceived learn to "lick [their] wounds and move on" (Elliott & Verdeyen, 2003, p. 142). This process involves the staff not getting "stuck" in feeling embarrassed or ashamed about having been duped in less serious incidents, but rather learning to "walk away, reflect on the experience, and consider alternative ways to prevent future occurrences of the same or similar manipulations" (Elliott & Verdeyen, 2003, p. 142). These correctional employees who have been manipulated or deceived should resist the urge to keep the incident private, as this will only encourage further manipulation, but should share their experience with a trusted colleague, and also document their experience appropriately. A good sense of humor will also serve correctional employees well, as it is often helpful to be able to laugh at both themselves and the particularly challenging aspects of their work environments (Elliott & Verdeyen, 2003).

Consequences of contraband, rule violations, inappropriate sexual relationships, and other boundary violations in correctional settings suggest that this area should remain a focus for those involved in setting institutional and public policy. In many institutions, violating appropriate boundaries with correctional or hospital staff is not a serious infraction and is even sometimes placed on par with failure to adhere to grooming standards (i.e., shaving, haircuts) or sleeping while at work. Due to the effects of these behaviors, it is recommended that more aggressive policies be written to address these issues (Dial & Worley, 2010). Additionally, policies to address aspects of the prison culture that encourage boundary violations should be considered. For example, Worley and colleagues (2010) recommended that prisons should restrict or eliminate supervision of inmates by officers of the opposite sex, allow tobacco in certain parts of correctional institutions (in order to reduce the need for inmates to manipulate staff in order to obtain such items), and provide inmates with tools to cultivate relationships outside of the facility (e.g., access to pay phones, frequent visits), to reduce their need and desire to foster inappropriate relationships with staff. Additionally, supervision of correctional employees should be improved, which would include changes such as wardens being physically present more often on housing units, closer monitoring of officers on night or weekend shifts who are more isolated and work at times when inmates are more likely to engage in manipulation, and rotating officers often during shifts so as to minimize the forming of relationships which are too close or unprofessional (Worley *et al.*, 2010). Increased supervision and consultation with correctional psychologists is also recommended. Appropriate support and education must be provided to both correctional officers and mental health staff to help prepare them for the unique challenges inherent in working in this setting.

Because inappropriate relationships often serve financial purposes for poorly-paid officers, the pay of correctional officers should be increased, to reduce their need to supply inmates with contraband for financial gain (Worley *et al.*, 2010). Additionally, during orientation and refresher trainings, correctional officers need to be reminded of the potential for losing their jobs, reputations, and possibly facing criminal action if they were to engage in this behavior. Amnesty programs could be developed for employees who have engaged in minor rule infractions to encourage them to come forward before the relationship and boundary violations go too far (Worley *et al.*, 2010).

In light of recent evidence suggesting that the means by which female inmates attempt to manipulate or deceive staff may be different than those utilized by male inmates, correctional employee training initiatives should be tailored to include gender-specific issues (Blackburn *et al.*, 2011). Finally, laws should be changed to make sexual relationships with inmates felonies, rather than misdemeanors (Beck *et al.*, 2010). Such changes would increase the likelihood that prosecutors would be willing to pursue cases of this sort (Beck *et al.*, 2010), as well as maximize the deterrent effect of such laws.

Suggestions for Future Research

Research regarding the nature, rates and consequences of correctional boundary violations has expanded, but there is still much to be learned. Future research should delineate whether the management strategies described in this section are differentially effective for inmates of varying genders, races, ages, and cultural groups (Blackburn *et al.*, 2011). Additionally, future research efforts should elucidate the ways in which inmates who violate boundaries differ from those who do not, and examine how these inmates are able to gain power over staff (Worley *et al.*, 2010). Future research could examine correctional officers' perception of how boundary violations and inappropriate relationships create security/safety problems in the institution. Research could also explore officers' opinions regarding how best to prevent such incidents (Worley *et al.*, 2010).

Another important area for future research concerns sexual relations between prison staff and inmates. Attempting to identify what types of staff characteristics are associated with such behavior could help in screening out these candidates at the beginning of the hiring process. Thus, future psychological harm to prisoners could be averted. Also, more in-depth studies of administrators' awareness of inmate sexual behaviors and their responses to it would provide a better understanding of exactly where officials stand on this issue and what needs to be done to educate them on the effects of sexual assaults. Struckman-Johnson and Struckman-Johnson (2002) suggest that certain characteristics in female inmates such as attractiveness, passivity, toughness, or sexual orientation could be studied to examine their correlation with being targeted as a victim of sexual assault. Additionally, they encourage future research into the long-term impact of sexual assault on the ability to form new social-sexual relationships outside of prison.

Future investigations should also examine the effectiveness of the management strategies discussed above, as well as the effectiveness of the recommended policy changes in reducing the number of inappropriate relationships and boundary violations among staff and inmates. Given that much of the research in this area has been conducted in large correctional institutions within the southern United States, future research in prisons and jails of varying security levels, geographical locations, and sizes should be conducted.

Prison Violence

Introduction

Christopher Scarver attacked Jeffrey Dahmer while he was cleaning a prison gymnasium bathroom, smashing his head with a metal bar borrowed from an exercise machine. Violence has become a central attribute of prison life. Dee Farmer, as another example, was convicted merely of credit card fraud, yet he suffered a savage attack at the hands of a fellow inmate. When Farmer refused an inmate's demand for sexual intercourse, the inmate punched and kicked Farmer. After threatening Farmer with a homemade knife, the attacker tore off Farmer's clothes and raped him. The attacker threatened to kill Farmer if he reported the incident. The Dahmer and Farmer incidents represent the controversial issue of poor prison conditions which cause prison violence. Numerous research studies indicate that inmate violence is the product of the psychologically stressful and oppressive conditions within the prison itself (Clements, 2004; Johnson, 2008; Gussak & Ploumis-Devick, 2004; McCorkle, Miethe, & Drass, 1995; Williams, 2003; Wilson, & Tamatea, 2010; Yoshikazu, 2010; Yuma, 2010). Measures of poor conditions, such as inadequate prison management and lack of prison programs due to overcrowding, are associated with high levels of prison violence.

Literature Review

Situations like those previously described are very common in prison life. The Farmer incident raises the question: If poor prison conditions are improved, does that indicate that psychological stress will decrease among inmates, causing a decrease in violence? In response to this question, there is growing consensus among recent research studies indicating that prisons with exceptional conditions, such as efficient prison management, numerous prison programs, and comfortable prison capacity, experience a decrease in prison violence compared to facilities with poor prison conditions (Clements, 2004; Johnson, 2008; Gussak & Ploumis-Devick, 2004; McCorkle *et al.*, 1995; Williams, 2003; Wilson & Tamatea, 2010; Yoshikazu, 2010; Yuma, 2010). Prison overcrowding and lack of satisfactory correctional management were conditions that contributed to the Dee Farmer attack. In Farmer's case, the assailant reacted to the psychologically stressful prison environment by attacking Dee Farmer. Effective prison management, suitable prison capacity, and programs designed to keep inmates busy contribute to relieving psychological tension in the prison. Art programs, for example, may contribute to improved quality of life and security in prison by providing inmates with some escape from the typical routine and stress inherent in day-to-day prison life (Clements, 2004; Gussak & Ploumis-Devick, 2004). Some evidence has emerged indicating that art programs may help to reduce inmates' disruptive and violent behaviors in prison (Gussak & Ploumis-Devick, 2004; Williams, 2003).

Research indicates that the social and environmental factors that primarily produce prison violence include: inmates' personal histories of violence; the youthfulness of the prison population; the lower socioeconomic class of most inmates; racial conflict between prisoners; inmate norms promoting violent behavior; and the psychological effects of prison conditions suffered by inmates. Additionally, reduced security from criminal victimization, the loss of autonomy, and the scarcity of goods and services also add to this stress. To lessen the physical and psychological effects of these deprivations, inmates sometimes undertake different illicit activities such as drug trafficking, murder, gambling, and selling protection from victimization. These illegal behaviors, in turn, require means for resolving disputes and thus invite the use of prison violence. The following vignette best exemplifies this process.

> J.T. owes C.L. several bottles of Scotch. C.L. reports that this debt covers gambling losses; J.T. insists he has been paying for protection. C.L. gives J.T. one month to settle, but J.T. is unable to do so. The best J.T. can do is supply several packs of cigarettes, which only covers a small portion of the amount owed. At the end of the one-month period, J.T. is violently assaulted and killed by V.P., who is often used by C.L. to "collect debts."

A psychological research prison study by McCorkle *et al.* (1995) found that poor prison management increases prison violence. Data were collected from 371 state prisons and included measures of both individual and collective violence. In this study, only adult male state correctional facilities were examined; federal prisons, institutions for youths and women, medical facilities, drug and alcohol centers, boot camps, work camps, and community correction facilities were excluded. Of the 371 state prisons, 99 were maximum-security, 140 medium-security, and 132 minimum-security. Institutions were asked to report major incidents for the period of 1 July 1989 to 30 June 1990. Three types of prison violence were examined: inmate assaults against inmates, inmate assaults against staff, and riots. **Riots** were defined as assaults with five or more inmates involved, which required the intervention of outside assistance and which resulted in serious injury and/or property damage. McCorkle *et al.* (1995) found that the average rate of inmate-on-inmate assaults reported by prisons for the year was approximately two per 100 prisoners. Staff assaults occurred at a rate of less than one per 100 inmates, and 8% of prisons had experienced a riot during the year.

Prison management variables included the guard-to-inmate ratio, the guard turnover rate, the ratio of White to Black correctional staff, program involvement, and institutional size as reported in 1990. McCorkle *et al.* (1995) found that several management variables were significant causes of individual-level violence. For example, higher White-to-Black guard ratios were identified with higher rates of both inmate and staff assaults. In a more recent study, Berg and DeLisi (2006) found that, in a large southwestern state, the most violent inmates were Hispanic and Native American males and African American and Native American females. The authors go on to suggest that there is reason to believe that this may be due to the influence of different rates of victimization between ethnicities. In other words, it is possible that the inmate violence seen in these ethnicities is actually an extension of the violence seen in their communities, Trulson and Marquart (2002) conducted a study whereby ten years of inmate-on-inmate assault data were used to compare the rates of violence among inmates racially integrated in a double cell versus inmates racially segregated in a double cell. The results indicated that the violence between integrated inmates was actually lower than between segregated inmates.

Prisons in which a major percentage of the inmate population involved itself in educational, vocational, and prison industry programs had a lower incidence of violence against staff and inmates. Therefore, a conclusion can be drawn that prisons depriving inmates of program involvement have a higher incidence of violence than prisons that encourage program involvement. Both individual and collective violence were more common in medium- and maximum-security institutions than in minimum-security facilities. Large prisons reported slightly lower rates of inmate-on-inmate assaults. This study (McCorkle *et al.*, 1995) found that external conditions play a role in influencing prison violence. For example, prisons in states with high unemployment experienced lower rates of inmate assaults than prisons in states with lower unemployment. One explanation is that when there is high unemployment, parole boards may be more restrained and less likely to grant early release. Under such conditions, there is less turnover in prison populations, a factor proposed by some to be a major cause of prison violence.

In a more recent study, Cunningham, Sorensen, Vigen, and Woods (2010) examined prison homicides occurring from 2000 to 2008 in the Texas Department of Criminal Justice. Their findings indicated that prison homicide is actually rare; only four inmates out of every 100,000 are murdered in the United States every year. The authors reported that Hispanic inmates were over-represented as perpetrators and victims. Perpetrators and victims were likely to have suspected or known gang affiliations and were overwhelmingly male. The results of the study indicated that perpetrators differed from their victims in that they were often younger in age, had higher IQ scores, were more educated, and were more likely to have sentences for armed robbery.

Inmates are not only exposed to physical violence during their incarceration, sexual victimization has gained attention in the past decade. In fact, in 2003, legislation known as the **Prison Rape Elimination Act (PREA)** was passed which required correctional administrators to prevent, identify, and prosecute acts of sexual assault and to provide services and programs to aid both victims and perpetrators (42 U. S. C. § 15602). According to a national survey conducted by the Bureau of Justice Statistics (2010), approximately 4.4% and 3.1% of prison and jail inmates (respectively) reported being sexually victimized one or more times within the past twelve months by another inmate or facility staff member. According to the same survey, extrapolating these results to the national prison population indicates that approximately 88,500 adult inmates in jails and prisons nationwide at the time of the study had been victimized. In studying perpetrators of sexual assault in the correctional context, Morash, Jeong, and Zang (2010) found that men who threatened, attempted, or achieved sexual penetration of another inmate were often younger in age, had spent more years in prison, and had histories of juvenile robbery and adult sexual assault convictions. According to the authors, sexual abuse in childhood, adult sexual assault convictions, and a life sentence predicted inmates' unwanted sexual touching of other men.

Gang affiliation has also gained more attention in the research as a factor contributing to violent behavior in correctional contexts. Illuminating the problem of gang violence in prisons, a National Geographic (2006) film reported that, in one prison, almost 200 attacks every year could be attributed to gang violence. A more recent study found that most prison officials reported an increase in gang member numbers over the five years preceding the study, and that these inmates were more disruptive and sophisticated (Winterdyk & Ruddell, 2010). Researchers have found that gang membership has a significant impact on prison management and is significantly related to increased violent behavior in correctional settings, even when controlling for individual factors like age and previous criminal history (Drury & DeLisi, 2011; Griffin & Hepburn, 2006; Wood, Moir, & James, 2009). According to Toch (2007), the limited success of most efforts to monitor or control gang activity in correctional settings may have led to the practice of segregating gang members.

Huebner (2003) surveyed 4168 male inmates and found that those who were involved in work programs were significantly less likely to assault staff. Additionally, African American respondents who were gang members with a longstanding history of criminal behavior were the most likely to assault staff and inmates. Finally, subjects who were older and educated were less likely to commit assaults (Huebner, 2003). Hollin and Palmer (2003) suggest that screening for drug and alcohol problems is an important prerequisite for working with violent offenders. These researchers recommend screening for intensity of service delivery and identifying target or goals for change upon the commencement of a prison term.

Johnson (2001) examines structural causes of violence among African American inmates in United States prisons. He indicates that media images of violent black men in the news, the utilization of underpaid prison labor, and the rise of prisoner militancy since the 1960s and 1970s are all structural causes of violence. Johnson (2001) contends that there has been a 510% increase in the number of incarcerated drug offenders from 1983 until 1993, many of whom are African American. In comparison, Harrison and Karberg (2004) found that the imprisonment rate for African American men was 4834 per 100,000 residents while White men were imprisoned at a rate of 681 per 100,000 residents.

In a study by Mills and Kroner (2003), alienation, impulse expression, and age were antisocial constructs that were related to institutional disruptions and infractions by violent offenders. A study examined the relationship between Axis II (personality) disorders and community and institutional violence among a sample of 261 incarcerated women (Warren, Burnette, South, *et al.*, 2002). Results revealed that a significant relationship occurred between antisocial personality disorder and institutional violence, as well as narcissistic personality disorder and incarceration for a violent crime. Harer and Langan (2001) examined data for 24,765 women and 177,767 men admitted to federal prison in 1991 through 1998. These researchers found that while in prison, women committed less violence, overall, and less serious violence than men. However, they also found that the same classification instrument predicted violent behavior equally well for both genders.

In a 2009 meta-analysis, Douglas, Guy, and Hart found that major mental illness was associated with increases in violence rates of 49% to 68%. This link in correctional environments is important as estimates suggest that inmates with major mental illness constitute 15% to 24% of prison populations (Lamb & Weinberger, 2005; Magaletta, Diamond, Faust, Daggett, & Camp, 2009). Others have estimated that there are three times as many individuals with major mental illness in correctional facilities than in psychiatric hospitals (Torrey, Kennard, Enslinger, Lamb, & Pavle, 2010). Though psychotic symptoms have been associated with violent behavior among inmates with major mental illness, other factors such as childhood conduct disorder, adult personality disorder, substance misuse, or **criminal thinking** (e.g., thought content and thought processes capable of promoting criminal acts) may mediate (alter) the relationship and make it more likely that violence will occur (Mullen, 2006; Taylor, Hill, Bhagwagar, Darjee, & Thompson, 2008; Walters, 2011; Walters, 2012).

Research has also attempted to explore the relationship between psychopathy and violent behavior in correctional settings, often utilizing the Psychopathy Checklist Revised (PCL-R: Hare, 2003) to classify inmates as psychopathic. Classification as a psychopath has a demonstrated relationship for risk of future violence. Other measures of psychopathy have emerged and gained some support in the research, including the Psychopathic Personality Inventory (PPI: Lilienfeld & Andrews, 1996; Lilienfeld & Fowler, 2006). The PPI is composed of two factors (PPI-I and PPI-II) that some have argued reflect primary and secondary psychopathy (Edens, Poythress, Lilienfeld, & Patrick 2007). Edens *et al.* (2007) explain that PPI-I captures characteristics of **primary psychopathy** (e.g., fearlessness, low social anxiety) which may predict higher levels of nonaggressive misconduct while PPI-II captures characteristics of **secondary psychopathy** (e.g., emotional maladjustment, interpersonal conflict, impulsivity) which may predict higher levels of aggressive misconduct. Some research has supported the prediction of violent behavior in correctional settings using the PPI-II factor (Edens *et al.*, 2007; Edens, Poythress, Lilienfeld, Patrick, & Test, 2008).

Some suggest that prison violence, both individual and collective, is the result of failed prison management, including security lapses, high staff turnover, a lack of discipline among guards, unsearched inmates, and lack of prison programs. Organizational and management factors can be important determinants of prison violence. Toch (2001) contends that supermax confinement or high-tech segregation settings create additional mental health problems in already violent offenders that result in the enhancement, not the reduction, of inmate violence potential. The increase in the prisoner population, which now numbers more than 1 million, has been relentless since the 1980s and shows no signs of diminishing. The consistent increase of the prison population since the late 1980s has been staggering. For example, the number of prisoners in the United States in 2003 was 2.1 million; 1.4 million in state and federal prisons, and 691,301 defendants in local jails (Harrison & Karberg, 2004). Prison statistics such as these raise the psychological issue: How can prison programs be effective to inmates in an overcrowded facility? In response to this question, some researchers engaged in a study focusing on the effects of prison overcrowding on correctional educational programs.

Forensic Psychology and Policy Implications

Life in prison entails facing a chronically stressful environment with its demanding regimentation, loss of control, and daily potential for violence. Prison educational programs offer inmates an escape from these stressors and a lower risk for violence. However, current criminal justice policies aimed at regulating prison populations have negative consequences for correctional education programs and the public. For example, an implemented population ceiling allows thousands of inmates early release and results in a rapid decrease in time served. Therefore, the opportunity to benefit and rehabilitate from educational programming eludes many prisoners. As a policy matter, returning unprepared and untrained prisoners to the community poses a threat to public safety. Prison educational programs are the most powerful methods to help advance prison governance, institutional stability, and control over inmate violence. For example, inmates who attend several hours of class each day are occupied rather than idle. Research suggests that inmates who are busy are not as likely to be security problems and present a lower risk for violence (Johnson, 2008; McCorkle *et al.*, 1995; Wilson & Tamatea, 2010; Yoshikazu, 2010; Yuma, 2010). However, when prison overcrowding forces policymakers to implement criminal justice initiatives − such as a population cap and a redistribution of funds to other prison necessities (additional cells, clothes, and food) − the results can have a disastrous impact on educational programming.

For example, depriving prisoners of such assistance creates a psychologically stressful environment. Inmates are not rehabilitated through programs nor kept busy with educational work. Abolition of educational initiatives would mean that other programs to keep the inmates active would need to be created, funded, and staffed. Therefore, prison stability and control over prison violence are hampered when educational programs are cut: inmates have increased idle time, which can produce violence and chaos. Research on correctional educational programs demonstrates that they help prison organizations run efficiently and keep inmates at a low risk for violence.

Correctional/forensic psychologists can play an important role in screening inmates for their potential for institutional violence. The HCR-20 and the Psychopathy Checklist: Screening Version (PCL:SV) were used to assess the prediction of institutional violence in 41 long-term sentenced offenders in two maximum security correctional institutions (Belfrage, Fransson, & Strand, 2000). Results demonstrated a high predictive validity for the clinical and risk management items of the HCR-20 but almost none for its historical items. Overall, the findings suggest that correctional institutional violence can be predicted adequately by the use of the HCR-20 and the PCL:SV.

Suggestions for Future Research

One method for minimizing incidents of violence is to use comprehensive environmental scanning systems to regularly monitor behaviors in prisons and identify potential "hot spots" for violence. The ultimate goal of these systems is to enhance the ability of correctional administrators and managers to better monitor the prison environment on a continuing basis. The environment is monitored by collecting and analyzing a variety of factors that provide information on the morale, behaviors, and perceptions of prison staff, administrators, and inmates.

Environmental scanning consists of four steps. First, a process is developed to identify emerging behaviors, such as increases or decreases in typical accepted prison tension indicators including assaults and fights. Second, the findings of the scanning process are organized in an information package and distributed to administrators. Third, upon reviewing the information, the administrators must decide whether the behaviors represent a threat to the prison (threats can emerge from factors such as increases in assaults, drug finds, and inmate misbehavior or decreases in such factors as inmate program participation, counseling contracts, or health care services). Fourth, they must determine if there is a need for intervention policies and/or procedures to address these behaviors.

Scanning systems have a critical role in prison violence prevention. First, potential prison problem areas can be detected before serious concerns emerge. Second, scanning systems force prison administrators to consider which factors best measure the well-being of their institution, the employees, and the inmate population. Third, scanning systems create a database for prison information and help correctional administrators better detect normal versus abnormal data entries. Finally, scanning systems force administrators to ask questions such as: Why did the trends emerge? Why are they shifting? Did any policy and/or personnel actions influence the trends? Should action be taken? These questions help corrections administrators make informed management decisions (Labecki, 1994). The comprehensive scanning systems enable administrators to better understand, predict, and design for the needs of offenders and programs, staffing, and security demands. Most importantly, a scanning system can help administrators distinguish between a psychologically acceptable and a psychologically oppressive and tension-filled environment.

Other programs such as art, work, or educational programs have shown promise in reducing inmate violence. Further research is needed to serve as evidence to argue for their continuation in the face of budget cuts and other correctional policy decision-making. Program involvement helps inmates stay out of trouble and reduces the violence in prisons. Conflict-resolution training teaches inmates the skills and resources to handle their own and other inmates' anger. It also teaches correctional officers the communication skills needed for positive interaction with inmates. Conflict-resolution training usually requires 15 hours of instruction. The course curriculum is designed to provide special skills in handling conflict with an emphasis on developing and improving skills in listening, problem solving, encouraging positive values, and mediation, plus an emphasis on anger control, forgiveness, and nonviolence. The conflict-resolution training objective is to improve communication, promote self-esteem, build relationships, and encourage respect for cultural differences and people's emotions. It also teaches techniques to resolve disputes without emphasizing winning or losing.

Historically, conflict-resolution training has been effective in prisons with highly aggressive and violent-prone inmates (Love, 1994). For example, conflict-resolution training was developed at the State Correctional Institution at Huntington, Pennsylvania, which houses some of the state's most aggressive inmates and where staff must deal with violence daily. Of the 2200 inmates, nearly a third are serving life sentences and many have extensive histories of assaultive behavior. In 1988, Community First Step, an inmate organization at SCI-Huntington, decided to bring the conflict-resolution program to that facility. The course was well received, and after 3 years, Community First Step invited prison officers to participate in a training session with inmates. They believed, correctly, that including officers would improve relationships between inmates and officers.

One Huntington inmate who was serving 10 to 20 years for a violent assaultive crime participated in the training with corrections officers. He noted that one of the officers who took part was a strict disciplinarian from a military background who believed that inmates were "nobodies." According to the inmate, after completing the conflict-resolution course, the officer was more humane and professional in his relationships with inmates (Love, 1994). The most powerful example of the effectiveness of conflict-resolution training occurred during the 1989 riots at the State Correctional Institution at Camp Hill. Inmates in the New Values drug-and-alcohol program, who had recently completed a course in conflict resolution, were the only inmates who did not participate in the disturbance. Also, these inmates were credited with helping officers so they would not be violently attacked. More research on the effectiveness of comprehensive scanning systems and conflict-resolution training in corrections is needed.

Further research into the role of major mental illness, as well as other mediating factors, on inmates' violent behaviors should be undertaken. How does a history of major mental illness when it is combined with significant criminal histories and the like increase the relationship to violent behavior or prisoner misconduct? Such research should include studies to clarify the role of each factor in contributing to violent behavior and their possible utility in predicting violent behavior. By identifying factors that may predict violence in correctional settings, it may be possible to develop new screening instruments, and/or further validate existing, screening instruments. This would enable inmates with major mental illness, who may be violent, to be placed into segregated populations or treatment programs. Psychopathy has continued to emerge as a potentially valuable construct in predicting violence in correctional settings; however, further research into the nature of psychopathy's relationship with violence is necessary to determine what elements can best predict future violence. Furthermore, actuarial violence risk measures specifically for institutional settings are needed.

Practice Update Section: Counseling/Treating Offender Populations in Corrections

Psychologists who work in correctional settings face a myriad of ethical and treatment-related challenges in working with difficult offender populations. The very environment itself can be a source of considerable stress for the inmates and sometimes the treatment provider. The policies and procedures of the institution are typically not conducive to a therapeutic environment. Clearly, the focus of incarceration remains on retribution, not rehabilitation.

Take for instance the inmate that is seen for individual counseling, who discloses suicidal ideation with a plan. The inmate describes the method he intends to use to harm himself and indicates that he is currently in possession of that means (e.g., a razor tucked inside his mattress). While it is necessary to immediately initiate suicide precautions and to prevent access to the weapon or razor described in the plan, a series of institutional policies must now be followed that will have quite punitive repercussions for the inmate. Some prison systems require that the inmate who poses an imminent risk for suicide be stripped naked to search for other potential weapons and to prevent any clothing from being used as a weapon to harm oneself. He may then be placed naked into a protective cell, where he must be observed by correctional staff. The razor the inmate possessed is considered contraband and he has now committed an infraction by having it in his possession. Committing an institutional infraction can have implications for parole hearings, inmate worker positions, and other privileges. It is likely the inmate will feel punished for expressing his suicidal ideation and plan to the psychologist and he may be reluctant or unwilling to report any future plans or wishes to harm himself. Additionally, feeling degraded and punished will do little to alleviate depression, hopelessness, or suicidal thoughts. When the environmental restraints to prevent suicide are lifted, the inmate might be less inclined to reach out for mental health services. Yet, the need for policies to protect a dense prison population, as well as ensure the security of the institution, is undeniable.

Correctional psychologists are typically understaffed and are required to perform a number of roles such as assessment and treatment, acting as research consultants for administrators, and training for correctional and medical staff. Specific assessment and treatment-related duties often include: psychological testing (e.g., differential diagnosis, malingering, cognitive deficits, etc.), inmate screenings, homicidal and suicidal risk assessments, crisis assessment and intervention, mental status examinations, competency to execute evaluations for death row inmates, reviewing infractions committed by mentally ill inmates, individual therapy, group therapy, sex offender treatment, substance abuse treatment, risk assessment for parole boards, and the like.

Although general clinical skills relating to assessment and treatment are essential, an understanding of institutional dynamics, policies and procedures, and characteristics and research specifically relating to offender populations is also critical to competently providing mental health services in a prison or jail.

Due to many inmates' history of violence and institutional security policies, group rooms or rooms for counseling and assessment must be clearly visible by correctional and/or nursing staff to ensure the safety of clinicians. Some institutions provide body alarms for mental health professionals to wear. Although the clinician wants to create a therapeutic alliance for individual or group therapy, safety must be paramount.

The level of confidentiality in a correctional institution can be quite different from the community, as inmates have much less privacy. Inmates must be clear on the limits of confidentiality that are inherent in a correctional or forensic setting, where often the protection of society or other individuals supercedes the individual. In cases where a psychologist is called in to assess an inmate who is engaging in bizarre or self-injurious behavior, a correctional staff is typically present. A psychologist who is conducting a psychological evaluation in the Administrative Segregation (AdSeg) or the Security Housing Unit (SHU) with an inmate who has been aggressive toward a staff or another inmate, is typically required to wear a protective vest and if the inmate has to be taken out of their individual cell, they are done so in ankle and wrist shackles, with the correctional officer present throughout the evaluation for the safety of the evaluator.

Mental health professionals working in jails or prisons also regularly encounter antisocial personalities or very manipulative and potentially dangerous clients. They quickly learn that what is reported to them frequently cannot be accepted at face value. It is very common for correctional staff to become "cynical, sarcastic, or negative" and these attitudes are very "detrimental to staff morale and therapeutic relationships" (Carr, Hinkle, & Ingram, 1991, p. 84). These researchers suggest the following tips for interacting with manipulative patients or inmates (pp. 84–85):

1. Be firm, but not abusive.
2. Set limits.
3. Don't make promises you can't keep.
4. Be clear about what you will and won't do.
5. For security reasons you cannot and therefore do not tell inmates everything or answer all their questions.
6. Distinguish between genuine and manipulative complaints using past history, evident gains, and personal experience.
7. Don't get into making deals. This puts patients in control.
8. Put the responsibility back on the patient.
9. Determine what is immediate and what can wait. Many patients will try to convince you that every concern they have is urgent and immediate.
10. Don't bend the rules unless it's a safety issue.
11. Get consultation. It's easy to be manipulated until you have some distance.
12. Try to determine the motive of the patient's behaviors and statements. Don't make assumptions.

13. Recognize that some patients are being manipulative because it is the only way they know how to get their needs met. Try to educate them regarding more adaptive coping mechanisms.
14. Try to determine the motive of the patient's behaviors and statements. Don't make assumptions.
15. Recognize that some patients are being manipulative because it is the only way they know how to get their needs met. Try to educate them regarding more adaptive coping mechanisms.

Correctional psychologists are charged with the provision of psychological services to a high-risk population with complicated treatment needs in a setting that is not conducive to rehabilitation. Appropriately trained correctional psychologists working with offender populations in jails and prisons are balancing ethical issues such as confidentiality, treatment needs, institutional security, and patient welfare.

Finally, Elliott and Verdeyen (2003) have offered the following "Ten Commandments" for individuals working with inmate or forensic populations: (1) Go home safe and sound at the end of the day (i.e., do not take unnecessary risks in an already risky setting, and be aware of your surroundings as well as how to call for help); (2) Establish realistic expectations (i.e., understand that many inmates have longstanding behavioral or personality traits which are difficult to change); (3) Set firm and consistent limits; (4) Avoid power struggles; (5) Manage interpersonal boundaries using the strategies described in this section; (6) Do not take things personally; (7) Strive for an attitude of healthy skepticism; (8) Do not fight the bureaucracy (i.e., follow policies and procedures, even if you disagree with them, and do not let inmates know which policies with which you do and do not agree); (9) Ask for help; and (10) Do not take your work home with you (i.e., engage in enjoyable activities with people not connected with the institution).

Related Websites

www.prisonpolicy.org
Website of the Prison Policy Initiative, which includes articles and recommendations regarding prison policies, including policies pertaining to the incarceration of the mentally ill.
www.aca.org/government/healthcare.asp#mentalillness
Website of the American Correctional Association, provides resources, statistics, and information pertaining to the incarcerated mentally ill.
http://nicic.gov/MentalIllness
Website of the National Institute of Corrections that provides articles and information pertaining to mental illness in correctional environments.
www.sanjeevhimachali.com/?p=401
Suicide Risk assessment is in need of providing mental health screenings, crisis intervention, and treatment for the prevention of suicide in inmates.
www.suicide.org
This website is designed to prevent suicide, bring awareness of suicides, and a website that offers support in need during a suicide crisis.

Continued

Related Websites—cont'd

www.save.org
This website is designed to educate individuals on suicide to prevent suicide, offer support to individuals in need, and also help deal with coping with a loss of someone who committed suicide.
www.tdcj.state.tx.us
This website offers an overview of sex offender treatment programs in the state of Texas.
www.doc.wa.gov
This website offers an overview of sex offender treatment programs in Washington State Prison system.
www.sexoffendertreatment.com
This is an online treatment program. It offers an outline of the program and what it entails.
www.ipt-forensics.com
This website provides an overview of court mandated treatments for sex offenders.
www.aapl.org
This website outlines and provides information on landmark cases.
www.ncjrs.gov
This website provides information on the legal limitations of correctional therapy and research.
http://desertwaters.com/?page_id=693
Provides resources and suggestions for correctional employees and their families, including information pertaining to manipulation attempts by offenders.
http://cipp.org/index1.html
The website for the Center for Innovative Public Policies, which contains information regarding policy recommendations regarding correctional and forensic facilities, including information regarding preventing and coping with staff boundary violations with inmates.
www.justice.gov
United States Department of Justice website.
http://bjs.ojp.usdoj.gov
Bureau of Justice Statistics website.

PART II

Juvenile Forensics

Courts and the Legal System: Delinquent Conduct

Key Issues

Defining the Age of Criminal Responsibility
- A review of landmark cases that set precedence in juvenile law.
- Trends in punishment verses treatment
- Become familiar with waivers used to transfer juveniles to adult courts
- Defining the age of criminal responsibility

Cyberbullying
- Forms of cyberbullying
- Current statistics regarding rates of cyberbullying
- Comparison with traditional forms of bullying
- Effects of cyberbullying
- Characteristics of cyberbullying victims and perpetrators

Psychology of School Violence
- Use of weapons in school violence
- Effects on students, teachers, staff, parents and the public
- The use of threat assessment techniques to predict and prevent school violence
- Effective prevention and intervention techniques
- Current legislation aimed at addressing school violence

Sentencing: Psychology of Juvenile Rehabilitation
- Background of the rehabilitative v. punitive debate.
- Examples of rehabilitative programs for juvenile offenders.

CHAPTER 6

Juvenile/Family Forensics

Chapter Outline

Overview

The role of psychology in the juvenile justice system brings a different set of pressing and complicated issues to the forensic field versus its adult counterpart. As various and recent media accounts depict, adolescent behavior can be no less gruesome and shocking than conduct committed by career criminals — this is particularly true with school shootings. While youth violent crime has typically been associated with minority gang members in urban areas, the Caucasian gunmen responsible for the small town school shootings in Columbine, Colorado; Jonesboro, Arkansas; and Santee, California make it clear that youth rage and violence can cross both geographic and racial boundaries. The domain of juvenile forensic psychology examines the conduct of children and adolescents and explains why they act deviantly and break the law. Although there are many more questions about adolescent (mis-)behavior than there are answers, the psychological sciences can help the court system make sense of what juveniles do and why.

There are four controversies investigated in this chapter. These topics include: (1) defining the age of criminal responsibility; (2) cyberbullying; (3) the psychology of school violence; and (4) sentencing: the psychology of juvenile rehabilitation. Certainly, many other contested subjects exist in the legal domain of juvenile and family forensics; however, these four issues represent key areas of considerable debate within the law and psychology communities. In addition, the issues explored in this chapter demonstrate where and how forensic psychological experts are called upon to assist the court system from the pretrial adjudication phase to the postconviction stage of a particular case, and how they can assist our school systems with threat assessments informed by research, as well as guiding prevention programs for students at risk of bullying or being bullied. Additionally, the devastating effects of bullying and the difficulties faced by school officials, parents, law enforcement and mental health professionals in this arena are explored, particularly when these effects escalate to potentially lethal school violence.

Adolescents can behave recklessly and deviantly. They can also engage in illicit conduct. What knowing decision-making capabilities do children exercise when breaking the law? How does psychology help us determine when youths are or are not responsible for their (criminal) actions? Is there a definable age of criminal responsibility?

Youths who violate the law can be held accountable for their behavior. Are children who engage in illicit conduct troubled or violent? How do the psychological sciences assist the court system in treating at-risk youths?

What prevention strategies exist to break the cycle of rage that can begin with bullying in all of its forms, including cyberbullying? What intervention and prevention strategies can prevent the most devastating consequences of bullying such as suicide or school shootings? What factors can lead to school shootings and how can these rare events be predicted and prevented? What are the causal factors leading to these (and other) forms of school violence? How can psychology and criminology help us understand the phenomenon of school shootings?

As the sections of this chapter demonstrate, there is an important role for forensic psychologists in the juvenile and adult criminal court arenas. The entire juvenile adjudication process could benefit from additional consultation with mental health specialists. Presently, therapists, administrators, and advocates in the psychological community are routinely called upon to help address the problems of at-risk youths and to divert them, where possible, away from the formal justice system. Solving many of the remaining questions in juvenile and family forensics requires careful and thoughtful research strategies. Indeed, as the sections of this chapter repeatedly make clear, evidenced-based practice is one viable direction by which psychologists can assist those court practitioners who work in the field.

Defining the Age of Criminal Responsibility

Introduction

> *There is evidence...that there may be grounds for concern that the child receives the worst of both worlds; that he (or she) get neither the protections accorded to adults nor the solicitous care and regenerative treatment postulated for children (383 U.S., at 556, 1966).*

The above statement was taken from the United States Supreme Court case of *Kent v. United States* (1966). In this case an intruder entered the apartment of a woman in the District of Columbia, raped her, and then took her wallet. The fingerprints at the apartment matched those of Morris Kent, a 16-year-old. He was soon taken into custody and interrogated from 3 pm to 10 pm the same evening. The next day Kent underwent further interrogation by the police. Kent's mother did not know that he was in custody until 2 pm on the second day. Kent's mother and her counsel visited Kent, at which time he was charged with housebreaking, robbery, and rape. Consider another example as depicted by Gray (2001, p. 7):

Few people in her South Philadelphia neighborhood understood why 11-year-old Miriam White snapped that afternoon two summers ago. They learned later that she had been hysterical after an argument with a family member and, seizing a kitchen knife and hiding it under her coat, had run out of the house and down the street. With the force of her frantic preadolescent body, Miriam, according to news reports, drove that knife blade deep into a stranger's chest. It cut through one of 55-year-old Rosemarie Knight's ribs and plunged six inches into her heart... Miriam later told the arresting officer, "I wanted to kill the lady. That's why I stabbed her in the heart."...According to court records, less than three weeks before she stabbed Rosemarie Knight, Miriam had been released from Horsham Clinic, an inpatient facility for children and adults with emotional and behavioral problems. She was back with her adoptive family, but receiving no community-based treatment services, she was having trouble adjusting. ...She told the psychiatrist that she left the house fully intending to stab somebody, but "a grown-up, not a teenager or a kid or a baby."..."I stabbed that lady," she told the psychiatrist. "I didn't think she had any kids." The doctor asked Miriam why it was important for the adult she chose to not have children. "Kids need their mothers," responded Miriam — an ironic comment given her own circumstance: As a toddler she had been taken by child-welfare authorities from her own birth mother who, like Miriam, was mentally ill... Today, in the Commonwealth of Pennsylvania, Miriam, now 14 years old, is the youngest person ever charged as an adult with murder and the youngest girl ever remanded to the Federal Detention Center in Philadelphia, an adult facility.

This section examines the issues stemming from these examples, especially the question of when juveniles are responsible for their actions and how juveniles should be treated in regards to these actions. This chapter also considers the respective roles criminal justice and psychology assume in creating, sustaining, and responding to the age of criminal responsibility. The age of criminal responsibility is addressed by looking at and providing examples of the juvenile and criminal court systems, relevant literature, case law, and current research.

At the turn of the century, juvenile offenders were separated from adult offenders because they were seen as treatable. Today, however, there is a general trend in society to hold juvenile offenders accountable for their actions (Granello & Hanna, 2003; Umbreit, 1995). Society is moving away from rehabilitation and restoration toward punishment and retribution. **Restorative justice** is focused on repairing the damage that has been done during the commission of a criminal act for both the victim and the offender. As a result of the shift in juvenile justice treatment philosophy, the majority of United States jurisdictions transfer juveniles to adult court through means of a waiver process. This process will be discussed later in this section. The courts' trend toward punishment creates a need for psychologists to determine when people are responsible for their actions and when they should be punished. When trying to determine the psychological age of responsibility, one cannot base the answer on a decision from a court, like the legal age of responsibility. Defining an age at which a youth should be transferred to adult court has not been validated scientifically, but evidence suggests that the youths who are transferred to adult systems are more likely to re-offend (Mason, Chapman, Chang, & Simons, 2003; Sellers & Arrigo, 2009). This creates some tension between these two fields. Notwithstanding, the fields of psychology and law are continually merging closer together. To understand cases like *Kent v. United States* (1966) and the age of criminal responsibility, we review the relevant legal and psychological literature.

Literature Review

According to Fritsch and Hemmens (1995), English common law held that children under the age of 7 were incapable of criminal responsibility. Children between the ages of 7 and 14 were still incapable, unless it could be established that they were able to understand the consequences of their actions. Juveniles over the age of 14 were considered fully responsible for their actions and would receive the same punishment as adult offenders. The *parens patriae* doctrine, which is derived from English common law, allows the state to intervene and act in the "best interests of the child" whenever it is deemed necessary (Reppucci & Crosby, 1993).

There is a general trend in society to lower the age of criminal responsibility and to punish rather than rehabilitate offenders. "This move away from rehabilitation has had a marked impact on every level of the criminal justice system, from the police to the courts to corrections" (Fritsch & Hemmens, 1995, p. 17). Research indicates that a possible explanation for the increase in public opinion favoring harsher punishment for these youthful offenders has been largely influenced by the high profile crimes such as mass school shootings with more than one victim and children who kill their parents (Piquero & Steinberg, 2010). Legislatures responded to the public's desire to "get tough" on crime by passing laws that have toughened the adult criminal justice system. These laws included making prison sentences longer, eliminating "good time" credits used toward an earlier parole, and replacing indeterminate with determinate sentencing. The trend of holding the offender accountable carried over from the adult criminal system into the juvenile justice system due to the rise in adolescent crime. The juvenile courts then shifted away from rehabilitation and moved toward punishment. This shift caused a large increase in the use of waivers by judges (Mason, Chapman, Chang, & Simons, 2003). Judicial waivers are used in 46 states (Griffin, 2009). In 1994, approximately 12,100 juvenile offenders were transferred to adult criminal courts, this declined by 33% in 1997 (D'Angelo, 2007). Judges use waivers to place juveniles into the adult justice system so that youth offenders can receive a more severe punishment. This procedure or waiver is also referred to as "certification," "transfer," "reference," "remand," or "declination" (D'Angelo, 2007; Sellers & Arrigo, 2009).

An April 2009 report from the Juvenile Justice Update found that every state had at least one provision for transferring juveniles to adult court (Griffin, 2009). "Twenty-eight states automatically exclude certain types of offenders from juvenile court jurisdiction, 15 permit prosecutors to file some cases directly to adult criminal courts, and 46 allow juvenile court judges' discretion on whether to send cases to adult courts" (p. 79). An April 2000 study by the National Council on Crime and Delinquency in Oakland found that among juveniles with no prison record, African Americans were six times more likely than their Caucasian counterparts to be waived from juvenile to adult court for comparable crimes, and were punished more harshly when convicted (Gray, 2001). Boys make up approximately 95% of the juveniles transferred and remanded to adult facilities in the United States; however, over 400 girls were sent to adult women's prisons in 1994 and 1996. It was notable that these

400 girls were disproportionately African American (Gaarder & Belknap, 2002; Puzzanchera, 2000). Allard and Young (2002, p. 65) state:

> *Because there is considerable racial disparity in the assignment of children to adult pros-*
> *ecution, the harshness, ineffectiveness, and punishing aspects of transfer from juvenile to*
> *adult court is doubly visited on children of color.*

More recently, the National Center for Juvenile Justice found that delinquency amongst African Americans increased by 33% in 2007 (Pazzanchera, Adams, & Sickmund, 2010). There has been a steady increase in the amount of female delinquency since 2007. The areas that have shown the greatest increase in female offending include property, drug-related, and **public order offenses** such as disorderly conduct, driving while intoxicated, or public intoxication (Pazzanchera, Adams, & Sickmund, 2010). According to the National Center for Juvenile Justice, 20% of arrests in 2000 involving youth who were eligible in their states for handling within the juvenile justice system were dealt with by law enforcement agencies; 71% were referred to the juvenile court; and 7% were referred directly to the criminal court (Federal Probation, 2003). Yet, others were referred to a welfare agency or to another police agency. According to the National Center for Juvenile Justice, of the 1,666,100 juvenile criminal cases in 2007, 54% of the youths were 16 years old or younger, 27% were females, and 64% were White (Pazzanchera, Adams, & Sickmund, 2010).

In the example of *Kent v. United States* (1966), the juvenile court judge ordered a judicial waiver to place 16-year-old Kent into the criminal court system and he was tried as an adult. Kent's counsel filed a "question of waiver" motion. This motion was filed in the juvenile court asking for a hearing to present reasons why Kent should be tried as an adult, but his motion was refused. In *Kent v. United States* (1966), the Supreme Court outlined the procedures for using waivers and extended several due process rights to juveniles that are involved in the waiver process. The waiver hearing must be a full hearing in which the juvenile has the right to have counsel present (Fritsch & Hemmens, 1995; Sellers & Arrigo, 2009).

In the 1980s many state legislatures passed laws that enacted waivers. These certifications transferred juvenile offenders of serious and violent crimes from the juvenile justice system into the criminal justice system. The legislatures believed that the juveniles would then receive a harsher punishment for their offenses. In one research study this intention of greater punishment was found to only be true in a small number of cases (Kinder *et al.*, 1995). In fact, the juvenile cases transferred to adult courts were far more likely to be pending or unresolved. Waivers are usually attached to the more serious and violent crimes like murder, rape, and aggravated assault because these offenses need more severe sanctions than the juvenile justice system can impose (D'Angelo, 2007). During 2008, juveniles were involved in 9% of the murder arrests in the United States, and approximately 25% of all other violent crimes including rape, robbery, and aggravated assault (Office of Juvenile Justice and Delinquency Prevention, 2009).

There are three types of waivers used: (1) **judicial waivers**; (2) **direct file statutes** (also known as prosecutorial discretion or concurrent jurisdiction); and (3) **exclusionary statutes** (D'Angelo, 2007). D'Angelo (2007, p. 148) also notes that these waivers are utilized when the juvenile offenders presented are deemed "untreatable." These are repeat offenders, or those juveniles who have committed serious crimes. These types of waivers are used in some fashion in all 50 states. The judicial waiver, which is most common, is implemented when "a juvenile court judge decides whether to transfer a juvenile case to criminal after a formal hearing" (Griffin, 2009, p. 7). Griffin (2009, p. 7) notes that this is a "traditional process," which is used to determine if the juvenile offender deserves the protection and support provided by the juvenile system. Statutory exclusion waivers involve "placing juveniles within the original jurisdiction of criminal courts" (p. 7). This determination is made based on circumstances such as the nature of the crime, and the age of the offender. The prosecutorial discretion waiver allows the prosecutor to determine if the case should be tried in either juvenile or criminal court (Sellers & Arrigo, 2009).

D'Angelo (2007) reported that in 1994 an estimated 12,100 juvenile offenders were transferred to criminal court; this is according to research by Puzzanchera in 2001 (p. 148). In this same research, it was noted that the principle behind judicial transfer of juvenile offenders is to punish those youthful offenders who are deemed "untreatable," these individuals have little hope of rehabilitation within the juvenile system (D'Angelo, 2007). This begs two questions: (1) If you are going to hold a juvenile accountable as an adult, then should the juvenile receive the same rights as an adult? (2) what are the relationships that exist between children's responsibilities and children's rights? The Supreme Court said that with the lowering of the age of responsibility, due process should be present in the juvenile justice system (Fritsch & Hemmens, 1995).

A major reason for the courts granting juveniles more rights is the belief that because of their age and inexperience they lack the ability and/or capacity to protect their own best interests (Fischer, Stein, & Heikkinen, 2009). Juvenile capabilities grow as a child develops and has age appropriate or customary life experiences. These capabilities will continue to mature throughout the adolescent's life. It is nearly impossible to put an age limit on the juvenile in the criminal justice system, as each case will have a different set of circumstances and should be tried on a case by case evaluation (Fischer, Stein, & Heikkinen, 2009). Allard and Young (2002, p. 65) state, "These transfers place children into a court setting in which they are at a disadvantage at every stage of the process." Theories regarding judgment in decision-making (or decisional competence) postulate that throughout adolescence, judgment is impaired because the development of several psychosocial factors that are thought to impact decision-making are less developed than the cognitive capacities that are required to make mature, rational decisions (Fried & Reppucci, 2001).

Nathaniel Abraham, a 13-year-old African American, was the youngest person in American history to be convicted of adult murder (Grisso, 2000). He committed the murder at age 11 as a sixth grader. Mr. Abraham shot and killed a stranger who was leaving a store and was convicted of second-degree murder. He was the first juvenile charged with murder to be prosecuted under a 1997 Michigan law also known as the Juvenile Waiver Law that allowed adult prosecutions of children of any age in a serious felony case. The law stood in stark contrast to traditional juvenile laws that allowed judges to use their discretion based on certain criteria to determine if a juvenile should be tried as an adult. During his trial, mental health experts testified that he was emotionally and mentally impaired. While a 13-year-old might have some of the basic cognitive skills to understand the nature and purpose of a trial, his rational and independent decision-making capacity might not be adequately matured, rendering him an ineffective participant in his legal defense (Grisso, 2000). Mr. Abraham was convicted as an adult but sentenced as a juvenile. He was sentenced to juvenile detention until his 21st birthday. He was released from juvenile custody in January of 2007. According to the Associated Press (2009), Mr. Abraham was found guilty on drug charges almost two years after his 2007 release. He had been caught with 254 ecstasy tablets outside a gas station that he was selling out of the back of his car. He is currently serving four to 20 years for this conviction and will be eligible for parole in August of 2011.

When determining the psychological age of responsibility, one cannot base the answer on a decision from a court, such as the legal age of responsibility. The age of responsibility differs from state to state, but federal law regards juveniles as adults at the age of 16. In *Thompson v. Oklahoma* (1988), the Supreme Court ruled that the Eighth Amendment to the U.S. Constitution prohibited the execution of a person who was under the age of 16 at the time of the offense. According to *Stanford v. Kentucky* (1989) and *Wilkins v. Missouri* (1989), executions were legal for crimes committed by juveniles aged 16 and 17 years. However, in March of 2005, the Supreme Court in *Roper v. Simmons* ruled that defendants under the age of 18 at the time of the crime cannot be sentenced to death. The majority opinion held that sentencing a youth to death was in direct violation of the Eighth and Fourteenth amendments.

The law has long recognized that children are less mature and less capable than adults in many legal areas. The law, however, is not clear about the degree to which certain capacities of responsibility vary with chronological age. For example, as we get older are we more responsible for all of our actions or only for specific age-based conduct? The law is also unclear as to how levels of cognitive and socioemotional development affect levels of responsibility (Fischer, Stein, & Heikkinen, 2009). When a juvenile judge sends a youth to the criminal court, the youth is then supposed to meet the adult standard of responsibility, including the ability to make informed decisions.

Psychologists maintain that a person can learn from his or her mistakes and succeed in life if placed in the right environment. It would be ideal for the courts, when holding a juvenile offender accountable, to consider if the juvenile had both a cognitive meaning (understanding impact of their behavior on the victim) and a behavioral meaning (taking action to make things right) for their conduct (Umbreit, 1995). Umbreit also argues that the justice system should start practicing interventions or "restorative justice" in which the victim, the offender, and the community actively solve problems together (see also Sellers & Arrigo, 2009). Psychologists would then be called in to assist the juvenile justice system with this proactive approach.

Forensic Psychology and Policy Implications

As more juveniles are being waived to adult courts, forensic psychologists will play an increasingly important role in educating the court about a juvenile's competency or capacity to function adequately in an adult system. It will be very important for the forensic psychologist to have a firm grasp on the differences between the juvenile court system and the adult criminal court system, including the nuances of the psycholegal questions and capacities required to function adequately in each. Psychologists who agree to provide guidance on matters of juveniles and the law must be able to provide insight into matters of social science as well (Fischer, Stein, & Heikkinen, 2009). We may be called to provide testimony about an adolescent's moral or cognitive development. A forensic evaluator could also be asked to speak to a juvenile's ability to plan and to make independent and rational decisions. It is important, however, for the courts to remember that juveniles are still growing and developing. It is essential to recognize that "different developmental capabilities are relevant to the analysis of different legal age boundaries" (Fischer, Stein, & Heikkinen, 2009, p. 602). There is no way to guarantee that what psychologists and courts believe is actually in the best interest of a youth. If society is going to hold a juvenile accountable as an adult, then the juvenile should receive the same rights as an adult. Additionally, when the court treats a youthful offender like an adult, does the court protect the youth and society (now and in the future)? In the legal system many unlawful acts also constitute moral violations; therefore, we must take into account how moral development affects the ability of a juvenile to understand why a particular action is "wrong" (Peterson-Badali & Abramovitch, 1993; Sellers & Arrigo, 2009).

Suggestions for Future Research

In order to provide useful information for legal decision-makers, future psychological research must be conducted with legal issues in mind. In this way, the findings will have a direct impact on the law. We need to continue to examine legal cases like *Kent v. United States* (1966) and integrate psychological knowledge about children's best interests and capacities to the decision-making process of the juvenile justice system. If research is conducted carefully with the inclusion of legal issues, the relationship between psychology and law can be woven together and will enable judges to make decisions that are in the best interest of the juvenile. Legal standards and their assumptions about children's capacities must be investigated from both legal and psychological perspectives (Fischer, Stein, & Heikkinen, 2009). Studying children's capacities and performance in a legal context, however, is difficult because children can only be compared with adults or other "normal" children (Mason, Chapman, Chang, & Simons, 2003). Future research and analysis of "impulse control and susceptibility to peer pressure" would provide valuable information about developmentally common adolescent decision-making (Fischer, Stein, & Heikkinen, 2009, p. 602). This information could help inform and facilitate any changes that need to be made in the laws affecting juveniles.

Throughout this section, the question of whether to rehabilitate or to punish an adolescent has continually surfaced. Thus, it is important to conduct research on the effects of punishment versus treatment so that juveniles who need help can effectively obtain it. It is crucial as well to study age-appropriate legal decision-making so that juveniles have the freedom to make legal decisions on their own while allowing them the opportunity to understand the law and their rights. It would also be beneficial to do research on the relationships that exist between children's responsibilities and children's rights. Research in this area is difficult because it is hard to determine at what age all juveniles can be allowed to make their own life decisions, considering each juvenile is unique. Studying age-appropriate decision-making raises other issues: Are we better decision-makers as our age increases, and is age the most important factor in determining responsibility? By studying the age of criminal responsibility, forensic psychologists can examine the effectiveness of the current juvenile justice system and make suggestions for change so as to improve the treatment of adolescent offenders.

Cyberbullying

Introduction

Traditional forms of bullying, as well as the challenges involved in designing and implementing solutions to prevent bullying, have plagued school systems, parents, and children for years, and they represent problems that span virtually all cultures (Calvete, Orue, Estevez, Villardon, & Padilla, 2010). However, with the advent and accessibility of new forms of technology, as well as the recent popularity and increased use of social networking sites, bullying has taken on a form that presents unique challenges and problems for those attempting to work with perpetrators and victims to eliminate this behavior. This form of bullying has received much attention in recent literature and has even been given a unique name "cyberbullying" (Campbell, 2005; Kapatzia & Syngollitou, 2007; Patchin & Hinduja, 2006; Raskauskas & Stoltz, 2007; Slonje & Smith, 2008; Smith, Mahdavi, Carvalho, & Tippett, 2006; Smith, Mahdavi, Carvalho, & Tippett, 2008). Various definitions have been proposed by leading authors for this phenomenon. One of the earliest definitions, offered by Hinduja & Patchin in 2007, is "willful and repeated harm inflicted through the medium of electronic text" (p. 112). Another definition, offered by Smith, Mahdavi, Carvalho, Fisher, Russell, & Tippett in 2008, is "an aggressive and deliberate behavior that is frequently repeated over time, carried out by a group or an individual using electronics aimed at a victim who cannot defend himself or herself easily" (p. 377). Still other authors have defined it more broadly, stating that cyberbullying occurs anytime an individual uses the Internet or cellular phones to torment victims (Kowalski & Limber, 2007). Regardless of the specific definition used, cyberbullying can have deleterious effects on victims, as well as perpetrators of these behaviors. Recent research has also discussed the various media children and adolescents utilize in carrying out acts of cyberbullying. The most common media used for this purpose include Internet-enabled personal computers and cellular phones, although perpetrators have particularly focused on social networking sites, such as MySpace and Facebook, as the locations to facilitate their bullying (Hinduja & Patchin, 2008). Given the vast number of homes, children, and adolescents with access to such devices, it is not surprising that cyberbullying is increasing. Indeed, Butterfield and Broad (2002) noted that:

> *Social changes always provide opportunities for the predatory behavior that is character-*
> *istic of a small number of people. With the new technologies which support the Internet,*
> *those who cannot adjust rapidly, and that is all of us, are at risk from those who can and*
> *will deploy technology as a criminal weapon" (p. 1).*

Hinduja & Patchin (2008) noted that "cyberbullying is the unfortunate by-product of the union of adolescent aggression and electronic communication, and its growth is giving cause for concern" (p. 131).

Many researchers have identified specific aspects and characteristics of electronic communication that contribute to the increased use of these media to bully others (Hinduja & Patchin, 2008; Calvete *et al.*, 2010; Katzer, Fetchenhauer, & Belschak, 2009; Twemlow, 2008). Hidjua & Patchin (2008) noted that "the elements of perceived anonymity on-line" (p. 134), as well as the "safety and security of being behind a computer screen, aid in freeing individuals from traditionally constraining pressures of society, consciences, morality, and ethics to behave in a normative manner" (p. 134). Additionally, because the identity of offenders may be obscured via the use of **pseudonymous mail** or user accounts (i.e., accounts which bear a false or fictitious name or accounts in which the user takes on the identity of someone who may or may not exist, and who may differ in age, gender, etc., from the actual creator/user of the account), offenders may feel more freedom to behave in ways that they would not under circumstances where they could be easily identified, as anonymity often implies the absence of consequences (Calvete *et al.*, 2010). It has been noted that the physical distance afforded by electronic communication may contribute to this discrepancy in face-to-face versus electronic communications (Hinduja & Patchin, 2008). For example, males may pretend to be females online, or vice versa; typically shy children may be emboldened to behave in more brazen ways, given the ability to remain anonymous (Katzer *et al.*, 2009). It has also been observed that electronic communication may simply be a means by which traditional forms of bullying may be diversified and intensified, and a way in which traditional bullies can continue their behavior even when physically absent from the victim (Twemlow, 2008). Hinduja & Patchin have stated that:

> *technological advances now provide bullies with the ability to marshal the power of on-line*
> *applications to infiltrate the home of victims by contacting them through electronic means.*

> *Cyberbullying, then, greatly expands the reach and augments the intensity of the interpersonal harm that occurs among this population (2008, p. 136).*

Further, at the time of this writing, laws making it illegal to use electronic communication to mistreat, harass, or tease others are still controversial due to First Amendment protections, which also likely contributes to the high prevalence of cyberbullying (Hinduja & Patchin, 2008). Finally, the general absence of regulatory bodies that monitor and supervise electronic communication, particularly communication involving minors, contributes significantly to this problem (Hinduja & Patchin, 2008). The difficulties in regulating online behavior are evidenced in the vignette below:

In 2006, 13-year-old Megan Meier, a Dardenne Prairie, Missouri resident, with the permission of her parents, accepted a "friend request" from a fellow MySpace user claiming to be a 16-year-old Josh Evans. Josh and Megan exchanged several messages, and her family and friends noticed that Megan, who had struggled with attention deficit disorder and depression, appeared to be happier and excited about Josh. She thought Josh was attractive and enjoyed receiving attention from him. On 15 October 2006, however, the tone of the messages changed. It is noted that the last message sent to Megan from the Josh Evans account read, "Everybody in O'Fallon knows who you are. You are a bad person and everybody hates you. Have a bad rest of your life. The world would be a better place without you." Megan responded, "You're the kind of boy a girl would kill herself over." She went upstairs to her bedroom, and when passing her father on the stairway, she expressed her distress about the situation. Twenty minutes later, her mother discovered that Megan had hung herself in her bedroom closet.

Efforts were made to revive her, but she died on 17 October 2006. Following her death, an FBI investigation found that the Josh Evans account was actually created by Lori Drew, the mother of an estranged friend of Megan's. Megan and this friend had recently had a disagreement. Drew reported that she had created the account to "mess with Megan".

Literature Review

As the devastating effects of cyberbullying are receiving national and international attention, researchers have attempted to determine the prevalence and frequency of this phenomenon. The National Children's Home (2005) conducted one of the earliest studies of the prevalence of cyberbullying in the United Kingdom. The organization found that 20% of children and adolescents between the ages of 11 and 19 indicated that they had been a victim of bullying via electronic means. Of these children, 73% were bullied by someone that they knew, while 26% indicated that the bully was a stranger (National Children's Home, 2005). Ten percent of this sample indicated that pictures of them had been taken with a camera phone that made them feel uncomfortable, embarrassed, or threatened. Another interesting finding from this study was that a significant portion of cyberbullying victims did not feel comfortable reporting their experiences to adults, as only 24% told a parent, 14% told a teacher, and 28% did not tell anyone (National Children's Home, 2005). Forty-one percent of respondents did, however, tell a friend. Participants indicated that they did not report the incidents for various reasons, including believing that the bullying was not a problem (31%); there was no one that they wanted to tell (12%); they did not think it would stop the bullying (11%); or they did not know where to go for help (10%). However, 23% reported that an opportunity to speak with a bullying expert would be helpful; 15% reported that speaking with a school staff member would have been helpful; and 13% reported that being directed to a website with tips on coping with bullying would be helpful (National Children's Home, 2005). This seminal study highlighted the growing need for programming to address the causes and effects of cyberbullying, and also illuminated the challenges facing those working with victims. It noted that incidents of cyberbullying often go unreported, although this was often due to a perceived lack of effective resources.

More recent findings have suggested various percentages of adolescents and children being victimized by cyberbullying. Studies of children and adolescents have yielded results ranging from 9.4% (Williams & Guerra, 2007) to 35.7% (Aricak, Siyahaan, Uzunhasanoglu, Saribeyoglu, Ciplake, Yilmaz, *et al.*, 2008). A recent study of college students indicated that 55.3% had been victims of cyberbullying, and 22.5% reported engaging in cyberbullying themselves (Dilmac, 2009), suggesting that older adolescents and young adults are not immune to this form of victimization. The number of students who are victims of frequent or severe cyberbullying are also troubling, as these have been estimated to range from 1.7% to 5.7% (Ortega, Calmaestra, & Mora-Mechan, 2008). The severe consequences of such victimization will be discussed in further detail below.

Research has indicated that cyberbullying accounts for a growing proportion of bullying behavior, as it was found that 10% of all bullying is now conducted via electronic means (Liang, 2010). Approximately one-fourth of cyberbullying instances represent repeated incidents and involved either distress to victims or required adult intervention (Wolak, Mitchell, & Finkelhor, 2007). Cases like that of Megan Meier demonstrate the damaging effects of repeated and cruel cyberbullying.

As educators, parents, policy makers, researchers, and students have focused more on cyberbullying, the specific media and tactics cyberbullies use to target their victims have been better understood. For example, Katzer, Fetchenhauer, and Belschak (2009) found that cyberbullies use methods including harassment, abuse, insult, teasing, and blackmail methods, which are similar to those utilized by traditional bullies. In addition, it has been noted that with the advent of camera phone technology, cyberbullies engage in acts termed "happyslapping," which includes filming offenses such as beatings, rapes, or setting victims afire, and then they are sent to others, posted on the Internet, or spread via electronic means such as email or chatrooms (Balci & Reimann, 2006, Calvete *et al.*, 2010). Researchers have also recognized that often cyberbullying is used as a means to perpetuate offline bullying, and some researchers (e.g., Wolak *et al.*, 2007) have suggested that unless it is accompanied by offline bullying, cyberbullying should be known simply as "online harassment." However, Wolak *et al.* (2007) acknowledged that when behavior occurs only online that references school events or "real life" settings, it also constitutes cyberbullying rather than online harassment.

Willard (2006, 2007) identified six types of cyberbullying, including: (1) flaming (i.e., sending electronic messages with hostile or vulgar language); (2) slandering (i.e., online disparagement, such as sending cruel images or rumors about others to spoil reputations or social relationships); (3) impersonation (i.e., "hacking," or infiltrating someone's account in order to send messages that make the victim lose face, cause trouble for or endanger the victim, or harm the victim's reputation or friendships); (4) defamation by spreading secrets or embarrassing information about someone; (5) deliberate exclusion of someone from an online group; or (6) cyber harassment (i.e., the repeated sending of messages that include threats of injury or that are very intimidating). As described, cyberbullying may take many forms, and several patterns emerge in the existing literature. For example, researchers have recently discovered that cyberbullies frequently target the same victims repeatedly and may use multiple methods and techniques to target a particular victim (Katzer *et al.*, 2009).

Cyberbullying is different from traditional bullying, has different effects on victims, and requires unique types of prevention and intervention programs (Wang, Iannoti, & Nansel, 2009). However, other researchers have observed that there is some overlap between cyberbullying and traditional forms of bullying (Katzer *et al.*, 2009; Campbell, 2005; Myers & Carper, 2008; Raskauskas & Stoltz, 2007), and that individuals who are prone to be victimized by traditional bullies are also more likely to fall prey to cyberbullies (Perren, Dooley, Shaw, & Cross, 2010; Hinduja & Patchin, 2008). Those children likely to be victims of cyberbullying have traits and characteristics that make them more likely to be targeted for traditional forms of bullying as well and vice versa (Hinduja & Patchin, 2008; Katzer *et al.*, 2009). Predictably, Hinduja and Patchin (2008) noted that individuals who bully others offline are more likely to engage in cyberbullying.

Researchers have found that individuals who are victims of cyberbullying are more likely to exhibit antisocial behaviors, experience feelings of depression (Perren *et al.*, 2010) and anxiety, and to have a reduced perception of school safety (Cheng, Chen, Liu, & Chen, 2011). With regard to other psychological traits, individuals lower in endurance and with fewer feelings of affiliation with peers are more likely to be victims of cyberbullying (Dilmac, 2009). Such stress and strain has been noted to increase victims' involvement in delinquent behaviors, as well as increasing the frequency of academic problems (Hinduja & Patchin, 2007). Victims of cyberbullying are more likely than non-victims to exhibit suicidal and parasuicidal behaviors (Klomek, Sourander, & Gould, 2011; Hinduja & Patchin 2010; Kim, Koh, & Leventhal, 2005; Roland, 2002; van der Wal, de Wit, Hirasing, 2009; Rigby & Slee, 1999; McMahon, Reulbach, & Keeley, 2010;

Kaltiala-Heino, Rimpela, & Marttunen, 1999; Brunstein, Klomek, Marrocco, & Kleinman, 2007). Moreover, individuals who are both victims and perpetrators of cyberbullying are at the greatest risk for **suicidal behaviors** and **gestures** (i.e., an act that is indicative of self-destructiveness, but the level of lethality is so low that it could not cause death; examples include cutting, and such gestures are usually made in front of at least one other person, or the person making the gesture anticipates or facilitates discovery shortly after the act) (Klomek, Sourander, & Gould, 2011). In a study of children with attention deficit/hyperactivity disorder (ADHD) and/or **Asperger Syndrome** (i.e., an autism spectrum disorder characterized by significant difficulties in social interaction, as well as restrictive and repetitive patterns of behavior and interests), researchers found that these populations experienced higher rates of victimization by electronic as well as traditional means, and that those who were victims of bullying had lower levels of physical and psychological health (Kowalski & Fedina, 2011). In a 2009 study, Katzer *et al.* noted that victims of cyberbullying were more likely to exhibit low self-concept, to have low levels of popularity, were at increased risk for engaging in cyberbullying of others; yet, they did not show an increased risk for exhibiting bullying behaviors offline. The authors suggested that this behavior may represent an attempt by these victims turned offenders to "fight back" or "let off steam" in the environment where they had previously been victimized (Katzer *et al.*, 2009, p. 32).

With regard to their Internet behavior, victims of cyberbullying were more likely to report frequenting "risky" Internet locations (e.g., right-wing extremist, pornographic, or hooligan chatrooms) (Katzer *et al.*, 2009). Contrary to popular belief, membership on a social networking site such as Facebook or MySpace does not place children and adolescents at increased risk for being cyberbullied (Sengupta & Chaudhuri, 2011). Rather, these researchers found that other characteristics, such as demographic and behavioral characteristics, rather than social networking in and of itself, were predictive of victimization by cyberbullying. Finally, with regard to parental support, Wang and colleagues (2009) found children and adolescents with more involved and supportive parents were less likely to be victimized by cyber or traditional bullies.

Research suggests that characteristics of individuals who are prone to becoming perpetrators of cyberbullying include the following associated factors: (1) increased displays of aggression via nonelectronic means (Dilmac, 2009); (2) previous history of depressive symptoms, suicidal ideation, and suicide attempts (Klomek *et al.*, 2011; Kumpulainen, Rasanen, & Henttonen, 1999; Sourander, Ronning, & Brunstein-Klomek, 2009); (3) increased number of friends (Wang *et al.*, 2009); (4) being in high school (as opposed to junior high) (Ybarra & Mitchell, 2004); (5) proactive forms of aggression in non-cyber setting (Calvete *et al.*, 2010); (6) beliefs associated with justifying violence (Calvete *et al.*, 2010); (7) previous exposure to violence (Calvete *et al.*, 2010); (8) less perceived social support from friends (Calvete *et al.*, 2010); and (9) rejection by peers (Calvete *et al.*, 2010).

Recent research has also focused on discerning whether differences exist with the gender of individuals who are more likely to be victims and/or perpetrators of cyberbullying. Results of this research have yielded mixed and sometimes conflicting results, as some studies have found that males are more likely to engage in cyberbullying (Calvete *et al.*, 2010; Dilmac, 2009; Wang *et al.*, 2009), while others have found that males and females are equally likely to engage in cyberbullying (Hinduja & Patchin, 2009), and that females may even be more likely to engage in cyberbullying. Hinduja and Patchin (2009) note that females are more likely than males to engage in relational or indirect and nonphysical forms of bullying, which is typical of cyberbullying. The research regarding cyberbullying victimization and gender is also mixed. Some investigations have suggested that males are more likely to be victimized (Raskauskas & Stoltz, 2007); other studies have yielded results indicating that the majority of cyberbullying victims are female (Campbell, 2010); still other inquiries have found no statistically significant gender differences (Williams & Guerra, 2007). These findings suggest that further research is necessary in order to determine whether gender differences exist with regard to engaging in and/or being a victim of cyberbullying.

Research examining the relationship between race and cyberbullying has also yielded mixed results. Some authors have found that African American adolescents are more likely to engage in cyberbullying behavior, but are less likely to be the victims of such bullying (Wang *et al.*, 2009). Others (Hinduja & Patchin, 2009) have found that such racial differences do not exist, and that African American or other members of minority groups are as likely as Caucasian adolescents and children to be involved in cyberbullying either as victims or perpetrators. As research on cyberbullying and its effects continues, attention will likely be paid to gender and race, in order to clarify these issues.

As tragedies like the suicide of Megan Meier have received national and international attention from the media, investigators have made some efforts to elucidate the effects and psychological consequences of cyberbullying. Evidence suggests that victims of cyberbullying, particularly those who endure ongoing victimization of this type, are at increased risk for negative psychological outcomes, including increased use of psychotropic medications, greater likelihood of receiving physical injuries that require medical attention, and increased levels of depression (Wang, Iannotti, Luk, & Nansel, 2010). Additionally, researchers have noted that those victimized via electronic bullying are more likely to experience academic difficulties, to engage in assaultive behaviors, or to abuse substances (Hinduja & Patchin, 2009).

Cyberbullying and suicide are a deadly and tragic combination that represents the worst possible outcome. As such, researchers are carefully scrutinizing this relationship. To date, investigators have concluded that self-harm behaviors and suicidal ideation are related to previous experiences as a victim of cyberbullying. This relationship is impacted by both the level of negative emotion experienced by the victim resulting from the bullying and by specific features of the victim's immediate environment and psychological health (Hay & Meldrum, 2010). Specifically, adolescents reared with an authoritative parenting style and who exhibit high levels of self-control are less likely to experience suicidal ideation and to exhibit suicidal behaviors

(Hay & Meldrum, 2010). An authoritative parenting style is likely to encourage appropriate coping, as well as early communication, before bullying escalates to a point where adolescents feel hopeless and/or engage in erratic or extreme behaviors. Moreover, adolescents with high measures of self-control are likely to spend more time weighing alternatives, as well as to think about the consequences of their actions such as suicidal behavior. Thus, it is not surprising that having both traits serves as an effective defense against one of the most detrimental effects of cyberbullying — suicidality. Although the specific outcomes and effects are still under empirical scrutiny, "what is clear is that cyber bullying has continued to exert a demonstrably harmful and at times fatal effect upon those targeted for such harassment" (Drogin & Young, 2008, p. 679).

Students' perspectives regarding cyberbullying, its effects, and ways that it can be prevented and its detrimental effects minimized, have also been the focus of recent research efforts. In one such study, a focus group, consisting of 148 middle and high school students, was asked a series of structured questions related to cyberbullying and its impact (Agatston, Kowalski, & Limber, 2007). Participants, particularly female participants, overwhelmingly stated that they felt cyberbullying was a serious problem; although, they also reported it was rarely discussed at their schools (Agatston *et al.*, 2007). Participants also indicated that they did not perceive school district personnel as helpful resources for combating cyberbullying even though many of the problems associated with cyberbullying bled over into the school day for them. Although they were familiar with some basic strategies for dealing with cyberbullying, most students were not aware of the ways that they could request that a problematic website or user be removed, or of how to appropriately respond as a bystander, when they witnessed another person being cyberbullied (Agatston *et al.*, 2007).

In another study utilizing the **focus group method** (i.e., a qualitative research method in which a group of people are asked questions regarding their experiences with and perceptions of a problem, in this case, cyberbullying, and are encouraged to openly and freely discuss their thoughts with other group members, in order to provide information to researchers), 38 students in the 5th through 8th grades were interviewed (Mishna, Saini, & Solomon, 2009). Results indicated that students felt cyberbullying was a serious problem, and some students indicated that it was a more serious problem than traditional bullying due to the anonymity associated with many forms of cyberbullying (Mishna *et al.*, 2009). In a similar study in three European countries, Italy, Spain, and Germany, researchers found that students were more likely to classify behavior as cyberbullying, and to report the behavior, if they were able to identify whether the action was done with the intention of harming the victim, if they knew whether the action resulted in harmful effects to the victim, and if the action represented a repeated, versus an isolated, instance of bullying (Nocentini, Calmaestra, Schltze-Kumbholz, Scheithauer, Ortega, & Menesini, 2010). See the International Issues textbox at the end of this chapter for more information.

As the potentially devastating effects of cyberbullying have become better understood, the focus of research has gradually begun to shift to designing and empirically validating interventions to prevent and combat these adverse consequences. Recent research focused on cyberbullying as a form of psychological trauma has suggested that **trauma-focused cognitive behavioral therapy** (TF-CBT) (i.e., an evidence-based treatment approach shown to help children, adolescents, and their caretakers overcome trauma-related difficulties, designed to reduce negative emotional and behavioral responses following child sexual abuse and other traumatic events) shows promise as an effective intervention for students who have been targeted by cyberbullies; although, it has also been noted that prevention efforts are important (Little, Akin-Little, & Medley, 2011).

Forensic Psychology and Policy Implications

Research regarding the effects of cyberbullying and ways to limits negative effects is slowly making its way to the desks of school administrators, other policymakers, and legislators. As this information has been more readily available, many recommendations regarding the most appropriate ways to deal with this ongoing problem have surfaced. Some authors have recommended that most efforts be exerted at the prevention level, that administrators should focus on identifying individuals at-risk for being victimized by cyberbullies prior to it happening, and to discuss with these students ways that they can either avoid cyberbullying or have strategies for addressing it early on should it happen to them (Anthony, Wessler, & Sebian, 2010; Little *et al.*, 2011).

Other researchers have recommended that such efforts be implemented on a group level, and have suggested that individual classrooms may be the most effective means by which to do this (Agatston *et al.*, 2007). Bauman (2010) has noted that, although it is important to address psychological needs of individual victims of cyberbullying, such interventions are largely ineffective. Additionally, group interventions seem most appropriate because cyberbullying occurs in a social or group context. Thus, interventions should treat bullies and victims in a group setting with trained adult group leaders, using a support group model (Bauman, 2010).

The specific elements that research suggests should be incorporated into these programs include: (1) interventions that deal with the normative beliefs about the use of violence; (2) assist cyberbullies in developing empathy for victims; and (3) strengthen interpersonal peer relationships among bullies and victims to promote positive social support (Calvete *et al.*, 2010). Along these lines, cooperative learning in small groups or common positive activities (such as organizing a trip or dance where all students take part) have been suggested as potentially useful programmatic initiatives (Calvete *et al.*, 2010). Indeed, research has supported the notion that the education system and school health care services are instrumental in the early detection of bullying and prevention of later negative outcomes (Klomek *et al.*, 2011). Due to the potentially irreversible and severe consequences, those working with cyberbullying victims and perpetrators should be aware of the relationship between this type of bullying and suicide, and efforts should include frequent assessment of suicidality, and interventions specifically designed to reduce these symptoms (Klomek *et al.*, 2011). It has also been noted that prevention programs designed to decrease traditional forms of bullying may be applicable and/or adaptable to cyberbullies and victims, although future research is needed to determine the empirical support for this claim (Katzer *et al.*, 2009).

Because cyberbullying occurs largely on the Internet, others have emphasized the importance of interventions targeted at regulating websites and online communication (Katzer *et al.*, 2009). Informing children with regard to "dangerous places" (e.g., websites, chatrooms, etc.) on the Internet, and training children to exhibit "media competence" is important, as often children access the Internet without direct supervision (Katzer *et al.*, 2009, p. 33). Although parental monitoring is recommended, and no intervention or prevention program can serve as a substitute for parental involvement and open communication between parents and children regarding cyberbullying (Wang & Iannotti, 2010), researchers understand that constant monitoring is often impossible; therefore, schools may need to be involved in monitoring and prevention efforts (Klomek *et al.*, 2011).

In addition to parental efforts, schools may benefit from the establishment of "**cyber police**" forces, which could assist in supervising popular chatrooms and serve as a point of contact and peer support for cyberbullying victims (Katzer *et al.*, 2009, p. 33). Virtual cyber police could also provide a similar point of contact and support online, when students are away from school and school-based helpers are not available (Katzer *et al.*, 2009). Indeed, Myers, McCaw, and Hemphill (2011) state that schools not only have a responsibility, but also the authority to regulate, censor, and sanction inappropriate cyber communication. If schools utilize awareness messages as part of cyberbullying intervention and/or prevention programs, it is recommended that these messages be accurate, and that they refrain from over-emphasizing the link between cyberbullying and suicide, as such overemphasis may actually increase rates of suicide by providing reinforcement for suicidal behavior (Klomek *et al.*, 2011). That is, showing videos or photos of adolescents or children who have ended their lives following bullying may in some ways "glorify" such behaviors to children and adolescents currently experiencing bullying, and may make these already vulnerable individuals more likely to choose suicide as a means by which to cope with the effects of cyberbullying.

It is also necessary for regulatory bodies to implement policies online, as most websites currently provide no such monitoring and allow cyberbullying to go undetected and unreported (Liang, 2010). To address this problem, Liang (2010) noted that a computer program could be designed to detect bullying content, and prevent such messages from being sent. Of course, such programs would only be effective if they were installed on the potential sender's computer. Based on current research and recommendations, it seems clear that efforts should focus on prevention as well as intervention, and involve every aspect of a child's or adolescent's social, academic, familial, and virtual environment.

Suggestions for Future Research

The research in the area of cyberbullying is relatively new, and several areas warrant more attention from future investigators. For example, further research is needed to determine the effectiveness of various modalities of cyberbullying intervention (e.g., Internet-based, school-based, computer-based, home-based, etc.) (Guan & Subrahmanyam, 2009; Wang & Iannotti, 2010). Also, the relationship between aggressive personality traits and tendencies to cyberbully should be further studied and elucidated, as it has been suggested that this relationship may differ from that seen with traditional bullying behaviors (Dilmac, 2009). These differences may have implications for treatment programs. With regard to victim characteristics and behaviors, future studies should examine the online behavior of victims to assist in the development of prevention strategies aimed at high-risk victim behaviors (Katzer *et al.*, 2009). Additionally, the current body of research could be expanded by including studies that involve multiple sources of data (e.g., peer, parent, and teacher reports, in addition to reports of victims/cyberbullies); such efforts could also provide information regarding the typical reactions of teachers and parents to cyberbullying (Calvete *et al.*, 2010).

More empirical analysis is necessary to determine the relationship between gender or racial differences, and being the perpetrator and/or victim of cyberbullying. The group effects on cyberbullying behavior are also currently poorly understood; future research efforts would do well to identify particular groups of adolescents who are more accepting of cyberbullying behavior via **qualitative research methods** (i.e., research methods which aim to provide a complete and detailed description of a phenomenon, typically through the use of in-depth interviews, which allow researchers to better understand a topic, usually one that is in the early stages of being studied) (Calvete *et al.*, 2010). Such information could then be utilized to identify those at higher risk for engaging in or accepting cyberbullying behaviors, and to develop more effective prevention and intervention programs. Further examination of individuals who are both perpetrators and victims of cyberbullying is recommended in order to better comprehend the consequences of cyberbullying for those who are both aggressors and victims (Calvete *et al.*, 2010). Finally, to allow greater understanding of the long-term consequences of cyberbullying, **longitudinal studies** of these issues, particularly of the relationship between cyberbullying and suicide, are necessary (Klomek *et al.*, 2011).

Psychology of School Violence

Introduction

School violence has received considerable attention in recent years as extreme instances of violence, such as mass shootings, have been the subject of increased public interest and media coverage. Although these incidents certainly constitute worst case scenarios for school violence, broader definitions of school violence have been offered by other authors. For example, Healey (2004) defined school violence as aggressive behavior based on the interaction among teachers, students, or other related staff within the school grounds and during school hours. School shootings, on the other hand, refer to "firearm violence occurring in educational institutions, especially the mass murder or spree killing of people within such an institution" (Preti, 2008, p. 544). Certainly, such instances of mass violence demand study. However, acts of verbal or physical aggression that happen at an educational institution and do not involve firearms or other weapons are also examples of school violence and are worthy of examination. Another form of school violence that has been identified by researchers is **stalking**, which is typically marked by the perpetrator seeking physical proximity to the victim and/or making repeated attempts to contact the victim. Stalking within an educational institution has been typically motivated by a desire for sexual contact with the victim, or by revenge or resentment, and is typically targeted at an acquaintance of the perpetrator (Purcell, Pathe, & Mullen, 2010). This section will examine characteristics of both perpetrators and victims of school violence, discuss current trends and patterns with regard to this phenomenon, and will elucidate procedures used by school personnel and law enforcement to identify those at risk for committing acts of school violence.

Although many in the public perceive school violence as a new phenomenon, research indicates that the first documented incident of school violence occurred on 29 April 1909, when an unidentified person fatally shot his former girlfriend on a university campus, and then killed himself. According to available information, the female victim had declined numerous marriage proposals by the perpetrator, and he came to the campus to change her mind (Drysdale *et al.*, 2010). Despite public and media perception that school violence is a new phenomenon, there are documented instances dating back to the early 20th century. Our perspective is likely skewed from the instantaneous and repeating, widespread media coverage focusing on extreme, but misrepresentative forms of school violence (Knoll, 2010a). Although school shootings are unique in their level of impact, potential and actual loss of life, and the amount of attention paid by the media and public, it has been noted by many authors that the most frequent instances of school violence take the form of traditional bullying (Yurtal & Artut, 2010). Traditional bullying is noteworthy because of the potential that it can lead to more extreme forms of violence. The most deadly instance of school violence occurred in 2007, and is illustrated in the following vignette:

On 16 April 2007, Seung Hui Cho, age 23, who was a student at Virginia Polytechnic University ("Virginia Tech") in Blacksburg, Virginia, carried out the deadliest school shooting in U.S. history. At around 7:15 am, Cho fatally shot a female student in her dormitory room in West Ambler Johnston Residential Hall and then shot the building's residential advisor. Approximately two and one half hours later, Cho entered Norris Hall, a lecture building, and shot numerous students and faculty before killing himself. In total, Cho killed 32 (27 students and five faculty members) and wounded 17. Some of the wounded individuals were struck by gunfire while others were injured trying to jump from the building. In the investigation that followed the shootings, it was revealed that Cho had been involved in at least three stalking incidents, including two which involved Virginia Tech campus police, prior to the shooting spree. It was also discovered that in the two and one half hour time span between the two shootings, Cho mailed a parcel with a DVD inside to NBC news, which contained video clips, photographs, and a manifesto explaining the reasons for his actions. Although NBC elected not to release the full contents of the package, in an effort to prevent copycat killings, they described the materials as containing "over the top profanity" and "incredibly violent images."

Literature Review

In the late 1990s, concern over school violence grew to such a degree that the Centers for Disease Control and Prevention proposed that such violence be conceptualized as a communicable disease (Tatem Kelley, Huizinga, Thorberry, & Loeber, 1997). At that time, adolescents exhibited the highest rates of crime and victimization of any age group (Snyder & Sickmund, 1999; Tatem

Kelley *et al.*, 1997), and approximately 37% of violent crime involving individuals age 12 to 15 occurred on school property (Friday, 1996). In the wake of this phenomenon, researchers began turning their attention to school violence, its effects, ways in which the level of threat posed by any particular individual could be identified, and appropriate prevention, intervention, and policy measures to address school violence and its resultant issues.

Although school violence is alarming to the public, research suggests that less than 1% of youth homicides occur at educational institutions (Cornell, 2006). Statistics regarding the rates of occurrence of school violence on university and college campuses have been compiled in recent years, and indicate that between 2004 and 2008, there were 174 murders, 46 negligent manslaughters, 13,842 forcible sex offenses, 222 non-forcible sex offenses, 19,900 robberies, 21,675 aggravated assaults, and 4045 instances of arson on college and university campuses in the United States (Drysdale, Modzeleski, & Simons, 2010). The authors further narrowed their focus by examining only incidents of violence which met four criteria: (1) the perpetrator selected a specific student, employee, or facility against which to carry out violence, or selected a random student, employee, or facility because they met the perpetrator's victim profile; (2) the victim(s) was/were selected prior to the act of violence or during the commission of violence due to the victim(s)' similarity or proximity to the target; (3) the subject employed or had the ability at the time of the offense to employ lethal violence; and (4) the incident occurred in the United states, was connected to an educational institution in some way, and occurred between 1 January 1900 and 31 December 2008. Of the 272 of these instances which were identified by the authors as targeted acts of violence, 84% occurred on the campuses of four-year universities, 14% at two-year institutions, 1% at post-secondary/technical schools, and 1% at post-graduate institutions at 218 distinct campuses (Drysdale *et al.*, 2010).

Statistics demonstrate that episodes of school violence in the United States are typically more deadly than in other countries. The number of victims per episode of school violence in this country range from 0 to 33, while the number of fatalities per episode in other countries are as follows: Canada − 1 to 14; Europe − 0 to 17; and other countries − 1 to 8 (Preti, 2008). Further, when compared to school shooters in other countries, perpetrators in Europe were much more likely to commit suicide during the attack than those in the United States, though a majority (60%) of perpetrators in United States also took their own lives (Preti, 2008). The figure on page 300 depicts rates of students reporting that they had carried a gun or other weapon to school or been in a physical fight at school within the year prior to the survey, and compares the rates of these reported behaviors by gender.

A study of Turkish students found that 50% of violence reported by students (which they had observed) occurred among their peers, while 24% involved a teacher assaulting a student, and 9% involved a director (i.e., a school administrator) assaulting a student (Yurtal & Artut, 2010). This study suggests school personnel in Turkey were often perpetrators of violence

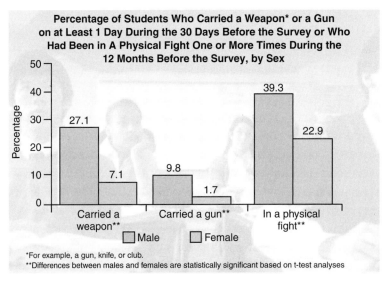

Percentage of Students Who Carried a Weapon* or a Gun on at Least 1 Day During the 30 Days Before the Survey or Who Had Been in A Physical Fight One or More Times During the 12 Months Before the Survey, by Sex

*For example, a gun, knife, or club.
**Differences between males and females are statistically significant based on t-test analyses

Data regarding rates of school violence and weapons use in the United States in 2009. Centers for Disease Control and Prevention, Youth Risk Behavior Surveillance System (YRBSS) 2009 National Youth Risk Behavior Survey Overview. Available from URL: www.cdc.gov/healthyyouth/yrbs/pdf/us_overview_yrbs.pdf.

against students. These students (ages 12 to 14) reported that 59% of the episodes of violence they witnessed occurred on the playground, 22% occurred in the classroom, 6% occurred in front of or outside of the school building, 5% occurred in an administrator's office, 3% occurred in the hallway, and the remaining 8% occurred in other settings within the institution (Yurtal & Artut, 2010).

One area of focus for researchers in the area of school violence has been the use of weapons in carrying out these acts of violence. Research conducted in the United States has indicated that the presence of weapons on school campuses is relatively rare, as 0.3% of university students reported carrying a gun on campus in the six months preceding the interview, while 4.2% reported carrying a knife, 0.3% reported carrying a bat, 2.1% had carried a mace or pepper spray, and 0.3% had carried a "rock sock" (i.e., a weapon often fashioned by inmates in which a hard object, such as a rock, lock, or book, is placed in a sock, allowing the sock to be swung at victims) (Fallahi, Shaw Austad, Fallon, & Leishman, 2009). Regarding the types of weapons used to carry out school violence in the United States, research indicates that 54% of incidents involved the use of firearms, 21% involved knives or other bladed weapons, 10% involved a combination of weapons, and 5% involved either manual strangulation or strangulation via some type of instrument (Drysdale *et al.*, 2010). According to Yurtal and Artut (2010), Turkish students aged 12 and 13 years who witnessed school violence described observing brute force 46% of the time, use of a knife 19% of the time, use of a stick 8% of the time, and the use of a gun 5% of the time (Yurtal & Artut, 2010). Although research suggests that it is only a minority of students who carry a weapon onto school campuses, the potential for lethal violence mandates that this issue continues to be targeted for prevention efforts.

Recent research has focused on determining the effects of school violence, including whether there are different effects for perpetrators, victims, and teachers, as well as the impact of school violence on the public in general. Researchers have found that the immediate impact of exposure to school violence may include: faintness or dizziness, hot or cold bodily sensations, tightness in the throat, stomach, or chest, and nausea or gastrointestinal distress (Daniels *et al.*, 2007). Further, victims have reported experiencing sleep disturbance, hypervigilance, interpersonal conflicts, avoidance of reminders of the event, inability to express feelings, withdrawal, and increased substance abuse in the aftermath of exposure (Daniels *et al.*, 2007). Emotional reactions to school violence can include: feelings of shock, anxiety, fear, **psychological numbness** (i.e., a decrease or elimination of normal psychological processes, such as emotional reactivity or cognition, particularly those processes that directly relate to a stressful or traumatic event), grief, and feelings of helplessness, hopelessness, and vulnerability (Daniels *et al.*, 2007). Finally, cognitive reactions reported by those exposed included: confusion or disorientation, poor concentration, complete or partial amnesia, flashbacks, self-criticism, preoccupation with protecting loved ones, and questioning of spiritual beliefs (Daniels *et al.*, 2007).

Researchers have found that individuals lacking in social support and those undergoing psychological distress prior to exposure to school violence were most likely to experience negative outcomes following such an experience (Littleton *et al.*, 2009). Additionally, these researchers discovered that the pattern of negative outcomes formed what they termed a "**resource loss spiral**" (p. 216) (i.e., a cyclical and worsening pattern wherein loss of connection to resources in one area leads to resource loss in other areas, and so on), suggesting that those experiencing loss of resources prior to the trauma were more likely to experience continued resource loss following the trauma. Once individuals began to experience loss of **psychological resources** (e.g., social support, coping skills, etc.) subsequent to trauma, that pattern of loss was more likely to continue even several months after the exposure (Littleton *et al.*, 2009). Conversely, individuals with more resources (e.g., social support) prior to the trauma exposure were more likely to actually gain, not lose, resources in the aftermath of exposure to school violence (Littleton *et al.*, 2009). The authors posited that this was because those "with greater resource reserves are more able and willing to engage in the actions necessary to experience resource gain following a threat to those resources," (p. 217). Individuals with greater resources were more likely to engage in active, rather than passive forms of coping with the traumatic event (Littleton *et al.*, 2009).

In the aftermath of the deadliest school shooting in history (i.e., the Virginia Tech "massacre"), researchers conducted surveys with college students either directly or indirectly exposed to the bloodshed to determine the impact of such an extreme and widely publicized act of violence (Fallahi *et al.*, 2009). According to the authors, students most often blamed the killer himself for the shootings; although 17.4% blamed the faculty and staff of the University; 13.4% blamed the killer's parents/upbringing; and 9.9% blamed mental illness and lack of treatment. Regarding ways that events such as the Virginia Tech shootings could be prevented, students were most likely to respond that better procedures for mental health treatment, assessments, and support were necessary (29.6%); that it was not possible to prevent these incidents (18.3%); that better gun control (10.7%) was necessary; or that more involvement between faculty/staff and students (5.1%) could prevent such events in the future (Fallahi *et al.*, 2009). The results of this study indicate that on average students and faculty experienced "moderately high" levels of shock following the event (p. 126); that most students believed that their parents were concerned for their safety following the incident; that females experienced more anxiety and fear than males following the shootings; and that students tended to favor gun control prior to the shootings and held this belief more fervently afterwards (Fallahi *et al.*, 2009). However, in spite of these feelings the researchers found that students were still more likely to fear being harmed while away from school property rather than while on school property and felt that tragedies such as the events at Virginia Tech were more likely to occur on another campus rather than their own (Fallahi *et al.*, 2009). Finally, students reported that "a Virginia Tech tragedy is likely to happen again, but less likely to happen on their own campus," and reported moderately strong beliefs that "the United States is a violent country" (Fallahi *et al.*, 2009, p. 128). Other researchers have found that individuals who are not exposed to incidents of school violence, as either the perpetrator or victim, have higher levels of general psychological adjustment, score higher on measures of global self-esteem and satisfaction with life, and score lower on measures of negative indicators of adjustment (Estevez *et al.*, 2009). Findings such as these suggest that extreme acts of school violence can impact the psychological functioning, beliefs, and perceptions of safety of those even indirectly exposed.

In a 2010 study, Griffiths examined the reactions of the public at large to incidents of school violence and found that due to media coverage of school violence carried out by members of the **"Goth" subculture**, often characterized by the wearing of light makeup and dark clothing, unusual hairstyles, body piercings, bondage items, etc., and a fascination with medieval, Victorian, and Edwardian history (e.g., the shootings at Columbine), the public was more likely to view those involved in the Goth subculture as "social outcasts" (p. 407) and as negative or problematic. This study suggests that society's beliefs are fueled by the media's misrepresentation of this subculture, particularly the over-estimation of the involvement of "Goth" students in carrying out violence. The FBI's Critical Incident Response Group (2000) identified myths about school violence and school shooters, which are magnified and perpetuated by the media: (1) school violence is an epidemic; (2) all school shooters are alike; (3) the school shooter is always a loner; (4) school shootings are exclusively revenge motivated; and (5) easy access to weapons is the most significant risk factor. In contrast to these commonly-held beliefs, the Critical Incident Response Group noted that "unusual or aberrant behaviors, interests, or hobbies" are more indicative of "the student destined to become violent" (p. 4). In light of these findings, the FBI has proposed a model of threat assessment in order to identify and intervene with those most at risk for carrying out school violence.

Risk assessment for future violence is generally a difficult and complex task, and it has been noted that when it involves predicting events such as school violence, which have a **low base rate** (i.e., an event that occurs very rarely, that is, very few members of the population will display the characteristic in question) (Mulvey & Cauffman, 2001), it becomes increasingly more difficult. The rates of both **false positives** (i.e., a person who is wrongly classified as being at risk for violence when they actually are not) and **false negatives** (i.e., a person who is wrongly classified as not being at risk for violence when they actually are) increases (Preti, 2008). Therefore, the rights of some individuals who are not in fact high risk may be needlessly restricted, or the system may not appropriately respond to someone who is at risk for committing violence, because the event in question happens so infrequently. Mulvey and Cauffman (2001), early researchers in the area of school violence threat assessment, noted that in addition to the low base rates of school violence, three additional challenges face those attempting to predict school violence: (1) viewing threats of violence within their social context, rather than in isolation; (2) predicting future behavior of adolescents is particularly difficult as their "characters are often not yet fully formed" (p. 798); and (3) interventions for working with violent-prone adolescents are still being developed, and their effectiveness evaluated. However, despite these challenges, researchers typically agree that risk must be viewed on a continuum, and that the more risk factors a person exhibits, the greater the risk of violence (Preti, 2008). Among the risk factors, research indicates the following warrant the greatest attention when assessing risk: (1) a history of aggression; (2) a decline in functioning (e.g., failure to meet familial, academic or social obligations, decreased ability to care for oneself); (3) a recent relational loss or stressful event; or (4) openly disclosing threats of suicide or targeted violence (Preti, 2008).

Researchers involved in examining and developing threat assessment techniques have recently delineated characteristics of perpetrators of school violence. For example, research has shown that perpetrators of school violence usually worked alone, were typically (94%) male, and ranged in age from 16 to 62 with an average age of 28 years (Drysdale, Modzeleski, & Simons, 2010). However, these figures may be misleading, as the average age may be falsely increased by "outliers" who are typically faculty or staff members, or nontraditional students, who commit school violence and are far older than the typical perpetrator of school violence. Perpetrators were more likely than others to express suicidal thoughts, plans, or make suicide attempts prior to engaging in violence and were more than twice as likely as nonperpetrators to have been bullied by their peers, to be described as loners, and to be poorly integrated into school activities (Preti, 2008). Females, although they represented a minority of perpetrators, were more likely than males to target victims of their same gender (Purcell *et al.*, 2010). In other words, it seems that females, although much less likely to commit school violence in general, are far more likely to target other females, while males are more likely to both commit school violence and to target members of the opposite sex. Such information can assist in the risk assessment process, by providing base rates of certain perpetrator and victim characteristics.

Research in the area of threat assessment has also focused on identifying the motivations of individuals who carry out acts of school violence. It has been noted that acts of violence are motivated by many factors, including: (1) providing a warning signal to others; (2) as a reaction to fear or punishment or some other anxiety; (3) as a demand for attention; (3) in order to taunt; (4) to intimidate; (5) to assert power or control; (6) to punish; (7) to manipulate or coerce; (8) to frighten; (9) to terrorize; (10) to compel someone to do something; (11) to strike back for a real or perceived injury, injustice, or slight; (12) to disrupt someone's or some institution's life; (13) to test authority; or (14) to protect oneself (FBI Critical Incident Response Group; Preti, 2008). Violence can be motivated by a number of emotions as well, including love, hate, fear, rage, or the desire for attention, revenge, excitement, or recognition (FBI Critical Incident Response Group, 2000).

In a 2010 study by Drysdale and colleagues, 227 incidents of school violence and their motives were examined, and it was found that 33.9% were prompted by problems in an intimate relationship, 13.7% represented retaliation for a specific action by the victim, 10.1% were prompted following refused advances resulting from the perpetrator's obsessions with the victim, 10.1% were carried out in response to academic stress or failure, 9.7% were acquaintance or stranger based sexual violence, 7.9% were prompted by psychotic symptoms, 6.2% were preceded by sanctions or dismissal at the perpetrator's place of employment, and the remaining 8.4% were prompted by either a need to kill victims of a specific demographic, efforts to draw attention to the perpetrator themselves or specific issues, or prompted by racism or other forms of bias. Although these motives have been identified, it has been noted by Purcell and colleagues (2010) that much research has focused on males, and females may vary in terms of their motivations to engage in acts of school violence and may specifically be more likely to act violently while stalking or bullying a victim. Data such as these are important, as they can provide critical information regarding base rates and motivations of acts of school violence, and may be incorporated into models used to predict the level of threat posed by any particular individual.

The FBI has recommended a model of threat assessment designed to assist in analyzing a person's potential for engaging in a specific act of school violence, which is comprised of four components (FBI Critical Incident Response Group, 2000). First, threat assessors must thoroughly examine the **personality** (e.g., ways in which the individual copes with conflict, expresses anger, demonstrates resiliency after a setback, feels about him- or herself, and responds to rules, authority figures, etc.) of the at-risk student identified. Then, the current and past **family dynamics** (e.g., the patterns of behavior, thinking, beliefs, traditions, roles, customs, and values that exist in a family) of the student must be examined, to identify both **static** (i.e., risk factors that cannot be changed via prevention or intervention measures, such as age, gender, previous history of violence, race, etc.) and **dynamic risk factors** (i.e., risk factors that can be changed via prevention or intervention measures, such as symptoms of mental illness, antisocial attitudes, or access to illicit substances and/or weapons). Third, the **school's dynamics** (e.g., behaviors which are formally and informally rewarded within a particular school/culture, how the student sees him- or herself fitting into the school culture), and the student's role in those dynamics must be examined. Finally, the **social dynamics** and context surrounding the student (e.g., patterns of behavior, thinking, beliefs, customs, traditions, and roles that exist in the larger communities of which a student is a part, such as beliefs about violence, drug use, and weapons) must also be studied.

In addition to identifying motivations and pre-attack behaviors, researchers have recently identified three distinct types of perpetrators of school violence. The first type, the "**pseudocommando**", "often kills indiscriminately in public during the daytime, but may also kill family members and a 'pseudo-community' he believes has mistreated him" (Knoll, 2010a, p. 87). School shooters such as Charles Whitman, who carried out a shooting spree on the campus of the University of Texas in Austin in the 1960s, are perhaps the most famous of these types of school shooters (Knoll, 2010a). Knoll (2010a) also notes that many school shooters engage in a pattern of violence known as the "**homicide-suicide**" pattern, when an individual commits a homicide and subsequently (usually within 24 hours) commits suicide. Such acts of violence represent a unique phenomenon, and although relatively rare, are typically carefully planned allowing for the application of a risk assessment model if they are identified in a timely and accurate fashion (Knoll, 2010a). Another type of perpetrator of school violence is the "**copycat killer**," who mimics the behavior of another, and typically carries out acts of violence following intense media attention regarding the methods and impact of other perpetrators of school violence (Preti, 2008). Copycat behaviors are common; for example, up to 350 students were arrested in the United States for charges of having some kind of threat against a school in the four weeks following the shootings in Columbine, Colorado (Drummond & Portner, 2008). Such typologies can assist law enforcement, school officials, and mental health professionals in constructing "reliable profiles that can be of assistance in promoting school safety" (Skiba, Reynolds, Graham, Sheras, Close Conoley, & Garcia-Vasquez, 2006, p. 9).

With regard to the specific techniques used in threat assessment, two underlying assumptions belie current models: (1) all threats and all threateners are not equal; and (2) most threateners are unlikely to carry out their threats, although all threats must be taken seriously and evaluated (FBI Critical Incident Response Group). Any threat assessment must begin by obtaining "specific, plausible details" regarding the identity of the victim or victims, the reason for making the threat, the means, weapon, and method by which it is to be carried out, the date, time, and place where the threatened act will occur, and concrete information about plans or preparations that have already been made (FBI Critical Incident Response Group, p. 7). Following collection of this information, specific information regarding the emotional context of the threat as well as the precipitating stressors experienced by the threatener must be gathered. The risk posed by a particular threat may then be classified as low, medium, or high (FBI Critical Incident Response Group). After collection of these types of data, including the intent and ability of a potential perpetrator to carry out an attack, efforts to manage the threat must be taken. These efforts can include: disrupting potential plans of attack, mitigating risk, and implementing strategies to facilitate long-term resolution of any problems or conflicts that have been identified (Drysdale *et al.*, 2010). Despite the advances regarding threat assessment, which have recently occurred, several caveats should be noted:

> *(1) No one or two traits or characteristics should be considered in isolation or given more weight than others; (2) behavior is an expression of personality, but one bad day may not reflect a student's real personality or usual behavior pattern; and (3) many of the behavioral traits [identified] are seen in depressed adolescents with narcissistic personality characteristics and other possible mental health problems. Despite the overlap between this list and diagnostic symptoms, evaluation under the four-pronged threat assessment model cannot be a substitute for clinical diagnosis of mental illness (FBI Critical Incident Response Group, p. 15).*

Once a threat has been identified and assessed, one of several prevention approaches may be implemented in order to neutralize or minimize the impact of the threat. Broadly, two types of prevention models exist: (1) **universal prevention models** that target and include all students, regardless of risk status; and (2) **selective prevention models** that focus only on a subset of high-risk students (National Institutes of Health – Public Access, 2009). Thus far, research has suggested that the latter is more effective in preventing acts of school violence (National Institutes of Health – Public Access, 2009). However, the utility of both forms of prevention efforts has been recognized by other authors, and it has also been noted that effective prevention should also target individuals who have already engaged in disruptive or violent behavior regardless of their current risk status (Skiba *et al.*, 2006). With regard to specific prevention models, several have been developed in recent years. One such model is the Coping Power Preventive Intervention for Aggressive Children, which is a multicomponent program for aggressive children designed to improve children's social cognitions, their pro-social and academically oriented behaviors, and to enhance parents' parenting skills (Lochman, Powell, Lewczyk, Boxmeyer, Qu, Wells, & Windle, 2009). The Peace Builders program is a universal, school-wide, violence prevention program for elementary schools. The program focuses on individual behavior change and incorporates an ongoing, long-term strategy to alter the culture of the entire school and has been shown to be effective in increasing students' social competence, increasing peace-building and pro-social behavior, and reducing aggressive behavior (Flannery, Vazsonyi, Liau, Guo, Powell, Atha, Vesterdal, & Embry, 2003).

In recent years, many schools have implemented controversial **zero tolerance prevention programs** in an effort to reduce the occurrence of school violence. Although the specifics of such programs vary, they share the common characteristics of mandating the enforcement of predetermined consequences most often severe and punitive in nature, which are intended to be applied regardless of the seriousness of the behavior, mitigating circumstances, or situational context (Skiba *et al.*, 2006). In addition, these programs are based on the following five key assumptions: (1) School violence is at a serious level and increasing, thus necessitating forceful, no-nonsense strategies for violence prevention; (2) through the provision of mandated punishment for certain offenses, zero tolerance increases the consistency of school discipline and thereby the clarity of the disciplinary message to students; (3) removal of students who violate school rules will create a school climate more conducive to learning for those students who remain; (4) the swift and certain punishments of zero tolerance have a deterrent effect upon students, thus improving overall student behavior and discipline; and (5) parents overwhelmingly support the implementation of zero tolerance policies to ensure the safety of schools, and students feels safer knowing that transgressions will be dealt with in no uncertain terms (Skiba *et al.*, 2006, pp. 3–5). Although such programs are increasingly popular, several problems have been identified regarding these methods. Skiba *et al.* (2006) indicate that students of color are disproportionately disciplined using these policies and the disproportionality is not solely due to economic disadvantage, higher rates of violence, or disruption committed by minority students. Additionally, zero tolerance policies may be developmentally inappropriate for adolescents, as they may "exacerbate both the normative challenges of early adolescence and the potential mismatch between the adolescent's developmental stage and the structure of secondary schools" (Skiba *et al.*, 2006, pp. 7–8). Specifically, these policies interfere with adolescents' ability to meet their unique developmental needs, such as forming close peer relationships, autonomy, identity formation, support from adults other than one's parents, and academic self-efficacy (Skiba *et al.*, 2006). School violence remains a relatively rare phenomenon and has actually remained stable or even decreased since approximately 1985 (Skiba *et al.*, 2006). Other problems noted include the following: such policies have not increased the consistency of school discipline, and that schools with higher rates of suspension and expulsion appear to have less satisfactory ratings of school climate, particularly regarding the degree to which the school's environment is conducive to learning. Further, school suspension predicts higher future rates of misbehavior and suspensions. Finally, data are mixed regarding whether parents actually support zero tolerance policies as wholeheartedly as proponents of such models suggest (Skiba *et al.*, 2006).

In light of research identifying methods by which school violence may be detected, prevented, and its impact minimized following acts which were not prevented, lawmakers have addressed these concerns via legislation. For example, in the wake of the Crime and Security Act of 1990, statistics were compiled regarding the level and types of crimes which occurred on school campuses in the United States (Drysdale *et al.*, 2010). The Act was amended in 1992, 1998, and 2000, and renamed the Jeanne Clery Disclosure of Campus Security Policy and Campus Crime Statistics Act, or the Clery Act, in memory of a student who was killed in her dormitory room in 1986, in an effort to provide students and their families with more information regarding the particular patterns of violence which occur on a given campus (Drysdale *et al.*, 2010). In 2008, following the Virginia Tech shootings, Congress further amended the Act, and established a requirement that campuses develop a campus emergency response plan, in which campuses must "immediately notify" the campus community as soon as an emergency is confirmed on the campus unless such notification would impede attempts to control the situation (Drysdale *et al.*, 2010). Such amendments and bills demonstrate the impact school shootings have had on public perception, as well as lawmakers' role in implementing policy changes which can prevent and minimize the impact of such incidents. Further policy and practice implications are listed below.

Forensic Psychology and Policy Implications

The growing understanding of factors contributing to school violence warrants several recommendations for public policy. First, it is recommended that prevention efforts be emphasized to minimize the likelihood that violence will occur at all, and to reduce negative impacts on potential perpetrators, victims, and the institutions and school systems in which violence would otherwise occur. For example, Yurtal and Artut (2010) have recommended that school violence prevention efforts combine with efforts to prevent and/or reduce bullying in schools as a result of the relationship that has been established between the two. Similar recommendations have been offered by Estevez, Murgui, and Musitu (2009), who indicate that prevention efforts with victims of bullying should focus on "developing self-esteem and reducing feelings of loneliness and depressive symptoms" (p. 479). They also suggest that efforts aimed at increasing general life satisfaction could be beneficial to both bullies and victims of bullying and could be effective in reducing school violence. Relatedly, Sweeting, Young, West, and Der (2006) note that those designing and implementing prevention programs should be aware that more vulnerable children are more likely to be the targets of victimization, and such knowledge should be used when selecting specific students with whom to intervene, as well as when designing specific treatment components.

It is recommended that those involved in prevention efforts (e.g., counselors, etc.) and the settings in which programs are to be implemented be screened (Lochman, Wells, Powell, Lewczyk, Boxmeyer, Qu, & Windle, 2009). These authors note that counselors who are agreeable, conscientious, noncynical, and those who are "not limited by excessive managerial control" (p. 481) are likely to be most effective, and that screening efforts should focus on identifying those high in these traits. In addition, training should be provided to principals and other administrators regarding how personality and school factors may impact implementation, as well as to increase the behaviors associated with these characteristics (i.e., agreeableness, conscientiousness, low cynicism, exerting low managerial control over subordinates) in order to maximize effectiveness and minimize barriers to implementation (Lochman *et al.*, 2009). In addition to these findings, it has also been noted that prevention programs are most effective when their goal is to "alter the entire school climate, not just individual risk factors" (Flannery, Liau, Powell, Vesterdal, Vazsonyi, Guo, Atha, & Embry, 2003, p. 305), when they are implemented for longer periods of time and with "no specified end point" (p. 305), and when the focus is on universal prevention with children beginning as early as kindergarten. Finally, any prevention program should include measures by which its effectiveness will be evaluated and demonstrated in order to ensure continued funding, and psychologists, who can offer specialized knowledge regarding research design and program evaluation, may be particularly helpful to school systems as consultants in achieving this goal (Evans & Rey, 2001). Finally, given evidence that many perpetrators of school violence exhibit signs of emotional distress and/or mental illness prior to engaging in acts of violence at school, increased access to mental health services has been recommended as a critical component of any prevention program (Preti, 2008; Knoll, 2010b).

Authors have also recently focused on the ways in which intervention programs that provide services after violence has already occurred may be made more effective. For example, as zero tolerance policies have been implemented more and more frequently, these programs have received increasing attention from researchers and policymakers alike. Despite their popularity, it has been noted that "zero tolerance policies have still not guaranteed safe school climates that ensure school learning" (Skiba, Reynolds, Graham, Sheras, Conoley, & Garcia-Vazquez, 2008, p. 12). In light of these findings, Skiba *et al.* (2008) recommend that such policies be applied more flexibly; that removal of students be reserved for only the most serious and severe of disruptive behaviors; that they be implemented in light of an understanding of adolescent development; and that teachers and others with regular contact with students remain the first line of communication with parents and caregivers regarding disciplinary incidents. Indeed, the National Institutes of Health (2009) summarized research that found that selective intervention methods, that identify and target the highest risk students, are the most productive, and likely the most cost-effective, method of intervening with students identified as high risk for engaging in school violence. Additionally, despite research that suggests that most students do not carry weapons of any form to school, the prevalence and use of weapons on school campuses is an important area of continued research and prevention efforts.

In instances where threats are not identified or prevented, intervention efforts may begin in order to minimize the lasting impact of the act(s) of violence. In general, it is recommended that individuals involved in this form of treatment/debriefing remain calm, nonanxious, engage in active listening in order to acknowledge, comfort, and soothe emotions, and to identify actions which can be implemented that day, the following day, or within the week to assist in coping (Daniels *et al.*, 2007). Further, counselors who are organized, thorough, planful, and able to be warmly positive and agreeable are more likely to be effective in this type of work (Lochman *et al.*, 2009). One model for such intervention is the Kent Educational Psychology Service (KEPS) consulting model. In this model, developed based on other models of critical incident debriefing, a focus on intensive training for those who will be working with victims is emphasized, and techniques developed for use with those experiencing bereavement and loss are implemented in the days following an incident (McCaffrey, 2004). In addition to training specific to the particular incident which has occurred, which by definition can only occur in the aftermath of such an incident, individuals who will be carrying out the program receive annual refresher courses on critical incident debriefing in general (McCaffrey, 2004). Programs such as these show promise in assisting students and other witnesses to school violence in coping with the effects of such trauma (McCaffrey, 2004).

Although much research has focused on assisting students exposed to school violence, other efforts have indicated that teachers and other school personnel who have been exposed to school violence may be most at need for intervention following an incident of school violence, and often help to set the tone for the recovery of the school system as a whole in the wake of violence (Daniels, Bradley, & Hays, 2007). The importance of interventions targeted at members of entire communities impacted by school violence has also been emphasized by Littleton, Axsom, and Grills-Taquechel (2009). These authors note that in addition to interventions targeted at those who directly witnessed school violence (e.g., teachers, administrators, students, law enforcement officers and other first responders), members of the broader community indirectly affected by school violence, may benefit from efforts to assist them in forming and restoring relationships with others and engaging in other important goal-directed behaviors to restore lost resources and spur their own recovery. Finally, given the possibility of copycat killings, some authors have produced specific guidelines for media outlets to help guide their coverage of high-profile acts of school violence, in order to minimize the likelihood of future acts attempting to replicate events which are given much attention in the media (Preti, 2008). It has been noted that:

> the media…has a duty to report such incidents in a way that does not grant the perpetrator the power of achieving his goal of sensationalized infamy, which may in turn influence others. Thus, it may be helpful for the media to consider a formalized set of reporting guidelines. For example, it has been suggested that the news media should avoid glorifying the perpetrator and not disclose his methods or the number of victims killed. Instead, the media should emphasize victim and community recovery efforts and deflect attention from the perpetrator (Knoll, 2010b, p. 270).

In instances wherein specific threats are received by school personnel, the FBI's Critical Incident Response Group (CIRG) recommends that the role of law enforcement be minimized and the role of school personnel be maximized in instances of threats determined to be low risk, and that the role of law enforcement personnel be increased as the validity of the threat increases. Further, this group recommends that schools clearly communicate their policies for handling threats of violence to students, and that a threat assessment coordinator be appointed at schools to help coordinate the school's response to all threats, regardless of deemed severity. Higher risk threats could then be referred to a multidisciplinary team in order for a response to be formulated. Caution must be exercised when dealing with threats; however, as the FBI's CIRG notes that "if a student feels unfairly or arbitrarily treated [s/he may become] even angrier and more bent on carrying out a violent act" (p. 26).

Suggestions for Future Research

Several areas warrant the ongoing investigation of school violence. For example, the CIRG of the FBI has indicated that more information is needed regarding the following:

1. Frequency and severity of psychopathic and narcissistic traits in school shooters.
2. The specific school dynamics that increase the risk of school violence.
3. The relationship between suicidal ideation and risk for school violence.
4. Comparing and contrasting the personality, backgrounds, and family characteristics of school shooters to those of adolescents involved in other forms of violence, as well as to adults who engage in workplace violence.

Additionally, to assist in effective prevention and threat assessment efforts, further information is needed regarding the pre-attack behaviors and warning signs exhibited by perpetrators of school violence (Drysdale *et al.*, 2010). Future research should examine the connection between mental illness and past violent and nonviolent behavior, as well as with risk for engaging in acts of school violence. Similarly, longitudinal studies of the relationship between bullying behavior and victimization, depressive symptomatology, and propensity for school violence are needed (Estevez *et al.*, 2009). Studies that further clarify the relationship between cultures of honor and school violence are needed to reveal ways in which educators and policymakers might identify at-risk students and the unique psychosocial issues contributing to this risk (Brown, Osterman, & Barnes, 2009). Further, given the relationship between stalking behavior and future school violence, longitudinal studies should also address the rates of violence in adults who were stalking perpetrators as adolescents, as well as the long-term effects of having been the victim of an adolescent stalker (Purcell *et al.*, 2010).

Finally, any research conducted regarding the educational system must be completed in light of increasing pressure to obtain funding by demonstrating effective and cost-effective methods. Thus, it has been noted that "as many schools contemplate zero-tolerance rules, installation of metal detectors, erosion of student privacy through random locker searches, and the creation of a more restrictive [i.e., jail-like] environment, researchers and experts in the field need to provide thoughtful and informed commentary on the probable ramifications of implementing these rules" (Osborne, 2004, p. 159). Further, as pressure to reduce costs and implement selective interventions only with those most in need increases, efforts should be made to "establish the proportion of high-risk youths within a school with whom to intervene in order to produce the optimum **ecological effects** (i.e., the impact prevention programs may have on the interaction between students and their social and physical environments, in this case, their educational institution and those within it) and to identify other strategies to strengthen the diffusion of that effect" (National Institutes of Health, 2009). Finally, comparing the cost effectiveness of alternative programs to more traditional zero tolerance policies should be an area of ongoing focus for researchers (Skiba *et al.*, 2006).

Sentencing: Psychology of Juvenile Rehabilitation

Introduction

The controversy surrounding the most appropriate way to deal with juvenile offenders remains unabated today. There are two opposing viewpoints which pervade the sentencing of youthful offenders. There are those who advocate a rehabilitative model when addressing juvenile crime, and those who advocate a retributive model. The **rehabilitative model** is based on the premise that youthful offenders are amenable to treatment and, if treated properly, will "age out" of criminal behavior. Those who promote the **retributive model** believe that juveniles who commit crimes are treated too leniently by the system and should receive more stringent punishment for their crimes. While rehabilitation used to be the primary goal of the juvenile justice system, over the past two decades there has been a shift to ensure retribution (Benekos & Merlo, 2008; Granello & Hanna, 2003; Gray, 2001; Scott & Steinberg, 2008; Sellers & Arrigo, 2009; Soler, 2002; Melton *et al.*, 2007; Zimring, 2005). The following case illustration depicts a high-profile case of a juvenile who committed a heinous crime, raising the question for many individuals throughout the nation what to do with a boy like Kip Kinkel. While some individuals perceive individuals such as Kip to be troubled teens in dire need of treatment, others think such youths deserve the ultimate punishment.

On 21 May 1998, a 15-year-old freshman named Kipland Kinkel allegedly committed a series of heinous crimes. The young boy walked into his high school cafeteria and opened fire on a room full of students. He fired a total of 52 rounds, which some have described as sounding like fireworks. Kinkel's rampage left two people dead and another 22 injured. As if his killing spree at school was not tragic enough, Kinkel shot and killed both of his parents prior to arriving at school that day.

Reviewing the boy's history reveals that Kinkel announced to his literature class that he dreamed of becoming a killer and expressed his admiration for the Unabomber. Additionally, the day before the shootings, Kinkel was arrested for possession of a gun at school. Rather than being incarcerated or receiving any psychological counseling or treatment, Kinkel was released to the custody of his parents the same day.

Literature Review

As illustrated in the case of Kinkel, juveniles are capable of committing crimes every bit as heinous as adults. However, determining what constitutes the most appropriate sentence for juvenile offenders is highly controversial. The execution of one's parents coupled with the attempted mass murder resulting in the deaths of two other juveniles, that Kinkel engaged in, would make any adult eligible for the death penalty. Although juveniles can no longer be executed in the United States due to the *Roper v. Simmons* (2005) decision that held that defendants under the age of 18 at the time of the crime cannot be sentenced to death, imposing a sentence for a 15-year-old oftentimes requires a great deal more consideration than imposing a sentence for an adult. The case of Kipland Kinkel highlights the numerous issues that ensue in the juvenile justice system. The overarching issue is whether juvenile offenders should be treated any differently than adult offenders based on developmental factors (e.g., brain development, maturity, etc.) As Sellers and Arrigo (2009) point out, courts routinely fail to consider adolescents' psychosocial and developmental maturity and their effects on legal decision-making and competency-related abilities. When the juvenile court was initially established, one of the most important features of the system was its focus on rehabilitation. Inherent in the rehabilitative model was the notion that the **disposition** (sentencing mandated by the court) would be made based on its appropriateness for the offender, not the offense (Kinscherff, 2006; Melton *et al.*, 2007). Therefore, when the juvenile justice system was established as a separate entity from the adult system, it was presumed that the juvenile offender was indeed different from the adult offender. However, the differences recognized between adult and juvenile offenders had both positive and negative impacts on the juvenile justice system, and led to a series of reform measures.

In landmark cases such as *Kent v. United States* (1966) and *In re Gault* (1967), juveniles were recognized as deserving many of the same constitutional rights that adult offenders were granted, and were therefore entitled to many of the same **due process protections** (the protections provided by the United State's Constitution to those accused of a crime) that

adults received during criminal proceedings. On the one hand, these cases acknowledged the rights of juveniles. On the other hand, they highlighted the commonality between juveniles and adults, making the position that the two should be treated fundamentally different in the legal system — something of a double standard. After the decision rendered in *In re Gault*, the juvenile court repeatedly encountered challenges to the due process clause as it pertains to juvenile offenders (*McKeiver v. Pennsylvania*, 1971; *In re Winship*, 1970). As a result, Grisso (2000, 1996b) notes that lawmakers became more and more supportive of retribution and less tolerant of any efforts to rehabilitate juvenile offenders. This trend still continues today as the "tough-on-crime" angle is often used to attract voters despite findings that retributive responses are often more expensive and less effective than rehabilitative approaches (Piquero & Steinberg, 2010; Scott & Steinberg, 2008; Sellers & Arrigo, 2009; Zimring, 2005). Following the reforms aimed at protecting the due process rights of juvenile offenders were the initiatives geared toward promoting **determinate sentencing**, or a specific term of confinement that is statutorily specified (American Bar Association, 1980). Thus, this period of reform sought to reduce the unpredictability inherent in the previous era of juvenile justice, which allowed for **discretionary sentencing** (sentencing by judges which order a sentence tailored to the needs of both the defendant and society) of youthful offenders. The move to determinate sentencing was temporarily supported by individuals with vastly different philosophies concerning the appropriate way to sentence youths. Grisso (1996b) states that individuals who supported the retributive philosophy endorsed the determinate sentencing reform because, from their perspective, juvenile offenders received their just desserts. Moreover, these individuals cite *some* clinician support for this approach due to the therapeutic effect of teaching juveniles responsibility for their actions.

Alternatively, it is also argued that those juveniles who are deemed "untreatable" would be best dealt with using determinate sentencing (D'Angelo, 2007). Likewise, individuals who advocated the rights of children supported this reform because it prevented the abuse of discretionary decision-making by juvenile court judges.

The current reform efforts are aimed at increasing the severity of the determinate sentencing for youths. As a result, the treatment of juvenile offenders is becoming a reflection of societal views. A national survey was conducted in 1991, which revealed that 99% of the public advocates punishment for violent offenders (Roberts, 2004; Schwartz, 1992). The public's attitude is reflected in action by the legislature as new laws are created to implement stiffer punishment for juvenile offenders. The 1992 Attorney General for the United States, William Barr, clearly stated that serious juvenile offenders are beyond rehabilitation and laws need to be enacted which provide the justice system with the flexibility needed to prosecute these youths as adults (Barr, 1992). Feld (1997) describes how the same public outcry and political pressures to waive the most serious juvenile offenders to criminal court are increasingly influencing juvenile courts to punish more severely the remaining juvenile delinquents. However, in a Canadian study, Sprott and Doob (2000) found that the widespread support for dealing with very young violent children (10 or 11 years old) in the juvenile justice system diminished substantially when those polled were given the choice of mental health and child welfare systems instead.

More recent studies have attempted to gauge the public's attitude toward rehabilitation and incarceration using a methodology called **contingent valuation** or a methodology that holds that "differences in respondents' willingness to pay for two policies of equal effectiveness must necessarily indicate a true preference for one over the other" (Nagin, Piquero, Scott, & Steinberg, 2006; Piquero & Steinberg, 2010, p. 1). Piquero and Steinberg (2010) utilized this methodology in a randomized telephone survey of residents in four states (i.e., Illinois, Louisiana, Pennsylvania, and Washington) in an effort to determine the public's preferences for rehabilitation and incarceration. They found that participants in their study were willing to pay almost 20% more in annual taxes to fund rehabilitative programs rather than pay for longer incarcerations. In keeping with their methodology, they inferred that this indicated more public support for rehabilitation.

As a result of these views, legal reforms in the juvenile justice system have primarily revolved around prosecuting juveniles in criminal court (Allard & Young, 2002; Granello & Hanna, 2003; Grisso, 1996b). By waiving the youth to the adult system, the juvenile essentially faces the same sentence as would an adult charged with a similar crime. Moreover, the process by which a juvenile is waived to adult court has been reformed over the years. Initially, in the course of a waiver, the juvenile court took into account the juvenile's individual characteristics and the youth's potential for rehabilitation. However, currently there are laws in some states which require a juvenile to be waived to adult court based solely on the crime committed (Allard & Young, 2002; Grisso, 1996b). Thus, the flexibility and discretion that was once used in determining sentences for juvenile offenders are becoming increasingly less popular and, in some cases, nearly impossible. Allard and Young (2002, p. 65) state:

> *The imposition of adult punishments, far from deterring crime, actually seems to produce an increase in criminal activity in comparison to the results obtained for children retained in the juvenile system. Reliance upon the criminal courts and punishment ignores evidence that more effective responses to the problems of crime and violence exist outside the criminal justice system in therapeutic programs.*

Policymakers in some states realize that community-based programs for juvenile offenders are more effective than facilities and institutions that are designed to incarcerate them (Allard & Young, 2002; Melton *et al.*, 1997; Scott & Steinberg, 2008; Zimring 2005). This is perhaps due to the fact that juvenile detention facilities frequently do not offer services aimed at rehabilitating the offender. Moreover, from a fiscal perspective, community-based programs are much more cost effective for juvenile offenders (Piquero & Steinberg, 2010). Furthermore, Straus (1994) presents a theoretical basis for diverting youths away from incarceration in the justice system. Straus reports that many individuals who advocate diversion programs believe that they will reduce the stigmatization associated with incarceration. Therefore, according to Straus, juvenile offenders can be better helped within their respective communities while being spared the detrimental effects of being labeled a delinquent.

There are numerous community programs which currently exist designed to provide juvenile offenders with an alternative to incarceration in a juvenile institution. These programs are often structured to address problems within the families of juvenile offenders, as well as psychological issues affecting the youths. Some of these programs include the following: peer support groups, work training programs, church-based programs, drop-in treatment centers, youth shelters, and inpatient treatment facilities. One such program is Functional Family Therapy (FFT), a prevention and intervention program for at-risk adolescents or those already engaging in problem behaviors that is designed to eliminate obstacles that may encourage behaviors such as delinquency and violence, substance abuse, and various conduct disorders and is provided in an average of twelve family sessions. FFT was studied by Sexton and Turner (2010) as a community-based intervention within the juvenile justice system of a western state. Juvenile offenders that had been designated for probation were randomly assigned to receive either FFT or the standard probation services in that jurisdiction. Their findings indicated that those juvenile offenders who received the FFT intervention showed a 21−35% reduction in recidivism compared to probation (Sexton & Turner, 2010). Sexton and Turner (2010) cautioned that adherence to the FFT model is necessary to attain these treatment effects. This list highlights the numerous opportunities for rehabilitative services that are available for youthful offenders. Thus, the dilemma concerning the most appropriate sentence to impose upon a particular juvenile remains at the discretion of the court judge unless the particular jurisdiction imposes mandatory sentences. It is highly likely that the controversy surrounding rehabilitation versus retribution of youthful offenders will continue to spark debate among the legislature, the media, and individuals in the fields of mental health and criminal justice.

Forensic Psychology and Policy Implications

The issues involved in the sentencing of juvenile offenders raise numerous implications for the field of forensic psychology. Forensic psychologists are being asked to complete evaluations of juvenile offenders to aid the courts with their decisions on dispositional placements (Hecker & Steinberg, 2003). The largest percentage of work that psychologists do for juvenile courts is the **predisposition evaluation**, which provides critical information about a juvenile to help inform the decisions of the court regarding postadjudication questions (Hecker & Steinberg, 2003; Grisso, 1998). Please refer to the practice update section at the end of this chapter for additional information regarding these evaluations.

With the gravity of offenses committed by young persons such as Kipland Kinkel, the public is intent on "solving" the problem of juvenile crime. Forensic psychologists are needed on both sides of the sentencing debate. On the one hand, those who promote the rehabilitation of juvenile offenders must be able to account for the recidivism rate among those who do receive such services. Perhaps the rehabilitative services that are currently available do not meet comprehensive guidelines, which would target social and structural changes in the families, as well as in the juvenile. Though some evidence for the efficacy of rehabilitative services for juvenile offenders has been emerging (Sexton & Turner, 2010) more evidence is likely to be necessary in order to sway legislators from imposing harsher sentences. Without data unambiguously documenting how rehabilitative programs serve to protect the community from future acts of violence, it is unlikely that the communities and the legislature will refrain from imposing more stringent retributive sentences on juveniles.

On the other hand, those who support the retributive model in sentencing juvenile offenders must be able to offer explanations as to why, because in an era of severe determinate sentencing, young boys such as Kip Kinkel continue to commit heinous crimes. According to Fox News (2007), there were 31 school shootings in the United States from 2000 to 2007. These cases do not provide evidence that determinate sentencing is reducing the severity or frequency with which juveniles commit crimes. Moreover, those who support the retributive model need to provide evidence that determinate sentencing does in fact curb recidivism among juvenile offenders. However, some current literature refutes this position by showing that youths who receive alternative dispositions versus incarceration have lower rates of recidivism (Piquero & Steinberg, 2010; Scott & Steinberg, 2008; Weaver, 1992; Zimring, 2005).

Suggestions for Future Research

The literature lacks longitudinal studies comparing the rehabilitative approach of juvenile sentencing to the retributive approach. Such studies are difficult to conduct due to the legalities involved in obtaining juvenile records; however, these inquiries are imperative for drawing conclusions regarding the effectiveness of either approach. Moreover, there are a few studies that attempt to detect the basis for the discretionary decisions made by juvenile court judges. It is crucial to understand why judges are sentencing some juveniles to life in prison, while others are sentencing juveniles with comparable crimes to juvenile detention facilities or treatment programs.

Research is emerging that examines existing rehabilitative programs; however, more research is necessary to reliably judge the effectiveness of these programs. These analyses would include: program evaluations, examining the scope of treatment services offered, the provision of specialized treatment programs, and the nature and quality of treatment juvenile offenders receive in such programs. Other research into treatment programs may focus on those providing services, specifically in terms of training, supervision, or other factors that may influence the effectiveness of the intervention. The contingent valuation methodology presents an interesting method of gauging the public's preference for rehabilitative versus retributive sentencing of juveniles. In an era where public spending is often justified on the grounds of public preference, research of this type may help to generate more funding for rehabilitative programs that have been shown to be more effective in lowering recidivism rates.

Practice Update Section: Issues in Juvenile and Family Forensics

This section will discuss some of the important issues concerning evaluations conducted by psychologists for the juvenile court system, specifically evaluations prior to placement. "Providing evaluative services within the framework of the juvenile court requires specialized knowledge and skill not typically received in most generalist clinical training programs" (Hecker & Steinberg, 2002, p. 304). Predisposition evaluations provide essential information to aid juvenile courts to make decisions about a juvenile's amenability to treatment and appropriate placement/treatment options. A clinician's specialized training in the psycholegal questions that arise in juvenile and criminal court contexts will be critical in appropriately addressing the referral question. Melton *et al.* (2007) suggest that the only time juveniles are referred for a competency to stand trial or a mental state at the time of the offense (insanity defense) evaluation, as they pertain to the adult criminal code, is when the juvenile may be transferred to adult court. Depending on the jurisdiction, requests for predisposition evaluations are left to the discretion of the judge, probation officers, and attorneys (Hecker & Steinberg, 2002).

General guidelines that have been suggested for predisposition evaluations typically indicate beginning with a thorough review of the juvenile's file. A detailed interview with the juvenile should be conducted including information on the juvenile's functioning over a number of situations relevant to the referral question. Topics correlated with recidivism and violence should be specifically queried; for example, substance abuse, history of violence, and mental heath history. Collateral contacts are also recommended to gather pertinent information, particularly if the juvenile is uncooperative and/or has a vested interest in presenting him- or herself in a more favorable or less favorable light. In addition to a thorough file review and clinical interview, the juvenile's intellectual, academic, and vocational abilities should be evaluated. This is to help make informed opinions about the juvenile's appropriateness for certain placements, and to ensure that any special educational needs are met as required by federal law (Hecker & Steinberg, 2002; Melton *et al.*, 2007). A personality measure may be warranted if relevant to the referral question; for example, whether or not the juvenile has a major mental illness that necessitates inpatient or other type of treatment setting, rather than a more peer-run, behavioral modification type of program. Psychologists should only use psychological tests or instruments to inform judgments, diagnoses, or recommendations about issues for which they have been validated (Heilbrun, 2001; Heilbrun, 1992; Hecker & Steinberg, 2002).

The mental health and cognitive needs of the juvenile should be addressed and reflected in appropriate treatment options provided in the recommendations section of the disposition evaluation. Careful consideration of the juvenile's family context is important in helping to determine the causes of the juvenile's delinquent behavior, or, perhaps, the level of support or detrimental effects provided by the family in the juvenile's rehabilitative goals (Hecker & Steinberg, 2002). Careful consideration of the resources available in the community is important in making realistic recommendations. Unfortunately, these resources are frequently limited. Reports to be used by court participants should be free of **psychological jargon** or words that are not typically understood by those who are not mental health professionals (e.g., affect, delusions, etc.) and should only provide information that is relevant to the psycholegal question. These reports are often quite different from general psychological evaluations completed in a nonforensic environment.

■ International Issues: Cyberbullying

In addition to the emphasis placed on cyberbullying in American literature, researchers abroad have recently turned their attention towards cyberbullying. Many trends in cyberbullying that have been highlighted in research conducted in the United States have been replicated internationally. For example, Nocentini, Calmaestra, Schltze-Kumbholz, Scheithauer, Ortega, and Menesini (2010) conducted a study designed to assess students' perceptions regarding the terms used to describe cyberbullying, behaviors related to and constituting cyberbullying, and components used to define cyberbullying (e.g., imbalance of power, intention to cause distress or harm, repetition of behaviors across time, anonymity of bully, and publicity of the bullying behavior). The study sample included 70 students from three European countries: Italy, Spain, and Germany. Students participated in nine focus groups, and the same interview guide and structure was used in all three countries. The study examined the words used to describe behaviors conducted online or via electronic devices (e.g., mobile phones) that represents cyberbully. The results indicated that German students were most likely to use a word akin to "cybermobbing;" Italian students were most likely to use words akin to "virtual" or "cyberbullying," and Spanish students were most likely to use the terms "harassment" or "harassment via Internet or mobile phone" to describe behaviors that would be classified in North America as cyberbullying. Further, as a whole, students in all three countries indicated that they did not believe impersonation alone constituted cyberbullying. However, these students indicated that they needed more information regarding whether the intention of the perpetrator was to harm or cause distress to the victim, the actual or potential effects of the behavior on the victim, and whether the behavior occurred in a singular incident or via repeated incidents across time. Specifically, students were more likely to classify a behavior as cyberbullying if the bully held an actual or perceived position of power over the victim; if the incidents occurred repeatedly, rather than as an isolated incident, or if the potential bully engaged in the behavior with the specific intention of causing harm or distress to the victim. Students also acknowledged that even if the bully's intention was not to cause harm or distress, if these effects were caused or very likely could have been given the intensity of the behaviors, the behavior was considered bullying regardless of the intention of the perpetrator. Furthermore, students indicated that they would be better able to assess the nature and severity of acts that might be considered cyberbullying if they had information regarding the anonymity of the perpetrator and the level of publicity of the act, with higher levels of either characteristics increasing the likelihood that a behavior would be identified as cyberbullying. Such studies demonstrate that cyberbullying and its effects are not a problem unique to the United States; rather it is an increasingly common problem with potentially devastating consequences, which are recognized by European students as well. Additionally, studies such as these provide evidence that the characteristics of cyberbullying exhibited by North American students are mirrored in cyberbullying behavior overseas.

■

Related Websites

www.deathpenaltyinfo.org
Provides information regarding the death penalty and juveniles.
www.ncjjservehttp.org
Provides statistical information about trends in juvenile crime.
www.ojjdp.gov
Provides statistical information about the trends in juvenile crime, and current laws surrounding them.
www.cyberbullying.us
Website of the Cyberbullying Research Center; includes statistics, headlines, resources, training opportunities, etc. related to cyberbullying.
www.cdc.gov/ViolencePrevention/youthviolence/schoolviolence/index.html
Information and resources regarding school violence published by the Centers for Disease Control and Prevention.
www.fbi.gov/stats-services/school-violence
Resources from the FBI regarding school violence, including statistics.
www.foxnews.com/story/0,2933,266371,00.html
A website summarizing the major school shootings from Oct. 1997 to Mar. 2007.
http://compassioninjuvenilesentencing.wordpress.com
A blog opposing the sentencing of juveniles to life without the possibility of parole.

Court and the Legal System: Civil Forensics

Key Issues

Family Law and Emotional Rights
- Child custody issues between divorcing biological parents, and between adoptive parents and biological parents
- The Best Interest standard and the affect it has on the children's emotional well-being
- The emotional affect divorce has on children long-term
- The court's role in looking out for the child's emotional well-being

Best Interests of the Child Doctrine
- History of child custody practices
- Criticisms of the Best Interests of the Child doctrine
- Courts' application of the best interests doctrine
- Evaluators' role in custody disputes

The Role of Psychologists in Custody Evaluations
- Standards and guidelines in custody evaluations
- Common practices among evaluators
- Instruments used in evaluations
- Ethical considerations

Children/Juveniles and the Reliability of their Courtroom Testimony
- History and evaluation of child witnesses
- Capacities for child witness competency

CHAPTER 7

Juvenile/Family Forensics

Chapter Outline

Overview

This chapter examines selected topics and practice issues in forensic psychology impacting juveniles and families related to child custody, as well as issues related to juveniles testifying in court — civil and particularly criminal court. Divorce in the United States has become an epidemic and psychologists are being called on in growing numbers to play a critical role in family courts in custody determinations. Although these issues address "family," at the heart of the issue, both legally and morally, is the best interests of the child. As such, four topical areas will be addressed that define all of the players in the often contentious child custody arena. However, the intention of this chapter is to bring the focus back to the child or juvenile at the center of the controversy. Research has consistently demonstrated that divorce

Introduction to Forensic Psychology. DOI: 10.1016/B978-0-12-382169-0.00007-4

and battles for custody are damaging to children. Even though the setting for this controversy is in family court, some would argue that the stakes and emotions run as high if not higher than those typically seen in criminal courts. The work of forensic psychologists conducting custody evaluations is subject to intense scrutiny by parents and their legal advocates. The legal system relies heavily on mental health professionals to help define the very ambiguous Best Interest of the Child Standard. Any psychologist who participates in this process should be very aware of the legal standards, have training in relevant areas, and most importantly have the positive adjustment and best interest of the child in question, as the focus of the recommendations. Additionally, juveniles can provide testimonial evidence in a court of law. How does the child's age impact the admissibility and/or veracity of his/her testimony? Can youths tell the difference between right and wrong? Do adolescents understand the consequences of giving sworn testimony in a legal proceeding?

This chapter gives an overview of the legal issues and professional guidelines involved in custody evaluations and determinations, as well as the impact of family law and custody issues on children and adolescents. In total, four subjects are examined. These topics include (1) family law and the "emotional rights" of children; (2) best interest of the child; (3) the psychologist's role in child custody evaluations; and (4) juveniles and the reliability of their court testimony. While the issues reviewed in this chapter do not exhaustively examine the issue of child custody determinations in juvenile/family court, the issues highlighted provide an important foundation for understanding the necessity for well trained, competent, mental health professionals working in this noncriminal subspecialty area of forensic psychology. The stakes can be very high for the professional, the parents, and certainly the children involved. The implications of allowing children to testify, whether it be in a civil matter such as a custody hearing or a criminal matter as the victim or witness to a crime, can be significant and the relevant issues need to be understood.

The legal system is very frequently being asked about the issue of child custody, when divorcing parents cannot agree on a coparenting plan or when one parent feels the other lacks adequate parenting skills or may pose a physical threat to the child. Judges, attorneys, and families often turn to mental health professionals to help educate the court and to provide recommendations about custody determinations as well as what is in the best interest of the child in question. The experience of divorce and adoption can be traumatic for families, especially when children are involved. How are children impacted by these events? What is the emotional impact of the custody dispute for children? How does family law, if at all, protect the emotional rights of children in custody disputes when divorce and/or adoption are at issue?

Child custody cases involve a decision about the placement of a youth with a particular parent or parental surrogate. Typically, judges rely upon the "best interest of the child" doctrine. What is this standard and how do psychologists interpret it? How, if at all, does the juvenile court system promote it? To what degree does the "best interest of the child" standard aid judges in child custody determinations? How do custody evaluators formulate their recommendations and how do they ensure that they are in the best interests of the child? Are there structured guidelines that most custody evaluators follow and are they consistent with the American Psychological Association's (APA, 1994) best practices in child custody evaluations? What assessment techniques are currently used and how much influence do forensic psychologists have on family court decisions? Finally, how common are ethical complaints and litigation against psychologists who conduct custody evaluations and what strategies can ensure that ethical and legal standards are being applied? The subjects examined in this chapter explore the way in which the legal system, with the aid of psychologists, make decisions about what is in the best interest of the child, how they formulate recommendations, and what potential impact these decisions have on parents and their children.

Family Law and Emotional Rights

Introduction

Children are involved in custodial disputes every day. According to the National Center for Health Statistics, 50% of American children will experience parental divorce (2008). Other children are involved in disputes between their biological and potentially adoptive, or psychological, parents (Levin & Mills, 2003; Radel, Bramlett, & Waters, 2010; Xiaojia, Misaki, Martin, Leve, Neiderhiser, Shaw, Villareal, Scaramella, Reid, & Reiss, 2008). Both divorce and adoption are events that are lifelong processes affecting the mental well-being of children (Lehrmann, 2010; Amato & Sobolewski, 2001; Sun & Yuanzhang, 2002; Leon, 2003). Children of divorced parents are more likely to have lower levels of social competency, poor academic performance, conduct difficulties, and lower self-esteem than children from intact homes (Lansford, 2009; Short, 2002; Katz & Gottman, 1997; Short, 1998). Laws have begun to recognize the emotional impact custody disputes can have on children, especially for custodial decisions for divorce (Gunroe & Braver, 2001; Bauserman, 2002; Lowenstein, 2002). However, children's **emotional rights** (consideration of children's feelings regarding their preference of living arrangement and contact with parents or guardians) are not always considered in legal decisions, especially for custody decisions in which spousal abuse occurred in the home, or in those cases in which adoption went wrong (Ballard, Holtzworth-Munroe, Applegate, & Beck, 2011; Logan, Walker, Horvath, & Leukefeld, 2003; Zuberbuhler, 2001; Austin, 2001). Though research has been conducted that shows children want to participate in the decision-making process and they can provide both accurate and meaningful information, children also do not want to be responsible for the outcomes of the case (Cashmore & Parkinson, 2008; Goodman & Melinder, 2007; Saywitz, Camparo, & Romanoff, 2010). Although all 50 states mandate that the child's best interests be the main determinant in custody decisions (APA, 2010; Otto & Edens, 2005), even when such standards are applied, some researchers indicate they may not, in reality, protect the child's emotional rights (Kurtz, 1997).

The "**best interest of the child**" standard is applied for child custody cases (Azar & Cote, 2002; Elrod, 2006; Kaltenborn, 2001; APA, 2010; Otto & Edens, 2005). Rather than allowing divorcing parents to make whatever decisions they want regarding the custody of their children, judges are now required to consider what portions of the divorce will affect the children and make certain their needs are met (Braver, Ellman, Votruba, & Fabricius, 2011). However, despite the Best Interest of the Child mandate for divorce custody decisions, a child's right to a loving family and emotional support is not always considered. For other custody decisions that are not the result of divorce, courts may use the **Parents Rights standard** (e.g., the parent's right to custody based on the fitness of the parent and their biological tie to the child) (Wynne, 1997). This standard does not even acknowledge the emotional rights of the child. The following vignette gives a case example of such a ruling.

Jessica Deboer was two when she was taken away from the only parents she had ever known. Baby Jessica's biological mother, Cara Clausen, signed away her parental rights to the Deboers only 40 hours after the birth of her daughter, despite the Iowa law bars against signing a release before at least 72 hours after the birth of a child. When the Deboer's attorney called and asked Cara who the father of the child was, she lied and named Seefeldt, an ex-boyfriend who signed away what he thought were his parental rights.

Two days after the Deboers received custody of baby Jessica, Cara told Dan Schmidt that he was really the father of the baby. When Jessica was 3 weeks old, Cara sued to have her parental rights restored, and Dan made a legal claim later the same month. The Deboers refused to give Jessica back without a fight, and when Iowa courts continued to rule against them, they took the case to Michigan, hoping to win on the question of the child's best interest. The Deboers won the case in Michigan, but the ruling was appealed when Iowa argued that Michigan did not have jurisdiction. The Iowa court did not consider the child's best interest, arguing that it was not required under Iowa law. By the time the court had determined a ruling, Jessica was 2 years old and did not know her biological parents.

Psychologists argue that nothing is more devastating than losing both parents as a toddler. Nevertheless, baby Jessica was returned to her biological parents. In August, 1993, the Deboers packed baby Jessica's things and tried to explain to her why she had to leave. When the van arrived to pick Jessica up, she began crying and screaming and continued to do so as the van drove away. Follow-up reports indicate baby Jessica, now named Anna, has adjusted well and is happy; however, there is no way to determine the long-term effects this court decision may have on her psychological well-being (Cowley, Springen, Miller, Lewis, & Titunik, 1993; Hansen, 1994b; Ingrasia & Springen, 1993, 1994).

Literature Review

In some states, family law clearly does not focus on the child's best interest when it comes to custody disputes between biological family and the custodial, psychological parent. The Best Interest of the Child standard is viewed as "flexible" and allows the court to customize its decision in deference to the facts of the case rather than impose a "one-size-fits-all rule" (Warshak, 2007). Wynne (1997) indicates that the case of Baby Jessica illustrates "that as a nation, Americans do not think enough of their children to consider their rights or interests or to discuss even if they have rights or interests" (p. 187). In fact, most states make a primary effort to give biological parents custody of the child as long as there is no evidence of parental unfitness (Condie & Condie, 2007; Debele, 2007; Otto & Edens, 2005). Even in states where the child's best interest standard is applied, there are different statutory orders of preference for the placement of the child. These preferences do not always take into consideration the child's emotional rights. For example, in California, the child is placed with a relative unless the court determines that such placement is not in the child's best interest. However, the law does not necessarily specify what the best interests are. Although some states do provide factors which should be considered in the best interest determination, much discretion is left to the judge (Kushner, 2006; Otto & Martindale, 2006; Sempek & Woody, 2010). As a result, the child's emotional well-being is not necessarily considered.

Saywitz, Camparo, and Romanoff (2010, p. 542) found that research over the last 25 years has shown that expectations about children are "knowledgeable about their own needs and experiences," and researched is focused on how to interview children and obtain reliable information during custody battles. Riggs (2003) notes that more recent trends focused on an increasing reliance on psychological research and testimony when determining custody and visitation privileges. However, she explains that the U.S. Supreme Court's majority decision in *Troxel v. Granville* prefers the rights of biological parents over the best interests or psychological interests of children. In many instances, the unilateral decision about what is in a child's best welfare is determined solely by adults. However, Smith and Gollop (2001) recommend that separating parents should keep their children informed, listen to them, elicit and respect their views, and consider their point of view while making decisions about their care and living arrangements.

Bracco's (1997) examination of Canada's Best Interest test illustrates the court's difficulty in determining the best interest of the child. Bracco explains that the test is a change in mentality from "every parent has the right to a child" to "every child has the right to a family." However, Bracco explains the difficulty with assessing the best interest; she poses the question of whether it is truly in the best interest of the child to keep adoptions in secrecy. In Canada, there is to be no contact between the adopted child and his or her biological parents.

The issue of children's emotional rights and family law is complex because laws differ from state to state (Kushner, 2006; Oppenheim & Bussiere, 1996). However, most researchers agree that family law does not adequately acknowledge children's emotional rights (Ballard *et al.*, 2011; Kushner, 2006; Bracco, 1997; Oppenheim & Bussiere, 1996). There tends to be a bias toward biological parents in determining custody between biological parents and a third party (Riggs, 2003; Shapiro, 1993; Wynne, 1997). This bias was evident in the Baby Jessica case. Wynne (1997) argues that the courts need to recognize and support a child's need for a "stable relationship with his or her psychological parent" (p. 189). In addition, Wynne asserts that in order for family reunification attempts to work, the courts need to reassert what they consider real family relationships. According to Wynne, the family reunification policy using a biological definition of family has resulted in abuse, neglect, and even the deaths of many children. Perhaps Wynne's argument can be best illustrated by the statement of Kimberly Mays, a 14-year-old girl who was switched at birth and whose biological parents sought custody. At a news conference, she stated "Biology doesn't make a family" (Shapiro, 1993, p. 13). Mays clearly identified her "psychological" father as her family and wanted to divorce her biological parents. Wynne (1997) described the importance of creating protections in the law that could potentially help protect children's emotional rights by forcing every state to consider the child as a person, rather than the property of his or her biological parents to include having the right to a safe home and loving family.

According to Davidson (2006, p. 70), "Few American laws have 'children's rights' in their title. This is in part because many believe that if children are afforded 'rights' that they will come at the expense of parental rights." The rights of parents and those independently possessed by children unfortunately can come into conflict. Fortunately, family law's shortcomings in addressing the emotional well-being of children have not been ignored. Over 50 years of judicial decisions speak to children's constitutional protections applied to a variety of situations (Davidson, 2006). The cases include issues such as those considering juvenile incarceration without access to legal counsel to those protecting children in foster care and, more recently, the prohibition of the juvenile death penalty.

Reforms in U.S. law addressing the "protection rights" of children, both at home and in the foster care system, have been accomplished by child advocates and attorneys winning victories in this arena (Davidson, 2006). One strong example of his includes the 2003 Washington Supreme Court's decision in *Braam v. State*. *Braam v. State* was based on over 20 years of federal court precedents upholding that foster children have substantive due process rights under the U.S. Constitution that must be honored by the states (2003). The rights include the right to be free from unreasonable risks of harm and a right to reasonable safety, which includes providing services to meet a foster child's basic needs.

According to Davidson (2006), the United States only has narrowly crafted "rights based" state laws for children (p. 71). For example, they include the rights of children in foster care placement (such as in New Jersey and Rhode Island) and include legislative protection of the rights of child crime victims (as in Illinois) (2006). Davidson (2006) describes a broad law in the Commonwealth of Puerto Rico; specifically, Puerto Rico's Bill of Rights of the Child protects persons from birth through the age of 21. It has 27 provisions that protect the rights of children in numerous areas. Additionally, New Jersey's Child Placement Bill of Rights Act was the impetus for a 2005 federal court decision. As cited in Davidson (2006, pp. 72–73):

Judge Brotman of the U.S. District Court for the District of New Jersey (*K.J. ex rel. Lowry v. Division of Youth & Family Services*) held that children maltreated in an adoptive home not only had a federal constitutional claim for deprivation of their substantive and procedural due process rights, but also a private right of action for damages under that specific New Jersey law. The court deemed it important that this statute gave children rights independent of their parents when placed outside the home by the state.

Individual "children's rights laws" at the state or federal level have had very limited impact on government actions (Davidson, 2006). Currently, there is little to be done for cases such as Baby Jessica's when both families appear to be loving. Although the changes in family law are underway for third-party custody disputes, laws already exist for custody disputes between biological parents. These laws, and the degree to which they consider the emotional well-being of children, are discussed next.

Some specifications have been outlined for custody decisions in divorce cases. The Uniform Marriage and Divorce Act of 1970 provides a list of factors judges should consider in child custody cases (Crosby-Currie, 1996). Because laws in every state differ, the factors vary from state to state. One factor that is considered in custody decisions in every state is the child's wishes. Despite the indication that utilizing the child's wishes in a custody determination was designed to protect the child's emotional best interests, some research indicates asking a child about his or her wishes regarding a custody dispute has a negative impact on the child's well-being (Currie-Crosby, 1996; Melton, Petrila, Poythress, & Slobogin, 2007). In fact research indicates custody disputes, regardless of whether the child is asked about his or her wishes, are detrimental to children (M. Bussey, 1996; Cashmore & Parkinson, 2008; Goodman &

Melinder, 2007). A longitudinal study that evaluated a child's relationships and residence preferences as custody criterion found that (1) a living arrangement that is commensurate with a child's wishes and relationships contributes to the child's welfare and represents a positive living arrangement in the family and social environment; (2) the child's personal relationships change and a timely change of residence that occurs with the changed emotional preferences of the child is beneficial; (3) a living arrangement that contradicts the child's attachments and preferences can lead to either adjustment, a course of suffering, or attempts to change the living situation (Kaltenborn, 2001).

Amato and Sobolewski (2001) used 17-year longitudinal data from two generations and examined the effects of divorce and marital discord on adult children's psychological well-being. Results indicated that divorce and marital discord are predictive of children's subsequent lower levels of psychological well-being. Marital discord had a negative impact on children's emotional bonds with their mother, whereas, both marital discord and divorce lessen or weaken children's emotional bonds with their fathers. Short (2002) compared 87 college students who experienced parental divorce between the ages of 8 and 18 with 67 students who experienced parental death during the same ages and 87 students whose parents have remained married. Adult children of divorced parents reported significantly more present life stress, family conflict, and less family cohesion and friend support than the comparison groups. Additionally, children of divorced parents reported greater levels of current antisocial behavior, anxiety, and depression than their peers were, related to the aforementioned factors. Research has also demonstrated that children with recent experiences of parental divorce are at a relatively high risk of behavioral and emotional problems (D'Onofrio, Emery, Maes, Silberg, & Eaves, 2007; Harland, Reijneveld, Brugman, Verloove-Vanhorick, & Verhulst, 2002).

Bussey (1996) used a systems perspective to examine the detrimental effects of divorce on children. Some of the system-wide interventions for children of divorce have included legal reform. Because of the abundance of psychological literature that indicates divorce has long-term detrimental effects on most children (D'Onofrio *et al.*, 2007; Short, 2002; Lee, 1997; Short, 1998; Vikström, Van Poppel, Van de Putte, 2011), some states have begun to change the legal process for divorce (Beck & Frost, 2006). For example, parent-targeted interventions are often mandatory instead of voluntary, and some states such as California, Connecticut, and Massachusetts have court-mandated mediation for all disputed cases (Beck & Frost, 2006). Family law has begun to work with psychologists in an effort to reduce the negative impact divorce has on children's emotional well-being. There are mediation programs to help the post separation adjustment of both the children and the parents. The program promotes coparenting in the form of mediation by using assessments, education, and counseling (Bacher, Fieldstone, & Jonasz, 2005; Boyan & Termini, 2005; Beck, Putterman, Sbarra, & Mehl, 2008; Sullivan 2008).

Zuberbuhler (2001) describes the Early Intervention Mediation research project that lasted for 15 months at the Court of Domestic Relations of Hamilton County, Ohio. The goal of the project was to measure the efficacy of early introduction of mediation into divorce proceeding to resolve custody issues. The research project included ordering half of all divorcing parents who could not agree on custody arrangements for their children to attend mediation within 6 weeks of filing for divorce, whereas the other half of divorcing parents under similar circumstances acted as the control group who followed existing court procedures. The results indicated that in 61% of divorce cases ordered to participate in mediation, the parenting or custody issues were fully resolved. Zuberbuhler (2001) suggests that emotionally and financially damaging litigation was avoided in these cases and the court reduced judicial hours.

Kelly (2003) describes focused mediation interventions with parents in ongoing custody disputes. She discusses a design that emphasizes areas of parental behavior that negatively affect children's adjustment; specifically, parent's conflict patterns, postseparation and postdivorce parenting relationships, appropriate communication patterns, and competent and desirable postdivorce parenting. Regarding the value of mediation in child custody disputes, Lowenstein (2002, p. 739) states: "The mediator's role is to help parents to value the contributions made by the other parent, to encourage parents always to put the children first, and to avoid allowing one parent's hostility and mistrust towards the other parent to undermine promoting the physical and psychological health of their children." Mediation is a "win–win" way to settle disputes between parents, who are hurting and angry over the divorce; mediation can also reduce the potential of the hostilities that come from adversarial legal negotiations and court proceedings (Sbarra & Emery, 2008).

Although research indicates that law and psychology have begun to intersect when it comes to custody disputes between biological parents, there have been criticisms regarding the adequacy of the law for such disputes. As discussed previously, states use the Best Interest of the Child standard when determining custody cases between biological parents. Kurtz (1997) argues that the Best Interest standard may be detrimental to both the child and the parents in cases of spousal abuse. The concern about victims of domestic violence going to mediation with their abuser is that the victim may feel coerced into a decision, and the child is not protected against future exposure to violence (Ballard *et al.*, 2011). Judges are not required to take spousal abuse into consideration when determining the custody of the child. When the laws changed to the Best Interest of the Child standard, courts were no longer required to assess parental behaviors. As a result, the courts are less concerned with the parental relationship as long as the relationship does not appear to have a physical impact on the child. In fact, because statutes do not require a judge to take parental abuse into account when determining custody, an abuser may be granted custody. Oftentimes, the abuser is the financial supporter for the family, and the judge may see it in the best interest of the child to be placed with a parent who can provide for him or her. Kurtz (1997) argues that legislation "must create a statutory presumption against awarding a spousal abuser custody of a child. Only then will the best interests of the child truly be met" (p. 2). Consider the following case illustration (Sachs, 2000, pp. 212–213):

When his infant son was six months old, this father pushed his wife off an overlook. She plunged into a ravine and survived, thanks to some bushes that cushioned the impact. Her husband evaded indictment. For the eight years this case was pending, the courts showed not a particle of compassion or concern for this mother. The first inexplicable affront to justice was awarding the father custody of the infant at the moment the mother was being discharged from the hospital to recover from her injuries. After finally winning her struggle for custody, the mother dared not attempt to curtail the father's visitation lest she put her son into play in a new custody suit. Still suffering flashbacks to the assault, the mother must stoically send off her son on alternate weekends to spend two nights with his brilliant, malicious father. The child invariably returns in an agitated, out-of-control state that subsides only in time for the next visitation. Why, we wonder, would the court not use its broad discretion to give this mother authority to raise her son free from the influence of a father known to be capable of murder and diagnosed by its own forensic specialist as a "sociopath?" (Sachs, 2000, pp. 212–213).

Sachs (2000) also describes the very detrimental effect that visitation with known spousal abusers can have on children. She indicates that protective parents are justified in their attempts to insulate their children from the destructive influence of an antisocial role model or coparent. Requests by these parents to reduce or cut off visitation with a parent known to be violent or criminal should be afforded respect by judges. Sachs (2000, p. 224) illustrates her point with the following cases of fatalities linked to visitation:

National Public Radio carried the story the morning of 23 December 1998 of the tragic death of a mother and child murdered by the father in an encounter after a supervised visitation outside a community center near Seattle. According to the reporter, the mother had obtained a protective order prohibiting her estranged husband from contact on the grounds that "he choked her, beat her and threatened to kill her. She found his gun and turned it in to the police. Still he retained the right to see his daughter." (In newspaper accounts following the murder, the father was quoted expressing regret that the bullets intended for his wife had also struck his child.)

In August 1998, a Brooklyn man was convicted of murdering his former wife, a policewoman, while she sat in his car holding their baby after a visitation she had agreed to arrange to appease his demand for time during the supervisor's vacation. After the verdict, members of the jury commented to spectators from the National Organization for Women that they had heard sufficient testimony about the father's harassing phone calls, constant stalking, and maneuvers to obtain an illegal gun that they felt he should have been forbidden to have contact with the baby. Several noted that he had been grinning inappropriately throughout the trial.

Family law has begun to take into consideration children's emotional well-being and their rights of emotional stability. However, the law has been criticized for not protecting the emotional interests of children in all situations. From the literature, it is apparent that the law has progressed further toward protecting children's emotional rights, when it comes to custody disputes between biological parents than it has for custody disputes involving third parties. Possibly, the changes in law for custody disputes between biological parents are further advanced because such disputes have existed longer and the detrimental effects to children have therefore been more publicized. Prior to the 1960s adoptions were closed. As a result, no disputes between biological parents and potentially adoptive parents existed. Now such cases are more common, and activists have proposed to legislation that they believe these would protect the child's emotional interests.

Forensic Psychology and Policy Implications

Davidson (2006) recommends that the United States needs more laws like those in Puerto Rico, Illinois, Rhode Island, and New Jersey. Additionally, he indicates that states and the federal government should be increasingly directed by laws that can be used to evaluate policies and procedures of government agencies and courts involved with families. He stated, "Laws should also be used to measure whether government is fulfilling its obligation to promote the healthy development of children — free of violence in their homes and neighborhoods (p. 73)." There are a variety of laws that strive to provide children the right to a safe home, the right to adequate health care, the right to an adequate education, and the right to the care of a loving family or a substitute that is as close to a loving family as possible. However, more needs to be done and the laws and court decisions available can be ambiguous. What one may consider adequate health care or a loving family may be quite different from another's opinion. Children's emotional rights cannot be protected unless amendments consider psychological research that indicates what children need emotionally. Had psychologists' opinions been considered in the Baby Jessica case, it is doubtful that she would have been taken from the only parents she knew.

Other researchers suggest defining the child's Best Interest standard more clearly and consistently (Kushner, 2006; Otto & Martindale, 2006; Sempek & Woody, 2010). The ambiguity of the Best Interest standard allows for the court to be flexible and meet the needs of each individual child; however, it does not protect children against the biases and prejudices of judges (Sachs, 2000; Finley & Schwartz, 2007). To reduce the ambiguity, Oppenheim and Bussiere (1996) suggest that blood relationships on children's well-being be assessed, and coherent laws based on the findings be enacted. In order to establish coherent laws, several questions such as "how much weight should be given to blood relationships in determining custody" and "under what circumstances should relatives be able to maintain a relationship with their kin following an adoption by a non-relative?" (pp. 480–481), need to be considered. Not only do Oppenheim and Bussiere address specific questions that must be answered prior to policy change, they provide guidelines with which each question should be answered. The researchers argue that the child's best interests should be considered more important than the interests of the adult parties, the court should protect the continuity of personal relationships, and the court should respect the importance of the child's relationships with the extended biological family that will encourage connections to family history and culture. If Oppenheim and Bussiere's policy recommendations had been accepted prior to the Baby Jessica case, the judge may have ruled that she remain in the Deboer's home and receive regular visits from her biological parents; it is difficult to determine the effects that such a ruling would have had on the child.

Family law experts are proposing measures which could help protect children from the negative emotional impact that results from unsatisfactory family law (Lowenstein, 2002; Sachs, 2000; Braver, Fabricus, & Ellman, 2003). In an effort to prevent adoption custody disputes, some activists have proposed to make adoptions closed, despite research indicating that positive ties to biological family can be beneficial for adoptees (Brooks, 2002; Bracco, 1997; Miall & March, 2005; Oppenheim & Bussiere, 1996; Xiaojia *et al.*, 2008). An open adoption could have prevented the Baby Jessica custody dispute completely. Perhaps if the biological mother was granted regular visits with her daughter, she may not have felt as if she were missing out on her daughter's life. Neil, Beek, and Schofield (2003) discuss postplacement contact with biological family members. These researchers state, "Children permanently separated from their birth families have to manage life-long issues of attachment, identity, and loss" (Neil *et al.*, 2003, p. 401). **Child development theories** (theories explaining the cognitive, emotional, physical, social, and educational growth of children) can help those working with juveniles better understand their emotions and behaviors. Bracco (1997) suggests that the law redefines what is considered family. She argues that adoption law is based on **patriarchal child development theories** (e.g., theories that support male-dominated families and have limited understanding into how the family has changed historically) and the current perception of the nuclear family may be too rigid. Bracco argues that policy changes in Canada should be made in which an adopted child's biological parents can have a role in raising the child. Although Bracco's arguments are primarily for adoption considerations and not necessarily custody disputes, her argument for redefining familial considerations relates to policy suggestions made by other researchers. Brooks (2002) discusses the tremendous potential of utilizing extended biological family members as a resource for at-risk children in a more creative and inclusive approach to adoption. Wynne (1997) suggests that courts work to redefine what are considered "real" family relationships. He argues that children's emotional needs will not be met until courts define family according to a psychological definition. This definition would place more emphasis on psychological ties with parents rather than on blood ties.

The analysis of policies concerning custodial disputes between biological parents and third parties is difficult because the policies concerning custody are confounded with adoption regulations. One cannot examine policy concerning custodial disputes without examining adoption law. A thorough examination of adoption law is beyond the scope of this section; however, the issue is important for the protection of children's emotional well-being and merits further examination.

Family law appears to be more adequate for custodial disputes involving biological parents. Psychological research has indicated that conflict in divorce situations is what is most detrimental to children (Amato & Sobolewski, 2001; Mitcham-Smith & Henry, 2007). States have changed statutes regarding custody to protect children emotionally. Although there is still room for family law to change in order to protect children to an even greater extent, the fact that courts and psychologists have begun working together to help determine the best interests of the child is promising. Only when special circumstances such as spousal abuse are considered do researchers make bold suggestions for policy change. Joint custody when one parent is abusive can be detrimental to the child, forcing him or her to maintain contact with the abusive parent. Spousal abuse is only one circumstance that may require a change in certain statutes regarding child custody. There are certainly many other circumstances in which current custody laws are insufficient; however, an examination of each circumstance is beyond the scope of this section. Spousal abuse provides one example of how current policies may not protect children's emotional well-being in every given situation. Though the National Conference of Commissioners on Uniform State Laws approved the Uniform Representation of Children in Abuse, Neglect, and Custody Proceedings Act in 2006, there is still room for improvement in the laws, and for representation for the child involved in the case (Lehrmann, 2010). This Act states that every child in an abuse and neglect case is entitled to legal representation, courts in private custody proceedings should have discretion to appoint a representative for a child when there is a need for one, and lay advocates can be valuable in assisting the courts in determining the child's best interest (Atwood, 2007).

Suggestions for Future Research

The ambiguity of the law suggests a lack of consensus among experts on the importance of blood ties versus psychological ties (Neil *et al.*, 2003; Oppenheim & Bussiere, 1996). Research is not consistent regarding what the best interests of the child are. While some research indicates that blood relationships are more important, other studies indicate that psychological relationships take precedence. Further research needs to be conducted to determine the psychological impact of not knowing one's biological parents, being raised by adoptive parents but maintaining a relationship with biological parents, and of being removed from one's psychological parents as a toddler and placed with biological parents. Psychologists have speculated about each of the above, but longitudinal research to determine the impact of each has not been undertaken. Such research will also provide social scientists with individual characteristics of children that may result in more or less emotional stability after living through a custodial dispute and possibly being taken from psychological parents. For example, research on divorce has shown that gender, degree of conflict in parental relationship, and the child's IQ all have an impact on the extent to which the divorce will have a negative impact on the child; however, research on adoption custody disputes of this nature has not been conducted.

There is ample research on the impact of divorce on children. This research has begun to contribute to change in family law regarding custody disputes. There are now Parenting Coordinators (PCs) that are sometimes used in divorce or separation situations that deal with concerns about the postseparation adjustment of children and parents (Mitcham-Smith & Henry, 2007; Deutsch, Coates, & Fieldstone, 2008). The PCs use conflict resolution that include assessments, education, mediation, evaluations, case management, child custody consulting, coparent counseling, monitoring, and enforcement (Bacher *et al.*, 2005; Boyan & Termini, 2005; Beck *et al.*, 2008; Sullivan 2008). The PCs have a background in social sciences, mental health, and/or law. Further research into this program, specifically, on the impact it has on the well-being of children of divorced or separating parents would be beneficial. Future research is needed on whether or not family law policy has caught up to the current cultural standards on views of the "ideal" family.

With the increased use of the mediation process, including some states mandating it for custody disputes, further research into the impact of this method on the children involved is needed. Also the issue of competency to participate in mediation needs to be addressed, and guidelines into determining competency are needed for the parents as well as the children. Further research is needed on domestic violence couples that participate in mediation and the outcome for the children in a longitudinal study in order to have laws in place for these situations in order for the court to use the best interest of the child standard.

Best Interests of the Child Doctrine

Introduction

The **Best Interests of the Child** doctrine was established in the legal system to determine the components of child custody that will provide the best environment for a child's adjustment and development (Smith & Gollop, 2001; Kelley, 1997). According to Haselschwerdt, Hardesty, and Hans (2011), judicial intervention is necessary to reach a custody decision in approximately 20% of divorcing couples in the U.S. The Best Interests of the Child doctrine is typically invoked during an adversarial divorce, which is the reason for most custody disputes (Otto & Martindale, 2006; Riggs, 2003; Logan, Walker, Jordan, Horvath, & 2002; Kelley, 1997; Skolnick, 1998). Divorce can have significant consequences for the child, and the purpose behind the Best Interests doctrine is to consider which adult can provide the most positive relationship with and the best environment for the child (Cartwright, 2006; Huurre, Junkkari, & Aro, 2006; Portnoy, 2006; Riggs, 2003; Pedro-Carroll, Nakhnikian, & Montes; Bauserman, 2002). Although positive aspects of the doctrine have been noted, including the idea that every decision can focus on an individual child's need and that it permits society to address shifting morals, values, and situations (Kelley, 1997), much of the literature highlights the standard's limitations. Consider the two case illustrations below:

Joe and Sarah have three children, ages 6, 10, and 13. The two youngest are girls, and the oldest is a boy. The parents have abused both drugs and alcohol. In addition, Joe went to prison several years ago for committing a sexual offense against a 12-year-old girl. Sarah remained married to Joe during this time but began having an affair with a coworker by whom she became pregnant. While Joe was in prison, their children were temporarily removed from Sarah's custody because of her drug use. However, she was able to straighten herself out and they were returned to her. When Joe was released from prison, he and Sarah did not initiate divorce proceedings; they shared joint custody of the two girls while the boy lived solely with his father. Joe does not have steady employment. He works odd jobs as a mechanic and lives with his girlfriend in a trailer in his parents' backyard. Sarah does not work at all and lives with her new fiancé in a one-bedroom apartment. They both claim to be drug free. Recently, Joe and Sarah became angry with one another, and Sarah filed for a divorce. In an effort to hurt Joe, she has sued for sole custody of the two girls, stating that Joe is a threat to them because of his prior sex offense. The question before the court is which parent will provide the best environment for the children.

Jeff casually dated Lydia, a girl from work, for four months. The relationship seemed to end naturally when Lydia took another job. Four years later when leaving for work in the morning, Jeff was served papers to appear for a paternity hearing. Jeff was never contacted about Lydia's pregnancy and wasn't made aware that he was likely the father of her child. The paternity test was compelled as a result of Lydia and her soon to be husband needing Jeff to sign over his legal rights to the child so she could be formally adopted by Lydia's fiancé. Test results determined Jeff was the father. A Texas state law that would force Jeff to pay back child support (over $14,000) if he refused to sign over his parental rights to his now four-year-old daughter, was used as leverage to compel him to sign over his rights. Jeff was faced with a dilemma with little notice and huge implications. After speaking with the man who had raised his daughter from birth, Jeff believed that signing over his rights was in his daughter's best interest. At the next hearing, Jeff told the family court judge he believed it was in the child's best interest to be raised by her mother and the only father she had ever known — Lydia's fiancé. However, he was very concerned that his daughter would be raised believing that he had abandoned her or didn't care about her well-being.

Although Jeff's financial means were limited, he asked the judge to set up a trust for the child to be available to her at age 18. Jeff was willing to sign over rights to the child because he perceived it to be in her best interest, but on the condition that this trust would include a $5000 bond signed over to his daughter, court transcripts of the family court hearings, as well as his monthly checks from the military based on an injury during service. Jeff did not want his daughter to believe that he didn't want her or wasn't willing to financially contribute to her care. The family court judge was stunned and told Jeff that in his 20 years of handling these types of cases, he had never had a parent be willing to sign over rights to the child for reasons centered on the best interest of the child, while also insisting on accepting some financial responsibility for that child. Despite her initial refusal to accept the conditions, Lydia eventually agreed to the arrangement. Jeff signed over his rights, but at the age of 18, his biological daughter will have the terms and circumstances of his rights' termination explained in court documents, as well inheriting a sum of money from Jeff that will help to fund her college education. It would only be at the daughter's discretion to decide if she wanted contact with Jeff at that time.

Literature Review

When deciding between Joe and Sarah as sole custodians of their children, many people might feel that neither should be awarded custody. However, the question before the court is to choose between these two individuals, and the judge must make the decision. In times past, a judge may have based his or her decision on very different criteria. For example, prior to the mid-19th century, children were perceived as property, and fathers were entitled to such property (Emery, Otto, & O'Donohue, 2005). Courts then began supporting the notion that children of young ages should be allowed to stay with their mothers until they were weaned. This was commonly referred to as The Tender Years presumption (Kushner, 2006; Otto & Martindale, 2006). It was not until 1925 that the Best Interests of the Child standard was initially proposed. This occurred in the case of *Finlay v. Finlay* (1925). A father was suing for custody of his child, and the court ruled that the concern should be for the child's welfare not for the argument between the parents. However, the Tender Years presumption continued to prevail until 1970, when it was officially supplanted by the Best Interests of the Child standard (Otto & Martindale, 2006).

A major complaint lodged against this relatively new standard is that it is very vague, allowing for **judicial bias** or the predisposition of a judge, arbitrator, or anyone making a judicial decision, against or in favor of one of the parties or a class of persons, that leads to different results in similar cases (Sempek & Woody, 2010; Skolnick, 1998). Dolgin (1996), for example, reported that many criticize the standard because it does not provide enough substantial guidance for courts to follow regarding child custody decisions. The author also suggested that using the Best Interests standard could lead to opposing decisions in child custody cases, depending on the presiding judge. Part of the problem is that there appears to be no widely recognized operational definition for the standard (Kushner, 2006; Otto & Martindale, 2006; Sempek & Woody, 2010). As Kushner (2006) explains, the methodological restraints in research with children in custody contexts can make it difficult to operationally define "best interests." Although every state has adopted a variation of the Best Interests of the Child doctrine, the codes and statutes in all of the states have very little in common regarding guidelines for this standard (Sempek & Woody, 2010). For example, many states allow the decision maker to consider factors that they believe to be relevant even if they are not included in the state's statutes (Otto & Martindale, 2006).

The criticisms about vagueness extend beyond the problem of judicial bias. There also appears to be a lack of agreement among mental health and legal professionals about the necessary requirements for the best interests of a child, which leads professionals to arrive at conflicting decisions in particular cases (Horvath, Logan, & Walker, 2002; Kelley, 1997; Kushner, 2006). Horvath *et al.* (2002) examined 60% of custody evaluations in one circuit court over a two-year period and found much variation in techniques used and a lack of consistency between guidelines and clinical practice. On an even broader level, the standard has been criticized because societal agreement about what is in the best interests of children does not exist (Goldstein, Solnit, Goldstein, & Freud, 1996; Skolnick, 1998). However, Braver, Ellman, Votruba, and Fabricius (2011) found that laypersons in their study believed that when parents shared equally in caretaking duties, then they should have equal custody. The authors also found that laypersons also believed that those in the legal system made decisions in favor of the mother more often than they should. Jeff's case raises questions about the rights of fathers who are never told about the existence of a child until years later. Azar and Cote (2002) contend that during the twentieth century both the rights of women and children evolved, as well as the needs of children beyond just physical ones. These researchers maintain that the expansion of child protection laws, the increased willingness and speed in terminating parental rights, and the increases in rights for other interested parties (e.g., grandparents) are proof that the pendulum is swinging away from parental rights to a greater emphasis on children's rights.

However, other researchers (Sachs, 2000; Dolgin, 1996) contend that the lack of guidance may lead judges to focus on the interests of the parents rather than on the interests of the child. In a review of judicial decisions, Marsh (2005) states that judges often struggle with balancing parents' statutory and constitutional rights. Marsh (2005) also went on to posit that the child's independent rights are vague and were rarely mentioned. A judge may do this by basing his or her decision on protecting the constitutional rights of the parents. Researchers contend that courts often examine other factors in addition to the best interests of the child (Otto & Martindale, 2006; Miller, 1993). These factors include the constitutional rights of those involved. Miller (1993) indicated that Supreme Court decisions reflect the idea that constitutional rights precede the Best Interests standard. This leads other courts to examine the interests of the adults over the children (Sachs, 2000). In the case of Joe and Sarah, a judge may have to consider Joe's constitutional rights of losing his children because of a crime he may never commit, even if this supersedes the best interests of the children. Kandel (1994) suggested that the Best Interests standard "does not rise to constitutional dimensions; it implicates neither substantive nor procedural due process rights. Further, it is subject to limitation in the interests of the state, the interests of the parents, and the interests of children themselves" (p. 349). He also indicated that the standard is more of an infringement on the rights of children than parents because a judge substitutes his or her opinion for the choice of the children. Sachs (2000) adamantly opposes judicial decisions to force joint custody or visitation with parents with a violent or criminal background against the best interests of the child. She states (pp. 223–224): "Judges do not seem to see the contradiction of upholding the law by forcing children to spend time with criminals. The callous disregard for children's feelings shown by some decision makers is troubling to witness."

In forming such an opinion, the judge does not have to consider psychological suggestions. In fact, Miller (1993) indicated that the Best Interests standard is defined differently both legally and psychologically, leading to further complications. For those working in mental health, the best interests of the child is the conclusive factor in recommending an appropriate placement, while for the courts, it is not; constitutional and legal factors rank higher than the Best Interests standard. Sachs (2000, p. 216) indicates: "Child advocates with no background in forensics are incredulous to learn that many judges, lawyers, and psychologists do not deem it necessary to weigh domestic violence as a factor in custody unless so instructed by state law." According to Kandel (1994), when the court does request psychological assistance, it does so to justify its decision. It appears that by creating "scientific validity" (p. 348) that this is the best choice; however, often the court asks mental health professionals the wrong question. Sachs (2000, p. 222) warns that some protective parents and judges are "cowed by the supposed unanimity among 'experts' that children should maintain relationships with both parents."

However, Kushner (2006) stated some judges see custody cases as stressful and slightly beyond their expertise. In these cases, Kushner explains that judges elicit the assistance of custody evaluators to provide assessments of the children's needs in a way that is understandable to the court. In a 2004 study of family court attorneys and judges, Bow and Quinnell found that 71% of respondents rated evaluations completed by court-appointed evaluators as extremely helpful. The most common complaint provided by the participants was that evaluations took too long to complete. Additionally, 15% of judges in the study were concerned about the evaluator's lack of objectivity, ignorance of relevant legal criteria and standards, and the absence of data to support the evaluation (Bow & Quinnell, 2004). This study revealed that, overall, family court judges and attorneys found consultation with forensic evaluators very useful.

Another factor that appears to bias judges' decisions is that since the early 20th century mothers have been given preference with regard to custody of their children, even though this has never been statutorily recognized (Kandel, 1994). Though the Best Interests standard prevails, most custody decisions still are made in favor of the mother possibly due to the persistence of the tender years philosophy (Kushner, 2006). There are four explanations provided by Warshak (1996) for this phenomenon: (1) women by nature make better parents and are more essential to children; (2) most mothers are better parents, not because they possess innate superiority, but because they have more experience than fathers in raising children; (3) custody should be a reward for the types of contributions a mother has made to her children; and (4) mothers suffer more emotionally than fathers from the loss of custody. Warshak also indicated that only one in 10 children resides with their fathers, and this has been a steady proportion for decades. Despite evidence showing that divorced fathers can provide nurturance for their children and can handle the responsibilities of child rearing, those who desire custody "must still prove mothers grossly negligent or abusive" (p. 399).

Otto and Martindale (2006) reported that all states have gender neutral child custody laws, which have superseded laws and precedents that favored mothers in custody disputes. However, he contends that the legal literature suggests that a maternal preference still exists. To further examine this issue, Stamps (2002) surveyed state judges in Alabama, Louisiana, Mississippi, and Tennessee (n = 149) by mail in order to ascertain their beliefs related to maternal preferences in custody decisions. Results of the study indicated that the judges surveyed demonstrated continuing maternal preference with regard to quality of parenting, children's adjustment following divorce, and the preferred custodian following divorce. If a judge believes that mothers are better caregivers for children, then it can be fairly simple to favor a particular parent by highlighting the negative behaviors of the other parent (Dolgin, 1996). In the case of Joe and Sarah, if the judge preferred that mothers retain custody, then the judge could focus on Joe's prior sexual offense as evidence that he would be an unfit caregiver.

Forensic Psychology and Policy Implications

Based on the arguments against the best interests of the child standard, there should be some type of uniformity in the guidelines (Horvath *et al.*, 2002; Hall *et al.*, 1996; Otto & Martindale, 2006). Guidelines that are more universally accepted that create more specificity for all professionals involved may decrease the bias associated with decision making (Banach, 1998; Otto & Martindale, 2006). Banach (1998) suggested that an operational definition be included in state statutes to create some uniformity. In addition, professionals should not rely solely on their own judgment but evaluate their decisions with other professionals to avoid biases. As Otto and Martindale (2006) suggest, those offering testimony in custody cases would serve their function better if they "only employed assessment and data-gathering techniques with demonstrated reliability and validity, limited opinions they offered to those for which there was empirical support, refrained from offering opinions on moral–legal matters that may enter custody decision making, and were wholly candid in representing the scientific basis for the techniques they employed and the opinions they offered" (p. 270).

Skolnick (1998) provided some suggestions to create more uniform criteria. She stated that a child's psychological well-being should be one consideration. This would include examining emotional ties the child has with the parents and the child's need for stability. Also, rules should be provided that prevent a judge from considering lifestyle choices or parental conduct that does not directly damage the relationship with the child. In Joe and Sarah's situation, this could be a difficult task to accomplish because they both engaged in behaviors that were potentially harmful to their children.

Goldstein *et al.* (1996) offered the notion of changing the Best Interests of the Child term to the Least Detrimental Alternative because it is more realistic and less subject to a magical idea of finding the best interest. They also suggested that child placement decisions should remain as free as possible from state intervention and be as permanent as possible because continuity is critical for children. The state should interfere only if it can provide the least detrimental alternative. Krauss and Sales (2000, p. 843) critically examined the roles of forensic evaluators and psychological researchers in determinations of the Best Interest of the Child standard in custody battles. These researchers maintain that current data do not support most "expert testimony" offered by mental health professionals in court. Instead, they argue that the Best Interest of the Child standard does not represent the needs of the legal system or the expertise of psychology, but rather the least detrimental alternative to the child standard more precisely meets the needs of both the legal and psychological arenas (Krauss & Sales, 2000). Others, however, opine that there is an existing research base concerning divorce, parenting, child development, and children's emotional and social adjustment that can be used in custody evaluations; the problem is that too few evaluators draw from this literature (Kelly & Johnston, 2005).

Creating new guidelines for this standard should include cooperation between legal and mental health professionals. Wall and Amadio (1994) indicated that child custody decisions must consider the entire family and the needs of each member to provide the most beneficial and continuous relationships between parents and children. They stated that if legal and mental health professionals could cooperate, this task would be easier to accomplish and the best interests of the family would be ascertained.

Suggestions for Future Research

Research needs to focus on exactly which factors to consider when making custody decisions based on the best interests of the child. Before specific guidelines can be proposed, however, they first have to be discovered. Conducting research on those areas of development and functioning most appropriate for children, at various ages, should be pursued by mental health professionals, specifically child development specialists. Further research into divorce and custody arrangement effects on children are also needed to better inform evaluators' decision-making and evaluation practices (Emery *et al.*, 2005; Kelly & Johnston, 2005). Bala and

Saunders (2003) report that there exists a lack of research concerning the effects that different living conditions and relationships have on children. Leon (2003, p. 258) suggests the following questions be addressed in future research: "How does parental divorce affect developmental outcomes? What risk and protective factors influence adaptation? How does early parental divorce affect later adjustment?"

Also, studying various decisions made by judges and determining which constitutional factors are important in these situations is warranted, especially since courts are not going to let psychological issues prevail over constitutional ones. There needs to be some clarification regarding those factors regularly considered and how different conditions change the factors that are deemed important (Banach, 1998: Otto & Martindale, 2006). Once these are learned, they can be incorporated into guidelines for those making child custody decisions.

In the area of gender bias decision-making, further research should be conducted on fathers who are awarded sole custody of their children in order to verify that they can be appropriate caregivers. Although findings exist in this area, additional studies are needed because courts continue to favor mothers in their decisions. This bias can adversely impact someone like Joe, who may have made a horrible mistake but could still be a good caregiver.

The Role of Psychologists in Custody Evaluations

Introduction

Approximately one half of all marriages end in divorce in the United States, impacting greater than one million children in a year (Edwards & Ray, 2008). Children are involved in 50% of divorce cases (Symons, 2010). Approximately 4% of divorce cases involve litigation over custody or visitation, resulting in about 40,000 children a year being at the center of a custody battle (Bernet, 2002; Donner, 2006). Contested custody disputes are purported to have the most detrimental psychological impact on the children involved and even the process of divorce itself can create a long-term, negative psychological impact on children (Krauss & Sales, 2000; Donner, 2006). When divorcing couples cannot agree on custody arrangements, custody disputes are often brought to family court, and mental health professionals are typically obtained to conduct custody evaluations. According to the American Psychological Association (2009), **child custody evaluations** are assessments by professionals that examine the relationship between a parent and a child with an emphasis on the psychological best interest of the child. Although custody evaluations can be conducted by a variety of mental health professionals, doctoral level psychologists with appropriate training are typically found to be amongst the most credible and thorough as reported by attorneys and judges (Zimmerman, Hess, McGarrah, Benjamin, Ally, Gollan, & Kaser-Boyd, 2009). The APA published recommended ethical guidelines for custody evaluations performed by psychologists and are considered the professional standard of competent practice (Symons,

2010). However, there is much concern that there are no structured guidelines for performing child custody evaluations or operationalizing and measuring what is in the **best interest of the child** (i.e., component of child custody that addresses environment, adjustment, and well-being of the child). The vast majority of parents who divorce do not require a custody evaluation by mental health professionals; however, a formal psychological custody evaluation may be particularly beneficial to the parents and the legal system in the following circumstances (Bernet, 2002, p. 784):

- One or both of the parents have a mental disorder that may affect the person's parenting skills;
- The child may have specific mental health needs that should be considered in developing the custody arrangements or parenting plan;
- The divorce has been unusually hostile and the custody evaluation is seen as a less adversarial approach to making decisions involving the children;
- The child's relative attachment to the parents seems like an important issue;
- It is suspected that one of the parents has tried to indoctrinate the child and alienate him or her from the other parent; or
- One parent has accused the other of physical or sexual abuse.

Depending on the age and maturity of the child, the child's wishes about who they would like to live with can also be a significant factor, particularly if custody of a teenager is in question. However, the evaluator must be aware of the many factors that could influence a child's proclamation of where he or she wants to live. Donner (2006) indicates that when a child is placed in the middle of a custody dispute he/she is being torn apart because of a **narcissistic**

injury (e.g., perceived threat to one's inflated sense of self-esteem or self-worth) to one or both parents, this can cause the parent to push the child away, forcing the child to choose between parents. Additionally, Sachs (2000) warns that seeking custody should not always be confused with being a fit parent. She indicated that some parents seek custody of their children for the wrong reasons which are certainly not in the best interest of the children, for example (Sachs, 2000, p. 217):

- To evade responsibility for paying child support.
- As a strategy to force the opposing parent into a reduced financial settlement.
- As a strategy — sometimes on advice of counsel — to add to the opponent's burden by expanding the scope and increasing the cost of litigation.
- To hold on to children with the intention of exploiting them sexually, physically, or emotionally.
- For self-gratification.
- To compensate for inner feelings of emptiness and isolation.
- For the satisfaction of defeating or tormenting the opposing parent.

Consider the following case example about Janina:

The ten-year-old Janina lived in her father's household at the time of the evaluation. She maintained good relationships with both parents, but showed preference for her mother and wished to live with her. Although the expert recommended that she should live with her mother, the court did not agree. In the first follow-up study about ten years after the child's psychiatric evaluation, the father refused to be interviewed. I was, however, able to conduct a lengthy interview with Janina, now almost 20 years old, and her mother on the occasion of a visit by Janina to her mother. Both regarded the custody decision in favour of Janina's father negatively. To the question as to why her father sought custody, the young woman replied that he wanted to use the custody dispute as revenge against his wife for leaving him; as a result of the divorce he had regarded Janina as his property… In the second interview, about six years after the first survey, …Janina felt that the fact that both of her parents had partners was particularly difficult for her. She told us that custody in favour of the mother would have resulted in the advantage of actually being cared for by her mother, but, as it was, during the time with her father, she was "cared for by a strange woman." In both interviews, she emphasized her good relationship with her mother, and how difficult it was only seeing her during the agreed visiting times. She also had painful memories of leaving her mother at the end of visits (Kaltenborn, 2001, p. 99–100).

Literature Review

All 50 states mandate that the child's best interests be the main determinant in custody decisions (APA, 2010; Otto & Edens, 2005). Over the last two decades, research has been conducted to attempt to determine whether or not there is consistency in standards of practice amongst mental health professionals conducting child custody evaluations. Otto and

Edens (2005) state that the adversarial nature of the courtroom and ambiguous guidelines make the task of conveying research, and evaluating results regarding child custody, an arduous task.

In an effort to help create a standard of practice, and in response to the numerous ethical complaints brought against psychologists, the American Psychological Association (APA) created practice guidelines for psychologists who perform custody evaluations (APA, 2010; Symons, 2010). The guidelines offer 16 principles for psychologists to follow while conducting custody evaluations for the court. These principles emphasized the importance of using multiple sources of data collection, explaining the limits of confidentiality and obtaining written informed consent; warned against overinterpreting or inappropriately using or interpreting assessment or psychological testing data for a custody evaluation; and highlighted the significance of parenting capacity, the psychological and developmental needs of the child, and the subsequent relevance to what would be in the best interest of the child involved (Symons, 2010). However, the guidelines are considered aspirational goals, not mandatory behavior on the part of psychologists participating in these evaluations. In other words, the guidelines do not require certain assessments and techniques or mandate certain expert opinions as ethical (Krauss & Sales, 2002). These researchers challenge that the constructs such as "parenting ability" set forth in the guidelines remain somewhat illusive and poorly defined.

Empirical psychological research exploring child custody decision-making has increased tremendously over the last 20 years (Symons, 2010). In an empirical study by Keilin and Bloom (1986), 82 mental health professionals who conducted child custody evaluations were surveyed. The participants included 78.1% doctoral level psychologists, 18.3% psychiatrists, 2.4% masters-level psychologists, and 1.2%. The results indicated that interviews were the primary means of data collection. However, the majority did use psychological testing. The Minnesota Multiphasic Personality Inventory (MMPI), Rorschach, and Thematic Apperception Test (TAT) were the assessment instruments most commonly used with adults and intellectual achievement, whereas projective testing was most commonly used with children (Keilin & Bloom, 1986). More recently, Novotney (2008) outlines the difficulties associated with child custody evaluations. She states that both the parents and the child(ren) should be evaluated and the administration of psychological testing is a useful information -gathering tool. Currently, the **Parent–Child Relationship Inventory** (PCRI) is showing promise in becoming a psychometric measure used in custody evaluations; reviews of this assessment have revealed that "all scales possessed internal consistency and test-retest reliability (Coffman, Guerin, & Gottfried, 2006, p. 209)." The PCRI is a instrument that is based on the parents' self-report of how they perceive their relationship with their child. Overall, the psychological tests commonly used have changed over the years and will be briefly discussed later in this analysis.

In a 2010 study by the American Psychological Association, it was found that psychologists participating in family law proceedings who practiced within the ethical guidelines of the APA were able to provide impartial decisions with direct application to the psychological best interests of the child. Researchers have found that psychologists view psychological testing as one source among many in an evaluation and do not overinterpret its significance (APA, 2010; Bow, Flens, Gould, & Greenhut, 2006; Archer, Stredny, & Zoby, 2006). Results from the APA (2010) study also indicated that the national survey of psychologists revealed that they were discriminative in their choice of testing instruments with a greater focus on objective assessment, particularly with the use of parent inventories and rating scales. Researchers caution that the report of participants' close adherence to APA guidelines can likely be attributed to the fact that these studies used a self-report format, allowing those surveyed to err on the side of presenting their more ideal standards of practice. Additionally, these researchers point out that the majority of individuals surveyed in the aforementioned studies were doctoral-level psychologists in private practice and that these individuals are not the only mental health professionals conducting these evaluations (APA, 2010).

In order to more accurately reflect the standard of practice of custody evaluators overall, Horvath *et al.* (2002) examined 60% of custody evaluations in one circuit court over a two-year period. These researchers found that in 63.6% of the cases, the final custody decisions were consistent with the recommendations of the custody evaluator. Overall, significant variability in the content and procedures of the child custody evaluations in the sample were found. In general, evaluators failed to conduct assessments of important factors such as domestic violence and child abuse, adequate evaluation of parenting skills, evaluation of parent's health status, and formal psychological testing. Horvath *et al.* (2002) found that approximately 40% of the evaluators sampled used only two methods of assessment to decide on a custody arrangement. In order to comply with APA guidelines and respect the significance of the impact of the evaluation on the parents and children, a variety of assessment techniques, including collateral sources (e.g. teachers, pediatricians, school records, etc.) should be utilized. Among private evaluators, doctoral level psychologists typically adhered most closely to the APA guidelines. Horvath *et al.* (2002) concluded that evaluators should use multiple sources of information to include family interviews, psychological testing, observations of each parent and child, a review of available records, interviews with other relevant collateral sources, and home visits in some instances if indicated.

According to Coffman, Guerin, and Gottfried (2006) the **Parent−Child Relationship Inventory** (PCRI) is a self-report instrument administered to both the mother and the father and it is intended to assess the parents' perceptions of their relationship with the child. Research indicates that this may be a helpful tool in custody evaluations. This tool measures on five scales: satisfaction with parenting; involvement; communication; limit setting; and autonomy (Coffman, Guerin, & Gottfried, 2006). The structure of the test is designed so that the questions reflect "parenting overlap (e.g., parents who evaluate communication with their child as effective also tend to report engagement in activities with their children)" thus providing an assessment "of the dyadic relationships parent have with their children" (p. 209).

Gourley and Stolberg (2000, p. 1) conducted a study to define the current standard of practice for those psychologists who were viewed as "credible" by family law attorneys. These researchers surveyed 20% of the licensed psychologists in the state of Virginia regarding their participation in custody evaluations and surveyed family law attorneys to obtain nominations regarding those psychologists regarded as credible. Finally, the "credible" psychologists were surveyed to determine their training as well as standards of practice. The majority of psychologists in the broader sample, as well as those nominated as credible custody evaluators, identified self-teaching through workshops, conferences, and professional reading materials being the primary method of training. Formal training and supervision in custody evaluations was rare and no licensing or accrediting bodies for this specialty area of forensic work exists. Psychologists can more generally be certified through boards such as the American Board of Professional Psychology (ABPP), although many well-regarded custody evaluators do not have this board certification and it does not signify any specialty training in this area. Forensic programs that provide specialized training in psycholegal issues are very new and many individuals currently practicing as custody evaluators learned by self-teaching.

Gourley and Stolberg (2000) found that one-third of the "credible" sample has some graduate training in custody evaluations, while the broader sample did not. These authors indicate that this finding is troublesome considering the lack of other areas in psychology where one could be considered an expert without formal training, including many hours of supervision by a more experienced professional. They also maintain that due to the lack of set guidelines to define who is considered an "expert," it is typically left to the discretion of the judge, who is not likely trained in behavioral science, child development, research design, or psychological testing or assessment. Gourley and Stolberg (2000, p. 22) state, "There are no guidelines, requirements, or licensing procedures established by most states or by the profession to help guide judges or the general public."

Overall, the surveyed psychologists in this study were in agreement about the relevant factors to be evaluated as set forth by research relating to child adjustment after divorce (Gourley & Stolberg, 2000). The results indicated that most psychologists give the most weight to the clinical interview or adapt instruments that measure psychopathology to inform on issues such as parenting and family functioning. A minority utilized home observations or surprise visits to obtain data on family functioning. The results of the study also indicated that while the majority of custody evaluators were in agreement about the critical factors to be assessed and the relative weight to assign to each, there was much less agreement on the techniques used to assess these factors (Gourley & Stolberg, 2000). The paucity of well-researched, standardized assessment instruments specifically designed to measure parenting skills, or other factors specifically related to the determination of child custody, was noted. This is still the case, although the PCRI described above attempts to focus on these (Coffman, Guerin, & Gottfried, 2006)

Quinnell and Bow (2001) found that, overall, psychologists are becoming more selective and discriminative in their administration of psychological tests in child custody evaluations. Presently, reliance on IQ testing or a singular battery of tests, despite the type of forensic referral question, is antiquated. Rather, there has been an increase in the use of parent rating scales and parenting inventories, which indicates greater efforts to measure parenting capacity. Furthermore, objective testing is used more frequently with adults. Projective testing is also being used but is largely discouraged in the forensic arena, generally due to the lack of psychometric or empirical support (Quinnell & Bow, 2001). Horvath *et al.* (2002) caution psychologists who routinely base custody recommendations on clinical interviews alone without including psychological testing or behavioral assessment instruments for hypothesis development. Horvath *et al.* (2002, p. 563) state, "There is a substantial risk to the intended objectivity of child custody recommendations when there are no independent anchors for opinions such as those that can be obtained through the use of validated instruments."

Based on their national survey of 198 psychologists, Bow and Quinnell (2001) found that the main referral sources for child custody evaluations were attorneys (41%) and judges (41%) with only a very small percentage directly from parents (4%). Eighty-four percent of the child custody evaluations were court ordered. The majority of psychologists surveyed (65%) indicated that they charged an hourly fee for child custody evaluations with the average hourly rate reported as $144, with the range of $75/hr to $400/hr. The majority of the remaining psychologists (33%) charged on a case by case basis. The most commonly reported costs for the evaluation by all survey psychologists were $2500 and $4000. On average, 24% of the child custody cases required expert testimony and 12% required depositions. The fee for expert testimony ranged from 0 to $400/hr, with a mean of $177/hr (Bow & Quinnell, 2001). When respondents were queried about the age at which they seriously considered a child's expressed preference for custody decision, the average age reported was 11.6 years, with 12 years being the most common response. When asked if they made specific recommendations about the ultimate issue or about custody/visitation, 94% responded affirmatively and 3% responded no, leaving the remainder to indicate "sometimes" (Bow & Quinnell, 2001, p. 265). Psychologists surveyed indicated that they recommend joint custody 73% of the time and sole legal custody in 27% of the cases evaluated. The three most important reasons provided for recommending sole custody included (2001, p. 265): (1) inability to coparent (e.g., lack of cooperation); (2) severe mental illness of a parent; and (3) abuse/neglect.

Results also significantly supported the notion that child custody evaluation participation is a high-risk specialty area for psychologists (Bow & Quinnell, 2001). Ten percent of the psychologists indicated they were involved in malpractice suits and 3% had been sued twice. Two of the participants had been sued three and five times. Thirty-five percent of those surveyed had received board complaints on at least one occasion based on child custody work. Ten percent reported two or more complaints and two psychologists had received 14 and 15 complaints based on child custody work. Many of the respondents added in their self-reports that the suits had been dismissed (Bow & Quinnell, 2001).

Controversial syndromes that are not formal diagnoses are becoming more popular or common in custody battles, while research in this area is still lacking. As a result, the psychologist must be increasingly diligent about adhering to professional and ethical guidelines to avoid malpractice suits when they conduct evaluations or provide expert testimony on issues surrounding child custody. **Parental alienation** can occur during a difficult divorce when there is a bitter custody dispute and one parent (alienating parent) uses the child as a weapon against the other parent (alienated parent) (Farkas, 2011). This phenomenon is also described as occurring when children are caught in the middle of divorce and often witness verbal abuse between parents, physical abuse, estrangement, and are forced into an alliance with one parent (Garber, 2011; Farkas, 2011). **Parental Alienation Syndrome** (PAS) is a controversial term that describes symptoms that occur as a result of parental alienation (Rand, 2011). Farkas (2011) further defines PAS as "The targeted parent-child relationship once encased with unconditional love is transformed by an unrelenting campaign of denigration, criticism, and hatred" (p. 20). Controversy over PAS exists because the literature lacks a clearly defined definition of PAS; for example, some of the literature contends that it is the rejection of a parent by a child, while other literature contends that it is the rejection of a child by a parent (Gordon, Stoffey, & Bottinelli, 2008; Bernet, von Boch-Galhau, Baker, & Morrison, 2010).

In a study by Baker and Chambers (2011), 105 graduate or undergraduate students whose parents had divorced were administered a computer-based survey that asked them to recall exposure to parental alienation behaviors. In this study at least 80% of the students surveyed had experienced at least one out of 20 of these behaviors. Twenty percent of these students endorsed that one parent attempted to create an alliance against the other parent.

Ellis and Boyan (2010) contend that these types of behaviors are not typical; however, when families present with problems that indicate parental alienation may be present, conventional methods of treatment or therapy are often ineffective. Walters and Friedlander (2010) suggest a **Multi-Modal Family Intervention** (MMFI) model. MMFI is based mainly on a broad-based social and cognitive learning theory and is typically psychoeducational and maintains that many problems begin from misinformation and missing information. In this context, MMFI consists of specialized clinical intervention that is geared at addressing the resistance/refusal of a child that is a result of the underlying parental alienation (Walters & Friedlander, 2010). Instruments such as the PCRI may be helpful in determining if parental alienation is present in the parent-child relationship (Coffman, Guerin, & Gottfried, 2006).

Psychologists are required to consider many ethical factors while conducting child custody evaluations. If a psychologist is prevented from completing a comprehensive evaluation due to circumstances out of their control (for example, if one parent refuses to participate), it is critical that he or she make limited recommendations and acknowledge the limited scope of their evaluation. Additionally, if the evaluator has only assessed the father and the child, he or she can only comment on the psychological status of the father and child, their attachment to one another, and the father's parenting skills, but not the status of the mother (Bernet, 2002). Typically, the evaluator could not make specific recommendations regarding custody, as a comparison between the father and mother could not be accurately made. Finally, if the child custody evaluator has been asked to participate in a one-sided evaluation, it is imperative to ascertain whether or not the parent who requested the evaluation and is bringing in the child actually has the legal standing to authorize the evaluation (Bernet, 2002). Without permission from the **custodial parent** (i.e., the parent who is given legal, physical custody of the child), such an evaluation would be unethical.

Forensic Psychology and Policy Implications

Bow and Quinnell (2001, p. 261) state that "child custody evaluations are among the most difficult in the forensic field" due in large part to hostility between the parents, extreme emotions for even minor issues, vague standards, and balancing ethical obligations to all. Some critics argue that the lack of a clear, definable definition of what constitutes the Best Interest of the Child standard allows far too much judicial discretion and permits judicial biases to influence custody decisions (Condie & Condie, 2007; Krauss & Sales, 2000; Otto & Edens, 2005). These researchers also suggest that the lack of guidance provided by the standard has led to a significant deference to mental health professionals when it comes to child custody evaluations in order to define what may be in the child's best interest. According to Davis and Dudley (1985, as cited in Krauss & Sales, 2002, p. 862), "It is hoped that mental health professionals will have what judges lack. The means to determine objectively what is the best interest of the child." The focus on the best interest of the child requires a thorough assessment of each parent's capacity to care for the child as the central feature of the evaluation (Condie & Condie, 2007).

In order to better achieve this goal and to adhere to a higher standard of practice, Zimmerman *et al.* (2009) suggest that formal training and licensing procedures should be created to better regulate custody evaluations. Training which includes coursework on theory and research relating to basic knowledge of state laws, proper advocacy, standards of care, inappropriate advocacy, and a procedure for postdoctoral supervision in custody evaluation by more seasoned, practicing custody evaluators should be required (Zimmerman *et al.*, 2009). Individuals who are conducting competency to stand trial evaluations or other criminal court-related evaluations are being more commonly held to this standard. More standardized procedures for conducting child custody evaluations should be established based on continuing research regarding critical, empirically supported variables (e.g., child adjustment, attachment issues, family functioning, etc.). Researchers suggest that there is a collective effort from mental health experts, judges, and attorneys in developing these guidelines and standards (Condie & Condie, 2007; Novotney, 2008). These researchers also highlight the importance of ongoing training and education of custody evaluators about critical areas that can significantly impact custody determinations such as domestic violence, substance abuse, and mental illness (Condie & Condie, 2007; Novotney, 2008).

There are also policy implications regarding parental alienation, despite the controversy regarding the use of PAS in court. When children are thrown in the middle of a very contentious divorce or separation where potentially destructive things are being said and/or done, the effects on the child can be damaging. Cookston and Fung's (2011) evaluation of Kid's Turn, a community-based divorcing parent education program, revealed that parents reported "improvements over time in interparental conflict, the number of topics parents argue about, parental alienation behaviors, parent anxiety and depression, and children's internalizing behaviors" (p. 348). School based, community based, or other types of programs or services that can be offered to help children through this difficult, life-changing experience, are needed as divorce is increasingly common.

Parents who suffer from severe mental illness may have significant hurdles in caring adequately for their children, requiring extra support, and/or treatment to facilitate their ability to parent (Krauss & Sales, 2000). Children with mental illness will also necessitate specialized care and resources and a level of parenting ability different from child with no evidence of a mental illness. Krauss and Sales (2000) indicate the importance of psychologists being the most able mental health professionals to assess for signs of mental illness and to draw conclusions about how these factors could likely affect parenting ability, a child's postdivorce adjustment, or the needs of the child.

In many custody cases, there are two parents who may appear equally capable of caring for the child in question. Yet, in others there may be only one capable parent, or two parents with significant barriers to healthy parenting or an appropriate home environment. Horvath *et al.* (2002) suggest that more custody evaluators should be encouraged to recommend special advocates be assigned when there are serious concerns about a child's physical and emotional needs. The special advocate can assist in ongoing monitoring of the child's welfare and report back to the court far beyond the participation of the custody evaluator.

Forensic psychologists need to conduct highly competent work in order to formulate what is in the best interest of the child in question, while also reducing their chances of ethical complaints and possible litigation. In order to reduce the risk of being the litigant in a malpractice suit or ethical or board complaints, Bow and Quinnell (2001, p. 267) suggest the following:

Such strategies include familiarity with the APA Guidelines (APA, 1994) and APA Ethical Principles (APA, 1992), obtaining court appointment, securing informed consent and waiver of confidentiality, maintaining impartiality, avoiding one-party evaluations and dual relationships, providing complete disclosure, preserving a well-documented file, and avoiding ex-parte communication. In some states, court-ordered custody work falls under the immunity of the court (Stahl, 1994); therefore, obtaining a court order may reduce the risk of a malpractice action in some states (as cited in Bow and Quinnell, 2001).

The stakes for a custody determination are high and the implications are far reaching. Forensic psychologists need to set a very high standard of training and expertise before taking on the enormous responsibility of custody evaluations.

Suggestions for Future Research

Krauss and Sales (2000) strongly suggest that the Best Interest of the Child standard be reevaluated and modified. These researchers indicate that the social sciences have been unable to demonstrate empirical foundations or support of current and past conceptualizations of the standard. Other researchers highlight the lack of standardized and objective measures available to assess parenting capacity and other constructs specifically related to child custody, rather than objective measures of psychopathology (e.g. MMPI-2, MCMI-III) that *could* have implications for parenting. Gourley and Stolberg (2000, p. 27) state, "Psychologists should be encouraged to develop research protocols that would allow families to be assessed in a clinic in a way that could provide data for criterion and construct validity of custody evaluation procedures, aid in the development of more objective measures of parenting and family functioning as they relate to custody evaluation, and provide training for psychologists and others performing custody evaluations."

Coffman, Guerin, and Gottfried (2006) suggest that further exploration into the nature of parent—child relationships be evaluated (i.e., adolescent and father versus adolescent and mother) as some indications have been found that communication styles differ and this impacts the results of the PCRI. These researchers also note that further research exploring alternative scales for the PCRI using **factor analysis** (i.e., statistical method used in behavioral science to examine possible patterns or relationships in large amounts of data) is needed.

Bow and Quinnell (2001) recommend research to explore the specific issues that are usually cited as the underlying causes for malpractice suits or ethical or board complaints. Having a better understanding of these issues could better prepare psychologists to reduce their risk of litigation. Quinnell and Bow (2001) also suggest further research regarding the situations in which specific assessment measures are used in order to better understand the role of psychological tests in custody evaluations. Bow, Flens, Gould, and Greenhut (2006) address significant concerns about the accuracy of computer-generated results on the MMPI-II and MCMI-II/III in child custody evaluations. Exploring the appropriate use of these psychological tests, including the potential misuse of computer-generated scoring, should continue in future research. It is critical that psychologists involved in these evaluations adhere to professional and ethical procedures, particularly in light of the tremendous impact their recommendations can have on families. Research by Zimmerman *et al.* (2009) suggest that clarifying the role of the psychologist in custody disputes would be important in avoiding legal actions against these providers. Future research in this area could provide relevant information to help psychologists reduce the number of complaints against them in divorce or custody evaluations.

Research and development of assessments geared towards the issue of PAS and parental alienation is seriously lacking. A thorough examination of the behaviors or emotions associated with parental alienation would aid in providing a clear definition of PAS and clarify its validity as a phenomenon in custody disputes. Future research should continue to evaluate the effectiveness of community-based programs in creating change in families after divorce as they emerge.

Finally, other researchers suggest future research to explore the assessment of a child's level of sophistication and decision-making abilities in order to assist judges and evaluators in deciding on how much weight to give a child's expressed wishes regarding custodial preference (Krauss & Sales, 2000). Psychologists should also continue to explore the issue of the most appropriate way to determine a child's preferences without further damaging a parent—child relationship and while minimizing the emotional impact on the child (Krauss & Sales, 2000; Melton, Petrilia, Poythress, & Slobogin, 2007).

Children/Juveniles and the Reliability of their Courtroom Testimony

Introduction

More and more often, children are becoming involved in the legal system to provide courtroom testimony, especially in sexual abuse cases (Troxel, Ogle, Cordon, Lawler, & Goodman, 2009; Whitcomb, 2003). For example, in 2006 over 18,000 children were involved in legal proceedings following a substantiated abuse or neglect report (U.S. Department of Health and Human Services, 2008). This, however, is only a fraction of the children involved in the legal system in some way each year. Frequently, children provide key testimony because their word is the only evidence available in many abuse cases (Blandón-Gitlin & Pezdek, 2009; McAuliff, 2009). The court must then determine whether the child is a reliable witness. As is discussed in this section, the court must examine various factors, such as the child's age, whether the child can tell the difference between the truth and a lie, and whether the child understands the consequences of the testimony he or she will provide.

Martha is a 12-year-old girl who has recently accused her old babysitter, a neighborhood friend named Mitch, of sexually abusing her, when she was 8 years old. She never told anyone about this while it was occurring because she said he had threatened to kill her dog. However, recently she was behaving in an inappropriate sexual manner, so her parents questioned her about her behaviors until she finally admitted what had occurred several years ago. Her parents pressed charges against Mitch, and they are expecting the case to go to trial because Mitch denied his guilt. Martha is the only witness for the prosecution, and she has been questioned many times about the alleged abuse. Some of the details of her story have changed, and she has expressed great fear about having to be in the courtroom with Mitch. Because of the inaccuracies in her story, the prosecutor wants the judge to determine if she is a competent witness. He has also requested the use of closed-circuit television so that Martha will not be in the room with Mitch when she testifies. The judge must determine whether Martha is a reliable witness by deciding if she can distinguish the truth from a lie and understand the meaning of taking an oath. She also must decide whether allowing Martha to testify via closed-circuit television would be a violation of Mitch's constitutional rights.

Literature Review

As reflected in the case illustration, having a child present testimony in court is not a simple, straightforward matter. There are many factors that need to be considered. Because prosecutors rely so much on children's testimony, especially in abuse cases, it is important to determine if children are competent to testify (Lamb, Hershkowitz, Orbach, & Espin, 2008; Trowbridge, 2003; Lyon, Saywitz, Kaplan, & Dorado, 2001). It used to be common practice to have children below a certain age deemed automatically incompetent. Yet, a 1770 case, *Rex v. Brasier*, held that there should be nothing automatic in determining competency, no matter how young the child (Myers, 1993b). *Wheeler v. U.S.* (1895) stated that no age marker should determine competency to testify. However, there are a few states that still use this approach. The approach used in most states today is that everyone is competent, which comes from the Federal Rules of Evidence – Rule 601. Some states also guarantee competence in sexual abuse cases (Myers, 1993b). Psychologists are frequently employed to evaluate child witnesses' competency. For example, Lamb, Hershkowitz, Orbach, and Espin (2008) cite children's developmental level, the nature of the events children are asked about, and the techniques used in questioning children as factors that can affect their capacities as a witness. Trowbridge (2003) indicates that most tests of child witness competency stress three basic concepts: perception, memory, and ability to communicate. Evaluation for the ability to differentiate between the truth and a lie and their ability to speak the truth, particularly when faced with the defendant, is another critical aspect of a child witness's competency (Trowbridge, 2003).

Whatever the state's approach, judges are ultimately responsible for determining children's competence, and they have broad **discretionary powers** (ability to issue certain orders based on their own judgment). Myers (1993b) also describes three main requirements that judges use to determine competency. The first is whether children have certain abilities. For example, they must be able to observe what occurs in the courtroom, but are not expected to necessarily completely comprehend what happens. In addition, they must possess adequate memory. According to Gudjonsson, Sveinsdottir, Sigurdsson, and Jonsdottir (2010), even children as young as 3.5 to 5 years of age are able to act as witnesses. Children must be able to communicate and be able to tell the truth from a lie, and understand the importance of telling the truth. In other words, they must understand the consequences of lying. Gudjonsson, Sveinsdottir, Sigurdsson, and Jonsdottir (2010) indicated that even 4-year-olds have the capacity to distinguish a lie from the truth, and that they are able to knowingly lie or tell the truth. Rule 602 of the Federal Rules of Evidence outlines that a competent witness must have personal knowledge about facts pertinent to their case and this also pertains to child witnesses. The final requirement is taking the oath. Walker (1993) stated that children can be found incompetent if they do not understand the meaning of the wording of the oath. In Martha's situation, the judge will have to determine if she possesses the capabilities described above and whether she understands the meaning of an oath.

If the prosecutor wants to proceed with Martha's case and use her as the sole witness, she/he must decide whether her testimony is reliable so that the jury will believe her. Evaluation of a child's reliability is extremely imperative and is determined by the stability of his or her account after consecutive interviews with the child (LaRooy, Lamb, & Pipe, 2009; Jaskiewicz-Obydzinska & Czerederecka, 1995). Jaskiewicz-Obydzinka and Czerederecka (1995) conducted a study with juvenile witnesses/victims of sexual abuse with the majority between the ages of 11 and 15. They found that in half of those examined, testimonial changes occurred. However, they found that the most common reason for these changes was the juvenile's low intellectual level. They concluded that in order to accept a child's testimony as reliable, psychological factors that include intellectual ability, significant fear of social evaluation, and increased self-criticism should be considered. More recent research into the effects of repeated interviews with child victims and witnesses has revealed that, in some cases, the witnesses may be better able to retain their memory of the event, when interviewed soon after their occurrence and when the interviews are closely timed together (LaRooy, Lamb, & Pipe, 2009).

In addition to Martha's conflicting stories, her age also presents a problem with establishing reliability. Gudjonsson, Sveinsdottir, Sigurdsson, and Jonsdottir (2010) reported that younger children tend to be viewed as more reliable than older children and adolescents in testifying about sexual abuse. People believe that children are not cognitively efficient and therefore could not possibly invent such stories, whereas adolescents are believed to be more likely/able to have fabricated their story. Some authors have found that children as young as three and a half can be capable of providing testimony (Gudjonsson, Sveinsdottir, Sigurdsson, & Jonsdottir, 2010). Beliefs of this kind may also be an example of jurors' expectancies for child witnesses. In a 2008 study, McAuliff, Maurice, Neal, and Diaz measured jurors' expectancies for child witnesses' behavior while testifying and instructed the jurors to rate the reliability of a child's testimony. The child's behavior, however, was scripted by the researchers to either conform to the jurors' expectations or to violate them. What the authors found was when children's behavior violated the jurors' expectancies, they were viewed as less credible than children who conformed to their expectations.

A "scientific case study" addressed the issue of reliability by using a detailed record of child sexual assault, documented by a "sex ring" leader. This was confiscated by police and compared to the child victims' reports (Bidrose & Goodman, 2000). Through police interviews and courtroom hearings, four girls, ages ranging from 8 to 15 years, testified about the sexual abuse they experienced at the hands of eight adult men (Bidrose & Goodman, 2000). The girls' allegations and reports were compared with evidence to include photographic and audiotaped records of the abuse. Overall, there was supportive evidence for approximately 80% of the allegations. The levels of proof for sexual act allegations were comparable for all four girls, regardless of age, but the youngest made more unsupported allegations of coercive behavior (Bidrose & Goodman, 2000).

Another factor affecting the reliability of children's testimony is the stress of the entire situation. Children must face an intimidating courtroom setting and discuss personal, traumatic events while confronting the alleged abuser (McAuliff, 2009; Montoya, 1999). Having this feared person in the courtroom could reduce the likelihood of the child disclosing entire descriptions of the events. Therefore, allowing the child to testify in the absence of the accused may provide more reliable testimony (Hall & Sales, 2008; Montoya, 1999; Pipe & Goodman, 1991).

Westcott and Page (2002) examined portions of cross-examinations with child witnesses (ages 8, 10, 14, and 15 years) who were alleged victims of sexual abuse in order to identify ways the child's role of victim and witness were challenged. These researchers found that the child witness could be portrayed as "unchildlike", less than innocent, as instigators, or accused of being poor witnesses, as being confused, untruthful, or having fallible memories. Overall, they suggest that poorly conducted cross-examinations can further traumatize a child witness (2002). Despite the increased stress of testifying in court, there is some evidence that this stress may dissipate over time. A 2005 **longitudinal study** (a study of the same participants over a time period) found that after 12 years, children who only testified once in court showed no more behavioral or emotional problems than children who never testified (Quas, Goodman, Ghetti, Alexander, Edelstein, Redlich, Cordon, & Jones, 2005). Those children who testified multiple times in more severe abuse cases, however, had more emotional problems than those who only testified once.

Tobey, Goodman, Batterman-Faunce, Orcutt, and Sachsenmaier (1995) suggested that if a child testifies in front of the defendant, then he or she might be psychologically traumatized because of facing their alleged abuser. They highlighted that this trauma could negatively affect the reliability and thoroughness of the testimony. It is for this reason that a number of legal interventions and protective measures have been introduced in order to lessen the children's stress and provide more reliable testimony (Hall & Sales, 2008). Tobey *et al.* (1995) stated that the use of closed-circuit technology eliminates the need for children to testify in such a traumatic situation. They could provide their testimony from outside the courtroom via television monitors. The opposition to this procedure is that it violates a defendant's Fourteenth Amendment right to due process because it interferes with the factfinder's capabilities of determining witness credibility and it violates a defendant's Sixth Amendment right to confront witnesses directly (Orcutt, Goodman, Tobey, & Batterman-Faunce, 2001; Goodman *et al.*, 1998.)

The Supreme Court has agreed with the opposition to testimony via television monitors to some extent. In *Coy v. Iowa* (1988), the Court ruled that the use of closed-circuit television (CCTV) did violate a defendant's Sixth and Fourteenth Amendment rights. However, two years later in *Maryland v. Craig* (1990), the Court decided in favor of allowing closed-circuit television in child sexual abuse cases where the child would be so traumatized as to be unable to reasonably communicate. The Supreme Court does agree that such technology is a violation of rights, but that the psychological effects related to a child's testimony outweigh those rights. However, following the decision in *Crawford v. Washington* (2004), in order for out of court statements, such as CCTV or statements made to police to be admitted into evidence, it may be necessary for child witnesses to appear in court so they can be subjected to cross-examination. According to some, the aforementioned forms of evidence would not meet the court's standards of reliability if they could not survive scrutiny under cross-examination (Goodman, Myers, Qin, Quas, Castelli, Redlich, & Rogers, 2006). Some courts have also ruled that a child victim's statements during a forensic interview constitute the same type of evidence that necessitates the child being present in court for cross-examination regarding their statements (*State v. Kennedy,* 2007: *Williams v. State,* 2007). In Martha's case, the judge would need to determine if she would be so traumatized as to incapacitate her communication abilities, in that it would warrant the use of closed-circuit television. Expert witnesses, frequently forensic psychologists, often evaluate a child and help to inform the court on this issue.

Goodman *et al.* (1998) conducted a study comparing children's testimony both in the courtroom and via closed-circuit television (CCTV). They found that CCTV reduced suggestibility for younger children and that these children made fewer errors related to misleading questions when compared to those testifying in the courtroom (see also Troxel *et al.* 2009). Closed-circuit television, overall, fostered more reliable testimony in children. The authors also concluded that in the CCTV situation, the defendant had no greater chance of being convicted, and the trial was not identified as being more unfair to the defendant. Jurors in this study reported that children testifying by CCTV were considered less believable, even though they actually were more accurate, than children testifying in the courtroom. More recent research has actually found that mock jurors were less convinced of a defendant's guilt after hearing hearsay evidence such as that provided by CCTV (Goodman *et al.*, 2006). Goodman *et al.*'s (2006) study found that children testifying live in court were perceived as more credible and elicited greater sympathy. Troxel *et al.* (2009) reported that the use of closed circuit television does not influence jurors' abilities to detect deception in children's testimony and that there is no support for the theory that jurors reach the truth better when children testify in open court versus testifying by closed circuit television.

There are many issues that can affect the reliability of children's testimony. It appears that the stress and trauma of testifying can reduce reliability in severe cases such as prolonged child abuse. In the case illustration, Martha likely has legitimate fears about facing her alleged abuser, and these fears could decrease the reliability of her testimony.

Forensic Psychology and Policy Implications

The issue of whether children are competent witnesses seems to rest solely with judges. This allows judges a great deal of discretion in making decisions that may have psychological implications. The requisite abilities for a child to be deemed competent are psychological in nature, yet judges may or may not involve mental health professionals in their decision-making process (Myers, 2009). Forensic psychologists should become more involved in these types of cases, especially when a judge is uncertain. Increasingly, forensic psychologists are assisting the courts to identify whether or not a child witness is competent and whether or not a child witness will be able to testify in the presence of the defendant (Trowbridge, 2003). If they do not provide expert testimony, they could at least educate the court on psychological issues relevant to competency for child witnesses. In the case illustration, a forensic psychologist could offer the judge information as to whether Martha possesses the necessary abilities to testify.

Another important implication is to reduce the level of trauma and stress that children endure when they must testify, especially in abuse cases. Psychologists may provide a great deal of assistance in helping a child to testify (Myers, 2009; Small & Melton, 1994). One approach offered is to prepare children by providing a tour of the courtroom and teaching them information about the legal system. This would need to be conducted in age-appropriate language and may reduce their anxiety and thus increase the reliability of their testimony (Gudjonsson *et al.*, 2010; Lamb *et al.*, 2008; Saywitz, 1995). Policies need to be developed to ensure that these children are not further traumatized, while at the same time keeping in mind the constitutional rights of the defendant. Although closed-circuit television appears to be one possible solution, it is not currently a standard procedure due to constitutional dilemmas. However, more solutions like this should be implemented so that children can provide reliable testimony. However, given jurors' perceptions of children and defendants when these techniques are used, attorneys should carefully weigh their options on a case-by-case basis and consider having child witnesses evaluated for existing trauma before pursuing one of these options.

Suggestions for Future Research

Much of the research on children's testimony has focused on suggestibility of child witnesses. Yet an important area related to reliability that should be examined is whether increased levels of suggestibility influence children's capability to offer reliable testimony (Gudjonsson *et al.* 2010; Ceci & Bruck, 1993). Since children are increasingly being relied upon to provide testimony, research must find the optimal techniques that limit the emotional stress that could compromise the reliability and credibility of their testimony (Gudjonsson *et al.* 2010; K. Bussey *et al.*, 1993). Research on this topic should also examine which of these situations will provide a fair trial. Lamb *et al.* (2008) emphasize that more research is needed to clarify the risks and benefits of repeated interviewing with child victims and witnesses. It seems that CCTV is one step toward minimizing child witnesses' stress while increasing the reliability of their testimony, yet there has not been enough empirical analysis to reach any definite conclusions (Batterman-Faunce & Goodman, 1993; Troxel *et al.*, 2009). Continued research needs to be done on CCTV as a possible solution to the problem of traumatizing children and whether it provides a fair trial. Another focus of research should examine how to prepare children to testify more competently and with minimal stress (Troxel *et al.*, 2009). If it is found that closed-circuit television is an unfair procedure, then children will have to continue to face their alleged abusers in court and to provide reliable testimony.

Practice Update Section: Child Custody Evaluations and Juvenile/Family Court

The work of forensic psychologists who interact with courts is subject to a high degree of scrutiny, perhaps none more than the child custody evaluator. This practice update section will summarize the article by Martindale (2001) entitled *Cross-examining mental health experts in child custody litigation*. The title alone is enough to raise anxiety levels but the points made serve to not only better prepare the attorney but also the mental health professional for cross-examination. The intense emotions and hostility that is often a part of heated custody battles serves to critically impair the objectivity of the parents involved. The "non-favored" litigant will not uncommonly register complaints with his or her attorney that the child custody evaluator did not consider all information that was presented; complains of irregular methods of evaluation; and insists that the evaluator was not impartial (p. 484). Although some parents seek custody for their own agendas far from the best interest of the child, the vast majority view themselves as the more capable parent and are profoundly disappointed, confused, and quite angry when the child custody evaluator recommends otherwise. Martindale (2001) maintains that the non-favored parent will often search for causes outside of their own potential parenting deficiencies or strengths of the other parent for the recommendation made by the evaluator. Some consider errors made by the evaluator as the likely culprit. Although this is a claim far too frequently made, in some instances they may have been placed at a disadvantage by a biased evaluator or one who was insufficiently trained to consider all relevant factors.

Cross-examination by the non-favored litigant's attorney is one opportunity to expose such biases or substandard practices. The forensic psychologist who conducts custody evaluations must be very mindful of the potential implications of their procedures and own preconceptions about "family" prior to engaging in this work. It is critical that the evaluator does not let their own biases prevent them from adequately assessing all factors and considering all hypotheses based on the data collected from each evaluation on a case-by-case basis. It is the job of the mental health expert to assist the trier of fact in making a custody determination. While it is the judge who makes the decision on the ultimate issue, research has demonstrated that the opinions offered by the evaluator often heavily influence the final decision.

During the discovery phase of the court process, the attorneys should have familiarized themselves with the evaluator's *curriculum vitae* and the agreement the evaluator made with the parties involved (Martindale, 2001). Martindale (2001) encourages attorneys to look for any training in the forensic specialty area of child custody, including conferences, workshops, and coursework. He states (p. 485): "It is inappropriate for a mental health professional whose background is treatment oriented to accept forensic assignments without first having secured education and training aimed specifically at preparing one for forensic work." As forensic psychology programs are relatively new, it is rare for a mental health professional to have originally received their education and training in a forensic specialty. If an evaluator lacks sufficient training on relevant issues by any of the previously mentioned methods, his or her credibility could be challenged at trial. The evaluator should also be very careful of listing "vanity boards" that do not conduct a thorough assessment of a candidate's expertise (e.g. work samples, oral and written exami-nations) on their vitae (p. 486). Attorneys are encouraged to follow up on claims of board certifications in order to gather information about the credentials-granting process.

The forensic mental health expert should also be very familiar with the subpoena process and the potential for their complete file, including evaluation notes, to be requested and the possibility of being part of the discovery process at trial. Martindale (2001) also suggests to attorneys to attempt to obtain a reasonable number of the expert's previous custody evaluation reports and to scan them for identical passages, as well as for inconsistencies in rationales for recommen-dations. He proceeds to suggest that if the descriptors used to describe the interaction of one litigant and their child is repeatedly used to describe other litigants, it is important to challenge the evaluator on "corner cutting" and whether or not they explored all relevant individual differences (p. 490).

Forensic psychologists are also cautioned to evaluate any other individuals who are presently playing a parent role or will likely in the future (e.g. a fiancé of one of the litigants). Martindale (2001) indicates that to do otherwise would be offering an opinion on insufficient information. One critical difference between the forensic evaluator and the more typical treatment provider is the necessity to investigate all self-reported information by the litigants by following up with collateral information (e.g. records, uninvested collateral sources, etc.). Particularly in custody evaluations, the litigants are quite motivated to present themselves in the most favorable light. The forensic evaluator is obligated to list in their reports all collateral sources used and the information gleaned from each within the body of the report.

The suggestions for the mental health expert to avoid impeachment at trial provided in this practice update section are far from exhaustive but highlight the degree of inquiry to be expected for the child custody evaluator. Refer to Chapter 1 for more information on expert testimony. Ultimately it is the child who may suffer the greatest consequences based on the opinions offered and decisions made on their behalf. "The best interests of the children are ill served when flawed reports go unchallenged and become the basis upon which the trier of fact rests her judicial decision" (Martindale, 2001, p. 504).

Related Websites

www.familylaw.org
This website has links for family law code for all 50 states, questions about custody section, and a complete display of the Uniform Child Custody Jurisdiction Act.
www.hg.org/family.html
This website defines family law, and also gives definitions for various terms that relate to the family law.
www.dc4k.org
Website providing resources for divorcing parents with children and assistance finding support groups for children of divorcing parents.
www.helpguide.org/mental/children_divorce.htm
Website providing information to help parents support their children during a divorce.

Related Websites—cont'd

http://parentsupportforchildsexualabuse.com
A website providing support and information regarding child sexual abuse and its effects on children and families.
www.d2l.org
A website providing information on child sexual abuse for individuals, families, and organizations as well as information on treatments.

Police and Corrections Practices

Key Issues

Dealing with Troubled Youths at School and in the Community
- Delinquency and truancy issues facing the adolescents of today
- The School Resource Officer and the affects this program has had on truancy and school violence

Policing Juvenile Gangs
- Review of anti-gang policing tactics
  - Intelligence databases
  - Civil gang injunctions
- Characteristics of gang members

Adolescent Female Prostitutes: Criminals or Victims?
- Discuss the agencies involved with adolescent female prostitution and how this special group of offenders is handled
- Define and examine teenage prostitution
- Discuss the victimization of adolescent females who are involved in prostitution
- Discuss issues related to human trafficking

Juveniles in Adult Jails
- Brief overview of legal precedence regarding placing juveniles in adult jail, relevant statistics, and the impact of adult jail on the adolescent offender

Juveniles on Death Row
- Brief history of the legality of juvenile capital punishment, related trends, and the influence of developmental and neurological factors

Juvenile Boot Camps
- Historical development of juvenile boot camps, the rationale behind their use, and a brief discussion of their effectiveness.

Suicide Among Incarcerated Juveniles
- Statistics relevant to juvenile offender suicide, risk factors for juvenile offender suicide, characteristics of adolescents who attempt suicide while in juvenile detention

CHAPTER 8

Juvenile Issues in Policing and Correctional Psychology

Introduction to Forensic Psychology. DOI: 10.1016/B978-0-12-382169-0.00008-6

Overview

Police involvement in the lives of juveniles has varied considerably throughout the history of the United States. What is unmistakable, however, is that disobedient youths can and do find themselves subject to law enforcement intervention. At the core of these interventions is a struggle over how to address the "best interests" of the child while, at the same time, maintain the public's concern for safety, order, security, and control. It is at this juncture that psychology assumes a pivotal role in the (successful) outcome of law enforcement interventions with juveniles.

Juveniles violate laws ranging from violating curfew to committing capital murder. The consequences of their behavior can include some form of incarceration. Psychologists may be in a position to raise doubts about the efficacy of correctional punishment for some adolescents and argue that juveniles who act delinquently are not criminals but, rather, are troubled youths. On the other hand, a forensic psychologist may be called upon to identify those youths who pose the greatest risk to society and how to best contend with their management in a correctional setting. The field of juvenile corrections, then, examines whether criminal justice or mental health responses are best suited to the needs and interests of juveniles who engage in illegal conduct. In addition, the domain of juvenile corrections explores the impact of correctional remedies for adolescents who break the law.

This chapter examines critical areas where the intersection of policing and adolescent behavior generates forensic psychological controversies and investigates controversies in the juvenile correctional arena. The issues examined in the pages that follow represent some of the more fiercely contested matters at the crossroads of juvenile justice, psychology, and corrections. Consistent with one theme organizing this textbook, while the reader is presented with a limited selection of topics to review and digest, the variety of issues considered demonstrates the breadth of the field and the need for experts trained in this subspecialty area. Topics explored in this chapter include: (1) dealing with troubled youths in school and in the community; (2) policing juvenile gangs; (3) adolescent female prostitution; (4) juveniles in adult jails; (5) juveniles on death row; (6) juveniles in boot camps; and (7) suicide among incarcerated youth. A practice update section will be offered to address the issues facing psychologists who practice in corrections or other juvenile facilities. Finally, international issues in juvenile forensic textboxes will be presented to discuss the international trends in the sentencing, rehabilitation, or punishment, including capital punishment of juvenile offenders and the devastating impact of human trafficking.

The issues investigated in this chapter barely scratch the surface of where and how the interface of policing, psychology, and juvenile justice affect the lives of police officers, youthful offenders, and the public at large. As with all chapters throughout this textbook, the intent here is to describe some of the more compelling crime and justice controversies identified in the field.

Police officers confront all sorts of troubled youths. For example, some adolescents engage in underage drinking, join gangs, are truant, or become suicidal. How do police officers in their crime control interventions promote the rehabilitation of the adolescent? How do officers promote the aims of punishment? Does the mental health of juveniles impact their legal status and if so, are appropriate treatment and placement options being applied?

Law enforcement personnel deal directly with youth gang members. What kind of anti-gang police tactics are used to inhibit membership? What sort of anti-gang control strategies are adopted to curb juvenile violence? What perceptions do non-gang-affiliated adolescents have about these police interventions?

Police officers also find themselves responding to youths who engage in some very physically and emotionally debilitating behavior. Addressing child sexual exploitation (e.g., adolescent female prostitution) is perhaps one of the most difficult forms of police intervention imaginable. How do officers cope with the sexual victimization of children? How do the principles of rehabilitation or retribution operate within this forensic problem? Are these juveniles hard-core criminals or unsuspecting victims? Delinquent adolescents can and do find themselves in adult jails. What type of crimes do juveniles commit and how are they different from their adult counterparts? What psychological problems do adolescents experience when placed in the adult jail system? What forms of (physical and sexual) violence do youths confront while in the adult system? Juveniles can be sentenced to death and a representative minority of convicted youths is awaiting execution. Does the age and/or mental state of the juvenile offender matter for purposes of sentencing determinations? What psychological difficulties do adolescents confront while awaiting execution? In response to the problems caused by adolescent delinquency, some correctional experts have advocated for juvenile boot camps that prepare youths to engage in productive, pro-social behavior. How do these facilities function and are they falling out of favor? Do juvenile boot camps promote the aims of rehabilitation and treatment or the aims of retribution and punishment? What impact, if any, do juvenile boot camps have on recidivism? Some incarcerated boys and girls commit suicide. What are the links between juvenile delinquency and suicide? What are the links between juvenile incarceration and suicide? What psychological prevention and intervention strategies exist to address the phenomenon of suicide among incarcerated youths?

The field of policing deviant, risky, and/or illicit juvenile conduct is by far more complex than is described in the pages that follow. In addition, the perceptions adolescents engender regarding law enforcement behavior and practices are also more intricate and subtle than can be addressed in this chapter. However, what is clear is the important role of psychology and the psychological sciences at the crossroads of policing and juvenile justice. As the individual sections in this chapter repeatedly point out, improving relations between officers and troubled youths is certainly needed. The impact of such efforts potentially could improve juvenile recidivism rates and promote more rehabilitative approaches with youths that often have significant trauma histories and complex mental health issues. One facet to this more civic-minded agenda entails additional research. The manner in which troubled youths, adolescent gangs, and child sexual exploitation relate to policing is not well-developed in the overlapping criminological and psychological literature. Thus, as the material developed in this chapter recommends, the future success of juvenile justice and law enforcement necessitates more cross-disciplinary efforts along these, and similar, lines of scholarly inquiry.

The juvenile forensic arena of corrections also shows us how the mental health and the criminal justice systems differentially respond to the problems posed by adolescent misconduct. Where the correctional community generally promotes retributive measures of justice (i.e., punishment), the psychological establishment typically advances rehabilitative measures of justice (i.e., treatment). As the sections of this chapter also reveal, there are a number of pressing issues affecting the lives of youths caught in the crossfire of "intervention politics." Thus, it is not surprising that forensic psychologists, cross-trained in the areas of corrections, adolescent delinquency, and psychology, are most especially competent to understand how the criminal justice and mental health systems *can* work in concert to meet the best interests of delinquent youths and society. Clearly, as the chapter implies, without such careful and thoughtful interventions developed and implemented by such forensic/psychological experts, we risk losing too many adolescents to the devastation of crime and violence. This is a loss that our society cannot afford to absorb or sustain.

Dealing with Troubled Youths at School and in the Community

Introduction

The youth of today are faced with a variety of problems that put them at risk. These problems include underage drinking and driving, drug abuse, pregnancy, suicide, truancy, gang activity, and prostitution. It is not uncommon to pick up a newspaper on any given day and find an article describing such behaviors. What follows is an illustration of how serious these problems can be.

Jill is a 14-year-old high school student who is currently facing criminal charges for being an accomplice to murder. Jill has a history of running with the wrong crowd. Many of the crowd's activities include drinking, doing drugs, and skipping school. She has a long history of truant behavior.

During the time Jill was away from school, she was burglarizing local neighborhood homes to support her drug habit. On one particular occasion, she was with her boyfriend, Mike, burglarizing a nearby residence. They were in the midst of robbing the house when the resident surprised them. Startled and scared, Mike pulled out his gun and shot the victim to death. Jill exemplifies how a life of drugs, truancy, and crime can lead to a tragic ending.

Historically, the tradition has been that the police assume ultimate responsibility for fighting crime and maintaining order. When dealing with delinquent adolescents, the aim has been to rehabilitate the juvenile, rather than to punish them. Criminal behavior typically peaks during late adolescence and early adulthood, approximately between the ages of 16 to 25 years old (Stolzenberg & D'Alessio, 2007). Despite common public misperception, juvenile crime is actually on the decline (Comes, Bertrand, Paetseh, & Hornick, 2003; Doob & Sprott, 1998; Drerup, Croysdale, & Hoffman, 2008; Foster, Jones, & Conduct Problems Prevention Research Group, 2005; Stevenson, Tufts, Hendrick, & Kowalski, 1999). Regarding females, those between the ages of 13 and 14 years old comprised the greatest prevalence within the juvenile justice system (Snyder & Sickmund, 2006). Adolescent violent acts have declined over the past 30 years and are continuing to do so. Reports of violent crimes and thefts have declined since the 1990s (Dinkes, Kemp, Baum, & Snyder, 2009). According to the Federal Bureau of Investigation in the *Uniform Crime Reports* (2008), of the 457,455 arrests made for violent crimes 73,970 (16%) were juvenile arrests, and of the 1,305,135 arrests made for property crimes, 339,990 (26%) of the arrests were juveniles.

The public's overestimation of the frequency and severity of juvenile crime is perpetuated by the media's nonstop coverage of extreme instances of school violence or other sensational cases of teen violence like the school shootings at Columbine, Colorado, and Paducah, Kentucky (Austin, 2003; Comes *et al.*, 2003; Knoll, 2010; Sullivan & Miller, 1999). However, despite an overall decline in juvenile crime, particularly in the late nineties, a growing number of juveniles are being jailed or are engaged in the criminal justice system in some way, as the focus in our juvenile justice system shifts further from the rehabilitative model (Granello & Hanna, 2003; Scott, 2010; Smith, 1998).

The perspective regarding rehabilitation versus retribution for these offenders is sometimes challenged by those who feel that the criminal justice system needs to resort to punishing offenders for their crimes. Police organizations nationwide are currently questioning the effectiveness of the early strategies of crime control, which date back to the turn of the century. At present these agencies are exploring ways to combat the problem of dealing with troubled youths, either through retributive or rehabilitative measures. Police strategies to address this issue vary with each jurisdiction. Some agencies are implementing programs that target specific at-risk behaviors such as drinking and driving and drug abuse. In this section, the focus is on truant youths and juvenile delinquency. Several examples, explaining how various law enforcement agencies nationwide confront these issues, are presented. Additionally, the prevalence of mental disorders in juvenile offenders is presented as well as the impact it has on their offenses and treatment.

Literature Review

As early as the 1800s, social reformers recognized the link between truancy and delinquency (Gavin, 1997). Truant behavior has been correlated with crimes such as burglary, vandalism, motor vehicle theft, and robbery. As a result of this relationship, law enforcement officials, community agencies, and school administrators have worked on developing various programs to address truant behavior as well as the resulting delinquent acts. The majority of these programs attempt to keep juveniles in school and to control daytime crimes. With a focus on rehabilitation, many of these programs strive to offer alternative choices for youths. The aim is to keep them out of the juvenile justice system. Depending on the policies and procedures of law enforcement and school agencies, combating truant behavior varies. The truant youths can be returned to school, taken home, or taken to local police departments where the parent or guardian is contacted.

When addressing the problems of truancy and delinquency, the responsibility lies with parents; school officials; law enforcement personnel; and local, state, and federal organizations. This makes truancy and adolescent crime a multifaceted problem. Thus, it is essential to have the cooperation and support from all participants in order to successfully combat the problem. In a study examining the principal factors of school violence, two of the five factors identified were (1) a decline in family structure and (2) family violence and drug use (Speaker & Peterson, 2000). Research has demonstrated a correlation between violence perpetrated by youth in the community and violence committed in the schools (Bradshaw, Rodgers, Ghandour, & Garbarino, 2009; Leone, Mayer, Malmgren, & Meisel, 2000). Austin (2003, p. 21) states, "Partnerships involving local law enforcement, business, social service agencies, teachers, administrators, and families create a sense of shared purpose and collaboration in reducing both school and community violence."

01/02/2005 04:19:49

In 1983, the Phoenix Arizona Police Department created a School Resource Officer (SRO) program in an attempt to reduce the number of truant children and juvenile delinquents. The program was funded through a 3-year federal grant. By the end of the grant period, the truancy rate at two pilot schools decreased by 73% and crimes committed on campus and in surrounding neighborhoods significantly decreased (Soto & Miller, 1992). As a result of the success, the school district agreed to continue to fund the project by paying 75% of each School Resource Officer's salary. The SRO program was expanded to include the servicing of 36 schools throughout the Phoenix area. More recently, during the 2009–2010 school year, the SRO Program at Gilbert High School in Gilbert, Arizona handled 602 incidents that included fights, traffic accidents, sexual assaults, trespassing, and police patrols. There were 13 drug offenses and it was noted that, overall, drug offenses were the most frequent incidents handled by police. SRO programs continue to grow and be used in schools across the country.

The officers involved with the SRO program volunteer their time, and in addition to keeping the schools safe, the officers are there to be mentors and role models to the students. Before being able to participate in the program, they must complete an extensive application process and pass a review procedure. Upon their acceptance, they receive intense training and education regarding juvenile issues. The officers work with state mental health agencies to receive training on working with individuals that have a mental illness. The SRO officers address problems both on and off school grounds. Their responsibilities include educating faculty and students on safety strategies to reduce crime, and to recognize signs of child abuse and neglect. The officers spend a great deal of time and energy attempting to establish a good working relationship with parents living in housing projects in nearby areas. This is done in an effort to educate the parents on the importance of monitoring their child's school habits and to encourage their children to stay in school. The SRO unit is also responsible for detecting, reporting, and investigating suspected cases of child abuse and neglect.

In a survey conducted by the National Association of School Resource Officers (2004), 78% of the school-based officers reported that they had taken a weapon away from a student in the past year; 8% reported that gang activity in their schools had decreased; fewer than 13% of the respondents stated that violent incidents on the school buses had decreased, and over 41% reported that they had cases involving students using their cell phones for improper reasons (i.e., cheating on exams, taking photos in restrooms and/or locker areas). In Anchorage, Alaska, 82% of the population believes a reduction of violent crime occurred due to the SRO program; 88% believe the program enhances safety in the schools, and 60% believe the program reduces the rate of juvenile crime (Myrstol, 2010). The goal and objective of the SRO program is to enforce truancy laws, educate school officials, and to build a trusting, working relationship with parents and children. These objectives are intended to serve as an effective crime prevention strategy in the hopes of combating criminal activity before it begins. Research has shown that there is a correlation between the presence of SROs and a decrease in school violence (Daniels, Bilksy, Chamberlain, & Haist, 2011). According to the National Crime Prevention Council (2011), the SRO program has been successful in thousands of communities across the United States in reducing violence.

Researchers have concluded that for the purpose of predicting future criminality, the most likely juvenile recidivists are those whose first referral involves truancy, burglary, motor vehicle theft, or robbery (Snider, as cited in Gavin, 1997). Various law enforcement agencies across the country have developed truancy interdiction programs to counter both short-term and long-term effects of truancy. Nationwide, the vast majority of truancy interdiction efforts produce significant reduction in crimes traditionally associated with juvenile offenders (Gavin, 1997).

The St. Petersburg Police Department in Florida decided to implement a truancy interdiction program in hopes of minimizing the relationship that exists between truancy and delinquency (Gavin, 1997). Currently, the St. Petersburg Police Department is subcontracting the program through the Police Athletic League of St. Petersburg (Needham, 2011). The ultimate goal of this initiative was to reduce the opportunities among elementary, middle and high school students to get into trouble by informing parents to encourage their children to stay in school. According to Gavin (1997), when first implemented, one of the first obstacles the St. Petersburg Police Department faced was what to do with these truant youths once officers apprehended them. Because St. Petersburg was a large jurisdiction, the time it took officers to personally return the child to their school consumed too much of their time and took away from other duties needing attention. The St. Petersburg police officials recognized the potential problem this would pose and realized that having officers return the truant youths directly to school would not actively involve the parents. They decided to establish a centralized truancy center where the truant youths waited for their parents to pick them up, ensuring that the parents took an active role in the situation.

Once the truant youths arrive at the center via the patrol officer, a receiving officer or a detective contacts both the school and the parents and proceeds to tend to the juvenile until the parents or guardians arrive. If the juvenile is on probation, the juvenile officer notifies the youth's case worker immediately. The initial process was intended by program developers to be very brief in nature so that the patrol officers could get back to patrolling. It is the responsibility of the parent or guardian to return their child to school. When they arrive at the center to pick up their child, the juvenile detective presents the parent or guardian with an accurate record of their child's attendance in an effort to make them realize the seriousness of the truant behavior. The parents are also presented with a letter signed by the chief of police and the school superintendent stressing the importance of ensuring that children go to school as well as a copy of the state statute mandating school attendance. The parents are advised that the law requires them to have their child in school and that failure to do so is a criminal act (Gavin, 1997). Before the child can be readmitted to school, their parent or guardian must bring a referral slip with the child to school. This, then, notifies school officials that the child was in custody. Many times, guidance counselors and school officials use this as an opportunity to meet with the child and parent or guardian. Presently, law enforcement officers can have students processed and assessed if they are truant during school hours by dropping the juveniles off at the center and assigning them to an attendance specialist who will contact the students' parents, the school, and conduct an assessment (Needham, 2011).

Another element of the interdiction program is geared toward counseling truant youths. The juvenile detective interviews the children and asks them about their truant behavior, their home life, and other variables that may be influencing their truant behavior. They also stress to the child the importance of staying in school and getting a good education. However, many of the juveniles in question could benefit from actual therapy or counseling from a mental health professional. Many times, the juvenile officers have recognized financial problems, or other issues, and have referred the family to the appropriate social service agency. When these situations arise, the officers give the parents lists and names of various community agencies that specialize in assisting with family problems. The program will work with the student and the family on the barriers to the student's attendance; make referrals to community resources when necessary and provide follow-up (Needham, 2011). In order to increase students' attendance, those with more than five unexcused absences will be assigned a subcontracted case manager through Family Resources, Inc. to work more intensively with the family and provide follow-up. The program provides services to any student found truant from Pinellas County (Needham, 2011).

The Los Angeles Unified School District (LAUSD) Local District 4, Los Angeles Police Department (LAPD), Rampart Division, Families in School, and California State University, Los Angeles instituted the Juvenile Intervention and Prevention Program (JIPP) in the fall of 2006 at the Belmont High School (Koffman, Ray, Berg, Covington, Albarran, & Vasquez, 2009). The program was designed to address "interdependent variables that affect academic, social, and mental health outcomes" in students that are high risk that have exhibited delinquent or predelinquent behavior (Koffman *et al.*, 2009, p. 240). This program concentrates on microinterventions in four areas: (1) biobehavioral; (2) psychosocial-emotional; (3) academic; and (4) family system support (Koffman *et al.*, 2009).

In order to participate in the program, students are selected by deans, administrators, and counselors at the school, as well as student attendance review boards, the Los Angeles attorney's office, and the California Department of Children and Family Services (Koffman *et al.*, 2009). Students participate in the program as an alternative to being suspended, and students can be referred for truancy and other misdemeanors by the juvenile courts (Koffman *et al.*, 2009). These students have been identified as high risk for dropping out, getting involved in gang activity, or becoming involved in the criminal justice system.

In the first two years of the program, there were over 387 students that participated, and 52% of the students graduated (Koffman *et al.*, 2009). The first six weeks of the program is the

Resistance phase in which biobehavioral physical training occurs to reduce the resistance to psychological and behavioral changes that will occur throughout the program (Koffman *et al.*, 2009). The students work on learning appropriate boundaries and build self-esteem through physical training. The next phase is the Empowerment phase in which public speaking, job interview skills are taught, and the "Pillars of Success" curriculum (i.e., lessons on trustworthiness, respect, responsibility, fairness, caring, and citizenship) (Koffman *et al.*, 2009). Leadership phase is next, in which the students learn leadership skills by working as peer mentors and leaders for the next group of JIPP students (Koffman *et al.*, 2009). The final stage of the program is within the family system where parents participate in an 18-week psychoeducational parenting class. The parents learn and change with the students in order to raise their children in a nonviolent and nurturing way by teaching respect, love, and compassion (Koffman *et al.*, 2009).

Since the program has begun, the number of days of suspensions has decreased by 50%, and the number of incidents of suspension has decreased by more than 90% (Koffman *et al.*, 2009). The suspension for disruptive or defiant behavior has decreased by more than 70% (Koffman *et al.*, 2009). The overall reduction in suspensions has allowed the students more instructional time in the classroom, and allows the campus (students and staff) to be a safe and secure environment.

In order for truancy interdiction programs to effectively address the issues of truancy and delinquency, it is imperative to have parental, community, school, and police support. Studies and analyses of crime and truancy rates in communities around the country confirm that today's truants commit a significant proportion of daytime crime (Gavin, 1997). Successful truancy interdiction programs serve both long-term and short-term objectives, keeping kids in school and preventing future criminal activity. By keeping youths off the streets, the police can reduce crime today, and by encouraging youths to stay in school, the police can help reduce dropout rates and prevent more serious criminal activity tomorrow (Gavin, 1997).

Psychologists, social workers, and teachers are also on the front lines of confronting truancy, delinquency, and violence in school settings. Austin (2003) examined effective interventions that help prevent school violence. The danger of zero tolerance policies created to rid schools of allegedly dangerous youth, or to send a strong message to first time offenders, has had some extremely detrimental effects on students, particularly those with mental illness. The 1997 amendments to the Individuals with Disabilities Education Act (IDEA) have actually enabled schools to unilaterally remove students for weapons or drug offenses, whether or not they are a manifestation of a student's disability (2003). There is a public panic that schools have become extraordinarily violent in recent years, when in fact they are safer than a child's home or neighborhood (Snyder & Sickmund, 1999). Historically, the probability that a student will be killed in school is less than 1 in 1 million (U.S. Department of Education, 1999). While zero tolerance policies are designed to protect students and staff from students who pose a threat to others, these policies are discriminating against students of color and those with behavioral disorders. Twenty percent of students suspended in 1999 were those with disabilities or those classified with a learning disorder or as emotionally disturbed, despite the fact that nationwide only 11% of students ages 6 to 21 are receiving special education (Austin, 2003). Research has indicated that removing students with emotional disabilities from school is the standard practice, rather than more preventive or proactive measures (Austin, 2003; Leone *et al.*, 2000; Stage, Jackson, Jensen, Moscovitz, Bush, Violette, Thurman, Olson, Bain, & Pious, 2008).

Students from ethnic minority groups are being disproportionally represented in suspension rates. Studies have also shown that African American students and Latino students are more likely to receive harsher punishments that are considered excessive when compared to their behavior (Bireda, 2000; Harvard Civil Rights Project, 2000; Austin, 2003; Monroe, 2005; Skiba, Horner, Chung, Rausch, May, & Tobin, 2008). While the zero tolerance policies give the appearance of getting tough on crime and making schools more safe, the youth that is expelled or suspended is likely at a greater risk for an escalation in deviant behaviors (American Psychological Association Zero Tolerance Task Force, 2008; Maeroff, 2000; Austin, 2003). Programs that focus on retribution and control are not effective in preventing school violence and can actually exacerbate criminal behaviors (Leone *et al.*, 2000; Walker & Bruns, 2006). Examples of the damaging effects of extreme, nondiscriminative, unilateral policies are presented in the following cases:

...a middle school student was observed using the file of a miniature Swiss Army knife to pare his fingernails. He was arbitrarily expelled from school for 1 year, in accordance with the school district's zero-tolerance policy for possessing a "weapon". ...a 7-year-old was suspended for bringing nail clippers to school in Illinois, and a 15-year-old was suspended for dying his hair blue (Zirkel, 1999 & Essex, 2000, as cited in Austin, 2003).

Forensic Psychology and Policy Implications

Police interactions with delinquent juveniles can be very difficult. The encounters they have with one another can have a profound effect on the juvenile's future. Police are often challenged by the role they play within the juvenile justice system. They vacillate between the need to help steer the youths away from a life of crime versus traditional police duties entailing crime prevention and maintaining order. When addressing issues of truancy and delinquency as well as the relationship that exists between the two, many police departments have focused on rehabilitative efforts to curtail the problem. In collaboration with other agencies, many of these programs have been effective.

Research does not support the effectiveness of zero tolerance policies in schools, but rather supports programs that reflect an understanding of the precipitating factors to school violence and then prevent their development in the very early stages (American Psychological Association Zero Tolerance Task Force, 2008; Austin, 2003; Braddock, 1999; Knoster & Kincaid; Stein & Davis, 2000). Austin (2003, p. 19) recommends that schools incorporate as many of the following components as possible in the development of school-wide violence-prevention programs: (1) using functional behavior assessment and behavior intervention plan effectively; (2) screening for risk factors; (3) teaching acceptance of diversity; (4) building self-esteem and teaching social skills; (5) resolving conflict through peer mediation; (6) involving the family and the community; and (7) focusing on the classroom as community. Psychologists can play a critical role in training others and/or implementing these components in a violence prevention program. The risk assessment training of a forensic psychologist would prove invaluable.

To support predelinquent intervention, it is essential to be able to identify youths who are at-risk for a life of delinquency and then to intervene. This can be accomplished by intervening early in the youth's development. Prevention efforts should focus on the environment of the child and the relationship they have with their parents. In the field of psychology, prevention is one of the fastest growing areas (Harpine, Nitza, & Conyne, 2010). Schools that have group prevention programs provide service to all ages, but with more attention on the adolescent age group. These programs focus on violence, drugs, bullying, suicide, dropping out, pregnancy, and truancy (Harpine *et al.*, 2010). Studies indicate that the child's home life is a key factor in delinquent behavior (Koffman *et al.*, 2009; Siegel & Senna, 1994). Without proper discipline and a nurturing and structured environment, the child's chances for healthy development are hindered, therefore making them more predisposed to engage in delinquent activities.

When efforts to reach the child early in development fail, it is imperative to implement treatment efforts in an attempt to reach the child before they engage in more serious offender behaviors. Mental health agencies and child welfare agencies as well as the juvenile justice system can either mandate treatment for the entire family or specifically work to assess the youth's behavioral problems.

Treatment options to address the needs of the family and the individual include alcohol and drug programs, child abuse and sexual abuse programs, or community-based programs where the focus is on a community-oriented approach. The community-oriented approach to the prevention of juvenile delinquency believes that youth crime is a community problem (Lundman, 1993; Scott & Steinberg, 2008; Zimring, 2005). Whether the programs developed are targeted for the family or the individual, it is essential to have the help of local, community, state, and federal entities as well as experts in the field working together to identify and address juvenile intervention and crime prevention.

In the efforts to address the issue of juvenile delinquency and early crime prevention, the literature has identified the issue of restrictive state statutes as being a hindrance in the process. Frequently, those in charge of such programs have a difficult time trying to implement programs due to restrictive or narrowly defined state legislative guidelines. In these instances, law enforcement agencies, psychologists, and social scientists should work with state legislatures to amend those statutes which are considered too restrictive. It is important to have a good working relationship with state legislatures so that they will help support and validate various truancy interdiction programs and proactive, mental health-based, violence prevention programs in the future.

Suggestions for Future Research

When addressing the issue of truant and delinquent youth, it is obvious that the problem is multifaceted. These issues have been a concern since the 1800s, yet with the increasingly violent nature of some current juvenile crime, the seriousness of the offenses, and public panic, new efforts are being examined to combat juvenile crime. Additional studies need to be undertaken to compare the effectiveness of zero tolerance policies on preventing or controlling school violence and longitudinal studies could be conducted to examine their impact on future antisocial behaviors. Other strategies for more effective school violence prevention should be implemented and their effectiveness examined.

A major area of interest for future research could address how various agencies throughout the United States are dealing with the issues of truancy and delinquency. One must keep in mind, however, that research addressing truancy in large cities incorporates more variables when compared to smaller communities. Further research and development of programs is needed in terms of resources needed and available in the community to begin and support such programs.

With the implementation of the JIPP program in California, further research is needed on the impact this program has on the students and families on a long-term basis. This program is new in that it targets the family support system, and gives parenting classes to these individuals. Studies to examine the effectiveness of this program are needed, and could provide valuable information about ways to implement this type of program in other communities.

One of the most important areas for future development is to accurately assess the repercussions these programs have on the community, the citizens, and the offenders. It cannot be emphasized enough how important it is to seek the help and support from many agencies in order to successfully combat the problems that face the youths of today. Programs and relationships need to be developed with social service organizations in order to provide effective services to juveniles. Further longitudinal research should focus on the affects of school-based prevention programs.

The police have the ultimate responsibility of enforcing the laws that govern juvenile offenders. With the help of social service organizations, such as youth service bureaus, mental health services, the school system, recreational facilities, and welfare agencies, coupled with parental involvement, truancy interdiction programs and violence prevention strategies can help keep kids in school as well as prevent future serious crimes. Jill's case presents a very tragic and real example of how truant behavior and juvenile delinquency led one person to confront the criminal justice system.

Policing Juvenile Gangs

Introduction

Juvenile gangs have continued to grow in size and are becoming increasingly violent. Throughout the United States in 2007, there were an estimated 788,000 members in 27,000 gangs (Egely Jr. & O'Donnell, 2009). Since active gang members account for the majority of violent adolescent offenders, the community and media pressure for law enforcement officers to suppress gang activity and membership has become intense (Thornberry, Krohn, Lizotte, Smith, & Tobin, 2003). For example, it is believed that gang members are responsible for taking the lives of almost 3100 people in southern California since 1999 (Thompson, 2007). The threat of gangs is no longer just an inner-city problem. Juvenile gangs have permeated every size of community, even branching out into rural areas (Evans, Fitzgerald, Weigel, & Chvilicek, 1999; National Gang Intelligence Center, 2009; Rojek, Petrocelli, & Oberweis, 2010). A study that examined factors associated with gang involvement among rural and urban juveniles found that there was no significant difference in gang membership or pressure to join gangs between the rural and urban samples (Evans *et al.*, 1999). However, there were differences in other gang violence indicators. Communities large and small are demanding action from law enforcement, and the police have had to take a more aggressive stance in their fight against gang activity. Anti-gang policing tactics such as **gang-tracking** databases and civil gang injunctions are being created and employed around the country in an attempt to suppress gang activity. If granted by the court, a civil gang injunction is a lawsuit that limits conduct by members of a gang that would otherwise be considered lawful. However, enforcement strategies alone fail to address the root causes of the juvenile gang epidemic. Understanding the factors that drive youths to join gangs is the first step in confronting the problem.

Supporters of such strategies maintain that they are effective forms of gang control while opponents hold that these tactics infringe upon youths' civil liberties, particularly ethnic minorities (Crawford, 2009; O'Deane & Morreale, 2011; Siegal, 1997). It is attitudes toward officers to flourish in areas where a fragile police—community relationship already exists. Police officers have the challenge of implementing these strategies without targeting juveniles who are not affiliated with gangs. Consider the following case illustration.

Sixteen-year-old Claudio Ceja of Anaheim, California is an 11th-grader at Loara High School. From 8:00 a.m. until 2:35 p.m. he attends class. From 4 p.m. to 6 p.m. he hands out fliers for a local business. From 6 p.m. to 9:30 p.m. he completes his homework before he goes to his second job at an Anaheim convention center. But the Anaheim police do not see Ceja as a hard-working young student. In the past few years, they have stopped, detained, and photographed Ceja five times and put his photograph in the city's gang-tracking computer database. Each time, Ceja told them he was not involved with a gang. But each time they ignored his claims, he says. Despite the police attention, Ceja has never been arrested or charged with any crime. "They seem to be doing it for the fun of it," says Ceja. "They take my picture, and they put it in a gang file. But I'm not a gangster. I don't want to be identified as one" (Siegal, 1997, p. 28).

Literature Review

Aggressive policing tactics and legal interventions into the lives of gang members, particularly those that criminalize activities that are typically lawful, are becoming more widespread. However, many argue that such tactics often lead to the harassment of law-abiding youths who may fit stereotypes of a gang member as in Claudio Ceja's case, creating a negative impact on community-police relations (Hoffman & Silverstein, 1995; Myers, 2008). Cases such as Ceja's illustrate the fine line between cracking down on gang members and further alienating at-risk youths.

As the literature demonstrates, anti-gang policing tactics serve as an imperfect attempt to treat the symptoms and not the causes of our juvenile gang epidemic. Two of the most common anti-gang policing tactics are gang-tracking databases and civil gang injunctions. These policing tactics attempt gang suppression or deterrence by their speed of enforcement, certainty of punishment, and severity of sanctions, while the targeting of these sanctions is extended through an increase in gang intelligence tracking (Crawford, 2009; Klein, 1995; Maxson, Hennigan, & Sloane, 2005).

Gang-tracking databases are being employed as an intelligence-gathering strategy as gangs become increasingly mobile and organized. These databases catalog territorial graffiti, tattoos, symbols, and specialized clothing (e.g., those indicating gang colors), which are visual symbols that can indicate gang affiliation in order to provide patrol officers with identification information (Brown, 2008; Owens & Wells, 1993). Gang intelligence information gathered or received by law enforcement or juvenile-related personnel are included in the database. Police departments that utilize these gang-tracking databases detain and photograph youths who are charged with gang activity as well as those who are only suspected of it, as in Ceja's case. Youths often deny gang membership, leaving officers to distinguish between delinquent behaviors and gang behavior.

Critics of these gang databases claim that minorities are disproportionately represented. Ed Chen, staff attorney with the American Civil Liberties Union (ACLU) of Northern California stated:

> There's a racially discriminating aspect to all these programs. In every case that we've seen, the targets are Latino or African American youth. They can concentrate on young black, brown, and sometimes yellow men. It's rarely used against non-minorities (Siegal, 1997, p. 31).

Despite claims of harassment by youths who are not affiliated with gangs, Torok and Trump (1994) state that crimes are often solved quickly or prevented altogether by stripping gang members of their anonymity. The U.S. Treasury Department's Bureau of Alcohol, Tobacco and Firearms (ATF) contends that not only do gang-tracking databases give accurate pictures of gang activities and membership but that a national intelligence network is necessary if law enforcement is to effectively confront violent gangs (Higgins, 1993). However, authors have more recently urged for these efforts to be aimed at keeping children out of gangs rather than entering them into databases (Brown, 2008). An example of an elaborate gang-tracking system was developed and implemented by the National Major Gang Task Force (NMGTF), an organization devoted to networking, training, and creating information-sharing about gangs and security threat group management in correctional settings (American Correctional Association, 2001). This system connects all 50 state correctional systems, the Federal Bureau of Prisons, major jails, law enforcement, and probation and parole officers across the nation (2001). Juvenile gang membership typically persists into adult gang membership. Subsequently, when their criminal behavior lands them in prison, a burgeoning, dangerous prison gang subculture also exists.

Civil gang injunctions are also being used as a preemptive strike against gang-related crime. A gang injunction is a court order that requires gang members to refrain from one or more acts

(Columbia, 2006). Using civil gang injunctions, prosecutors can prohibit members of a particular street gang from participating in criminal activities such as graffiti or possessing weapons as well as engaging in conduct which facilitates criminal activity that is typically not illegal. Gang injunctions also give police officers substantial leeway in dealing with gangs by allowing them to arrest members they know or suspect of being included in the injunction; sometimes before these members are able to commit a crime (O'Deane, 2007). According to the Los Angeles City Attorney Gang Prosecution Section (1995), "…aggressive enforcement of an injunction enables law enforcement to effectively prevent imminent criminal activity by arresting persons for prohibited patterns of conduct which are known to precede and facilitate these crimes" (p. 325). For example, those members of the gang named in the injunction could be enjoined (prohibited) by a court from activities like wearing pagers, dressing in gang attire, flashing "handsigns," approaching and soliciting business from pedestrians and passing vehicles, or gathering at specified locations such as a city park. This is a proactive technique that is designed to enable uniformed officers to arrest gang members before a drug deal is consummated or any other gang-related crime is committed. In a survey of five neighborhoods prior to and following the issuance of a gang injunction, Maxson, Hennigan, and Sloane (2005) found that, in the short term, injunction neighborhoods experienced less gang presence, less gang intimidation, and less fear of confrontation with gang members. The authors explained that these effects were short-lived, however, as the only benefit still present at intermediate and long-term periods was a relative decrease in fear of crime. Other authors have pointed out that some gangs are less likely to be affected by an injunction as they may be too loosely associated or more mobile with less well defined territories (Baylis, 2005; Valdez, 2005). The Bureau of Justice Assistance (2006) suggests that, in the case of gangs with more mobility, other law enforcement strategies may be more effective than gang injunctions; for example, electronic surveillance or undercover operations.

Heinkel and Reichel (2002) explored the use of the driver's license as a new strategy that does not lead to harassment or violate constitutional rights, which can effectively reduce gang activity in both smaller and larger cities. Examination of the driver's license status of 383 gang members (ages 16 to 34) found that 77% did not have a valid license. Gang members were significantly more likely to be driving without a valid license, more so males than females. The strategy would require police officers to reduce potential gang activity by engaging in rolling drivers' license checks on known gang members and by stopping those individuals identified in the license check as driving without a license and taking them into custody when allowed by statute or department policy (2002).

While critics of civil gang injunctions argue that injunctions violate gang members' civil rights (Crawford, 2009), others argue that "it is the duty of public officials to require gang members to respect the rights of others; if not, they will have their own rights limited within the parameters of the gang injunction" (O'Deane, & Morreale, 2011, p. 3). Other critics question if the desire for safe streets overrides constitutionally protected rights, such as the right to free assembly and the concern of where gang members will congregate after being pushed from one park or neighborhood to another (Crawford, 2009; Maxson, Hennigan, & Sloane, 2005; Reza, 2006). Research suggests that the underlying causes for juvenile gang participation or prevention are largely ignored by enforcement strategies alone. According to a report by the Center for Mental Health in Schools at the University of California, Los Angeles (UCLA; 2007), "poor school performance, feeling unsafe on the way to and at school, and association with peers who engage in delinquency are among the strongest correlates found in research on factors related to gang membership."

Traditional law enforcement agencies tend to have only a reactive plan to managing street gangs (Etter, 2003). Individuals who consider themselves to be members of an organized gang are more likely to participate in all kinds of delinquent behaviors (Alleyne & Wood, 2010; Barnes, Beaver, & Miller, 2010; Bjerregaard, 2002; Dishion, Véronneau, & Myers, 2010; Melde, Taylor, & Esbensen, 2009; Sharkey, Sheckhtmeyster, Chavez-Lopez, Norris, & Sass, 2011). Juvenile street gangs are a serious problem that cannot be understood, managed, or prevented by reactive law enforcement strategies alone. A lesser studied segment of the gang culture is that of female gang members, despite their growth in the United States (Snethen, 2010). A study that focused on young Mexican American girls (aged 14 to 18 years) who were not formal gang members but participated in street-based activities of male gangs and risky behaviors such as sexual relations, partying, substance use, and crime found that these behaviors resulted in a number of negative outcomes (Cepeda & Valdez, 2003). The study indicated that the females' problems went beyond individual characteristics and were impacted by the social, cultural, and economic conditions of their environment. A study that examined the differences between female and male juvenile gang members, using a sample of 5935 eighth graders in a multisite evaluation, found that girls reported greater isolation from family and friends than do boys (Esbensen, Deschenes, & Winfree, 1999). Others, however, have found little difference between adolescent males and females in terms of risk factors for gang membership (Bell, 2009). Snethen (2010) suggests the mother-daughter relationship can provide a protective resource, preventing adolescent girls from joining gangs. Research has also indicated that when youth are physically and sexually abused, their likelihood of gang involvement is four times greater than those who do not suffer abuse (Thompson & Braaten-Antrim, 1998).

In order to effectively address the problems at the root of gang membership, mental health professionals and law enforcement must first understand that within their own subculture, gang membership can be adaptive for the at-risk youth (Alleyne & Wood, 2010; Barnes, Beaver, & Miller, 2010; Dishion, Véronneau, & Myers, 2010; Melde, Taylor, & Esbensen, 2009; Sharkey, Sheckhtmeyster, Chavez-Lopez, Norris, & Sass, 2011). In a study of 395 adjudicated juveniles, over half (n = 194) of the male youths and almost half of the females (n = 29) reported being affiliated with a gang (Granello & Hanna, 2003; Evans, Albers, Macari, & Mason, 1996). The study further indicated that male juveniles involved in a gang had lower rates of suicidal ideation and suicide attempts as those males who were not involved in a gang. This is an example of how gang membership can have some adaptive functions no matter how misguided (Hanna *et al.*, 1999; Katz, Webb, Fox, & Shaffer, 2010; Sharkey, Shekhtmeyster, Chavez-Lopez, Norris, & Sass, 2011).

Forensic Psychology and Policy Implications

The current trend in gang policy involves gang suppression and deterrence, while some argue that prevention and rehabilitation possibilities are neglected. Law enforcement is certainly under significant pressure to address the problem, as gang members disproportionately contribute to serious crimes, particularly homicide (Decker & Scott, 2002). According to the Los Angeles City Attorney Gang Prosecution Section (1995), little effort is being made to change the social conditions that make juvenile gangs a viable option for a growing number of youths. Almost 15 years later, and, yet, this statement remains largely true.

Civil gang injunctions and gang-tracking databases are representative of this thrust in gang policy. In order to increase the effectiveness of gang injunctions, Maxson, Hennigan, and Sloane (2005) suggest that the police should use injunctions strategically. Specifically, they suggest that law enforcement should consider the size of the injunction area and the type of gang being targeted. Opponents question their effectiveness and maintain that the civil rights of gang members are being infringed upon. Once an individual is named in a gang injunction, it seems that being removed from it can be exceedingly difficult. In fact, McGreevy and Banks (2006) reported that, as of the writing of their article, no gang member in Los Angeles had ever been successful in having their name removed from an injunction. This being the case, Crawford (2009) emphasizes that it is necessary for jurisdictions utilizing civil gang injunctions to implement a clearly defined process for inactive gang members to have their names removed from gang injunctions.

According to Klein (1995), the gang subculture discourages the acceptance or assignment of legitimacy to police, prosecution, and court definitions of acceptable behaviors. Additionally, he states that deterrence strategies may not only inhibit the expression of fear of sanctions, but encourage the bravado that accompanies antisocial or criminal activities while increasing group cohesiveness. Recognizing the limitations of enforcement strategies alone, gang policies need to encompass more comprehensive programs addressing the root causes of juvenile gangs.

Research indicates that aggressive policing strategies might curb the incidence of gang activity in a particular area for a period of time; however, factors influencing juveniles to join gangs have tremendous psychological and sociological origins. Various factors such as a sense of belonging; the need for recognition and power; a sense of self-worth and status; the desire for a place of acceptance; a search for love, structure, and discipline; the need for physical safety and protection; and, in some instances, a family tradition motivate juveniles to join gangs (Walker, Schmidt, & Lunghofer, 1993). Juveniles who are drawn to gangs generally live in a subculture where attachments to families, friends, and teachers are lacking and involvement in pro-social activities are minimal or nonexistent. As a result, the stringent enforcement of gang laws or policing tactics may only decrease gang activity in one neighborhood while displacing it into another.

Forensic psychologists have a critical role in a more comprehensive strategy of gang suppression. With specialized training in the psychological aspects of a gang, as well as the criminological theories and sociocultural factors that influence gang membership and activity, forensic psychologists can work in conjunction with various law enforcement agencies and school districts to identify and counsel those youths who are at risk or who are actively involved in a gang. Conflict resolution and conflict mediation strategies are being utilized by forensic psychologists working with juvenile gang members. These strategies are being used to provide these youths with the skills and insight to nonaggressively manage conflict. A structured network of aggressive policing and prosecuting illegal gang activity serves as a deterrent to active gang members. Providing educational programs, conflict resolution strategies, and professional psychological services to both juvenile gang members and those juveniles at risk of joining a gang could more effectively address the problem of juvenile gangs. Programs to provide education and occupational opportunities to at-risk youth could help to curb the economic and environmental correlates of gang participation.

As juvenile membership continues to grow, the examination of the issues that make gangs so attractive to our youths could make a more lasting and significant impact on the gang epidemic. Research demonstrates that gangs satisfy important needs for many youths who are denied access to power, privileges, and resources. These same youths find it difficult to meet many psychological and physical needs, as well as feeling alienated and neglected at home (Glick, 1992). In the face of such strong motivating influences, being arrested or incarcerated is infrequently a deterrent.

Aggressive enforcement of anti-gang tactics is only one component of an overall comprehensive gang strategy that includes intelligence gathering, school intervention, graffiti abatement, vertical prosecution, community support, conflict resolution strategies, and professional psychological services. Wraparound programs should exist that not only address the problems of the individual, but that also involves the family and the community. Juvenile gangs are a complex problem requiring a complex solution. After first understanding the reasons that compel juveniles to join gangs, the need for a coordinated response is imperative.

Suggestions for Future Research

Very little research exists regarding the role of forensic psychologists working with at-risk youths or juvenile gang members. As more comprehensive programs are implemented, including prevention and rehabilitation components, comparative studies need to be undertaken to test their effectiveness. For example, which conflict resolution or mediation strategies best enable these youths to nonaggressively manage conflict? What types and durations of psychological services are the most effective? Research examining the effects of various psychoeducational and recreational programs are needed. In addition, the effects of involving families and siblings in the psychological interventions of at-risk youths should be investigated. Once programs are in place, arrest records, school dropout rates, and other forms of acting out can be monitored to determine the effectiveness of the various services being offered to the youths.

Maxson *et al.* (2005) suggest that future research into civil gang injunctions should focus on their effectiveness in multiple contexts; for example, with different gang structures or different community environments. The authors also highlight the need for future longitudinal studies of gang injunctions to determine their long-term effects on community residents.

Research regarding the attitudes and perceptions that the police hold about juvenile gangs is limited. As gangs become greater in number and increasingly violent, the effect that working with this volatile population has on police officers is a vital concern. Their perceived threat of danger and the demeanor of gang members can greatly impact officers' interactions with these youths as well as the direction of anti-gang tactics. Additionally, the levels of stress and its effects on officers who work in gang units is an area in need of examination. Finally, as Claudio Ceja's case demonstrates, more effective means to identify juvenile gang members should be continually explored.

Adolescent Female Prostitutes: Criminals or Victims?

Introduction

The criminal justice response to juvenile prostitution is composed of distinct departments with conflicting philosophies. Varying aspects of child exploitation are handled by different divisions of law enforcement. Typically, the juvenile division works closely with child protective service agencies and handles child abuse and neglect cases or those cases that involve intrafamilial abuse (Cooper *et al.*, 2005). Sexual exploitation cases such as adolescent prostitution are usually assigned to the vice division. The issue of human trafficking is most often handled on a federal level due to the nature of the crime (i.e., bringing persons across state lines for the purpose of sexual exploitation) (Newman, 2006). While juvenile divisions generally embrace a rehabilitative model, viewing these prostitutes as victims, the vice division police officers tend to favor a punitive approach, perceiving these juveniles as criminals.

Flowers (1995) defines teen prostitution as the "use of or participation of persons under the age of 18 in sexual acts with adults or other minors where no force is present, including intercourse, oral sex, anal sex, and sadomasochistic activities where payment is involved" (p. 82). Kennedy, Klein, Bristowe, Cooper, and Yuille, (2007) explain that payment is not only defined by money but with anything of exchangeable value such as drugs, food, shelter, or clothing. Although adult female prostitution is being explored as a form of work in feminist theory, the adolescent prostitute is still excluded from this perspective. She is viewed as a victim of deviant adult behavior and frequently of her own past.

Often, these individuals have suffered physical, emotional, and sexual abuse within their family unit. The ranks of juvenile prostitutes abound with runaways or "throwaways." A study on the later effects of child sexual abuse in females in pre- or early adolescence, found that victims of abuse were described as struggling with feelings of depression, death, and suicidal ideation, experiencing lower self-esteem, running away from home, having multiple sexual partners, having an increased risk of becoming pregnant, and/or an increased risk of contracting sexually transmitted diseases, including HIV and AIDS (Farrow, 2005). According to Farrow (2005), intervention by officers usually occurs in the form of an arrest or harassment with little regard for treatment or rehabilitation. Although these individuals engage in a variety of other criminal or delinquent behaviors, they have very complex mental health needs that are not being adequately addressed through the juvenile justice system. Consider the following case illustration.

Kara is a 15-year-old Caucasian female living in a large metropolitan area. Kara comes from a single-parent household, her father having left before she was born. She has never met or spoken with him. From as far back as she can remember, her mother has had various "boyfriends" living with them in the two-bedroom apartment that also houses Kara's two younger brothers. As Kara's mother has been employed infrequently, and her various "boyfriends" have contributed little financially to the family, they have often been confined to modest, if not altogether poor, living circumstances. At times, they have nearly been evicted as rent money has not always been available.

Beginning in early childhood, at age 5 or 6, Kara was subjected to hurtful and psychologically devastating verbal abuse. While her mother rarely struck her physically, her violent outbursts were often directed at Kara. Starting at age 7, she was sexually molested by her mother's live-in "boyfriend." Perhaps the most damaging element of his attacks was her mother's refusal to believe the sexual abuse was occurring.

At the age of 13, Kara took to the streets to "get away" from her troubles at home. Having no money, shelter, or food, Kara was quick to accept the help offered to her by other young girls living on the streets. These girls gave Kara the sort of friendship and "care-structure" that was not available to her at home. As Kara would come to find out, however, these girls were prostitutes, utilizing the only resource they believed they had to survive. At the age of 14, Kara began prostituting herself.

Now Kara has been discovered by the local police. While she has had no prior contact with the police and is otherwise a "good citizen," she has nonetheless engaged in activities that are illegal. Kara assures the police that she has chosen this way of life both knowingly and in a rational manner. She insists that she will continue to prostitute herself, as it allows her to "get the things she wants" and "not have to go back home." What are the police to do in Kara's situation?

Literature Review

Cases like Kara's illustrate the conflict facing law enforcement when dealing with adolescent prostitutes. They are faced with an individual breaking the law, yet what options are available to this child? Despite the abundance of research and various perspectives on adult female prostitution, adolescent female prostitution is an entirely different phenomenon. For example, with regard to adult prostitution, feminist theories look at issues such as power relationships between men and women and the lack of opportunities in the labor market for these women (Jesson, 1993). Sereny (1984) explains that juvenile prostitution addresses the power differential between adults and children who have not yet entered the workforce. Although the literature available on policing adolescent prostitution in the United States is sparse, it is clear that the behavior of these juveniles cannot be appropriately considered using theories of adult female prostitution.

The scope of juvenile prostitution in the United States is alarming. Cases like Kara's are far too common. According to the National Incident-Based Reporting Systems (NIBRS), out of the 13,814 prostitution incidents between 1997 and 2000, 200 (1.4%) were juvenile offenders (Finkelhor & Ormrod, 2004). The research suggests a variety of contributing factors and motivations that led to adolescent prostitution. The literature overwhelmingly suggests that prior to entering prostitution, the vast majority of these girls suffered physical, emotional, or, most frequently, sexual abuse (Cooper *et al.*, 2005; Farrow, 2005; Kennedy *et al.*, 2005; Sheridan & VanPelt, 2005). The story of Kara illustrates how many teenagers flee from a dangerous household to a dangerous lifestyle on the streets as a prostitute. The Huckleberry House Project concluded that 90% of the adolescent female prostitutes studied were sexually molested (Flowers, 1998).

Research examining adolescent prostitution in Canada and the Philippines found that runaways from abusive homes were particularly susceptible to pimps and drug dealers on the streets (Bagley, 1999). Wilson and Widom (2009) found that childhood neglect was also a risk factor for entry into juvenile prostitution. Researchers indicated that the children on the streets alone are more vulnerable to the lures offered by pimps or other juveniles. "Early childhood abuse and neglect appear to place children at increased risk of becoming prostitutes, which reinforces the importance of viewing prostitution in a victimization context" (Widom & Kuhns, 1996, p. 1611).

Researchers have repeatedly found that sexual abuse leads to running away and the combination of the two is critical in the juvenile's risk for entering prostitution (Edinburgh &

Saewyc, 2008; Wilson & Widom, 2008; Farley, 2003). Researchers agree that there is a strong correlation between running away and juvenile prostitution. Many of these girls who leave home to escape abuse or to seek independence and excitement quickly become prostitutes to pay for drugs, food, shelter, and the like (Farley, 2003; Kennedy *et al.*, 2007). Some are lured by the sweet-talking pimp offering love, protection, and companionship. Edinburgh and Saewyc (2008) suggest that the majority of women enter street prostitution when they are vulnerable and impressionable. Other studies suggest that the primary reason these adolescents become involved in prostitution is to support a drug habit (Wilson & Widom, 2008).

Mitchell, Finkelhor, and Wolak (2010) examined how law enforcement agencies process young female prostitutes in the United States. Out of the 1450 arrests in a one year period, 138 were examined and three categories of offenders were identified: (1) third-party exploiters; (2) solo prostitution; and (3) conventional child sexual abuse with payment. Based on these categories, the juveniles were divided into categories based on the police agencies "orientation toward the juvenile" (p. 18). These categories include: (1) juveniles as victims (53%); (2) juveniles as delinquents (31%); and (3) juveniles as both delinquents and victims (16%) (p.18). Results of this study indicate that police perception of the juvenile offender influences whether the juvenile is treated as a victim, or delinquent.

According to the U.S. Department of Justice, Federal Bureau of Investigation's *Uniform Crime Reports* for 1995 (1996), 504 females under 18 years old were arrested for prostitution and commercialized vice, and approximately 108,840 females under the age of 18 were arrested as runaways. Far more female adolescents were arrested for loitering (34,011), vagrancy (313), and suspicion (322) than for prostitution and vice. Historically, research shows that officers will arrest these adolescent girls under various other status offenses in order to prevent stigmatizing them as "prostitutes." In addition to prostitution, these girls frequently engage in diverse criminal and delinquent activities. Flowers (1995) found that the crimes most typically committed by these juvenile prostitutes include theft, robbery, drug dealing, and the use of drugs. Greater than 80% of the arrests of both females and males were between the age range of 15−17 years of age.

Overall, officers exercise a great deal of discretion in their decisions to arrest or not arrest and on what charge (Finkelhor & Ormrod, 2004). The literature is consistent in that the overwhelming majority of juvenile females arrested for prostitution are Caucasian (Finkelhor & Ormrod, 2004; Wilson & Widom, 2009). African Americans compose a distant second-largest category of juvenile prostitutes (Wilson & Widom, 2009). However, a study was conducted that explored the association between severity of childhood trauma and adult prostitution behaviors with a sample of 676 heterosexual women with drug addiction in San Antonio, Texas. The findings indicated that black women reporting severe degrees of emotional abuse, emotional neglect, or physical neglect were more likely to engage in prostitution behavior than Hispanic or white women with similar levels of trauma (Medrano, Hatch, Zule, & Desmond, 2003). Juvenile prostitutes can come from all socioeconomic backgrounds. Research by Farrow (2005) indicates that youth who live within the fringes of society are most often those who are homeless, runaways, throwaways, school drop-outs, "counterculture youth," and those who have been institutionalized (i.e., delinquent) and more susceptible to the deviant lifestyle that accompanies prostitution regardless of the socioeconomic status from which they came (p. 337).

A number of pieces of federal legislation have been enacted since the 1970s to crack down on the sexual exploitation of children. According to Weisberg, states are creating "criminal statutes that fail to punish adolescent prostitutes either by omitting any mention of sanctions or specifically excluding adolescents involved in prostitution from any liability" (as cited in Flowers, 1998, p. 152). Weisberg (1985) further explains that in civil legislation, many states look at adolescent prostitution as a form of child abuse/sexual exploitation, rather than as a result of delinquent behavior. In both cases, the adolescent prostitute is viewed as victim, not as an offender.

Governor David A. Paterson (2008) from New York signed a package of bills into law, which included the "Safe Harbor for Exploited Youth Act." It requires districts in New York to provide crisis intervention services and community-based programming for exploited youth in order to enhance child protection services. Prior to the enactment of this bill, individuals under the age of 18 who were arrested for prostitution or other sexually-related illegal activities entered the criminal justice system with the legal presumption that they were juvenile delinquents. This bill decriminalizes child prostitution, recognizing these children as victims, not criminals, and provides them with necessary social services.

"As a society we must do everything in our power to prevent sexual exploitation, but when it does occur we must be prepared to assist our youth with appropriate outreach services. For too long we have been disciplining young children who are the victims of brutal sexual exploitation instead of providing them with the necessary services to reintegrate them into society and ensure they receive adequate crisis intervention," said Governor Paterson (2008). When the bill was signed Governor Patterson further stated, "This law establishes a Safe Harbor Act which will ensure that sexually exploited youth receive counseling and emergency services as well as long term housing solutions."

Current research considers juveniles who are "induced to perform labor or commercial sex act[s] through force, fraud or coercion" victims of human trafficking and are therefore protected under the Trafficking Victims Protection Act of 2000 (TVPA) (U.S. Department of Justice, 2011). The TVPA states "any person under the age of 18 who performs a commercial sex act is considered a victim of human trafficking regardless of whether force, fraud, or coercion was present"(U.S. Department of Justice, 2011). Currently USDJ reports that there are approximately 2515 suspected incidents of human trafficking.

As previously mentioned, most cases of juvenile prostitution are handled by either a police department's vice squad or juvenile division. Historically, the various units and police officers involved in a juvenile prostitution case create the lack of a coordinated response (Weisberg, 1985). He maintains that vice squad officers perceive these juveniles as delinquents as a result of their involvement with various types of crime and their "streetwise" demeanor. In addition, he explains that frequently officers are unaware of the resources available in the community to help these adolescents. Their typical response is to arrest. In contrast, Weisberg suggests that the juvenile division officers are much more in tune with a rehabilitative approach and have the capability to make the appropriate referrals to community organizations and treatment programs. He levies the criticism that officers who simply arrest are failing to provide any long-lasting solution to the problems posed by juveniles. Recently, Mitchell, Finkelhor, and Wolak's (2010) study continues to support the notion that an officer's perception of the juvenile's behavior has significant impact on whether the adolescent is treated like a delinquent or victim.

Some researchers suggest that it is not an officer's lack of knowledge about community resources for adolescent female prostitutes but rather their belief that these programs are not effective in making either short- or long-term changes in the lives of these juveniles (Finkelhor & Ormrod, 2004). All too commonly, the same youths are being rearrested on charges related to prostitution time and time again. Weisberg (1985) suggests that these officers are left with a lack of faith in the courts and treatment programs for these individuals. The literature suggests that officers are also frustrated by the quick release of adolescents from juvenile hall who are arrested for status offenses such as running away. In Kara's case, she is blatantly telling officers that she will return to prostitution as soon as she is released. Officers are regularly left with the discretion to treat the adolescent female prostitute as either a criminal or a victim. In both instances officers are habitually dissatisfied with the outcome, as the same juveniles are cycled through the system.

Forensic Psychology and Policy Implications

Adolescent female prostitution is in many cases an unfortunate result of abuse or neglect. Young women with various emotional scars are left feeling worthless, degraded, and depressed. Research indicates that many of these young women have been treated for mental disorders or substance abuse in inpatient care facilities and have higher rates of suicidal ideation or attempts (Farrow, 2005). Many of these juveniles have a variety of emotional problems that cause them to seek out and participate in prostitution (Wilson & Widom, 2009).

This is clearly a population that would benefit from mental health services. Unfortunately, the link between officers and mental health professionals is not established in many cases. Some officers are not aware of the available resources or do not recognize the juvenile prostitute as having been victimized. The literature suggests that adolescent females selling sex are often the most alienated from social services, despite their obvious need for help (Community Care,

2003). Forensic psychologists would be particularly able to see the underlying psychological correlates to the criminality of these juveniles. The plethora of emotional and psychological problems often experienced by adolescent female prostitutes is not being addressed and the cycle of crime and arrest is perpetuated. Moreover, having more protections against child sexual abuse would best prevent the problem of female adolescent prostitution. If it is known that such abuse has occurred, the victim should first be placed in a safe environment and provided with counseling to help them cope with the effects of the abuse.

Finkelhor and Ormrod (2004) suggest that when in contact with the criminal justice system, these juveniles are exposed to practices that suggest they are mainly being punished for sexual promiscuity. They maintain that treatment is at best secondary. Historically, Schaffer and DeBlassie (1984) suggested that those in authority in law enforcement are "security-oriented" and the law enforcement personnel who are interested in rehabilitation are no more than tolerated, having very little impact on policy. According to Finkelhor and Ormrod (2004), those officers who find themselves dealing with juvenile prostitutes lack resources to offer rehabilitation and find themselves forced into arresting these adolescents in order to protect them. Programs to address these needs could be implemented, with the critical factor being adequate training and education for line officers to recognize those in need of these services. The training offered to both juvenile division officers and vice officers could be more uniform. Although vice squad officers are extensively trained in the different components of prostitution, the special needs of the troubled adolescent often go unrecognized. Officers who see these juveniles on the street committing various crimes could easily miss the child victim that many of these teenagers used to be.

Future Research

There is a paucity of research regarding policing female adolescent prostitution. While the research on adult female prostitution is abundant, more research must consider the unique aspects of juvenile prostitution. The literature overwhelmingly suggests that there are special emotional and psychological issues that must be considered with this population. However, there is no research indicating what differences occur between those adolescent prostitutes who receive psychological services from their contact with the criminal justice system and those who do not. Program evaluations comparing police departments that take a more rehabilitative approach with juvenile prostitutes in comparison with those who take more of a retributive approach are needed. Recidivism rates and suicide rates could be compared. Additional research on how officers view juvenile prostitutes, as criminals or victims, would also be of great value. Research is needed on those juvenile prostitutes who come from middle- and upper-class backgrounds. This is a growing phenomenon with seemingly different precipitating factors. Research indicating the efficacy of the Safe Harbor law is lacking in the recent literature. Recent changes in legislature and laws have had an impact on how officers view the juvenile victims. Future research exploring how these laws have impacted the trend in human trafficking would be beneficial. Overall, female adolescent prostitution is an area needing further research.

Juveniles in Adult Jails

Introduction

Thousands of adolescents are placed in adult jails each year. The conditions in which these adolescents are held, and the circumstances they encounter, pose serious threats to their physical and mental well-being. Children's advocates have long been aware of the dangers that adolescents face in this environment, and their concerns have prompted litigation to end the incarceration of juveniles in adult jails. Despite many years of litigation to abolish the holding of adolescents in adult facilities, approximately 40 states continue to do so, placing thousands of juveniles in dangerous situations a year. Oftentimes, when juveniles are imprisoned with adults in an attempt to reform their behavior, they leave the jail even less equipped to deal with the outside world than before incarceration (Tomasevski, 1986).

There are numerous cases depicting specific problems of incarcerating juveniles in adult jails. Adolescents are particularly vulnerable to suicide when confronted with the adult jail environment. The following example illustrates the problem of keeping juveniles in isolation.

Kathy Robbins was a 15-year-old girl who was arrested for running away from home in 1984. She was taken to Glenn County Jail in California, where she was strip-searched and placed in a small dark cell with a solid steel door. She was held in virtual isolation for 4 days until her hearing date. At her hearing, she begged the judge to send her home.

The court ordered that her case be continued and that Kathy remain incarcerated in the jail until such time.

That afternoon, Kathy committed suicide by hanging herself with a sheet from the guardrail of the top bunk. Disturbing information concerning Kathy Robbins was disclosed during the case of *Robbins v. Glenn County* (1986). Kathy had physical evidence of previous suicide attempts, yet no measures were taken in jail to supervise Kathy or ensure her safety. She was only allowed one brief visit with her mother and was not given any reading material that her mother had provided. Further, the jail staff had refused to take her phone messages from her mother. Most troubling in this case is the fact that space was available at a local group home while Kathy was incarcerated in the jail.

It should be noted that girls who are so traumatized by the experience of being held in an adult jail are not the only ones who resort to suicide. Every year there are cases of young boys who commit suicide while being subjected to the conditions in adult jails. Oftentimes for boys, suicide follows their victimization in a rape assault by adult inmates. Whereas boys are subjected to rape victimization by adult prisoners, girls are often victims of rape by the jail staff, as can be seen from the following examples.

In *Doe v. Burwell*, a 15-year-old girl from Ohio had left home for 1 day without her parents' permission. In order to "teach her a lesson," the juvenile court judge ordered her to be incarcerated in the county jail for 5 days. During her 4th night in jail, she was raped by a deputy jailer.

A 14-year-old runaway girl was held in a county jail in Pennsylvania when she was raped by the deputy sheriff as well as by two male inmates. One of the inmates was a convicted murderer who was awaiting sentencing. The sheriff released the inmates in order for them to participate in the rape of the young girl (Chesney-Lind, 1988).

In *Yellen v. Ada County* (1985), a 15-year-old boy was incarcerated in an adult jail for failing to pay $73 in traffic fines. He was held for a 14-hour period during which time he was brutally tortured by other inmates and eventually beaten to death.

Literature Review

Examining the psychological and criminological literature provides us with a better understanding of the pervasive and severe problems encountered when incarcerating juveniles in adult jails. **The Juvenile Justice and Delinquency Prevention Act** originally passed in 1974, prevents youth under age 18 from being incarcerated in adult facilities unless the state defines "adult" as younger than 18, or if the juvenile was convicted of a felony or is awaiting trial for a felony offense (Hartney, 2006). The Act makes exceptions, for example, for short periods in rural areas or while awaiting a court appearance, and in these instances juvenile inmates are to be kept entirely separate from adults. Soler (2002) cites the increased prosecution of juveniles as adults and incarceration of juveniles in adult jails, while a serious lack of mental health resources and services in the correctional system exist. There was a 208% increase in the number of youth under age 18 serving time in adult jails on any given day between 1990 and 2004 (Snyder & Sickmund, 2006). As juvenile crime increased, longer sentences and the transfer of juvenile offenders to the adult system gained momentum in the 1980s and 1990s. The number of youth under age 18 in adult jails rose sharply through the 1990s to a high of almost 9500 in 1999 and then reduced to an average of just over 7200 since 2000 (Snyder & Sickmund, 2006). Federal correctional institutions held 39 inmates under age 18 in 1990, but none in 2004. Federal law requires that all persons under age 18 convicted of a federal offense be placed in appropriate juvenile facilities, and not in adult facilities (Hartney, 2006).

The Center for Disease Control and Prevention's 2007 report on the transfer of youth from the juvenile to the adult justice system indicates that in 44 states and the District of Columbia, juveniles as young as 14 can be tried in the adult criminal justice system. Forty states either permit or require the incarceration of juveniles in adult facilities before trial. The report argues that children and adolescents should not be held as responsible for their actions as adults based on research that shows the developmental differences between adolescents and adults. These findings indicate that the prefrontal cortex, a part of the brain that is involved in planning complex cognitive behaviors such as reasoning, advanced thinking, as well as the expression of personality and appropriate social behavior (e.g., impulse control), is one of the last areas of the brain to mature. The developmental differences between adults and adolescents highlight the importance of examining the impact of having juveniles in adult jails as well as the role of forensic psychologists in helping to inform and educate the criminal justice system about the potential implications.

In most states if a motion for a waiver hearing is held the court will use criteria set forth by the Supreme Court case of *Kent v. United States* (1966) in which a juvenile judge sent a 16-year-old boy to adult court without a hearing, and the Supreme Court ruled that this violates the Fourteenth Amendment of right to due process. In more recent years, state legislatures have increasingly reduced judges' discretion in sending particularly heinous juvenile offenders to adult court, mandating that all adolescents of a certain age accused of a certain crime be sentenced as adults and sent to adult jails (Beinart, 1999). The Coalition for Juvenile Justice advocated for increased access to mental health services designed specifically for the problems of incarcerated youth in their 2000 annual report (Thomas & Penn, 2002). The Risk-Sophistication-Treatment-Inventory (RST-I) is designed to address three important psychological constructs of the juvenile's level of violence risk, the level of maturity or sophistication, and the degree to which the juvenile can be rehabilitated by treatment (Salekin & Grimes, 2002). Most states require an evaluation that is used to determine if a juvenile is able to be rehabilitated or if treatment is a viable option within the juvenile justice system before the juvenile is transferred to adult court (Scott, 2010), while some states require that a juvenile is transferred to an adult court for criminal prosecution in which the juvenile meets criteria in age or offense or if a prior record exists (Griffin, 2009). The specific recommendations include the need for wraparound services, improved planning and coordination between agencies, and further research (Thomas & Penn, 2002).

According to the Annual Survey of Jails in 1989, there were approximately 53,994 juveniles held in adult jails and the numbers were growing. However, more recent studies indicate the proportion of juveniles under age 18 among total adult jail populations is dropping (Snyder & Sickmund, 2006). Individuals under the age of 18 accounted for 1.4% of the total population of state jails in 1994, 1.2% in 2000, and 1% in 2004. Only a small percentage of the juveniles held in jails were charged with violent crimes (Soler, 1988). Murray (1983) reports that of the nearly half a million adolescents in adult jails, only 14% of them had been charged with a serious offense such as homicide, rape, or burglary. Findings summarized in the Center for Disease Control and Prevention's 2007 report on the transfer of youth from the juvenile to the adult justice system indicate that transfer policies have generally resulted in increased arrest for subsequent crimes, including violent crime, among juveniles who were transferred compared with those retained in the juvenile justice system.

A lawsuit was filed against the City of Long Beach and the County of Los Angeles in *Baumgartner v. City of Long Beach* (1987) when a taxpayer was outraged that the cities incarcerated more than 4000 juveniles each year in the Long Beach City Jail. Nearly 1000 of the adolescents had not been charged with an offense. Instead, these juveniles were victims of abandonment, neglect, and abuse by their parents and, thus, were removed from their homes. While proper placements in foster or group homes were pending for these juveniles, they remained locked up in jail with adult inmates. This environment further placed these abused adolescents in the face of danger. Additionally, a nursery equipped with cribs and toys was located in the jail where infants were placed until such time as proper placements could be arranged for them (Soler, 1988; Steinhart, 1988). Another 1000 of the youths were status offenders, while less than 10% were charged with violent offenses. All of the adolescents were kept in dark cells behind bars.

The adult jail environment is not conducive to the detainment of juveniles. Tomasevski (1986) presents the results from a comprehensive study conducted by the Defense for Children International in 1983, in an attempt to create awareness about the problem of detaining juveniles in adult facilities. Adolescents who are held in the adult facilities are subjected to circumstances, which are direct threats to their emotional and physical health. In order to "protect" adolescents in such an environment, they are often separated from the adult inmate population. The result of this action is isolation, often resembling solitary confinement. Tomasevski's (1986) international study of adolescents in adult prisons revealed that the United States displayed the most evidence of virtual solitary confinement.

When juveniles are required to remain separate from adult prisoners by "sight and sound," they are oftentimes completely isolated from human contact. Adolescents are particularly vulnerable to depression and suicide when they are isolated and fearful. Further, the correctional officers are not trained to identify the signs of depression in adolescents, and, therefore, intervention frequently does not occur in time.

As demonstrated by the case of Kathy Robbins, we see the depression that juveniles suffer and the desperate measures they take when held in isolation. When adolescents in jail are not isolated, they encounter severe problems of a different nature. Juveniles are particularly vulnerable to sexual and physical abuse by staff and adult inmates. Adolescents are abused more frequently and driven to desperation more quickly in correctional facilities (Ziedenberg & Schiraldi, 1998). Many juveniles can be rehabilitated with treatments such as pharmacotherapy (prescribed psychiatric medication), individual psychotherapy, cognitive-behavioral therapy, family therapy, group therapy, drug and alcohol treatment, residential placement, vocational rehabilitation, treatment for sex offenders, boot camps, and work programs (Scott, 2010).

Females in jail are held under more restrictive conditions than males (Chesney-Lind & Shelden, 1992). Often, they are housed in a subsection of a male facility. For this reason, they are rarely granted equal opportunity for recreation, education, or work-release programs as their male counterparts (Mann, 1984). Women will often spend most, if not all of their time inside their cell. This is difficult for adult women, but it is particularly trying for young girls. It is particularly dangerous for girls who often have backgrounds involving sexual and physical abuse. The repeated trauma makes them especially susceptible to depression and even suicide (Browne & Finkelhor, 1986). A pilot study revealed that psychoeducational group intervention for incarcerated girls (aged 13−17 years old) may be effective in alleviating depression and trauma symptoms (Pomeroy, Green, & Kiam, 2001). Chesney-Lind and Shelden (1992) report that girls in jail tend to be younger, commit less serious offenses (primarily status offenses), and, despite their less severe offenses, remain in custody for approximately the same length of time as their male counterparts.

Forensic Psychology and Policy Implications

The incarceration of adolescents in adult jails is a social, political, and human rights problem. Despite the high profile nature and wide media coverage of the most extreme instances of juvenile violence, the rate of juvenile violent crime has consistently decreased since 1994 (Snyder & Sickmund, 2006). However, during this period of overall decline in adolescent violence, juvenile female violent crime arrests have increased (especially for assault), marking an important change in the types of youth entering the juvenile justice system and in their programming needs (Snyder & Sickmund, 2006). As efforts increase to curb the rate of juvenile crime, the special needs and rights of adolescents must not be ignored. Adolescent detention facilities are especially equipped to address the special needs of youthful offenders. Specialized treatment programs are designed to offer juveniles an opportunity for rehabilitation. To hold youths in adult facilities is to deny them this opportunity, as well as to potentially subject them to severe psychological distress, physical and sexual abuse, and an environment where they are influenced by career and violent offenders. Nevertheless, society apparently supports the stricter, more punitive approach to dealing with juvenile offenders. Tomasevski (1986) described the Canadian Adult Prisoners' association response regarding adult facilities as places that should not house juveniles. Those youths who do not succumb to molestation or get hurt tend to become tougher than when they entered the facility; their young age and their exposure to adult facilities only ensures that they will return. The November 2007 report from the Center for Disease Control and Prevention found that teens sent to adult facilities commit more crimes on average than those sent to juvenile facilities. This report described a study in New Jersey found that juveniles transferred to adult facilities are 39% more likely to be rearrested for a violent offense than are teens in juvenile detention. This report also cited a study in Pennsylvania that found juveniles housed in adult prisons for a violent offense had a 77% greater likelihood of being rearrested for a new violent offense than teens in juvenile detention. Juveniles incarcerated as adults in Minnesota were 26% more likely to be reconvicted. Finally, a study in Florida found consistent results for adolescents arrested for violent felonies. While there is a small subsection of juvenile offenders who are extremely violent and potentially **psychopathic** (e.g., lacking remorse, empathy, versatile criminal history, etc.), the majority of youthful offenders would be extremely vulnerable and inappropriately housed in an adult jail. Forensic psychologists can play an important role in evaluating for and educating about the developmental differences present in these juveniles. Psychologists who work in adult jails would need to be particularly vigilant in assessing for suicidal thoughts and intent in juveniles incarcerated in these facilities.

Suggestions for Future Research

There has not been a great deal of recent research conducted on juveniles incarcerated in adult jails, and most research that has been conducted is centered on male juveniles with little researched on the outcome for female juveniles. The long-term effects of such an environment on juveniles needs to be examined from a psychological as well as a criminological perspective. Specifically, follow-up studies on adolescents who have been held in adult facilities would provide useful information regarding their psychological functioning, as well as their subsequent criminal behavior. Further, such analyses could then be compared to youthful offenders who were held in juvenile facilities. Would adolescents released from adult jails have lower recidivism rates than teens detained in the juvenile justice system? This would provide a clear illustration of the ramifications of incarcerating juveniles with adults as opposed to other adolescents. Future studies could explore what characteristics place a juvenile at higher risk of suicide in an adult jail. The Center for Disease Control and Prevention (2007, p. 9) recommend the following for future research: "Do youth receive more rehabilitative programming in juvenile institutions than in adult institutions? Has the programming in adult corrections changed in response to the influx of youthful offenders? Do youth in adult correctional institutions have extensive contact with adult offenders and, if so, does that have negative effects on them or promote more subsequent offenses?" Additionally, the differences among state laws have not been assessed systematically, making comparisons from review findings limited. Future research should also focus on the economic costs of transferring juveniles to the adult criminal justice system versus retaining them in the juvenile system (Roman & Butts, 2005).

Further research into implementing psychological and rehabilitation therapy would explore alternatives to punishing these juveniles with adults as an adult who committed the crime. Additionally, the exploration into alternative placements for juveniles needs to continue. Future research on the prevalence of mental illness among juvenile offenders is needed and specific attention should be paid to the differences in symptom presentation in adolescents versus adults. Finally, future research might entail an analysis about the actual impact of the increasing number of adolescents being housed in adult jails and if this is serving any type of deterrent effect.

Juveniles on Death Row

Introduction

Capital punishment has remained an unabated controversy for decades. The constitutionality of the death penalty, the cost of capital cases and executions, and the impact the death penalty has on deterring crime in our society have all been repeatedly questioned. This controversy is further complicated by the issue of sentencing juveniles to death. The United States was one of only a few nations to allow the execution of juvenile offenders. The other nations include: Iran, Nigeria, Pakistan, Saudi Arabia, and Yemen (Blum, 2002). The United States was not only one of the six countries that permitted adolescent capital punishment, it was the leading country. Fifty-eight juveniles in the United States were serving their sentences on death row as of March, 1997 (Streib, 1998). Moreover, juveniles on death row typically exhibit neurological damage, psychoses, and suffered severe physical and/or sexual abuse as younger children (Lewis *et al.*, 1988). The following case illustrates the complexities involved when a juvenile capital punishment.

James Terry Roach was executed on 10 January 1986, in South Carolina, the same state in which he was born. Terry was raised by an ill mother and a father who was absent most of the time. Terry suffered from mental retardation with an IQ near 70. He dropped out of school early, became involved with drugs, and was diagnosed with a personality disorder. When Terry was 16 years old, he lived in a home with unemployed antisocial people who were involved in extensive drug use. Due to Terry's limited mental capacities, he was easily influenced by others. When Terry was 17 years old, he was convinced by an older housemate to spend the day riding around in a car while drinking beer and using marijuana and PCP. The boys came upon a 17-year-old male with his 14-year-old girlfriend, both from prominent families in the community. On a signal from his friend, Terry fatally shot the male three times. The boys then took the girl to a secluded area where they repeatedly raped her. Terry's friend then shot and killed the girl and he later returned to mutilate her body.

The community was outraged by the crimes, especially given the prominent status of the victims' families. The death penalty was sought and received for both Terry and his friend. It should be noted that Terry's court-appointed attorney was disbarred two years after his representation of the case for irregularities in his practice. However, his handling of Terry's case was deemed constitutionally adequate. Despite letters to the governor pleading for clemency from Mother Theresa and former President Carter, Terry's execution was carried out. Although Terry had reached the chronological age of 25 at the time of his execution, his mental age remained fixed at 12 (*Roach v. Aiken*, 1986).

Literature Review

The case of Terry Roach depicts both the gravity of crimes that are committed by the tragedy of executing an individual who only has the mental capacity of a 12-year-old boy. In March of 1997, juveniles on death row constituted approximately 2% of that total population (Streib, 1998). All of these offenders were males who received death sentences for murder. Of these 58 juveniles, 49% were African American, 17% Latino, and 34% Caucasian. This is consistent with the high percentage of minority executions that are found in adult capital punishment cases as well. Moreover, 59% of the executed juvenile offenders were convicted of murdering a Caucasian adult. Since the 1970s, 221 juvenile offenders have received death sentences in the United States and 21 have been executed (Blum, 2002). Blum (2002) states that greater than 80% of the juvenile death sentences since that time were either reversed or commuted as compared to 40% of adult death sentences.

From a criminological stance, punishment for crime serves one of three primary purposes: (1) deterrence; (2) retribution; or (3) rehabilitation. For obvious reasons, the death penalty cannot serve a rehabilitative function. However, rehabilitation is the premise of the juvenile justice system in America. Therefore, the basic assertion of the juvenile justice system (i.e., rehabilitation of juvenile offenders) was inherently incompatible with the death penalty.

In two separate decisions in the 1980s, the U.S. Supreme Court upheld the death penalty for crimes committed at the age of 16 or 17 but ruled that it was unconstitutional to impose the death penalty for crimes that were committed at age 15 or below (Blum, 2002). A study examining public opinion on the death penalty for juvenile and adult offenders found that 14% of the 535 individuals surveyed were willing to execute juveniles who were 15 years or younger at the time they committed the crime (Vogel & Vogel, 2003). There was less support for executing juveniles than adults and 28.2% of those surveyed strongly opposed the execution of juveniles, while 42.5 % of the subjects that supported the use of the death penalty for juveniles would support life without parole as an alternative (Vogel & Vogel, 2003).

Capital punishment has been further examined in its relationship to deterrence of criminal activity. The Federal Bureau of Investigation Uniform Crime Reports indicate that since the death penalty was reinstated in 1976, the number of death-row inmates and executions have increased substantially. There has, however, been virtually no change in the commission rate of murders (FBI, 1997). Furthermore, comparisons between those states which utilize the death penalty and those that do not, reveal that the majority of death-penalty states have higher rates of murder. This finding supports those who oppose the death penalty because it shows how capital punishment fails to deter crime (FBI, 1997).

Particularly in the case of Terry Roach, it is highly unlikely that his execution will deter others like him. His attorney addressed the improbability of a deterrence effect, stating that Terry (and those with similar problems) did not have the ability to think more than a few hours in advance and could likely not even conceive of possibilities for his actions such as arrest or execution (Streib, 1987). This is consistent with developmental theory, which acknowledges that adolescents have a deficient understanding of mortality. This furthers the previous discussion on rehabilitation in the juvenile justice system. According to his attorney, Terry lacked the ability to think about the consequences of his actions. This is common among adolescents and certainly something to be expected from an intellectually disabled adolescent. The public outrage at Terry's sentence illustrates the general perception that the punishment did not fit the offender. Constitutional law focuses primarily on the fact that the death penalty for juvenile offenders is in violation of the Eighth Amendment. In 1976, the landmark Supreme Court case of *Gregg v. Georgia* held that the death penalty does not violate the Eighth Amendment to the constitution. Although the essence of this case does not involve the age of the offender, the concern over an offender's age did emerge. In this ruling, the Court maintained that the jury must consider characteristics of the offender that might mitigate against a capital punishment ruling. Among such characteristics mentioned was the age of the offender. Special consideration of the constitutionality of the death penalty for juveniles was addressed in *Eddings v. Oklahoma* (1982). This case involved a 16-year-old defendant who was potentially facing capital punishment. Regarding the age of the offender, the Court found that a person's youthfulness is worthy of consideration as a mitigating factor. In *Eddings*, the Supreme Court avoided making a determination on the constitutionality issue and sent the case back for resentencing; however, Justices Burger, Blackmun, Rehnquist, and White stated that there was no constitutional basis to bar the death penalty for the 16-year-old defendant. The Supreme Court continues to avoid ruling on the federal constitutionality of sentencing juveniles to death; rather, the legality of the death penalty for juveniles remains a determination for individual jurisdictions. In *Thompson v. Oklahoma* (1988), the Supreme Court ruled that it was not unconstitutional to execute juveniles who were 15 years old or younger at the time of their offense. In 1989, the Supreme Court ruled in *Stanford v. Kentucky* that sentencing juveniles to the death penalty did not violate the constitution for those who were 16 or 17 years old at the time of their offense.

The 6 June, 1989, decision in *Perry v. Lynaugh,* that explicitly allowed the continued execution of intellectually disabled offenders, was overturned 13 years later on 20 June 2002, with the *Atkins v. Virginia* decision (Weeks, 2003). The majority opinion held that the Eighth Amendment prohibited the continued execution of the intellectually disabled because it constituted "cruel and unusual" punishment. The Supreme Court ruling in *Roper v. Simmons* (2005) stated that the execution of juveniles under the age of 18 when their crime was committed also violated the Fourteenth and Eighth Amendments. The Supreme Court addressed whether under the Constitution it is permissible to execute an offender who was older than 15 but younger than 18 at the time of his or her crime. The Court was asked to reconsider its 1989 conclusion in *Stanford v. Kentucky*. Christopher Simmons had exhausted his appeals when the Supreme Court decided in *Atkins v. Virginia* (2002) that the Eighth and Fourteenth Amendments prohibit the execution of a "mentally retarded person." Simmons argued that the *Atkins'* reasoning regarding the developmentally disabled being "categorically less culpable than the average criminal" should also mean that the Constitution prohibits the execution of a juvenile. The Missouri Supreme Court set aside Simmons' death sentence, upholding the current criminal justice trend of abolishing the execution of juveniles.

It is interesting to note that historically these same juveniles who were sentenced to death were not legally old enough to vote, enter into a contract, marry, or sit on the juries like those who convict them (Streib, 1987). Perhaps for this reason, the age of minority for sentencing juveniles to death in many states was already 18. However, not all states held age 18 as the threshold, and some states did not abide by a minimum age for capital punishment at all. In 1962, the death penalty existed in 41 states, in which the minimum age was 7 in 16 states, age 8 in three states, age 10 in 3 states, and ages 12–18 in 19 states (Streib, 1987). This has changed considerably over the past four decades. According to Blum (2002), only 22 states allowed capital punishment for crimes committed before the age of 18. Four states had death penalty eligibility for those 17 and above, 11 states for 16 and above, and seven states had no minimum age specified (Weeks, 2003). Virginia laws that allowed capital punishment for minors may have been the precipitating factor in sending D.C. sniper suspects John Allen Muhammad, 41, and John Lee Malvo, 17, first to Virginia to face trial, when the majority of their victims were shot in Maryland (Blum, 2002). In both the federal system and in Maryland, individuals must be at least 18 to face capital punishment, while Washington, D.C. has no death penalty (2002).

Streib (1987) reported that younger juveniles on death row experienced greater fear as well as a strong sense of abandonment. Streib described such juveniles as exhibiting uncontrollable crying, severe depression, and "childlike pleas for rescue to a parent or authoritative adult" (p. 158). The case illustration of Terry Roach, the 17-year-old intellectually disabled boy, demonstrates how the public viewed him as evil for his heinous crimes. A study conducted by Lewis *et al.* (1988) examined 14 juveniles on death row concerning their psychological characteristics and disorders. The researchers reported that the typical juvenile offender on death row had serious injuries to the central nervous system, exhibited psychotic symptoms, and had been physically and sexually abused.

A study evaluating the precursors to lethal violence found that when examining the social and family histories of 16 men sentenced to death in California, institutional failure had occurred in 15 cases, including 13 cases of severe physical or sexual abuse while in foster care or under state youth authority jurisdiction (Freedman & Hemenway, 2000). Schaefer and Hennessy (2001) reported that neuropathy, psychiatric illness, substance abuse, and child abuse may be found in greater proportions in executed capital offenders versus among other violent incarcerated offenders. Finally, studies continue to question the developmental maturity of juveniles. Magnetic Resonance Imaging (MRI) studies have allowed scientists to propose that the human brain may not be fully mature until a person reaches his or her mid-twenties (Tamber, 2003). The frontal lobe, which controls executive functioning tasks such as planning, inhibition, and abstraction or more complex cognitive functions, is the last part to develop (Tamber, 2003).

Forensic Psychology and Policy Implications

The appropriateness of imposing the death penalty on juveniles was explored from a criminological, sociological, and psychological perspective. When combining views from experts representing the American Society of Criminology, the Academy of Criminal Justice Sciences, and the Law and Society Association, the death penalty has not proven itself to be a deterrent to crime (Radelet & Akers, 1995). Therefore, the death penalty has not served its primary function in society. With the abolition of the juvenile death penalty, the juvenile justice system can now focus on strategies and programs for the goal of rehabilitation that they believe is the most appropriate for youthful offenders. Cases such as Terry Roach illustrate the need for special considerations in sentencing juveniles, particularly when capital punishment is involved. Terry's attorney stated that his client lacked the ability to think about the consequences of his actions. By killing such children, society abandoned its responsibility to teach appropriate ways to control behavior as well as the skills needed to think and understand consequences for one's conduct. In Texas, the Texas Youth Commission (TYC) does have a program, the Capital Offender Program, in place for violent offenders, particularly capital offenders, for the purpose of rehabilitation. The program began at the Giddings State Home and School, and focuses on the emotions of the offender that motivated them to commit the criminal act (Mikhail, 2006). The Capital Offender Program is 20 weeks of a variety of therapeutic activities such as role playing that encourage the offender to take responsibility for their criminal act, and the offender also is exposed to the living victims of their crime (Mikhail, 2006). While the Capital Offender Program does have potential to help juvenile offenders, difficulties with this program include the ineligibility of juvenile offenders who are transferred to adult court. Emotional or psychological benefits from the program are likely to be lost when the juvenile transfers to an adult prison and serves a lengthy sentence, which could be up to 40 years (Mikhail, 2006).

Suggestions for Future Research

Future research will need to focus on the impact of increased long-term sentences instead of the death penalty for juveniles convicted for the most violent of crimes. The rehabilitation of juvenile offenders and new, evidenced-based programming should continue to be a goal of on-going research. Longitudinal or long-term research should be conducted on programs like the Capital Offender Program to evaluate recidivism rates after a rehabilitation program specifically designed for violent juvenile offenders. The developmental differences between juveniles and adults should continue to be investigated, particularly with respect to the consequences of juveniles being transferred to adult courts and given very adult sentences. How these differences affect the psychological benefits and therapeutic opportunities that should be offered to juvenile offenders warrants future research. When adolescents who would have previously been given the death penalty receive lengthy prison sentences, are there beneficial treatments or therapies that could return these individuals to society as a productive and contributing member of society?

Juvenile Boot Camps

Introduction

Juvenile boot-camp facilities have become an increasingly popular response to adolescent crime in the United States. Often referred to as shock incarceration, boot camps are based on the premise that instilling regimen and discipline in young offenders will decrease subsequent criminal behavior. Controversy exists as to whether recidivism reduction has actually been achieved with the implementation of boot camps throughout the United States. Some experts argue that the implementation of boot-camp programs does nothing to change the environment from which the juvenile emerges, and, therefore, once the program has ended, the juvenile's return to the same environment perpetuates their engagement in criminal behavior. For this reason, it has been argued that boot-camp facilities do not curb long-term recidivism rates among juvenile offenders. The hypothetical case of Johnny illustrates a common trend among boot-camp participants.

Johnny is a 16-year-old boy who was recently arrested for the first time. He was caught breaking into a house while under the influence of a controlled substance. Because this was Johnny's first offense, he was sentenced to the local juvenile boot camp which had recently been built in his small town. While at the boot camp, Johnny's day began at 5:00 a.m. and ended at 9:00 p.m. His 16-hour day consisted of rigorous calisthenics, strict discipline, difficult work, job training, and educational programs. Johnny became very comfortable with the routine and was a role-model to new recruits. After 90 days in the boot camp, Johnny was released to his parents. He would remain on probation for the next month, during which time he was not to leave his house except to go to school and meet with his probation officer.

Johnny's first night at home reminded him of what his life was like prior to boot camp. His parents were both intoxicated and began yelling at one another within the first hour Johnny was home. Johnny decided to tell his parents about his experience at boot camp and the changes he intended to make in his life. Johnny's father, irate at his son for interrupting, began to beat Johnny and tell him how worthless he was. The physical and verbal abuse lasted for one hour at which time the neighbors called the police for the disturbance. Johnny, afraid of the police seeing his bloody and bruised body, ran away. The next day Johnny was arrested for violating his probation.

Literature Review

A rapid growth of boot camps for adult offenders evolved in the United States in the 1980s. At the time, there were questions as to whether such programs would be appropriate for youthful offenders. The growing number of cases of troubled youth that die while participating in rigorous boot-camp programs bring this question into sharp focus (Janofsky, 2001). The Office of Juvenile Justice and Delinquency Prevention (OJJDP) sought to explore whether adult boot camps could in fact be adapted to suit the needs of juveniles. The OJJDP funded a study in 1992 to examine three existing boot-camp programs in order to determine the possible adaptations that would be required to make them suitable for juvenile offenders (Bourque *et al.*, 1996). Throughout the 1990s, numerous juvenile boot camps have been developed as an alternative to traditional incarceration.

Boot-camp facilities provide a militaristic regimen of strenuous physical conditioning and strict discipline. Specifically, boot camps are intended to provide a cost-effective means of dealing with delinquent youths, instill morality and ethics, strengthen academic achievement, and hold adolescents accountable for their actions while providing them with the tools necessary to prevent reoffense. It is questionable whether boot camps are in fact providing juveniles with the necessary tools to curb recidivism. As illustrated in the case of Johnny, it may not be enough to simply provide these youths with the skills and expect them to leave the boot camp and be able to function in their natural environment.

Military-style residential treatment programs for adolescents were introduced in the early 1990s as a spin off of boot camps for incarcerated men (Benda, 2005). They have evolved significantly since that time, and, presently, there are at least 50 public and privately administered juvenile boot-camp programs in the United States and several in other countries (Weis & Toolis, 2008). Typically, juvenile boot camps are operated for first-time juvenile offenders without histories of serious violent crime. They are meant to be a form of punishment, ranging in severity between traditional juvenile detention and probation (Wilson, MacKenzie, & Mitchell, 2005).

Peterson (1996) reports that the pilot programs evaluated by the OJJDP reveal that there was no significant difference in recidivism between those in the boot-camp programs and those in control programs. Similarly, in a study conducted by MacKenzie and Souryal (1994), an evaluation of boot-camp programs in eight states revealed that such programs did not reduce recidivism rates for juvenile offenders in five of the eight states investigated. In the three states that did show lower recidivism rates for participants in the boot-camp programs, juveniles were provided intensive follow-up supervision (Reid-MacNevin, 1997). However, supporters of boot-camp facilities suggest that recidivism rates are not appropriate measures of a successful program (Osler, 1991). More recently, Wilson and MacKenzie's 2005 meta-analysis or study that combined the results of several related studies (cited in Steiner and Giacomazzi, 2007) found boot camps to be ineffective in reducing recidivism or the likelihood of relapse into criminal behavior. In a recent (2007) study of a Northwestern boot-camp program, Steiner and Giacomazzi found recidivism rates among their sample to be unaffected though graduates of the program were less likely to violate their probation. However, they did find that juveniles adjudicated for a nonviolent offense were less likely to commit another offense and suggested the possibility of only sending nonviolent offenders to boot-camp facilities.

A study examining the reoffense patterns of 162 youth who were transferred to, and sentenced to, adult court during 1999 through June of 2001 revealed that the youths receiving adult probation or boot camp were 1.74 to 2.29 times more likely to reoffend than were youth receiving juvenile sanctions (Mason, Chapman, Chang, & Simons, 2003). A juvenile boot camp that was implemented in a public school setting was named Specialized Treatment and

Rehabilitation (STAR). Although operated jointly by the school, the juvenile court, and the juvenile probation department, this program has also demonstrated very little impact on recidivism (Trulson, Triplett, & Snell, 2001). The Acting Assistant Attorney General for Civil Rights in the state of Georgia has stated that boot camps are not only ineffective, but can be harmful to some adolescents (Tyler, Darville, & Stalnaker, 2001).

Several explanations have been offered describing why boot camps do not have a general effect on recidivism. From a criminological perspective, boot camps are theoretically based on deterrence theory. As noted by Reid-MacNevin (1997), "correctional research has shown time and again that deterrence-based criminal justice interventions do not work" (p. 156). This philosophy of deterrence has been repeatedly tested within the criminal justice system through such programs as Scared Straight. These programs assume that juvenile delinquents can be scared and intimidated into engaging in pro-social behavior and respecting authority (Welch, 1997). Unfortunately, such programs have consistently reported unsuccessful deterrence effects. In 1992, Lipsey conducted a meta-analysis of 443 studies between 1950 and 1992, which revealed that deterrence programs such as boot camps had negative effects on juvenile delinquents. Therefore, research has not only shown that boot camps do not lower the rate of reoffending by juveniles, but more importantly, that youths may be negatively effected by such programs.

The literature suggests that boot camps are more costly than most other traditional options and they are much less effective than what the public perceives (Tyler *et al.* 2001). The OJJDP has reported that most boot camps run an average of 10 times the cost of a juvenile on probation (Tyler *et al.*, 2001). More recently, Meade and Steiner (2010) found that boot camps for juveniles appear to reduce the number of confinement beds jurisdictions require, often resulting in cost savings (Meade & Steiner, 2010).

Meade and Steiner's (2010) study involved an examination of the frequency of state-run boot camps for juvenile delinquents and a review of the existing evaluations of boot-camp programs designed for adolescents. Findings revealed that boot camps are less common than they were in the 1990s. According to this study, boot camps, by themselves, typically do not have an effect on participants' tendency to relapse into criminal behavior. Boot camps do seem to improve individuals' attitudes and other behaviors within programs (Meade & Steiner, 2010).

From a psychological perspective, research has examined the image of masculinity, which is portrayed in boot-camp programs. Morash and Rucker (1990) suggest that the confrontation and demanding nature of boot camps illustrate aggression and thus produce aggressive behavior among participants. This can be explained through social learning theory, which maintains that behavior is acquired through modeling the behavior of others. Such learning is particularly found among adolescents. Therefore, according to Morash and Rucker, the goal of teaching juveniles pro-social behavior is not being achieved in correctional boot camps.

Trulsen *et al.* (2001) postulate that boot camps are popular with the public and political leaders because it presents a strong appearance of being tough on juvenile crime. However, they note that boot camps are not reaching the goal of reducing juvenile crime.

As noted by Correia (1997), boot camps are implemented in an artificial environment and, therefore, any behavioral changes that are made by an offender will most likely not be reinforced when the juvenile returns to his or her natural environment in society. Learning theory maintains that it is essential for a behavior to be performed in one's natural environment for a permanent change in conduct to occur. Furthermore, Correia (1997) explains that criminal behavior is strongly influenced by environmental factors. Thus, if changes are not made to an individual's natural environment, any progress made while at boot camp is unlikely to continue postrelease. In the case of Johnny, it is unlikely that any of his progress made at boot camp will present and sustain itself in his home environment. Within the first two hours of being released, Johnny's life returned to what it was prior to his participation in the boot-camp program. The California Department of Corrections closed its boot camp in 1997, due to its expense and failure to reduce recidivism (Parenti, 2000).

According to Peterson (1996), differences between boot-camp participants and control-group participants did emerge in various arenas. Substantial improvement in academic achievement occurred among participants in the boot-camp program. On average, youths increased their achievement scores in reading, language, spelling, and math by at least one academic grade level. Moreover, a significantly higher number of graduates from the boot-camp program became employed while in aftercare. Aftercare is a dimension of the program that follows one's participation in the residential component of the boot camp and entails stringent monitoring for six to nine months in the community.

In order to ensure maximum effectiveness of boot-camp programs, target populations are selected for participation. The criteria initially established included juvenile males who did not have violent criminal histories. Most juveniles who were selected for such programs had been convicted of property or drug offenses. Therefore, the applicability of boot camps was purposefully limited. The OJJDP maintains that the boot-camp focus remains within the rehabilitation model of the juvenile justice system. The lack of positive results emerging from recidivism studies begs the question: Are boot camps truly serving their rehabilitative function?

Forensic Psychology and Policy Implications

Millions of dollars a year are used in funding the development of new boot-camp programs for juvenile offenders each year. With such an investment, it is imperative that programs provide the rehabilitation services they propose. Psychologists have acquired a great deal of knowledge in terms of the family environment and the psychological characteristics of the offender that lead to subsequent delinquency. Given this knowledge, it is apparent that boot-camp programs do not fully address the complexity of the issues involved in juvenile criminality. The environment to which the adolescent will return postrelease from the boot camp is lacking in attention. Although boot camps can be effective in teaching discipline and providing structure, they are not designed to deal with the underlying emotional issues that result in problematic behavior.

Developmental theory shows us that children do not adapt well to drastic changes in their environment. This is exactly what occurs when a child does not receive any means of discipline in the home, aside from perhaps physical abuse (as in the case of Johnny), and then is placed in a militaristic, rigid environment for 90 days. When three months have elapsed, the child is once again placed in an unstructured environment and expected to maintain the regimen that he or she has "learned." According to behavioral theory, the behavior will not generalize to the natural environment because the ecological cues are completely different and the person's conduct is neither required nor reinforced. For these reasons, it appears that psychologists can provide a great deal of insight into the methods for improving existing boot-camp programs; this would allow for the comprehensive impact of environmental influences on human behavior and child development. It also appears that boot camps utilizing treatment and aftercare as part of the rehabilitation process may help to lower recidivism among juvenile offenders. Furthermore, criminal justice research has illustrated for years that programs based on deterrence are not effective in reducing recidivism. With the vast amount of literature supporting this notion, policymakers should question why millions of dollars continue to be spent to build new boot-camp facilities. Such programs have yet to prove they decrease juvenile recidivism. Indeed, at times, they have deleterious effects on adolescents.

Suggestions for Future Research

Outcome studies would provide a more thorough understanding of the lasting effects of boot camp placement on subsequent offending. Future research would do well to focus on which aspects of existing boot-camp programs are working and which are not. Some beneficial results may be found by adjudicating only those adolescents who have committed nonviolent crimes to boot-camp facilities. In some instances, academic achievement increases among those who participate in boot camps. However, there are no studies examining the psychological well-being of the children when they enter as opposed to when they leave the program. Future research should focus on the impact of boot camps that incorporate treatment and aftercare versus those with a discipline and structure focus only. Additionally, research needs to explore potential program development including a family and community reunification component so that situations such as Johnny's can be better addressed. Continued investigation into the short-term versus long-term effects of military style residential treatment programs on adolescents' attitudes, behavior, as well as social and emotional functioning is recommended. Weis and Toolis (2008) suggest future directions for research to include the use of voluntary boot-camp programs for adolescent boys and girls with budding conduct problems.

Suicide Among Incarcerated Juveniles

Introduction

Suicide claims the lives of thousands of adolescents each year. Currently, suicide is the third leading cause of death among youths. Moreover, it is important to note that for every adolescent who completes suicide, hundreds of others attempt it. Among the youths at high risk for suicide are those who are incarcerated. The isolation, despair, guilt, and hopelessness felt by many incarcerated juveniles is portrayed through suicidal ideation, nonfatal self-injurious (parasuicidal) behavior, and, ultimately, the desperate act of taking one's own life. The research and clinical intervention concerning life-threatening behavior among incarcerated juveniles is relatively sparse. The link between delinquency and suicide, as well as between incarceration and suicide, has been clearly documented in the literature. However, currently there are no concentrated efforts to address this issue in terms of prevention or intervention measures. The following cases illustrate the gravity of the situation, depicting both a male and female juvenile who resorted to suicide while incarcerated.

Within 1 year at Westchester County Jail in New York City, two juveniles committed suicide while incarcerated. Nancy Blumenthal was 17 years old when she hanged herself in her cell from her own bedsheet. She was being held in jail while she awaited trial for robbery charges. Her bail had been revoked. Nancy was placed on a suicide watch while she participated in a court-ordered psychiatric evaluation. Following the evaluation, she was placed in the psychiatric ward where she could be observed every 30 minutes. During the investigation of her suicide, it was discovered that Nancy had been taking the antidepressant Zoloft for 2 years prior to her incarceration. During her month in jail, however, she was taken off of the drug.

Ivan Figueroa was another 17-year-old who committed suicide in the same jail within 3 months of Nancy's death. Similarly to Nancy, Ivan hanged himself in his jail cell. He had been in jail for 4 days and was awaiting trial for rape and assault charges. When he was first arrested, he too was placed on a suicide watch. He was subsequently returned to the general inmate population and soon committed suicide (Anonymous, 1997).

Literature Review

Cases like Nancy's and Ivan's remind us that suicide among incarcerated juveniles exists, needs to be examined and, ultimately, prevented. Adolescent suicide in general has been a focal point of research over the past three decades. As a result of such close scrutiny, the mental health field is far better equipped to assess, treat, and prevent suicidal behavior than ever before. It appears, however, that examination of suicidal behavior occurring among incarcerated juveniles is a particular concern that has not received a great deal of research attention. Incarcerated adolescents have unique environmental, social, and interpersonal factors that render them especially susceptible to suicidal ideation and behavior. Yet, as the literature illustrates, this population has not been studied nor has it received the amount of clinical intervention for suicide as has the general adolescent population.

The alarming suicide rate among adolescents has resulted in considerable research regarding the incidence, prevalence, and causes of life-threatening behavior. According to the National Center for Health Statistics (1997), adolescent suicide had more than tripled compared to the prior three decades. Some studies incorporate individuals ages 15–24 in their investigations of adolescent suicide. Padgitt (1997) states that within this age group, there were approximately 10,000 reported teen suicides a year and estimates that there were between 100,000 and 200,000 adolescent suicide attempts annually. Further, others noted that every 78 seconds an adolescent attempts suicide and every 90 seconds one succeeds (National Center for Health Statistics, 1996). Delinquent juveniles are at a very high risk for suicide with death rates four times higher than in the general population (Plattner, The, Kraemer, Williams, Bauer, Kindler, Feucht, Friedrich, & Steiner, 2007). These researchers indicate that psychological risk factors for suicidal behavior in nonforensic adolescent populations are well defined, while those associated with suicidality in delinquent juveniles remain less clear. Research has repeatedly shown that boys are far more likely than girls to complete suicide; however, there is little gender difference in terms of suicidal thoughts.

Although there is extensive research regarding adolescent suicide, there is relatively limited research conducted on suicide among incarcerated adolescents (Evans, Albers, Macari, & Mason, 1996). Within the existing literature, there are conflicting results regarding the prevalence or frequency of suicide among confined juveniles. Some suggest that one reason for this may be due to the under-reporting of such occurrences by detention facility officials (Flaherty, 1983). Flaherty notes that it is a sensitive and embarrassing issue for officials to discuss, particularly when suicides occur within their facilities. Therefore, many results are skewed in the direction of underestimating the incidence rate.

A 1997 report on prison suicides by the British Prison Reform Trust found that while individuals aged 15 to 21 composed only 13% of the prison population, they represented 22% of all the suicide deaths (Ziedenberg & Schiraldi, 1998). In a more recent report (2004) report, Sickmund indicates that 16 of the 27 deaths of adolescents in custody in the 12 months prior to a 2004 census were due to suicide, Despite studies demonstrating considerable mental health treatment needs among adolescents in the juvenile justice system, much less is known about young offenders transferred to adult criminal court (Murrie, Henderson, Vincent,

Rockett, & Mundt, 2009). According to the study by Murrie *et al.* (2009), juveniles in adult prison reported higher rates of symptoms than did those in juvenile correctional facilities. Even as the mental health needs of youths in the juvenile justice system are becoming increasingly recognized, this study reveals that mental health treatment needs appear to be even more evident in the relatively small subgroup of adolescents transferred to the adult criminal justice system and incarcerated in adult prison.

A distinction needs to be made between completed suicide and parasuicide. Completed suicide refers to the suicidal act resulting in an individual's death, whereas parasuicide refers to nonfatal intentional self-harm. Research has shown that younger inmates are more vulnerable to parasuicide (Ivanoff, Jang, & Smyth, 1996). Others suggest that an increase in the incidence of parasuicide among younger inmates may be attributed to impulsivity (Brown, Linnoila, & Goodwin, 1992). One study reported that in a sample of 11,000 juveniles in detention facilities, 18,000 acts of attempted suicide, suicidal gestures, or self-mutilation occurred within the institution.

Research that examined 81 adolescents (aged 13−16) in a short-term juvenile facility and a matched group of 81 adolescent psychiatric inpatients compared the correlates of suicide risk between these two high risk groups (Sanislow, Grilo, Fehon, Dwain, Axelrod, McGlashan, 2003). The adolescents in both groups reported similar levels of distress on measures of suicide risk, depression, impulsivity, and drug abuse. After controlling for depression, impulsivity and drug abuse remained significantly associated with suicide risk for the juvenile detention group only (2003).

Previous research has linked delinquency to physical and sexual abuse (Albers & Evans, 1994; de Wilde, Kienhorst, Diekstra, & Wolters, 1992; Kenny, Lennings, & Munn 2008). More specifically, studies have reported that incarcerated juveniles are at an increased risk for suicide due to their high incidence of substance abuse as well as physical and sexual abuse (Battle, Battle, & Tolley, 1993; Chapman & Ford, 2008). In a study conducted by Evans *et al.* (1996), no difference was found between gang and nongang members in terms of reported physical abuse; however, nongang members reported higher levels of suicidal ideation. In this same study, gang members who had a history of sexual abuse had higher levels of suicidal ideation than their nongang counterparts.

Contrary to the previously mentioned research, results have emerged which conclude that incarcerated juveniles are at less risk for suicide. Flaherty (1983) reported that youths in juvenile detention facilities committed suicide at a lower rate than adolescents in the general population. Kenny, Lennings, and Munn (2008) indicate that an adolescent's risk for suicide may increase or decrease upon entering custody depending on their perception. For those who view detention as being therapeutic, suicide risk may be reduced as their psychological distress is lessened. For those who experience humiliation and confinement, there may be an increase in suicidal or self-injurious behavior. However, this study also reported that juveniles detained in adult jails were at a far greater risk for completing suicide. Flaherty found that 17 of the 21 suicides were committed by youths who were held in adult jails in complete isolation. This was clearly the situation in the case illustration of Kathy Robbins. As demonstrated by this section's case examples, the most common means of committing suicide among incarcerated juveniles is hanging.

A recent study examined the lifetime history of suicide attempts in incarcerated youths (n = 289 adolescents) and psychological factors related to suicidal and self-mutilative behaviors during incarceration (Penn, Esposito, Schaeffer, Fritz, & Spirito, 2003). Of the 289 adolescents, 12.4% reported a prior suicide attempt and 60% of the attempts were made using violent methods. The results of the study suggested that incarcerated juveniles have higher rates of suicide attempts with more violent methods than juveniles in the general population (Penn *et al.*, 2003).

Several characteristics distinguish young offender suicides from the general population of inmate suicides. A study by Liebling (1993) revealed that youthful inmates were more likely to commit suicide after their conviction, but prior to their sentencing. Most suicides among the young inmates occurred during the first month of custody. Additionally, Liebling concluded that young inmates who committed suicide were less likely to have ever received psychiatric treatment.

Previous research found that Caucasian delinquents made more serious and lethal suicide attempts than African American delinquents or delinquents of mixed ethnicity (Alessi, McManus, Brickman, & Grapentine, 1984). Alessi *et al.* further reported that offenders diagnosed with serious mood disorders (e.g., depression or bipolar disorder) or borderline personality disorder (a pervasive pattern of instability in interpersonal relationships, self-image, emotions, and marked impulsivity) (APA, 2000) attempted suicide at a much greater rate. These results are consistent with suicidal behavior among individuals suffering from these disorders in the general population. Wool and Dooley (1987) reported the explanations given by younger inmates who attempted suicide while in custody. The most frequent explanations included the following: a close relationship was threatened; a visit did not take place; and the prison environment was intolerable. When these adolescent needs are not fulfilled, many youths enter a state of emotional crisis. Sometimes this manifests itself as a cry for help or self-injury, other times the child literally escapes from the crisis through the desperate act of suicide.

Forensic Psychology and Policy Implications

Juvenile suicide is a tragic end to a young life. Psychologists have studied the predictors and the reasons for suicide for many years. Specific studies have been conducted on adolescent suicide and how it differs from its adult counterpart, as well as on subgroups of adolescents who are at a greater risk for suicide. The research clearly draws a link between delinquency and suicide as well as incarceration and suicide. It should be of no surprise that a combination of delinquency and incarceration places a youth at high risk for suicidal ideation and behavior. In the case of Nancy and Ivan, two suicides committed within three months of one another should alert correctional facilities, mental health agencies, and the public to the severity of suicidal behavior among incarcerated juveniles.

Within the field of psychology there is an increased awareness of suicide prevention strategies and an ability to implement crisis intervention with suicidal individuals. If incarcerated youths are at such a high risk for suicide, why is little being done to prevent such occurrences? Relying on the results of empirical studies, we find that specific youths can be identified who are particularly vulnerable. We also know that adolescents who commit suicide while incarcerated often do so within the first month of custody. Thus, in order to provide the necessary preventive measures, these individuals need to be identified and given counseling and crisis intervention as soon as they arrive in custody. Some authors advocate for the use of multiple assessment and triage approaches utilizing the suicide risk factors identified for this population and for interventions targeting psychological distress and the abuse the adolescents may have endured in the past. When dealing with a human life and, in particular, a young vulnerable life, the focus must be on addressing the problem of suicidality before it occurs. Society places a strong emphasis on research and intervention with suicidal individuals, yet virtually ignores the issue of suicide among incarcerated adolescents. This suggests that some believe that the lost life of an incarcerated youth does not equal that of a nonincarcerated youth. As long as this bias exists, so too will the problem of suicide among incarcerated adolescents. Within the field of suicide risk assessment, some authors such as Stathis *et al.* (2008) recommend the development of **validated instruments** (psychological tests that have been determined through research to measure what they are supposed to measure) to aid in the detection and treatment of suicide risk among incarcerated adolescents as well as the development of national guidelines for the assessment of suicide risk in this population.

A study conducted by Penn, Esposito, Stein, Lacher-Katz, and Spirito (2005) measured juvenile correctional officers' knowledge and attitudes regarding suicide risk factors and mental health and substance abuse issues through administration of the Mental Health Knowledge and Attitude Test (MHKAT) before and after a staff training on suicide prevention. These officers exhibited marked improvement in their awareness of and need for mental health treatment of incarcerated juveniles. Findings suggest that correctional staff are open to increasing knowledge of critical mental health issues and these are the individuals who are in the best position to observe early warning signs in those youth who pose the highest risk of suicide. Moreover, the frequency of their interactions with the incarcerated juveniles provide many opportunities for intervention and prevention.

Suggestions for Future Research

Over the past three decades, research on adolescent suicide in the general population has expanded; however, relatively scant research exists which examines suicidal ideation and behavior among incarcerated adolescents. Suicide prevention programs need to be designed and implemented in juvenile detention facilities. Moreover, these programs need to be empirically studied (based on or characterized by observation and experiment instead of theory alone) in order to determine the proper method of identifying those individuals in need, as well as the location and time for the prevention program to be most beneficial. Chapman and Ford (2008) have found some preliminary evidence for the inclusion of brief measures of psychological trauma and traumatic stress symptoms in the assessment of suicide risk among **adjudicated** (under a court's jurisdiction usually as a result of having engaged in delinquent behavior) adolescents. Other authors (Stathis *et al.*, 2008), however, point out that since many chronic risk factors for suicide are so common among incarcerated adolescents, some other factors such as the adolescent's current mental state and the presence of risk and **protective factors** (issues that lessen suicide risk) may be deserving of further research. Incarcerated settings for juveniles that have crisis intervention and regular psychological services need to be compared with those that do not offer such assistance.

As Kenny, Lennings, and Munn (2008) suggest, the detention environment itself should also be studied to determine what elements are associated with self-harm and suicide. The direction of future research should also include correctional staff knowledge, attitudes, and perceptions about incarcerated juveniles' mental health needs, including suicide prevention in correctional settings. As more facilities incorporate this type of training and programming, studies of the retention, implementation, and maintenance of this new knowledge and practice by direct care staff over time and the best possible type and frequency of new staff training and continuing education are indicated (Penn *et al.*, 2005). Finally, studying the similarities and differences among adolescents who attempt or commit suicide within an incarceration facility with those who engage in suicidal behavior in the community, would help provide a more thorough understanding of what treatment needs best serve this vulnerable population.

Practice Update Section: Issues in Juvenile Corrections

Early intervention and prevention is clearly the best approach for reducing juvenile crime from status offenses to capital murder. However, forensic/correctional psychologists are being asked to evaluate and treat increasingly violent and mentally ill juveniles. More often than not, these adolescents have slipped through the cracks or the services indicated were just not available. In general, adolescents in the juvenile court system do not have an enforceable right to treatment and are only entitled to whatever services are available in their jurisdiction (Haller, 2000). Frequently, psychologists are asked to evaluate a juvenile and make recommendations regarding their disposition to their caseworker, probation officer, and/or other participants in the juvenile court system. Clinicians are encouraged by referring agencies to be realistic in their recommendations based on what services can be obtained in the community. With little money or resources being provided for intervention, or mental health programs, for delinquent or troubled youth, the options are often limited. Unfortunately, what is offered often falls short of what is recommended. There is a growing need for mental health services that involve not only the adolescents, but their families and community resources as well. The Department of Justice, Office of Juvenile Justice and Delinquency Prevention has identified additional research on the prevalence of mental disorders in juvenile offenders, the development of mental health screening assessment protocols, and improved mental health services, as the three main factors in addressing the mental health needs of delinquent youth (Thomas & Penn, 2002).

The mentally ill and often dually diagnosed juvenile offenders present unique issues for follow-up. More often than not, symptoms of mental illness in children and adolescents will manifest behaviorally, as compared to their adult counterparts. For example, depression in children and adolescents is frequently exhibited through irritability and anger, rather than the depressed mood more typically associated with depression in adults (American Psychiatric Association, 2000). Additionally, there are a number of behavioral disorders associated with childhood and adolescence. Juveniles who act out as a result of emotional disturbance may be charged with status offenses for running away, truancy, or more serious charges, based on their actions. Psychologists may be asked to evaluate juveniles whose crimes are a cry for help, as a result of emotional and family problems. Suicide and parasuicidal behaviors are a serious concern in jail and prison settings, particularly with juveniles. Psychologists are typically involved in the screening, prevention, and assessment of risk for these behaviors. When juvenile offenders are incarcerated in adult jails or prisons, the screening and follow-up on these issues are even more critical. In addition to other factors, juvenile offenders are at a far greater risk for being sexually assaulted or other types of violent victimization. The Juvenile Suicide Assessment (JSA) is an instrument for the assessment and management of suicide risk with incarcerated juveniles. This instrument can help mental health professionals identify both factors that increase and decrease an incarcerated juvenile's risk for suicide (Gallousis & Francek, 2002).

There are a growing number violent crimes perpetrated by juveniles, where a complete lack of empathy for victims, remorse, or responsibility for one's own actions is apparent. This is a disturbing trend that will create an ever-increasing demand for adolescent violence risk assessments. A number of highly publicized school shootings and the D.C. sniper case have demonstrated the devastation that an extremely violent youth can create. Unfortunately, most juvenile offenders suffer the gravest of consequences for their exceedingly rare, more psychopathic behavior, not unlike their adult counterparts who also engage in this type of extreme and lethal violence.

International Issues

Human Trafficking

Human trafficking is a growing phenomenon in which children and women are being imported into or exported out of the U.S. for the purpose of sexual exploitation. Though not all acts of human trafficking are for the purpose of sexual exploitation, the majority of them are. In a study by Hodge (2008) it was found that of the people trafficked into the U.S., 50% are children. Additionally, 70% of these are females who have been sexually exploited. To understand the phenomenon of human trafficking, it is important to know what it is, whom it affects, and how it affects society. Human trafficking for the purpose of sexual exploitation is a growing trend, and police officers as well as those in the mental health professions should become familiar with its impact on the criminal justice system.

Human Trafficking as defined in the United States is "the recruitment, harboring, transportation provision, or obtaining of a person for the purposes of a commercial sex act" (P.L. 106-386: § 103 (9)).

The definition of a **commercial sex act** according to the U.S. government is "any sexual act in which anything of value is given or received by any person (P.L. 106-386: § 103 (3) as cited in Hodge, 2008, p. 144). In an article by Kureshi (2007), human trafficking is defined similarly as "the recruitment or transportation of persons for work by using threats of violence, deception or debt bondage" (p. 26). Human trafficking for the purpose of sexual exploitation is the third largest known source of revenue for organized crime; narcotics and arms trafficking are the largest (Hodge, 2008). Internationally, human trafficking is one of the fastest growing criminal trades and it affects women and children, as well as their families.

Women and children who find themselves victims of the sex trade industry are often sold for prostitution, pornography, or other types of sexually dominated crimes. Research indicates that these individuals have increased rates of PTSD, depression, and dissociative disorders, making these individuals victims as well as offenders (Farley & Briscoe-Smith, 2010). The U.S. Department of Justice discusses the problems encountered by law enforcement officials when they arrest a prostitute only to find that she is part of a bigger network. Finding evidence of trafficking is a first step in apprehending the bigger network of offenders that are taking part in organized crime (Newman, 2006). Gathering the evidence and the inclusion of all local and federal agencies is the key to ending this type of crime. Human trafficking and its international reach as a criminal enterprise, results in extremely detrimental effects to society.

Hodge (2008) indicates that human trafficking is a "transnational phenomenon...each year some 600,000 to 800,000 people are trafficked across international borders" with about 14,500—17,500 of these winding up in the United States (p. 144). It is estimated by the United Nations that some 4 million people disappear as a result of human trafficking and nearly 70% are trafficked into the sex trade (Kureshi, 2007). When you consider how many children go missing and the estimated numbers above, it is astounding. Internationally, children are often abducted and sold to traffickers; others are sold by family members or friends (Kureshi, 2007). Organized crime can play a critical role in brokering those who work in the sex trade industry. Human trafficking is not often carried out by one individual (although this does still exist); it requires a network of individuals to facilitate such a business. Hodge (2008) indicates that with the rise in human trafficking, the level of organization has increased. Once thought to be loosely organized groups, these individuals have become a complex and organized network. This network consists of recruiters, transporters, and pimps. With such specialized and organized networks, the effect this has had on society is substantial. The prevalence of human trafficking and its impact on victims and society, it is easy to understand why more resources have been designated to this area of crime. The need for psychologists who can address the unique trauma experienced by victims is clear.

Evolution of Juvenile Justice

At one time the United States was the only country that "officially sanctioned the execution of juveniles" (Petrilia, 2009, p. 369). With the increase in incidents of violent juvenile offending, many of our Western European countries have joined the U.S. in imposing stiffer penalties for juvenile offending. With this in mind, there has been an increase in alternative punishment taking the form of rehabilitation for this group of offenders. Many countries, such as Germany, the Netherlands, England, Sweden, Italy, and more have experienced an increase in violent juvenile crime. This has led to the implication of policies and guidelines with the idea of stiffer punishment and rehabilitation, without the death penalty as a form of punishment. According to Petrilia (2009), these standards include the United Nations Standard Minimum Rules for the Administration of Juvenile Justice, United Nations Standard Minimum Rules for Non-Custodial Measures, and the United Nations Rules for the Protection of Juveniles Deprived of Their Liberty, which prohibit using the death penalty as a means of punishment for children younger than 18.

■

Related Websites

www.deathpenaltyinfo.org/
Death Penalty Information Center.
www.campaignforyouthjustice.org/documents/November2007Newslettersent.pdf
The Campaign for Youth Justice is a national campaign dedicated to ending the practice of trying, sentencing and incarcerating youth under the age of 18 in the adult criminal justice system.
www.nccd-crc.org/nccd/pubs/2006may_factsheet_youthadult.pdf
Views from the National Council on Crime and Delinquency — Youth Under Age 18 in the Adult Criminal Justice System.
www.nasro.org/mc/page.do?sitePageId=123707&orgId=naasro
This website is the National Association of School Resource Officers. On this site you can view handouts that the attendees received at the 2011 conference. www.schoolsecurity.org/resources/nasro_survey_2004.html

Continued

Related Websites—cont'd

This site is the National Association of School Resource Officers. On this site you can view links to all the various training and duties that an SRO officer goes through, as well as view surveys taken by the officers to assess how the program is doing.

www.nationalgangcenter.gov

Website providing information and reports from academic and government sources regarding juvenile gangs.

www.ncgangcops.org/gangs.html

North Carolina Gang Investigators Association website; provides information and photos on several known gangs.

www.bjs.ojp.usdoj.gov

This website provides guidelines, practice manuals for professionals, and statistics related to prostitution and sex crimes.

PART III

Family Forensics

Court and the Legal System: Criminal Forensics

Key Issues

Family Violence: Homicide
- Discuss the characteristics of families in which family violence occurs
  - What factors place families at higher risk
- Characteristics of family violence offenders
  - Who is more likely to engage in this behavior
- The nature of the offense itself

Maternal Filicide: Mothers who Kill their Children
- Brief overview of the categories of motives for mothers who kill their children
  - Define categories of child homicide
  - The role of mental illness
  - How the legal system responds
- Characteristics of these mothers who kill their children
- Difficulties encountered in their treatment
  - Confronting grief and symptoms
- Preparing and coping with society's reaction
- Coming to terms with religious beliefs and past delusions

Domestic Violence
- Discuss predominant patterns of abusers and their families of origin
- The nature and prevalence of intimate-partner violence
  - Gender, racial, and other demographic issues
  - The impact on victims
  - How psychology plays a role in intervention and prevention

Family Violence and the Cycle of Crime
- The long-term effects of family violence
  - Discuss the impact on children
  - Risk and protective factors for repeating the cycle
- How to help children raised in these homes

CHAPTER 9

Violence in the Family

Chapter Outline

Overview

Violence within the family also presents a multitude of difficult issues within the mental health and court systems. This chapter explores how trauma and violence affect the behavior of family members, and how the courts respond to such abuse. Domestic violence, particularly when physical, sexual, and emotional battering is involved, can be extremely painful for families. How does domestic violence impact couples, their children, and the family unit? Are there patterns to abuse in domestic violence cases? If so, can such patterns be traceable to one's family of origin? What is the role of the forensic psychologist in the area of domestic violence?

Introduction to Forensic Psychology. DOI: 10.1016/B978-0-12-382169-0.00009-8

There are four controversies investigated in this chapter. These topics include: (1) family violence: homicide; (2) maternal filicide; (3) domestic violence; and (4) family trauma and the cycle of crime. Certainly, many other contested subjects exist in the legal domain of family forensics; however, these four issues represent key areas of considerable debate within the law and psychology communities. The devastating effects of family violence and the difficulties faced by law enforcement and mental health professionals in this arena are explored.

What prevention strategies, as developed in forensic psychology, exist to help break the intergenerational cycle of abuse or understand its consequences? People are at a greater risk to be victimized by a family member than by a stranger. Several manifestations of family violence include infanticide (killing of a child less than one year but more than one day), parricide (killing of one's parent), and spousal abuse. What are the causal factors leading to these (and other) forms of family violence? How can law and psychology help us understand the phenomenon of family homicide? The field of mental health law affects the behavior and rights of individuals in families.

As the sections of this chapter demonstrate, there is an important role for forensic psychologists in adult criminal court arenas, particularly when difficult issues such as a mother killing her children or a history of trauma are central to the legal proceedings and are difficult to comprehend. The domain of forensic psychology examines those situations where questions persist about the behavior, attitudes, and beliefs of parents and/or children in the family context. Some of these concerns are extremely serious, in that immediate trauma, abuse, violence, and even life are at stake.

Family Violence: Homicide

Introduction

When most people think of violence, they think of an innocent victim being attacked by a total stranger. The media exacerbates these fears by depicting the perpetrator as an unknown, unidentifiable psychopath that sneaks around hunting for prey. An obvious means of avoiding contact with such a person is to stay away from the "bad" neighborhoods where such crimes are more likely to occur. The safest place appears to be the confines of your own home, behind locked doors and set alarms. The reality, though, is that the risk of dying at the hands of an acquaintance or family member far exceeds the threat of being killed by a complete stranger.

Familial violence, more specifically **familial homicide**, is much more common than most people would like to believe. This section explores the various forms of familial homicide such as intimate partner murder (e.g., femicide), **parricide** (killing of one's parent), and the causal factors that lead to such incidents. **Filicide** (the killing of one's child), specifically **maternal filicide**, will be discussed in greater detail in the next section.

According to the (2005) **Bureau of Justice Statistics** report focusing on murders within families, 22% of all murders committed in 2002 were committed against family members, which is a 6% increase from 1988. The breakdown of these findings indicated that 9% of the victims were murdered by their spouses, 6% by parents, and 7% were murders by other family members. Between 1993 and 2002, family murder accounted for about 1% of crimes involving family violence. During this same time, children under the age of 13, who were killed by a parent, totaled about 23% of murder victims by a family member (U.S. Bureau of Justice, 2005). The following vignette is an illustration of family violence.

After an exhausting day of caring for the children, cleaning the house, and working at her part-time job, Carla was laying down for a quick nap. Sleeping a bit longer than expected, Carla was late preparing dinner. When her husband Charlie came home, he was infuriated by her tardiness, laziness, and insensitivity to his needs. He had just lost a big contract at work and did not appreciate her lack of consideration. Feeling it his obligation to set her straight, which he had continually done in the past, Charlie picked up a pot of boiling water from the stove and threw it in Carla's face. Screaming for help, Carla charged toward the door where Charlie proceeded to hit her over the head with the pot. Carla died 3 days later from a subdural hematoma.

Also consider the high profile case of Mary Winkler:

Mary Winkler alleged she suffered years of physical and emotional abuse, including sexual degradation, at the hands of her husband. On 22 March 2006 in a small Tennessee town, Mary shot her husband in the back with a 12-gauge shotgun killing him and then fled with her three daughters. Mathew Winkler was a pastor at the Church of Christ and, according to Mary, he spent years punching, pinching, and shoving her. Mary reported that she was forced to dress up like a prostitute and have sex with her husband, while he was humiliating and demeaning her. She also alleged that Mathew would beat their children with a belt and she was becoming increasingly concerned about her children's welfare. According to Mary's statement to the police, she and her husband had been arguing throughout the evening about several things, including family finances. She admitted some of the problems were her fault.

Mary Winkler had lost money in what was characterized by her lawyers as a scam. Winkler had become involved in the "Nigerian scam," which promises a great deal of money to victims who send money to cover the processing expenses. She had deposited checks that came from "unidentified sources" in Canada and Nigeria into bank accounts belonging to her and her husband. The checks amounted to more than $17,000. Mary reported that her husband's treatment of her had become increasingly belittling and she described snapping on the night of the murder.

Prosecutors charged Mary with first degree murder. The jury believed Mary when she told her story of terror and the years of abuse she endured at the hands of her husband. They found her guilty of voluntary manslaughter, a lesser crime. Mary was sentenced to 210 days. Mary then served her remaining time (67 days after time served in jail credited) in a mental health facility receiving treatment for PTSD and depression. She was put on probation for the rest of her sentence. In August 2008, Winkler was granted full custody of her three daughters and lives as a free woman. There was considerable debate surrounding this case regarding the blurred lines between victim(s) and perpetrator(s).

Literature Review

Domestic homicides are one of the most common forms of familial violence. According to the **Presidential Task Force on Violence in the Family**, in 1996 as many as 1300 battered women were killed by their abusers (Ewing, 1997). Forty percent of all homicides in the United States are the result of domestic violence (Browne & Herbert, 1997). The U.S. Bureau of Justice Statistics (2002) indicated that the number of women killed by intimate partners was stable for two decades, declined from 1993 through 1995, and then remained stable through 2000. "Femicide, or the homicide of women, is the leading cause of death in the United States among young African American women aged 15 to 45 years, and the seventh leading cause of premature death among women overall" (Campbell *et al.*, 2003, p.1089). Intimate partner homicides are responsible for approximately 40% of femicides in the United States but only for a small percentage of male homicides (5.9%). Finally, the majority (67% to 80%) of intimate partner homicides include the physical abuse of the female by the male prior to the murder, no matter if it is the male or the female partner that is killed (Campbell *et al.*, 2003).

Campbell *et al.* (2003) stress the importance of identifying and intervening with at-risk battered women as a critical way to decrease intimate partner homicide.

Domestic violence is nothing new to society but has gained public attention due to the shift in opinions regarding domestic relations. It should be noted that either gender can be the aggressor in intimate partner violence in either heterosexual or homosexual relationships. In historical context, women were seen as the property of their husbands and, therefore, occasional beatings for their disobedience were expected. Rarely, if ever, were men charged with a crime for beating or killing their wives. Even with the increased awareness of domestic violence, many women were left legally powerless and vulnerable to the abuse. While domestic violence crosses gender lines, research has demonstrated that women are abused by intimate male partners more frequently than any other type of family violence, and that this abuse crosses all racial, ethnic, religious, and age groups (Leonard, 2000). Women who sought the protection of law enforcement found themselves beating against closed doors or, if they were helped, it was only with the granting of a restraining order. In reality, though, a piece of paper will not be effective when an angered spouse has a mission (Snow, 1997). In all fairness, the elevated number of domestic violence cases is not entirely due to shortcomings within a faulty system. At times, the victims in domestic violence cases refuse to press charges against their abusers, given the ramifications they face once the assailant is released and a myriad of other potential consequences. Because of the way our legal system is structured, a person is rarely detained for attempted murder if he simply makes threats. If the victim presses charges, the perpetrator will experience at most a night or two in jail, which will more than likely enrage him even more.

Research has consistently found that there is an elevated risk of intimate partner homicide for women who have separated or left the relationship versus those who remain (Johnson & Hotton, 2003). An 11 city study that examined the risk factors for femicide in abusive relationships found that preincident risk factors associated with increased risk of intimate partner femicide included the perpetrator's access to a gun and previous threat with a weapon, perpetrator's stepchild in the home, and estrangement, particularly from a controlling partner (Campbell *et al.*, 2003). If the perpetrator has access to a gun, the risk for homicide increases. According to the Bureau of Justice Statistics (2010), 678 women who were victims of intimate partner homicide were killed by the use of a gun during the commission of the crime in 2005. Farr (2002) found that women who had survived an attempted domestic homicide shared patterns in their experiences. For example, the year prior to the attack was typically fraught with a build-up in tension from on-going contact with an angry, controlling batterer. Generally, the batterer was an alcoholic or drug addict, a gun owner, and was actively engaging in stalking the victim if the couple was estranged (Farr, 2002). The vast majority of the women had either left or announced to the perpetrator that she was leaving him. Most of the women felt afraid of the perpetrator but prior to the incident did not believe that he was capable of killing her. These women were often left feeling isolated and alone after the attacks and in need of mental health services (Farr, 2002).

In recent times, shelters and special interest groups have been organized to help women and men in battering relationships. It is suspected that the number of male victims is underestimated due to under-reporting the abuse. Unfortunately, as the number of shelters has increased, so too have the number of domestic homicides. Once the perpetrator targets his victim, there is little that law enforcement is able to do to prevent the crime from eventually occurring (Snow, 1997).

Considering the lack of effective support available for victims of domestic abuse, the victims themselves have begun to take matters into their own hands. Although husbands are more likely to be the perpetrators in domestic homicides, wives commit a portion of these murders. From 1976 to 2005, about one-third of female murder victims were killed by an intimate, while approximately 3% of male murder victims were killed by an intimate, which has dropped 1% since 2000 (U.S. Bureau of Statistics, 2010). Although less common, women also perpetrate domestic violence. In a study examining the treatment needs of females arrested for domestic violence, female offenders were noted to be demographically similar and few differences were noted in their childhood experiences (Henning, Jones, & Holdford, 2003). However, women were more likely to have previously attempted suicide; whereas a greater proportion of the men had conduct problems as children and substance abuse problems as adults (Henning *et al.*, 2003).

The fate of women who kill their abusive husbands has become the topic of many debates in recent years. Some would consider these women to be acting in self-defense, while others would argue that there are other avenues that battered women should take. In terms of Carla, the woman in the vignette presented above, if she had grabbed a knife to protect herself prior to Charlie reaching for the pot of water, and Charlie died as a result of his wounds, should she be charged with and convicted of murder?

In situations such as this, women have tried a variety of strategies for defending their fate during trial. Some have plcd insanity, self-defense, guilt, and **battered woman's syndrome**. It has been hypothesized that women who are the constant recipients of physical and verbal abuse by their spouses suffer from a mental disorder known as battered woman's syndrome. Several expert psychologists and psychiatrists have defended this theory. Their testimony enables jurors to "understand why the women endured such allegedly serious abuse for so long, why they did not leave their abuser, and why they felt it was necessary to use deadly force at a time when she was not being battered" (Ewing, 1997, p. 34). Of course, those women who have killed their abusers at the time of their abuse are more likely to find success in a self-defense plea as opposed to women who kill while not in immediate danger. Although battered woman's syndrome is becoming increasingly popular in the mental health arena, it has yet to receive substantial support in the courtroom.

In the case of *People v. Aris* (1989), Dr. Lenore Walker, a clinical and forensic psychologist, testified in Ms. Aris' defense on the premise of the battered woman's syndrome. The jury found Ms. Aris guilty because her husband was sleeping at the time of the offense and therefore her actions could not be considered self-defense (*People v. Aris*, 1989). There is no consistency in the sentencing of these women and verdicts depend largely on the jury of each particular case and the differences from crime to crime. Currently, few women are acquitted based upon battered woman's syndrome.

Just as it is disturbing to think of a mother killing her own child, which will be explored in the next section of this chapter, it is difficult to fathom a child killing the parent(s) who gave him or her life. Nevertheless, parricide, the killing of one's parent(s), is more common than one would expect. Parricide was highly publicized by the Menendez trial in Southern California where Eric and Lyle Menendez were charged with killing their wealthy parents for the purpose of receiving their inheritances. The defense team claimed that the boys killed their parents in an act of self-defense, given the continual abuse they received from their father. Nevertheless, after much debate, the boys were charged with the murders, but spared from the death penalty.

Similar to battered women, some children kill their parent(s) because of a history of abuse suffered by them, or witnessed toward the other parent. Further, some youths kill in self-defense during an episode of their abuse; others kill on random occasions as a result of their continual abuse. In terms of Carla, the scenario may have had a different conclusion had her son entered the kitchen and witnessed his father beating his mother as described. Out of fear and anger, the son could have run into his parents' room, grabbed the loaded gun from his father's nightstand, and returned to the kitchen to shoot and kill his father. Heide (1992) claims that "these children, typically adolescents, were psychologically abused by one or both parents and often witnessed or suffered physical, sexual, and verbal abuse as well" (p. 3).

Baxter, Duggan, Larkin, *et al.* (2001) compared those individuals committed to high security care who committed parricide and those who killed strangers. These researchers found that those who committed parricides were more likely to suffer from schizophrenia but less likely to have had a disrupted childhood and criminal history than those individuals who committed stranger homicide. The individuals in the parricide group had made a previous attack on their victim in 40% of cases (Baxter *et al.*, 2001).

Other factors associated with parricide are mental illness, antisocial personalities, and greed. These can be sole factors but are most likely exhibited as combinations. Greed is rarely found to be a full explanation for why children commit parricide, although some cases have been reported. Children whose immediate motivation for killing their parents is greed will most likely have evidence of antisocial characteristics, abusive pasts, or mental illness. In these instances, the child is usually convicted on terms associated with insanity. In those cases where greed was found to be the sole determinant for the murder, other determinants such as antisocial personality were most likely not effectively explored or not accepted by the jury (Ewing, 1997). This does not mean, however, that the children were not suffering from some sort of disorder in addition to greed.

Forensic Psychology and Policy Implications

A consistent theme throughout most of the above forms of familial homicide is the issue of abuse. For some, the killing of their abuser becomes the only means of protection from receiving further abuse. The legal system has provided little help for victims of abuse. Even if the victims are fortunate enough to receive legal intervention through documentation or incarceration of the abuser, the reality is that the system provides little to no protection once the abuser is released.

It is quite difficult to intervene or prevent an obsessed abuser from continuing to harm or from eventually killing their victim. Campbell *et al.* (2003) suggest more proactive measures such as increasing employment opportunities, preventing substance abuse, and restricting abusers' access to guns as ways to reduce the rates of intimate partner femicide, as well as the overall homicide rates. However, law enforcement should treat abuse as a priority. The fact that domestic violence calls are common and dangerous for law enforcement officers should not be a justification for not responding to calls. Instead, the increased number of domestic violence calls should indicate that a special domestic violence unit is needed to deal with this escalating problem. With the push of special interest groups advocating victims' rights, many police and sheriffs' departments have organized units to specifically combat this epidemic. In addition to a law enforcement response, the Austin Police Department dispatches a crisis unit comprised of mental health professionals that aid in interviewing and supporting family violence victims.

Child abuse has received a great deal of public attention because society currently views it as its responsibility to care for those who cannot care for themselves. Policies have been established so that fewer children will have to experience abuse from their parents. Programs exist, but they are so crowded and understaffed that too many children are "falling through the cracks." This partially explains why many homicides committed in this country are parricides. Psychopathic personalities and greed are also likely to blame in some of the most notorious cases like the Menendez brothers.

Being abused should not be a justification for killing someone. Much of the debate surrounding sentencing for these perpetrators has centered on this issue.

There are mixed feelings about how to punish someone who takes another's life but does so for the purpose of saving their own. If there were effective programs, community outlets, and judicial supports for victims of abuse, then murder would be less likely to be the end result. Currently, the mental health field provides support for the plea of self-defense in relation to abuse cases, but it has been faintly accepted by the judicial system.

Suggestions for Future Research

Research needs to be conducted so that more effective programs can be established in order to decrease the occurrence of abuse and possible murder. As it stands, programs are not necessarily the problem, but the lack of funding and inadequate staffing inhibits these programs from being as effective as they could be. Frequently, money is hard to raise when benefits are not immediate or apparent. Abuse intervention at crucial moments will help to decrease the number of familial homicides in that it will eliminate murders by abusers, as well as retaliations by the abused.

Many victims who kill their abusers are sentenced to prison terms similar to those of other violent offenders. They are placed in the same units as the other predatory offenders simply because their crime was murder. This can create many problems for the individual, as well as environmental problems within the prison. The individual whose crime was motivated by self-defense tends not to have the same predatory personality as other violent offenders, and therefore they may encounter unnecessary problems. With the increase of mental health care for inmates in the state of California, for example, special groups have been developed specifically for incarcerated individuals whose crimes involve issues of abuse (*Coleman v. Wilson*, 1995). More programs such as these need to be instituted on a national level, and further research needs to be conducted regarding the effects of incarceration on these individuals.

The impact of economic downturns on **familicide** (the murder of an entire family or several family members by a family member) should be further studied, as well as why fathers are much more likely to engage in this form of family annihilation. Additionally, while rare overall, there seems to be an increasing number of adolescents who kill their parent(s) or conspire to kill their parents for motives such as the misguided belief that this would allow them to continue with a forbidden relationship. What factors contribute to children with no prior history of violence and few overt risk factors to commit such an unspeakable act? While large samples of these offenders would be difficult to obtain, research including case study analysis could help to better inform both risk and mitigating factors to parricide. Without the proper understanding of these forms of familial homicide, and how they originate, the risk of more unnecessary deaths is inevitable.

Maternal Filicide: Mothers who Kill their Children

Introduction

It may seem paradoxical, but it is not vice that leads to the death of the infant, rather it is morbid and mistaken maternal solitude (Baker, 1902, p. 16).

This section will address **maternal filicide**, the phenomenon of a mother killing her child as a result of **postpartum** (period following childbirth) **depression** or **postpartum psychosis** (being out of touch with reality) or other forms of psychotic illness such as schizophrenia, delusional disorder, bipolar disorder, or as a result of severe depression. Discussion of prevalence, motives, and the disposition of offenders will be offered. Specifically, filicide resulting from severe mental illness will be explored by using the case example of Andrea Yates to illustrate how unidentified and untreated or undertreated mental illness can contribute to the occurrence of these tragic acts.

Maternal filicide is in direct contradiction to society's firmly held notion that all mothers instinctually and unconditually love, nurture, and protect their children. Women who kill their children as a result of acute psychosis do not generally kill for the motives typically associated with murder such as punishment, revenge, and secondary gain (the expected benefit of the criminal act). They often believe that they are being instructed by God or are in some way saving their children from unspeakable torment or disease and are driven by delusions (irrational beliefs despite all evidence to the contrary) and other perceptual disturbances. What are the legal implications for this type of crime? Whether or not these women belong in prison or a forensic psychiatric hospital and to what extent the media and public opinion influence their disposition will be examined. This section will discuss treatment implications for mental health professionals who will provide services to these women in a forensic setting (e.g., in jail or in a maximum-security forensic hospital). Women who kill their children due to psychosis often become very depressed and potentially suicidal after receiving psychiatric treatment in jail or a forensic hospital. Additionally, these women face unique issues such as grieving the loss of their children by their own hands, likely divorce, alienation from loved ones, and coming to terms with their mental illness under the harshest of circumstances. When their psychosis remits, these mothers are left asking, "How could I have done such a thing?" Consider the case of Andrea Yates:

On 20 June 2001, in Clearlake, Texas, Andrea Yates drowned all five of her children in the family bathtub after her husband Rusty left for work. Ms. Yates had a long-standing history of mental illness including four hospitalizations since 1999, two attempted suicides, and she had had an outpatient prescription for Haldol (an antipsychotic medication used to help control hallucinations and other symptoms of psychosis) (Gesalman, 2002; Manchester, 2003). She was suffering a severe postpartum psychosis with numerous delusions and hallucinations. She was an intelligent and gentle woman who by all accounts was a devoted mother who homeschooled her children and provided them with Bible studies. She had been pregnant or breastfeeding almost continually for the seven years prior to the murder of her children (Spinelli, 2004). In addition to caring for Noah (age seven), John (age five), Paul (age three), Luke (age two), and Mary (six months), she was also caring for her beloved father, who was slipping away due to Alzheimer's disease. She was caring for her frail mother and her newborn, mourning the loss of her father, and home schooling her elder three children all while suffering from postpartum psychosis (Oberman, 2003). She had a family history of diagnosed and treated bipolar disorder and major depression (O'Malley, 2004; Spinelli, 2004). Each time she gave birth, she experienced a postpartum depression and her mental illness worsened with each subsequent birth. Her first reported psychotic episode occurred after the birth of Noah in 1994. At the time, she refused to tell anyone of her experience because she had delusions that Satan would hear her and harm her children. With subsequent deliveries she became more depressed, psychotic, overwhelmed, and impaired. She attempted suicide on two occasions after her fourth birth because she was trying to resist demonic voices or command hallucinations instructing her to kill her infant (Spinelli, 2004).

Ms. Yates's treating psychiatrist discontinued her Haldol two weeks prior to the event, resulting in her becoming very psychotic. She reported that Satan commanded her to kill her children to save them from the fires and torment of hell. She had delusional beliefs that she was influenced by the devil and that she had irreversibly damaged her children and the only way to protect their innocence and ensure their entrance to heaven, was that she must kill them. It appears that everyone around her failed to appreciate the severity of her illness. Andrea Yates was charged with capital murder with a maximum possible penalty of death, which the prosecution aggressively sought. The jury returned after three and a half hours with a verdict of guilty. During the sentencing phase, it took the jury only 35 minutes to decide on a sentence of life in prison. During her first trial, the Texas jury rejected her insanity defense despite the overwhelming psychiatric evidence.

In January of 2005, after Andrea had already been incarcerated for four years with deteriorating mental health, a Texas appeals court overturned her conviction based on the misleading and prejudicial information provided by an expert witness for the prosecution. She was granted a new trial with a much different outcome. The second trial resulted in a Texas jury finding her Not Guilty by Reason of Insanity. As much new information has come to light regarding Ms. Yates's mental illness and its impact on her ability to appreciate the wrongfulness of her actions, there seems to have been an appreciable shift in public opinion. She was a woman in deep torment due to her illness and the loss of her children, who was in need of intensive psychiatric treatment and therapy, not the harshest of punishments handed down to the most violent of offenders.

Literature Review

Child murder is so tragic and evokes such a strong response from the media and our communities that the women who commit these heinous acts are often demonized with little understanding of their actual plight. Women who murder their children vary in their motives and a rush to judgment and punishment often further exacerbates a horrible tragedy. The killing of children by their parents is an almost unthinkable crime, particularly when the mother is the perpetrator. It is so antithetical to what it means to be mother, nurturing and the ultimate protector of her children. Another form of homicidal violence that occurs within the family is the killing of children by their parents. Fifty-seven percent of the murders of children under the age of 12 have been committed by the victims' parents with the average age being seven years old (Bureau of Justice Statistics, 2005; Dawson & Langan, 1994). According to the U.S. Bureau of Statistics (2002), out of all the children under age five who were murdered between 1976 and 2000, 31% were killed by fathers; 30% were killed by mothers; 23% were killed by male acquaintances; 7% were killed by other relatives; and 3% were killed by strangers. The Bureau of Justice Statistics (2005) suggests that 19% of parent—child murders involved only one parent committing multiple murders.

The statistics on adult murder show that male perpetrators and victims outnumber females by a ratio of 5:1 or 6:1 (Jason, 1983; Marks & Kumar, 1993; Stanton & Simpson, 2002). Men predominate as perpetrators of family homicides, involving both spouse and children (Liem & Koenraadt, 2008). When infants are killed within the first 24 hours, it is almost always by their mothers with equal number of male and female victims. For babies and children killed after one year, studies demonstrate that slightly more of the perpetrators are male or the numbers are almost even between male and females perpetrators and children are most frequently killed by one of their parents (Stanton & Simpson, 2002).

"**Filicide**" is often used as a generic term to describe the killing of children by their parents or step-parents and can include **neonaticide, infanticide, and filicide** (Stanton & Simpson, 2002). Dr. Philip Resnick, a forensic psychiatrist, was the first to categorize filicides based on the age of the child, when they were killed (1969, 1970). He categorized "neonaticide" as the killing of a child directly after birth or within the first 24 hours after birth. These perpetrators are typically young women who deny they're pregnant to themselves and others, and fear, not psychotic illness, motivates the crime (Oberman, 2003). Infanticide is the killing of a child up to one year old, by a parent who has not fully recovered from pregnancy and who typically suffers from some degree of mental disturbance often associated with postpartum mental illness (Bourget & Labelle, 1992). Filicide is the killing of a child older than one year and is very frequently associated with psychosis in the female perpetrator (Manchester, 2003). Filicide is often associated with mental illness in the parent and suicide. Although filicide is a form of homicide, rates of infanticide are more congruent with suicide rates rather than murder rates (Putkonen, Weizmann-Henelius, Lindberg, *et al.*, 2009).

Pitt and Bale (1995) highlighted the characteristic differences between parents who commit infanticide as opposed to neonaticide. The results indicated that mothers in the neonaticide group were significantly younger than the mothers in the infanticide or filicide groups. The mothers in the infanticide or filicide groups were more likely to suffer from depression or psychoses and have histories of attempted suicide. "Eighty-eight percent of the infanticide mothers were married, while 81% of the neonaticide mothers were unwed" (Pitt & Bale, 1995, p. 378). Resnick (1970) found that the mothers involved in neonaticide are younger, often unmarried, and less frequently psychotic than mothers who commit filicide. He indicated that most neonaticides are carried out because the child isn't wanted due to illegitimacy, rape, or social stigma, rather than altruistic reasons. "Studies have documented that neonaticide offenders are often single young women who deny the pregnancy and kill their newborn infants in an effort to avoid the social and parental pressure against an illegitimate child" (Manchester, 2003, p. 724).

Resnick's (1969) seminal work reviewed 131 (88 mothers, 43 fathers) child murder cases from the international literature from 1751 to 1967 and proposed a classification system for filicide. He devised five categories based on motives for murder. His categories are: (1) **altruistic filicide**; (2) **acutely psychotic filicide**; (3) **unwanted child filicide**; (4) **accidental filicide**; and (5) **spouse revenge filicide**. He also introduced or coined "**neonaticide**" as a separate phenomenon and operationally defined it at that time.

It is uncommon for women to kill their children as a result of coldhearted, callous disregard, revenge, or some other self-serving motive. It is far more common that maternal filicide results from severe mental illness. Sadoff (1995) indicated that there is little evidence that these mothers kill in a callous, calculated manner but rather as a result of depression, psychosis, or in a disassociative state, or state of fear or panic. Certainly, psychosis is more common when women kill children that are over one year of age (filicide) as compared to any other form of child murder. Resnick (1969) classified more than half the women in his study as "altruistic filicide" or murders committed out of love. In this view, the murder would be seen as a rational act in the context of the mother's delusional perception of the world. (p. 10). Resnick (1970) found that psychosis was the primary factor in two-thirds of the women in his sample that committed filicide. These women kill their children based on altruistic beliefs of being merciful or ending real or imagined (delusional) suffering. Andrea Yates has reported that she believed she was possessed and was a "Jezebel" and that her poor mothering threatened her children's ability to go to heaven. She saw only two choices: either kill her children while some innocence remained, therefore allowing them entrance in heaven, or continue to damage them and ensure their eternal damnation. In her delusional state, her love for her children and her belief that she was saving them from certain eternal suffering led her to follow through on the grotesque act of drowning all five of her children. Some severely depressed and suicidal mothers will murder their child in order to protect the child from the suffering associated with growing up motherless in a harsh, cruel world that will only cause them the same pain that she endured.

In some instances, women experiencing ongoing **grandiose delusions** and a strong religious background may believe that she is being commanded by God to kill her children as a testament to her faith and to ensure entrance into heaven for both herself and her children. She may, in her delusional state and within the context of her strong religious upbringing, believe that she should not only do God's bidding without questioning, but that she has done a good thing that is in the best interest of her child. Certainly, the story of Abraham being instructed by God to kill his son has been referenced and may even serve as a model for this type of delusional belief. Consider many evangelical religions that encourage speaking in tongues, being filled by the Holy Spirit, and directly communicating with God. While these religions are in no way responsible for the actions or mental illness of these women, the norms of the church may make her perceptual disturbances more difficult to identify. In each of the aforementioned examples, these women's beliefs are not reality based and are directly resulting from their mental illness. Little is understood about the tragic, tortured, and often very psychotic motives that underlie these deaths.

There are a variety of reasons why parents kill their children. Explanations range from postpartum depression, particularly postpartum psychosis and schizophrenia. Postpartum depression is a mental disorder that occurs with new mothers shortly after they give birth. According to the American Psychiatric Association's Diagnostic and Statistical Manual of Mental Disorders, Fourth Edition-Text Revision (DSM-IV-TR) (2000), the most severe form of postpartum depression, postpartum psychosis, often presents episodes of delusions in which the mother feels that the infant is possessed, or presents hallucinations that tell her to kill the child. Not all incidents of postpartum depression present delusions or hallucinations, but often there are suicidal ideations and obsessional thoughts of violence toward the child.

Whereas **the postpartum blues** are very common, only about 0.2% of childbearing women will experience postpartum psychosis, which typically emerges within two to four weeks after childbirth and frequently requires hospitalization (Sit, Rothschild, & Wisner, 2006; Dobson & Sales, 2000; Manchester, 2003).

Women with a family history or a genetic predisposition for a mental illness or a personal history of mental illness, a mood disorder in particular, are far more vulnerable to the flood of hormones associated with the postpartum period or the period after childbirth (Kim, Choi, & Ha, 2008; Glover & Kammerer, 2004; Payne, MacKinnon, Mondimore, *et al.*, 2008). Early screening, identification, and intervention with those women at risk or who are already experiencing symptoms is imperative.

In a study (n = 100) evaluating new mothers' experiences of intrusive thoughts of harm related to the newborn, Fairbrother and Woody (2008) found that postpartum intrusive thoughts of accidental harm to the infant were universal. Close to half of their sample reported unwanted thoughts of intentionally harming their infant. Accidental harm thoughts were more frequent and time consuming, but less distressing. Researchers found that high parenting stress and low social support were predictive of thoughts of intentional harm; however, there was little evidence that these thoughts typically translate to aggressive parenting (Fairbrother & Woody, 2008). The shocking and tragic consequences of the most severe instances of postpartum psychosis (maternal filicide) stand in stark contrast to the thoughts of accidental or intentional harm that never lead to actual harm to the child.

Forensic Psychology and Policy Implications

Stanton and Simpson (2006) explored recovery experiences derived from a semi-structured interview study of six women who committed filicide in the context of major mental illness. The women described incomplete but horrific memories they avoided thinking about. Intense self-hate and punishment feelings were common. Better understanding their mental illness and how it could have so completely impaired their thinking and judgment is critical in helping them to make some sense out of what has happened. Psychotic women who kill their children from motives such as saving or relieving their children from spiritual and other physical torture, suffering, and doom, or the belief that God instructed it are qualitatively much different from coldblooded murderers. Some argue that these women have lost their children and do not pose a significant threat to others as long as they are maintained on their medication and have a firm understanding of their mental illness and are committed to ongoing management of their mental illness. No measure of punishment such as extended incarceration or death will compare to the guilt they feel for what they have done. This way of thinking would not apply to the psychopathic killer who kills for personal or material gain or seemingly without a conscience. The psychopathic killer has only remorse for being caught and has no regard for the victim who has been objectified, murdered, and thrown away. The mentally ill maternal filicide offender who was devoted to her child does not demand the same type of justice as the quite different psychopathic or even revenge- or anger-motivated offenders.

Early identification of signs of depression and psychosis is imperative in the prevention of maternal filicide (Sharma, *et al.*, 2009). Preemptive action in these cases serves the best interest of the child and the mother. Identifying those women at risk, and providing early and appropriate treatment and ongoing management of the mental illness is critical. Education should be provided for mental health professionals, family members, general practitioners, emergency room doctors and nurses, pediatricians, obstetricians, police, child protective services personnel, members of the clergy, and social workers. A number of women who commit maternal filicide will come into contact with mental health professionals before the event, and the possibility of homicidal impulses or ideation should never be overlooked in depressed individuals, particularly mothers (Bourget & Labelle, 1992).

Many individuals do not trust mental health professionals and will balk at the idea of seeking mental health care. The contact with the medical personnel may be the solitary interface with a woman at high risk for maternal filicide. It is imperative that medical professionals are well aware of this literature and properly educate the women and families involved, as well as referring them to a mental health profession or seek immediate civil commitment if the mother is actually expressing homicidal impulses toward her children. The mother who is experiencing a major mental illness will likely have significant difficulty monitoring her parenting effectiveness and level of risk (Stanton *et al.*, 2000). Those in contact with at-risk women should not be lulled into believing that a mother's devotion to her children would automatically preclude her from harming her baby or child. According to Stanton *et al.*, 2000, "Evident devotion to the child and parenting is not likely to be a protective factor" (p. 1459).

The response of the courts to maternal filicide has a history of vacillating between leniency and retribution. What is the appropriate degree of culpability to attach to mentally ill mothers who kill their children for what they believe are altruistic reasons? The current response of society, the media, and the criminal justice system is typically quite punitive as demonstrated by the initial trial of Andrea Yates despite her well documented history of severe mental illness. Prosecutors sought the death penalty for Andrea Yates, although the jury rejected it. Community outrage and public opinion have a tremendous impact on jurors' verdicts and the severity of sentences. Finkel, Burke, and Chavez (2000) indicate that public opinion changes over time based on cultural, legal, moral, historical, and psychological trends, as well as the cogent influence of media saturation of high-profile cases. Additionally, mandatory sentencing has become more common for the most serious offenses. Judges have much less discretion to include taking into consideration mitigating factors, particularly the severe mental illness of mothers who are found guilty of murder.

People are very suspicious of insanity defenses, and successful Not Guilty by Reason of Insanity verdicts are rare and frequently result in lengthy incarceration in maximum-security forensic hospitals (Finkel *et al.*, 2000). Refer to the *Practice Update Section* for more information about treatment issues for maternal filicide offenders.

Suggestions for Future Research

Future research on larger samples of filicidal women would facilitate a more robust and reliable set of predictive criteria to identify those women at higher risk for maternal filicide (Lewis & Bunce, 2003). They also suggest that research on women who do not kill children or have those impulses, but are mentally ill and are exposed to similar psychosocial stressors, would also be important in this endeavor. In order to achieve larger samples, international cooperation could facilitate a large scale database. There is a lack of screening instruments that are created specifically for use before and/or after childbirth in women with diagnosed or suspected histories of mood or psychotic disorders. McKee and Shea (1998) found from their sample of 20 women who had been charged with killing their children and been referred to a forensic psychiatric hospital for pretrial evaluation, 78% of the multichild families had sibling survivors that would likely require treatment for issues like post-traumatic stress disorder or major depression. They noted the complete absence of research on sibling survivors of filicidal parents and clearly this is an important area for future research.

Domestic Violence

Introduction

Domestic violence is a pervasive social problem which plagues couples and families and has been described by some authors as having reached epidemic proportions both nationally and internationally (Alhabib, Nur, & Jones, 2010). A disproportionate amount of heterosexual domestic violence is male-to-female and generally affects anywhere from 2 to 28 million women. However, many men are also the victims of domestic violence and more research is needed in this area. This variability may be attributed to the ambiguity regarding what constitutes spousal abuse or battery or that due to stigma or gender role stereotypes, men may be less likely to report. Hence, definitions of domestic violence are likely to vary among existing counties, states, and nations. It is important to note that there is contradictory literature, with some revealing that women are as likely as men to perpetrate violence against an intimate partner and others showing that it is overwhelmingly men who perpetrate violence against their female partners (Dobash & Dobash, 2004).

It is readily apparent that women are at an appreciably higher risk in their homes due to the potential volatility that exists in their relationships with their intimate partners.

The preponderance of research literature aims to tease out distinct characteristics of the abusers. However, perpetrators cannot be succinctly typified into one global category because they are essentially a heterogeneous group. There is an increased likelihood for partner-assaultive men to report childhood histories of physical abuse. Furthermore, the laws and policies pertinent to domestic violence offenders are continually evolving and are subject to change with new legislation. Currently, limited efforts are being made to address issues such as prevention, intervention, and the implementation of new laws and policies. The following case studies were selected to illustrate the seriousness of this issue.

In one case, a jury of eight women and four men rejected Ms. Malott's claim of self-defense based on battered woman syndrome and convicted her of second-degree and attempted murder. She was sentenced to life in prison with no possibility of parole for at least 10 years (Bindman, 1991).

In a second case, On 26 December 1993, Marsha Brewer Stewart was found with a knife in her chest. Police say she was murdered by her husband, Gregory. Just 7 months earlier, Marsha had defended her husband in a suburban Chicago courtroom by testifying that he had not attempted to murder her. She had dismissed the episode as a drunken fit of rage. Police and prosecutors begged her not to post his bond or move back in with him. Like many other women, she forgave him. On December 26, Marsha called the police in a desperate plea for help. By the time a squad car arrived, Marsha was dead. Hours later, her husband was charged with murder (Shalala, 1994).

Literature Review

Cases such as Ms. Malott's and Ms. Stewart's exemplify that domestic violence, all too often, leads to disastrous consequences for the couple and their children. Early intervention can be facilitated by neighbors, community members, and a legal system that implements stringent arrest policies for the accused perpetrators. However, how can victims, police officers, and the courts identify such abusers? As alluded to earlier, a plethora of research has been geared toward identifying characteristics of male spousal abusers. Thus far, researchers have been unable to consistently identify a profile which is inclusive of most abusers, in terms of personality, psychopathology, and demographics. In this section the predominant patterns of abusers and their families of origin are discussed. Furthermore, issues pertinent to court mediation and legal interventions regarding the deterrence of abusers are explored. The primary objective is to provide clarification on the preceding issues.

Dobash and Dobash (2004) presented quantitative and qualitative findings from 190 interviews with 95 couples in which men and women reported separately upon their own violence and upon that of their partner. These researchers compared men's and women's violence. Their findings suggested that intimate partner violence is primarily an unbalanced problem of men's violence to women. More specifically, this study demonstrated that women's violence is not equal to men's in terms of frequency, severity, consequences and the victim's sense of safety and well-being. However, the male victim's of intimate violence must not be forgotten in terms of victim's assistance and relevant policy.

The increasing prevalence of cases such as Ms. Malott's and Ms. Stewart's has engendered vast research regarding the incidence of such abuse and the characteristics of abusive individuals. A study by Coleman *et al.* (2007) estimates that 29% of women have experienced an episode of partner violence since the age of 16. By 1996, battery by a spouse or intimate partner was the single most common reason for women entering emergency rooms, exceeding the rate of childbirth, automobile accidents, muggings, and all other medical emergencies (Mills, 1996). Cross-cultural research indicates that American women are not alone in this regard. Historically, a cross-cultural study of family violence found that domestic abuse occurs in over 84% of the 90 societies examined (Levinson, 1988). In countries such as Canada, Guatemala, Chile, Columbia, Belgium, and parts of Europe, domestic violence figures range from 4 to 60%. A recent meta-analysis of 134 studies on the prevalence of domestic violence perpetrated against women reveals that the prevalence of lifetime domestic violence varies in the United States from 1.9% in Washington to 70% of Hispanic Latinas in the Southeast U.S. (Alhabib, Nur, & Jones, 2010). These alarming statistics have mobilized a number of battered women and feminists nationwide to address the issue of domestic violence.

In an effort to reveal theoretical and treatment implications, vast research has focused on describing the characteristics of abusers. Historically, Hastings and Hamberger (1988) suggested that the preponderance of identified male batterers showed evidence of a personality disorder. These researchers found that in comparison to age-matched, nonviolent males, batterers showed higher levels of dysphoria, anxiety, and somatic complaints. The batterers in their sample presented as more alienated, moody, labile, and passive—aggressive. Alcoholic batterers showed the highest levels of pathology, followed by non-alcohol-abusive batterers. Both batterer subgroups showed a greater disadvantage in terms of higher unemployment rates; lower education; and higher rates of reported, experienced, and witnessed violence victimization in the family of origin. In general, their findings provide support for the notion that batterers are a heterogeneous group and cannot be adequately explained by a unified "batterer profile."

Another study examining the instances of partner violence in young men with early onset alcoholism who had committed suicide, found that half of the men had histories of domestic violence (Conner, Duberstein, & Conwell, 2000). Those who were violent in their intimate relationship were found to have an earlier age of onset of alcoholism.

The literature on psychopathology and anger suggests that both significantly contribute to interpersonal violence. Greene, Coles, and Johnson (1994) conducted a cluster analysis with data gathered from 40 court-referred abusers. The Minnesota Multiphasic Personality Inventory-2 (MMPI-2) and the State-Trait Anger Expression Inventory (STAXI) were utilized as measures of personality functioning and the expression of anger among abusers in the sample. The MMPI-2 scores demonstrated that domestic violence offenders indicated some degree of depression, antisocial attitudes, distrust, anxiety, and other psychopathologies. Results confirmed four clusters of violent offenders, with the most pathological cluster being angrier than their non-pathological counterparts. Furthermore, these results were also consistent with the literature in that there was not a single, homogeneous "abuser" profile.

Researchers have also emphasized the importance of traumatic childhood experiences, such as severe physical abuse, in an effort to classify abusers. Murphy, Meyer, and O'Leary (1993) examined associations between family of origin violence, levels of current abusive behavior, and self-reports of psychopathology in a clinical sample of male abusers. Compared to nonviolent men in discordant and well-adjusted relationships, partner-assaultive men were significantly more likely to report childhood histories of physical abuse as well as physical abuse of the mother in the family of origin. When compared to batterers without such histories, those who were severely abused in childhood displayed more evidence of psychopathology on the Millon Clinical Multiaxial Inventory-II (MCMI-II), and expressed higher levels of aggression directed toward their current partner. These results suggest that violence in the family of origin, and in particular a history of severe childhood physical abuse, can differentiate partner-assaultive men (Murphy *et al.*, 1993).

Whitfield, Anda, Dube, and Felitti (2003) studied the relationship of childhood physical abuse, sexual abuse, or growing up with a battered mother, to the risk of being a victim of intimate partner violence for women or a perpetrator for men. The Adverse Childhood Experiences Study had 8629 participants and was conducted in a large HMO. Results indicated that each of the three violent childhood experiences increased the risk of either victimization or perpetration of intimate partner violence about two-fold. For those persons who had all three forms of violent experiences, the risk increased 3.5-fold for women and 3.8-fold for men.

Literature on the legal attempts to punish perpetrators of domestic violence has become more prevalent during the past three decades. Some of the legal responses include an increased reliance on civil protection orders and numerous options for prosecuting batterers, including, most notably, mandatory arrest. Police officers are more likely to arrest the perpetrator when the victim is visibly injured or when there is probable cause to believe a crime has been committed (Mills, 1996). Although mandatory arrest tends to reduce domestic violence, abusers' high recidivism rates continue to adversely affect the lives of many women. The new law, Uniform Interstate Enforcement of Domestic-Violence Protection Orders Act, makes it easier and safer for domestic violence victims to travel from state to state (Saunders, 2003). This law mandates that a court must enforce all terms of a protection order from another state, even if the terms are typically prohibited in their jurisdiction. This law has been enacted in California, Delaware, Idaho, Indiana, Montana, and Texas with 20 other states planning to implement it in 2003 (Sauders, 2003).

Civil protection orders, which enjoin a batterer from further violence, may curtail domestic violence. In most states, civil protection orders can be used either in conjunction with criminal proceedings or in civil court (Keilitz, 1994). However, Mills (1996) contends that the problem with civil protection orders, prosecution, and arrest policies is that they require women to terminate their abusive relationships and subject them to even more serious attacks by their batterers. Many studies show that battered women who attempt to leave the abuser may be at a higher risk of being harmed or killed (Campbell, Sharps, Laughon *et al.*, 2003). Ironically, criminal strategies which aim to curb abuse and violent relationships through legal interventions may instead place victims in more dangerous predicaments. A descriptive study that retrospectively examined 485 victim surveys gathered in a domestic violence advocacy center over 12 months, sought to explore the reasons why a victim of domestic violence would return to the abusive relationship (Gillig, Sitaker, & McCloskey, 2003). The reasons for returning included lack of money (45.9%), the lack of a place to go (28.5%), and the absence of police assistance (13.5%). These obstacles were considered to directly impact the safety of the victim (Gillig *et al.*, 2003).

Forensic Psychology and Policy Implications

Domestic violence is a widespread problem that affects families from every socioeconomic level in our society. Psychologists, judges, and lawmakers have struggled with devising an efficient means of preventing, assessing, and deterring perpetrators of such violence. While studies have undoubtedly placed an emphasis on identifying the primary characteristics of abusers, the research suggests that batterers are a relatively heterogeneous group. The heterogeneous nature of the batterers unequivocally hinders efforts geared toward prevention and rehabilitation.

The literature also clearly indicates the increased likelihood of abusers to endorse psychopathological symptoms and express bouts of anger and hostility. Hence, it is readily apparent that domestic violence offenders are likely to need extensive counseling for varying degrees of psychopathology as well as anger management interventions to modulate their intense feelings of anger. Also, victims are at an increased risk to develop psychopathological symptoms, including mood disorders and post-traumatic stress. Accordingly, group or individual counseling is likely to be a necessary component when working with victims of domestic violence. However, attrition continues to be a major problem for domestic violence rehabilitation programs (Gerlock, 2001). A study on domestic violence rehabilitation attrition with 62 male batterers (aged 20–62 years) and 31 female victims found that those who completed the program were more likely to be young and court monitored. In addition, they had lower levels of stress and post-traumatic stress, and higher levels of mutuality in their relationships (Gerlock, 2001).

Mandatory arrest laws and civil protection orders are currently being utilized by many states to reduce domestic violence. There is, however, an implicit precursor within these statutes, which requires women or men to end their relationships with their abusers and subsequently places them at an increased risk of being attacked. For example, these women should be encouraged to not directly confront their abusers about their intentions to leave, as this action is related to increased violence or even **femicide (e.g., the killing of a woman)** (Campbell *et al.*, 2003). It remains evident that battered women and men need to be provided with information about arrest policies and protection orders. This need is directly referenced in congressional testimony which also emphasizes the need to provide victims with the knowledge, skills, and resources needed to reach financial independence from an abusive partner (Watersong, 2010). Furthermore, the same testimony also speaks to the need for legal employment protections if victims of domestic violence decide to take steps to ameliorate their difficulties with violent partners, it is imperative that they are provided with adequate protection from their abusers. If issues such as these are thoroughly considered and implemented, scenarios like that of Ms. Malott's and Ms. Stewart's may be avoided. Conversely, if domestic violence continues to be under-prioritized, the issue is likely to go unabated and remain an intractable problem.

Finally, if those making and implementing policies and making decisions about public and private resources are unaware of the ever growing number of male victims of domestic violence, "the very nature of this problem has real consequences for what might be done for those who are its victims and those who are its perpetrators" (Dobash & Dobash, 2004, p. 324). Male victims should not be left without resources and support and female perpetrators should be held accountable; however, Dobash and Dobash (2004) indicate that their findings provide support for the current efforts of legislators, policymakers and advocates and suggest that the current general direction of public policy and expenditure is appropriate.

Suggestions for Future Research

Over the past two decades, research on domestic violence offenders has expanded. However, there has been limited in-depth research about women's violence to male partners or a consensus as to what constitutes "violence" in the available research. Without some agreement as to the concept of violence, the comparisons in the domestic violence literature about the gender of the perpetrators and victims are difficult to make (Dobash & Dobash, 2004). Continued exploration into impact of gender and sexual orientation and who constitutes the victim and the perpetrator in intimate partner violence is recommended. More research that explores the impact of domestic violence on men in either heterosexual or homosexual relationships is needed. Additionally, more studies that attempt to identify the true prevalence of this problem in particular are recommended. Despite a growing literature on domestic violence, relatively scant research exists which assesses the legal and psychological impact of the victims in question. Recent research has emphasized how empowering the victim throughout their involvement with the legal system can serve as a more reliable predictor of improvement in depression and quality of life than reabuse, expectations of the court, and even the legal outcome (Cattaneo & Goodman, 2010). Further research is needed to learn what legal and psychological interventions can be implemented to better serve those who are victimized by such abuse, particularly with reference to what specific practices contribute to a victim's sense of empowerment. The studies will need to ascertain the efficiency and effectiveness of such interventions and analyze the feasibility of devising remedial methods which can also be implemented.

As research on the profiles of abusers gains more validity, treatment studies can be included to ascertain what type of treatment works best with what type of abuser. It would be beneficial to study whether varying treatment modalities differ in terms of effectiveness and, if so, more efficient interventions may evolve. Furthermore, researchers are also encouraged to examine more closely the options available for handling domestic violence situations including mandatory arrest, protection orders, and options for prosecuting batterers. For example, states which utilize mandatory arrest laws, or any other laws pertinent to domestic violence, can be compared to those which do not. Studies such as these are likely to enhance the opportunities and resources available to victims of domestic violence.

Family Trauma and the Cycle of Crime

Introduction

An increasing number of children are living in chaotic familial and community environments. Conservative estimates indicate that over 1 million children are abused and neglected each year in the United States alone (National Center on Child Abuse and Neglect, 1994). In 2008, 772,000 children were victims of child abuse or neglect (United States Department of Health and Human Services, 2008). The United States is one of the most violent countries in the world and the lifetime exposure rates of young adults for victimization ranges from 76% to 82% and 93% to 96% for witnessing violence (Scarpa, 2003). The National Center on Child

Abuse and Neglect (2008) reports that an estimated 21.7 in 1000 children are victims of abuse or neglect with more than half of that being girls (51.3% and 48.3% boys). According to Guadalupe and Bein (2001, p. 157), "A long history of violence and social and institutional oppression in U.S. society has reinforced violent behavior among children and youth." These children are often exposed to exorbitant levels of trauma characterized by parental neglect, physical abuse, sexual abuse, and domestic violence, as well as the detrimental effects of inconsistent discipline from parental figures. The biological, psychological, and social repercussions of children growing up with such trauma are numerous. According to Scarpa (2003), young adults with high levels of violence exposure by way of either victimization or witnessing, report more psychological difficulties to include depressed mood, aggressive behavior, post-traumatic stress disorder symptoms, and interpersonal problems. Of particular interest, however, is the significance of family trauma and its relation to intergenerational cycles of antisocial and criminal behavior. The relationship between one's traumatic upbringing and the perpetuation of criminal behavior in adolescence and adulthood has been clearly noted in the literature. Empirical evidence does suggest that the growing numbers of adolescent and adult criminal offenders come from backgrounds plagued with varying levels of trauma. However, currently there are no concentrated efforts made to address this issue in terms of prevention and effective intervention measures. The following case illustrates how a young male, who lived in a chaotic familial environment, resorted to violence.

Fifteen-year-old Arnold was arrested and incarcerated after he fatally stabbed his mother's boyfriend of 2 months. As a young child, Arnold had been exposed to numerous distressing events. On many occasions he observed his biological father physically assaulting his mother. Arnold's father physically abused him and often used objects such as belts, electric cords, and wooden planks. As a young child, Arnold was left alone in the house for days at a time without any guidance or supervision. Subsequently, Arnold began having numerous difficulties both at home and at school. His teachers reported that during class, he seemed distracted and irritable and he would often engage in physical altercations with other classmates. He began to exhibit increasingly dangerous and reckless behaviors; spoke perseveratively about weapons, stabbings, and the physical abuse he had witnessed; and expressed vague fears that he himself would come to harm others. The night of the stabbing, Arnold witnessed his mother and her boyfriend arguing in the living room. Arnold was unable to tolerate his mother's boyfriend's argumentative behavior and Arnold impulsively reached for a kitchen knife and proceeded to stab him. Arnold was charged with assault with a deadly weapon and is currently awaiting sentencing.

Literature Review

As a result of Arnold's case, and those that are similar, it is apparent that the perpetuation of violence within families needs to be thoroughly examined and, ultimately, prevented. The results of exposure to severe familial violence are not randomly distributed within the population. Some children are substantially more likely to have such experiences associated with where they reside and with whom they live. Inner-city youth are exposed to especially chaotic environments, often marked by poverty and violence (Sklarew, Krupnick, Ward-Wimmer, & Napoli, 2002). Children who have risk factors in their lives such as domestic violence, parental substance abuse, and living in poverty are certainly at an increased risk for exposure to trauma and violence. Many children are unable to adapt or cope with intense feelings of helplessness, hopelessness, grief, and violent fantasies. In addition these children typically manifest an underlying depression and PTSD symptoms often expressed through aggression and self-destructive behaviors (Sklarew *et al.*, 2002; Wraith, 2000). Children can experience such violence within a number of different contexts; however, it is likely that the family, and especially a child's relationship with caregivers, is one of the most important of these contexts. The following literature review explores the risk factors involved in the cycle of crime. Preventive measures geared toward breaking the intergenerational cycle of crime are also discussed.

A common setting for violence is the home. Problems of parental abuse, neglect, and spousal abuse account for a major component of the physical and emotional trauma suffered by children. It is therefore not only important, but also necessary, to examine the effects of familial violence, abuse, and neglect on the development of children who live within these contexts. Historically, in Helfer and Kempe's (1986) study, 82% of a group of adolescent offenders were found to have a history of abuse and neglect, and 43% recalled being knocked unconscious by one of their parents. Their sample of violent adolescents were victims of, as well as witnesses to, severe physical abuse. The sample provided a clear indication of how extreme physical disciplinary practices in the home correlated with aggressive and destructive delinquency. A study that examined abuse perpetrated by siblings, as compared to parental abusers, found that abuse by siblings, like abuse by parents, may be associated with a cycle of violence in the life of the victim (Simonelli, Mullis, Elliott, & Pierce, 2002).

McCord's (1991) study came from a larger longitudinal investigation of males who had been in a program designed to prevent delinquency. McCord (1991) examined families in which fathers were criminals and those in which fathers were not criminals, and found significant differences that help explain the cycle of violence among sons of criminals. Results indicated that sons of criminals were more, rather than less, likely to become criminals. The data suggested that aggressive parental models increased the likelihood that their sons would be involved in criminal activities. Furthermore, maternal affection, self-confidence, and consistent nonpunitive discipline or supervision helped protect their sons from engaging in criminal behavior. This discovery leads to the tentative conclusion that intervention techniques designed to develop competence among parents may be particularly effective when the targets are children at high risk (McCord, 1991).

Who are the children at high risk and how do these risk factors perpetuate a cycle of violence? Blumenthal (2000) describes a pattern where a child's early examples of how to function in relationships with others is damaged and the child learns to identify with the aggressor and repeats early childhood traumas in adulthood. Attachment theory provides some explanation of how a child in this environment develops a pattern of preemptive aggression. In other words, the child learns that the world is a hostile place made up of victims and victimizers and they must strike first to protect themselves in future relationships or interactions with others (Shipley & Arrigo, 2004). One longitudinal study completed by Widom (1992) looked specifically at the cycle of violence. Widom (1992) tracked 1575 cases from childhood through young adulthood and compared the arrest records of the two groups. One group contained 908 subjects who experienced some form of substantiated childhood abuse or neglect and a comparison group of 667 children who were not officially recorded as abused or neglected. Both groups were matched for age, race, sex, and socioeconomic status. Clear and succinct operational definitions of abuse and neglect allowed *if necessary* a separate examination of physical abuse, sexual abuse, and neglect.

Results indicated that children who had been abused or neglected were 58% more likely to be arrested as juveniles, 38% more likely to be arrested as adults, 38% more likely to be arrested for a violent crime, and 77% more likely to be arrested if they were females. Abuse and neglect cases on average were nearly one year younger at first arrest, committed twice as

many crimes, and were arrested 89% more frequently than the control group. A noteworthy conclusion was that a child who was neglected was just as likely as a child who was abused to be arrested for a violent crime. The aforementioned study further exemplifies how childhood abuse and neglect can precipitate violent behavior in adolescence and adulthood. In order to test the hypothesis that victimized children grow up to victimize other children, a nationally representative data set made up of 6,002 participants was examined (Heyman & Slep, 2002). Results found that exposure to both physical violence and a witnessing of domestic violence between parents significantly increased the risk of adulthood family violence for women.

The mood disturbances often experienced by the youthful offender who has suffered from abuse and neglect can also impact the cycle and expression of violence. Children who experience depression, anxiety, post-traumatic stress, and the like often have a difficult time controlling aggressive displays and are more prone to anger; therefore, they are more likely to carry out criminal behaviors (Viljoen, Elkovitch, & Ullman, 2008). Viljoen, Elkovitch, and Ullman (2008) list several areas of positive behaviors and actions that can mitigate the potential for criminal behavior as: pro-social attitudes, intelligence, and resilient personality traits. High self-efficacy and resilience are cited as strong indicators that a youth may not carry on the cycle of violence. These traits can act as protective factors against violence for children exposed to traumatic circumstances.

Researchers have also explored the family backgrounds of criminal offenders. Briscoe (1997) examined the familial histories of youths who were committed to the **Texas Youth**

Commission (TYC). The TYC is a state agency which is responsible for the most seriously delinquent and disturbed youths. The findings indicated that the vast majority of the youths in TYC had histories of abuse and neglect. A majority of youth offenders had family members with histories of violence, substance abuse, criminal behavior, and mental impairments. Approximately 71% of these delinquent youths came from chaotic environments and 80% of the subject's parental figures lacked adequate disciplinary skills. This youth offender study further highlights the relationship between traumatic childhood experiences and increased the likelihood of engaging in delinquent behavior.

A similar study (Levinson & Fonagy, 1999) examined 22 male patients in a prison sample and matched them with a group of psychiatric controls. Their crimes included attempted burglary, theft, property damage, car theft, gross indecency, importation of drugs, armed robbery, kidnapping, rape, and murder. They were interviewed with a structured clinical interview for Diagnostic and Statistical Manual of Mental Disorders (1983), Third Edition, Revised (DSM-III-R) disorders. They all had at least one clinical disorder and 91% had at least one personality disorder; 50% had a DSM-III-R diagnosis of Borderline Personality Disorder. A number of striking findings indicated that among this group of 22 criminals, extreme deprivations in childhood, severe physical abuse, and neglect were commonly and convincingly reported. Although this was only a pilot investigation, the results are promising to the extent that they link histories of abuse with the perpetuation of criminal behavior and psychopathology.

Forensic Psychology and Policy Implications

The crisis of family trauma and the perpetuation of violence affect tens of thousands of families nationwide. Increasingly, children are not only witnessing, but experiencing, varying degrees of violence in their homes and communities. This exposure to violence changes the way children view the world and may change the value they place on life itself (Groves, Zuckerman, Marans, & Cohen, 1993). It can certainly affect their ability to learn, to establish and sustain relationships with others, and to cope with life's stressors. Yet there is a general lack of knowledge and understanding in terms of how growing up in such chaotic environments affects young children's social, emotional, and cognitive development. Factors such as the public's lack of understanding about the effects of **family trauma** only serve to hinder efficient and effective intervention methods.

The literature clearly points to a link between family trauma and an intergenerational cycle of violence and crime. Children who grow up in unstructured, chaotic, and abusive homes are at an increased risk of engaging in violent or antisocial behavior. Thus, it is imperative that policy-makers endorse services for children and families which interface with police, schools, courts, community programs, and health care settings. Solutions must encompass preventing trauma, treating trauma, early intervention, and swift and clear repercussions for chronic or violent behavior. It is crucial to reach children who experience such trauma long before they arrive at an age where they act out their experiences in a violent manner. Another inherent component to helping traumatized children is to provide information and counseling to the caregivers in the children's lives. Psychologists should play a vital role in treatment and evaluation of these issues. Children who have witnessed and/or experienced violence should be provided with therapy to not only address grief- and anger-related issues, but also to help them build adaptive coping strategies to help them to prevent the perpetuation of the cycle of violence.

Trauma informed care is a growing trend and psychologists working with these populations should be trained in not only altering behavior, but to also address the underlying motivations and causes of the behavior. These children are more likely to come in contact with the family court system and/or mental health system. Violence risk assessments are a likely referral, as well as dispositional evaluations or those that help to inform juvenile courts or agencies about the best recourse or placements and treatments for the juvenile in question. Mental health professionals should play an active role in prevention or intervention programs that focus on problem-solving, communication skills, conflict resolution skills, and anger management skills (DuRant, Barkin, & Krowchuk, 2001). Studies have shown that intervention programs for youthful offenders have reduced recidivism by 10%, with some of the more effective programs yielding a 20–30% success rate (Viljoen, Elkovitch, & Ullman, 2008).

Suggestions for Future Research

Research has suggested that while the majority of those who perpetrate violence have a history of abuse or trauma as a child, most childhood victims of abuse do not perpetrate violence or abuse in adulthood. Research needs to continue to examine what mitigating factors prevent the majority of abuse survivors from perpetuating the cycle. What are the intermediating variables that lead from abuse to violence in adulthood for those who do become perpetrators (Fagan, 2001)? Future investigations of family trauma must investigate how familial trauma affects children, and how it impacts communities and society in general. The present findings provide some important insights into these issues; however, a great deal of research still needs to be conducted. If family trauma perpetuates itself, producing a vicious cycle of violence, then it is imperative to explore what interventions can break this cycle. There is an ongoing discussion about how significant a childhood history of abuse and neglect is compared to biological or genetic factors in the development of psychopathic tendencies. Studies are needed which elucidate more fully the range and effects of familial trauma and, more so, assess the effects of early treatment measures. Future research into the nature of individual protective factors that may contribute to resilience versus criminal behavior is needed to determine the likelihood of future violence. We therefore need a closer look at the extent to which some interventions may be more effective than others in terms of differences between parental education, counseling for families in crisis, or stricter accountability measures for perpetrators of such violence. In addition, a gamut of preventive measures need to be explored and utilized in order to thwart the cyclical nature of family trauma and violence. Finally, future research could help to elucidate the harmful effects of extreme stress in childhood on brain development (Koenen, Moffitt, Caspi, & Taylor, 2003).

Practice Update Section: Issues in Family/Criminal Forensics

Although paradoxical, the motivation of mentally ill mothers who kill for altruistic reasons is compassionate. As these women become stabilized through aggressive mental health treatment, they are often shocked and bewildered that they could have so dangerously miscalculated their situation or believed so fully their delusions. These mentally ill mothers are dealt a crushing blow when they become stabilized and realize the gravity of what they have done. Their experience of remorse, disbelief, and horror is often the most severe punishment inflicted upon them and this burden.

These women are at high risk of experiencing **suicidal ideation** or attempting suicide. In addition to medication management for their mood and psychotic symptoms, receiving support and having a mental health professional to talk to about what they are experiencing is important. Obviously, when these women are pretrial, what she should or would be advised or able to discuss about her situation is extremely limited.

In addition to her own grief, the maternal filicide offender will need support in encountering head-on the grief of others associated with the children or family. Mental health professionals must be aware of the range of reactions from surviving family and friends including anger, fear, sadness, confusion, and the like and how their emotions and actions will impact the mental health of the mother/patient. As the curtain of psychosis, depression, or mania lifts and the mother is left with the realization that her offspring are dead and she is responsible, the grief is usually unbearable. These women must face bereavement as a result of murder and therapists can be overwhelmed by the enormity of their suffering (Stanton & Simpson, 2006).

Mental health education is absolutely essential. Helping her to understand all of the signs, symptoms, and triggers of her illness, particularly those that led to the offense, is mandatory to get her mentally well, to reduce risk for relapse, and to protect society. She will need to understand and follow up with her treatment for the rest of her life to ever have an opportunity to safely reintegrate into society. These women struggle desperately with the question, "How could this have happened?"

For those women who had a strong religious component to their delusions, there often remains an anger and distrust of God or their previous faith. If at the time of the crime they believed they were serving the will of God or were instructed to not question the action of killing their children, they may fear any strong relationship with God or trust themselves to unquestioning faith in whatever they may have believed before. To be clear, religion does NOT cause mental illness, but for those women who are susceptible or who are mentally ill, it is quite possible that their religious ideas or beliefs will mask or become intertwined with their psychotic symptoms. This is a very personal and complicated issue but a reality for those women whose symptoms that led to the deaths of their children had strong religious meaning or components. This also has implications for educating church officials and congregations about signs of mental illness, including postpartum illnesses.

Whether the female offender is in prison or a psychiatric hospital, there is an inescapable stigma attached to killing children and they may suffer harsh reactions or treatment, particularly in a prison setting. This type of treatment, shame, and deep sadness are often rekindled when a story reemerges in the media, through television or in print. It is common for graphic details, pictures, and the names of all involved to be widely publicized. Coping with the reality of media coverage, including when and if they are ever released to the community is another reality for which to prepare. Helping these women to cope with their tragedies and to have some hope for the future is a difficult but important role for mental health professionals involved in their treatment.

■ International Issues: Maternal Filicide

The United States has extremely restrictive laws that govern infanticide or filicide cases the same as any other homicide. The United States does not have an infanticide statute.

Traditionally, the older the child, the more likely the conviction rate. British law has specific infanticide laws that govern infanticide, which some view as overly lenient that take into consideration the very enormous possible impact of childbirth, depression, and other issues relating to the postpartum period. Britain's law more closely equates infanticide to manslaughter with regard to penalties, rather than murder, which is much more common in the United States. In Great Britain, the Infanticide Act of 1922 and 1938 both maintained that postpartum psychosis was an appropriate cause to reduce charges for neonaticide and infanticide from murder to manslaughter. The diminished responsibility defense utilized in New South Wales allows for probation or for an individual to be sent to a psychiatric facility for treatment rather than to prison (Schwartz & Isser, 2001). Finland has legislation comparable to that of the British Infanticide Act of 1922, proposing women who are vulnerable in the postpartum period often receive no sentence and are referred for mental health treatment (Kauppi *et al.*, 2008).

In approximately 30 countries throughout the world, to include Britain, Canada, and Australia, murder charges are ruled out for a lesser charge for women who kill their children within the first year after giving birth. This legislation implies that childbirth may have had a destabilizing effect on mothers, and that the infant homicide may have happened due to the resulting unstable psychological conditions, presenting a case for diminished responsibility for the crime (Marks, 2001). Their stance does not promote devaluing the lives of the infants, but rather reflects a greater understanding and mitigation for postpartum illnesses. Clearly, this should not take the place of prevention and education. Insanity defenses based on postpartum depression are not often successful. According to Gold (2001, p. 346), "This is, in no small part, because altruistic homicide, even in a psychotically disorganized individual, is voluntary, often premeditated, planned logically, and accomplished methodically, always in full consciousness, and perfectly remembered."

Laporte *et al.* (2003, pp. 96–97) stated that the most cogent arguments against sentencing women with postpartum depression to terms of incarceration are as follows: "(1) an illness beyond their control caused these women's homicidal acts; (2) they have already suffered enough; (3) they have lost their offspring and have to live with the guilt related to their behavior; and (4) they do not represent a threat to others as long as they do not have other children" (Ewing, 1997; Pitt & Bale, 1995).

Related Websites

www.ncdsv.org/publications_domhomicide.html
Website on domestic violence and homicides.

Continued

Related Websites—cont'd

www.vpc.org/press/0609wmmw.htm
Violence Policy Center: info on female homicides by males.
www.aardvarc.org/dv/malevictims.shtml
Website with resources about male victims of domestic violence, etc.
www.domesticviolence.org
Website includes information about victims and abusers, common myths, and cycle of violence, as well as information to help provide victims information on how to get support and how to plan for his or her safety.
www.ncbi.nlm.nih.gov/pmc/articles/PMC2174580
Website which provides the article: "Child murder by mothers: patterns and prevention" coauthored by Resnick (2007).
www.ncbi.nlm.nih.gov/pmc/articles/PMC2922347
Website from PubMed that gives an overview of filicide.

Court and the Legal System: Civil Forensics

Key Issues

Impact of Mental Health Law Doctrines on Families: Paternalism and *Parens Patriae*
- The *parens patriae* doctrine
- Civil commitments
- Problems with *parens patriae* and civil commitment

Termination of Parental Rights
- Legislation and public policies regarding termination of parental rights, as well as criticisms and resultant problems of such policies
- Characteristics of children and parents most likely to be impacted by termination of parental rights
- Roles of mental health professionals in this area including the critical components of psychological evaluations in this domain

Gay/Lesbian Rights and Definitions of the Family
- The nontraditional family structure of same-sex parents and their rights in terms of adoption
- Concerns expressed in the debate of allowing same-sex partners to adopt children, and the process of second parent adoption

Family Forensics

Chapter Outline

Overview

This chapter examines selected controversies and issues in forensic psychology impacting families. For purposes of this chapter, the use of the term "family" is broadly defined. When the legal and psychological communities promote policies and/or therapeutic interventions that affect how parents and their children are to interact, then the structure and process of what it means to be in a family are called into question. In some instances, the law dictates which individuals are allowed to become a family, while in others the law allows individuals to retain their parental rights.

This chapter addresses the legal rights of families and the implications of neglectful and abusive care on children. Some sections consider how trauma and violence affect the behavior of family members and how the courts respond to such abuse. In total, three subjects are examined. These topics include (1) the role of paternalism and *parens patriae* in mental

health law on the family; (2) the termination of parental rights; and (3) gay/lesbian rights and definitions of the family. While the issues reviewed in this chapter do not exhaustively canvass the family forensic field, the topics chosen are, nonetheless, controversial, significant, and demonstrate the pressing need for skilled practitioners in this subspecialty area of law and psychology.

The doctrines of paternalism and *parens patriae* are two legal principles demonstrating the power that the state possesses and exercises in the lives of persons suffering from psychiatric illness. How do paternalism and *parens patriae* work? What influence do these doctrines exert on families? How are these legal principles used in relation to civil commitment? Repeated exposure in childhood to family trauma and abuse can be devastating for young boys and girls. How does exposure to such violence affect a person in adulthood? What are the behavioral and situational risk factors involved in cycles of crime? What is our response to children who experience abuse and neglect and the pathogenic care they are receiving? At what point is the termination of parental rights in the best interest of these children? What are the implications for the parents and children involved in termination of parental rights hearings? What role do forensic psychologists play in this process? In today's society, gay and lesbian citizens have redefined the meaning of family life and the family unit. Are children of nonheterosexual couples at any greater psychological risk when growing up in homosexual families? How does law and psychology assist us in our understanding of gay and lesbian family rights?

The legal system has a vested interest in protecting the rights and ensuring the responsibilities of families and their respective members. Often, the issue is about understanding how the law, with the assistance of psychology, can better address the changing and emerging needs of different families. The forensic specialist assumes a pivotal role in the intervention and policy process. As the individual sections of this chapter make clear, the field of family forensics requires additional research into the nature of family life in general, as well as the social, psychological, and legal factors that limit parents and their children from experiencing the joys of such a healthy existence in particular.

Impact of Mental Health Law Doctrines on Families: Paternalism and Parens Patriae

Introduction

At 6 years of age, a child was admitted indefinitely to a state hospital. The child's parents sought treatment for their son because of his aggressive and uncontrollable behavior. His diagnosis was "hyperkinetic reaction of childhood." Four years later, the parents relinquished their parental control to the county, whereupon the boy was placed in a mental hospital. Not long after, the youth filed a lawsuit requesting that the court "place him in a less drastic environment suitable to his needs" (*Parham v. J.R.*, 1978).

Although this occurred several decades ago, this example demonstrates the ramifications of what may occur when a person is deemed incapable of making his/her own decisions and placed under the guardianship of the state. The majority of these individuals are juveniles, the elderly, and persons who are found to be "out of sound" mind/mentally ill. This is the basic premise at work in the doctrines of *paternalism* and *parens patriae*. In these cases, the government has traditionally intervened with the police power and **parens patriae** justifications*;* namely, that the intervention of the state in the life of an individual determined to be a serious threat to him/herself and/or others is warranted and necessary (Belbot, 2007; Geller, Fischer, Grudzinskas, Clayfield, & Lawlor, 2006; Mrad & Nabors, 2007). The historical context of the *parens patriae* doctrine comes from the authority of English kings to act or take responsibility for the presumed best interest of a disabled or impaired subject (Quinn, 2002). Today, it is often the police who manage the mentally ill when they are in crisis. According to Lamb, Weinberger, and DeCuir (2002, p. 1266), there are two principles that provide the justification for the police to take responsibility for the mentally ill which include: "their power and authority to protect the safety and welfare of the community and their *parens patriae* obligations to protect individuals with disabilities"

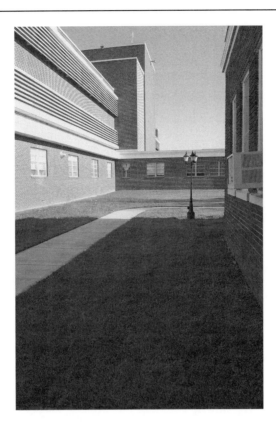

(also: Seitler, 2008). What occurs when it is the family of the mentally ill individual who seeks out treatment over the objections of their mentally ill loved one? Within this framework, this section explores the development of *parens patriae* and paternalism in the realm of involuntary hospitalization and how, specifically, it has influenced the role of the family in such issues.

In the 1860s, E. P. W. Packard was committed to a mental institution by her husband. Mrs. Packard, who was not in need of such care, was nevertheless institutionalized due to an 1851 Illinois statute that stated:

> *Married women and infants who, in the judgment of the medical superintendents of the state asylum…may be entered or detained in the hospital at the request of the husband of the woman or guardian of the infant, without the evidence of insanity require (J. E. Myers, 1983–1984, p. 376).*

Upon her release, Mrs. Packard began a nationwide campaign to adjust this law and others like it. Through her efforts, several bills were eventually passed that restricted the institutionalization of any person not found to be "insane or distracted by a verdict of a jury" (Myers, 1983–1984, p. 376).

Literature Review

Much of Western civilization perceives the family as a unit in which its members have a duty to protect those who cannot care for themselves. This perception rests upon the assumption that adults, due to maturity and experience, are more knowledgeable than children and are better equipped to make decisions for their offspring. This concept was fundamental in establishing the historical notions of *parens patriae (literally translated as "parent of his or her country:" Black, 2009, p. 488)* and paternalism, whereby the state, similar to knowing family adults, is entrusted with the responsibility of caring for those persons in need of mental health care. Within a legal context, this concept embodies the public policy power of the state to intercede on behalf of those unable to care for themselves or protect their well-being as a result of mental illness, disability, or against an abusive or neglectful parent, guardian, or caretaker. Slobogin and Fondacaro (2000) propose three separate models to rationalize the deprivation of personal freedoms by governmental institutions which include: (1) the punishment model that deprives liberty as a sanction for blameworthy behavior; (2) the prevention model to prevent harm by way of deterrence or restraint; and finally (3) the protection model, which deprives civil liberty in order to ensure independent decision-making. Police power and the *parens patriae* doctrine as they apply to the involuntary hospitalization of individuals serve two of these rationales — prevention and protection. *Parens patriae* hospitalizations serve these purposes by intervening in situations where an individual suffers some form of impairment (due to mental illness for example) to the extent that they do not possess the capacity to make or communicate responsible decisions, in situations where they are unable to provide for their own basic needs, or situations where the individual presents a threat to their own safety or the safety of others (Lavelle & Tusaie, 2011; Schopp, 2001).

Analysis of parental obligation to care for family members depicts a different picture. In reality, as the increasing number of child and elder abuse cases indicates, this familial belief system is not always practiced. "Some parents may at times be acting against the interests of their children" (*Bartley v. Kremens*, 1975, p. 1041). According to Hamilton (2006), states have become more willing to utilize the *parens patriae* doctrine to intervene in intact families in order to protect children who may be at risk (Hamilton, 2006). In terms of involuntary hospitalization, some parents, or other family members, may not have the desire or energy to care for their unruly children or cognitively impaired, elderly parent. In addition, there are instances in which family members are motivated by financial gain, such as inheritance or property control, culminating in the institutionalization of another relative. Hence, they request that the individual child or elder be admitted into a mental hospital despite the consequences that may transpire. Essentially, involuntary hospitalization may not be the most appropriate treatment for a given individual.

To demonstrate the susceptibility of involuntary hospitalization, one can analyze the first-mentioned case of J.R. As unmanageable as J.R. may have been, placing him in an institution was not appropriate for his needs, according to the court's opinion (*Parham v. J.R.*, 1978). However, as a juvenile, J.R. was not able to overcome the request of his parents and psychologists when the initial decision to commit him was made. Prior to the *Parham* decision, there was virtually no judicial input that existed to ensure that the liberties and rights of the mentally ill were considered when a relative requested the hospitalization of a child family member.

Before the 1970s, involuntary hospitalization or civil commitment was an informal arena that was perceived as medical, not legal (Reisner & Slobogin, 1990). Hearings questioning whether a person should have been committed rarely occurred, if at all, until after the person had been confined. Since individuals with mental illness were considered incapable of knowing what was best for them, their opinions were not weighed heavily in court. In other words, if a family member requested a relative's hospitalization, and there was a doctor's consent, then regardless of the wishes of the individual, he/she would most likely be committed. Once committed, the person was labeled mentally ill and it became difficult to cast off the stigma. Consequently, the probability of wrongfully or erroneously committing an individual to a psychiatric hospital was highly likely, given the nature of mental health policies defining commitment at that time. According to Sheehan (2009), the rate of involuntary hospitalizations has increased 16 to 40% among several Western nations (Sheehan, 2009).

A recent study surveyed state statutes, which restricted the civil rights of the mentally ill or those found mentally incompetent (Hemmens, Miller, Burton, & Milner, 2002). The study examined the restriction of civil rights in five areas, which included: jury service, voting,

holding public office, marriage, and parenting. The results of a 1999 study were compared to those of a 1989 study in order to examine trends in the restriction of civil rights for those with mental illness. The study revealed that the restriction of their civil rights continues with an increase in the restriction of **familial rights**, specifically marriage and parenting (Hemmens *et al.*, 2002).

Involuntary hospitalization is not without its opponents. Some believe that it is wrong, while others justify its use only under specific conditions and criteria. Overall, there is agreement that the use of involuntary hospitalization should be reduced due to its potential negative consequences (Agnetti, 2009). Those who oppose the involuntary hospitalization and treatment of persons with mental illness typically focus on civil liberties, human rights, stigma, self-determination, and the definition of mental illness (Agnetti, 2008). Lavelle and Tusaie (2011, p. 276) summarize some of the most common arguments for and against involuntary medication:

- Arguments against forced medication:
    - Forcing someone to do something against their will is inherently wrong.
    - People often refuse medications because of side-effects or other bona fide reasons.
    - Coercion drives people away from the mental health system and builds distrust.

- Arguments supporting forced medication:
  - Society has a paternal obligation to care for citizens who cannot care for themselves and to provide for the safety of others affected by those who cannot see the harm they may cause.
  - Lack of awareness of mental illness is a persistent symptom for many patients.
  - Offering services is often not enough when patients lack insight, compelling them to take medication may be necessary.

Provisions in the mental health field regarding the issue of commitment or hospitalization have only been developed within the past few decades. Previously, questions were not raised regarding the intentions of the family members who suggested it. Now that the courts are more actively involved in the process, there is a more watchful eye over family members, hospital administrators, and their motivations for civil confinement. Public defenders and specialists are assigned by the court to defend those individuals who are evaluated for hospitalization. This procedure is essential in those instances when family members do not look out for the best interest of a specific relative (e.g., as we have seen in cases such as *Parham v. J.R.*, 1978).

Currently, a judicial-type hearing is held prior to confinement during which time decisions surrounding hospitalization and the best medical care are addressed. These judicial guidelines are necessary, considering the unjust institutionalization some individuals faced as a result of past unethical standards for hospitalization. Yet, some major problems have developed with these new restrictions in relation to *parens patriae* and paternalism.

One difficulty with this transition can be observed when families that act in the best interest of a given member are penalized due to the actions of other members who harmfully suggest the hospitalization of a certain relative. New policies can marginalize the voices of good-intentioned families when deciding what is best for their relatives. Currently, psychologists and judges make judgments with respect to the rights of individuals who are committed. However, these individuals place a professional standard on involuntary hospitalization determinations. Ultimately, these decisions lack a more personal understanding from those family members who represent the true needs of the hospitalized patient. Shaw, Hotopf, and Davies (2003) found that discharges from psychiatric hospitals by the nearest relative against psychiatric advice were not related to poor clinical outcomes.

There are aspects of familial relations that are beneficial for determining what is best for an individual. For example, family members may possess a better awareness about the type of programs and activities to which an individual could respond. This is because family members have a personal connection with the individual. Court-appointed servants, however, lack this subjective knowledge about the committee. Thus, their decisions often do not embody all of a given situation's dynamics, and solely reflect documented information.

Despite the obvious advantages, good-intentioned family members, representing the interests of another individual, have often found it virtually impossible to get the care they feel would be most effective for their relative. As a result, the voices of invested family members frequently have been silenced. For these family members, in order to obtain the care they deem proper, several legal barriers must be hurdled. Then, too, there is the risk that the courts will not respect the wishes of family members for a variety of political and economic reasons (e.g., the case of Mrs. Packard). However, in many ways, psychiatric hospitals are becoming increasingly aware of making their care patient- and recovery-centered, which encourages family involvement when the patients consent to it.

Many debates exist which argue over whether the current implementation of *parens patriae* and paternalism in the involuntary hospitalization arena is any better than it was decades ago, considering the effect it has had on the family. In the process of protecting the mentally ill from family members who did not represent the best interests of the patient, relatives who are genuinely concerned now have to prove their well-meaning intentions to commit a relation, in order for that person to receive proper care. This practice is far removed from the historical assumption that family members will look out for the best interest of their relatives.

Forensic Psychology and Policy Implications

It is difficult to balance the views of the individual, family, and the state when dealing with the issue of involuntary hospitalization. First and foremost, the individual should always have his/her liberties protected, yet, in most instances the individual is incapable or too young to fight for such rights. This is why the doctrines of *parens patriae* and paternalism were established. However, when the state is given the power to act as a parent for an individual, the decisions made are going to reflect the politics and economics of that time. There needs to be some consistency in how these doctrines are implemented and what foci should be taken. As it stands, we have come to a point where the interests of the mentally ill are determined by public defenders and specialists. These specialists need to be appointed by the courts and not by advocates on either side of the debate. The experts, whether psychologists or doctors, need to be impartial to the situation at hand. Furthermore, the family needs to be recognized when decisions are made regarding an individual. For example, when forming treatment plans for patients admitted on an involuntary commitment, it can be very helpful to consult with family members concerning possible treatment options and important historical information when possible and with the appropriate patient consent. Facilities such as North Texas State Hospital, which consists of a general psychiatric campus in Wichita Falls, Texas and the only maximum-security forensic campus for the state of Texas in Vernon, provide short-term accommodations for indigent families, who travel to visit their hospitalized family member. In providing more protection for individuals suffering from mental illness, the impact of the family can become less of a force in the entire process. It seems that while trying to protect the individual from family members with ill intentions, others are categorized as being guilty of exploiting the mentally ill when they are not. Even when an individual has been involuntarily hospitalized, treatment providers should be active partners with that individual and their family (when appropriate) in determining and working toward recovery/wellness goals. Despite the circumstances of their hospitalization, wellness and autonomy should be at the heart of treatment for those who have been civilly committed for hospital care.

Suggestions for Future Research

When the doctrines of *parens patriae* and paternalism were first introduced, our society was very different. Since then, we have been trying to fit these antiquated notions into our modern values and beliefs. It seems as though we have done a successful job, considering the slim probability of pleasing everyone. Yet, it appears as if we have gone too far in making generalizations about the role of the family in this process. Some would argue that it is better to be pessimistic than optimistic in regard to predicting the motivations for people's actions. We have become so paranoid with this new system that we have drifted from making decisions based on human factors and are more concerned with making choices based on the judicial system.

Further research is needed to determine if current legal proceedings regard the patient as the most important figure. Along with that, since the family has become less of a voice in this process, it may be beneficial to investigate the ramifications of losing such a personal figure in the decision-making process. Research should also be undertaken exploring the involvement of family members and the patient as partners in the treatment planning process. Doing so may benefit treatment compliance and shorten the length of stay for involuntarily hospitalized patients.

Termination of Parental Rights

Introduction

In cases where the abuse and neglect of children are evident, the state may find it necessary to petition for the **termination of parental rights** (i.e., legal process through which the legal relationship between parent and child is ended, legally allowing the child to be placed for adoption in order to be placed in a more stable environment) in order to act in the best interests of the child. It is estimated that at any given time, approximately 84,000 children are awaiting adoption in the United States following the termination of their parents' rights, and this number has increased steadily over the last several years (Administration for Children, Youth, and Families, 2008). Some view this as an extreme measure by the state to forever sever the legal bonds between the biological parent(s) and child (Wattenberg, Kelley, & Kim, 2001; Lauter, 2007; Williams, 2008; Vesneski, 2011; Condie & Condie, 2007). Serious risk factors are evident in both the decision to reunite a child with an abusive or neglectful parent or to terminate their parental rights. Forensic psychologists are being called upon for parental rights termination consultation (Condie & Condie, 2007). Psychologists are frequently utilized to conduct assessments and to provide testimony in these hearings (Bogacki & Weiss, 2007). Experts are often presented by all parties involved.

In 1980, Congress passed the **Adoption Assistance and Child Welfare Act (AACWA)**, the goal of which was to preserve families that had engaged in child abuse and neglect (Erickson, 2000). During the last decade, there has been a shift from an emphasis on rehabilitation and reunification to a focus on the safety of the child being paramount with provisions for expedited termination of parental rights and speedier adoptions. This paradigm shift occurred in part as a result of the wave of serious child abuse and death cases in the 1980s and 1990s. The attempts at rehabilitation were marginal at best and many children languished in the foster care system. When President Clinton signed the 1997 **Adoption and Safe Families Act (ASFA)**, the focus shifted to permanency planning within an expedited time frame (Wattenberg *et al.*, 2001). Much debate still exists as to what is in the best interests of the child and at what point should legal ties to the biological parent be dissolved (Miller, 2010; Hawkins-Leon & Worthy, 2008; Rockhill, Green, & Furrer, 2007; Murphy, Quartly, & Cuthbert, 2009; Davidson, 2008). Some argue that while the intent of the shift is understandable, it may just encourage an already overburdened family court system, in some instances, to terminate parental rights without close enough scrutiny or just cause. It may also result in increased spending on litigation of these cases without effectively protecting children and encouraging safe and healthy families (Gainsborough, 2009).

This legislation has also been criticized because of its poor explanation to parents affected by it, and that it turns a blind eye to the challenges placed on parents by poverty (Meyer, McWey, McKendrick, & Henderson, 2010), addiction (Hannett, 2007), and emotional distress. Courts are criticized for frequently allowing inadequate representation for parents in these cases, which have significant consequences, and for not providing sufficient resources to assist families who are reunited and transitioning back to family life (Miller, 2010). Additionally, critics have indicated that these laws may disproportionately and unfairly impact parents with substance abuse disorders or other mental illnesses (Meyer *et al.*, 2010; Hannett, 2007). According to Douglas and McCarthy (2011), legislative changes regarding these issues are predicted by the amount of media coverage paid to individual cases, rather than the actual rates of child maltreatment. They also note that legislative changes have been ineffective in decreasing child abuse or even fatalities (Douglas & McCarthy, 2011).

When one considers the extreme cases of child abuse or neglect that end in death, the court erring on the side of caution and terminating parental rights is not difficult to imagine. Media accounts during the 1980s and 1990s described stories of children who had been reunited with their families, only to be later killed by the abusive parent (Erickson, 2000). Consider the following case illustration (Dawson, 2010).

In a recent case our judicial system was tested and failed. Katie Tagle sought a restraining order on 21 January 2010 against her ex-boyfriend Stephen Garcia to stop him from having unsupervised visitation with their nine-month-old child. She told the judge Garcia threatened to kill the infant. The judge thought she was lying. The court transcript records Judge Robert Lemkau as saying, "One of you is lying…" And later, "Mr. Garcia claims it's total fabrication on your part." Garcia also referred to it as "little stunts and games" that "she used" to deny him access to his son. Even when she mentioned the evidence of the threats, the judge stated, "Well, ma'am, there's a real dispute about whether that's even true or not." And finally, "My suspicion is that you're lying…" He denied her the order (as did two other judges). Garcia took their nine-month-old son that day and drove off into the mountains. Ten days later, they were both found dead in the cab of his pickup truck from gunshot wounds to the head. In his suicide letter, Garcia addressed family, friends, and Katie Tagle. He explained his motivation for the murder-suicide and expressed his loving feelings for Katie Tagle but was contemptuous of Tagle's family. In his letter, he wrote in all capital letters that they were to blame for his and the infant's deaths. In the letter, he referred to Tagle as his "true love" and expressed his wish that they could have had the infant's first birthday party. Garcia shared 50—50 custody with Tagle, but expressed in his suicide note a desire to have full custody of his son and to have Tagle back with him, so that they could be a "whole family again."

Yet another tragic case example is that of Elisa (Erickson, 2000, p. 84):

For example, the cover story "A Shameful Death" in *Time* magazine on 11 December 1995 documented the case of Elisa Izquierdo, a six-year-old child who had been returned to an abusive mother by social services only to be brutally tortured and murdered. Elisa's mother, a crack addict, came to believe that her father had put Elisa under a spell that had to be beaten out of the child. Elisa was also repeatedly sexually assaulted with a toothbrush and a hairbrush. Elisa's mother confessed to killing her by throwing her against a concrete wall. "She confessed that she made Elisa eat her own feces and that she mopped the floor with her head. The police told reporters that there was no part of the six-year-old's body that was not cut or bruised" (Van Biema, 1995, p. 36; cited in Erickson, 2000, p. 84).

Those involved in research and policy called for reform of the child welfare system. Gelles, in *The Book of David* (1996), eloquently argued that AACWA was not protecting vulnerable children. Like Elisa, 15-month-old David was killed by his mother, and also like Elisa it was a death that should not have occurred given the known history of child abuse in the family. Gelles described how the model of family preservation that was based on rehabilitation of parents was failing to protect children. He questioned the assumption that all parents were motivated to change their behavior, arguing that many parents simply agreed to participate in rehabilitative programs in order to avoid further court action. Gelles stated the need to "abandon the fantasy that child welfare agencies can balance the goals of protecting children and preserving families, adopting instead a child-centered policy of family services" (1996, p. 148; cited in Erickson, 2000, p. 84).

Literature Review

These cases demonstrate the extreme example of what can go horribly wrong with reuniting a child with an abusive family or parent. **Parental rights termination** refers to proceedings in which the "state alleges that even after the provision of relevant services, the parent remains unable or unfit to care for the child. The court is concerned with the behaviors and capacities of the adult in his or her role as a parent, and the harm that may, or has, come to the child" (Condie & Condie, 2007, p. 294). It has also been defined as a permanent severing of ties between a parent and child that results in a loss of custody and any legal authority over the child's welfare in the future, as well making the child eligible for adoption (Johnson, Baker, & Maceira, 2001). Researchers indicate that the state's responsibility to petition for parental rights termination and the court's ability to grant the order draws from the *parens patriae* doctrine, which places the state in a position to maintain societal interests (Pruit & Wallace, 2011; Johnson *et al.*, 2001).

In the late 20th century, there was a shifting focus on the federal government's position on what action should be taken to protect children who experienced abuse or severe neglect while in the care of their families (Erickson, 2000). Prior to the mid-1970s, the federal government had little involvement in child welfare policy. By the mid-1970s, child welfare policies in the United States was focusing more and more on removing children from unsafe homes and placing them in the foster care system. In 1980, with the passage of the AACWA, the government acknowledged the obligation the states owed to parents whose children were in foster care to provide rehabilitative and prevention services and a time line to help with the process of reunification as the primary goal (Erickson, 2000). The services included group and individual counseling, substance abuse treatment, parenting classes, and regular visitation of the parent with the abused or neglected child in the home of the foster parent. This legislation was aimed at targeting the growing drift in foster care, specifically those children caught in limbo. Initially, it appeared that this was successful with a decline in the foster care population from 1980 until 1986. However, from 1986 until 1993, the foster care population grew from 280,000 to 445,000 (House Ways & Means Committee, 1998).

In addition to the overall criticisms of the ineffectiveness of this approach, researchers argued that there was little empirical evidence to support these rehabilitative approaches as effective under these circumstances (Erickson, 2000). Costin, Karger, and Stoesz (1996) explained that the belief was that once the parents of these children understood the causes of their behavior, they would then change it. Early critics blasted that this model ignored the myriad of more complex environmental factors that contributed to this cycle of violence for many of the families involved (Erickson, 2000; Costin *et al.*, 1996). More recently, critics have noted that children removed from abusive or neglectful homes and placed in foster care are often exposed to further maltreatment "in the very placements designed for care and treatment" (Overcamp-Martini & Sutton, 2009, p. 55).

Indeed, children of parents whose parental rights have been terminated are more likely to face homelessness, joblessness, drug addiction, early pregnancy, mental health problems, and prison time (O'Donnell, 2010). They are also more likely to experience depression, impaired coping abilities, and other psychological dysfunction (Schneider & Phares, 2005), suggesting that the detrimental long-term effects the system is trying to address via parental rights termination are not being adequately addressed or avoided (O'Donnell, 2010). In light of these criticisms, the federal government's role in directly overseeing these systems and placements has decreased in favor of individual states' providing oversight within their own systems (Overcamp-Martini & Sutton, 2009). Although the more recent changes represent an improvement, a more "middle of the road" approach has been suggested, which would encourage "collaborative system review between state protective services and federally funded protection and advocacy programs" (Overcamp-Martini & Sutton, 2009, p. 55).

In 1993, Congress allowed 930 million dollars to be used over five years for family preservation by way of the **Family Preservation and Support Program**, which was designed to prevent out-of-home placements for children who were abused or neglected (Erickson, 2000). "**Permanency planning**" (i.e., a movement which developed in the 1970s to either return children to their biological homes or terminate parental rights quickly and place the child for adoption) has been a consistent concept throughout the past four decades, but the means by which policy, the government, and the courts believe this should happen has shifted (Becker, Jordan, & Larsen, 2007). Both the 1980 and 1993 legislation addressed this issue by way of reasonable efforts at family reunification or preservation. Once again, critics of the 1993 legislation compared it to the 1994 Violence Against Women Act and noted that the legislation for children only received half of the money, and that the legislation did not include a proarrest strategy for parents who physically abused their children (Erickson, 2000; Costin *et al.*, 1996). The child abuse and neglect policy mandated home-based services, including psychological treatment for parents who abused their children, while the **Violence Against Women Act** mandated arrest for husbands who were physically abusive toward their wives. Researchers ask the question, "Why does violence against women result in arrest, whereas violence against children leads to treatment?" (Erickson, 2000, p. 85).

Ultimately, the critics of the AACWA were instrumental in shaping the 1997 Adoption and Safe Families Act (ASFA) (Johnson, *et al.*, 2001). ASFA strives to improve on the deficits of the previous legislation by expediting parental rights termination or reunification if possible, providing financial incentives to the states for adoption placements, and by making the safety and welfare of the child the paramount issue rather than family preservation. All 50 states had passed legislation that had enacted ASFA by the end of 1999 (Erickson, 2000). This legislation attempts to reunify families using reasonable efforts; however, the time line is well defined and much shorter. ASFA also promotes concurrent planning or that states may pursue alternative placements, while attempting reunification, in order to speed up placement if parental conduct changes or is deemed unfit. ASFA mandates a state to file a termination of parental rights petition if a child has been placed in foster care for at least 15 of the last 22 months (Erickson, 2000). Termination is usually pursued in cases of: (1) parental incapacity to care for the child by reason of mental illness, substance abuse, or mental defect; (2) extreme disinterest in or abandonment of the child; (3) extreme or repeated abuse or neglect; (4) conviction of a crime carrying a sentence of long-term incarceration with chances of parole being low; (5) failure of parent to improve in response to interventions; and (6) limitations on the length of the time the child may remain in state-sponsored placement (Condie & Condie, 2007).

There are three exceptions in place that do not require the petition be filed, which include: (1) a relative is caring for the child; (2) the agency documents a compelling reason why termination is not in the best interests of the child; or (3) if the state failed to provide reasonable efforts or services to safely reunite the child with their family within that time frame (Erickson, 2000). However, "reasonable efforts" are not operationally defined and the standard is not clearly set out. Three exceptions also exist wherein reasonable efforts for family preservation are not required and include: (1) the parent has forced the child to experience an aggravating circumstance to include torture, abandonment, or sexual abuse; (2) a person has killed another one of his or her children or has in some way conspired or aided another person in doing so; and finally (3) reasonable efforts are not mandated when the parental rights have been terminated for a sibling of the child in question (Erickson, 2000). Clear and convincing evidence is the burden of proof required to demonstrate that a child cannot safely remain with his or her parents and that a safer option which is in the best interest of the child exists (Wattenberg *et al.*, 2001).

Some criticized ASFA for failing to take into consideration the ability for children to form multiple attachments and that severing parental ties quickly can have enduring negative effects (Garrison, 1996; Erickson, 2000). As long as the child is in foster care, visitation by parents is possible. Another criticism is the assumption that expediting termination of parental rights will lead to adoption. Some researchers have found that the number of adoptions can not keep up with the larger number of children whose parental rights have been terminated, with many of these children just aging out of the system (Erickson, 2000).

According to the results of a recent survey of judges involved in termination of parental rights cases by Ellis, Malm, and Bishop (2009), judges reported their observations that many children were not adopted prior to reaching the age of majority, and expressed concerns that terminating parental rights when children were unlikely to be adopted simply created "legal orphans" (p. 1), and did relatively little to minimize the harm to these already vulnerable children. Further, judges reported that their decisions to terminate parental rights were complicated when older children did not wish to be adopted or separated from their families, as well as by concerns that children would lose all ties to their birth families, after having known and been with them for the majority of their developmental years (Ellis *et al.*, 2009). The judges felt that these concerns could be addressed through **open adoptions** (i.e., an adoption in which the biological and adoptive parents know each other's identity, and in some cases maintain some level of contact with one another, which may include limited contact of the biological parents with their child), post-adoption contact agreements, and court-mandated treatment efforts (Ellis *et al.*, 2009).

Since the Family Preservation and Support Program was discontinued in 2002, many states have implemented and continued their own policies and programs to "prevent the unnecessary placement of children in foster care" by providing parents with supervised treatment opportunities prior to the removal of children from the home (Bagdasaryan, 2005, p. 615). Although studies with nonexperimental designs have indicated that these programs are largely effective in meeting this goal, experimental studies have yielded mixed results, which have led researchers to examine specific conditions under which such programs may be most effective. Results indicate that services provided for longer durations are more likely to result in successful completion than shorter programs (Bagdasaryan, 2005). Families who successfully completed family preservation programs indicate the following: parents emerge feeling, although they still require professional support, their family situations are more manageable; they feel more equipped to interact appropriately with their children, despite expressing uncertainty about their parenting abilities; and that successful program completion had no significant impact on the number and quality of social contacts (Van Puyenbroeck, Loots, Grietens, Jacquet, Vanderfaeillie, & Escudero, 2009).

Other researchers have found that parents with a mental disorder or **developmental disability** (i.e., lifelong disabilities attributable to mental and/or physical impairments that are evident prior to age 18, such as mental retardation) were less likely to successfully complete these programs (Becker *et al.*, 2007). However, placement of children in **therapeutic foster care** (i.e., the placement of children with foster families who have been specially trained to care for children with certain medical or behavioral needs, such as medically fragile children, children with emotional or behavioral disorders, and HIV+ children) increased the likelihood of successful completion (Becker *et al.*, 2007). Such findings suggest that, although preservation efforts may be effective, more research is needed to determine traits of families and programs to increase their effectiveness, and to extend this effectiveness to such outcome measures as the number and quality of social contacts by parents.

Another difficulty regarding parental rights termination hearings is that many of the parents involved are indigent and have marginal representation from attorneys who may have little experience dealing with these issues (Johnson *et al.*, 2001; Miller, 2010). Additionally, the child welfare agency that is attempting to provide services to them is also collecting evidence at the same time that might be used against the parents at trial, resulting in ethical dilemmas. Furthermore, Johnson *et al.* state (2001, p. 17), "If a judge errs in terminating the parental rights, the consequences are minimal in that the aggrieved, typically indigent, parent and child can only suffer quietly. While if the judge errs in the direction of returning a child to a parent who later harms the child, the response from the press and the public will be substantial."

Research has demonstrated that parents who are involved with termination of parental rights typically have a long history of multiple problems including mental illness, substance abuse, lower intellectual functioning, involvement with the criminal justice system, limited formal education, poverty, and their own childhood history of out of home placement, as well as abuse and neglect (Wattenberg *et al.*, 2001; Meyer *et al.*, 2010; Lightfoot, Hill, & LaLiberte, 2010; Kundra & Alexander, 2009; Larrieu, Heller, Smyke, & Zeanah, 2008; McWey, Henderson, & Alexander, 2008). The characteristics of parents who are facing a termination of parental rights petition is an example of the previously discussed **cycle of violence** (i.e., a cyclical pattern of abuse in which high emotions lead to abuse, which increase emotions and the likelihood of abuse for retributional or vengeful reasons).

The children involved were generally very young, typically lived in poverty-stricken, chaotic homes, and spent an extended amount of time in the system, when placed out of the home (Wattenberg *et al.*, 2001). Past research has noted that a number of children from these home environments manifest a variety of disorders, including gross behavioral problems and below average IQs (Borgman, 1981). Additionally, mothers with fewer years of education, who had been abused themselves as children, had a history of psychiatric difficulties, abused substances, had been convicted of a crime in the past, and who had experienced domestic partner violence were more likely to have their parental rights terminated (Larrieu *et al.*, 2008). Fathers, on the other hand, were more likely to have their parental rights terminated if they lacked social support or financial resources, had a mental health or substance abuse diagnosis, or had ever been incarcerated (Olmstead, McWey, & Henderson, 2011).

Critics of parental rights termination also point out that this strategy does little to benefit the older child with strong attachments to their parents as well as scant desire and probability to be adopted (Johnson *et al.*, 2001; Noonan & Burke, 2005). Research over the last three decades has consistently demonstrated that children often remain fiercely loyal and attached to their parents, even when they have experienced serious abuse or neglect (see, e.g., Noonan & Burke, 2005; Johnson *et al.*, 2001; Johnson, 1999; Johnson, 1996; Garrison, 1996; Borgman, 1981). Johnson *et al.* (2001, p. 16) state, "For instance, an early adolescent female responded to the state's petition to terminate her parental ties to her birth-mother by running away from her foster home of seven years and returning to the home of her psychiatrically impaired mother." The termination of parental rights not only has implications for the child's abusive or neglectful parent(s), but for the child's relationship with siblings and extended family as well (Johnson *et al.*, 2001).

Regarding placement of children, research has demonstrated that there are circumstances which either hinder or prevent permanent placement (Cushing & Greenblatt, 2009). According to Cushing and Greenblatt (2009), male children are less likely than females to be adopted quickly or at all and children with emotional or behavioral problems were less likely to be adopted. Other factors that reduced the likelihood of adoption included a greater length of time since the termination of parental rights and if the child's case worker had changed frequently (Cushing & Greenblatt, 2009).

Janko (1994) highlights the role of environmental or sociocultural factors that contribute to the problem of abuse and neglect and that also need to be addressed in order to reduce this problem overall and to more successfully reunify families with some expectation of success. Whether or not certain environmental circumstances, such as having "adequate money, food, housing, health care, and available adults to share care-giving responsibilities" can either add stress or relief to parents (Janko, 1994, p. 3).

An early study examined the records of 97 children ages six and under whose parental rights were terminated in Minnesota between 1991 and 1997 (Wattenberg *et al.*, 2001). The study was initiated to identify risk factors or a "risk pool" of families who are likely to have a high probability of parental rights termination. The racial makeup of the sample data was approximately 48% Caucasian and 34% African American, as the two largest groups. About 64% of the mothers were Caucasian, 21% were African American, and 9.3% were American

Indian, with the remaining 5.7% being multiracial. More than half of the mothers had their first child before the age of 18 with approximately 12% having their first child when they were age 15 or younger. The median age of the mothers at termination was age 26. More than 80% of the mothers in the sample had multiple disorders, including substance abuse currently or in the past (57.7%); disorders such as major mental illness (i.e., depression, bipolar disorder, schizophrenia, or personality disorders) (47.5%); developmental disabilities (12%); and almost one-third had a childhood history of abuse or out of home placement. Greater than one-quarter were involved with the correctional system and more than one-fifth had experienced one or more relationships with a history of domestic violence (Wattenberg *et al.*, 2001). Substance abuse was identified as the problem that led to a termination of parental rights judgment in the majority of cases. Overall, 80% of cases documented varied, overlapping conditions resulting in a chaotic and unsafe living environment (Wattenberg *et al.*, 2001).

Forty-one of the 97 cases did not have any information regarding the father of the child. Out of the 56 remaining case files, greater than 60% of the fathers also had multiple problems (Wattenberg *et al.*, 2001). Greater than one-third had a current or past substance abuse problem; 25% had a criminal record; approximately 20% engaged in domestic violence with their partner; 15% had a history of childhood abuse and/or placement, and 14% were incarcerated at the time of the termination hearing.

Children of color were over-represented in the sample taking into consideration the demographics of Minnesota with 57.7% Caucasian, 25.8% African American, and 13.4% American Indian. The Latino/Chicano children and Asian American children were more evenly represented in the sample at 2.1% and 3.3% respectively. Approximately 20% of the sample were biracial. Almost two-thirds or 63.7% of the children were the age of three or younger at the termination of parental rights. Greater than 75% of the children in the sample had siblings also in the process with more than one-third having had three or more siblings. Approximately 80% of the children had most recently lived with nonfamilial or nonrelative foster homes. Almost 60% of the children were identified as having disabilities to include: emotional disturbance (26.8%), physical disability (9.3%), developmental disability (7.2%), learning disability (5.2%), and other conditions (11.4%). Evidence of sexual abuse was present in 18.5% of the cases. More than one-quarter of the children had been born either drug or alcohol exposed (Wattenberg *et al.*, 2001).

Finally, the "reasonable efforts" at family preservation included counseling (52.6%), substance abuse treatment (48.5%), and parenting classes (47.4%). Mental health assessments occurred in 36.1% of the families and chemical dependency assessments in 29.9% of the cases. Parenting assessments occurred in 21.6% of the cases, home-based services (18.6%), and domestic violence treatment (14.4%). Direct services to children included special education (20.6%), therapy (15.5%), and developmental and psychological assessment

(13.4%). However, the vast majority of children had no documented services (Wattenberg *et al.*, 2001). The role that psychologists can play in this process is substantial. Certainly, additional services for these at-risk children are desperately needed.

More recent research has extended and updated the findings of the Wattenberg *et al.* (2001) study. These researchers have found that Hispanic and African American children placed in foster care are at lower risk than their Caucasian counterparts for having their parent(s)' rights terminated. They also discovered that children with a disability were less likely to be reunited with their parents, and their parents were more likely to have their rights terminated (Noonan & Burke, 2005). Parents of older children were less likely to have their parental rights terminated, and children who had been placed in foster care more often were less likely to be reunified with their parents and more likely to have their parents' rights terminated (Noonan & Burke, 2005). Finally, results have indicated that parents with mental illness, developmental disabilities, **learning disabilities** (i.e., disorders which affect a person's ability to learn in specific area(s), such as reading, writing, arithmetic, listening, speaking, or reasoning), and other cognitive deficits were more likely to have proceedings initiated to terminate their parental rights, and more likely to actually have their rights terminated at the conclusion of these proceedings (Bogacki & Weiss, 2007).

As psychologists and other mental health professionals have become increasingly involved in cases of parental rights termination, evaluation procedures have been more precisely defined and investigated in the literature. However, more work is needed in this area. Researchers currently recommend that evaluations include a thorough **clinical interview** (i.e., an interview in which a mental health professional collects information regarding a person's background, history, and current functioning to assist in diagnosis, treatment planning, or, in this case, in

order to assist the court in answering a legal question). This clinical interview should minimally address the following: (1) the psychosocial history of the parents and all children; (2) history of substance use or abuse among the parents and alternative caregivers; (3) assessment for risk factors for future domestic violence against the children or other adults in the home by parents; and (4) risk of ongoing neglect to the child(ren) (Condie & Condie, 2007). In addition, all evaluations in this area should include efforts to corroborate information from objective third party sources, as well as subjective and objective measures of response styles such as **under-reporting** (i.e., efforts by an evaluee to minimize their current or past difficulties, or to appear more well-adjusted than they actually are) (Condie & Condie, 2007).

Evaluation of **psychological bonding**, or a "reciprocal, two-way process" which occurs between parent and child, and which is marked by a "strong emotional connectedness…that endures over space and time, and is necessary for physical survival and emotional well-being" (Barone, Weitz, & Witt, 2005, p. 397), is also a critical component of evaluations to determine whether a parent's rights should be terminated. These evaluations are called **bonding evaluations** (i.e., "a specialized type of assessment whose goal is to determine the nature of the child's attachment to birth parents and foster parents, especially to address the question of who occupies the position of greatest centrality in the child's emotional life" [Barone *et al.*, 2005, p. 402]). According to Barone *et al.* (2005), bonding evaluations may involve the following techniques: (1) an initial review of records and background information pertaining to biological and foster parents and all children involved; (2) an interview with all caregivers to evaluate their perceptions of their relationship with the child(ren); (3) an observation of the child(ren) interacting with all current and potential caregivers; and (4) a brief interview with the child(ren), assuming they are old enough to participate in such an interview. At each step in the evaluation, the evaluator should be looking for information pertaining to: (1) comfort level the child and the parent have with each other; (2) comfort-seeking and guidance-seeking behavior by the child; (3) degree to which the parent and child initiate interaction with each other; (4) nature of the parent–child interaction; (5) amount of time the parent and child spend smiling at each other and/or making eye contact; (6) degree of upset by the child if a brief separation occurs and the child is asked to wait with the evaluator for a brief interview; (7) willingness of the child to explore the environment with the parent in the same room; (8) whether or not the child will approach others for comfort and/or guidance when the parent is present; and (9) ease with which the child is able to make his or her needs known to the parent and the degree of responsiveness to such expression by the parent (Barone *et al.*, 2005).

Forensic Psychology and Policy Implications

Child welfare policy and practice in the United States continues to be criticized. The resources available to this system are overwhelmed by the number of children and families who experience abuse and neglect. Wattenberg *et al.* (2001) describe the need for courts, child welfare workers, and mental health professionals to identify early on those families who are unlikely to be reunited with children, so that resources can be effectively used early on to investigate other permanency options. Recent evidence suggests that children who are placed with a foster care family who eventually adopted them after termination of parental rights adjust better than children whose foster families do not adopt them. Therefore, it is recommended that children who are unlikely to be reunified with a parent be placed with foster families likely to adopt them (Cushing & Greenblatt, 2009).

There are risks inherent in both the foster care system and in the abusive or neglectful parental home. Burford, Pennell, MacLeod, Campbell, and Lyall (1996) stated, regarding the Canadian system, "Disclosures of widespread abuse in foster care and in children's institutions during the past decade have laid bare as false belief that placing a child into protective custody or substitute care is a guarantee of safety or long-range well-being for that child" (cited in Johnson *et al.*, 2001, p. 26). What is also striking is the lack of therapeutic resources currently provided to these very high-risk children. Not only have they experienced abuse and/or neglect, but their parental bonds are being severed and no matter how toxic the relationship, it is often quite traumatic for the children involved. Although the cycle of violence is present in the national consciousness, our society puts little resources toward prevention and intervention programs for these children. Our near sightedness prevents us from contemplating the far more expensive human and financial costs our lack of action will create in the future. Wattenberg *et al.* (2001) cautions that the "reasonable efforts" phrasing in the AACWA legislation from the 1980s did not provide a workable guideline for how much intervention or services is adequate in the attempt for reunification.

For those children who cannot or should not be reunited with their biological families, expediting the adoption process by shortening stays in foster care would reduce costs and would bring the security of a permanent home to numerous children each year (Festinger & Pratt, 2002). Additionally, recent models have proposed a "**halfway house**" approach, which involves parents attempting to be reunified with their children living under supervised conditions, while working towards treatment goals (Carolan, Burns-Jager, Bozek, & Chew, 2010). These authors suggest that these types of programs may be especially helpful for women with trauma and/or substance abuse histories.

Erickson (2000) suggests that interventions should increase social supports for high risk families, rather than just focusing on the psychological problems of the parent accused of abuse or neglect. As a whole, our society must recognize the impact of prolonged marginalization, poverty, and inequality. These broad societal changes, however, will not come quickly enough to aid the parent facing parental rights termination in a little over one year or the children whose lives are in danger in an abusive home. Some critics also question the policy on not criminally prosecuting more parents who do not feed or physically beat their children. Erickson (2000) speculates that perhaps our society values our indigent children less or wishes to limit governmental control over the institution of the family. Child welfare policies could be focused toward strengthening families and their connections to the larger community (Costin *et al.*, 1996). For example, it has been recommended that intervention programs created to prevent the need for termination of parental rights for parents with mild cognitive or intellectual deficits be designed to place decreased demand on these parents, while still ensuring the safety of children (Bogacki & Weiss, 2007).

Mental health professionals, particularly psychologists who will testify as experts, should have extensive training in assessing the parent–child relationship. The evaluating psychologist will likely also be asked to opine about whether or not the parent's behavior or condition is likely to change in the foreseeable future. Training in assessing the nuances of whether or not the parent(s) are likely to comply with reunification requirements is also recommended (Wattenberg *et al.*, 2001). The forensic expert will frequently testify regarding the potential risks and benefits of either termination or reunification. Some mental health professionals should also have a more prominent role in providing developmental and mental health assessments for these children, while others take on the treatment role of providing individual or group therapy for the myriad of problems and stressors they face. Evaluators should also assess parents for cognitive deficits, in order to provide specific recommendations regarding the likelihood of reunification, as well as possible treatment interventions to facilitate reunification (Bogacki & Weiss, 2007). Testimony should also provide a balanced view of the strengths and weaknesses of the parent(s) so that reunification, when possible, can occur successfully (Bogacki & Weiss, 2007). In order to guide professionals working in this area, specific competency and practice standards should be developed (Kalich, Carmichael, Masson, & Blacker, 2007). Finally, this area of forensic psychology practice may impact the objectivity of evaluators and courts, depending upon the personal values of the evaluator, particularly regarding appropriate childrearing practices. Therefore, efforts should be made by legislatures to ensure statutes do not unnecessarily reflect these value judgments and by evaluators to ensure they remain objective in answering the psycholegal question.

Suggestions for Future Research

Future research should attempt to discern a better understanding of the interaction of high risk factors such as substance abuse, mental illness, poverty, intellectual disabilities, domestic violence, and a history of childhood abuse in a family's involvement in the child welfare system and in the criminal and family courts (Wattenberg *et al.*, 2001). Additionally, a better understanding of these factors could aid in the development of more appropriate programming and therapeutic interventions for these families. Wattenberg *et al.* (2001) also recommend further examination of multicultural issues in the service delivery to at-risk families. Research should be explored to determine the effectiveness of concurrent planning in expediting permanent placements for children whose parental rights are terminated. Studies should also be conducted to help refine our risk assessments of children in both reunification and termination situations in order to more fully appreciate the detrimental effects either of these scenarios might have on a particular child. A better understanding of a child's attachment to an abusive parent and their ability to form multiple attachments can aid in the development of permanency planning that is truly in the best interest of the child.

Future research should also develop guidelines to assist mental health professionals in conducting or facilitating the final visit between parents and children after parental rights have been terminated (Lauter, 2007). Studies to examine the outcomes of these various approaches are needed. Additionally, future research should examine how different players in the family justice system view the parenting capabilities of parents with intellectual disabilities. Lightfoot *et al.* (2010) suggest examining the impact of placing language concerning disabilities in state statutes on termination of parental rights' decision-making. Recent evidence indicates that minorities are disproportionately represented amongst those whose parental rights are terminated (Vesneski, 2011).

Future research should examine the role that diversity in a jurisdiction might play in determining the content of termination laws. Additionally, future studies are needed to compare the rates of parental rights termination, in particular, jurisdictions examine the impact of more or less vaguely worded statutes have (Vesneski, 2011). Although current research indicates that factors such as substance abuse, mental health problems, and incarceration increase a parent's risk of having their rights terminated, future research should examine which combination of risk factors are particularly predictive of termination (Meyer *et al.* 2010). Investigations to clarify how judges and attorneys utilize termination of parental rights evaluations are recommended (Kalich *et al.*, 2007).

It has been suggested that terminating the parental rights of children who lack an identified adoptive family may facilitate faster adoption and placement due to the wider array of recruitment strategies available for finding adoptive parents (Ellis *et al.*, 2009). This possibility should be explored in future studies. Future work should also examine the feelings and experiences of children following termination of parental rights. Studies could explore the effects of multiple foster care placements on the well-being of these children as compared to the potential effects of remaining with the parent(s) whose rights were terminated (Durousseau, 2008). Finally, it would be beneficial to compare the grieving and emotional processes of children whose parents have their rights terminated to children who lose contact with a parent because of death, divorce, or parental absence (Schneider & Phares, 2005). Clearly, much can be learned to better support children through this difficult and potentially traumatic process.

Gay/Lesbian Rights and Definitions of the Family

Introduction

The dynamics of contemporary families have shifted away from the "ideal" context of the nuclear family. Single-parent households are becoming increasingly commonplace and, more importantly, there has been an increase in the formation of gay and lesbian families. The political debate and policies surrounding **civil marriage rights** (same-sex couples can be legally recognized as a legally registered couple but are not guaranteed the same rights and responsibilities as a heterosexual married couple) for same-sex couples have a psychological and social impact on the gay, lesbian, and bisexual community as well as their families (Fingerhut, Riggle, & Rostosky, 2011). The impact on the gay, lesbian, and bisexual community "converge in demonstrating that the denial of civil marriage rights is a significant public health issue with important policy implications" (Fingerhut *et al.*, 2011, p. 225). In 2004, the state of Massachusetts legalized gay marriages, allowing homosexual couples to receive the legal benefits and protections that heterosexual couples have always been afforded. In June of 2011, New York passed legislation allowing same-sex marriages, while Rhode Island passed legislation that allows same-sex civil unions (National Conference of State Legislatures, 2011). Dillen (2003) describes the oppression of gay and lesbian individuals by the heterosexual, White, and middle class.

Currently, Massachusetts also prohibits discrimination against individuals who apply to become adoptive parents, and enables adults to adopt a partner's child through second parent adoption (Shelley-Sireci & Ciano-Boyce, 2002; Patterson, 2009). Many jurisdictions across America have recently allowed openly lesbian and gay adults to successfully complete second parent adoptions (Richmond, 2009; National Gay and Lesbian Task Force, 2008; Goldberg & Smith, 2011). However, overall, little attention is paid to how parental rights have often been denied to lesbian, gay, or transgender individuals. Common misconceptions about gay and lesbian families only serve to hinder the development of laws and policies which favor artificial insemination, adoption, and foster care. For example, some people believe that children of homosexuals are apt to acquire parental sexual proclivities as well as to be subjected to additional sexual harm based on stereotypes and misinformation.

Concerns also arise as far as children in nonconventional families experiencing difficulties with gender identity, gender roles, and having an increased likelihood of moving toward a homosexual orientation. A second category of concerns is that children living with homosexual parents may be stigmatized, teased, or otherwise traumatized by peers. Some courts have expressed fears that children in the custody of gay or lesbian parents will be more vulnerable to psychological maladjustment or will exhibit interpersonal difficulties and subsequent behavior problems. These are just some of the pertinent issues which are discussed within the context of gay and lesbian families. The following case illustrates the family dynamics of a young girl raised by lesbian parents.

Sarah is a 10-year-old in the fourth grade. She is healthy, bright, curious, and determined. She was born to Marsha into a White family consisting of two parents, Marsha and Jane. The donor of the sperm, Bill, is a heterosexual man who is a friend of Marsha and Jane and liked the idea of physically participating in helping his friends create a family. Marsha and Jane have all along chosen to counter external threats to their family by being out as lesbians. They live in a large city in a part of town friendly to lesbian-headed families. Marsha is active at Sarah's school, working to educate the teachers about lesbian and gay parents and the needs of the children. They belong to a local lesbian-and-gay parents group and attend gatherings as a family. In addition, they have consciously tried to give Sarah tools for interacting with the larger world. They talk to her about homophobia, helping her recognize it so she can learn to separate someone else's prejudice from a statement about her personally. However, to her parents' dismay, Sarah is signaling a need to know about her biological roots. Her parents have feelings in common with many parents whose families are created through adoption or donor insemination. They want Sarah to be only their child. Sarah's parents want to protect her from the pain and confusion that may be generated by needing to integrate the complex roots of her identity. On the other hand, her parents want Sarah to feel whole and integrated. They want to do all they can to prepare Sarah by giving her the support and the skills to maneuver through a complex process (Barrett, 1997).

Literature Review

Sarah's case elucidates some of the dynamics which may arise in gay and lesbian families. For example, gay and lesbian families have to continually struggle with prejudicial notions such as homophobia and gross stereotyping. On the basis of their sexual orientation, homosexual parents are continually labeled as unfit parents who are incapable of rearing well-adjusted children. Yet there is an absence of literature indicating any significant difficulties experienced by children brought up in households of lesbian or gay parents relative to those experienced by children growing up in comparable heterosexual households (Tye, 2003; Franklin, 2003; Welsh, 2011). Munsey's (2010) study demonstrated that children adopted by same-sex couples were as well adjusted as children adopted by heterosexual parents. The existing body of research suggests that gay and lesbian parents are as likely as heterosexual parents to provide home environments that are conducive to positive developmental outcomes among children growing up within them. The following literature review further exemplifies the preceding premise and counters many commonly held misconceptions of gay and lesbian families.

Approximately 22% of same-sex couples in the United States are raising children aged 18 years or younger (The Williams Institute, 2010), and it is estimated that 65,500 children are adopted with a lesbian or gay parent (Census, 2007). According to the Census (2007), by 2005 there was an estimated 270,313 children living with same-sex couples. In 2003, it was estimated that there were between 1.2 and 3 million individuals who were in homosexual partnered household relationships in the United States (Tye, 2003). In contrast, the American Civil Liberties Union (2002) indicated that estimates of the prevalence of children being raised by gay parents varies significantly with the high end being as many as nine million. A national study found that out of a random sample, 8% of lesbians and gay men were parents or a legal guardian of a child under the age of 18, and 49% of participants indicated that although they were not currently parents they would like to be (Henry J. Kaiser Family Foundation, 2001). Many lesbians and gay men who became parents within heterosexual marriages before adopting homosexual identities are also becoming parents after coming out. Therefore, it is likely that the preceding estimates minimize the actual number of homosexual parents. Franklin (2003) describes the growing trend of the planned gay and lesbian family. She describes the impact of such public figures as Melissa Etheridge and Rosie O'Donnell, as well as the crisis in the U.S. child welfare system with greater than a half a million children in long-term foster care, as contributing to the growing awareness and increasing acceptance of the homosexual family through adoption or assisted fertilization.

Additionally, the diversity of their family systems are described to include donor insemination, frequently used by lesbian couples, whereby one woman carries the child and the other obtains legal parental rights through a second parent adoption process. Some lesbian couples adopt through the public adoption system, which is the most likely means used by gay men to parent (Franklin, 2003; Richmond, 2009; Wells, 2011). However, some gay men may opt to use a surrogate mother in order to have children (Patterson, 2009).

Heterosexual individuals are typically expected to become parents and many do so without planning, which is very different from the way many homosexual couples become parents (Franklin, 2003; Wells, 2011). Franklin (2003, p. 51) discusses how the minority of lesbian and gay men who become parents are a "self-selected, highly motivated" group who often endured a great deal of thought and planning, as well as financial expense prior to becoming parents. These individuals are also highly sensitive to outside criticism and negative expectations, so they may strive to be "super parents" (p. 51). More recently, Goldberg and Smith (2009) found that gay men might view their parenting skills in a more positive light than heterosexual males because homosexual men do not view their partner as the more highly skilled parent. Lesbians may view themselves less positively than heterosexual women because they are comparing themselves to another female parental figure (Goldberg & Smith, 2009). Thus, it is imperative for social scientists and the general public to take a closer look at the dynamics of gay and lesbian families. Tasker and Golombok's (1995) longitudinal study of 25 young adults from lesbian families and 21 young adults raised by heterosexual single mothers revealed that those raised by lesbian mothers functioned well in adulthood in terms of psychological well-being, family identity, and relationships. The commonly held assumption that lesbian mothers will have lesbian daughters and gay sons was not supported by the findings.

Furthermore, young adults from lesbian family backgrounds were no more likely to remember general teasing or bullying by their peers than were those from heterosexual single-parent homes. With respect to teasing about their sexuality, young adults from lesbian families were more likely to recall having been teased about being gay or lesbian themselves. No significant differences were found between young adults from lesbian and heterosexual single-mother households in the proportion who had experienced sexual attraction to someone of the same gender. Moreover, the majority of young adults from lesbian backgrounds identified themselves as heterosexual. No significant difference between young adults from lesbian and heterosexual single-parent homes were found for anxiety level as assessed by the Trait Anxiety Inventory. The groups did not differ with respect to depression level as assessed by the Beck Depression Inventory. The study clearly indicates that this sample of young adults who were raised in lesbian households did not experience any detrimental effects as a result of their familial upbringing (Tasker & Golombok, 1995). Adolescents of same-sex homes report that there is teasing that is focused on their parent's sexual orientation (Patterson, 2009). Overall, current research not only fails to substantiate assumptions of significant detrimental effects to children of homosexual parents, but also identifies specific strengths, such as more egalitarian and authoritative parenting styles and children who are more emotionally attuned (Franklin, 2003; Johnson & O'Connor, 2002; Patterson & Chan, 1999).

A study examined the experience of lesbian adoptive parents as compared to heterosexual adoptive parents (Shelley-Sireci & Ciano-Boyce, 2002). Eighteen lesbian adoptive parents, 44 heterosexual adoptive parents, and 49 lesbian parents who utilized donor fertilization were surveyed to assess the similarities in the adoption process. Results indicated that the adoption process was similar for parents of both sexual orientations, but lesbian parents perceived more discrimination and were more likely to be guarded with information during the home study (Shelley-Sireci & Ciano-Boyce, 2002). On the basis of a literature review on the children of lesbian and gay parents, Patterson (1994) concluded that the development of these children was well within normal limits. Patterson studied 37 4- to 9-year-olds and found only two differences between children of lesbian and heterosexual parents: (1) children of lesbian parents reported more symptoms of stress, but also (2) a stronger sense of well-being. Lesbian mothers who did not conceal their sexual orientation and who maintained supportive relationships with extended family members and adults in the community were better able to protect their children from prejudicial experiences. The author concluded that the common misconception that children of gay men and lesbians were more likely to adopt a homosexual orientation was completely unfounded.

Flaks, Ficher, Masterpasqua, and Joseph (1995) compared 3- to 10-year-old children born to 15 lesbian families through donor insemination with those of 15 matched heterosexual families. The families were White, well educated, and drawn from a fairly affluent population. As demonstrated by their performance on a broad range of parent and child outcome measures, couples of both sexual orientations were assessed in terms of parental awareness skills and child-care problems and solutions. Compared with fathers but not with mothers in heterosexual couples, lesbian couples exhibited more parental awareness skills and identified more child-care problems and solutions. The results of this study should generalize well to young children of affluent, stable, and committed lesbian couples who have used anonymous donor insemination. The traditional hypothesis that the healthy development of children requires two heterosexual parents is certainly called into question. The results within this sample show few differences among children of lesbian and heterosexual couples in terms of their psychological and social adjustment.

How important are family structural variables, such as the number of parents in the home and the sexual orientation of parents, as predictors of children's development? Chan, Raboy, and Patterson's (1998) study of 80 families, all of whom had conceived children using the resources of a single sperm bank, included 55 families headed by lesbians and 25 families headed by heterosexual parents. Children averaged 7 years of age and biological mothers averaged 42 years of age. Results showed that children were developing in a normal fashion and that their adjustment was unrelated to structural variables such as parental sexual orientation or the number of parents in the household. Variables associated with family interactions and processes were, however, significantly related to children's adjustment. Not surprisingly, parents who were experiencing higher levels of stress, higher levels of interparental conflict, and lower levels of love for each other had children who exhibited more behavioral problems. The results are consistent with the general hypothesis that children's well-being is more a function of parenting and relationship processes within the family than the function of household composition. More recently, research has shown no significant difference on measures of anxiety, depressive symptoms, self-esteem, delinquency, victimization, or use of substances (tobacco, alcohol, or marijuana) in adolescents living with female same-sex couples (Wainright & Patterson, 2006; Wainright, Russell, & Patterson, 2004). However, there is a lack of research on the children's experience of being raised in a same-sex household (Wells, 2011).

Forensic Psychology and Policy Implications

For many individuals, getting married and raising children are central aspirations; however, these basic rights have been denied to lesbian and gay citizens in many states across America, although in recent years more state legislation is allowing for same-sex marriages and same-sex couples to adopt. Common misconceptions allude to the notion that lesbians and gay men are unfit parents or that children suffer irreparable harm if brought up in the households of lesbian or gay parents. Psychologists are being called upon to research the effects of being raised in same-sex households compared to children being raised in heterosexual households. Current research shows no negative impact on children raised in a same-sex household, but further longitudinal research is needed. Psychologists are being asked to look at the psychological and social development of children in same-sex couple households (Welsh, 2011). Evidence from recent research indicates otherwise and suggests that children raised within lesbian- or gay-headed households are generally well adjusted. In cases such as Sarah's, her parents countered external threats to their family by educating Sarah and providing her with the support and encouragement that she needed.

A question then arises as to why half of the states in America consider parental sexual orientation relevant to child custody, visitation rights, foster care, and adoption rights? State laws on child custody, visitation, and adoption are based on what is in the "best interest of the child." Unfortunately, this particular clause opens the door to consideration of a parent's sexual orientation and may introduce a certain level of subjectivity as far as court decisions about child custody, visitation rights, and adoption cases. Most states, however, utilize the Best Interests standard by considering the parent's homosexual conduct, only as far as it can be shown that this has some adverse effect on the child. Indeed, the evidence to date suggests that home environments provided by gay and lesbian parents are as likely as those provided by heterosexual parents to support and to enable children's psychosocial growth (Patterson & Redding, 1996; Munsey, 2010).

In some jurisdictions, same-sex couples are able to adopt a child through a second parent adoption, which allows one parent to adopt the child after the first parent has successfully adopted the child. In child custody disputes, courts have issued conflicting rulings regarding the rights (i.e., custody and visitation) and the responsibilities (i.e., child support) of the non-biological parents (Miller, 2011). Miller (2011) looked at the typology of five factors that typically influence the judges' decisions; these factors include (1) interpretation of parenting status; (2) legislative intent; (3) parental intent; (4) legal documents establishing parenthood; and (5) the child's best interest. Accordingly, social scientists can work to expand the body of research on lesbian and gay families and can make efforts to ensure that the results become available to the public and policy makers through appropriate publications. Not only can scientific evidence help alleviate misconceptions about lesbian- or gay-headed households; it can also facilitate changes in judicial or legislative decision-making processes. Thus, as certain elements change within the legal system, securing child custody cases and gaining adoption rights may eventually be a less arduous process for gay or lesbian families.

Suggestions for Future Research

Goldfried (2001) stresses the importance of future research on many gay, lesbian, and bisexual issues such as life span development, teenage suicide, substance abuse, victimization and abuse, and family and couple relationships. Research on lesbian and gay families is still relatively new, and additional work is needed if we are to expand our understanding of the lives of homosexual parents and their children. While the controversial issue of same-sex marriages continues to make progress in becoming legally recognized, issues surrounding child custody and adoption for same-sex couples are also issues in the political forefront. Future research that explores the predominant child-rearing styles of such families and their effects on children's adjustment in comparison to heterosexual families is certainly needed. James (2002, p. 475) states, "The changing face of gay and lesbian parenting demands that researchers, educators, clinicians, and policy makers explore the issues of gay and lesbian adoptive parents and their children in their own right, not assuming that they are necessarily the same as those faced by other lesbian and gay families."

Less research is conducted on children of gay fathers than on children with lesbian mothers. There is limited research assessing the development of children of gay or lesbian parents during adolescence and adulthood. Longitudinal studies which follow gay or lesbian families over a certain time period are also needed. However, the costly and time-intensive nature of such studies has, to date, hindered such efforts. Nonetheless, longitudinal studies with representative samples of homosexual and heterosexual families, including observational as well as questionnaire and interview assessments, would be better able to enhance our understanding of parents and children within these contexts. Research in this area would help expand our understanding of families such as Sarah's and many others headed by gay fathers and would elucidate more fully the dynamics of such families. Future research needs to address the voice of the children, and their experience of growing up with same-sex parents and what factors impact their experience both inside and outside of the home (Welsh, 2011). Finally, more research is needed regarding the transgender community's family experiences, including marriage or civil unions, as well as the issues faced with having and raising children.

Practice Update Section: Family Issues in Court and Civil Forensics

Forensic psychologists can become involved in parental rights termination litigation in a variety of ways. Anytime a psychologist is addressing an issue as contentious as parental rights, he or she must be very well trained and prepared for their work to be carefully scrutinized. A psychological examiner in this situation should be very familiar with pertinent research and the forensic standard of practice in assessing the issue at hand. Even more importantly, the forensic evaluator should have a firm grasp and understanding of the relevant laws in his or her jurisdiction. Johnson *et al.* (2001) describes the engagement of psychologists in termination of parental rights proceeding as early on as the initial stages of removing a child from the home and foster care placement. Psychologists may be asked to educate the family court regarding the risk of future harm to the child, the parent's probability of complying with reunification requirements, clinical issues relating to the negative impact of the abuse/neglect on the child, or the potential impact of a parent's myriad of problems on their ability to care for the child. Psychologists are also asked to provide intervention services to parents and children in some cases, albeit, far too few in light of current research. In order to provide relevant and beneficial services, the mental health professional should have a good understanding of the needs and risk factors of the parties involved.

Johnson *et al.* (2001, p. 22) also describe the critical role forensic psychologists often play in providing evidence and testimony that is critical to the state's case in providing "persuasive proof" that the parent is unfit, that reasonable efforts for rehabilitation were made, and/or the termination of parental rights is in the best interests of the child. Then the battle of the experts is likely to ensue, whereby the parent's representing counsel retains a psychologist to conduct assessments to contradict the important facts regarding the state's case.

The child often has an appointed legal guardian that can use his or her own psychological expert witness. Alternatively, the judge can appoint an expert, or a specialist can be retained by foster parents. In the latter instance, this is particularly the case when foster parents are attempting to adopt the child in question (Johnson *et al.*, 2001). It is crucial for psychologists participating in this process to be informed about the legal criteria in their jurisdiction, as well as the relevant case law.

Parental rights termination proceedings typically involve two parts: the initial phase that focuses on why the parent is unfit, and applicable legal grounds for termination. These stages are then followed by discussion of dispositional issues and the potential impact of the varying options on the child's well-being. Johnson *et al.* (2001) warns that far too often there is an assumption that parental rights termination is warranted without a careful look at the potential risks involved. These researchers state (2001, p. 23): "These risks are not only the loss of the relationship with the parent but also the loss of ties to siblings and extended family, risk of languishing indefinitely as a ward of the state, risks of maltreatment and abuse in foster care or institutional setting, and risks of adoption disruption. If the interests of children are to be pursued vigorously, it is critical that psychological examiners are aware of and conduct inquiry to inform the courts of these various risks, as well as risks associated with maintaining parental ties." Forensic psychologists acting in this capacity have a tremendous burden to adhere to ethical, legal, and overall, high professional standards. With so much as stake, accepting consultation for parental rights termination cases should not be taken lightly.

Related Websites

www.childwelfare.gov/systemwide/laws_policies/statutes/groundtermin.cfm
Provides information regarding various states' statutes regarding termination of parental rights, as well as articles and resources pertaining to termination of parental rights.
www.ncsc.org/Topics/Children-Families-and-Elders/Adoption-Termination-of-Parental-Rights/Resource-Guide.aspx
Contains links to multiple websites with resources pertaining to adoption, termination of parental rights, and foster care.
www.nclrights.org/site/PageServer?pagename=issue_families
This site offers news on cases that rule in favor for homosexual individuals' rights concerning custody, stranger adoption, and second parent adoption.
http://humanrights.einnews.com/category/gay-and-lesbian-rights
This site offers various news about rights concerning parental rights of gays and lesbians.
www.megalaw.com/top/mentalhealth.php
This site offers information on mental health law from multiple states.

Police and Law Enforcement

Key Issues

Police as Mediators in Domestic Disputes
- The role of police officers as mediators in domestic disputes
- Police practices and tactics
- Existing policies regarding offenders
- Recommendations
- Prevention strategies

Police Stress
- Causes and consequences of police stress
- Operational and organizational stressors, substance use, the impact of using a firearm, the police as targets of violence, suicide, and the stigma associated with police officers seeking mental health counseling

Police and the Mentally Ill
- Examine changes in policy for officers who are handling mentally ill subjects
- Discuss the police officer's role in handling the mentally ill
- Discuss procedures for the commitment of a mentally ill offender by police

Police Training: Communication Skills and Conflict Resolution
- Ways in which police officers must utilize effective communication skills, as well as various factors which increase the likelihood that violent or forceful means must be used to contain or control a situation
- Training curricula used for Texas law enforcement officers will be reviewed, as an example of the emphasis placed on communication skills by law enforcement agencies
- The application of communication skills in crisis negotiations

The Psychology of Terrorism: Motivations, Implications, and Healing
- Overview of the definition of terrorism, its emotional impact on people and society, its psychological consequences, and the need and role of psychological first-aid (PFA) responders
- A brief description of the impact of the attacks on the World Trade Center and the Pentagon on 11 September, 2001, as well as the ongoing Israeli and Palestinian conflict, will be used to illustrate the impact of terrorism on mental health symptoms, quality of life, and emergency mental health systems in the United States and abroad

CHAPTER 11

Family/Community Issues in Policing

Chapter Outline

Introduction to Forensic Psychology. DOI: 10.1016/B978-0-12-382169-0.00011-6
493

Overview

At the crossroads of policing and psychology are controversies that affect adult and juvenile offenders as well as society in general. This chapter explores areas of inquiry in the field of law enforcement and family or community issues. As developed in this chapter, family/community issues in policing refers to how psychological sciences are or can be used to understand the manner in which police officers address domestic dilemmas in their own lives or in the lives of citizen suspects. The overlapping fields of policing and psychology are not limited to crime and justice controversies afflicting adult and juvenile offenders. There are also many issues that impact society in general. The domain of community issues in forensic psychology and law enforcement encompasses those topics in which the relationship between the police and the public is called into question and more closely examined. There are many facets to this relationship. Psychology is one medium that allows us to understand where and how police, families, and the public interface.

Although the field of forensic psychology has grown rapidly during the last several decades, most research settings and professional organizations focus on the national-level concerns relevant to specific jurisdictions (Eaves, 2002). Increased awareness of international aspects of forensic practice will encourage an attitude of globalization versus isolationism. Conducting research between nations without consideration of borders on topics such as terrorism will facilitate a more thorough and sophisticated understanding of issues germane to forensic psychology. Overall, this comparative approach will help facilitate and contribute to a safer society. As such, the psychology of terrorism is also discussed in this chapter emphasizing an area of practice in psychology and policing that can have a tremendous impact on our communities.

In this chapter, five controversial matters are investigated. These topics include: (1) officers as mediators in domestic disputes; (2) police stress; (3) police and the mentally ill; (4) police training in communication skills and conflict resolution; and (5) the psychology of terrorism. While certainly not exhaustive, the five issues investigated in this section represent some of the more controversial concerns at the forefront of the family and community area of policing and psychology.

Law enforcement personnel are called upon to resolve domestic disputes. To this extent, the police function as mediators attempting to peacefully settle family strife. What police methods are used to mediate family squabbles? What are the prevention strategies officers employ to quell protracted domestic violence?

Police work is stressful. This stress assumes many forms and impacts the family of which the officer is a member. How does substance abuse, the use of firearms, work-related violence, and stigma contribute to an officer's experience of stress? How, if at all, do law enforcement personnel express their concerns about these experiences in their home life?

The stress of police work also directly impacts an officer's family members. This is not surprising since crime, suffering, and death are routine components of law enforcement. How do occupational stressors (e.g., shootings) create family trauma and turmoil? What is the impact of an officer's authoritarianism, cynicism, and violence on his/her family members? What support, if any (e.g., grief therapy), is provided to surviving spouses of officers killed in the line of duty? How do family members cope in the aftermath of an officer's suicide?

The police increasingly find themselves responding to citizen encounters with the mentally ill. What preconceived notions, if any, do officers harbor regarding the psychiatrically disordered? How do officers deal with the mentally ill? Does police academy training sufficiently prepare cadets to interface with the psychiatrically ill?

Recent strategies designed to improve the law enforcement presence in various urban, rural, and suburban neighborhoods have relied upon community-oriented policing techniques. What are these techniques? Is this strategy a viable solution to fighting crime? Is it a law enforcement trend with limited effectiveness? How does the public perceive community-oriented policing?

Police departments find that communication skills and conflict resolution training are integral dimensions to effective police–citizen encounters. What kind and degree of training do officers receive? How do these skills affect victims and offenders?

As technology grows, so do the boundaries that used to restrict our global community's exchange of ideas and competencies. Terrorist acts in recent years have also increased our international awareness of the plight and progress of other nations. An exchange of expertise and data will be critical in improving our ability to identify, prevent, and protect ourselves against terrorists. The international community can also take lessons from one another about the process of healing and the provision of mental health services to those affected directly and indirectly by terrorism. What is the psychology of terrorism? How can a sense of safety, security, and dignity be restored to those who have experienced a mass terror attack? What is the role of psychology in the provision of emergency mental health services and after-care for those affected by the trauma? Do residents of different countries or regions react differently to terrorist attacks and are they affected by media coverage of terrorism internationally?

The controversies considered in this section suggest that law enforcement and psychology are undeniably linked in matters that affect the domestic life of officers, their families, and the public. Terrorism not only affects the immediate victims, but the fear that is left in its wake affects our communities and families. Law enforcement is at the center of efforts to protect communities both nationally and abroad. In an era where much is made about violence, crime, and how our law enforcement responds to it, it is essential that we not forget or overlook how matters of peace and justice also operate at the intersection of policing and psychology.

In addition, more research at the crossroads of psychology and policing would help educate future generations of forensic experts with interests in these and related issues. Indeed, if forensic psychology is to affect the organization, culture, and practice of policing in society, then responding to crime and justice controversies such as those canvassed in this chapter is not only necessary but essential.

Police as Mediators in Domestic Disputes

Introduction

Domestic violence has occurred, and even been condoned, among certain cultures throughout history. In fact, the often-heard phrase "**rule of thumb**" actually refers to the old practice that a man could not beat his spouse with an object greater than the width of his thumb. It is unarguable that domestic violence is a pervasive societal problem and affects not only victims and their offenders, but also the police who must deal with such a delicate, emotionally laden, and often controversial subject. The following case illustration is a typical, yet compelling, scenario of a domestic violence situation.

An officer is patrolling in his squad car when he receives a call from dispatch to respond to a complaint of domestic violence. The officer recognizes the address and mumbles to himself in an irritating manner, "Why, should I even bother to respond?"

This address with this same complaint has occurred numerous times since his joining the police force some 13 years ago. This scenario happens about once a month. Typically, a complaint is received from Mrs. Jones that her husband is being verbally and often physically abusive and that she requires assistance immediately. However, each time an officer confronts this situation, Mrs. Jones refuses to cooperate with the arresting or prosecuting procedures, stating that her call to the police was premature, a mistake, and does not wish to prosecute despite her blackened eyes and bruised cheeks. Often, Mr. Jones is not present in the home, making it a waste of valuable time to try and find him.

Situations such as these are commonplace for the police officer who responds to domestic violence calls. Depending on the policy and procedures of the police department's jurisdiction, officers are instructed to deal with these situations differently. Some law enforcement departments have a mandatory arrest policy for the perpetrator as well as the victim. In a time of increased public concern and increased police involvement, officers are faced with the task of having to handle domestic disputes via mandatory arrest or through mediation. Far too often, domestic violence calls can be the most physically dangerous for the responding officers as compared to other types of calls.

01/01/2005 07:22:26

A significant amount of literature exists on the dynamics, causes, prevention strategies, policing methods, and other topics related to this subject. **Mediators** are most often police officers who deal with these types of situations on a daily basis. The focus of this section is on the role of police officers as mediators in domestic disputes. A variety of aspects related to mediation in domestic disputes are examined, including police practices and tactics, existing policies regarding offenders, recommendations, and prevention strategies.

Literature Review

Research indicates that about half of victims call for police service in **domestic disturbances** in which intimate partners have engaged in loud or abusive arguments, or even physical violence (Barnett, Miller-Perrin, & Perrin, 2011). As a result, police officers are forced to attend to such disputes in an effort to maintain order as well as to protect potential victims from imminent physical injury. Depending on the particular officer, they may or may not feel comfortable assisting in domestic violence calls due to lack of training or knowledge in the area of domestic violence and dispute resolution. Research indicates that police have historically been reluctant to intervene in domestic disputes and a number of beliefs may influence officers' decisions to make an arrest in a domestic violence situation (Barnett, Miller-Perrin, & Perrin, 2011; Danis, 2003; Bayley & Garofalo, 1989). It has been the attitude of many officers that social workers are better suited to deal with the social problem of domestic violence versus law enforcement. Despite the idealism of this philosophy, it is the inherent duty of law enforcement to maintain order, as well as to enforce the law. For the last three decades, a variety of legal challenges, and an increase in public awareness and outcry about domestic violence, has resulted in changes in law enforcement policies to include: required training in domestic violence, misdemeanor arrests without warrants; enforcement in some jurisdictions of civil restraining orders (otherwise known as protective orders) as well as requirements for officers to provide information and referrals for victim services (Buzawa & Hotaling, 2006; Danis, 2003; Ptacek, 1999).

One way the legal system has begun to intervene in domestic violence cases is the use of **protective orders** which forbid abusers from having contact with their victims. It is thought that protective orders can help victims of domestic violence feel safer, which has been supported by some research (Logan & Walker, 2009; Vigdor & Mercy, 2006). In fact, a 2003 survey found that female victims in Seattle who had pursued protective orders believed that their safety had been enhanced in terms of fewer injuries and fewer threats (Holt, Kernic, Wolf, & Rivara, 2003). In actuality though, research has also shown that protective order violation is a common occurrence with almost 51% of violators re-abusing victims (Klein, Willson, Crowe, & DeMichele, 2005). Despite the possible benefits of protective orders, only a small number of victims obtain them (Tjaden, & Thoennes, 2000). The results of one study make it clear that law enforcement personnel can play an effective role in helping victims obtain protective orders as the authors found that 43% of victims with protective orders obtained them with the encouragement of police officers (Ptacek, 1999).

The police response to domestic violence is regarded as a controversial and ever-changing social problem. Traditional responses to such disputes have several distinct characteristics. They include case screening, avoidance of intervention by police, and bias against arrest. Research indicates that historically less than 10% of domestic violence incidents were reported to the police (Buzawa & Buzawa, 1997). This suggests that due to socioeconomic and racial factors, only a small minority of incidents were ever reported. Research has shown that domestic violence assaults resulting in emergency room treatment were four times higher than estimates of domestic violence incidents reported to law enforcement agencies (Danis, 2003; Rand, 1997). Violence in middle to higher socioeconomic groups was often communicated to medical or religious personnel. The research also suggests that victims of domestic violence were often advised to contact social service entities instead of expecting the assistance of police officers (Danis, 2003). One study found that in a sample of cases, over two-thirds of domestic violence incidents were "solved" without the dispatch of officers (Buzawa & Buzawa, 1997). Because of the pervasive lack of social concern, these practices were unofficially accepted. According to Barnett, Miller-Perrin, and Perrin (2011), many unintended consequences can occur as a result of police intervention to include additional violence by the perpetrators, mutual arrests, and the possible lack of cultural sensitivity to victims and perpetrators.

Historically, in regard to police attitudes and perceptions of domestic violence, research consistently shows that most police officers, regardless of individual or departmental characteristics, strongly dislike responding to domestic violence calls (Buzawa & Buzawa, 1997; DeJong, Burgess-Proctor, Elis, 2008). There are several reasons for this, which include organizational impediments, lack of training, police attitudes, and fear of injury. Some attitudes and beliefs that may cause an officer to be hesitant to make an arrest are listed below:

- If assaults are the victim's fault, they are justified (Ford, 1999).
- If she stays with her abuser, there is no real victim (Waaland & Keeley, 1985).
- If abused women are manipulative and unbelievable (Rigakos, 1995).

- Police involvement is not the best way to stop domestic violence (Feder, 1998).
- If real police work is catching "real" criminals or responding to domestic violence calls it is not "real" police work (Mastrofski, Parks, Reiss, & Worden, 1998).
- If intervening in domestic violence is the most dangerous work police can be involved with (Garner & Clemmer, 1986).

Prior to the 1970s and 1980s, almost all 50 states limited police in arresting for misdemeanor and domestic violence assaults. Police could only intervene with an arrest if they directly witnessed the assault. This policy affected police officers' perceptions regarding their role in domestic disputes. Many felt that their role was merely peripheral. Without being able to make arrests, they were limited in their abilities. In addition to organizational constraints, many officers have experienced a lack of training in the areas of domestic violence and conflict mediation. This further impedes their efforts to effectively combat the issue. A 2003 study examining 485 victim surveys from a domestic violence victim advocacy center, over a period of 12 months, found that reasons for a woman returning to an abusive relationship included lack of money (45.9%), lack of a place to go (28.5%), and lack of police help (13.5%) (Anderson, Gillig, Sitaker, *et al.*, 2003).

Traditionally, police departments denied the importance of their role in domestic violence because of society's view, organizational and legislative constraints, as well as a general lack of training and knowledge in the area; however, modern policies have changed dramatically. The catalyst to such change involved pioneering legislation in the state of Pennsylvania that was enacted in 1977. As a result, all 50 states, including the District of Columbia, passed domestic violence reforms. Depending on the jurisdiction, arrests were encouraged or even mandated by legislation. New statutory-specific domestic violence offenses have been incorporated into the criminal code. In contrast to traditional policing, punitive solutions are currently being emphasized as well.

Today some jurisdictions have **mandatory arrest laws** in which both the victim and the offender are taken into custody. Mandatory arrest laws were studied by Mignon and Holmes (1995). Their research indicated that police officers were much more likely to arrest offenders when mandatory arrest laws were in place, particularly in cases of violation of restraining orders. In addition, it was discovered that two-thirds of offenders were not arrested, and that physical assaults provided the strongest evidence for arrest. The greater the injury to the victim, the more likely the offender was to be arrested. A more recent review by Eitle (2005) using a sample of 57,000 cases concluded that mandatory arrest has only led to an arrest rate of 50%, indicating that officers still exercise their own discretion when making an arrest decision. Buzawa and Hotaling (2006) outlined certain statutory requirements that officers are required to fulfill when making an arrest:

- Inform victims of their legal rights.
- Offer assistance in obtaining a protective order.

- Inform victims of community services.
- Inquire about suspect's prior abuse.
- Inquire if suspect has access to weapons.

Some police departments have moved toward using **dual arrests** in domestic violence situations; meaning that both parties involved are arrested, regardless of who is the primary aggressor or in situations in which police officers cannot determine who the aggressor is. An unintended consequence of the dual arrest policy is the increase in arrests of women who are thought to actually be victims (Miller & Meloy, 2006). Some estimates of women arrested for domestic violence under dual arrest policies range from 17.4% to 30.8% (Hirschel, Buzawa, Pattavina, & Faggiani, 2007). Another researcher found that, in a sample of women arrested and court-ordered to counseling for domestic violence, only 12% qualified as primary aggressors (Kernsmith, 2005). The consequences of these arrests are that women may be left feeling blameworthy for the incident and their arrest, when they may have, in reality, been a victim. Furthermore, arresting victims can actually place them in greater danger by making them more hesitant to protect themselves physically if they believe they will be arrested for it (Downs, Rindels, & Atkinson, 2007). Hutchinson (2003) found that women are significantly more likely to call the police when their male partners abuse both alcohol and drugs, and when they are frequently intoxicated.

The police officer who responds to a domestic violence call must, in some way, play the role of a psychologist. Upon arriving at the scene of a domestic dispute, the officer must discriminate between conflicting stories, examine the psychological status of the victim, evaluate the potential dangerousness of the alleged offender, and provide support and comfort to the victim. Police officers may face civil liability for inappropriate responses if those responses are apathetic, or for untimely responses to 911 calls, failure to enforce a state statute, or if their responses are motivated by animus against women (Blackwell & Vaughn, 2003).

Quantitatively, it has been found that a variety of factors contribute directly to an officer's decision to make an arrest. In order of importance they are: (1) use of violence against police officers; (2) commission of a felony; (3) use of a weapon; (4) serious injury to the victim; (5) likelihood of future violence; (6) frequent calls for police assistance from the household; (7) alcohol-/drug-intoxicated assailant; (8) disrespect for police officers; (9) previous injury to victim or damage to property; (10) previous legal action (restraining order); and (11) victim insisting on arrest (Buzawa & Buzawa, 2003; Dolon, Hendricks, & Meagher, 1986). It is clear that the police officer must consider a large array of factors, either consciously or unconsciously, when faced with a domestic dispute. In addition to these influences, other variables, such as personal attributes and officers' perceptions regarding their role in domestic violence, will ultimately influence his or her decision to make an arrest.

Forensic Psychology and Policy Implications

The establishment of policies related to domestic violence took center stage in the feminist movement of the 1970s. During this time, it was demanded that policies and laws should be reformed so as to further protect a woman from her abusive partner (Stalans & Lurigio, 1995a,b). Some authors take an educative stance and advise that more victims should be made aware of the benefits of protective orders in domestic violence situations (Kethineni & Beichner, 2009). Today, research exists that has attempted to make restitution, and has influenced the further reformation of public policy relating to domestic disputes.

Research indicates that mandatory arrest laws, overall, significantly contribute to increased arrest rates for domestic violence offenders. In 2008, 23 states had mandatory arrest policies on record for dealing with domestic violence; given the problems associated with mandatory arrests, it may be beneficial to further reduce this number. It may be more beneficial to establish more specialized police units to respond to domestic disturbances.

Danis (2003) discusses the importance of developing counseling intervention programs for batterers that reduce drop-out and no-show rates, address cultural differences, develop outcome measures, and apply interventions specific for different batterer subtypes. Required court appearances have been found to reduce these drop-out and no-show rates (Gondolf, 2000).

As mentioned, the establishment of more informed and rigorous training programs for police officers is seen as the most important step in controlling or mediating domestic dispute situations. These programs should include mental health training that could be conducted by police psychologists to aid officers in more effectively interfacing with victims of domestic violence. Training, coupled with the implementation of available legal and social resources, is the method of choice for the Albuquerque Police Department. Legal and social resource availability such as domestic violence shelters, medical care, counseling, and even escorted transportation and assistance in the removal of items from the victim's residence, have shown to be powerful in developing immunity from civil liability, as well as being a comforting force to victims of domestic violence (Ellsberg, 2006; Shefer Crawford, Strebel, Simabayi, Dwadwa-Henda, Cloete, Kaufman, & Kalichman, 2008). Psychologists who have expertise in treating domestic violence victims are needed to not only provide services to victims, but also to consult with police departments on this complicated issue.

Suggestions for Future Research

There are a number of areas ripe for research in the field of domestic violence mediation. Research is needed that examines public support for different interventions in the criminal justice system. Victim counseling efficacy and financial/legal service usefulness have yet to be examined. Public perception and support for plea bargaining of offenders is under-researched, as are victims' views of the criminal justice system as related to domestic violence (Stalans, 1996). Some research has found that 30% of victims were critical of police officers' responses to domestic violence and cited their threats of dual arrest or making jokes about the violence (Stephens & Sindin, 2000). Further research is still necessary. Police attitudes toward domestic violence have been examined, albeit rarely, in the professional literature. However, comprehensive studies examining the relation between certain police personality characteristics such as cynicism and other possible causal or relational links to domestic violence responses are unstudied. Since domestic violence calls constitute such a large percentage of police responses, the dynamics of domestic abuse can also affect the police officer and not just the offender or victim.

Other research could examine the effects of chronic spousal abuse on victims' psychological symptom development and their refusal to prosecute offenders. Also, more studies are needed that examine the psychological profiles of officers who deal with domestic violence situations.

Due to the process of change and controversies in domestic violence, the particular style of policing used by different officers within a department, as well as between departments, varies to a greater extent than before (Barnett, Miller-Perrin, & Perrin, 2011; Buzawa & Buzawa, 1997). Traditionally, police have avoided responding to domestic disputes, but due to societal change, police have been forced to deal with domestic disputes at increased frequencies. Because of the controversies associated with police responses to domestic violence, it is imperative that they receive adequate training to effectively deal with this issue. Simpson (2003, p. 631) states, "Continued empirical examination is vital to the understanding of how police may influence the reporting behavior of domestic violence victims." When looking at the case illustration of Mrs. Jones, the repeat nature of her domestic disputes and lack of follow-up may become very frustrating for the officers who respond. Depending on the departmental policy, the officer may have certain limitations, which may further frustrate him or her. Training by psychologists as mediators may help the officer learn effective methods to help reduce the frequency of incidents, as well as to recommend other options for Mrs. Jones. By utilizing other agencies within the community, the officer may act as a liaison for victims of repeated violence.

Police Stress

Introduction

Many different definitions from many different disciplines have attempted to define the term "stress." However, with such inherent issues as constant danger, severe intensity of job responsibilities, threat of personal injury, grueling shift changes, and a myriad of rules and regulations, police work may in some ways typify the very meaning of stress. Not surprisingly, then, police officers experience a tremendous amount of stress, often leading to tragic circumstances such as substance abuse, termination from the police force, or even suicide.

Imagine for a moment that you are a police officer. You have been assigned to work the graveyard shift this particular night, a shift you have not worked for about 2 weeks. Your assignment for the night is to patrol a particularly dangerous area of town. You have had only a few hours sleep due to the abrupt shift change, and you are certainly not feeling very alert. As luck would have it, you receive a call over the radio stating that you are to investigate a complaint of gang activity in the area you are patrolling. Without hesitation, you arrive at the scene, and are greeted by a number of men holding a variety of weapons. As you step out of the car, you cannot help but think that this confrontation may very well cost you life or limb.

Literature Review

Incidents such as that just described may cause feelings of fear, resistance, and acute stress. Researchers have examined the topic of police stress to help us understand the dynamic process involved with a law enforcement officer's job requirements and its association to the amount of stress experienced.

A survey conducted by Violanti and Aron (1995) demonstrated that police officers experience two basic types of stressors: organizational practices and the inherent nature of police work. **Organizational stressors** refer to events stemming from police administration, which are found to be bothersome or intolerable to members of the police force. They include such issues as authoritarian structure, lack of participation in decision-making processes, and unfair discipline. Inherent nature stressors, or **operational police stressors** (Page & Jacobs, 2011), refer to those occurrences that may threaten to harm the police officer either physiologically or psychologically. Included in this category are such items as high-speed chases, dealing with crises, and personal physical attacks (Violanti & Aron, 1993). Another examination of police stress literature found that there are several different types of stressors which include four main categories: (1) intra-interpersonal (i.e., personality-related stressors); (2) occupational (i.e., job-related stressors); (3) organizational; and (4) health consequences of police stress (Abdollahi, 2002).

In Violanti and Aron's (1993) study, they found that killing someone in the line of duty was found to be the most stressful event one could experience as a police officer. Experiencing a fellow officer being killed was found to be the second most stressful experience. Both of these stressors could be considered inherent to the nature of police work. The highest ranked organizational stressor was found to be shift work, followed by inadequate support, incompatible patrol partner, insufficient personnel, excessive discipline, and inadequate support by supervisors. Interestingly, seven of the top 20 stressors were found by the authors to be organizational/administrative. The authors further broke down stressors by job ranking and experience. Those with 6 to 10 years of police experience were found to have the highest levels of overall stress (organizational and inherent combined). The ranking of desk sergeant was found to be most associated with overall stress, as were those officers who were between the ages of 31−35 years, Caucasian, and those who were female. In a more recent study, Page and Jacobs (2011) examined stress and coping strategies in rural law enforcement agencies. They found that organizational police stress was predictive of general life stress, but operational stressors were not. The authors hypothesized that this may be due to recognizing and accepting these stressors as inherent in the nature of the work but viewing the organizational stressors as unnecessary yet unavoidable. Likewise, Shane (2010; cited in Page and Jacobs) found that organizational stressors were more stressful than operational stressors in large urban departments. Similarly, Buker and Wiecko (2007; cited in Stuart, 2008, p. 507) found that organizational and administrative factors are "more important indicators of job stress than the police work itself." It is further noted that the officers "rarely mention danger, violence, or human misery as sources of stress unless specifically asked" (p. 507).

Substance Abuse

Remembering the vignette described earlier, one can only imagine the cumulative effects that years of police work can have on one's psychological functioning. Given the many varied sources of police stress, it is of little surprise that officers often utilize unhealthy ways of coping with these stressors. One of the most common, yet under-reported, ways police officers cope with these stressors is through the use/abuse of drugs and alcohol.

Of particular interest is the number of officers who abuse alcohol as a means of dealing with their stressful lives. Researchers claim that reported alcohol abuse may be under-reported due to fear of retribution or demotion within the police department (Ballenger, Best, Metzler, Wasserman, Mohr, Liberman, *et al.*, 2011). Further, the authors state that known alcohol abusers are "hidden" in positions where they cannot detrimentally influence the department or the public's interaction with the department. Davey, Obst, and Sheehan (2001) in a study of Australian state police officers found that 30% were at risk of harm from excessive alcohol consumption. Furthermore, they found that officers would frequently attribute their drinking patterns to celebration and socializing with peers, justifying it to themselves as more acceptable. However, factors relating to stress emerged as the most predictive of scores indicating possible alcohol use disorders on the Alcohol Use Disorders Identification Test-AUDIT (Davey *et al.*, 2001). In a more recent study of 747 police officers, Ballenger, Best, Metzler, Wasserman, Mohr, Liberman, *et al.* (2011) found the following: "(a) 7.8% of the entire sample met criteria for lifetime alcohol abuse or dependence; (b) 18.1% of males and 15.9% of females endorsed experiencing adverse lifetime consequences from alcohol use; and (c) 11.0% of males and 16.3% of females reported excessive drinking in the past week" (p. 8). Interestingly, the authors note greater current alcohol use was not associated with greater exposure to critical incidents and current symptoms of post-traumatic stress disorder (PTSD). They did find, however, that increased lifetime adverse consequences from alcohol use were associated with lower education, routine work stress, and an increased level of current psychiatric symptoms.

Violanti (2004) described a model of how a police officer may be driven to drink as a result of job-related stress. Job demands can lead to a number of possibilities for the police officer. These demands can be dealt with by using various coping techniques, some of which may lead to feelings of stress or alcohol/drug use. Probably most common, rather than a direct route, is a combination of pathways eventually leading to alcohol/drug use. Cohan and O'Connor (2002) found that among police officers, job stress was mainly associated with negative affect and alcohol consumption.

With proper psychological coping mechanisms, the abuse of alcohol and other substances can be avoided. Indeed, it is the destruction or breakdown of the coping mechanisms available to the officer that most often leads to the abuse of alcohol/drugs. Consequently, alcohol/drug abuse may lead to unsatisfactory job performance, resulting in reprimand, which may then lead to increased use of alcohol/drugs, thus forming a maladaptive cycle of dysfunctional behavior.

The Impact of Using a Firearm

At this point, it is likely that one will ask themselves what the single most contributing factor leading to the abuse of substances within police work might be. As mentioned earlier, there are numerous factors which contribute to police stress. These factors can be broken down into finite categories of stressors. Not surprisingly, research reveals that the use of a firearm by a police officer to kill someone is often the single most stressful event experienced by a police officer (Violanti & Aron, 1995).

The use of a firearm by a police officer often leads to a number of detrimental psychological states. Much like a soldier using a firearm to defend oneself or others, the police officer may experience flashbacks, perceptual distortions, isolation, emotional numbing, sleep difficulties, depression, or a heightened sense of danger following the event. Sleep disturbance is another common symptom. A study that examined critical incident exposure and sleep quality in police officers found that duty-related critical incident exposure to on-line policing and work environment stress associated with routine administrative and organizational elements were the main predictive variables to subjective sleep disturbances (Neylan, Metzler, Best, *et al.*, 2002). Cumulative critical incident exposure was related to nightmares, whereas general work environment stress was strongly associated with poor global sleep quality. Interestingly, however, a recent study (LaFauci Schutt & Marotta, 2011) found that trauma exposure frequency was a poor predictor of whether or not an individual developed PTSD. Exposure to the threat of death or to death events is required in the manifestation of PTSD (Sugimoto & Oltjenbruns, 2001). Researchers acknowledge that death-related stressors are inherent in law enforcement. Sugimoto and Oltjenbruns contend that police personnel who continue to work while actively experiencing symptoms of PTSD may be at risk of reduced self-control, escalated use of force, and other behaviors related to irritability or outbursts of anger which are related to PTSD.

In fact, it is often after the use of a firearm that many officers decide to leave their profession, due to the traumatic psychological nature of the event (Solomon & Horn, 1986). The experience of acute stress in police work can lead to chronic stress, burnout, professional resignation, and other somatic or physical health concerns (Anshel, 2000). When combining these operational stressors with the organizational stressor of completing hours of paperwork dealing with the rationale for the use of the firearm, the entire impact of such an ordeal burdens the officer with a great deal of stress.

Police as Targets of Violence

In 2009, 48 law enforcement officers were feloniously killed in the line of duty and 10.3 officers per 100 were assaulted (United States, 2010). Perhaps no other single event is more stressful than the threat of personal bodily harm. Immersing yourself in the imagined scenario described at the beginning of this section may have induced feelings of stress. Considering this, one can certainly understand the level of stress an officer faces when the nature of the profession threatens violence against him or her every day.

A study conducted by McMurray (1990) revealed that of the 161 police officers surveyed from Washington, DC and/or Newark, New Jersey police departments, 90% indicated that they felt assaults against the police had increased over the past year. These same officers also felt that support services within their departments were inadequate. An interesting and distinct pattern emerged when the officers were asked to rank events that most disturbed them following an assault. Seventy-four percent explained that not knowing that the assault was coming was most disturbing to them. This was followed by feelings of powerlessness (53%) and nonsupport from onlookers (48%), from the courts (47%), from police officials (35%), from fellow officers (26%), from friends (23%), and lack of support from family (8%). It is clear that the lack of a support structure on both professional and personal levels are substantial sources of distress for the police officer who has been assaulted (McMurray, 1990).

The law enforcement category indicated that 90% of officers stated they were as aggressive in law enforcement after the assault as prior to it (McMurray, 1990). Half of the officers surveyed indicated that they would be more likely to use force if a situation called for it prior to their being assaulted. McMurray further states that while an aggressive officer may cause fewer officer injuries, this may also have implications for placing the community and police department at undue risk if unwarranted or excessive force is implemented against the citizens.

Concluding the discussion on police as targets of violence necessitates a summary of the detrimental effects of being assaulted while on active duty as a police officer. One need not be a psychologist or criminologist to understand that being assaulted, especially unexpectedly, can result in a tremendous amount of stress and emotional turmoil. Everything from recurring nightmares to a "quick-trigger syndrome" may develop as a result of being a victim of assault. Considering that the police officer places him- or herself in a potentially hostile environment every day, it is no wonder that some officers harbor feelings of violation and psychological disarray.

Suicide

In general, it is thought that the suicide rate for law enforcement officers is two to three times the rate in the general population, and three times as many officers commit suicide as are killed in the line of duty (Miller, 2005). However, some (Miller) believe that this figure may actually be an underestimate as a result of some deaths being undetermined. There is no doubt that the ultimate and most tragic result of an inability to cope with police stress is suicide. An occupation surrounded with constant death, deceit, antisocial behaviors and personalities, defiance, ridicule, criticism, boredom, rigid hierarchical structures, and lack of social support may result in suicide in some cases. Historically, Baker and Baker's (1996) study reported that in 1994, 11 New York City police officers committed suicide. However, only two officers were actually killed by criminals in New York City that same year. It is clearly an unacceptable and distressing ratio when police are killing themselves at a rate greater than that by criminals. Another study examined the suicide rates of New York City police officers from 1977 to 1996 and compared them to the suicide rates of New York's general population (Marzuk, Nock, Leon, *et al.*, 2002). The police suicide rate was 14.9% per 100,000 residents, compared with the general population's 18.3% per 100,000. Overall, it was found that the rate of suicide among New York City's police officers is equal to or even less than that of the city's resident population (Marzuk *et al.*, 2002).

An article by Arrigo and Garsky (2001) investigated a police officer's decision to commit suicide. The authors state that a combination of occupational stress, nonsupportive family structure, and alcoholism may contribute to suicidal ideation in the police officer. Occupational stress in the police force is what the authors describe first as a contributing factor in police suicide. The inherent and chronically stressful nature of police work accumulates in the form of such feelings as helplessness and hopelessness. Also, organizational stressors such as those described earlier lead to feelings of suppressed hostility, frustration, and a sense of having little influence. In addition to occupational stress, family strife is cited by Arrigo and Garsky (2001) as being another significant source of stress. A number of important and often undesirable responsibilities such as shift work and disabling injuries occur with police work. These and other factors have a tremendous impact on the officer's family, who must deal with these issues daily. A police officer's job requires a large amount of time and energy in order ensure that he or she is doing their job properly and "by the book." As a result, police officers' spouses are often neglected in the process. Also, police officers' training often attempts to instill such psychological coping techniques as detachment from emotional situations. All too often this detachment is reflected in the personal lives of the officers. This results in a breakdown of family communication and a lack of emotional intrigue, attachment, or romance within the marriage, thus causing a loss of family support and more stress. Miller (2005, p. 102) notes that in most cases of suicide "there has been a cumulative effect of several stressors, often involving a combination of relationship and work problems."

The final component described is that of a police officer's use of alcohol and its effects on the decision to commit suicide. It is a well-known fact that many people use alcohol as a means to escape a reality that they would rather not experience or to at least detach themselves from it. As described in the section on police officers' use of alcohol, the typical officer's use is higher than that of the general population. When one examines the nature of police work, it is not difficult to understand this phenomenon.

Alcohol is often used by police officers as a sleep-inducing agent to help deal with biological rhythm disruptions associated with shift work. It is also used to help control deep-seated cynicism, another coping strategy employed by police officers who have become disenchanted with the operation of the police department in which they work.

Baker and Baker (1996) described the warning signs associated with the police officer who may commit suicide. According to these authors, supervisors should look for clusters of symptoms such as a recent loss, sadness, frustration, disappointment, grief, alienation, depression, loneliness, physical pain, mental anguish, and mental illness. Mohandie and Hatcher (1999) describe verbal and physical cues that may be warning signs of suicide in law enforcement officers. The authors briefly describe these cues, which are related to the warning signs described by Baker and Baker. The reader is directed to the articles by Mohandie and Hatcher and Miller (2005), who also discuss these verbal and physical cues. Other signs should also be examined, the most obvious being a previous suicide attempt or other type of **self-mutilation**, physically harming oneself without the intent of committing suicide. When an officer does commit suicide, police departments often have difficulty dealing with the loss (Loo, 2001). Police psychologists can play an invaluable role in the process of healing.

Stigma in Asking for Help

As with many other occupations, law enforcement includes its own unwritten code of conduct and subculture. A traditionally masculine occupation, many male police officers feel the need to keep psychological distress signs to themselves for fear of being viewed as "soft." Likewise, female police officers often do not wish to display their negative psychological states for fear that they will be viewed as weak in character. Many police officers also refuse to reveal their emotional concerns or disruptions for fear that they will not obtain one of the very few promotional positions available within the department (Shane, 2010; Stuart, 2008; Arrigo & Garsky, 2001; Miller, 2005). This often results in a police officer's understanding that asking for help may result in such things as forced leave, demotion, or simply ridicule and lack of respect by colleagues. As a result, emotions, feelings, and sometimes faulty or unhealthy thinking patterns remain bottled up inside for indefinite amounts of time, causing such states as depression.

Depression is characterized as a mood disorder that may encompass a person's entire range of functioning: increased or decreased appetite or sleep, bouts of crying, feelings of worthlessness, guilt, difficulty concentrating, difficulty making decisions, and thoughts of suicide and death. Clearly, this psychological state can detrimentally affect the police officer's ability to competently and objectively perform his or her duties. Realizing this, the police officer often chooses silence as a means of avoiding these issues.

Understanding this, supervisors must take a more active role in identifying problems that officers may have. It is not enough to simply tell the officers that they are available if anyone has a problem or issue and would like to discuss it. Supervisors must actively question the officers and provide periodic check-ups that will give them a better opportunity to assess if an officer is dealing with an issue or experiencing a large amount of stress and is in need of counsel.

Further complicating the matter is that law enforcement officers are frequently resistant to outsiders and lack knowledge of mental health services (Page & Jacobs, 2011). In their study, Page and Jacobs (2011) found that social support from a significant other, family, and friends was beneficial in helping rural police officers cope with general life stress. However, only social support from friends was beneficial in helping cope with operational and organizational sources of police stress. Regarding the use of some form of counseling, 8% identified a full-time counselor in their department, 41% reported the availability of a police chaplain, 55% indicated that an Employee Assistance Program (EAP) was available, and 73% were aware of community mental health agencies. Despite the awareness of these available sources, 71% of the officers reported that they would prefer to talk to a peer than a therapist.

Forensic Psychology and Policy Implications

A variety of topics were discussed in this section, and a multitude of policy implications exist for each topic. Police stress is a problem that has existed since the inception of law enforcement and will certainly not disappear any time in the near future. Despite this, however, surprisingly few policies have been implemented in order to not only protect the police officer from the detrimental effects of exposure to stressors, but also to prevent and treat stress-related syndromes.

Resiliency, an individual's ability to recover from stressful or traumatic experiences, is commonly thought to be a protective factor in how successfully an individual exposed to a traumatic incident is able to effectively cope. Miller (2008) advocates for resiliency training for law enforcement officers. He argues that this training would enable the officer to deal with an incident with more confidence and effectiveness. He also recommends the use of resilience-based interventions following a traumatic incident.

As discussed earlier, police officers' abuse of substances such as drugs and alcohol are used as a means to escape the stresses associated with their occupation and to escape their harsh realities. Therefore, policy implications surrounding the use/abuse of alcohol and/or drugs within the police force must deal with the very root of the problem in addition to the abuse of substances itself. In other words, helping the officer to utilize more effective coping mechanisms and encouraging him or her to discuss more openly his or her concerns will, in effect, reduce the need to use alcohol or drugs as a means of dealing with these same issues or problems.

It is also surprising that perhaps the most stressful event one could experience as a police officer, using a firearm, incorporates virtually no policies to help the officer cope and deal effectively with the potential psychological trauma associated with this situation. Aside from the hours of paperwork required of the officer after the use of a firearm, the officer is left to him- or herself to cope with the post-traumatic stress associated with this event. Luckily, many police agencies are now incorporating psychological care, including critical incidents debriefing, in order to assist the officer in coming to an understanding of the psychological consequences of their actions. Still, more formal policies need to be enacted as standard procedure after a police officer uses a firearm to ensure their psychological well-being.

Many policy implications stem from police officers who have been victims of assault. McMurray (1990) described a number of useful policy implications associated with this topic. For instance, he states that supervisors need to be trained to deal with post-traumatic stress associated with assault, crisis intervention, and "how to listen." In addition, assaulted police officers should be allowed time off with pay following an assault until he or she is deemed fit to return to work. Further, the paperwork associated with the event should be performed by another officer familiar with the case. Similarly, Tehrani and Piper (2011), in their interviews with police personnel, found that they felt it would be useful if they received training to help identify stress, burn-out, and trauma reactions in both themselves and others. Furthermore, they also identified the need for supervisors to be trained in ways to help their team talk openly about the emotional impact of their work and to challenge negative behaviors.

Many officers interviewed in McMurray's (1990) study claim that the police department only concerns itself with physical, not psychological, injuries. Likewise, police personnel interviewed by Tehrani and Piper (2011) expressed similar concerns regarding the need for psychological screening and counseling. Psychological screening should become mandatory following an event involving an assault. Finally, as noted above, many officers claim that they are not even sure what resources, if any, are available to them following a traumatic event. This should result in a policy requiring officers to understand at all times what psychological resources are available as well as encouraging them to use those resources whenever necessary.

Issues surrounding police suicide are lacking and in need of development. Since troubled officers often resist seeking help, supervisors should instill the notion that no officer will suffer economic or promotional consequences. Further, all information given to supervisors must remain confidential, and this policy must be relayed to the officers. In addition, any information given to a supervisor by an officer should ultimately lead to a referral to a professional source, such as a psychologist or other counselor (Baker & Baker, 1996). Also, psychological interventions should be made available at any time an officer deems it necessary. Crisis counseling, specifically for police officers, is often nonexistent, causing the officer to rely on the same resources available to the public. This may leave officers with a feeling of hesitancy if they believe the treatment will be lengthy or costly. Therefore, the intervention supplied to officers free of charge by the police agency, being proactive in dealing with the build-up of stressors, would also be beneficial. Miller (2005) suggests that in addition to pre-employment screening, periodic assessments should be implemented as part of policy. He notes that this would allow an efficient, and nonstigmatizing, referral for psychological counseling to be proactive in dealing with psychological difficulties.

Arrigo and Garsky (2001) advocate three main policies that may help deter the officer from engaging in self-mutilation or suicide. The first of these is stress management and stress-reduction techniques. The authors recommend that a special class explaining how to cope with anxiety and stressors, in addition to reducing them, needs to be incorporated into all training programs. The aspects of the course could include such topics as nutrition and dieting, physical health, fitness, humor, play, amusement strategies, and others.

Given the findings by Page and Jacobs (2011) that law enforcement officers would prefer to talk to a peer rather than a mental health professional, in addition to stress management and stress-reduction techniques, group "rap" or process sessions should be made available to all police officers. This would incorporate group sessions emphasizing peer support dealing with issues such as the death of a partner or the use of deadly force. This training, according to Arrigo and Garsky (2001), should occur early in the candidate's training and regularly while in the police force. The intention of this policy is to help demystify the concept of counseling for the police officers, hopefully leading to more voluntary use of these services.

Finally, Arrigo and Garsky (2001) advocate police mentoring. While some types of these mentoring programs already exist within the police force, this type of instruction may not be governed by a standard of quality. This could lead to negative influences regarding policing, stress build-up, and possibly even suicidal ideation. Skilled mentoring could allow for more disciplined officers incorporating a higher degree of respect for colleagues and others.

Police officers' reluctance in asking for help has already, to some degree, been discussed. With the promise of confidentiality, absence of ridicule, and no detrimental advancement or employment threats, officers should not feel hesitant in asking for help. Inclusion of even a few of these policies would no doubt make for a less dangerous, more psychologically (and physically) healthy lifestyle for police officers. With the opportunity for officers to vent frustrations and use appropriate emotional outlets, better decision making will no doubt take place, resulting in more efficient policing techniques and procedures and fewer inappropriate and dangerously hostile outbursts by officers.

Suggestions for Future Research

The subject of police stress encompasses a large array of topics and information. As a result, many opportunities for future research in this area are available. Police officers' use of alcohol, for example, has been blamed on the rigid structure associated with the police department as well as with often faulty coping mechanisms such as police cynicism. However, others argue that it is within the individual alone that such habits develop.

As discussed, the use of a firearm is judged by many officers as an extremely stressful event. However, a small percentage of officers actually have engaged in such behavior. Future research is needed in order to determine the psychological ramifications associated with the occurrence (or perceived view of the occurrence) of such an event.

Future research is also needed in the area of assaulted police officers. Relatively few studies exist examining issues such as attitudes toward the perpetrator, self-esteem reductions associated with being physically injured, attitudes toward counseling and psychological treatment, and the psychology of anticipating physical confrontations. If officers were able to be trained to anticipate the intentions of a would-be attacker, less injury might result.

Regarding the risk of developing PTSD after incidents such as use of a firearm or being assaulted, recent research has found that the number of incidents an individual is exposed to is a poor predictor of symptomatology (LaFauci Schutt & Marotta, 2011). The authors suggest that the severity, amount of direct exposure during an incident, or time spent at the site of the incident may have a more significant impact. They also suggest that after an individual reaches a threshold of incidents, future incidents have less of an impact or a differential impact. Given these findings, it would be beneficial to further investigate variables such as these, which may increase an individual's susceptibility or resiliency to developing PTSD.

Research in the area of police suicide is an area in dire need of additional research. Studies examining the impact of suicide on family members, friends, the community, criminals, and other police officers are clearly lacking. Developing and validating measures for the periodic screening of police officers would be beneficial in ensuring that individuals at high risk for suicide or whose psychological symptoms may be worsening received the appropriate referrals and help. More importantly, research dealing with teaching police officers more effective psychological coping mechanisms, both during their initial training and as part of annual refreshers, is needed. Also, research regarding the inherent elements of police work and how to reduce their detrimental psychological impact is needed in order to help reduce the rate of police suicides.

Police work is by no means a stress-free job. A myriad of potential stressors plague the officer daily. This section attempts not only to enumerate, but to explain some of these sources of police stress and their consequences. Police officers are not immune to the effects of psychological and physical manifestations of stress. A clear understanding is needed in order to allow law enforcement agencies and the officers themselves to function to the best of their abilities.

Police and the Mentally Ill

Introduction

A police officer's job is one riddled with a variety of pitfalls and potential dangers. As if maintaining control over "normal" populations is not difficult enough, law enforcement agents often find themselves having to deal with populations that cannot, or are incapable of, rational and reasonable thought. This is due in large part to the stigma that is associated with the mentally ill. Society tends to be less tolerant of those who are mentally ill; this is due to the myth that individuals have control over their thoughts, behaviors, and emotions. Society tends to have an aversion to the terms "disability" or "disease," when it pertains to mental illness. Some individuals with mental illness will create a façade of positive mental health, which can promote a build-up of unhealthy coping styles (i.e., alcohol and drug abuse) in an attempt to continue the masquerade of happiness and adjustment. When these stresses become more than they can bear, it becomes more likely these individuals will encounter troubles with law enforcement. These contacts can be a result of violent or lethal offenses (Cant, 2007). Unfortunately, individuals who have untreated mental disorders have increasingly been interfacing with law enforcement, after having made some specific threat or engaged in some inappropriate or illegal action. The development of a mental health liaison between the mentally ill offender and the criminal justice system is proving to be an important element in bridging the gap between the two systems (Sadler, 2009). Consider the following example of how a mentally ill individual may come face-to-face with the law.

A police officer receives a call and is told that there is an involuntary commitment request at a large psychiatric institution downtown. The officer calls for an ambulance to arrive at the scene before he arrives. By the time he has reached the institution, he is greeted by a malady of interested pedestrians, disarrayed staff members, and a hostile-looking man holding a butter knife he apparently stole from the kitchen. The man in question is pacing and mumbling something to himself, apparently severely agitated. It looks to the police officer like any movement toward the patient may result in a violent outburst. Due to the fact that the patient is in possession of a potentially dangerous weapon, the situation must be handled with extreme caution, diligence, and cunning in order to prevent the patient from hurting himself or anyone else.

The manner in which the police officer handles the above situation is critical for a variety of reasons. For example, would a wrong or inappropriate statement made by the officer invoke some sort of rage response? Would other patients observing the ordeal become agitated as well after seeing such an encounter, thus resulting in other psychotic outbreaks? If the patient refused to submit, how will physical restraints be applied? Will anyone get hurt in the process? These questions and others are faced by officers every day. However, a surprising paucity of literature exists on exactly how an officer should deal with the mentally ill in the line of duty (Lamb, Weinberger, & Gross, 2004). This section attempts to answer these questions as well as address other related issues regarding the public's perception of the mentally ill and law enforcement, how police should handle mentally ill patients, the psychological makeup of the mentally ill lawbreaker, the co-occurring or comorbid diagnosis often given to jailed mentally ill inmates, and public policy implications dealing with the appropriate manner in which to effectively deal with the mentally ill.

Literature Review

As a result of deinstitutionalization and a dramatic increase of individuals with severe mental illness in the community, police officers are often the first line responders to the mentally ill in crisis and potential gatekeepers for mental health services (Lamb, Weinberger, & Gross, 2004). Knowledge and attitudes of police officers toward the mentally ill have traditionally been that of ignorance and misunderstanding. In the past police officers have tended to have somewhat cynical attitudes toward this same population; with the change in policing standards from enforcement and response to community policing, their attitudes are shifting (Sellers, Sullivan, Veysey, & Shane, 2005). Additionally, with the evolution of most police agencies towards that of community policing, more officers are placed into situations that involve mentally ill subjects, officers' attitudes towards the system that is supposed to aid them in assisting these subjects is also disfavored (Sellers *et al.*, 2005). This is not surprising, considering the tremendous amount of stress experienced by police officers every day.

The failure of police academies and training programs to adequately address issues related to mental health have conceivably fostered the ignorance toward this specific population. By examining 84 medium and large law enforcement agencies, Hails and Borum (2003) found that departments varied greatly in the amount of police training on mental health topics, with a median of 6.5 hours for basic recruits and one hour of in-service training. Around one-third of the departments had some degree of specialized responding for handling calls involving individuals with mental illness. Twenty-one percent had a special unit within the department to aid in these types of calls and 8% had the availability of a mobile mental health crisis team

(Hails & Borum, 2003). The literature indicates the creation of these specialized departments and special response units have proven not only to create a specialized workforce, but to also provide field officers with an individual who has an understanding of both the law and how it is applied to the mentally ill. This liaison would be specially trained in de-escalation of violence for the safety of the officer and the suspect, as well as giving the mentally ill individual an advocate who is considering what is in their best interest (Sadler, 2009). While often officers are called upon for transportation to acute psychiatric units or emergency rooms, other situations arise that call for more finite and definitive policing skills necessary to adequately handle the mentally ill.

Research demonstrates that people with mental illness and substance abuse disorders are major contributors to police-identified criminal violence (Lamb, Weinberger, & Gross, 2004; Cant, 2007; Chappell, 2010). It further indicates that although public perception of the prevalence may be slightly exaggerated, it is becoming more commonplace, and more aggressive (Chappell, 2010). Overall, public perceptions of mentally ill persons as criminally dangerous are exaggerated. However, this is not to say that the mentally ill, particularly those who are fearful or paranoid as a result of psychosis, do not commit violent acts. **Severe mental illness** (i.e., mania, psychosis, delusions, and hallucinations) and substance abuse are often co-occurring and result in higher incidence of violence (Cant, 2007). When a mental illness is combined with substance use disorder(s) (e.g., alcohol, cocaine, or methamphetamine abuse), the risk of violence substantially increases.

The most extreme, although rare examples, involve mass murderers such as Jarred Loughner (Gabrielle Gifford's attacker in Arizona), Cho Sueng-Hue (Virginia Tech. Shooter), Charles Whitman (University of Texas Tower Shooter), and others who were struggling with symptoms of schizophrenia (i.e., delusions, paranoia) (Colloff, 2006; Cloud, 2011; Goodstein & Glaberson, 2000). In a reevaluation of a 50-year-old case study of 100 rampage murderers by the New York Times (cited in Goodstein & Glaberson, 2000), it was found that the majority of these offenders did not just "snap," rather, there was a gradual progression from the onset of symptoms of mental disorder to the time of the attack. In 34 of the 100 cases, family members or friends were aware of the danger and sought help but, according to them, police, school administrators, and/or mental health workers failed to act on their concerns. The study closely examined the precursory violence prevalence found the following: (1) 63 of the 100 (102 killers involved) had made general threats of violence prior to the acts; (2) 55 regularly expressed explosive anger or frustration; and (3) 35 had a history of violent behavior and assaults (Goodstein & Glaberson, 2000). Many of these offenders had previous interactions with the criminal justice or mental health systems.

Lamb, Weinberger, and Gross (2004) caution that the unnecessary criminalization of the mentally ill can occur if police officers do not appropriately perform and balance their roles as protectors of those with disabilities as well as the welfare of the community. The cursory training an officer receives does not encapsulate the complexities of dealing with the mentally ill offender who is experiencing delusions or paranoia which can often involve police officers and the distress that the mentally ill offenders are experiencing as a result of the stressful situation they may find themselves in. It is important that the officer be extremely aware of the dangers they are facing when dealing with these types of offenders (Chappell, 2010). These dangers include, but are not limited to: increased risk for suicide, increased risk for a suicide by cop scenario, and elevated agitation and aggression. The meeting of force with force cannot only re-traumatize the mentally ill subject (as they are often victims themselves); it can lead to an escalation in violence. Lamb, Weinberger, and Gross (2004) strongly emphasize the importance of criminal justice and mental health collaboration through mental health training for officers, mobile crisis units, knowledge of appropriate community mental health resources, and identification of the mentally ill.

Research has shown that there are differences between police departments in big cities and smaller communities in helping officers to avoid shootings involving emotionally disturbed persons (Fyfe, 2000). While larger cities have seen a decline, more midsized cities have not shown a decrease in these tragedies that impact the mentally ill, the community, and police officers. Fyfe (2000) contends that big cities are more sophisticated in handling situations with emotionally disturbed persons because of increased exposure and knowledge about the mentally ill. More recently, these numbers seem to be changing; this could be in large part due to the lack of funding provided to state facilities that provide public mental health services. Hart (2010) indicates that in Houston, Texas, approximately 25,000 crisis intervention calls were handled by the police with 47 of these becoming suicide by cop situations just in the last year. The recent increase in these types of calls is being correlated to the lack of state funding to mental health hospitals.

A Canadian study by Cant (2007) examines the creation of a mental health support team (MHST), which was developed as a result of several "high profile incidents involving police and mentally ill people" (p. 31). She discovered that mentally ill individuals who are experiencing a mental health crisis often encounter law enforcement, and for these individuals, the MHST was an effective tool for officers. She stated by "combining the knowledge of a social worker and law enforcement, this cooperation allowed for a more 'proactive' form of police intervention as compared to a 'reactive' policing solution" (p. 32). A program like this can have a significant impact as police officers may spend about 10% of their time interfacing with individuals with mental health problems, with "60% of officers responding at least once a month to a mental health-related issue" (McLean & Marshall, 2010, p. 63).

Steadman, Stainbrook, Griffin, *et al.* (2001) explained that some communities had developed pre-booking diversion programs that depended on specialized crisis response sites, where the police officers could drop off individuals in psychiatric crisis and return to duty. These programs were designed to facilitate collaboration between law enforcement and mental health professionals, while helping individuals to receive appropriate treatment and to not over-burden the jails.

Research by Lamb, Weinberger, and Gross (2004) demonstrates that police officers tend to have certain preconceived notions regarding mental illness. Those with mental illness are viewed as the offenders in a situation rather than the victim, and, as a result, they are potentially exposed to additional victimization (Wood & Edwards, 2005). Wood and Edwards (2005) also found that mentally ill patients are more likely to be violently assaulted than the general public; females who suffer from mental illness are more likely to be sexually victimized, and mentally ill men are more likely to be victims of robbery or assault. It is not uncommon for this victimization to occur within the community, as well as by mental health workers and police.

In evaluating the effectiveness of a mental health training intervention with the police force in England, a total of 109 police officers attended training workshops and completed pre- and post-surveys including knowledge, attitudes, and behavioral interventions (Pinfold, Huxley, Thornicroft, *et al.*, 2003). It was noted that positive impact on police work, particularly improvements in communication between officers and persons with mental illness, was reported in one-third of the cases. Although stereotypes linking the mentally ill and violent behavior overall was not successfully challenged, it was demonstrated that short educational interventions produced change in the officers' attitudes towards the mentally ill and left officers feeling more informed and confident to interact with persons with mental illness (Pinfold *et al.*, 2003).

Forensic Psychology and Policy Implications

Given the current state of police attitude, inference, and beliefs regarding the mentally ill, what can be done to improve the knowledge base surrounding this issue? Programs developed to bridge the gap between law enforcement and mental health are increasing, and more specialized training, programs, and liaison positions are being created, but there is still a long way to go. What information does exist tends to be limited in scope. Certain programs have been implemented, with varying degrees of success, in an attempt to assist law enforcement officers to more effectively and humanely work with those with mental illness and to better inform law enforcement procedures and policies. Mentally ill persons very often find themselves in jail for committing an act, which has broken the law in some way. Often, the mentally ill are incarcerated in a jail setting, not because they are criminals, per se, but because there are no other available resources to utilize at the time of the offense (Sellers, Sullivan, Veysey, & Shane, 2005).

Lamb, Weinberger, and Gross (2004) found that due to the various degrees and co-occurrence of mental disorders and substance use, mentally ill offenders are an especially challenging population for law enforcement officers. Co-disordered arrestees require mental health policy development in three key areas: improving the treatment of the co-disordered when they are in crisis, improving the jails' identification of and response to the co-disordered mentally ill and developing community treatment facilities to address the needs of the co-disordered mentally ill. These same researchers concluded that there is little choice but to reform the current health care delivery system in order to accommodate and properly treat the mentally disordered in jail.

Alleviating problems such as those just described may start at a more basic level by invoking mandatory mentally ill training sessions for police officers. Such training would address the reluctance of officers to deal with mentally ill offenders, as well as enhance the officers' ability to provide services for these special offenders. These training sessions are designed to keep the mentally ill from initially ending up in jail, making it more difficult to remove them from those conditions after the fact. Educational sessions would appear to be a useful concept in this regard.

These results beg the question of whether police officers should be mandated to learn more in-depth information regarding the mentally ill so as not to make faulty decisions regarding their treatment. Policy implications relating to these findings are good evidence that programs of this nature should be implemented.

Suggestions for Future Research

Areas related to future research are, not surprisingly, wide open. The articles described here are valuable contributions to the study of the police and the mentally ill. Virtually any other scientific information which could advance the understanding of police officers' perceptions regarding the mentally ill is in need.

More specifically, additional pre- and post-test evaluations of police officers' training in, and understanding of, the mentally disordered would be of value in detecting the understanding of the police officers' learning curve on the mentally ill in the United States and in other countries, replicating the study in the United Kingdom. Further, data obtained from mentally ill persons themselves would permit a converse view of the treatment of the mentally ill by police officers or law enforcement in general. Further research into detainment procedures for agencies and officers and the effect these procedures have on a mentally ill offender would provide valuable information to enhance training programs for officers who interact with the mentally ill. Research exploring officers' attitudes toward arresting mentally ill offenders versus hospitalization is lacking. This would allow for further understanding of the effective and ineffective manners in which to handle different types of police situations involving the mentally ill.

Finally, research on the effectiveness of various educational programs is recommended in order to promote advancement of officers' understandings of the mentally ill. Conceivably, once greater understanding is achieved, better decisions regarding crisis intervention and the physical handling of patients may lead to the de-escalation of potentially dangerous situations, thus making the police force's ability to deal with the mentally ill that much more effective. Recently, information about programs such as specialized mobile units, and liaison type positions have began to surface. The literature is promising, and more studies should explore the elements and effectiveness of these programs. For instance, what specifically works and does not work in these programs, and how can they be applied to create a more effective system to assist the police in handling mentally ill offenders?

Police Training: Communication Skills and Conflict Resolution

Introduction

The nature of a police officer's job requires routine interaction with members of the public. Often, these encounters entail the resolution of some existing, or potentially existing, conflict (Diaz, 2009). Through domestic disturbance inquiries, interaction with victims and offenders, interviewing witnesses, answering citizen questions, making arrests, and giving citations, to name a few, communication with the public and, thus, occasional conflict, is inevitable and potentially harmful in consequence (Eisikovits, Buchbinder, & Bshara, 2008). The occupation of policing, more than many other professions, requires that one be capable of and effective in communicative abilities and processes that settle conflict. As a result, training and education in conflict resolution and interpersonal communication play pivotal roles in the effective administration of law enforcement practice.

In addition to the development of these two skills, officers who are capable of assessing volatile situations, identifying the most appropriate tactics to control them, and utilizing best techniques to resolve these dangerous encounters, further the public order interests of society. This section discusses some of the relevant issues pertaining to police officers and conflict resolution skills. This includes an examination of recent research addressing effective **crisis negotiation** (i.e., techniques utilized by law enforcement to communicate with individuals who are threatening violence, including barricaded subjects, hostage takers, workplace violence, or persons threatening suicide). Frequently used tactics, as well as tactics which are not commonly employed by police officers — that arguably would be more effective in some situations — are also addressed. The following vignette demonstrates the very different outcomes that might be achieved when ineffective or effective communication strategies are utilized by officers:

Two officers were dispatched to [a] halfway house where resident Henry had been causing a disturbance. The staff wanted him expelled. The first officer to arrive gave him an intense lecture. Henry, feeling unjustly chastised, walked off and went outside. The officer grabbed him by the back of the shirt and told him he was not finished talking to him. Henry pushed the officer and the officer pushed back. A backup officer arrived at the scene and stepped in between the two men just before the situation got out of control. Through the use of verbal skills he calmed Henry and helped his fellow officer regain composure. He then persuaded the staff members into allowing Henry to remain at the center. Henry agreed to modify his behavior. The result? Because of good communication skills on the second officer's part, everyone was appeased (Woodhull, 1993).

Literature Review

Police officers spend a great deal of their time communicating with others; in fact, it is estimated that an officer may spend as much as 80% of his or her on-duty time in this activity (Collins, Lincoln, & Frank, 2005). Officers must be able to engage in written and verbal communication that is clear, succinct, and calm, often in situations that are emotionally evocative. Job descriptions for police officers frequently include communication skills as a prerequisite for employment in such positions, and also indicate that officers will receive in-depth training in communication skills once they are selected for employment (Henrico County Police Department, 2011). In addition to communicating with citizens and others while making arrests or investigating crime scenes, officers must also communicate via written reports which comply with agency and legal standards. They may also be frequently called upon to testify in court as part of their job duties, a situation where effective communication is also critical. Finally, given recent controversies surrounding false confessions, it has been recommended that officers be extensively trained in building rapport and communicating effectively during interrogations in order to minimize the likelihood of obtaining a false confession (Collins *et al.*, 2005; Beune, Giebels, & Sanders, 2009). Thus, police officers are aware of the large portion of time that is spent in communicating with the public. Further, they recognize the importance of being adequately trained in that area. Administrators and educators also agree that police officers need to be trained in interpersonal communication, although adequate training is often not provided to officers (Woodhull, 1993; Henrico County Police Department, 2011; Collins *et al.*, 2005; Diaz, 2009).

The necessity of communicative abilities, and failure of existing training programs to acknowledge the importance of communication and conflict skills, has long been illustrated by its emphasis in officer training curricula. Woodhull (1993) noted that police officers "undergo more intense training than perhaps any other professionals" (p. 4). Officers are extensively trained in the use of firearms and subsequently required to demonstrate proficiency in firearm use. Most officers, however, will rarely, if ever, use their weapons in the line of duty. In contrast, officers will inevitably spend most of their time communicating, but are not as extensively trained in such skills (Collins *et al.*, 2005). This contradiction was alluded to over 2000 years ago by Aristotle, who claimed that people should not train themselves in fist-and-weapon tactics while neglecting to train themselves in verbal tactics (Woodhull, 1993). As communication characterizes the human being, effective communication can develop understanding, while ineffective communication can result in violence (Woodhull, 1993). Thus, even before the day of the modern police officer, the importance of communication versus physical tactics in human encounters was well understood. Given the extent of communication in a police officer's job, and the significance of effective skills, we need to examine some of the reasons why conflict occurs between police and citizens.

The police are asked to maintain public order, including defusing volatile or potentially volatile situations. As noted earlier, these situations may involve criminal, disorderly, intoxicated, and/or mentally ill citizens; individuals who are angry about more general police practices or motivated by political views; and a host of other situations. The instability of citizens in these encounters creates significant risk to the officers, the citizen, and the bystanders, and the officers' handling of these situations greatly influences the public's perception of and confidence in the police, for better or for worse (Wrightsman, Nietzel, & Fortune, 1994; Hohl, Bradford, & Stanko, 2010). Often, these disputes between police officers and the public exist because of differing opinions about the duties of police officers. The *role* of police officers is an area where there has been much disagreement among scholars, the public, and the police. There is general agreement that the police officer's job consists of multiple duties, including situations where no crime has occurred. In addition to law enforcement practices (crime detection, making arrests, questioning individuals about criminal activity, etc.), the police must concern themselves with keeping peace, maintaining order, and servicing the public in general (Sprafka & Kranda, 2008; Waddington, 2007). While the disagreement often revolves around exactly what duties the police are responsible for, there is little debate that the job includes dealing with many different types of problems (Brooks, 1997; Sprafka & Kranda, 2008; Waddington, 2007).

Public encounters may result in conflict when the officer's perception of his or her duties or role differs from the citizen's perception (Bennett & Hess, 1996; Areh, Dobovsek, & Umek, 2007; Hohl *et al.*, 2010). A prime example is the otherwise upstanding citizen who is cited or ticketed for a traffic violation and replies, "Why are you bothering me when there are real criminals running around on the streets? Don't you have anything better to do with your time?" Such complaints are common in police work and often open the door for conflict. Once one understands the motivating factors behind conflict situations, the next step is to understand the other side. In other words, what are some basic tactics of conflict resolution and how are they employed by police officers?

A growing number of communities, including New York City, as well as members of the international community, are beginning to use mediation programs to facilitate the potential resolution of complaints made by citizens against the police (Berger, 2000; Buchner, Bobb, Root, & Barge, 2008; Aertsen, 2009; Meyer, Paul, & Grant, 2009; Waddington, 2007). Early in the implementation of such programs, Berger (2000) indicated that the lack of an understanding of police duties, poor communication by both the police and the public, or simple misunderstandings, were at the root of most police-community conflicts. Berger (2000, p. 211) believed that "the mediation process itself can work in a transformative way, improving strained relations between the police and the general population." Since that time, as empirical investigations have been conducted to examine the effectiveness of these programs, their success in yielding increasingly favorable resolution of conflicts between officers and the public at large has been proven (Buchner *et al.*, 2008; Aertsen, 2009; Meyer *et al.*, 2009; Waddington, 2007).

Conflict resolution tactics include a large group of behaviors which are intended to either gain compliance in an interaction or resolve the interaction in a way which is satisfactory to both parties (Waddington, 2007; Meyer *et al.*, 2009). Such tactics are necessary when two parties have goals or desires in an encounter which are incompatible, yet the interaction must end in some sort of compromise. This scenario describes the great majority of interactions involving the police and the public. The question becomes, "What tactics do police officers generally employ in public situations, and what other (better) options are available to them?"

Early researchers discovered that officers implement a wide variety of conflict resolution tactics, and that the tactic selected and used depends on a number of factors. For example, Wilson and Gross (1994) noted that officers may select tactics based upon the citizens' socioeconomic status, gender, ethnicity, and age. Chosen tactics have also been related to the degree of citizen compliance and perception of intoxication (Worden, 1989), as well as to the neighborhood in which the encounter occurs and the specific police department's attitude toward tactics for gaining compliance (Smith & Klein, 1984). More specifically, it has recently been discovered that officers are more likely to use coercive tactics when the encounter occurs in a socially disadvantaged neighborhood than in other locales (Sun, Payne, & Wu, 2008). Toch (1985) and others have implied that the attitude of specific officers upon entering an interaction can increase the likelihood of a conflict occurring or even escalating. Some officers, whose chosen goal is to obtain compliance from the citizen, may behave in a way that increases the probability of a negative (confrontative or escalated) interaction.

These officers may perceive coercive tactics as the most effective available strategy for dealing with the situation. This is supported by research which indicates that officers who are more interpersonally and physically aggressive are more likely to engage in behavior resulting in confirmed allegations of abuse or of escalating tense situations (Hassell & Archbold, 2010). On the other hand, officers who prefer problem-solving tactics, as well as those who are less likely to be interpersonally or physically aggressive, would be less likely to increase the existing tension in interactions with citizens (Hassell & Archbold, 2010). Problem solving is one method of *nonconventional* conflict resolution to which we now turn our attention.

Common, or conventional, methods of conflict resolution for police officers include legitimate use of physical force, arrest, coercion and/or threats to arrest, and avoidance (Cooper, 1997). These tactics are commonly employed in conflict situations and, admittedly, are necessary on occasion. The issue is whether more appropriate tactics are available that would allow an officer to address a volatile (or potentially volatile) situation in a more productive and less injurious way. In one of the early investigations of these methods, Cooper (1997) referred to methods which do not involve force, coercion, or arrest as ***non-conventional* conflict-resolution methods**. These methods include mediation, arbitration, third-party negotiation, facilitation, reconciliation, counseling, problem solving, and problem management. He contended that these methods are suitable for addressing situations such as "disputes or conflicts characterized as public, barricade situations, community-based, and interpersonal" conflict (p. 88). Further, the effectiveness of such techniques on a global scale requires not only increased usage, but also perfecting the *manner* in which they are used.

As empirical attention has turned towards evaluating the effectiveness of these methods, their usefulness and efficacy has been demonstrated by many investigators (Buchner *et al.*, 2008; Aertsen, 2009; Meyer *et al.*, 2009; Waddington, 2007). A more in-depth discussion of the various methods previously outlined is not necessary here. The point worth noting is that there are a number of conflict-resolution tactics available to police officers which may not be typically employed, but are useful in appropriate situations. The increasing utilization of such tactics by law enforcement can have a positive impact in multiple ways, including decreasing the need for use of many intrusive and potentially dangerous methods, improving the public's opinion of police officers, and reducing the risk of harm to officers and society.

The importance of effective communication skills is reflected in the growing emphasis placed on developing this skill set by Texas Commission on Law Enforcement Officer Standards and Education (2007), an agency which develops training curricula for law enforcement officers across the state. During their initial training, officers complete a fifteen-part module consisting of lecture, role plays, and written assessments of their communication abilities. Officers are taught that effective communication begins with effective observation and "sizing up" of the situation, as an effective solution cannot be arrived at if the situation is misappraised from the outset. Officers are also taught that even prior to their interaction with another person, they should be aware of any behavior that is out of the ordinary, the ways in which others are grouping themselves, changes in noise levels, which may indicate problems, and changes in the physical appearance of others.

Additionally, officers are taught that an officer who is an effective communicator: (1) is fair; (2) gives orders respectfully; (3) provides support and back-up for other officers; (4) makes others feel appreciated; (5) makes others feel as though everyone is working toward a common purpose; (6) is predictable and consistent; (7) listens before speaking; (8) has knowledge of his or her own job duties; and (9) is a good role model for others. Emphasis is also placed on officers' physical proximity to those with whom they are communicating, as officers must strike a balance between keeping a safe distance and being close enough to effectively communicate with others. With regard to eye contact, officers are instructed regarding the different purposes of both direct and indirect eye contact, and to use direct eye contact when they wish to convey authority or when they wish to obtain accurate information, but to balance direct eye contact with indirect eye contact so that the officer and the person(s) with whom they are communicating feel comfortable. Emphasis is also placed on **posturing,** or the way in which the officer holds and positions his or her body during communication. Officers are instructed to stand erect, to eliminate distracting behaviors such as fidgeting or leaning against walls or ledges, and to lean slightly towards the person with whom they are interacting (Texas Commission on Law Enforcement Officer Standards and Education, 2007).

Officers are also provided training regarding the development of their listening skills (Texas Commission on Law Enforcement Officer Standards and Education, 2007). Officers are trained to suspend judgment and not to respond until the other party has completed their statement, to pick out key words, which may communicate the mental or physical state of the person speaking, to appraise the intensity of what's being said in order to determine the appropriate level of force that may be necessary in a response, and to reflect on the mood conveyed by the person speaking. Officers are also encouraged to develop the following traits that epitomize good communicators: (1) being a good listener; (2) exhibiting genuine concern for others and their concerns; (3) not over-reacting; (4) displaying non-threatening posture; (5) asking appropriate questions; and (6) exhibiting a relaxed demeanor, even in high-stress situations. Officers are also taught to ask themselves the following questions when reflecting back on an interaction with a member of the public, in order to reflect on what they said, as well as the importance of things which may have been omitted; (1) How did the individual look? (e.g., relaxed, nervous, angry); (2) What did they say?; (3) What didn't they say? (Texas Commission on Law Enforcement Officer Standards and Education, 2007).

Officers often have to make requests of strangers; these requests often represent things which the individual may not want to do. Therefore, training also frequently focuses on ways in which officers can communicate requests and orders to maximize the likelihood of compliance and minimize risk to the officer and the public (Texas Commission on Law Enforcement Officer Standards and Education, 2007). Officers' orders should be: (1) specific; and (2) given using a polite but direct tone which becomes stronger and more direct when necessary. Officers also receive training in positive reinforcement, and are instructed to offer verbal and tangible reinforcements when their orders or requests are obeyed, in order to buttress their relationship with the individual with whom they are communicating. Although this represents an overview of the training Texas law enforcement officers receive regarding communicating with others, it is reflective of the increasing emphasis placed on effective communication by law enforcement agencies (Texas Commission on Law Enforcement Officer Standards and Education, 2007).

Perhaps nowhere are communication skills more essential for law enforcement personnel than in situations where **crisis negotiations** (e.g., a technique for law enforcement to communicate with those who are threatening violence, including barricaded subjects, hostage takers, persons threatening suicide, or workplace violence offenders) are necessary. Despite the high stress associated with these situations and propensity for loss of multiple lives, the continued development of effective negotiation techniques has resulted in successful outcomes for approximately 82% of the approximately 100,000 crisis negotiation situations that occur annually in the United States (Van Hasselt, Baker, Romano, Schlessinger, Zucker, Dragone, *et al.*, 2006). Psychologists and other mental health professionals have long been involved in developing methods for crisis negotiations (Gelles & Palarea, 2010).

The psychologist may play varying roles, depending upon the phase of negotiations in which their services are sought. For example, during the pre-incident phase, a psychologist may provide psychological screening and selection of individuals likely to be successful as negotiators, provide training on psychological topics such as active listening skills, persuasion techniques, or crisis intervention, or participate in training exercises with officers likely to encounter situations involving crisis negotiations (Gelles & Palarea, 2010). The importance of psychologists in training of law enforcement officers cannot be understated, as research has indicated that incorporating mental health professionals into such training and including role-playing activities increases the effectiveness of officers in real-life negotiation incidents (Van Hasselt *et al.*, 2006). If a psychologist is called upon after an incident has begun, they may: (1) monitor the negotiations; (2) provide information regarding the behavior and communications of the subject; (3) manage the stress level of the negotiator; (4) act as a liaison with collateral sources and other professionals to support ongoing assessment of the subject; (5) assess the interface between the mental state of the subject and the unfolding situation; (6) assess the original motivation for the crisis situation and the evolving motivations underlying each communication; (7) analyze intelligence gathered through interviews with family members and other data sources regarding the subject's patterns of behavior and violence risk; and (8) apply threat assessment models to determine if the subject is making a specific threat and the likelihood that the threat will be carried out (Gelles & Palarea, 2010). Following an incident, a psychologist may: (1) provide stress management education to those involved; and/or (2) provide team debriefings and counseling to crisis team members (though this should be done by a psychologist who was not involved in the incident itself to avoid a dual relationship and subsequent ethical violations) (Gelles & Palarea, 2010). It is recommended that, in order to maintain their competence to engage in such activities, psychologists receive intensive training with law enforcement negotiation teams and experienced crisis negotiation psychologists; such activities represent a specialized discipline with forensic psychology and involve high stake situations where lives can be lost if effective practice is not ensured; therefore, crisis negotiation should not be undertaken lightly (Gelles & Palarea, 2010).

Psychologists and law enforcement personnel have used a variety of methodologies to negotiate with subjects in crisis situations (Rowe, Gelles, & Palarea, 2006; Grubb, 2010). One such model is the SAFE model (Hammer, 2007). This model identifies four triggers typically characteristic of crisis negotiations, from which its acronym was derived: (1) **Substantive demands** (the instrumental wants/demands made by the parties, e.g., subject and negotiator); (2) **Attunement** (the relational trust established between the parties); (3) **Face** (the self-image of each of the parties that is threatened or honored); and (4) **Emotion** (the degree of emotional distress experienced by the parties). Negotiators identify the specific triggers for a subject in each of these categories, then match their communication style accordingly, in order to de-escalate the situation somewhat. After some de-escalation occurs, the negotiator(s) use verbal skills to shift the subject's triggers in a desired direction to achieve a safe outcome (Hammer, 2007). This model has been shown effective in situations involving armed individuals attempting to escape capture (Royce, 2005), domestic disturbances, and suicidal individuals (Hammer, 2007).

Regardless of the model of negotiation used, researchers have demonstrated the importance of juxtaposing high-probability and low-probability requests in order to increase the likelihood of successful resolution. A **high-probability request** is one with which the subject is likely to comply (e.g., a request for information regarding the number of hostages, a request to not shoot any of the hostages in the leg), whereas a **low-probability request** is one with which the subject is unlikely to comply (e.g., surrendering to law enforcement, releasing all hostages). Findings of recent research indicate that negotiations are most effective when several high-probability requests are made over time with subject compliance, and with relationship-building communication occurring between requests. Only after compliance with several such requests are subjects likely to comply with a low-probability request, and when this occurs, the result will usually successfully resolve the incident (Hughes, 2009). Research has also consistently demonstrated that inexperienced negotiators may immediately make low-probability requests of subjects, making it unlikely that a successful resolution of the crisis situation will happen (Hughes, 2009). These findings emphasize the necessity of extensive training for those wishing to become negotiators, as behaviors which may seem intuitively helpful may actually exacerbate an already dangerous situation.

Forensic Psychology and Policy Implications

Given the extent and nature of conflict between police and citizens, as well as the large majority of time officers spend in communicative encounters, the need for training is undeniable. It is apparent that existing policy for training officers in communication skills, as well as extended training throughout their careers, is currently inadequate in many departments. In the case of Henry, the first officer to arrive on the scene was clearly not effective in communicative abilities. His communication, in fact, escalated the conflict rather than brought it to a peaceful resolution. Based on the story, we can assume that initially the first officer's attempt to communicate with Henry was ineffective for a number of reasons. Namely, his "intense lecture" immediately left Henry feeling like the officer was against him, versus with him or for him. Naturally, Henry's perception was that the officer was there to lecture him and punish him rather than peacefully resolve the conflict between Henry and the staff. Later, when Henry felt "chastised" and walked away, the officer responded with an even more authoritarian attitude, bringing threats and physical force into the interaction. At this point, the encounter could have easily become unnecessarily inflated to the point of violence and the arrest of Henry. Luckily, the second officer arrived on the scene in time to calm the situation. The communication and conflict-resolution skills of the second officer became vitally important, and a potentially explosive conflict was controlled.

Police officer training academies should spend a considerable amount of time instructing their officers on the importance of effective and de-escalating communication, as these skills will be most frequently used by officers. Conflict resolution skills will often become their first line of defense when encountering agitated and potentially violent citizens. Mental health professionals may be helpful in this aspect of the officer's training, as well as in assisting departments in selecting candidates with the most potential for becoming effective communicators during times of intense stress. As mental health professionals are more involved in training and assisting officers in high impact situations such as hostage negotiation, ethical and practice guidelines should be developed to guide these individuals in their professional activities (Gelles & Palarea, 2010). Even in circumstances that are routinely encountered by police officers and typically do not lead to violence (e.g., traffic stops), increasing officers' communicative abilities can improve the public's perceptions of officers and their roles in their communities (Areh, Dobovsek, & Umek, 2007).

Approaching a situation as did the first officer in Henry's case will regrettably create unnecessary consequences for citizens and police. The more aware the public becomes of such behaviors, and the more communicative conflicts that citizens themselves have with officers, the more likely society is to doubt and disrespect the police. For police to enjoy the kind of relationship it aspires to maintain with citizens, communicating effectively becomes as important as other duties. Whenever possible, resolving volatile or conflict situations without the use of unnecessary force, threat, or arrest should be the goal of every police officer. Consequently, natural communicative ability and effective training become a necessity. Recent authors have also noted that mentoring of "rookie" officers by more experienced staff seems to be a promising method by which to disseminate and model effective communication strategies taught in training academies (Sprafka & Kranda, 2008).

More recently, psychology has made important contributions to police-citizen conflict situations. Generally, psychologists are called upon to educate the police about matters such as dealing with the mentally ill, hostage situations, domestic violence situations, and other crises (Detrick & Chibnall, 2008; Diaz, 2009). Psychology has proven an effective tool for developing approaches to such situations but has more to offer than just training. The knowledge of human relations and general communication skills establishes a place for psychology in the education and training of police officers. Further, psychology avails itself well to the establishment and ongoing evaluation of training programs. Forensic psychology, in its mutual regard for psychological and criminal justice matters, has established a place for itself in police administration and consultation. Recently, more departments are realizing the value that psychology can bring, and are beginning to employ psychologists in roles outside of the traditional clinical and crisis situations. Police departments are beginning to realize the importance of officers having the necessary communicative skills (like the second officer in the scenario with Henry) and thus are looking to increase training in such areas in the future.

In addition to these procedural and administrative changes, it has been recommended that independent and external oversight agencies be formed to evaluate the effectiveness of training, as well as to investigate cases in which officers resorted to physical intervention before effectively or thoroughly engaging in effective verbal communication (Diaz, 2009). As officers increasingly encounter members of culturally diverse groups, training curricula should include information about how officers may vary their communication style in order to increase their effectiveness with specific groups (Eisikovits *et al.*, 2008; Wolff & Cokely, 2007). Consultation with psychologists and other mental health professionals, as well as with members of and experts on specific cultural groups, may be particularly helpful in this regard (Wolff & Cokely, 2007).

Suggestions for Future Research

Given the increasing public awareness and citizen complaints regarding police use of force, brutality, and "attitude," such nonconventional tactics are worthy of additional research and consideration on the policy level. Certainly, additional research needs to be done on the effectiveness of nonconventional tactics and their applicability to various situations. The lack of officer training in nonconventional techniques and communication skills in general, makes them difficult to employ and even more difficult to measure in terms of their effectiveness. Situations such as Henry's provide convincing evidence of the positive benefits of communication and nonthreatening and nonforceful measures by the police.

Additionally, future research efforts should identify whether certain communicative strategies are differentially effective when implemented with members of various cultural groups, and to identify particular strategies which are effective for various cultural groups officers are likely to encounter. In light of recommendations that departments utilize mentoring to continue training once officers begin their patrols (Sprafka & Kranda, 2008), future studies should examine ways in which mentors and mentees can best be matched to optimize their working relationships. The fact that, as of yet, appropriate education and training is often not supplied renders only speculative accounts of the effectiveness and usefulness of these methods.

The Psychology of Terrorism: Motivations, Implications, and Healing

Introduction

Many countries around the world, such as Ireland, South Africa, Israel, Spain, Japan, and Lebanon to name only a few, have been the target of terrorist threats and attacks for years. Yet, the horrific terrorist attack on the United States on 11 September, 2001 had a profound impact on the worldview of terrorism. The sheer magnitude of casualties and destruction forced many countries, especially the United States, to realize the international community's

vulnerability to terrorism. In the wake of the devastation, United States citizens have been forced to shift from an isolationist perspective to a global perspective. Subsequent attacks, such as the 11 March, 2004 terrorist bombings on commuter trains in Madrid, Spain, and the 7 July, 2005 suicide bombings on three underground trains and a bus in London, further heightened awareness that the need exists to unite as a global community to better comprehend and prevent terrorism, as well as to heal from its debilitating effects that permeate many facets of life.

Acts of terrorism are psychological by nature. They are typically intended to disrupt ways of life and effect political change by sending ripples of fear throughout a society, far outreaching the relatively small numbers of physical victims killed or injured in the actual bombings, shootings, or other displays of violence. Often, those killed or injured are random targets selected to create a media fervor and to send shock waves of panic and distress into the political, economic, and social sectors of a country targeted (i.e., United States, Israel). This section will provide a broad, sweeping overview of the definition of terrorism, its emotional impact on people and society, its psychological consequences, and the need and role of **psychological first-aid (PFA)** responders, given these tragic and horrific events. As described by Bryme, Jacobs, Layne, *et al.* (2006), PFA is an evidence-informed, supportive intervention designed to help individuals and families in the aftermath of disasters and acts of terrorism. Additionally, a brief description of the impact of the attacks on the World Trade Center and the Pentagon on 11 September, 2001, as well as the ongoing Israeli and Palestinian conflict, will be used to illustrate the impact of terrorism on mental health symptoms, quality of life, and emergency mental health systems in the United States and abroad. The importance of care for caregivers also is stressed. Stout (2002) warns that terrorism is a very complicated and complex issue that is not easily comprehended or reduced to clear, understandable components. As such, this section will be necessarily broad and brief. It will review only some of the controversial issues relevant to forensic psychologists and will highlight topics addressing a response to and/or the prevention of terrorism, as well as treatment of trauma survivors.

Although countries such as the United States and New Zealand are relatively new to developing mental health response programs and protocols to terrorist attacks, mental health professionals in Israel have been working with those who have either directly or indirectly suffered from terrorism for years. Consider the following case examples:

> Judy is a mental health professional who was traveling on a bus shot at by Palestinian terrorists. Although the bus was bulletproof and no one was injured, Judy developed heavy somatic pains and depression, which prevented her from working for more than half a year. Judy was diagnosed as suffering from depression and PTSD. She entered psychotherapy, which allowed her gradually to get back to work. In conversations with her supervisors, she expressed the effects of the trauma that continued to influence her. About a year after the incident, she attended a staff meeting in which the discourse "Hardship as an opportunity for personal growth" was presented. This alternative discourse resonated with Judy. She told us it was a new revelation for her. This discourse informed her of the possibility of being in control of the meaning of the incident and not falling victim to it.
>
> This revelation enabled her to take a ride back home at dusk in a private car for the first time since the shooting incident (Shalif & Leibler, 2002, p. 63).
>
> In the case of a suicide bomb attack in a shopping mall, Joy saw many injured people in terrible states, as well as body parts scattered around. When talking to me (Y.S.) after the event, she was very upset and told me that she "almost went crazy." I asked her what kept her from running away or "going crazy." She then remembered that a woman who had been trying on some clothing handed over her baby at the very moment that the bomb exploded.
>
> She realized that her responsibility to the baby helped her to stay "together" and not to run away or "fall to pieces." When asked why this experience had that effect on her, she mentioned the issue of responsibility. The conversation that ensued turned toward the topic of how a sense of responsibility toward vulnerable others can help us deal with even the most terrible situations (pp. 68–69).

Literature Review

The State Department defines "**terrorism**" as "premeditated, politically motivated violence perpetrated against noncombatant targets by subnational groups or clandestine agents, usually intended to influence an audience" (U.S. Department of State, 2000); while the FBI defines it as "the unlawful use or threat of violence against persons or property to intimidate the government, the civilian population, or any segment thereof, in furtherance of political or social objectives" (U.S. Department of Justice, 1999a). Terrorism also has been characterized as psychological warfare whereby the "explicit goal of the terrorist act is to create a condition of fear, uncertainty, demoralization, and helplessness as a coercive and/or punitive force" (Everly, 2003, p. 57). The actual physical targets of a terrorist attack are only a means to an end to break the will and spirit of the perceived enemy and to irrevocably alter their lifestyle. These casualties are typically only symbolic targets and the message of fear is perpetuated through round the clock media coverage (Shamir & Shikaki, 2002). After the events of 11 September, 2001, there is growing concern and question about how terrorism is defined and who is at risk. Shamir and Shikaki (2002, p. 537) suggest that there is no universally accepted description of terrorism and that the majority of definitions offered by the international community are colored by "self-serving motivations." Nevertheless, Arnold *et al.* (2003) propose a universal definition for the purposes of medical and public health. These authors describe terrorism as:

> *the intentional use of violence — real or threatened — against one or more non-combatants and/or those services essential for or protective of their health, resulting in adverse health effects in those immediately affected and their community, ranging from a loss of well-being or security to injury, illness or death (p. 49).*

Conventional wisdom maintains that terrorists are not able to combat or overcome their enemy by way of military force. Consequently, their only recourse is terrorism and psychological warfare. Yet, some scholars warn that most Western countries attempt to separate the means from the intended goals and define terrorism based on the targeting of civilians. This belief causes many Third World and Muslim countries to fear that the complete separation of goals from methods will result in all national liberation, resistance, and guerilla movements to be defined as terrorist organizations (Shamir & Shikaki, 2002). Many terrorist groups justify their activities as retaliation when they see no other alternative. Although society collectively conjures up the image of Osama Bin Laden upon the mention of terrorism, care in who and what we define as terrorism is exemplified through the words of Nelson Mandela, South Africa's first democratically elected president. As he explained:

> *I argued that the state had given us no alternative to violence… Violence would begin whether we initiated it or not. Would it not be better to guide this violence ourselves, according to the principles where we saved lives by attacking symbols of oppression, and not people?" (Mandela, 1994, p. 322).*

The word terrorism has strong negative connotations and implications and must be used carefully. Clearly, the leadership efforts of Nelson Mandela cannot be classified with those of Osama Bin Laden.

Shamir and Shikaki (2002, p. 553) describe the old adage that "one man's 'terrorist' is another man's 'freedom fighter'" as demonstrated by the Israeli–Palestinian debate on the matter. Connolly (2003) takes a psychoanalytic approach and uses the psychological mechanisms of dehumanization and splitting to explain the terrorist's justifications for his or her actions. In many cases, the other or the target is seen as oppressive, evil, or less than human. Therefore, the **means** (i.e., acts of violence) clearly justify the **ends** (i.e., the end of oppression). Frequently, terrorist acts are fueled by **religious fanaticism** (i.e., intense, uncritical devotion to a particular religion) with the belief that they are on a crusade. Similarly, Post (2010) suggests that, at least for Palestinians, the terrorists likely view their behavior as "defensive aggression, required by the aggression of the occupiers" (p. 246). According to Reich (1998), feelings of hatred, revulsion, and revenge motivate many terrorists. For example, the attacks by Al Qaeda were justified by Islamic fundamentalism and religious fanaticism with Western culture and any who consorted with Westerners being demonized. Tausch, Becker, Spears, Christ, Saab, Singh, and Siddiqui (2011) examined the roles of anger, contempt, and efficacy as it relates to normative versus nonnormative action. They found that nonnormative action (e.g., terrorist strategies) is associated with low efficacy and contempt and that anger and high efficacy are associated with normative actions. Thus, individuals who are angry and believe that they can affect change through normative action are less likely to resort to violence than individuals who feel contempt and perceive that they are powerless to affect change. Terrorists typically are acting as groups or cells or in groups that share common goals or beliefs (Lawal, 2002). Lawal maintains that terrorists will act as individuals (i.e., suicide bomber) when they are extremely inspired by their group and that, as such, these violent displays still can be classified as collective acts.

Research indicates that the true impact of terrorism cannot be measured by casualties, but rather by the impact of fear on the individual's thoughts, feelings, behavior, and personal freedom (Davis, 2002; Hoffman, Diamond, & Lipsitz, 2011; Woods, 2011). There are many other consequences of terrorism. Economic costs were evidenced after the September 11 attacks by a decline in the stock market, as well as appreciable financial problems with the airline and travel industries. In essence, our way of life changed. As Silver (2011, p. 1) points out:

> We are different now. Most of us willingly tolerate long lines at the airport, empty our pockets, and remove our shoes, belts, and jackets, sending them through X-ray machines for scrutiny. We open our bags before entering sporting events, theaters, and musical performances. We sometimes gaze askance at young men carrying backpacks on public transportation.

The bombings on the commuter trains in Madrid, Spain just days before their national elections may have significantly contributed to the defeat of the incumbent party, known to be a firm ally with the United States during the war with Iraq. This is one example of how acts of terrorism can weaken political unity. Everly (2003, p. 58) describes four salient terrorist threats to the United States at this time: (1) threats of physical destruction and death; (2) perceived threat of injury/death to individuals, families, and communities; (3) threat of sociological turmoil; and (4) the threat of economic recession, with the potential for particular industrial sectors to collapse. By undermining the most basic human needs of safety and security, terrorists can infiltrate many aspects of society and can obliterate day-to-day living in the targeted country.

The etiology of terrorism is unclear and although theories abound, there is no agreed-upon understanding of this phenomenon. Crenshaw (1998) maintains that terrorists' actions are based on logical thinking and strategic choices with the intent of accomplishing a reality-based goal. Bandura (1998) suggests that terrorists have become morally detached and are driven more by psychological forces. Arena and Arrigo (2005) argue that terrorism is linked to group identity and the need to take on roles, advance symbols, and locate personal meaning consistent with this identity. Yet, other researchers suggest that the factors contributing to aggressive actions taken by terrorists are a complex combination of biological processes in combination with cultural/environmental situations and psychological correlates. For example, Davis (2002) describes the interaction of frustration, intense negative emotions, poor impulse control, and social and group norms that support and validate violence as contributing to the phenomenon of terrorism. He further describes the research from social psychology that suggests that attack, threat, and even a perceived threat are the most reliable predictors of or catalysts for aggression. When an individual or group responds with preemptive aggression toward a perceived threat, the person does not identify the behavior as aggressive but, rather, as legitimized conduct (Davis, 2002).

Terrorists typically perceive a hostile world that is not responsive to their needs, religions, ideologies, or miseries (Post, 2010; Shamir & Shikaki, 2002; Tausch *et al.*, 2011). To illustrate, the ideologies of many current terrorist movements of Middle Eastern origin advance the belief that the government of Saudi Arabia is corrupt and only remains in power because of its support from Western governments. Additionally, they maintain that Israel unfairly occupies land and oppresses the Palestinians precisely because of Western (especially U.S.) assistance (Davis, 2002). With these observations on the phenomenon of terrorism in mind, one thing is certain: there is no silver bullet or singular psychology to account for this behavior; rather, there is a complex picture entangled with culture, politics, real and perceived social injustices, social and environmental factors, and, in some cases, psychopathology (Stout, 2002).

According to the National Counterterrorism Center (United States, 2011), **suicide bombers**, (i.e., individuals who carry out a terrorist attack using bombs and who do so with the intent of dying in the attack) are the most lethal type of terrorist attack. While suicide attacks accounted for approximately 2% of all terrorist attacks in 2010, suicide bombings are responsible for 13.5% of terrorism-related fatalities. Spencer (2002) notes that suicide bombers are not typically suffering from a diagnosable mental illness but instead are engaging in "altruistic suicide." He describes "**altruistic suicide**" as "self-inflicted death owing to powerful beliefs, resulting in individuals losing their sense of autonomy" (p. 436). Moreover, as he describes it, "When a central belief that life is but a temporary prelude to everlasting utopian existence is one of these regulatory norms, the definition of suicide itself becomes ambiguous, and the role of psychiatry as a valid therapeutic intervention is also questionable" (p. 436).

Recently, Merari, Diamant, Bibi, Broshi, and Zakin (2010) performed clinical interviews and psychological testing on three groups of Palestinians — unsuccessful suicide bombers, a control group of terrorists arrested for participating in nonsuicide missions, and a group of organizers of suicide operations. The authors found that while there was no single personality profile of would-be suicide bombers, the majority displayed significantly less **ego strength** than the organizers. According to Bellak, Hurvich, and Gediman (as described in Merari *et al.*, p. 93), ego strength is reflected in an individual's ability to efficiently cope with both internal and external stress and to regulate one's emotions in such a way as to "act independently with self control, to establish and maintain focus and attention, to actualize pre-conceived plans, to think logically...." They also found some of the would-be suicide bombers exhibited symptoms of depression and/or post traumatic stress disorder, including a significant number who displayed **subclinical suicidal characteristics** (e.g., an individual may be experiencing symptoms of depression and have thoughts of suicide, but does not have an active plan to commit suicide). Nevertheless, the majority of the would-be suicide bombers did not display suicidal tendencies. The authors note, however, personality factors alone cannot account for the willingness of some individuals to carry out suicide attacks since these missions are typically organized by groups.

Israel was established in 1948 and since that time its residents or civilian population have experienced many periods of terrorist attacks (Shalif & Leibler, 2002). Bleich, Gelkopf, and Solomon (2003) report that by 30 April, 2002, 472 individuals, including 318 civilians, had been killed by terrorist attacks and 3846 had been injured, including 2708 civilians, in Israel. The Israel Ministry of Foreign Affairs (2007) reported that between 2000 and 2006, 1116 individuals, including 786 civilians, had been killed by terrorist attacks and 8800 individuals, including 5531 civilians, had been wounded. According to Shalif and Leibler, the first **Intifada**, or uprising, of the Palestinians against the Israeli occupation of the West Bank and the Gaza Strip occurred from 1987 to 1993, following the signing of the Oslo Accord between the government of Israel and the Palestine Liberation Organization (PLO). During this time, there was an increase in the terrorist attacks on Jewish residents of Judea, Samaria, and the Gaza coastal region, and terrorist bombings in populated areas such as shopping malls, city buses, and markets. The second Intifada began in October of 2000 and created increasing levels of terrorism to include repeated suicide bombings (Shalif & Leibler, 2002). The case examples of Judy and Joy represent the trauma experienced by many individuals who live in this region.

This Middle Eastern region has been plagued by violence for many, many years and has experience with psychological first-aid responders. Shalif and Leibler (2002, p. 61) write:

> *Every municipality in Israel employs school psychologists who specialize in counseling, testing, group interventions, and crisis intervention. News broadcasts that inform the population about a mass civilian disaster are most often accompanied by the announcement of available services provided by school psychologists in the area.*

These authors stress the importance of involving community support to those affected by terrorism as a foundation of crisis intervention in Israel. Debriefing groups are very common and mental health professionals act as consultants to the community (Shalif & Leibler, 2002). As these investigators explain, the communities themselves are the primary source of empowerment for its members. Researchers find that those who experience or are affected by act of terrorism engage in "meaning-making" as a strategy for coping (Shalif & Leibler, 2002). Davis and McKearney (2003) found that individuals who are faced with loss and trauma are motivated to perceive their lives as highly meaningful and interpret their purpose in life as a sign of well-being, based on a self-protective process. This ability to face trauma with a positive outlook is an important key to adaptive coping. Culture and religion are important components of this process of making sense out of tragedy. Those who experience the trauma associated with terrorism can have a wide variety of reactions. Notwithstanding the reaction (e.g., fear, anxiety), it should be normalized in an effort to avoid marginalizing individuals, given their unique responses to it (Shalif & Leibler, 2002).

Strous, Stryjer, Keret, Bergin, and Kotler (2003) explored the effects of terrorism in Israel on the subjective mood and behavior of medical and psychiatric inpatients in Israel. To accomplish this, they surveyed 42 medical and 36 psychiatric inpatients with 54 staff members at the two hospitals serving as the control population. The results indicated that the level of worry in response to security instability in the region was the highest in clinical staff, was midrange in medical patients, and was lowest in psychiatric inpatients with schizophrenia. Those who did report that their mood was affected were of similar severity. Strous *et al.* (2003) suggest that the lower level of anxiety or worry in psychiatric patients might have been linked to their inability to make sense out of the situation. This study highlights the need to assist mental health caregivers in order to facilitate the provision of optimal psychiatric care of others under conditions that affect the emotional (and trauma) needs of clinical personnel.

Bleich *et al.* (2003) conducted a nationally representative telephone-based survey of Israeli residents undertaken from April through May of 2002 in order to ascertain the prevalence of post traumatic stress disorder (PTSD) symptoms and the methods of coping used to deal with exposure to terrorism and its ongoing threat. There were 512 participants, consisting of 250 men (48.9%) and 262 women (51.1%) and 444 Jews (86.6%) and 68 Arabs (13.2%). The interviews were conducted by telephone using a structured questionnaire. Overall, the results indicated that 84 (16.4%) Israeli adults surveyed had been personally involved in an attack in the year and a half prior to the survey; 113 (22.1%) of the respondents indicated that a friend or family member was wounded or killed in an attack, and 78 (15.3%) reported that they knew someone who survived an attack uninjured (Bleich *et al.*, 2003). Moreover, the results indicated that nearly two-thirds of the sample (60%) feared for their lives and more than two-thirds (67.9%) stated that they feared for the lives of their friends and family.

Respondents in the Bleich *et al.* (2003) study also reported trauma-related and stress-related mental health symptoms. Greater than one-third (37.4%) reported having at least one trauma-related symptom for at least one month, with an average of four symptoms reported per person. The most commonly reported symptoms were avoidance/numbing (55.5%), followed by hyperarousal symptoms (49.4%), and reexperiencing trauma-related scenes (37.1%). Additionally, 26.9% of the respondents reported at least one disassociative symptom, 46.3% reported being distressed by symptoms, and 22.7% reported that their work or social functioning was impaired. Greater than half (58.6%) reported feeling depressed or gloomy and 28% reported feeling "very" depressed. Overall, 9% of the participants met the *DSM-IV* criteria for PTSD.

Similarly, Canetti, Galena, Hall, *et al.* (2010) interviewed adults in the West Bank, Gaza Strip, and East Jerusalem and found that 23.3% of the respondents met criteria for PTSD and 28.2% met criteria for major depression. Salguero, Fernández-Berrocal, Iruarrizaga, *et al.* (2011) reviewed the literature and determined the risk of developing major depressive disorder after a terrorist attack is between 20 and 30% in direct victims and 4 and 10% in the general population in the first few months following the attack. Bleich *et al.* (2003) reported that the number and severity of trauma-related symptoms reported in their sample are comparable to those found among a national sample of U.S. residents after the September 11 terrorist attack on the World Trade Center, as well as comparable to a sample of New York residents, overall. However, the prevalence of trauma-related symptoms reported for persons in the immediate vicinity of the World Trade Center one to two months after the attack was greater (20%) (Galea, Ahern, Resnick, *et al.*, 2002).

The terrorist attacks that took place on 11 September, 2001 in both New York City and Washington, D.C. left approximately 3000 people dead and several thousands of people in grief, anger, and shock (Taylor, 2002). Numerous official and unofficial agencies were involved in the counseling response to this enormous tragedy. During the first eight weeks after the attacks across the United States, the American Red Cross alone had 135,800 mental health and grief contacts (Taylor, 2002). Schuster, Stein, Jaycox, *et al.* (2001) indicate that the World Trade Center terrorist attacks on the United States affected Americans far beyond New York City with substantial symptoms of stress. Clearly, the saturation of the 9/11 events — particularly through sustained media coverage — had a significant impact on the emotions and feelings of people's security throughout the United States. Back, Küfner, and Egloff (2010) analyzed the use of emotional words used in text pagers on September 11. Contrary to what might be expected, they found that sadness was not the primary emotion with which individuals reacted to the attacks. They also found that individuals experienced a number of peaks in anxiety throughout the day, from which they recovered quickly. With regards to anger, they found that anger was present from the time of the impact of the first airplane and steadily increased over the course of the day.

In response to the first anniversary of September 11, one New Yorker observed the following (cited in Jordan, 2003, p. 110):

> We remembered the many lives we lost on the 11th, last year. The children that lost one parent, or worse, were orphaned that day. But you know, today we once more all became one country. There's no race, no ethnicity, and no poor or rich, we are all Americans. And we grew united out of the dust of the 11th.

Jordan (2003) discusses not only the tremendous impact of the actual events of 11 September, 2001, but also the intense emotional reactions to the first year anniversary. She describes the need to deal with anniversaries of trauma proactively to help minimize the potential escalation of stress responses or other emotional reactions and to help the individual move toward closure and to move forward in the grieving process. The first anniversary was described as being the most difficult for individuals who had "(a) group affiliation with a victim; (b) shared characteristics, interests, or attributes with a victim; (c) previously demonstrated poor coping skills; (d) exhibited extreme or atypical reactions; (e) a personal history of trauma…and concurrent adverse reactions (e.g., family problems, health problems, psychiatric history)" (Roberts, 2000, cited in Jordan, 2003, p. 111). Mental health professionals should reassure those clients affected by an anniversary of a trauma that the intensity and duration of the experience varies from person to person and that their reactions are normal insofar as they are not: "(a) contemplating harming themselves or others, (b) resorting to using alcohol and other substances to numb the pain, and (c) abusing or being abused" (Jordan, 2003, p. 112).

Mental health professionals are not immune to the psychological trauma associated with terrorism and fear. Although mental health professionals are aware of the long-term potential of burnout, particularly forensic psychologists who typically come into contact with the darker side of human nature, psychologists responding to the emergency work at the World Trade Center and the Pentagon could not have been prepared for the physical and emotional effects of their task (Taylor, 2002). Those involved in emergency work were vulnerable to compassion fatigue, secondary traumatic stress, or "**vicarious traumatization**" (Taylor, 2002, p. 105). Vicarious traumatization is said to have occurred when an individual who is providing treatment to a trauma victim begins to experience symptomatology as a result of their empathy towards the victim. Similarly, Cukor, Wyka, Jayasinghe, *et al.* (2011)

investigated PTSD symptoms in utility workers who were deployed to the World Trade Center and found that 10–34 months later, 20% of the individuals reported symptoms that were consistent with either a diagnosis of PTSD or **subclinical** (i.e., not meeting full diagnostic criteria) PTSD. The American Psychological Association advised responding psychologists to attend to self-care strategies and to seek professional support. Crime scene photos and police records detailing gruesome crimes would have insufficiently desensitized forensic psychologists to the death, destruction, and gruesome sights and smells that they experienced from the mass casualties at the World Trade Center in New York.

According to the National Center for PTSD in the United States (2001), the prevalence rates for PTSD are 4–5% from natural disasters, 28% from mass shooting, 29% from a plane crash into a hotel, and 34% from bombing. Galea *et al.* (2002) found that after the 11 September, 2001 terrorist attack on the United States, there was a rise in PTSD symptomatology in the United States. The Longitudinal Aging Study in Amsterdam demonstrated the long-range effects of the September 11 attacks (Van Zelst, De Beurs, & Smit, 2003). These terrorist attacks caused a rise in the PTSD symptomatology on the elderly Dutch population. Victims of the September 11 attacks experienced anxiety about the future, engaged in avoidance and fear of public transportation, and were fearful of being random targets in crowded areas such as sports events (American Red Cross, 2001; Pawlukewicz, 2003).

Eisenberg and Silver (2011) suggest that the way individuals are affected by terrorism and political violence may be different than the way individuals are affected by natural disasters, partly because acts of terrorism by their nature are deliberate. Similarly, Post (2010) proposes that rather than experiencing post traumatic stress disorder, **chronic stress disorder** (i.e., stress that is caused by ongoing trauma and/or stress rather than by an isolated incident) may be more likely in situations where ongoing stress and trauma is really the issue. Hoffman, Diamond, and Lipsitz (2011, p. 790) note, "In situations of ongoing terror, many individuals show signs and behaviors which may appear consistent with a diagnosis of PTSD. However, these signs may be better understood as responses to ongoing threat and anger rather than a pathological consequence of past exposure to trauma."

Everly (2003, p. 57) indicates that the fight against terrorism must occur on three levels: "(1) prevention of the terrorist attacks themselves; (2) mitigating the adverse impact of the persistent threats of terrorist acts, as well as terrorist attacks when they do occur; and (3) psychological treatment of the lingering adverse effects of threatened or actualized terrorist attacks." He refers to the third level as "psychological counterterrorism" (p. 57). Everly stresses the importance of the psychology of terrorism as being paramount in its understanding and as being foundational for rebuilding a community devastated by its effects, not only structurally but psychologically as well. This approach is essential to restoring a sense of humanity. Therefore, the role of psychologists in assisting law enforcement personnel with profiling guidance or otherwise apprehending terrorists, with providing crisis counseling to trauma survivors, and with conducting research relating to counterterrorism, are all of critical importance.

Forensic Psychology and Policy Implications

Everly (2003) describes psychological efforts to prevent terrorism as falling into four domains. These include the following: (1) efforts to remove terrorism as a tactical option by encouraging the global community to view it with extreme legal, moral, and political disdain so as not to render it viable; (2) efforts to remove it as a strategic option by not negotiating with terrorists under any circumstances; (3) responding to terrorism with immediate and overwhelming force, wherein the costs outweigh the gains; and (4) establish a global climate where justice is perceived to be accessible to all. Similarly, Tausch *et al.* (2011) note that "the challenges faced by policymakers lie in creating inclusive political institutions that provide minority groups with the means to participate in the democratic decision-making process (p. 145);" thus, increasing their sense of efficacy and preventing contempt as a means of discouraging nonnormative action.

Everly (2003, p. 58) also describes psychological efforts to mitigate the negative impact of terrorism. These include: (1) the provision of pre-incident training and education; (2) the provision of "acute psychological first aid;" (3) the provision of community "town meetings" as a means to provide important updates, stress management information, and to build personal and community empowerment; and (4) the implementation of a multifaceted system of crisis intervention and emergency mental health services. Finally, Everly (2003) outlines psychological efforts to treat and rehabilitate those affected by way of using individual and group psychotherapy (with psychotropic medications where indicated), and even acute inpatient hospitalization in the most severe cases, especially where less restrictive means were ineffective or contraindicated. Effective strategies to mitigate the negative impact of terrorism is especially important since there is some research to suggest that children may be adversely affected by the reactions of those around them (DeVoe, Klein, Bannon, Jr., & Miranda-Julian, 2011).

The United States has several agencies that aid trauma victims and survivors. Examples include the American Red Cross (ARC), the Critical Incident Stress Management group (CISM) and the Green Cross. The Green Cross was established in 1995 after the Oklahoma City bombing, and focuses on post-disaster work. This organization responds mostly in connection with employee assistance programs, and provides a comprehensive three-tiered training service for its staff with ascending degrees of certification based on progressive coursework and supervision (Taylor, 2002). The ARC, CISM, and the Green Cross all address the following: (1) clinical signs and symptoms of acute and chronic trauma; (2) differentiation between reactions attributable more to recent trauma rather than an unresolved psychiatric disorder or normal grief; (3) identification of the kinds of support victims may require at various stages of disaster recovery and designations as to where this support should be provided; (4) consideration of the spiritual impact of behavior; (5) description of procedures that encourage survivors to adaptively manage their trauma into manageable memories; and (6) requiring that potential volunteers be adequately self-disciplined and responsive to organizational demands in order to fulfill their duties while minimizing embarrassment, stress, and fatigue (Taylor, 2002).

The enormity of the terrorist attacks on the United States forced many other nations to consider their vulnerability to terrorism and their response preparedness with emergency mental health care. With respect to the New Zealand mental health system, Taylor (2002) notes that this country is overburdened, sparsely located, and virtually unfamiliar with components of immediate disaster trauma. Moreover, Taylor (p. 106) indicates that the immediate goal of crisis responders is to help victims return to their "psychological status quo." In his assessment of critical aspects to consider when developing a crisis plan in New Zealand, Taylor (p. 106) observes the following: "As members of a multicultural society in which for many citizens English is a second language, and in a country that increasingly is becoming a popular tourist destination, they will need either to be multilingual or have access to interpreters to facilitate contact with casualties." Multicultural issues were also very significant in the United States — in New York City particularly — as some residents of Middle Eastern descent experienced further revictimization when they were looked upon with suspicion and anger by their fellow residents.

Some educational institutions in the United States and Great Britain are beginning to address issues specific to terrorism and trauma psychology. In 2006, the Division of Trauma Psychology (Division 56) was formed within the American Psychological Association to advance their professional and research concerns. While forensic psychologists are expanding their role in consulting with law enforcement agencies to profile potential terrorists, some psychologists specialize in crisis counseling with trauma victims only. The Australasian Society for Traumatic Stress Studies and the Australasian Critical Incident Stress Association aid their members in sharing personal experiences, professional expertise, and research ideas (Taylor, 2002).

Psychologists responding to scenes of disaster should be aware of safety concerns for survivors and try to connect individuals with their family and support groups within their cultural and religious networks. Pamphlets with appropriate contact information, as well as education relating to possible reactions that may arise, should be made available. Taylor (2002) stresses the importance of psychologists working with trauma survivors to take time and to not press for the removal of psychological defenses such as avoidance and hyperarousal too soon. It is also important to differentiate between acute versus chronic symptomatology, especially in situations of ongoing threat. Furthermore, the clinician is encouraged to refer victims to general practitioners for medication or for more intensive professional care services if no significant improvement is made. The attacks on September 11 resulted in work groups, group debriefings/process groups, and spiritual gatherings offered at hospitals, schools, mental health clinics, job sites, community centers, and the like (Pawlukewicz, 2003). Research suggests that giving individuals an opportunity to discuss their experiences shortly after the trauma may reduce symptoms of PTSD.

Finally, there are several policy implications regarding research on terrorism. In recent years, there has been much controversy surrounding the participation of psychologists in interrogations which prompted the Ethics Committee of the American Psychological Association (2009) to issue a position statement prohibiting the involvement of psychologists in the techniques involving torture. However, research on interrogation techniques is lacking (Schouten, 2010). Psychologists can also be useful in developing and improving methods to gather and analyze intelligence and "for understanding the origins and causes of terrorist behavior, for predicting who is likely to engage in such acts, and for understanding the radicalization process" (Schouten, 2010, p. 373).

Davis (2002, p. 47) states, "Language differences are the greatest barrier to worldwide sharing of information." He indicates that few psychological databases regarding terrorism are available in English, which is the language spoken by the majority of psychologists worldwide. He encourages policy makers to have these data bases translated into other languages for wider accessibility. Psychologists who are researching terrorism should familiarize themselves with cultural meanings and contexts of the groups under scrutiny in order to better understand them and contribute to the field. In addition, psychologists can help to educate the public with accurate and reliable information about terrorism in order to help increase vigilance and empowerment. As Davis (p. 49) explains it, "With increased alertness, initiative, and vigilance, ordinary people can find ways to maintain privacy and other norms of an open society while still countering the dangers of terrorism."

Suggestions for Future Research

Future research should compare the efficacy of terrorist profiles developed by forensic psychologists based on psychological and criminological research to that of the FBI and other intelligence agencies. Terrorists are part of groups that are shrouded in secrecy. Future research should continue to focus on exploring the individual psychological correlates leading to terrorism, as well an the interfacing social, political, economic, religious, and other ideological influences that contribute to developing the blueprint for a terrorist individual or the motivation for a terrorist act. Social science research should be conducted and used to help aid policy makers with regard to foreign affairs and to better inform our intelligence-gathering agencies. Additionally, continued research comparing the demographics and prevalence (or lack thereof) of mental illness in those who act as suicide bombers is needed.

Additional studies evaluating the impact of more recent trends regarding extreme violence on attitudes of isolationism versus globalization among Western, European, and other countries must be undertaken.

As noted above, the traumatic effects of terrorism and other traumatic events (e.g., natural disasters) may vary. Future research should focus on ways of effectively identifying and treating the psychological effects of terrorist attacks in situations where the threat of such attacks is real and ongoing. For example, Hoffman, Diamond, and Lipsitz (2011) point out that our traditional conceptualization of PTSD is based on the assumption that an individual's symptoms are pathological and based on past experience(s). However, typical criteria, such as avoidance behavior, may actually be functional in circumstances where the "situations avoided carry real and imminent danger" (p. 792). Furthermore, Brymer *et al.* (2006) point out that while PFA strategies are evidenced based, more systemic empirical research is needed.

It is also important to assess and interpret the process of effective coping and "meaning-making" for individuals who have faced significant trauma. More long-term or longitudinal studies regarding the impact of security threats on a person's mental health, specifically symptoms related to anxiety, depression, and PTSD of vulnerable populations (e.g., the mentally ill, children, or the elderly), should be conducted in relation to the prevalence of these psychiatric/psychological problems as found in the general population.

Practice Update Section: Issues in Family/Community Policing

In 1996, Amber Hagerman, a nine-year-old girl from Arlington, Texas was abducted and murdered. Congress and President Bush recently passed the National Amber Alert Plan as an extension of the Amber Alert emergency response system. The Amber Plan is likely the most far-reaching and impactful extension of community policing. According to the Federal Communications Commission (2003), its purpose is to galvanize communities across the country to add millions of extra eyes and ears to aid law enforcement in the safe return of the child and apprehension of the suspect. Once police have confirmed a missing child report, an alert is sent to radio stations, television stations, and cable companies. These sources interrupt programming and repeat news bulletins about abducted children typically with descriptions of the children, suspect vehicles, and the like. The Amber Alerts are used only in the most serious child abduction cases when the police believe the child is in danger of serious bodily harm. The Amber Alert program is credited with the resolution of at least eight abductions since its inception in 1997. Under revised guidelines, the new Amber Plan is only activated if the missing child is under age 15, disabled, or believed to be in danger (Burns, 2001). As of October 2003, 46 states have adopted the Amber Plan. The Amber Plan is likely one of the most aggressive and wide reaching policing strategies to be implemented in the fight against child abduction and murder. Now law enforcement is incorporating more community resources into the fight against child victimization.

Police officers face a number of job-related stressors that are very traumatic and unique to law enforcement: take for instance child abduction and murder. Some police officers experience being attacked or wounded by an assailant, fearing for their lives, viewing horrific crime scenes, interacting with living victims, and with the families of those who are deceased. Certainly, no one could imagine the horrors faced by law enforcement officers who responded to the 9/11 attacks on the World Trade Center and the Pentagon. Both the physical and psychological demands placed on some law enforcement officers can have a profound impact on the mental and physical health of an officer. Psychological services addressing both proactive and reactive measures should be firmly in place in police departments around the country. Critical incident debriefing is one such reactive measure. Tobin (2001) contends that critical incident stress debriefing (CISD) is only useful when a major incident has happened, typically when there has been significant loss of life. He recommends that CISD be used sparingly, with highly trained personnel, who also act as peer supporters of the at-risk population. This is a very important service that a police psychologist who is properly trained in issues relating to policing, psychology, and trauma can provide. Tobin (2001) indicated that CISD helps to reduce anger that is often felt toward those in authority and promotes unit cohesiveness when effective. He further warns of the legal liability if done improperly.

Buchanan, Stephens, and Long (2001) conducted a study that examined the number of traumatic events experienced by police recruits and serving police officers. These authors suggested that the number of traumatic events experienced as young adults, including incidents such assault, disasters, and motor vehicle accidents, is an important variable in determining vulnerability to developing psychological symptoms if exposed to future trauma. These are potentially important factors for police psychologists to take into consideration when considering the potential psychological impact of a job-related critical incident.

Van Patten and Burke (2001) found that the child homicide investigator experienced significantly higher levels of stress when compared with ordinary adults. Additionally, the traumatic scene of a child homicide was the most significant predictor of stress. Police departments and police psychologists should be particularly mindful of the extreme stress experienced by homicide investigators, particularly child homicide investigators. In addition to critical incident debriefing as a reactive measure, individual counseling and other proactive measures such as stress reduction education and programs should also be implemented.

Related Websites

www.tcfv.org
Texas Council on Family Violence website: provides information on domestic violence prevention, treatment, and law enforcement.
www.fbi.gov/about-us/cjis/ucr/ucr
The FBI's Uniform Crime Reports, including crime statistics and information about law enforcement officers killed or injured in the line of duty.
http://bjs.ojp.usdoj.gov
The Bureau of Justice Statistics, including information about law enforcement, crimes, courts, corrections, and victims.
www.npr.org
This website has the story of a Tennessee officer who shot and killed a mentally ill man.

Continued

Related Websites—cont'd

---

www.latimes.com
Discusses the story of a mentally ill man who was severely beaten by police.
www.ncjrs.gov/pdffiles1/jr000244c.pdf
Examines and outlines policy changes and police roles in the detainment and handling of mentally ill offenders.
www.tcleose.state.tx.us/content/training_instructor_resources.cfm
Provides information used in officer training in Texas.
www.hostagenegotiation.com/index.cfm
The website of the International Association of Hostage Negotiators. Includes resources pertaining to hostage negotiations, including videos of actual negotiations.
www.safehostage.com
Website describing the SAFE model of crisis negotiation.
www.apatraumadivision.org
The homepage for the Division of Trauma Psychology, Division 56, of the American Psychological Association.
www.nctsnet.org
The homepage for the National Child Traumatic Stress Network. It includes information for the general public about understanding child and adolescent trauma. It also includes information about various types of trauma and helpful resources for various audiences including parents and schools. The *Psychological first aid: Field operations guide* (2nd edn) is also available on this website.
www.greencross.org
Homepage of the Green Cross Academy of Traumatology.
www.redcross.org
Homepage of the American Red Cross.
www.apa.org/news/press/statements/ethics-statement-torture.pdf
The American Psychological Association Ethics Committee position statement on the use of torture.
www.apa.org/news/press/statements/open-letter-membership.pdf
Open letter from the Board of Directors of the American Psychological Association regarding members' participation in interrogations.
www.state.gov/s/ct
The United States Department of State, Office of the Coordinator of Counterterrorism website.

Corrections and Prison Practices

Key Issues

Psychological Stress and Correctional Work
- The prevalence and nature of psychological stress among correctional officers
- Correlates of stress in correctional settings
- Programs intended to help alleviate officers' stress

Intellectually Disabled Inmates
- Prevalence of intellectually disabled offenders and their characteristics
- Methods of identifying and treating intellectually disabled inmates

Society's Reaction to Sex Offenders
- The number of convicted sex offenders has tripled since 1996
- Megan's Law: Why federal legislation passed the law, and what it means for society
- What it means for sex offenders who reenter society, how they are stigmatized and how it affects recidivism rates
- How society chooses to handle sex offenders in society

Women Working in Male Prisons
- A look at how women are accepted by male colleagues, inmates, and society when working in a correctional setting

"Make Believe" Families
- Brief history at the familial support female inmates create while incarcerated
- This section looks at the reasons why these familial support groups are created, and how the families are viewed by correctional officers

Women in Prison and Mother–Child Separation
- A brief look at the psychological implications of programs that allow women in prison to have their child to live with them for a length of time

Community Reentry Programs and Family Reunification
- This section will briefly review the history of reentry and reunification programs, and then discuss current programs, including literature regarding their effectiveness, as well as barriers to the effective implementation of reentry and reunification programs

CHAPTER 12

Family/Community Issues in Corrections/ Correctional Psychology

Chapter Outline

Introduction to Forensic Psychology. DOI: 10.1016/B978-0-12-382169-0.00012-8

Overview

Psychologists are called upon to address a myriad of problems that directly affect the adult prison populations. In addition, psychologists are relied upon to assess other correctional dilemmas regarding the intellectual, personality, and behavioral characteristics of offenders and those who work in the institutions, as well as to interpret society's responses to particular offender groups and general correctional practices. This is the domain of family- and community-oriented corrections. Unlike its adult and juvenile counterparts, the family/community corrections field explores many of the social variables that inform noncriminal inmate behavior, ongoing prison practices, and the public's responses to both.

This chapter includes six topical themes, representing the breadth of the field affecting correctional/forensic psychology. It is not possible to present a complete and thorough cataloging of issues and/or controversies contained in this subspecialty area. However, those subjects examined in the pages that follow include some of the more interesting and pressing concerns at the interface of corrections, psychology, and civil justice. Topics investigated include: (1) psychological stress and correctional work; (2) intellectually disabled prisoners; (3) society's response to sex offenders; (4) women working in male prisons; (5) "make-believe" families; (6) women in prison and mother–child separation; and (7) community reentry programs and family reunification.

The conditions under which correctional work occurs are emotionally and physically demanding. Symptoms of chronic fatigue, depression, cynicism, burnout, and the like are not uncommon for many correctional officers. What is the psychological impact of work-related stress for correctional personnel? How do employees cope with it, and what prevention and intervention programs exist to curb the excesses of stress? A representative minority of prisoners are intellectually disabled. How are the rehabilitative and retributive philosophies of corrections managed for prisoners with intellectual disabilities? What special services and/or programs exist for these inmates? How are prisoners screened and assessed for mental retardation, and what role exists for correctional psychologists to assist in the evaluation process? A number of societal responses have been proposed to address the problems posed by convicted sex offenders. Some of these include chemical castration, community notification, civil commitment, and formalized registration. How, if at all, do these interventions prevent future victimization? What is the relationship between these societal responses and recidivism? Do proposals such as these violate the constitutional rights of sex offenders who have already paid their debt to society? Increasingly, women correctional officers work in male prisons. How are such officers perceived by their male correctional officer counterparts? How do women COs cope with the hostility, sexual harassment, and discrimination they experience on the job? How do female COs and correctional psychologists cope with the stress of working in male prisons?

People have a fundamental need to express intimacy and affection. The same is true for persons in prison, especially women. One response to this need is to create "make believe" families. What emotional needs do surrogate or "play" families fill for women in prison? What specific roles do prisoners assume in these kinship systems? How do pseudofamilies operate in the correctional milieu? Women in prisons represent a special group of offender. Who are they demographically? Many female prisoners are mothers. To what extent do mothers in prison feel shame, guilt, and grief as a result of their (criminal) life choices? How do they cope with the grief that comes from the loss of parental bonding and parenting? What are the emotional and health care consequences to both mothers and their children when the parent is incarcerated? How do children (and mothers) deal with the anxiety of separation? How can correctional/forensic psychologists help ease the pain of separation caused by criminal confinement? What services exist (i.e., support groups) to address these psychological problems? What advocacy work is being done to improve the standards for prison visitation by family members? What programs are available to help offenders transition from correctional settings back to the community? What are the unique problems and challenges they face? Does proactive attention to community reentry programs impact recidivism?

At the intersection of corrections, psychology, and family studies are an array of issues and controversies affecting the lives of persons incarcerated and their loved ones. Correctional/forensic psychologists are uniquely trained to explore these dynamic issues and assist prison systems in meeting the challenges posed by this population. The domain of community/family corrections places the psychologist in a position to investigate noncriminal behavior, attitudes, beliefs, and so on pertaining to prisoners, correctional personnel, institutional practices, and the public's responses to them. As the sections of this chapter demonstrate, we know little about the family/community aspect of correctional/forensic psychology. Future investigators would do well to engage in research to advance our knowledge of prisoners, children of inmates, correctional workers, and society's understanding of offender behavior.

Psychological Stress and Correctional Work

Introduction

The American Heritage Dictionary defines **stress** as "a mentally or emotionally disruptive or disquieting influence" (Berube, 1982; p. 1205). This definition does not fully describe the types of stress that correctional officers experience on a day-to-day basis, as they are under a continual threat of physical danger. They experience hostility from the inmates and often the public. They respond to political changes in attitudes toward the role of institutional corrections. They work daily "with the central task of supervising and securing unwilling and potentially violent populations" (Armstrong & Griffin, 2004, p. 577). Finally, they completely depend on their coworkers to provide for their safety (Finn, 1998; Grossi and Berg, 1991). Working in such an atmosphere every day can lead to some very debilitating consequences, including depression, chronic fatigue, physical illness, and even post-traumatic stress disorder (PTSD). The following illustration describes a stressful situation that officers often must face.

The day began like any other at the prison. The day staff came in and were briefed on any problems or incidents of which they needed to be aware, and then they began their duties of moving the prisoners through their daily routines. After a few hours, when the work was becoming tedious and correctional officers began to relax, three inmates attacked a guard walking by and managed to get his gun away from him. They used him as a hostage and demanded that the other officers give up their guns. The officers had to comply to avoid having their coworker killed. The inmates were able to gain control of the prison unit by holding approximately 30 employees hostage. The correctional officers that were able to avoid becoming hostages locked themselves in the administrative offices but could not escape from the prison. This highly intense and stressful situation lasted for over 2 hours with the officers under constant fear for their lives. The incident ended without any serious injuries but with a great deal of property damage (Bergmann and Queen, 1987). The officers who had to endure this hostage situation were exposed to a type of stress that most people will never experience in their lifetime. Even the officers that were not held hostage felt the effects of the stress because they had to return to work in this environment wondering if such an incident might happen again.

Literature Review

Although the above illustration is a severe example, it represents the type of stressful situation that correctional officers are potentially faced with and must learn to accept as part of their job. Research shows that most correctional officers do feel this stress. In a study that asked officers to rate their levels of day-to-day job-related stress, only 26.2% reported feeling low levels of stress. Most of the officers experienced medium to high levels of stress every day, with 10.0% reporting very high levels of work stress (Robinson, 1992). Generally, the type of stress that officers experience is related to the work that they do; that is, guarding the inmates. With overcrowded prisons, officers have a more difficult time controlling inmates, especially when the inmates know that they will be there for a long time and do not fear punishment (Martinez, 1997; Finn, 1998). The case illustration shows how it is possible for prisoners to become uncontrollable just by outnumbering the officers. Robinson (1992) reported that the most frequently cited source of stress by correctional officers is related to security. Twenty-seven percent of the officers reported a fear of offenders and a lack of security procedures. Their second and third most reported sources of stress were a lack of communication in the prison and a heavy workload. In addition Robinson determined that officers' job commitment was affected by stress. He found that officers who reported higher levels of work-related stress had lower levels of commitment to their jobs.

Lambert, Hogan, and Barton (2002) stated that correctional staff job stress has grown dramatically due to increasing prison populations and differing ideologies. These researchers found that role ambiguity and work creating family conflict decreased overall job satisfaction. A study examined correctional officer stress and burnout by surveying 250 correctional officers from a Southwestern state (Morgan, Van Haveren, & Pearson, 2002). Results indicated that older and more educated correctional officers experienced a greater sense of personal accomplishment, whereas younger and less experienced officers experienced greater depersonalization and emotional exhaustion, as well as decreased levels of personal accomplishment.

A literature review by Schaufeli and Peeters (2000) examined job stress and burnout of correctional officers. The empirical literature elucidated the most notable stressors to be role problems, work overload, demanding social contacts (with inmates, coworkers, and supervisors), and poor social status. Finn (1998) describes several factors that have contributed to increased correctional officer stress to include inmate overcrowding, increased inmate assaults against staff, longer inmate sentences resulting in less fear of punishment, and more prison gangs. Furthermore, Finn (1998) identifies organizational and work-related categories of stressors, as well as stressors from outside of the system. The four most common organizational conditions found that most frequently cause stress are understaffing, overtime, shift work, and supervisor demands. Role conflict and role ambiguity were less consistent organizational stressors. Research indicates that the most common work-related stressors include threat of inmate violence, actual inmate violence, inmate demands and attempts at manipulation, and problems with coworkers (Finn, 1998). Finally, stress from outside the criminal justice system most commonly included a poor public image or negative societal stereotypes of correctional officers and low pay. Finn (1998) found that the effects of correctional officer stress can include impaired physical health from heart disease to eating disorders, excessive use of sick time, burnout, high staff turnover, reduced safety (e.g. sloppy searches, increased use of force), early retirement, and impaired family life (e.g. displacing aggression, isolating).

Job burnout has also been found to be significantly related to an increased risk for health and substance abuse problems as well as decreased job performance (Carlson & Thomas, 2006; Garner, Knight, & Simpson, 2007). Burnout has also been seen to play a role in heightened psychological withdrawal from the job, increased absenteeism, and turnover (Carlson & Thomas, 2006; Garland, 2002; Neveu, 2007). Research focusing on correlations between burnout and demographic characteristics of officers has produced mixed and often conflicting results (Carlson, Anson, & Thomas, 2003; Carlson & Thomas, 2006; Garland, 2004; Garner, Knight, & Simpson, 2007; Morgan, Van Haveren, & Pearson, 2002).

More recent research has found that role stress has a significant impact on correctional staff job stress, job satisfaction, and job satisfaction (Armstrong & Griffin, 2004; Dowden & Tellier, 2004; Griffin, 2004; Hogan, Lambert, Jenkins, & Wambold, 2006; Lambert & Paoline, 2005; Lambert, Reynolds, Paoline, & Watkins, 2004; Tewksbury & Higgins, 2006). Research into the correlates of role stress have found that officers' input into decision making, supervision, formulization, integration, and instrumental communication all influence a correctional officer's level of role stress (Lambert, Hogan, & Tucker, 2009). Allowing officers to provide input into the decision-making processes of the organization is likely to lead to decreased job stress and **role stress** (the stress resulting from ill-defined or poorly structured job-related duties) as well as increased organizational commitment and job satisfaction (Lambert, Hogan, & Tucker, 2009; Lambert, Paoline, & Hogan, 2006). Those officers who perceive their supervisors as fair, accessible, and encouraging are less likely to experience role stress or job stress, and are more likely to show increased levels of job satisfaction and organizational commitment (Lambert, 2004; Lambert, Hogan & Tucker,

2009). **Formalization**, or the provision of guidance to staff concerning what needs to be done and how to do it, tends to decrease role stress while increasing job satisfaction and organizational commitment (Lambert, Hogan, & Tucker, 2009; Lambert, Paoline, & Hogan, 2006). The integration of staff has been seen to decrease role stress and increase job satisfaction by decreasing conflict between groups of staff members (Lambert, Barton, *et al.*, 2002; Lambert, Hogan, &Tucker, 2009). **Instrumental communication**, which involves providing clarification of tasks, processes, procedures, problems, or changes, has been found to be related to lower levels of role stress and higher levels of job satisfaction and organizational commitment (Lambert, Barton, *et al.*, 2002; Lambert, Hogan, & Allen, 2006; Lambert, Hogan, & Tucker, 2009).

Martinez (1997) identified two different types of stress focusing on frequency that correctional officers experience in the course of their duties. The first was described in the previous case illustration. This was an **episodic stressor** where a traumatic incident happened to, or was witnessed by, a guard. The other type of stress is what the author refers to as **chronic stress**. This is stress that officers encounter every day. It is the routine of doing the same thing over and over. This can be very damaging psychologically if the officers do not have the appropriate abilities to deal with it. It may even lead to a psychological disability. For example, in the case of *Fasanaro v. County of Rockland* (1995), the petitioner was a correctional officer who began to suffer from a **stress-related disability**. The doctor who evaluated him indicated that the pressures from his job had become too much for him and recommended that the officer take a leave of absence. This case arose because he was denied disability benefits. The court ruled in favor of the correctional officer and stated that if stress exists at work, then any stress-related anxiety disorders and disabilities can be causally related to the job and the employee should be allowed to collect **Worker's Compensation** (a form of insurance that provides medical care for employees who are injured in the course of employment).

A stress-related anxiety disorder is just one possible consequence for correctional officers. A more serious consequence may be suicide. Kamerman (1995) found that speaking about correctional-officer suicide is a taboo. After examining New York City statistics for a five-year period, he reported that correctional-officer suicides were at least as great a problem as police suicides, and that the number of suicides were most likely greater than what was actually reported. In little over a year, a correctional facility in New York had three correctional officers commit suicide. Kamerman proposed that the overcrowded prisons and the building of new facilities without the necessary funding for additional correctional officers will only increase the pressures faced by these personnel. Kamerman further indicated that the lack of research on officer suicides reflects the public's diminished concern for the stress that correctional officers confront. However, clearly, the effects will continue to manifest themselves in extreme ways such as mental disability and suicide.

The traumatic events occasionally experienced by correctional officers, as in the case illustration, can also have debilitating consequences. Bergmann and Queen (1987) report that there are three characteristics which must be present for an event to be traumatic. There must be an extremely high level of stress, a denial of the importance of the event or a shock-like response, and a normal set of feelings or consequences following the event. They labeled this normal set of feelings as an **acute stress response** where individuals may withdraw from important people and activities, reexperience the event through flashbacks, feel depressed, have sleep difficulties and nightmares, feel anxious and hypervigilant, feel guilty, and have difficulty returning to work.

Davis (1995) also described stress related to traumatic incidents. He described a traumatic incident as being a routine day where suddenly a fight breaks out among the inmates, and one inmate cuts the other in the neck and creates a gaping wound with blood spraying everywhere. According to the author, possible consequences for the correctional officers are confusion, sweating, depression, anger, grief, and changes in eating and sleeping behaviors. Both Bergmann and Queen (1987) and Davis (1995) identified long-term side-effects from stress, including alcoholism, divorce, unemployment, violent relationships, and suicide if the correctional officers did not receive appropriate mental health services.

These traumatic incidents can also cause **post-traumatic stress disorder (PTSD)**, or a condition of persistent mental and emotional stress occurring as a result of injury or severe psychological shock, in certain employees. In the case of *Wertz v. Workmen's Compensation Appeal Board* (1996), the plaintiff worked at a prison during a prison riot. He suffered PTSD and was awarded total disability benefits. When he returned to a modified duty position at the prison, his PTSD symptoms began to increase again, forcing him to leave his job permanently. Despite the fact that there were no riots when he returned to work, he was still awarded disability payments because his psychological stress was related to the workplace.

Although many studies have examined the nature and extent of stress experienced by correctional officers, few have researched ways to reduce this stress. As can be seen from the Worker's Compensation lawsuits, stress can have some serious consequences and lead to additional expenses for institutions. A study that did examine methods for reducing stress researched the benefits of exercise programs for correctional officers (Kiely & Hodgson, 1990). The authors found that the exercise programs were a success, although they relied on self-reports for their data. The staff was able to see how they benefited from the exercise programs and therefore were in favor of them. They reported higher staff morale, improved attitudes, increased confidence, and greater physical fitness which improved resistance to stress. The authors did find that correctional officers had a difficult time recognizing stress in themselves or others, and therefore concluded that heightening their awareness of potential stressors along with preventive actions such as exercise would be the best way to minimize the negative consequences of stress. Their overall findings revealed the benefits of physical fitness as a way of reducing stress and aiding correctional officers in overcoming the effects of stress-related illnesses. Finn (1998) reported that there are programs or stress services to help prevent and treat correctional officer stress. He identified four categories of programs: academy training, in-service training, critical incidents stress management, and individual counseling. However, he pointed out that the criticism most often levied at these programs is their lack of specificity to correctional environments and the related stressors. In other words, those correctional systems that offer these types of programs often examine stress in general and provide generic coping strategies without real-life utility to the unique circumstances faced by correctional officers.

Another variable that intuitively would seem to reduce stress is peer support. However, Grossi and Berg (1991) found that peer support actually increased work stress. They hypothesized that in a prison setting, correctional officers may have to compromise their personal values and integrity in order to obtain peer support, particularly when overlooking infractions made by other officers. This would produce more feelings of stress instead of less. It may be that other forms of support could be stress reducing, such as the role of administration or family support. However, these variables were not examined in this study.

A more recent study of the Power to Change Performance stress and health risk reduction program found that emotion self-regulation and communication techniques together with a biofeedback component showed promise in reducing officers' stress (McCraty, Atkinson, Lipsenthal, & Arguelles, 2009). In addition, this intervention includes five training modules. First, participants learn about risk factors and how they relate to their health and wellness. The second module, Freeze-Frame, involves a refocusing technique that enables the participant to more effectively intervene in the moment once a stress reaction has been triggered. Coherent Communication, the third module, focuses on facilitating clear and constructive communication between people. The fourth module, Power Tools for Inner Quality, involves creating a caring culture and increasing job satisfaction. The fifth and final module, Work Place Applications, involves applying the tools from the previous modules in an organizational context so as to increase planning and decision-making effectiveness. The authors caution though that their study suffered important methodological flaws that should be addressed in future research. Specifically, they admit that their study included too few subjects to provide sufficient statistical power. Additionally, cross-contamination effects on the two groups of participants would not allow for meaningful between-group comparisons. Finally, the authors suggest that using a longer follow-up period could be expected to yield greater reductions in health risk factors and greater financial savings.

Forensic Psychology and Policy Implications

After examining the effects that stress has on correctional officers, it is clear that programs need to be developed to help them handle work tension before they burn out

(Carlson, Anson, & Thomas, 2003; Keinan & Malach-Pines, 2007). Several authors have suggested that workshops and training sessions along with improved support systems are needed to help combat job burnout (Carlson, Anson, & Thomas, 2003; Keinan & Malach-Pines, 2007; Lambert, Hogan, & Altheimer, 2010). One type of program that has received a considerable amount of attention is critical incident stress debriefing. This is a stage method whereby individuals are taken back through the incident to explore their thoughts and feelings with one another regarding the incident. The group processing of such a fact-finding—thinking—feeling model, combined with relaxation training, as well as individual counseling aimed at reducing flashbacks of the incident, can help prevent the development of PTSD or assist in reducing the intensity of the experience (Finn, 1998; McWhirter and Linzer, 1994). According to "Battle Staff Burnout" (1997), critical incident stress debriefing with correctional staff should be done within 1 or 2 days after the event and should include all personnel. The article also recommended creating a policy for debriefing that includes the following points: clear definitions of debriefing, an outline of what critical incidents would require debriefing, rules of confidentiality, and an outline of responsibilities.

Other recommendations for preventing long-term consequences of traumatic stress were outlined by Bergmann and Queen (1987). Departments should organize their response before a traumatic incident occurs. Psychological responses of survivors should be included in the policies and procedures for handling prison disturbances. Departments should make sure that post-trauma services are only provided by qualified and trained staff. Finally, creative ways must be found to finance post-traumatic services.

Another important policy matter that needs to be addressed is correctional officer suicide. Training programs need to be implemented to handle all officers' confrontations with death. There should be institutional training for suicide prevention focused on correctional officers and inmates. The gains from such training initiatives could extend beyond suicide prevention (Kamerman, 1995). Correctional psychologists should also be available for individual counseling regarding stress, depression, and the like. Finn (1998) reported that most correctional officers only have their Employee Assistance Programs (EAPs) to turn to and that many officers feel that their EAPs will not protect their confidentiality and are unfamiliar with correctional officer stress. Correctional and forensic psychologists who are trained to understand both the systemic or organizational problems within the prison system and general clinical psychology would be the best equipped to effectively work with correctional personnel on these issues.

A final policy consideration for correctional officer stress is funding. As mentioned previously, with overcrowded prisons and the building of new facilities, correctional staff have not been able to keep up with the growth. Instead of funneling more funds into building prisons, attention needs to be placed on providing services for correctional officers, including adequate numbers of staff. The problem of crime is not going to disappear with the addition of new prisons, but the problem of stress-related disease and disability could be greatly reduced if correctional officers were to receive the appropriate mental health services.

Suggestions for Future Research

The major area in which research is lacking concerns the benefits of stress-reduction programs for correctional officers. Although exercise was found to decrease stress and provide additional advantages, a more rigorous empirical study needs to be conducted. This could take a holistic approach examining ways to create healthy workplaces in terms of overall organizational structure, as well as expanding personal coping mechanisms such as the exercise programs (Kiely & Hodgson, 1990). Also, a more systematic study of critical-incident stress-debriefing programs, including follow-up investigations (McWhirter & Linzer, 1994; Finn, 1998) and their direct applications in a correctional setting, would provide further evidence that such programs are beneficial. Lambert, Hogan, and Tucker (2009) propose that more research should be undertaken in an effort to identify and understand the correlates of role stress. Other creative ways for reducing the job-related stress of institutional work need to be examined. One such possibility may be to examine the types of contact staff have with inmates in search of a relationship with job burnout. Interventions designed to help correctional staff prevent and cope with burnout is another area worthy of study (Lambert, Hogan, & Altheimer, 2010). Finally, more research must be conducted on correctional officer suicide. This could foster a better understanding of the causes of suicide, and the effects suicide has on those who are left to deal with it.

Intellectually Disabled Inmates

Introduction

The prevalence of prisoners who are intellectually disabled is relatively small, consisting of approximately 2% or less of inmates in state and federal prisons and this has remained relatively stable for the past 20 years (Fazel, Xenitidis, & Powell, 2008; Conley, Luckasson, & Bouthilet, 1992). However, this small population of inmates provides a great challenge to the correctional system given their need for specialized services. The dilemma that exists concerns the handling of prisoners diagnosed with mental retardation. There is a concern for public safety due to their criminal behavior and there is a concern for providing appropriate services (Haney, 2006; Exum, Turnbull, Martin, & Finn, 1992). As a result, there is a constant struggle to maintain a balance between habilitation and punishment that does not occur with the typical offender.

Richard, a 28-year-old with mental retardation, was sentenced to prison for 3½ to 7 years for criminal mischief. This was his fifth arrest over a period of 3 years, and the judge did not know what else to do but place Richard in prison. Richard was living in a community home but had to be released because he resisted the services provided by staff, who also were at a loss as to what would be best for him. During a period of six months in prison, Richard committed four infractions. The disciplinary review board lost patience with him and decided to take away six months of good time for his last infraction of fighting with other inmates. The correctional officers are aware that Richard is not like other prisoners, but they do not know how to help him stay out of trouble. Richard also does not know how to stay out of trouble and feels that he must continue fighting in order to keep harassment from other inmates to a minimum. He worries that he will not be safe if he lets his guard down (Exum *et al.*, 1992).

Literature Review

Fazel, Xenitidis, and Powell (2008) estimate that 0.5 to 1.5% of offenders have been diagnosed with an intellectual disability. Morlok (2003) found that within the United States, the number of intellectually disabled offenders varies from state to state. For example, Louisiana reported that there were only seven such offenders in their correctional system while New York estimated housing 1206 intellectually disabled offenders. With the rise in correctional populations all over the country, there also has been an increase in inmates like Richard who have functional disabilities and low IQs falling in the mentally retarded range (Fazel *et al.*, 2008; Hall, 1992). Individuals with intellectual disabilities are over-represented in the criminal justice system, as compared to their prevalence in the general population (Haney, 2006; Hayes & Farnill, 2003; Hayes, 2002; Hayes, Shackell, Mottram, & Lancaster, 2007). Because of this, prisons have had to develop appropriate services and programs to assist these individuals. Before an inmate can be given these special services, he or she must first be diagnosed as mentally retarded. Accurate diagnosis of mental retardation has important implications for correctional administrators, probation and parole, and community services (Hayes & Farnill, 2003). The American Association of Intellectual and Developmental Disabilities (2010) has provided a definition of **intellectual disability**:

> *Intellectual disability is a disability characterized by significant limitations both in intellectual functioning and in **adaptive behavior** as expressed in conceptual, social, and practical adaptive skills. This disability originates before age 18.*

Screening and evaluating an inmate prior to placing the person in a housing unit is perhaps the most important aspect in developing appropriate services for a prisoner with intellectual disabilities (Hayes, 2002; Exum *et al.*, 1992). This is the stage where intellectual disability characteristics can be determined for prisoners. Hayes (2002) stresses the importance of early detection in order to provide these individuals with appropriate services, protection, diversion, and rehabilitation.

Bowker and Schweid (1992) reported a profile of the intellectually disabled offender. Ninety-one percent were male, 57% were African American, 48% were between the ages of 20 and 24, 73% were single, 13% completed high school, 67% were repeat offenders, and the mean full-scale IQ was 68. A program in Florida reported that a majority of the intellectually disabled inmates were male, African American, and under age 30. Due to the higher number of African American intellectually disabled inmates, Ho (1996) conducted a study which examined race as a factor in predicting those inmates who would be diagnosed as mentally retarded. The researcher found that the effect of race did not make any significant addition to the prediction. "Regardless of race, the offender who had a low IQ or a severe deficit in adaptive behavior was most likely to be diagnosed as having severe retardation" (Ho, 1996, p. 343). Ho reported that IQ was the strongest determinant for predicting mental retardation among offenders.

While the majority of research into intellectually disabled offenders has focused on males, a more recent study has focused on investigating some of the characteristics of female offenders with intellectual disabilities. This study found that female offenders represent 9% of referrals for intellectual disability evaluation (Lindsay, Smith, Quinn, Anderson, Smith, Allan, & Law, 2004). The authors also found that 61% had experienced some form of sexual abuse and 38.5% had experienced physical abuse (Lindsay *et al.*, 2004). With respect to recidivism for intellectually disabled female offenders, the study found that after five years 22% had re-offended; however, after excluding prostitution, the recidivism rate dropped to 16.5% (Lindsay *et al.*, 2004). The authors also found higher levels of mental illness (67%) among intellectually disabled female offenders (Lindsay *et al.*, 2004).

The type of instrument used to measure **intelligence**, defined by Wechsler as:

> *the capacity to act purposefully, think rationally, and to deal effectively with [one's] environment*

is an important factor to consider because the way in which inmates are screened can affect the prevalence of mental retardation diagnoses (Wechsler, 1944). Often a group test is administered to incoming offenders because it saves time. Yet, Spruill and May (1988) found that group testing overestimates the prevalence of mental retardation. They found that if inmates were administered an individual intelligence test, such as the Wechsler Adult Intelligence Scale (WAIS), then there was a lower prevalence of retardation. Upon questioning inmates who had been tested, they learned that many were very anxious upon entering prison, and the group testing did not allay their anxieties. The inmates also reported that they did not understand why they were being tested and, therefore, some did not try to do their best on the tests. Furthermore, group administrations of tests such as the WAIS are often counter to the standard administration guidelines that call for individual administration (Lichtenberger & Kaufman, 2009). Hayes and Farnill (2003) have proposed using the Kaufman Brief Intelligence Test (K-BIT) to assess intelligence and the Vineland Adaptive Behavior Scales (VABS) to assess for deficits in adaptive behavior. The WAIS is one of the most frequently used and, when appropriately administered, most valid and reliable tests of intelligence (Lichtenberger & Kaufman, 2009).

Hayes, Shackell, Mottram, and Lancaster (2007) used the Wechsler Adult Intelligence Scale-Third Edition (WAIS-III) and VABS to determine the prevalence of mental retardation in a United Kingdom prison population. They found that the occurrence of intellectual disabilities was higher than expected given the previous research in the UK.

Despite the problems associated with using group screenings to determine IQ or possible intellectual disabilities, prisons still do administer group screening tests because of the sheer volume of inmates that must be processed. Morlok's 2003 study found that 19 states used some form of IQ test to identify intellectually disabled offenders while 63% of the corrections departments in their sample used some form of life skills or functioning indicator. In a 2003 study, Morlok surveyed 41 state corrections departments (nine did not participate) on their programs and procedures for dealing with intellectually disabled offenders. Of the 41 states, 44% had specialized programs or living units for lower-functioning offenders. These programs often provide offenders with schooling, work opportunities, and treatment classes such as anger management or sex offender classes. The other 56% of states in the study did not have programming for those with intellectual disabilities and instead would group them with the mentally ill if programs existed for them.

Once an inmate has been identified as having mental disabilities, what types of services are available? Hall (1992) describes two state approaches to treating this population. The South Carolina Department of Corrections has a Habilitation Unit. This is a minimum-security unit reserved for those with developmental disabilities. Services such as special education, life-skills training, vocational preparation, recreation, counseling, and prerelease preparation are offered. These programs are run by a team of professionals which includes psychologists, special education teachers, and vocational specialists. The primary goal is to provide appropriate training which will improve the inmate's socialization skills. Therefore, the inmate will be prepared to live on the outside and hopefully not return. It appears that this program is still active, but no additional details were available.

The other program described by Hall (1992) is the Georgia State Prison Mental Retardation Unit. Unlike South Carolina's program, this is run through a maximum-security facility. The prisoners typically are repeat offenders who have committed violent crimes. Similar to South Carolina, this program teaches socialization and life-skills development. However, the goal is not to prepare the inmate for the outside world but to emphasize **institutional adaptation**. An effort is made to train the inmate on how to live inside the prison without committing further crimes. Barron, Hassiotis, and Barnes (2002) identify those offenders with intellectual disabilities as a group with complex needs who have the potential to create a continuing risk to their communities. These researchers suggest that despite the number of offenders with intellectual disabilities, little is known about treatment effectiveness or outcomes. Finally, they contend that these offenders often receive inadequate services due to not being identified in the criminal justice system and that there is a tremendous lack of research into treatment effectiveness or about this population in general (Barron *et al.*, 2002; Barron, Hassiotis, & Banes, 2004; Tudway & Darmoody, 2005).

Historically, a special program for prisoners with mental retardation has been implemented in the Texas Department of Corrections (Santamour, 1990). Once an inmate is identified as possibly disabled, the prisoner is sent to a special unit for evaluation. Multidisciplinary teams made up of doctors, social workers, educators, psychologists, vocational trainers, and security conduct the evaluations and work with inmates in the program. If the decision is made to admit the person into the program, then housing is available in one of five units designed to fit particular needs. One unit consists of **dual-diagnosis** inmates who have been diagnosed with mental retardation and another psychological disorder. The prisoners housed in this unit also tend to act aggressively. A second unit houses inmates identified as being particularly vulnerable to abuse and therefore in need of extra protection. A third unit houses those inmates who are aggressive or disruptive and have histories of belligerent behavior. A fourth unit consists of those who have only mental retardation and no other identified problems. A fifth unit is reserved for model prisoners with mental retardation who are allowed the highest level of privileges. Once an inmate has been identified and housed, then an individualized habilitation and education plan is developed by the treatment team. This plan emphasizes four areas: (1) habilitation, which includes academic, vocational, and social skills; (2) social support, which includes counseling by psychologists and trained correctional officers who work as case managers; (3) institutional security; and (4) continuity of treatment, which prepares the inmate for the outside world when his or her release date approaches.

More recently, authors have found little evidence supporting the use of adapted mainstream models, or models originally intended for use with populations without disabilities, to assess or treat inmates with intellectual disabilities (Barron, Hassiotis, & Banes, 2004; Tudway & Darmoody, 2005). However, one area that has shown promise is the assessment and treatment of sexual offenders with intellectual disabilities. Authors have found that **cognitive distortions**, or attitudes consistent with sexual offending, are frequently seen in this population (Lindsay, Michie, Whitefield, Martin, Grieve, & Carson, 2006). In a 2006 study, Craig, Stringer, and Moss found support for a program targeting cognitive distortions amongst other things in treating sexual offenders with learning disabilities. This seven-month program consists of four components: (1) sex education and the law; (2) identifying and reconstructing cognitive distortions; (3) investigation of the offending cycle; and (4) relapse prevention and victim empathy skills. The program utilized the group setting and included various methods including pictures, interactive exercises, videos, quizzes, and structured group discussions. The authors found that the participants had significantly improved socializations skills and, after twelve months, no reports of sexual reoffending had been made (Craig, Stringer, & Moss, 2006).

The Good Way model of reentry programming that targets adult and youth offenders with intellectual difficulties and sexually abusive behaviors has recently been implemented and researched in Australia and New Zealand (West, 2007). The program teaches offenders to identify both the "good side" and the "bad side" of themselves, and then encourages offenders to act consistently with the "good side," that is, in a "good way." The consequences of these decisions are then emphasized to participants, who also examine times when they have chosen the "bad way" and the consequences of those decisions. The program utilizes practical, constructive neutralizations with its participants, whose intellectual disabilities may prevent them from processing their offenses, choices, and reactions on deeper levels (West, 2007). To date, studies examining the effectiveness of the Good Way model in reducing recidivism and facilitating successful community transition have not been conducted.

When an inmate is released from prison, he or she may still require special services. Therefore, an Ohio county had developed a Mentally Retarded Offender (MRO) Unit in their probation department (Bowker & Schweid, 1992). The criterion for being assigned to this unit is a score of 75 or lower on the Wechsler Adult Intelligence Scale, which must be administered by a licensed psychologist. This unit is run on a case management model where the probationer receives individualized services determined by the probation officer, the clinical director of the MRO unit, and others as deemed necessary. The supervision levels for these probationers range from "super-high," which means contact with the probation officer once a week, to "extended," which means only monthly contacts via mail with the probation officer. A probation officer working in this unit generally carries a caseload of approximately

55—65 individuals compared to the regular officers' caseloads of approximately 200. Due to the case management model, the MRO Unit officers take a much more active role in their probationers' postrelease services. If Richard, from the case illustration, had been assigned to such a unit, then more appropriate services may have been found for him, and he might have remained in the community instead of being sent to prison.

The programs that have been described all focus on aspects such as habilitation and vocational and social skills. Yet, are these skills important or even necessary for an inmate with intellectual disabilities? A study conducted by Munson (1994) suggested that there are three important processes that take place once an offender is released into a community. These include beginning an appropriate occupation, selecting a home, and developing appropriate and positive leisure skills. He hypothesized that offenders who were provided career development training would score significantly higher than a control group on self-esteem and participation and commitment in the worker, homemaker, and leisure roles. His participants were youthful offenders who had been diagnosed with mental retardation and/or learning disabilities as well as behavioral problems. He found that the offenders in the group who received career development training increased their self-esteem, while it decreased for those in the control group. Also, participation and commitment in the homemaker role increased more for the group receiving training than the control group. Although commitment to the worker and leisure roles did not show a significant difference between groups, the training did increase the offenders' commitment to finding and maintaining a home, and it did increase their self-esteem. These two benefits could provide enough incentive for released offenders to remain in the community and avoid criminal activities, which is the ultimate goal of most training programs.

Bowker and Schweid (1992) provide another reason for implementing specialized programs within prisons. Offenders with intellectual disabilities, such as Richard in the case illustration, often become victims of physical attacks and psychological abuse (Fazel, Xenitidis, & Powell, 2008). Beail (2002) states that people with intellectual disabilities are also victims of violent crimes. They can be manipulated for goods or blamed for infractions by more intelligent inmates. This type of behavior only becomes worse with overcrowding, and many prisons are overcrowded. If separate units are not created for those with intellectual disabilities, then they must be housed with the mentally or physically ill, where they will not receive the types of services they need.

Placing inmates with intellectual disabilities in the general population of a prison can create many conflicts. If the inmate breaks the rules, as Richard continuously did, then correctional officers may place him or her in disciplinary isolation based on the policy and procedures of the institution without consideration of the individual differences and cognitive challenges that may have impacted the rule violation. The stress of the punishment may only frustrate the intellectually disabled inmate further, and he or she may verbally or physically act out this frustration because of a lack of understanding about what is happening. The aspects of prison life may actually place the intellectually disabled prisoner at risk, despite attempts to help the person (Haney, 2006; Hall, 1992). This is why it is so important to develop separate units and programs for this population.

Forensic Psychology and Policy Implications

Although programs for intellectually disabled inmates do exist, not all prisons have them, not all of the programs are adequate, and calls for reform are still forthcoming (Talbot, 2009). For example, Talbot (2009) calls for better identification of intellectually disabled inmates and more support and effective treatments for them. Policy makers need to develop programs, which focus on the special needs of these inmates, especially their slower learning capabilities and limited ability to understand the rules of the prison. Policies should be developed that decrease mainstreaming them into the general population and increase the creation of special facilities (Barron, Hassiotis, & Banes, 2004; Spruill & May, 1988; Tudway & Darmoody, 2005). Policies also need to be developed to create interagency communications, which would smooth the way for a continuum of care from prison into the community (Hall, 1992). Psychologists, social workers, probation officers, and correctional staff should begin working together to assist prisoners in habilitating and transitioning back into the community so that they refrain from future criminal activities. Without this type of teamwork, offenders like Richard will keep cycling back through the system because they do not know how to live effectively in their communities. Mental health professionals and other correctional staff who work with the intellectually disabled should have training regarding their special needs (Talbot, 2009). Communication with these individuals should be commensurate with their intellectual abilities, for example, simplistic language should be used with repetition of ideas or concepts provided in a concrete manner. Correctional staff should also be acutely aware of the potential for manipulation of these inmates by **higher functioning** inmates, or inmates with a greater capacity for rational thought or less adaptive skill deficits. In addition, they should be informed that in some instances behavior being interpreted as oppositional may actually be a result of a lack of understanding of instructions.

Suggestions for Future Research

Further research needs to be conducted on what types of programs are appropriate for inmates with intellectual disabilities and those with additional problems or disabilities (Hall, 1992; Talbot, 2009). Because of the difficulties inherent in group testing, more effective methods of screening for intellectual disabilities should be studied further. The tests currently used for identifying mental retardation (i.e., IQ, adaptive functioning) among inmates should be examined for validity with different ethnic groups (Ho, 1996; Morgan, Marsiske, & Whitfield, 2008). If these tests are culturally biased, then the reported higher prevalence of

African American inmates with intellectual disabilities may not be accurate. Inmates who really are not intellectually disabled, but have been raised with different cultural values and ideals, may be receiving services that are not suitable for them. Research also should be conducted on community-based programs that have had success in housing and habilitating prior offenders so that more effective initiatives can be developed to help this population stay out of prison. Additional research is needed on what are the most effective treatment strategies with individuals with intellectual disabilities.

Society's Reaction to Sex Offenders

Introduction

There are currently more than 600,000 convicted sex offenders in the United States (U.S. Department of Justice, 2008). According to Sandler and Freeman (2010), females comprise approximately four to five percent of this population with men making up the majority. These offenders are perhaps the most detested individuals in today's society. Since the late 1980s, there have been numerous movements calling for tougher penalties for sex offenders by law enforcement, legislatures, and communities. These movements support chemical castration, community notification, formalized registration, and civil commitment. At first glance, such actions may appear as proper precautions to ensure the safety of society against further victimization by convicted sex offenders. However, these actions also need to be examined in terms of whether they serve their intended function of curbing recidivism. Further, one needs to question whether the constitutional rights of the offender are violated. The case of Jose illustrates the repercussions that recent implementation of community notification laws have on both sex offenders and their families.

Jose is a 19-year-old Latino male who has been participating in sex offender-specific treatment for the past 6 months. Jose attends high school and works 30 hours a week in order to pay for his treatment. One Monday night during a group therapy session, Jose disclosed the devastation that he and his family have encountered as a result of his sexual offense, and, specifically, the mandated registration and community notification laws. Jose revealed how he was recently confronted by five men whom he considered friends. They located Jose's name on the CD-ROM which contains information about all registered sex offenders. Accessible information included Jose's name, picture, zip code, and a description of his offense. Jose tearfully described how his friends did not stop after confronting just him. They also confronted Jose's sister, who, they learned, was his victim. They then took it upon themselves to notify Jose's girlfriend (who subsequently left him), Jose's place of employment (which subsequently fired him), and students at his school. Feeling extremely scared and alone, Jose then disclosed that he was intending to commit suicide.

Literature Review

The case of Jose is an example of a young man who has completed a jail sentence for his offense and is currently receiving outpatient sex-offender treatment while he is on probation. Despite these punishment and rehabilitation efforts, society imposes additional requirements for the protection of the community against individuals such as Jose. These additional requirements are explored in terms of their respective advantages and disadvantages within the literature. The three issues examined are the registration and community notification laws, the statute for Sexually Violent Predators, and chemical castration.

Sex-offender registration and community notification

The death of 7-year-old Megan Kanka sparked a nationwide movement to release information about the location and identity of sex offenders in the community. New Jersey was the first state to pass "Megan's Law" after the young girl was raped and murdered by a convicted child molester who had moved into her neighborhood. Currently, "Megan's Law" is upheld under federal legislation and is upheld in every state. The purpose of the law is to equip the community with information necessary for the protection of children against child molesters (Beck, Clingermayer, Ramsy, & Travis, 2004). According to this law, the identification of the victim is not to be released. However, as illustrated in the case of Jose, the victim's name does not need to be present in order for identification to occur. A description of the sexual offense is provided, which can, at times, be sufficient for victim identification. Although in Jose's case his name was provided, victim identification can occur after it was stated that the sexual offense was committed against his sister. Regardless of the public's opinion on the rights (or lack thereof) of sex offenders, most would agree that the rights of victims, and particularly their identities, need to be protected.

In terms of the practical application of this law, it is important to examine whether it serves its intended purpose of protecting children from sexual abuse as well as reducing recidivism among sexual offenders. Since Megan's Law was passed in 1996, laws to supplement Megan's Law have been created. In 2006, President Bush enacted the Adam Walsh Child Protection and Safety Act (www.govtrack.us). Several foundations aid in the maintenance of websites that provide services for sex-offender location under Megan's Law (www.klaaskids. org). Beck, Clingermayer, Ramsy, and Travis (2004) contend that there is not scientific evidence that community notification and registration laws are effective in protecting society from sexual reoffending. A study at a 240-bed state inpatient psychiatric hospital in Nebraska indicated the sex offenders in this sample showed little familiarity with community notification laws and perceived some aspects of these laws as unfair (Elbogen, Patry, & Scalora, 2003). The literature provides a great deal of information concerning sexual offenses and offenders, which can help to address whether the law will meet its goals. Perhaps the most important issue is that most sexual offenses are not committed by strangers in the community;

rather, most sexual offenses are perpetrated by members of the family. This illustrates one misperception by society that sexual offenders are crazed predators who are waiting to pounce on the first child they see. This misconception is easier for the public to understand than the fact that, by far, most offenses are incestuous in nature. As noted by Williams (1996), it is the stereotypic image of a sex offender that creates fear and misunderstanding within society. However, it is precisely such fear and misunderstanding that provide the basis for an emotional response by legislatures, as witnessed by the sex-offender registration and community notification laws.

A total of 133 mental health professionals who work with sex offenders were surveyed regarding their opinions of public sex-offender registry websites (Malesky & Keim, 2001). Results indicated that greater than 80% of the participants did not believe that sex-offender registry websites would affect the number of children who were sexually abused each year and 70% of respondents believed that that a listing of sex offenders would actually create a false sense of security for parents. Over 60% of the mental health professionals surveyed believed that sex offenders listed on the websites would become targets of vigilantism in their communities (Malesky & Keim, 2001). Edwards and Hensley (2001) state that the stigma and backlash from the community may discourage offenders from reporting their behaviors and seeking counseling. Some researchers argue that the gains in public awareness come at a high cost for corrections by way of personnel, time, and budgetary resources (Zevitz & Farkas, 2000a).

A study was conducted to explore the experience of residents who attended community notification meetings regarding the notification of convicted sex offenders (Zevitz & Farkas, 2000b). Results indicated that these meetings could perform an important role in managing behavior of known sex offenders in the community but could come at the cost of increased community anxiety. Zevitz and Farkas (2000b) report that the anxiety is related to how those in attendance were notified of the meeting, how clearly the purpose was conveyed, and how organized the presentation during the meeting was given. Younglove and Vitello (2003, p. 25) point out the paradox of discretionary community notification by stating "perception of public safety is increased only by decreasing perception of public safety."

Sexually Violent Predator Act

Another way in which society chooses to deal with sexual offenders is by following their incarceration with civil commitment. The definition of a **Sexually Violent Predator** varies slightly across states; however, the basic premise is the same. California has defined the statute in the following way:

A person who has been convicted of one or more sexually violent offenses against two or more victims for which he or she received a determinate sentence and who has a diagnosed mental disorder that makes the person a danger to the health and safety of others in that it is likely that he or she will engage in sexually violent criminal behavior (Cohen, 1997).

The purpose of the law is to identify, locate, apprehend, and prosecute habitual sexual offenders (Cohen, 1997). Wood, Grossman, and Fichtner (2000) report that the intent of sexually violent predator laws is to reduce sexually violent crimes through treatment and involuntary confinement. Civil commitment for sexually violent predators has been implemented in 15 states, with the newest approach occurring in Texas since 1999, where civil commitment is implemented on an outpatient basis (Molett *et al.*, 2001; Bailey, 2002). When examined more closely, there are numerous issues inherent in this statute that call into question its constitutionality. There has long been a debate as to whether sex offenders need treatment or imprisonment. The Sexually Violent Predator Act, which became effective in California on 1 January, 1996, allows the state to subject the offender to both. In essence, this Act permits an indefinite civil commitment to be imposed on an offender after a full prison sentence has been served and prior to his release from prison. The *ex post facto* clause of the United States Constitution prohibits retroactive application of penal statutes. Given that the Sexually Violent Predator Act is a civil law, analysis of *United States v. Ward* (1980) extends the *ex post facto* clause to civil cases. In this case, it was found that civil laws violate the *ex post facto* law if the statute is "so punitive either in purpose or effect as to negate its intention." This applies to the Sexually Violent Predator Act in that the said intent was to provide mental health treatment to the offender; however, the underlying goal was to extend the confinement of the individual.

In a similar fashion, the Sexually Violent Predator Act is in conflict with prohibitions against double jeopardy. **Double jeopardy** is said to have occurred if one of three situations is present: (1) a second prosecution for the same offense after acquittal; (2) a second prosecution for the same offense after conviction; and (3) multiple punishments for the same offense. In terms of the Sexually Violent Predator Act, violations of the latter two occur. The major defense that has been used in court to claim that this Act does *not* constitute double jeopardy is that a civil commitment is not punitive in character (*Department of Revenue of Montana v. Kurth Ranch*, 1994). One must determine whether the motivation for the commitment is truly for the offender to receive treatment or whether the purpose is to keep the offender confined in a secure facility apart from the rest of society. Further, if treatment is needed for the individual, such treatment needs to be provided immediately upon this determination, rather than after a prison sentence has been completed. Young v. Weston (9th Cir. 1999), which was an appeal of a writ of habeas corpus on indefinite commitment under the Washington State's Sexually Violent Predator Statute, was reversed and remanded (Walcott, 2000). The appeals court held that the conditions of confinement and the quality of treatment at a special center violated the ex post facto and double jeopardy clauses of the U.S. Constitution. However, in the case of *Hubbart v. Superior Court of Santa Clara County*, the court upheld California's Sexually Violent Predator Act (Scott & Yarvis, 2000).

Supporters of the Texas outpatient civil commitment statute contend that it is an effective and low cost, less restrictive means to protect the community and treat the sexual offender, with the cost of outpatient civil commitment being about $30,000 per person/year as compared to more than $200,000 for inpatient commitment in other states (Garib, 2011). Outpatient civilly committed sex offenders in Texas are managed by a team made up of a case manager (supervision), mental health professionals, public safety officer (global positioning satellite monitoring), and other professionals (Meyer *et al.*, 2003). These researchers have found that out of 21 committed individuals, seven are in treatment, one passed away, 10 are in custody after violating the conditions of commitment that constitute a felony, and three await release from prison.

Chemical castration

Perhaps the most drastic measure that has been implemented as a means of protecting society against sex offenders is the chemical castration law. In addition to psychotherapy, some researchers contend that pharmacotherapy is another important tool or treatment option for sex offenders, particularly for paraphilias (Briken, Hill, & Berner, 2003). According to Maletzky and Field (2003, p. 391), there are three classes of medications currently used to reduce sex drive: "(1) hormonal agents acting peripherally, predominantly medroxyprogesterone acetate (MPA) (Depo-Provera); (2) hormonal agents acting centrally, predominantly leuprolide (Leupron); and (3) serotonin-active antidepressants, such as fluoxetine (Prozac) and paroxetine (Paxil). Again, the chemical castration law varies slightly from state to state; however, the fundamentals of the law remain the same. In California, two-time sex offenders can be required to take Depo-Provera upon parole. Depo-Provera is a hormone-suppressing drug which lowers testosterone levels, thereby decreasing a man's sex drive. The court has also allowed for discretion in using this procedure for first-time sex offenders. In support of the chemical castration law, research suggests that chemical castration has the best long-term results (Critten & West, 2006). A study completed by Critten and West (2006) found that the recidivism rate for sex offenders who had undergone chemical castration was, at 13.4%, lower than those who had not received treatment, at 16.6%. This suggests that treatment can effectively reduce recidivism among sexual offenders.

Arguments have been made in the literature that chemical castration is not only unconstitutional but also ethically wrong (Critten & West, 2006). The American Civil Liberties Union of Florida historically has argued that the use of chemical castration is unconstitutional for several reasons (Spralding, 1997). First, chemical castration interferes with an individual's rights to procreate and to refuse treatment.

Second, Depo-Provera is not FDA-approved for chemical castration. Third, judges, not physicians, will be making the ultimate decision as to whether an offender should be given the drug and when the drug can be discontinued. Fourth, there are serious side-effects from

Depo-Provera which include diabetes, gallstones, hypertension, fatigue, weight gain, nightmares, and muscle weakness. For this reason, the chemical castration law can be viewed as judges practicing medicine without a license.

Perhaps one of the most important opposing arguments to the chemical castration law is that it will not curb recidivism in many offenders. The treatment strategy that has the best effect on curbing recidivism among sexual offenders is cognitive-behavioral therapy that incorporates a relapse prevention plan or a self-regulation model depending on the specific type of sex offender in question (Polaschek, 2003; Gibbons, 2003; Laws, 1989). A more recent study indicates a recidivism rate of about 13% for all types of sex offenders who received cognitive-behavioral therapy and about 12% for child sexual offenders who were up to "five years post-release" (Critten & West, 2006). Some basic empirical animal research also does not support the use of chemical castration to deter deviant sexual aggression in humans (Moore, 2001). Chemical castration does nothing to treat the psychological roots of sexually aberrant behavior. Numerous sexual offenders do not offend as a result of an overactive sex drive. Many offenders commit sexual offenses for reasons that have nothing to do with sex such as power, control, and anger.

Forensic Psychology and Policy Implications

There is a great need for forensic psychologists to provide information to the public and legislature regarding sexual offenders and their recidivism and treatment. It appears that several of the recent actions taken against sexual offenders will be ineffective in accomplishing the goal of protecting society. Cordoba and Chapel (1983) acknowledge that historically society is more willing to allow sex offenders back into the community if they have undergone antiandrogen therapy (chemical castration). Critten and West (2006) indicate that today, sex offenders are "treated as outcasts of our communities," and society is reluctant to allow them back into our communities regardless of treatment (p. 143). It is important, however, to examine whether such measures are based simply on emotion and community misperceptions or whether thorough research was conducted to support their implementation. It appears that there is a direct conflict between society's outcry for severe punishment of sex offenders and mental health experts who maintain that there is effective treatment for such individuals. Notification programs such as those outlined in Megan's Law give members of the community a chance to protect themselves, although some research indicates that it increases the likelihood that the offender will be victimized (Beck *et al.*, 2004). Given this conflict, the legislature has attempted to satisfy both sides through legally sanctioned penal and civil commitments.

Chemical castration, community notification, registration, and the Sexually Violent Predator Act are all aimed at protecting society from sex offenders who are likely to recidivate upon release from prison. In lobbying the chemical castration bill in California, proponents stated that recidivism would drop from almost 100 to 2% (Moses, 1996). In reviewing the literature on recidivism among sexual offenders, no study documents that recidivism occurs in almost 100% of the cases (Proulx *et al.*, 1997; Critten & West, 2006). This illustrates the public's misperceptions about sexual offenders and specifically about their likelihood for reoffense. Furthermore, policy makers should be educated on the fact that public awareness needs to be focused primarily on the family, where many sexual offenses occur. Numerous studies have shown the effectiveness of cognitive behavioral treatment for sexual offenders in reducing recidivism. With this in mind, attention needs to be focused on funding prison and parole treatment programs, which are designed specifically for this population.

Suggestions for Future Research

Sexually violent predator laws are all relatively new in the United States. Longitudinal analyses need to be conducted, examining recidivism rates before and after the laws. This will provide a more accurate measure of whether the laws are meeting their goal of curbing recidivism. In order to illustrate the discrepancy between society's perceptions of sex offenders, studies should be conducted which directly compare the statistical data gathered in the department of corrections with society's perceptions of recidivism among sex offenders and the effectiveness of treatment for this population. It is likely that the results will show that the legislature supports the misperceptions within society versus the data available from corrections and mental health professionals. Several studies indicate there is an upward trend in the rate of female sexual offenders (Wijkman, Bijleveld, & Hendricks, 2010; Sandler & Freeman, 2010). There is a need for research in the area of female sexual offenders to include types, prevalence, recidivism, and society's perception of female offenders. Research differentiating between fear of victimization and perceived risk of victimization to the offender is needed. This will provide insight into what the offender faces as a result of the notification systems and if this notification places a sort of "scarlet letter" on the offender.

Women Working in Male Prisons

Introduction

Today when you walk into a male prison it is not uncommon to see women there, not as inmates but as correctional officers (COs) guarding the male prisoners. Prior to the passage of Title VII of the Civil Rights Act of 1964, this would have been a rare sight. Women were delegated to work in all-female institutions and juvenile corrections (Etheridge, Hale, & Hambrick, 1984). Fortunately, Title VII prohibited sex discrimination by state and local governments, so female corrections officers began to move into the male prison system. Unfortunately, the question arose about the capability of women being able to handle the physical and emotional strains that are involved in working with corrections (Lambert,

Paoline, Hogan, & Baker, 2007). Historically, some female COs have found it challenging to coexist with the male COs in an atmosphere of hostility, harassment, and nonsupportiveness. As more women have entered the workforce in previously male-dominated professions, hostility has lessened but not disappeared.

The following example illustrates the process that female COs sometimes face when trying to fit into the male prison system.

When Jane first began her career as a correctional officer, she chose to work in a female prison because there were more job openings and she felt more comfortable working with this population. After several years, she decided to move to an all-male prison because she had two kids to help support and needed the pay raise this job would bring. Although she was very familiar with the job requirements of a CO and had never worked in a male prison, she was aware that every prison had its own rules.

On her first day, she went in with a friendly, open attitude. She smiled and introduced herself to her new coworkers. She noticed that she was the only female CO in her unit. She got a couple of nods and one person even grunted hello. Nobody returned her friendly attitude, though. She knew the name of the CO who was to train her, but it took her half an hour to find him because he started his rounds without waiting for her. Upon finding him, he immediately ordered her to be quiet and watch everything he did. Several times that day she asked him questions about the job, and he often did not give her a sufficient answer or ignored her altogether. After one question, he accused her of being stupid and of not knowing anything about being a correctional officer.

During her lunch break, none of the male COs would sit with her. She overheard them talking and laughing about her, and one even cornered her and asked her to go out for a drink after work. After telling him she was married, he just laughed and said he was sure her husband expected such things since she worked with "real men." When Jane left work after that first day, she felt very discouraged and was afraid to return.

After thinking it over, she vowed to go back with a different attitude. She began to act more assertively and to not let her male coworkers demean her. She began to use more offensive language and joked around with the men so that she would fit in better. Gradually, the men began to accept her, but only after she showed she could be tough like them and not act feminine. She had to change her personality to fit their beliefs about how a CO should act. Her problem then became one of trying to leave her work personality at work. Her comments were that, "It's a macho environment and I have to act aggressively to succeed. I work here all day, talk loud, act tough. I go home at night and find myself talking in a deep, loud voice to my kids" (Jurik, as cited in Martin and Jurik, 1996, p. 197). So, Jane found that she could fit into the male prison system, but at the cost of giving up her own identity to conform to her male counterparts.

With the tragic death of Correctional Officer Jayme Biendl, the debate of whether or not females should work in male prisons has been reignited. Fear of women being unable to fend off stronger, male inmates and questions about the safety of female COs when surrounded by violent and aggressive offenders are at the center of this discussion. Consider Officer Biendl's case below:

Officer Biendl, an 8-year veteran, was assigned to the prison chapel at the Monroe Correctional Facility in Washington State. On Saturday 29 January, 2011, Byron Scherf, an inmate serving a life sentence, went missing during a headcount went to church services at the prison's chapel. Around 8:30 in the evening, after the church services ended, Scherf stated that he had waited for everyone else to leave the area and then he attacked Officer Biendl (KOMO News, 2011). According to a transcript of an interview Scherf gave to detectives, he took Officer Biendl's shoulder and belt radios away from her before she could successfully call for help. The transcript shows that Scherf stated he wrestled with Officer Biendl trying to choke her with his hands, but when that was unsuccessful he "spotted the microphone cable on the stage of the prison chapel, wrapped it around her neck and used that to strangle her" (KOMO News, 2011). Around 10 p.m., an inventory of equipment showed that a set of keys and radios were missing. Officers headed to the assigned post of Officer Biendl where she was discovered unresponsive, CPR was attempted, and she was pronounced dead at the scene by paramedics. Officer Biendl had been strangled with no signs of sexual assault, but she was not discovered until almost an hour and a half after Scherf strangled her. Scherf is a repeat sex offender most recently convicted of kidnapping and raping a woman at knifepoint and then setting her on fire with gasoline.

Literature Review

Both male and female COs should be allowed to work in correctional settings without fear of harassment by their coworkers. Correctional officers are placed in potentially life and death situations by managing and routinely interacting with some of the most violent offenders. Safety in prisons must be paramount, and much like police officers in the community, COs rely on one another for safety and support. The death of Officer Biendl is the worst case scenario.

The first signs of discrimination began after Title VII was passed. All-male prisons tried to prohibit women from even being hired by using the BFOQ clause, which states that sex discrimination can occur if it is a **Bona Fide Occupational Qualification** (Pollock-Byrne, 1990). *Dothard v. Rawlinson* (1977) is an example of this. The state of Alabama prohibited a woman from working in an all-male prison because it claimed the violence of the state prisons would be dangerous for women. The state used the BFOQ clause as their justification. The U.S. Supreme Court upheld the state's case, although it did overturn the use of height and weight restrictions in hiring unless it could be shown how it related to the job. Although this seems like a negative outcome for women, it was really a narrow ruling applying only to Alabama. Historically, other states have had a difficult time proving that height, weight, or gender influence what is necessary to be a corrections officer (Pollock-Byrne, 1990).

01/01/2005 07:14:21

Although prisons have not been able to prevent women from being hired, some male correctional officers have not welcomed them into their subculture. Fry and Glaser (1987) conducted a study on female COs and found that they were not viewed positively by the male guards. In fact, they found that the male officers' resistance was the greatest problem the female COs faced in male prisons. Martin and Jurik (1996) found, more specifically, that it is in the area of actual security work in men's prisons where women are least likely to be included. According to the U.S. Department of Justice (2008), at the end of 2005, the male to female ratio of employees working in state and federal correctional facilities was 2 to 1. In federal correctional facilities women only made up 13% of the correctional officer staff, in state facilities 26% of correctional officers were women, and in private facilities 48% of correctional officers were women (U.S. Dept. of Justice, 2008). Since their numbers are so low, it is not surprising that female COs being recognized and treated as equals can be problematic. Jane's situation captures this dilemma.

However, more recent research suggests that maybe the perceptions of female correctional staff are not as negative as they once were. Hemmens, Stohr, Schoeler, and Miller (2002) conducted a survey of 467 prison workers employed by a variety of institutions and found that the perceptions of female correctional staff were generally positive. The majority of subjects viewed several sexually harassing behaviors inappropriate, such as: sexual jokes or teasing, insults, personal comments, rumors of sexual inappropriateness with fellow staff or inmates, or sexual relations between staff and inmates. Individuals who worked at maximum-security facilities had the lowest perceptions of female correctional staff's abilities, while those who worked at women's facilities had the highest view of their capabilities. Subjects over the age of 50 had the lowest perceptions of female correctional staff and females had better impressions of the work of other female staff. Finally, previous military service also negatively impacted positive impressions of female correctional workers (Hemmens *et al.*, 2002).

From their first day, women COs are faced with fitting in with their coworkers. This problem does not always go away with time. Female COs can face opposition and sometimes sexual harassment from the male guards; however, opposition can take many different forms. Although male coworkers at times show overt hostility, they also engage in more subtle ways of undermining female COs. They can put pressure on women by constantly questioning or scrutinizing their performance, particularly in front of inmates or other COs (Martin & Jurik, 1996). They sometimes reverse decisions made by women, thereby undermining women's authority over prisoners. For women in supervisory positions, their male subordinates engage in subtle and blatant forms of resistance such as rolling their eyes, inattentiveness, and feigning an inability to hear orders. They can also undermine a woman's authority by "going over her head," thus causing her to lose the respect of her superiors due to ineffective management (Martin and Jurik, 1996).

Sexual harassment can be another technique male COs use to keep women in an unequal status. Women become victims of rumors and allegations of sexual misconduct. There are overt propositions made by male COs and even more subtle behaviors such as joking, teasing, and name calling (Martin & Jurik, 1996). In the case illustration, Jane was propositioned by her coworker and then ridiculed when she refused his advances. Historically, women COs have reported that male officers proposition them in front of male inmates (Pollock-Byrne, 1990). It seems as if this might encourage the inmates to behave in a similar manner. In a study of San Quentin Prison, it was found that women COs were sexually harassed at work and by phone at home. The overtly sexist language and conduct was openly tolerated (Owen, as cited in Martin and Jurik, 1996). This sexual harassment makes relationships with male COs "difficult in that a balance always has to be struck between being friendly and being thought of as sexually available — being 'one of the boys' or designated as the fraternity whore" (Pollock-Byrne, 1990, p. 118). Martin and Jurik (1996) state that further problems arise when female COs refuse their counterparts' protection and sexual advances and attempt to show their competence. The male COs will label them as "too mannish, 'man-haters', bitches, or lesbians" (Martin & Jurik, 1996, p. 174).

Women have had some success in trying to stop sexual harassment. For example, in *Bundy v. Jackson* (1981), a woman prison counselor was being harassed by her male supervisors. When she rejected their advances, they prevented her from advancing in her job. When she charged them with sexual harassment, the court ruled in her favor, saying that her employer had allowed a hostile and discriminating work environment that violated Title VII (Martin & Jurik, 1996). Despite cases like this, Martin and Jurik (1996) say that sexual harassment in all-male prisons still occurs. The correctional field has been slow to prevent this type of behavior. Women fear that if they complain it may cause a negative evaluation of their job performance or even job loss.

Another aspect of opposition that female COs must face is that male COs evaluate women's job performances more negatively than they do their own (Martin & Jurik, 1996). A study by Fry and Glaser (1987), which gave questionnaires to staff, reported that the men found women COs to be less capable than themselves in duties that related to security and safety. Szockyj (1989) stated a similar finding in that male COs viewed themselves as more effective in handling situations that involved physical strength and preferred male back-up over female back-up. Male COs view women as too physically and emotionally weak to work in all-male prisons, and, therefore, they cannot do their jobs adequately in violent situations and will be injured (Martin and Jurik, 1996). There is also a fear that women will get too friendly with the inmates, so female officers' intentions with the prisoners are scrutinized, although male officers' intentions are rarely monitored (Martin & Jurik, 1996).

Female officers can be perceived as threatening an established subcultural code; they can threaten a self-image held by male officers that correctional work is dangerous and therefore only suitable for men. In other words, women are a status threat to men. Men may treat women in a sexually harassing way to deny women acceptance on the job; therefore, their status as men will not be diminished (Crouch, 1985). If women can perform the guard job as well as men, the job can no longer be used as a way of defining their masculinity. It is interesting to note that Boothby and Clements (2000) conducted a national survey of correctional psychologists (n = 830) and found that the majority were Caucasian males. Are the attitudes different for female correctional psychologists?

Another explanation is that women COs conduct their job in a different way than men. Female COs are successful at diffusing potentially violent situations in the early phases of confrontations and are reported to have an overall calming effect on the male inmates (Cheeseman & Worley, 2006). They spend more time focusing on communication and interacting in a less authoritarian manner with the inmates. This suggests that interacting in a respectful manner will make it more likely that the detainees will voluntarily comply with orders and the women will not have to use force or intimidation. Cheeseman and Worley's study found that inmates may like having female COs "because of their 'softer' and more humane intervention style" (2006). In a maximum security prison setting inmates gave female COs a higher rating on job than medium security prisons, and minimum security prison inmates gave the lowest score for job competency in female COs (Cheeseman & Worley, 2006). Most are acting under the principle that you can command respect by giving respect to others. Male COs may perceive this behavior as sympathy toward inmates and feel that female guards are incapable of handling the job properly. Grekul (1999) indicates that those correctional officers who hold views sympathetic to inmates often feel that they are an isolated minority and are extremely different from their coworkers.

Research exploring correctional officer burnout indicated that female correctional officers were less likely than their male colleagues to interact with inmates in a detached, impersonal way (Morgan *et al.*, 2002). Despite the harassment and exclusion female COs feel from some of their male coworkers, Lambert *et al.* (2007) found that female COs had more job satisfaction than male COs. It is important to point out that many male COs are not hostile toward female coworkers. Yet, for those women who are confronted with hostile attitudes and practices by their male peers, a prison setting can be an unsettling and unsafe place on many levels.

Although there is no agreed-upon reason why some male COs treat female officers with such opposition, what can be agreed upon is that women in "male" fields such as corrections face many hindrances, including expressed and subtle hostilities, exclusion from the male CO subculture, and sexual harassment (Cheeseman & Worley, 2006).

Forensic Psychology and Policy Implications

The hostility endured by female COs in all-male prisons can be a significant social problem. The harassment women face "is a source of mistrust, resentment and job-related stress" (Martin & Jurik, 1996, p. 178). This reinforces the concept of women as outsiders and subordinates. Research suggests that role conflict or the challenge of balancing custodial responsibilities (e.g. maintaining security) and treatment roles (e.g. helping inmates to rehabilitate, or modeling pro-social interactions) is a significant source of stress for correctional officers (Finn, 1998). Female officers may believe they must ignore and stifle their femininity, which is a part of who they are. Jane found that in order to fit in with her male coworkers she had to develop a macho persona. This behavior can lead to a negative self-image, which can have adverse effects on health and family interactions. It could even influence a female officer's ability to do her job effectively, perpetuating the negative stereotypes. Thus, it can be a self-fulfilling prophecy: female COs are treated as subordinates, causing them to do their job in a way they are uncomfortable with, thereby forcing them to be seen as incompetent, which leaves them in subordinate positions. Etheridge *et al.* (1984) emphasized that a major barrier to advancement by women is the expectancies held by the women themselves. Additionally, women can be the harshest critics of other women, creating obstacles for each other, while others are a critical source of empathy and support. In a correctional environment, persons who work in the institution as either an officer or a psychologist will be faced with the overall culture of the institution as well as the subcultures amongst the COs and the inmates.

Because the numbers of female COs in all-male prisons are relatively small, they may be considered token employees, making them highly visible and potentially adding pressure on the job. They must represent the ability of all female COs, proving that they can do the job as well as their male counterparts. This can cause female COs to be wary of making mistakes, so they imitate the male officers, which may not be the most effective way to perform their job.

The fact that sexual harassment is still occurring in all-male prisons underscores an important political dynamic for women working as correctional officers. This type of behavior interferes with basic civil rights and therefore should be assessed by policy makers in an attempt to prevent women from having to endure degrading experiences in their place of business. Sexual harassment further reinforces the notion that women are subordinate and not worthy of being treated as equals in the job environment. Policy analysts must address this false sentiment. It is quite important to note that homosexual officers of either gender could potentially face parallel issues and challenges working in this type of environment.

Female correctional/forensic psychologists who are working in prison systems often encounter similar attitudes and misconceptions. Not only are female psychologists working in a masculinized system, but they are in a profession that is misunderstood and regarded with suspicion. Too often, women who hold this position are viewed as a "bleeding heart" or a "push over" who is babying the inmates, or perhaps take on an overly harsh approach to over-compensate for this perception. Correctional officers too often misunderstand the role of the correctional psychologist and underestimate her training in working with frequently manipulative and dangerous clients. Psychologists in prison systems may encounter passive aggressive antics by correctional officers such as "forgetting" to process a request for inmates to attend group therapy or by harassing inmates who are trying to pass through security with approved group materials (e.g., notebooks, homework assignments). Correctional/forensic psychologists can play an active role in providing in-service training to correctional officers educating them about mental illness and about your role as a mental health professional in a correctional environment. The role of a private practice psychologist in the community differs in many ways that most security staff would not be aware of.

The argument that women are not as capable of protecting themselves against the violent male offender population is a continuing battle. The tragic death of Officer Jayme Biendl raises the issue of female COs' safety in male prisons. However, any officer or psychologist isolated from other correctional staff and alone with a prisoner would be at a much higher risk of serious violence by an inmate if the interaction turned violent.

Suggestions for Future Research

Although work-related sexual harassment was dealt with to a certain extent during the first few decades after Title VII was passed, this issue is yet to be resolved. The effects of stricter, more defined sexual harassment laws in regard to women working in all-male prisons is a major area of needed research. Are women COs more willing to bring these situations out into the open now that sexual harassment is in the public eye? Do women now garner better results in getting this behavior to stop without having to sacrifice their jobs or level of respect by their coworkers?

Another area of inquiry should focus on the effects this profession has on the female's family members. Developing a tougher, more aggressive personality could have a major impact on a female correctional officer's family. It could change the dynamics of the marital relationship or have an impact on the way she raises her children. In Jane's situation, she had a difficult time leaving her work personality at work. She spoke to her children the way she spoke to the inmates and guards. Consequently, does being a CO cause women to redefine their entire identity in order to succeed in the correctional setting or do women who already have more masculine personalities or relate easily with men in a nonsexualized manner gravitate toward these positions? Are women with more **stimulus-seeking** (i.e., looking for excitement, easily bored) personalities more prone to seek out correctional officer or psychology positions? Do these women have personality styles that make this line of work more attractive than general practice? Research is needed in this area.

How are female correctional officers perceived by their male counterparts? How are forensic psychologists perceived by COs both male and female? Do the perceptions of mental illness and the necessity of treatment differ between male and female COs in prisons? Are incidents of stress and burnout higher for the female psychologist in a correctional setting? Is she afforded less credibility or respect than her male counterparts? Are female psychologists more or less at risk for inmate assault? This is an area that is little researched and could provide valuable information to aid with recruitment, job satisfaction, and job retention.

Cheeseman and Worley (2006) suggest that if correctional agencies offered gender-specific training at preservice and in-service trainings, then female COs would be more equipped with handling the population in which they work. Is any difference in training for female staff such as more or different techniques or possibly different types of maneuvers for safety required or is this further perpetrating negative stereotypes? Additional research is also needed into other minority populations (e.g., homosexual officers, racial minorities) working in prison environments that may face similar or quite distinct challenges working in a correctional institution.

"Make Believe" Families

Introduction

When men and women who commit crimes are sent to prison, it is easy for many people to say that they are being punished and should not be entitled to those things to which ordinary citizens are entitled. However, some criminals spend many years confined in the prison environment, and they still experience the same emotions and feelings as when they were not imprisoned. It is unrealistic to assume that these inmates can shut themselves off from wanting intimacy and affection, especially in such a lonely environment where the need for affection is perhaps greater (Bedard, 2009). Male and female prisoners recreate their desires and needs inside of the correctional facility, yet they do so in different ways. In female prisons, women create caring relationships (Bedard, 2009; MacKenzie, Robinson, and Campbell, 1989) which have been referred to as **kinship systems** (Giallombardo, 1966), **"play" families** (MacKenzie *et al.*, 1989), **surrogate families** (Church, 1990), **pseudofamilies** (Pollock-Byrne, 1990; Huggins, Capeheart, & Newman, 2006; Bedard, 2009) and **dyads** (Huggins et al., 2006).

Kelly was 28 years old when she was convicted of selling drugs on the streets. She was sentenced to 5 years in a state correctional facility. Kelly had spent a few weeks in the local jail before, but she had never been to prison. She had heard all sorts of stories about prison and was not sure what to expect when she arrived. She was scared and felt very alone. She had no family to speak of, and her so-called friends were other drug dealers and addicts whom she could not rely on to be supportive during her time of need. On Kelly's first day in prison, she was placed in a cell with a 23-year-old inmate named Sabrina. Although Sabrina was 5 years younger than Kelly, she seemed much older and wiser. Sabrina instantly began sharing her feelings with Kelly in an attempt to have Kelly talk about her fears. Sabrina stated that it would make things easier if Kelly would talk about them. Kelly immediately felt a connection to Sabrina, which she had never experienced with anyone before. In a very short amount of time, Kelly began to view Sabrina as a mother figure and even began calling her "mom." She also was surprised to learn that Sabrina was married to another female who was housed in a different unit. This inmate's name was Christina, but everyone called her Chris. Kelly soon began to call her "Dad" because Chris behaved like a father and treated Kelly like her own daughter. Over time, the three of them interacted like a family and Kelly was able to adjust to prison life with their help and support.

Literature Review

As exemplified in Kelly's case, women who are sentenced to serve time in prison find ways to cope with their environment. One way many of these women accomplish this is by modeling real families (Watterson, 1996; Beer, Morgan, Garland, & Spanierman, 2007). They use these "play" mothers, fathers, daughters, and lovers to make up for losing their real parents, children, and lovers (Morgan, 1997; Burke, 1992; Beer *et al.*, 2007). Other family member roles that could be filled include grandparents, sisters, and brothers to complete the family they are separated from during incarceration (Beer *et al.*, 2009). The inmates do not necessarily enter prison to consciously create these families, but when they are scared and lonely they either retreat into their own misery or create new relationships which develop into substitute families (Beer *et al.*, 2007; Bedard, 2009; Watterson, 1996). The families are often created to be the emotional and economical support that the inmate is lacking because female inmates are often incarcerated further from home than male inmates, and the families can be created for protection in the prison environment (Beer, Morgan, Garland, & Spanierman, 2007).

As one of the early researchers in this area, Giallombardo (1966) defined a prison family as "a group of related kin linked by ties of allegiance and alliance who sometimes occupy a common household and are characterized by varying degrees of solidarity" (p. 163). She expressed the notion that many of these women come together in homosexual relationships to create a marriage unit. Some of the prisoners take on the role of a man and adopt masculine traits such as wearing their hair short, wearing pants, and expressing typical societal male characteristics of strength and authority. Other inmates take on the feminine role of wife or mother and wear makeup and more feminine clothing (Giallombardo, 1966; Watterson, 1996; Bedard, 2009). However, these families are not necessarily created to be sexual in nature, but as a way to cope with the feelings of isolation from their families due to being incarcerated (Bedard, 2009).

Pollock-Byrne (1990) described the male and female roles as being stereotypical where the males are domineering and leading and the females are nurturing and pleasing. Because the inmates play these roles in such a stereotypical fashion, those playing the male role may seem so masculine that they are referred to as "he" and "him". These "men" also may become carried away with their roles and treat their wives as slaves, ordering them around. The women who go along with this behavior probably have been involved in similar relationships while outside of prison. Therefore, it is a habit for them to do anything in order to keep their man (Watterson, 1996). Despite the sometimes negative consequences of developing prison marriages, these relationships actually serve to meet the inmates' needs for affection, and they provide closeness and a sense of belonging (Beer *et al.*, 2007). The women turn to each other for comfort and create these homosexual relationships and surrogate families (Beer *et al.*, 2007; Bedard, 2009; Morgan, 1997; Church, 1990). The marriages may not even have anything to do with sex. In fact, some women may never consummate their marriage in a sexual manner (Watterson, 1996). Instead, possibly for the first time ever, the women base their relationships on kinship and intimacy as opposed to sex (Pollock-Byrne, 1990).

Relationships among female prisoners may not be restricted to homosexual unions. Entire families organize themselves by choice and give each other titles (Beer *et al.*, 2007; MacKenzie *et al.*, 1989). Women of varying ages assume roles of mothers, daughters, aunts, and fathers. As in Kelly and Sabrina's situation, age does not necessarily dictate what role the women play. These families are not bound by ethnic categories either. Many families will include members of several ethnicities (Church, 1990). Pollock-Byrne (1990) reported that the mother–daughter dyad is the most common familial relationship. A prison mother may have several daughters, and if she has a prison husband, then he may become their father, as Chris did for Kelly. Pollock-Byrne also indicated that when playing the role of mother in prison, the inmate may be a better parent to her role-playing daughter than she ever was to her real children on the outside. For the inmates playing the role of the child, their prison mother serves as a type of role model and may become like a real mother, who helps instead of neglects them (Watterson, 1996b). In Kelly's situation, Sabrina became a real mother for her.

Whether this is true in all situations, prison families, especially the roles of parent and child, are viewed as very special. The relationships consist of consideration and warmth (Giallombardo, 1966). The families are similar to regular friendships where the inmates support each other in order to decrease the stress of life in prison. Coming together as a family allows them to feel a sense of security, ease, and connection with others (Watterson, 1996). The family also serves as a form of protection for each member. If a member of the family is in physical danger from some other inmate, then the "father" or "brother" can protect that person (Giallombardo, 1966; Watterson, 1996).

Some researchers suggest that these prison families may serve a purpose for only some women. MacKenzie *et al.* (1989) conducted a study and found that many women newly admitted to prison were involved in play families. However, those who had been in prison for a great deal of time did not partake in this phenomenon. The researchers suggested that these play families may assist inmates in adjusting to prison life, but then once acclimated, this need for safety and security disappears. Pollock-Byrne (1990) discussed something similar. She stated that when an inmate approaches her release date or when she maintains close ties to her real family, then the need for a pseudofamily is not as strong as for those inmates who are alone and have no outside connections. Kelly is an example of this latter type of inmate. Without those outside relationships, the prison families become real families. Pollock-Byrne (1990) also suggested that with increased efforts at family programming and community support, female inmates are able to preserve their outside connections, which therefore decreases the need for a prison family.

In a study conducted by Ansay (as cited in Silverman & Vega, 1996), it was found that the most common group in prison was more like a gang than a family. Approximately 6 to 12 inmates who were serving long sentences comprised these gang groups and had labels such as "associates" and "cousins," thus providing more support for the notion that prison families may not be as common as they once were.

Genders and Player (1990) questioned prison staff about these inmate families, and their responses appeared to concur with what inmates reported. They suggested that relationships were more about finding affection and emotional support than they were about engaging in sexual behaviors. The staff reported that many women engaged in lesbian behaviors at some time during their imprisonment. In fact, the staff indicated that this was an eventual phase for women serving long terms in prison; however, these women were not thought to be lesbians when not imprisoned. Morgan (1997) contends that the lesbian relationships fostered in prison are often not the angry, violent ones portrayed on TV but a relationship based on a need for support and companionship. Prison administrators have indicated that they believe that fewer than 5% of female inmates have engaged in lesbian relationships outside of prison (Watterson, 1996).

Prison staff also reported that problems with these families can occur when a couple breaks up because jealous feelings and even suicidal thoughts can erupt (Genders & Player, 1990). Watterson (1996) indicated that problems occur when a female inmate "drops her belt" (p. 294). This is when the woman reverts back to her female role after playing a male role. It creates problems because there are not enough female inmates who want to play the male role. The woman is then seen as a phony and this is threatening to other inmates. A more recent study suggested the negative attention drawn from correctional officers prevented inmates from becoming emotionally involved with each other due to fear of being singled out or viewed as a problematic inmate (Severance, 2005). Inmates involved in a pseudofamily group are more likely to have an increased amount of disciplinary actions than inmates not involved in a family group (Huggins *et al.*, 2006).

Despite the difficulties prison families can create, it appears as though they do offer something for which these women are searching. As one inmate stated, "…inside this place, when I do something with a girl, usually I feel like someone's comforting me and just making me feel good. It's not really a sex thing, even when it's sex, because in here you feel so damn little and alone…" (Watterson, 1996, p. 285).

Forensic Psychology and Policy Implications

An important consideration in these make-believe families is to understand why the inmates find them necessary. As the literature has suggested, female inmates find that they are an important source of support and a necessity in adjusting to the prison environment. Psychologists and mental health workers should play a significant role in helping inmates and correctional staff identify this need. Policies should be implemented to assist these women in their initial adjustment to prison. Psychologists must make correctional staff aware of the types of issues these women confront upon entry into the prison system so that staff can assist them during the transition. This could prevent some acting-out behaviors that the women might otherwise exhibit out of fear and insecurity.

Policies also should be developed to prevent women from being labeled as lesbians and placed in separate housing units if these prisoners do not view themselves in such a manner. If female inmates assume a role in a homosexual relationship only while in prison, then when nearing release, they should be assisted in coming to terms with this. They also will need assistance in transitioning back into heterosexual relationships and into their real families.

Another dimension to consider when dealing with female inmates is their natural families on the outside. Policies should be developed to help women maintain connections with their friends and families, especially since female inmates tend to be incarcerated further from their home then male inmates, so that the need to create make-believe ones will not be necessary. If a woman enters prison and does not have any connections to anyone outside of prison, then correctional staff and psychologists should assist her in developing ties to the community in the form of education, vocation, and community service. In this way, the inmate may have something to look forward to upon release and not feel so alone upon having to leave her prison family.

Suggestions for Future Research

In recent years, limited research has been conducted on female inmates' make-believe families. Much of the research was conducted in the late 1960s and 1970s, with a few scattered studies in the early 1990s. If this is a phenomenon which is no longer as prevalent in prisons, then studies should be conducted to determine why this is so and what may have taken its place. If women no longer feel the need for these families, then what are they doing to adjust to prison life? More current investigations need to be implemented. If the phenomenon of make-believe families has decreased, are homosexual relationships that develop during incarceration becoming the new trend? Additionally, research into the prevalence of more traditional prison gangs in female institutions should be conducted. With acts of female violence increasing, are relationships for women in prison trending toward prison gang structures or are make-believe family structures more common?

An area of research that has been neglected is learning how men adjust to and cope with prison life. If they do not create surrogate families in prison, then it is important to learn what they do instead? Are their mechanisms for coping effective, and, if not, then what can be done to assist them? If men are able to maintain ties with their real families, then it would be helpful to know how they manage to do so. In this way, maybe female prisons can implement the policies and programs that assist men in continuing their relationships with their families.

Women In Prison and Mother–Child Separation

Introduction

While it has been widely recognized that the United States has the highest incarceration rate in the world, women prisoners have not received as much attention from the media, the legislature, and the fields of psychology and criminology as have their male counterparts. Yet the recent trend toward retributive justice dramatically affects the incarceration rates of women. This is primarily because most women in prison are incarcerated as a result of nonviolent offenses (Luke, 2002; Watterson, 1996; Schen, 2005). The vast majority of female offenders commit drug-related crimes. While the increase in prison populations may create a sense of security in the community, there are numerous detrimental effects which result from incarcerating less serious offenders. Among the most important issues regarding incarcerated women is their status as mothers. Therefore, confinement serves to emotionally and physically separate mothers from children, which in turn creates a host of debilitating effects on both the women and their children. Additionally, the majority of women prisoners have a substance abuse problem for which they do not receive treatment while imprisoned (Boudin, 1998; Luke, 2002; Reichart, Adams, & Bostwick, 2010). The lack of services provided to women prisoners contributes greatly to their perpetual criminal behavior, and this is connected to their drug addiction.

Adolescents with parents who have been arrested are at much greater risk to be arrested two or more times during adolescence, particularly if the parent arrested was the mother (Eddy & Reid, 2001). Children of inmates are often-overlooked victims. Moreover, this group is not small. The U.S. Department of Justice (2008) reported that midyear through 2007, 809,800 prisoners out of the 1,518,535 total prisoners were parents of minor children. Approximately 744,200 of those prisoners with minor children are fathers and 65,600 are mothers. Minor children in the U.S. with parents in prison accounted for 2.3% of minors (U.S. Dept. of Justice, 2008). In 2008, the U.S. Department of Justice reported that 22% of children of state inmates and 16% of children of federal inmates were aged 4 years old or younger. According to the U.S. Department of Justice (1999) in 1998 approximately 950,000 women were involved with either federal, state, or local corrections, including those incarcerated in jails and prisons and out on parole. Brownell (1997) reported that at least 75% of female inmates have children, with the average of two children per prisoner. According to the U.S. Department of Justice (2008), the number of children with a mother in prison has increased 131% since 1991. African American children were reported to be seven and a half times more likely to have a parent in prison than Caucasian children, and Hispanic children were two and a half times more likely to have a parent in prison than Caucasian children (U.S. Dept. of Justice, 2008). Having a parent become incarcerated can be very traumatic and can lead to severe consequences for most children, including "anxiety, **hyperarousal** (muscular or emotional tension brought on by hormones being released during a fight-or-flight response), depression, bedwetting, eating and sleeping disorders, behavior and conduct disorders, attention disorders, and prolonged developmental regression" (Center for Children of Incarcerated Parents, as cited in Adalist-Estrin, 1994, p. 165). As examined in this section, the mother—child separation can have negative consequences for the mother as well.

When Annie was sent to prison for 1 to 3 years, she was 8-months pregnant. Upon giving birth in prison, her baby was taken away from her and sent to live with Annie's mother, who was interested in becoming a foster parent. Annie became depressed after being separated from her baby and upon realizing that she may lose custody. She is worried about the baby living with her mother because Annie reported being physically abused by this woman while growing up. Despite this, she feels there are no other alternatives: she cannot rely on the baby's father to help her because he beat and threatened her both before and during her pregnancy. Annie's depression has escalated to the point of her mentioning ways to commit suicide (Brownell, 1997).

Leslie is a first-time offender who is incarcerated. She has a 9-year-old son who was living with her prior to her incarceration. Her son now lives with his father from whom Leslie is separated. The father does not want their son to go to the jail but agreed to allow visitation. The son wants to visit his mother, yet he is afraid of the jail. Leslie is worried that her son will no longer respect her and that she may be causing psychological damage to him. Although she wants to see her son, she does not want him to see her in jail because she fears this will create more damage than has already been done (Hairston, 1991b).

Literature Review

Women comprise one of the fastest growing prison populations in the United States (U.S. Dept. of Justice, 2008; Reed & Reed, 1998; Haywood, Kravitz, Howard, *et al.*, 2000). In the 9-year period between 1986 and 1995, the number of incarcerated women in the United States increased by more than 250% (Beck & Gilliard, 1995). In 2001, women were 6.6% of the State prison inmates, up from 6% in 1995 (U.S. Department of Justice, 2003). In 2006, there were 112,498 women incarcerated, which was a 33% increase from 1998 (Reichart, Adams, & Bostwick, 2010). The criminal justice system is much more likely to sentence a woman to prison now than ever before (Watterson, 1996b). According to the U.S. Department of Justice (2003) the prevalence of imprisonment in 2001 was higher for black females (1.7%) and Hispanic females (0.7%) than for white females (0.3%). Further, women are receiving much longer prison sentences at both the state and the federal levels (Watterson, 1996). However, this is not to suggest that women are becoming more violent or committing more crimes than they were previously; rather, the criminal justice system has broadened the scope of criminal behavior for which it deems incarceration a necessary remedy. Due largely to the "War on Drugs," California prisons actually showed a decrease in their percentage of violent offenders from 1985 to 1991, while their percentage of substance abuse offenders doubled (California Department of Corrections, 1991). The majority of women prisoners are incarcerated as a result of drug-related crimes. Women of color are disproportionately represented within groups of women incarcerated for both possession and trafficking drugs (Loper, 2002). Davis (2000, p. 151) maintains that "women in prison are among the most wronged victims in the war on drugs." Thus, it is clear why this population has been particularly affected by the new laws, which require stiffer sentences for drug offenses.

Given the recent influx of women prisoners nationwide, it is important to look at the overall impact that such a movement has on society. First, there are numerous psychological considerations that pertain to incarcerated women that do not pertain to incarcerated men. Boudin (1998) identifies central issues that women prisoners encounter during their period of confinement. Since the vast majority of women inmates are mothers, the issue of parenting permeates throughout all of these core concerns. Boudin claims that a woman's personal traumatic experiences that occurred prior to incarceration have dramatic effects on her life choices before, during, and after confinement. The U.S. Department of Justice (1994) reports that over 40% of incarcerated women report a history of physical or sexual abuse. The U.S. Department of Justice (2003) reports that 48% of jailed women indicated that they had been physically or sexually abused prior to admission with 27% having been raped. Fletcher, Rolison, and Moon (1993) report that the typical female prisoner was sexually abused in childhood by a male member of her immediate family. While Boudin (1998) agrees that there is a high prevalence of physical, sexual, and emotional abuse in the lives of women prisoners, she reports that there are very few opportunities for women to receive help in resolving such matters during the time they are incarcerated. Greene, Haney, and Hurtado (2000) describe how mothers who are frequently incarcerated for nonviolent, drug-related offenses experienced poverty, physical and sexual abuse, and drug addition, and the cycle is often repeated by their children.

Many incarcerated mothers report that the worst part of being incarcerated is having to be separated from their children (Church, 1990; Hairston, 1991b; Luke, 2002). As the case illustrations show, there are many issues involved when dealing with children of incarcerated parents. Indeed, children are not the only ones who can experience the negative consequences of being separated. In Leslie's instance, the incarcerated mother may feel embarrassed and guilty about being in jail and having to subject her children to such an environment. These mothers may not even want their children to visit them in jail or prison (Hairston, 1991b). Even if they want to see their children, other factors may prevent them from attending visiting days. Often women's prisons are in places far away from children's homes and in areas difficult to reach by public transportation, making it difficult for traveling (Church, 1990; Kiser, 1991). Many incarcerated mothers experience intense guilt, loss, and sadness and fear for the loss of custody of their children (Luke, 2002).

Luke (2002) discusses the shift in focus of the U.S. child welfare policy with the implementation of the **Adoption and Safe Families Act of 1997** to shorten time periods before the termination of parental rights is sought. She indicates that while the intent of these new laws and policies are to better protect children from abusive or neglectful homes, it does not take into consideration the circumstances of the many mothers who are incarcerated for crimes unrelated to their parenting and often as a result of harsh penalties for low-level drug offenses. A recent study found that many women engaged in economic crimes such as drug dealing as a solution to hunger or homelessness (Ferraro & Moe, 2003).

Similar to Annie's case, sometimes the children are placed with foster families during the mother's incarceration, and the foster parents may not want the child to visit the mother because of their own desires to adopt the child (Osborne, 1995). Sometimes even the mother's own relatives do not want the children to visit her in prison (Kiser, 1991). A survey conducted by Hairston (1991b) found that 71% of incarcerated mothers had not had any visitation with their children during their period of confinement.

Watterson (1996b) reports that 75% of the jails in 1994 did not allow contact visits between prisoners and their children. When such visits are allowed, it is often a traumatic experience for everyone involved. Children have a difficult time with the intimidating environment of a prison. They often do not understand why they have limited or no contact with their mothers, and they have difficulty saying goodbye to their mothers once the visit is over. For the mother, once a contact visit is granted, she knows that in order to be with her child she may be subject to the humiliation of a strip-search immediately after the visit.

> [T]he reality is that she knows before she begins that after seeing her children and family and perhaps feeling very good about herself, she will have to take off all her clothing and stand naked in front of the guards, who will check under her arms and breasts for contraband. She'll have to open her mouth and let them look under her tongue and in her cheeks. Then she has to squat, pull apart her buttocks and cough, so the guard in charge can check her vagina and anus for any hidden objects (Watterson, 1996, p. 214).

For this reason, contact visits can simultaneously be a rewarding and positive experience as well as a humiliating and punishing one. Acknowledging the importance of interaction between mothers and children, programs were developed in the 1980s to support such contact. However, in the 1990s such programs were largely discontinued due to a loss of state and federal funding (Watterson, 1996). The Women's Prison Association (2008) found that prison nursery programs either already exist or will soon be implemented in California, Illinois, Indiana, Ohio, Nebraska, New York, South Dakota, Washington, and West Virginia.

In 2007 an innovative prison-based program, the Moms and Babies program, was developed by the Illinois Department of Corrections. This program allows qualified pregnant inmates to keep their infants with them at the Decatur Correctional Center. Mothers scheduled for release within 24 months of their delivery date are eligible to be screened for the program. The selected mother and her infant will have their own room in the correctional facility, specially designed to accommodate the needs of mother and child. The program also contains an Infant Development Center where infants are cared for while their mothers attend programming classes and perform job assignments within the prison. The program is designed to support the incarcerated mother in developing a bond with her infant. The program is one of the first of its kind and is designed to not only foster healthy relationships between mother and child, but also to reduce the potential criminal behavior patterns for the children, as research has demonstrated that children reared with a parent in prison are more likely to engage in criminal behavior as adults. The program has been described as a "holistic approach for the female offender and her newborn and the opportunity for the offender to increase her personal and paternal growth and development," and is "designed to emulate the dynamics consistent with an indigent, single, expecting mother in the community while ensuring proper protocol is followed for a correctional environment" (Illinois Department of Corrections, 2008).

When children lose their mother to incarceration, there are many negative consequences. Luke (2002, p. 933) indicated:

> *Behavioral and emotional problems, school problems, fear, anxiety, anger, sadness, and guilt are within the normal range of experiences for children of incarcerated parents, as are abuse of chemicals at a young age, early sexual activity, teen pregnancy, truancy, and juvenile delinquency.*

The California Research Bureau (2000) found that:

> *Children whose parents have been arrested and incarcerated face unique difficulties. Many have experienced the trauma of sudden separation from their sole caregiver, and most are vulnerable to feelings of fear, anxiety, anger, sadness, depression and guilt. They may be moved from caretaker to caretaker. The behavioral consequences can be severe, absent positive intervention — emotional withdrawal, failure in school, delinquency and risk of intergenerational incarceration. Yet these children seem to fall through the cracks.*

Kiser (1991) found that children felt they were to blame for their mother's offense and became very depressed. They continued to experience these negative emotions years after the mother's incarceration and some even attempted suicide. Falk (1995) noted that children feel powerless when they have to sit by and watch their mothers go to jail. While the separation is now unavoidable, the attachment between the mother and child is critical as a protective factor for the child's future development. The author stated that these children experience grief emotions such as anger, denial, and depression. They may withdraw from others, or they may begin to act out and become aggressive. Research suggests that children experience emotions such as insecurity, lack of trust, confusion, and loneliness (White, Galietta, & Escobar, 2006; Feinman, 1994). White *et al.*'s (2006) study found that one-third of mothers reported that their children were having behavioral problems. These emotions can show themselves in mental and physical illnesses and a drop in school grades. Additionally, children with parents who are incarcerated are up to six times more likely to be incarcerated during their lifetime, as compared to peers without a family history of incarceration (Luke, 2002; Myers, Smarsh, Amlund-Hagen, & Kennon, 1999).

If a child loses his or her mother to incarceration, then who takes care of the child? White *et al.* (2006) found that 39% of children with incarcerated mothers were in the physical custody of their father and 31% of children were in the custody of their maternal grandmother. These children often live with relatives, often grandparents, or friends of the mother. If these are not possibilities, then state-financed foster families care for them (Falk, 1995; Osborne, 1995). Occasionally, siblings have to be separated and live in different homes (Falk, 1995), thus increasing the loss they experience. Feinman (1994) reported that some states have laws which allow the state to determine whether an incarcerated mother is unfit and to take away her children via a foster home or adoption. Once again, this creates additional loss for the child.

According to a fact sheet provided by the Chicago Legal Aid to Incarcerated Mothers (1997), nearly 90% of male prisoners report that while they are incarcerated, their children are being cared for by the children's mothers, whereas only 25% of similarly confined women report that their children are being cared for by their fathers. The result is that thousands of children end up in "the system." At times, relatives will care for the children of incarcerated mothers; however, all too often the children are placed in foster homes, separated from their siblings, and denied visitation with their mothers. Fifty-four percent of the mothers in a study conducted by Bloom and Steinhart (1993) reported that their children had never visited them while they were in prison. Participants in this study attributed the distance between their place of residence and their mother's place of incarceration as a primary reason for the lack of visitations. Thus it becomes obvious how the incarceration of mothers has a great impact on society overall, not solely on the lives of the women in prison.

There are several solutions that could be implemented so that the child will not have to go through the trauma of enduring the incarceration of one's mother. The implementation and funding of programs is an important preventive measure to reduce the number of emotionally damaged children with an increased risk of future substance abuse, criminality, and incarceration. Perhaps the most comprehensive solution is one that permits children to live with their mothers while in prison for a certain length of time (Feinman, 1994; Jaffe, Pons, & Wicky, 1997). Jaffe *et al.* (1997) report that the negative impact of this solution is that a child will have to experience the prison environment. Others opposed to this solution feel that prison is not a place for raising children and that these youths would learn to become criminals by associating with their offending mothers (Feinman, 1994). Jaffe *et al.* (1997) suggest the positive impact of this solution is that it emphasizes the mother–child bond and the important part it plays in a developing child. Being with one's mother is critical for a developing child and having her taken away during the early years could create some very negative consequences.

Some correctional institutions have implemented programs to allow children to remain with their incarcerated mothers. In the city of New York, the Legal Aid Society brought a lawsuit against the Department of Corrections based on the notion that separating a mother and newborn child is an action of cruel and unusual punishment under the Eighth Amendment. Apparently, there was a New York State law which allowed infants to remain in state prisons until the age of 1 year, so the Legal Aid Society wanted that law applied to the city jail. The court agreed with this argument, and, since 1985, incarcerated mothers have been allowed to have their newborn children remain with them in a special area of the jail designed for such a purpose (Women's Prison Association, 2008; Feinman, 1994). The Bedford Hills Correctional Facility in New York has been a model prison for such programs as it was the first women's prison to implement a nursery for mothers and their infants (Brownell, 1997; Women's Prison Association, 2008). Positive results have been reported in relation to these nursery programs. They decrease tensions and increase obedience and morale among female inmates, as well as positively affecting staff.

A similar program in Nebraska was implemented in order to decrease the effects of separation between a mother and her child due to incarceration. Children younger than 18 months old can remain at the correctional facility with their mothers in a nursery equipped for six infants. Children between the ages of one year old to six years old are allowed to spend up to five nights a month at the prison with their mother (Dahm, Nebraska Correctional Center for Women, 2005). The mothers must take prenatal courses, and other inmates can become involved by babysitting or providing support for the mothers (Hromadka, 1995).

Most programs that allow children to live with their mothers in prison have been developed for only very young children. Illinois Department of Corrections' (2007) Moms and Babies program is one such program; however, to be eligible for this program the offender has to have a projected release date before the child is 24 months old. There have been attempts to create other options for older children through visitation programs. Having children visit their mothers is viewed as an important ingredient to maintaining attachment bonds (Adalist-Estrin, 1994). Despite this, there are still few initiatives which provide visitation for children on a consistent basis (Moses, 1995). However, some alternatives that have been developed include expanded visitations, longer visitation hours, and overnight to week-long visits (Adalist-Estrin, 1994).

The Minnesota Correctional Facility at Shakopee is credited with having the most extensive and well-developed parenting programs of this kind in the country (Luke, 2002; Alley, 1998). Incarcerated mothers are offered a number of specialized parenting classes and two extended visitation programs (Luke, 2002). The two extended visitation programs include: the Children's Program, for children up to 11, and the Parenting Teens Program, for inmates with children ages 12 through 17 years old (Luke, 2002). "The philosophy of the parenting programs at the MCF Shakopee, the state's only prison for adult women, is that the family unit is important and should be maintained and enhanced, whenever possible, for the sake of both parents and children. The MCF-Shakopee has various parenting programs to support this philosophy" (Minnesota Department of Corrections, 2010). These programs are designed to increase cohesiveness between parent and child; enhance parenting skills in a safe environment, and to provide the inmate an opportunity to assess their capabilities and desire to parent their children. Once again, these types of programs also compel good behavior by inmates who desire to see their children. The Children's Program consists of extended, well-structured, overnight weekend visits with one and sometimes two of their children, depending on space. The Parenting Teens Program consists of monthly "teen days" or visits from teenage children contingent upon the inmate participating in weekly support group meetings for parents of teens. In addition to parenting skills, these groups also serve to provide a support network for mothers who are suffering as a result of being separated from their children. The teens and their mothers often play in the gym, work on crafts, watch a movie, or just spend time talking alone during the scheduled "teen day" visits (Luke, 2002).

Forensic Psychology and Policy Implications

The number of women incarcerated in the United States is increasing with every new law that requires stiffer sentences for minor offenses. Although the vast majority of women prisoners are incarcerated as a result of drug-related crimes, few programs exist inside the prisons to provide the treatment that such women need to assist them in recovering from their addictions. Research has repeatedly shown that incarceration alone does not alter the subsequent criminal behavior of drug-abusing offenders (Moon, Thompson, & Bennett, 1993; National Institute of Corrections, 1991). Policy reforms are drastically needed, given that most women prisoners are substance abusers, most prisons do not offer substance abuse treatment, and incarceration without a treatment component does not curb recidivism for offenders who abuse drugs or alcohol. Programs or psychotherapy groups designed to address their histories of abuse are also scarce or nonexistent.

Although efforts have been made to improve programs for children and their incarcerated mothers, there are still many issues that remain unresolved. For instance, as Falk (1995) pointed out, because of their restrictions, many of these projects exclude one or more children of the same family from visiting their mother. This could create a new set of problems for the family. It may be unreasonable for all of a woman's children to live with her in the prison, but programs should be developed where all the children in one family can visit their mother for extended periods of time.

Since incarcerated women have suggested that being separated from their children is the most difficult aspect of their confinement, support services designed specifically to assist them in adjusting to this separation should be developed further (Luke, 2002; Hairston, 1991b). Annie would have benefited greatly from assistance on how to cope with being separated from her child. As women are more likely than men to return to a primary caregiver role for their children upon their release from prison, and children's stability appears to be more adversely affected by the incarceration of a mother than that of a father, reentry programs for females must address mothering and reunification issues (Moses, 2006). In a 2006 study, Grella & Greenwell found that incarcerated mothers with higher self-efficacy, decision-making ability, social conformity, and childhood problems exhibited less risky attitudes towards parenting, while mothers with depression, fewer years of education, and those of non-White ethnicity exhibited more risky parenting attitudes. Based on these findings, the authors recommend that reentry programs focus on these psychological needs of women to encourage successful resumption of their parenting roles.

Correctional/forensic psychologists can also be instrumental in developing programs, which support contact between imprisoned mothers and their children. Programs are being developed and sustained in some states that support mothers having their children live with them. Research on the benefits of these programs for the mothers, children, and community may help support the continued development of these programs in other states. What is the effect of these programs on the recidivism rates of the mother? With the expertise of both criminological and psychological approaches to the issues at hand, psychologists have valuable services to offer in this area.

Psychologists can also work with correctional staff and facilities on how best to implement and run programs where children would live within the prison or come for overnight visitation. Not all staff will be knowledgeable about how to provide a positive environment for children, so child development specialists should be involved in the programming. Also, the correctional facilities need to develop visitation areas which promote family bonding (Hairston, 1991b) and help children overcome their fears of going to the prison for visitation. As Leslie's case shows, children are afraid of jails and prisons and may not want to see their mothers for this reason. Psychologists could also facilitate psychotherapy groups for women in need of support, as a result of their separation from their children.

Once programs and services have been developed within the correctional institution, then policies should be developed to assist these same women when released from prison. Continuing programs once the women are released could have tremendous benefits; yet, this rarely occurs. As in Annie's situation, these mothers may be struggling with someone who is seeking to terminate their parental rights, and they may need assistance with this process. Correctional facilities could have social workers on staff whose role it is to help these women transition back into their families. Luke (2002) strongly recommends that changes in current child welfare policy be made in order to reflect the unique needs of children of incarcerated parents.

Considering the costs of mother–child programming is a reality, particularly during these economic times; however, over the long run, and when combined with other community efforts, it could make a difference in decreasing the prevalence of adolescent delinquency and adult criminal behavior (Eddy & Reid, 2001). It could also decrease the costs related to incarceration. Children of incarcerated parents are currently faced with a myriad of emotional, social, financial, and other problems that are inadequately addressed by limited or inadequate programming and support.

One area that has been neglected is the development of more comprehensive programs for fathers who become incarcerated. In some situations, the father may have been the sole caretaker, and, therefore, his children would experience the same sense of grief over the loss of the parent. Even if the children have a mother at home, they still have a connection with their father and should be able to visit him in order to maintain that connection. Male correctional facilities could assist with this by also improving their visitation areas and allowing for extended visits by the children. If the father is the sole caretaker of a young child, then policies for developing live-in programs at male prisons also should be developed.

Suggestions for Future Research

Compared to the literature on male prisoners, the research on women confined is relatively scarce. Female prisoners have only recently received concentrated attention as a separate cohort from their male counterparts. While the existing research strongly supports contact between women prisoners and their children, studies are needed that compare those women who do receive such visits with those who do not in terms of their psychological well-being, their behavioral conduct within the prison, and their future criminal behavior. One of the primary goals of the criminal justice system is the reduction of future criminal behavior. Therefore, recidivism studies need to be conducted that compare women who receive substance abuse treatment and other forms of treatment; for example, psychotherapy/group therapy that addresses trauma history while incarcerated with those who do not. Further research into recidivism rates of mothers in programs that allowed children to live with them while incarcerated or had overnight visits would be valuable in helping to inform other states about the utility of initiating mother–child programs. For many reasons, alternative sentencing programs need to be examined for women who have committed nonviolent offenses. If such programs are found to be equally effective at reducing recidivism among women offenders as are correctional placements, then their implementation would be economically and psychologically sensible.

Limited information is available about the children of incarcerated patients. Studies are needed to gather information about the development of these children across the lifespan (Eddy & Reid, 2001). According to Eddy and Reid (2001) critical questions such as the difference between the characteristics of families who succeed despite incarceration versus the characteristics of those who struggle need to be asked and answered. Information gleaned from this type of research can help guide the design and implementation of programming that will be the most beneficial to parent and child.

Another area of research is to determine which situations are beneficial and which are detrimental for children who continue contact with their incarcerated parents. In some instances, seeking termination of parental rights may be in the best interest of the child, but a better understanding of what those instances are should be explored. Similarly, the effects on children of visiting or not visiting their incarcerated parent, as well as what factors make the visitation more successful in the short and long term should be studied further. Additional research should be conducted regarding the possible effects on children who live with their mothers in correctional institutions. More information is needed, particularly regarding whether this is beneficial or detrimental to youths. Currently some programs allow children of one year to six years old to spend the night with their incarcerated mothers. What effect does this limited contact with their mother have on the child? Is there any difference on the impact to the child depending upon the age or developmental stage of that child?

Finally, research should examine what the effects are on children who have a father who becomes incarcerated, even if that father is not the sole provider. Do these children experience the same sense of loss as losing a mother? Are the bonds as strong with a father as they are with a mother? The father plays an important role in his children's lives, and more information needs to be learned about what kind of an effect his absence creates.

Community Reentry Programs and Family Reunification

Introduction

Currently, the challenges facing our criminal justice system that have contributed to an upsurge in the number of inmates being released from correctional facilities each year include increasing correctional population, reduced funding for prison programs and community social services, and weakening of the traditional support structures within communities and neighborhoods (Seiter & Kadela, 2003). Many of these individuals discharge under the purview of a **community supervision program**. In 2008, for example, almost 5.1 million adults, nearly one in every 45 Americans, were under community supervision (Glaze & Bonzcar, 2009). This has created an increased demand for research regarding components of effective programs, as well as delineating the needs of special populations within the correctional system (e.g., women, sexual offenders, parents, individuals with mental illness, substance abusers). As research efforts have increased, so have the number of inmates successfully completing probation and parole programs. In 2006, 58% of inmates successfully completed their probationary terms; this increased to 63% by 2008 (Glaze & Bonzcar, 2009). For parolees, the completion rate has increased from 46% in 2007 to 49% in 2008 (Glaze & Bozcar, 2009). Though a significant portion of probationers and parolees still fail to successfully complete their terms, these figures suggest that community supervision programs are a critical component of an offender's successful reentry into their communities, and ongoing research is necessary to ensure that these figures continue to rise.

The challenges faced by inmates upon release, as well as the positive impact of a **community reentry program** (i.e., programs designed to assist adults and juveniles in transitioning from correctional facilities back to their communities; these programs may include components such as probation or parole, or mental health treatment), is illustrated in the following statement, produced by an inmate who completed the Mentally Ill Offender Community Transition Program in the state of Washington:

> "When I was incarcerated at the Washington Correctional Center for Women I had no idea what I was going to do for my future, in fact to me it was hopeless.
>
> I was incarcerated for a very serious crime. To make this situation more complicated I was facing some very serious mental health problems and medical problems. I had no idea how I was going to pay my rent, pay my bills or even feed myself. I felt that no company would hire me, and that I was going to wind up homeless or living with my dysfunctional family. I also had no way to pay for the medical services that I have acquired since my release from prison. The prison had said that the medical problems didn't exist, but after seeing specialists there were even more problems than anticipated. The 6002 Program assisted me with medication management and medications, one on one therapy, a case manager, and group therapy. My case manager assisted me with getting on GAU services with DSHS, and eventually Social Security. They have paid most of my rent. I am responsible for paying 30% of my benefits towards my rent, the rest of it is provided by the program. I am also encouraged to look at my future and to move towards it. My case manager helps me with filling out the complicated forms for these programs and to check on how I am adjusting to the community. She has helped make sure that I am not alone isolating in my room. Instead she encourages me to reintegrate into society. She also keeps a close eye on how I am emotionally handling this reintegration. She helps me do a monthly budget to make sure I don't overspend my benefits. One of the most important tasks that my case manager does is a home visit at least twice a month. This makes me feel like she really cares how my home life is going.
>
> Since my release I am working a part time job, in stable housing, having my medical issues addressed, and soon to be seeking more permanent housing. Even though some of this had come from me, without the assistance from the program, I feel I would have never come this far. Thank you for your time" (Washington State Department of Social & Health Services, 2002, p. A-14).

Literature Review

Reentry programs must be designed in light of the special needs of offenders, as well as the unique sociological and psychological effects of incarceration. For example, 24% of inmates report recent mental health problems, a percentage which far exceeds that found in the general population, and as many of 87% of inmates with severe mental disorders also have co-occurring substance use disorders (Bureau of Justice Statistics, 2006). Inmates may also exhibit restlessness, agitation, concentration and memory impairment, irritability, anger, frustration, intolerance, **apathy** (i.e., a state of indifference, or the suppression of emotions such as concern, excitement, motivation and passion), social withdrawal, **dysphoria** (i.e., an emotional state characterized by anxiety, depression, or unease), mood and **affective lability** (i.e., rapid shifts in outward emotional expression), generalized anxiety and panic attacks, and irrational suspicion or **paranoia** (i.e., a thought process heavily influenced by anxiety or fear, which often includes delusions that others are attempting to harm a person) as the result of prolonged incarceration (Beven, 2005). The effect or symptoms associated with prolonged incarceration may cause offenders with existing mental illness to deteriorate or represent the development of mental illness in those without a previous diagnosis. Thus, it is recommended that community reentry programs include transitional services that may provide "a single point of contact to help with crisis management, appointments with mental health providers, liaison and advocacy with service providers, courts, and community supervision; and to provide monitoring and surveillance for early warning signs of relapse and criminal behavior" (Peters & Bekman, 2007, p. 7). Indeed, offenders themselves identify "restarting and readjustment problems" as the most difficult challenges they face when attempting to return to their communities, followed by material problems (e.g., housing, transportation) and family problems (Sandhu, Dodder, & Davis, 1990). Thus, reentry programs face unique challenges, and must address a diverse array of problems, typically requiring professionals from multiple disciplines and areas of expertise. Additionally, problems with community reentry have been shown to contribute to larger social problems, including health inequities in low-income communities (Freudenberg, Daniels, Crum, Perkins, & Richie, 2005), further demonstrating the importance of effective programming, and the widespread consequences when programs are underfunded, poorly designed, or improperly implemented.

Researchers have provided several general suggestions for those working with offenders who are either preparing for release or in the early stages of release/community supervision. It has been suggested that **discharge planning** (i.e., the process of preparing an inmate for release, which may begin as early as six months prior to release, and involves securing housing, medical care, mental health services, and other community-based services for the discharging inmate) should begin as soon as an offender enters the correctional system, though this is often at odds with traditional correctional models that often indicate that "the duty to provide care should end at the back door and to the prison as it begins at the front door" (Cohen & Gerbasi, 2005, p. 277). Fortunately, a gradual shift in this paradigm has recently begun, which has extended the duty of institutions to provide care and the rights of offenders to receive care beyond the time a person is physically incarcerated (Cohen & Gerbasi, 2005). This movement has come in the wake of cases that have demonstrated a facility's legal obligation to provide discharging offenders with sufficient medication to sustain their supply for a reasonable period or until the offender can connect with services and ensure continued care (*Wakefield v. Thompson*, 1999). Although neither community treatment plans nor housing or access to health care were specifically mandated by *Wakefield*, the decision did represent a "very small step from the back door [of correctional institutions] into the community, [and] legal developments often surge after such a small step" (Cohen & Gerbasi, 2005, pp. 277–278). In 2005, just such a surge occurred with the case of *Brad H. v City of New York*. Although the decision was based in New York State law and is not binding in other jurisdictions, it did allow increased access to medications, **Medicaid** (i.e., a government program which provides health care services, including mental health services, to low income families), community services, public benefits, housing, and transportation. In 2000, *Lugo v. Senkowsky* expanded on the decision in *Wakefield*, and held that inmates who underwent surgery while in correctional custody were entitled to follow up care related to that procedure even after release from prison. Although not directly related to community supervision and reentry, the case set an important precedent regarding the "continuing obligation" of correctional facilities to provide care to inmates after their discharge (Cohen & Gerbasi, p. 278). Such rulings both reflect and contribute to a growing emphasis on community-based and reentry-focused offender rehabilitation.

A diverse array of programs and services fall under the umbrella of prisoner reentry; some authors even suggest that every correctional facility could be considered a reentry program, as reentry efforts should and often do, beginning with the booking process (Seiter & Kadela, 2003). However, these authors developed a more specific, two-part definition of community reentry programs. Such programs include any correctional programs "that focus on the transition from prison to community [prerelease, work release, halfway houses, or specific reentry programs]" and those which have "initiated treatment [substance abuse, life skills, education, cognitive/behavioral, sex/violent offender] in a prison setting and have linked with a community program to provide continuity of care" (Seiter & Kadela, 2003, p. 368). These programs have in common the goals of enhancing success of offenders' reentry into society (Illinois Department of Corrections, 2008), preserving limited financial resources (Parker, 2006), and assisting offenders into a transition to productive and crime-free lives.

History of reentry programs

The history of reentry programs can be traced to the mid-1900s, when states implemented the use of parole boards to monitor and approve the release of all prisoners (Clear & Cole, 1977). As the number of parolees steadily increased into the 1970s, prisons began creating formal programs to prepare inmates for return to their communities (Seiter & Kadela, 2003). Such programs consisted of educational and vocational programs, substance abuse and other counseling services, therapeutic communities, residential programs, and prison industry work programs, and placed a clear and consistent emphasis on rehabilitation and reintegration (Seiter & Kadela, 2003). In the early 1980s, a "tough-on-crime" attitude, as well as the widespread belief that reentry efforts were ineffective, contributed to a shift from a rehabilitative focus to one of punishment, deterrence, and incapacitation (Seiter & Kadela, 2003). Such a shift corresponded with changes in sentencing and supervision policies, including a tendency towards "zero tolerance" policies and a preference for determinate sentencing in many jurisdictions (Seiter & Kadela, 2003). Despite the current political atmosphere, due to the increasing number of incarcerated offenders, as well as funding and housing challenges, the number of offenders enrolled in community reentry programs is currently on the rise (Glaze *et al.*, 2009). Subsequent to this increase, increasing efforts have been made to develop structured programs, some of which target specific types of offenders or problems. Some of these programs are described below.

Specific types of reentry program

Reentry programs can be broadly categorized as being either prison-based, jail-based, or community-based (Peters & Beckman, 2007). Because of the accessibility of inmates, **prison-based programs** (i.e., community reentry programs which prepare the inmate for discharge while they are incarcerated in a prison) are typically characterized by a comprehensive approach, a focus on engagement, motivation, and readiness for treatment, ongoing assessment which allows for tailoring of treatment, and an emphasis on the continuity of care (Peters & Beckman, 2007). These programs are typically highly structured, allow for much repetition and overlap of information, and assist inmates in the identification of community resources that will extend and complement the program after the inmate's release (Peters & Beckman, 2007). With regard to specific techniques utilized, prison-based programs typically use supportive feedback rather than confrontation, address medication and symptom management, include substance abuse treatment (e.g., 12-step programs), address criminal thinking patterns, utilize study groups, peer mentors, and peer support groups, and provide frequent reinforcement for positive behaviors (Peters & Beckman, 2007).

Jail-based reentry programs (i.e., community reentry programs which prepare the inmate for discharge while they are incarcerated in a jail) differ in significant ways from prison-based programs, primarily due to the relative brevity of incarceration in jails (Peters & Beckman, 2007). In contrast to prison-based programs, jail-based programs emphasize immediate and basic needs, focus on the integrated delivery of both substance abuse and mental health services, include preparation for release throughout an inmate's stay, and involve direct and more frequent collaboration with community agencies to enhance continuity of care (Peters & Beckman, 2007). These goals are accomplished via identification and screening processes, acute stabilization efforts, comprehensive medical and psychological assessment, integration of mental health and substance abuse treatment, and an emphasis on accessing and restoring an inmate's benefits (e.g., SSI, SSDI).

Many reentry programs focus on offenders with mental illness. One such program, the Reasoning and Rehabilitation (R&R) Programme, developed in London, is based on two principles: (1) offenders are under-socialized and lack the values, attitudes, reasoning, and social skills required for pro-social adjustment; and (2) such skills can be taught (Clarke, Cullen, Walwyn, & Fahy, 2010). The program consists of 36 two-hour sessions designed to provide inmates with an increased repertoire of skills and behaviors as alternatives to criminal behavior, and is a cognitive skill intervention similar to others that have been shown to reduce recidivism in offenders (McGuire, 2000). The R&R program has previously been shown to result in a 14% reduction in recidivism in nondisordered offenders (Tong & Farrington,

2006), and has since been shown to increase problem-solving and coping abilities in psychotic male offenders (Clarke, Cullen, Walwyn, & Fahy, 2010). Thus, the program successfully provides mentally disordered inmates with skills they can utilize following their release. Such efforts appear to be connected to a reduction in criminal activity as well as increased adaptation to community life.

The Mentally Ill Offender Community Transition Program (MIOCTP) was developed and implemented in Washington State with the goals of reducing incarceration costs, increasing public safety, and improving the offender's chance of succeeding in the community (Washington State Department of Social & Health Services, 2002). The program consists of a variety of components, including individual and group mental health and substance abuse treatment, drop-in and day treatment, special evaluations and consultations, medication prescription and monitoring, specialized sex-offender treatment, case management, and supervised housing. The inmates participating in the program are primarily diagnosed with psychosis, depression, bipolar disorder, or substance use disorder. Results of a pilot study examining the effectiveness of the program indicated that participants had reduced rates of corrections violations, felony recidivism, and substance abuse relapse. These data suggest the effectiveness of this program in preparing offenders with mental illness for successful transition to the community (Washington State Department of Social & Health Services, 2002).

The Illinois Department of Corrections has been recognized for its efforts in developing focused and successful prison-based reentry programs (Illinois Department of Corrections, 2008). Two such programs, the Sheridan National Model Drug Prison and Reentry Program and the National Model Meth Prison and Reentry Program, provide inmates with intensive drug treatment, vocational training, job preparation, and mental health services prior to the end of the incarceration. Such treatment then continues after release with intense supervision of offenders as they return to their communities (Illinois Department of Corrections, 2008). In addition to these programs, the Department's Incarcerated Veterans Transition Program supports reentry by identifying the unique needs and strengths of veteran offenders. This program functions in conjunction with community resources, including the Illinois Department of Veterans Affairs, the Illinois Department of Employment Security and the Federal Department of Labor, and reentry preparation typically begins approximately 18 months prior to an inmate's release via educational modules, employment workshops and counseling, and linkage to other benefits and programs available to veterans (Illinois Department of Corrections, 2008).

The Department has also developed and hosted Reentry Summits statewide at its correctional facilities. This initiative promotes relationships between incarcerated offenders, community service providers, policy experts and government agencies. Offenders are educated on topics including finance and economics, religions, spirituality, mental health, physical well-being, employment, housing, and education, and resource fairs introduce offenders to agencies which can help connect them with resources after their release. Department officials also explain the requirements and expectations of parolees, to increase the likelihood of successful completion (Illinois Department of Corrections, 2008). Perhaps the most innovative prison-based program, the Moms and Babies program, was started in 2007. This program allows qualified pregnant inmates to keep their infants with them at the Decatur Correctional Center in Illinois. This program is detailed in the "Women in Prison and Mother–Child Separation" subsection of this chapter.

The department's Operation Spotlight Parole Reform Program is a community-based program that expanded the state's parole program in an effort to increase public safety, and serves the needs of parolees in the time following their release from prison. The program provides enhanced supervision for inmates post-release via increased monitoring and graduated sanctions. As of 2008, more than 35,000 inmates were enrolled in the program, and eight supervision centers had been opened in high-impact regions. Each center serves an estimated 8000 parolees annually, with the goal of reducing their risk to communities and providing case management services to assist them in successfully transitioning back to society (Illinois Department of Corrections, 2008).

The comprehensive and diverse reentry efforts by Illinois' Department of Corrections have yielded promising results. For example, following the implementation of these programs, Illinois has boasted "the lowest conviction rates for parolees in state history" (Illinois Department of Corrections, 2008, p. 31), as well as a 23% decline in total arrests among parolees. Additionally, participants in the Department's program have a 40% lower recidivism rate than comparison groups, and the Department of Corrections has experienced its slowest rate of prison population growth since its establishment in 1970, resulting in an estimated savings to taxpayers of $64 million since 2004 (Illinois Department of Corrections, 2008). The programs have also improved the rate of aftercare admission and completion and enhanced community-based partnerships with the Department (Olson, Rozhon, & Powers, 2009). Although they are initially more expensive to implement, outcomes such as these reflect the long-term savings and increases in public safety which can be accomplished via intensive reentry planning and support.

Although the implications of unsuccessful reintegration are perhaps the most serious for serious and violent offenders, few programs focus specifically on the needs of these offenders. One such program is the Serious and Violent Offender Reentry Initiative (SVORI), a nationwide effort supported by the federal government (Bouffard & Bergeron, 2007). The programming consists of a compilation of components which individually are known to be effective in working with violent offenders (e.g., matching services to inmate needs, combining community supervision and rehabilitative services). Results from Bouffard and Bergeron's 2007 investigation indicate that the program resulted in a 60%

lower likelihood of re-arrest for participants, although probation revocation rates were similar to those of a comparison group who did not participate in SVORI programming. Thus, though the program appears promising, there are mixed results with regard to its effectiveness.

As the number of women in correctional facilities has increased and the differing needs of female versus male offenders have been elucidated, programs have been designed specifically to address the unique reentry and reunification needs of female inmates. Female inmates preparing to transition from correctional facilities may need additional resources relative to their male counterparts. Such resources may include violence prevention efforts, treatment for post-traumatic stress disorder, educational services, child advocacy, and family reunification (Richie, 2001). One program designed to address these unique needs is Health Link that is utilized with drug-using jailed women in New York City to reduce drug use, HIV risk behavior, and re-arrest rates. The program consists of four levels of care: direct services (i.e., case management while in the jail and for one year following release), technical assistance, training, and financial support for community providers serving ex-offenders, staff support to facilitate the coordination of services and to advocate for resources, and policy analysis and advocacy to identify and reduce barriers to successful reintegration (Richie, 2001).

Reentry programs for juveniles have also been the focus of recent research and development efforts, though to a lesser degree than programs designed for adult offenders. One of the first programs, designed for juveniles, ages 11 to 28 years, Project ADAPT, is based on a social developmental model, and integrates knowledge of risk factors for adolescent drug use and crime. This approach combines behavioral skills training, supportive network development, and involvement in pro-social activities to facilitate successful reintegration, particularly with regard to abstinence from illicit substances (Haggerty, Wells, Jenson, & Catalano, 1989). In Alaska, juveniles nearing release are transferred to the McLaughlin Youth Center's Transitional Services Unit, which houses a team of facility staff, probation officers and on-site community partners who provide reintegration and aftercare services to youth. The Unit partners with local resources, including the Boys & Girls Clubs, Big Brothers Big Sisters, Alaska Children's Services, and the Alaska Native Justice Center. The reentry program represents one of the first designed specifically for implementation with juveniles, and is a "theory driven, risk and needs assessment based, and empirically grounded approach to transitioning youth from confinement into the community" (State of Alaska Department of Health & Social Services, 2005). Relative to the programs and research available regarding adult reentry, programs designed for use with juvenile offenders are currently lacking; however, programs are being developed that show considerable promise. It is recommended that juvenile reentry programs place great emphasis on assisting participants in avoiding criminal associates, as this is associated with lower rates of re-arrest and incarceration, particularly in juveniles (Abrams, 2007).

Do reentry programs work?

Recent research has focused on the effectiveness of community reentry programs. Petersilia (2004) noted programs that took place mostly in the community (rather than in an institution), were at least six months in duration, focused on high-risk offenders, used cognitive-behavioral techniques, and matched therapist and program to the specific learning styles and characteristics of individual offenders were associated with greater effectiveness. Listwan and colleagues (2006) recommend that assessment of prisoner needs begins prior to discharge and the identification of risk, need, and responsivity characteristics be emphasized when selecting participants for reentry programs. Additionally, Listwan *et al.* (2006) recommend that follow-up assessments be conducted to determine whether the program effectively reduced the risk of recidivism and careful attention be paid to the **criminogenic needs** (i.e., areas which have been shown to increase an offenders' rate of re-offending, and can be changed, such as: family dysfunction, antisocial attitudes and associates, substance abuse, lack of employment/occupational skills) of offenders, in order to maximize the effectiveness of reentry efforts. After an extensive analysis of the effectiveness of reentry programs' literature, Seiter and Kadela (2003) reached the five following conclusions: (1) vocational training and/or work release programs work in terms of both reductions in recidivism and an increase in job-readiness; (2) drug treatment programs are effective in facilitating effective community transition; (3) educational programs are not effective in reducing recidivism but do increase educational achievement scores of offenders; (4) reentry programs specifically targeted at sexual offenders are a promising new area of treatment (though data are not conclusive at this point), and, finally; (5) halfway houses are effective, as are prerelease centers and programs in reducing recidivism rates and easing the transition to the community.

Barriers to effective implementation of reentry programs

It has been noted that "the issue of prison reentry is one that covers a broad base of social and governmental networks" (Seiter & Kadela, 2003, p. 362). The effective and efficient implementation of these programs is affected by the following factors: the type of sentences and release mechanisms currently in place, the types of programs provided by the departments of corrections, the types and intensity of supervision provided by overseeing boards, familial support available to offenders, community funding of social services, and the economic status and availability of jobs (Seiter & Kadela, 2003). These factors mean that offenders attempting to transition to their communities and those assisting them in this transition are faced with a daunting task influenced by many factors over which they have little or no control. Policy implications and recommendations of this information are discussed below.

Forensic Psychology and Policy Implications

The benefits of successful community reintegration — both to society at large and individual offenders — cannot be understated. Policy should reflect an increasing emphasis on well-implemented and empirically-based reentry efforts, which can result in significantly reduced risk of recidivism and decreased costs. In order to maximize the effectiveness of such programs, and to protect public safety, several policy recommendations are warranted. Inmates should be screened for mental illness upon arrival in a correctional facility, and it should also be determined whether they receive benefits for a mental illness (Peters & Bekman, 2007). In contrast to current policy that requires inmates' benefits be terminated during incarceration, inmates' benefits should only be suspended so they may be reinstated expeditiously as the individual's release date approaches (Peters & Bekman, 2007). Correctional facilities and professionals working in reentry programs should ensure that all inmates have valid identification prior to release (Peters & Bekman, 2007). Such changes, though seemingly minor, could have significant impact on the ease and success with which offenders transition to their respective communities.

Based on research on the effectiveness of various types of reentry programs, correctional administrators should increase the use of vocational training, work-release programs, drug rehabilitation programs, education programs, halfway house programs, and pre-release programs (Seiter & Kadela, 2003). This will ensure effective reintegration of offenders, while ensuring that scarce financial and human resources are not squandered on ineffective methods. When presenting proposals for reentry programs to administrators and/or government officials, emphasis should be placed on the cost-effectiveness of these programs, and their success in reducing costs associated with recidivism. Correctional facilities should incorporate discharge planning and community reentry into standard programming available to all inmates, and inmates should be permitted and encouraged to take an active role in planning for their release.

Finally, all reentry programs should comply with the American Association of Community Psychiatrists' 2010 recommendations regarding post-release planning. These recommendations are as follows: (1) efforts should be made to divert mentally ill offenders from correctional settings; (2) release planning should begin at admission; (3) for homeless individuals, referrals to treatment shelters should be made when possible; (4) funding for care following release should be arranged well before the release date; (5) release planning should be multidisciplinary; (6) probation or parole officers should receive information about all referrals for an offender; (7) inmates should have input into their release plans; (8) an inmate's family should have input into the release plan; (9) arrangements should be made with an outpatient team or agency for follow-up care; (10) community service providers should have access to the jail to maximize continuity of care; (11) assignments of treatment providers shall be made collaboratively with input from the inmate, the jail providers and the community agency; (12) inmates should meet via face-to-face contact an individual from the community agency who will assist in their aftercare; (13) medications should be provided for an adequate period of time post-release; (14) the responsibility to assume care between release and the first outpatient appointment should be communicated to all involved in an offender's care; (15) transportation arrangements should be made for the first outpatient appointment; (16) child care arrangements for this appointment should also be made, as needed; (17) a tracking mechanism should be in place for those who do not attend their first outpatient appointment; (18) the release treatment plan should be documented in the jail chart as well as the chart at the community agency; (19) rigorous Quality Assurance must be maintained; and finally (20) an oversight group should be established to monitor implementation.

Suggestions for Future Research

Although research efforts investigating community reentry programs are increasing, further efforts are needed to elucidate the following issues: effective methods of integrating treatment for co-occurring mental illnesses and substance use disorders, methods for successfully adapting community-based methods to correctional settings to prepare inmates for release, and the impact of specialized interdisciplinary treatment teams on relevant measures of successful reentry (Peters & Bekman, 2007). Additionally, efforts should be made to determine which methods should be implemented in custody-based versus community-based settings in order to maximize treatment effectiveness. Future research regarding the effectiveness of reentry programs should include measures of cost-effectiveness in order to meet practical demands of facility administrators and to demonstrate the "real world" usefulness of such programs. In addition to these issues, reentry programs addressing specific types of offenders should continue to be developed and their effectiveness investigated. Populations which could be a focus of such efforts include minority groups, offenders with intellectual disabilities, repeat offenders, and first-time offenders.

Practice Update Section: Issues in Corrections/Correctional Psychology

Boothby and Clements (2002) indicate that while the number of psychologists choosing to work in correctional settings are increasing, little research is done to evaluate their job experiences or job satisfaction. The number of correctional psychologists has doubled in the last 20 years with the majority being Caucasian males (Boothby and Clements, 2000). These researches surveyed 800 correctional psychologists and discovered that, overall, these psychologists had a moderate level of job satisfaction (Boothby and Clements, 2002). Safety, job security, and relationships with clients were ranked as the job characteristics that were the most satisfying, while opportunities for advancement and professional growth were ranked as the least satisfying. Finally, psychologists who worked for federal prisons or less crowded institutions were comparatively more satisfied with their jobs (Boothby and Clements, 2002). Although working with violent offenders, psychologists working in a forensic hospital or correctional institution may have increased feelings of security due to the presence of security staff, cameras, and other safety measures taken in these settings. Psychologists working in community mental health centers are typically not afforded many of these same protections or security measures, while sometimes working with potentially dangerous clients.

A study examining the priorities of psychological services in a correctional environment identified assessment, harm prevention, other clinical services, as well as being a role model, and evaluating and training other staff as important duties to be developed (Byrne, Byrne, and Howells, 2001). Boothby and Clements (2000) found that administrative duties have grown and now consume about one-third of a psychologist's professional time in correctional settings. This can be a source of frustration for some psychologists who feel that there is already a shortage of psychologists to offer clinical services such as group therapy or psychological testing. Some prisons require that staff psychologists review infractions committed by inmates with a docu-mented mental illness to determine the impact of the mental illness on their actions. In essence, these reviews are similar to a miniature mental state at the time of the offense evaluations for institutional infractions. Procedures such as these in some correctional environments are a result of previous litigation regarding the treatment of mentally ill inmates.

In the past, psychologists who worked in a correctional environment were regarded with suspicion by individuals who may have questioned their ability to work in a private practice arena. While the security and benefits of a prison-based job is alluring to some, the specialized practice of correctional/forensic psychology has attracted many highly qualified clinicians who have specialty training with offender populations. Psychologists who are trained with a specialty in forensic psychology are often skilled and knowledgeable about treatment interventions designed for criminal populations. They are trained in subject matter and skill areas focused on psycholegal issues and in the dynamics of correctional or courtroom settings, enabling them to function more effectively in these contexts. The correctional client is different from the client in the community and the organizational dynamics (e.g. chain of command, security issues); in addition the correctional settings are also quite different. Private practitioners routinely interface with insurance companies and typically deal with pro-social clientele rather than violent offenders, correctional officers, and wardens. There are differing implications as set forth by the Standards for Psychology Services in Jail and Prisons regarding informed consent, confidentiality, and "duty to warn" (American Association for Correctional Psychology, 2000). The American Association for Correctional Psychology (2000) revised their 1980 Standards in order to promote the highest quality of mental health services to those in custody and to increase the scope of the correctional psychologists' role to include policy making, psychological screening of security staff, and consultation. Understanding the differences in roles between the correctional/ forensic psychologist, the community, and the general clinical psychologist can have important implications for the recruitment and retention of psychology staff in correctional settings.

■ International Issues: Characteristics of Female Sex Offenders in the Netherlands

A study by Wijkman, Bijeveld, and Hendriks (2010) analyzed characteristics of female sex offenders in the Netherlands. This study examined and titled different classifications of female sex offenders within a relatively small sample. One hundred and eleven adult female sex offenders, who are involved with the justice authorities in the Netherlands, were the sample for this study. In 77% of the cases the women had sexually abused children, and two-thirds of these women did not act alone, they had a "male co-offender" (p. 135). Several key aspects of the perpetrators' background, mental state, and marital status were studied.

In this study, several "problematic background" features were identified. These features include mental disorders, violent parents, and the most prominent of these features is a history of sexual abuse. In this study the average age of female sex offenders was between 26 and 32, most of them are Caucasian, and about one-third of them were married. It is interesting to note, 85% of the women who were married indicated that they entered into a marriage out of a desire to "escape the family home" (p. 137). Notably another key feature is an adolescent history of drug and alcohol abuse. Mental disorders that were prominent in these women include depression, PTSD, anxiety, cognitive disorders, and personality disorders. A distinctive feature in the mental history, associated with mental illnesses, was psychosis and social isolation.

The victims in these cases were most often a relative or an acquaintance and the extent of the sexual abuse was often genital fondling, oral sex, and penetration. The victims' ages range between 6 and 12 years old. It is also notable that the majority of the victims are females in this study.

Although they were working with a small sample, Wijkman, Bijeveld, and Hendriks (2010) were able to cluster the female sex offenders into three separate classifications. These classifications include the *teacher-lover type, the intergenerationally predisposed type, and the male-coerced type* (p. 139). The **teacher-lover type** is the woman who denies abuse, but considers herself romantically involved with the victim. The **intergenerationally predisposed type** is the woman who has a significant history of sexual abuse, physical abuse, and acts on her crimes without a co-offender, or male counterpart. The **male-coerced type** is the woman who has endured sexual abuse herself, and is forced into the commission of a sexual offense by her male counterpart.

Although information in regards to female sexual offenders is scarce, this study demonstrates that there is a need for future research on this topic, and provides some information into the characteristics of female sex offenders.

■

Related Websites

www.criminaljusticeoffice.org/story.html
Information about Correctional Officer Stress.
www.bls.gov/oco/ocos156.htm
Information about the nature of correctional officers' work and the training and qualifications needed.

Related Websites—cont'd

www.thearc.org/page.aspx?pid=2458
General information on intellectually disabled offenders.
www.aaidd.org
American Association on Intellectual and Developmental Disabilities.
klasskids.org
Provides information about Megan's Law.
govtrack.us
Provides information about supplemental laws to Megan's Law.
Objectives are attached.
http://womenincorrections.blogspot.com/2008/07/male-female-or-correctional-officer.html
This website is a website for correctional officers to post about their experiences and duties that are involved in being a correctional officer. There are also blogs from correctional officers, both male and female, that share their experience about when females began being allowed to work in male prisons.
www.insidecca.com/inside-cca/honoring-women-corrections
This website is about honoring women who worked in corrections during a time when females were not welcome in a predominately male environment.
www.ncjrs.gov/pdffiles/172858.pdf
This website is designed for female offenders and issues they face with employment, helping inmates set and achieve goals, and focus on family focused programming.
www.wpaonline.org
This site is designed for female inmates and their families, deal with their legal history. The site is to provide peer support for the female offender while the offender develops self-reliant skills.
www.tasc-il.org/preview/corrections.html
Provides information regarding current reentry programs offered by the Illinois Department of Corrections.
www.ojp.usdoj.gov/BJA/grant/reentry.html
Information from the United States Bureau of Justice regarding training opportunities, links to information on specific reentry programs, and organizations involved in implementing and designing community reentry programs.

References

Abadinsky, H., & Winfree, L. (1992). *Crime and justice: An introduction* (2nd edn.). Chicago: Nelson-Hall.

Abdollahi, M. K. (2002). Understanding police stress research. *Journal of Forensic Psychology Practice, 2*(2), 1−24.

Abram, K. M., Teplin, L. A., & McClelland, G. M. (2003). Comorbidity of severe psychiatric disorders and substance use disorders among women in jail. *American Journal of Psychiatry, 160*, 1007−1010.

Abrams, L. S. (2007). Youth offenders' perceptions of the challenges of transition. *Journal of Offender Rehabilitation, 44*, 31−53.

Acklin, M. W. (2002). Forensic psychodiagnostic testing. *Journal of Forensic Psychology Practice, 2*(3), 107−112.

Adalist-Estrin, A. (1994). Family support and criminal justice. In S. L. Kagan, & B. Weissbourd (Eds.), *Putting families first America's family support movement and the challenge of change* (pp. 161−185). San Francisco: Jossey-Bass.

Aderhold, B., Boulas, J., & Huss, M. T. (2011). *Guide to graduate programs in forensic and legal psychology.* Accessed September 13, 2011, at. www.ap-ls.org/education/Guide%20to%20Graduate%20Programs%20in%20Forensic%20and%20Legal%20Psychology%202-18-11.pdf.

Adler, J. R. (1999). Strengthening victims' rights in domestic violence cases: An argument for 30-day mandatory restraining orders in Massachusetts. *Boston Public Interest Law Journal, 8*, 303−332.

Administration for Children, Youth, and Families. (2008). *Trends in foster care and adoption.* Washington, DC. Retrieved from. www.acf.hhs.gov/programs/cb/stats_research/afcars/trends_02-07.pdf.

Adoption and Safe Families Act. Public Law. (1997). No. 105-89, 101−501, 111 Statute 2115.

Aertsen, I. (2009). Restorative police practices in Belgium: A research into mediation processes and their organization. *Journal of Police Studies, 2*(11), 65−82.

Agatston, P. W., Kowalski, R., & Limber, S. (2007). Students' perspectives on cyber bullying. *Journal of Adolescent Health, 41*(6), S59−S60.

Agnetti, G. (2009). The consumer movement and compulsory treatment: A professional outlook. *International Journal of Mental Health, 37*(4), 33−45.

Albers, E., & Evans, W. (1994). Suicide ideation among a stratified sample of rural and urban adolescents. *Child and Adolescent Social Work Journal, 11*(5), 379−389.

Alessi, N. E., McManus, M., Brickman, A., & Grapentine, L. (1984). Suicidal behavior among serious juvenile offenders. *American Journal of Psychiatry, 141*, 286−287.

Alexander, M. A. (1997). *Sex offender treatment probed anew. Unpublished manuscript.*

Alhabib, S., Nur, U., & Jones, R. (2010). Domestic Violence Against Women: Systematic Review of Prevalence Studies. *Journal of Family Violence, 25*, 369−382.

Alison, L., Bennell, C., Mokros, A., & Ormerod, D. (2002, Mar). The personality paradox in offender profiling: A theoretical review of the processes involved in deriving background characteristics from crime scene actions. *Psychology Public Policy, & Law, 8*(1), 115−135.

Allard, P., & Young, M. C. (2002). Prosecuting juveniles in adult court: The practitioner's perspectives. *Journal of Forensic Psychology Practice, 2*(2), 65−77.

Allen, H., & Simonsen, C. E. (1989). *Corrections in America.* New York: Macmillan.

Alleyne, E., & Wood, J. L. (2010). Gang involvement: Psychological and behavioral characteristics of gang members, peripheral youth, and nongang youth. *Aggressive Behavior, 36*(6), 423–436.

Amato, P. R., & Sobolewski, J. M. (2001). The effects of divorce and marital discord on adult children's psychological well-being. *American Sociological Review, 66*(6), 900–921.

American Academy of Psychiatry and the Law. (2005). *Ethics guidelines for the practice of forensic psychiatry.* Bloomfield, CT: AAPL.

American Association for Correctional Psychology. (2000, Aug). Standards for psychology services in jails, prisons, correctional facilities, and agencies. *Criminal Justice & Behavior, 27*(4), 433–494.

American Association of Community Psychiatrists. (2010). *AACP position statement on post-release planning.* Retrieved from. http://communitypsychiatry.org/publications/position_statements/postrelease.aspx.

American Association of Mental Retardation. (2002). *Mental retardation: Definition, classification, and systems of supports* (10th ed.). Washington, D.C: American Association on Mental Retardation.

American Association on Intellectual and Developmental Disabilities. (2010). *Definition of intellectual disability.* Retrieved April 28, 2011, from. http://aamr.org/content_100.cfm?navID=21.

American Bar Association. (1980). *Juvenile justice standards on dispositions.* Cambridge, MA: Ballinger Press.

American Civil Liberties Union Lesbian & Gay Rights Project (2002). *Too high a price: The case against restricting gay parenting.* Available from: 125 Broad Street, 18th Floor, New York, NY 10004, lgbthiy@aclu. org. American Correctional Association. (2001). ACA welcomes its newest affiliate. *Corrections Today, 63*(3), 18.

American Psychiatric Association. (1987). *Diagnostic and Statistical Manual of Mental Disorders* (3rd edn. revised). Washington, DC: Author.

American Psychiatric Association. (2000). *Diagnostic and Statistical Manual of Mental Disorders* (Revised 4th edn.). Washington, DC: APA

American Psychological Association. (1992). Ethical principles of psychologists and code of conduct. *American Psychologist, 47*(12), 1597–1611.

American Psychological Association. (2002). Ethical principles of psychologists and code of conduct. *American Psychologist, 57*, 1060–1073.

American Psychological Association. (2009). *Guidelines for child custody evaluations in family law proceedings. APA:* Washington, DC: Author. Retrieved from www.apapracticecentral.org/news/guidelines.pdf.

American Psychological Association. (2010). Guidelines for child custody evaluations in family law proceedings. *American Psychologist, 65*(9), 863–867.

American Psychological Association. (2010). *Ethical Principles of Psychologists and Code of Conduct. American Psychological Association.* Retrieved August 23, 2011. From. http://www.apa.org/ethics/code/index.aspx.

American Psychological Association. (2011). *Specialty Guidelines for Forensic Psychologists. American Psychology-Law Association.* Retrieved August 23, 2011. From. www.ap-ls.org/aboutpsychlaw/SGFP_Final_Approved_2011.pdf.

American Psychological Association Zero Tolerance Task Force. (2008). Are zero tolerance policies effective in the schools? An evidentiary review and recommendations. *American Psychologist, 63*(9), 852–862, American Red Cross (2001). Available. www.trauma-pages.com.

American Suiciodology Association. (2006). *U.S.A. suicide: 2006 official final data.* Washington, DC: American Association of Suicidology. Retrieved on September 7, 2011 from www.suicidology.org/c/document_library/ get_file?folderId=228&;name=DLFE-142.pdf.

Andrews, D. (2009). *The Level of Service Assessments: A question of confusion, selectivity, and misrepresentation of evidence in Baird.* Orlando, Florida: Paper presented at the meeting of the International Community Corrections Association. Available online at. www.iccaweb.org/documents/D.Andrews_Service.Assessments. pdf.

Anonymous. (1997). Hell on Block 1G. *Westchester County Weekly.* [On-line]. Available. www.westchesterweekly. com/articles/suicied2.html.

Anshel, M. H. (2000, Sep). A conceptual model and implications for coping with stressful events in police work. *Criminal Justice & Behavior, 27*(3), 375–400.

Anthony, B. J., Wessler, S. L., & Sebian, J. K. (2010). Commentary: Guiding a public health approach to bullying. *Journal of Pediatric Psychology, 35*(10), 1113−1115.

Appelbaum, K. L. (1994). Criminal-justice related competencies in defendants with mental retardation. *The Journal of Psychiatry and the Law, 22,* 483−497.

Appelbaum, P. S. (2009). Mental retardation and the death penalty: After Atkins. *Psychiatric Services, 60*(10), 1295−1297.

Archer, R. P., Buffington-Vollum, J. K., Stredny, R. V., & Handel, R. W. (2006). A survey of psychological test use patterns among forensic psychologists. *Journal of Personality Assessment, 87*(2), 84−94.

Archer, R. P., Stredny, R. V., & Zoby, M. (2006). Introduction to forensic uses of clinical assessment instruments. In R. P. Archer (Ed.), *Forensic uses of clinical assessment instruments* (pp. 1−18). Mahwah, NJ: Lawrence Erlbaum Associates Publishers.

Areh, I., Dobovsek, B., & Umek, P. (2007). Citizen's opinions of police procedures. *Policing, 30*(4), 637−650.

Arias, E. A., Schlesinger, L. B., Pinizzoto, A. J., Davis, E. F., Fava, J. L., & Dewey, L. M. (2008). Police officers who commit suicide by cop: A clinical study with analysis. *Journal of Forensic Sciences, 53(6)* 1455−1457.

Aricak, T., Siyahaan, S., Uzunhasanoglu, A., Saribeyoglu, S., Ciplak, S., Yilmaz, N., et al. (2008). Cyberbullying among Turkish adolescents. *Cyberpsychology & Behavior, 11,* 253−261.

Armstrong, G., & Griffin, M. (2004). Does the job matter? Comparing correlates of stress among treatment and correctional staff in prisons. *Journal of Criminal Justice, 32,* 577−592.

Armstong, K., O'Callahan, W., & Marmar, C. R. (1991). Debriefing Red Cross disaster personnel: The multiple stressor debriefing model. *Journal of Traumatic Stress, 4,* 581−593.

Arnold, J. L., Örtenwall, P., Birnbaum, M. L., Sundnes, K. O., Aggrawal, A., Arantharaman, V., Al Musleh, A. W., Asai, Y., Burkle, F. M., Jr., Chung, J. M., Vega, F. C., Debacker, M., Corte, F. D., Delooz, H., Dickinson, G., Hodgetts, T., Holliman, J., MacFarlane, C., Rodoplu, U., Stok, E., & Tsai, M. (2003). A proposed universal medical and public definition of terrorism. *Prehospital and Disaster Medicine, 18,* 47−52.

Arrigo, B. (1993). Paternalism, civil commitment, and illness politics: Assessing the current debate and outlining a future direction. *Journal of Law and Health, 7*(3/4), 131−168.

Arrigo, B. (1996). *The contours of psychiatric justice: A postmodern critique of mental illness, criminal insanity, and the law.* New York: Garland.

Arrigo, B. (2002). *Punishing the mentally ill.* Albany, NY: State University of New York Press.

Arrigo, B. A., & Bullock, J. L. (2008). The psychological effects of solitary confinement of prisoners in supermax units: Reviewing what we know and recommending what should change. *International Journal of Offender Therapy and Comparative Criminology, 52*(6), 622−640.

Arrigo, B., & Claussen, N. (2003, Jun). Police corruption and psychological testing: A strategy for preemployment screening. *International Journal of Offender Therapy & Comparative Criminology, 47*(3), 272−290.

Arrigo, B., & Garsky, K. (1997). Police suicide: A glimpse behind the badge. In R. Dunham, & G. Alpert (Eds.), *Critical issues in policing* (pp. 609−626). Prospect Heights, IL: Waveland Press.

Arrigo, B., & Tasca, J. (1999). Right to refuse treatment, competency to be executed, and therapeutic jurisprudence: Toward a systemic analysis. *Law and Psychology Review, 23*(1), 1−47.

Arseneault, L., Cannon, M., Fisher, H. L., Polanczyk, G., Moffitt, T. E., & Caspi, A. (2011). Childhood trauma and children's emerging psychotic symptoms: A genetically sensitive longitudinal cohort study. *The American Journal of Psychiatry, 168*(1), 65−72.

Associated Press. (2009, January 20). *Nathaniel Abraham accused of assaulting prison guards.* Accessed September 13, 2011, on. http://theoaklandpress.com/articles/2011/01/20/news/cops_and_courts/ doc4d37a7b6ab58d149663467.txt.

Association of Psychology Postdoctoral and Internship Centers (APPIC). (2011). Accessed September 13.01.11, at www.appic.org.

Atkins, E. L., Podboy, J., Larson, K., & Schenker, N. (2007). Forensic psychological consultation in U.S. death penalty cases in state and federal courts. *American Journal of Forensic Psychology, 25,* 9−20.

Atkins, E. L., & Stein, R. A. (1993). When the boundary is crossed: A protocol for attorneys and mental health professionals. *American Journal of Forensic Psychology, 11*(3), 3−21.

Atkinson, J. M., & Garner, H. C. (2002, Jul). Least restrictive alternative – Advance statements and the new mental health legislation. *Psychiatric Bulletin, 26*(7), 246–247.

Atwood, B. A. (2007). *The new uniform representation of children in Abuse, Neglect, and Custody Proceedings Act: Bridging the divide between pragmatism and idealism.* Family Law Quarterly, *Arizona Legal Studies Discussion Paper No 06–41.*

Austin, V. L. (2003). Fear and loathing in the classroom: A candid look at school violence and the policies and practices that address it. *Journal of Disability Policy Studies, 14*(1), 17–22.

Austin, W. G. (2001, Oct). Partner violence and risk assessment in child custody evaluation. *Family Court Review, 39*(4), 483–496.

Ax, R. K., Fagan, T., Magaletta, P. R., Morgan, R. D., Nussbaum, D., & White, T. W. (2007). Correctional assessment and treatment: Issues and innovations. *Criminal Justice and Behavior, 34,* 879–892.

Azar, S., & Cote, L. (2002, May–Jun). Sociocultural issues in the evaluation of the needs of children in custody decision making: What do our current frameworks for evaluating parenting practices have to offer? *International Journal of Law & Psychiatry, 25*(3), 193–217.

Bacher, N., Fieldstone, L., & Jonasz, J. (2005). The role of parenting coordination in the family law arena. *Journal of American Family Law, 19*(2), 84–96.

Back, M. D., Küfner, A. C. P., & Egloff, B. (2010). The emotional timeline of September 11, 2001. *Psychological Science, 2,* 1417–1419.

Bagdasaryan, S. (2005). Evaluating family preservation services: Reframing the question of effectiveness. *Children and Youth Services Review, 27*(6), 615–635.

Bagley, C. (1999). Adolescent prostitution in Canada and the Philippines. *International Social Work, 42*(4), 445–455.

Bailey, R. K. (2002). The civil commitment of sexually violent predators: A unique Texas approach. *Journal of the American Academy of Psychiatry & the Law, 30*(4), 525–532.

Baillargeon, J., Penn, J. V., Thomas, C. R., Temple, J. R., Baillargeon, G., & Murray, O. J. (2009). Psychiatric disorders and suicide in the nation's largest state prison system. *Journal of American Academy Psychiatry Law, 37,* 188–193.

Baird, C. (2009). *A question of evidence: A critique of risk assessment models used in the justice system.* Madison WI: National Council on Crime & Delinquency. Available electronically at www.nccd-crc.org/need/pubs/2009_a_question_evidence.pdf.

Baker, J. (1902). Female criminal lunatics. *Journal of Mental Science, 48,* 13–28.

Baker, A., & Chambers, J. (2011). Adult recall of childhood exposure to parental conflict: Unpacking the black box of parental alienation. *Journal of Divorce & Remarriage, 52*(1), 55–76.

Baker, T. E., & Baker, J. P. (1996, October). Preventing police suicide. *FBI Law Enforcement Bulletin,* 25–27.

Bala, N., & Saunders, A. (2003). Understanding the family context: Why the law of expert evidence is different in family law cases. *Canadian Family Law Quarterly, 20,* 277–338.

Balci, G., & Reimann, A. (2006). *Violent video tapes on mobiles phones. Beaten, raped, and videotaped.* Retrieved April 30, 2011, from www.spiegel.de/politik/deutschland/0, 1518, 418326,00.hrml.

Ballard, R. H., Holtzworth-Munroe, A., Applegate, A. G., & Beck, C. J. A. (2011). Detecting intimate partner violence in family and divorce mediation: A randomized trial of intimate partner violence screening. *Psychology, Public Policy, and Law, 17*(2), 241–263.

Ballard, R. H., & Nyman, M. (2009). Interdisciplinary law and psychology training at Indiana University. *Family Court Review, 47*(3), 485–492.

Ballenger, J., Best, S. R., Metzler, T. J., Wasserman, D. A., Mohr, D. C., Liberman, A., et al. (2011). Patterns and predictors of alcohol use in male and female urban police officers. *The American Journal of Addictions, 20,* 21–29.

Banach, M. (1998). The best interests of the child: Decision-making factors. *Families in Society, 79,* 331–340.

Bardwell, M. C., & Arrigo, B. A. (2002). Competency to stand trial: A law, psychology, and policy assessment. *Journal of Psychiatry & Law, 30*(2), 147–269.

Barnes, J. C., Beaver, K. M., & Miller, J. M. (2010). Estimating the effect of gang membership on nonviolent and violent delinquency: A counterfactual analysis. *Aggressive Behavior, 36*(6), 437–451.

Barnes, J. E. (2000). Insanity defense fails for man who threw woman onto track (cover story). *New York Times*. 03/23/2000, 149(51336), pA1.

Barnett, J. E., Wise, E. H., Johnson-Greene, D., & Bucky, S. F. (2007). Informed consent: Too much of a good thing or not enough? *Professional psychology: Research and practice, 38*(2), 179−186.

Barnett, O. W., Miller-Perrin, C. L., & Perrin, R. D. (2011). Abused heterosexual partners. In O. W. Barnett, C. L. Miller-Perrin, & R. D. Perrin (Eds.), *Family Violence Across the Lifespan: An Introduction* (3rd edn.). Los Angeles, CA: Sage Publications, Inc.

Barnhart, T. E. (2007). *The art of manipulation*. Retrieved August 14, 2011, from. www.corrections.com.

Baroff, G. S. (1996). The mentally retarded offender. In J. W. Jacobson, & J. A. Mulick (Eds.), *Manual of diagnosis and professional practice in mental retardation*. Washington, DC: American Psychological Association.

Barone, N. M., Weitz, E. I., & Witt, P. H. (2005). Psychological bonding evaluations in termination of parental rights cases. *The Journal of Psychiatry & Law, 33*, 387−411.

Barr, W. P. (1992). Violent youths should be punished as adults. In M. D. Biskup, & C. P. Cozic (Eds.), *Youth violence*. San Diego, CA: Greenhaven Press.

Barrett, S. E. (1997). Children of lesbian parents: The what, when, and how of talking about donor identity. *Children's Rights, Therapists' Responsibilities, 20*, 43−55.

Barron, P., Hassiotis, A., & Barnes, J. (2002). Offenders with intellectual disability: The size of the problem and therapeutic outcomes. *Journal of Intellectual Disability Research, 46*(6), 454−463.

Barron, P., Hassiotis, A., & Banes, J. (2004). Offenders with intellectual disability: A prospective comparative study. *Journal of Intellectual Disability Research, 48*(1), 69−76.

Bartol, C. R., & Bartol, A. M. (2008). *Juvenile delinquency and antisocial behavior: A developmental perspective*. New York: Prentice Hall.

Bartram, D., & Coyne, I. (1998). Variations in national patterns of testing and test use: The ITC/EFPPA international survey. *European Journal of Psychological Assessment, 14*(3), 249−260.

Bassman, R. (2005). Mental illness and the freedom to refuse treatment: Privilege or right. *Professional Psychology: Research and Practice, 36*(5), 488−497.

Batterman-Faunce, J. M., & Goodman, G. S. (1993). Effects of context on the accuracy and reliability of child witnesses. In G. S. Goodman, & B. L. Bottoms (Eds.), *Child victims, child witnesses: Understanding and improving testimony* (pp. 301−330). New York: Guilford Press.

Battle, A. O., Battle, M. V., & Tolley, E. A. (1993). Potential for suicide and aggression in delinquents at juvenile court in a southern city. *Suicide and Life Threatening Behavior, 23*(3), 230−244.

Bauman, S. (2010). Groups and bullying. *Journal for Specialists in Group Work, 35*(4), 321−323.

Bauserman, R. (2002). Child adjustment in joint-custody versus sole-custody arrangements: A metanalytic review. *Journal of Family Psychology, 16*(1), 91−102.

Baxter, H., Duggan, C., Larkin, E., Cordess, C., & Page, K. (2001, Sep). Mentally disordered parricide and stranger killers admitted to high-security care: A descriptive comparison. *Journal of Forensic Psychiatry, 12*(2), 287−299.

Baylis, M. (2005, October 12). Gang injunction not suited to Santa Maria police say. *Santa Maria Sun*. Retrieved from. http://santamariatimes.com/news/local/article_e8c8acf7-4edf-571b-ba27-0bb4bf38ef77.html.

Beail, N. (2002). Constructive approaches to the assessment, treatment and management of offenders with intellectual disabilities. *Journal of Applied Research in Intellectual Disabilities, 15*(2), 179−182.

Beauregard, E., Lussier, P., & Proulx, J. (2007). Criminal propensity and criminal opportunity. In R. Kocsis (Ed.), *Criminal profiling: International theory, research, and practice*. Totowa, NJ: Humana Press Inc.

Beck, A. (2008). Systematic interventions with sexual offending. In J. Houston, & S. Galloway (Eds.), *Sexual offending and mental health* (pp. 248−262). London, UK: Jessica Kingsley Publishers.

Beck, A. J., & Gilliard, D. K. (1995). *Prisoners in 1994*. Washington, DC: Bureau of Justice Statistics Bulletin.

Beck, A. J., Harrison, P. M., Berzofsky, M., Caspar, R., & Krebs, C. (2010). *Sexual victimization in prisons and jails reported by inmates, 2008−09*. Washington, DC: Bureau of Justice Statistics.

Beck, C. J. A., & Frost, L. E. (2006). Defining a threshold for client competence to participate in divorce mediation. *Psychology, Public Policy, and Law, 12*(1), 1−35.

Beck, C., Putterman, M., Sbarra, D., & Mehl, M. (2008). Parenting coordinator roles, program goals and services provided: Insights from the Pima County, Arizona Program. *Journal of Child Custody, 5*(1/2), 122−139.

Beck, V., Clingermayer, J., Ramsey, R., & Travis, L. (2004). Community response to sex offenders. *The Journal of Psychiatry & Law, 32*, 141−168.

Becker, M. A., Jordan, N., & Larsen, R. (2007). Predictors of successful permanency planning and length of stay in foster care: The role of race, diagnosis, and place of residence. *Children and Youth Services Review, 29*(8), 1102−1113.

Bedard, L. E. (2009). The pseudo-family phenomenon in women's prisons. *Women in Corrections*. Retrieved from. http://www.correctionsone.com/women-in-corrections/articles/1956587-The-pseudo-family-phenomenon-in-womens-prisons/.

Beer, A., Morgan, R., Garland, J., & Spanierman, L. (2007). The role of the romantic intimate relationships in the well being of incarcerated females. *Psychological Services, 4*, 250−261.

Beggs, S. M., & Grace, R. C. (2011). Treatment gain for sexual offenders against children predicts reduced recidivism: A comparative validity study. *Journal of Consulting and Clinical Psychology, 79*(2), 182−192.

Beinart, P. (6/14/1999). Bill of goods. *New Republic, 220*(24), 6.

Belbot, B. (2007). Mandatory mental health treatment and juveniles. In M. D. McShane, & F. P. Williams (Eds.), *Youth violence and delinquency: Monsters and myths*, Vol. 3 (pp. 97−112). Westport, CT: Praeger Publishers/ Greenwood Publishing Group.

Belfrage, H., Fransson, G., & Strand, S. (2000). Prediction of violence using the HCR-20: A prospective study in two maximum-security correctional institutions. *Journal of Forensic Psychiatry, 11*(1), 167−175.

Bell, K. E. (2009). Gangs and gender. *Crime and Delinquency, 55*(3), 363−387.

Bellak, L., Hurvich, M., & Gediman, H. (1973). *Ego functions in schizophrenics, neurotics, and normals*. New York: Wiley.

Benda, B. (2005). Ecological factors in recidivism: A survival analysis of boot camp graduates after three years. *Journal of Offender Rehabilitation, 35*, 63−85.

Benekos, P. J., & Merlo, A. V. (2008). Juvenile justice: The legacy of punitive policy. *Youth Violence and Juvenile Justice, 6*, 28−46.

Benner, A. (1994). The challenge for police psychology in the twenty first century: Moving beyond efficient to effective. In J. T. Reese, & R. Solomon (Eds.), *Organizational Issues* (pp. 363−374). Washington, DC: Federal Bureau of Investigations.

Bennett, W., & Hess, K. (1996). *Management and supervision in law enforcement* (2nd edn.). St. Paul, MN: West Publishing.

Berg, M. T., & DeLisi, M. (2006). The correctional melting pot: Race, ethnicity, citizenship, and prison violence. *Journal of Criminal Justice, 34*(6), 631−642.

Berger, V. (2000, Jul). Civilians versus police: Mediation can help to bridge the divide. *Negotiation Journal, 16*(3), 211−235.

Bergmann, L. H., & Queen, T. R. (1987). The aftermath: Treating traumatic stress is crucial. *Corrections Today, 49*, 100−104.

Bernet, W. (2002, Oct). Child custody evaluations. *Child & Adolescent Psychiatric Clinics of North America, 11*(4), 781−804.

Bernet, W., von Boch-Galhau, W., Baker, A. J., & Morrison, S. L. (2010). Parental alienation, DSM-V, and ICD-11. *American Journal of Family Therapy, 76*(112), 76−187.

Bernstein, R. (2008). Commentary on the "choice" between seclusion and forced medication. *Psychiatric Services, 59*(2), 212.

Bersoff, D. (1999). Preparing for two cultures: Education and training in psychology and law. In R. Roesch, S. Hart, & J. Ogloff (Eds.), *Psychology and law: State of the discipline* (pp. 375−401). New York: Plenum.

Berube, M. S. (1982). *The American Heritage dictionary* (2nd edn.). Boston: Houghton Mifflin.

Beutler, L. E., Nussbaum, P. D., & Meredith, K. E. (1988). Changing personality patterns of police officers. *Professional Psychology: Research and Practice, 19*(5), 503−507.

Beutler, L. E., Storm, A., Kirkish, P., Scogin, F., & Gaines, J. A. (1985). Parameters in the prediction of police officer performance. *Professional Psychology: Research and Practice, 16*, 324−335.

Beven, G. E. (2005). Offenders with mental illnesses in maximum and supermaximum security settings. In C. L. Scott, & J. B. Gerbasi (Eds.), *Handbook of correctional mental health* (pp. 209−228). Arlington, VA: American Psychiatric Publishing.

Bidrose, S., & Goodman, G. S. (2000, May−Jun). Testimony and evidence: A scientific case study of memory for child sexual abuse. *Applied Cognitive Psychology, 14*(3), 197−213.

Binder, R. L. (2002). Liability for the psychiatrist expert witness. *American Journal of Psychiatry, 159*(11), 1819−1825.

Binder, A., & Scharf, P. (1980). The violent police-citizen encounter. *Annals of the American Academy of Political and Social Science, 452*, 111−121.

Bireda, M. R. (2000). Education for all. *Principal Leadership, 1*(4), 8−13.

Birger, M., Bergman-Levy, T., & Asman, O. (2011). Treatment of sex offenders in Israeli prison settings. *Journal of American Academic Psychiatry Law, 39*, 100−103.

Bisson, J., McFarlane, A., Rose, S., Ruzek, J. I., & Watson, P. J. (2000). Psychological debriefing for adults. In E. B. Foa, T. M. Keane, & M. J. Friedman (Eds.), *Effective treatments for PTSD: Practice guidelines from the international society for traumatic stress studies* (pp. 83−105). New York: Guilford.

Bjerregaard, B. (2002, Sep). Self-definitions of gang membership and involvement in delinquent activities. *Youth & Society, 9*(4), 45−56.

Black, K. (2009). Trashing the presumption: Intervention on the side of the government. *Environmental Law, 39*(2), 481−505.

Blackwood, K., & Guyer, M. (2009). Involuntary medication to render a defendant competent to stand trial. *Journal of the American Academy of Psychiatry and the Law, 37*(1), 122−124.

Blandón-Gitlin, I., & Pezdek, K. (2009). Children's memory in forensic contexts: Suggestibility, false memory, and individual differences. In B. L. Bottoms, C. J. Najdowski, & G. S. Goodman's (Eds.), *Children as victims, witnesses, and offenders: Psychological science and the law* (pp. 233−252). New York: Guilford Press.

Blau, T. H. (1998). *The psychologist as expert witness* (2nd edn.). New York: John Wiley & Sons, Inc.

Bloom, B., & Steinhart, D. (1993). *Why punish the children? A reappraisal of the children of incarcerated mothers in America.* San Francisco: National Council on Crime and Delinquency.

Blum, J. (2007). Identifying and treating mental illness: One jail system's story. *Corrections Today, 69*(4), 30−32.

Blum, V. (2002). Allowing execution of juveniles gives Virginia its edge in case. *The Legal Intelligencer, 227*(97), 1−3.

Blume, J. H., Johnson, S. L., & Seeds, C. (2009). Of Atkins and men: Deviations from clinical definitions of mental retardation in death penalty cases. *Cornell Journal of Law and Public Policy, 18*(3), 689−733.

Blumenthal, S. (2000). Developmental aspects of violence and the institutional response. *Criminal Behaviour & Mental Health, 10*(3), 185−198.

Bo, S., Abu-Akel, A., Kongerslev, M., Haahr, U. H., & Simonsen, E. (2011). Risk factors for violence among patients with schizophrenia. *Clinical Psychology Review, 31*(5), 711−726.

Bogacki, D. F., & Weiss, K. J. (2007). Termination of parental rights: Focus on defendants. *The Journal of Psychiatry and Law, 35*, 25−45.

Bohrer, S., & Chaney, R. (2010). *Police investigations of the use of deadly force can influence perceptions and outcomes.* Accessed September 13, 2011. http://www2.fbi.gov/publications/leb/2010/january2010/police_feature.htm.

Bonner, R. L. (1992). Isolation, seclusion, and psychological vulnerability as risk factors for suicide behind bars. In A. L. Berman, R. W. Maris, J. T. Maltsberger, & R. I. Yufit (Eds.), *Assessment and Prediction of Suicide* (pp. 389−419). New York: Guilford.

Boothby, J. L., & Clements, C. B. (2002, Jun). Job satisfaction of correctional psychologists: Implications for recruitment and retention. *Professional Psychology: Research & Practice, 33*(3), 310−315.

Boothby, J. L., & Clements, C. B. (2000, Dec). A national survey of correctional psychologists. *Criminal Justice & Behavior, 27*(6), 716−732.

Bordenave, F. J., & Kelly, D. C. (2010). Death penalty and mentally ill defendants: Two state Supreme Courts hold that mental illness is not a per se bar to execution. *Journal of the American Academy of Psychiatry and the Law, 38*(2), 284–286.

Borgman, R. (1981). Antecedents and consequences of parental rights termination for abused and neglected children. *Child Welfare, 60*, 391–403.

Borton, I. M. (2009). Effects of race, sex, and victims' reasons for victim-offender dialogue. *Conflict Resolution Quarterly, 27*(2), 215–235.

Borum, R., & Grisso, T. (1995). Psychological test use in criminal forensic evaluations. *Professional Psychology: Research and Practice, 26*(5), 465–473.

Borum, R., & Reddy, M. (2001). Assessing violence risk in Tarasoff situations: A fact-based model of inquiry. *Behavioral Science & the Law, 19*(3), 375–385.

Boudin, K. (1998). Lessons from a mother's program in prison: A psychosocial approach supports women and their children. *Women & Therapy, 21*(1), 103–125.

Bouffard, J. A., & Bergeron, L. E. (2007). The implementation and effectiveness of a serious and violent offender reentry initiative. *Journal of Offender Rehabilitation, 44*, 1–29.

Bourget, D., & Labelle, A. (1992). Homicide, infanticide, and filicide. *Psychiatric Clinics of North America, 15*(3), 661–673.

Bourque, B. B., Cronin, R. C., Felker, D. B., Pearson, F. R., Han, M., & Hill, S. M. (1996). *Boot camps for juvenile offenders: An implementation evaluation of three demonstration programs [On-line].* Available: askncjrs@aspensys.com Message: NCJ 157316.

Bow, J., Flens, J., Gould, J., & Greenhut, D. (2006). An analysis of administration, scoring, and interpretation of the MMPI_2 and MCMI-2 and MCMI_II/III in child custody evaluations. *Journal of Child Custody: Research, Issues, and Practices, 2*(4), 1–22.

Bow, J. N., & Quinnell, F. A. (2001, Jun). Psychologists' current practices and procedures in child custody evaluations: Five years after American Psychological Association. *Professional Psychology: Research & the Law, 32*(3), 261–268.

Bowker, A. L., & Schweid, R. E. (1992). Habilitation of the retarded offender in Cuyahoga County. *Federal Probation, 56*, 48–52.

Boyan, S. M., & Termini, A. M. (2005). *The psychotherapist as parent coordinator in high-conflict divorce: Strategies and techniques.* Binghamton, NY: Haworth Clinical Practice Press.

Bracco, K. (1997). Patriarchy and the law of adoption: Beneath the best interests of the child. *The Alberta Law Review, 35*, 1035–1055.

Braddock, D. (Ed.), (1999). *Positive Behavior Support for People with Developmental Disabilities: A Research Synthesis.* Washington, DC: American Association on Mental Retardation.

Bradshaw, C. P., Rodgers, C. R. R., Ghandour, L. A., & Garbarino, J. (2009). Social-cognitive mediators of the association between community violence exposure and aggressive behavior. *School Psychology Quarterly, 24*(3), 199–210.

Braver, S. L., Ellman, I. M., Votruba, A. M., & Fabricius, W. V. (2011). Lay judgments about child custody after divorce. *Psychology, Public Policy, and Law, 17*(2), 212–240.

Braver, S. L., Fabricius, W. V., & Ellman, I. M. (2003, Jun). Relocation of children after divorce and children's best interests: New evidence and legal consideration. *Journal of Family Psychology, 17*(2), 206–219.

Bresler, S., Scalora, M. J., Elbogen, E. B., & Moore, S. Y. (2003). Attempted suicide by cop: A case study of traumatic brain injury and the insanity defense. *Journal of Forensic Science, 48*(1), 1–5.

Briken, P., Hill, A., & Berner, W. (2003, Aug). Pharmacotherapy of paraphilias with long-acting agonists of luteinizing hormone-releasing hormone: A systemic review. *Journal of Clinical Psychiatry, 64*(8), 890–897.

Briscoe, J. (1997). Breaking the cycle of violence: A rational approach to at-risk youth. *Federal Report, 61*, 3–13.

Brodsky, S. L. (2004). *Coping with cross-examination and other pathways to effective testimony.* Washington, DC, US: American Psychological Association.

Brodsky, S. L., & Galloway, V. A. (2003). Ethical and professional demands for forensic mental health professionals in the post-Atkins era. *Ethics and Behavior, 13*, 3–9.

Brodsky, S. L., Caputo, A. A., & Domino, M. L. (2002). The mental health professional in court: Legal issues, Research foundations, and effective testimony. In B. Van Dorsten (Ed.), *Forensic Psychology: From Classroom to Courtroom* (pp. 17–33). New York: NY: Kluwer Academic/Plenum Publishers.

Brodsky, S. L., Zapf, P. A., & Boccaccini, M. T. (2005). Competency for execution assessments: Ethical continuities and professional tasks. *Journal of Forensic Psychology Practice, 5*(4), 65–74.

Brooks, L. (1997). Police discretionary behavior: A study of style. In R. Dunham, & G. Alpert (Eds.), *Critical issues in policing* (3rd edn.). Prospect Heights, IL: Waveland Press.

Brooks, S. L. (2002). Kinship and adoption. *Adoption Quarterly, 5*(3), 55–66.

Brown, C. H., Bennett, M. E., Li, L., & Bellack, A. S. (2011). Predictors of initiation and engagement of initiation and engagement in substance abuse treatment among individuals with co-occurring serious mental illness and substance use disorders. *Addictive Behaviors, 36*(5), 439–447.

Brown, G. L., Linnoila, M. I., & Goodwin, F. K. (1992). *Impulsivity, aggression, and associated affects: Relationship to self-destructive behavior and suicide.* New York: Guilford Press.

Brown, J. G. (1994). The use of mediation to resolve criminal cases: A procedural critique. *Emory Law Journal, 43*, 1–45.

Brown, R. R. (2008). The gang's all here: Evaluating the need for a national gang database. *Columbia Journal of Law and Social Problems, 42*, 293–333.

Brown, J. M., & Campbell, E. A. (1994). *Stress and policing: Sources and strategies.* New York: John Wiley & Sons.

Brown, R. P., Osterman, L. L., & Barnes, C. D. (2009). School violence and the culture of honor. *Psychological Science, 20*(11), 1400–1405.

Browne, A., & Finkelhor, D. (1986). Impact of child sexual abuse: A review of the research. *Psychological Bulletin, 99*(1), 66–77.

Browne, K., & Herbert, M. (1997). *Preventing family violence.* New York: Wiley.

Brownell, P. (1997). Female offenders in the criminal justice system: Policy and program development. In A. R. Roberts (Ed.), *Social work in juvenile and criminal justice settings* (2nd edn.). (pp. 325–349) Springfield, IL: Charles C. Thomas.

Brunstein, K. A., Klomek, A., Marrocco, F., & Kleinman, M. (2007). Bullying, depression, and suicidality in adolescents. *Journal of the American Academy of Child and Adolescent Psychiatry, 46*, 40–49.

Brymer, M., Jacobs, A., Layne, C., Pynoos, R., Ruzek, J., Steinberg, A., Vernberg, E., & Watson, P. (2006). *National Child Traumatic Stress Network. Psychological first aid: Field operations guide* (2nd edn.). Retrieved August 30, 2011. www.nctsnet.org/sites/default/files/pfa/english/1-psyfirstaid_final_complete_manual.pdf.

Buchanan, A. (2006). Psychiatric evidence on the ultimate issue. *Journal of the American Academy of Psychiatry and the Law, 34*, 14–21.

Buchanan, A. (2007). Capacity, consent, and mental health legislation: Time for a new standard? *British Journal of Psychiatry, 190*(2), 176–177.

Buchner, B., Bobb, M. J., Root, O., & Barge, M. (2008). *Evaluation of a pilot community policing program: The Pasadena police-community mediation and dialog program.* Washington, DC: US Department of Justice.

Buene, K., Giebels, E., & Sanders, K. (2009). Are you talking to me? Influencing behavior and culture in police interviews. *Psychology, Crime, & Law, 15*(7), 597–617.

Buker, H., & Wiecko, F. (2007). Are causes of police stress global? Testing the effects of common police stressors on the Turkish National Police. *Policing: An International Journal of Police Strategies and Management, 30*, 291–309.

Bullock, J. L. (2002). Involuntary treatment of defendants found incompetent to stand trial. *Journal of Forensic Psychology, 2*(4), 1–33.

Bureau of Justice Assistance Bulletin. (2006). *Effective Gang Enforcement.* Retrieved February 5, 2006, from. www.ncjrs.gov/html/bja/gang/bja3.html.

Bureau of Justice Statistics. (2006a). *Special report: Mental health problems of prison and jail inmates.* Washington, DC: U.S. Department of Justice.

Bureau of Justice Statistics. (2006b). *Prisoners in 2005*. Washington, DC: U.S. Department of Justice.

Bureau of Justice Statistics. (2010). *Homicide trends in the United States*. Retrieved from BJS: Bureau of Justice Statistics on Nov. 28, 2010. http://bjs.ojp.usdoj.gov/homicide/tables/totalstab.cfm.

Bureau of Justice Statistics. (2010). *Sexual victimization in prisons and jails reported by inmates 2008-09*. Retrieved September 2, 2011 from. http://bjs.ojp.usdoj.gov/content/pub/pdf/svpjri0809.pdf.

Burford, G., Pennell, J., MacLeod, S., Campbell, S., & Lyall, G. (1996). Reunification as an extended family matter. *Community Alternatives: International Journal of Family Care, 8*(3), 33−55.

Burke, C. (1992). *Vision narratives of women in prison*. Knoxville: University of Tennessee Press.

Burns, T., Fazel, S., Fahy, T., Fitzpatrick, R., Rogers, R., Sinclair, J., Linsell, L., Doll, H., & Yiend, J. (2011). Dangerous Severe Personality Disordered (DSPD) patients: Characteristics and comparison with other high-risk offenders. *The International Journal of Forensic Mental Health, 10*(2), 127−136.

Bursten, B. (1981). The psychiatrist-witness and legal guilt. *American Journal of Psychiatry, 139*, 784−788.

Bussey, K., Lee, K., & Grimbeck, E. J. (1993). Lies and secrets: Implications for children's reporting of sexual abuse. In G. S. Goodman, & B. L. Bottoms (Eds.), *Child victims, child witnesses: Understanding and improving testimony* (pp. 147−168). New York: Guilford Press.

Bussey, M. (1996). Impact of kids first seminar for divorcing parents: A three-year follow-up. *Journal of Divorce and Remarriage, 26*, 129−149.

Butcher, J. N. (2011). *A beginner's guide to the MMPI-2* (3rd edn.). Washington, DC: US: American Psychological Association.

Butler, B. (2008). The role of death qualification in venirepersons' susceptibility to victim impact statements. *Psychology, Crime, and Law, 14*(2), 133−141.

Butler, B. M., & Moran, G. (2002, Apr). The role of death qualification in venirepersons' evaluations of aggravating and mitigating circumstances in capital trials. *Law & Human Behavior, 26*(2), 175−184.

Butler, B., & Moran, G. (2007a). The impact of death qualification, belief in a just world, legal authoritarianism, and locus of control on venirepersons' evaluations of aggravating and mitigating circumstances in capital trials. *Behavioral Sciences & the Law, 25*, 57−68.

Butler, B., & Moran, G. (2007b). The role of death qualification and need for cognition in venirepersons' evaluations of expert scientific testimony in capital trials. *Behavioral Sciences & the Law, 25*, 561−571.

Butler, T., Andrews, G., Allnutt, S., Sakashita, C., Smith, & Basson, J. (2006). Mental disorders in an Australian prison: Comparison with a community sample. *Australian and New Zealand Journal of Psychiatry, 40*(3), 272−276.

Butterfield, L., & Broad, H. (2002). *Children, young people, and the internet*. Available at. www.netsafe.org.nz/articles/articleschildren.aspx. Accessed April 30, 2011.

Buzawa, E. S., & Buzawa, C. G. (2003). *Domestic Violence: The Criminal Justice Response* (3rd edn.). Thousand Oaks, CA: Sage.

Buzawa, E. S., & Hotaling, G. T. (2006). The impact of relationship status, gender, and minor status in the police response to domestic assaults. *Victims & Offenders, 1*, 323−360.

Byrne, S., Byrne, M. K., & Howells, K. (2001). Defining the needs in a contemporary correctional environment: The contribution of psychology. *Psychiatry, Psychology, & Law, 8*(1), 97−104.

California Department of Corrections. (1991). *California prisoners and parolees 1990*. Sacramento: State of California.

California Research Bureau. (2000). California research bureau reports: Children of incarcerated parents. *Family and Corrections Network*. Accessed September 13, 2011, at. www.fcnetwork.org/reading/simmons.html.

Calvete, E., Orue, I., Estevez, A., Villardon, L., & Padilla, P. (2010). Cyberbullying in adolescents: Modalities and aggressors' profile. *Computers in Human Behavior, 26*, 1128−1135.

Camara, W. J., & Merenda, P. F. (2000, Dec). Using personality tests in preemployment screening: Issues raised in Soroka v. Dayton Hudson Corporation. *Psychology, Public Policy, & Law, 6*(4), 1164−1186.

Campbell, J., Sharps, P., Laughon, K., Webster, D., et al. (2003, Jul). Risk factors for femicide in abusive relationships: Results from a multisite case control study. *American Journal of Public Health, 93*(7), 1089−1098.

Campbell, M. A. (2005). Cyber-bullying: An old problem in a new guise? *Australian Journal of Guidance & Counseling, 15*(1), 68–76.

Campbell, M. A. (2010). Research on cyberbullying. *Australian Journal of Guidance & Counseling, 20*(2). iii-iv.

Campfield, K., & Hills, A. (2001). Effect of timing of critical incident stress debriefing (CISD) on posttraumatic symptoms. *Journal of Traumatic Stress, 14*(2), 327–340.

Canetti, D., Galea, S., Hall, B. J., Johnson, R. J., Palmieri, P. A., & Hobfoll, S. E. (2010). Exposure to prolonged socio-political conflict and the risk of PTSD and depression among Palestinians. *Psychiatry, 73*, 219–231.

Cant, I. (2007). The secondary family: The result of strong community partnering. *Mental Health Review Journal, 12*(3), 30–32.

Canton, R. (2008). *Addressing offending behavior: Context, practice, and values. Devon.* United Kingdom: Willan Publishing.

Cantor, J. D. (2005). Of pills and needles: Involuntarily medicating the psychotic inmate when execution looms. *Indiana Health Law Review, 2*, 119–131

Carlson, J., Anson, R., & Thomas, G. (2003). Correctional officer burnout and stress: does gender matter? *The Prison Journal, 83*, 277–288.

Carlson, J., & Thomas, G. (2006). Burnout among prison caseworkers and corrections officers. *Journal of Offender Rehabilitation, 43*(3), 19–34.

Carolan, M., Burns-Jager, K., Bozek, K., & Chew. (2010). Women who have their parental rights removed by the state: The interplay of trauma and oppression. *Journal of Feminist Family Therapy, 22*, 171–186.

Carr, K., Hinkle, B., & Ingram, B. (1991). Establishing mental health and substance abuse services in jails. *Journal of Prison & Jail Health, 10*(2), 77–89.

Cartwright, C. (2006). You want to know how it affected me? Young adults' perceptions of the impact of parental divorce. *Journal of Divorce & Remarriage, 44*(3-4), 125–143.

Case of Roland, K. (June 27, 1997). *Landgericht Nuernberg-Fuerth.* KLs 600 Js 37934/97.

Cashmore, J., & Parkinson, P. (2008). Children's and parent's perceptions on children's participation in decision making after parental separation and divorce. *Family Court Review, 46*(1), 91–104.

Cattaneo, L. B., & Goodman, L. A. (2010). Through the lens of therapeutic jurisprudence: The relationship between empowerment and well-being for intimate partner violence victims. *Journal of Interpersonal Violence, 25*(2), 481–502.

Ceci, S. J., & Bruck, M. (1993). Suggestibility of the child witness: A historical review and synthesis. *Psychological Bulletin, 113*, 403–439.

Centers for Disease Control and Prevention. (2007). Effects on violence of laws and policies facilitating the transfer of youth from the juvenile to the adult justice system: A report on recommendations of the task force on community preventive services. *MMWR, 2007*(56(No. RR-9)), 1–10, Accessed 03/11/2011 at. www.cdc.gov/mmwr/pdf/rr/rr5609.pdf.

Cepeda, A., & Valdez, A. (2003, Jan). Risk behaviors among young Mexican American gang-associated females: Sexual relations, partying, substance use, and crime. *Journal of Adolescent Research, 18*(1), 90–106.

Chan, R. W., Raboy, B., & Patterson, C. J. (1998). Psychosocial adjustment among children conceived via donor insemination by lesbian and heterosexual mothers. *Journal of Child Development, 69*, 443–451.

Chapell, D. (2010). From sorcery to stun guns and suicide: The eclectic and global challenges of policing and the mentally ill. *Police Practice and Research, 11*(4), 289–300.

Chapman, J. F., & Ford, J. D. (2008). Relationships between suicide risk, traumatic experiences, and substance use among juvenile detainees. *Archives of Suicide Research, 12*, 50–61.

Chappelle, W., & Rosengren, K. (2001). Maintaining composure and credibility as an expert witness during cross-examination. *Journal of Forensic Psychology Practice, 1*(3), 51–68.

Cheeseman, K. A., & Worley, R. (2006). Women on the wing: perceptions about female correctional officer job competency in a southern prison system. *The Southwest Journal of Criminal Justice, 3*(2), 86–106.

Cheng, Y., Chen, L., Liu, K., & Chen, Y. (2011). Development and psychometric evaluation of the school bullying scales: A Rasch measurement approach. *Educational and Psychological Measurement, 71*(1), 200–216.

Chesney-Lind, M. (1988). Girls in jail. *Crime and Delinquency, 34*, 150–168.

Chicago Legal Aid to Incarcerated Mothers. (1997). *Women in prison: Fact sheet* [On-line], Available: www.c-l-a-i-m.org/factsheet.htm.

Chopra, M. P., Weiss, D., Stinnett, J. L., & Oslin, D. W. (2003, Mar-Apr). Treatment-related decisional capacity. *American Journal of Geriatric Psychiatry, 11*(2), 257–258.

Christopher, P. P., Boland, R. J., Recupero, P. R., & Phillips, K. A. (2010). Psychiatric residents' experience conducting disability evaluations. *Academic Psychiatry, 34,* 211–215.

Church, G. J. (1990). The view from behind bars. *Time, 135,* 20–22.

Clarke, A. Y., Cullen, A. E., Walwyn, R., & Fahy, T. (2010). A quasi-experimental pilot study of the Reasoning and Rehabilitation Programme with mentally disordered offenders. *The Journal of Forensic Psychiatry and Psychology* 491–500.

Clear, T., & Cole, G. (1997). *American corrections.* Belmont, CA: Wadsworth.

Clements, P. (2004). The rehabilitative role of arts education in prison: Accommodation or enlightenment? *International Journal of Art Design Education, 23*(2), 169–178.

Clements, C. B., Althouse, R., Ax, R. K., Magaletta, P. R., Fagan, T. J., & Wormith, J. S. (2007). Systemic issues and correctional outcomes. *Criminal Justice and Behavior, 34*(7), 919–932.

Clements, C. B., & Wakeman, E. E. (2007). Raising the bar: The case of doctoral training forensic psychology. *Journal of Forensic Psychology Practice, 7*(2), 53–63.

Cloud, J. (2011). A mind unhinged. *Time Special Report: Guns. Speech. Madness. Where we go from Arizona, 177*(3), 32–39.

Cloyes, K. G., Wong, B., Latimer, S., & Abarca, J. (2010). Women, serious mental illness and recidivism: A gender-based analysis of recidivism risk for women with SMI released from prison. *Journal of Forensic Nursing, 6,* 3–14.

Coalition of Juvenile Justice. (2009). *Grants at-a-glance, 1–17.* Accessed on 08-29-11. www.michigan.gov/documents/ProgSumm_4th_Edition_CJJ_106148_7.pdf.

Coffman, J., Guerin, D., & Gottfried, A. (2006). Reliability and validity of the parent-child relationship inventory (PCRI): Evidence from a longitudinal cross-informant investigation. *Psychological Assessment, 18*(2), 209–214.

Cohen, D. A. (1997). *Sexual psychopaths* [On-line], Available: http://members.tripod.com/»dazc/sexopat.htm#watiz.

Cohen, F., & Dvoskin, J. (1992, Jul-Aug). Inmates with mental disorders: A guide to law and practice. *Mental & Physical Disability Law Reporter, 16*(4), 462–470.

Cohen, F., & Gerbasi, J. B. (2005). Legal issues regarding the provision of mental health care in correctional settings. In C. L. Scott, & J. B. Gerbasi (Eds.), *Handbook of correctional mental health* (pp. 259–285). Arlington, VA: American Psychiatric Publishing.

Colb, S. F. (2003). The conviction of Andrea Yates: A narrative of denial. *Duke Journal of Gender Law & Policy, 10,* 141–148.

Coleman, K., Jansson, K., Kaiza, P., & Reed, E. (2007). *Homicides, Firearms Offenses and Intimate Partner Violence 2005/2006.*

Crime in England and Wales, Supplementary Volume. (2005/2006). *56 Home Office Statistical Bulletin.* London: Home Office.

Coles, E. M., & Veiel, H. O. F. (2001). Expert testimony and pseudoscience: How mental health professionals are taking over the courtroom. *International Journal of Law & Psychiatry, 24*(6), 607–625.

Collins, R., Lincoln, R., & Frank, M. (2005). The need for rapport in police interviews. *Humanities and Social Sciences Papers.* Available at. http://works.bepress.com/robyn_lincoln/14.

Collof, P. (2006). *96 Minutes. Texas Monthly, August 2006.* Retrieved from. www.texasmonthly.com.

Columbia. (2006). *The Columbia Encyclopedia Injunction Defined* (6th edn.). Columbia University Press.

Columbia Encyclopedia. (2006). *The Columbia Encyclopedia Injunction Defined* (6th edn.). Columbia University Press.

Comes, J. T., Bertrand, L. D., Paetseh, J. J., & Hornick, J. P. (2003, Spr). Self-reported delinquency among Alberta's youth: Findings from a survey of 2,001 junior and senior high school students. *Adolescence, 38*(149), 75–92.

Community Care. (2003, 5/1). Prostitution study points to alienation. *Community Care, 1470,* 11−18.

Condie, L., & Condie, D. (2007). Termination of parental rights. In A. Goldstein (Ed.), *Forensic psychology: Emerging topics and expanding roles.* Hoboken, NJ: John Wiley and Sons Inc.

Conley, R. W., Luckasson, R., & Bouthilet, G. N. (1992). *The criminal justice system and mental retardation.* Baltimore, MD: Paul H. Brookes.

Conlon, L., Fahy, T., & Conroy, R. (1999). *PTSD in ambulant RTA victims: Prevalence, predictors and a randomized controlled trial of psychological debriefing in prophylaxis.* Unpublished manuscript.

Connell, M. A. (2003). A psychobiographical approach to the evaluation for sentence mitigation. *The Journal of Psychiatry and Law, 31,* 319−354.

Cookston, J. T., & Fung, W. W. (2011). The kids' turn program evaluation: Probing change within a community based intervention for separating families. *Family Court Review, 49*(2), 348−363.

Cooper, C. (1997). Patrol police officer conflict resolution processes. *Journal of Criminal Justice, 25*(2), 87−101.

Cooper, S. W., Estes, R. J., Giardino, A. P., Kellogg, N. D., & Veith, V. I. (2005). *Medical, Legal, & Social Aspects of Child Exploitation.* St Louis, MO: G.W. Medical Publishing, Inc.

Cordoba, O. A., & Chapel, J. L. (1983). Medroxyprogesterone acetate antiandrogen treatment of hypersexuality in a pedophiliac sex offender. *American Journal of Psychiatry, 140,* 1036−1039.

Cornelius, G. F. (2009). *The art of the con: Avoiding offender manipulation* (2nd edn.). Manassas Park, VA: Impact Publications.

Cornell, D. G. (2006). *School violence: Fears versus facts.* Mahwah, NJ: Erlbaum.

Cornell, D. G., & Hawk, G. L. (1989). Clinical presentation of malingerers diagnosed by experienced forensic psychologists. *Law and Human Behavior, 13*(4), 375−383.

Correia, M. E. (1997). Boot camps, exercise, and delinquency. *An analytical critique of the use of physical exercise to facilitate decreases in delinquent behavior, 13,* 94−113.

Corrigan, P. W., & Kleinlein, P. (2005). The impact of mental illness stigma. In P. W. Corrigan (Ed.), *On the stigma of mental illness: Practical strategies for research and social change* (pp. 11−44). Washington, DC: American Psychological Association.

Cortina, J. M., Doherty, M. L., Schmitt, N., Kaufman, G., & Smith, R. G. (1992). The "Big Five" personality factors in the IPI and MMPI: Predictors of police performance. *Personnel Psychology, 45,* 119−140.

Costanzo, M., & Leo, R. A. (2007). Research and expert testimony on interrogations and confessions. *Expert psychological testimony for the courts* 69−98, Available at: http://papers.ssrn.com/sol3/papers.cfm?abstract_id=1521647.

Costin, L. B., Karger, H. J., & Stoesz, D. (1996). *The politics of child abuse in America.* New York, NY: Oxford University Press.

Cothran, M., & Jacquin, J. (2011). Brief discussion on inductive/deductive profiling. *Investigative Psychology, 22*(1), 15−25.

Cowley, G., Springen, K., Miller, S., Lewis, S., & Titunik, V. (1993, August 16). Who's looking after the interests of the children? *Newsweek* 54−55.

Cox, D. (2009). When to start the process. In C. M. Nezu, J. Finch, & N. P. Simon (Eds.), *Becoming board certified by the American Board of Professional Psychology* (pp. 475−556). New York: Oxford University Press.

Cox, J. F., & Morschauser, P. C. (1997). A solution to the problem of jail suicide. *Crisis, 18*(4), 178−184.

Craig, L. A., Stringer, I., & Moss, T. (2006). Treating sexual offenders with learning disabilities in the community. *International Journal of Offender Therapy and Comparative Criminology, 50*(4), 369−390.

Craigie, Jillian (2011). Competence, practical rationality, and what a patient values. *Bioethics, 25*(6), 326−333.

Cramer, R. J., Brodsky, S. L., & DeCoster, J. (2009). Expert witness confidence and juror personality: Their impact on credibility and persuasion in the courtroom. *Journal of the American Academy of Psychiatry and Law, 37*(1), 63−74.

Crawford, L. (2009). No way out: An analysis of exit processes for gang injunctions. *California Law Review, 97,* 161−193.

Crisanti, A. S., & Love, E. J. (2002, Nov-Dec). From one legal system to another? An examination of the relationship between involuntary hospitalization and arrest. *International Journal of Law & Psychiatry, 25*(6), 581—597.

Crisanti, A. S., & Love, E. J. (2001, Jul-Oct). Characteristics of psychiatric inpatients detained under civil commitment legislation: A Canadian study. *International Journal of Law & Psychiatry, 24*(4—5), 399—410.

Critten, M., & West, D. (2006). The lowest of the low? Addressing the disparity between community view, public policy, and treatment effectiveness for sex offenders. *Law and Psychology, 30,* 79—88.

Crosby-Currie, C. (1996). Children's involvement in contested custody cases: Practices and experiences of legal and mental health professionals. *Law and Human Behavior, 20,* 289—310.

Crouch, B. M. (1985). Pandora's box: Women guards in men's prisons. *Journal of Criminal Justice, 13,* 535—548.

Cukor, J., Wyka, K., Jayasingthe, N., Weathers, F., Giosan, C., Leck, P., Roberts, J., Spielman, L., Crane, M., & Difede, J. (2011). Prevalence and predictors of posttraumatic stress symptoms in utility workers deployed to the World Trade Center following the attacks of September 11, 2001. *Depression and Anxiety, 28,* 210—217.

Cummings, D. L., & Thompson, M. N. (2009). Suicidal or manipulative? The role of mental health counselors in overcoming a false dichotomy in identifying and treating self-harming inmates. *Journal of Mental Health Counseling, 31*(3), 201—212.

Cunningham, M. D., & Reidy, T. J. (2001). A matter of life or death: Special considerations and heightened practice standards in capital sentencing evaluations. *Behavioral Sciences and the Law, 19,* 473—490.

Cunningham, M. D., Sorenson, J. R., Vigen, M. P., & Woods, S. O. (2010). Inmate homicides: Killers, victims, motives, and circumstances. *Journal of Criminal Justice, 38*(4), 348—358.

Cushing, G., & Greenblatt, S. B. (2009). Vulnerability to foster care drift after the termination of parental rights. *Research on Social Work Practice, 19*(6), 694—704.

Daéid, N. (1997). Differences in offender profiling in the United States of America and the United Kingdom. *Forensic Science International, 90,* 25—31.

Daftary-Kapur, T., Dumas, R., & Penrod, S. D. (2010). Jury decision-making biases and methods to counter them. *Legal and Criminological Psychology, 15,* 133—154.

Dahm, J. J. (2005). *Nebraska Correctional Center for Women Program.* Retrieved on September 7, 2011 from http://www.corrections.nebraska.gov/nccw.html.

D'Angelo, J. (2007). The complex nature of juvenile court judges' transfer decisions: A study of judicial attitudes. *The Social Science Journal, 44,* 147—159.

Daniel, A. E. (2006). Preventing suicide in prison: A collaborative responsibility of administrative, custodial, and clinical staff. *Journal of the American Academy of Psychiatry and the Law, 34,* 165—175.

Daniels, J. A., Bilksy, K. D. P., Chamberlain, S., & Haist, J. (2011). School barricaded captive-takings: An exploratory investigation of school resource officer responses. *Psychological Services, 8*(3), 178—188.

Daniels, J. A., Bradley, M. C., & Hays, M. (2007). The impact of school violence on school personnel: Implications for psychologists. *Professional Psychology: Research and Practice, 38*(6), 652—659.

Davey, J., Obst, P., & Sheehan, M. (2001, May). It goes with the job: Officers' insights into the impact of stress and culture on alcohol consumption within the policing occupation. *Drugs: Education, Prevention & Policy, 8*(2), 141—149.

Davidson, D. (2008). Federal law and state intervention when parents fail: Has national guidance of our child welfare system been successful? *Family Law Quarterly* 481—510.

Davidson, H. (2006). Children's rights and American law: A response. *Emory International Law Review, 20,* 69—80.

Davis, A. Y. (2000, Sep). Women in prison. *Essence, 31*(5), 150—152.

Davis, D., & Follette, W. C. (2002). Rethinking the probative value of evidence: Base rates, intuitive profiling, and the "postdiction" of behavior. *Law & Human Behavior, 26*(2), 133—158.

Davis, M. (1995). Critical incident stress debriefing: The case for corrections. *The Keeper's Voice* [On-line], *16.* Available: http://www.acsp.uic.edu/iaco/kv160145.htm.

Dawson, J. (2010). Reproductive rights, parental rights, and family violence: A dangerous intersection. *Reproductive & Sexual Health and Justice: News, Analysis, & Commentary.* Retrieved from www.rhrealitycheck.org/blog/2010/03/17/reproductive-rights-parental-rights-family-violencedangerous-intersection.

Dawson, J. M., & Langan, P. A. (1994). *Murder in families*. Washington, DC: Bureau of Justice Statistics.

Dear, G. E., Thomson, D. M., & Hills, A. M. (2000, Apr). Self-harm in prison: Manipulators can also be suicide attempters. *Criminal Justice & Behavior, 27*(2), 160–175.

Debele, G. A. (2007). Custody and parenting by persons other than biological parents: When non-traditional family law collides with the constitution. *North Dakota Law Review*, (83), 1227–1272.

Decker, S. (2002). *Policing gangs and youth violence (Ed)*. Belmont, CA: Wadsworth.

Declue, G. (2005). Three things we have learned from studying investigative interviews by police that should be used to guide investigative interviews by military and intelligence agencies. *Open Access Journal of Forensic Psychology, 1*, E81–E89.

DeJong, C., Burgess-Proctor, A., & Elis, L. (2008). Police officer perceptions of intimate partner violence: An analysis of observational data. *Violence and Victims, 23*(6), 683–696.

De La Fuente, L., De La Fuente, E. I., & Garcia, J. (2003, Jun). Effects of pretrial juror bias, strength of evidence and deliberation process on juror decisions: New validity evidence of the Juror Bias Scale scores. *Psychology, Crime & Law, 9*(2), 197–209.

DeMatteo, D., Marczyk, G., Krauss, D., & Burl, J. (2009). Educational and training models in forensic psychology. *Training and Education in Professional Psychology, 3*, 184–191.

DeMatteo, D., Marczyk, G., & Pich, M. (2007). A national survey of state legislation defining mental retardation: Implications for policy and practice. *Behavioral Sciences and the Law, 25*, 781–802.

Denno, D. W. (2003). Who is Andrea Yates? A short story about insanity. *Duke Journal of Gender Law & Policy, 10*, 1–60.

Dernevik, M., Grann, M., & Johansson, S. (2002). Violent behaviour in forensic psychiatric patients: Risk assessment and different risk-management levels using the HCR-20. *Psychology, Crime, & Law, 8*, 93–111.

Detrick, P., & Chibnall, J. T. (2002). Prediction of police officer performance with the Inwald Personality Inventory. *Journal of Police & Criminal Psychology, 17*(2), 9–17.

Detrick, P., & Chibnall, J. T. (2008). Positive response distortion by police officer applicants: Association of Paulhus Deception Scales with MMPI-2 and Inwald Personality Inventory Validity scales. *Assessment, 15*(1), 87–96.

Detrick, P., Chibnall, J. T., & Call, C. (2010). Demand effects on positive response distortion by police officer applicants on the revised NEO Personality Inventory. *Journal of Personality Assessment, 92*(5), 410–415.

Detrick, P., Chibnall, J. T., & Rosso, M. (2001, Oct). Minnesota Multiphasic Personality Inventory-2 in police officer selection: Normative data and relation to the Inwald Personality Inventory. *Professional Psychology: Research & Practice, 32*(5), 484–490.

Deutsch, R., Coates, C., & Fieldstone, L. (2008). Parenting coordination: An emerging role. In C. Coates, & L. Fieldstone (Eds.), *Innovations in interventions with high conflict families* (pp. 187–223). Madison, WI: Association of Family and Conciliation Courts.

DeVoe, E. R., Klein, T. P., Bannon, W., Jr., & Miranda-Julian, C. (2011). Young children in the aftermath of the World Trade Center attacks. *Psychological Trauma, Theory, Research, Practice, and Policy, 3*, 1–7.

Dewa, C., & Lin, E. (2000, Jul). Chronic physical illness, psychiatric disorder and disability in the workplace. *Social Science & Medicine, 51*(1), 41–50.

De Wilde, E. J., Kienhorst, I. C., Diekstra, R. F., & Wolters, W. H. (1992). The relationship between adolescent suicidal behavior and life events in childhood and adolescence. *American Journal of Psychiatry, 149*(1), 45–51.

Dexter, H., Cutler, B., & Moran, G. (1992). A test of voir dire as a remedy for the prejudicial effects of pretrial publicity. *Journal of Applied Social Psychology, 22*(10), 819–832.

Dial, K. C., & Worley, R. M. (2008). Crossing the line: A quantitative analysis of inmate boundary violators in a southern prison system. *American Journal of Criminal Justice, 33*, 69–84.

Diaz, E. I. (2009). Police oversight. In J. deRivera (Ed.), *Handbook on building cultures of peace* (pp. 287–301). New York: Springer Science.

Diaz-Aguado, M. J. (2006). Peer violence in adolescents and its prevention from the school. *Psychology in Spain, 10*, 75–87.

Dillen, A. (2003, Oct). Queer family values: Debunking the myth of the nuclear family. *Archives of Sexual Behavior, 32*(5), 489–490.

Dilmac, B. (2009). Psychological needs as a predictor of cyber bullying: A preliminary report on college students. *Kuram ve Uygulamada Eglitim Billimleri, 9*(3), 1307–1325.

Dinkes, R., Kemp, J., Baum, K., & Snyder, T. D. (2009). *Indicators of School Crime and Safety: 2009* (NCES 2010–012/NCJ 228478). Washington, DC: National Center for Education Statistics, Institute of Education Sciences, U.S. Department of Education, and Bureau of Justice Statistics, Office of Justice Programs, U.S. Department of Justice.

DiPietro, A. L. (1993, July). Lies, promises, or threats: The voluntariness of confessions. *FBI Law Enforcement Bulletin*, 27–31.

Dishion, T. J., Véronneau, M., & Myers, W. (2010). Cascading peer dynamics underlying the progression from problem behavior to violence in early to late adolescence. *Development and Psychopathology, 22*(3), 603–619.

Dobash, R. P., & Dobash, R. E. (2004). Women's violence to men in intimate relationships: working on a puzzle. *The British Journal of Criminology, 44*(3), 324–349.

Dobson, V., & Sales, B. (2000). The science of infanticide and mental illness. *Psychology, Public Policy, & Law, 6*, 1098–1109.

Dolan, L., Bowyer, D., Freeman, C., & Little, K. (1999). *Critical incident stress debriefing after trauma: Is it effective?* Unpublished raw data.

Dolgin, J. L. (1996). Why has the best interest standard survived? The historic and social context. *Children's Legal Rights Journal, 16*, 2–10.

Donaldson, T., & Abbott, B. (2011). Prediction in the individual case: An explanation and application of its use with the static -99R in sexually violent predator risk assessments. *American Journal of Forensic Psychology, 29*(1), 5–35.

Donner, M. (2006). Tearing the child apart: The contribution of narcissism, envy, and perverse modes of thought to child custody wars. *Psychoanalytic Psychology, 23*(3), 542–553.

D'Onofrio, B. M., Turkheimer, E., Emery, R. E., Maes, H. H., Silberg, J., & Eaves, L. J. (2007). A children of twins study of parential divorce and offspring psychopathology. *Journal of Child Psychology and Psychiatry, 48*(7), 667–675.

Doob, A. N., & Sprott, J. B. (1998, Apr). Is the "quality" of youth violence becoming more serious? *Canadian Journal of Criminology, 40*(2), 185–194.

Douglas, E. M., & McCarthy, S. C. (2011). Child maltreatment fatalities: Predicting rates and the efficacy of child welfare policy. *Journal of Policy Practice, 10*(2), 128–143.

Douglas, J. E., & Burgess, A. E. (1986, December). Criminal profiling: A viable investigative tool against violent crime. *FBI Law Enforcement Bulletin*, pp. 9–13.

Douglas, K. S., Guy, L. S., & Hart, S. D. (2009). Psychosis as a risk factor for violence to others: A meta-analysis. *Psychological Bulletin, 135*(5), 679–706.

Dowden, C., & Tellier, C. (2004). Predicting work-related stress in correctional officers: a meta-analysis. *Journal of Criminal Justice, 32*, 31–47.

Downs, W. R., Rindels, B., & Atkinson, C. (2007). Women's use of physical and nonphysical self-defense strategies during incidents of partner violence. *Violence Against Women, 13*, 28–45.

Drake, R. E., Skinner, J. S., Bond, G. R., & Goldman, H. H. (2009). Social security and mental illness: Reducing disability with supported employment. *Health Affairs, 28*(3), 761–770.

Drerup, L. C., Croysdale, A., & Hoffman, N. G. (2008). Patterns of behavioral health conditions among adolescents in a juvenile justice system. *Professional Psychology: Research and Practice, 39*(2), 122–128.

Dripps, D. A. (1988). Supreme court review. Foreward: Against police interrogation – and the privilege against self incrimination. *Journal of Criminal Law and Criminology, 78*(4), 699–734.

Drogin, E. Y., & Young, K. (2008). Forensic mental health aspects of adolescent "cyber bullying": A jurisprudent science perspective. *Journal of Psychiatry & Law, 36*(4), 679−690.

Drummond, S., & Portner, J. (1999). Arrests top 350 in threats, bomb scares. *Education Week on the Web, 18* (12-14). Available at www.edweek.org/ew/articles/1999/05/26/37threat.h18.html. Accessed May 8, 2011.

Drury, A. J., & DeLisi, M. (2011). Gangkill: An exploratory empirical assessment of gang membership, homicide offending, and prison misconduct. *Crime & Delinquency, 57*(1), 130−146.

Druss, B. G., Marcus, S. C., Rosenheck, R. A., Olfson, M., Tanielian, T., & Princus, H. A. (2001). Understanding disability in mental and general medical conditions. *American Journal of Psychiatry, 157*, 1485−1491.

Drylie, J. J. (2008). Research on suicide by cop. In J. M. Violanti, & J. J. Drylie (Eds.), *Copicide: Concepts, cases, and controversies of suicide by cop.* Springfield, IL: Charles C. Thomas Publisher.

Drylie, J. J., & Violanti, J. M. (2008). *Copicide: Concepts, cases, and controversies of suicide by cop.* Springfield, IL: Charles C. Thomas Publisher.

Drysdale, D., Modzeleski, W., & Simons, A. (2010). Campus Attacks: Targeted violence affecting institutions of higher education. U.S. Secret Service, U.S. Department of Homeland Security, Office of Safe and Drug-Free Schools, U.S. Department of Education, and Federal Bureau of Investigation, U.S. Department of Justice.

D'Silva, K., & Ferriter, M. (2003). Substance use by the mentally disordered committing serious offences − A high-security hospital study. *Journal of Forensic Psychiatry & Psychology, 14*(1), 178−193.

Dudley, R., Siitarinen, J., James, I., & Dodgson, G. (2009). What do people with psychosis think caused their psychosis? A Q methodology study. *Behavioural and Cognitive Psychotherapy, 37*(1), 11−24.

DuRand, C. J., Burtka, G., Federman, E., Haycox, J., & Smith, J. (1995). A quarter century of suicide in a major urban jail: Implications for community psychiatry. *American Journal of Psychiatry, 152*(7), 1077−1080.

DuRant, R. H., Barkin, S., & Krowchuk, D. P. (2001). Evaluation of a peaceful conflict resolution and violence prevention curriculum for sixth-grade students. *Journal of Adolescent Health, 28*(5), 386−393.

Durousseu, R. (2008). Termination of parental rights: Recall of attachment experiences among adults who were legally separated from their parents. *Dissertation Abstracts International* 7808.

Duvall, J. C., & Morris, R. J. (2006). Assessing mental retardation in death penalty cases: Critical issues for psychology and psychological practice. *Professional Psychology: Research and Practice, 37*(6), 658−665.

Dvoskin, J. A., & Guy, L. S. (2008). On being an expert witness: It's not about you. *Psychiatry, Psychology and Law, 15*, 202−212.

Eddy, J. M., & Reid, J. B. (2001). *The antisocial behavior of the adolescent children of incarcerated parents: A developmental perspective.* Accessed September 13, 2011, at. http://aspe.hhs.gov/hsp/prison2home02/eddy.htm.

Eddy, J. M., & Reid, J. B. (2001). *From prison to home: The effect of incarceration and reentry on children, families, and communities the antisocial behavior of the adolescent children of incarcerated parents: A Developmental Perspective.* Available at http://aspe.hhs.gov/hsp/prison2home02/eddy.htm.

Edens, J. F., Poythress, N. G., Lilienfeld, S. O., & Patrick, C. J. (2008). A prospective comparison of two measures of psychopathy in the prediction of institutional misconduct. *Behavioral Science and Law, 26*(5), 529−541.

Edinburgh, L., & Saewyc, E. (2008). A novel, intensive home-visiting intervention for runaway, sexually exploited girls. *Journal for Specialists in Pediatric Nursing, 14(1)*, 41−48.

Edwards, O., & Ray, S. (2008). An attachment and school satisfaction framework for helping children raised by grandparents. *School Psychology Quarterly, 23*(1), 125−138.

Edwards, W., & Hensley, C. (2001). Contextualizing sex offender management legislation and policy: Evaluating the problem of latent consequences in community notification laws. *International Journal of Offender Therapy and Comparative Criminology, 45*(1), 83−101.

Egley, A., Jr., & O'Donnell, C. E. (2009). Highlights of the 2007 national youth gang survey. *OJJDP Fact Sheet* April 2009.

Ehrenreich, J. H. (2002). *A guide for humanitarian, health care, and human rights workers.* Old Westbury: Center for Psychology and Society, State University of New York.

Eisenberg, J. R. (2001). The role of the forensic psychologist in death penalty litigation. *Workshop handout presented at the American Academy of Forensic Psychology, San Antonio, TX.*

Eisenberg, N., & Silver, R. C. (2011). Growing up in the shadow of terrorism: Youth in America after 9/11. *American Psychologist, 66*, 468–481.

Eisikovits, Z., Buchbinder, E., & Bshara, A. (2008). Between the person and the culture: Israeli Arab couple's perceptions of police intervention in intimate partner violence. *Journal of Ethnic & Cultural Diversity in Social Work, 17*(2), 108–129.

Eitle, D. (2005). The influence of mandatory arrest policies, police organizational characteristics, and situational variables on the probability of arrest in domestic violence cases. *Crime and Delinquency, 51*, 573–597.

Elbogen, E. B., & Johnson, S. C. (2009). The intricate link between violence and mental disorder: Results from the national epidemiologic survey on alcohol and related conditions. *Archives of General Psychiatry, 66*(2), 152–161.

Elbogen, E. B., Patry, M., & Scalora, M. J. (2003). The impact of community notification laws on sex offender treatment attitudes. *International Journal of Law & Psychiatry, 26*(2), 207–219.

Elias, R. (1986). *The politics of victimization.* New York: Oxford University Press.

Ellsberg, M. (2006). Violence against women and the Millennium Developmental Goals: Facilitating women's access to support. *International Journal of Gynecology & Obstetrics, 94*, 325–332.

Elliot, B., & Verdeyen, V. (2003). *Game over! Strategies for redirecting inmate deception.* Manassas Park, VA: Impact Publications.

Elliott, W. N. (2006). Power and control tactics employed by prison inmates: A case study. *Federal Probation, 70*(1). Retrieved from www.uscourts.gov/uscourts/FederalCourts/PPS/Fedprob/2006-06/inmatetactics.html.

Ellis, E. M., & Boyan, S. (2010). Intervention strategies for parent coordinators in parental alienation cases. *The American Journal of Family Therapy, 38*(3), 218–236.

Ellis, R., Malm, K., & Bishop, E. (2009). The timing of termination of parental rights: A balancing act for children's best interests. *Child Trends Research Brief, 2009*(40), 1–13.

Ellsberg, M. (2006). Violence against women and the Millennium Developmental Goals: Facilitating women's access to support. *International Journal of Gynecology & Obstetrics, 94*, 325–332.

Elrod, L. D. (2006). Moving in the right direction? Best interest of the child emerging as the standard for relocation cases. *Journal of Child Custody, 3*(3–4), 29–61.

Emery, R. E., Otto, R. K., & O'Donohue, W. T. (2005). A critical assessment of child custody evaluations: Limited science and a flawed system. *Psychological Science in the Public Interest, 6*(3), 1–29.

Endrass, J., Rossegger, A., Urbaniok, F., Laubacher, A., & Vetter, S. (2008). Predicting violent infractions in a Swiss state penitentiary: A replication study of the PCL-R in a population of sex and violent offenders. *BMC Psychiatry, 8,* 74.

Enelow, A. J., & Leo, R. J. (2002). Evaluation of the vocational factors impacting on psychiatric disability. *Psychiatric Annals, 32*(5), 293–297.

Erickson, P. E. (2000, Spr). Federal child abuse and child neglect policy in the United States since 1974: A review and critique. *Criminal Justice Review, 25*(1), 77–92.

Esbensen, F. A., Deschenes, E. P., & Winfree, T. L. (1999). Differences between gang girls and gang boys: Results from a multisite survey. *Youth & Society, 31*(1), 27–53.

Estevez, E., Murgui, S., & Musitu, G. (2009). Psychological adjustment in bullies and victims of school violence. *European Journal of Psychology and Education, XXIV(4)*, 473–483.

Etheridge, R., Hale, C., & Hambrick, M. (1984). Female employees in all-male correctional facilities. *Federal Probation, 48*, 54–65.

Etter, G. W. (2003, Spr). Strategic planning for law enforcement agencies: Management as a gang fighting strategy. *Journal of Gang Research, 10*(3), 13–23.

Evans, C. (2006). What violent offenders remember of their crime: Empirical explorations. *Australia & New Zealand Journal of Psychiatry, 40*, 508–518.

Evans, W., Albers, E., Macari, D., & Mason, A. (1996). Suicide ideation, attempts and abuse among incarcerated gang and nongang delinquents. *Child and Adolescent Social Work Journal, 13*, 115–126.

Evans, W. P., Fitzgerald, C., Weigel, D., & Chvilicek, S. (1999). Are rural gang members similar to their urban peers? Implications for rural communities. *Youth & Society, 30*(3), 267–282.

Evans, G. D., & Rey, J. (2001). In the echoes of gunfire: Practicing psychologists' responses to school violence. *Professional Psychology: Research and Practice, 32*(2), 157–164.

Everington, C., & Keyes, D. W. (1999, Jul-Aug). Mental retardation: Diagnosing mental retardation in criminal proceedings: The critical importance of documenting adaptive behavior. *Forensic Examiner, 8*(7–8), 31–34.

Everly, G. S., & Mitchell, J. T. (1997). *Critical incident stress management (CISM): A new era and standard of care in crisis intervention.* Ellicott City, MD: Chevron.

Evers, T. (1998). A healing approach to crime: Victim-offender mediation. *The Progressive Inc., 9*(62), 30–36.

Ewing, C. P. (1997). *Fatal families: The dynamics of intrafamilial homicide.* Thousand Oaks, CA: Sage.

Exum, J. G., Turnbull, H. R., Martin, R., & Finn, J. W. (1992). Points of view: Perspectives on the judicial, mental retardation services, law enforcement, and corrections systems. In R. W. Conley, R. Luckasson & G. N. Bouthilet (Eds.), *The criminal justice system and mental retardation* (pp. 1–16). Baltimore: Paul H. Brookes.

Exworthy, T., Mohan, D., Hindley, N., & Basson, J. (2001). Seclusion: Punitive or protective? *Journal of Forensic Psychiatry, 12*(2), 423–433.

Fagan, A. A. (2001, Aug). The gender cycle of violence: Comparing the effects of child abuse and neglect on criminal offending for males and females. *Violence & Victims, 16*(4), 457–474.

Faigman, D. L., & Monahan, J. (2009). Standards of legal admissibility and their implications for psychological science. In J. L. Skeem, K. S. Douglas, & S. O. Lillenfeld (Eds.), *Psychological science in the courtroom: Consensus and controversy* (pp. 3–25). New York: Guilford Press.

Fairbrother, N., & Woody, S. R. (2008). New mothers' thoughts of harm related to the newborn. *Archives Women's Mental Health, 11,* 221–229.

Falk, J. A. (1995). Project exodus: The corrections correction. In L. Combrinck-Graham (Ed.), *Children in families at risk: Maintaining the connections* (pp. 375–392). New York: Guilford Press.

Fallahi, C. R., Shaw Austad, C., Fallon, M., & Leishman, L. (2009). A survey of perceptions of the Virginia Tech tragedy. *Journal of School Violence, 8,* 120–135.

Farkas, M. (2011). An introduction to parental alienation syndrome. *Journal of Psychosocial Nursing and Mental Health Services, 49*(4), 20–26.

Farley, M. (2003). Prostitution and the invisibility of harm. *Women & Therapy, 26*(3–4), 247–280.

Farley, M., & Briscoe-Smith, A. (2010). *Evaluation and Treatment of Women and Girls Trafficked for Prostitution.* American Psychological Association 2010 Convention Presentation. (n.p.).

Farr, K. A. (2002, Jun). Battered women who were "being killed and survived it": Straight talk from survivors. *Violence & Victims, 17*(3), 267–281.

Farrow, J. (2005). Psychosocial Context Leading Juveniles to Prostitution and Sexual Exploitation. In S. W. Cooper, R. J. Estes, A. P. Giardino, N. D. Kellogg, & V. I. Veith (Eds.), *Medical, Legal, & Social Aspects of Child Exploitation. Vol. 1.* St Louis, MO: G.W. Medical Publishing, Inc.

Fava, G. A. (2001, May-Jun). Physicians, medical associations and death penalty. *Psychotherapy & Psychosomatics, 70*(3), 168.

Fay, J. (2000). A narrative approach to critical and subcritical incident debriefings. *Dissertation Abstracts International.* (UMI No. 2000-95008-019). Retrieved September 17, 2010, from Dissertations and Theses database.

Fazel, S., Xenitidis, K., & Powell, J. (2008). The prevalence of intellectual disabilities among 12000 prisoners: A systematic review. *International Journal of Law and Psychiatry, 31*(4), 369–379.

Feder, L. (1998). Police handling of domestic and nondomestic assault calls: Is there a case for discrimination? *Crime and Delinquency, 44,* 335–349.

Federal Bureau of Investigation (FBI). (1985a, August). The men who murdered. *FBI Law Enforcement Bulletin,* 2–11.

Federal Bureau of Investigation (FBI). (1985b, August). Crime scene and profile characteristics of organized and disorganized murderers. *FBI Law Enforcement Bulletin,* 18–25.

Federal Bureau of Investigation. (2008). *Uniform Crime Report, 2008. Washington, DC: United States Department of Justice, Federal Bureau of Investigation.*

Federal Bureau of Prisons. (2007). *Suicide prevention program.* (Program Statement 5324.08) Retrieved August 28, 2011, from www.bop.gov/policy/progstat/5324_008.pdf.

FBI Critical Incident Response Group. (2000). *The school shooter: A threat assessment perspective.* Retrieved May 8, 2011, from www.fbi.gov/stats-services/publications.

Federal Probation. (2000, Jun). It has come to our attention. *Federal Probation, 64*(1). [On-line]. Available: http://web22.epnet.com/citation.asp.

Feelgood, S., Cortoni, F., & Thompson, A. (2005). Sexual coping, general coping, and cognitive distortions in incarcerated rapists and child molesters. *Journal of Sexual Aggression, 11*(2), 157—170.

Feinman, C. (1994). *Women in the criminal justice system* (3rd edn.). Westport, CT: Praeger.

Feld, B. C. (1997, Fall). Abolish the juvenile court: Youthfulness, criminal responsibility, and sentencing. *Journal of Criminal Law & Criminology, 88*(1), 68—69.

Felthous, A., & Kachigian, C. (2001). To warn and to control: Two distinct legal obligations or variations of a single duty to protect. *Behavioral Sciences & the Law, 19*(3), 355—373.

Ferraro, K. J., & Moe, A. M. (2003, Feb). Mothering, crime, and incarceration. *Journal of Contemporary Ethnography, 32*(1), 9—40.

Festinger, T., & Pratt, R. (2002). Speeding adoptions: An evaluation of the effects of judicial continuity. *Social Work Research, 26*(4), 217—224.

Fingerhut, A. W., Riggle, E. D. B., & Rostosky, S. S. (2011). Same-sex marriage: The social and psychological implications of policy and debates. *Journal of Social Issues, 67*(2), 225—241.

Finkel, N. (2006). Insanity's disconnect, the law's madness, and the irresistible impulses of experts. In M. Costanzo, D. Krauss, & K. Pezdek (Eds.), *Expert Psychological Testimony for the Courts.* Wales: Psychology Press.

Finkel, N. J., Burke, & Chavez, L. J. (2000). Commonsense judgments of infanticide: Murder, manslaughter, madness, and miscellaneous. *Psychology, Public Policy, and Law, 6*(4), 1113—1137.

Finkelhor, D., & Ormrod, R. (2004). Prostitution of juveniles: Patterns from NIBRS. *Juvenile Justice Bulletin.* June 1—12. Available at www.ncjrs.gov/pdffiles1/ojjdp/203946.pdf.

Finkelman, J. M. (2010). Litigation consulting: Expanding beyond jury selection to trial strategy and tactics. *Consulting Psychology Journal: Practice and Research, 62*(1), 12—20.

Finley, G. E., & Schwartz, S. J. (2007). Father involvement and long-term young adult outcomes: The differential contributions of divorce and gender. *Family Court Review, 45*(4), 573—587.

Finn, P. (1998, Dec). Correctional officer stress: A cause for concern and additional help[a]. *Federal Probation, 62*(2), 65—75.

Fiorillo, A., De Rosa, C., Del Vecchio, V., Jurjanz, L., Schnall, K., Onchev, G., et al. (2011). How to improve clinical practice on involuntary hospital admissions of psychiatric patients: Suggestions from the EUNOMIA study. *European Psychiatry, 26*(4), 201—207.

First, M., & Halon, R. (2008). Use of DSM paraphilia diagnoses in sexually violent predator commitment cases. *Journal of American Academic Psychiatry Law, 36*, 443—454.

Fischer, K. W., Stein, Z., & Heikkinen, K. (2009). Narrow assessments misrepresent development and misguide policy: Comment on Steinberg, Cauffman, Woolard, Graham, and Banich (2009). *American Psychologist, 64*(7), 595—600.

Fischoff, S. (2003, Sep). Stack and sway: The new science of jury consulting. *Political Psychology, 24*(3), 628—631.

Flaherty, M. G. (1983). The national incidence of juvenile suicide in adult jails and juvenile detention centers. *Suicide and Life Threatening Behavior, 13*, 85—93.

Flaks, D. K., Ficher, I., Masterpasqua, F., & Joseph, G. (1995). Lesbians choosing motherhood: A comparative study of lesbian and heterosexual parents and their children. *Developmental Psychology, 31*, 105—114.

Flannery, D. J., Vazsonyi, A. T., Liau, A. K., Guo, S., Powell, K. E., Atha, H., Vesterdal, W., & Embry, D. (2003). Initial behavior outcomes for the PeaceBuilders universal school-based violence prevention program. *Developmental Psychology, 39*(2), 292—308.

Fletcher, B. R., Rolison, G. L., & Moon, D. G. (1993). The woman prisoner. In B. R. Fletcher, L. D. Shaver, & D. G. Moon (Eds.), *Women prisoners: A forgotten population* (pp. 15–26). Westport, CT: Praeger.

Flowers, R. B. (1995). *Female crime, criminals and cellmates: An exploration of female criminality and delinquency.*

Flowers, R. B. (1998). *The prostitution of women and girls.* Jefferson, NC: McFarland.

Flynn, J. R. (1984). The mean IQ of Americans: Massive gains 1932 to 1978. *Psychological Bulletin, 95*, 29–51.

Flynn, J. R. (1987). Massive IQ gains in 14 nations: What IQ tests really measure. *Psychological Bulletin, 101*, 171–191.

Flynn, J. R. (2000). The hidden history of IQ and special education: Can the problems be solved? *Psychology, Public Policy, and Law, 12*, 191–198.

Flynn, J. R. (2006). Tethering the elephant: Capital cases, IQ, and the Flynn effect. *Psychology, Public Policy, and Law, 12*, 170–189.

Ford, D. A. (1999). *Coercing victim participation in domestic violence prosecutions.* Paper presented at the Sixth International Family Violence Research Conference. Durham, NH.

Foster, E. M., Jones, D. E., & Conduct Problems Prevention Research Group. (2005). The high costs of aggression; public expenditures resulting from conduct disorder. *The American Journal of Public Health, 91*(10), 1767–1772.

Franklin, K. (2003). Practice opportunities with an emerging family form: The planned lesbian and gay family. *Journal of Forensic Psychology Practice, 3*(3), 47–64.

Franzese. (2002). *Suprema Corte di Cassazione, Sezioni Unite Penali.* September 11, no. 30328.

Freedman, A., & Radden, J. (2006). Judicial uses of forced psychotropic medication. *International Journal of Mental Health, 35*(1), 3–11.

Freedman, D., & Hemenway, D. (2000, Jun.). Precursors of lethal violence: A death row sample. *Social Science & Medicine, 50*(12), 1757–1770.

Freeman, A., & Alaimo, C. (2001). Prevention of suicide in a large urban jail. *Psychiatric Annals, 31*(7), 447–452.

French, L. A. (2005). Mental retardation and the death penalty in the USA: the clinical and legal legacy. *Criminal Behavior and Mental Health, 15*(2), 82–86.

Freudenberg, N., Daniels, J., Crum, M., Perkins, T., & Richie, B. E. (2005). Coming home from jail: The social and health consequences of community reentry for women, male adolescents, and their families and communities. *American Journal of Public Health, 95*, 1725–1736.

Friday, J. C. (1996). Weapon-carrying in school. In A. M. Hoffman (Ed.), *Schools, violence, and society* (pp. 21–31). Westport, CT: Praeger.

Fried, C. S., & Reppucci, N. D. (2001, Feb.). Criminal decision making: The development of adolescent judgment, criminal responsibility, and culpability. *Law & Human Behavior, 25*(1), 45–61.

Friedman, R. A. (2006). Violence and mental illness: How strong is the link? *New England Journal of Medicine, 355*, 2064–2066.

Fritsch, E., & Hemmens, J. D. (1995). Juvenile waiver in the United States 1979–1995: A comparison and analysis of state waiver statutes. *Juvenile and Family Court Journal, 46*(3), 17–35.

Frost, L. E., de Camara, R. L., & Earl, T. R. (2006). Training, certification and regulation of forensic evaluators. *Journal of Forensic Psychology Practice, 6*, 77–91.

Frumkin, B. I. (2010). Evaluations of competency to waive Miranda rights and coerced or false confessions: Common pitfalls in expert testimony. In G. D. Lassiter, & C. A. Meissner (Eds.), *Police interrogation and false confessions: Current research, practice, and policy recommendations.* Washington, DC: American Psychological Association.

Fry, L. J., & Glaser, D. (1987). Gender differences in work adjustment of prison employees. *Journal of Offender Counseling, Services, and Rehabilitation, 12*, 39–52.

Gaarder, E., & Belknap, J. (2002). Tenuous borders: Girls transferred to adult court. *Criminology, 40*(3), 1–33.

Gabbard, G. O., & Crisp-Ham, H. (2011). Teaching professional boundaries to psychiatric residents. *Focus, 9*(2), 217–220.

Gacono, C. B. (2002). Forensic psychodiagnostic testing. *Journal of Forensic Psychology Practice, 2*(3), 1–10.

Gainsborough, J. F. (2009). Scandals, lawsuits, and politics: Child welfare policy in the U.S. states. *State Politics and Policy Quarterly, 9*(3), 325–355.

Gallousis, M., & Francek, H. (2002, Sum.). The juvenile suicide assessment: An instrument for the assessment and management of suicide risk with incarcerated juveniles. *International Journal of Emergency Mental Health, 4*(3), 181–200.

Garber, B. (2011). Parental alienation and the dynamics of the enmeshed parent-child dyad: Adultification, parentification, and infantilization. *Family Court Review, 49*(2), 322–335.

Garib, M. (2011, Apr.). Punishing pedophiles: Criminal commitment or criminal imprisonment rather than prison followed by outpatient civil commitment. *Health Law Perspectives,* 1–4.

Garland, B. (2002). Prison treatment staff burnout: consequences, causes, and prevention. *Corrections Today, 64*(7), 116–120.

Garland, B. (2004). The impact of administrative support on prison treatment staff burnout: An explanatory study. *The Prison Journal, 84,* 452–471.

Garner, B. A. (Ed.), (2009). *Black's law dictionary.* St. Paul, MN: West Publishing.

Garner, B. R., Knight, K., & Simpson, D. D. (2007). Burnout among corrections-based drug treatment staff: Impact of individual and organizational factors. *International Journal of Offender Therapy and Comparative Criminology, 51*(5), 510–522.

Garner, J. H., & Clemmer, E. (1986). *Danger to police in domestic disturbances: A new look.* Washington, DC: U. S. Department of Justice.

Garrison, M. (1996). Parent's rights versus children's rights: The case of the foster child. *New York University Review of Law and Social Change, 22*(2), 371–396.

Gavin, T. (1997, March). Truancy: Not just kids' stuff anymore. *FBI Law Enforcement Bulletin.*

Ge, X., Natsuaki, M. N., Martin, D. M., Leve, L. D., Neiderhiser, J. M., Shaw, D. S., et al. (2008). Bridging the divide: Openness in adoption and postadoption psychosocial adjustment among birth and adoptive parents. *Journal of Family Psychology, 22*(4), 529–540.

Geller, J. L., Fischer, W. H., Grudzinskas, A. J., Clayfield, J. C., & Lawlor, T. (2006). Involuntary outpatient treatment as "deinstitutionalized coercion": The net-widening concerns. *International Journal of Law and Psychiatry, 29*(6), 551–562.

Gelles, M. G., & Palarea, R. (2010). Ethics in crisis negotiation: A law enforcement and public safety perspective. In C. H. Kennedy, & T. J. Williams' (Eds.), *Ethical practice in operational psychology: Military and national intelligence applications.* Washington, DC: American Psychological Association.

Genders, E., & Player, E. (1990). Women lifers: Assessing the experience. *The Prison Journal, 80,* 46–57.

Gerkin, P. M. (2009). Participation in victim–offender mediation: Lessons learned from observations. *Criminal Justice Review, 34*(2), 226–247.

Gerrig, R. J., & Zimbardo, P. G. (2002). *Psychology and Life, 16th edn.* Boston: Pearson Education.

Gerson, A., & Fox, D. D. (1999). Boundary violations: The gray area. *American Journal of Forensic Psychology, 17*(2), 57–61.

Gesalman, A. B. (2002). Signs of a family feud: The trial of Andrea Yates tests the insanity defense as relatives try to cope: An 'unspeakable' crime. *Newsweek,* January, *21,* 2002.

Giallombardo, R. (1966). *Society of women: A study of a women's prison.* New York: Wiley.

Gibbons, P. (Ed.). (2003 Mar). Managing sex offenders: Is there a role for psychiatry? *Irish Journal of Psychological Medicine, 20*(1), 4–5.

Gilbert, F., & Daffern, M. (2011). Illuminating the relationship between personality disorder and violence: Contributions of the General Aggression Model. *Psychology of Violence, 1*(3), 230–244.

Gioia, D., & Brekke, J. S. (2003). Use of the American with Disabilities Act by young adults with schizophrenia. *Psychiatric Services, 54*(3), 302–304.

Gist, R., & Devilly, G. J. (2010). Early intervention in the aftermath of trauma. In G. M. Rosen, & C. B. Frueh (Eds.), *Clinician's guide to pasttraumatic stress disorder* (pp. 153–175). Hoboken, NJ: John Wiley & Sons, Inc.

Glaze, Lauren E., & Bonczar, Thomas P (2009). *Bureau of Justice Statistics: Probation and parole in the United States, 2008*. Washington, DC: US Department of Justice NCJ 228230.

Glick, B. (1992). In New York: Governor's task force tackles growing juvenile, gang problem. *Corrections Today, 54*, 92−97.

Glover, V., & Kammerer, M. (2004). The biology and pathophysiology of peripartum psychiatric disorders. *Primary Psychiatry, 11*(3), 37−41.

Gold, L. H. (2001). Clinical and forensic aspects of postpartum disorders. *Journal of the American Academy of Psychiatry and the Law, 29*, 344−347.

Gold, L. H., Anfang, S. A., Drukteinis, A. M., Metzner, J. L., Price, M., Wall, B. W., et al. (2008). AAPL practice guideline for the forensic evaluation of psychiatric disability. *Journal of the American Academy of Psychiatry and the Law, 36*, S3−S50.

Goldberg, A. E., & Smith, J. Z. (2011). Stigma, social context, and mental health: Lesbian and gay couples across the transition to adoptive parenthood. *Journal of Counseling Psychology, 58*(1), 139−150.

Golding, S. L. (2008). Evaluations of adult adjudicative competency. In R. L. Jackson (Ed.), *Learning forensic assessment* (pp. 75−108). New York: Taylor and Francis Group, LLC.

Golding, S. L., & Roesch, R. (1988). Competency for adjudication: An international analysis. In D. N. Weisstub (Ed.), *Law and mental health: International perspectives, Vol. 4* (pp. 73−109). NY: Pergamon.

Goldfried, M. R. (2001, Nov). Integrating gay, lesbian, and bisexual issues into mainstream psychology. *American Psychologist, 56*(11), 977−988.

Goldstein, A. M. (2001). Expert opinions. *AP-LS News, 21*, 8−14.

Goldstein, A. M. (2002). Criminal sentencing: Case 3 principle: Decline referral when impartiality is unlikely. In K. Heilbrun, G. R. Marczyk, & D. DDeMatteo (Eds.), *Forensic Mental Health Assessment: A Casebook* (pp. 134−150). New York: Oxford University Press.

Goldstein, H. (1990). *Problem-oriented policing*. New York: McGraw-Hill.

Goldstein, J., Solnit, A. J., Goldstein, S., & Freud, A. (1996). *The best interests of the child: The least detrimental alternative*. New York: Free Press.

Goldstein, L., & Glaberson, W. (2000). The Well-Marked Roads to Homicidal Rage. *New York Times, April 10*, national edition, sec. 1. (n.p.) Retrieved from. www.nytimes.com.

Goldstein, R. L. (1999). Commentary on "Attorneys' pressures on expert witness." *Journal of the American Academy of Psychiatry & the Law, 27*(4), 554−558.

Gondles, J. A. (2000). Special needs offenders: Everyone's concern. *Corrections Today, 62*(7), 6.

Goodman, G. S., & Melinder, A. (2007). Child witness research and forensic interviews of young children: A review. *Legal and Criminological Psychology, 12*, 1−19.

Goodman, G. S., Myers, J. E. B., Qin, J., Quas, J. A., Castelli, P., Redlich, A. D., & Rogers, L. (2006). Hearsay versus children's testimony: Effects of truthful and deceptive statements on jurors' decisions. *Law and Human Behavior, 30*, 363−401.

Goodman, G. S., Tobey, A. E., Batterman-Faunce, J. M., Orcutt, H., Thomas, S., Shapiro, C., & Sachsenmaier, T. (1998). Face-to-face confrontation: Effects of closed circuit technology on children's eyewitness testimony and jurors' decisions. *Law and Human Behavior, 22*, 165−203.

Goodness, K. R., & Renfro, N. S. (2002). Changing a culture: A brief program analysis of a social learning program on a maximum-security forensic unit. *Behavioral Sciences and the Law, 20*(5), 495−506.

Gordon, R. M., Stoffey, R., & Bottinelli, J. (2008). MMPI-2 Findings of primitive defenses in alienating parents. *The American Journal of Family Therapy, 36*, 211−228.

Gothard, S., Viglone, D., Meloy, J., & Sherman, M. (1995). Detection of malingering in competency to stand trial evaluations. *Law and Human Behavior, 19*, 493.

Gourley, E. V., & Stolberg, A. L. (2000). An empirical investigation of psychologists' custody evaluation procedures. *Journal of Divorce & Remarriage, 33*(1−2), 1−29.

Graham, J. R. (2005). *MMPI-2: Assessing personality and psychopathology* (4th edn.). Oxford: University Press.

Granello, P. F., & Hanna, F. J. (2003, Winter). Incarcerated and court-involved adolescents: Counseling an at-risk population. *Journal of Counseling & Development, 81*(1), 11−19.

Graney, D. G., & Arrigo, B. A. (2002). *The Power Serial Rapist: A Criminology-Victimology Typology of Female Victim Selection.* Springfield, Illinois: Charles C. Thomas: Publisher Ltd.

Grassian, S., & Friedman, N. (1986). Effects of sensory deprivation in psychiatric seclusion and solitary conferment. *International Journal of Law and Psychiatry, 8*(1), 49–65.

Graves, W. (1996). Police cynicism: Causes and cures. *FBI Law Enforcement Bulletin, 65*, 16–20.

Gray, K. (2001). Juvenile justice. *Essence, 32*(5), 147–153.

Gray, L., & Harding, A. (1988). Confidentiality limits with clients who have the AIDS virus. *Journal of Counseling and Development, 66*, 219–223.

Gray, N. S., Taylor, J., Fitzgerald, S., MacCulloch, M. J., & Snowden, R. J. (2007). Predicting future reconviction in offenders with intellectual disabilities: The predictive efficacy of VRAG, PCL-SV, and the HCR-20. *Psychological Assessment, 19*(4), 474–479.

Greene, J., Pranis, K., & Frost, N. A. (2006). *Hard hit: The growth in the imprisonment of women.* New York: Institute on Women & Criminal Justice.

Greene, S., Haney, C., & Hurtado, A. (2000). Cycles of pain: Risk factors in the lives of incarcerated mothers and their children. *Prison Journal, 80*(1), 3–23.

Greenspan, S. (2006). Issues in the use of the "Flynn effect" to adjust IQ scores when diagnosing MR. *Psychology in Mental Retardation and Developmental Disabilities Newsletter, 31*(3), 3–7.

Greer, K. R. (2000). The changing nature of interpersonal relationships in a women's prison. *The Prison Journal, 80*, 442–468.

Grekul, J. (1999, Oct). Pluralistic ignorance in a prison community. *Canadian Journal of Criminology, 41*(4), 513–535.

Grella, C. E., & Greenwell, L. (2006). Correlates of parental status and attitudes toward parenting among substance-abusing women offenders. *The Prison Journal, 86*, 89–113.

Griffin. (2009). Different from adults: An updated analysis of juvenile transfer and blended sentencing laws, with recommendations for reform. *Juvenile Justice Update, 15*(2), 7.

Griffin, M. (2004). Job satisfaction among detention officers: Assessing the relative contribution of organizational climate variables. *Journal of Criminal Justice, 29*, 219–232.

Griffin, M. L., & Hepburn, J. R. (2006). The effect of gang affiliation on violent misconduct among inmates during early years of confinement. *Criminal Justice and Behavior, 33*(4), 419–448.

Griffiths, R. (2010). The gothic folk devils strike back! Theorizing folk devil reaction in the post-Columbine era. *Journal of Youth Studies, 13*(3), 403–422.

Grisso, T. (1991). A developmental history of the American Psychology-Law Society. *Law and Human Behavior, 15*, 213–231.

Grisso, T. (2003). *Evaluating competencies: Forensic assessments & instruments* (2nd edn.). New York: Kluwer Academic/Plenum.

Grisso, T. (1996a). Pretrial clinical evaluations in criminal cases: Past trends and future directions. *Criminal Justice and Behavior, 23*(1), 90–106.

Grisso, T. (1996b). Society's retributive response to juvenile violence: A developmental perspective. *Law and Human Behavior, 20*(3), 229–247.

Grisso, T. (2000, Apr). The changing face of juvenile justice. *Psychiatric Services, 51*(4), 425–426, 438.

Grisso, T. (2005). Chapter 9, *Competence to Consent to Treatment.* In *Perspectives in Law and Psychology*, 16.

Groscup, J. L., Penrod, S. D., Studebaker, C. A., Huss, M. T., & O'Neil, K. M. (2002). The effects of Daubert on the admissibility of expert testimony in state and federal criminal cases. *Psychology, Public Policy, & Law, 8*(4), 339–372.

Grossi, E. L., & Berg, B. L. (1991). Stress and job dissatisfaction among correctional officers: An unexpected finding. *International Journal of Offender Therapy and Comparative Criminology, 35*, 73–81.

Groves, B., Zuckerman, B., Marans, S., & Cohen, D. (1993). Silent victims: Children who witness violence. *JAMA, Journal of the American Medical Association, 269*, 262–264.

Grubb, A. (2010). Modern day hostage (crisis) negotiation: The evolution of an art form within the policing arena. *Aggression and Violent Behavior, 15*(5), 341–348.

Grudzinskas, A. J., Clayfield, J. C., Roy-Bujnowski, K., Fisher, W. H., & Richardson, M. H. (2005). Integrating the criminal justice system into mental health service delivery: The Worcester Diversion Experience. *Behavioral Sciences and the Law, 23*, 277–293.

Guadalupe, J. L., & Bein, A. (2001). Violence and youth: What can we learn? *International Journal of Adolescence & Youth, 10*(1–2), 157–176.

Guan, S. A., & Subrahmanyam, K. (2009). Youth Internet use: Risks and opportunities. *Current Opinion in Psychiatry, 22*(4), 351–356.

Gudjonsson, G. H., & Copson, G. (1999). The role of the expert in criminal investigation. In J. L. Jackson, & D. A. Bekerian (Eds.), *Offender profiling, theory, research and practice* (pp. 61–67). Chichester, UK: Wiley.

Gudjonsson, G., Sveinsdottir, T., Sigurdsson, J. F., & Jonsdottir, J. (2010). The ability of suspected victims of childhood sexual abuse (CSA) to give evidence. Findings from the children's house in Iceland. *Journal of Forensic Psychiatry and Psychology, 21*(4), 569–586.

Gunroe, M. L., & Braver, S. L. (2001). The effects of joint legal custody on mothers, fathers, and children controlling for factors that predispose a sole maternal versus joint legal award. *Law & Human Behavior, 25*(1), 25–43.

Gussak, D., & Ploumis-Devick, E. (2004). Creating wellness in correctional populations through the arts: An interdisciplinary model. *Visual Arts Research, 29*(1), 35–43.

Guthiel, T. G. (2005). Boundary issues. In J. M. Oldham, J. Skadol, & B. Bender (Eds.), *The American Psychiatric Publishing Textbook of Personality Disorders*. Arlington, VA: American Psychiatric Publishing.

Guthiel, T. G., & Gabbard, G. O. (1993). The concept of boundaries in clinical practice: Theoretical and risk management dimensions. *American Journal of Psychiatry, 150*, 188–196.

Haggerty, K. P., Wells, E. A., Jenson, J. M., & Catalano, R. F. (1989). Delinquents and drug use: A model program for community reintegration. *Adolescence, 24*, 439–456.

Haimowitz, S., Urff, J., & Huchshorn, K. (2006). *Restraint and seclusion a risk management guide*. Retrieved from www.dshs.state.tx.us.

Hairston, C. F. (1991). Mothers in jail: Parent-child separation and jail visitation. *Affilia, 6*, 9–27.

Halim, S., & Stiles, B. L. (2001, Feb). Differential support for police use of force, the death penalty, and perceived harshness of the courts: Effects of race, gender, and region. *Criminal Justice & Behavior, 28*(1), 3–23.

Hall, A. S., Pulver, C. A., & Cooley, M. J. (1996). Psychology of best interest standard: Fifty state statutes and their theoretical antecedents. *American Journal of Family Therapy, 24*, 171–180.

Hall, H., & Poirier, J. G. (2001). *Detecting malingering and deception: Forensic distortion analysis* (2nd edn.). Boca Raton, FL: CRC Press.

Hall, J. N. (1992). Correctional services for inmates with mental retardation: Challenge or catastrophe? In R. W. Conley, R. Luckasson, & G. N. Bouthilet (Eds.), *The criminal justice system and mental retardation* (pp. 167–190). Baltimore, MD: Paul H. Brookes.

Hall, S., & Sales, B. D. (2008). *Courtroom modifications for child witnesses: Law and science in forensic evaluations*. Washington, DC: American Psychological Association.

Hall, T., Cook, N., & Berman, G. (2010). Navigating the expanding field of law and psychology: A comprehensive guide to graduate education. *Journal of Forensic Psychology Practice, 10*(2), 69–90.

Haller, L. H. (2000, Oct). Forensic aspects of juvenile violence. *Child and Adolescent Psychiatric Clinics of North America, 9*(4), 859–881.

Halpern, J., Gurevich, M., Schwartz, B., & Brazeau, P. (2009). Interventions for critical incident stress in emergency medical services: A qualitative study. *Stress and Health, 25*, 139–149.

Hamilton, V. (2006). Principles of U.S. family law. *Fordham Law Review, 75*(1), 31–73.

Hammer, M. R. (2007). *Saving lives: The S.A.F.E. model for resolving hostage and crisis incidents*. Westport, CT: Praeger Security International.

Haney, C. (1995). The social context of capital murder: Social histories and the logic of mitigation. *Santa Clara Law Review, 35*, 547–609.

Haney, C. (2003). Mental health issues in long-term solitary and "supermax" confinement. *Crime & Delinquency, 49*(2), 124–156.

Haney, C. (2006). *Reforming punishment: Psychological limits to the pains of imprisonment, the law and public policy*. Washington, DC: American Psychological Association.

Hanna, E. J., Hanna, C. A., & Keys, S. G. (1999). Fifty strategies for counseling defiant, aggressive, adolescents: Reaching, accepting, and relating. *Journal of Counseling & Development, 77*, 395–404.

Hannett, M. J. (2007). Lessening the sting of ASFA: The rehabilitation-relapse dilemma brought about by drug addiction and termination of parental rights. *Family Court Review, 45*(3), 524–537.

Hansen, M. (1994b, November). Fears of the heart. *American Bar Association Journal*, 58–63.

Hansen, M. (1997). Repairing the damage: Citizen boards tailor sentences to fit the crimes in Vermont. *American Bar Association Journal, 83*(20), 1–2.

Hanson, R. K., & Bussiere, M. T. (1996). *Sex offender risk predictors: A summary of research results* [On-line]. Available: www.csc-scc.gc.ca/crd/forum/e082/e082c.htm.

Hanson, R. K., Steffy, R. A., & Gauthier, R. (1993). Long-term recidivism of child molesters. *Journal of Consulting and Clinical Psychology, 61*(4), 646–652.

Hare, R. D. (2003). *Hare psychopathy checklist-revised manual* (2nd edn.). Toronto: MHS.

Hare, R. D., & Neumann, C. S. (2008). Psychopathy as a clinical and empirical construct. *Annual Review Clinical Psychology, 4*, 217–246.

Harer, M. D., & Langan, N. P. (2001, Oct). Gender differences in predictors of prison violence: Assessing the predictive validity of a risk classification system. *Crime & Delinquency, 47*(4), 513–536.

Harland, P., Reijneveld, S. A., Brugman, E., Verloove-Vanhorick, S. P., & Verhulst, F. C. (2002, Dec). Family factors and life events as risk factors for behavioral and emotional problems in children. *European Child & Adolescent Psychiatry, 11*(4), 176–184.

Harpine, E. C., Nitza, A., & Conyne, R. (2010). Prevention groups: Today and tomorrow. *Group Dynamic: Theory, Research, and Practice, 14*(3), 268–280.

Harris, A. J. R., & Hanson, R. K. (2010). Clinical, actuarial and dynamic risk assessment of sexual offenders: why do things keep changing? *Journal of Sexual Aggression, 16*(3), 1–15.

Harris, C. J. (2009). Police use of improper force: A systematic review of the evidence. *Victims and Offenders, 4*(1), 25–41.

Harris, C. J. (2010). Longitudinal patterns of internally generated complaints filed against a large cohort of police officers. *Policing & Society, 20*(4), 401–415.

Harris, G., Rice, M., & Cormier, C. (2002, Aug). *Law and Human Behavior, 26*(4), 377–394.

Harris, G., Rice, M., Quinsey, V., Lalumiere, M., Boer, D., & Lang, C. (2003, Sep). A multisite comparison of actuarial risk instruments for sex offenders. *Psychological Assessment, 15*(3), 413–425.

Harrison, P. M., & Karberg, J. (2004). *Prison and jail inmates at midyear 2003*. Washington, DC: US Department of Justice, Office of Justice Programs, Bureau of Justice Statistics.

Hart, P. (2010). Cop drama. *Texas Monthly, August, 2010*, 68–76.

Hartney, C. (2006, June). *Youth under age 18 in the adult criminal justice system*. www.nccd-crc.org/ncd/pubs/2006may_factsheet_youthadult.pdf.

Harvard Civil Rights Project. (2000). *Opportunities suspended: The devastating consequences of zero tolerance and school discipline policies: Report from a national summit on zero tolerance*. Washington, DC: HCRP. (ERIC Document Reproduction Service No. ED454314).

Haselschwerdt, M. L., Hardesty, J. L., & Hans, J. D. (2011). Custody evaluators' beliefs about domestic violence allegations during divorce: Feminist and family violence perspectives. *Journal of Interpersonal Violence, 26*(8), 1694–1719.

Hatcher, S. S. (2010). Recognizing perspectives on community reentry from offenders with mental illness: Using the Afrocentric framework and concept mapping with adult detainees. *Journal of Offender Rehabilitation, 49*(8), 536–550.

Hauser, R., Schweri, E., & Hartmann, K. (2005). *Schweizerisches Strafprozessrecht* (6th edn.). Basel, Switzerland: Helbing & Lichtenhahn.

Hawkins-Leon, C. G., & Worthy, A. (2008). Ten years out of step and out of line: Florida's statutory ban of "lesbi-gay adoption" violates the adoption and safe families act of 1997 (AFSA). *University of Maryland*

Law Journal of Race, Religion, Gender and Class, 8. Retrieved from http://papers.ssrn.com/sol3/papers. cfm?abstract_id=1422721.

Hay, C., & Meldrum, R. (2010). Bullying victimization and adolescent self-harm: Testing hypotheses from general strain theory. *Journal of Youth and Adolescence, 39*(5), 446–459.

Hayes, L. M. (1989). National study of jail suicides: Seven years later. *Psychiatric Annals, 31*(7), 447–452.

Hayes, L. M. (1998). Suicide prevention in correctional facilities: An overview (pp. 245–256. In M. Puisis (Ed.), *Clinical Practice in Correctional Medicine.* St. Louis, MO: Mosby.

Hayes, S. C. (2002). Early intervention or early incarceration? Using a screening test for intellectual disability in the criminal justice system. *Journal of Applied Research in Intellectual Disabilities, 15*(2), 120–128.

Hayes, S. C., & Farnill, D. (2003, Apr). Correlations for the Vineland adaptive behavior scales with Kaufman brief intelligence test in a forensic sample. *Psychological Reports, 92*(2), 573–580.

Hayes, S., Shackell, P., Mottram, P., & Lancaster, R. (2007). The prevalence of intellectual disability in a major UK prison. *British Journal of Learning Disabilities, 35*(3), 162–167.

Haywood, T. W., Kravitz, H. M., Goldman, L. B., & Freeman, A. (2000, Jul). Characteristics of women in jail and treatment orientations: A review. *Behavior Modification, 24*(3), 307–324.

Hazelwood, R., & Warren, J. (2000). The sexually violent offender: Impulsive or ritualistic? *Aggression and Violent Behavior, 5*(3), 267–279.

Healey, J. B. (2004). Violence and bullying in schools: New theoretical perspective and the Macarthur model for comprehensive and customized intervention. Unpublished doctoral dissertation. University of Western Sydney.

Heath, I. (2000). May state treat, over his objection, a capital murder inmate who, as a result of mental illness, is found to be a danger to self and others, when a concurrent effect of the treatment is the restoration is the restoration of competency to be executed. *Journal of the American Academy of Psychiatry & the Law, 28*(2), 247–248.

Hecker, T., & Steinberg, L. (2002, June). Psychological evaluation at juvenile court disposition. *Professional Psychology: Research and Practice, 33*(3), 300–306.

Heide, K. M. (1992). *Why kids kill parents: Child abuse and adolescent homicide.* Columbus: Ohio State Press.

Heilbrun, K. (2005). *The task force and resolution: Background, proceedings, and current status.* The ABA task force on mental disability and the death penalty symposium, annual meeting of the American Psychology-Law Society, La Jolla, CA.

Heilbrun, K. (2001). *Principles of Forensic Mental Health Assessment.* New York: Kluwer Academic/Plenum Publishers.

Heilbrun, K. (1992). The role of psychological testing in forensic assessment. *Law and Human Behavior, 16*(3), 257–272.

Heilbrun, K., Radelet, M. L., & Dvoskin, J. (1992). The debate on treating individuals incompetent for execution. *American Journal of Psychiatry, 149*(5), 596–605.

Heilbrun, K., Rosenfeld, B., Warren, J., & Collins, S. (1994). The use of third-party information in forensic assessments: A two-state comparison. *Bulletin of the American Academy of Psychiatry and Law, 22,* 399–406.

Heinkel, J. O., & Reichel, P. L. (2002). The driver's license: A suggested gang suppression strategy. *Journal of Gang Research, 9*(4), 45–56.

Helfer, R. E., & Kempe, C. H. (Eds.), (1986). *Child abuse and neglect: The family and the community.* Cambridge, MA: Ballinger.

Hemmens, C., Miller, M., Burton, V. S., & Milner, S. (2002, Apr). The consequences of official labels: An examination of the rights lost by the mentally ill and mentally incompetent ten years later. *Community Mental Health Journal, 38*(2), 129–140.

Hemmens, C., Stohr, M. K., Schoeler, M., & Miller, B. (2002, Nov-Dec). One-step up, two steps back: The progression of perceptions of women's work in prisons and jails. *Journal of Criminal Justice, 30*(6), 473–489.

Henderson, C. (2007). Gaols or de facto mental institutions? Why individuals with a mental illness are over-represented in the criminal justice system in New South Wales, Australia. *Mental Health Issues in the Criminal Justice System, 45*(1–2), 69–80.

Henning, K., Jones, A., & Holdford, R. (2003, Aug). Treatment needs of women arrested for domestic violence: A comparison with male offenders. *Journal of Interpersonal Violence, 18*(8), 839—856.

Henrico County Police Department. (2011). *Communications officer job description.* Accessed August 28, 2011 at www.co.henrico.va.us/police/police-employment/communications-officer.html.

Henry, J., Kaiser Family Foundation. (2001). *Inside-Out: A report on the experiences of lesbians, gays and bisexuals in America and the public's views on issues and policies related to sexual orientation.* Available online at www.kff.org

Herbert, P. (2002). The duty to warn: A reconsideration and critique. *Journal of the American Academy of Psychiatry & the Law, 30*(3), 417—424.

Heyman, R., & Slep, A. M. S. (2002, Nov). Do child abuse and interparental violence lead to adulthood family violence? *Journal of Marriage & Family, 64*(4), 864—870.

Higgins, S. E. (1993). Interjurisdictional coordination of major gang interventions. *The Police Chief, 60*(6), 46—47.

Hilsenroth, M., & Stricker, G. (2004). A consideration of challenges to psychological assessment instruments used in forensic settings: Rorschach as exemplar. *Journal of Personality Assessment, 83,* 141—152.

Hinduja, S., & Patchin, J. W. (2007). Offline consequences of online victimization: School violence and delinquency. *Journal of School Violence, 6*(3), 89—112.

Hinduja, S., & Patchim, J. W. (2008). Cyberbullying: An exploratory analysis of factors related to offending and victimization. *Deviant Behavior, 29*(2), 129—156.

Hinduja, S., & Patchin, J. W. (2010). Bullying, cyberbullying, and suicide. *Archives of Suicide Research, 14,* 206—221.

Hirschel, J. D., Buzawa, E., Pattavina, A., & Faggiani, D. (2007). *Explaining the prevalence, context, and consequences of dual arrest in intimate partner cases* (NCI Publication No. 218355). Washington, DC: U.S. Department of Justice, National Institute of Justice.

Ho, T. (1996). Assessment of retardation among mentally retarded criminal offenders: An examination of racial disparity. *Journal of Criminal Justice, 24,* 337—350.

Hobbs, M., Mayou, R., Harrison, B., & Warlock, P. (1996). A randomised trial of psychological debriefing for victims of road traffic accidents. *British Medical Journal, 313,* 1438—1439.

Hodge, D. (2008). Sexual trafficking in the United States: A domestic problem with transnational dimensions. *National Association of Social Workers, 53*(2), 143—152.

Hodgkinson, P., & Stewart, M. (1991). *Coping with catastrophe: A handbook of disaster management.* London: Routledge.

Hoffman, Y. S. G., Diamond, G. M., & Lipsitz, J. D. (2011). The challenge of estimating PTSD prevalence in the context of ongoing trauma: The example of Israel during the Second Intifada. *Journal of Anxiety Disorders, 25,* 788—793.

Hoffman, P., & Silverstein, M. (1995). Safe streets don't require lifting rights. In M. W. Klein, C. L. Maxon, & J. Miller (Eds.), *The modern gang reader.* Los Angeles: Roxbury.

Hogan, N., Lambert, E., Jenkins, M., & Wambold, S. (2006). The impact of occupational stressors on correctional staff organizational commitment: a preliminary study. *Journal of Contemporary Criminal Justice, 22,* 44—62.

Hohl, K., Bradford, B., & Stanko, E. A. (2010). Influencing trust and confidence in the London metropolitan police: Results from an experiment testing the effect of leaflet drops on public opinion. *British Journal of Criminology, 50*(3), 491—513.

Hollin, C. R., & Palmer, E. J. (2003, Sep). Level of service inventory-revised profiles of violent and nonviolent prisoners. *Journal of Interpersonal Violence, 18*(9), 1075—1086.

Holt, V. L., Kernic, M. A., Wolf, M., & Rivara, F. P. (2003). Do protection orders affect the likelihood of future partner violence and injury? *American Journal of Preventative Medicine, 24,* 16—21.

Hong, G. K. (2002). Psychiatric disabilities. In M. G. Brodwin, F. A. Tellez, & S. K. Brodwin (Eds.), *Medical, psychosocial, and vocational aspects of disability* (pp. 107—118). Athens, GA: Elliott and Fitzpatrick.

Hope, L., Memon, A., & McGeorge, P. (2004). Understanding pretrial publicity: Predecisional distortion of evidence by mock jurors. *Journal of Experimental Psychology, 10*(2), 111—119.

Horvath, L. S., Logan, T. K., & Walker, R. (2002, Dec). Child custody cases: A content analysis of evaluations in practice. *Professional Psychology: Research & Practice, 33*(6), 557–565.

House Ways & Means Committee. (1998). *Green book*. Washington, DC: Committee Print.

Howell, R. (2004). The importance of relating the crime to mental illness in the issue of sanity. In E. Geiselman (Ed.), *Psychology of Murder*. Carlsbad, CA: ACFP.

Hromadka, P. (1995). Innovative York program allows babies to stay with inmate moms. *Nebraska Nurse, 28*, 14.

Hu, J. M., Yang, M., Huang, X., Liu, X. H., & Coid, J. (2010). Forensic psychiatry assessments in Sichuan Province, People's Republic of China. *Journal of Forensic Psychiatry and Psychology, 21*(4), 604–619.

Hubbard, K. L., Zapf, P. A., & Ronan, K. A. (2003, Apr). Competency restoration: An examination of the differences between defendants predicted restorable and not restorable to competency. *Law & Human Behavior, 27*(2), 127–139.

Huber, M., Balon, R., Labbate, L., Brandt-Youtz, S., Hammer, J., & Mufti, R. (2000, Jun). A survey of police officers' experience with Tarasoff warnings in two states. *Psychiatric Services, 51*(6), 807–809.

Huebner, B. M. (2003, Mar-Apr). Administrative determinants of inmate violence: A multilevel analysis. *Journal of Criminal Justice, 31*(2), 107–117.

Huggins, D. W., Capeheart, L., & Newman, E. (2006). Deviants or scapegoats: An examination of pseudofamily groups and dyads in two Texas prisons. *The Prison Journal, 86*, 114–139.

Hughes, J. (2009). A pilot study of naturally occurring high-probability request sequences in hostage negotiations. *Journal of Applied Behavioral Analysis, 42*(2), 491–496.

Huprich, S. K., Fuller, K. M., & Schneider, R. B. (2003, Jul). Divergent ethical perspectives on the duty-to-warn principle with HIV patients. *Ethics & Behavior, 13*(3), 263–278.

Hutson, H. R., Anglin, D., Yarbrough, J., Hardaway, K., Russell, M., Strote, J., et al. (1998). Suicide by cop. *Annals of Emergency Medicine, 32*, 665–669.

Huurre, T., Junkkari, H., & Aro, H. (2006). Long-term psychosocial effects of parental divorce: A follow-up study from adolescence to adulthood. *European Archives of Psychiatry and Clinical Neuroscience, 256*(4), 256–263.

Illinois Department of Corrections. (2008). *Annual report*. Springfield, IL: IDC.

Inciardi, J. A. (1993). *Criminal justice*. Orlando, FL: Harcourt Brace Jovanovich.

Ingrassia, M., & Springen, K. (1993, May 3). Standing up for fathers. *Newsweek*, 52–53.

Ingrassia, M., & Springen, K. (1994, March 21). She's not baby Jessica anymore. *Newsweek*, 60–65.

International Association for Forensic and Correctional Psychology. (2010). Standards for psychology services in jails, prisons, correctional facilities and agencies. *Criminal Justice and Behavior, 37*(7), 752–807.

International Justice Project. (2005). *Juvenile offenders on death row*. Accessed September 13, 2011, at www.internationaljusticeproject.org/juvStats.cfm.

Inwald, R. (2008). The Inwald Personality Inventory (IPI) and Hilson Research inventories: Development and rationale. *Aggression and Violent Behavior, 13*(4), 298–327.

Inwald, R., Knatz, H., & Shusman, E. (1983). *Inwald Personality Inventory manual*. New York: Hilson Research.

Israel Ministry of Foreign Affairs. (2007). *The Nature and Extent of Palestinian Terrorism, 2006*. Retrieved September 14, 2011. www.mfa.gov.il/MFA/Terrorism-Obstacle+to+Peace/Palestinian+terror+since+2000/Palestinian+terrorism+2006.htm.

Ivanoff, A., Jang, S. J., & Smyth, N. (1996). Clinical risk factors associated with parasuicide in prison. *International Journal of Offender Therapy and Comparative Criminology, 400*, 135–146.

Jackson, M. (2001). The psychological effects of administrative segregation. *Canadian Journal of Criminology, 43*(1), 109–116.

Jackson, R., & Richards, H. (2008). Evaluations for the civil commitment of sexual offenders. In R. Jackson (Ed.), *Learning forensic assessment* (pp. 183–209). New York: Taylor Francis Group.

Jaffe, P. D., Pons, F., & Wicky, H. R. (1997). Children imprisoned with their mothers: Psychological Implications. In S. Redmonds, V. Garrido, J. Perez, & R. Barberet (Eds.), *Advances in psychology and law: International contributions* (pp. 399–407). Berlin: de Gruyter.

James, D. J., & Glaze, L. E. (2006). *Mental health problems of prison and jail inmates*. Washington, DC: U.S. Department of Justice, Office of Justice Programs, Bureau of Justice Statistics.

James, D. V., Kerrigan, T. R., Forfar, R., Farnham, F. R., & Preston, L. F. (2010). The Fixated Threat Assessment Centre: preventing harm and facilitating care. *The Journal of Forensic Psychiatry and Psychology, 21*(4), 521–536.

James, S. E. (2002, Jul). Clinical themes in gay- and lesbian-parented adoptive families. *Clinical Child Psychology & Psychiatry, 7*(3), 475–486.

Janko, S. (1994). *Vulnerable children, vulnerable families: The social construction of child abuse.* New York, NY: Teachers College Press.

Janofsky, J. S. (2001). Reply to Schafer: Exploitation of criminal suspects by mental health professionals is unethical. *Journal of the American Academy of Psychiatry & the Law, 29*(4), 449–451.

Jarrett, M., Bowers, L., & Simpson, A. (2008). Coerced medication in psychiatric inpatient care: Literature review. *Journal of Advanced Nursing, 64*(6), 538–548.

Jaskiewicz-Obydzinska, T., & Czerederecka, A. (1995). Psychological evaluation of changes in testimony given by sexually abused juveniles. In G. Davies, & S. Lloyd-Bostock (Eds.), *Psychology, law, and criminal justice: International developments in research and practice* (pp. 160–169). Berlin: de Gruyter.

Jason, J. (1983). Child homicide spectrum. *American Journal of Disease of Childhood, 137*, 578–581.

Jesson, J. (1993). Understanding adolescent female prostitution: A literature review. *British Journal of Social Work, 23*, 517–530.

Johnson, H., & Hotton, T. (2003, Feb). Losing control: Homicide risk in estranged and intact relationships. *Homicide Studies: An Interdisciplinary & International Journal, 7*(1), 58–84.

Johnson, J. G. (2001). Violence in prison systems: An African American tragedy. *Journal of Human Behavior in the Social Environment, 4*(2–3), 105–128.

Johnson, L. M. (2008). A place for art in prison: Art as a tool for rehabilitation and management. *Southwest Journal of Criminal Justice, 5*(2), 100–120.

Johnson, M. B. (1996). Examining risks to children in the context of parental rights termination proceedings. *New York University Review of Law and Social Change, 22*(2), 397–424.

Johnson, M. B. (1999). Psychological parent theory reconsidered: The New Jersey JC case, part II. *American Journal of Forensic Psychology, 17*(2), 41–56.

Johnson, M. B., Baker, C., & Maceira, A. (2001). The 1997 Adoption and Safe Families Act and parental rights termination consultation. *American Journal of Forensic Psychology, 19*(3), 15–28.

Johnson, M. B., & Hunt, R. C. (2000). The psychological interface in juvenile Miranda assessment. *American Journal of Forensic Psychology, 18*(3), 17–35.

Johnson, S., & O'Connor, E. (2001). *The gay baby boom: A psychological perspective.* New York: New York University Press.

Johnstone, B., Schopp, L., & Shigaki, C. (2000). Forensic psychological evaluation. In R. Frank, & T. Elliot (Eds.), *Handbook of rehabilitation psychology.* Washington, DC: American Psychological Association.

Jones, J. (2007). Persons with intellectual disabilities in the criminal justice system. *International Journal of Offender Therapy and Comparative Criminology, 51*(6), 723–733.

Jones, N. T., Sheitman, B., Edwards, D., Carbone, J., Hazelrigg, M., & Barrick, A. L. (2011). Psychiatric and criminal histories of persons referred for pretrial evaluations: Description and policy implications. *Journal of Forensic Psychiatry and Psychology, 22*(1), 99–109.

Joseph, K. L. (1996). Victim-offender mediation: What social and political factors will affect its development? *Ohio State Journal of Dispute Resolution, 11*(207), 1–14.

Junker, G., Beeler, A., & Bates, J. (2005). Using trained inmate observers for suicide watch in a federal correctional setting: A win-win solution. *Psychological Services, 2*, 20–27.

Kääriäienen, J., Lintonin, T., Laitinen, A., & Pollock, J. (2008). The code of silence: Are self-report surveys a viable means for studying police misconducts? *Journal of Scandinavian Studies in Criminology and Crime Prevention, 9*, 86–96.

Kagle, J., & Kopels, S. (1994). Confidentiality after Tarasoff. *Health and Social Work, 19*(3), 217–222.

Kain, C. (1988). To breach or not to breach: Is that the question? A response to Gray and Harding. *Journal of Counseling and Development, 66*, 224–225.

Kalich, L., Carmichael, B. D., Masson, T., & Blacker, D. (2007). Evaluating the evaluator: Guidelines for legal professionals in assessing the competency of evaluations in termination of parental rights cases. *The Journal of Psychiatry & Law, 35*, 365–397.

Kaltenborn, K. (2001, Feb). Children's and young people's experience in various residential arrangements: A longitudinal study to evaluate criteria for custody and residence decision making. *British Journal of Social Work, 31*(1), 81–117.

Kaltiala-Heino, R., Rimpela, M., & Marttunen, M. (1999). Bullying, depression, and suicidal ideation in Finnish adolescents: School survey. *British Journal of Medicine, 319*, 348–351.

Kamerman, J. (1995). Correctional officer suicide. *The Keeper's Voice* [On-line], *16*. Available: www.acsp.uic.edu/iaco/kv160307.htm.

Kandel, R. F. (1994). Just ask the kid! Towards a rule of children's choice in custody determinations. *University of Miami Law Review, 49*, 299–376.

Kapatzia, A., & Syngollitou, E. (2007). *Cyberbullying in middle and high schools: Prevalence, gender, and age differences. Unpublished manuscript based on master's thesis of A. Kapatzia.* Greece: University of Thessoloniki.

Kassin, S. M. (2008). False confessions: Causes, consequences, and implications for reform. *Current Directions in Psychological Science, 17*(4), 249–253.

Katz, C. M., Webb, V. J., Fox, K., & Shaffer, J. N. (2010). Understanding the relationship between violent victimization and gang membership. *Journal of Criminal Justice, 39*(1), 48–59.

Katz, L. F., & Gottman, J. M. (1997). Buffering children from marital conflict and dissolution. *Journal of Clinical Child Psychology, 26*, 157–171.

Katzer, C., Fetchenhauer, D., & Belschak, F. (2009). Cyberbullying: Who are the victims? *Journal of Media Psychology, 21*(1), 25–36.

Kauppi, A., Kumpulainen, K., Vanamo, T., Merikanto, J., & Karkola, K. (2008). Maternal depression and filicide-case study of ten mothers. *Archives of Women's Mental Health, 11*, 201–206.

Keilin, W. G., & Bloom, L. J. (1986). Child custody evaluation practices: A survey of experienced professionals. *Professional Psychology: Research and Practice, 17*, 338–346.

Keinan, G., & Malach-Pines, A. (2007). Stress and burnout among prison personnel: Sources, outcomes, and intervention strategies. *Criminal Justice and Behavior, 34*, 380–398.

Kelley, J. B. (2003, Apr). Parents with enduring child disputes: Focused interventions with parents in enduring disputes. *Journal of Family Studies, 9*(1), 51–62.

Kelley, J. B. (1997). The best interests of the child: A concept in search of meaning. *Family and Conciliation Courts Review, 35*, 377–387.

Kelly, J. B. (2003). Changing perspectives on children's adjustment following divorce: A view from the United States. *Childhood, 10*(2), 237–254.

Kelly, J. B., & Johnston, J. R. (2005). Commentary on Tippins and Whitman's Empirical and ethical problems with custody recommendations: A call for clinical humility and judicial vigilance. *Family Court Review, 43*, 233–241.

Kennedy, D. B., Homant, R. J., & Hupp, R. T. (1998). Suicide by Cop. *FBI Law Enforcement Bulletin*, 21–27.

Kennedy, M. A., Klein, C., Bristowe, J. T. K., Cooper, B. S., & Yuille, J. C. (2007). Routes of recruitment: Pimps' techniques and other circumstances that lead to street prostitution. *Journal of Aggression, Maltreatment, & Trauma, 15*(2), 1–19.

Kenny, D. T., Lennings, C. J., & Munn, O. A. (2008). Risk factors for self-harm and suicide in incarcerated young offenders: Implications for policy and practice. *Journal of Forensic Psychology Practice, 8*(4), 358–382.

Kernsmith, P. (2005). Treating perpetrators of domestic violence: Gender differences in the applicability of the theory of planned behavior. *Sex Roles, 52*, 589–596.

Kethineni, S., & Beichner, D. (2009). A comparison of civil and criminal orders of protection as remedies for domestic violence victims in a Midwestern county. *Journal of Family Violence, 24*, 311–321.

Kevles, D. J. (1985). *In the name of eugenics: Genetics and the uses of human heredity.* New York: University of California Press.

Keyes, D., Edwards, W., & Perske, R. (1998). *Mental retardation and the death penalty* [On-line], Available: www.essential.org/dpic/dpicmr.html.

Kiely, J., & Hodgson, G. (1990). Stress in the prison service: The benefits of exercise programs. *Human Relations, 43*, 551—572.

Kilchling, M., & Loeschnig-Gspandl, M. (2000). Legal and practical perspectives on victim/offender mediation in Austria and Germany. *International Review of Victimology, 7*(4), 305—332.

Kim, J. H., Choi, S. S., & Ha, K. (2008). A closer look at depression in mothers who kill their children: is it unipolar or bipolar depression? *Journal of Clinical Psychiatry, 69*(10), 1625—1631.

Kim, Y. S., Koh, Y. J., & Leventhal, B. (2005). School bullying and suicidal risk in Korean middle school students. *Pediatrics, 115*, 357—363.

Kimber, A. M. (2005). Psychotic journeys of the green mile. *Thomas M. Cooley Law Review, 22*, 27—54.

Kimietowicz, Z. (2009). Mentally ill prisoners continue to face death penalty in Japan, Amnesty says. *British Medical Journal, 339*, 3729.

Kinder, K., Veneziano, C., Fichter, M., & Azuma, H. (1995). A comparison of the dispositions of juvenile offenders certified as adults with juvenile offenders not certified. *Juvenile and Family Court Journal, 46*(3), 37—42.

Kingshott, B. F. (2009). Suicide by proxy: Revisiting the problem of suicide by cop. *Journal of Police Crisis Negotiations, 9*(2), 108—118.

Kinscherff, R. (2006). Forensic assessment of amenability to rehabilitation in juvenile delinquency. In S. Sparta, & G. P. Koocher (Eds.), *Forensic mental health assessment of children* (pp. 311—329). New York: Oxford University Press.

Kirschman, E. (1997). *I love a cop: What police families need to know.* New York: Guilford Press.

Kiser, G. C. (1991). Female inmates and their families. *Federal Probation, 55*, 55—63.

Kleider, H. M., & Parrott, D. J. (2008). Aggressive shooting behavior: How working memory and threat influence shoot decisions. *Journal of Research in Personality, 43*, 494—497.

Klein, A., Wilson, Wilson, A., Crowe, A., & DeMichelle, M. (2005). *Evaluation of the Rhode Island probation specialized domestic violence supervision unit* (NJC Publication No. 222912). Washington, DC: National Institute of Justice.

Klein, M. W. (1995). Attempting gang control by suppression: The misuse of deterrence principles. In M. W. Klein, C. L. Maxon, & J. Miller (Eds.), *The modern gang reader.* Los Angeles: Roxbury.

Klomek, A. B., Sourander, A., & Gould, M. S. (2011). Bullying and suicide: Detection and intervention. *Psychiatric Times, 28*(2).

Knapp, S., & VandeCreek, L. (2001). Ethical issues in personality assessment in forensic psychology. *Journal of Personality Assessment, 77*(2), 242—254.

Knoll, J. L. (2010a). The "pseudocommando" mass murderer: Part I, the psychology of revenge and obliteration. *Journal of the American Academy of Psychiatry and the Law, 38*(1), 87—94.

Knoll, J. L. (2010b). The "pseudocommando" mass murderer: Part II, the language of revenge. *Journal of the American Academy of Psychiatry and the Law, 38*(2), 263—272.

Knoll, J. L. (2010c). Suicide in correctional settings: Assessment, prevention, and professional liability. *Journal of Correctional Health Care* 1—17.

Knoster, T., & Kincaid, D. (1999). Effective school practice in educating students with challenging behaviors. *TASH Newsletter, 11*(25), 8—11.

Kocsis, R. N. (2003). Criminal psychological profiling: Validities and abilities? *International Journal of Offender Therapies and Comparative Criminology, 47*(2), 126—144.

Kocsis, R. N. (2006). *Criminal Profiling: Principles and Practice.* Totowa, NJ: Humana Press.

Kocsis, R. N. (2003, Feb). An empirical assessment of content in criminal psychological profiles. *International Journal of Offender Therapy & Comparative Criminology, 47*(1), 37—46.

Kocsis, R. (2009a). Criminal Profiling. In R. Kocsis (Ed.), *Applied criminal psychology: A guide to forensic behavioral sciences.* Springfield, IL: Charles Thomas.

Kocsis, R. N., Cooksey, R. W., & Irwin, H. J. (2002, Oct). Psychological profiling of sexual murders: An empirical model. *International Journal of Offender Therapy & Comparative Criminology, 46*(5), 532—554.

Kocsis, R. N., Irwin, H. J., Hayes, A. F., & Nunn, R. (2000, Mar). Expertise in psychological profiling. *Journal of Interpersonal Violence, 15*(3), 311−331.

Kocsis, R., & Palermo, G. (2007). Contemporary problems in criminal profiling. In R. Kocsis (Ed.), *Criminal profiling: International theory, research, and practice*. Totowa, NJ: Humana Press Inc.

Koenen, K. C., Moffitt, T. E., Caspi, A., Taylor, A., & Purcell, S. (2003, Jun). Domestic violence is associated with environmental suppression of IQ in young children. *Development & Psychopathology, 15*(2), 297−311.

Koetting, M. G., Grabarek, J., Van Hasselt, V. B., & Hazelwood, R. R. (2003). Criminally committed inpatients in a residential forensic pre-release treatment program: An exploratory study. *Journal of Offender Rehabilitation, 37*(2), 107−122.

Koffman, S., Ray, A., Berg, S., Covington, L., Albarran, N. M., & Vasquez, M. (2009). Impact of a comprehensive whole child intervention and prevention program among youths at risk of gang involvement and other forms of delinquency. *Children and Schools, 31*(4), 239−245.

KOMO, Staff (2011). Documents: Inmate confesses to killing corrections officer Biendl. *KOMO News*. Retrieved from http://www.komonews.com/.

Koocher, G. P., & Keith-Spiegel, P. (2008). Privacy, confidentiality, and record keeping. In G. Koocher, & P. Keith-Spiegel (Eds.), *Ethics in psychology and the mental health professions: Standards and cases* (3rd edn.). New York: Oxford University Press.

Kornfeld, A. D. (1995). Police officer candidate MMPI-2 performance: Gender, ethnic, and normative factors. *Journal of Clinical Psychology, 51*(4), 536−540.

Kovera, M. B., Dickinson, J. J., & Cutler, B. L. (2003). Voir dire and jury selection. In A. M. Goldstein (Ed.), *Handbook of psychology: Forensic Psychology, Vol. 11* (pp. 161−175). New York, NY: John Wiley & Sons, Inc.

Kowalski, R. M., & Fedina, C. (2011). Cyber bullying in ADHD and Asperberger syndrome populations. *Research in Autism Spectrum Disorders*.

Kowalski, R. M., & Limber, S. P. (2007). Electronic bullying among middle school students. *Journal of Adolescent Health, 41*(6), S22−S30.

Krauss, D. A., & Sales, B. D. (2000). Legal standards, expertise, and experts in the resolution of contested custody cases. *Psychology, Public Policy, & Law, 6*(4), 843−879.

Krisberg, B., & DeComo, R. (1993). Juveniles taken into custody: Fiscal year 1991 report. *Office of Juvenile Justice and Delinquency Prevention*. Washington, DC: United States Department of Justice.

Kroes, W. H. (1976). *Society's victim: The policeman*. Springfield, IL: Charles C. Thomas.

Kucharski, T. L., & Duncan. (2007). Differentiation of mentally ill criminal defendants from malingering on the MMPI-2 and PAI. *American Journal of Forensic Psychology, 25*(3), 21−42.

Kumpulainen, K., Rasanen, E., & Henttonen, I. (1999). Children involved in bullying: Psychological disturbance and the persistence of the involvement. *Child Abuse and Neglect, 23*, 1253−1262.

Kundra, L. B., & Alexander, L. B. (2009). Termination of parental right proceedings: Legal considerations and practical strategies for parents with psychiatric disabilities and the practitioners who serve them. *Psychiatric Rehabilitation Journal, 33*(2), 142−149.

Kureshi, S. (2007). Stolen lives breaking the silence on sex trafficking. *Islamic Magazine, 19*, 25−31.

Kurtz, L. (1997). Comment: Protecting New York's children: An argument for the creation of a rebuttable presumption against awarding a spouse abuser custody of a child. *Albany Law Review, 60*, 1345−1376.

Kushner, M. A. (2006). Is best interests a solution to filling potholes in child custody planning? *Journal of Child Custody, 3*(2), 71−90.

Labecki, L. A. (1994). Monitoring hostility: Avoiding prison disturbances through environmental screening. *Corrections Today, 56*(5), 104−111.

LaFauci Schutt, J. M., & Marotta, S. A. (2011). Personal and environmental predictors of posttraumatic stress in emergency management professionals. *Psychological Trauma: Theory, Research, Practice, and Policy, 3*, 8−15.

Lamb, D., Clark, C., Drumheller, P., Frizzell, K., & Surrey, L. (1989). Applying Tarasoff to AIDS-related psychotherapy issues. *Professional Psychology: Research and Practice, 20*, 37−43.

Lamb, H. R., & Weinberger, L. E. (2005). The shift of psychiatric inpatient care from hospitals to jails and prisons. *Journal of the American Academy of Psychiatry and the Law, 33*(4), 529–534.

Lamb, H., Weinberg, L., DeCuir, W., & Walter, W. (2002, Oct). The police and mental health. *Psychiatric Services, 53*(10), 1266–1271.

Lamb, H. R., Weinberger, L., & Gross, B. (2004). Mentally ill persons in the criminal justice system: Some perspectives. *Psychiatric Quarterly, 75*(2), 107–126.

Lamb, H. R., Weinberger, L. E., Marsh, J. S., & Gross, B. H. (2007). Treatment prospects for persons with severe mental illness in an urban county jail. *Psychiatric Services, 58*(6), 782–786.

Lamb, M. E., Hershkowitz, I., Orbach, Y., & Espin, P. W. (2008). *Tell me what happened: Structured investigative interviews of child victims and witnesses.* Chichester: John Wiley & Sons.

Lambert, E. (2004). The impact of job characteristics on correctional staff. *The Prison Journal, 84*, 208–227.

Lambert, E., Barton, S., Hogan, N., & Clarke, A. (2002). The impact of instrumental communication and integration on correctional staff. *The Justice Professional, 15*, 181–193.

Lambert, E., Hogan, N., & Allen, R. (2006). Correlates of correctional officer job stress: The impact of organizational structure. *American Journal of Criminal Justice, 30*, 227–246.

Lambert, E., Hogan, N. L., & Altheimer, I. (2009). The association between work-family conflict and job burnout among correctional staff: A preliminary study. *American Journal of Criminal Justice, 35*, 37–55.

Lambert, E. G., Hogan, N. L., & Altheimer, I. (2010). An exploratory examination of the consequences of burnout in terms of life satisfaction, turnover intent, and absenteeism among private correctional staff. *The Prison Journal, 90*(1), 94–114.

Lambert, E. G., Hogan, N. L., & Barton, S. M. (2002, Fal). The impact of work-family conflict on correctional staff job satisfaction: An exploratory study. *American Journal of Criminal Justice, 27*(1), 35–52.

Lambert, E. G., Hogan, N. L., & Tucker, K. A. (2009). Problems at work: Exploring the correlates of role stress among correctional staff. *The Prison Journal, 89*(4), 460–481.

Lambert, E., & Paoline, E. (2005). The impact of jail medical issues on job stress and job satisfaction of jail staff: An exploratory study. *Punishment and Society, 7*, 259–275.

Lambert, E., Paoline, E., & Hogan, N. (2006). The impact of centralization and formalization on correctional staff job satisfaction and organizational commitment. *Criminal Justice Studies: A Critical Journal of Crime, Law, and Society, 19*, 23–44.

Lambert, E. G., Paoline, E. A., III, Hogan, N. L., & Baker, D. N. (2007). Gender similarities and differences in correctional staff work attitudes and perceptions of the work environment. *Western Criminology Review, 8*(1), 16–31.

Lambert, E., Reynolds, M., Paoline, E., & Watkins, C. (2004). The effects of occupational stressors on jail staff job satisfaction. *Journal of Crime and Justice, 27*, 1–32.

Lancet. (2/22/2003). Execution: an unwanted side-effect. *Lancet, 361*(9358), 621.

Lansford, J. E. (2009). Parental divorce and children's adjustment. *Perspective on Psychological Science, 4*, 140–152.

Lanyon, R. I. (1986). Psychological assessment procedures in court-related settings. *Professional Psychology: Research and Practice, 17*(3), 260–268.

Laporte, L., Poulin, B., Marleau, J., & Roy, R. (2003). Filicidal women: Jail or psychiatric ward? *Canadian Journal of Psychiatry, 48*(2), 94–98.

Large, M., Nielssen, O., & Elliott, G. (2009). Reliability of psychiatric evidence in serious criminal matters: fitness to stand trial and the defence of mental illness. *Australian and New Zealand Journal of Psychiatry, 43*(5), 446–452.

LaRooy, D., Lamb, M. E., & Pipe, M. E. (2009). Repeated interviewing: A critical evaluation of the risks and the potential benefits. In K. Kuehnle, & M. Connell (Eds.), *The evaluation of child sexual abuse allegations: A comprehensive guide to assessment and treatment* (pp. 327–364). Hoboken, N.J: John Wiley & Sons.

Larrieu, J. A., Heller, S. S., Smyke, A. T., & Zeanah, C. H. (2008). Predictors of permanent loss of custody for mothers of infants and toddlers in foster care. *Infant Mental Health Journal, 29*(1), 48–60.

Lauter, R. (2007). Facilitating impossible goodbyes: A proposal for conducting the final visit after termination of parental rights (Doctoral dissertation, Antioch University New England). *Dissertation Abstracts International*, 6740.

Lavelle, S., & Tusaie, K. (2011). Reflecting on forced medication. *Issues in Mental Health Nursing, 32*(5), 274–278.

Laws, R. D. (1989). *Relapse prevention with sex offenders*. New York: Guilford Press.

Laws, R. D. (2003, Mar). The rise and fall of relapse prevention. *Australian Psychologist, 38*(1), 22–30.

Laws, R. D., & O'Donohue, W. T. (Eds.), (2008). *Sexual deviance: Theory, assessment and treatment*. New York: Guilford Press.

Lee, C., Slade, P., & Lygo, V. (1996). The influence of psychological debriefing on emotional adaptation in women following early miscarriage: A preliminary study. *British Journal of Medical Psychology, 69*, 47–58.

Lee, D. T. (2003). Community-treated and discharged forensic patients: An 11-year follow-up. *International Journal of Law & Psychiatry, 26*(3), 289–300.

Lee, H., & Vaughn, M. (2010). Organizational factors that contribute to police deadly force liability. *Journal of Criminal Justice, 38*, 193–206.

Lee, M. (1997). Post-divorce interparental conflict, children's contact with both parents, children's emotional processes, and children's behavioral adjustment. *Journal of Divorce and Remarriage, 27*, 61–82.

Lee, R. W., & Gillam, S. L. (2000). *Clinical Supervisor, 19*(1), 123–136.

Leese, M., Thomas, S., & Snow, L. (2006). An ecological study of factors associated with rates of self-inflicted death in prisons in England and Wales. *International Journal of Law and Psychiatry, 29*, 355–360.

Lehrmann, D. H. (2010). Advancing children's rights to be heard and protected: The model representation of children in abuse, neglect, and custody proceedings act. *Behavioral Sciences & the Law, 28*(4), 463–479.

Leo, R. A. (1996). Criminal law: Inside the interrogation room. *Journal of Criminal Law and Criminology, 86*(2), 266–303.

Leo, R. J. (2002). Social Security Disability and the mentally ill: Changes in the adjudication process and treating source information requirements. *Psychiatric Annals, 32*(5), 284–292.

Leon, C. S. (2011). Sex offender punishment and the persistence of penal harm in the U.S. *International Journal of Law and Psychiatry, 34*(3), 177–185.

Leon, K. (2003, Jul). Risk and protective factors in young children's adjustment in parental divorce: A review of the Research. *Family Relations: Interdisciplinary Journal of Applied Family Studies, 52*(3), 258–270.

Leonard, E. D. (2000, Jan-Jul). Battered women prisoners as agents of social change: Cross-cultural implications. *Caribbean Journal of Criminology & Social Psychology, 5*(1–2), 154–164.

Leone, P. E., Mayer, M. J., Malmgren, K., & Meisel, S. M. (2000). School violence and disruption: Rhetoric, reality, and reasonable balance. *Focus on Exceptional Children, 33*(1), 1–20.

Leong, G. B., Weinstock, R., Silva, J. A., & Eth, S. (1993). Psychiatry and the death penalty: The past decade. *Psychiatry Annals, 23*, 41–47.

Lerman, D. N. (2006). Second opinion: Inconsistent deference to medical ethics in death penalty jurisprudence. *Georgetown Law Journal, 95*, 1941–1950.

Levin, A. (2006). APA calls for halt to executions of mentally incompetent convicts. *Psychiatric News, 41*(2), 13–44.

Levin, A. (2008). Psychiatrists lack crystal balls to predict patient violence. *Psychiatric News, 43*(12), 4.

Levin, A., & Mills, L. G. (2003, Oct). Fighting for child custody when domestic violence is at issue: Survey of state laws. *Social Work, 48*(4), 463–470.

Levinson, A., & Fonagy, P. (2004). Offending and attachment: The relationship between interpersonal awareness and offending in a prison population with a psychiatric disorder. *Canadian Journal of Psychoanalysis, 12*, 225–251.

Levy, R., & Rubenstein, L. (1996). *The rights of people with mental disabilities*. Carbondale: Southern Illinois University Press.

Lewis, C. F., & Bunce, S. C. (2003). Filicidal mothers and the impact of psychosis on maternal filicide. *Journal of the American Academy of Psychiatry and the Law, 31*, 459–470.

Lewis, D. O., Pincus, J. H., Bard, B., Richardson, E., Prichep, L. S., Feldman, M., & Yeager, C. (1988). Neuropsychiatric, psychoeducational, and family characteristics of 14 juveniles condemned to death in the United States. *American Journal of Psychiatry, 145*, 584–589.

Liang, W. (2010). Cyberbullying: Let the computer help. *Journal of Adolescent Health, 47*(2), 209.

Lichtenberger, E. O., & Kaufman, A. S. (2009). *Essentials of WAIS-IV Assessment.* Hoboken, NJ: John Wiley & Sons, Inc.

Liebling, A. (1993). Suicides in young prisoners: A summary. *Death Studies, 17*(5), 381–409.

Liem, M., & Koenraadt, F. (2008). Filicide: a comparative study of maternal versus paternal child homicide. *Criminal Behaviour and Mental Health, 18*, 166–176.

Lightfoot, E., Hill, K., & LaLiberte, T. (2010). The inclusion of disability as a condition for termination of parental rights. *Child Abuse & Neglect, 34*, 927–934.

Lilienfeld, S. O., & Andrews, B. P. (1996). Development and preliminary validation of a self-report measure of psychopathic personality traits in noncriminal populations. *Journal of Personality Assessment, 66*(3), 488–524.

Lilienfeld, S. O., & Fowler, K. (2006). The self-report assessment of psychopathy. In C. Patrick (Ed.), *Handbook of psychopathy* (pp. 107–132). New York, NY: Guilford.

Lin, C. (2003, Jun). Ethical exploration of the Least Restrictive Alternative. *Psychiatric Services, 54*(6), 866–870.

Lindsay, M. S., & Dickson, D. (2000). Negotiating with the suicide by cop subject. *Suicide by cop: Inducing officers to shoot: Practical direction for resolution, recognition, and recovery.* New York: Looseleaf Law Publications.

Lindsay, M., & Lester, D. (2008). Criteria for suicide-by-cop incidents. *Psychological Reports, 102*, 603–605.

Lindsay, W. R., Michie, A. M., Whitefield, E., Martin, V., Grieve, A., & Carson, D. (2006). Response patterns on the questionnaire on attitudes consistent with sexual offending in groups of sex offenders with intellectual disabilities. *Journal of Applied Research in Intellectual Disabilities, 19*, 47–53.

Lindsay, W. R., Smith, A. H. W., Quinn, K., Anderson, A., Smith, A., Allan, R., & Law, J. (2004). Women with intellectual disability who have offended: Characteristics and outcome. *Journal of Intellectual Disability Research, 48*(6), 580–590.

Litschge, C. M., & Vaughn, M. G. (2009). The mentally ill offender treatment and crime reduction act of 2004: Problems and prospects. *The Journal of Forensic Psychiatry and Psychology, 20*(4), 542–558.

Littelton, H. L., Axsom, D., & Grills-Tequechel, A. E. (2009). Adjustment following the mass shooting at Virginia Tech: The roles of resource loss and gain. *Psychological Trauma: Theory, Research, Practice, and Policy, 1*(3), 206–219.

Little, S. G., Akin-Little, A., & Medley, N. S. (2011). Interventions to address school crises and violence. In M. A. Bray, & T. J. Kehle (Eds.), *The Oxford handbook of school psychology, The Oxford library of psychology.* New York: Oxford University Press.

Litz, B., & Adler, A. (2005). *A controlled trial of group debriefing.* Unpublished raw data.

Liu, K. W. D., Hollis, V., Warren, S., & Williamson, D. L. (2007). Supported-employment program processes and outcomes: experiences of people with Schizophrenia. *AJOT: American Journal of Occupational Therapy, 61*(5), 543–554.

Lochman, J. E., Powell, N. P., Lewczyk Boxmeyer, C., Qu, L., Wells, K. C., & Windle, M. (2009). Implementation of a school-based prevention program: Effects of counselor and school characteristics. *Professional Psychology: Research and Practice, 40*(5), 476–482.

Logan, T., & Walker, R. (2009). Civil protection order outcomes. *Journal of Interpersonal Violence, 24*, 268–291.

Logan, T. K., Walker, R., Jordan, C. E., & Horvath, L. S. (2002, Dec). Child custody evaluations and domestic violence: Case comparisons. *Violence & Victims, 17*(6), 719–742.

Logan, T. K., Walker, R., Horvath, L. S., & Leukefeld, C. (2003). Divorce, custody, and spousal violence: A random sample of circuit court docket records. *Journal of Family Violence, 18*(5), 269–279.

Loper, A. B. (2002, Fal). Adjustment to prison of women convicted of possession, trafficking, and nondrug offenses. *Journal of Drug Issues, 32*(4), 1033–1050.

Lord, D. D. (2001, Mar-Apr). Jury selection: Part one. *Forensic Examiner, 10*(3–4), 27–30.

Lord, E. A. (2008). The challenges of mentally ill female offenders in prison. *Criminal Justice and Behavior, 35*(8), 928−942.

Lord, V. B. (2004). *Suicide by cop: Inducing officers to shoot.* Flushing, NY: Looseleaf Law Publications.

Lorigio, A. (2007). Psychiatrists, mental illness, and violence. *Aggression and Violent Behavior, 12*(5), 542−551.

Lorr, M., & Strack, S. (1994). Personality profiles of police candidates. *Journal of Clinical Psychology, 50*(2), 200−207.

Los Angeles City Attorney Gang Prosecution Section. (1995). Civil gang abatement: A community based policing tool of the office of the Los Angeles City Attorney. In M. W. Klein, C. L. Maxon, & J. Miller (Eds.), *The modern gang reader.* Los Angeles: Roxbury.

Love, B. (1994). Program curbs prison violence through conflict resolution. *Corrections Today, 56*(5), 144−156.

Lowenstein, L. F. (2002a). Joint custody and shared parenting: Are courts listening? *Family Therapy, 29*(2), 101−108.

Lowenstein, L. F. (2002b). The value of mediation in child custody disputes (recent research 1996-2001). *Justice of the Peace, 166*(38), 739−744.

Luke, K. P. (2002, Nov-Dec). Mitigating the ill effects of maternal incarceration on women in prison and their children. *Child Welfare League*(6), 929−948, LXXX1.

Lundman, R. (1993). *Prevention and control of juvenile delinquency* (2nd edn.). New York: Oxford University Press.

Lurigio, A. J. (2007). Serious mental illness and arrest: The generalized mediating effect of substance use. *Crime and Delinquency, 53*(4), 581−604.

Lurigio, A., Rollins, A., & Fallon, J. (2004). The effects of serious mental illness on offender reentry. *Federal Probation, 68*(2), 45−52.

Lyon, T. D., Saywitz, K. J., Kaplan, D. L., & Dorado, J. S. (2001, Feb). Reducing maltreated children's reluctance to answer hypothetical oath-taking. *Law & Human Behavior, 25*(1), 81−92.

MacDonald-Wilson, K., Rogers, E. S., & Anthony, W. A. (2001). Unique issues in assessing work function among individuals with psychiatric disabilities. *Journal of Occupational Rehabilitation, 11*(3), 217−232.

MacKenzie, D. L., & Souryal, R. (1994). Results of a multisite study of boot camp prisons. *Federal Probation, 58,* 60−66.

MacKenzie, D. L., Robinson, J. W., & Campbell, C. S. (1989). Long-term incarceration of female offenders: Prison adjustment and coping. *Criminal Justice and Behavior, 16,* 223−228.

Maeroff, G. I. (2000). *A symbiosis of sorts: School violence and the media* (Choices Briefs No. 7). New York: Columbia University. (ERIC Document Reproduction Service No. ED445138).

Magaletta, P. R., Diamond, P. A., Faust, E., Daggett, D. M., & Camp, S. D. (2009). Estimating the mental illness component of service need in corrections: Results from the mental health prevalence project. *Criminal Justice and Behavior, 36*(3), 229−244.

Magaletta, P. R., Patry, M. W., Wheat, B., & Bates, J. (2008). Prison inmate characteristics and suicide attempt lethality: An exploratory study. *Psychological Services, 5*(4), 351−361.

Maggio, M., & Terenzi, E. (1993). The impact of critical incident stress: Is your office prepared to respond? *Federal Probation, 57*(4), 10−16.

Malesky, A., & Keim, J. (2001). Mental health professionals' perspectives on sex offender registry web sites. *Sexual Abuse: Journal of Research & Treatment, 13*(1), 53−63.

Maletzky, B. M., & Field, G. (2003, Jul-Aug). The biological treatment of dangerous sexual offenders, A review and preliminary report of the Oregon pilot Depo-Provera program. *Aggression & Violent Behavior, 8*(4), 391−412.

Manchester, J. (2003). Beyond accommodation: Reconstructing the insanity defense to provide an adequate remedy for postpartum psychotic women. *The Journal of Criminal Law & Criminology, 93*(2−3), 713−752.

Manguno-Mire, G., Thompson, W., Bertman-Pate, J., Burnett, D., & Thompson, H. (2007). Are release recommendations for NGRI acquittees informed by relevant data? *Behavioral Sciences and the Law, 25,* 43−55.

Mann, C. (1984). *Female crime and delinquency.* Birmingham: University of Alabama Press.

Marcus, D. K., & Buffington-Vollum, J. K. (2008). Countertransference and sexual offenders' cognitive distortions. *Scientific Review of Mental Health Practices*(6), 40–50.

Marcus, D. K., & Buffington-Vollum, J. K. (2005). Countertransference: A social relations perspective. *Journal of Psychotherapy Integration, 15,* 254–283.

Marczyk, G., Heilbrun, K., DeMatteo, D., & Bell, B. (2003). Using a model to guide data gathering, interpretation, and communication in capital mitigation evaluations. *Journal of Forensic Psychology Practice, 3,* 89–102.

Marini, I. (2003). What rehabilitation counselors should know to assist Social Security beneficiaries in becoming employed. *Work: Journal of Prevention, Assessment & Rehabilitation, 21*(1), 37–43.

Marks, M. (2001). Parents at risk of filicide. In G. F. Pinard (Ed.), *Clinical assessment of dangerousness: Empirical contributions* (pp. 158–180). New York: Cambridge University Press.

Marques, J. K. (1999, Apr). How to answer the question Does sexual offender treatment work? *Journal of Interpersonal Violence, 14*(4), 437–451.

Marsh, J. C., & Dingcai, C. (2005). Parents in substance abuse treatment: Implications for child welfare practice. *Children and Youth Services Review, 27*(12), 1259–1278.

Marshall, L. E. (2001, Jul). Excessive sexual desire disorder among sexual offenders: The development of a research project. *Sexual Addiction & Compulsivity, 8*(3–4), 301–307.

Marshall, S. L. (1944). *Island victory.* New York: Penguin Books.

Martin, D. (1989). Human immunodeficiency virus infection and the gay community: Counseling and clinical issues. *Journal of Counseling and Development, 68,* 67–71.

Martin, M. A., Allan, A., & Allan, M. M. (2001). The use of psychological tests by Australian psychologists who do assessments for the courts. *Australian Journal of Psychology, 53*(2), 77–82.

Martin, M., Marchand, A., & Boyer, R. (2009). Traumatic events in the workplace: Impact of psychopathology and healthcare use of police officers. *Journal of Emergency of Mental Health, 11,* 165–176.

Martin, S. E., & Jurik, N. C. (1996). *Doing justice, doing gender: Women in law and criminal justice occupations.* Thousand Oaks, CA: Sage.

Martindale, D. A. (2001). Cross-examining mental health experts in child custody litigation. *Journal of Psychiatry & Law, 29*(4), 483–511.

Martinez, A. R. (1997). Corrections officer: The other prisoner. *The Keeper's Voice* [On-line], *18.* Available: www.acsp.uic.edu/iaco/kv1801/180108.shtml.

Martone, C. A., Nemoianu, A., Shuarman, R. S., Singh, A., & Dolan Strano, A. (2008). Forensic psychiatry—criminal law. In D. Kupfer, M. S. Horner, D. Brent, D. Lewis, C. Reynolds, M. Thase, & M. Travis (Eds.), *Oxford American Handbook of Psychiatry* (pp. 855–885). Oxford, NY: Oxford University Press.

Marzuk, P., Nock, M., Leon, A., Portera, L., & Tardiff, K. (2002, Dec). Suicide among New York City police officers, 1977-1996. *American Journal of Psychiatry, 159*(12), 2069–2071.

Masho, S., Odor, R., & Adera, T. (2005). Sexual assault in Virginia: A population-based study. *Women's Health Issues, 15,* 157–166.

Mason, C., Chapman, D., Chang, S., & Simons, J. (2003). Impacting re-arrest rates among youth sentenced in adult court: An epidemiological examination of the juvenile sentencing advocacy project. *Journal of Clinical and Adolescent Psychology, 32*(2), 205–214.

Mason, T., Worsley, A., & Coyle, D. (2010). Forensic multidisciplinary perspectives of Tarasoff liability: A vignette study. *Journal of Forensic Psychiatry and Psychology, 21*(4), 549–554.

Mastrofski, S. D., Parks, R. B., Reiss, A. J., & Worden, R. E. (1998). *Policing neighborhoods: A report from Indianapolis.* Washington, DC: U.S. Department of Justice.

Maxson, C. L., Hennigan, K. M., & Sloane, D. C. (2005). It's getting crazy out there: Can a civil gang injunction change a community? *Criminology and Public Policy, 4*(3), 501–530.

Mayou, R., Ehlers, A., & Hobbs, M. (2000). Psychological debriefing for road traffic accident victims: Three year follow-up of a randomised controlled trial. *British Journal of Psychiatry, 176,* 589–593.

McAuliff, B. D. (2009). Child victim and witness research comes of age: Implications for social scientists, practitioners, and the law. In B. L. Bottoms, C. J. Najdowski, & G. S. Goodman (Eds.), *Children as victims, witnesses, and offenders: Psychological science and the law* (pp. 233−252). New York: Guilford Press.

McAuliff, B. D., Maurice, K. A., Neal, E. S., & Diaz, A. (2008). *She should have been more upset…: Expectancy violation theory and jurors' perceptions of child victims.* Jacksonville, FL: Paper presented at the annual meeting of the American Psychology-Law Society.

McCaffrey, T. (2004). Responding to crises in schools: A consultancy model for supporting schools in crisis. *Educational and Child Psychology, 21*(3), 109−120.

McCord, J. (1991). The cycle of crime and socialization process. *Journal of Criminal Law and Criminology, 82*, 211−228.

McCorkle, R. C., Miethe, T. D., & Drass, K. A. (1995). The roots of prison violence: A test of the deprivation, management, and not-so-total institution models. *Crime and Delinquency, 41*(3), 317−331.

McCraty, R., Atkinson, M., Lipsenthal, L., & Arguelles, L. (2009). New hope for correctional officers: an innovative program for reducing stress and health risks. *Applied Psychophysiological Biofeedback, 34*, 251−272.

McCreary, D. R., & Thompson, M. M. (2006). Development of two reliable and valid measures of stressors in policing: The Operational and Organizational Police Stress Questionnaires. *International Journal of Stress Management, 13*, 494−518.

McDonnell, M., & Phillips, R. T. M. (2010). Physicians should treat mentally ill death row inmates, even if treatment is refused. *Journal of Law, Medicine, and Ethics, 38*(4), 774−788.

McGrath, R. (1991). Sex-offender risk assessment and disposition planning: A review of empirical and clinical findings. *International Journal of Offender Therapy and Comparative Criminology, 35*(4), 328−350.

McGrath, R. J., Cumming, G., Livingston, J. A., & Hoke, S. E. (2003). Outcome of a treatment program for adult sex offenders: From prison to community. *Journal of Interpersonal Violence, 18*(1), 3−17.

McGrath, R. J., & Torres, A. (2008). Forensic psychology, forensic psychiatry, and criminal profiling: The mental health professionals contribution to criminal profiling. In B. E. Turvey (Ed.), *Criminal Profiling: An Introduction to Behavioral Evidence Analysis*. New York: Academic Press.

McGreevy, P., & Banks, S. (2006, 23 March). On paper, leaving a gang is difficult. *Los Angeles Times*. Available at http://articles.latimes.com/2006/mar/23/local/me-gang23.

McGuire, J. (2000). *Cognitive-behavioural approaches: An introduction to theory and research*. London: Home Office.

McGuire, T. J. (2000). Correctional institution based sex offender treatment: A lapse behavior study. *Behavioral Sciences & the Law, 18*(1), 57−71.

McKee, G. R., & Shea, S. J. (1998). Maternal filicide: A cross-national comparison. *Journal of Clinical Psychology, 54*(5), 679−687.

McKenzie, I. K. (2006). Forcing the police to open fire. *Journal of Police Crisis Negotiations, 6*(1), 5−25.

McLean, N., & Marshall, L. (2010). A front line police perspective of mental health issues and services. *Criminal Behavior and Mental Health, 20*, 62−71.

McMahon, E. M., Reulbach, U., & Keeley, H. (2010). Bullying victimization, self harm and associated factors in Irish adolescent boys. *Social Science Medicine, 71*, 1300−1307.

McMurray, H. L. (1990). Attitudes of assaulted police officers and their policy implications. *Journal of Police Science and Administration, 17*(1), 44−48.

McNally, V. J. (1999). FBI's employee assistance program: An advanced law enforcement model. *International Journal of Emergency Mental Health, 1*(2), 109−114.

McSherry, B. (2001). Expert testimony and the effects of mental impairment: Reviving the ultimate issue rule. *International Journal of Law & Psychiatry, 24*(1), 13−21.

McWey, L. M., Henderson, T. L., & Alexander, J. B. (2008). Parental rights and the foster care system: A glimpse of decision making in Virginia. *Journal of Family Issues, 29*(8), 1031−1050.

McWhirter, E. H., & Linzer, M. (1994). The provision of critical incident stress debriefing services by EAPs: A case study. *Journal of Mental Health Counseling, 16*, 403−414.

Meade, B., & Steiner, B. (2010). The total effects of boot camps that house juveniles: A systematic review of the evidence. *Journal of Criminal Justice, 38*(5), 841–853.

Medrano, M. A., Hatch, J. P., Zule, W. A., & Desmond, D. P. (2003). Childhood trauma and adult prostitution behavior in a multiethnic heterosexual drug-using population. *American Journal of Drug & Alcohol Abuse, 29*(2), 463–486.

Melde, C., Taylor, T. J., & Esbensen, F. (2009). I got your back: An examination of the protective function of gang membership in adolescence. *Criminology: An Interdisciplinary Journal, 47*(2), 565–594.

Melton, G. B., Petrila, J., Poythress, N. G., & Slobogin, C. (2007). *Psychological evaluations for the courts: A handbook for mental health professionals and lawyers*. New York: Guilford.

Meltzer, H. (2010). The mental-ill health of prisoners. In G. L. Cooper, J. Field, & J. Goswami (Eds.), *Mental Capital and Well-Being*. Hoboken, NJ: Wiley-Blackwell.

Melville, J. D., & Naimark, D. (2002). Punishing the insane: The verdict of guilty but mentally ill. *Journal of the American Academy of Psychiatry & the Law, 30*(4), 553–555.

Merari, A., Diamant, I., Bibi, A., Broshi, Y., & Zakin, G. (2010). Personality characteristics of self martyrs/suicide bombers and organizers of suicide attacks. *Terrorism and Political Violence, 22*, 87–101.

Meyer, A. S., McWey, L. M., McKendrick, W., & Henderson, T. L. (2010). Substance using parents, foster care, and termination of parental rights: The importance of risk factors for legal outcomes. *Children and Youth Services Review, 32*, 639–649.

Meyer, C. B. (2002). Das Taeterprofil aus interdisziplinaerer Sicht, unter besonderer Beruecksichtigung des Strafprozessrechts. In M. Cottier, D. Rueetschi, & K. Sahlfeld (Eds.), *Information & Recht* (pp. 135–172). Basel/Genf/Muenchen: Helbing & Lichtenhahn.

Meyer, C. B. (2007). Criminal profiling as expert evidence? An international case law perspective. In Richard N. Kocsis (Ed.), *Criminal Profiling: International Theory Research and Practice* (pp. 207–247). Totowa, NJ: Humana Press.

Meyer, J. F., Paul, R. C., & Grant, D. R. (2009). Peacekeepers turned peacemakers: Police as mediators. *Contemporary Justice Review, 12*(3), 331–344.

Meyer, W. J., Molett, M., Richards, C. D., Arnold, L., & Latham, J. (2003, Aug). Outpatient civil commitment in Texas for management and treatment of sexually violent predators: A preliminary report. *International Journal of Offender Therapy and Comparative Criminology, 47*(4), 396–406.

Miall, C. E., & March, K. (2005). Community attitudes toward birth fathers' motives for adoption placement and single parenting. *Family Relations, 54*(4), 535–546.

Michelson, J. (2006). Unspeakable justice: The Oswaldo Martinez case and the failure of the legal system to adequately provide for incompetent defendants. *William and Mary Law Review, 48*, 2075–2089.

Mikhail, D. (2006). Refining and resolving the blur of guilt for juvenile capital offenders in Texas: A world without the juvenile death penalty. *Victims and Offenders, 1*, 99–121.

Miller, C. E., & Barrett, G. V. (2008). The coachability and fakability of personality-based selection tests used for police selection. *Public Personnel Management, 37*(3), 68–69.

Miller, G. (1993). The psychological best interests of the child. *Journal of Divorce and Remarriage, 19*, 21–36.

Miller, L. (2005). Police officer suicide: Causes, prevention, and practical intervention strategies. *International Journal of Emergency Mental Health, 7*, 101–114.

Miller, L. (2008). Stress and resilience in law enforcement training and practice. *International Journal of Emergency Mental Health, 10*, 109–124.

Miller, L. (2010). Good intentions, mixed outcomes. *Rise*. Retrieved from www.risemagazine.org/featured_stories/good_intentions_mixed_outcomes.html.

Miller, M. K. (2011). How judges decide whether social parents have parental rights: A five-factor typology. *Family Court Review, 49*(1), 72–83.

Miller, M., & Morris, N. (1988). Predictions of dangerousness: An argument for limited use. *Violence and Victims, 3*(4), 263–283.

Miller, R. (1990). Involuntary civil commitment. In R. Simon (Ed.), *Annual review of psychiatry and the law*. Washington, DC: American Psychiatric Press.

Miller, R. D. (2003). Testimony by proxy: the use of expert testimony to provide defendant testimony without cross-examination. *Journal of Psychiatry & Law, 31*(1), 21–41.

Miller, S. L., & Meloy, M. L. (2006). Women's use of force: Voices of women arrested for domestic violence. *Violence Against Women, 12,* 89–115.

Mills, A., Lathlean, J., Bressington, D., Forrester, A., Van Veenhuyzen, W., & Gray, R. (2011). Prisoners' experiences of antipsychotic medication: Influences on adherence. *Journal of Forensic Psychiatry & Psychology, 22*(1), 110–125.

Mills, J., & Kroner, D. G. (2003, Jun). Antisocial constructs in predicting institutional violence among violent offenders and child molesters. *International Journal of Offender Therapy & Comparative Criminology, 47*(3), 324–334.

Milner, J. S., & Campbell, J. C. (1995). Prediction issues for practitioners. In J. C. Campbell (Ed.), *Assessing dangerousness: Violence by sexual offenders, batterers, and child abusers.* Thousand Oaks, CA: Sage.

Minnesota Department of Corrections. (2010). *Parenting programs: Minnesota correctional facility (MCF) Shakopee.* Accessed September 13, 2011, at www.doc.state.mn.us/publications/documents/08-10SHKparentingprogramsummary.pdf.

Minzi-Levi, M., & Shields, M. (2007). Serial sexual murderers and prostitutes as their victims: difficulty profiling perpetrators and victim vulnerability as illustrated by the Green River case. In M. Shields (Ed.), *Brief treatment, crisis intervention.* Oxford, UK: Oxford University Press.

Mire, G. (2007). Are release recommendations for NGRI acquittees informed by relevant data? *Behavioral Sciences and the Law* (25), 43–55.

Mishna, F., Sainin, M., & Solomon, S. (2009). Ongoing and online: Children and youth's perceptions of cyber bullying. *Children and Youth Services Review, 31*(12), 1222–1228.

Mitcham-Smith, M., & Henry, W. J. (2007). High-conflict divorce solutions: Parenting coordination as an innovative co-parenting intervention. *The Family Journal, 15*(4), 368–373.

Mitchell, J. T. (1983). When disaster strikes: The critical incident stress debriefing process. *Journal of Emergency Services, 8,* 36–39.

Mitchell, J. T. (1988a). The history, status and future of critical incident stress debriefing process. *Journal of Emergency Medical Services, 8*(1), 36–39.

Mitchell, J. T. (1988b). Development and functions of a critical incident stress debriefing process. *Journal of Emergency Medical Services, 13*(12), 43–46.

Mitchell, K., Finkelhor, D., Jones, L., & Wolak, J. (2010). Use of social networking sites in online sex crimes against minors: An examination of national incidence and means of utilization. *Journal of Adolescent Health, 47*(2), 183–190.

Mohandie, K., & Hatcher, C. (1999). Suicide and violence risk in law enforcement: Practical guidelines for risk assessment, prevention, and intervention. *Behavioral Science and the Law, 17,* 357–376.

Mohandie, K., & Meloy, J. R. (2000). Clinical and forensic indictors of "suicide by cop." *Journal of Forensic Sciences, 45*(2), 384–389.

Mohandie, K., Meloy, J. R., & Collins, P. I. (2009). Suicide-by-cop among officer-involved shooting cases. *Journal of Forensic Sciences, 54*(2), 456–462.

Molett, M. T., Arnold, L., & Meyer, W. J. (2001, Nov). Commitment as an adjunct to sex offender treatment. *Current Opinion in Psychiatry, 14*(6), 549–553.

Monahan, J. (1981). *The clinical prediction of violent behavior.* Beverly Hills, CA: Sage.

Monahan, J. (2002). The MacArthur studies of violence risk. *Criminal Behaviour & Mental Health, 12*(4), S67–S72.

Monahan, J. (2003). Violence risk assessment. In I. B. Weiner (Series Ed.) & A. M. Goldstein (Vol. Ed.), *Handbook of psychology: Vol. 11. Forensic psychology* (pp. 527–540). New York: Wiley.

Monahan, J., Steadman, H. J., Clark Robbins, P., Appelbaum, P., Banks, S., Grisso, T., et al. (2005). An actuarial model of violence risk assessment for persons with mental disorders. *Psychiatric Services, 56,* 810–815.

Monahan, J., Steadman, H., Silver, E., Appelbaum, P., Robbins, P., Mulvey, E., Roth, L., et al. (2001). *Rethinking Risk Assessment: The MacArthur Study of Mental Disorder and Violence.* New York: Oxford University Press.

Monroe, C. R. (2005). Why are "bad boys" always black? Causes for disproportionality in school discipline and recommendations for change. *The Clearing House, 79*, 45–50.

Monson, C. M., Gunnin, D. D., Fogel, M. H., & Kyle, L. L. (2001). Stopping (or slowing) the revolving door: Factors related to NGRI acquittees' maintenance of a conditional release. *Law & Human Behavior, 25*(3), 257–267.

Montoya, J. (1999). Child hearsay statutes: At once over-inclusive and under-inclusive. *Psychology, Public Policy, and Law, 5*(2), 304–322.

Moon, D. G., Thompson, R. J., & Bennett, R. (1993). Patterns of substance use among women in prison. In B. R. Fletcher, L. D. Shaver, & D. G. Moon (Eds.), *Women prisoners: A forgotten population* (pp. 45–54). Westport, CT: Praeger.

Moore, T. O. (2001). Testosterone and male behavior: Empirical research with hamsters does not support the use of castration to deter human sexual aggression. *North American Journal of Psychology, 3*(3), 503–520.

Moran, G. (2001). Trial consultation: Why licensure is not necessary. *Journal of Forensic Psychology Practice, 1*(4), 77–85.

Moran, M. J., Sweda, M. G., Fragala, M. R., & Sasscer-Burgos, J. (2001). The clinical application of risk assessment in treatment-planning process. *International Journal of Offender Therapy and Comparative Criminology, 45*(4), 421–435.

Morash, M., & Rucker, L. (1990). A critical look at the idea of boot camp as a correctional reform. *Crime and Delinquency, 36*, 204–222.

Morash, M., Jeong, S. J., & Zang, N. L. (2010). An exploratory study of the characteristics of men known to commit prisoner-on-prisoner sexual violence. *The Prison Journal, 90*(2), 161–178.

Morgan, A. A., Marsiske, M., & Whitfield, K. E. (2008). Characterizing and explaining differences in cognitive test performance between African American and European American older adults. *Experimental Aging Research, 34*(1), 80–100.

Morgan, D. (1997). Restricted love. *Women & Therapy, 20*(4), 75–84.

Morgan, J. E. (2009). Competency to stand trial and the insanity defense. In J. E. Morgan, & J. J. Sweet (Eds.), *Neuropsychology of Malingering Casebook* (pp. 401–412). New York: Psychology Press.

Morgan, R. D., Van Haveren, R., & Pearson, C. A. (2002). Correctional officer burnout: Further analyses. *Criminal Justice & Behavior, 29*(2), 144–160.

Morlok, E. (2003). Analysis of mentally retarded and lower-functioning offender correctional programs. *Corrections Today.* Retrieved June 22, 2011 from www.allbusiness.com/public-administration/justice-public-order/1143300-1.html.

Morrison, E., Morman, G., Bonner, G., Taylor, C., Abraham, I., & Lathan, L. (2002). Reducing staff injuries and violence in a forensic psychiatric setting. *Archives of Psychiatric Nursing, 16*(3), 108–117.

Morse, S. J. (1978). Crazy behavior, morals, and science: An analysis of mental health law. *Southern California Law Review, 51*, 527–564.

Morse, S. J. (2003). Involuntary competence. *Behavioral Sciences & the Law, 21*(3), 311–328.

Moses, E. (1996). *Ogles proposes castration law.* [On-line] Available: www.bhip.com/news/9ogles.htm.

Moses, M. C. (1995). *A synergistic solution for children of incarcerated parents.*

Moses, M. C. (2006). Correlating incarcerated mothers, foster care and mother-child reunification. *Corrections Today,* 98–100.

Mossman, D. (2007). Predicting restorability of incompetent criminal defendants. *The Journal of American Academy of Psychiatry and the Law, 35*, 34–43.

Mossman, D., Noffsinger, S. G., Ash, P., Frierson, R. L., Gerbasi, J., Hackett, M., et al. (2007). AAPL practice guideline for the forensic psychiatric evaluation of competence to stand trial. *Journal of the American Academy of Psychiatry and the Law, 35*(4), S3–S72.

Mrad, D. F., & Nabors, E. (2007). The role of the psychologist in civil commitment. In A. M. Goldstein (Ed.), *Forensic psychology: Emerging topics and expanding roles* (pp. 232–259). Hoboken, NJ: John Wiley & Sons Inc.

Mueller, C., & Wylie, M. (2007). Examining the effectiveness of an intervention designed for the restoration of competency to stand trial. *Behavioral Sciences and the Law, 25*, 891–900.

Mueser, K. T., Lu, W., Rosenberg, S. D., & Wolfe, R. (2010). The trauma of psychosis: Posttraumatic stress disorder and recent onset psychosis. *Schizophrenia Research, 116*(2–3), 217–227.

Mullen, P. (2006). Schizophrenia and violence: From correlations to preventative strategies. *Advances in Psychiatric Treatment, 12*(4), 236–248.

Mulvey, E. P., & Cauffman, E. (2001). The inherent limits of predicting school violence. *American Psychologist, 56*(10), 797–802.

Mumola, C. (2005). *Suicide and homicide in state prisons and local jails*. Washington, DC: U.S. Department of Justice, Office of Justice Programs.

Munsey, C. (2010). Adopted children thrive in same-sex households, study shows. *Monitor on Psychology, 41*(9), 48.

Munson, W. M. (1994). Description and field test of a career development course for male youth offenders with disabilities. *Journal of Career Development, 20*, 205–218.

Murphy, C. M., Meyer, S. L., & O'Leary, K. D. (1993). Family of origin violence and MCM I-II psychopathology among partner assultive men. *Violence and Victims, 8*, 165–175.

Murphy, J. J. (1972). Current practices in the use of the psychological testing by police agencies. *Journal of Criminal Law, Criminology, and Police Science, 63*, 570–576.

Murphy, K., Quartly, M., & Cuthbert, D. (2009). In the best interests of the child: Mapping the (re)emergence of pro-adoption politics in contemporary America. *Australian Journal of Politics and History, 55*(2), 201–218.

Murrie, D., Henderson, C. E., Vincent, G. M., Rockett, J. L., & Mundt, C. (2009). Psychiatric symptoms among juveniles incarcerated in adult prison. *Psychiatric Services, 60*(8), 1092–1097.

Myers, B. J., Smarsh, T. M., Amlund-Hagen, K., & Kennon, S. (1999). Children of incarcerated mothers. *Journal of Child and Family Studies, 8*(1), 11–25.

Myers, J. E. (1983–1984). Involuntary civil commitment of the mentally ill: A system in need of change. *Villanova Law Review, 29*, 367–433.

Myers, J. E. B. (1993b). The competency of young children to testify in legal proceedings. *Behavioral Sciences and the Law, 11*, 121–133.

Myers, J. E. B. (2009). Expert psychological testimony in child sexual abuse trials. In B. L. Bottoms, C. J. Najdowski, & G. S. Goodman's (Eds.), *Children as victims, witnesses, and offenders: Psychological science and the law* (pp. 233–252). New York: Guilford Press.

Myers, J. J., & Carper, G. T. (2008). Cyber-bullying: The legal challenge for educators. *Education Law Reporter, 238*, 1–15.

Myers, J. J., McCaw, D. S., & Hemphill, L. S. (2011). *Responding to cyberbullying: An action tool for school leaders*. Thousand Oaks, CA: Corwin Press.

Myers, T. (2008). The unconstitutionality, ineffectiveness, and alternatives of gang injunctions. *Michigan Journal of Race and Law, 14*, 285–301.

Myrstol, B. A. (2010). *"School Resource Officers: Public perspectives and perceptions" (PowerPoint slide presentation, 5 Feb). Slide presentation presented to the Western Society of Criminology*. Honolulu: Hawaii. (Available from Justice Center, University of Alaska Anchorage.) http://justice.uaa.alaska.edu/research/2010/1008.sro/1008.01.schoolresourceofficers.html.

Nagin, D. S., Piquero, A. R., Scott, E., & Steinberg, L. (2006). Public preferences for rehabilitation versus incarceration of juvenile offenders: Evidence from a contingent valuation survey. *Criminology and Public Policy, 5*, 301–326.

National Center for Health Statistics. (1996). *A generation at risk*. [On-line] Available: www. rainbows.org/Rain5a.htm.

National Center for Health Statistics. (1997). *Teen suicide rate*. [On-line] Available: http://home.ptd. net/»buzz/fam-cide.htm.

National Center for Health Statistics. (2008). *Marriage and divorce*. Retrieved July 24, 2011, from www.cdc.gov/nchs/fastats/divorce.htm.

National Center on Child Abuse and Neglect. (1994). *Child maltreatment 1992: Reports from the states to the National Center on Child Abuse and Neglect.* Washington, DC: U.S. Department of Health and Human Services.

National Children's Home. (2005). *Putting U in the picture: Mobile bullying survey.* Available at www.nch.org/uk/uploads/documents/mobile_bullying_%20report.pdf. Accessed April 30, 2011.

National Conference of State Legislatures. (2011). *Same-sex marriage, civil unions and domestic partnerships.* Retrieved on September, 12, 2011 from www.ncsl.org/default.aspx?tabid=16430.

National Crime Prevention Council. (2011). *Strategy: School Resource Officers.* Arlington, VA: Author. Retrieved on September 4, 2011 at www.ncpc.org/topics/school-safety/strategies/strategy-school-resource-officers.

National Gang Intelligence Center. (2009). *National Gang Threat Assessment 2009.* Washington, DC: NGIC.

National Gay and Lesbian Task Force. (2008). *Adoption laws in the United States map.* Retrieved August 1, 2011, from www.thetaskforce.org/reports_and_research/adoption_laws.

National Geographic. (2006). *Lockdown: Gang War.* Des Moines, IW: National Geographic.

National Institute of Corrections. (1991). *Intervening with substance-abusing offenders: A framework of action* (Report No. 296−934/40539). Washington, DC: U.S. Government Printing Office.

National Institutes of Health − Public Access. (2009). The ecological effects of universal and selective violence prevention programs for middle school students: A randomized trial. *Journal of Consulting and Clinical Psychology, 77*(3), 526−542.

Needham, P. (2011). *"South County Truancy Interdiction Center: FY 08-09 key indicators." Juvenile Welfare Board-The Children's Services Council at Pinellas County at* www.jwbpinellas.org/south-county-truancy-interdiction-center.

Neil, E., Beek, M., & Schofield, G. (2003). Thinking about and managing contact in permanent placements: The differences and similarities between adoptive parents and foster careers. *Clinical Child Psychology & Psychiatry, 8*(3), 401−418.

Neveu, J. P. (2007). Jailed resources: Conservation of resources theory as applied to burnout among prison guards. *Journal of Organizational Behavior, 28,* 21−42.

Newman, G. (2006). The exploitation of trafficked women. *Problem-Oriented Guides for Police, Problem-Specific Guides Series, 38.* Retrieved from www.cops.usdoj.gov.

New York Office of the Governor, Office of the Governor David A Paterson. (2008). *Governor Paterson and legislative leaders announce agreement on legislation to improve quality assurance reviews for persons with mental illness involved in violent incidents.* [Press Release] Retrieved from www.ny.gov/governor/press/press_0620083_print.html.

Neylan, T., Metzler, T., Best, S., Weiss, D., Fagan, J., et al. (2002, Mar-Apr). Critical incident exposure and sleep quality in Police officers. *Psychosomatic Medicine, 64*(2), 345−352.

Nicholson, R., & Kugler, K. (1991). Competent and incompetent criminal defendants: A quantitative review of comparative research. *Psychological Bulletin, 109*(3), 355−370.

Nicholson, R. A., & Norwood, S. (2000, Feb). The quality of forensic psychological assessments, reports, and testimony: Acknowledging the gap between promise and practice. *Law & Human Behavior, 24*(1), 9−44.

Nies, K. J. (2005). Symptom validity testing and post traumatic stress disorder: Nothing but the truth. In R. L. Heilbronner's (Ed.), *Forensic Neuropsychology Casebook* (p. 41). New York, NY: Guilford Press.

Nocentini, A., Calmaestra, J., Schultz-Krumbholz, A., Scheithauer, H., Ortega, R., & Menesini, E. (2010). Cyberbullying: Labels, behaviours, and definition in three European countries. *Australian Journal of Guidance & Counseling, 20*(2), 129−142.

Noonan, K., & Burke, K. (2005). Termination of parental rights: Which foster care children are affected? *The Social Science Journal, 42*(2), 241−256.

Novotney, A. (2008). Custody collaborations: Lawyers and psychologists work together to keep children's best interests in mind. *Monitor on Psychology, 39*(7), 49−51.

Nugent, W., Umbreit, M. S., Wiinamaki, L., & Paddock, J. (2001, Jan). Participation in victim-offender mediation and reoffense: Successful replications? *Research on Social Work Practice, 11*(1), 5−23.

Nussbaum, D., Hancock, M., Turner, I., Arrowood, J., & Melodick, S. (2008). Fitness/competency to stand trial: A conceptual overview, review of existing instruments, and cross-validation of the Nussbaum Fitness Questionnaire. *Brief Treatment and Crisis Intervention, 8*(1), 43–72.

Oberman, M. (2003). Mothers who kill: Cross-cultural patterns in and perspectives on contemporary maternal filicide. *International Journal of Law and Psychiatry, 26*, 493–514.

O'Brien, A. (2010). Fusion of mental health and incapacity legislation. *Contemporary Nurse, 34*(2), 237–247.

O'Deane, M. (2007). *Gang Investigators Handbook.* Boulder, CO: Paladin Press.

O'Deane, M. D., & Morreale, S. A. (2011). Evaluation of the effectiveness of gang injunctions in California. *The Journal of Criminal Justice Research, 2*(1), 1–32.

O'Donnell, R. J. (2010). A second chance for children and families: A model statute to reinstate parental rights after termination. *Family Court Review, 48*(2), 362–379.

Office of Juvenile Justice and Delinquency Prevention. (2009, Dec). Juvenile Arrests 2008. *Juvenile Justice Bulletin,* 1–12.

Olley, J. G. (2010). Knowledge and experience required for experts in Atkins cases. *Applied Neuropsychology, 16*(2), 135–140.

Olmstead, S. B., McWey, L. M., & Henderson, T. (2011). In the child's best interest: Terminating the rights of fathers with children in foster care. *Journal of Family Issues, 32*(1), 31–54.

O'Malley, S. (2004). *Are you there alone?: The unspeakable crime of Andrea Yates.* New York: Simon & Schuster.

Oppenheim, E., & Bussiere, A. (1996). Adoption: Where do relatives stand? *Child Welfare League of America, 5*(47), 1–488.

Oppenheimer, K., & Swanson, G. (1990). Duty to warn: When should confidentiality be breached? *Journal of Family Practice, 30*(2), 179–184.

Orcutt, H., Goodman, G., Tobey, A., Batterman-Faunce, J., & Thomas, S. (2001, Aug). Detecting deception in children's testimony: Factfinder's abilities to reach the truth in open court and closed-circuit trials. *Law & Human Behavior, 25*(4), 339–372.

Ortega, R., Calmeastra, J., & Mora-Merchan, J. (2008). Cyberbullying: un estio exploratorio en education secundaria. *International Journal of Psychology and Psychological Therapy, 8*, 183–192.

Ortiz, J. (2010, August 27). Grief counseling requests rise in wake of state worker suicides. *The Sacramento Bee,* Retrieved April 30, 2011, from www.sacbee.com/2010/08/27/2986251/grief-counseling-requests-rise.html.

Osborne, J. W. (2004). Identification with academics and violence in schools. *Review of General Psychology, 8*(3), 147–162.

Osborne, O. H. (1995). Jailed mothers: Further explorations in public sector nursing. *Journal of Psychosocial Nursing, 33*, 23–28.

Osinowo, T. O., & Pinals, D. A. (2003). Competence to stand trial. *Journal of the American Academy of Psychiatry & the Law, 31*(2), 261–264.

Osler, M. W. (1991). Shock incarceration: Hard realities and real possibilities. *Federal Probation, 55*, 34–42.

Otto, R. K., & Edens, J. (2005). Parenting capacity. In T. Grisso (Ed.), *Evaluating Competencies: Perspectives in Law and Psychology.* New York: Kluwer Academic Press.

Otto, R. K., Edens, J. F., & Barcus, E. H. (2000, Jul). The use of psychological testing in child custody evaluations. *Family & Conciliation Courts Review, 38*(3), 312–340.

Otto, R. K., & Martindale, D. A. (2006). The law, process, and science of child custody evaluation. In M. Costanzo, D. Krauss, & K. Pezdek's (Eds.), *Expert psychological testimony for the courts* (pp. 251–275). Mahwah, NJ: Erlbaum.

Otto, R. K., Poythress, N. G., Nicholson, R. A., Edens, J. F., Monahan, J., Bonnie, R. J., et al. (1998). Psychometric properties of the MacArthur Competence Assessment Tool – Criminal Adjudication (MacCAT-CA). *Psychological Assessment, 10*, 435–443.

Overcamp-Martini, M. A., & Nutton, J. S. (2009). CAPTA and the residential placement: A survey of state policy and practice. *Child and Youth Care Forum, 38*(2), 55–68.

Owen, C., Tarantello, C., Jones, M., et al. (1998). Violence and aggression in psychiatric units. *Psychiatric Services, 49,* 1452–1457.

Owens, R. P., & Wells, D. K. (1993). One city's response to gangs. *The Police Chief, 60*(2), 25–27.

Page, K. S., & Jacobs, S. C. (2011). Surviving the shift: Rural police stress and counseling services. *Psychological Services, 8,* 12–22.

Palermo, G. B. (2002, Aug). Criminal profiling: The uniqueness of the killer. *International Journal of Offender Therapy & Comparative Criminology, 46*(4), 383–385.

Palermo, G. B. (2007). The mind of the sexual predator. *Current Opinion in Psychiatry, 20,* 497–500.

Palmer, B., Nayak, G., Dunn, L., Appelbaum, P., & Jeste, D. (2002, Mar-Apr). Treatment-related decision-making capacity in middle-aged and older patients with psychosis: A preliminary study using the MacCAT-T and HCAT. *American Journal of Geriatric Psychiatry, 10*(2), 207–211.

Pannebaker, J. W., & Susman, J. (1988). Disclosure of traumas and psychosomatic disease. *Canadian Psychologist, 26,* 82–95.

Papapietro, D. J. (2008). Commentary: Psychotherapy in a forensic hospital. *Journal of the American Academy of Psychiatry and the Law, 36*(4), 567–571.

Parenti, C. (2000, Oct.). When 'touch love' kills. *Progressive, 64*(10), 31–34.

Parker, G. (2006). Community reintegration of prisoners with mental illness. *Psychiatric Services, 57,* 1512–1513.

Parsons, S., Walker, L., & Grubin, D. (2001). Prevalence of mental disorder in female remand prisons. *Journal of Forensic Psychiatry, 12*(1), 194–202.

Patchin, J. W., & Hinduja, S. (2006). Bullies move beyond the schoolyard: A preliminary look at cyberbullying. *Youth Violence and Juvenile Justice, 4*(2), 148–169.

Paterson, D. A. (Governor) (2008). *Governor Paterson signs law to protect sexually exploited youth: "Safe Harbor" Law to provide support and social services to victims.* Press Release (Sep, 26, 2008). Retrieved from www.governor.ny.gov/archive/paterson/press/press_0926082.html.

Patterson, C. (1994). Children of the lesbian baby boom: Behavioral adjustment, self-concepts, and sex-role identity. In B. Greene, & G. Herek (Eds.), *Contemporary perspectives on gay and lesbian psychology: Theory, research, and applications* (pp. 156–175). Beverly Hills, CA: Sage.

Patterson, C. J. (2009). Children of lesbian and gay parents: Psychology, law, and policy. *American Psychologist, 64,* 727–736.

Patterson, C. J., & Chan, R. W. (1999). Families headed by lesbian and gay parents. In M. E. Lamb (Ed.), *Parenting and child development in "nontraditional"families* (pp. 191–219). Mahway, NJ: Lawrence Erlbaum Associates, Inc.

Patterson, C. J., & Redding, R. E. (1996). Lesbian and gay families with children: Implications of social science research for policy. *Journal of Social Issues, 52,* 29–50.

Patterson, G. T. (2001). Reconceptualizing traumatic incidents experienced by law enforcement personnel. *The Australian Journal of Disaster, 5*(2).

Patterson, R. F., & Hughes, K. (2008). Review of completed suicides in the California Department of Corrections and Rehabilitation, 1999 to 2004. *Psychiatric Services, 59,* 676–682.

Payne, J. L., MacKinnon, D. F., Mondimore, F. M., et al. (2008). Familial aggregation of postpartum mood symptoms in bipolar disorder pedigrees. *Bipolar Disorders, 10,* 38–44.

Pedro-Carroll, J., Nakhnikian, E., & Montes, G. (2001, Oct). Assisting children through transition: Helping parents protect their children from the toxic effects of ongoing conflict in the aftermath of divorce. *Family Court Review, 39*(4), 377–392.

Penn, J. V., Esposito, C. L., Schaeffer, L. E., Fritz, G. K., & Spirito, A. (2003, Jul). Suicide attempts and self-mutilative behavior in a juvenile correctional facility. *Journal of the American Academy of Child & Adolescent Psychiatry, 42*(7), 762–769.

Penner, N., & Oss, M. E. (1996, November). Barred on the inside: Mental illness in prisons. *Open Minds.*

Perlin, M. (2004). "Salvation" or "lethal dose"? Attitudes and advocacy in right to refuse treatment cases. *Journal of Forensic Psychology Practice, 4*(4), 51–69.

Perlin, M. (2005). And my best friend, my doctor, won't even say what it is I've got: The role and significance of counsel in right to refuse treatment cases. *San Diego Law Review, 42*, 735.

Perlin, M. (2008). *Competence in the law: From legal theory to clinical application.* Hoboken, NJ: John Wiley & Sons, Inc.

Perlin, M., Gould, K., & Dorfman, D. (1995). Therapeutic jurisprudence and the civil rights of institutionalized mentally disabled persons: Hopeless oxymoron or path to redemption. *Psychology, Public Policy, and the Law, 1*(1), 80–119.

Perren, C. S., Dooley, J., Shaw, T., & Cross, D. (2010). Bullying in school and cyberspace: Associations with depressive symptoms in Swiss and Australian adolescents. *Child and Adolescent Psychiatry and Mental Health, 4*, 4–28.

Perrou, B. (2004). *Crisis intervention: Studies in progress: A working document.* Los Angeles, CA: Public Safety Research Institute.

Perske, R. (2000, Dec). Deception in the interrogation room: Sometimes tragic for persons with mental retardation and other developmental disabilities. *Mental Retardation, 38*(6), 532–537.

Peters, J. M., & Murphy, W. D. (1992). Profiling child sexual abusers: Legal considerations. *Criminal Justice and Behavior, 19*(1), 38–53.

Peters, R. H., & Bekman, N. M. (2007). Treatment and reentry approaches for offenders with co-occurring disorders. *Jail Suicide/Mental Health Update, 16*, 1–12.

Petersilia, J. (2004). What works in prisoner reentry? Reviewing and questioning the evidence. *Federal Probation, 68*, 4–8.

Peterson, E. (1996). *Juvenile boot camps: Lessons learned.* [On-line] Available www.ncjrs.org/txtfiles/fs-9636.txt.

Peterson-Badali, M., & Abramovitch, R. (1993). Grade related changes in young people's reasoning about plea decisions. *Law and Human Behavior, 17*, 537–552.

Petrila, J., & Otto, R. K. (2003). Civil and criminal trial matters. In J. Petrila, & R. K. Otto's (Eds.), *Law and mental health professionals* (pp. 325–353). Washington D.C: American Psychological Association.

Pfeifer, J. E., & Brigham, J. C. (1993). Ethical concerns of nonclinical forensic witnesses and consultants. *Ethics and Behavior, 3*, 329–343.

Pinals, D. (2005). Where two roads met: Restoration of competence to stand trial from a clinical perspective. *New England Journal of Civil and Criminal Confinement, 31*, 81–108.

Pinals, D. A. (2009). Informed consent: Is your patient competent to refuse treatment? *The Journal of Family Practice, 8*(4), 33–43.

Pipe, M. E., & Goodman, G. S. (1991). Elements of secrecy: Implications for children's testimony. *Behavioral Sciences and the Law, 9*, 33–41.

Piquero, A., & Steinberg, L. (2010). Public preferences for rehabilitation versus incarceration of juvenile offenders. *Journal of Criminal Justice, 38*, 1–6.

Pitt, S., & Bale, E. (1995). Neonaticide, infanticide, and filicide: A review of the literature. *Bulletin of the American Academy of Psychiatry and Law, 23*, 375–386.

Plattner, B., The, S. S. L., Kraemer, H. C., Williams, R. P., Bauer, S. M., Kindler, J., et al. (2007). Suicidality, psychopathology, and gender in incarcerated adolescents in Austria. *Journal of Clinical Psychiatry, 68*(10), 1593–1600.

Podlas, K. (2006). "The CSI-Effect": Exposing the media myth. *Fordham Intellectual Property, Media and Entertainment Law Journal, 16*, 429–465.

Polaschek, D. L. L. (2003, Aug). Relapse prevention, offense process models, and the treatment of sexual offenders. *Professional Psychology: Research & Practice, 34*(4), 361–367.

Poletiek, F. H. (2002). How psychiatrists and judges assess the dangerousness of persons with mental illness: An 'expertise bias'. *Behavioral Sciences & the Law, 20*(1–2), 19–29.

Pollock-Byrne, J. M. (1990).*Women, prison, & crime.* Belmont, CA: Wadsworth. Pomeroy, E. C., Green, D. L., & Kiam, R. (2001, Apr). Female juvenile offenders incarcerated as adults: A psychoeducational group intervention. *Journal of Social Work, 1*(1), 101–115.

Pope, K. S., Butcher, J. N., & Seelen, J. (2006). *MMPI/MMPI-2/MMPI-A in court: Assessment, testimony, and cross-examination for expert witnesses and attorneys* (3rd edn.). Washington, D.C.: American Psychological Association.

Portnoy, S. M. (2006). New roles for psychologists: Divorce coaching and training lawyers in client management. *NYS Psychologist, 8*(4), 9–13.

Post, J. M. (2010). Commentary on "Exposure to prolonged socio-political conflict and the risk of PTSD and depression among Palestinians": Bio-psychosocial foundations of contemporary terrorism. *Psychiatry, 73*, 244–247.

Poythress, N. G., & Feld, D. B. (2002). "Competency restored" – what forensic hospital reports should (and should not) say when returning defendants to court. *Journal of Forensic Psychology Practice, 2*(4), 51–57.

Poythress, N., Nicholson, R., Otto, R. K., Edens, J. F., Bonnie, R. J., Monahan, J., & Hoge, S. K. (1999). *The MacArthur Competence Assessment Tool – Criminal Adjudication: Professional manual*. Odessa, FL: Psychological Assessment Resources.

Prentky, R., & Burgess, A. (1990). Rehabilitation of child molesters: A cost benefit analysis. *American Journal of Orthopsychiatry, 60*, 108–117.

Prentky, R. A., Janus, E., Barabee, H., Schwartz, B. K., & Kafka, M. P. (2006). Sexually violent predators in the courtroom. *Psychology, Public Policy, and the Law, 12*(4), 357–393.

Preti, A. (2008). School shooting as a culturally enforced way of expressing suicidal hostile intentions. *The Journal of the American Academy of Psychiatry and the Law, 36*, 544–550.

Pritchard, I. A. (2011). How Do IRB Members Make Decisions? A Review and Research Agenda. *Journal of Empirical Research on Human Research Ethics: An International Journal, 6*(2), 31–46.

Proulx, J., Pellerin, B., Paradis, Y., McKibben, A., Aubut, J., & Ouimet, M. (1997). Static and dynamic predictors of recidivism in sexual aggressors. *Sexual Abuse: A Journal of Research and Treatment, 9*(1), 7–27.

Pruitt, L. R., & Wallace, J. L. (2011). Judging parents, judging place: Poverty, rurality, and the termination of parental rights. *Missouri Law Review, 77*(1).

Ptacek, J. (1999). *Battered women in the courtroom: The power of judicial responses*. Boston, MA: Northeastern University Press.

Pulley, S. (2000). *Critical incident stress management*. Available: www.emedicine.com/ererg/topic826.htm.

Purcell, R., Pathe, M., & Mullen, P. (2010). Gender differences in stalking behaviour among juveniles. *The Journal of Forensic Psychiatry and Psychology, 21*(4), 555–568.

Pursley, R. D. (1994). *Introduction to criminal justice*. New York: Macmillan.

Putkonen, H., Weizmann-Henelius, G., Lindberg, N., Eronen, M., & Hakkanen, H. (2009). Differences between homicide and filicide offenders; results of a nationwide register-based case-control study. *BioMed Central Psychiatry, 9:*27, Available at www.biomedcentral.com.

Puzzanchera, C. M. (2000). *Delinquency cases waived to criminal court, 1988–1997*. OJJDP Fact Sheet, U.S. Department of Justice.

Puzzanchera, C., Adams, B., & Sickmund, M. (2010). *Juvenile court statistics 2006-2007*. Pittsburg, PA: National Center for Juvenile Justice.

Pyszaora, N. M., Baker, A. F., & Kopelman, M. D. (2003). Amnesia for criminal offenses: A study of life sentence prisoners. *Journal of Forensic Psychiatry and Psychology, 14*, 475–490.

Quas, J. A., Goodman, G. S., Ghetti, S., Alexander, K. W., Edelstein, R. S., Redlich, A. D., et al. (2005). *Childhood sexual assault victims: Long-term outcomes after testifying in criminal court. Monograph of the Society for Research in Child Development*. New York: Wiley-Blackwell.

Quattrocchi, M. R., & Schopp, R. F. (2005). Tarasaurus rex: A standard of care that could not adapt. *Psychology, Public Policy, and Law, 11*, 109–137.

Quinn, K. M. (2002). Juveniles on trial. *Child & Adolescent Psychiatric Clinics of North America, 11*(4), 719–730.

Quinnell, F. A., & Bow, J. N. (2001). Psychological tests used in child custody evaluations. *Behavioral Sciences & the Law, 19*(4), 491–501.

Quinsey, V. L. (1998). Comment on Marshall's "A monster, victim, or everyman." *Sexual Abuse: A Journal of Research and Treatment, 10*, 65—69.

Quinsey, V. L., Harris, G. T., Rice, M. E., & Cormier, C. A. (2006). *Violent offenders: Appraising and managing risk.* Washington, DC: American Psychological Association.

Radden, J. (2001). Boundary violation ethics: Some conceptual clarifications. *Journal of the American Academy of Psychiatry and the Law, 29*(3), 319—326.

Radel, L. F., Bramlett, M. D., & Waters, A. (2010). Legal and informal adoption by relatives in the U.S.: Comparative characteristics and well-being from a nationally representative sample. *Adoption Quarterly, 13*(3—4), 268—291.

Radelet, M. L., & Akers, R. L. (1995). *Deterrence and the death penalty: The views of the experts.* [On-line] Available http://sun.soci.niu.edu/critcrim/dppapers/mike.deterrence.

Radelet, M. L., & Borg, M. J. (2000, Feb.). Comment on Ubreit and Vos: Retributive versus restorative justice. *Homicide Studies: An Interdisciplinary & International Journal, 4*(1), 88—92.

Radelet, M. L., & Miller, K. S. (1992). The aftermath of Ford v. Wainwright. *Behavioral Sciences and the Law, 10*, 339—351.

Rand, D. (2011). Parental alienation critics and the politics of science. *American Journal of Family Therapy, 39*(1), 48—71.

Raphael, S., & Stoll, M. A. (2010). *Assessing the contribution of the deinstitutionalization of the mentally ill to growth in the U.S. incarceration rate, 57.* Retrieved from http://ist-socrates.berkeley.edu/~raphael/IGERT/Workshop/mental%20illness%20raphael%20and%20stoll%20march%202010.pdf.

Raskauskas, J., & Stoltz, A. D. (2007). Involvement in traditional and electronic bullying among adolescents. *Developmental Psychology, 43*, 564—575.

Raso. (2005). Suprema Corte di Cassazione, Sezioni Unite Penali. March 8, no. 9163.

Redding, R. E., Floyd, M. Y., & Hawk, G. L. (2001). What judges and lawyers think about the testimony of mental health experts: A survey of the courts and bar. *Behavioral Sciences & the Law, 19*(4), 583—594.

Redding, R. E., & Reppucci, N. D. (1999, Feb.). Effects of lawyers' socio-political attitudes on their judgments of social science in legal decision making. *Law & Human Behavior, 23*(1), 31—54.

Redlich, A. D., & Drizin, S. (2007). Police interrogation of youth. In C. L. Kessler, & L. J. Kraus (Eds.), *The mental health needs of young offenders: Forging paths towards reintegration and rehabilitation.* Cambridge, UK: Cambridge University Press.

Reed, J. (1999). Current status of the admissibility of expert testimony after Daubert and Joiner. *Journal of Forensic Neuropsychology, 1*(1), 49—69.

Reed, D. F., & Reed, E. L. (1998). Children of incarcerated parents. *Social Justice, 24*(3), 152—169.

Reichert, J., Adams, S., & Bostwick, L. (2010). Victimization and help-seeking behaviors among women incarcerated in Illinois prisons. *Illinois Criminal Justice Information Authority,* i-64.

Reid, W. H. (2003). Expert evaluation, controversial cases, and the media. *Journal of Psychiatric Practice, 9*, 388—391.

Reid, W. H. (2006). Sanity evaluations and criminal responsibility. *Applied Psychology in Criminal Justice, 2*(3), 114—146.

Reid-MacNevin, S. A. (1997). Boot camps for young offenders. *Journal of Contemporary Criminal Justice, 13*, 155—171.

Reisner, R., & Slobogin, C. (1990). *Law and the mental health system: Civil and criminal aspects.* St. Paul, MN: West Publishing.

Reppucci, N. D., & Crosby, C. A. (1993). Law, psychology, and children: Overarching issues. *Law and Human Behavior, 17*, 1—10.

Reske, H. J. (1995). Victim-offender mediation catching on: Advocates say programs, typically for nonviolent offenses, benefit both parties. *American Bar Association Journal, 81*(14), 1—4.

Resnick, P. J. (1969). Child murder by parents: A psychiatric view of filicide. *American Journal of Psychiatry, 126*, 73—82.

Resnick, P. J. (1970). Murder of the newborn: A psychiatric review of neonaticide. *American Journal of Psychiatry, 126,* 1414–1420.

Reza, H. G. (2006, July 26). O.C. Gang's movements are limited by injunction. *Los Angeles Times Saturday Home Edition.* Retrieved from http://articles.latimes.com/2006/jul/15/local/me-streetgang15.

Richie, B. E. (2001). Challenges incarcerated women face as they return to their communities: Findings from life history interviews. *Crime & Delinquency, 47,* 368–389.

Richmond, D. (2009). Parentage by intention for same sex partners. *Journal of the Center for Families, Children, and the Courts,* 125–138.

Rigakos, G. S. (1995). Constructing the symbolic complainant: Police subculture and the nonenforcement of protection orders for battered women. *Violence and Victims, 10,* 227–247.

Rigby, K., & Slee, P. (1999). Suicidal ideation among adolescent school children, involvement in bully-victim problems, and perceived social support. *Suicide and Life Threatening Behavior, 29,* 119–130.

Riggs, S. A. (2003). Response to Troxel v. Granville: Implications of attachment theory for judicial decisions regarding custody and third-party visitation. *Family Court Review, 41*(1), 39–53.

Roach, K. (2000, Jul). Changing punishment at the turn of the century: Restorative justice on the rise. *Canadian Journal of Criminology, 42*(3), 249–280.

Roberts, J. V. (2004). Public opinion and youth justice. *Crime and Justice, 34,* 495.

Robinson, D. (1992). Commitment, attitudes, career aspirations and work stress: The experiences of correctional staff. *Focus on Staff* [On-line], *4.* Available http//198.103.98.138/crd/forum/e04/e04li.htm.

Robinson, R. C., & Mitchell, J. T. (1993). Evaluation of psychological debriefings. *Journal of Traumatic Stress, 6*(3), 367–3382.

Rocca, P., Villari, V., & Bogetto, F. (2006). Managing the aggressive patient in the psychiatry emergency. *Progress in Neuropsychopharmacol & Biological Psychiatry, 30,* 586–598.

Rockhill, A., Green, B. L., & Furrer, C. (2007). Is the adoption and safe families act influencing child welfare outcomes for families with substance abuse issues? *Child Maltreatment, 12*(1), 7–19.

Roesch, R., Zapf, P. A., Golding, S. L., & Skeem, J. L. (1999). Defining and assessing competency to stand trial. In A. K. Hess, & I. B. Weiner (Eds.), *The handbook of forensic psychology* (2nd edn.) (pp. 327–349). New York: Wiley.

Rogers, F., Bagby, R., & Dickens, S. (1992). *Structured interview of reported symptoms: Professional manual.* Odessa, FL: Psychological Assessment Resources.

Rogers, R., & Ewing, C. P. (2003). The prohibition of ultimate opinions: A misguided enterprise. *Journal of Forensic Psychology Practice, 3*(3), 65–75.

Rogers, R., Grandjean, N., Tillbrook, C. E., Vitacco, M. J., & Sewell, K. W. (2001). Recent interview-based measures of competency to stand trial: A critical review augmented with research data. *Behavioral Sciences & the Law, 19*(4), 503–518.

Rogers, R., & Johansson-Love, J. (2009). Evaluating competency to stand trial with evidence-based practice. *Journal of the American Academy of Psychiatry and the Law, 37,* 450–460.

Rogers, R., & Shuman, (2005). *Fundamentals of forensic practice: Mental health and criminal law.* New York: Springer.

Rogers, R., Tillbrook, C. E., & Sewell, K. W. (2004). *Evaluation of competency to stand trial – Revised (ECST–R) and professional manual.* Odessa, FL: Psychological Assessment Resources.

Rojek, J., Petrocelli, M., & Oberweis, T. (2010). Recent patterns in gang prevalence: A two state comparison. *Journal of Gang Research, 18*(1), 1–17.

Roland, E. (2002). Bullying, depressive symptoms, and suicidal thoughts. *Educational Research, 44,* 55–67.

Rolon, Y. M., & Jones, J. C. (2008). Right to refuse treatment. *Journal of the American Academy of Psychiatry & Law, 36*(2), 252–255.

Roman, J., & Butts, J. A. (2005). *The economics of juvenile jurisdiction: A white paper from the research roundtable on estimating the costs and benefits of the separate juvenile justice system.* Washington, DC: Urban Institute.

Romero, A. P., Rosky, C. J., Badgett, M. V. L., & Gates, G. J. (2007). *Census snapshot: United States, The Williams Institute.* Available at www.law.ucla.edu/williaminstitute/publications/USCensusSnapshot.pdf.

Rose, S., Brewin, C. R., Andrews, A., & Kirk, M. (1999). A randomized controlled trial of psychological debriefing for victims of violent crime. *Psychological Medicine, 29,* 793−799.

Rowe, K. L., Gelles, M. G., & Palarea, R. E. (2006). *Crisis and hostage negotiation.* New York: Guilford Press.

Roy, S. (1993). Two types of juvenile restitution programs in two midwestern counties: A comparative study. *Federal Probation, 57,* 48−53.

Royce, T. (2005). The negotiator and the bomber: Analyzing the critical role of active listening in crisis negotiations. *Negotiation Journal, 21*(1), 5−27.

Russell, H. E., & Beigel, A. (1982). *Understanding human behavior for effective police work.* New York: Basic Books.

Ruva, C., McEvoy, C., & Becker-Bryant, J. (2007). Effects of pre-trial publicity and jury deliberation on juror bias and source memory errors. *Applied Cognitive Psychology, 21,* 45−67.

Ryan, A. H., & Brewster, M. E. (1994). PTSD and related symptoms in traumatized police officers and their spouses/mates. In J. T. Reese, & E. Scrivner (Eds.), *Law Enforcement Families* (pp. 217−226). Washington, DC: Federal Bureau of Investigations.

Saathoff, G. B., & Buckman, J. B. (1990). Diagnostic results of psychiatric evaluations of state police officers. *Hospital and Community Psychiatry, 41*(4), 429−432.

Sachs, N. P. (2000, Fal). Is there a tilt toward abusers in child custody decisions? *The Journal of Psychohistory, 28*(2), 203−228.

Sacks, J. Y. (2004). Women with co-occurring substance use and mental disorders (COD) in the criminal justice system: A research review. *Behavioral Sciences and the Law, 22*(4), 449−466.

Sadler, C. (2009). A force for good. *Nursing Standard, 24*(15−17), 18−19.

Sadoff, R. L. (1995). Mothers who kill their children. *Psychiatric Annals, 25,* 601−605.

Salguero, J. M., Fernández-Berrocal, P., Iruarrizaga, I., Cano-Vindel, A., & Galea, S. (2011). Major depressive disorder following terrorist attacks: A systemic review of prevalence, course and correlates. *BMC Psychiatry, 11,* 1−11.

Salters-Pedneault, K., Ruef, A. M., & Orr, S. P. (2010). Personality and psychophysiological profiles of police officer and firefighter recruits. *Personality and Individual Differences, 49*(3), 210−215.

Sandhu, H. S., Dodder, R. A., & Davis, S. P. (1990). Community adjustment of offenders supervised under residential vs. non-residential programs. *Journal of Offender Rehabilitation, 16,* 139−162.

Sandler, J., & Freeman, N. (2009). Female sex offender recidivism: A large-scale empirical analysis. *Sexual Abuse: A Journal of Research and Treatment, 21*(4), 455−473.

Sandler, J., & Freeman, N. J. (2010). Female sex offenders and the criminal justice system: A comparison of arrests and outcomes. *Journal of Sexual Aggression, 17*(1), 61−76.

Sanislow, C. A., Grilo, C. M., Fehon, D. C., Axelrod, S. R., & McGlashan, T. H. (2003, Feb). Correlates of suicide risk in juvenile detainees and adolescent inpatients. *Journal of the American Academy of Child & Adolescent Psychiatry, 42*(2), 234−240.

Santamour, M. B. (1990). Mentally retarded offenders: Texas program targets basic needs. *Corrections Today, 52,* 52, 92, 106.

Say, R. E., & Thomson, R. (2003, Sep). The importance of patient preferences in treatment decisions − challenges for doctors. *BMJ: British Medical Journal, 327*(7414), 542−545.

Saywitz, K., Camparo, L. B., & Romanoff, A. (2010). Interviewing children in custody cases: Implications of research and policy for practice. *Behavioral Sciences & the Law, 28*(4), 542−562.

Sbarra, D. A., & Emery, R. E. (2008). Deeper into divorce: Using actor-partner analyses to explore systemic differences in co-parenting conflict following custody dispute resolution. *Journal of Family Psychology, 22*(1), 144−152.

Scalora, M. J., & Garbin, C. (2003). A multivariate analysis of sex offender recidivism. *International Journal of Offender Therapy & Comparative Criminology, 47*(3), 309−323.

Scarpa, A. (2003, Jul). Community violence exposure in young adults. *Trauma Violence & Abuse, 4*(3), 210–227.

Schaefer, K. D., & Hennessy, J. J. (2001). *Intrinsic and environmental vulnerabilities among executed capital offenders, revisiting the Bio-Psycho-Social Model of criminal aggression.*

Schaffer, B., & DeBlassie, R. R. (1984). Adolescent prostitution. *Adolescence, 19*(75), 689–696.

Schalock, R. L., Luckasson, R. A., & Shogren, K. A. (2007). Perspectives: The renaming of mental retardation: Understanding the change to the term intellectual disability. *Intellectual and Developmental Disabilities, 45*(2), 116–124.

Schaufeli, W. B., & Peeters, M. C. W. (2000, Jan). Job stress and burnout among correctional officers: A literature review. *International Journal of Stress Management, 7*(1), 19–48.

Schen, C. R. (2005). When mothers leave their children behind. *Harvard Review of Psychiatry, 13*(4), 233–243.

Schennach-Wolff, R., Jager, M., Seemuller, F., Obermeier, M., Messer, T., Laux, G., et al. (2009). Defining and predicting functional outcome in schizophrenia and schizophrenia spectrum disorders. *Schizophrenia Research, 113*(2–3), 210–217.

Schiele, D. R. (2003). Dissociation and unconsciousness as a defense in the criminal case. In R. E. Geiselman (Ed.), *The psychology of murder: Readings in forensic science*. Carlsbad, CA: ACFP Press.

Schneider, K. M., & Phares, V. (2005). Coping with parental loss because of termination of parental rights. *Child Welfare, 84*(6), 819–842.

Schopp, R. F. (2001). Incompetence and commitment. In R. F. Schopp (Ed.), *Competence, condemnation, and commitment: An integrated theory of mental health law* (pp. 81–108). Washington, DC: American Psychological Association.

Schouten, R. (2010). Terrorism and the behavioral sciences. *Harvard Review of Psychiatry, 18*, 369–378.

Schwartz, I. M. (1992). Juvenile crime-fighting policies: What the public really wants. In I. M. Schwartz (Ed.), *Juvenile justice and public policy: Toward a national agenda*. Lanham, MD: Lexington Books.

Schwartz, L. L., & Isser, N. K. (2001). Neonaticide: An appropriate application for therapeutic jurisprudence? *Behavioral Sciences and the Law, 19*, 703–718.

Schweitzer, N. J., & Saks, M. J. (2007). The CSI Effect: Popular fiction about forensic science affects the public's expectations about real forensic science. *Jurimetrics, 47*, 357–364.

Scott, C. L. (2010). Juvenile waiver and state-of-mind assessments. In E. Benedek, P. Ash, & C. Scott (Eds.), *Principles and practice of child and adolescent forensic mental health* (pp. 347–360). Arlington, VA: American Psychiatric Publishing.

Scott, C. L. (2010). Legal issues regarding the provision of care in a correctional setting. In C. L. Scott (Ed.), *Handbook of correctional mental health* (pp. 63–90). Arlington, VA: American Psychiatric Publishing.

Scott, C. L., & Resnick, P. J. (2006). Violence risk assessment in persons with mental illness. *Aggression and Violent Behavior, 11*(6), 598–611.

Scott, C. L., & Yarvis, R. M. (2000). Hubbart v. Superior Court of Santa Clara County. *Journal of the American Academy of Psychiatry & the Law, 28*(1), 82–85.

Scott, E., & Steinberg, L. (2008). *Adolescence and crime: Rethinking juvenile justice*. Cambridge, MA: Harvard University Press.

Scrivner, E. M. (1994). Controlling police use of excessive force. *Series: National Institute of Justice Research in Brief* [On-line]. Available: www.ncjrs.org/txtfiles/ppsyc.txt.

Seeman, M. V., & Seeman, B. (2011). Ethics in a clinic for women with psychosis. *Journal of Medical Ethics*. Retrieved from http://jme.bmj.com/content/early/2011/03/29/jme.2010.042069.abstract.

Seiter, R. P., & Kadela, K. R. (2003). Prisoner reentry: What works, what does not, and what is promising. *Crime & Delinquency, 49*, 360–388.

Seitler, B. (2008). Once the wheels are in motion: Involuntary hospitalization and forced medicating. *Ethical Human Psychology and Psychiatry, 10*(1), 31–42.

Sellbom, M., Fischler, G. L., & Ben-Porath, Y. S. (2007). Identifying MMPI-2 predictors of police officer integrity and misconduct. *Criminal Justice and Behavior, 34*(8), 985–1004.

Sellers, B. G., & Arrigo, B. A. (2009). Adolescent transfer, developmental maturity, and adjudicative competency: An ethical and justice policy inquiry. *Journal of Criminal Law and Criminology, 99*(2), 435–487.

Sellers, C., Sullivan, C., Veysey, B., & Shane, J. (2005). Responding to persons with mental illnesses: Police perspectives on specialized and traditional practices. *Behavioral Sciences and the Law, 23*, 647–657.

Sempek, A. N., & Woody, R. H. (2010). Family permanence versus the best interests of the child. *American Journal of Family Therapy, 38*, 433–439.

Sengupta, A., & Chadhuri, A. (2011). Are social networking sites a source of online harassment for teens: Evidence from survey data. *Children and Youth Services Review, 33*(2), 284–290.

Sereny, G. (1984). *The invisible children*. London: Pan Books.

Seto, M. C., & Lalumiere, M. L. (2010). What is so special about male adolescent sexual offending? A review and test of explanations through meta-analysis. *Psychological Bulletin, 136*(4), 526–575.

Severance, T. A. (2005). "You know who you can go to": Cooperation and exchange between incarcerated women. *The Prison Journal, 85*(3), 343–367.

Severson, M. M., & Bankston, T. V. (1995). Social work and the pursuit of justice through mediation. *Social Work, 40*, 683–690.

Sexton, T., & Turner, C. W. (2010). The effectiveness of functional family therapy for youth with behavioral problems in a community practice setting. *Journal of Family Psychology, 24*(3), 339–348.

Shane, J. M. (2010). Organizational stressors and police performance. *Journal of Criminal Justice, 38*, 807–818.

Shapiro, B. L. (1993). Non-traditional families in the courts: The new extended family. *Journal of the American Academy of Matrimonial Law, 11*, 117.

Shapiro, J. (1993, August 9). Bonds that blood and birth cannot assure. *US News and World Report*, p. 13.

Sharkey, J. D., Shekhtmeyster, Z., Chavez-Lopez, L., Norris, E., & Sass, L. (2011). The protective influence of gangs: Can schools compensate? *Aggression and Violent Behavior, 16*(1), 45–54.

Sharma, V., Burt, V. K., & Ritchie, H. L. (2009). Bipolar II postpartum depression: detection, diagnosis, and treatment. *American Journal of Psychiatry, 166*(11), 1217–1221.

Shaw, P., Hotopf, M., & Davies, A. (2003). In relative danger? The outcome of patients discharged by their nearest relative from sections 2 and 3 of the Mental Health Act. *Psychiatric Bulletin, 27*(2), 50–54.

Shea, S. C., & Barney, C. (2007). Macrotraining: A "how-to" primer for using serial role-playing to train complex clinical interviewing tasks such as suicide assessment. *Psychiatric Clinics of North America, 30*, e1–e29.

Sheehan, K. (2009). Compulsory treatment in psychiatry. *Current Opinions in Psychiatry, 22*(6), 582–586.

Sheehan, K. A., & Burns, T. (2011). Perceived coercion and the therapeutic relationship: A neglected association. *Psychiatric Services, 62*(5), 471–476.

Shefer, T., Crawford, M., Strebel, A., Simabayi, L. C., Dwadwa-Henda, N., Cloete, A., Kaufman, M. R., & Kalichman, S. C. (2008). Gender, power and resistance to change among two communities in the Western Cape, South Africa. *Feminism & Psychology, 18*, 387–402.

Sheridan, D. J., & VanPelt, D. (2005). Intimate partner violence in the lives of prostituted adolescents. In S. W. Cooper, R. J. Estes, A. P. Giardino, N. D. Kellogg, & V. I. Vieth (Eds.), *Medical, legal & social science aspects of child sexual exploitation: A comprehensive review of child pornography, child prostitution, and Internet crimes against children* (pp. 423–435). St. Louis, MO: GW Medical Publishing.

Sherman, L. W., & Strang, H. (2007). *Restorative Justice: The Evidence*. UK: The Smith Institute.

Shipley, S. L. (in press). Competency to stand trial: Legal foundations and practical applications. In J. B. Helfgott (Ed.), *Criminal Psychology- Three Volume Set*. Westport, Connecticut: Praeger Publishers.

Shipley, S., & Arrigo, B. (2001). The confusion of psychopathy (II): Implications for forensic (correctional) practice. *International Journal of Offender Therapy and Comparative Criminology, 45*(4), 407–420.

Shipley, S. L., & Arrigo, B. A. (2004). *The female homicide offender: Serial murder and the case of Aileen Wuornos*. Upper Saddle River, NJ: Pearson Education/Prentice Hall.

Shipley, S. L., & Arrigo, B. A. (2008). Serial killers and serial rapists: Dichotomy or continuum – an examination of commonalities and comparison of typologies. In R. Kocsis (Ed.), *Serial Murder and the Psychology of Violence* (pp. 119–140). Totowa, NJ: Humana Press, Inc.

Shipley, S. L., & Arrigo, B. A. (2011). Sexual offenses against adults. In P. Sturmey, & M. McMurran (Eds.), *Forensic Case Formulation* (pp. 195–214). West Sussex, UK: John Wiley & Sons, Ltd.

Short, J. L. (1998). Evaluation of a substance abuse prevention and mental health promotion program for children of divorce. *Journal of Divorce and Remarriage, 28*, 139–155.

Short, J. L. (2002). The effects of parental divorce during childhood on college students. *Journal of Divorce & Remarriage, 38*(1–2), 143–156.

Schouten, R. (2010). Terrorism and the behavioral sciences. *Harvard Review of Psychiatry, 18*, 369–378.

Shuman, D. W., & Sales, B. D. (2001). Daubert's Wager. *Journal of Forensic Psychology Practice, 1*(3), 69–78.

Sickmund, M. (2007). Deaths of juveniles in custody. *Corrections Today, 69*(1), 68–69.

Siegal, N. (1997). Ganging up on civil liberties: Anti-gang policing and civil rights. *The Progressive, 61*(10), 28–31.

Siegel, L. J., & Senna, J. J. (1994). *Juvenile delinquency, theory, practice, and law* (5th edn.). St. Paul, MN: West Publishing.

Sijbrandij, M., Olff, M., Reitsma, J., Carlier, I., & Gersons, B. (2006). Emotional or education debriefing after psychological trauma; Randomised controlled trial. *British Journal of Psychiatry, 189*, 150–155.

Silten, P. R., & Tullis, R. (1977). Mental competency in criminal proceedings. *Hastings Law Journal, 28*, 1053–1074.

Silver, R. C. (2011). An introduction to "9/11: Ten years later." *American Psychologist, 66*, 427–428.

Silverman, I. J., & Vega, M. (1996). *Corrections: A comprehensive view*. St. Paul, MN: West Publishing.

Simon, R. I., & Shuman, D. W. (2011). Psychiatry and the law. In R. E. Hales, S. C. Yudofsky, & G. O. Gabbard (Eds.), *Essentials of Psychiatry*. Washington, DC: American Psychiatric Association.

Simonelli, C., Mullis, T., Elliot, A., & Pierce, T. (2002, Feb). Abuse by siblings and subsequent experiences of violence within the dating relationship. *Journal of Interpersonal Violence, 17*(2), 103–121.

Sisak, M. R. (2011). Judge: Banks incompetent, can't be executed. *The Times Tribune*. Retrieved September 11, 2011, from http://thetimes-tribune.com/judge-banks-incompetent-can-t-be-executed-1.784178#axzz1Xegbq4mM.

Sit, D., Rothschild, A. J., & Wisner, K. L. (2006). A review of postpartum psychosis. *Journal of Women's Health, 15*(4), 352–368.

Skeem, J. L., Golding, S. L., Cohn, N. B., & Berg, G. (1998). The logic and reliability of evaluations of competence to stand trial. *Law and Human Behavior, 22*, 519–547.

Skeem, J. L., & Monahan, J. (2011). Current directions in violence risk assessment. *Current Directions in Psychological Science, 20*(1), 38–42.

Skiba, R., Horner, R., Chung, C. G., Rausch, M. K., May, S. L., & Tobin, T. (2008). *Race is not neutral: A national investigation of African American and Latino disproportionality in school discipline*. Paper presented at the annual meeting of the American Educational Research Association, New York.

Skiba, R., Reynolds, C. R., Graham, S., Sheras, P., Close Conoley, J., & Garcia-Vasquez, E. (2006). Are zero tolerance policies effective in the schools? An evidentiary review and recommendations. *School Psychology Quarterly, 23*(1), 852–862.

Sklarew, B., Krupnick, J., Ward-Wimmer, D., & Napoli, C. (2002, Jul). The school-based mourning project: A preventive intervention in the cycle of inner-city violence. *Journal of Applied Psychoanalytic Studies, 4*(3), 317–330.

Skolnick, A. (1998). Solomon's children: The new biologism, psychological parenthood, attachment theory, and the best interests standard. In M. A. Mason, & A. Skolnick (Eds.), *All our families: New policies for a new century* (pp. 236–255). New York: Oxford University Press.

Slobogin, C. (1994). Involuntary community treatment of people who are violent and mentally ill: A legal analysis. *Hospital and Community Psychiatry, 45*(7), 685–689.

Slobogin, C. (2003). Pragmatic forensic psychology: A mean's of "scientizing" expert testimony from mental health professionals? *Psychology, Public Policy, & Law, 9*(3–4), 275–300.

Slobogin, C. (2000, Jul-Aug). Mental illness and the death penalty. *Mental & Physical Disability Law Reporter, 24*(4), 667–677.

Slobogin, C., & Fondacaro, M. (2000). Rethinking deprivations of liberty: Possible contributions from therapeutic and ecological jurisprudence. *Behavioral Sciences & the Law, 18*(4), 499−516.

Slonje, R., & Smith, P. K. (2008). Cyberbullying: Another main type of bullying? *Scandinavian Journal of Psychology, 49*(2), 147−154.

Slovenko, R. (2002). The role of psychiatric diagnosis in the law. *Journal of Psychiatry and Law, 30*(3), 421−444.

Small, M. A., & Melton, G. B. (1994). Evaluation of child witnesses for confrontation by criminal defendants. *Professional Psychology: Research and Practice, 25*(3), 228−233.

Smith, A. B., & Gollop, M. M. (2001, Jun). What children think separating parents should know. *New Zealand Journal of Psychology, 30*(1), 23−31.

Smith, B. (1998). Children in custody: 20-year trends in juvenile detention, correctional, and shelter facilities. *Crime & Delinquency, 44*, 526−543.

Smith, D., & Klein, J. (1984). Police control of interpersonal disputes. *Social Problems, 31*(4), 468−481.

Smith, P., Mahdavi, J., Carvalho, M., Fisher, S., Russell, S., & Tippett, N. (2008). Cyberbullying: Its nature and impact in secondary school pupils. *The Journal of Child Psychology and Psychiatry, 49*, 376−385.

Smith, P., Mahdavis, J., Carvalho, M., & Tippett, N. (2006). An investigation into cyberbullying, its forms, awareness, and impact, and the relationship between age and gender in cyberbullying. *A report for the Anti Bullying Alliance*. Retrieved April 9, 2011, from http://www.anti-bullyingalliance.org.uk.

Snell, T. S. (2010). *Capital punishment, 2009 − Statistical tables. Retrieved from the Bureau of Justice Statistics website:* http://bjs.ojp.usdoj.gov/index.cfm?ty=dpbdetail&iid=2215.

Snethen, G. (2010). Preventing female gang involvement: Development of the joint-interest core and balance model of mother-daughter leisure functioning. *Aggression and Violent Behavior, 15*(1), 42−48.

Snook, B., Eastwood, J., Gendreau, P., Goggin, C., & Cullen, R. (2007). Taking stock of criminal profiling: A narrative review and meta-analysis. *Criminal Justice and Behavior, 34*(4), 437−453.

Snow, C. R. (1997). *Family violence: Tough solutions to stop the violence*. New York: Plenum Press.

Snow, J., & Weed, R. (1998). Mental health forensic issues in Georgia: The role of the expert witness. *Georgia Journal of Professional Counseling, 6*(1), 53−65.

Snow, W. H., & Briar, K. H. (1990). The convergence of the mentally disordered and the jail population. In *Clinical Treatment of the Criminal Offender* (pp. 147−162). The Haworth Press, Inc.

Snyder, H. N., & Sickmund, M. (2006). *Juvenile offenders and victims: 2006 national report*. Washington, DC: US DOJ, Office of Justice Programs, Office of Juvenile Justice and Delinquency Prevention. Accessed 02/27/2011 at www.ojjdp.ncjrs.gov/ojstatbb/nr2006.

Snyder, H. N., & Sickmund, M. (1999). *Juvenile offenders and victims: 1999 national report*. Washington, DC: Office of Juvenile Justice and Delinquency Prevention.

Snyder, R. T. (2001). *The protestant ethic and the spirit of punishment*. Grand Rapids, Michigan: William B. Erdmans Publishing Company.

Sobol, J. J. (2010). Social ecology and police discretion: The influence of district crime, cynicism, and workload on the vigor of police response. *Journal of Criminal Justice, 38*(4), 481−488.

Social Security Administration. (2001). *Disability evaluation under Social Security*. Washington, DC: U.S. Government Printing Office. SSA publication no. 64−039.

Soler, M. (2002). Health issues for adolescents in the justice system. *Journal of Adolescent Health: Official publication of the Society for Adolescent Medicine, 31*(Suppl. 6), 321−333.

Soler, M. (1988). Litigation on behalf of children in adult jails. *Crime and Delinquency, 34*, 190−208.

Solomon, R., & Horn, J. (1986). Post-shooting traumatic reactions: A pilot study. In J. Reese, & H. Goldstein (Eds.), *Psychological services for law enforcement*. Washington, DC: U.S. Government Printing Office.

Soto, G., & Miller, M. (1992, August). Keeping kids in school. *Police Practices*.

Sourander, A., Ronning, J., & Brunstein-Klemek, A. (2009). Childhood bullying behavior and later psychiatric hospital and psychopharmacologic treatment: Findings from the Finnish 1981 birth cohort study. *Archives of General Psychiatry, 66*, 1005−1012.

Sousa, W., Ready, J., & Ault, M. (2010). The impact of TASERs on police use-of-force decisions: Findings from a randomized field-training experiment. *Journal of Experimental Criminology, 6*(1), 33−55.

Speaker, K. M., & Peterson, G. J. (2000). School violence and adolescent suicide: Strategies for effective intervention. *Educational Review, 52*(1), 65−73.

Spehr, A., Hill, A., Habermann, N., Briken, P., & Berner, W. (2010). Sexual murderers with adult or child victims: Are they different? *Sexual Abuse, 23*(2), 290−314.

Spinelli, M. G. (2004). Maternal infanticide associated with mental illness: Prevention and the promise of saved lives. *American Journal of Psychiatry, 161*(9), 1548−1557.

Sprafka, H., & Kranda, A. H. (2008). Institutionalizing mentoring in police departments. *Police Chief, 75*(1), 46−49.

Spralding, L. H. (1997). Chemical castration: A return to the dark ages. *American Civil Liberties Union.* [On-line]. Available www.shadow.net/aclu/t-chem.htm.

Sprott, J. B., & Doob, A. N. (2000, Apr). Bad, sad, and rejected: The lives of aggressive children (N1). *Canadian Journal of Criminology, 42*(2), 1−8.

Spruill, J., & May, J. (1988). The mentally retarded offender: Prevalence rates based on individual versus group intelligence tests. *Criminal Justice and Behavior, 15*, 484−491.

Stage, S. A., Jackson, H. G., Jensen, M. J., Moscovitz, K. K., Bush, J. W., Violette, H. D., et al. (2008). A validity study of functionally-based behavioral consultation with students with emotional/behavioral disabilities. *School Psychology Quarterly, 23*(3), 327−353.

Stahl, P. M. (1994). *Conducting child custody evaluations.* Thousand Oaks. CA: Sage.

Stamps, L. E. (2002). Maternal preference in child custody decisions. *Journal of Divorce & Remarriage, 37*(1−2), 1−11.

Stanard, R., & Hazler, R. (1995). Legal and ethical implications of HIV and duty to warn for counselors: Does Tarasoff apply? *Journal of Counseling and Development, 73*, 397−400.

Stanton, J., & Simpson, A. (2002). Filicide: A review. *International Journal of Law and Psychiatry, 25*, 1−14.

Stanton, J., Simpson, A., & Wouldes, T. (2009). A qualitative study of filicide by mentally ill mothers. *Child Abuse and Neglect, 24*, 1451−1460.

State of Alaska Department of Health and Social Services. (2005). *Juvenile justice "transitional" program a promising national model for re-integrating incarcerated youth back to community.* Retrieved from www.hss.state.ak.us/press/2005/pr062905mclaughlintransitionalsvcs.htm.

Stathis, S., Litchfield, B., Letters, P., Doolan, I., & Martin, G. (2008). A comparative assessment of suicide risk for young people in youth detention. *Archives of Suicide Research, 12*, 62−66.

Steadman, H., McGreevy, M., Morrissey, J., Callahan, L., Robbins, P., & Cirincione, C. (1993). *Before and after Hinckley: Evaluating insanity defense reform.* New York: Guilford Press.

Stein, M., & Davis, C. A. (2000). Direct instruction as a positive behavioral support. *Beyond Behavior, 10*(1), 7−12.

Steiner, B., & Giacomazzi, A. L. (2007). Juvenile waiver, boot camp, and recidivism in a northwestern state. *The Prison Journal, 87*(2), 227−240.

Steinhart, D. (1988). California legislature ends the jailing of children: The story of a police reversal. *Crime and Delinquency, 34*, 169−189.

Stephens, B. J., & Sindin, P. G. (2000). Victims' voices: Domestic assault victims' perceptions of police demeanor. *Journal of Interpersonal Violence, 15*, 534−547.

Stevenson, K., Tufts, J., Hendrick, D., & Kowalski, M. (1999, Sum). Youth and crime. *Canadian Social Trends* 17−21.

Stout, R. G., & Farooque, R. S. (2008). Claims of amnesia for criminal offenses: Psychopathology, substance abuse, and malingering. *Journal of Forensic Sciences, 53*, 1218−1222.

Straus, M. B. (1994). *Violence in the lives of adolescents.* New York: W. W. Norton.

Streib, V. (1998). *Juveniles and the death penalty: Brief facts and figures* [On-line]. Available www.prince.essential.org/dpic/juvchar.html.

Strier, F. (2001). Why trial consultants should be licensed. *Journal of Forensic Psychology Practice, 1*(4), 69−76.

Stolzenberg, L., & D'Alessio, S. (2007). Co-offending and the age crime curve. *Journal of Research in Crime and Delinquency, 45*, 65−86.

Struckman-Johnson, C., & Struckman-Johnson, D. (2002, Aug). Sexual coercion reported by women in three Midwestern prisons. *Journal of Sex Research, 39*(3), 217−227.

Stuart, H. (2008). Suicidality among police. *Current Opinion in Psychiatry, 21*, 505−509.

Sugimoto, J. D., & Oltjenbruns, K. A. (2001). The environment of death and its influence on police officers in the United States. *Omega: Journal of Death & Dying, 43*(2), 145−155.

Sullivan, M. J. (2008). Coparenting and the parenting coordination process. *Journal of Child Custody, 5*(1/2), 4−24.

Sullivan, M. L., & Miller, B. (1999). Adolescent violence, state processes, and the local context of moral panic. In J. M. Heyman (Ed.), *States and illegal practices* (pp. 261−283). New York: Berg.

Sullivan, S. M. (2010). Private force, public goods. *Connecticut Law Review, 42*, 853−897.

Sun, I. Y., Payne, B. K., & Wu, Y. (2008). The impact of situational factors, officer characteristics, and neighborhood context on police behavior: A multilevel analysis. *Journal of Criminal Justice, 36*(1), 22−32.

Sun, Y., & Li, Y. (2002, May). Children's well-being during parents' marital disruption process: A pooled time-series analysis. *Journal of Marriage & Family, 64*(2), 472−488.

Sweeting, H., Young, R., West, P., & Der, G. (2006). Peer victimization and depression in early-mid adolescence: A longitudinal study. *British Journal of Educational Psychology, 76*, 577−594.

Symonds, M. (1970). Emotional hazards of police work. *American Journal of Psychoanalysis, 30*, 155−160.

Symons, D. (2010). A review of the practice and science of child custody and access assessment in the United States and Canada. *Professional Psychology: Research and Practice, 41*(3), 267−273.

Szockyj, E. (1989). Working in a man's world: Women correctional officers in an institution for men. *Canadian Journal of Criminology, 31*, 319−328.

Talbot, J. (2009). No one knows: Offenders with learning disabilities and learning difficulties. *International Journal of Prisoner Health, 5*(3), 141−152.

Tamber, C. (2003, 04/29). Minors on death row may have new hope. *The Legal Intelligencer, 228*(82).

Tasker, F., & Golombok, S. (1995). Adults raised as children in lesbian families. *American Journal of Orthopsychiatry, 65*, 203−215.

Tatem Kelley, B., Huizinga, D., Thornberry, T. P., & Loeber, R. (1997). *Epidemiology of serious violence*. Washington, D.C.: Office of Juvenile Justice and Delinquency Prevention.

Tausch, N., Becker, J. C., Spears, R., Christ, O., Saab, R., Singh, P., & Siddiqui, R. N. (2011). Explaining radical group behavior: Developing emotion and efficacy routes to normative and nonnormative collective action. *Journal of Personality and Social Psychology, 101*, 129−148.

Taylor, P. J., Hill, J., Bhagwagar, Z., Darjee, R., & Thompson, D. G. (2008). Presentations of psychosis with violence: Variations in different jurisdictions: A comparison of patients with psychosis in the high security hospitals of Scotland and England. *Behavioral Sciences and the Law, 26*(5), 585−602.

Teaster, P. B., & Roberto, K. A. (2002, Jun). Living the life of another: The need for public guardians of last resort. *Journal of Applied Gerontology, 21*(2), 176−187.

Tehrani, N., & Piper, N. (2011). Traumatic stress in the police service. In N. Tehrani (Ed.), *Managing trauma in the workplace: Supporting workers and organizations* (pp. 17−32). New York: Routledge.

Tehrani, N., & Westlake, R. (1994). Debriefing individuals affected by violence. *Counseling Psychology Quarterly, 7*(3), 251−259.

Teplin, L. A., Abram, K. M., & McClelland, G. M. (1996). Prevalence of psychiatric disorders among incarcerated women. I. Pretrial jail detainees. *Archives of General Psychiatry, 53*(6), 505−512.

Teplin, L. A., Abram, K. M., & McClelland, G. M. (1997). Mentally disordered women in jail: Who receives services? *American Journal of Public Health, 87*(4), 604−609.

Terrill, W., & Reisig, M. D. (2003, Aug). Neighborhood context and police use of force. *Journal of Research in Crime & Delinquency, 40*(3), 291−321.

Territo, L. (1989). *Crime and justice in America*. St. Paul, MN: West Publishing.

Testa, M., & West, S. G. (2010). Civil Commitment in the United States. *Innovations in Clinical Neuroscience, 7*, 30−40.

Tewksbury, R., & Higgins, G. (2006). Prison staff and work stress: The role of organizational and emotional influences. *American Journal of Criminal Justice, 30,* 247−266.

Texas Code of Criminal Procedure Article 46B.025. (2006). Retrieved on 03-15-11, www.statutes.legis.state.tx.us/docs/CR/htm/CR.46B.htm.

Texas Commission on Jail Standards. (1996). State standards and suicide prevention: Lone Star. *Jail/Suicide/Mental Health Update, 6,* 9−11.

Texas Commission on Law Enforcement Officer Standards and Education. (2005). *Intermediate Use of Force.* Retrieved from www.tcleose.state.tx.us/content/training_instructor_resources.cfm.

Texas Commission on Law Enforcement Officer Standards and Education. (2007). *Interpersonal communications in the correctional setting.* Austin, TX: TCLEOSE.

Thakker, J., Collie, R., Gannon, T., & Ward, T. (2008). Rape assessment and treatment. In R. Laus, & W. O'Donohue (Eds.), *Sexual deviance* (pp. 356−383). New York: Guilford Press.

The Psychological Corporation. (1997). *WAIS-III/WMS-III technical manual.* San Antonio: Harcourt Brace.

Theobald, N., & Haier-Markel, D. (2009). Race, bureaucracy, and symbolic representations: Interactions between citizens and police. *Journal of Public Administration Research and Theory, 19*(2), 409−426.

Thomas, C. R., & Penn, J. V. (2002, Oct). Juvenile justice mental health services. *Child and Adolescent Psychiatric Clinics of North America, 11*(4), 731−748.

Thompson, K. M., & Braaten-Antrim, R. (1998). Youth maltreatment and gang involvement. *Journal of Interpersonal Violence, 13*(3), 328−345.

Thompson, L. (2007). Ganging up on city hall. *LA Weekly.* Retrieved August 6, 2011 from www.laweekly.com/news/news/ganging-up-on-city-hall/15863.

Thompson, R. A. (2004). *Crisis intervention and crisis management: Strategies that work in schools and communities.* New York: Brunner-Routledge.

Thornberry, T. P., Krohn, M. D., Lizotte, A. J., Smith, C. A., & Tobin, K. (2003). *Gangs and Delinquency in Developmental Perspective.* Cambridge, U.K: Cambridge University Press.

Tiedeman, M., & Ballon, D. (2009). *Annual report on conditions inside Los Angeles County Jail.* Los Angeles: American Civil Liberties Union of Southern California.

Tillbrook, C., Mumley, D., & Grisso, T. (2003). Avoiding expert opinions on the ultimate legal question: The case for integrity. *Journal of Forensic Psychology Practice, 3*(3), 77−87.

Tjaden, P., & Thoennes, N. (2000). *Extent, nature, and consequences of intimate partner violence* (NCJ Publication No. 181867). Washington, DC: U.S. Department of Justice.

Tobey, A. E., Goodman, G. S., Batterman-Faunce, J. M., Orcutt, H. K., & Sachsenmaier, T. (1995). In M. S. Zaragoza, J. R. Graham, G. C. N. Hall, R. Hirschman, & Y. S. Ben-Porath (Eds.), *Memory and testimony in the child witness* (pp. 214−239). Thousand Oaks, CA: Sage.

Tobin, J. (2001). The limitations of critical incident stress debriefing. *Irish Journal of Psychological Medicine, 18*(4), 142.

Toch, H. (1985). The catalytic situation in the violence equation. *Journal of Applied Social Psychology, 15*(2), 468−481.

Toch, H. (2001, Sep). The future of supermax confinement. *Prison Journal, 81*(3), 376−388.

Toch, H. (1992). *Violent men: An inquiry into the psychology of violence.* Washington, DC: American Psychological Association.

Tolman, A. O. (2001). Clinical training and the duty to protect. *Behavioral Sciences & the Law, 19*(3), 387−404.

Tolman, A. O., & Mullendore, K. B. (2003, Jun). Risk evaluations for the courts: Is service quality a function of specialization? *Professional Psychology-Research & Practice, 34*(3), 225−232.

Tomasevski, K. (1986). *Children in adult prisons: An international perspective.* London: Palgrave Macmillan.

Tong, L. S. J., & Farrington, D. P. (2006). How effective is the "Reasoning and Rehabilitation" programme in reducing reoffending? A meta-analysis of evaluations in four countries. *Psychology, Crime, & Law, 12,* 3−24.

Torok, W. C., & Trump, K. S. (1994). Gang intervention: Police and school collaboration. *FBI Law Enforcement Bulletin, 63*(5), 13−17.

Torres, A. N., Boccaccini, M. T., & Miller, H. A. (2006). Perceptions of the validity and utility of criminal profiling among forensic psychologists and psychiatrists. *Professional Psychology: Research and Practice, 37*(1), 51–58.

Torrey, E. F., Kennard, A. D., Eslinger, D., Lamb, R., & Pavle, J. (2010). *More mentally ill persons are in jails and prisons than hospitals: A survey of the states.* Alexandria, Virginia: National Sheriffs Association.

Trowbridge, B. (2003). Psychologists' roles in evaluating child witnesses. *American Journal of Forensic Psychology, 21*(3), 27–70.

Troxel, N. R., Ogle, C. M., Cordon, I. M., Lawler, M. J., & Goodman, G. S. (2009). Child witnesses in criminal court. In B. L. Bottoms, C. J. Najdowski, & G. S. Goodman (Eds.), *Children as victims, witnesses, and offenders: Psychological science and the law* (pp. 233–252). New York: Guilford Press.

Trulson, C., & Marquat, J. W. (2002, Jun). The caged melting pot: Toward an understanding of the consequences of desegregation in prisons. *Law & Society Review, 36*(4), 743–781.

Trulson, C., Triplett, R., & Snell, C. (2001, Oct). Social control in a school setting: Evaluating a school-based boot camp. *Crime & Delinquency, 47*(4), 573–610.

Tudway, J. A., & Darmoody, M. (2005). Clinical assessment of adult sexual offenders with learning disabilities. *Journal of Sexual Aggression, 11*(3), 277–288.

Turco, R. N. (1990, September). Psychological profiling. *International Journal of Offender Therapy and Comparative Criminology,* 147–154.

Twemlow, S. W. (2008). Assessing adolescents who threaten homicide in schools: A recent update. *Clinical Social Work Journal, 36*(2), 127–129.

Tye, M. C. (2003, Jan). Lesbian, gay, bisexual, and transgender parents: Special considerations for the custody and adoption evaluator. *Family Court Review, 41*(1), 92–103.

Tyler, J., Darville, R., & Stalnaker, K. (2001). Juvenile boot camps: A descriptive analysis of program diversity and effectiveness. *Social Science Journal, 38*(3), 445–461.

Tyler, T. R. (2006). Viewing CSI and the threshold of guilt: managing truth and justice in reality and fiction. *The Yale Law Journal, 115*(5), 1050–1085.

UCLA. (2007). *Dropout prevention.* Los Angeles, CA: UCLA.

Umbreit, M., & Armour, M. P. (2010). *Restorative justice dialogue: An essential guide for research and practice.* New York: Springer Publishing Company.

Umbreit, M. S. (1993). Crime victims and offenders in mediation: An emerging area of social work practice. *Social Work, 38,* 69–73.

Umbreit, M. S. (1995). Holding juvenile offenders accountable: A restorative justice perspective. *Juvenile and Family Court Journal, 46*(2), 31–42.

Umbreit, M. S., Coates, R. B., & Roberts, A. W. (2000, Spr). The impact of victim-offender mediation: A crossnational perspective. *Mediation Quarterly, 17*(3), 215–229.

Umbreit, M. S., Coates, R. B., & Vos, B. (2001, Dec). The impact of victim-offender mediation: Two decades of research. *Federal Probation, 65*(3), 29–35.

Umbreit, M. S., & Vos, B. (2000, Feb). Homicide survivors meet the offender prior to execution. *Homicide Studies: An Interdisciplinary & International Journal, 4*(1), 63–87.

Umbreit, M. S., & Bradshaw, W. (1997). Victim experience of meeting adult vs. juvenile offenders: A crossnational study. *Federal Probation, 61,* 33–39.

Uotila, E., & Sambou, S. (2010). Victim-offender mediation in cases of intimate relationship violence – Ideals, attitudes, and practices in Finland. *Journal of Scandinavian Studies in Criminology and Crime Prevention, 11*(2), 189–207.

U.S. Department of Health and Human Services. (2009). *Child maltreatment 2007.* Washington, D.C.: U.S. Government Printing Office.

U.S. Department of Justice. (1994). *Special report: Women in prison* (Report No. NCJ-145321). Washington, DC: Bureau of Justice Statistics.

U.S. Department of Justice, Bureau of Justice Statistics. (2005). *Family violence statistics.* Washington, D.C.: U.S. Department of Justice, Bureau of Justice Statistics.

U.S. Department of Justice. (2008a). *Census of state and federal correctional facilities, 2005.* Washington, D.C.: James J. Stephan.

U.S. Department of Justice. (2008b). *Parents in prison and their minor children.* Washington, D.C.: USDJ.

U.S. Department of Justice. (2010). *Law enforcement officers killed and assaulted, 2009.* Retrieved August 27, 2011. www2.fbi.gov/ucr/killed/2009/index.html.

U.S. Department of Justice, Bureau of Justice Statistics. (2002). *Homicide trends in the U.S.: Intimate homicide.* [On-line]. Available www.ojp.usdoj.gov/bjs/homicide/intimates.htm.

U.S. Department of Justice, Bureau of Justice Statistics. (2003). *Incarcerated parents and their children* [On-line]. Available www.ojp.usdoj.gov/bjs/abstract/iptc.htm.

U.S. Department of Justice, Bureau of Justice Statistics. (1999b). *Women offenders (NCJ-175688).* Washington, DC: Snell. Available from www.ojp.usdoj.gov/bjs/pub/press/wo.pr.

U.S. Department of Education. (1999). *The condition of education 1999.* Washington, D.C.: National Center for Educational Statistics. (ERIC Reproduction Service No. ED 430 324).

U.S. Department of Justice, Federal Bureau of Investigation. (1996). *Crime in the United States: Uniform Crime Reports 1995.* Washington, DC: U.S. Government Printing Office.

U.S. National Counterterrorism Center. (2011). *NCTC 2010 Report on Terrorism.* Retrieved September 02, 2011. www.nctc.gov/witsbanner/docs/2010_report_on_terrorism.pdf.

Valdez, A. (2005). *Gangs: A Guide to Understanding Street Gangs* (4th edn.). San Clemente, Ca: Law Tech Publishing.

van der Wal, M. F., de Wit, C. A., & Hirasing, R. A. (2003). Psychosocial health among young victims and offenders of direct and indirect bullying. *Pediatrics, 111,* 1312–1317.

Vandiver, D., & Kercher, G. (2004). Offender and victim characteristics of registered female sexual offenders in Texas: A proposed typology of sexual offenders. *Sexual Abuse: A Journal of Research and Treatment, 16*(2), 121–137.

Van Hasselt, V. B., Baker, M. T., Romano, S. J., Schlessinger, K. M., Zucker, M., Dragone, R., et al. (2006). Crisis (hostage) negotiation training. *Criminal Justice and Behavior, 33,* 56–69.

Van Hasselt, V. B., Romano, S. J., & Vecchi, G. M. (2008). Role playing: Applications in hostage and crisis negotiation skills training. *Behavior Modification, 32*(2), 248–263.

Van Ooursouw, K., Merckelbach, H., Ravelli, D., Nijman, H., & Mekking-Pompen, I. (2004). Alcoholic blackout for criminally relevant behavior. *Journal of the American Academy of Psychiatry and Law, 32,* 364–370.

Van Puyenbroeck, H., Loots, G., Grietens, H., Jacquet, W., Vaderfaeille, J., & Escudero, V. (2009). Intensive family preservation services in Flanders: An outcome study. *Child & Family Social Work, 14*(2), 222–232.

Vasilopoulos, N. L., Cucina, J. M., & Hunter, A. E. (2007). Personality and training proficiency: Issues of bandwidth-fidelity and curvilinearity. *Journal of Occupational and Organizational Psychology, 80,* 109–131.

Vaughan, P. J., & Stevenson, S. (2002). An opinion survey of mentally disordered offender service users. *The British Journal of Forensic Practice, 4*(3), 11–20.

Vesneski, W. (2011). State law and the termination of parental rights. *Family Court Review, 49*(2), 364–378.

Victim Offender Mediation Association (VOMA). (2006). VOMA connections. *Justice Connections, 23,* 1–12.

Vigdor, A. R., & Mercy, J. A. (2006). Do laws restricting access to firearms by domestic violence offenders prevent intimate partner homicide? *Evaluation Review, 30,* 313–346.

Vikstrom, L., Van Poppel, F., & Van de Putte, B. (2011). New light on the divorce transition. *Journal of Family History, 36*(2), 107–117.

Viljoen, J. L., Elkovitch, N., & Ullman, D. (2007). Assessing risk for violence in adolescents. In B. Jackson (Ed.), *Learning forensic assessment* (pp. 385–414). New York: Erlbaum.

Violanti, J. M. (2004). Predictors of police suicide ideation. *Suicide and Life Threatening Behavior, 34,* 277–283.

Violanti, J. M., & Aron, F. (1993). Sources of police stressors, job attitudes, and psychological distress. *Psychological Reports, 72,* 899–904.

Violanti, J. M., & Aron, F. (1995). Police stressors: Variations in perception among police personnel. *Journal of Criminal Justice, 23*(3), 287−294.

Violanti, J. M., & Drylie, J. J. (2008). *Copicide: Concepts, cases, and controversies of suicide by cop*. Springfield, IL: Charles C. Thomas Publisher.

Violanti, J. M., Fekedulegn, D., Charles, L. E., Andrew, M. E., Hartley, T. A., Mnatsakanova, A., & Burchfiel, C. M. (2009). Suicide in police work: Exploring potential contributing influences. *American Journal of Criminal Justice, 34*(1−2), 41−53.

Violanti, J. M., Marshall, J. R., & Howe, B. (1985). Stress, coping, and alcohol use: The police connection. *Journal of Police Science and Administration, 13*(2), 106−110.

Vitacco, M. J., & Packer, I. K. (2003). Civil commitment. *Journal of the American Academy of Psychiatry & the Law, 31*(2), 264−266.

Vitacco, M., & Rogers, R. (2010). Assessment of malingering in correctional settings. In C. L. Scott (Ed.), *Handbook of correctional mental health* (2nd edn.) (pp. 255−276). Arlington, VA: American Psychiatric Publishing, Inc.

Vogel, B. L., & Vogel, R. E. (2003, Mar-Apr). The age of death: Appraising public opinion of juvenile capital punishment. *Journal of Criminal Justice, 31*(2), 169−183.

Waaland, P., & Keeley, S. (1985). Police decision making in wife abuse: The impact of legal and extralegal factors. *Law and Human Behavior, 9*, 355−366.

Waddington, D. P. (2007). *Policing public disorder: Theory and practice*. Portland, OR: William Publishing.

Wainright, J. L., & Patterson, C. J. (2006). Delinquency, victimization, and substance use among adolescents with female same-sex parents. *Journal of Family Psychology, 20*, 526−530.

Wainright, J. L., Russell, S. T., & Patterson, C. J. (2004). Psychosocial adjustment and school outcomes of adolescents with same-sex parents. *Child Development, 75*, 1886−1898.

Wakefield, H., & Underwager, R. (1993). Misuse of psychological tests in forensic settings: Some horrible examples. *American Journal of Forensic Psychology, 11*, 55−75.

Walcott, D. M. (2000). Sexually violent predator commitment successfully challenged on basis of conditions of confinement and treatment. *Journal of the American Academy of Psychiatry & the Law, 28*(2), 244−245.

Walcott, D. M., Cerundolo, P., & Beck, J. C. (2001). Current analysis of the Tarasoff duty: An evolution towards the limitation of the duty to protect. *Behavioral Sciences & the Law, 19*(3), 325−343.

Walker, A. G. (1993). Questioning young children in court: A linguistic case study. *Law and Human Behavior, 17*, 59−81.

Walker, J. S., & Bruns, E. J. (2006). The *wraparound* process: Individualized, community-based care for children and adolescents with intensive needs. In J. Rosenberg, & S. Rosenberg (Eds.), *Community mental health: Challenges for the 21st century* (pp. 47−57). New York: Routledge.

Walker, M., Schmidt, L., & Lunghofer, L. (1993). Youth gangs. In M. I. Singer, L. T. Singer, & T. M. Anglin (Eds.), *Handbook for screening adolescents at psychosocial risk* (pp. 504−552). New York: Lexington Books.

Wall, J. C., & Amadio, C. (1994). An integrated approach to child custody evaluation: Utilizing the Best Interest of the child and family systems frameworks. *Journal of Divorce and Remarriage, 21*, 39−57.

Walters, G. D. (2011). Taking the next step: Combining incrementally valid indicators to improve recidivism predictions. *Assessment, 18*(2), 227−233.

Walters, G. D. (2012). *Crime in a psychological context: From career criminals to criminal careers*. Thousand Oaks, CA: Sage.

Walters, M., & Friedlander, S. (2010). Finding a tenable middle space: Understanding the role of clinical interventions when a child refuses contact with a parent. *Journal of Child Custody: Research, Issues, and Practices, 7*(4), 287−328.

Wang, J., & Iannotti, R. J. (2010). Cyberbullying: Let the computer help, authors reply. *Journal of Adolescent Health, 47*(2), 209−210.

Wang, J., Iannotti, R. J., Luk, J. W., & Nansel, T. R. (2010). Co-occurrence of victimization from five subtypes of bullying: Physical, verbal, social exclusion, spreading rumors, and cyber. *Journal of Pediatric Psychology, 35*(10), 1103–1112.

Wang, J., Iannotti, R. J., & Nansel, T. R. (2009). School bullying among adolescents in the United States: Physical, verbal, relational, and cyber. *Journal of Adolescent Health Care, 45*(4), 368–375.

Ward, T., & Hudson, S. M. (1998). A model of the relapse process in sexual offenders. *Journal of Interpersonal Violence, 13*(6), 700–725.

Ward, T., & Hudson, S. M. (2000). A self regulation model of relapse prevention. In D. R. Laws, S. M. Hudson, & T. Ward (Eds.), *Remaking Relapse Prevention with Sex Offenders: A Sourcebook*. London: Sage Publications.

Warren, J. I., Burnette, M., South, S. C., Chauhan, P., Bale, R., & Friend, R. (2002). Personality disorders and violence among female prison inmates. *Journal of the American Academy of Psychiatry & the Law, 30*(4), 502–509.

Warshak, R. A. (1996). Gender bias in child custody decisions. *Family and Conciliation Courts Review, 34*, 396–409.

Warshak, R. A. (2007). Punching the parenting time clock: The approximation rule, social science, and the baseball bad kids. *Family Court Review, 45*(4), 600–619.

Washington State Department of Social & Health Services. (2002). *Mentally ill offender community transition program: Annual report to the legislature*.

Watersong, A. W. (2010). Economic Justice, Vermont Network Against Domestic and Sexual, (n.d.) Violence Against Women. *FDCH Congressional Testimony*, Retrieved from MasterFILE Premier Database.

Watson, P. (2004). Mental health interventions following mass violence. *Stresspoints, 12*, 4–5.

Watson, P. J., Friedman, M. J., Ruzek, J. I., & Norris, F. H. (2002). Managing acute stress response to major trauma. *Current Psychiatry Reports, 4*, 247–253.

Wattenberg, E., Kelley, M., & Kim, H. (2001, Jul-Aug). When the rehabilitation ideal fails: A study of parental rights termination. *Child Welfare, 80*(4), 405–431.

Watterson, K. (1996). *Women in prison: Inside the concrete womb* (Rev. ed). Boston: Northeastern University Press.

Way, B. B., Miraglia, R., Sawyer, D. A., Beer, R., & Eddy, J. (2005). Inmate suicide and time spent in special disciplinary housing in New York state prisons. *International Journal of Law and Psychiatry, 28*, 207–221.

Weaver, R. S. (1992). Violent youth need rehabilitation, not harsh punishment. In M. D. Biskup, & C. P. Cozic (Eds.), *Youth violence*. San Diego, CA: Greenhaven Press.

Webber, M. (2005). Die Rechtsmedizin-Koenigin des Beweises oder Hure der Strafjustiz? *Recht, 25*, 147–150.

Weber, M. C. (2008). AAPL guideline for forensic evaluation of psychiatric disabilities: a disability law perspective. *The Journal of the American Academy of Psychiatry and the Law, 36*, 558–562.

Wechsler, D. (1944). *The measurement of adult intelligence* (3rd edn.). Baltimore: Williams & Wilkins.

Weeks, R. M. A. (2003). Comparing children to the mentally retarded: How the decision in *Atkins v. Virginia* will affect the execution of juvenile offenders. *B.Y.U. Journal of Public Law, XVII*, 441–486.

Weiner, I. B. (2003). Prediction and postdiction in clinical decision making. *Clinical Psychology: Science & Practice, 10*(3), 335–338.

Weinstein, H. C. (2002). Ethics issues in security hospitals. *Behavioral Sciences & the Law, 20*(5), 443–461.

Weis, R., & Toolis, E. (2008). Military style residential treatment for disruptive adolescents: A critical review and look to the future. In A. M. Columbus (Ed.), *Advances in Psychology Research*, Vol. 56 (pp. 1–44). Hauppauge, NY: Nova Science Publishers.

Weisberg, D. K. (1985). *Children of the night: A study of adolescent prostitution*. Lexington, MA: Lexington Books.

Weisner, D. A. (2006). From Tarasoff to Ewing: Expansion of the duty to warn. *American Journal of Forensic Psychology, 24*, 45–55.

Weiss, M. (1997). A legal evaluation of criminal competency standards. *Journal of Contemporary Criminal Justice, 1*(3), 213–223.

Weiss, P. A., Hitchcock, J. H., Weiss, W. U., Rostow, C., & Davis, R. (2008). The Personality Assessment Inventory Borderline, Drug, and Alcohol Scales as predictors of overall performance in police officers: A series of exploratory analyses. *Policing and Society, 18*(3), 301−310.

Welch, M. (1997). A critical interpretation of correctional bootcamps as normalizing institutions: Discipline, punishment and the military model. *Journal of Contemporary Criminal Justice, 13*(2), 184−205.

Welch, M., & Gunther, D. (1997). Jail suicide and prevention: Lessons from litigation. *Crisis Intervention, 3*, 229−244.

Wells, G. (2011). Making room for daddies: Male couples creating families through adoption. *Journal of GBLT Family Studies, 7*(1−2), 155−181.

Welsh, M. G. (2011). Growing up in a same-sex parented family: The adolescent voice of experience. *Journal of GBLT Family Studies, 7*(1−2), 49−71.

Werth, J. L. (2001, Fal). U. S. involuntary mental health commitment statutes: Requirements for persons perceived to be a potential harm to self. *Suicide & Life-Threatening Behavior, 31*(3), 348−357.

West, B. (2007). Using the Good Way model to work positively with adults and youth with intellectual difficulties and sexually abusive behaviour. *Journal of Sexual Aggression, 13*, 253−266.

Wcstcott, H. L., & Page, M. (2002, May-Jun). Cross-examination, sexual abuse and child witness identity. *Child Abuse Review, 11*(3), 137−152.

Wheeler, J., George, W., & Stephens, K. (2005). Assessment of sexual offenders. In D. Donovan, & G. Marlatt (Eds.), *Assessment of addictive behaviors* (pp. 392−424). New York: Guilford Press.

Whitcomb, D. (2003, Apr). Legal interventions for child victims. *Journal of Traumatic Stress, 16*(2), 149−157.

White, M. D., Galietta, M., & Escobar, G. (2006). Technology-driven literacy programs as a tool for re-connecting incarcerated mothers and their children: Assessing their need and viability in a federal prison. *Justice Policy Journal, 3*(1), 1−20.

Widom, C. S. (1992). The cycle of violence. *Journal of Marriage and the Family, 43*, 331−337.

Widom, C., & Kuhns, J. (1996). Childhood victimization and subsequent risks for promiscuity, prostitution, and teenage pregnancy: A prospective study. *Am. J. Public Health, 86*(11), 1607−1612.

Wijkman, M., Bijleveld, C., & Hendricks, J. (2010). Women don't do such things! Characteristics of female sex offenders and offender types. *Sex Abuse, 22*(2), 135−156.

Willard, N. E. (2006). *Cyberbullying and cyberthreats: Responding to the challenge of online social cruelty, threats, and distress.* Eugene, OR: Center for Safe and Responsible Internet Use.

Willard, N. E. (2007). *An educator's guide to cyberbullying and cyberthreats.* Available from http://www.cyberbully.org/cyberbully/docs/cdcteducator.pdf. Retrieved 15 February 2008.

Williams, A. T. (2008). Rethinking social severance: Post-termination contact between birth parents and children. *Connecticut Law Review, 41*(2), 609−612.

The Williams Institute. (2010). *United States census snapshot: 2010.* Retrieved on September 12, 2011 from http://services.law.ucla.edu/williamsinstitute/pdf/Census2010Snapshot_US.pdf.

Williams, K. (2010). Disability and the performance paradox: Can social capital bridge the divide? *British Journal of Industrial Relations, 48*(3), 534−559.

Williams, K. R., & Guerra, N. G. (2007). Prevalence and predictors of internet bullying. *Journal of Adolescent Health, 41*(6), 14−21.

Williams, R. M. (2003). Introduction. In R. M. Williams (Ed.), *Teaching the arts behind bars* (pp. 3−13). Boston, MA: Northeastern University Press.

Williams, S. M. (1996). A national strategy for managing sex offenders. *Forum on Corrections Research, 8*(2), 33−35.

Wilson, C., & Gross, P. (1994). Police-public interactions: The impact of conflict resolution tactics. *Journal of Applied Social Psychology, 24*(2), 159−175.

Wilson, D., & MacKenzie, D. (2005). Boot camps. In B. Welsh, & D. Farrington (Eds.), *Preventing crime: What works for children, offenders, victims, and places* (pp. 73−86). Belmont, CA: Wadsworth.

Wilson, D. B., MacKenzie, D., & Mitchell, F. N. (2005). Effects on correctional boot camps on offending. *Campbell Systematic Reviews, 1*, 1−45.

Wilson, H., & Widom, C. (2008). An examination of risky sexual behavior and HIV in victims of child abuse and neglect: A 30-year follow-up. *Health Psychology, 27*(2), 149–158.

Wilson, H., & Widom, C. (2009). A prospective examination of the path from child abuse and neglect to illicit drug use in middle adulthood: The potential mediating role of four risk factors. *Journal of Youth Adolescence, 38*, 340–354.

Wilson, N. J., & Tamatea, A. (2010). Beyond punishment: Applying PRISM in a New Zealand maximum security prison. *The International Journal of Forensic Mental Health, 9*(3), 192–204.

Winick, B. J. (1992). Competency to be executed: A therapeutic jurisprudence perspective. *Behavioral Sciences and the Law, 10*, 317–337.

Winick, B. J. (2009). Determining when severe mental illness should disqualify a defendant from capital punishment. In R. Schopp, R. Wiener, B. Bornstein, & S. Willborn (Eds.), *Mental disorder and criminal law: Responsibility, punishment, and competence.* University of Miami Legal Studies Research Paper No. 2009-18. Available at SSRN: http://ssrn.com/abstract=1372320.

Winterdyk, J., & Ruddell, R. (2010). Managing prison gangs: Results from a survey of U.S. prison systems. *Journal of Criminal Justice, 38*(4), 730–736.

Winzenried, U. (1989). "Criminal profiling," Die Schweizer Polizei profitiert aus FBI-Ermittlungsmethode. *Kriminalistik, 43*, 434–435.

Wolak, J., Mitchell, K. J., & Finkelhor, D. (2007). Does online harassment constitute bullying? An exploration of online harassment by known peers and online-only contacts. *Journal of Adolescent Health, 41*(Suppl. 6), S51–S58.

Wolber, G. (2008). The unrestorable incompetent defendant: Length of attempted restoration and factors contributing to a decision of unrestorable. *American Journal of Forensic Psychology, 26*(3), 63–77.

Wolff, K. B., & Cokely, C. L. (2007). To protect and to serve? An exploration of police conduct in relation to the gay, lesbian, bisexual, and transgender community. *Sexuality & Culture, 11*(2), 1–23.

Wolfgang, M. E. (1959). Suicide by means of victim-precipitated homicide. *Journal of Clinical and Experimental Psychopathology, 20*, 335–349.

Women's Prison Association. (2008). *Mother's, infants, and imprisonment: A national look at prison nurseries and community-based alternatives.* New York: Author. Retrieved at www.wpaonline.org.

Wood, J., & Edwards, K. (2005). Victimization of mentally ill patients living in the community: Is it a life-style issue? *Legal and Criminological Psychology, 10*, 279–290.

Wood, J., Moir, A., & James, M. (2009). Prisoners' gang-related activity: The importance of bullying and moral disengagement. *Psychology, Crime & Law, 15*(6), 569–581.

Wood, R., Grossman, L., & Fichtner, C. (2000). Psychological assessment, treatment, and outcome with sex offenders. *Behavioral Sciences & the Law, 18*(1), 23–41.

Woodhull, A. (1993). *Police communication in traffic stops.* Rochester, NY: Schenkman Books.

Woods, J. (2011). The 9/11 effect: Toward a social science of the terrorist threat. *The Social Science Journal, 48*, 213–233.

Woodworth, M., & Porter, S. (2000). Historical foundations and current applications of criminal profiling in violent crime investigations. *Expert Evidence, 7*(4), 241–264.

Wool, R. J., & Dooley, E. (1987). A study of attempted suicides in prisons. *Medicine Science Law, 27*(4), 297–301.

Worden, R. (1989). Situational and attitudinal explanations of police behavior: A theoretical reappraisal and empirical assessment. *Law and Society Review, 23*(4), 667–711.

Worley, R., & Cheeseman, K. A. (2006). Women on the wing: Inmate perceptions about female correctional officer job competency in a southern prison system. *The Southwest Journal of Criminal Justice, 3*(2), 86–102.

Worley, R. M., Marquart, J. W., & Mullings, J. L. (2003). Prison guard predators: An analysis of inmates who established inappropriate relationships with prison staff. *Deviant Behavior, 24*, 175–198.

Worley, R. M., Tewskbury, R., & Frantzen, D. (2010). Preventing fatal attractions: Lessons learned from inmate boundary violators in a southern penitentiary system. *Criminal Justice Studies, 23*(4), 347–360.

Wortzel, H. (2006). The right to refuse treatment. *Psychiatric Times, 23*(14), 30.

Wortzel, H. S., Binswanger, I. A., Anderson, C. A., & Adler, L. E. (2009). Suicide among incarcerated veterans. *Journal of American Academy Psychiatry Law, 37*, 82−91.

Wrightsman, L., Nietzel, M., & Fortune, W. (1994). *Psychology and the legal system* (3rd edn.). Pacific Grove, CA: Brooks/Cole.

Wynne, E. E. (1997). Children's rights and the biological bias in biological parent versus third-party custody disputes. *Child Psychiatry and Human Development, 27*, 179−191.

Yang, M., Wong, S. C. P., & Coid, J. (2010). The efficacy of violence prediction: A meta-analytic comparison of nine risk assessment tools. *Psychological Bulletin, 136*(5), 740−767.

Yates, K. F., & Denney, R. L. (2008). Neuropsychology in the assessment of mental state at the time of the offense. In R. L. Denney, & J. P. Sullivan (Eds.), *Clinical neuropsychology in the criminal forensic setting* (pp. 204−237). New York: Guilford Press.

Ybarra, M. L., & Mitchell, J. K. (2004). Online aggressor/targets, aggressors and targets: A comparison of associated youth characteristics. *Journal of Child Psychology and Psychiatry, 45*, 1308−1316.

Young, B., Boccaccini, M. T., Conroy, M. A., & Lawson, K. (2007). Four practical and conceptual assessment issues that evaluators should address in capital case mental retardation evaluations. *Professional Psychology: Research and Practice, 38*(2), 169−178.

Young, M. E. (2009). The therapeutic relationship. In M. E. Young (Ed.), *Learning the art of helping: Building blocks and techniques* (4th edn.). Columbus, OH: Pearson Education.

Younglove, J. A., & Vitello, C. J. (2003). Community notification of "Megan's Law" from a therapeutic jurisprudence perspective: A case study. *American Journal of Forensic Psychology, 21*(1), 25−38.

Yuan, C., Wang, Z., Inslicht, S. S., McCaslin, S. E., Metzler, T. J., Henn-Haase, C., et al. (2011). Protective factors for posttraumatic stress disorder symptoms in a prospective study of police officers. *Psychiatry Research, 188*(1), 45−50.

Yufik, A. (2005). Revisiting the Tarasoff decision: Risk assessment and liability in clinical and forensic practice. *American Journal of Forensic Psychology, 23*, 5−21.

Yuma, Y. (2010). The effect of prison crowding on prisoners' violence in Japan: Testing with cointegration regressions and error correction models. *Japanese Journal of Psychology, 81*(3), 218−225.

Yurtal, F., & Artut, K. (2010). An investigation of school violence through Turkish children's drawings. *Journal of Interpersonal Violence, 25*, 50−62.

Zapf, P. A. (2007). Competency for execution. In R. Jackson (Ed.), *Learning forensic assessment* (pp. 239−261). Boca Raton, FL: CRC Press.

Zapf, P., Green, D., & Rosenfeld, B. (2011). Competency to stand trial and criminal responsibility research. In B. Rosenfeld, & S. D. Penrod (Eds.), *Research Methods in Forensic Psychology* (p. 156). Hoboken, NJ: John Wiley & Sons, Inc.

Zappalá, A., & Bosco, D. (2007). The phenomenon of serial murder and the judicial admission of criminal profiling in Italy. In R. N. Kocsis (Ed.), *Criminal Profiling: International Theory, Research, and Practice* (pp. 263−272). Totowa, NJ: Humana Press.

Zevitz, R. G., & Farkas, M. A. (2000b). Sex offender community notification: Examining the importance of neighborhood meetings. *Behavioral Sciences & the Law, 18*(2−3), 393−408.

Zevitz, R. G., & Farkas, M. A. (2000a). The impact of sex-offender community notification on probation/parole in Wisconsin. *International Journal of Offender Therapy and Comparative Criminology, 44*(1), 8−21.

Ziedenberg, J., & Schiraldi, V. (1998, Aug). The risks juveniles face. *Corrections Today, 60*(5), 22−25.

Zimmerman, J., Hess, A., McGarrah, N., Benjamin, G., Ally, G., Gollan, J., & Kaser-Boyd, N. (2009). Ethical and professional considerations in divorce and child custody cases. *Professional Psychology: Research and Practice, 40*(6), 539−549.

Zimring, F. E. (2005). *American juvenile justice.* New York: Oxford University Press.

Zuberbuhler, J. (2001, Apr). Early intervention mediation: The use of court-ordered mediation in the initial stages of divorce litigation to resolve parenting issues. *Family Court Review, 39*(2), 203−206.

Cases

18 U.S.C. § 3592 (a)(8)

42 U. S. C. § 15602

Atkins v. Virginia, 536 U. S. 304 (2002).

Barefoot v. Estelle, 103 S. Ct. 3383, 463 U.S. 880 (1983)

Bartley v. Kremens, 402 F. Supp. 1039 (1975)

Baston v. Kentucky, 476 U.S. 79 (1986)

Baumgartner v. City of Long Beach, Civil No. C-54782 (L.A. Super. 1987)

Braam v. State, 81 P.3d 851 (Wash. 2003)

Brad H. v City of New York, 712 NYS.2d 336 (Sup. Ct. 2000); 716 NYS.2d 852 (N.Y. App. Div. 2000)

Brown v. Board of Education of Topeka, 347 U.S. 483 (1954)

Buchanan v. Kentucky, 483 U.S. 402 (1987)

Buck v. Bell, 274 U.S. 200 (1927).

Bundy v. Jackson, 641 F. 2d 934 (D.C. Cir. 1981)

Chambers v. Mississippi, 410 U.S. 284 (1973)

Clemons v. Alabama, CR-01-1355 (Ala. Crim. App. 2005).

Coleman v. Wilson, 912 F. Supp. 1282 (1995)

Coy v. Iowa, 108 S. Ct. 2798 (1988).

  Crawford v. Washington, 124 S.Ct. 1354 (2004).

Daubert v. Merrell, 509 U.S. 579, 591 (1993)

Davis v. United States, 512 U.S. 452-464 (1994)

Delo v. Lashley (1993). 507 U.S. 272.

Department of Health and Mental Hygiene v. Kelly 397 Md. 399; 918 A.2d 470; 2007 Md. LEXIS 102

Department of Revenue of Montana v. Kurth Ranch, 511 U.S. 128 L.Ed. 2d 767, 777 (1994)

Dodd v. Hughes, 81 Nev. 43, 398 P.2d 540 (1965)

Dothard v. Rawlinson, 433 U.S. 321 (1977)

Drope v. Missouri, 420 U.S. 162 (1975)

Durham v. United States, 214 F.2d 862 (D.C. Cir. 1954)

Dusky v. United States, 362 U.S. 402 (1960)

Eddings v. Oklahoma, 455 U.S. 104 (1982)

Estelle v. Smith,451U.S. 454 (1981)

Ewing v. Goldstein (2004), 15 Cal. Rptr. 3d 864.

Ex parte Jose Garcia Briseno, 135 S.W.3d 1 (2004).

Faretta v. California, 422 U.S. 806 (1975)

Fasanaro v. County of Rockland, 166 Misc. 2d 152, 632 N.Y.S. 2d 453 (NY 1995)

Finlay v. Finlay, 240 N.Y. 429, 148 N.E. 624 (1925)

Fla. Stat. § 921.137.

Ford v. Wainwright, 477 U.S. 399 (1986)

Foucha v. Louisiana, 504 U.S. 71 (1992)

Frith's Case, 22 Howes' State Trials 307, 318 (1790)

Frye v. United States, 293 F. 1013 (D. C. Cir 1923)

Garrett v. Collins, 951 F. 2d 57, 58 (5th Cir. 1992)

General Electric Co. v. Joiner (1997)

Godinez v. Moran, 509 U.S. 389 (1993) – U.S.S.C.

Graham v. Connor, 490 U.S. 386 (1989).

Gregg v. Georgia, 428 U.S. 1301 (1976)

Hitchcock v. Dugger (1987). 481 U.S. 393.

Hirschfeld v. Stone, 193 F.R.D. 175 (S.D.N.Y. 2000)

Indiana v. Davis (898 N.E.2d. 281 (Ind. 2008))

Indiana v. Edwards, 554 U.S. 164 (2008)

In re Gault, 387 U.S. 1 (1967)

In re Winship, 397 U.S. 358 (1970)

Jackson v. Indiana, 406 U.S. 715 (1972)

JEB v. Alabama ex rel. TB, 511 US 127, (1994).

Jenkins v. United States, 307 F.2d 637 (D.C. Car. 1962).

Kent v. United States, 383 U.S. 541 (1966)

Knecht v. Gillman, 488 F. 2d 1136 (1973)

Kumho Tire Co., Ltd., et al., v. Carmichael et al. No. 97-1079. (1999).

Lugo v. Senkowsky, 114 F.Supp.2d 111 (N.D. N.Y. 2000).

Maryland v. Craig, 110 S. Ct. 3157 (1990)

McKeiver v. Pennsylvania, 403 U.S. 528 (1971)

Miller-El v. Dretke, 545 U.S. 231 (2005).

Missouri v. Davis, 653 S. W. 2d 167, Mo. Sup. Ct. (1983)

Montana v. Austed, 641 P.2d. 1373 Mont. Sup. Ct. (1982)

Morgan v. Rabun 128 F.3d 694; 1997 8th Circuit

Morrow v. Maryland, 423 A. 2d 251, Md. Ct. Spec. App. (1980)

Panetti v. Quarterman (2007), 551 U.S. 930.

Parham v. J. R., 442 U.S. 584 (1978)

Pate v. Robinson, 383 U.S. 375 (1966)

Penry v. Lynaugh, 109 S. Ct. 2934 (1989)

People v. Aris, N.E. 005418 Cal. App. Lexis 1187 (1989)

People v. Morgan (1999) 719 N.E.2d 681.

Perry v. Louisiana, 111 S. Ct. 449 (1990)

R. v. Mohan (1994), 2 S.C.R. 9.

Ritchie v. Indiana, 468 N. E. 2d 1369, Ind. Sup. Ct. (1984)

Roach v. Aiken, Warden et al., 474 U.S. 1039 (1986)

Robbins v. Glenn County, No. CIVS-85-0675 RAR (U.S.D.C., E.D. Ca. 1986)

Rock v. Arkansas, 107 S. Ct. 2704 (1987)

Roper v. Simmons, 543 US 551 (2005)

Santobello v. New York, 404 U.S. 257 (1971)

Schall v. Martin, 104 S. Ct. 2403 (1984).

Sell v. U.S., 539 U. S. 166 (2003)

Singleton v. State, 90-CP-36-66 (Newberry County) (1991)

Skipper v. South Carolina (1986). 461 U.S. 1.

Snyder v. Louisiana, 552 U.S. 472 (2008).

Stanford v. Kentucky, 492 U.S. 361 (1989)

State v. Kennedy, 957 So.2d 757, 2005-1981 (La. 2007).

State v. Michael (1987). 530 So.2d 929.

Swain v. Alabama, 380 U.S. 202 (1965)

Tarasoff v. Regents of the University of California, 551 P.2d 334 (1976)

Tennard v. Dretke, 542 U.S. 274 (2004).

Tennessee v. Garner, 471 U.S. 1 (1985)

Thompson v. Oklahoma, 487 U.S. 815 (1988)

Troxel v. Granville, 530 U.S. 57 (2000)

United States v. Binion, 132 Fed. Appx. 89, 8th Circuit (2005)

United States v. Greer, 158 F. 3d 228, 5th Circuit (1998)

United States v. Salerno, 481 U.S. 739 (1987).
United States v. Timmins, 9th Circuit (2002)
United States v. Ward, 448 U.S. 242, 248 (1980)
Va. Code Ann. § 19.2-264.3:1.1.
Wakfield v Thompson, 177 F.3d 1160 (9th Cir. 1999).
Walker v. True, 399 F.3d 315 (2005).
Washington v. Harper, 494 U.S. 210, 110 S. Ct. 1028 (1990)
Wertz v. Workmen's Compensation Appeal Board, 683 A.2d 1287 (Pen. 1996)
Wheeler v. United States, 159 U.S. 523 (1895)
Wiggins v. Smith (02-311) 539 U.S. 510 (2003) 288 F.3d 629
Wilkins v. Missouri, see Stanford v. Kentucky, 492 U.S. 361 (1989)
Williams v. State, 970 So.2d 727 (Miss. App. Sep 4, 2007).
Wilson v. United States, 391 F. 2d 460, D.C. Cir. (1968)
Wright v. Walls, 288 F. 3d 937, 7th circuit (2002).
Young v. Weston, 11 F. 3d 38 (9th Cir. 1997).

Index

Page numbers followed by "b" indicate boxes; "f" figures; and "t" tables.